JDITING

CONCEPTUAL FOUNDATIONS AND PRACTICE

McGraw-Hill Series in Management Information Systems

Gordon B. Davis, *Consulting Editor*

Davis and Olson: Management Information Systems: Conceptual Foundations, Structure, and Development
Dickson and Wetherbe: The Management of Information Systems
Dickson and Wetherbe: Management of Information Systems Casebook
Everest: Database Management: Objectives, System Functions, and Administration
Lucas: The Analysis, Design, and Implementation of Information Systems
Lucas: A Casebook for Management Information Systems
Meadow and Tedesco: Telecommunications for Management
Philippakis and Kazmier: The New COBOL: An Illustrated Guide
Scott: Principles of Management Information Systems
Senn: Analysis and Design of Information Systems
Weber: EDP Auditing: Conceptual Foundations and Practice

OF RELATED INTEREST

Dordick: Understanding Modern Telecommunications
Jones: Programming Productivity
Newman: Designing Integrated Systems for the Office Environment

EDP AUDITING

CONCEPTUAL FOUNDATIONS AND PRACTICE

SECOND EDITION

Ron Weber
University of Queensland
Australia

McGRAW-HILL BOOK COMPANY

New York   St. Louis   San Francisco   Auckland   Bogotá
Hamburg   London   Madrid   Mexico   Milan   Montreal   New Delhi
Panama   Paris   São Paulo   Singapore   Sydney   Tokyo   Toronto

EDP AUDITING
Conceptual Foundations and Practice
INTERNATIONAL EDITION

Exclusive rights by McGraw-Hill Book Co. — Singapore for manufacture and export. This book cannot be re-exported from the country to which it is consigned by McGraw-Hill.

9 0 FSP 9 4 3

Library of Congress Cataloging-in-Publication Data
Weber, Ron.
  EDP auditing.

  (McGraw-Hill series in management information systems)
  Includes index.
  1. Electronic data processing—Auditing.   I. Title.   II. Series.
QA76.9A93W43   1988   657'.453   87-3397
ISBN 0-07-068832-X

This book was set in Times Roman by the College Composition Unit in cooperation with The William Byrd Press, Inc.
The editor was Robert Lynch.
The cover was designed by Scott Chelius.
The production supervisor was Friederich Schulte.

When ordering this title use ISBN 0-07-100341-X

Printed in Singapore

For my parents

CONTENTS

PREFACE

A friend and colleague once said to me: "To be a good auditor you have to be better at business than your client." I've often pondered that remark, for on the one hand it is a compelling notion, yet on the other it sets an impossible ideal for auditors to achieve. Perhaps in the more traditional areas of auditing we, as auditors, are gaining confidence in the soundness of our methodologies. Admittedly, the lawsuits still prevail, but the problems seem to be in the application of the methodologies rather than in the methodologies themselves.

In the domain of modern auditing, however, we have an Achilles heel: our methodologies for the control and audit of computer systems are still in their infancy. Further, the rate at which new computer technology is developed and introduced seems to outstrip the rate at which we can develop viable audit methodologies. It is the area of EDP auditing that currently represents the great challenge to auditors.

EDP auditing is the process of collecting and evaluating evidence to determine whether a computer system safeguards assets, maintains data integrity, achieves organizational goals effectively, and consumes resources efficiently. Safeguarding assets involves ensuring that they are protected from damage or destruction, unauthorized use, and being stolen. Data integrity is a state: it means data is accurate, complete, and consistent. Asset safeguarding and data integrity always have been the concern of auditors. However, the definition of EDP auditing proposed also encompasses a concern for the effectiveness with which EDP systems meet their objectives and the efficiency with which data is processed. Since EDP expenditure often is a major item in an organization's balance sheet and income statement, currently management is more frequently asking auditors to evaluate these aspects of EDP systems.

Some Pedagogical Issues

Before writing this book, I thought long and hard about the approach I should use to present the subject matter of EDP auditing. It seems to me there are two approaches. With the first approach, which I will call the "exposures approach," the writer focuses primarily on the types of losses that can occur in computer systems. The secondary focus is on the controls used to reduce these losses. With the second approach, which I will call the "controls approach," the primary focus is on the controls and the secondary focus is on the losses that the controls reduce.

Why can't *both* exposures and controls be the primary focus? Both certainly have major importance from an audit perspective. The problem is that there is not a one-to-one relationship between exposures and controls. A single control can reduce the loss from multiple exposures. Thus, if the writer focuses on *exposures*, some subject matter on controls will be repeated; alternatively, if the writer focuses on *controls*, some subject matter on exposures will be repeated. As my students have not hesitated to point out, the writer who does not carefully control the duplication of material that results will bore the reader quickly. The only solution, I believe, is for the writer to adopt either exposures or controls as the primary focus; the secondary focus then becomes the material that must be duplicated as efficiently as possible so presentation of the subject matter of EDP auditing is complete.

In this book, I chose to focus on *controls* for three major reasons. First, I trust that students who have had a first course in auditing will be familiar with the major types of exposures facing an organization (these do not change with computers); I assume they are reading this book because their knowledge of computer control technology is not so well developed. Second, my experience is that students feel more comfortable with the controls approach; they seem to find it less "messy" than the exposures approach. I am unsure why this is the case, but I think it has to do with controls requiring a smaller "chunk" of understanding than exposures. Third, a major purpose of this book is to integrate the burgeoning literature on computer controls that appears in *both* the auditing and computer science areas. It dismays me that each area still tends to ignore the other; each has much to contribute to the other.

The controls approach has its problems. The subject matter on computer controls is somewhat more volatile than the subject matter on exposures. Some control technology is still evolving; for example, several problems remain to be solved relating to the use of cryptography in communications networks. But I believe there to be more than enough stability in the control technology to make the approach that I have adopted worthwhile.

Structure of the Book

The parts (and chapters) of the book follow a natural sequence. The first part motivates the EDP audit function within an organization. The second and third parts describe the computer control frameworks that should exist in an organization at the management level and application system level, respectively. By first evaluating the management control framework, the EDP auditor determines the extent and scope of testing needed at the application system level. Techniques of evidence collection are discussed in the fourth part of the book; and the fifth part discusses how the evidence collected can be evaluated. The final part discusses EDP audit management.

One point must be made on the subject matter of the chapters. As a potential reader, you may look for chapters on the specialized areas of EDP audit: online realtime systems, database management systems, service bureaus, etc. You may be disappointed to find these chapters missing. However, through experience I am convinced that this is not the best way to initially present the subject matter of EDP auditing. Many of the controls and audit methodologies needed for online systems are the same for database management systems, and so forth. This is not to deny there are specialized controls and specialized audit techniques for these specialized areas. However, organizing the basic subject matter of EDP auditing by these specialized areas results in substantial duplication of material and frustrations for both the instructor and student. The secret of being a good EDP auditor is to be capable of assembling the fundamental controls and EDP audit methodologies in a manner appropriate for a specific computer installation, be it a simple batch system or a complex database management system.

Using the Book

I intend this book to be of use primarily to both students and practitioners of EDP auditing. However, I hope it will also prove useful to EDP managers, systems analysts, and programmers who have responsibility for designing and implementing controls in systems.

The book presumes the reader has at least a basic knowledge of auditing, computer data processing, and a programming language. Thus, it is not intended for beginners in the field. The beginner should first study one of the many excellent introductory texts in the areas of auditing and computers.

At the college level, the book provides sufficient material for a solid semester's work at the upper undergraduate or graduate level. The instructor may wish to leave out some chapters—for example. Chapter 25 on organization and management of the EDP audit function—and give more emphasis to others. The chapter bibliographies are a source of additional reading for students if the instructor wants to spend more time on particular chapters.

Besides the usual lecture method, the instructor might like to try using the book employing a case study approach. The students are made responsible for studying the chapter materials; the class periods are used to discuss the exercises and cases at the end of each chapter.

Besides the exercises and cases, each chapter in the book also contains a set of review questions and multiple choice questions. In general, answers to the review questions can be found in the chapter. At times, however, a little thought may be required. Answers to the multiple choice questions can be found at the end of the chapter. The exercises and cases are more demanding. Often I have tried to make the student think from an exposures perspective, thereby compensating for my primary focus on controls in the chapter. The exercises and cases also may require the student to integrate material covered in earlier chapters. To assist the instructor, there is also an instructor's manual available containing suggested solutions to the assignment material.

I strongly recommend that the instructor supplement the assignment material with further case studies and some computer problems. The case studies should be more comprehensive than the short cases contained in the book so the student is forced to integrate the text material. They might be on specific types of systems; for example, an online banking system or a service bureau. A variety of computer problems can be set; for example, using a generalized audit software package to examine the quality of data on a file or using a test data generator to assist validating the logic of a program.

I hope that as a user of the book, you conclude that the benefits exceed the costs. I would appreciate your feedback, whether it be positive or negative, so that a third edition (if it occurs) might better meet your needs.

Changes in the Second Edition

The second edition of this book is an extensive revision of the first edition. The chapter material has been updated to include discussions on new data processing and new control technologies that have emerged since the publication of the first edition. For example, material on microcomputers, high-level programming languages, electronic funds transfer systems, inference controls, and expert systems has been incorporated in this new edition of the book.

Previous material in the book has also been expanded and reorganized. A new chapter on security management has been added to cover material that was treated somewhat superficially in the first edition in the chapter on operations management. Previous chapters on audit trail and backup and recovery controls have been deleted. The material in these chapters has been relocated to other chapters where it is better integrated with material on related controls. The single chapter in the first edition on access and communication controls has been broken up into two chapters in the second edition. This action was needed to provide adequate coverage of substantial new control technology that has emerged in these areas, primarily as a result of the increasing use of electronic funds transfer systems. The material on evidence collection tools has been expanded to reflect recent work in expert systems, modeling software, spreadsheet software, and decision support software. The material on organization and management of the EDP audit function has been moved to the final part of the book to allow the reader to move more quickly to the substance of EDP auditing.

There are changes, also, in the end-of-chapter materials. The review questions and exercises and cases have been expanded considerably. In particular, the exercises and cases should provide a rich and varied source of items for discussion and debate. A set of multiple choice questions also now accompanies each chapter. The answers to these questions are at the end of each chapter. Thus, students have extensive material to test their understanding of the chapter contents.

ACKNOWLEDGMENTS

Once again I gratefully acknowledge the assistance and support provided to me by Professor Gordon B. Davis, the editor of the series in which this book belongs. Across 13 years his wise counsel and gentle guidance have been a source of inspiration, and I owe him a debt I cannot repay.

I am grateful, also, to a large number of people who provided me with comments and suggestions on the first edition of the book. In particular, I would like to acknowledge the detailed suggestions made by Professor Clinton E. White, Jr., Mr. Guy Gable, and the late Mr. D.V.A. Campbell.

Part of the second edition was written while I was on sabbatical leave during the first six months of 1986 at the Univerity of British Columbia. I gratefully acknowledge the considerable assistance provided to me by Ms. Monica Holtforster, Touche Ross and Co., Vancouver, in allowing me access to library materials that otherwise I could not have obtained on a timely basis.

I would also like to thank the following reviewers for their useful comments and suggestions: Karen Hooks, University of Southern Florida; and Frederick L. Neuman, University of Illinois at Urbana.

Finally, to the three women in my life—my wife, Kay, and my daughters, Amy and Georgia—go my deepest thanks. The debt I owe them for their love, support, and patience is awesome.

Ron Weber

EDP AUDITING
CONCEPTUAL FOUNDATIONS
AND PRACTICE

PART ONE

INTRODUCTION

EDP auditing is a function that has been developed to assess whether computer systems safeguard assets, maintain data integrity, and achieve the goals of an organization effectively and efficiently. Parties both internal and external to an organization are concerned with whether computer systems fulfill these objectives. The management of an organization attempts to use resources in an optimal manner within the constraints established by the society; for example, management may pursue a profit-maximizing objective subject to the legal constraint that it maintain the privacy of data provided to it by individual members of the society. External parties, whether they be shareholders, unions, or pressure groups, also have vested interests in how organizations use

Chapter	Overview of contents
1 Overview of EDP Auditing	Discusses the need for control and audit of computers; defines EDP auditing; examines the underlying support disciplines; evaluates the effects of EDP on internal control
2 Conducting an EDP Audit	Examines the effects of the system of internal controls on the audit approach; discusses the relationship between expected losses and errors and irregularities; discusses the nature of computer controls; provides an overview of the steps in an EDP audit; describes some of the major EDP audit decisions

computers. Their concerns vary from wealth maximization to possible work displacement to a loss of personal privacy.

The first two chapters of this book introduce the EDP audit function. They discuss the motivations for an EDP audit function and the objectives of EDP auditing and present an overview of the EDP audit process.

OVERVIEW OF EDP AUToITING

CHAPTER OUTLINE

3

FOUNDATIONS OF EDP AUDITING
Traditional Auditing
Information Systems Management
Behavioral Science
Computer Science
SUMMARY
REVIEW QUESTIONS
MULTIPLE CHOICE QUESTIONS
EXERCISES AND CASES
ANSWERS TO MULTIPLE CHOICE QUESTIONS
REFERENCES

Whereas 30 years ago we fulfilled most of our data processing needs manually, today computers perform much of the data processing required in both the private and public sectors of our economy. The need to maintain the integrity of data processed by computers pervades our lives. We have increasing fears that our substantially increased data processing capabilities are not well controlled. The media makes much of computer abuse. We have concerns about the privacy of data we exchange with organizations such as the tax department, medical authorities, and credit granting institutions. Probably all of us have suffered the frustrations of trying to get an organization to update its computer-maintained name and address file.

Uncontrolled use of computers has a widespread impact on a society. Inaccurate information causes misallocation of resources within the economy. Frauds are perpetrated because of inadequate system controls. Unfortunately, the person who suffers most is often the person who can least afford to suffer, for example, the small shareholder and the low-income earner. Perhaps more subtle is the growing distrust of institutions that gather and process large volumes of data. A sense of lost individuality now exists: the "big brother" of 1984 is upon us.

NEED FOR CONTROL AND AUDIT OF COMPUTERS

Computers continue to be used more extensively to process data. Initially they were available only to large organizations that could afford their high purchase and operations costs. The advent of minicomputers and the rapid decrease in the cost of computer technology then enabled medium-sized organizations to take advantage of computers for their data processing. Nowadays, the widespread availability of powerful microcomputers and their associated packaged software has resulted in the extensive deployment of computers for use by individuals in the workplace and at home. Given the intensively competitive marketplace for computer hardware and software technology, the rapid diffusion of computers in our economies will continue.

Since computers play such a large part in assisting us to process data and make decisions, it is important that their use be controlled. Figure 1-1 shows seven major reasons for establishing a function to examine controls over computer data processing. The following sections examine these reasons in more detail.

Organizational Costs of Data Loss

Data is a critical resource necessary for an organization's continuing operations. Everest [1985] proposes that data provides the organization with an image of itself, its environment, its history, and its future. If this image is accurate, the organization increases its abilities to adapt and survive in a changing environment.

Consider the case of a large department store that has its accounts receivable file destroyed. Unless its customers are honest, and also remember what they have purchased from the store, the firm can suffer a major loss in cash receipts and its long-run survival may be affected. Consider, also, the department store losing its accounts payable file. It is unable to pay its accounts on time and can suffer a loss of credit rating as well as any discounts available for early payment. If it contacts creditors requesting assistance, the department store relies on the honesty of the creditors in notifying it of the amounts owed. Furthermore, creditors must now question the competence of the department store's management and may be unwilling to extend credit in the future.

Such losses can arise through lax controls existing over computers. Management may not provide adequate backup for computer files; thus, the loss of a file through computer program error, sabotage, or natural disaster means the file cannot be recovered and the organization's continuing operations are impaired.

FIGURE 1-1
Factors influencing an organization toward control and audit of computers.

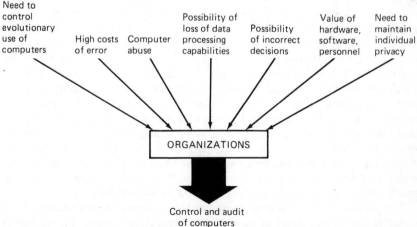

Need to control evolutionary use of computers

High costs of error

Computer abuse

Possibility of loss of data processing capabilities

Possibility of incorrect decisions

Value of hardware, software, personnel

Need to maintain individual privacy

ORGANIZATIONS

Control and audit of computers

Incorrect Decision Making

The importance of accurate data depends on the types of decisions made by individuals having some interest in an organization. For example, if management makes strategic planning decisions, most likely they will tolerate some errors in the data, given the nature of strategic planning decisions—their long-run perspective and surrounding uncertainty. However, management control and operational control decisions usually require accurate data. These latter decisions involve detection, investigation, and correction of out-of-control processes. Inaccurate data may cause costly, unnecessary investigations to be undertaken, or result in out-of-control processes remaining undetected.

Other people besides management have interests in an organization. Shareholders need accurate financial statements to enable them to make their investment decisions. Governments, labor, and pressure groups such as environmentalists also need accurate data to make decisions about an organization. However, accurate data is a necessary but not sufficient condition to prevent misallocation of resources within an economy.

Besides the implications of incorrect data for decision making, incorrect *decision rules* in a computer system also can have significant detrimental effects on an individual or an organization. Consider, for example, the increasing availability and use of expert systems (artificial intelligence systems that aid judgment) and the potential impact of erroneous knowledge bases in these systems. A medical diagnostician who relied on such systems may make a fatal judgment error if the system provides incorrect advice. Perhaps at a more mundane level, an incorrect interest calculation routine may result in an organization making substantial overpayments to its customers.

Computer Abuse

The major stimulus for development of the EDP audit function within organizations often seems to be computer abuse. Parker [1976, p. 12] defines computer abuse to be "any incident associated with computer technology in which a victim suffered or could have suffered loss and a perpetrator by intention made or could have made gain." Recently, some spectacular cases of computer abuse have caused management and more academics and researchers to be concerned with the problem. However, after extensive studies of computer abuse, Parker [1976] regards it to be only the third most serious problem confronting an organization using computers. The most serious problem is errors and omissions causing losses to organizations. Next is disruption to computer data processing caused by natural disasters such as fire, water, and power failures. Control techniques for handling these two types of problems are better developed than those for computer abuse.

The losses which result from computer abuse seem to be higher than those which result when abuses of manual data processing systems occur. Parker

[1976] reports two studies made of general bank fraud and embezzlement (not involving the computer) and computer bank fraud and embezzlement. The average loss per case for general bank fraud and embezzlement was $104,000 and the average loss per case for computer bank fraud and embezzlement was $617,000. Even with the problems of collecting data on fraud and embezzlement, figures that show computer-related fraud and embezzlement to be approximately six times higher than general fraud and embezzlement are cause for concern.

Controlling computer abuse is often made more difficult by the inadequacy of the law. It may be difficult to prosecute someone who makes unauthorized use of computer time because the law does not consider the computer to be a "person" and only a person can be deceived unlawfully. Some successful prosecutions have been reduced to actions based on unlawful use of electricity or the telephone system (see Tettenborn [1981]). Similarly, the law relating to unauthorized access to information is problematical. In some countries the law of theft may not cover information. Thus, an organization may not be successful in an action against someone who makes an unauthorized copy of a confidential customer file for sale to competitors. These deficiencies in the law are now motivating some governments to enact remedial legislation (see, for example, Steier [1984]).

Because computer abuse has had such an important influence on the development of EDP auditing, the reader should be familiar with some of the major cases of computer abuse. The exercises and case studies at the end of this chapter describe four of the more famous cases. The bibliography that follows includes several references that contain extensive discussions and analyses of computer abuse.

Value of Computer Hardware, Software, and Personnel

Besides data, computer hardware, software, and personnel are critical organizational resources. Some organizations have multimillion dollar investments in hardware. Even with adequate insurance, the intentional or unintentional loss of hardware can cause considerable disruption. Similarly, software often constitutes a considerable investment of an organization's resources. If the software is corrupted or destroyed, the organization may be unable to continue operations if it cannot recover promptly. If the software is stolen, confidential information may be disclosed to competitors; or, if the software is a proprietary package, lost revenues or lawsuits may arise. Finally, personnel are always a valuable resource, particularly in light of an ongoing scarcity of well-trained computer professionals.

High Costs of Computer Error

Computers now automatically perform many critical functions within our society. For example, they control robots on an assembly line, monitor the condition of patients during surgery, calculate and pay interest on investment accounts, direct the flight of a nuclear missile, and steer a ship on its course. Consequently, the costs of a computer error can be high. An error in an Australian government computer system resulted in a $126 million overpayment of pharmaceutical benefits. Data errors in a computer system used to control flight paths resulted in the death of 257 people when an airplane crashed into a mountain in Antarctica. An individual was jailed incorrectly for five months because of erroneous data contained about him in a computer system.

Privacy

Much data is now collected about us as individuals: taxation, credit, medical, educational, employment, residence, etc. This data also was collected before computers. However, the data processing capabilities of the computer, particularly the rapid throughput, integration, and retrieval capabilities, cause many people to now wonder whether the privacy of individuals (and organizations) is being eroded. Some people conceive that ultimately there will be a large database on all individuals containing substantial information about them keyed on some universal identifier.

Aside from any constitutional aspect, many nations deem privacy to be a human right. They consider it to be the responsibility of those people concerned with computer data processing to ensure computer use does not evolve to the stage where different data about people can be collected, integrated, and retrieved quickly. A further responsibility exists to ensure data is used only for the purposes intended.

Controlled Evolution of Computer Use

Technology is neutral, neither good nor bad. It is the *use* of technology that produces social problems. Major decisions still have to be made on how computers should be used within the society; for example, to what extent should the implementation of computer technology be allowed to displace the work force?

It is a function of governments, professional societies, and pressure groups to be concerned with evaluating the use of technology; but, it is also well-accepted that individual organizations should have a social conscience that includes the use of computer technology.

EDP AUDITING DEFINED

EDP auditing is the process of collecting and evaluating evidence to determine whether a computer system safeguards assets, maintains data integrity, achieves organizational goals effectively, and consumes resources efficiently. Thus, EDP auditing supports the attainment of traditional audit objectives:

attest objectives (those of the external auditor) that have asset safeguarding and data integrity as their focus, and management objectives (those of the internal auditor) that encompass not only attest objectives but also effectiveness and efficiency objectives. The EDP audit process can be conceived as a force that helps organizations to better attain these objectives (Figure 1-2).

Asset Safeguarding Objectives

The assets of a computer installation include hardware, software, people, data files, system documentation, and supplies. Like all assets they must be protected by a system of internal control. Hardware can be damaged maliciously. Proprietary software and the contents of data files can be stolen. Supplies of negotiable forms can be used for unauthorized purposes. Because of the concentration of assets within the physical locality of the computer installation, asset safeguarding is an especially important objective.

Data Integrity Objectives

Data integrity is a fundamental concept in EDP auditing. It is a state implying data has certain attributes: completeness, soundness, purity, veracity. Without data integrity being maintained, an organization no longer has a true representation of itself or of real world events. However, maintaining data integrity can only be achieved at a cost. The benefits obtained should exceed the costs of the control procedures needed.

Two major factors affect the value of a data item to an organization: (*a*) the value of the informational content of the data item for individual decision makers and (*b*) the extent to which the data item is shared among decision

FIGURE 1-2
Impact of the EDP audit function on organizations.

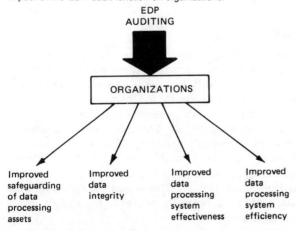

EDP
AUDITING

ORGANIZATIONS

| Improved safeguarding of data processing assets | Improved data integrity | Improved data processing system effectiveness | Improved data processing system efficiency |

makers. The value of the data item determines how important it is to maintain the integrity of the data item.

The informational content of a data item depends on its ability to reduce the uncertainty surrounding a decision. The value of this uncertainty reduction in turn depends on the payoffs associated with the decision to be made. These notions have been well-developed within statistical decision theory (see, for example, Marschak and Radner [1972]).

If data is shared, corruption of data integrity affects not just one user but multiple users. The value of a data item is some aggregate function of the value of the data item to the individual users of the data item. Thus, in a shared data environment, maintenance of data integrity becomes more critical.

System Effectiveness Objectives

An effective data processing system accomplishes its objectives. Evaluating effectiveness implies knowledge of user needs. To evaluate whether a system reports information in a way that facilitates decision making by its users, the auditor must know the characteristics of the user and the decision-making setting.

Effectiveness auditing typically occurs after a system has been running for some time. Management requests a postaudit to determine whether the system is achieving its stated objectives. This evaluation provides input to the decision on whether to scrap the system, continue its running, or modify it in some way.

Effectiveness auditing also can be carried out during the design stages of a system. Systems designers have a difficult task ensuring users communicate their needs and understand and accept the proposed design. If a system is complex and costly to implement, management may want an independent evaluation of whether the design is likely to fulfill user needs. The auditor may be responsible for performing this independent evaluation for management.

System Efficiency Objectives

An efficient data processing system uses minimum resources to achieve its required output. Data processing systems consume various resources: machine time, peripherals, channels, system software, labor. These resources are scarce and different application systems compete for their use.

The question of whether a data processing system is efficient often has no clear-cut answer. The efficiency of any particular application system cannot be considered in isolation from other application systems. Problems of suboptimization occur if one system is "optimized" at the expense of other systems. For example, minimizing an application system's run time may require dedication of a channel to that system. However, the system may not utilize the channel fully and the slack resource normally available for use by other application systems is no longer available.

Data processing system efficiency becomes especially important when a computer no longer has excess capacity. The performance of individual application systems typically degrades (for example, slower response times occur) and management must decide whether efficiency can be improved or extra resources must be purchased. Since extra hardware and software are expensive, management needs to know whether available capacity has been exhausted because individual application systems are inefficient or existing allocations of computer resources are causing bottlenecks. Again, because auditors are independent, management may ask them to perform or to assist in the evaluation.

EFFECTS OF EDP ON INTERNAL CONTROLS

Asset safeguarding, data integrity, system effectiveness, and system efficiency can be achieved only if an organization's management sets up a system of internal control. Traditionally, major components of an internal control system have included separation of duties, clear delegation of authority and responsibility, recruitment and training of high-quality personnel, a system of authorizations, adequate documents and records, physical control over assets and records, management supervision, independent checks on performance, and periodic comparison of recorded accountability with assets. In an EDP system these components must still exist; however, use of EDP affects the *implementation* of these components in several ways. The following sections briefly examine some of the major areas of impact.

Separation of Duties

In a manual system, separate individuals should be responsible for initiating transactions, recording transactions, and custody of assets. As a basic control, separation of duties prevents or detects errors and irregularities. In a computer system, however, the traditional notion of separation of duties does not always apply. For example, a program may reconcile a vendor invoice against a receiving document and print a check for the amount owed to a creditor. Thus, the program is performing functions that in manual systems would be considered incompatible. Nevertheless, it may be inefficient and, from a control viewpoint, useless to place these functions in separate programs. Instead, separation of duties must exist in a different form. Once it has been determined that the program executes correctly, the capability to run the program in production mode and the capability to change the program must be separated.

In minicomputer and microcomputer environments, separation of incompatible functions may be even more difficult to achieve. Some minicomputers and microcomputers allow users to change programs and data easily; furthermore, they provide no record of these changes. If the minicomputer or microcomputer does not have an inbuilt capability to provide a secure record of changes, it may be difficult to determine whether incompatible functions have been performed by system users.

Delegation of Authority and Responsibility

A clear line of authority and responsibility is an essential control in both manual and computer systems. In a computer system, however, delegating authority and responsibility in an unambiguous way may be difficult because some resources are shared among multiple users. For example, one of the objectives of using a database management system is to provide multiple users with access to the same data, thereby reducing the control problems that arise with maintaining redundant data. When multiple users have access to the same data and the integrity of the data is somehow violated, it is not always easy to trace who is responsible for corrupting the data and who is responsible for identifying and correcting the error. Some organizations have attempted to overcome these problems by designating a single user as the *owner* of the data. This user assumes ultimate responsibility for the integrity of the data.

Authority and responsibility lines are also being blurred by the rapid growth in end-user computing. With the availability of fourth-generation languages, more users are developing, modifying, and maintaining their own application systems instead of having this work performed by the information systems department (see Martin [1982]). While these developments have substantial benefits for the users of computing services in an organization, unfortunately they exacerbate the problems of exercising overall control over computing use.

Competent and Trustworthy Personnel

The technology of data processing is now exceedingly complex—much more complex than in the days of manual systems. Highly skilled personnel are needed to develop, modify, maintain, and operate today's computer systems. Thus, the existence of competent and trustworthy personnel becomes even more important when computer systems are used to process an organization's data, since a relatively small number of individuals assume major responsibility for the integrity of the data.

Unfortunately, assuring an organization has competent and trustworthy data processing personnel has been a difficult task. Historically, well-trained and experienced data processing personnel have been in short supply. Therefore, organizations sometimes have been forced to compromise in their choice of staff. Moreover, it is not always easy for an organization to assess the competence and integrity of its EDP staff. High turnover in the data processing industry has been the norm, and the rapid evolution of technology inhibits management's ability to evaluate an employee's skills. Data processing personnel also lack a well-developed system of ethics, and the profession often seems populated by individuals who delight in subverting controls.

System of Authorizations

Management issues two types of authorizations to execute transactions. General authorizations establish policies for the organization to follow; for example, a fixed price list is issued for personnel to use when products are sold. Specific authorizations apply to individual transactions; for example, acquisitions of major capital assets may have to be approved by the board of directors.

In a manual system, auditors evaluate the adequacy of procedures for authorization by examining the work of employees. In a computer system, authorization procedures often are embedded within a computer program. For example, the order entry module in a sales system may determine the price to be charged to a customer. Thus, when evaluating the adequacy of authorization procedures, auditors have to examine not only the work of employees but also the veracity of program processing.

In a computer system it is also more difficult to assess whether the authority assigned to individuals is consistent with management's wishes. For example, it may be hard to determine exactly what data can be accessed by users when they are provided with a generalized retrieval language. Users may be able to formulate queries on a database in such a way that they can *infer* the contents of confidential information. Indeed, substantial research is now being undertaken on controls that prevent the privacy of data being violated via queries that allow inferences to be made. Chapter 15 examines inference controls in more detail.

Adequate Documents and Records

In a manual system, adequate documents and records are necessary to provide an audit trail of activities within the system. In computer systems, documents may not be used to support the initiation, execution, and recording of some transactions. For example, in an online order entry system, customers' orders received by telephone may be entered directly into the system. Similarly, some transactions may be activated automatically by a computer system; for example, an inventory replenishment program may initiate purchase orders when stock levels fall below a set amount. Thus, no visible audit or management trail may be available to trace the transaction.

The absence of a visible audit trail is not a problem for the auditor provided that systems have been designed to maintain a record of all events and there is a means of accessing these records. In well-designed computer systems, audit trails are often more extensive than those maintained in manual systems. Unfortunately, not all computer systems are well designed. Some minicomputer and microcomputer software packages, for example, provide inadequate access controls and logging facilities to ensure preservation of an accurate and complete audit trail. When this situation is coupled with a decreased ability to separate incompatible functions, serious control problems can arise.

Physical Control over Assets and Records

Physical control over access to assets and records is critical in both manual systems and computer systems. Computer systems differ from manual systems, however, in the way they concentrate the data processing assets and records of an organization. For example, in a manual system, a person wishing to perpetrate a fraud may have needed access to records that were maintained at different physical locations. In a computer system, however, all the necessary records may be maintained at a single site—the data processing installation. Thus, the perpetrator does not have to go to physically disparate locations to execute the fraud.

This concentration of data processing assets and records also increases the loss that can arise from computer abuse or a disaster. For example, a fire that destroys a computer room may result in the loss of all major master files in an organization. If the organization does not have suitable backup, it may be unable to continue operations.

Adequate Management Supervision

In a manual system, management supervision of employee activities is relatively straightforward because the managers and the employees are often at the same physical location. In computer systems, however, data communications may be used to enable employees to be closer to the customers they service. Thus, supervision of employees may have to be carried out remotely. Supervisory controls must be built into the computer system to compensate for the controls that usually can be exercised through observation and inquiry.

Computer systems also make the activities of employees less visible to management. Since many activities are performed electronically, managers must ensure they periodically access the audit trail of employee activities and examine it for unauthorized actions. Again, the effectiveness of observation and inquiry as controls has decreased.

Independent Checks on Performance

In manual systems, independent checks are carried out because employees are likely to forget procedures, make genuine mistakes, become careless, or fail intentionally to follow prescribed procedures. Checks by an independent person help to detect any errors or irregularities that occur. In a computer system, provided that program code is authorized, accurate, and complete, the system will always follow the designated procedures. Thus, independent checks on the performance of programs are unnecessary. Instead, the control emphasis shifts to assuring the veracity of program code. Insofar as many independent checks on performance are no longer appropriate, auditors must now evaluate the controls established for program development, modification, and maintenance.

Comparing Recorded Accountability with Assets

Periodically, data and the assets that the data purports to represent should be compared to determine whether incompleteness or inaccuracies in the data exist or shortages in the assets have occurred. In a manual system, independent staff prepare the basic data used for comparison purposes. In a computer system, however, programs are used to prepare this data. For example, programs may sort an inventory file by warehouse location and prepare counts by inventory item at the different warehouses. If unauthorized modifications occur to the programs or the data files that the programs use, an irregularity may not be discovered. Again, internal controls must be implemented to ensure the veracity of program code, since traditional separation of duties no longer applies to the data being prepared for comparison purposes.

EFFECTS OF EDP ON AUDITING

When EDP systems first appeared, many auditors were concerned that the fundamental nature of auditing may have to change to cope with the new technology. It is now clear this is not the case. Auditors still provide a competent, independent evaluation as to the correspondence between some set of economic activities and established standards or criteria. Nevertheless, EDP systems have impacted the two basic functions of auditing: evidence collection and evidence evaluation.

Changes to Evidence Collection

Collecting evidence on the reliability of an EDP system is more complex than collecting evidence on the reliability of a manual system. Auditors confront a diverse and sometimes complex range of internal control technology that did not exist in manual systems. For example, accurate and complete operation of a disk drive requires a set of hardware controls not used in a manual system. Similarly, system development controls include procedures for testing programs that would not be found in the development of manual systems. Auditors must understand these controls if they are to be able to collect evidence competently on the reliability of the controls.

Unfortunately, understanding the control technology is not easy. Hardware and software continue to evolve rapidly, and although there is some time lag, the associated controls evolve rapidly also. For example, with increasing use of data communications for data transfer, substantial research is now being undertaken on the development of cryptographic controls to protect the privacy of data. Auditors must keep up with these developments if they are to be able to evaluate the reliability of communications networks.

The continuing evolution of control technology also makes it more difficult for auditors to *collect* evidence on the reliability of controls. It may be impossible for auditors to obtain the evidence using manual means. Thus, auditors need EDP systems themselves if they are to be able to collect the necessary evidence. The development of generalized audit software occurred, for example, because auditors needed access to data maintained on magnetic media. Similarly, new audit tools may be required in due course to evaluate the reliability of controls in data communications networks. Unfortunately, the development of these audit tools usually lags the development of the technology that must be evaluated. In the meantime, auditors are forced to compromise in some way when they perform the evidence collection function.

Changes to Evidence Evaluation

Given the increased complexity of EDP systems and internal control technology, it is also more difficult for auditors to evaluate the consequences of control strengths and weaknesses for the overall reliability of systems. Auditors first must understand when a control is acting reliably or malfunctioning. Next, they must be able to trace the consequences of the control strength or weakness through the system. In a shared data environment, for example, this may be a difficult task. A single input transaction may update multiple data items that are used by diverse, physically disparate users. Somehow auditors must be able to trace the consequences of an error in the transaction input for all users.

In some ways auditors are also under greater stress when they perform the evidence evaluation function for computer systems. As noted earlier, the consequences of errors in a computer system can be more serious than the consequences of errors in a manual system. Errors in manual systems tend to occur stochastically; for example, periodically a clerk prices an inventory item incorrectly. Errors in computer systems tend to be deterministic; an erroneous program always will execute incorrectly. Moreover, errors are generated at high speed, and the cost to correct and rerun programs may be high. Whereas fast feedback can be provided to clerks if they make errors, errors in computer programs can involve extensive redesign and reprogramming. Thus, internal controls that ensure high-quality computer systems are designed, implemented, and operated are critical. The onus is on auditors to ensure these controls are sufficient to maintain asset safeguarding, data integrity, system effectiveness, and system efficiency and that they are in place and working.

FOUNDATIONS OF EDP AUDITING

EDP auditing is not just a simple extension of traditional auditing. Recognition of the need for an EDP audit function came from two directions. First, auditors realized that computers had impacted their ability to perform the attest function. Second, both corporate and information processing management recognized computers were valuable resources that needed controlling like any other valuable resource within the organization.

Figure 1-3 shows EDP auditing to be an intersection of four other areas or

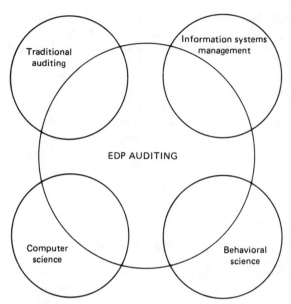

FIGURE 1-3
EDP auditing as an intersection of other disciplines.

disciplines. EDP auditing borrows much of its theory and practical methodologies from traditional auditing, information systems management, behavioral science, and computer science.

Traditional Auditing

Traditional auditing brought to EDP auditing a wealth of knowledge and experience concerning internal control techniques. A computer system has both manual and machine components. There are clerical activities such as data preparation activities supporting a computer system. These activities should be subject to internal control principles such as separating duties, having competent and trustworthy personnel, and establishing clear definitions of duties, just as a manual system should be subject to these principles. Applying these principles attempts to ensure the integrity of data before it reaches the computer facility, and in the subsequent distribution of the computer output.

Traditional auditing also impacts the computer component of a data processing system. Concepts such as control totals are relevant to the update and maintenance of files by computer programs. Computer programs must ensure all transaction data is processed and that it is processed correctly in the same way a manual system must ensure these things. Many of the controls used in traditional auditing can be carried over directly into computer data processing activities.

The general methodologies for evidence collection and evidence evaluation used by EDP auditors are rooted in traditional auditing (see, further, Chapter 2). The long evolution and extensive experience of traditional auditing highlight the critical importance of objective, verifiable evidence and independent evaluation of systems.

Perhaps most important, traditional auditing brings to EDP auditing a control philosophy. It is difficult to articulate the nature of this philosophy. However, one can glean elements by reading auditing literature or examining the work of auditors. The philosophy involves examining data processing with a critical mind, questioning a system's ability to safeguard assets, maintain data integrity, and achieve its objectives effectively and efficiently.

Information Systems Management

The early history of computer data processing shows some spectacular disasters when implementing computer systems. There were massive cost overruns and failures to achieve stated objectives. Recently, many researchers have been concerned with better ways of developing and implementing information systems. As a result, several advances have occurred. Techniques of project management have been carried across into the information systems area. Documentation, standards, budgets, and variance investigation are now emphasized. Better ways of developing and implementing systems have been developed. For example, the structured programming and chief programmer team approaches to software development seem to result in software being developed faster, with fewer errors, and with easier maintenance in the future. These advances impact EDP auditing because they ultimately affect asset safeguarding, data integrity, system effectiveness, and system efficiency.

Behavioral Science

Lucas [1975] concluded after a study of 2000 users in 16 different organizations that the major reason computer systems fail is through ignoring organizational behavior problems in the design and implementation of information systems. The failure of an information system can impact asset safeguarding, data integrity, system effectiveness, and system efficiency. Thus, the EDP auditor must know those conditions that lead to behavioral problems and possible system failure. Behavioral scientists, especially organization theorists, have contributed much to understanding people problems within organizations. Some researchers are now applying the findings of organization theory to information systems development and implementation. They emphasize the need for systems designers to consider *concurrently* the impact of a computer system on task accomplishment, the technical system, and the quality of work life of individuals within the organization, the social system.

Computer Science

Computer scientists also have been concerned with asset safeguarding, data integrity, system effectiveness, and system efficiency (see, further, Hoffman [1977] and Denning and Denning [1979]). For example, research has been carried out on how to develop error-free software and ways to maintain overall hardware/software system integrity. The theoretical basis for structured programming developed in computer science. Reliability theory and control theory have been the basis for designing secure operating systems, secure system software, and error-free hardware.

The high-level technical knowledge of computer science provides both benefits and problems for EDP auditing. On the one hand, it allows the auditor to be less concerned about the reliability of certain components in a data processing system. On the other hand, if the knowledge is abused, it may be very difficult for the auditor to detect the abuse. Fraud perpetrated by a skilled systems programmer may be almost impossible to detect by an auditor who does not have a corresponding level of technical knowledge.

SUMMARY

EDP auditing is an organizational function that evaluates asset safeguarding, data integrity, system effectiveness, and system efficiency in computer systems. It has arisen for seven major reasons: (a) the consequences of losing the data resource; (b) the possibility of misallocating resources because of decisions based on incorrect data; (c) the possibility of fraud and embezzlement if computer systems are not controlled; (d) the high value of computer hardware, software, and personnel; (e) the high costs of computer error; (f) the need to maintain the privacy of individuals; and (g) the need to control the evolutionary use of the computer.

Asset safeguarding, data integrity, system effectiveness, and system efficiency can be achieved only if a sound system of internal control exists. Use of a computer for data processing does not affect the basic objectives of internal control; however, it affects how these objectives must be achieved.

The use of computers for data processing impacts both the evidence collection and evidence evaluation functions of auditors. Computer control technology is more complex than manual system control technology; consequently, it is more difficult to understand controls and to collect evidence on the reliability of controls. Similarly, it is more difficult to understand the implications of a control strength or weakness for the overall reliability of a system.

EDP auditing borrows much of its theory and methodologies from other areas. Traditional auditing contributes knowledge of internal control practices and overall control philosophy. Information systems management provides methodologies necessary to achieve successful design and implementation of systems. Behavioral science indicates when and why information systems are likely to fail because of people problems. Computer science contributes knowledge about control theory and the formal models that underlie hardware and software design as a basis for maintaining data integrity.

REVIEW QUESTIONS

1-1 Why is there a need for control and audit of computer systems?

1-2 For each of the following groups, give a specific example of how incorrect data processing by a company's computer system may lead to incorrect decisions being made:

  a Management

  b Shareholders

  c Labor unions

  d Environmentalists

  e Tax department

  f Affirmative action group

1-3 What are the implications of a company losing its:

  a Personnel master file

  b Inventory master file

1-4 Why is the integrity of the decision rules being incorporated into computer systems becoming increasingly important?

1-5 Should we be any more concerned about computer fraud and embezzlement versus other forms of business fraud and embezzlement?

1-6 In general, how adequate is the law in terms of being able to prosecute someone who undertakes computer abuse?

1-7 Why are controls still needed to protect hardware, software, and personnel, even though substantial insurance coverage may have been taken out by an organization?

1-8 What characteristics of computer systems often lead to high costs being incurred because of computer system errors?

1-9 Why does the computer cause us to have increased concerns about the privacy of individuals?

1-10 Give an example of the computer being used for data processing where you consider it to be:

  a Socially desirable

  b Socially undesirable

1-11 What are the four major objectives of EDP auditing? Explain the meaning of each one of them.

1-12 What are the major assets in a computer installation?

1-13 Define data integrity. What factors affect the importance of data integrity to an organization?

1-14 What is the difference between system effectiveness and system efficiency? Why is the EDP auditor concerned with both system effectiveness and system efficiency?

1-15 Briefly explain the nature of the impact of using computers on the overall objectives of internal control.

1-16 What problems arise for ensuring that incompatible functions are separated in a computer installation?

1-17 How does resource sharing in a computer system affect the internal control objective of having clear lines of authority and responsibility? Give an example.

1-18 How does the growth of end-user computing affect the internal control objective of having clear lines of authority and responsibility?

1-19 Why is the need for competent and trustworthy personnel even more important when an organization uses computers for its data processing?

1-20 When computer systems are used, how does the auditor evaluate the system of authorizations used by an organization?

1-21 How does the use of computers impact the audit trail within a data processing system?

1-22 With the increasing use of computers for data processing, is the audit trail disappearing? Explain.

1-23 Briefly explain how assets may be lost by a person having unauthorized access to a payroll program.

1-24 How does a computer system affect the concentration of assets within an organization? What implication does the effect have for internal controls?

1-25 Relative to a manual system, in a computer system is it easier or harder to implement adequate management supervision of employees? Explain.

1-26 How do independent checks on employee performance differ between a manual system and a computer system?

1-27 How does an organization compare recorded accountability with assets when computer systems are used? What controls must be exercised to ensure the veracity of this process?

1-28 How does the continuing evolution of computer hardware and software technology affect an auditor's ability to (a) understand controls and (b) collect evidence on the reliability of controls?

1-29 What impact does the use of computers have on the nature and conduct of the evidence evaluation function carried out by auditors?

1-30 Briefly explain the contribution of the following areas to EDP auditing:
a Traditional auditing
b Information systems management
c Computer science
d Behavioral science

MULTIPLE CHOICE QUESTIONS

1-1 Incorrect data in a computer system is likely to have more serious consequences for a(an):
a Strategic planning system
b Expert system
c Personal decision support system
d Management control system

1-2 Loss of which of the following files is likely to have more serious consequences for a manufacturing organization:
a Inventory file
b Material requirements planning file
c Job routing file
d Bill-of-materials file

1-3 Computer abuse is:
a Malicious damage carried out to hardware and software
b Any incident associated with computer technology whereby a victim suffered loss and a perpetrator gained
c A fraud perpetrated by modifying software or hardware
d Misrepresentation by the media of how computers are used

1-4 Relative to general bank fraud and embezzlement, computer bank fraud and embezzlement seems to be about:
a Twice the size
b The same amount
c Six times larger
d Half the size

1-5 The evolution of technology needs to be controlled because:
a Using new technology always has undesirable consequences unless it is controlled
b It tends to increase the monopolistic power of those companies that can afford to purchase the technology
c Though computer technology is neutral, its use can produce social problems
d It places too much power in the hands of technocrats

1-6 From an EDP audit perspective, which of the following is the most valuable asset in a data processing department:
a Hardware
b Database
c Personnel
d Software

1-7 An objective of EDP auditing is:
a Asset safeguarding
b Preserving data integrity
c Achieving system efficiency
d All of the above

1-8 An effective data processing system:
a Accomplishes its objectives
b Maintains data integrity at all costs
c Is the most efficient system that could be implemented
d Has an expected life of several years

1-9 In a computer system, separation of duties:
a Can always be attained in the same way as in a manual system
b May have to be implemented in different forms compared with manual systems
c Is less important than in a manual system because programs make fewer errors than clerks
d Usually is easy to automate, especially in minicomputer systems

1-10 Compared with a manual system, the consequences of error in a computer system often are more serious because:
a Errors in computer systems tend to be stochastic
b Computer systems process more data than manual systems
c Errors in computer systems are generated at high speed, and the cost to correct and rerun programs may be high
d Users of computer systems always believe the output produced is correct

1-11 Compared with a manual system, in a computer system:
  a Basic internal control objectives change
  b The methodologies for implementing controls change
  c Control objectives are more difficult to achieve
  d All of the above

1-12 Clear lines of authority and responsibility are sometimes difficult to achieve in a computer system because:
  a Resources are shared and ownership is sometimes difficult to assign
  b Duties constantly change as a result of the rapid evolution of technology
  c Data processing personnel tend to object to traditional organizational principles
  d End-user computing is making this internal control principle irrelevant

1-13 Assuring data processing personnel are competent and trustworthy has been a difficult task because:
  a Historically, data processing personnel have been in short supply
  b Data processing personnel have lacked a well-developed system of ethics
  c Data processing personnel often perform tasks that are exceedingly complex
  d All of the above

1-14 In a computer system, it is often difficult to evaluate the system of *general* authorizations because general authorizations have been:
  a Dispersed to more users
  b Combined with specific authorizations
  c Embedded in computer programs
  d Displaced by hardware controls

1-15 In an EDP system, the audit trail is:
  a Still always present in hard-copy form
  b Disappearing as more online systems are used
  c Produced automatically during the update process
  d Sometimes more extensive than the audit trail in manual systems if it is designed properly

1-16 Compared with a manual system, data processing assets and records in a computer system tend to be:
  a More concentrated at a single location
  b Dispersed across many more locations
  c Concentrated to about the same extent
  d More concentrated at different locations but less valuable

1-17 Compared with a manual system, supervision of employee activities in a computer system is:
  a Easier, because observation and inquiry of employee activities is easier
  b Harder, because many activities are performed electronically and remotely
  c Easier, because unauthorized activities can always be detected automatically from the audit trail
  d Harder, because EDP employees are less tolerant of management supervision

1-18 In a computer system, independent checks on performance are often unnecessary because a procedure is performed by a computer program. Similarly, computer programs rather than independent staff often prepare reports that enable data and assets to be compared for accountability purposes. As a result, which of the following controls in a computer system becomes important to the auditor:
  a Equipment controls to ensure hardware does not malfunction

1 Backup and recovery controls

2 Controls over the development, maintenance, and modification of program code

3 Personnel controls that ensure only high-quality staff are hired

1-19 Which of the following has *not* been an effect of EDP systems on auditing:

a Evidence collection tends to be harder to carry out

b Understanding the control technology tends to be harder

c It is often harder to trace the effects of a control weakness

d The fundamental objectives of auditing have changed

1-20 A major contribution of computer science to the discipline of EDP auditing has been:

a The insight into how generalized audit software should be developed

b An understanding of why behavioral problems occur with information systems implementation

c An understanding of how project management techniques can contribute to information systems success

d The development of theoretical bases underlying the ways in which software and hardware reliability can be improved

EXERCISES AND CASES

1-1 Further research on computer abuse is useful because it helps provide answers to the following questions:

a *Who* perpetrates abuses?

b *How* are abuses perpetrated?

c *Why* are abuses perpetrated?

d What *controls* would have prevented or detected abuses?

e What *audit procedures* would have detected the abuse?

Required: Undertake some reading on computer abuse, and on the basis of your reading write a brief report providing some answers to the above questions.

1-2 Equity Funding Corporation

In 1973, the largest single company fraud known was discovered in California. The collapse of the Equity Funding Corporation of America involved an estimated $2 billion fraud. The case is extremely complex and it took several years before the investigation was complete. However, some of the pertinent findings derived from the Trustee's Bankruptcy report follow.

Equity Funding was a financial institution primarily engaged in life insurance. In 1964, its top management commenced to perpetrate a fraud that would take almost 10 years to discover. The intent of the fraud was to inflate earnings so that management could benefit through trading their securities at high prices.

The fraud progressed through three major stages: the "inflated earnings phase," the "foreign phase," and the "insurance phase." The inflated earnings phase involved inflating income with bogus commissions supposedly earned through loans made to customers. Equity Funding had a funded life insurance program whereby customers who bought mutual funds shares could obtain a loan from the company to pay the premium on a life insurance policy. After some years the customer would sell off the mutual fund holdings to repay the loan, and hopefully the mutual fund shares would have appreciated sufficiently so only a partial sale of shares would be required. Thus, the customer had the cash value of the insurance policy and the remaining mutual fund shares as assets from the investment.

The inflated earnings obtained via bogus commissions were supported by manual entries made on the company's books. Even though supporting documentation did not exist for the entries, the fraud managed to miss the scrutiny of the company's auditors. However, the inflated assets did not bring about cash inflows, and the company started to suffer severe cash shortages because of real operating losses.

To remedy the cash shortage situation, the fraud moved into the second stage called the foreign phase. The company acquired foreign subsidiaries and used these subsidiaries in complex transfers of assets. Funds were brought into the parent company to reduce the funded loans asset account and falsely represent customer repayments of their loans. However, even this scheme proved inadequate.

The third stage of the fraud, called the insurance phase, involved the resale of insurance policies to other insurance companies. This is normal practice in the insurance business when one company needs cash immediately and another company has a cash surplus. Equity Funding created bogus policies and in the short run attempted to solve its cash problems by selling these policies to another insurance company. In the long run, however, the purchasing company expected cash receipts from premiums on the policies. Since the policies were bogus, Equity Funding had to find the cash to pay the premiums. Thus, it was a matter of time before the fraud could no longer be concealed. Interestingly, the fraud was revealed by a disgruntled employee involved in the fraud who had been fired by Equity Funding management.

The computer was not used in the fraud until the insurance phase. The task of creating the bogus policies was too big to be handled manually. Instead, a program was written to generate policies and these policies were coded as the now infamous "Class 99."

The trustee's report reveals two clear-cut conclusions. First, the fraud was unsophisticated and doomed to failure. Second, Equity Funding's auditors were grossly negligent. The fundamental principles of good auditing were not applied. The fraud was the financial ruin of many families.

Required: Write a brief report outlining some traditional audit procedures which, if they had been used, should have detected the fraud. Be sure to explain why you believe the procedures you recommend would have been successful.

1-3 Jerry Schneider

One of the more famous cases of computer abuse involves a young man called Jerry Schneider. Schneider always had a flair for electronics and by the time he left high school he had already formed his own firm to market his inventions. His firm also sold refurbished Western Electric telephone equipment. In 1970, he devised a scheme whereby Pacific Telephone in Los Angeles would supply him with good equipment—free!

Pacific Telephone used a computerized equipment ordering system. Equipment sites placed orders using a Touch-Tone card dialer. The orders were then keypunched onto cards and the computer updated the inventory master file and printed the orders. The orders were then supplied to a transportation office that shipped the supplies.

Schneider intended to gain access to the ordering system and have Pacific Telephone deliver supplies to him thinking they were supplying one of their legitimate sites. He used a variety of techniques to find out the working of the system and breach security. He sifted through trash cans and found discarded documents that provided him with information on the ordering system. He posed as a magazine writer and gathered information directly from Pacific Telephone. To support his activities he bought a Pacific Telephone delivery van at an auction, "acquired" the master key for supply deliver locations in the Los Angeles area, and bought a Touch-Tone telephone card dialer with a set of cards similar to those used by the equipment sites to submit orders.

Schneider took advantage of the budgeting system used for ordering sites. Typically, these sites had a budget allocated larger than they needed. Providing this budget was not exceeded, no investigation of equipment ordering took place. Schneider managed to gain access to the online computer system containing information on budgets and determined the size of orders that would be tolerated.

For seven months Pacific Telephone delivererd him equipment that he resold to his customers and to Pacific Telephone. He kept track of the reorder levels for various Pacific Telephone inventories, depleted these inventories with his ordering, and then resold the equipment back to Pacific Telephone.

Schneider's downfall occurred when he revealed his activities to an employee. He was unable to keep up with the pace of his activities and so he confided in an employee to obtain assistance. When the employee asked for a pay raise, Schneider fired him and the employee then went back to Pacific Telephone and told them of the fraud.

There are varying reports on how much Schneider took from Pacific Telephone. Parker [1976] estimates it was possible equipment worth a few million dollars was taken. For the fraud Schneider received a two-month jail sentence followed by three years probation. Interestingly, upon completing the jail term he set up a consulting firm specializing in computer security.

Required: Write a brief report outlining some basic internal control procedures which, if they had been applied, should have prevented or detected Schneider's activities. Be sure to explain why the application of the internal control procedures you recommend would have been successful.

1-4 Union Dime Savings Bank

Banks seem especially prone to computer abuse. Roswell Steffen used a computer to embezzle $1.5 million of funds at the Union Dime Savings Bank in New York City. In an interview with Miller [1974] after he was discovered, he claimed: "Anyone with a head on his shoulders could successfully embezzle funds from a bank. And many do." Steffen was a compulsive gambler. He initially "borrowed" $5000 from a cash box at the bank to support his gambling with a view to returning the money from his earnings. Unfortunately, he lost the $5000 and he spent the next three and one-half years trying to replace the money, again by "borrowing" from the bank to gamble at the racetrack.

As the head teller at Union Dime, Steffen had a supervisory terminal in the bank's online computer system that he used for various administrative purposes. He took money from the cash box and used the terminal to manipulate customer account balances so the discrepancies would not be evidenced in the bank's daily proof sheets.

He used several techniques to obtain money. He first concentrated on accounts over $100,000 that had little activity and had interest credited quarterly. He used the supervisory terminal to reduce the balances in these accounts. Occasionally an irate customer complained about the balances so Steffen then faked a telephone call to the data processing department, informed the customer it was a simple error, and corrected the situation by moving funds from another account.

Other sources of funds included two-year certificate accounts and new accounts. With two-year certificate accounts, he prepared the necessary documents but did not record the deposit in the bank's files. Initially he had two years to correct the situation but matters became more complicated when the bank started to pay interest on these accounts quarterly. With new accounts, he used two new passbooks from the bank's supply of prenumbered books. Upon opening an account, he entered the transaction using the account number of the first passbook but recorded the entry in the second passbook. He then destroyed the first passbook. Perpetrating the fraud became very complex and he made many mistakes. However, the bank's internal control system and audit techniques were sufficiently weak that he could explain away discrepancies and continue. He was caught because police raided Steffen's bookie and noticed a lowly paid bank teller making very large bets.

Required: Write a brief report outlining some basic internal control procedures which, if they had been applied, should have prevented or detected Steffen's activities. Be sure to explain why the application of the control procedures you recommend would have been successful.

1-5 Stanley Rifkin

Stanley Rifkin was a free-lance computer consultant who had been employed by a firm that did consulting work for Security Pacific Bank in California. In early October 1978, he visited a diamond broker in Los Angeles and placed an order for about 42,000 carats of polished gemstones. The retail value of the stones was about $13 million; however, Rifkin contracted to pay $8 million as the cash wholesale price. An order was then placed by the broker on Russalmaz, the Soviet government's diamond exporting company.

To finance his purchase, Rifkin decided to defraud Security Pacific. First he gained access to the bank's wire transfer room. He did not arouse the suspicion of employees since he had worked there on earlier consulting assignments. Next he gained access to three critical data items: the security code needed to authorize a particular day's funds transfer orders, the personal identification code used by one of the bank's employees to gain access to the system, and the number of an account that had a substantial deposit balance. At the end of the day when he knew bank employees would be tired and less likely to detect an impropriety, he initiated the procedures to transfer $10.2 million to a bank account in Zurich. He then authorized the required payment of $8 million to Russalmaz.

After making the payment, Rifkin flew to Zurich under a fake passport to pick up the diamonds. He smuggled them back into the United States and commenced to pawn them. His downfall occurred when he made contact with someone in Rochester, New York, during an attempt to sell the remaining diamonds. The contact was a lawyer with whom he had been associated, and he disclosed to the lawyer how he had committed "the perfect crime." Ethically, the lawyer was bound to take the matter further with the authorities. The FBI traced the sequence of transfers and apprehended Rifkin in a friend's apartment with the diamonds. Rifkin executed the transfers on October 25. However, it was not until early November that Security Pacific found out the money was missing, supposedly in response to some inquiries from the FBI. Once the fraud was detected, it was easy to identify Rifkin as the culprit since the bank taped all telephone transfer orders. The diamond broker in Los Angeles identified Rifkin's voice on the tape. When questioned about their inability to promptly identify the unauthorized transfer of funds, the bank responded that there was nothing unusual about the $10.2 million transfer that had occurred.

Required: It might be argued that the physical access controls in the bank's system were weak. Nevertheless, Rifkin was a skilled, intelligent individual who had acquired a position of trust among the bank employees, and consequently the system might always be vulnerable in spite of strong preventive controls. What *detective* controls would you recommend, therefore, to enable an unauthorized electronic funds transfer to be identified quickly?

ANSWERS TO MULTIPLE CHOICE QUESTIONS

1-1 d	1-6 c	1-11 b	1-16 a
1-2 a	1-7 d	1-12 a	1-17 b
1-3 b	1-8 a	1-13 d	1-18 c
1-4 c	1-9 b	1-14 c	1-19 d
1-5 c	1-10 c	1-15 d	1-20 d

REFERENCES

Allen, Brandt. "The Biggest Computer Frauds: Lessons for CPAs," *Journal of Accountancy* (May 1977), pp. 52–62.

American Institute of Certified Public Accountants. *Statement on Auditing Standards No. 3: The Effects of EDP on the Auditor's Study and Evaluation of Internal Control* (New York: American Institute of Certified Public Accountants, 1974).

American Institute of Certified Public Accountants. *The Auditor's Study and Evaluation of Internal Control in EDP Systems* (New York: American Institute of Certified Public Accountants, 1977).

American Institute of Certified Public Accountants. *Report of the Special Advisory Committee on Internal Accounting Control* (New York: American Institute of Certified Public Accountants, 1979).

Blish, Eugene A. "Computer Abuse: A Practical Use of the AICPA Guide," *EDPACS* (September 1978), pp. 6–12.

Boritz, J. Effrim. *Computer Guide '79* (Canada: Morka Publications, 1979).

Denning, Dorothy E., and Peter J. Denning. "Data Security," *Computing Surveys* (September 1979), pp. 227–249.

Everest, Gordon C. *Database Management: Objectives, System Functions, and Administration* (New York: McGraw-Hill, 1985).

Hoffman, Lance J. *Modern Methods for Computer Security and Privacy* (Englewood Cliffs, NJ: Prentice-Hall, 1977).

Krauss, Leonard I., and Aileen MacGahan. *Computer Fraud and Countermeasures* (Englewood Cliffs, NJ: Prentice-Hall, 1979).

Leibholz, Stephen W., and Lois D. Wilson. *Users' Guide to Computer Crime: Its Commission, Detection and Prevention* (Radnor, PA: Chilton Book Company, 1974).

Lucas, Henry C. *Towards Creative System Design* (New York: Columbia University Press, 1975).

McKnight, Gerald. *Computer Crime* (New York: Walker Publishing Company, 1973).

McNeil, John. *The Consultant* (New York: Coward, McCann and Geoghegan, 1978).

Marschak, Jacob, and Roy Radner. *Economic Theory of Teams* (New Haven and London: Yale University Press, 1972).

Martin, James. *Application Development without Programmers* (Englewood Cliffs, NJ: Prentice-Hall, 1982).

Miller, Curt. "Union Dime Picks Up the Pieces in $1.5 Million Embezzlement Case," *Bank Systems and Equipment* (June 1973), pp. 34–35, 92.

Miller, Curt. "How I Embezzled $1.5 Million—And Nearly Got Away with It," *Bank Systems and Equipment* (June 1974), pp. 26–28. An interview with Roswell Steffen.

Parker, Donn B. *Crime by Computer* (New York: Charles Scribner's Sons, 1976).

Parker, Donn B., Susan Nycum, and S. Stephen Oura. *Computer Abuse* (Stanford, CA: Stanford Research Institute, 1973). Available from National Technical Information Service, U.S. Department of Commerce, Springfield, VA 22151, Order No. PB-231-320.

Parker, Donn B., and Susan H. Nycum. "Computer Crime," *Communications of the ACM* (April 1984), pp. 313–315.

Phister, Montgomery. *Data Processing Technology and Economics*, 2d ed. (Bedford, MA: Digital Press, 1979).

Price Waterhouse. *Accounting Controls in a Minicomputer Installation* (New York: Price Waterhouse, 1979).

Steier, Rosalie. "From Washington: Congress Tackles Computer Abuse," *Communications of the ACM* (January 1984), pp. 10–11.

Tettenborn, Andrew. "Some Legal Aspects of Computer Abuse," *The Company Lawyer*, vol. 2, no. 4, 1981, pp. 147–154.

Ware, Willis H. "Information Systems Security and Privacy," *Communications of the ACM* (April 1984), pp. 315–321.

Weiss, Harold. "The Latest from Equity Funding," *EDPACS* (December 1974), pp. 1–9.

CONDUCTING AN EDP AUDIT

It is a sobering experience to be in charge of the EDP audit of a data processing installation that has several hundred programmers and analysts, a large computer, and thousands of files. Obviously all data processing installations are not this size. However, in all but the smallest installation, it is normally impossible for the auditor to perform a detailed check of all the data processing carried out. How, then, can the EDP audit be performed so that the auditor obtains reasonable assurance the installation safeguards its EDP assets, maintains data integrity, and achieves system effectiveness and efficiency?

This chapter provides an overview of the approach used to conduct an EDP audit. First, it describes some techniques for simplifying and providing order to the complexity faced by auditors when making evaluation judgments on computer systems. Next, it discusses the basic steps to be undertaken in the conduct of an EDP audit. Finally, it examines some of the major decisions that auditors must make when planning and implementing an EDP audit.

DEALING WITH COMPLEXITY

Conducting an EDP audit is an exercise in dealing with complexity: somehow auditors must accomplish their objectives given the myriad of systems that now confront them. Since this is a common problem faced by many professionals, researchers have attempted to develop guidelines that reduce the complexity of judgment tasks (see, for example, Simon [1982] and Miller [1978]). These guidelines underlie the following major steps to be undertaken when conducting an EDP audit:

1 Given the purposes of the EDP audit, factor the system to be evaluated into subsystems.

2 Identify the components that perform the basic activities in each subsystem.

3 Evaluate the reliability with which each component executes its activities.

4 Determine the reliability of each subsystem and the implications of each subsystem's level of reliability for the overall level of reliability in the system.

The following sections discuss these steps in some detail since they provide the major conceptual foundations on which the remainder of this book is based.

Subsystem Factoring

The first step in obtaining an understanding of a complex system is to break it up into subsystems. A subsystem is a "unit" within the system that performs a basic *function* needed by the overall system for it to be able to attain its fundamental objectives. It is a logical concept rather than a physical concept.

The process of decomposing a system into subsystems is called "factoring." Factoring is an iterative process that terminates when auditors feel they have broken the system down into small enough parts that each part can be understood and evaluated. In other words, each subsystem is decomposed into its constituent subsystems which, in turn, are decomposed again until auditors can comprehend sufficiently the subsystem with which they are dealing. The system to be evaluated can then be described as a hierarchy of subsystems with each subsystem performing a function needed by some higher-level subsystem.

To undertake the factoring process, some basis for identifying subsystems is needed. One basis has been suggested already, namely, that the essence of a subsystem is the *function* it performs. Auditors should look first, therefore, for the fundamental functions that a system performs to accomplish its overall objectives. Different functions delineate different subsystems. For example, the overall objective of an organization (system) may be to make a profit. A critical function in the system is the receipt of customer orders. This function delineates the order entry subsystem, which is distinct from, say, the subsystem that prepares the payroll as its basic function. The order entry subsystem, in turn, can be broken down into further subsystems on the basis of function.

Besides function, two other guidelines underlie the way in which subsystems should be identified and delineated: (*a*) each subsystem should be relatively independent of other subsystems (loosely coupled); and (*b*) each subsystem must be internally cohesive in the sense that all the activities performed by the subsystem are directed toward accomplishing a single function. The theory of coupling and cohesion has been extensively developed (see, for example, Yourdon and Constantine [1979]). From an audit viewpoint, however, the pragmatic issue is that subsystems are difficult to understand and their reliability is difficult to evaluate unless they have these characteristics. An understanding of complex systems can be obtained only if each of their parts can be studied relatively independently, and this requires that the subsystems studied must be loosely coupled and internally cohesive. When auditors decompose a system into subsystems, therefore, they should evaluate the extent of coupling and cohesion in the subsystems they choose. If the subsystems are not loosely coupled and internally cohesive, they should attempt a different factoring. If no factoring seems to delineate subsystems that have these characteristics, probably the reliability of the system cannot be evaluated. Indeed, it has long been recognized that some systems cannot be audited. The theory of coupling and cohesion provides a rationale for this situation.

At least conceptually, auditors might choose to factor systems in several different ways. It has been found, however, that two ways have been especially useful when conducting EDP audits. The first way is according to the *managerial functions* needed to accomplish information processing. The second way is according to the *application functions* needed to accomplish information processing. Neither decomposition is irrevocable, and in due course others might prove better. Nevertheless, since they underlie the audit approaches advocated by most professional bodies, the following sections discuss them in more detail.

Management Subsystems The EDP management subsystems in an organization attempt to ensure that the development, implementation, operation, and maintenance of information systems proceed in a planned and controlled manner. They function to provide a stable environment in which information systems are built and operated on a day-to-day basis. Several levels of management subsystems have been identified corresponding to the organizational hierarchy and major functions performed within a data processing installation:

Management subsystem	Description of subsystem
Top management	Top management of the organization must ensure the data processing installation is well managed. It is responsible primarily for long-run policy decisions on how computers will be used in the organization.
EDP management	EDP management has overall responsibility for the planning and control of all computer activities. It also provides inputs to top management's long-run policy decision making and translates long-run policies into short-run goals and objectives.
Systems development management	Systems development management is responsible for the design, implementation, and maintenance of individual application systems.
Programming management	Programming management is responsible for programming new systems, maintaining old systems, and providing general systems support software.
Data administration	Data administration is responsible for the control and use of an organization's data including the database and library of application system files.
Security administration	Security administration is responsible for the physical security of the data processing installation.
Operations management	Operations management controls the day-to-day operations of data processing systems. It is responsible for data preparation, the data flow through the installation, production running of systems, maintenance of hardware, and sometimes maintenance of program and file library facilities.

When an EDP audit is conducted, auditors typically identify and evaluate controls in the management subsystems first for two reasons. First, management (subsystem) controls are fundamental controls in that they apply across all application systems; thus, the absence of a management control is a serious concern for the auditor. Conceptually, they constitute several layers of "onion skins" around applications (Figure 2-1). Forces that erode asset safeguarding, data integrity, system effectiveness, and system efficiency must penetrate each layer to get to a lower layer. To the extent that the outer layers of controls are intact, it is more likely the inner layers of controls will be intact. Second, it is often more efficient for auditors to evaluate management controls before application controls. If the auditor evaluates a management control once, it usually does not have to be evaluated again since it should function across all applications. For example, if the auditor finds an installation enforces high-quality documentation standards, it is unlikely the auditor will have to review the quality of documentation for each application system.

Application Subsystems   Traditionally, auditors have adopted a "cycles" approach when conducting their evaluation of the data processing systems in an

FIGURE 2-1
Management controls as onion skin layers around application controls.

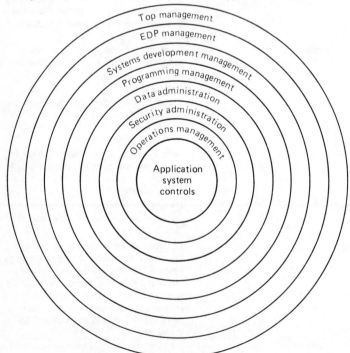

organization (see, for example, Arens and Loebbecke [1984]). Cycles vary across industries, but a typical set for a commercial or manufacturing enterprise includes (*a*) sales and collections, (*b*) payroll and personnel, (*c*) acquisitions and payments, (*d*) conversion, inventory, and warehousing, and (*e*) treasury. Each cycle is then factored into one or more application systems. For example, the sales and collections cycle comprises an order entry application system, a billing application system, and an accounts receivable application system. Application systems, in turn, are then factored into subsystems. The set of application subsystems includes:

Application subsystem	Description of subsystem
Boundary	Comprises the components that establish the interface between the user and the system
Input	Comprises the components that capture, prepare, and enter transaction data into the system
Communication	Comprises the components that transmit data among all systems in the system, and between one system and another system
Processing	Comprises the components that perform computation, classification, ordering, and summarization of data in the system
Database	Comprises the components that define, add, access, modify, and delete data in the system
Output	Comprises the components that retrieve and present data to users of the system

After auditors have identified the subsystems in an application, they then trace each major *class* of transactions through each subsystem and evaluate the reliability of controls exercised over the transactions. For each subsystem, the auditor attempts to evaluate its overall reliability with respect to each major class of transactions. Once auditors *fix* an evaluation judgment in their minds about the reliability of each subsystem, they can commence to aggregate their judgments for each subsystem to the application system level to enable them to make a judgment about the overall reliability of the application system. This process can then be extended to the cycles level and ultimately to a judgment about the overall reliability of data processing systems within the organization (Figure 2-2).

Component Identification

Subsystem functions are executed via components, the *physical* units that perform the basic activities needed to accomplish a function. The following components are used in computer systems:

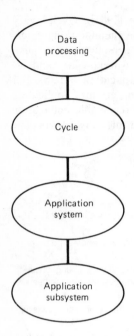

FIGURE 2-2
System levels in transaction processing.

1 Hardware, e.g., central processors, visual displays, printers
2 Software, e.g., application programs, database management systems, operating systems
3 People, e.g., data entry clerks, operators, end-users
4 Transmission media, e.g., cards, reports, source documents

Auditors obtain an understanding of how a subsystem functions by determining the components in the subsystem, the activities each component performs, and the interrelationship of components with one another. For example, three components in an input system might be a data entry clerk, a visual display unit, and an input program. To understand how the input subsystem works, auditors must understand what activities the data entry clerk performs, how the visual display is used, and how the input program interacts with the data entry clerk.

Component identification should always follow subsystem identification. There are two reasons. First, whereas auditors can rely on the relative stability of subsystems over time, components are in a constant state of flux. The basic functions of a 1950s input subsystem, for example, are still the same as those of a 1980s input subsystem; in both cases data must be captured and entered into the system. Substantial changes have occurred, however, to the components used in input subsystems: card readers have been replaced by visual display units, input programs are more user friendly, and source documents often are no longer used. Indeed, science strives continually to improve the component technology so that subsystem functions are performed more effectively and more efficiently. Auditors can cope better with technological changes if they rely on the inherent stability of subsystems and see the changes manifested in the components rather than the subsystems.

Second, people (auditors) seem better able to understand systems if they initially focus on subsystems rather than components (see, further, Miller [1978, pp. 30–31]). To be able to obtain an understanding of the overall system, auditors must be capable of aggregating their understanding of the *parts* of a system. Recall that subsystems should have three characteristics: they should be organized hierarchically, they should be loosely coupled with other subsystems, and they should be internally cohesive. These characteristics allow auditors to understand each subsystem somewhat in isolation from other subsystems and then to be able to aggregate their understanding. Components do not have these characteristics to the same extent. For example, two clerks might be tightly coupled when opening mail containing cash receipts; one carefully checks the other to prevent an impropriety. It is difficult to accumulate an understanding of the system by evaluating components if the components cannot be considered independently. Indeed, it is a useful exercise to try to assess the reliability of, say, an accounts receivable system by focusing only on components—card readers, clerks, processors, printers, etc.—rather than on subsystems.

Clearly identifying the components in a subsystem is not always an easy task, however, because the mapping between subsystems and components may not be one-to-one. A subsystem may use multiple components; for example, an input subsystem uses a card reader and a clerk. A subsystem may use only one component; for example, the database subsystem uses a single dedicated database machine. A component may service multiple subsystems; for example, the operating system performs access control functions in the boundary subsystem and memory management functions in the processing subsystem. Notwithstanding these difficulties, however, auditors must understand the mapping between subsystems and components for any particular configuration since they ultimately have to assess the reliability of a subsystem as a function of the reliability of the components that perform activities in the subsystems.

Component Reliability

A system achieves the goals of asset safeguarding, maintaining data integrity, and achieving system effectiveness and efficiency if each of its subsystems is reliable. Each subsystem is reliable only if the components that perform the basic activities in the subsystem are reliable. Once the components have been identified, therefore, auditors must evaluate their reliability with respect to each type of error or irregularity that might occur.

The reliability of a component is a function of the controls that act on that component. A control is a *pattern* of activities or actions executed by one or more components to prevent, detect, or correct errors or irregularities that affect the reliability of components. Note, components may exercise control activities on themselves or on other components. For example, clerks may review their own work to determine whether they have made pricing errors; alternatively, one clerk may review pricing activities performed by another clerk. The set of all control activities performed in a system constitutes the *control subsystem* within a system. Its function is to establish, execute, modify, and maintain control activities so the overall reliability of the system is at an acceptable level.

Controls improve the reliability of components by reducing the *expected losses* from the failure of a component. Expected losses can be reduced in two ways: (*a*) by reducing the probability of component failure and (*b*) by reducing the amount of the loss if component failure occurs. Thus, the value of a control can be assessed in terms of its cost to implement, operate, and maintain and the extent to which it reduces expected losses.

In a computer system many different types of controls are used to enhance component reliability. Recall that Chapter 1 pointed out how auditing has become more complex as the diversity of control technology increases. Some of the major classes of controls that auditors must evaluate are:

1 *Authenticity controls:* Authenticity controls attempt to verify the identity of the individual or process wanting to undertake some action in a system. Examples: passwords, personal identification numbers, digital signatures.

2 *Accuracy controls:* Accuracy controls attempt to ensure the correctness of data and processes in a system. Examples: program validation check that a numeric field contains only numerics, overflow check, financial control total, hash total.

3 *Completeness controls:* Completeness controls attempt to ensure that no data is missing and that all processing is carried through to its proper conclusion. Examples: program validation check to verify a field is not blank, record sequence numbers, financial control total.

4 *Redundancy controls:* Redundancy controls attempt to ensure that a data item is processed only once. Examples: batch cancellation stamps, record sequence numbers, circulating error files, financial control total.

5 *Privacy controls:* Privacy controls attempt to ensure that data is protected from inadvertent or unauthorized disclosure. Examples: encryption, passwords, data compaction, inference controls.

6 *Audit trail controls:* Audit trail controls attempt to ensure that a chronological record of all events that have occurred in a system is maintained. This record is needed to answer queries, fulfill statutory requirements, deter irregularities, detect the consequences of error, and allow system monitoring and tuning. Two types of audit trail must be maintained. The *accounting audit* *trail* shows the source and nature of data and processes that update the database. The *operations audit trail* maintains a record of attempted or actual resource consumption within a system.

7 *Existence controls:* Existence controls attempt to ensure the ongoing availability of all system resources. Examples: database dump and logs for recovery purposes, duplicate hardware, preventive maintenance, checkpoint and restart controls.

8 *Asset safeguarding controls:* Asset safeguarding controls attempt to ensure that all resources within a system are protected from destruction or corruption. Examples: fire extinguishers, physical barriers, passwords, file libraries.

9 *Effectiveness controls:* Effectiveness controls attempt to ensure that systems achieve their goals. Examples: regular monitoring of user satisfaction, postaudits, monitoring of frequency of use, periodic cost-benefit analyses.

10 *Efficiency controls:* Efficiency controls attempt to ensure that a system uses minimum resources to achieve its goals. Examples: logs of resource consumption, performance monitoring using hardware and software monitors, regular interviews with system users.

Note, each type of control usually appears in each subsystem. For example, an audit trail must exist as a control in the input subsystem and as a control in the processing subsystem; it must be possible to determine the past events that occurred in both subsystems. Similarly, existence controls must be established for all subsystems. If a system fails, it must be possible to reconstruct each subsystem via backup and recovery facilities.

Note, also, the above classes of controls are not mutually exclusive. A single control may fall into several categories. For example, consider a traditional control such as separation of duties. Separation of duties is an activity (action) exercised by management (a component) that may prevent, detect, or correct several types of errors or irregularities; it may discourage the submission of unauthorized transactions (authenticity control) or detect a genuine pricing error (accuracy control). By knowing the various classes of controls that exist, however, auditors have a checklist that facilitates their evaluation of the reliability of each component.

When evaluating the effects of a control on component reliability, auditors consider various attributes of the control. They seek to determine whether the control chosen is appropriate, given the nature of the processing activities that the component performs in the system. Clearly, one critical attribute is whether the control is in place and working. However, there are other attributes that impact this evaluation. One such attribute is the level of *generality* versus *specificity* of the control with respect to the various types of errors and irregularities that can occur. General controls inhibit the effects of a wide variety of errors and irregularities. In addition, their generality allows them to be more robust to change. For example, separation of duties reduces expected losses from many types of errors and irregularities, and the particular ways in which duties are separated often remain constant across system change. This generality has a cost, however; it means the control is usually less effective against particular kinds of errors and irregularities that occur. Controls in the management subsystems tend to be general controls because the components in these subsystems execute a wide variety of activities. Controls in the applications subsystems tend to be specific controls because the components in these subsystems execute activities having limited variety.

A second attribute that auditors may consider when evaluating the effectiveness of a control is whether the control acts to prevent, detect, or correct errors. The auditor focuses here on *when* controls are exercised as data flows through a computer system. *Preventive* controls stop errors or irregularities from occurring; for example, good forms design reduces the likelihood of clerks' making errors when they code source documents. *Detective* controls identify errors and irregularities after they occur; for example, an input validation program identifies data outside an allowable range of values. *Corrective* controls remove or reduce the effects of errors and irregularities after they have been identified; for example, communications software may request data be retransmitted if it has been corrupted. In general, it is more desirable to prevent errors and irregularities from occurring in the first place. But given they do occur, they must be detected; and given they are detected, they must be corrected. Auditors expect to see a higher "density" of preventive controls being exercised over components that execute activities early in system processing; conversely, they expect to see more detective and corrective controls later in system processing.

A third attribute that auditors may consider is the *number of components* used to execute the control. For example, an input validation test that examines whether a field is numeric uses few components: a program and the processor on which it operates. A backup and recovery control that restores an online, realtime, distributed system, however, will probably use many components to execute its activities: various distributed hardware, software, etc. Multicomponent controls are more complex and more error-prone, but they are usually needed to handle complex errors and irregularities. If multicomponent controls are being used, auditors must evaluate whether they are appropriate given the nature of the activities executed by the component whose reliability they increase.

Finally, the auditor may consider the *number of subsystems* impacted by a control. This is a function of whether the control acts on a component that is a *shared* component, that is, one that executes activities in multiple subsystems. In general, controls over shared components need to be more reliable and consequently need to be more complex. For example, the operating system is a component used by many subsystems. Controls to ensure the integrity of the operating system are critical, therefore, since an error or irregularity can have widespread consequences. The control technology that has evolved to protect the integrity of operating systems is now exceedingly complex.

Evaluating System Reliability

As discussed previously, assessing overall system reliability is a process of progressively making reliability evaluation judgments as the auditor proceeds from lower levels to higher levels in the system hierarchy. Table 2-1 illustrates the first decision to be made when evaluating an application subsystem. (A similar table could be constructed when evaluating management subsystems.) For a major class of transactions at the subsystem level, the reliability of the subsystem must be evaluated with respect to each type of error or irregularity that can occur. The columns of the matrix represent the different types of errors and irregularities that may be present, the rows represent the controls established to reduce expected losses from these errors or irregularities, and the elements of the matrix represent some type of reliability assessment relating a specific control to a specific error or irregularity. As shown in the matrix, it is often useful to group controls by the components whose reliability they improve, particularly if auditors trace the flow of data through components via a flowchart. The matrix and the flowchart can then be cross-referenced.

TABLE 2-1
INPUT SUBSYSTEM EVALUATION FOR CUSTOMER ORDER TRANSACTION CLASS

Errors/irregularities \\ Controls	Unauthorized customer	Unauthorized terms and credit	Incorrect quantity	Incorrect price	Untimely processing
Order-entry operator well-trained	M	M	M	M	M
Input screen layout (quality) screen organization			M	M	M
field captions and entry fields			M	M	M
field alignment, justification, spacing			M	M	M
headings and messages			M	M	M
Input program valid customer check	H				
authorized credit		H			
inventory available			M		
Sales manager override report	M	M		L	L

Note: H = high reliability; M = moderate reliability; L = low reliability.

Table 2-2 illustrates the second decision to be made. For each major class of transactions and each application system, a reliability decision must be made. The columns of the matrix represent the different types of errors and irregularities that can occur, the rows represent the application system subsystems, and the elements represent a reliability assessment relating each subsystem to each type of error and irregularity. This process of aggregation is then continued to a higher level. For example, the next level might be for a transaction cycle in the business; the rows in the matrix would show the application systems that make up the cycle.

This type of evaluation matrix can be constructed in various ways. For example, instead of using errors and irregularities as the columns, various *control objectives* might be used—for example, sales transactions must be authorized, and invoice extensions must be calculated accurately. Some audit firms have prepared extensive lists of control objectives for each cycle within an organization (see, for example, Arthur Andersen & Co. [1978]). Control objectives are simply the converse of errors and irregularities; it is always possible to translate an error or irregularity into a control objective or vice versa.

Like the system levels, errors and irregularities or control objectives must also be aggregated as the auditor moves up the hierarchy. Eventually the auditor must work out the general consequences of a particular type of error or irregularity. At the topmost level, Mair et al. [1976] identify nine major causes of loss that arise from errors and irregularities:

TABLE 2-2

EVALUATION OF CUSTOMER ORDER TRANSACTION CLASS FOR ORDER ENTRY
APPLICATION SYSTEM

Errors/ irregularities Subsystem	Unauthorized customer	Unauthorized terms and credit	Incorrect quantity	Incorrect price	Untimely processing
Boundary	H				
Input	H	H	H	H	M
Communication	M				
Processing			L	L	
Database					
Output	L		L	L	L

Note: H = high reliability; M = moderate reliability; L = low reliability.

1 Erroneous record keeping
2 Unacceptable accounting
3 Business interruption
4 Erroneous management decisions
5 Fraud and embezzlement
6 Statutory sanctions
7 Excessive costs or lost revenues
8 Loss or destruction of assets
9 Competitive disadvantage

Each of these causes of loss is a function of lower-level causes of loss (errors or irregularities). Unfortunately, the nature of these functional relationships between higher-level causes of loss and lower-level causes of loss is often complex because, as with components and subsystems, the mappings are not one-to-one. Figure 2-3 shows, for example, that erroneous management decisions are caused in part by inaccurate and incomplete data. These two causes in turn are a function of lower-level causes—for example, clerical errors or program errors. But the lower-level causes may affect multiple high-level causes; so the transition from lower levels to higher levels is rarely clear-cut. Nevertheless, in spite of these shortcomings, the process of factoring a complex system into simpler parts, obtaining an understanding of these parts, and then aggregating the parts is central to the way auditors now collect evidence on and evaluate the reliability of systems.

FIGURE 2-3
Loss and its causes as a hierarchy.

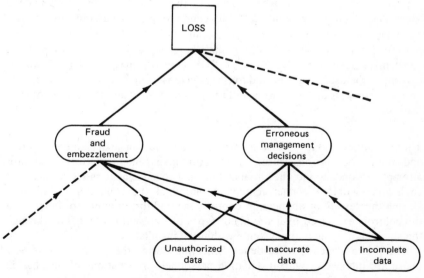

OVERVIEW OF STEPS IN AN EDP AUDIT

Bearing in mind, then, the lessons of the previous sections on how an EDP audit might be approached, Figure 2-4 flowcharts the major steps in an EDP audit. The general approach shown in the flowchart is representative of the approaches advocated by many of the professional audit organizations (see, for example, American Institute of Certified Public Accountants [1984, 1977a]). It has been formulated in light of substantial experience in performing EDP audits.

The following sections describe briefly each step in an EDP audit. Though Figure 2-4 and the ensuing discussion imply a sequential progression of audit steps, some of the steps may be carried out concurrently. For example, for efficiency purposes data required for the preliminary review evaluation and detailed review evaluation may be collected at the same time.

The Preliminary Review Phase

The first step in an EDP audit is the preliminary review of the computer installation. The objective of the preliminary review is to obtain the information necessary for the auditor to make a decision on how to proceed with the audit. At the conclusion of the preliminary review, the auditor can proceed in one of three ways:

1 Withdraw from the audit; there may be problems of independence because the auditor may lack the technical competence to perform the audit.

2 Perform a detailed review of the internal control system with the expectation that reliance can be placed upon the internal control system and the scope and extent of substantive testing can be reduced as a consequence.

3 Decide not to rely on the internal control system. There are two possible reasons for this decision. First, it may be more cost-effective to perform substantive tests directly. Second, EDP controls may duplicate controls existing in the user area. The auditor may decide it is more cost-effective to rely on these *compensating* controls and proceed to review and test these controls instead.

The preliminary review phase incorporates a review of management controls and application controls. During the review of management controls the auditor attempts to understand the organization and management practices used at each level within the management hierarchy of the computer installation. During the review of application controls the auditor attempts to understand the controls exercised over the major types of transactions that flow through the significant application systems within the installation.

The primary means of evidence collection during the preliminary review phase are interviews with installation personnel, observations of installation

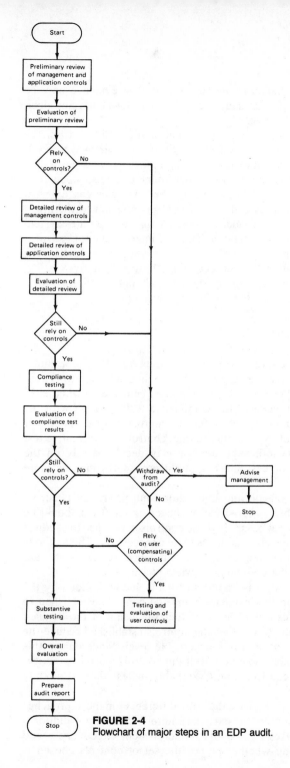

FIGURE 2-4
Flowchart of major steps in an EDP audit.

activities, and reviews of installation documentation. The evidence may be documented by completing questionnaires, constructing flowcharts and decision tables, and preparing narratives.

The preliminary review carried out by internal auditors differs from the preliminary review carried out by external auditors in three ways. First, internal auditors typically need to undertake less preliminary review work than external auditors, especially in terms of management controls, since they should be familiar with the installation already. Second, whereas external auditors focus primarily on causes of loss and controls relevant to the attest decision, internal auditors have a broader perspective that incorporates system effectiveness and efficiency considerations. Third, if internal auditors suspect serious weaknesses exist in the internal control system when they complete the preliminary review phase, rather than proceed directly to substantive testing, they still may carry out detailed testing of the internal control system with a view to making specific recommendations for improvement.

The Detailed Review Phase

The objective of the detailed review phase is to obtain the information necessary for the auditor to have an *in-depth* understanding of the controls used in a computer installation. Once again a decision must be made on whether to withdraw from the audit, proceed to the compliance testing phase with the expectation that reliance can be placed upon the internal control system, or proceed directly to a review of user (compensating) controls or substantive test procedures. For some applications the auditor may decide to rely on the internal control system; for others, alternate audit procedures may be more appropriate.

Again, both management controls and application controls are reviewed. As discussed earlier in the chapter, if possible, management controls should be reviewed first, as pervasive weaknesses in these controls may cause the auditor to deem further review of application controls to be unnecessary. The methods of obtaining and documenting evidence in the detailed review stage are primarily those used during the preliminary review phase.

In the detailed review phase, it is important for the auditor to identify the causes of loss existing within the installation and the controls established to reduce the effects of these causes of loss. At the conclusion of the detailed review the auditor must evaluate whether the controls established reduce the expected losses from these causes to an acceptable level. Since during this phase the auditor still does not know how well the controls work in practice, the evaluation assumes the controls function reliably, unless there is already evidence to the contrary.

As with the preliminary review phase there are differences in the approaches adopted by the internal auditor and the external auditor. The internal auditor is more likely to consider causes of loss that affect system effectiveness and efficiency. Besides evaluating whether or not the set of controls chosen is sufficient to reduce expected losses to an acceptable level, the internal auditor also often considers whether or not the set of controls chosen is "optimal"; that is, the system may be overcontrolled or it may be possible to achieve a satisfactory level of control using fewer or less costly controls. If the internal auditor considers the system of internal controls to be unsatisfactory, again, rather than proceed directly to review and testing of compensating controls or substantive test procedures, compliance testing still may be undertaken as a basis for making specific recommendations for improvement.

The Compliance Testing Phase

The objective of the compliance testing phase is to determine whether or not the system of internal controls operates as it is purported to operate. The auditor seeks to determine whether or not alleged controls in fact exist and whether or not they work reliably.

Besides the manual evidence collection techniques described previously, often the auditor must use computer-assisted evidence collection techniques to determine the existence and reliability of controls. For example, to evaluate the validation controls in an input program, the most cost-effective way may be to use a test data generator to produce test data for input to the program.

At the conclusion of the compliance testing phase, the auditor again must evaluate the internal control system in light of the evidence collected on the reliability of individual controls. The general process of evaluation and the choices of further audit procedures available are the same as those for the previous phases.

Review and Testing of User (Compensating) Controls

In some cases the auditor might decide not to rely on internal controls within the computer installation because users exercise controls that compensate for any weaknesses in the EDP internal control system. For example, even though weak controls may exist over the transit of source data to the computer installation, users may carefully reconcile their own control totals with those produced as output from application system programs.

From an external audit viewpoint, evaluating compensating controls may be a more cost-effective way of completing the audit. The internal auditor may be concerned, however, that compensating controls do not represent a needless duplication of controls; in other words, it may be worthwhile to eliminate either some user controls or some computer controls.

The Substantive Testing Phase

The objective of the substantive testing phase is to obtain sufficient evidence so the auditor can make a final judgment on whether or not material losses have occurred or could occur during computer data processing. The external auditor expresses this judgment in the form of an opinion as to whether a material misstatement of the accounts exists. Usually the internal auditor is concerned with a broader perspective: given the state of the internal control system, have losses occurred or could they occur in the future because of weaknesses in the controls used to safeguard assets and to achieve data integrity, system effectiveness, and system efficiency?

Davis et al. [1983] identify five types of substantive tests that can be used within a data processing installation:

1 Tests to identify erroneous processing
2 Tests to assess the quality of data
3 Tests to identify inconsistent data
4 Tests to compare data with physical counts
5 Confirmation of data with outside sources

Many of these tests require computer support; for example, generalized audit software can be used to select and print confirmations. However, the fundamental processes involved in carrying out substantive testing and issuing the audit report for computer systems are the same as those for manual systems.

SOME MAJOR AUDIT DECISIONS

By presenting only an overview of the major steps in an EDP audit, the previous section glossed over the difficulties involved in making some of the major decisions required when carrying out an EDP audit. Since these decisions can impact substantially the audit approach adopted for a specific system, the following sections highlight the nature of these decisions and some of the considerations involved in making the decisions.

The Evaluation Judgment

Perhaps the most difficult decision for auditors to make during an EDP audit is the evaluation judgment. The evaluation judgment must be made at the end of the preliminary review phase, at the end of the detailed review phase, at the end of the compliance testing phase, and at the end of the substantive testing phase. It impacts whether the auditor will continue with the audit, whether the internal control system can be relied upon, what controls are critical to the audit and how they should be tested for compliance, what extent of substantive testing is needed, and, finally, whether or not the system has satisfactorily safeguarded assets, maintained data integrity, and achieved system effectiveness and efficiency.

Since the evaluation decision is a *judgment* decision, there is no single accepted method of making the decision. However, Table 2-3 shows a conceptual representation of the judgment decision to be made. The columns of the matrix are causes of loss, in this case, circumstances that would cause a loss if they occurred during the data capture stage of an application system. The rows are controls exercised over the causes to reduce the expected loss. The elements of the matrix might be some rating of the effectiveness of each control at reducing the expected loss from each cause, the reliability of the control with respect to each cause in light of compliance testing results, or the marginal benefits and costs of exercising the control. In Table 2-3 the elements simply show the existence of a relationship between the different controls and causes of loss.

In terms of the matrix, conceptually the auditor performs three types of evaluations: a columnar evaluation, a row evaluation, and a global evaluation. The *columnar* evaluation involves asking the question: For a given cause of loss, do the controls exercised over the cause reduce the expected loss from the cause to an acceptable level? As discussed previously, the auditor asks this question prior to and after testing the reliability of controls.

TABLE 2-3
MATRIX CONCEPTUALIZATION OF CONTROLS THAT REDUCE EXPECTED LOSSES DURING DATA CAPTURE (RECOGNITION AND MEASUREMENT OF AN ECONOMIC EVENT)

Control \ Cause of loss	Recognition/ measurement inaccurate	Recognition/ measurement incomplete	Event not recognized/ measured	Measurement/ recognition unauthorized
Hire high-quality staff	✔	✔	✔	✔
Ensure staff are trained	✔	✔	✔	
Ensure division of duties exists	✔	✔	✔	✔
Procedures well-designed	✔	✔	✔	
Procedures well-documented	✔	✔	✔	
Supervise staff properly	✔	✔	✔	✔
Well-designed tasks	✔	✔	✔	
Pleasant work environment	✔	✔	✔	
Restrict physical access				✔

✔ Denotes functional relationship.

The *row* evaluation involves asking the question: Do the benefits of having a control exceed the costs? To facilitate this evaluation, the elements of the matrix might contain the net marginal benefits (marginal benefits less marginal costs) of each control with respect to each cause of loss.

The *global* evaluation involves asking the question: What is the optimal set of controls for the organization? The answer to this question requires somehow a joint evaluation of columns and rows to be made. Whereas from a columnar perspective it may not be worthwhile to have a control, from a row perspective the benefits of the control when it is exercised over *all* causes of loss may exceed its cost.

With respect to the global evaluation question, there are still two more complicating factors. First, the marginal benefits and costs of a control often depend on what controls are being exercised already; that is, the benefits and costs of a control are conditional. Second, there is an overriding constraint on how many controls should be introduced into a system. This constraint applies when for all controls that still might be exercised, the marginal benefits of any one control exceed the marginal costs of that control.

The matrix conceptualization of the evaluation judgment also can be used to illustrate the different functions of the external and internal auditor. The external auditor is concerned primarily with columnar evaluation: Has the expected loss from a cause of loss been reduced to a satisfactory level? Further, the external auditor focuses on those causes of loss relating to lack of safeguards over assets or violation of data integrity. Whether or not the choice of controls is optimal in a global sense is a secondary consideration.

The internal auditor performs all three types of evaluation. Columnar evaluations include also causes of losses relating to ineffective and inefficient systems. The internal auditor is concerned, furthermore, with whether the marginal benefits of a control exceed the marginal cost (row evaluation) and whether the choice of controls is optimal from a global viewpoint (joint row and columnar evaluation).

Unfortunately, *how* a columnar, row, or global evaluation should be performed is still a research area. With respect to the columnar evaluation, some professional bodies have designated minimum control standards, that is, control standards that must be met for the auditor to consider controls over a cause of loss as being satisfactory (see, further, Canadian Institute of Chartered Accountants [1970] and EDP Auditors Foundation, Inc. [1983]).

Timing of Audit Procedures

One of the important decisions the auditor must make when planning an EDP audit is the timing of audit procedures to be performed. The timing of EDP audit activities has been a controversial area. Some auditors argue little change is needed to the traditional schedule of interim work, end-of-period work, and postperiod-end work. Nevertheless, they recognize that audit use of the computer for evidence collection purposes often requires substantial advance preparation, for example, scheduling computer time for audit purposes, preparation of audit programs and test decks, and obtaining files for testing (see, also, Davis et al. [1983]). Other auditors argue fundamental changes are needed to the timing of audit procedures when computer systems must be evaluated. These auditors emphasize audit participation in the design phases of an EDP system. If this latter view is accepted, audits will be performed at three stages in the life of a system: (*a*) during the design phase, (*b*) during the operations phase, and (*c*) during postaudits (Figure 2-5).

There are two major reasons given for design phase participation by EDP auditors. First, changing a system to include necessary controls after it has been implemented can be expensive. Second, it is often difficult, if not impossible, for the auditor on the basis of a periodic review to understand a system that has taken several thousand work-hours to design and implement. To avoid these problems, some EDP auditors argue both external and internal auditors should, at a minimum, review and evaluate the design of computer controls at various major checkpoints in the system development process.

The major concern about design phase participation by EDP auditors has been the potential effects on the auditor's independence. Controversy surrounds whether or not design phase participation impairs an auditor's ability to evaluate a system from a detached, objective viewpoint, particularly if the initial design reflects closely the auditor's recommendations.

Rittenberg [1977] surveyed internal and external auditors, EDP management, and top management to investigate the perceived effects of design phase participation on auditor independence. In general he found these groups believed design phase participation decreased auditor independence, but there

FIGURE 2-5
Auditor involvement in the systems life cycle.

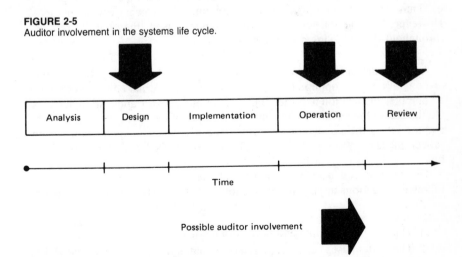

were several ways in which auditor independence could be strengthened to compensate, at least partially, for the effects of design phase involvement:

1 Increase the auditor's technical knowledge of EDP

2 Assign different auditors to design phase audit work and postinstallation audit work

3 Recruit auditors with more extensive EDP experience

4 Set up an EDP audit section within the internal audit department specializing in EDP auditing

5 Obtain greater top management support

The groups surveyed believed the first two methods of increasing auditor independence were especially important, namely, increasing the technical knowledge of EDP auditors and assigning different auditors to the postaudit of a system.

Audit Use of the Computer

Another important decision the auditor must make when planning the audit is whether to use the computer to assist the audit or whether to audit without using the computer. The two approaches are commonly called "auditing around the computer" and "auditing through the computer."

The terms are unfortunate since they derive from the period when auditors were auditing around the computer because of technical incompetence rather than arriving at a decision through a cost-benefit analysis of the two approaches. Thus the term "auditing around the computer" has negative connotations. However, because the terms are still commonly used, they will be retained throughout the following discussion.

Auditing around the Computer   Auditing around the computer involves arriving at an audit opinion through examining the internal control system for a computer installation and the input and output *only* for application systems. On the basis of the quality of the input and output of the application system, the auditor infers the quality of the processing carried out. Application system processing is not examined directly. The auditor views the computer as a black box.

The auditor can usually audit around the computer when either of the following situations applies to application systems existing in the installation:

1 The system is simple and batch oriented.

2 The system uses generalized software that is well-tested and used widely by many installations.

Sometimes batch computer systems are just an extension of manual systems. These systems have the following attributes:

1 The system logic is straightforward and there are no special routines resulting from the use of the computer to process data.

2 Input transactions are batched and control can be maintained through the normal methods, for example, separation of duties and management supervision.

3 Processing primarily consists of sorting the input data and updating the master file sequentially.

4 There is a clear audit trail and detailed reports are prepared at key processing points within the system.

5 The task environment is relatively constant and few stresses are placed on the system.

For these well-defined systems, generalized software packages often are available. For example, software vendors have developed payroll, accounts receivable, and accounts payable packages. If these packages are provided by a reputable vendor, have received widespread use, and appear error-free, the auditor may decide not to test directly the processing aspects of the system. The auditor must ensure, however, that the installation has not modified the package in any way and that adequate controls exist over the source code, object code, and documentation to prevent unauthorized modification of the package.

Not all generalized software packages make application systems amenable to auditing around the computer. Some packages provide a set of generalized functions that still must be selected and combined to accomplish application system purposes. For example, database management system software may provide generalized update functions, but a high-level program still must be written to combine these functions in the required way. In this situation the auditor is less able to infer the quality of processing from simply examining the system's input and output.

The primary advantage of auditing around the computer is simplicity. Auditors having little technical knowledge of computers can be trained easily to perform the audit, though they should be managed by a computer audit specialist.

There are two major disadvantages to the approach. First, the type of computer system where it is applicable is very restricted. It should not be used for systems having any complexity in terms of size or type of processing. Second, the auditor cannot assess very well the likelihood of the system degrading if the environment changes. The auditor should be concerned with the ability of the system to cope with a changed environment. Systems can be designed and programs can be written in certain ways so that a change in the environment will not cause the system to process data incorrectly or for it to degrade quickly. These aspects will be discussed in later chapters.

Auditing through the Computer For the most part the auditor now is involved in auditing through the computer. The auditor can use the computer to test: (a) the logic and controls existing within the system and (b) the records produced by the system. Depending upon the complexity of the application system being audited, the approach may be fairly simple or require extensive technical competence on the part of the auditor.

There are several circumstances where auditing through the computer must be used:

1 The application system processes large volumes of input and produces large volumes of output that make extensive direct examination of the validity of input and output difficult.

2 Significant parts of the internal control system are embodied in the computer system. For example, in an online banking system a computer program may batch transactions for individual tellers to provide control totals for reconciliation at the end of the day's processing.

3 The logic of the system is complex and there are large portions that facilitate use of the system or efficient processing.

4 Because of cost-benefit considerations, there are substantial gaps in the visible audit trail.

The primary advantage of this approach is that the auditor has increased power to effectively test a computer system. The range and capability of tests that can be performed increases and the auditor acquires greater confidence that data processing is correct. By examining the system's processing, the auditor also can assess the system's ability to cope with environmental change.

The primary disadvantages of the approach are the high costs sometimes involved and the need for extensive technical expertise when systems are complex. However, these disadvantages are really spurious if auditing through the computer is the only viable method of carrying out the audit.

Selecting Application Systems for Audit

As a general rule the auditor should select for audit those application systems most critical to the continued existence of the organization. Since budget constraints usually apply, the auditor wants to select those application systems where the highest payoff will be obtained. The following sections provide some guidelines for selecting application systems for audit.

User Audits as a Selection Basis A useful way of finding out which application systems have problems is to perform a user audit. When application systems do not function correctly, users are affected because reports are late or incorrect, source data coding is difficult, error resubmission is onerous, etc. The control clerks in the user area responsible for gathering and batching source data, error correction, and error resubmission often know the fundamental weaknesses in an application system. User management can provide information on any problems experienced with the quality and timeliness of reports produced by the system.

The auditor also needs to investigate carefully a further aspect of the user environment. Sometimes an application system has detrimental effects on the quality of work life of its users. This can produce a variety of problems that impact asset safeguarding, data integrity, and system effectiveness and efficiency. At one extreme users attempt to directly sabotage the system. At the other extreme they simply show disinterest in the system. Eventually the application system degrades through lack of active user support. Sometimes these problems are covert and are difficult to identify.

The auditor can carry out the user audit in a formal or informal manner. If the user audit is part of the evaluation of an application system's effectiveness, user opinions may be solicited through questionnaires or structured interviews. If the auditor is simply carrying out a user audit to identify potential application systems for further investigation, the approach may be more informal. However, even if the approach is informal. it still needs to be planned and the results documented in working papers. The auditor's problem always is to ask those questions that elicit a response enabling problems to be identified. Asking the "right" questions requires forethought and planning.

Application System Characteristics as a Basis for Selection Perry [1974] provides other guidelines that the auditor can use to choose a specific application system for audit. The table on p. 56 is based upon his initial list.

Beside the audit of application systems where problems are apparent, internal auditors should perform a cyclical review of systems that seem to function well. This review examines ways of improving these systems.

SUMMARY

Conducting an EDP audit is an exercise in dealing with complexity. To cope with this complexity, the auditor needs to factor the system to be evaluated into subsystems, identify the components that perform the basic activities in each subsystem, assess the reliability of each component, evaluate the reliability of the subsystems, and progressively aggregate the judgments on each subsystem to arrive at a global judgment on the overall reliability of the system.

The steps involved in carrying out an EDP audit are similar to those involved in carrying out the audit of a manual system. First, the auditor performs a preliminary review of the computer installation to obtain an understanding of

Selection guideline	Explanation
Financial system	The auditor should give major attention to those systems providing financial control over the assets of the corporation, e.g., cash receipts and disbursements, payroll, accounts receivable and payable.
High-risk system	Some application systems are riskier than others because: 1 They are susceptible to various kinds of losses, e.g., fraud and embezzlement. 2 Their failure may cripple the organization, e.g., failure to process payroll causes employees to strike. 3 They interface with other systems, and errors generated permeate these other systems.
High potential for competitive damage	Some systems give an organization a competitive edge in the marketplace, e.g., an effective strategic planning system. Others through patents, copyrights, etc., are major sources of revenue for the organization. Others through their loss would destroy the image of the organization.
Technologically advanced system	If a system utilizes advanced technology, e.g., a database management system, distributed hardware and software, or technology with which the installation has little experience, it is more likely the system will be a source of control problems.
High-cost system	Systems that are costly to develop are often complex systems presenting many control problems.

how the installation is managed and the major application systems being processed. Second, if the auditor expects to rely on the internal control system, a detailed review is carried out. Third, the auditor tests the reliability of those controls critical to the audit judgment. Fourth, substantive test procedures are performed. Finally, an audit opinion must be given. After all steps, the auditor evaluates the internal control system and decides whether to proceed with the audit or take alternative steps.

Throughout the EDP audit several difficult decisions must be made. Each evaluation of the reliability of the internal control system requires a complex joint evaluation of piecemeal evidence. The auditor must make a decision on whether to become involved at the design phase. Whether or not to audit through or around the computer must be evaluated carefully. The critical systems on which the audit will focus also must be chosen.

REVIEW QUESTIONS

2-1 What is meant by "subsystem factoring"? Why does an auditor factor a system into subsystems? On what basis should an auditor factor a system into subsystems?

2-2 What is meant by "loose coupling" and "strong internal cohesion" of subsystems? Why are these desirable goals in the factoring process?

2-3 Briefly explain the difference between management controls and application controls. Give an example of each type of control and explain why it is either a management or an application control.

2-4 For each of the following activities, identify the level of management that has primary responsibility for performing the activity:

a Control and use of the organization's database

b Maintenance of old application systems

c Provision of general systems support software

d Implementation of long-run computer policy decisions

2-5 Why might a serious weakness in management controls result in the auditor's not examining application controls?

2-6 Classify each of the following controls by application subsystem (e.g., input, communication, processing):

a A control to prevent unauthorized access to computing resources

b A control to ensure that erroneous data is corrected and reentered into the computer system

c A control to ensure data recorded on a form is authorized

d A control to prevent the user of a query language from making unauthorized inferences about private data in the database

e A control to ensure that messages are not lost when they are transmitted from one computer to another computer

2-7 What is meant by "fixing" the evaluation judgment?

2-8 Briefly explain the cycles approach to conducting an EDP audit.

2-9 Briefly explain the difference between a subsystem and a component.

2-10 Why should the auditor focus on subsystems first and then on components?

2-11 What is meant by a control? Is a control a system or a component?

2-12 Briefly explain the relationship between controls, causes of loss, and expected loss. Be sure to define precisely what you mean by expected loss. Give an example to illustrate the relationship.

2-13 Classify each of the following controls by type (e.g., authenticity, accuracy, audit trail):

a Password

b Encryption

c Hash total

d Batch cancellation stamp

e Database dump

2-14 Why is the auditor interested in the generality versus the specificity of a control?

2-15 Briefly explain the difference between preventive, detective, and corrective controls. Give an example of each. Why is it sometimes useful to classify controls in this way?

2-16 Why might the auditor consider the number of components needed to execute a control?

2-17 When does a control impact the reliability of multiple subsystems?

2-18 Briefly explain the relationship between control objectives and errors and irregularities. Give an example to illustrate the relationship.

2-19 What is meant by a hierarchy of causes of loss? Why is it useful to conceptualize the causes of loss as a hierarchy? What problems exist with conceptualizing the causes of loss in this way?

2-20 Briefly explain the nature and purpose of the preliminary review phase. Are there any differences in the way internal and external auditors might perform the preliminary review?

2-21 Explain the nature of compensating controls. Give an example of a compensating control and show how its existence might affect the audit approach.

2-22 Briefly explain the relationship between the detailed review phase and the compliance testing phase of an EDP audit.

2-23 What courses of action might the auditor take after completing the compliance testing phase of an EDP audit?

2-24 List three types of substantive tests that the EDP auditor may perform and give an example of how the test may be performed.

2-25 List the major differences between the way an internal auditor might perform the various phases in an EDP audit and the way an external auditor might perform the phases.

2-26 Briefly explain how the means of evidence collection change between the detailed review and compliance testing phases in an EDP audit. Why do they change?

2-27 If the relationship between controls and causes of loss is conceptualized as a matrix, briefly explain how the row evaluation, columnar evaluation, and global evaluation relate to audit objectives.

2-28 Briefly explain why the evaluation judgment usually is very difficult for the auditor to make.

2-29 Why do some auditors argue they must become involved in design phase auditing? What problems can arise when the auditor gets involved at the design stage of a system? How might these problems be overcome?

2-30 Why does an EDP audit often involve more advance preparation than the audit of a manual system? Be sure to point out the specific areas where more advance preparation often is necessary.

2-31 Give an example of a system where auditing around the computer would be appropriate and an example where auditing through the computer would be necessary. Explain why the approaches are appropriate for the examples you give.

2-32 Briefly explain how user audits can help the auditor to identify application systems where the payoff from an audit may be high.

2-33 Consider a manufacturing company. Give two examples of EDP application systems that would be important from the viewpoint of the external auditor and two that would be relatively unimportant.

MULTIPLE CHOICE QUESTIONS

2-1 Factoring is the process of:
a Identifying the components of a system
b Identifying the interfaces between subsystems
c Decomposing a system into component activities
d Decomposing a system into subsystems

2-2 Which of the following is *not* a guideline for the factoring process:
a Focus on functions rather than activities
b Ensure subsystems are tightly coupled
c Proceed in a hierarchical manner
d Ensure subsystems are internally cohesive

2-3 Which of the following is *not* a management subsystem:
 a Audit trail subsystem
 b Data administration subsystem
 c Security administration subsystem
 d System development management subsystem

2-4 Which of the following is *not* an application subsystem:
 a Hardware
 b Boundary
 c Input
 d Database

2-5 When auditors attempt to understand data processing systems, which *order* of decomposition are they most likely to follow:
 a Applications, cycles, transactions, controls
 b Cycles, applications, controls, transactions
 c Cycles, applications, transactions, controls
 d Transactions, applications, cycles, controls

2-6 Which of the following is likely to be the most stable over time:
 a Components
 b Output
 c Subsystems
 d Controls

2-7 When auditors *fix* their evaluation judgments, they should:
 a Focus primarily on components
 b Aggregate their judgments on the basis of transaction type
 c Review the judgment as each higher level in the hierarchy of subsystems is reached
 d Focus only on the global judgment as they consider higher levels in the system hierarchy

2-8 Which of the following is *not* a component:
 a Database management system
 b Backup and recovery procedure
 c Data entry clerk
 d Printer

2-9 A control is:
 a A component that prevents errors
 b A pattern of activities that prevents, detects, or corrects errors
 c A subsystem
 d Both b and c above

2-10 Controls act to:
 a Eliminate expected losses
 b Reduce the probability of a cause of loss occurring
 c Prevent the cause of the loss occurring
 d Reduce the probability of the cause of loss occurring and/or reduce the amount of loss if the cause of loss does occur

2-11 Expected losses are defined as:
 a Losses anticipated in the normal course of business
 b The losses that occur when an error or irregularity occurs
 c The losses that occur when an error or irregularity occurs multiplied by the probability of the error or irregularity occurring

    d Losses anticipated when a system does not meet effectiveness and efficiency objectives

2-12 Match the following:

I Postaudit	A Effectiveness control
II Database dump and log	B Authenticity control
III Password	C Accuracy control
IV Overflow check	D Existence control

    a I-A; IV-C; II-D; III-B
    b III-A; I-B; II-D; IV-C
    c IV-A; III-C; I-B; II-D
    d II-C; IV-A; III-B; I-D

2-13 Match the following:

I Encryption	A Completeness control
II Hash total	B Efficiency control
III Checkpoint and restart	C Privacy control
IV Hardware monitoring	D Existence control

    a IV-C; II-D; I-A; III-B
    b II-A; I-C; III-D; IV-B
    c III-D; IV-C; II-A; I-B
    d I-A; III-D; IV-B; II-C

2-14 The classification of controls as preventive, detective, or corrective is useful to the auditor because:

    a Only preventive and detective controls are relevant to the audit decision

    b It highlights when the controls are exercised during the flow of data through a computer system

    c Corrective controls can only ever be considered as compensating controls

    d It helps the auditor identify which controls are missing

2-15 Which of the following is a high-level cause of loss:

    a A data coding error made by an input clerk

    b A logic error in a utility program

    c Business interruption caused by a corrupted master file

    d A formatting error in a management report program

2-16 The objective of the detailed review phase is:

    a To obtain an in-depth understanding of the controls used in a computer installation

    b To test the reliability of controls critical to the audit decision

    c To decide on the substantive test approach to be used

    d To obtain a preliminary understanding of the controls to be tested for compliance

2-17 Auditors may decide to test compensating controls because:

    a They possess insufficient technical knowledge to test computer controls

    b It may be more cost-effective to rely on compensating controls

    c They have decided to proceed directly to substantive testing

    d The internal control system cannot be relied upon anyway

2-18 Which of the following is *not* a substantive test:

    a A test to compare data with a physical count

    b A test to assess the quality of data

c A test to compare data with an outside source

d A test to determine whether a data definition standard has been followed

2-19 In a matrix conceptualization of the evaluation judgment where the rows are controls and the columns are causes of loss, the global evaluation judgment involves determining:

a Whether the benefits of each control exceed the costs

b Whether the most cost-effective set of controls has been chosen to reduce expected losses to an acceptable level

c Whether each potential loss has been reduced to an acceptable level

d Whether a material error may exist in the accounts

2-20 Auditing around the computer might be used when:

a There are significant gaps in the audit trail in the computer system

b The internal controls in the computer system cannot be relied upon

c Processing consists primarily of sorting the input file and updating the master file sequentially

d The auditor lacks technical expertise to perform a direct evaluation of computer controls

2-21 A user audit often is a useful way of selecting a specific application system for audit because:

a It enables the auditor to check users' understanding of their computer system

b It is generally a more cost-effective way of selection compared with using application system characteristics as a basis for selection

c A user audit does not require formal planning, and it can be carried out informally

d Users often can provide important information on the strengths and weaknesses in an application system

EXERCISES AND CASES

2-1 Many audit organizations now follow the "cycle" approach when evaluating an internal control system (see, for example, American Institute of Certified Public Accountants [1979] and Arthur Andersen & Co. [1978]). This approach involves classifying transactions by cycles, converting the broad objectives of internal control into specific objectives for these classifications of transactions, and evaluating the controls in place in light of these objectives. Five major cycles of a business can be identified: revenue, expenditure, production or conversion, financing, and external financial reporting. For the revenue cycle the American Institute of Certified Public Accountants [1979] lists the following eight objectives:

1 The types of goods and services to be provided, the manner in which they will be provided, and the customer to whom they will be provided should be properly authorized.

2 Credit terms and limits should be properly authorized.

3 The prices and other terms of sale of goods and services should be properly authorized.

4 Sales-related deductions and adjustments should be properly authorized.

5 Deliveries of goods and services should result in preparation of accurate and timely billing forms.

6 Sales and related transactions should be recorded at the appropriate amounts and in the appropriate period and should be properly classified in the accounts.

7 Cash receipts should be accounted for properly on a timely basis.

8 Access to cash receipts and cash receipts records, accounts receivable records, and billing and shipping records should be suitably controlled to prevent or detect within a timely period the interception of unrecorded cash receipts or the abstraction of recorded cash receipts.

The Canadian Institute of Chartered Accountants [1970] gives four control objectives for the processing phase in a computer system:

1 Ensure the completeness of data processed by the computer.

2 Ensure the accuracy of data processed by the computer.

3 Ensure that all data processed by the computer is authorized.

4 Ensure the adequacy of management (audit) trails.

Required: Write a short report showing how the two sets of objectives can be reconciled.

2-2 You are on the staff of an external audit firm that audits a small-medium size financial institution. One day you receive a copy of a letter from the president of the financial institution to the partner-in-charge of the audit. The letter indicates that the client is considering replacing its existing computer with 20 desk-top minicomputers and converting its application systems to the minicomputers. You are alarmed at this "radical" move and its audit implications so you go to the partner-in-charge to request time to investigate the proposed changes and, if need be, suggest some design alternatives. The partner-in-charge hesitates when you make your request. She explains that she believes you should not become involved at this stage because it will affect the firm's independence. However, she concedes there may be problems with the changes proposed and she asks you to prepare a brief for her.

Required: Write a report to the partner outlining some of the control and audit problems that may arise with the proposed changeover to the minicomputers and suggest why you should become involved with the client at this stage.

2-3 The accounting department of a small company is responsible for payment of creditors. It receives a copy of each purchase order issued, a receiving document when the goods arrive, and the vendor's invoice. All documents are date-stamped upon receipt and filed securely. When the receiving document and vendor's invoice arrive, a clerk matches details and checks the accuracy of items and computations on the documents. A second clerk then prepares a disbursement voucher and a check for payment and gives the check, the voucher, and the supporting documents to a manager who examines them before signing the check.

Required: List the control objectives for the above operations. Prepare a controls matrix where the columns show causes of loss and the rows show the controls in existence to reduce expected losses. The elements of the matrix should show which controls act on the causes of loss. How well does the system of internal control allow the control objectives to be accomplished?

2-4 You are a staff EDP auditor in a public accounting firm. The firm has just acquired a new client—a small manufacturing organization. The client uses a minicomputer for its data processing.

All of the application systems are straightforward batch systems with well-defined input and output. However, the client uses a database management system that was purchased initially for its bill-of-materials application system. Furthermore, all application systems now use the DBMS.

Required: You are on the first audit of the new client. The partner-in-charge asks you to advise him on whether to plan the audit through the computer or around the computer. Write a short report giving your recommendations and the reasons for your recommendations.

2-5 You have just been engaged as the external auditor for a medium-sized automotive servicing organization. The organization obtains most of its revenue in three ways: (*a*) it services motor vehicle fleets, (*b*) it sells spare parts, and (*c*) it converts vehicles from petroleum to LP gas consumption.

The organization uses a local area network of three microcomputers running the following application software packages:

1 General ledger
2 Debtors/invoicing
3 Creditors
4 Payroll
5 Spare parts/inventory
6 Job costing
7 Bill-of-materials

All applications are relatively straightforward. Job costing and bill-of-materials, for example, are used to support workshop activities: a supervisor specifies the type of service required for a vehicle, and the bill-of-materials application identifies the standard parts and labor required for the job.

The three microcomputers are placed in different locations: (*a*) workshop—to enter data about a job or enquire about a job, spare part, etc.; (*b*) accounting—to process data related to debtors, creditors, payroll, and general ledger and to prepare management reports; and (*c*) spare parts—to provide over-the-counter service to customers and workshop personnel. The operating system used to support the microcomputers allows concurrent but controlled access to a central database. All the software used by the organization is well-known, well-tested, and supplied by a reputable vendor. The general manager assures you that no modifications have been made to the software. Indeed, he indicates there is no one on the staff of the organization with the EDP knowledge needed to carry out modifications to the software.

Required: Outline how you would approach the audit of this organization. In particular, indicate how the use of generalized application software that supposedly has not been modified will affect your audit strategy.

ANSWERS TO MULTIPLE CHOICE QUESTIONS

2-1 d	2-6 c	2-11 c	2-16 a
2-2 b	2-7 d	2-12 a	2-17 b
2-3 a	2-8 b	2-13 b	2-18 d
2-4 a	2-9 d	2-14 b	2-19 b
2-5 c	2-10 d	2-15 c	2-20 c
			2-21 d

REFERENCES

American Institute of Certified Public Accountants. *Auditor's Study of Internal Control in EDP Systems* (New York: American Institute of Certified Public Accountants, 1977a).

American Institute of Certified Public Accountants. *Management, Control and Audit of Advanced EDP Systems* (New York: American Institute of Certified Public Accountants, 1977b).

American Institute of Certified Public Accountants. *Report of the Special Advisory Committee on Internal Accounting Control* (New York: American Institute of Certified Public Accountants, 1979).

American Institute of Certified Public Accountants. *Statement on Auditing Standards No. 48: The Effects of Computer Processing on the Examination of Financial Statements* (New York: American Institute of Certified Public Accountants, 1984).

Arens, Alvin A., and James K. Loebbecke. *Auditing: An Integrated Approach*, 3d ed. (Englewood Cliffs, NJ: Prentice-Hall, 1984).

Arthur Andersen & Co. *A Guide for Studying and Evaluating Internal Accounting Controls* (Chicago: Arthur Andersen & Co., 1978).

Canadian Institute of Chartered Accountants. *Computer Control Guidelines* (Toronto, Canada: The Canadian Institute of Chartered Accountants, 1970).

Davis, Gordon B., Donald L. Adams, and Carol A. Schaller. *Auditing and EDP*, 2d ed. (New York: American Institute of Certified Public Accountants, 1983).

EDP Auditors Foundation, Inc. *Control Objectives* (Carol Stream, IL: EDP Auditors Foundation, Inc., 1983).

Jancura, Elise G. *Audit & Control of Computer Systems* (New York: Petrocelli/Charter, 1974).

Jancura, Elise G., and Fred L. Lilly. "SAS No. 3 and the Evaluation of Internal Control," *Journal of Accountancy* (March 1977), pp. 69–74.

Loebbecke, James K., and George R. Zuber. "Evaluating Internal Control," *Journal of Accountancy* (February 1980), pp. 49–56.

Mair, William C., Donald R. Wood, and Keagle W. Davis. *Computer Control & Audit*, 2d ed. (Altamonte Springs, FL: The Institute of Internal Auditors, Inc., 1976).

Miller, James Grier. *Living Systems* (New York: McGraw-Hill, 1978).

Perry, William E. "Selecting an EDP System for Audit," *EDPACS* (April 1974), pp. 1–8.

Perry, William E. *Selecting EDP Audit Areas* (Altamonte Springs, FL: EDP Auditors Foundation, 1980).

Perry, William E. *Planning EDP Audits* (Altamonte Springs, FL: EDP Auditors Foundation, 1981).

Porter, W. Thomas, and William E. Perry. *EDP: Controls and Auditing*, 4th ed. (Belmont, CA: Kent Publishing Company, 1984).

Rittenberg, Larry E. "The Impact of Internal Auditing During the EDP Application Design Process on Perceptions of Internal Audit Independence." Unpublished Ph.D. Dissertation, University of Minnesota, Minneapolis, MN, 1975.

Rittenberg, Larry E. *Auditor Independence and Systems Design* (Altamonte Springs, FL: The Institute of Internal Auditors, 1977).

Simon, Herbert A. *The Sciences of the Artificial*, 2d ed. (Cambridge, MA: The M.I.T. Press, 1982).

Watne, Donald A., and Peter B. B. Turney. *Auditing EDP Systems* (Englewood Cliffs, NJ: Prentice-Hall, 1984).

Yourdon, Edward, and Larry L. Constantine. *Structured Design: Fundamentals of a Discipline of Computer Program and Systems Design* (Englewood Cliffs, NJ: Prentice-Hall, 1979).

PART TWO

THE MANAGEMENT CONTROL FRAMEWORK

The auditor's primary objective in examining the management control framework for a computer installation is to see that management manages well. A recurring theme throughout this book is that the quality of management influences both the quality of controls at the detailed level and the extent to which assets are safeguarded and data integrity, system effectiveness, and system efficiency will be achieved.

Examining and evaluating the management control framework is important for two reasons. First, the auditor can use the evaluation as a basis for determining the nature and extent of detailed testing to be carried out on individual application systems. Second, the quality of the management control framework influences the likely quality of computer data processing in the future. The auditor can form an opinion on whether application systems are likely to degrade in the future.

The task of evaluating management controls is not easy, however. Perhaps the greatest difficulty is to know how the presence or absence of a management control might affect asset safeguarding, data integrity, system effectiveness, and system efficiency. Consider, for example, the audit of the computer systems that support a small social club. If the club does not have an information systems master plan, it is unlikely that this lack will have serious ramifications for, say, maintenance of data integrity. If a major organization that is about to embark upon a policy of decentralizing its computer operations does not have a master plan, however, the auditor will have serious concerns. Thus, the importance of management controls varies across situations, probably more so than the importance of application controls. Somehow auditors must develop the ability to recognize when a management control is important and when it is not. In essence they must be capable of generating scenarios that articulate the implications of missing or weak management controls for the reliability of the systems they audit.

The next six chapters present the essence of good EDP management practices. Auditors cannot evaluate management unless they know what management *should* be doing; thus, it behooves EDP auditors to gain expertise in the management of computers.

Chapter	Overview of contents
3 Top Management and EDP Management	Discusses top management's and EDP management's role in planning, organizing, staffing, directing, and controlling the EDP function
4 System Development	Provides a contingency perspective on normative models of the system development process that the auditor can use for purposes of evidence collection and evidence evaluation
5 Programming Management	Provides a contingency perspective on normative models of the programming life cycle; discusses alternative ways of organizing and managing the programming team; examines various software development aids
6 Data Administration	Discusses the functions performed by the data and database administrators; examines the control problems posed by the data and database administration roles
7 Security Administration	Discusses how to conduct a security program; identifies major security threats and remedial measures; examines disaster recovery and insurance
8 Operations Management	Discusses the functions of operations management: computer operations; communications network control; data preparation; production work flow control; file library; documentation library; performance monitoring

CHAPTER 3

TOP MANAGEMENT AND EDP MANAGEMENT

CHAPTER OUTLINE

MULTIPLE CHOICE QUESTIONS
EXERCISES AND CASES
ANSWERS TO MULTIPLE CHOICE QUESTIONS
REFERENCES

One finding consistently appears in empirical studies that examine why computer systems succeed or fail: the active participation of top management and the existence of high-quality EDP management are essential for the continuing successful development and implementation of computer systems.

How can the auditor evaluate top management and EDP management involvement in a computer installation? One useful way is to evaluate each of the functions management must perform: planning—determining the goals of the installation and the means of achieving these goals; organizing—providing facilities and grouping activities and personnel to accomplish required tasks; staffing—selecting and training personnel required to accomplish tasks; directing—coordinating activities, providing leadership and guidance, and motivating personnel; and controlling—comparing actual performance with budgeted performance as a basis for adjusting actions.

Each section in this chapter outlines how the auditor can evaluate these functions. It is assumed that the reader already is familiar with the fundamentals of good management (see, for example, Koontz et al. [1984]); thus, the chapter highlights those aspects of management that are somewhat different for the EDP function.

EVALUATING THE PLANNING FUNCTION

Top management and EDP management must address two fundamental planning questions. First, should the organization start to use or continue to use computers for its data processing requirements? Second, if the organization uses computers for its data processing, how should they be used?

Table 3-1 shows the major plans formulated for a computer installation, whether they are typically short-run or long-run, and the group responsible for their development. The various plans needed follow the life cycle of an installation. When management first contemplates using computers, a feasibility study is performed to examine the costs and benefits of the long-run use of computers in the organization. A decision to use computers results in a preinstallation plan, which is a short-run plan needed to guide the changeover process. These two plans may be needed again at a later stage in the installation's life when new hardware and software are purchased. The ongoing operations of the installation require a master plan to provide long-run directions and various short-run project plans to guide the development of individual systems. Finally, the installation needs a disaster recovery plan that is typically short-run since it depends on the particular hardware/software configuration and the systems developed at a point in time.

TABLE 3-1
MAJOR PLANS NEEDED FOR A COMPUTER INSTALLATION

Plan	Brief description	Time period covered	Responsible group
Feasibility study	Investigates costs and benefits of long-run use of computers and recommends whether or not the organization should use computers	Long run	Steering committee
Changeover plan	Specifies the tasks and activities to be carried out during changeover to computer data processing, a new hardware/software configuration, or a new organization structure	Short run	Steering committee
Master plan	Strategic plan for a computer installation setting out its long-run objectives and the tasks necessary for accomplishing these objectives	Long run	Steering committee
Project plan	Forms the basis of the budget for developing a specific system and ensures the project is consistent with the goals and objectives set out in the master plan	Short run	EDP management
Disaster recovery plan	Plan needed to restore the installation's files and data processing capabilities within the required time in the event of a disaster	Short run	EDP management

Function of a Steering Committee in Planning

Top management participates in the planning function for a computer installation via a steering committee. A steering committee should be formed at the outset when an organization first contemplates using a computer for its data processing. The steering committee plays an important part in the initial feasibility study, the purchase of a computer and its setup, and later decisions on further hardware, software, and systems needed.

Strategic planning is the primary function of the steering committee. The steering committee must produce a master plan for the computer installation that guides the installation's long-run development and allows EDP management to establish short-run objectives and policies. However, Ditri et al. [1971] argue the committee has five other functions to perform:

1 Establishes the size and scope of the EDP function
2 Sets priorities within these bounds
3 Assures a viable communications system exists between EDP and its users
4 Monitors the accomplishments of the computer installation
5 Measures the results of EDP projects in terms of return on investment, etc.

A steering committee seems to work best if it comprises only a small number of members. The chairperson must be the senior organization executive ultimately responsible for the computer installation. The EDP manager should act as secretary to the committee. Other members of the committee are senior management from major user areas. At various times temporary members of the committee exist to provide specialist advice on technical matters. The committee also should have as a member the internal audit manager.

Feasibility Study

Management requires a feasibility study for any major planning decision in the life of a computer installation. For example:

1 Should a computer be used for the organization's data processing requirements?
2 Should a new application system be implemented or a major change be made to an old application system?
3 Should new hardware and software be purchased and, if so, what should be the required features of the hardware and software?
4 Would a major structural change to an organization increase its data processing capabilities?

In one sense a feasibility study is a *tool* of the planning process rather than a plan itself. In another sense it constitutes a plan since it documents the deliberations of management and provides recommendations and guidelines for implementing these recommendations.

To illustrate the process of undertaking a feasibility study, consider a decision on whether or not to use a computer. Two major steps are involved. First, a *preliminary survey* must be undertaken to determine quickly whether computer data processing may be worthwhile and whether a comprehensive feasibility study is warranted. Second, if it seems computer data processing is worthwhile, a *feasibility study proper* must be undertaken.

Carrying out a preliminary survey involves the three major steps shown in the table at the top of the following page.

Major step	Examples of activities involved
Planning the survey	Setting objectives; setting time schedules–interim and final; setting resource constraints–time, staff, financial; identifying organizational constraints; staffing the task force group
Data gathering	Characteristics of existing systems–input and output, processing, volumes and timings of data, peakloads; strengths and weaknesses of existing systems; new systems that need developing; old systems that need modification or scrapping; potential areas of computer use; costs and benefits of computer use; resource considerations; organizational changes needed; long-run impact of computer use
Report preparation and recommendations	Whether or not to use computers; areas of computer use; constraints that should be applied; resources needed; basic direction to be followed for acquisition, implementation, and use; time schedule for acquisition and implementation

Management must form a task force group to perform the preliminary survey. The task force group should have well-defined terms of reference, be properly staffed and managed, and receive adequate support. It usually functions best if its size is small so group interaction problems are reduced.

If, on the basis of the preliminary survey, management decides to proceed to the feasibility study proper, the task force group size usually is expanded and the steps performed during the preliminary survey repeated; however, the analysis and evaluation now are more in depth and rigorous. The final report must recommend whether computer data processing should be introduced or not. If the report recommends using computers, it also should provide information on the means of computer processing to use—whether it should be in-house or provided by a service center; the computer facilities required—hardware, software, personnel, floor space, etc.; and the means of converting to computer data processing.

The description of the computer facilities required provides the basis for preparing a *manual of specifications*. The manual of specifications is a statement of requirements distributed to hardware and software vendors for use in preparing their proposals.

Perhaps the most difficult aspect of a feasibility study is deciding whether a data processing investment will provide an acceptable rate of return. In theory, evaluating a data processing investment is straightforward: the net cash flows over the life of the investment are estimated and discounted at the required rate of return; if the net present value is not negative, the investment is acceptable (see, for example, Bierman and Smidt [1975]). Unfortunately, for several reasons the practice is fraught with complexities. First, data processing investments often must be evaluated in terms of major intangible benefits and costs—for example, improved customer relationships, better management decision making, and increased trade union conflict. Second, calculating the discount rate to be used is difficult. Finance theory prescribes that it be the risk-adjusted rate of return, but as discussed further in Chapter 23, the data required to calculate the risk adjustment may be difficult to obtain. Third, many data processing projects are now interdependent, and their financial viability is difficult to evaluate in isolation from other projects. For example, data processing systems are changing from being stand-alone, application-oriented systems to being database-oriented systems supporting multiple users. Given the database is a shared resource, how should the costs of establishing and maintaining data be allocated to the respective users?

As a consequence of these complexities, the financial evaluation technique chosen should depend on the uncertainty surrounding the project and the extent to which it affects other projects. For example, if the project being considered is the development of a traditional batch application system, conventional return-on-investment evaluation techniques can be applied. If the project being considered is a decision support system, other evaluation techniques might be used. For example, Keen [1981] advocates a technique called "value analysis." It involves providing a small threshold dollar amount that enables a prototype system to be developed, and then in light of experience with the prototype, progressively expanding or contracting expenditures to refine and further develop the system or terminate its use. Parker [1982] advocates a similar technique for data-managed systems. Chapters 22 and 23 examine these matters further.

Changeover Plans

Changeover plans specify the tasks that must be accomplished, their interdependencies, and the constraints that apply when the organization undertakes some major change related to its data processing; for example, acquisition and installation of a new computer, establishing a new hardware/software configuration, or changing the organization structure. From a control viewpoint the important aspect of a changeover plan is that it forces management to articulate the necessary activities involved. Consequently, the changeover is likely to proceed in a more orderly manner. To illustrate a changeover plan, some of the typical activities included in a plan for setting up a computer installation would be:

1 Completion of hardware/software specifications
2 Evaluation and selection of hardware/software
3 Physical planning and site preparation
4 Final testing and acceptance of hardware/software
5 Delivery and installation of hardware/software
6 Design of an organization structure for the computer installation

Whereas the changeover plan budgets resources for these activities at a global level, specific project plans then have to be prepared for each activity to show how it is to be accomplished.

Master Plan

A major responsibility of the steering committee is the preparation of a master plan for the computer installation. A master plan is the rolling plan for the next several years' (two–five years) activities. It may cover a fairly long or fairly short period depending on the rate of change within the organization. Some organizations by their very nature experience frequent changes both internal and external to the organization that make long-run planning difficult, for example, research and development organizations. Other organizations are relatively stable and the task of planning is not so onerous.

The master plan focuses on whether computers should continue to be used for the organization's data processing and, if so, how they should be used. Given computers will continue to be used, the steering committee must decide on new areas of application. These new areas of application may in turn require decisions to be made on new hardware/software configurations and major structural changes within the organization.

There are four major components of a master plan: (*a*) a summary of the organizational strategic plan, (*b*) the information systems strategic plan, (*c*) the information systems requirements plan, and (*d*) the information systems applications and facilities plan. The following sections give a brief description of each component and the means by which each is prepared. Note that the preparation of the master plan occurs in stages (Figure 3-1).

Organizational Strategic Plan The organizational strategic plan provides the overall charter under which all units in the organization, including the information systems function, must operate. It is the primary plan prepared by top management of the organization that guides the long-run development of the organization. It includes a statement of mission, a specification of strategic objectives, an assessment of environmental and organizational factors that impact the attainment of these objectives, a statement of strategies for achieving the objectives, a specification of constraints that apply, and a listing of priorities.

The steering committee must examine carefully the organizational strategic plan and identify those aspects of the plan that are pertinent to the information systems function. Relevant parts of the plan should be summarized (or expanded) and included in the master plan. The organization's strategic plan is the starting point for deriving all other components of the information systems master plan.

Information Systems Strategic Plan The steering committee has the responsibility for translating the organizational strategic plan into a strategic plan for the information systems function; the steering committee must determine what implications the overall objectives have for the development of information systems within the organization. For example, a financial institution may determine that to improve customer service, it must diversify from traditional-

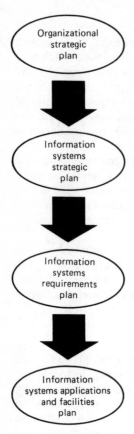

FIGURE 3-1
Four-stage model of information systems master plan.

money management activities into leisure and pleasure activities. One implication of this overall objective may be that the organization has to develop information systems to support holiday travel. Consequently, the steering committee may designate the development of travel information systems as a major priority for future developmental work. In addition, it may set certain constraints and dictate certain design strategies to be followed in developing these systems; for example, all travel systems have to be developed within two years, customers' financial data must be integrated with their travel data to facilitate overall management of their affairs, and the software developed must be amenable to a later shift toward decentralized operations.

Unfortunately, how the steering committee formulates the information systems strategic plan from the organizational strategic plan is not a clear-cut process. Nevertheless, a few formal approaches are starting to emerge, and auditors might examine whether any of these approaches could be useful to the organizations they are evaluating. Three such approaches are:

1 *Strategy set transformation*: This approach has been advocated by King [1978]. It focuses on identifying the claimant groups in an organization (e.g., creditors, shareholders, managers), their respective goals, and the organizational strategy that affects each group. Alternative information systems strategies for meeting the needs of each group are then devised and evaluated.

2 *Strategic grid approach*: This approach has been advocated by McFarlan and McKenney [1983]. It identifies the position of the information system activity relative to the rest of the organization. Four possibilities exist: (*a*) strategic—information systems are critical to the current and future strategies of the organization; (*b*) factory—information systems are critical to well-defined organizational functions but not to future strategic applications; (*c*) support—information systems are useful but not critical to daily organizational functions; (*d*) turnaround—information systems are in transition from a support state to a strategic state. By analyzing where current and planned information systems are placed in the grid, the steering committee can determine how closely corporate planning and information systems planning need to be integrated and whether a changed direction is needed for the information systems function.

3 *Customer resource life cycle approach*: This approach has been advocated by Ives and Learmonth [1984]. An organization provides goods or services that are resources acquired by its customers. The organization can use information systems strategically to support its customers in the various phases of the resource life cycle; for example, an information system might be implemented for customers to determine their product requirements.

Whatever the methodology used, ultimately the steering committee must specify both the long- and short-run goals for the information systems department and determine the priorities to be assigned to each goal.

Information Systems Requirements Plan   The information systems requirements plan defines an information system architecture for the information systems department. The architecture specifies the major organizational functions (processes) needed to support planning, control, and operations activities and the data classes associated with each function. The functions are grouped according to some criterion; for example, they create or use the same data class or they lend themselves to being performed by a single physical unit in the organization. For the financial institution previously considered, various marketing functions may be identified: market definition, market research, advertising and promotion, etc. The data classes needed to support these functions would include market surveys, trend analysis, and customer demographics.

Several "enterprise" analysis techniques are available to assist in the preparation of an information systems architecture:

Technique	Description
Critical Success Factors (CSF)	Executives are interviewed to determine their goals, the key areas in an organization where performance must be satisfactory if these goals are to be attained, and the measures needed to assess performance (see Rockart [1979]).
Business Systems Planning (BSP)	BSP is a top-down approach to developing an information systems architecture. It comprises four major steps: define business objectives, define business processes, define data classes, and define the IS architecture (see IBM [1981]).
Business Information Analysis and Integration Technique (BIAIT)	BIAIT provides seven key questions to be asked of an organization. Based on the answers to these questions, a normative set of information requirements are proposed (see Carlson [1979]).
Business Information Control Study (BICS)	BICS is a methodology that combines various aspects of the BSP and BIAIT approaches (see Zachman [1982]).
Ends/Means (E/M) Analysis	E/M analysis involves specifying the objectives to be achieved, the means of achieving these objectives, and relevant effectiveness and efficiency measures (see Bowman et al. [1983]).

Again, which technique should be used to formulate the information systems architecture is not always a clear-cut decision. Davis [1982] argues the choice is determined by the uncertainty surrounding the information requirements determination process. Some techniques are more appropriate when there are high levels of uncertainty, others when the level of uncertainty is low.

Once the architecture has been formulated, the steering committee must assign priorities to the various components in the architecture. These priorities direct the information systems management to those areas where the architecture must be refined and expanded and application systems must be developed, modified, or replaced.

Information Systems Applications and Facilities Plan   On the basis of the information systems architecture and its associated priorities, information systems management can develop an information systems applications and facilities plan. This plan includes:

1 Specific application systems to be developed and an associated time schedule
2 Hardware and software acquisition/development schedule
3 Personnel acquisition and development schedule
4 Financial resources required

5 Facilities required

6 Organizational changes required

The decisions documented in the information systems applications and facilities plan guide the short-run activities undertaken by the information systems department so they are consistent with the long-run goals of the organization.

Project Plan

A project plan forms the basis of a budget for a particular project; for example, EDP management should use project plans to monitor the progress of application system development and implementation activities. System development, programming, and operations management typically perform the detailed work needed for project planning. EDP management, or in some cases the steering committee if a major project is involved, reviews and approves the final plan.

The major activities involved in project planning are:

1 Identify tasks to be performed.

2 Identify relationships between tasks.

3 Determine time constraints on the project.

4 Determine resource requirements of each task.

5 Determine any other constraints applying.

6 Sequence tasks.

Several techniques have been developed to facilitate project planning activities; for example, work breakdown structure (WBS), project planning (GANTT) charts, program evaluation and review technique (PERT), critical path method (CPM), graphical evaluation and review technique (GERT), and network simulation (see, further, Cleland and King [1975]).

A project plan should be submitted to the same kind of economic analysis undertaken during feasibility studies. Management must take into account the risk of the project and use discounted cash flow procedures to determine if the return on the investment is acceptable.

Disaster Recovery Plan

A data processing installation can suffer disaster for many reasons: hurricanes, fire, sabotage, fraud, hardware failure. Management must plan for such disasters if the organization is to be capable of continuing its operations when disaster occurs. Since the resources in an installation usually are in a constant state of flux—new applications are being developed, existing systems are being modified, personnel are turning over, new hardware is being acquired, etc.—

the disaster recovery plan must be updated on a regular basis. Indeed, its existence and currency are a major concern for the auditor. Chapter 7 examines disaster recovery planning in more detail.

EVALUATING THE ORGANIZING FUNCTION

The planning process establishes goals and objectives for a computer installation. The organizing process structures personnel, facilities, and information flows to enable these goals and objectives to be achieved.

On one point organization design theorists are clear. If organizations are to achieve goals effectively and efficiently, organization structures simply cannot be allowed to evolve. Organization design must be an ongoing, conscious, rational decision process within organizations.

Organizational Structure Issues

What should be the form of the organizational structure adopted within a computer installation? Traditionally, two types of hierarchical structure have been used (Figure 3-2): (*a*) a functional form—systems analysts are grouped together, programmers are grouped together, etc.; and (*b*) a project form—though some support staff may be grouped functionally, systems analysts, programmers, etc., are grouped together by application areas or specific projects.

There are various advantages and disadvantages to these structures. Using the functional form, advantages accrue through greater task specialization. Using the project form, advantages accrue because personnel are closer to the user area. Nevertheless, in spite of their historical prominence, these two hierarchical structures are not the only ways to organize a computer installation. Organization theorists argue in some cases alternate structures may be desirable; furthermore, sound theory now exists to support the choice of structures that improve the effectiveness and efficiency of organizations.

The basis for these contentions is *contingency theory*. Contingency theory evolved from empirical studies carried out on organizations over a long period of time. Based on these studies the theory states: first, there is no single best way to organize; and second, not all ways of organizing are equally effective.

The results of a number of studies show the primary variable affecting the choice of a particular organization structure is *task uncertainty*. Lawrence and Lorsch [1969] found successful organizations increasingly *differentiate* their subunits in response to higher task uncertainty, yet at the same time they *integrate* these subunits to achieve the coordination necessary for successful completion of a task. Successful organizations facing stable environments tend to have mechanistic types of organization structures with well-defined hierarchies of authority, standards, etc. Successful organizations facing unstable environments tend to have "organic" types of organization structures with delegation of decision making, less formal lines of authority and responsibility, etc.

Task uncertainty affects the amount of information an organization must process. As task uncertainty increases, the organization needs more informa-

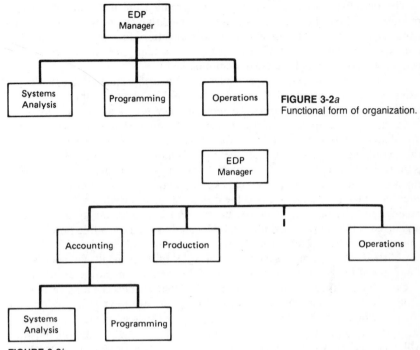

FIGURE 3-2a
Functional form of organization.

FIGURE 3-2b
Project form of organization.

tion to cope with this uncertainty. Different organizational structures facilitate information processing in different ways. Galbraith [1977] provides a detailed discussion of how the following organization design strategies can be used to improve an organization's information processing capabilities:

Strategy	Explanation
Environmental management	Instead of modifying its own structure, the organization attempts to modify its environment and reduce uncertainty. Strategies include cooperation, contracting, coopting, and coalescing.
Creation of slack resources	The organization reduces its level of performance and consequently reduces the number of exceptions occurring.
Creation of self-contained tasks	Tasks are decomposed into subtasks and units are provided with all the resources necessary to accomplish the subtasks.
Investment in vertical information systems	The capacity of existing communication channels is increased, new channels are created, and new decision mechanisms are introduced.
Creation of lateral relations	Lateral decision processes are employed to cut across lines of authority, e.g., liaison roles, task forces, teams, matrix organization.

The first two strategies are designed to reduce the need for information processing. The last three strategies are designed to increase the organization's capacity to process information. If the organization does not choose at least one strategy when faced with greater task uncertainty, reduced performance and slack resources will be created automatically.

To illustrate these concepts, consider two types of project groups that might exist within a mature EDP installation: one involved in the design and implementation of a straightforward application system, and the other involved in the initial developmental work to support the organization's move toward a distributed database system. In the former group there is low task uncertainty; thus, contingency theory predicts the group is more likely to be successful if it is organized along traditional project lines—a clear hierarchy of authority, rigorous standards, well-defined checkpoints, etc. For the latter group, however, contingency theory predicts the group will be more successful if it adopts an organic type of organization structure. For example, the group might be organized rather loosely and physically located to promote a free flow of ideas among its members. To reduce uncertainty, new information channels might be established; for example, members of user groups might be coopted as members of the project group and a special committee might be established.

Contingency theory provides a framework that enables the auditor to think about how well management has chosen an organization structure for the computer installation. The auditor must attempt to gauge the task uncertainty facing the computer installation, the amount of information the organization will need to cope with this uncertainty, and whether the organization structures chosen are appropriate for the information processing needs of the computer installation.

Centralization versus Decentralization

A major organization design issue often facing top and EDP management is whether to centralize or decentralize computer facilities. The issue arises for three major reasons. First, if a centralized computer installation continues to grow, it may become awkward and unwieldy to manage. Second, top management may have made a centralization/decentralization decision for the organization as a whole. If top management decides to create divisions scattered around the country, the computer installation may have to respond by decentralizing its own facilities. Third, many organizations now find themselves confronting this decision unexpectedly. With the widespread availability of cheap minicomputers and microcomputers, it is often difficult to prevent managers from purchasing machines for tneir department's use. Decentralization of information processing occurs by default. If development, implementation, and operation of information systems are to be controlled and coordinated, formal guidelines for decentralization must be established.

There are alternative ways of centralizing and decentralizing computer operations (see, also, Davis and Olson [1985] and King [1983]):

Centralized functions	Decentralized functions
1 All functions	
2 Overall coordination	All other functions, i.e., development, implementation, and operations
3 Hardware/software operations	Systems development and implementation
4 Hardware/software operations, and systems implementation	Systems development
5 Systems development and implementation	Hardware/software operations

The centralization/decentralization decision can have an important impact on data integrity and system effectiveness and efficiency. Consider, for example, the following:

Organization strategy	Advantages	Disadvantages
Decentralize systems analysis	Better systems designed through greater awareness of user needs	Greater difficulties in standardizing and integrating systems
Centralize programming	Economies of scale	Slower response to changes needed
Decentralize hardware	Fewer data errors because data can be input directly from remote locations	Loss of processing power through use of smaller machines
Centralize software	Greater standardization	Software not attuned to the needs of individual users

Miller [1978] argues that the tendency of all living systems (including organizations) is toward specialization of function and decentralization. This allows the subsystems within the system to be more robust to change; as a consequence, the system is better able to survive. If the system is not to become pathological, however, decentralization must be accompanied by an increase in integrating mechanisms so the system still can control its subsystems.

If Miller's theory of living systems is correct, computer systems will tend to become more decentralized. Auditors should focus on whether or not decentralization moves have been accompanied by an increase in integrating mechanisms;

for example, the establishment of new information channels and increased emphasis on planning and budgeting.

Selecting Hardware/Software Facilities

Another aspect of organizing is choosing suitable hardware/software facilities. Selecting hardware/software facilities involves two major steps: first, preparing a manual of specifications for distribution to hardware/software vendors; and second, evaluating vendor proposals and selecting a final hardware/software configuration.

The manual of specifications is prepared to communicate to vendors the needs of the computer installation. It forms the basis for the vendor's proposal. From a control viewpoint the manual of specifications must: (a) clearly state the needs of the installation and (b) act as a turnaround document to ensure uniformity in proposals tendered and thereby facilitate evaluation. Table 3-2 shows the contents of a manual of specifications.

TABLE 3-2
CONTENTS OF A MANUAL
OF SPECIFICATIONS

1 Description of the organization
2 Data processing requirements
  a Major application systems to be developed
  b Workloads
  c Suggested processing methods
3 Hardware requirements
  a CPU
  b Peripherals
  c Data preparation
4 Software requirements
  a Compilers
  b Systems software
  c Generalized packages
  d Database management
5 Support required
  a Maintenance
  b Training
  c Backup
6 Adaptability requirements
  a Upgrading of hardware/software
  b Changeover facilities for other machines
7 Constraints
  a Processing
  b Delivery dates for hardware/software
8 Changeover requirements
  a Test time
  b Test facilities
9 Pricing schedule

The bases to be used for evaluating vendor proposals should be planned formally. Test data may have to be prepared. Management also must decide on the relative weightings to give different criteria in the evaluation. Chapter 21 provides an extended discussion of the different techniques that can be used for evaluating hardware and software.

Methods Standards

To guide and control its activities, a computer installation must have: (*a*) methods standards and (*b*) performance standards. Methods standards establish uniform practices, procedures, rules, etc., to be followed in an installation. Performance standards establish yardsticks for measuring the performance of a computer installation. Methods standards as an *organizational* technique are discussed briefly in this section. Performance standards as a *control* technique are discussed later in the chapter.

Within a computer installation, methods standards have four major purposes:

1 Facilitate communication between interdependent parties, for example, between systems analysts and programmers.
2 Reduce the effects of personnel turnover; new staff are not affected by the idiosyncracies of their predecessors.
3 Reduce the effects of technological change, for example, by facilitating hardware/software changeover.
4 Form the basis for performance standards by providing a common measurement base.

As a general rule, standards should be pervasive and be formally documented in the computer installation's standards manual. Brandon [1963] provides a detailed discussion of the standards required for activities in various areas: systems analysis, programming, and operations. A major problem in formulating standards is determining their appropriate level. Very detailed standards are costly to develop and maintain and personnel made responsible for them become loathe to update them. The standards manual can become outdated quickly. Superficial standards are also useless since they provide inadequate guidance for performing tasks.

EVALUATING THE STAFFING FUNCTION

Staff are some of the critical elements in the overall computer control structure. The quality of staff directly influences the quality of systems produced by the installation.

The master plan indicates staffing needs into the future. Two factors emphasize the need for ongoing staff planning. First, historically, good computer personnel have been in short supply. This situation seems unlikely to change in the near future. Second, some staff needed in a computer installation have highly technical skills. Acquiring these staff can be very difficult. Staff planning involves taking an inventory of the current staff capabilities, determining future staff requirements, assessing the likely turnover of staff, and determining how positions will be filled.

Personnel Acquisition

To hire the right person for a job, it is important both management and the applicant for the job understand clearly the requirements of the job. For each position in the computer installation, a formal documented job specification must exist defining the nature of the job, its duties, and opportunities for advancement. The job specification forms the basis of advertising the job and evaluating applicants for the job.

Personnel can be recruited internally or externally to the organization. There are various advantages and disadvantages to each method. Internal recruitment enhances morale and captures existing experience within the organization. External recruitment may result in a better match between the job specification and the applicant's skill set. It also injects new knowledge into the organization.

Management can obtain data to evaluate applicants through interviews, aptitude tests, references, résumés, and scholastic records. Some basic control procedures that should be applied include:

1 Background checking of references, résumés, scholastic records, etc.
2 Screening applicants for mental and physical health
3 Bonding of key employees
4 Explanation of organization protocol to be observed, e.g., matters not to be discussed in public
5 General organization indoctrination

Personnel Development

Personnel development involves (*a*) establishing promotional and personal growth opportunities for employees and (*b*) education. These activities maintain employee morale and the skill set necessary for carrying out the computer installation's tasks.

Providing promotional and personal growth opportunities can be a special problem in computer installations. On the one hand employees are often young, have experienced rapid promotion, and are quickly left with few opportunities for advancement. On the other hand the technical expertise of the "older" systems analyst or programmer makes them immobile within the organizational hierarchy. These problems have not been well-addressed.

Regular staff reviews should be carried out for three reasons: (a) to assess whether an employee warrants promotion, (b) to identify opportunities for the employee's personal growth, and (c) to identify the employee's strengths and weaknesses. Employees should understand clearly the nature of the staff review and the basis on which they will be evaluated. Management should discuss with them their overall ratings so there is scope for appeal and counsel them.

Sometimes staff reviews give insufficient emphasis to identifying opportunities for the employee's personal growth. If promotional opportunities are scarce, personal growth may be the only means of preventing high staff turnover. Management must seek more responsible and challenging positions for employees, yet at the same time determine whether employees have earned the necessary trust and have the required skill set for these positions.

Because of the high rate of obsolescence in computer technology, training and continuing education are critical for the successful ongoing operations of the computer installation. There is a tendency during high-pressure periods to forgo training. The long-run implications of this decision can be disastrous for employee morale and coping with new technology.

Training must not be haphazard. Those areas where employee expertise is lacking should be identified. Proposed coursework should be carefully evaluated. Employees attending training sessions should disseminate the knowledge acquired upon returning to the installation.

Personnel Termination

Personnel termination may be voluntary or involuntary. In either case, certain control procedures should be exercised. The severeness of the procedures depends on whether the employee is disgruntled or not. Examples of these control procedures are:

1 Upon an employee's giving notice, if the employee is a key person, management should be immediately informed. The employee's supervisor should be contacted to determine reasons for leaving.

2 Upon termination, a checklist should be prepared so that (a) keys and ID badges are recovered, (b) employee passwords are cancelled, (c) distribution lists are changed, (d) all reports, books, documentation, etc., are returned, and (e) any equipment issued is returned.

3 The terminating employee should provide training for the replacement employee.

4 If the employee is disgruntled, the employee should be assigned to noncritical areas.

5 Exit interviews should be given so that (a) any areas of discontent are determined, (b) reminders are given on secrecy oaths, etc., and (c) potential problems are identified.

EVALUATING THE DIRECTING FUNCTION

Directing is a complex management function designed to motivate employees. Koontz et al. [1984] propose the *purpose* of directing to be achieving harmony of objectives; that is, an individual's objectives must not conflict with group objectives. The *process* of directing is based upon three major principles: first, unity of command whereby individuals should report to a single supervisor to avoid conflict in instructions and promote a greater feeling of responsibility for results achieved; second, direct supervision whereby management should supplement objective methods of supervision with direct personal contact; and third, appropriate variation of supervisory techniques to suit different people, tasks, and organizational environments.

Evaluating top management's and EDP management's ability to direct people may seem an abstruse type of activity for the EDP auditor to perform. Clearly, many EDP auditors have insufficient training in the behavioral sciences to be able to perform an in-depth evaluation. Nevertheless, EDP auditors (whether they be external or internal auditors) must still attempt to gauge (if only superficially) management's ability to direct. Ineffective directing can lead to system failure as surely as erroneous design specifications can lead to system failure: EDP staff may not understand their overall purposes, they may be poorly motivated, they may not communicate the results they achieve, etc.

How can the auditor evaluate how well top management and EDP management perform the directing function? In a few pages, this question can barely be addressed. It requires the auditor to understand areas fundamental to effective directing: how to motivate subordinates, how to give leadership, and how to communicate clearly the work requirements to subordinates.

Human Motivation

The research and writings on human motivation are immense (see, especially, Dunnette [1976]). There has been a steady progression of motivation theories advanced: Maslow's hierarchy of needs theory, Herzberg's motivator-hygiene theory, Vroom's expectancy theory. However, a contingency theory of motivation now seems to be well-accepted: there is no one best way of motivating people; the best way depends on individuals and their environment. Consider, for example, two systems analysts in a computer installation, both of whom are well-paid. On the basis of some motivation theories, a manager may feel that it is necessary to provide "challenging" work to motivate them. However, contingency theory emphasizes that it is still necessary to take into account the individual differences of both analysts. One analyst, for example, may have a high propensity for dealing with uncertainty; the other may feel acute stress and anxiety when faced with high uncertainty. Clearly it would be unwise to assign the latter analyst to a project that involved high levels of task uncertainty, even though the project may be a challenging one. If this is done, the outcome may be a poorly designed and implemented project; furthermore, an inappropriate match of tasks and personnel can mean staff turnover occurs.

The auditor usually has neither the time nor the expertise to go through a computer installation and evaluate from a motivation viewpoint the match of individuals with the jobs they perform. What the auditor can do, however, is examine variables that often indicate when motivation problems exist, for example, staff turnover statistics, frequent failure of projects to meet their budget, and absenteeism levels.

Leadership

Koontz et al. [1984] argue a manager who adopts an effective leadership style exhibits certain characteristics: awareness—they understand the essentials of motivation and leadership; empathy—they can place themselves in the position of others; objectivity—they can examine and evaluate events unemotionally; and self-knowledge—they are aware of the results their actions evoke.

Leadership styles vary along a continuum from authoritarian to democratic. As with motivation, organization theorists advocate a contingency theory of leadership: there is no one best leadership style for all people and all situations; it depends on personalities and tasks. For example, if a project team is developing a decision support system for strategic planning purposes and a high level of task uncertainty exists, a democratic style of leadership probably will be more successful than other leadership styles; in fact, at different times leadership of the group may switch to the person having most expertise with the problem being addressed at that point in time. Even within the group, some individuals require more guidance than others. They may be inexperienced or lack confidence in their abilities; thus, a more authoritarian style of leadership may be needed with these personnel.

Again, the auditor usually has neither the time nor the expertise to perform an in-depth evaluation of management's ability to choose the appropriate leadership style in a given situation. Instead, as with motivation, the auditor must be aware of indicators that suggest poor leadership: staff turnover, projects failing to meet budgets, etc.

Communications

Because so much of the work in a computer installation requires precision, effective and efficient communications between management and subordinate staff are critical. Messages must be clearly understood, the integrity of messages must be assured, and any message sent must obtain the attention of the receiver.

The auditor has both formal and informal sources of evidence for evaluating how well top and EDP management communicate with their subordinate staff. Many of the formal sources of evidence have been covered earlier in the chapter: master plans, project plans, methods standards, etc. The minutes of meetings also are an important source of formal evidence on the success or lack thereof of communications within an installation.

The informal sources of evidence include interviews with installation staff, the existence of a sense of purpose among members of a project group, general awareness by the staff of other developments within the installation even though they may not be directly involved with these developments, etc. Often the auditor assimilates this type of evidence as more formal evidence collection tasks are being performed.

EVALUATING THE CONTROLLING FUNCTION

The controlling function involves determining when the actual activities of the computer installation deviate from the planned activities. In essence the remainder of this book is concerned with how well management performs the controlling function. Nevertheless, when evaluating top and EDP management, auditors focus on only a subset of the control activities that should be performed in a computer installation; namely, those aimed at assuring the installation accomplishes its objectives at a global level.

Stage Growth Hypothesis

Nolan [1973] hypothesizes that the growth pattern of EDP facilities within an organization follows an S shape. This pattern is traced by graphing the budget of a computer installation over time (Figure 3-3). He argues that from a control viewpoint the turning points in the S-shaped curve represent critical times in an installation's life. Four stages exist in his stage growth model (see, also, Nolan [1979]):

Stage	Characteristics of stage
Initiation	Installation of a computer; computer often located in the primary user department; controls are lacking: only a loose budget exists, no transfer pricing scheme is used; projects are assigned priorities on a FIFO basis

Stage	Characteristics of stage
Contagion	Sales-oriented management intent on showing the usefulness of the computer; higher status given to EDP manager; lax controls engender rapid applications development; few standards; informal project control and a loose budget
Control	Control-oriented management; computer moves out of primary user department; proliferation of controls to contain runaway budget; establishment of steering committee, standards, project control, postaudits; transfer pricing scheme introduced
Integration	Resource-oriented planning and control; EDP becomes a separate functional area; some decentralization of systems analysts and programmers into user areas; increasing specialization of function within computer installation; advanced systems introduced, e.g., online realtime systems; refinement of controls and transfer pricing scheme; establishment of a master plan

Lucas and Sutton [1977] conducted an empirical study that produced evidence contrary to the stage growth model. Using regression methodology they found straight-line and exponential curves provided better fits of budget data over time than an S-shaped curve. Nevertheless, they concluded the stage growth model was still useful as a means of anticipating problems that occur as an installation passes through the various stages. Rather than use the installation's budget as an indicator of the stage reached, they suggested the state of the

Figure 3-3
The S-shaped curve of the stage growth hypothesis. (*From Nolan [1973]. Copyright 1973, Association for Computing Machinery, Inc., reprinted by permission.*)

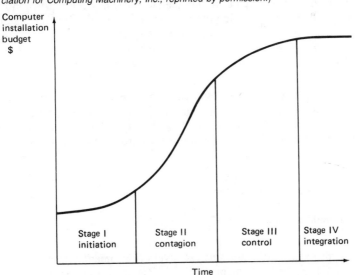

installation's applications portfolio may be a better predictor. As the installation matures, its mix of application systems changes to include more strategic planning systems.

From an audit viewpoint Nolan's "theory" is important because it focuses on the state of controls within a computer installation as it passes through the various stages. If external auditors can determine the stage reached by an installation, they can predict the likely control problems existing in the installation. Internal auditors can use the theory as the basis for designing controls appropriate to the various stages and alerting management as to the likely problems that will exist. Nevertheless, the theory also has its critics (see, for example, Benbasat et al. [1984] and King and Kraemer [1984]).

The Means of Control

Management exercises control over the computer installation's activities through the normal means: plans and budgets, measuring actual performance, and determining variances from budgets. A study by McKinsey and Company [1968] demonstrates the importance of controlling computer resource usage. They found that companies which plan EDP activities and audit the results are more successful users of computers than companies which do not perform these control activities. The following sections briefly examine some essential control elements in a computer installation.

Performance Standards   Together with a project plan, performance standards form the basis of constructing budgets for information system projects. Performance standards describe the resource usage that should be expected from undertaking different activities within the computer installation. Brandon [1963] provides a detailed discussion of performance standards for four major areas within a computer installation: (*a*) equipment use, (*b*) systems analysis, (*c*) programming, and (*d*) operations. Performance standards also must be formulated for other areas, for example, database administration.

Documentation Standards   In an empirical study of why information system projects succeed or fail, Dickson and Powers [1973] found documentation standards to be an important factor affecting the time taken to complete a project. London [1977] argues documentation standards serve four purposes:

1 Inter-task/phase communication
2 Quality control and project control
3 Historical reference
4 Instructional reference

Management's problem is to determine the level of documentation needed in the installation. Preparing documentation is a time-consuming activity (see, also, Chapter 8). The benefits should outweigh the costs. The Canadian Institute of Chartered Accountants [1970] provides a detailed description of the types of documentation it regards as necessary within a computer installation (see, also, U.S. Department of Commerce [1976, 1979]).

Checkpoint Reviews   Most projects can be broken up into a set of relatively self-contained steps. For example, the development of a new system comprises the following major phases: feasibility study, analysis, design, programming, implementation. At the completion of each phase a checkpoint can be defined. When the checkpoint is reached, management can review progress on the project and determine whether further work should be done. If checkpoint reviews are conducted diligently, they provide an important means of detecting problem areas in the conduct of a project.

Project Control Aids   Although checkpoint reviews enable progress to be evaluated after each major phase is completed, some means of providing an early warning of project deviations are needed. Traditional project control techniques can be used since they enable ongoing progress to be monitored; for example, management can use a GANTT chart to plot actual resource expenditure against budgeted resource expenditure and a PERT chart to determine the implications of missed deadlines for the final completion date of a project.

Postaudits   Besides the audits carried out by the EDP audit group, EDP management should carry out regularly its own audits as a fundamental control procedure. The computer installation audit team has the same control objectives as the EDP audit team; however, it differs from the EDP audit team in two respects. First, it does not have to maintain independence; thus, it can be more involved in the detailed analysis, design, and implementation of a system. Second, as a corollary of the first difference, the team members can be picked specially for the audit because of their in-depth knowledge of the system to be audited.

Controlling Users of Computer Services

There are two ways of controlling users of the data processing installation's services. First, some type of review committee can examine users' requests for services. Second, a transfer pricing or chargeout scheme can be used. Both schemes have strengths and limitations; consequently, both might be used to provide stronger control over users.

If a review committee evaluates users' requests for computing services, it needs some type of mechanism to evaluate priorities. Wetherbe and Dickson [1979] advocate using Zero-Based Budgeting (ZBB). If ZBB is used, the first step is to reduce all information systems activities to a zero base. Next, all potential information systems activities are identified and structured into sequentially dependent incremental service levels. For each service level, estimates must be made of the expected benefits and resource consumption. Finally, the review committee must establish priorities. Initially, projects might be ranked using a technique such as Delphi (see, further, Wedley [1977]). Cumulative resource consumption can then be calculated. Once the level of information systems funding available has been determined, those activities that will be supported can be chosen.

The primary strength of the ZBB approach is that it highlights applications that have outlived their usefulness. Furthermore, it allows strong centralized control to be exercised over information systems activities without placing onerous requirements on users to quantify the benefits and costs of applications for the review committee. Nevertheless, its ability to control day-to-day resource consumption is a moot issue; indeed, some type of chargeout mechanism may still be needed. Moreover, ZBB can become complex to conduct, perhaps even more complex than chargeout.

Use of a transfer pricing or chargeout scheme to control users involves determining the units of service offered by the data processing installation (e.g., CPU seconds, disk storage space, lines printed) and an associated fee schedule. Users are charged for the services they consume. In this way the costs of running the data processing installation are recouped, and hopefully managers are motivated to carefully plan and control their data processing expenditures.

The major problem with a transfer pricing scheme is determining the chargeout price that will cause managers to act optimally in terms of the overall objectives of the organization. Some transfer prices cause suboptimization because managers seeking to maximize their own profits do so by reducing the overall profit of the organization. The "theoretically correct" transfer price has been a thorny problem for researchers. Except in fairly constrained cases—for example, when perfect competition exists—the correct transfer price to use is unclear. In some cases economic theory suggests a complex system of taxes and subsidies may be needed. However, the behavioral ramifications of different transfer prices have not been researched extensively. Abdel-Khalik and Lusk [1974] and Drury and Bates [1979] provide useful summaries of much of the literature.

Of direct relevance to the pricing of computer services is a study carried out by Nolan [1977]. Nolan examined the effects of different transfer pricing schemes on user/manager attitudes toward computer-based information systems. He surveyed user/manager attitudes at 13 research sites using different kinds of transfer pricing schemes and found "advanced" chargeout systems to be associated with relatively high user/manager attitudes and a marked increase in EDP usage. Interestingly, one characteristic of advanced chargeout systems was their simplicity. Users looked unfavorably upon complex transfer pricing schemes that they were unable to understand.

SUMMARY

The auditor's evaluation of top management and EDP management is a difficult task. It requires the auditor to have a sound knowledge of the principles of good management. Furthermore, it requires the auditor to be able to determine when the performance of a particular managerial function is essential if asset safeguarding, maintenance of data integrity, system effectiveness, and system efficiency are to be achieved. In some cases—for example, small organizations or organizations facing low environmental uncertainty—the function may be relatively unimportant from a control perspective. In other cases—for example, organizations developing a diverse and complex range of systems—proper performance of the function may be critical.

A useful way of evaluating top management and EDP management is to examine the various functions they perform: planning, organizing, directing, staffing, and controlling. For each of these functions, normative guidelines exist that can be used as a basis for evaluation. The auditor should first determine what aspects of the function are critical to the organization from a control perspective and then evaluate performance of the function against these normative guidelines.

REVIEW QUESTIONS

3-1 Why is it important that the auditor be capable of evaluating the quality of top management and EDP management of an organization in relation to the computer installation?

3-2 How is the framework of managerial functions—planning, organizing, staffing, directing, and controlling—useful to the auditor?

3-3 Briefly describe each of the major plans that must be formulated for a computer installation.

3-4 What are the functions of the steering committee of a computer installation? Who should comprise the steering committee?

3-5 Briefly describe three situations in the life cycle of a computer installation when a feasibility study might be needed. What aspects of feasibility studies are of interest to the auditor? How can the auditor evaluate whether feasibility studies are carried out properly?

3-6 Briefly describe two aspects of the changeover to a new computer installation that pose major threats to an organization's data integrity. What aspects of a changeover plan would the auditor examine to determine whether these threats have been properly considered?

3-7 Briefly describe the four major components of a master plan.

3-8 Which component of the information systems master plan might be prepared using the following techniques:

a Critical success factors

b Strategy set transformation

c Customer resource life cycle approach

    d Business systems planning
    e Ends/means analysis
3-9 Briefly explain the nature and purpose of the following plans:
    a Project plan
    b Disaster recovery plan
3-10 Why is the auditor interested in the organizing capabilities of management? What evidence would the auditor collect to determine whether management is competent at organizing the computer installation?
3-11 What impact has the widespread availability of minicomputers and microcomputers had on the centralization/decentralization decision?
3-12 What are the advantages and disadvantages of:
    a Decentralizing systems analysis
    b Centralizing programming
3-13 When purchasing hardware and software, why is it important to prepare a manual of specifications? Outline the contents of a manual of specifications. Why should the manual of specifications be prepared to act as a turnaround document?
3-14 What are methods standards? What are the purposes of having methods standards in a computer installation? What is the relationship between methods standards and performance standards? Outline some methods standards you think would be needed for (*a*) systems analysis and (*b*) programming.
3-15 Why should a computer installation have a standards manual? What impact does the absence of a standards manual have on carrying out an audit?
3-16 What evidence should the auditor seek to determine whether the management of a computer installation performs the staffing function competently?
3-17 Outline the controls that should exist for personnel acquisition, development, and termination. What factors determine whether or not these controls should be applied?
3-18 What principles underlie the management function of directing? What evidence should the auditor seek to determine whether EDP management has a fundamental understanding of these principles?
3-19 How does EDP management's understanding of human motivation, theories and styles of leadership, and principles of communication impact the effectiveness and efficiency with which computer systems can be developed?
3-20 Explain Nolan's stage growth hypothesis. What is the relevance of the stage growth hypothesis to the auditor?
3-21 Explain the relationship between performance standards, budgeting, and control.
3-22 What are the purposes of documentation? Briefly explain the types of documentation that should exist in a computer installation. What evidence should the auditor seek to determine whether documentation standards are being applied?
3-23 How can the following techniques be used to control an EDP project:
    a Checkpoint reviews
    b GANTT chart
    c PERT chart
3-24 Why should management periodically carry out audits of the computer installation? How are these audits different from those carried out by internal or external auditors?
3-25 What is a transfer price? How do transfer prices assist in controlling the computer installation? What does empirical evidence suggest the basic design guidelines for transfer prices should be?

MULTIPLE CHOICE QUESTIONS

3-1 The primary function of a steering committee is:
a Strategic planning for a computer installation
b Preparing a changeover plan when an organization decides to use computers
c Evaluating specific project plans for systems
d Conducting any major feasibility study when it is needed

3-2 A feasibility study should be conducted when:
a A decision must be made on the best way of sequencing tasks during system development
b An assessment must be made of whether or not the disaster recovery plan works
c The consequences of decentralizing data processing functions must be assessed
d A decision must be made on whether or not a new operations schedule will increase throughput

3-3 Which of the following elements is usually *not* included in a changeover plan prepared when an organization sets up a computer installation:
a Physical planning and site preparation
b Acceptance testing procedures for hardware/system software
c Design of an organization structure for the installation
d Technological developments that will affect the installation over the next three–five years

3-4 The *major* purpose of a master plan is to:
a Specify the major tasks that must be accomplished when a changeover occurs from one hardware/software configuration to another
b Provide the rolling plan for the next several years' activities in a computer installation
c Identify the impact of any technological advances that may occur five–ten years in the future
d Show how the computer installation will meet its budget for the next financial year

3-5 The information systems requirements plan is derived directly from the:
a Information systems applications and facilities plan
b Information systems strategic plan
c Master plan
d Organizational strategic plan

3-6 When formulating an information systems strategic plan, an approach which focuses on identifying the claimant groups in an organization, their respective goals, and the organizational strategy that affects each group is:
a Critical success factors approach
b Strategic grid approach
c Strategy set transformation approach
d Customer resource life cycle approach

3-7 An information systems requirements plan specifies:
a The hardware/software configuration needed to support application systems
b The applications systems needed to support the strategic plan
c An information systems architecture for the information systems department
d The resource needs of the information systems department over the next three–five years

3-8 Which of the following techniques is unlikely to be used in formulating an information systems requirements plan:
a Ends/means analysis
b Critical success factors
c Business Information Analysis and Integration Technique
d Strategy set transformation

3-9 A major activity to be conducted during project planning is:
a Specifying the hardware/software configuration for the computer installation
b Determining whether the project has a positive net present value
c Identifying constraints that apply to tasks that must be performed
d Determining whether the project is technically, behaviorally, and economically feasible

3-10 A contingency theory of organization states:
a There is no single best way to organize and not all ways of organizing are equally effective
b As task uncertainty increases, differentiation must be reduced and integration increased
c Organic types of organization structures are not appropriate when there is high environmental uncertainty
d Both (a) and (b) above

3-11 Which of the following is a strategy designed to *reduce* the need for information flows in an organization:
a Creation of lateral relations
b Investment in vertical information systems
c Tighter coupling of subsystems
d Creation of slack resources

3-12 A disadvantage of decentralization often is:
a It is more difficult to standardize and integrate systems within an organization
b Software is less attuned to the needs of individual users
c Response to needed changes is slower
d Data input errors from remote locations increase

3-13 The major purpose of a manual of specifications is to:
a Detail the methods and performance standards in an installation
b Communicate to vendors the hardware/software needs of an installation
c Reduce the effects of personnel turnover by providing the necessary documentation for system maintenance
d Act as a turnaround document when communicating a system design to users

3-14 A major problem in formulating methods standards is:
a Knowing which activities need methods standards
b Ensuring they are integrated with the performance standards already developed
c Choosing the documentation style to be used in writing up the standards
d Choosing an appropriate level so they are neither too global nor too detailed

3-15 Careful staff planning within a computer installation is necessary because:
a Computer staff are much more costly to develop than staff in other departments within an organization
b Typically the computer installation is attempting more projects than it can handle
c Historically computer staff have been in short supply and acquiring skilled staff can be very difficult

d Unfortunately, computer staff as a profession have often shown themselves to be unreliable

3-16 If programmers resign because they are disgruntled, they should be:
   a Asked to finish their existing projects as soon as possible
   b Asked to train a new employee to take over their job so continuity of work is achieved
   c Assigned to a noncritical task immediately
   d Assigned to maintenance work only and not new development work

3-17 Which of the following is *not* fundamental to the *process* of directing:
   a Appropriate variation of supervisory techniques to suit different people, tasks, and organizational environments
   b A participative style whereby subordinates help determine how harmony of objectives should be achieved
   c Unity of command—individuals should report to a single superior only
   d Direct supervision whereby objective supervisory techniques should be supplemented with direct personal contact

3-18 After an empirical study of Nolan's stage growth model, Lucas and Sutton concluded:
   a The model was invalid and worthless
   b The contagion stage was missing or very short in the installations they studied
   c A log-normal curve provided a better fit of budget data over time
   d An installation's application portfolio may be a better predictor of the stage reached in the organization's life than the installation budget

3-19 After a study of transfer pricing schemes used at 13 research sites, Nolan concluded:
   a Advanced chargeout systems tended to be simple
   b User-managers had better attitudes toward computer use when no chargeout system was used
   c Computer chargeout schemes tended to fail because of behavioral problems
   d Transfer prices that used a system of taxes and subsidies were the most common chargeout schemes used

3-20 During an information systems project, a Gantt chart is primarily used as a:
   a Checkpoint review
   b Documentation standard
   c Project control aid
   d Postaudit technique

3-21 An advantage of using zero-based budgeting (ZBB) as a means of controlling users of computer services is:
   a It is easy to use
   b It allows control of day-to-day resource consumption
   c It is more likely to gain acceptance among user managers than a transfer pricing scheme
   d It highlights applications that have outlived their usefulness

EXERCISES AND CASES

3-1 Consider a medium-sized manufacturing organization that is a mature user of computers. For the organization you consider, fill in the elements of the following controls matrix where the elements represent your opinion on the likely cost-ef fectiveness (in general) of the various categories of controls (rows of the matrix) at achieving various control objectives (columns of the matrix). Note, assume a score of 5 means controls within a category have high cost-effectiveness and a score of 1 means controls within a category have low cost-effectiveness. Also, be sure to give a brief explanation of each of your ratings.

Objectives / Controls	Asset safeguarding	Data integrity	System effectiveness	System efficiency
Planning				
Organizing				
Staffing				
Directing				
Controlling				

3-2 Make a list of those controls described in the chapter that would *not* be of major interest to external auditors, that is, controls that are not especially cost-effective at reducing the expected losses from lack of asset safeguarding in the computer installation or lack of data integrity. Briefly explain each of your choices.

3-3 Remote Resources Inc., is a large diversified and decentralized mining company. For some time the company has operated a bauxite mining site on the Gulf of Carpentaria in Queensland, Australia. The site is very remote. It is surrounded by tropical jungle and the road to the nearest major city, Cairns, is impassable during the wet season, lasting from about December through April. The main means of access are by air—a three-hour flight from Cairns (only small aircraft can be used)—and by sea—a four-day boat trip from Cairns. However, even these means of access can't be used when cyclones are about; consequently, at times the mining site can be cut off for about a week or more.

It has become increasingly difficult to hire competent staff to perform the clerical, administrative, and accounting functions at the site. Thus, the head office of the company is contemplating installing a small computer at the site to process several accounting applications such as payroll and inventory as well as providing the mining engineers with computational support.

Required: You are on the internal audit staff of Remote Resources Inc. The internal audit manager has asked you to prepare a brief report outlining a disaster recovery plan for the proposed installation. Be sure to point out some of the major difficulties involved with disaster recovery at the mining site.

3-4 Harrison University is a large university with about 30,000 students offering a wide range of courses in the humanities and the physical, social, behavioral, health, agricultural, biological, and engineering sciences. The existing computing facilities are divided between two groups: an academic computing center and an administrative computing center. Each group has its own hardware, software, personnel, etc., and operates independently of the other group. The academic computing center services all teaching and research needs; the administrative computing center services all other computing needs—payroll, student records, budgeting, financial planning, etc.

Currently the facilities of the administrative computing center are heavily overloaded. A steering committee of the university has been formed to examine the problem. The steering committee has been given wide terms of reference. In recent years, the university has found it increasingly difficult to find sources of private funding and to obtain federal funding. The president of the university has asked the steering group to consider the possibility of amalgamating the academic and administrative computing groups, selling off the existing hardware, and purchasing a large machine that will service both groups. She feels that centralizing computer facilities may produce economies of scale. During the interim period, since the academic computer has substantial excess capacity, she also questions whether some administrative applications might not be shifted to the academic computer.

Required: You are a member of the internal audit staff of the university. The chairman of the steering committee has asked the manager of internal audit for his views on the proposed changes, and he has asked you to brief him. Prepare a memo outlining the advantages and disadvantages of the change from an internal audit viewpoint.

3-5 You are the head of internal audit for a medium-sized organization. One day you receive a memo from the controller of your organization requesting some assistance with the decision on upgrading computer facilities within your organization.

The controller's concern is that he believes the data processing manager is not giving adequate consideration to all the tenders submitted by the different vendors. Apparently she is arguing that the only tender worth considering is the one submitted by the vendor who supplies the existing hardware and software used by your organization. The reason is that she contends the changeover to another vendor would be too costly.

Required: The controller asks you to send him a brief memorandum outlining the steps you will take to investigate the issue. He also asks you to list the information you will need to be able to carry out the evaluation.

3-6 Innovation, Inc. is a company specializing in research and development. It accepts short-term research and development projects from other companies and aims to obtain results quickly. It has been very successful at achieving this objective (current sales $100 million).

You are a field auditor in a firm of external auditors that has just taken over the audit of Innovation. When carrying out the audit of their computer installation, you find there is no master plan for the installation. This concerns you, as Innovation uses computers extensively to support its activities. It has two large machines for both scientific and commercial activities. When you interview the manager of the computer installation on this problem, he informs you it is impossible to prepare a master plan for the installation because of the uncertainty surrounding Innovation's activities.

Required: What implications does the absence of a master plan have for the conduct of the audit? How would you now proceed?

3-7 PUFTS (Public Funds Transfer Services) Ltd is a new, rapidly expanding organization that offers public electronic funds transfer facilities to financial institutions. For example, it provides a public data communications network that enables its customers to share automatic teller machines (ATMs) and point-of-sale devices (POSs). Using the network, an account holder in any customer financial institution can enter transactions at a terminal device attached to the network and have these transactions routed to their host institution.

PUFTS is currently undertaking an intensive research and development program to develop new hardware and software to support public electronic funds transfer systems. Approximately 30% of current expenditures are devoted to research and development. The projects are high risk, but the potential payoffs are also high.

The board of directors of PUFTS comprises representatives from each of the five organizations that are the major shareholders in PUFTS plus the managing director of PUFTS. The makeup of the board is as follows:

1 John Jones	Director from NBS, a merchant bank
2 Georgia Williams	Director from first National Bank; strong background in accounting
3 Helen Smith	Director from Cost-Less Clothes, a major retailer using POS; strong background in marketing
4 Ian Reeves	Director from SFSL, a savings and loan association; strong background in accounting
5 Arthur Webb	Director from Second Federal Bank; strong background in general management
6 Amy Coulster	Managing Director of PUFTS; strong background in computer science, especially data communications

To date, PUFTS has not made a profit. However, after reviewing budgets prepared by Amy Coulster, the board is convinced that a profit will be made for the first time in the coming financial year. Coulster has argued that losses have been incurred because of the substantial investments in research and development, and payoffs from these expenditures are only just beginning to occur. PUFTS has only just "gone public," and you are an EDP auditor in the external audit firm hired to perform the audit. During your review of EDP management controls, you note there is no steering committee. When you raise this matter with Coulster, she argues that PUFTS is too small for a steering committee. Moreover, she argues that the board fulfills the role of a steering committee and that since most of the technological innovations are her own ideas, she is able to brief the board fully on any matters that concern them. Coulster argues emphatically that PUFTS cannot afford to have a steering committee given its current size, and that she can provide the technical briefings required by the board.

Required: What impact, if any, does the absence of a steering committee have on the way you will approach the audit? What recommendations, if any, would you provide to the board in light of the absence of a steering committee?

ANSWERS TO MULTIPLE CHOICE QUESTIONS

3-1 a	3-6 c	3-11 d	3-16 c
3-2 c	3-7 c	3-12 a	3-17 b
3-3 d	3-8 d	3-13 b	3-18 d
3-4 b	3-9 c	3-14 d	3-19 a
3-5 b	3-10 a	3-15 c	3-20 c
			3-21 d

REFERENCES

Abdel-Khalik, A. Rashad, and Edward J. Lusk. "Transfer Pricing—A Synthesis," *The Accounting Review* (January 1974), pp. 8–23.

Benbasat, Izak, Albert S. Dexter, Donald H. Drury, and Robert C. Goldstein. "A Critique of the Stage Hypothesis: Theory and Empirical Evidence," *Communications of the ACM* (May 1984), pp. 476–485.

Bierman, Harold, and Seymour Smidt. *The Capital Budgeting Decision,* 4th ed. (New York: Macmillan, 1975).

Bowman, Brent J., Gordon B. Davis, and James C. Wetherbe. "Three Stage Model of MIS Planning," *Information and Management,* vol. 6, 1983, pp. 11–25.

Brandon, Dick H. *Management Standards for Data Processing* (Princeton, NJ: D. Van Nostrand, 1963).

Canadian Institute of Chartered Accountants. *Computer Control Guidelines* (Toronto, Canada: The Canadian Institute of Chartered Accountants, 1970).

Canning, Richard G. "Developing Strategic Information Systems," *EDP Analyzer* (May 1984), pp. 1–12.

Carlson, W. M. "Business Information Analysis and Integration Technique (BIAIT)— The New Horizon," *Data Base* (Spring 1979), pp. 3–9.

Cleland, David I., and William R. King. *Systems Analysis and Project Management,* 2d ed. (New York: McGraw-Hill, 1975).

Davis, Gordon B. "Strategies for Information Requirements Determination," *IBM Systems Journal,* vol. 21, no. 1, 1982, pp. 4–30.

Davis, Gordon B., and Margrethe H. Olson. *Management Information Systems: Conceptual Foundations, Structure, and Development,* 2d ed. (New York: McGraw-Hill, 1985).

Dickson, Gary W., and Richard F. Powers. "MIS Project Management: Myths, Opinion and Reality," in F. Warren McFarlan, Richard L. Nolan, and David P. Norton, eds., *Information Systems Administration* (New York: Holt, Rinehart & Winston, 1973), pp. 401–412.

Ditri, Arnold E., John C. Shaw, and William Atkins. *Managing the EDP Function* (New York: McGraw-Hill, 1971).

Drury, Donald H., and John E. Bates. *Data Processing Chargeback Systems: Theory and Practice* (Hamilton, Ontario: The Society of Management Accountants of Canada, 1979).

Dunnette, Marvin D., ed. *Handbook of Industrial and Organizational Psychology* (Chicago: Rand McNally, 1976).

Galbraith, Jay R. *Organization Design* (Reading, MA: Addison-Wesley, 1977).

Gillenson, Mark L., and Robert Goldberg. *Strategic Planning, Systems Analysis, and Database Design* (New York: Wiley, 1984).

IBM Corporation. *Information Systems Planning Guide*, 3d ed. (White Plains, NY: International Business Machines, 1983), Publication No. GE20-0527-3.

Ives, Blake, and Gerard P. Learmonth. "The Information System as a Competitive Weapon," *Communications of the ACM* (December 1984), pp. 1193–1201.

Keen, Peter G. W. "Value Analysis: Justifying Decision Support Systems," *Management Information Systems Quarterly* (March 1981), pp. 1–15.

King, John Leslie. "Centralized versus Decentralized Computing: Organizational Considerations and Management Options," *Computing Surveys* (December 1983), pp. 319–349.

King, John Leslie, and Kenneth L. Kraemer. "Evolution and Organizational Information Systems: An Assessment of Nolan's Stage Model," *Communications of the ACM* (May 1984), pp. 466–475.

King, William R. "Strategic Planning for Management Information Systems," *Management Information Systems Quarterly* (March 1978), pp. 27–37.

Koontz, Harold, Cyril O'Donnell, and Heinz Weihrich. *Management: A Systems and Contingency Analysis of the Managerial Functions*, 8th ed. (New York: McGraw-Hill, 1984).

Lawrence, Paul R., and Jay W. Lorsch. *Developing Organizations: Diagnosis and Action* (Reading, MA: Addison-Wesley, 1969).

London, Keith R. *Documentation Standards*, 2d ed. (New York: Petrocelli/Charter, 1977).

Lucas, Henry C., and Jimmy A. Sutton. "The Stage Hypothesis and the S-Curve: Some Contradictory Evidence," *Communications of the ACM* (April 1977), pp. 254–259.

McFarlan, F. Warren, and James L. McKenney. "The Information Archipelago—Maps and Bridges," *Harvard Business Review* (September-October 1982), pp. 109–119.

McFarlan, F. Warren, and James L. McKenney. *Corporate Information Systems Management* (Homewood, IL: Irwin, 1983).

McFarlan, F. Warren, James L. McKenney, and Philip J. Pyburn. "The Information Archipelago—Plotting a Course," *Harvard Business Review* (January-February 1983), pp. 145–156.

McKinsey & Company, Inc. "Unlocking the Computer's Profit Potential," *The McKinsey Quarterly* (Fall 1968), pp. 17–31.

Miller, James Grier. *Living Systems* (New York: McGraw-Hill, 1978).

Nolan, Richard L. "Managing the Computer Resource: A Stage Hypothesis," *Communications of the ACM* (July 1973), pp. 399–405.

Nolan, Richard L. "Effects of Chargeout on User/Manager Attitudes," *Communications of the ACM* (March 1977), pp. 177–184.

Nolan, Richard L. "Managing the Crises in Data Processing," *Harvard Business Review* (March-April 1979), pp. 115–126.

Parker, M. M. "Enterprise Information Analysis: Cost-Benefit Analysis and the Data-Managed System," *IBM Systems Journal*, vol. 21, no. 1, 1982, pp. 108–123.

Rockart, John F. "Chief Executives Define Their Own Data Needs," *Harvard Business Review* (March-April 1979), pp. 81–93.

U.S. Department of Commerce/National Bureau of Standards. *Guidelines for Documentation of Computer Programs and Automated Data Systems,* Federal Information Processing Standards Publication 38, February 15, 1976.

U.S. Department of Commerce/National Bureau of Standards. *Guidelines for Documentation of Computer Programs and Data Systems for the Initiation Phase,* Federal Information Processing Standards Publication 64, August 1, 1979.

Wedley, W. "New Uses of Delphi in Strategy Formulation," *Long Range Planning* (December 1977), pp. 70–78.

Wetherbe, James C., and Gary W. Dickson. "Zero-Based Budgeting: An Alternative to Chargeout," *Information and Management,* vol. 2, 1979, pp. 203–213.

Zachman, J. A. "Business Systems Planning and Business Information Control Study: A Comparison," *IBM Systems Journal,* vol. 21, no. 1, 1982, pp. 31–53.

SYSTEM DEVELOPMENT

REVIEW QUESTIONS
MULTIPLE CHOICE QUESTIONS
EXERCISES AND CASES
ANSWERS TO MULTIPLE CHOICE QUESTIONS
REFERENCES

What distinguishes a good system from a bad system? This is a question that has plagued information systems researchers for many years. In some ways the development of good systems is still an art. The formal guidelines are meager and insight and experience still play an important part in determining the quality of the resulting design.

This chapter discusses the activities that should be performed in the system development process. A normative model is described that allows the auditor to structure the evidence collection process. The model also provides the basis for evaluating how well system development activities are performed in a computer installation.

AUDITING THE SYSTEM DEVELOPMENT PROCESS

There are two ways in which the auditor may evaluate the system development process: first, as a member of the system development team (see, also, Chapter 2); and second, in an ex post review capacity when the system development process, in general, is evaluated. The objectives of the audit and the methods used to gather evidence are different for these two types of audit.

When the auditor *participates* in the system development process, the objectives are to ensure for a *specific* application system that controls are built into the system to safeguard assets, ensure data integrity, and achieve system effectiveness and efficiency. The auditor collects evidence primarily by observing the activities of the other members of the development team. This evidence then is evaluated against the auditor's normative model of the system development process.

When the auditor carries out an ex post audit, the objectives are to reduce the extent of substantive testing needed for application systems and to make recommendations for improving the system development process in general. The audit proceeds according to the general approach described in Chapter 2. First, the auditor uses interviews, observations, and a review of standards to obtain general and then detailed information on the system development process. Second, an evaluation of this information forms the basis for hypothesizing strengths and weaknesses that may exist and designing compliance tests. Third, the auditor selects a sample of application systems to determine whether the hypothesized strengths and weaknesses do, in fact, exist.

NORMATIVE MODELS OF THE SYSTEM DEVELOPMENT PROCESS

The auditor seeks answers to two basic questions when auditing the system development process. First, do system design personnel perform all the activities necessary for the design and implementation of high-quality information systems? Second, are these activities performed well? To answer these questions the auditor needs some basis for thinking about, evaluating, and approaching the audit of the system development process. System development personnel have the same problem. They need a basis, framework, or model to guide their approach to system development. The quality of the systems they design and implement depends on the adequacy of their model for *prescription* and *description* of system development activities.

System Development Life Cycle Approach

Traditionally, system development personnel have thought about the system development process in terms of a life cycle consisting of nine major phases (see, for example, Hartman et al. [1968]):

Phase	Explanation
Feasibility study	Applying cost-benefit criteria to the proposed application
Information analysis	Determining user information requirements
System design	Designing files and information processing functions to be performed in the system
Program development	Designing, coding, compiling, testing, and documenting programs
Procedures and forms development	Designing and documenting procedures and forms for system users
Acceptance testing	Final testing of the system and formal approval and acceptance by management and users
Conversion	Changeover from the old system to the new system
Operation and maintenance	Ongoing running of the system and subsequent modifications and maintenance in light of problems detected
Postaudit	Periodic review of the system

The life cycle approach does not imply all these phases must be carried out serially. Some of the phases may proceed concurrently; for example, procedure and forms development may proceed at the same time as program development occurs. Some phases may require several iterations; for example, as programs are developed the system design may have to be modified to improve processing efficiency.

The life cycle approach arose out of early efforts to apply project management techniques to the system development process. There had been a history of system failure because of massive cost overruns, inadequate economic evaluations, inadequate system design, management abdication, poor communication, inadequate direction, etc. The life cycle approach helps overcome some of these problems. By clearly defining tasks in terms of the life cycle, the project management and control techniques described in Chapter 3 can be applied. To develop high-quality systems, each phase of the life cycle should be planned and controlled, comply with developed standards, be adequately documented, be staffed by competent personnel, have project checkpoints and signoffs, etc. (see, further, Biggs et al. [1980]).

Sociotechnical Design Approach

Another set of problems motivated the sociotechnical design approach to information system development. Though the system life cycle approach might have helped alleviate the technical and managerial problems encountered with systems, behavioral problems still persist. Systems degrade through lack of use, apathy, and sometimes outright sabotage. The sociotechnical approach arose because an understanding was needed of *why* behavioral problems occur and *how* they might be remedied.

A sociotechnical system design process attempts to jointly optimize two systems: (*a*) the *technical system,* where the objective is task accomplishment and (*b*) the *social system,* where the objective is to achieve a high quality of working life for the users of the system (Figure 4-1). Sociotechnical design theorists argue many of the behavioral problems arising from system implementation occur because system designers neglect the social system. Bostrom and Heinen [1977*a*] believe there are seven reasons why this is the case:

1 *System designers' implicit theories:* System designers make assumptions about people, organizations, and the change process that impact their modes of action. These theories are inadequate; for example, research shows many system designers hold a theory X view of man, which results in their designing tightly structured job situations that lower the quality of working life of system users.

2 *System designers' concept of responsibility:* Research shows system designers perceive they are responsible for the system development process. Behavioral scientists argue change agents (system designers) cannot accept responsibility for another person's change; they can only facilitate or inhibit change.

3 *Limited frameworks—nonsystemic view:* System designers have a limited view of work systems; their primary focus is the information system. There may be many secondary effects of information system development, for example, job de-enrichment.

4 *Limited goal orientation:* System designers seek to optimize the technical system; their focus is task accomplishment and not quality of working life issues.

5 *Limited design referent group:* System designers have middle management as their primary design referent group. They have little concern for

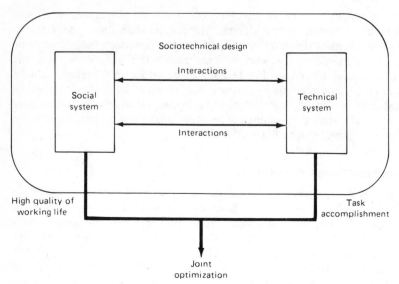

FIGURE 4-1
The objectives of sociotechnical design.

secondary users, for example, clerks who may be responsible for the primary input to the system.

6 *Rational/static view of the system development process:* Information system training emphasizes the application of formal project control techniques to a rational design process that proceeds in clearly defined steps. Behavioral scientists argue the design process should be fluid and iterative because a change process causes power shifts, conflicts, etc.

7 *Limited change technologies:* Typically, system designers are trained in management science/operations research. They know little about behavioral science; consequently, they often know little about how to deal with social problems.

Use of a sociotechnical design approach forces system designers to take a broader and richer view of the design process than the view that Bostrom and Heinen argue designers now have of the design process. The approach consists of five major phases (Figure 4-2):

Phase	Explanation
Diagnosis and entry	Problem identification; determining whether the organization is amenable to change; analysis of the social and technical systems and coordinating mechanisms; determining the strategic requirements of the system

Phase	Explanation
Management of the change process	Ensuring throughout the design process that the organization is amenable to change; facilitating adaptation to change
System design	Design of both the technical and social system
Adjustment of coordinating mechanisms	Changes in one subsystem may necessitate changes in another subsystem; e.g., a reward system may have to be adjusted because the information system supports a new job design
Implementation	Installation of the new sociotechnical system

The sociotechnical design approach to the system development process does not negate the importance of project management techniques and the traditional life cycle approach. The major criticisms made are that the life cycle approach is incomplete and nonsystemic. System development is a much more comprehensive process than suggested by the life cycle approach.

Political Approach

The political approach to information systems development underscores the need for system designers to take into account the ways in which information systems can change the distribution of power within organizations. Markus [1981] points out that new systems can change existing organizational power

FIGURE 4-2
Major phases in the sociotechnical design process.

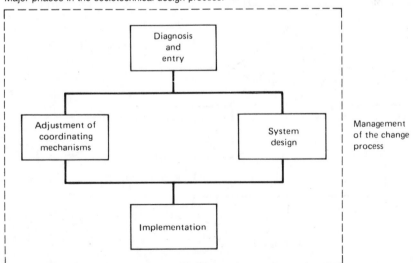

structures in three ways. First, systems provide access to information that may facilitate or inhibit a person's decision making abilities. Since power is a function of decision making capabilities, changes to information channels may modify the power structure. Second, systems may alter one person's ability to influence the behavior and performance of another person. For example, the system may provide access to performance data that was previously unavailable for evaluation reviews. Third, systems can be used as a source of symbolic power. Managers may promote an image that they can influence outcomes via the system, even if this is not really the case.

When the political approach to information systems development is adopted, a critical task is to study the history of the organization. By studying the history of the organization, the designer can evaluate whether the desired system will leave the existing power structure intact or necessitate change to the power structure. Development and implementation strategies must vary depending upon the impact that the proposed system will have on the existing power structure (Figure 4-3).

FIGURE 4-3
The political approach and user involvement in the system development process.

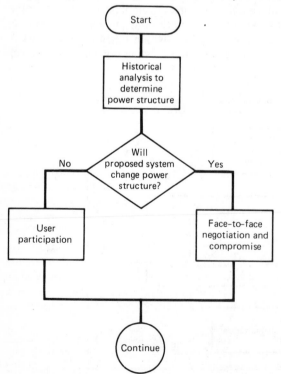

If the proposed system will leave the existing power structure intact, user participation in the design process is an important means of ensuring congruence between the system and the organization. Users will attempt to have the system design manifest the existing power structure. Serious problems can arise if an important user group is omitted from the design deliberations, since their concerns may not be incorporated into the design.

If the proposed system necessitates changes to the existing power structure, design and implementation is more difficult. Indeed, user participation may be counterproductive because users feel they are being manipulated in situations where the conclusions are foregone. Alternatively, they may attempt to change the design to be congruent with their own political motives. Participation needs to be replaced by meaningful negotiations between designers and users where compromise is the accepted objective. Keen [1981] argues that explicit contracts for change must be obtained; moreover, designers must seek out resistance early, build personal rapport, co-opt users from the start, and attempt face-to-face negotiations. Notwithstanding these tactics, for some system development projects consensus may be impossible, and the designer may confront users who employ counterimplementation strategies to sabotage the system. How these difficulties can be overcome successfully is still unclear, but designers may have to invoke their own power base by having a "fixer" who is a senior organizational sponsor.

Prototyping Approach

Historically, the primary responsibility for system development has been in the hands of a skilled computer professional, although users may have played a prominent role. This situation is changing with the increasing availability of high-level, end-user programming languages (see, for example, Martin [1982]). For several reasons it is likely this trend will continue. First, many data processing installations face a development backlog of several years (see, for example, Alloway and Quillard [1983]). When the backlog is coupled with an ongoing shortage of experienced data processing personnel, alternative means of developing systems must be found. Second, as transaction processing and management control systems have become commonplace, organizations have begun to develop strategic planning systems. High levels of uncertainty often surround the development of these systems, and software is needed that supports an experimental approach where design iteration is the norm. Third, in the context of the earlier discussion on organizational power, many managers seek to have system development under their own control rather than to relinquish it to the data processing installation. Moreover, they perceive opportunities to employ end-user computing strategically to enhance their organizational position.

At least in principle, the prototyping approach to system development is straightforward (see, for example, Mason and Carey [1983] and Jenkins and Naumann [1982]). It involves developing an initial prototype system, gaining

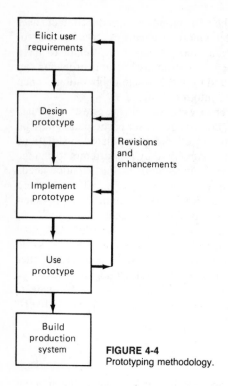

FIGURE 4-4
Prototyping methodology.

experience with the system, modifying the system in light of this experience, and continuing to iterate through this cycle until an acceptable solution is found (see Figure 4-4). High-level programming languages are used because they facilitate rapid iteration through successive designs. If efficiency is a major problem when the final system is derived, the system may then be programmed in a lower-level language. Often, however, this action is not warranted because the ongoing stability of the system is suspect or the costs of reprogramming the system exceed the costs of purchasing additional hardware to support the inefficiencies.

From an audit viewpoint, one of the more significant changes in the prototyping approach is the transition of responsibility for developmental work that may occur away from the data processing personnel to end-user personnel. With the availability of high-level programming languages, end users may be able to undertake their own development and programming work independently of the data processing department. Alternatively, they may use data processing personnel only in an advisory capacity. Some organizations have now established *information centers* that are staffed by personnel skilled in high-level development tools such as fourth generation languages. The information center

CHAPTER 4: SYSTEM DEVELOPMENT **115**

exists to provide advice and support for end users who are undertaking their own system development work (see, for example, Hammond [1982] and Rivard and Huff [1984]).

Contingency Approach

Proponents of the contingency approach to system development argue that there is no one best way to develop systems; instead, the best development approach will vary depending on the circumstances at hand. Thus, the various phases of the system development life cycle may be performed differently for different system development efforts. For example, Davis [1982] argues that the strategy which should be used to elicit user information requirements depends upon the level of uncertainty surrounding the requirements determination process. If the level of uncertainty is low, an asking strategy can be used. If the level of uncertainty is moderate, information requirements may be derived from an existing system or synthesized from the utilizing system. At high levels of uncertainty, information requirements must be discovered from experiments with an evolving system; that is, a prototyping approach should be used.

Similarly, Naumann et al. [1980] argue that different strategies must be used to provide assurance that the information requirements elicited from system users are accurate and complete. Again, the choice of strategy depends upon the level of uncertainty surrounding the project as a function of project size, the level of structuredness, the extent of user task comprehension, and the proficiency of the designer. As the level of uncertainty changes from low to high levels, the requirements assurance strategy changes from (a) an acceptance of user statements of requirements, to (b) a linear assurance process, to (c) an iterative assurance process, to (d) an experimental assurance process.

Still other phases of the system development life cycle or, indeed, the overall system development approach may vary depending upon the values of various contingent variables. For example, if power structure changes are imminent when a new system is implemented, the political approach should be adopted. If jobs will be changed as a consequence of a new system, a sociotechnical design approach should be adopted. If both will occur, a combination of political and sociotechnical design strategies may be needed.

EVALUATING THE MAJOR PHASES IN THE SYSTEM DEVELOPMENT PROCESS

Given these alternative models of the system development process, what basis should auditors use, therefore, to evaluate the process? In some ways, evaluating the process seems futile. How can auditors obtain assurance about the quality of system development if responsibility for development is dispersed across many end-users employing high-level programming languages? Unless the organization exercises some means of overall coordination and control of users, it is difficult to see how application system testing can be reduced based upon a review of system development controls. Similarly, in an ex post review audit, what sources of evidence do auditors use if development approaches vary across systems? When the traditional life cycle approach was employed, the standards manual was an important source of evidence. But now, what does a standards manual look like when a contingency approach to system development is adopted? These are difficult issues that are far from being resolved.

One approach to addressing these problems is to argue that auditors can rely on the *presence* of each phase in the system development process, if not the conduct, timing, and sequence of the phases. In other words, whatever the system development approach used, certain phases will always occur. However, how the phases are performed, the timing and sequence of each phase, and the number of iterations of each phase may vary across system development efforts, depending upon such factors as political considerations and the level of uncertainty surrounding the system. If auditors are participating as a member of the system design team, they must be capable of evaluating the choices made on the system development approach to be used and the activities to be carried out in each phase. Alternatively, if they are conducting an ex post review, somehow they must obtain assurance that system development personnel, whether they be computer professionals or end-users, understand and follow the contingency approach to system development. Next, they must evaluate the choices made across a sample of systems that have already been implemented. In either case, auditors have an onerous responsibility to know how systems should be developed under the different approaches and to be capable of evaluating the circumstances under which a particular approach is appropriate.

The following sections describe the activities to be performed in a model of the system development process that comprises 12 major phases:

1 Problem definition

2 Management of the change process

3 Entry and feasibility assessment

4 Analysis of the existing system

5 Organizational and job design

6 Information processing system design

7 Software acquisition and development

8 Procedures development

9 Acceptance testing

10 Conversion

11 Operation and maintenance

12 Postaudit

If the auditor is concerned only with asset safeguarding and data integrity, the first five phases are given only a cursory evaluation. Often it is only when the information processing system design phase begins that controls to ensure asset safeguarding and maintenance of data integrity assume particular importance in the system development process. Nevertheless, since an ineffective and inefficient system can lead eventually to a degradation in controls that ensure asset safeguarding and maintenance of data integrity, even in an attest audit the first five phases cannot be ignored.

Problem Definition

The need for change may be recognized in two ways. First, management may conceive a project through the development and maintenance of a master plan for the data processing installation. Second, management or users may recognize a problem area or an opportunity and initiate a proposal for change. Irrespective of how the need for change is recognized, a formal document should be prepared describing (a) the definition of the problem and (b) the terms of reference. The definition of the problem describes those factors that motivate the need for change. The terms of reference describe the boundaries of the system to be examined, the proposed objectives of the new system, resource constraints, organizational constraints, and a strategy for developing the system.

Once the problem definition and terms of reference have been prepared, management must give formal approval to proceed. The level of management approval required should depend upon the size and scope of the proposed project. If the project is small and its scope is limited, user management may be given the authority to approve the project. If the project is large and it has a widespread impact, top management via the steering committee may need to give approval to the project. Once formal approval is given, someone, whether they be an information analyst from the data processing department or a user skilled in high-level programming languages, has authority to "enter" the organizational area where change is needed and to undertake a feasibility assessment of the proposed changes.

During the problem recognition phase, auditors have three concerns. First, they must evaluate whether top management has established a system of authority and responsibility for project approval that will lead to systems being developed within the organization that achieve asset safeguarding, maintain data integrity, and accomplish effectiveness and efficiency objectives. As a corollary, they must ensure this system is in place and working. Second, they must determine that documentation exists which formally approves intervention by a designer and sets out the problem and terms of reference for the designer. Third, they should be concerned about who initiated the intervention. Fewer behavioral problems are likely to arise if the potential users of the system initiate the intervention.

Management of the Change Process

This phase in the system development process runs parallel to all other phases. The change process starts at the initial conception of the system and continues until the new system is running and the organization has adjusted to the new system. Management of the change process has two aspects: formal project control aspects and change facilitating aspects.

Chapter 3 discussed briefly the elements of project management: budgeting, exception reporting, checkpoints, user signoffs, etc. The application of formal project management techniques is critical to the successful development and implementation of systems. Nevertheless, the way in which these techniques are applied should vary, depending upon the type of system being implemented. For example, if the system is a straightforward operational control system, checkpoints may be well defined and signoffs may bind users to a period of constancy with respect to the system architecture. If a strategic planning system is being developed using a prototyping approach, however, checkpoints and signoffs may indicate stages where detailed reviews of progress are undertaken, but changes to the system architecture are an accepted part of the prototyping approach.

Management of the change facilitating aspects of system development is critical. Ginzberg [1981a] found that an organization's commitment to the project and its commitment to change were key issues in successful system development, irrespective of the type of system being designed and implemented. Current prescriptive models for facilitating change in the system development process tend to be some adaptation of the Lewin/Schein or Kolb/Frolman models of organizational change (see Ginzberg [1981b]). Three major classes of activities are required:

Class of activities	Explanation
Unfreezing the organization	Preparing the organization for change; providing feedback to the organizational members on their attitudes and behaviors, using techniques such as education, participatory decision making, and command
Moving the organization	Changeover to the new system
Refreezing the organization	Helping system users adapt to their new roles by providing positive feedback on their new attitudes and behaviors

Behavioral problems are likely to arise unless the designer unfreezes and refreezes the organization when a new system is implemented or an old system is modified substantially. Unfreezing activities help avoid having to *impose* change upon organization members. Refreezing activities make it more difficult for organization members to revert to their old attitudes and behavior patterns.

Various techniques can be used to unfreeze and refreeze an organization. Mumford and Henshall [1979] describe the techniques they used to implement a new online accounting system in Rolls-Royce Limited. To unfreeze the organization they formed a design team that included members from user departments, held workshops to educate members of the design team in techniques of analysis and design of work systems, conducted a series of extensive meetings with all staff to explain the aims of the project and the role of the design team, and solicited feedback from all organization members potentially affected by the proposed change. To refreeze the organization they set up a steering committee to provide positive support and encouragement to the design team and user departments; they also implemented the new system on a gradual basis so the benefits of the system could be documented and users' expectations, attitudes, and values could adjust to assimilate and evaluate the changes.

The unfreezing and refreezing techniques used will depend on the nature of the system being implemented. For example, as discussed previously, attempting to unfreeze an organization by having users participate in the system design process may be pointless if the system will have a marked effect on the existing power structure within the organization. Similarly, the resources devoted to unfreezing and refreezing an organization may be small if a system development effort has been motivated by end-users in response to a problem they are confronting and they, themselves, undertake the design and implementation work using a high-level programming language.

The auditor can obtain evidence on whether or not designers undertake unfreezing and refreezing activities by reviewing standards, examining the minutes of meetings and workshops, interviewing designers and users, determining the role of project steering committees, etc. The existence of users' own private information systems sometimes indicates refreezing activities may not have been undertaken.

Entry and Feasibility Assessment

The change process commences by the designer initiating entry to the organizational areas that will be affected by the new system. The objective of entry is to establish a commitment to change. Depending upon the effects of the system on the existing power structure, the designer attempts either to foster among users a spirit of collaborative analysis and evaluation of the existing system or to negotiate a contract for change. Other factors also affect how entry is attempted. If the designer is the end-user who motivated the new system, clearly a commitment to change exists already. If the proposed system potentially impacts the structure of jobs or reward systems, successful entry often is an onerous task. If the proposed system simply replaces an existing computer system, entry may be a minor task; indeed, users may consider that their time is being wasted if the designer involves them in an extensive series of workshops, presentations, and group meetings. Again, the designer must identify the relevant contingencies and choose an appropriate entry strategy.

However entry is accomplished, sociotechnical design theorists emphasize the importance of the task and how it is carried out by the designer, especially when the proposed system significantly impacts the social system. Though management may want a new system, users of the system may not desire change. Unless the designer successfully accomplishes entry, further progress cannot be made or the system must be imposed upon users. Failure to enter may result in the designer having to withdraw and the proposal for the new system having to be scrapped, at least temporarily.

If entry is successful, the designer can then carry out a preliminary study to evaluate the feasibility of the new system. There are four bases for evaluating feasibility:

Basis for evaluation	Issues
Technical feasibility	Is the available technology sufficient to support the proposed project? Can the technology be acquired or developed?
Operational feasibility	Can the input data be collected for the system and is the output usable?
Economic feasibility	Does the project have a positive net present value?
Behavioral feasibility	What impact will the system have on the users' quality of working life?

As discussed in Chapter 3, the specific techniques used to evaluate the feasibility of the systems vary, depending upon the type of system being proposed. If there is substantial uncertainty surrounding the system, an approach such as Keen's [1981] value analysis might be used. If the level of uncertainty surrounding the system is low, traditional return-on-investment evaluation criteria might be used.

The completion of the initial feasibility assessment constitutes an important checkpoint. At this time management must decide whether the project should proceed. Nevertheless, even if a decision is made to continue, the feasibility of the system should be reassessed periodically throughout the system development life cycle. As new information is gathered, the evaluation can be more complete and management may need to reconsider its decision on the viability of the system.

With respect to the entry and feasibility assessment phase, the auditor's primary objectives are to determine whether a new system or a modification to an existing system was imposed upon users, and to ensure that an application is converted to the computer only if the benefits exceed the costs. There should be evidence in the form of reports, minutes of meetings, etc., to show that the designer successfully accomplished the unfreezing process and that a feasibility study was undertaken carefully.

Analysis of the Existing System

When a new system is proposed, the designer needs to understand the organizational context in which the system will operate and the old system if one exists already. This understanding must encompass the existing social and technical systems, the coordinating mechanisms, and the overall requirements for the new system.

The analysis of the existing system serves two purposes. First, it provides the basis for managing the change process. For example: knowledge of the coordinating mechanisms (e.g., reward system) for the social and technical systems establishes how these mechanisms must be adjusted when a new system is implemented; knowledge of the users' flexibility or rigidity to change impacts the rate at which change can be implemented successfully. Second, it provides the basis for determining the *strategic* requirements for the new system. These strategic requirements establish the goals and policies for the new system that guide the elicitation of detailed requirements and the design process. They include both task accomplishment and quality of working life considerations.

Analysis of the existing system involves four major tasks:

1 Study the present organization
2 Study the product and information flows
3 Formulate strategic requirements for the new system
4 Evaluate the present system

The conduct of these tasks can vary considerably, depending upon whether a system is already in place and working, the nature of the proposed system, and the extent of its likely impact on the organization. For example, if the proposed system is a decision support system to assist top financial managers in undertaking strategic planning, aside from informal information flows and private information systems maintained by each manager, there may be no existing system to study. Similarly, if the proposed system will have a substantial impact on the quality of working life of users or the power structure within the organization, formulating the strategic requirements for the new system may be a very difficult task involving extensive negotiation, iteration, and user involvement. In this light, therefore, the following sections provide a brief overview of the activities that might be undertaken to accomplish each task.

Study the Present Organization The designer studies the present organization to gain an understanding of the existing social and technical systems and coordinating mechanisms and the willingness of the organization to change. Figure 4-5 shows the variable sets in an organization that can be manipulated to create alternative organizational designs. Manipulation of one variable set may require changing another variable set if task accomplishment or the quality of working life is not to degrade.

From a design viewpoint the critical variable set is the set of coordinating mechanisms. Usually the designer can do little about the tasks that must be

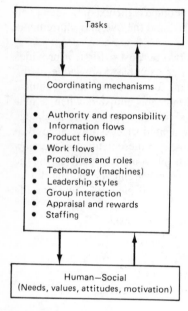

FIGURE 4-5
Variable sets that can be manipulated to create alternative organizational designs.

accomplished and the needs, values, etc., of individuals in the organization. However, the set of coordinating mechanisms can be manipulated to achieve a "best" match between task accomplishment objectives and human-social objectives. Miles [1975] illustrates the choices that can be made with respect to some of the major coordinating mechanisms:

Coordinating mechanisms	Example range of choices
Direction	Unilateral versus joint determination of goals and objectives; close and direct supervision versus supportive supervision allowing self-direction and control
Organizational and job design	Hierarchically structured, highly specialized teams versus loosely structured, self-paced heterogeneous teams; highly specialized tasks versus tasks encompassing a wide range of activities
Selection, training, appraisal, and development	Selection and training focusing on traits and abilities versus the long-run needs of the organization and the individual; supervision versus joint appraisal of progress; unilateral versus joint determination of targets and objectives
Communications and control	Vertical flows of information versus diffusing needed information directly to the decision point; transmission of information to distant points versus systems with a short feedback loop

Coordinating mechanisms	Example range of choices
Reward systems	Systems based on longevity or merit alone versus systems that acknowledge both loyalty and performance; unilateral versus joint determination of the nature of rewards and the paths by which they can be attained

By studying the present organization the designer sees the design choices that have been made. This not only suggests ways of improvement but also indicates the likely impact that changing one variable set will have on another variable set.

Study the Product and Information Flows Since the information system usually is the major concern of the designer, it is important that any existing information systems be understood so that information needs and the strengths and weaknesses of the existing systems can be determined. In some cases the information system supports a product flow. Understanding the product flow helps the designer to understand the information system and to formulate the information requirements of a new design.

Several formal methodologies have been developed to assist the designer to understand the existing product and information flows. Perhaps the most popular is structured analysis (see, for example, De Marco [1978], Weinberg [1979], and Gane and Sarson [1979]). Structured analysis is a top-down, breadth-first approach to studying a system that is supported by a set of tools to document data flows, define data, and describe logic and policy. It is a data-driven methodology in the sense that designers focus on the flow of data through a system rather than, say, the procedures executed in the system or the flow of control.

The central tool of structured analysis is the data flow diagram (DFD). A DFD is a pictorial representation of the flow of data through a system. It comprises four basic elements: (*a*) data flows—represented by named vectors; (*b*) processes—represented by circles, rounded-edge rectangles, or "bubbles"; (*c*) files or data stores—represented by straight lines or open-ended rectangles; and (*d*) external entities or data sources/sinks—represented by squares. Constructing a DFD usually involves a two-step process. First, a *physical* DFD is drawn showing how the logical flow of data is currently implemented. Second, a *logical* DFD is derived showing "what" is done and not "how" it is done.

To illustrate how a DFD can be used, consider Figure 4-6, which shows a DFD for an order entry system. Each bubble in the DFD is decomposed into further levels of detail. For example, Figure 4-7 presents a more detailed description of the data flow in bubble 4: Price Order. By recursively breaking down the bubbles into further levels of detail, top-down, breadth-first decomposition occurs—the notion of "leveling" the DFD in structured analysis terms.

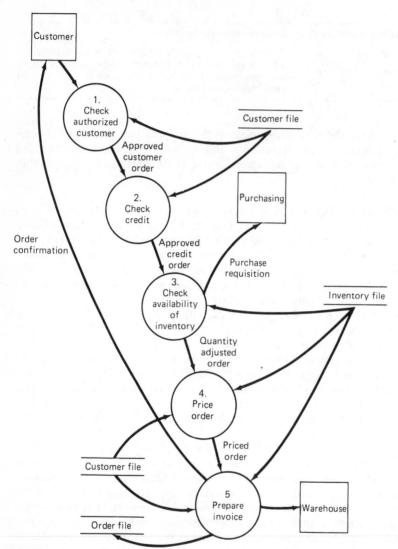

FIGURE 4-6
Data flow diagram for order entry system.

   The elements in a DFD require further definition if the nature of the system is to be clear. When the bubbles have been "exploded" to their lowest-level bubbles, the logic of these lowest-level bubbles must be described. Three techniques are used: decision tables, decision trees, and structured English. Figure 4-8 shows how the logic for bubble 4.2 in Figure 4-7 might be represented using these three techniques. Decision tables and decision trees

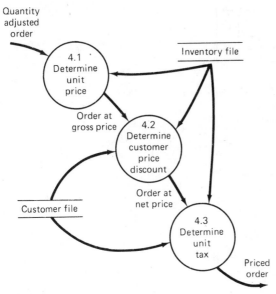

FIGURE 4-7
Lower level data flow diagram for "price order" bubble.

tend to be used when the procedures to be defined primarily describe conditional logic. Structured English tends to be used when the procedures to be defined describe sequence logic.

The data flows and data stores must also be described in a data dictionary. Figure 4-9 shows how the data flow "order" might be partially described using the data dictionary conventions given by De Marco [1978]. Before defining the data, however, proponents of structured analysis argue the data flows and data stores should be placed in their "simplest" form using the techniques of "normalization" derived from relational database management systems theory (see, for example, Gane and Sarson [1979]). In addition, data structure diagrams might be constructed to show the access paths available to various data items maintained in files in the database.

Once the existing information system has been understood via the DFD, any associated materials or product flows can be examined. Gane and Sarson [1979, pp. 43–46] show how a materials flowchart can be integrated with a DFD to provide an overall understanding of the system.

Still other structured analysis techniques can be used by designers (or auditors) to understand the existing product and information flows. For example, a technique called a Warnier-Orr diagram can be used to map data structure considerations and functional considerations onto a single chart (see Orr [1977]). An analysis approach called SADT (system analysis and design

Type of customer	W	W	R	R
Type of inventory	A	B	A	B
Discount (%)	10	15	5	10

(a)

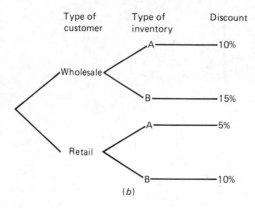

(b)

```
IF order is from wholesale customer
and IF order is for Type-A inventory item
    THEN item-discount is 10%
    ELSE order is for Type-B inventory item
        SO item-discount is 15%
ELSE order is from retail customer
SO IF order is for Type-A inventory item
    THEN item-discount is 5%
    ELSE order is for Type-B inventory item
        SO item-discount is 10%
```

(c)

FIGURE 4-8
Representation of procedural logic for DFD bubble: (a) decision table; (b) decision tree; (c) structured English.

FIGURE 4-9
Partial definition of order in data dictionary.

```
Order      = Order-Number + Customer-Name
             + Mailing-Address + Shipping-Address
             +{Order-Line}+ Carrier +
             Order-Date +{Customer-Instruction-Line}


Order-Line = Line-Number + Product-Number + Product-Description
             + Quantity + Unit-of-Measure
```

technique) extends a DFD to include control flow considerations and the components used to perform the functions represented by each bubble (see, for example, Ross [1977]). Colter [1984] provides a comparative evaluation of these techniques. He points out that each technique can be useful under different circumstances. Furthermore, he argues that all structured analysis techniques tend to provide weak specifications of input/output details. Thus, traditional analysis techniques that document input/output details still have their place.

Formulate Strategic Requirements   A major purpose of studying the existing system is to formulate the strategic requirements of the new system. The strategic requirements specify the *overall* goals and objectives to be accomplished. They are identified based on perceived deficiencies in the existing system or perceived opportunities for enhanced task accomplishment and quality of working life.

Sociotechnical design theorists stress the importance of carefully eliciting the strategic requirements for a system *before* system design commences. They argue that many system failures can be attributed to inadequate performance of this activity. Both management and users must be consulted, as their strategic requirements often differ. Management's strategic requirements tend to be primarily task accomplishment oriented. They may be vague; for example, increase the wealth of the shareholders. They may be more specific; for example, provide information that will allow 5% penetration of a market, or produce a product below a given cost subject to various constraints relating to the amount of pollutant emitted. The users' strategic requirements tend to involve quality of working life issues: economic security, self-esteem, job satisfaction, control and influence, leisure. Users may be concerned with maintaining a set of flexible and differentiated tasks rather than having rigid, narrowly defined tasks. Or they may be concerned with maintaining a set of simple tasks so their work is less stressful and they have more time and energy for leisure activities. A union may be concerned with maintaining its share of power in the management of an organization. Of course, managers may consider quality of working life issues, particularly if they are also system users; and users may consider task accomplishment issues, particularly if the system is critical to the ongoing viability of the organization.

Formulating strategic requirements at the outset gives recognition to the fact that information systems *can* be neutral technology. For a given job design, for example, it is possible to design and implement different information systems. The strategic requirements form the basis for evaluating the alternatives. Forcing people, job designs, organization structures, etc., to fit information systems can be a root cause of behavioral problems.

Evaluate the Present System   In light of information obtained from the previous activities, the existing system (to the extent that one exists) can be evaluated. Though this activity was performed during the initial feasibility assessment phase, the gathering of more detailed information provides the basis for reassessing the proposed system. Again, the specific design that will be chosen is still unclear; however, knowledge of the strategic requirements for the system helps the designer determine a set of design alternatives that are likely to be feasible.

Organizational and Job Design

Traditionally, system design has meant the design of the information processing system only. There has been an implied expectation that users will adapt to the demands of the system. In some cases this expectation will be realized; in other cases behavioral problems will result that lead to implementation failure.

During the elicitation of strategic requirements for the new system, the designer must determine the desired relationships between the organizational structure, job design, and the information processing system design. An information processing system can be used strategically as a mechanism for change. For example, management may authorize the design and implementation of a decision support system to bring about changes in the way managers do their job. Ginzberg [1978] points out that in these circumstances implementation success is dependent upon the designer carefully working out the level of change required and adopting appropriate change facilitating strategies (see, also, Chapter 23).

Often, however, information processing systems should be designed to *support* organizational and job designs; that is, the organizational and job designs dictate the shape of the information system, not vice versa. To illustrate this design philosphy, Hedberg [1975] provides two examples of how computer systems were designed to support particular organizational and job designs that attempted to enrich the quality of working life without decreasing task performance. The first is a new car assembly plant where the traditional assembly line was broken up and the logistics of the production system changed to support small semiautonomous groups of 15 to 20 members. Each team was responsible for one complete function of the car, for example, the electrical system. The computer system was designed to support this decentralized structure. Online terminals provided continuous quality control information back to worker groups. The second is a registration system for immigration authorities. The introduction of a new online registration and retrieval system foreshadowed increased task accomplishment, at least initially, but decreased quality of working life. The clerks directly involved in using the system participated in the strategic design of the system. The final design of the terminal system facilitated various forms of rotation of duties which, compared with the old system, provided a more stimulating work environment (see, also, Mumford and Weir [1979]).

In this light, therefore, the following sections provide an overview of three major activities that must be undertaken in organizational and job design:

1 Elicitation of detailed requirements
2 Design of the organization structure
3 Design of the job structure

Again, the conduct and extent of these activities will depend upon the level of change desired as determined in the formulation of the strategic requirements for the system.

Elicitation of Detailed Requirements   When an organization formulates its goals and objectives, one of the first steps to be undertaken is an analysis of the tasks to be performed to accomplish these goals and objectives. The nature of these tasks suggests the type of organization structure that will facilitate their accomplishment and, in the context of an organization structure, the type of job design needed. For example, as discussed in Chapter 3, if there is substantial uncertainty surrounding the task, a loose, organic organization structure may be needed; conversely, if the tasks are straightforward, a formal, mechanistic organization structure may work best. The job design must be congruent with the organization structure chosen; for example, it is pointless to have a rigidly structured job in an organization structure set up to facilitate free flows of information between the organization and its environment and among the employees in the organization. Nevertheless, these considerations must be mediated by the quality of working life goals of the employees who will perform the tasks. It is pointless, for example, to set up a challenging, demanding job structure for employees who are unhappy with high-stress loads.

How the designer elicits the detailed task accomplishment and quality of working life objectives that drive the organization and job designs varies considerably. For example, if the designer is the user employing a high-level programming language to implement a decision support system, the elicitation of detailed task accomplishment and quality of working life objectives may be a brief, informal activity undertaken mainly by introspection. On the other hand, if a major transaction processing system for the organization is being designed, skilled organizational psychologists and job analysts may be required to assist the designer not only in the elicitation of detailed requirements but also in the formulation of organizational and job designs.

Design of the Organization Structure   Once a preliminary set of task accomplishment and quality of working life requirements has been obtained, various organizational designs can be considered and evaluated. Chapter 3 described some of the fundamental relationships between the task requirements and the organizational design that must be considered; for example, if the task is uncertain and it requires substantial amounts of information if it is to be performed properly, an organization structure must be chosen that facilitates information processing. Recall, contingency theory says that there is no one best organization design to cover all situations and that not all ways of organizing are equally effective. The design process is made even more complicated when quality of working life requirements must be considered. Again, a requirement for highly enriched jobs may preclude certain types of organization structures. Inevitably the design process is iterative whereby detailed requirements are reconsidered in light of possible organization designs and job designs.

Design of the Job Structure   As with organization designs, there is no one best job design across all situations. Miles [1975] identifies three major types of job designs that might be used:

Model of job design	Explanation
Job design under the traditional model	Individuals are assumed to be more interested in what they earn rather than what they do. Jobs contain a limited number of tasks requiring similar skills and the same learning period. There is separation between thinking and doing.
Job design under the human relations model	Job prescriptions under this model are the same as for the traditional model. The difference is the focus on the context in which the job is performed, i.e., the conditions of the job. Task accomplishment is still the primary objective; however, the manager must be concerned with human needs to facilitate task accomplishment.
Job design under the human resources model	This is the most complex model. Employees accept responsibility for their own self-direction and control. The manager's role is to guide and to assist employees to this position. Satisfaction is a by-product rather than a direct target of management activities.

How does the designer (and the auditor) know what job design is "right" in a given situation? Unfortunately, resolving this question still constitutes a major research area. For the same task, different employees sometimes prefer different job designs. For example, Hackman [1979b] reports the findings of a study that examined the change in job satisfaction levels of six Detroit auto workers who worked on a traditional assembly line, after they had worked for a month in the highly "enriched" team assembly jobs in a Swedish automobile plant. At the end of the month, five of the six workers stated that they preferred the traditional assembly line job design.

A useful model for considering how jobs might be designed has been proposed by Hackman [1979a]. He argues that high task accomplishment and high job satisfaction are a function of the experienced meaningfulness of work, the experienced responsibility in a job, and knowledge of results. These variables in turn are a function of five core job dimensions that can be manipulated by the designer: (a) skill variety—the extent to which the job requires different talents; (b) task identity—the extent to which an identifiable and complete job must be accomplished; (c) task significance—the extent to which the job impacts others; (d) autonomy—the extent to which the job allows freedom, independence, and discretion; and (e) feedback—the extent to which employees know the consequences of their performance. Instruments are available that allow each of these dimensions to be measured and evaluated. To the extent that a job is deficient on a particular dimension, it can be redesigned.

Information Processing System Design

For the auditor acting as a participant in the system development process, the information processing system design phase is one of major involvement. From a system effectiveness viewpoint the auditor is concerned with whether the design meets strategic requirements. From an efficiency viewpoint the auditor is concerned with the resources that will be needed to run the system. From an asset safeguarding and data integrity viewpoint the auditor is concerned with the controls designed into the system.

During this phase the auditor also evaluates the ongoing auditability of the system. The auditor may deem it necessary to build certain audit capabilities into the system in the form of audit modules. These modules capture data or examine conditions of interest to the auditor concurrently with production running of the system. Chapter 19 provides a detailed discussion of the nature and purposes of these audit modules and the ways in which they might be designed and implemented.

When evaluating the information processing system design phase, either as a participant in the design process or in an ex post review capacity, the auditor must examine six major activities:

1 Elicitation of detailed requirements
2 Design of the data/information flow
3 Design of the database
4 Design of the user interface
5 Physical design
6 Design of the hardware/software configuration

As with the previous phases, these activities may vary considerably depending on the type of system being designed and implemented. Nevertheless, the following sections provide an overview of how they might be performed.

Elicitation of Detailed Requirements Davis [1982] identifies four ways of eliciting detailed information requirements for a system:

1 Asking the users of the system
2 Deriving the requirements from an existing system
3 Synthesizing the characteristics from the utilizing system
4 Discovering from experimentation with an evolving system

The primary factor affecting the choice of the elicitation approach is the level of uncertainty surrounding the system to be developed. In turn, the level of uncertainty is a function of whether or not a set of usable requirements is available, the ability of users to specify their requirements, and the ability of designers to elicit and evaluate requirements. If on all measures the level of uncertainty is low, it may be possible simply to ask users what they need. As the level of uncertainly increases, however, the simpler elicitation strategies become ineffective; there may be no existing system on which to base requirements, or the utilizing system may be unstable and poorly understood. At the highest levels of uncertainty, an experimental approach to eliciting requirements must be used.

Design of the Data/Information Flow   The design of the data and information flows is the primary step in the *conceptual design* of the new system. It is undertaken in light of any organizational and job design that has resulted and the detailed information requirements that have been elicited. Three decisions must be made:

1 The flow of data and information and the transformation points must be determined.

2 The frequency and timing of the data and information flows must be determined.

3 The extent to which data and information flows will be formalized must be determined.

With respect to the first decision, the designer may be influenced by existing flows of data and information, the organizational and job design that has been proposed, the information needs of users expressed during the elicitation process, or the results of experimentation with alternative data and information flows. The flow of data and information through the proposed system must be charted, and the transformations needed to manipulate data or to convert data into information must be specified. A tool such as a data flow diagram (described earlier in the chapter) can be used for these purposes.

The frequency and timing of the data and information flows affect when data must be submitted to the system, when it must be processed, and when output must be provided. Several factors may influence this decision. The nature of the job may dictate immediate output requirements; for example, a user is monitoring a continuous production process. The service level to be provided to customers may dictate a fast response to enquiries is required. High levels of uncertainty surrounding the task may mean that more frequent reports are required (see Galbraith [1977]).

The extent to which data and information flows can be formalized affects the assignment of data and information processing to users or the computer. As the level of formalization increases, responsibility can transfer from people to the machine. In the past, designers have tended to focus only on the formal data and information flows. In many systems, however, the informal flows may be critical. For example, much of the data needed for a decision support system may be provided via informal data flows.

Design of the Database The design of the database involves determining its *scope* (context) and *structure*. The scope of the database ranges from local to global. A major factor affecting the scope of the database is the extent of interdependence among organizational units. The greater the interdependence, the greater the need for a global database to prevent suboptimization by subunits. Organizations with highly interdependent subunits also have more incentive to share data resources, for example, by using a database management system. However, as the database becomes more global, cost increases.

Choosing the "optimal" structure for the database is an extremely complex decision. There are many interacting variables, and the problem must be solved subject to certain constraints such as the retrieval time required and the storage space available. Some of the major design considerations are:

1 Response time required

2 Frequency of record addition, deletion, and modification

3 Storage space required—primary versus secondary

4 Ease of programming

5 Data integrity constraints

6 Data redundancy permissible

The structural design of the database involves four decisions:

Decision	Explanation
Choice of the infological structure	The infological structure shows the user's view of the data. It is a logical representation indicating the entities and their interrelationships and the attributes of these entities and relationships to be stored in the database. Different users may require different logical "views" of the same data. The total representation of data in the database is sometimes called the schema; the subset that a particular user may view is sometimes called the subschema.
Choice of the data structure	The infological structure, which is a high-level representation of the data, must be mapped into a more formal structure that is amenable to computer processing. This more formal, but still logical, structure is called a data model or data structure. It shows the choice of data items, groups of data items, and relationships between groups to be established in the database. Four data structures that are often used are a flat file, tree, network, and relation.

Decision	Explanation
Choice of the storage structure	How to linearize and partition the data structure so it can be represented on storage media. Choice of the external access paths, e.g., direct addressing, indexing, hashing. Choice of the internal access paths, e.g., sequential search, binary search. Choice of a structure, e.g., chain, multilist, inverted list, B-tree.
Choice of the physical representation	How to represent the storage structure on the physical media, e.g., across tracks, cylinders, disks.

Methodologies for designing databases are currently in a state of flux. Some organizations are attempting to design the database somewhat independently of the application systems that use the data. They argue that the patterns of access to data are now difficult to determine since users may employ high-level languages to gain access to and to manipulate the data. Thus, it is important to try to design the database from the viewpoint of the whole enterprise rather than the viewpoint of applications. Other organizations design the database after the information flow has been determined since they argue good design can occur only in light of knowing the functions to be performed in a system. Still other organizations attempt to design the database concurrently with the design of the information flow. They argue that the design of the functions to be performed by the system and the design of the data to be accessed and manipulated is an iterative process because both designs are interrelated. Finally, there is still substantial debate over the "right" infological structure, data structure, storage structure, and physical representation to be used. The bibliography to this chapter contains several references for further reading.

Design of the User Interface   The design of the user interface involves determining the ways in which users will interact with a system. Given the diversity of technology now available to support the user interface, the design process can be complex and multifaceted. Some of the elements that may have to be designed are:

1 Source documents to capture raw data
2 Hard-copy output reports
3 Screen layouts for dedicated source document input
4 Inquiry screens for database interrogation
5 Command language for the decision support system
6 Interrogation languages for the database
7 Graphic and color displays
8 Voice output to guide users or answer queries
9 Screen layouts for manipulation by a light pen or mouse
10 Icons for pictorial representation of output

From an audit perspective, the design of the user interface can be a critical activity, as it affects the extent to which users will make errors when interacting with the system. For example, a poorly designed source document may result in users capturing data incorrectly; similarly, poorly designed graphics output can result in users making erroneous decisions because the output misleads them. Chapters 9, 10, 11, and 15 examine the design of the user interface in more detail.

Physical Design So far the design activities that have been described address primarily the logical or conceptual aspects of the system. Ultimately the logical design must be converted to a physical design if it is to run on a machine. The physical design process involves breaking up the logical design into units which, in turn, can be decomposed further into implementation units such as programs and modules.

If the logical design has been expressed via a logical data flow diagram, Page-Jones [1980] advocates breaking up the system into jobs by identifying and drawing three types of physical boundaries on the DFD:

Type of boundary	Explanation
Hardware .	It may be cost-effective to implement different parts of the system on different machines; e.g., data may be captured and validated using a microcomputer while database update may be better accomplished on a mainframe.
Batch/online/realtime	Some parts of the system may require only periodic actions, e.g., generation of hard-copy reports. Other parts may require an immediate response, e.g., answers to customer telephone queries on inventory availability. Still other parts require data to be updated immediately, e.g., funds investment in a system to support short-term money market operations.
Cycle (periodicity)	Functions to support generation of, say, a monthly report can be separated from functions that update inventory availability.

Once the job boundaries have been identified, the jobs can be partitioned into job steps. In general, system complexity is reduced if a job is partitioned into as few job steps as possible since more job steps produce a need for more intermediate files. Figure 4-10 shows job step partitioning for a sales reporting system. A cycle boundary exists between the submission of sales data from salespersons and the preparation of sales reports because the submission of sales data occurs more frequently than the preparation of sales reports. Thus, receipt and validation of data is a separate job from the preparation of reports. The preparation of reports is then partitioned into two separate job steps because of the availability of a commercial sort package and a commercial report package that will update files and prepare reports. Job steps, in turn, are partitioned into programs and load units.

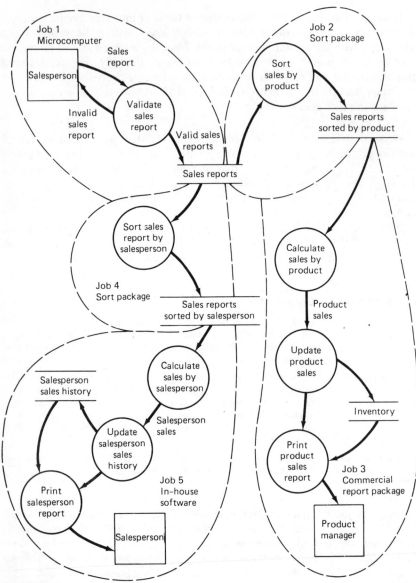

FIGURE 4-10
Packaging of logical system design into jobs.

Still other ways of undertaking physical design may be used. For example, if the logical design emerges from experimentation with a high-level language, the physical design may occur by default. If the designer deems it not to be worthwhile to reprogram the resulting system in a low-level language, the architecture of the high-level language dictates the form of the physical design. Similarly, it may be clear that the logical design can be accommodated using a generalized application package. Again, the architecture of the package will dictate the physical design, except to the extent that the user must choose parameter values when the package is initially configured.

Design of the Hardware/Software Configuration In some cases the new system requires hardware and system software not currently available in the organization. For example, a decision support system may require high-quality graphics output that cannot be supported with the existing hardware and software; user work stations may have to be purchased to support an office automation system; a minicomputer may have to be purchased to provide the extra processing resources consumed by a system programmed in a high-level language. Chapter 3 described the methodology to be followed in determining hardware and system software needs, preparing a manual of specifications, and undertaking an evaluation of alternative proposals.

Software Acquisition and Development

After the system design phase is complete, software acquisition or development may have to be undertaken. In some cases generalized software packages may be purchased to perform all or some of the job steps in the system. These packages have to be configured and perhaps modified and adapted. In other cases the system may exist in a prototype form at the conclusion of the design phase. Attempts may be made to tune the prototype so it runs more efficiently. In still other cases new programs must be developed from scratch. Various activities must be undertaken: design, coding, compiling, testing, and documenting. Chapter 5 discusses these activities further.

During this phase the audit staff themselves may be involved in acquiring or developing software for any audit modules to be embedded in the system. If generalized audit software is to be purchased, they must specify the tasks that the software must accomplish and test the software to ensure its suitability. If audit programs must be developed, they must be involved in at least the design and testing phases; coding, compiling, and documenting might be performed by professional programmers.

Procedures Development

During the procedures development phase the designer specifies the activities that users and computer operators must undertake to support the ongoing operation of the system and to obtain useful output. In general, the objective is to provide minimum specification of procedures. What needs to be done should be clearly specified; where possible, how it should be done should be left to the person responsible for the task. Overspecification of procedures can result in a stultifying job that leads to a degradation in controls.

Procedures development involves four major tasks:

Task	Explanation
Design of procedures	To the extent that procedures must be specified, they must be matched with the job/task design. What triggers the task and the task input and output must be identified.
Testing of procedures	Users and operators must evaluate the adequacy of the design. They may suggest modifications in light of their experience during the test.
Implementation of procedures	Conformity with system procedures represents the most direct way that individuals have to change their behavior when a new system is implemented. Management of the change process can be especially critical during this task.
Documentation of procedures	User and operator procedures must be formally documented in manuals. Where possible, procedures manuals should be written in a consistent and formal style such as PLAYSCRIPT (see Haga [1968]).

As with the previous phases, procedures development may be a formal, linear process or it may be somewhat informal and iterative, depending upon the uncertainty surrounding the phase. The auditor's primary concern is to see well-documented user and operator manuals that provide a sound basis for the day-to-day control over system operations.

Acceptance Testing

The purpose of acceptance testing is to identify as far as possible any errors and deficiencies in the system prior to its final release for implementation. Errors and deficiencies can exist in the software supporting the system, the user interface, procedures manuals, the job design, the organizational design, etc. Acceptance testing is carried out to identify these errors or deficiencies before they have a widespread impact on users or the organization.

The conduct of acceptance testing can vary considerably, depending upon the type of system being implemented and the activities undertaken during system development. For example, if substantial amounts of program code have been written, acceptance testing must attempt to ensure the code is authorized, accurate, and complete. If generalized software has been purchased and the software has an extensive user base or it has been "certified" by a public accounting firm, acceptance testing may focus primarily on deficiencies in the job design or user procedures. If the system has been developed using a high-level language, testing may be iterative as various system prototypes are tried and discarded.

In most cases, acceptance testing cannot be comprehensive; that is, all aspects of the system cannot be tested. There are five reasons. First, it is difficult to conceive of every execution path through a system of moderate complexity. Second, deficiencies in the system may become apparent only with extensive use of the system. For example, users may realize they have an inadequate job design or an inadequate procedures manual only after they gain experience with the system. Third, it is difficult to conceive of every condition under which the system must operate. Exceptional circumstances may arise, such as an abnormal system load or a rare combination of transactions, which were not anticipated in the design of acceptance tests. Fourth, in some cases it is difficult to know whether a result is correct, anyway. For example, a complex algorithm may have been implemented in a decision support system. Whether the algorithm is a correct model of reality may be uncertain. Fifth, even with the availability of testing tools such as test data generators (see Chapter 5), acceptance testing can be costly. At some point the costs of extra testing outweigh the expected benefits. Because of these difficulties, it is better to design and implement systems without errors or deficiencies in the first place rather than to attempt to remove errors through the acceptance testing process.

There are three major types of acceptance testing:

Type of Testing	Explanation
Program testing	Programmers who develop individual programs must test the processing accuracy and efficiency of their programs.
System testing	Testing the overall information processing system with emphasis on the interfaces between programs within the system.
User testing	Testing the *total* system including the job design, organizational design, user interface, procedures, programs, etc. Provides the basis for management and users signing off on the final system.

From an audit viewpoint an important aspect of testing is the planning and design of test data and the documentation of test results. Careful planning and design is necessary since resources for testing are not unlimited, and the objective is to obtain the maximum benefits possible. The auditor should check that test documentation shows:

1 How the testing process was planned
2 How test data was designed and developed
3 What test data was used
4 What results were obtained
5 Action taken as a result of errors identified
6 Subsequent modifications to test data

One of the outcomes of the testing phase should be a test bed of data for individual programs and the overall system that should be properly documented and maintained. A test bed facilitates later testing of modifications and maintenance to the system by making available a standard set of test data with known, documented results.

Conversion

Conversion involves changing over from the existing system, if one exists, to the new system. Depending upon the nature of the system being developed, it may be a minor step or it may involve major efforts that extend over a long time period. For example, if users have developed a small decision support system using a high-level programming language, conversion may occur progressively as they experiment with various system prototypes. There may be no existing system, aside from informal, private information systems that provide meager support for their decision making activities. The transition to the new system occurs almost by default. Alternatively, the implementation of a major organizationwide application system often requires extensive planning and control of the conversion phase. Significant disruption to the day-to-day activities of the organization may be unavoidable.

If some type of system exists already, conversion to a new system can occur in one of three ways. First, the old system may be totally stopped and the new system takes over immediately. Second, both systems may run in parallel for a period (but performing different functions) with output from both systems being used. Third, both systems may run in parallel (performing the same functions) with the old system output being used. In this last case, parallel running provides the basis for validating the design and implementation of the new system.

Changeover to a new system may involve four activities:

Activity	Explanation
Personnel training	Primary and secondary users of the system need training. For example, primary users such as management need training in the use of system output. Secondary users such as clerks need training in the preparation of input. Operators and programmers need training if new hardware and software has been purchased.
Installation of new hardware	If new hardware and software has been purchased, it must be installed.
Conversion of files and programs	This can be a complex and lengthy process, particularly when there is a changeover from a manual system. Taking up manual system files may involve several months of work. Maintaining two systems in parallel may place substantial strain on the users of the system.
Scheduling of operations and test running	Scheduling involves timing of input, processing, and output. The schedules should be tested for a period and any needed adjustments made before the final schedule is frozen and documented.

The auditor is especially concerned with several aspects of the conversion phase. If substantial disruption is likely to occur, asset safeguarding, data integrity, effectiveness, and efficiency are at risk. For example, a programmer may take advantage of a situation where there is insufficient time to review a program modification to install unauthorized code; or a data entry clerk may introduce unauthorized transactions into the system when there are large backlogs of data to be processed and errors to be corrected. Conversion can also be a time when tempers become frayed and users become severely disillusioned with the system such that they inhibit its implementation. Often tradeoffs must be made between the integrity of data taken up on the system and the need to get the system running; for example, data validation criteria may be relaxed because of the large number of errors identified with a view to getting the system operational and later undertaking error correction.

Careful planning of the activities to be undertaken during the conversion phase is essential for most systems. Controls to ensure asset safeguarding, data integrity, effectiveness, and efficiency must be designed and implemented. For example, control totals might be used to ensure data being converted from one storage medium to another is not corrupted. In addition, the conversion phase then must be carefully monitored so that the problems can be identified promptly and remedial action taken.

Operation and Maintenance

During the operation of a system, three types of changes may be needed. First, logic errors may be discovered that require correction. Second, changes in the system (user) environment may necessitate system modification. Third, changes may be made to improve processing efficiency. Whatever the reason for maintenance, the auditor's primary concern is that a formal change process exists to authorize and control needed changes to the system. This formal change process is more important in systems that are used widely throughout the organization and which perform basic and critical functions. Even in small systems developed by users for their own purposes, however, formal change procedures may still be important. Small, localized systems may support users who are making critical decisions affecting the overall welfare of the organization. The introduction of erroneous modifications into these systems can have widespread consequences, therefore. Maintenance activities on these systems need to be approved and carefully monitored.

Postaudit

Periodically a system needs to be reviewed and evaluated to determine how well it is meeting its objectives. A review team might comprise representatives from management, users, and audit. It should seek to obtain answers to such questions as:

1 How has the system impacted task accomplishment and the quality of working life of the users?

2 Do the benefits of the system exceed the costs?

3 Are there any major problem areas with the system?

4 Can modifications be made to improve effectiveness, efficiency, and data integrity?

5 What has been learned from the system so that the system development process can be improved?

The postaudit is the basic means of ensuring that a system adapts to organizational and user changes. Chapters 22, 23, and 24 discuss in more detail the activities that might be performed during a postaudit. The existence of an ongoing series of postaudits provides the auditor with evidence that the organization is making a serious attempt to recognize deficiencies, identify opportunities, and adapt its systems accordingly.

MANAGING THE SYSTEM DEVELOPMENT PROCESS

It should be apparent from the discussion so far that effective management of the system development process will be a difficult affair. The previous sections have pointed out the range of system development approaches that might be undertaken and the diversity of ways in which system development activities might be performed. This final section of the chapter addresses two further issues: (a) organizing the system development team and (b) controlling user-developed systems. Both issues have important implications for the auditor.

Organizing the System Development Team

Traditionally, organizing the system development team involved a choice between a team set up along functional lines and a team set up along project lines. Contingency theory predicted that functional teams worked better when the task was routine and straightforward whereas project teams worked better when the task was uncertain (see Chapter 3). In both cases, however, the teams comprised skilled data processing professionals, perhaps aided by user representatives if quality of working life, organizational design, or job design considerations arose.

With the advent of high-level programming languages and the widespread availability of packaged software, the choice of an organizational structure for the system development team is not as clear-cut, nor is it a choice that is easily controlled by data processing management or top management. There has been a gradual transition of control over systems into user areas. User managers are not only demanding control over traditional resources, they are also seeking control over the information systems and data processing resources needed by their areas.

Because end-user computing offers many benefits, it will be impossible to prevent the growth of user-developed systems in organizations (see, for example, Rockart and Flannery [1983]). Thus, organizations must attempt to formalize how user system development teams are organized and controlled; otherwise, systems may be developed that are not consistent with the overall goals of the organization. Several possibilities exist. Someone in the user area might be trained in system development methodologies, especially project management skills. A data processing professional might act in an advisory capacity to the user system development team. Organizations might set up an information center staffed by personnel skilled in user system development methodologies (see Hammond [1982]). However, in their survey of organizations employing end-user computing, Rockart and Flannery [1983] found that end-users were seeking *distributed* support: they wanted someone to act as a focal point when assistance was needed; furthermore, this person had to be "local."

Whatever the approach taken to organizing end-user system development teams, it is important that a strategy be formulated and promulgated throughout the organization. As with previous approaches to system development, presumably no single approach will be best for all systems. Consequently, the auditor must evaluate how a particular approach is chosen rather than requiring a single approach to be enforced for all systems.

Controlling User-Developed Systems

After long experience, an extensive set of controls has now built up around the traditional system development process in an attempt to ensure high-quality systems are designed and implemented. Many data processing professionals are now concerned that user-developed systems will not be subjected to these same controls. If this is the case, Rockart and Flannery's [1983] results show there is cause for concern. Many of the user-developed systems they surveyed were critical to the ongoing viability of the organization. The systems often had some of the following characteristics: (*a*) they performed important, day-to-day operational functions; (*b*) they had multiple users, sometimes crossing departmental boundaries; (*c*) they performed complex analytical tasks; (*d*) they required users to supply their own data, either keyed in from existing reports or derived from other sources and keyed in to the system.

User-developed systems create certain exposures for the organization, therefore (see, also, Benson [1983] and Davis [1981]). If they are not subjected to *public* scrutiny, there may be an error in the processing logic which results in decisions being made that severely impair the ongoing viability of the organization. Furthermore, *private* data capture and *private* information systems run contrary to the objectives that organizations have been striving to achieve via database management systems: improved data shareability, evolvability, availability, and integrity (see Chapter 6). Private information systems also run the risk of being developed in ignorance of other systems in the organization, thereby resulting in duplicated efforts or incompatible systems.

Again, the solution to these problems lies in formulating and formalizing a control strategy and promulgating this strategy throughout the organization.

Some of the issues that must be addressed are:

1 Security standards for end-user hardware and software
2 Backup and recovery standards for end-user systems
3 Corporate database access privileges for end-user systems
4 Standards for authorization and evaluation of critical end-user systems development
5 Adaptation of internal audit functions to cover end-user systems
6 Education requirements for end-user system developers
7 Organizational standards to guide purchase of end-user hardware and software such as microcomputers, word processors, database management systems
8 Certification of "public" end-user developed systems
9 Role of the data processing department in end-user system developments
10 Transfer pricing policy for end-user system resource consumption
11 Criteria by which end-user systems are to be justified and evaluated for feasibility

Once policies have been determined, however, they must be exercised through the line managers whose staff will be involved in developing end-user systems. Given that end-user systems are meant to provide decentralized computing flexibility for their users, it is unlikely that any centralized control authority will be successful. Nevertheless, insofar as policies for *overall* coordination and control are formulated and enforced, the exposures that arise with end-user systems can be reduced.

SUMMARY

The auditor can be involved in the system development process in two ways. First, in a participative capacity the auditor evaluates the quality of the system development process for a particular system, ensures needed controls are built into the system, and implements any audit modules required to monitor the system. Second, in a review capacity the auditor evaluates, in general, the quality of the overall system development process. This review allows judgments to be made on the likely quality of individual application systems developed and the extent of substantive testing of application systems that will be needed.

Both activities require the auditor to have a thorough knowledge of the system development process. The auditor must know what activities should be performed, how they should be performed, and when they should be performed if the resultant system is to safeguard assets, maintain data integrity, and be effective and efficient. In particular, the auditor must be able to evaluate from a contingency perspective the choices made by a designer during each phase of the system development process.

The way in which the system development process is managed also has an important impact on the quality of the systems that are produced. System development teams need to be structured differently, depending upon the level of uncertainty surrounding the system to be designed and implemented. If users develop their own systems, problems arise in exercising effective control over the system development process to ensure production of high-quality systems from an organizational perspective as well as from an end-user perspective.

REVIEW QUESTIONS

4-1 What are the two ways that the auditor may become involved in the system development process? How do the audit objectives of the two methods of audit involvement differ? How do the evidence collection methods differ?

4-2 Why does the auditor need a normative model of the system development process? How might the adequacy of normative models of the system development process be evaluated?

4-3 Two ways of thinking about the system development process are the life cycle approach and the sociotechnical design approach. What are the major *differences* between the two approaches? What are the major *similarities* between the two approaches? Can the two approaches be reconciled?

4-4 What is meant by middle management being the primary design referent group for system designers? Why do Bostrom and Heinen [1977a] claim this "condition" has been one of the primary reasons for behavioral problems in information system development?

4-5 The sociotechnical design approach negates almost every major feature of the traditional life cycle approach to system development. Comment.

4-6 Briefly explain the nature of the political approach to information system development. If the political approach to information system development is used, when is it important to have user involvement in the design process? When is it important to have face-to-face negotiation and compromise?

4-7 How does the prototyping approach to system development differ from the traditional life cycle approach? Briefly describe the *five* major phases of the prototyping approach.

4-8 Briefly explain the nature of the contingency approach to information system development. What is the primary variable that determines the particular approach to be used?

4-9 Why might different normative models of the system development process be appropriate for the auditor to use at different times? Give an example to help your explanation.

4-10 The primary concern of the auditor when evaluating the system development process is the application of the appropriate methodology to the design and implementation of information systems. Why is it difficult for the auditor to sort out what aspects of a system development methodology deal with data integrity objectives, what aspects deal with system effectiveness objectives, and what aspects deal with system efficiency objectives? How do these difficulties in being able to differentiate the objectives of activities carried out during system development impact the audit?

4-11 How might the need for a new system be recognized? What control techniques would the auditor look for when examining the ways in which system development activities are initiated?

4-12 Briefly explain the impact the following may have on the quality of the system development process:

a Standards
b Documentation
c Quality of the system development staff
d Checkpoints and signoffs

4-13 If the system development staff does not freeze and unfreeze the organization when developing a new system, what are the possible implications for data integrity in the new system? How might an audit be carried out on the way in which the change process is managed?

4-14 What are the bases on which the feasibility of a system should be assessed? What bases are the most important from an audit perspective?

4-15 Briefly explain the nature of a coordinating mechanism in an organization. Why are coordinating mechanisms of primary interest to the system designer and the auditor?

4-16 What is meant by the strategic design of a system? What is the relationship between system effectiveness and the strategic design of a system? How would an auditor carry out an ex post review audit of the strategic design phase of the system development process?

4-17 In what ways might the auditor fruitfully participate in the system design process? Give special attention to the ways in which the auditor might be involved in the adjustment of coordinating mechanisms between the social and technical systems.

4-18 Briefly explain the nature of structured analysis. During what phase of the system development process is structured analysis most likely to be used?

4-19 What is a data flow diagram? What elements of an information system are represented by the following data flow diagram symbols:

a Named vectors
b Squares
c Circles
d Open-ended rectangles

4-20 How are decision trees, decision tables, and structured English used as tools in structured analysis? In what circumstances is one tool likely to be used in preference to another tool?

4-21 Briefly explain how a data dictionary is used during structured analysis.

4-22 What is the relationship between organizational and job design and information system design? How does this relationship illustrate the "neutrality" of information systems?

4-23 What relevance has contingency theory for the auditor trying to evaluate a job design, an organization design, and the impact of these designs on system effectiveness and system efficiency? How would an auditor carry out an ex post audit of the job and organization design phases of the system development process?

4-24 Identify *four* ways of eliciting the detailed information system requirements for a system. What is the primary factor affecting the choice of the elicitation approach used?

4-25 Briefly explain the effects of increasing task uncertainty on the frequency and timing of information flows and the extent to which the information flow is formalized. How might information systems be designed to respond to these effects?

4-26 Briefly outline the audit steps that might be followed to evaluate the adequacy of standards for database design in the system development process.

4-27 Identify *five* elements that may have to be considered in the design of the user interface in an information system. Focus on an online realtime update system rather than a batch system.

4-28 If a data flow diagram is used to assist the process of physical information system design, give three ways in which physical boundaries might be identified and drawn on the diagram.

4-29 What aspects of procedure and forms design activities impact the extent to which an application system maintains data integrity?

4-30 Briefly describe the major activities in acceptance testing. Why is documentation an important part of acceptance testing? What should be documented during acceptance testing?

4-31 What is meant by a "test bed" of data? How is a test bed created and maintained? List the advantages and disadvantages of a test bed.

4-32 Why must data validation procedures sometimes be relaxed during system changeover? If validation procedures are relaxed, what procedures should the auditor follow?

4-33 What are the purposes of a postaudit of an operational system? Why should an auditor who participated in the system development process not participate in the postaudit of the system?

4-34 How has the advent of high-level programming languages affected the organization of system development teams?

4-35 Identify *five* control issues that should be addressed when systems are developed by end-user teams.

MULTIPLE CHOICE QUESTIONS

4-1 In an ex post review audit of the system development process, the auditor:

a Evaluates a specific system to determine whether the necessary controls have been included in the design

b Carries out a substantive test of the system development process for all accounting application systems within the installation

c Evaluates the system development process, in general, as a basis for reducing the extent of substantive testing needed

d Focuses only on asset safeguarding and data integrity objectives relating to an attest audit

4-2 The auditor uses a normative model of the system development process as a basis for:

a Determining the activities that should be carried out during system development

    b Determining what activities are usually undertaken during system development

    c Describing the activities that are, in fact, performed during system development

    d Predicting the system development activities undertaken in the installation being audited

4-3 A major difference between the life cycle approach and sociotechnical system design approach to system development is:

    a The sociotechnical system design approach deemphasizes project control techniques

    b The sociotechnical system design approach gives more emphasis to joint design of the technical and social systems

    c The life cycle approach is more structured

    d The life cycle approach uses action research to develop the strategic design for a system

4-4 Which of the following is given by Bostrom and Heinen as a reason why behavioral problems have occurred with the traditional approach to system design:

    a Designers have attempted to apply too broad a range of technologies to design problems

    b Designers have not accepted sufficient responsibility for the change process

    c Designers have inadequate theories about people, organizations, and the way change can be accomplished

    d Designers try to satisfy too many types of users with the designs they propose

4-5 Under the political approach to information system development, user participation in the design process is an important means of ensuring congruence between the system and the organization when:

    a The system will alter the existing power structure in the organization

    b Face-to-face negotiation will be needed

    c A "fixer" must be called in to resolve conflict among users

    d The proposed system will leave the existing organizational power structure intact

4-6 Design prototyping is more likely to be needed when:

    a The application system to be designed is a traditional accounting system

    b The designer believes users will react negatively to the system to be implemented

    c The life cycle approach to system development is chosen

    d There is substantial uncertainty surrounding the system to be designed

4-7 Under the contingency approach to system development, the major factor affecting the requirements elicitation strategy chosen is the:

    a Extent of conflict among users

    b Level of uncertainty surrounding the system

    c Nature of the job and organizational design proposed

    d Likelihood of the sociotechnical design approach being unsuccessful

4-8 With respect to the various phases in the system development life cycle, which of the following is *least* likely to vary:

    a Conduct of each phase

    b Sequence in which the phases are performed

    c Presence of each phase

    d Resources needed to perform each phase

4-9 Which of the following is the *most likely* sequence of phases in the system development process:
   a Analysis of the existing system, software acquisition and development, organizational and job design
   b Acceptance testing, procedures development, management of the change process
   c Entry and feasibility assessment, organizational and job design, information processing system design
   d Entry and feasibility assessment, problem definition, analysis of the existing system

4-10 During the problem definition phase, the terms of reference describe:
   a Boundaries of the system to be examined
   b Organizational and resource constraints
   c Proposed objectives of the new system
   d All of the above

4-11 Management of the change process is the phase in the system development process that:
   a Proceeds concurrently with all other phases
   b Stops after unfreezing has occurred and restarts when refreezing commences
   c Occurs between the problem recognition and entry and feasibility assessment phases
   d Distinguishes the sociotechnological design approach from all other approaches to system development

4-12 During the entry phase the system designer:
   a Explains to users various alternative designs that can be implemented
   b Attempts to determine what problem is the real motivation for the system development effort
   c Assists users to formulate the strategic design
   d Attempts to unfreeze the organization

4-13 A reward system is an example of a:
   a Task accomplishment variable
   b Coordinating mechanism
   c Human-social variable
   d Quality of working life variable

4-14 In a data flow diagram, processes are represented by:
   a Open-ended rectangles
   b Squares
   c Named vectors
   d Circles or rounded-edge rectangles

4-15 Which of the following is most likely to be used to describe sequence logic:
   a Decision table
   b Data flow diagram
   c Structured English
   d Decision tree

4-16 Which of the following is *not* an example of a strategic system requirement:
   a Use a high-level language to program the system
   b Produce a product below a given cost
   c Increase task variety
   d Maintain the existing organizational power structure

4-17 Which of the following requirements elicitation techniques is most appropriate when the level of uncertainty surrounding the system to be designed is the lowest:
  a Making a discovery from experimentation
  b Asking the users of the system
  c Synthesizing the characteristics from the utilizing system
  d Deriving the requirements from an existing system

4-18 System design using action research means:
  a The designer facilitates a collaborative mode whereby users jointly share the responsibility for design decisions
  b Design alternatives are generated by the designer and users approve or disapprove the design
  c No design action is taken until the problem is thoroughly researched
  d Prototype designs are implemented and evaluated before a decision is made on the final design

4-19 Which of the following coordinating mechanisms tends *not* to be the focus of information systems design:
  a Communications and control
  b Organization design
  c Direction
  d Job design

4-20 During the system design phase an auditor participating in system development attempts to:
  a Evaluate whether the system is auditable
  b Determine whether necessary controls have been designed into the system
  c Ensure the refreezing methodology has been designed
  d Both a and b above

4-21 With respect to designing the information flow during system development:
  a The length of the interval between information processing should be increased as task uncertainty increases
  b Formalization speeds up communications, but it increases the number of symbols needed to communicate a message
  c Not all information lends itself to formalization
  d Frequency and timing decisions should be considered independently

4-22 A global database design is more likely to result if:
  a An organization already has a database management system
  b Subunits within the organization are highly interdependent
  c Decision making is to be decentralized
  d The storage structure design dictates a database is needed

4-23 The primary difference between program testing and system testing is:
  a Program testing is more comprehensive than system testing
  b System testing focuses on testing the interfaces between programs, whereas program testing focuses on individual programs
  c System testing is concerned with testing all aspects of a system including job designs and reward system designs
  d Programmers have no involvement in system testing, whereas designers are involved in program testing

4-24 During conversion the primary purpose of parallel running is to:
  a Provide the basis for validating the design and implementation of the new system

b Determine which of the systems being run in parallel is more effective and efficient

c Provide the basis for carrying out comprehensive system and user tests

d Determine whether there are any bugs in the new hardware/system software configuration that has been chosen

4-25 Which of the following characteristics of user-developed systems has been identified in empirical research:

a Usually have only a single user

b Typically obtain data from a centralized database

c Often perform important, day-to-day operational functions

d All of the above

EXERCISES AND CASES

4-1 Repeat Exercise 3.1 where the elements of the controls matrix constitute *proper performance* of the activities within each phase of the system development process. In other words, you are to rate how important it is (in general) to properly perform the activities in each phase of the system development process if the four control objectives (columns of the matrix) are to be achieved.

Controls	Asset safeguarding	Data integrity	System effectiveness	System efficiency
Problem recognition				
Management of the change process				
Entry and feasibility assessment				
Diagnosis and information analysis				
System design				
Program development				
Procedure and forms development				
Acceptance testing				
Conversion				
Operation, maintenance, and audit				

4-2 The vice-president of production has requested that top management have the information systems department investigate the feasibility of a computer system to improve the scheduling of production. She is convinced that though her production managers are extremely competent, they do not always make the best production scheduling decisions. One of the system designers from the information system department starts the process of entry by requesting that the production managers participate in a series of workshops that will examine the strengths and weaknesses of the total scheduling system. Even though attendance at the workshop is voluntary, most of the production managers still attend. After six workshops over a period of four months, the system designer reports to management that the production managers are convinced a computer system will solve many of their problems. The vice-president of production is convinced the project should go ahead. However, because top management is uncertain about the eventual success of the system, they come to you as the internal audit manager to ask your advice. They value your independence.

Required: Prepare a brief report advising top management on how they should proceed.

4-3 Sunmatics started out as a small manufacturing firm producing solar energy equipment. With the impending shortage of energy, demand for its production has grown and the company has trebled in size over a period of five years. As a result of problems experienced with inventory control, a computer system has been designed to assist reordering and keeping control over inventory. There are about 800 components used in the various solar energy equipment manufactured. Currently, inventory records are maintained on bin cards. Inventory levels constantly change as production workers obtain components for their needs.

Required: The system development team is meeting to consider changeover procedures for the inventory file. You are the internal auditor participating in the system development effort. How would you recommend the file changeover be accomplished? What controls would you recommend be set up to maintain data integrity during changeover?

4-4 Finerfoods, Inc., is a large decentralized and diversified organization that primarily manufactures and sells grocery items. Various divisions of the company are widely dispersed geographically. In the past, divisions have been responsible for all aspects of their data processing operations. Recently, top management has questioned whether or not it would be more efficient to have a centralized group of analysts and programmers develop and implement standard systems that could be distributed and used by all divisions within the company. The vice-president of information systems is strongly objecting to the proposed change. He argues that the primary reason information systems in the company have been so successful is that they have been designed not only to accomplish task objectives but also to achieve a high quality of working life for users of the system. He contends that data processing departments in the division should be left to develop and implement their own systems since they are best able to develop systems that will support the organization and job design of their users. However, top management is questioning whether the costs of having individual divisions develop their own systems can be justified.

Required: As the manager of internal audit for the company, the president of the company asks you to prepare a report outlining your thoughts on the costs and benefits of the proposed change. He asks you to give him your opinion on the validity of the arguments made by the vice-president for information systems.

4-5 You are the chief internal auditor for Corbault Corporation, a large decentralized, diversified manufacturing organization. As a result of concerns about controls over hardware and software purchases throughout the corporation, the controller asks you to investigate a major subsidiary of the corporation. Your investigation reveals that the subsidiary has purchased over $1 million worth of microcomputer hardware and software and that many managers are actively engaged in developing their own systems. The hardware and software purchases have escaped detection by top management as individual purchases have involved only small expenditures. In total, however, the expenditures are considered to be substantial. Most of the purchases have occurred during the last three years.

The controller's initial reaction is to prohibit any further purchases of microcomputer hardware and software throughout the corporation. She is concerned about the large expenditures. More importantly, however, she is concerned about the ways in which user-developed systems are being employed in the corporation and their potential impact on operations, especially if the systems are poorly designed. Nevertheless, before taking the matter further, she asks your advice on what should be done to exercise effective control over hardware and software purchases and end-user developed systems in the corporation.

Required: Write a brief report to the controller outlining possible strategies to address her concerns. Your report should list the relative advantages and disadvantages of each strategy you identify.

ANSWERS TO MULTIPLE CHOICE QUESTIONS

4-1 c	4-7 b	4-13 b	4-19 c
4-2 a	4-8 c	4-14 d	4-20 d
4-3 b	4-9 c	4-15 c	4-21 c
4-4 c	4-10 d	4-16 a	4-22 b
4-5 d	4-11 a	4-17 b	4-23 b
4-6 d	4-12 d	4-18 a	4-24 a
			4-25 c

REFERENCES

Alloway, R. M., and J. Quillard. "User Managers' Systems Needs," *Management Information Systems Quarterly* (June 1983), pp. 27–42.

Benson, David H. "A Field Study of End User Computing: Findings and Issues," *Management Information Systems Quarterly* (December 1983), pp. 35–45.

Biggs, Charles L., Evan G. Birks, and William Atkins. *Managing the Systems Development Process* (Englewood Cliffs, NJ: Prentice-Hall, 1980).

Boland, Richard J. "The Process and Product of System Design," *Management Science* (May 1978), pp. 887–898.

Bostrom, Robert P., and J. Stephen Heinen. "MIS Problems and Failures: A Socio-Technical Perspective—Part I: The Causes," *Management Information Systems Quarterly* (September 1977*a*), pp. 17–32.

Bostrom, Robert P., and J. Stephen Heinen. "MIS Problems and Failures: A Socio-Technical Perspective—PART II: The Application of Socio-Technical Theory," *Management Information Systems Quarterly* (December 1977*b*), pp. 11–28.

Cherns, Albert. "Principles of Sociotechnical Design," *Human Relations*, vol. 29, no. 8, pp. 783–792.

CODASYL Development Committee. "An Information Algebra Phase 1 Report," *Communications of the ACM* (April 1962), pp. 190–204.

Colter, Mel A. "A Comparative Examination of Systems Analysis Techniques," *Management Information Systems Quarterly* (March 1984), pp. 51–66.

Couger, J. Daniel, Mel A. Colter, and Robert W. Knapp. *Advanced Systems Development/Feasibility Techniques* (New York: Wiley, 1982).

Davis, Gordon B., and Margrethe H. Olson. *Management Information Systems: Conceptual Foundations, Structure, and Development*, 2d ed. (New York: McGraw-Hill, 1985).

Davis, Gordon B. "Caution: User-Developed Decision Support Systems Can Be Dangerous to Your Organization," Working Paper MISRC-WP-82-04, Management Information Systems Research Center, University of Minnesota, Minneapolis, MN, 1981.

Davis, Gordon B. "Strategies for Information Requirements Determination," *IBM Systems Journal*, vol. 21, no. 1, 1982, pp. 4–30.

DeMarco, Tom. *Structured Analysis and System Specification* (Englewood Cliffs, NJ: Prentice-Hall, 1978).

Galbraith, Jay R. *Organization Design* (Reading, MA: Addison-Wesley, 1977).

Gane, Chris, and Trish Sarson. *Structured Systems Analysis: Tools and Techniques* (Englewood Cliffs, NJ: Prentice-Hall, 1979).

Ginzberg, Michael J. "Redesign of Managerial Tasks: A Requisite for Successful Decision Support Systems," *Management Information Systems Quarterly* (March 1978), pp. 39-52.

Ginzberg, Michael J. "A Prescriptive Model for System Implementation," *Systems, Objectives, Solutions*, vol. 2, no. 3, 1981*a*, pp. 33–46.

Ginzberg, Michael J. "Key Recurrent Issues in the MIS Implementation Process," *Management Information Systems Quarterly* (June 1981*b*), pp. 47–59.

Hackman, J. Richard. "Work Design," in Richard M. Steers and Lyman W. Porter, *Motivation and Work Behavior*, 2d ed. (New York: McGraw-Hill, 1979*a*), pp. 399–426.

Hackman, J. Richard. "The Design of Work in the 1980's" in Richard M. Steers and Lyman W. Porter, *Motivation and Work Behavior*, 2d ed. (New York: McGraw-Hill, 1979*b*), pp. 458–573.

Haga, Clifford I. "Procedures Manuals," *Ideas for Management* (Cleveland: Systems and Procedures Association, 1968), pp. 127–154.

Hammond, L. W. "Management Considerations for an Information Center," *IBM Systems Journal*, vol. 21, no. 2, 1982, pp. 131–161.

Hartman, W., H. Matthes, and A. Proeme. *Management Information Systems Handbook: Analysis, Requirements Determination, Design and Development, Implementation and Evaluation* (New York: McGraw-Hill, 1968).

Hedberg, Bo. "Computer Systems to Support Industrial Democracy," in Enid Mumford and Harold Sackman, eds., *Human Choice of Computers* (New York: American Elsevier, 1975).

Hopwood, Anthony. *Accounting and Human Behavior* (London: Haymarket Publishing, 1974).

Kaiser, Kate M., and Bostrom, Robert P. "Personality Characteristics of MIS Project Teams: An Empirical Study and Action-Research Design," *Management Information Systems Quarterly* (December 1982), pp. 43–60.

Keen, Peter G. W., and Michael S. Scott Morton. *Decision Support Systems: An Organizational Perspective* (Reading, MA: Addison-Wesley, 1978).

Keen, Peter W. "Information Systems and Organizational Changes," *Communications of the ACM* (January 1981), pp. 24–33.

Kling, Rob. "Social Analyses of Computing: Theoretical Perspectives in Recent Empirical Research," *Computing Surveys* (March 1980), pp. 61–110.

Langefors, Borje. *Theoretical Analysis of Information Systems*, Vols. I and II (Sweden: Studentlitteratur, Lund, 1970).

Macy, Barry A., and Philip H. Mirvis. "A Methodology for Assessment of Quality of Work Life and Organizational Effectiveness in Behavioral Economic Terms," *Administrative Science Quarterly* (June 1976), pp. 212–226.

Mair, William C., Donald R. Wood, and Keagle W. Davis. *Computer Control and Audit*, 2d ed. (Altamonte Springs, FL: The Institute of Internal Auditors, 1976).

Markus, M. Lynne. "Implementation Politics: Top Management Support and User Involvement," *Systems, Objectives, Solutions*, vol. 1, no. 4, 1981, pp. 203–215.

Markus, M. Lynne. "Power, Politics, and MIS Implementation," *Communications of the ACM* (June 1983), pp. 430–444.

Markus, M. Lynne. *An Organizational Angle on Systems: Their Bugs and Features* (Marshfield, MA: Pitman, 1984).

Martin, James. *Application Development without Programmers* (Englewood Cliffs, NJ: Prentice-Hall, 1982).

Mason, R. E. A., and T. T. Carey. "Prototyping Interactive Information Systems," *Communications of the ACM* (May 1983), pp. 347–354.

Miles, Raymond E. *Theories of Management: Implications for Organizational Behavior and Development* (New York: McGraw-Hill, 1975).

Mumford, Enid, and Don Henshall. *A Participative Approach to Computer Systems Design* (New York: Wiley, 1979).

Mumford, Enid, and Mary Weir. *Computer Systems in Work Design—ETHICS Method* (New York: Wiley, 1979).

Naumann, J. David, and A. Milton Jenkins. "Prototyping: The New Paradigm for Systems Development," *Management Information Systems Quarterly* (September 1982), pp. 29-44.

Naumann, J. David, Gordon B. Davis, and James D. McKeen. "Determining Information Requirement: A Contingency Method for Selection of a Requirements Assurance Strategy," *The Journal of Systems and Software*, vol. 1, 1980, pp. 273-281.

Nunamaker, J. F., Benn R. Konsynski, Thomas Ho, and Carl Singer. "Computer-Aided Analysis and Design of Information Systems," *Communications of the ACM* (December 1976), pp. 674–687.

Orr, Kenneth T. *Structured Systems Development* (New York: Yourdon Press, 1977).

Page-Jones, Meiler. *The Practical Guide to Structured Systems Design* (New York: Yourdon Press, 1980).

Rittenberg, Larry E. *Auditor Independence and Systems Design* (Altamonte Springs, FL: The Institute of Internal Auditors, 1977).

Rivard, Suzanne, and Sid L. Huff. "User Developed Applications: Evaluation of Success from the DP Department Perspective," *Management Information Systems Quarterly* (March 1984), pp. 39–50.

Robey, Daniel, and D. L. Farrow. "User Involvement in Information System Development: A Conflict Model and Empirical Test," *Management Science* (January 1982), pp. 73–85.

Robey, Daniel, and M. Lynne Markus. "Rituals in Information System Design," *Management Information Systems Quarterly* (March 1984), pp. 5–15.

Rockart, John F., and Lauren S. Flannery. "The Management of End User Computing," *Communications of the ACM* (October 1983), pp. 776–784.

Ross, D. T. "Structured Analysis (SA): A Language for Communicating Ideas," *IEEE Transactions on Software Engineering* (January 1977), pp. 16–34.

Senko, Michael E. "Data Structures and Data Accessing in Data Base Systems: Past, Present, Future," *IBM Systems Journal* (July 1977), pp. 208–257.

Severance, Dennis G. "The Evaluation of Data Structures in a Data Base System Design," *Proceedings of the 1974 IEEE International Conference* (March 1974a), pp. 1–6.

Severance, Dennis G. "Identifier Search Mechanisms: A Survey and Generalized Model," *Computing Surveys* (September 1974b), pp. 175–194.

Severance, Dennis G., and A. G. Merten. "Performance Evaluation of File Organizations through Modeling," *Proceedings of the 1972 ACM Conference* (August 1972), pp. 1061–1072.

Severance, Dennis G., and Ricardo Duhne. "A Practitioner's Guide to Addressing Algorithms," *Communications of the ACM* (June 1976), pp. 319–326.

Severance, Dennis G., and John V. Carlis. "A Practical Approach to Selecting Record Access Paths," *Computing Surveys* (December 1977), pp. 259–272.

Turner, Jon A. "Observations on the Use of Behavioral Models in Information Systems Research and Practice," *Information and Management*, vol. 5, 1982, pp. 207–213.

Weinberg, Victor. *Structured Analysis* (New York: Yourdon Press, 1978).

Woodward, Joan. *Industrial Organization: Theory and Practice* (Oxford: Oxford University Press, 1965).

Woodward, Joan. *Industrial Organization: Behavior and Control* (Oxford: Oxford University Press, 1970).

CHAPTER **5**

PROGRAMMING MANAGEMENT

Recall from Chapter 4 that some of the outputs from the information processing system design phase are a physical design showing the program job step to be accomplished, a design for the user interface, a design for the database, and a hardware/software configuration design. In the software acquisition and development phase of the system development process, working programs must be produced or purchased that are congruent with these designs.

The ways in which congruence in designs might be achieved have been the subject of substantial research in the programming area. Better congruence means the costs of programming will be lower since programs can be designed and implemented more easily, they can be modified and maintained more easily, and they are more likely to accomplish their objectives. These have become critical goals for three reasons. First, the demand for software continues to grow at about 21–23% per year (Boehm [1976, 1981]). Unless major increases in programmer productivity or a substantial increase in the number of information systems professionals occurs, the already significant software development backlog will increase. Second, to some extent hardware developments are now constrained by software developments. Vendors recognize they cannot sell hardware unless the appropriate software support is also available. Third, the growth of new software is inhibited by the extent of effort that must be expended on maintaining existing software. Various researchers report that 40–80% of software costs involve maintenance activities (see, for example, Mills [1976], Elshoff [1976], Lientz and Swanson [1978, 1980], and Canning [1978b]).

This chapter discusses those practices that lead to high-quality programs being produced. The first section of the chapter provides an overview of the program life cycle. It focuses on normative methodologies for developing, implementing, and maintaining programs. The second section examines alternative ways of organizing and managing programming teams. It highlights the advantages and disadvantages of the different structures that can be used. The third section discusses the special control problems associated with managing a system programming group and some ways in which these problems might be overcome. Finally, several software development and maintenance aids are reviewed.

THE PROGRAM LIFE CYCLE

As discussed in Chapter 4, program development is a major phase within the system development process. The primary objective of the phase is to produce high-quality programs. Yourdon [1975] identifies seven characteristics of high-quality programs:

1 The program works
2 The design is simple
3 Development costs are minimal

4 Testing costs are minimal

5 Maintenance costs are minimal

6 The program should be amenable to change

7 The program should run efficiently

For programs to have these characteristics, the programming phase must be well-managed. Since the programming phase itself can be considered to have a life cycle, this means that execution of the various phases within the program life cycle must be planned and controlled.

The following sections provide normative guidelines for *five* major phases in the program life cycle: (*a*) planning, (*b*) analysis and design, (*c*) coding, (*d*) testing, and (*e*) operation and maintenance. Depending on such factors as whether the software is to be purchased or developed in house or whether a fourth-generation language is to be used instead of a third-generation language, the conduct of activities in each phase may vary considerably. For example, if a high-level programming language is to be used, program analysis and design can proceed at a higher level of abstraction since the language enables more global functions to be performed. Nevertheless, as Boehm [1981] points out, irrespective of the technology used, organizations ignore the need for careful planning and control of each phase at their peril.

Planning

During the planning phase of the program life cycle, management must address a large number of decisions on how the development and implementation of software will proceed. The extent and importance of these decisions will vary, depending on such factors as the risk surrounding the project, the availability of well-developed standards, whether the organization is acting as a software contractor, and whether a software package can be acquired. Nevertheless, some of the important planning decisions that must be made are:

Decision	Nature
Resource requirements	Management must determine the resources required to complete each phase of the program life cycle.
Design approach	Depending upon the level of uncertainty, management may choose a prototyping approach or some variation of the top-down or bottom-up design approaches.
Implementation approach	The software may be written in house, contractors may be employed, or packages may be purchased. Decisions must be made on the languages to be used and the coding disciplines to be applied.

Decision	Nature
Integration and testing approach	Testing may require special resources, e.g., simulators or special hardware to monitor performance. Responsibility for integration and testing must be assigned.
Software quality assurance measures	Procedures for ensuring the software complies with its specifications must be determined. The group responsible for quality assurance must be determined.
Change control	Procedures for initiating, authorizing, and implementing changes to the software must be specified.
Project team organization	The way in which the various project teams will be organized must be chosen.

Perhaps the most difficult of all these decisions is the determination of resources needed to complete the various phases in the program life cycle. It is difficult because it is a critical decision, in that it provides the basis for establishing milestones against which progress can be evaluated, yet techniques for estimating resources needed are still evolving. Boehm [1984] identifies five major software cost estimation techniques that can be used:

1 *Algorithmic models:* These models estimate resources needed based on a set of variables hypothesized to be the primary determinants of cost, for example, the estimated number of source instructions to be written, the number of data items to be processed, the programming language to be used, the experience and continuity of the programming team, and the volatility of the requirements definition. Several of the major models available are Putnam's [1978] SLIM model, Boehm's [1981] COCOMO model, and RCA, Ltd's PRICE S model (see Freiman and Park [1979]). These models tend to estimate resource requirements at the macro level.

2 *Expert judgment:* This technique involves using one or more experts to estimate the resources needed to undertake the programming project. Various subsidiary techniques, such as Delphi or brainstorming, might be used to obtain consensus among the experts.

3 *Analogy:* If a similar software project has been undertaken already, resource requirements for the proposed project may be estimated based on previous resource expenditures.

4 *Top-down estimation:* The project is first subdivided into its various tasks, and resource requirements for each task are then estimated. The resultant hierarchy is called a work breakdown structure (WBS). The various tasks in the hierarchy then can be sequenced and scheduled (see Howes [1984]).

5 *Bottom-up estimation:* If the various tasks in the software project are fairly well defined at the outset, resource needs for these tasks can be estimated and aggregated to obtain the resource needs for the whole project.

Whatever the technique used to estimate resource needs, ultimately a software plan must show the set of tasks to be accomplished at a level of detail sufficient to allow adequate monitoring to occur, the sequence in which these tasks must be performed, the resources budget for each task, and a schedule for each task showing when it must be started and completed. This plan provides the basis for monitoring actual resource expenditure against budgeted resource expenditure and for identifying the implications of slippages in the completion of a task.

Analysis and Design

Each job step in the physical information processing system design must be translated into one or more working programs. To some extent the means by which this task is accomplished is still a heuristic process. Somehow the program designer must produce a set of specifications that accommodates the database design, user interface design, functional information processing requirements, and hardware/software configuration. Nevertheless, substantial progress has been made on formalizing the analysis and design process. The methodologies that have been developed are based upon the techniques devised for organizing and understanding complex systems that were discussed in Chapter 2.

The following sections provide an overview of three major approaches used to program analysis and design: (*a*) functional decomposition, (*b*) data flow design, and (*c*) data structure design. These approaches use a *top-down approach* to design. Overlap among the three approaches is considerable; nevertheless, there are also some important differences. Furthermore, they are not the only approaches used for analysis and design (see, for example, Bergland [1981] and Zave [1984]). Insofar as these other approaches are still in the research stages, however, they are not discussed below, as the auditor is unlikely to encounter them in practice.

Functional Decomposition Functional decomposition involves applying the divide-and-conquer technique to programming problems. In other words, the problem is progressively broken up into smaller pieces until the smaller pieces can be solved; the pieces are then reassembled to form the whole. In the programming domain, designers first focus on the overall function to be performed by the program. This function is broken down into subfunctions and the process occurs iteratively until the subfunctions can be understood sufficiently well that they can be translated into programming code. In the programming literature this technique goes under various names: top-down design, composite design, step-by-step refinement, the levels of abstraction approach.

To illustrate functional decomposition, consider a general ledger system. The highest level function "Update general ledger" might be subdivided into three lower-level functions (Figure 5-1*a*). Each of these functions can be

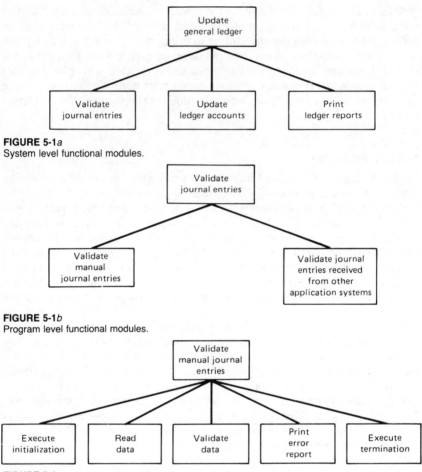

FIGURE 5-1a
System level functional modules.

FIGURE 5-1b
Program level functional modules.

FIGURE 5-1c
Subprogram level functional modules.

subdivided again into lower-level functions. For example, "Validate journal entries" might be broken up into a function to validate manually coded entries (adjustments) and a function to validate entries provided as the output of other systems such as accounts receivable, inventory, order entry, etc. (Figure 5-1b). Further subdivision then occurs (Figure 5-1c). Ultimately a hierarchy of functions and subfunctions is produced. The functions and subfunctions then become modules within programs.

There are several guidelines for designers to follow when performing the decomposition. First, they should focus on *what* is to be done rather than *how* it is to be done. Myers [1975] argues that the function description for a program module must contain a verb; thus, "get master record" is a valid description

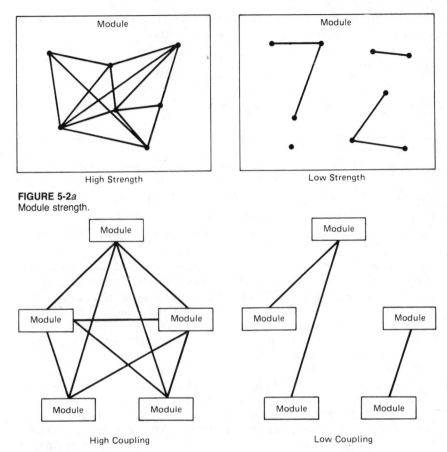

FIGURE 5-2a
Module strength.

FIGURE 5-2b
Module coupling.

but "master record routine" is not. This requirement forces designers to continue to focus on a module's function.

Second, at each level in the hierarchy, designers should focus on only a small number of elements or modules. This guideline recognizes the limited capacity of humans to process information (see, also, Chapters 10 and 11). By disregarding other levels, modules, and elements in the hierarchy, designers are better able to define the functions for the small set of modules under consideration. If possible, that part of the design under consideration should fit on a single work page.

Third, designers should attempt to conceive modules that have high *strength* or *cohesion* (Figure 5-2a). In other words, the elements in a module should have a singular purpose. The "goodness" of a module can be evaluated by assessing the level of its cohesion. Myers [1975] identifies seven such levels on the basis of the nature of the interdependency that exists between module elements. From highest to lowest strength they are:

Interdependency	Explanation
Functional	All elements in the module perform only a single function.
Informational	Elements in the module perform multiple functions but only on a single data structure.
Communicational	Elements in the module reference the same data set or pass data among themselves.
Procedural	Elements in the module perform different functions but the functions are related via a common procedure.
Classical	Elements in the module perform a class of functions that are related in time.
Logical	Elements in the module perform a class of functions.
Coincidental	No meaningful relationships exist between the elements in the module.

The process of decomposition increases the cohesion of modules. The elements of high-level modules have only weak interdependencies, for example, classical or logical interdependencies. The elements of the lowest-level modules should have only functional interdependencies. When modifications are made to modules with functional cohesion, the effects of the modification can be localized to the module that has to be changed, thereby making the change easier to understand and easier to implement.

Fourth, designers should attempt to reduce the extent of *coupling* between modules (Figure 5-2*b*). Again, the purpose of this guideline is to reduce the effects of changes. If modules are loosely coupled, changes to one module are unlikely to propagate to another module. Like cohesion, the extent of coupling is a function of the nature of the interdependency that exists between modules. Myers [1975] identifies six types of interdependency. Ranked according to their ability to reduce coupling between modules they are:

Interdependency	Explanation
Data coupling	Only data elements are passed as arguments between modules.
Stamp coupling	A data structure is passed as an argument between modules.
Control coupling	Control elements (flags, switches) are passed as arguments between modules.
External coupling	Modules access the same data elements that exist in a shared storage area.
Common coupling	Modules access the same data structure that exists in a shared storage area.
Content coupling	One module directly references the contents of another module.

Ideally, all modules have only one entry point and one exit point, and entry and exit are accomplished only via receiving or passing data elements, that is, via data coupling.

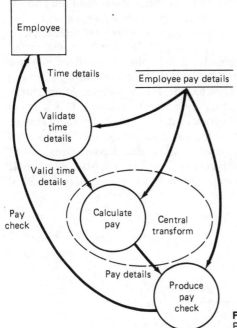

FIGURE 5-3a
Payroll DFD with central transform indicated.

The primary disadvantage of the functional decomposition approach to program design is that the results are unpredictable and variable. Inevitably there seem to be multiple ways of undertaking the decomposition. Consequently, two designers may produce different designs. Nevertheless, functional decomposition allows higher-quality programs to be produced than under the traditional ad hoc approach to design, and recent research has been attempting to define more clearly the ways in which decomposition should be undertaken.

Data Flow Design Data flow design is simply functional decomposition undertaken with respect to the data flow that occurs through a system (see Yourdon and Constantine [1979] and Page-Jones [1980]). Each module in a data flow design either transforms the structure of data or it transforms the information content of data. For example, it may reformat data items or it may validate a data item. Thus, the function in a data flow design is always some type of data transformation.

There are two primary strategies for undertaking data flow design. The first is called "transform analysis." Transform analysis commences by identifying the central transform in a data flow diagram (DFD). The central transform is the bubble, or set of bubbles, that performs the primary function in a DFD. It can be identified by tracing forward the afferent or input data flows to the stage where they are in their most logical form and by tracing backward the efferent or output data flows to the stage where they are in their most logical form. The set of bubbles that links the most logical input form with the most logical output form is the central transform. By "picking up" the DFD by its central transform and letting all the other bubbles dangle, the shape of the program structure chart emerges. The central transform constitutes the highest-level module, the modules on the left of the chart deal with input transformations, and the modules on the right deal with output transformations. This first-cut structure chart needs to be refined in various ways. For example, there may be several candidate bubbles in the central transform for the top-level bubble, and other modules may have to be added such as those that handle errors.

To illustrate transform analysis, Figure 5-3*a* shows a DFD for a simple payroll application with the central transform marked. Figure 5-3*b* shows the

FIGURE 5-3*b*
Structure chart for payroll DFD.

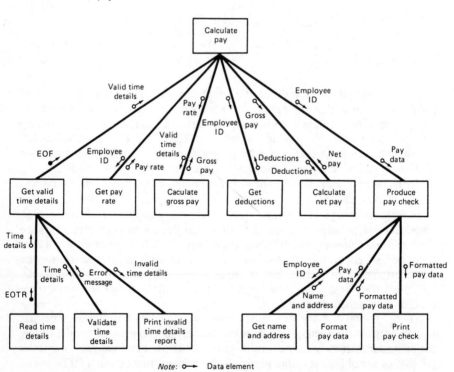

Note: ○—→   Data element
●—→   Control element

corresponding program structure chart. Note how the central transform "Calculate Pay" constitutes the top-level module in the structure chart. The left side of the chart shows the afferent or input stream of data; the right side shows the efferent or output stream.

The second data flow design strategy is called "transaction analysis." Transaction-centered designs tend to be used when systems process many different transaction types which must be validated in different ways and which subsequently may update different master files. This situation often occurs in business systems.

Figure 5-4a shows a DFD for part of an order entry system that will motivate a transaction-centered design. Figure 5-4b shows the associated structure chart. Note that the decision diamond at the bottom of the "Determine Transaction Type" module in Figure 5-4b signifies that the choice of which lower-level modules to invoke depends on the value of the transaction type data item.

Although the data flow approach to program design represents a major step toward improved programming methodologies, it has been criticized on two bases (see Bergland [1981]). First, like the functional decomposition approach, there is no assurance that different programmers would derive the same designs for a problem. Second, it is a moot point as to how well the data flow approach

FIGURE 5-4a
Transaction-centered DFD.

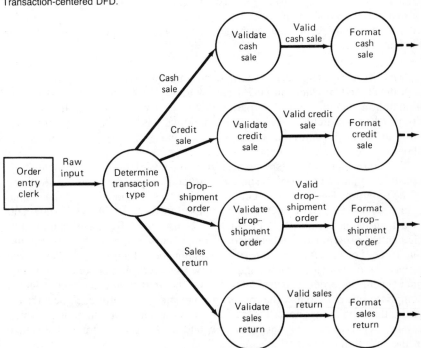

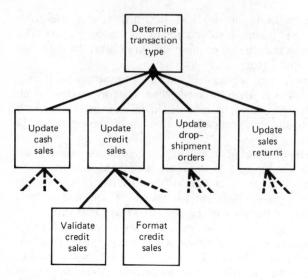

FIGURE 5-4b
Structure chart for transaction-centered DFD.

models the problem environment. To the extent that the resultant program design is not a good model of the problem environment, small changes in the environment may result in large changes in the program. This issue is discussed further below.

Data Structure Approach   The data structure approach to program design was developed by Jackson [1975] and Warnier [1974]. It is founded on the assumption that the "best" program design is one that models its problem domain. The structure of the problem domain is manifested in the data structures that the program must process. Thus, the design of the program should correspond to these data structures.

To establish this correspondence, Jackson [1975] provides a set of four constructs that can be used to show the structure of the data and the structure of the program. The first construct is an *elementary* component. It is the atomic component—that is, it cannot be decomposed further. A "MOVE" statement or a field declaration via a "PICTURE" clause in COBOL are examples of elementary program and data structure components, respectively. The remaining three constructs are composite components. Figure 5-5a shows the *sequence* component, which comprises two or more components occurring, once each, in order. Figure 5-5b shows the *iteration* component, which comprises one component that occurs zero or more times for each occurrence of the iteration component. Figure 5-5c shows a *selection* component, which comprises two or more components, only one of which occurs for each instance of the selection component.

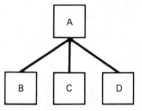

```
Program:   MOVE X to Y
           ADD Y to Z
           PERFORM MN

Data:      01   INPUT-REC
             02   CDCODE PIC 9.
             02   CUSTNO PIC 9999.
             02   CUSTNM PIC X(20).
```

FIGURE 5-5a
A sequence construct.

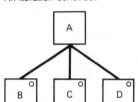

```
Program:   PERFORM MFUPDATE
           UNTIL INKEY = TERMIN.

Data:      01   PRICES
             02   INDIV-PR OCCURS 100 TIMES.
               03   PRCD PIC 9(3).
               03   PRVAL PIC 9(9).
```

FIGURE 5-5b
An iteration construct.

```
Program:   IF INCD = 3
             ADD X to Y
           ELSE PERFORM ERROR-MOD.

Data:      01   CURRENCY-AMT.
             02   CURRENCY-CD PIC-X.
             02   DOLL-CENTS   PIC 9(4)V99.
             02   YEN REDEFINES DOLL-CENTS PIC 9(6).
             02   FRANC-CENTS REDEFINES
                    DOLL-CENTS   PIC 9(4)V99.
```

FIGURE 5-5c
A selection construct.

To illustrate the data structure design approach, consider a simple accounts receivable application where a program reads a file of customer charges and payments and updates the customer account. The program produces a report showing the audit trail of transactions, the net amount debited or credited to each account, and the total of debits and credits to all accounts. Figure 5-6 shows the data structure for the input file, the data structure for the report, and the way in which the program structure must establish a one-to-one correspondence between the input and output data structures. Figure 5-7 shows the resulting program structure.

The essence of the data structure approach is the dependence of the data structure on the problem to be solved. If the problem to be solved changes, the data structure must be changed to reflect the new problem structure, and the program structure must be altered accordingly. For example, assume that management now wants to flag all debit transactions that exceed $1000. Figures 5-8a, 5-8b, and 5-8c show the modified input data structure, modified output data structure, and modified program structure, respectively. Note, there has

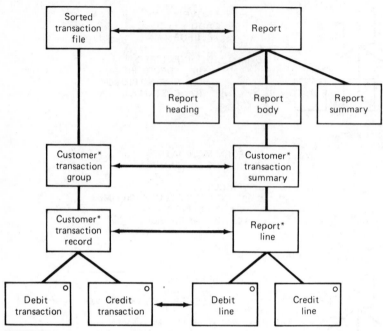

FIGURE 5-6
Correspondence between input and output data structures.

been no alteration to the *physical* form of the input data; nevertheless, the input data structure must be altered to reflect the changed problem structure. As long as the data structures continue to represent the problem structure and the program structure continues to represent the data structures, Jackson [1975] argues it will be relatively easy to validate and maintain the program.

It should be realized that the above examples show simple situations where the data structure solutions are straightforward. With more complex problems, the solutions often are not so clear-cut. For example, Jackson [1975] identifies a situation where reconciling the various data structures in a program may be difficult because there is no one-to-one correspondence between the input and output data structures. This situation often occurs when multiple sequential files must be processed that are not in the same order, or when the physical structure of one file precludes a correspondence being established. When a "structure clash" occurs, one solution is to establish an intermediate file that allows the conflicting data structures to be reconciled. However, this solution increases the size of the program and, given the nature of most current programming languages, results in inefficient processing. To overcome these problems, Jackson [1975] proposes a technique called "program inversion" whereby one process is called as a subroutine by another process. These matters are left for further study.

As with the other approaches to program design, the data structure approach also appears to have limitations. Yourdon and Constantine [1979] argue that the approach seems to work best on relatively small systems. With large systems, multiple structure clashes occur that make for awkward and unwieldy solutions. Nevertheless, they argue that a design produced via transform or transaction analysis might first be converted into a data structure design before coding occurs. With the advent of fourth- and fifth-generation programming languages, however, the notion of system size is changing. Given the power of these languages, systems previously considered large may now be considered small. Consequently, the data structure design approach may have more widespread applicability.

Coding

During the coding phase, programmers translate a program design into a linear sequence of statements that conform to the syntactic and semantic rules of some programming language. Like program analysis and design, this phase has

FIGURE 5-7
Program structure for data structures.

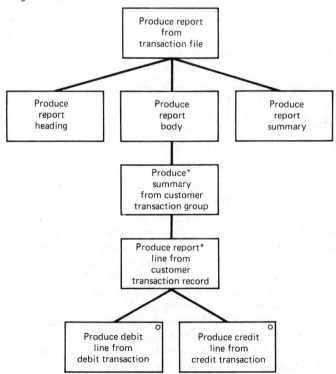

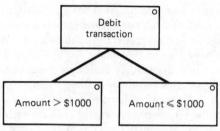

FIGURE 5-8a
Modified input data structure.

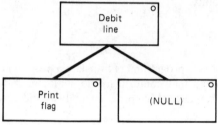

FIGURE 5-8b
Modified output data structure.

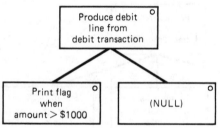

FIGURE 5-8c
Modified program structure.

become increasingly formalized. The following sections discuss some of the bases that now guide how programmers write code.

Top-Down Coding Just as the top-down philosophy drives the functional decomposition, data flow, and data structure approaches to program analysis and design, so it also drives some of the current approaches to coding programs. In its "pure" form, top-down coding means each module is coded immediately after it is designed. Thus, higher levels in the hierarchy of modules will be coded even before the lower levels are designed.

Whether the pure form of top-down coding should be followed, however, is a moot point. Opponents of the approach argue that design revisions to the higher-level modules will be inevitable because the programmer is working with incompletely defined lower-level modules. They underscore the iterative

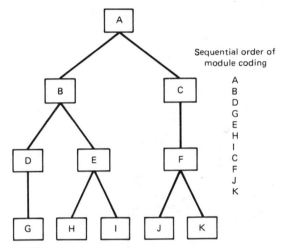

FIGURE 5-9
Preorder traversal of program design hierarchy for sequential coding of modules. (*Adapted from Yourdon [1975]; by permission of Prentice-Hall, Inc.*)

nature of design. Consequently, the initial code written will be invalidated. Moreover, with current programming languages it is difficult, if not impossible, to compile and test modules incrementally as they are designed and coded.

A less extreme form of top-down coding has the programmer proceeding down the hierarchy in some order and coding the modules at each level. However, program design is complete before coding commences. The installation should adopt a standard for traversing the design hierarchy; for example, Yourdon [1975] suggests a preorder traversal might be used for sequential coding of the modules (Figure 5-9).

Structured Programming   Irrespective of the method used to traverse the design hierarchy or the time at which coding commences, all code should be prepared according to a particular discipline. This discipline is characterized by its prohibition of the use of the "GO TO" statement. The discipline is called "structured programming" and sometimes "GO-TO-LESS" programming.

The theory supporting structured programming derives from the work of researchers such as Dijkstra [1972] and Böhm and Jacopini [1966]. In a fundamental paper, Böhm and Jacopini demonstrated that all programs could be constructed from three basic control structures, none of which required a "GO TO" mechanism (Figure 5-10).

1 Simple sequence (SEQUENCE)
2 Selection based on a test (IF-THEN-ELSE)
3 Conditional repetition (DO-WHILE)

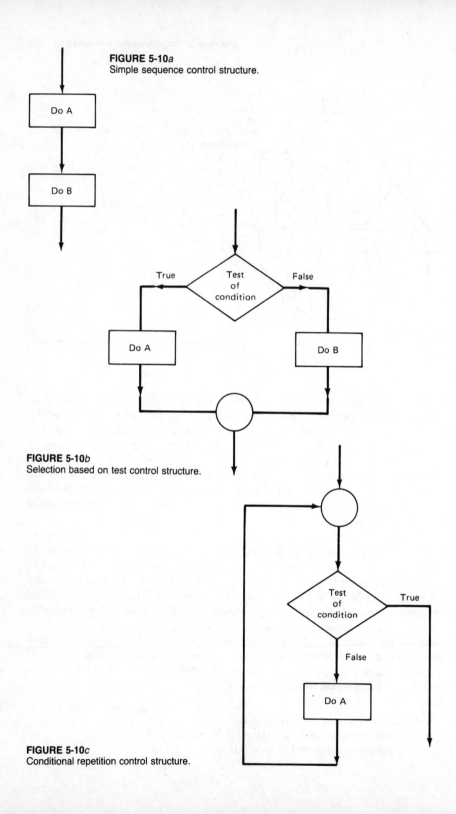

FIGURE 5-10a
Simple sequence control structure.

FIGURE 5-10b
Selection based on test control structure.

FIGURE 5-10c
Conditional repetition control structure.

Currently, none of the widely used programming languages have implemented these control structures in a rigorous manner. For example, COBOL implements the structures in the following ways:

1 Simple sequence
  Examples: **a** MOVE ZEROS TO AMOUNT.
  b MULTIPLY HOURS BY RATE GIVING PAY.
2 Selection Based on a Test
  Examples: **a** IF HOURS GREATER THAN 50
  MOVE 'ERROR'
  TO ERROR MESSAGE
  ELSE
  MOVE ZEROS TO AMOUNT.
  b GO TO
  SALES-A
  SALES-B
  SALES-C
  DEPENDING ON SALES-TYPE.
3 Conditional Repetition
  Examples: **a** PERFORM READ-JOURNAL UNTIL REC-TYPE
  EQUALS 99.
  b PERFORM ADD-ROUTINE UNTIL TOTAL-VALUE
  GREATER THAN 1000.

However, the implementations violate some of the "principles" of structured programming. One version of the IF-THEN-ELSE control structure uses a GO TO clause. For the DO-WHILE control structure the PERFORM clause does not pass the data to be operated upon as arguments to the module to be performed. Myers [1976] discusses the deficiencies of PL/1, FORTRAN, COBOL, APL, RPG, and ALGOL in more depth.

Pseudocode A major argument advanced (discussed further below) for adopting the pure form of top-down coding is that it facilitates carrying out top-down testing of a design. As the top levels in the hierarchy are coded, the design can be inspected for errors.

Unfortunately it is generally impossible to express the top levels of the design in code that would be compilable in any of the currently available programming languages. For example, some high-level functions in a job costing program might be:

1 Accumulate job costs for each engineer
2 Accumulate job costs for each project
3 Accumulate job costs for each district

These functions could not be expressed concisely in a language such as COBOL.

To help overcome this problem some organizations use a pseudocode to express these high-level functions (see, for example, Van Leer [1976]). A pseudocode or metacode is simply an informal language used to express a program design.

However, not just any language should be used for a pseudocode. If an organization uses a pseudocode to aid its program design process, it should be careful to specify the syntactic and semantic rules of the pseudocode. For example, a quality pseudocode would permit only the control structures allowed in structured programming and use an indented format to show the flow of control. It should be easy to translate the pseudocode into compilable code.

Some Structured Programming Conventions In the past, flowcharts have constituted a major part of the documentation of a program. Structured programming tends to deemphasize flowcharts as a documentation tool and requires the program code to be self-documenting. Flowcharts are still used but primarily as a development tool when the code initially is being written. They are discarded when the program is released into production. Whereas programmers can forget to update flowcharts, they cannot avoid updating code when program modifications take place. Providing programmers follow certain coding conventions, structured programs are meant to be readable and understandable without flowcharts. The self-documenting features of structured programs arise because:

1 The program is constructed as a hierarchy of modules with higher-level modules calling or performing lower-level modules.
2 Each module has only one entry point and one exit point.
3 Each module is limited to about 50–100 source statements.
4 There is no use or very restricted use of the GO TO statement.
5 Meaningful data names are used.
6 Comments are used liberally to document the functions of a module and the nature of its interface.
7 Line indentation follows rules; for example:
   a Each sentence begins on a new line.
   b Subsequent lines belonging to a sentence are indented.
   c Statements following conditional tests, such as the DO part of the DO-WHILE control structure and the THEN and ELSE parts of the IF-THEN-ELSE control structure, are indented.

Testing

The objective of program testing is to validate the logic paths within a program. In a program of moderate size (say, 3000 source statements long), carrying out a test of every logic path through the program would be enormously time consuming and very costly. At best, tests can be performed only on a sample of logic paths through the program; hopefully, the more important logic paths. Even so, Canning [1974b] reports that testing and debugging usually takes from 40–70% of the initial program development time.

Much of the stimulus for top-down design and programming has come from researchers who are concerned with developing formal proofs of program correctness. If it is possible to prove a program is correct in the same way it is possible to prove a theorem in mathematics, then brute force approaches (test data) to validating logic paths would no longer be necessary. Further, as Dijkstra [1972] has pointed out, testing can show only the presence of bugs; it cannot show their absence.

Unfortunately, the practical application of proofs of program correctness is still some time off. However, substantial insights have been gained into how the program testing process should be carried out. The following sections outline the newer approaches to testing programs. To provide the auditor with a normative basis for evaluating programming management, the focus is on the philosophies underlying the approaches. Chapter 18 discusses the more procedural aspects of testing: the design of test data, use of test data generators, etc.

Top-Down Testing   Historically, programmers have used a bottom-up approach to testing. First, modules in a program are tested; then the program is tested; finally the system is tested. Even the modular approach to programming uses a bottom-up testing procedure (see Canning [1974a]). Programmers test modules, then combine modules and test the interfaces between modules.

The primary motivation for adopting a top-down testing approach is the recognition that the most critical errors in a program are those that occur in the interfaces between modules. Errors in the interfaces affect at least two modules. Errors internal to a module are localized. Top-down testing involves testing the interfaces between modules first; then the modules themselves are tested.

The pure form of top-down testing has testing in progress at the same time top-down design and top-down coding are in progress. At first glance it is difficult to see how testing can commence when the top-level modules—the system level modules—are being designed and coded. For example, in a simple system the first level of modules might be:

1 Validate and edit data
2 Update master files
3 Print reports

The corresponding pseudocode in the mainline control module might be:
CALL VALIDATION AND EDIT ROUTINE.
CALL MASTER FILE UPDATE ROUTINE.
CALL REPORT ROUTINE.
When coding is complete, each of these routines may constitute programs or even multiple programs. However, if testing commences at this stage of design

and coding, these lower-level modules have not even been developed; that is, there is no logic for the test data to traverse.

To overcome this problem the top-down testing technique uses dummy modules or program "stubs." For example, the "VALIDATION AND EDIT ROUTINE" may contain one command only: "EXIT." Alternatively, the module may print some message to indicate it has been called satisfactorily, or perform some simple transformation on data passed as arguments to the module.

Carrying out a test when even the first-level modules exist as stubs may seem ludicrous. However, Yourdon [1975] argues a test at this time at least allows the job control commands for the system to be validated. For some systems correctly formulating these commands may not be easy. In any case the top-down testing approach is not meant to be rigid. Programmers should exercise their intuition and experience to determine at what levels in the hierarchy of modules tests are worthwhile.

Structured Walk-Throughs The proponents of top-down design, top-down coding, and top-down testing argue programmers should not perform these tasks in isolation. Their designs, code, and tests should be reviewed by peer groups, especially at the planning stage.

One technique used for review purposes is a structured walk-through. Structured walk-throughs involve programmers responsible for the design, code, or test plan leading a group of about six other programmers, who usually are on the project team, through the work they have performed. The review group focuses on detecting design flaws, coding errors, or test plan deficiencies. The product of the review process is a list of errors to be corrected, and not a list detailing how the errors are to be corrected. Often a program librarian takes responsibility for preparing formal notes and disseminating information on the errors detected to project team members.

Design and Code Inspections Structured walk-throughs are simply an extension of the desk-checking approach used by programmers to detect errors in their program logic. Still a further formalization of structured walk-throughs is a design and code inspection.

Design and code inspections consist of five steps (see Fagan [1976]):

Inspection step	Explanation
Overview	The designer or programmer who performed the work to be inspected provides the review team with an overview of what has been done.
Preparation	Individual review team members study the documentation for the design or program so they understand in detail the work performed.
Inspection	The review team gathers together to find errors in the work done. A "moderator" (usually a person from an unrelated project) guides the review process and prepares a written report on the inspection and its findings.
Rework	The person who performed the work must resolve all the errors identified.

Inspection step	Explanation
Follow-up	The moderator performs a follow-up to check the errors identified have been corrected. If major rework is involved, the moderator may reconvene the review team to inspect the changes made.

The major difference between structured walk-throughs and design and code inspections is the level of formality involved in carrying out the review process. In a structured walk-through, the conduct of the inspection primarily is left up to the review team members. In a design and code inspection, prescribed procedures must be followed. At a more detailed level, further differences are (see, also, Fagan [1976]):

1 Whereas the designer or programmer responsible for the work being reviewed leads a structured walk-through, a trained moderator leads a design and code inspection team.

2 There are defined participant rules for each review team member in a design and code inspection; in a structured walk-through this is not the case.

3 Design and code inspections make use of formal tools to guide the inspection process, for example, checklists for "how to find errors" and ranked distributions of error types for error-prone modules.

4 Design and code inspections use preprinted forms for documenting the results of a review team meeting. These forms also provide the basis for follow-up to determine whether or not rework has been carried out correctly.

5 Typically, structured walk-throughs occur only at three stages in the development of a system: (*a*) after preliminary design of the module hierarchy, (*b*) after detailed design of individual modules, and (*c*) after coding (but prior to compilation) of the modules. Design and code inspections occur at every stage in the program development process where it is possible to define a checkpoint, that is, a point where specific exit (output) criteria can be specified.

6 Structured walk-throughs have little or no follow-up procedures; the follow-up procedures in design and code inspections are extensive.

In general, it seems that the more formal the inspection process, the more likely it is to be successful. However, inspections add overheads to the programming process; thus, their benefits and costs should be carefully evaluated.

Operation and Maintenance

As programs carry out their day-to-day execution, three types of maintenance may be needed to keep them operational: (*a*) repair maintenance—logic errors may be discovered that have to be corrected; (*b*) adaptive maintenance—user needs may change and the program has to be altered accordingly; and (*c*) perfective maintenance—the program may be tuned to decrease its resource consumption.

The procedures whereby maintenance is carried out to programs often are a major concern to the auditor. If controls over maintenance activities are not exercised, unauthorized, inaccurate, or incomplete code may be introduced into a production program. Procedures should exist whereby changes to production programs must be approved formally, and the process of designing, coding, testing, and implementing the modifications is controlled carefully. Chapter 8 discusses these issues further.

In due course, systems and programs may have to be reworked. The extent of ongoing maintenance required may be so great that the existing system no longer seems cost-effective. Unfortunately, there are few formal guidelines to assist management in this decision. They must rely primarily on their intuition and experience. Nevertheless, some research has been carried out on the dynamics of program evolution that at least suggests the sorts of things on which programming management ought to focus when making this decision. For example, Belady and Lehman [1976] studied the evolutionary dynamics of several operating systems. One of their objectives was to derive some measure of system complexity that could be used by programming management to decide when complete structural redesign of a program was necessary. Though their research involved only very large programs, they found several general patterns existing in the evolutionary process:

Evolutionary pattern	Explanation
Smooth growth in size	With each new release of the operating systems, the rate of growth in size (measured by the change in the number of new modules added to the system) was constant.
Exponential growth in complexity	Complexity (measured by the fraction of modules handled) increased exponentially at each release.
Decreased growth rate with age	System size (measured by number of modules) increased at a decreasing rate over time.
Exponential growth in release intervals	The time between successive releases of the operating systems increased exponentially.

The research cannot give a definite answer on when structural redesign is necessary; however, it suggests some useful variables which management can monitor as indicators of when structural redesign should be considered, namely:

1 Age of the program

2 Size of the program

3 Interval between production releases

4 Extent of change to program at each release

Since the research indicates these variables tend to exhibit different types of smooth relationships with one another, any marked deviation from these predetermined relationships may mean structural redesign is necessary (see, further, Canning [1978b]).

ORGANIZING THE PROGRAMMING TEAM

In 1971 IBM completed a project for the *The New York Times*. The system designed and implemented was an online retrieval system for the newspaper's file of clippings. Throughout the project IBM used a programming team organized on radically different lines to the traditional ways programming teams are organized. For the size of the project—about 83,000 lines of source code—the results were impressive (see Baker [1972]):

1 The system was delivered on time after 22 elapsed months and 11 worker-years of effort.

2 Only 21 errors were found in the five weeks of acceptance testing allowed for the system. Each error could be fixed within a single day. Most of the errors occurred in the lower-level modules which had been written during the last two months of the project.

3 Only a further 25 errors were found during the system's first year of operation.

4 Each principal programmer on the project averaged one detected error and 25,000 lines of source code per worker-year.

5 Approximately half the subprograms consisting of about 200–400 lines of source code were correct at the first compilation.

6 One week after coding was complete the file maintenance subsystem was delivered. It operated for 20 months before any errors were discovered.

The success of this project and other similar projects highlights the importance of the organization structure adopted for a programming team as a factor affecting programmer productivity and the quality of systems designed and implemented. The following sections examine four different types of organization structure proposed for programmers and their strengths and weaknesses. Again, the objective is to provide the auditor with a basis for evaluating these structures in terms of how well they facilitate the design and implementation of high-quality programs.

Traditional Organization Structures

Chapter 3 discussed the traditional organization structures used within an EDP installation, which also are applied to programmers: function-based structures and project-based structures. Programmers may be members of a central pool of programmers. The programming manager simply assigns work to individual programmers as it becomes available. Alternatively, programmers may be-members of a project team; they work for some time on a suite of programs needed for an application. Often, they also are responsible for maintaining the programs in the application system.

As discussed in Chapter 3, modern organization theory focuses on task uncertainty as the primary factor affecting the choice of an organization structure. Task uncertainty in turn affects the amount of information the organization must process. If the organization needs to process only small amounts of information to accomplish its tasks, in general, a mechanistic organization structure will suffice. Alternatively, if an organization faces high task uncertainty and must process large amounts of information, in general, an organic organization structure will be needed.

Function-based organization structures tend to be more mechanistic than project-based organization structures. If the computer installation has its programmers organized along functional lines, the auditor should question whether or not the task uncertainty faced by programmers is low. Programmers must be given a precise set of program specifications. Further, the specifications must comply with well-defined standards. The programmer also must produce a program that meets well-defined standards. If programmers have to rely on substantial interaction with other personnel to accomplish their tasks, it is unlikely a functional organization structure will be successful. However, if programming tasks are small or well-defined, a functional organization structure imposes few overhead costs, since programmers do not have to interact with other personnel.

Several benefits accrue from organizing programmers along project lines. First, programmers develop expertise in an application area, so there are few startup costs when new programs must be developed or old programs must be maintained. In some cases the application area requires programmers to have expert knowledge in the area anyway. Second, having programmers identify themselves with projects encourages a commitment to the project. Third, project teams can be organized to facilitate communication among members of the team. This communication is especially important if there is high task uncertainty. In this respect, a project team structure is often used when a prototyping approach to system development is being employed. The team may comprise members from the user group and the data processing department. Nevertheless, project-based structures tend to be more loosely organized than function-based structures. Thus, they often are more difficult to control, particularly when their numbers are drawn from areas that cut across established authority and responsibility lines. In a prototyping project team comprising members from the user department and the data processing department, for example, confusion can arise over who is ultimately responsible for successful completion of the system.

Chief Programmer Teams

The particular organization structure used by IBM on the *New York Times* project is known as a chief programmer team. A chief programmer team is simply a specific form of a project-based organization structure.

Figure 5-11 shows the structure of a chief programmer team. The functions of the various personnel who are members of the team are:

Team member	Functions
Chief programmer	Ultimately responsible for the system on which the team works; must be an expert, highly productive programmer; responsible for designing, coding, and integrating the critical parts of the system; assigns work to the backup and support programmers.
Backup programmer	A senior programmer responsible for providing full support to the chief programmer; must be capable of assuming the chief programmer's duties at any time.
Support programmer	Needed for large projects that could not be handled by the chief programmer and backup programmer alone; provides specialist support and assists in the coding and testing of lower-level modules.
Librarian	Responsible for maintaining the program production library (discussed below); submits input and collects output for programmers; files output from compilations and tests; keeps source code and object code libraries up to date.

This structure is designed to reduce the need for information processing among the team members and to increase their capacities to process information. It achieves these objectives in three ways.

First, a chief programmer team structure reduces the number of communications channels needed among team members by minimizing the number of personnel on the team. However, as a consequence, the structure places more onerous productivity requirements on each team member to compensate for the loss of worker resources.

Second, each member of the chief programmer team performs specialized tasks. The chief programmer primarily is responsible for designing, coding, and testing the system. The backup programmer and support programmers provide specialized support; for example, they may advise the chief programmer on the intricacies of the operating system. The librarian relieves the chief programmer, backup programmer, and support programmers of the routine, clerical

FIGURE 5-11
Chief programmer team organization structure.

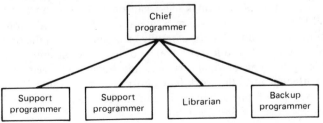

duties associated with the system. Thus, the structure aims at improving productivity by having team members do what they do best.

Third, the team's capacity to process information is increased by having the librarian perform a lateral coordinating role. Central to this role is a program production library consisting of two parts: an internal part and an external part (see, also, McGowan and Kelly [1975]). The internal part comprises source code, object code, linkage commands, job control statements, etc. It is maintained solely by the librarian, not the programmers. The external part comprises folders containing compilation results, test results, and other supporting documentation. The programmers work only with the external library, making whatever changes they need on program listings or coding sheets, and the librarian implements these changes. Each team member has access to the external library; thus, code, test results, etc., are public. Programmers are encouraged to examine each other's work so errors or potential interface problems are identified.

Mantei [1981] argues that chief programmer teams will be most successful when the task is well defined. Centralized structures like a chief programmer team inhibit the information flows that are needed to generate innovative alternatives when the task is uncertain. Nevertheless, by controlling interaction among group members, chief programmer teams are more likely to meet tight deadlines than decentralized groups.

Adaptive Teams

Weinberg [1971] proposes another type of team structure for programmers: an adaptive team. Like chief programmer teams, adaptive teams comprise only a small number of individuals, say, 6–10 programmers. The structure of the team is meant to cater to two sets of needs: (a) the organization's requirements for quality programs to be produced and (b) the social/psychological needs of each programmer in the team.

Adaptive teams differ from chief programmer teams in three ways. First, adaptive teams have no hierarchy of authority. The leadership of the team rotates among its members. The person having greatest skill with the activity undertaken usually assumes the leadership for the duration of that activity. Second, in an adaptive team, tasks are assigned to members of the team rather than defined positions. In the assignment of tasks the objective is to exploit the strengths and avoid the weaknesses of a particular team member. Thus, there is no notion of a chief programmer with a defined role, a backup programmer with a defined role, etc.; an adaptive team is self-organizing. Third, an adaptive team has no formal librarian role to perform a lateral coordinating function. Instead, team members are responsible for carefully examining and evaluating one another's work. The intent is to foster a feeling of joint responsibility for the quality of the programming product. At the same time team members cannot have an ego attachment to the work they perform if open evaluation is to exist; hence, this type of programming is sometimes called "egoless" programming.

An adaptive team gives recognition to the fact that substantial individual differences exist among programmers in their abilities to perform various types of programming tasks (see, for example, Sackman et al. [1968]). It also is structured to allow the free flow of information among team members. Thus, adaptive teams are suited to programming tasks where a high level of uncertainty exists. Nevertheless, Mantei [1981] argues adaptive teams have several limitations. First, because an adaptive team is a form of decentralized organization structure, it will generate more communications than a centralized team. Although this increase is an advantage in a long-term, difficult project, it is a disadvantage when a project is subject to tight time constraints. Second, groups engage in riskier behavior than individuals because the effects of failure can be dispersed; thus, an adaptive team may adopt risky solutions to a programming problem. Third, adaptive teams may discourage innovative programming solutions. Decentralized groups tend to exhibit greater conformity than centralized groups because they enforce uniformity of behavior and punish deviations from the norm.

Controlled Decentralized Team

A fourth type of organization structure for programmers is a controlled decentralized team. This structure has a group of junior programmers reporting to senior programmers who in turn report to a project leader. Information flows occur within a group and upward through the senior programmer to the project leader. Thus, the controlled decentralized team attempts to reap the benefits of both the chief programmer and adaptive team structures.

Mantei [1981] argues that controlled decentralized teams are best used when the programming task is large and difficult. Large tasks cannot be accomplished by chief programmer teams, whatever the productivity of the team members. Moreover, complex problems can best be solved by decentralized groups, and the group structure of the controlled decentralized team facilitates problem solving. Nevertheless, controlled decentralized teams do not work well when the programming task cannot be subdivided nor are they suited to projects that must meet tight deadlines.

MANAGING THE SYSTEM PROGRAMMING GROUP

There are two types of programmers in a computer installation: application programmers and system programmers. The former are responsible for developing and maintaining programs for application systems. The latter develop and maintain system software, that is, software that provides general functions useful to a wide range of application software.

Control Problems

Both the nature of system software and the nature of system programming activities present control problems for management. System software is a shared resource; thus, errors or irregularities in the software may be propagated through any application systems that use it. Furthermore, system software often must operate in privileged mode if it is to be able to perform its functions; that is, the operating system allows it to have a special execution status that enables it to circumvent many standard controls. This privileged status can be abused. For example, system software might be used to gain unauthorized access to private data that can be sold to competitors or to allow jobs to execute without being charged for resource consumption via the normal job accounting software. In the latter case, for example, system programmers may be carrying out private consulting activities and using the machine as a free resource.

Controlling system programmers is a difficult task. They are highly skilled individuals who often work alone or in small groups. Thus, it is difficult to exercise traditional controls over their activities, such as separation of duties and independent checks on performance. Moreover, they often work in crisis situations where the need to get a job running overrides the need to maintain established control procedures. For example, the communications software may crash during a peak load period, and a system programmer may be required to devise a "fix" so terminals can be reactivated and customers once again can be serviced.

Control Measures

In many installations, there has been a tendency to regard the system programming group as uncontrollable. Indeed, it is sometimes argued that the imposition of controls over system programmers will cause their work to deteriorate; they are sensitive, creative, often erratic individuals who do not take kindly to restrictions.

Auditors should be skeptical of these claims. Organizations that hold to these beliefs run the risk of major losses occurring. Well-controlled system programming groups *do* exist. These groups experience neither high staff turnover nor poor quality work. Although it is difficult to exercise strong and varied controls over system programmers, at least some of the following control measures can be instituted:

1 *Hire only high-quality staff.* Compared to application programmers, management might undertake more in-depth background checking and interviewing when hiring system programmers.

2 *Separate duties to the extent possible.* If more than one system programmer is employed, duties should be separated to the extent possible. For example, responsibilities for designing and coding a program might be separated from responsibilities for testing a program.

3 *Develop and document methods and performance standards.* System programmers should know what is expected of them in terms of how they perform their jobs. They should not be left to devise their own approaches, which may run contrary to the organization's control objectives.

4 *Restrict the powers of system programmers.* System programmers should not be allowed to "tinker" with the operating system during production time. Moreover, they should be allowed to develop and test system software that runs in privileged mode only during special test periods. In general, during production periods, system programmers should have only the same powers as application programmers.

5 *Keep a manual and machine log of system programmer activities.* Periodically these logs should be scrutinized to determine whether any unauthorized activities have occurred.

6 *Employ consultants to evaluate system programming work.* Periodically outside experts might be hired to examine and evaluate the work of system programmers.

7 *Have application programmers evaluate system programmers.* Although application programmers may not be capable of writing high-quality system software, they may be able to evaluate the quality of work performed by the system programming group, at least to some extent.

Even with these control measures in place and working, ultimately the best control may be to indoctrinate system programmers in the organization's policies. If system programmers see high ethical behavior on the part of management and an expectation that all employees should follow this norm, it is more difficult for them to rationalize any abuse of their powers.

SOFTWARE DEVELOPMENT AIDS

The reliability of programs and the productivity of programmers can be increased through the use of various software development aids that are available. When evaluating programming management the auditor can check to see the extent to which these aids are used as an indicator of the likely quality of programs produced by the programming group. The following sections provide an overview of these aids. The discussion highlights how these aids facilitate the program development process and some of the control problems experienced in using these aids.

Analysis and Design Aids

Analysis and design aids facilitate the decomposition process whereby a programming task is broken into subtasks so the problem can be better understood and a better solution designed and implemented. One major analysis and design aid, the structure chart, was discussed earlier in the chapter. The following sections examine briefly two other major analysis and design aids.

HIPO Chart Beside the structure chart, perhaps the best-known analysis and design aid is IBM's HIPO (hierarchical plus input-process-output) chart (see Stay [1976]). Figure 5-12 shows an example of a HIPO chart for a payroll application system. The chart has two components: (*a*) a hierarchy chart that shows how functional modules are decomposed into lower-level functional modules and (*b*) for each module an input-process-output chart that shows the input, processing, and output for each function. Note, also, the numbering system used in Figure 5-12 to assign identifiers to each diagram.

Although the HIPO chart has many strengths as an analysis and design aid, Canning [1979*b*] argues it has two limitations. First, he argues HIPO does not really lead into the design method. It does not have the data analysis proceeding concurrently with the functional analysis. Second, the charts are not compact. They are wordy and somewhat difficult to redraw. Since top-down design is an iterative process, any analysis and design aids developed to facilitate the process must enable easy revision.

Nassi-Shneiderman Charts Nassi-Shneiderman charts have been devised as a visual aid to the construction of structured algorithms (see Nassi and Shneiderman [1973]). Figure 5-13 shows the Nassi-Shneiderman chart representations of the sequence, selection, and repetition structures. In addition, a fourth representation is shown for the "case" construct, which is simply a convenient way of representing the selection construct when there are many conditions. Traditional flowcharts also can be used when designing structured algorithms; however, in a large flowchart the three control constructs are sometimes difficult to identify, whereas with a Nassi-Shneiderman chart they are always clear.

Coding Aids

Coding aids have five purposes:

1 Reduce the effort required to code a program
2 Speed up the coding process
3 Increase the documentation content of program code
4 Increase the amount of standardized code used
5 Improve the accuracy of coding

The following sections review seven types of coding aids that currently are available.

Shorthand Preprocessors Languages such as COBOL are verbose. Shorthand preprocessors allow the programmer to write an abbreviated form of code; they then translate this abbreviated form into the full language syntax.

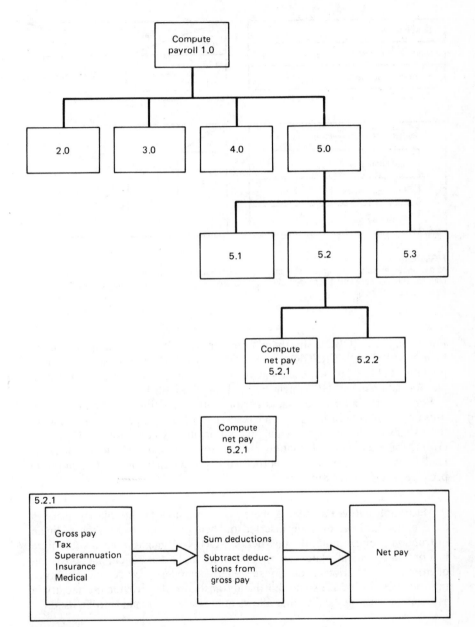

FIGURE 5-12
HIPO chart.

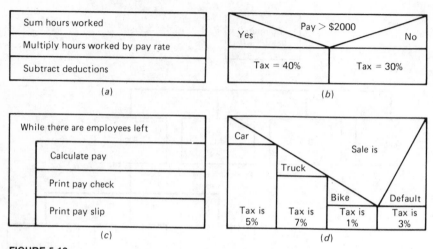

FIGURE 5-13
Nassi-Shneiderman representation of structured constructs: (a) sequence construct representation; (b) selection construct representation; (c) repetition construct representation; (d) case construct representation.

For example, a COBOL shorthand preprocessor might allow the programmer to use "P" for "PERFORM" and "M" for "MOVE." Besides a set of predefined abbreviations, users can define their own abbreviations; for example, for data names "GP" might be used for "GROSS-PAY."

Some shorthand preprocessors perform other functions. If the installation uses only a subset of a language (see below), it will ensure programmers adhere to this subset. Some check syntax and automatically correct certain types of errors, for example, punctuation errors. Some format code to enhance its readability. The shorthand preprocessor is sometimes part of a librarian package (see Chapter 8).

Macro/Subroutine Facility A macro or subroutine facility allows users to have a standard set of code inserted in their programs by writing a single instruction. For example, the instruction "DO N-P" might insert a subroutine in a program that calculates net pay, given a standard argument list consisting of gross pay and various deductions. Modern compilers provide macro/subroutine facilities. However, some shorthand translators also provide this facility in association with the facility that allows abbreviated commands to be used.

Decision-Table Preprocessors Decision-table preprocessors convert decision tables inserted in the code of a program into the source code of the compiler language in which the program is written. The characteristics of decision-table preprocessors vary. Beside limited entry tables, some allow extended entry tables to be used. Often the decision table is included in the source code generated as a note or comment to aid documentation. Some preprocessors check for redundancy and contradiction in the table.

Providing the programmer codes the decision table correctly, the source code generated by the preprocessor will be correct. The code generated may be somewhat inefficient, but most preprocessors attempt to optimize the code they generate. For an experienced user of decision tables, in general, it is faster to code a decision table than the associated source code. Further, the code generated is standardized, readable, and maintainable through changes to the decision table.

Copy Facility A copy facility allows large sections of code to be copied from a library into a program. For example, coding the DATA DIVISION of a COBOL program can be very laborious. Using the COPY facility, only one programmer needs to code the DATA DIVISION. It then can be stored on a library and other programmers can copy those sections of the DATA DIVISION needed in their program. COPY facilities exist in most modern compilers, librarian packages, and shorthand preprocessor packages.

Online Coding Facility An online coding facility allows programmers to code and compile programs while working in an interactive mode with a computer. The facility provides appropriate instructions for entering, modifying, and deleting code, storing source and object programs, listing programs, etc. Some facilities compile source code on a line-by-line basis; thus, the programmer has almost immediate feedback on any syntax errors made.

There is some debate over the benefits and costs of using an online coding facility. In general, an online coding facility allows faster development of programs. Further, because turnaround is faster, programmers are better able to maintain their momentum. This may improve their problem-solving abilities. However, online coding can lead to sloppy programming. Programmers may not take sufficient time to think out their program design and structure their code.

A primary concern for the auditor should be the access controls instituted in an online coding facility. Since programmers can retrieve programs, modify them, and restore them, scope exists for unauthorized modification of programs. The auditor should check to see that programmers cannot obtain unauthorized access to production programs or programs being developed. Chapter 9 discusses access controls in more detail.

Text Editors Text editors allow parameter-specified modifications of source code. For example, a programmer may wish to change a data name from "G-PAY" to "GROSS-PAY." By using a text editor command such as C/G-PAY/GROSS-PAY/, all instances of G-PAY in the source code will be changed to GROSS-PAY. The text editor also can be used to print out where G-PAY occurs in the program. Thus, changes can be made quickly and accurately.

Tidy Facility   A tidy facility can be used to "clean up" the source code of a program. For example, by specifying the appropriate parameter values, all "IF" statements in a program can be indented to make the code more readable. Similarly, nested "DO" or "PERFORM" statements can be indented to show more clearly the various levels.

Debugging/Testing Aids

In any computer installation the auditor should expect to see at least two basic debugging/testing aids in use: (*a*) memory dumps and (*b*) traces. Memory dumps show the state of internal memory at a point in time. When chasing a program bug, a programmer may need to examine the contents of a particular register or field at some point in the program's execution, for example, when the program references a location outside its assigned boundaries. Traces show the status of memory locations at various stages throughout a program's execution, for example, as a counter is incremented by the program. Typically, the machine vendor supplies software for memory dumps and traces. For example, different packages will be available to format memory dumps for programs written in different languages. Special verbs such as "TRACE" or "MONITOR" may be included in a compiler to perform a trace function.

There are two major reasons why debugging and testing aids should be used during the program life cycle. First, program testing and debugging is an extremely time consuming and difficult task. Brooks [1971] argues that debugging and testing problems are major causes of software being late. He estimates testing and debugging time normally take about 50% of program development time. Second, testing and debugging aids facilitate correct program maintenance. Boehm [1973] estimates programmers have only a 50% chance of correctly changing 10 source statements in a program; if 50 source statements are changed, the probability of success is only 20%.

The following sections discuss eight types of debugging and testing aids that are available. Chapter 18 also discusses some of these aids, as they are useful to the auditor when designing test data for audit evidence collection. The aids have several purposes:

1 Facilitate understanding of program logic
2 Assist test data development
3 Assess accuracy of test results
4 Ensure comprehensive testing of execution paths
5 Aid identification of logic errors
6 Handle the mechanics of program testing
7 Provide documentation of the testing process

Cross-Reference Listers   Cross-reference listers show where in a program or set of programs a data name, procedure name, or literal is used. Programmers making changes to programs can determine quickly what parts of a program the change affects without having to perform a serial search of the program code. The lister associates with each named item the line numbers where it appears in a program. The cross-reference list may be ordered alphabetically by item name and appear at the end of the source code listing. Alternatively, it may be embedded in the source code listing so that line numbers appear by the item name where it is defined in the program. Beside each line number some cross-reference listers also print the operation performed on the item, for example, the symbol "M" to indicate a MOVE and the symbol "P" to indicate a PERFORM.

Traces/Monitors Naftaly et al. [1972] identify two types of traces: intraprogram traces and extraprogram traces. Intraprogram traces are extensions to the source language, for example, the TRACE and MONITOR commands discussed previously. Extraprogram traces are separate object programs that must be link-edited to the object programs they monitor. Extraprogram traces are activated by a hardware interrupt. The trace takes a snapshot of the state of memory when an interrupt occurs so the programmer can identify whether an invalid instruction or invalid data caused the interrupt. The trace then attempts to correct the instruction or data that caused the interrupt so the program can proceed.

Test Data Generators Test data generators perform three major functions: (a) automatic generation of data items having certain attributes, (b) automatic creation of records for these data items, and (c) automatic creation of data (file) structures for these records. By specifying the appropriate parameter values, the programmer can have data generated in several ways; for example (see, also, Adams [1973]):

Data generation method	Explanation
Constants	The data item has a constant value in all records containing the item.
Range	Instances of the data item have values generated within a range.
Random	Random values are assigned to the data item.
Computation	The value of a data item is an arithmetic function of other data item values generated.
Logical	The value of a data item depends on whether a test carried out on other data items produces a true or false result.
List	Data item values are selected from a list.

Again, by specifying the appropriate parameter values, the programmer can select either fixed-length or variable-length records for the data items and have the records structured as a sequential file, indexed sequential file, etc.

Flowcharters Flowcharters use as input the source code of a program and produce as output a flowchart for the program (Figure 5-14). The value of the flowchart produced depends both on how well the program is documented and on what the capabilities of the flowcharter are. The flowcharter simply transcribes the data names and procedure names used in a program onto the flowchart it produces. If meaningful data names and procedure names are not used, the flowchart produced also will be less useful as an aid to understanding the program's logic. Flowcharters differ on the basis of a number of attributes, for example, whether or not they use ANSI symbols, how they paginate, how they group source statements together, how they handle GO TO's or PERFORM's, how they cross-reference the flowchart to the source listing.

Output Analyzers Output analyzers check the accuracy of the results produced by a test run. There are three types of checks that an output analyzer can perform. First, if a standard set of test data and test results exists for a program, the output of a test run after program maintenance can be compared with the set of results that should be produced. Second, as programmers

FIGURE 5-14
Output of automatic flowcharter. (*US Navy.*)

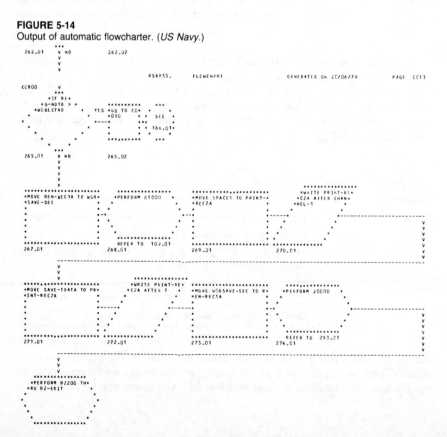

prepare test data and calculate the expected results, these results can be stored on a file and the output analyzer compares the actual results of a test run with the expected results. Third, the output analyzer can act as a query language; it accepts queries about whether certain relationships exist in the file of output results and reports compliance or noncompliance.

Online Debugging Facility   An online debugging facility allows programmers to monitor the status of their programs while the programs are executing. Programmers type in commands to the facility at a terminal and receive responses as the program executes.

The facility provides four major functions. First, programmers can examine memory locations in their programs. If the memory location is a data field that changes as the program executes, the changing status is printed out. Second, programmers can change the contents of a memory location; a data field or instruction can be modified while the program is executing. Third, control points can be set in the program. When the program reaches a control point, it either stops and awaits further instructions or indicates the particular control point reached. Fourth, programmers can have memory locations searched for particular values.

An online debugging facility is a very powerful and useful tool, but it also presents some major control problems. It is critical the facility is used only for programs that are being developed or maintained. If it is used on production programs, unauthorized code can be inserted in the program or unauthorized modification of data can take place. Further, the change may be temporary, only while the memory resident version of the program executes a particular instruction at a point in time. Access controls must exist to restrict the computing resources on which the facility can operate, and an audit trail must be kept of all uses of the facility.

Execution Path Monitors   An execution path monitor detects whether or not execution paths in a program have been traversed by test data designed by the programmer. The monitor reads a source program and inserts flags at all branch points within the program. The modified program then is compiled and the test run carried out. If an execution path is tested, the flag for that path is set. When testing is complete, the execution path monitor provides a report on all unset flags; that is, it shows those paths within the program that were not traversed by the test data (Figure 5-15). The programmer then can design further test data to traverse these paths.

Test Managers   A test manager is a control program that calls and executes the resources needed to carry out test runs for a program or set of programs and manages the production of the output test results. For example, for a single program the test manager might retrieve stored test input data, call the program to be tested, call and execute an execution path monitor, execute the program

PROGRAM TSAR			TEST DATA VALIDATION REPORT			PAGE NO. 1 29/C6/79		
SEQ NO.	TRUE PATH	FALSE PATH	SEQ NO.	TRUE PATH	FALSE PATH	SEQ NO.	TRUE PATH	FALSE PATH
008400	0 **	2	011200	0 **	12	C12000	8	0 **
012800	12	0 **	013600	12	0 **	014400	12	0 **
015200	12	0 **	C16000	12	0 **	016800	12	0 **
018900	0 **	2	02000C	33	3	C20300	0 **	3
020700	0 **	3	020900	1	2	022000	0 **	2
022800	0 **	34	024000	1	1	025300	0 **	0 **
025900	0 **	3	026300	0 **	3	026600	1	2
027700	0 **	2	029430	(101)	135	029440	(0) **	101
029460	101	135	029470	0 **	101	029490	37	98
029500	C **	37	029520	37	98	029530	0 **	37
029550	14	84	029560	0 **	14	029580	14	84
029590	0 **	14	Number of Tests of Path			Path Not Tested		

**** END OF REPORT

FIGURE 5-15
Output of execution path monitor. (*Main Roads Department Queensland, Australia.*)

to be tested, simulate the operation of various input devices such as online enquiry terminals, capture and secure output, call and execute an output analyzer, and order and print output test results. Thus, a test manager performs many functions that otherwise would have to be performed by a computer operator.

Execution Aids

Execution aids improve the run-time efficiency of programs. There are two types of execution aids: (*a*) language subsets and (*b*) code optimizers.

Language Subsets Compiler languages provide a very general set of instructions. Depending on the way in which these instructions are implemented and the characteristics of the machine on which the compiler operates, some of these instructions may execute inefficiently. For example, for some COBOL compilers the COMPUTE verb takes substantial time to execute.

There are two objectives of preparing a subset of a compiler language for use in an installation: (*a*) to identify a set of instructions that execute efficiently and (*b*) to identify a set of instructions that are sufficient to construct any program. Coding flexibility is traded off for improved efficiency. To prevent programmers from using instructions other than those in the subset, a shorthand preprocessor can be used.

Code Optimizers Code optimizers operate on either the source code or object code of a program to remove inefficient code without changing the intent of the program. In the case of source code optimizers a diagnostic report sometimes is prepared showing the nature of the inefficiencies. Code optimizers typically reduce both the memory requirements of a program and execution time.

SUMMARY

Recent advances in software engineering have provided the auditor with normative models that can be used to evaluate the program development process. These models involve top-down analysis and design, structured coding, and top-down testing. They are based on a theory of complexity: a theory that identifies the characteristics of complex systems that survive.

Associated with software engineering advances have been attempts to find better organization and management structures for programming teams. One particular organization structure, the chief programmer team, seems to have been especially successful in allowing programmers to produce high-quality software. By reducing the need for information, yet at the same time increasing the ability of the team to process information, the structure allows the team to cope with the uncertainty surrounding the programming task.

A major problem in programming management is controlling the activities of system programmers. The nature of system programming is such that many opportunities exist to perpetrate frauds. Ultimately, controls over system programming can be exercised only through a sound system of management controls.

When evaluating the programming process the auditor should determine whether or not various program development aids are being used. These aids allow programmers to develop high-quality software. There are four types of program development aids: analysis and design aids, coding aids, testing and debugging aids, and execution aids. The use of some of these aids must be controlled since they provide opportunities to breach data integrity.

REVIEW QUESTIONS

5-1 What are the major phases in the program life cycle? What events indicate the termination of each phase? Why can the program development process be called a life cycle?

5-2 Give three attributes of a high-quality program. From an audit viewpoint, what is meant by a "high-quality" program?

5-3 What is the overall purpose of the planning phase in the program development life cycle? List *four* major decisions that have to be made during the planning phase.

5-4 Briefly describe how the following program resource requirements estimation techniques differ:

  a Expert judgment versus analogy

  b Top-down estimation versus bottom-up estimation

5-5 Why are theories of complexity relevant to the programming process? What help do these theories provide to programming practitioners?

5-6 Briefly explain the nature of functional decomposition. How are the concepts of module strength and module coupling related to the technique of functionaldecomposition? When evaluating a program, how can the auditor gauge the extent of its module strength and the extent of its module coupling?

5-7 In data flow design of programs, briefly explain the difference between transform analysis and transaction analysis. For both types of design approaches, give an example where the design approach would most likely be used.

5-8 What is the claimed advantage of the data structure approach to program design over the functional decomposition and data flow approaches? What is the underlying principle that drives the data structure approach to program design?

5-9 In the data structure approach to program design, briefly explain the nature of the following three components:
a Sequence component
b Iteration component
c Selection component

5-10 Why do programming researchers currently advocate a top-down approach to program analysis and design? Give two advantages that a top-down approach has over a bottom-up approach. Can you think of a disadvantage?

5-11 Why in the analysis and design process should the designer focus on only a small number of modules? How can the auditor determine whether this design principle is being followed in an installation?

5-12 When evaluating an installation's documentation standards for the program analysis and design phase, on what attributes of a documentation standard should the auditor focus? In terms of the top-down approach to analysis and design, does the flowchart have desirable or undesirable characteristics as a documentation standard?

5-13 There is no difference between structured programming and modular programming. Comment.

5-14 What impact does the "GO TO" statement have on the module strength and module coupling of a program? Why is it unnecessary ever to use a "GO TO" statement in a program?

5-15 What is the purpose of a pseudocode in the coding phase of the program life cycle? Give two desirable attributes of a pseudocode.

5-16 Is adherence to the three control structures of structured programming a sufficient condition for well-documented code in a program? If not, explain.

5-17 Why have programming researchers been concerned with developing formal proofs of program correctness as opposed to developing better ways of testing programs? What is meant by the statement: Testing can only show the presence of bugs; it cannot show their absence?

5-18 What is the difference between the top-down approach to testing and the bottom-up approach to testing? How is the top-down approach based on a theory of complexity?

5-19 Briefly discuss the relationship between desk checking, structured walk-throughs, and design and code inspections. Why does it appear that structured walk-throughs have been more successful at finding design flaws and program bugs than desk checking, and why do design and code inspections appear to be more successful than structured walk-throughs?

5-20 Briefly explain the difference between repair maintenance, adaptive maintenance, and perfective maintenance. Why is the auditor concerned with controls over all types of program maintenance?

5-21 What relevance does the research on the dynamics of program evolution have for management of the operation and maintenance phase of the program life cycle? Why is it important to know when a program should be scrapped and redesigned and when it should be modified and maintained?

5-22 Why has there been heightened interest in the way programming teams should be organized? Are the organization structures currently proposed using a functional approach or a project team approach? Explain why you think this is the case.

5-23 Give three advantages that a chief programmer team structure has over traditional organization structures for programming teams. Give one potential disadvantage of the chief programmer team approach.

5-24 Briefly explain the role of the librarian in a chief programmer team. What duties does the librarian have with respect to the program production library? How does the librarian role inhibit unauthorized program modifications?

5-25 Give two motivations for organizing programmers as an adaptive team. What are the differences between a chief programmer team and an adaptive team? Give an example of a programming project where you think an adaptive team might be more successful than a chief programmer team.

5-26 Briefly explain the nature of a controlled decentralized programming team. Give an example of a programming project where you think a controlled decentralized team would be more successful than other types of programming team structures.

5-27 Give two reasons why it is difficult to control the work of system programmers. How might application programmers be used to control the work of system programmers?

5-28 Why is it important to try to indoctrinate system programmers with the organization's policies and for management to exhibit high standards of ethical behavior?

5-29 What are the purposes of a HIPO chart and a Nassi-Shneiderman chart? How might a Nassi-Schneiderman chart be used in conjunction with a HIPO chart?

5-30 How can a shorthand preprocessor be used to enforce a coding standard prohibiting use of the "GO TO" statement? What other coding standards can a shorthand preprocessor be used to enforce?

5-31 What control problems arise when online coding and debugging facilities are used?

5-32 Briefly explain the limitations of flowcharters as an aid to testing and debugging programs. What aspect of the testing and debugging process does a flowcharter facilitate?

5-33 Briefly explain how a test data generator and an execution path monitor can be used in conjunction with one another. Is an execution path monitor likely to identify a section of unauthorized code in an object program?

5-34 Briefly explain the functions a test manager might perform when tests on a set of programs are carried out.

5-35 How useful are execution aids for monitoring data integrity within an installation? How useful are they for ensuring programs are effective; that is, programs achieve their objectives?

MULTIPLE CHOICE QUESTIONS

5-1 In terms of total software costs, maintenance costs appear to constitute about:
a 5–20%
b 20–40%

 c 40–80%

 d 80–90%

5-2 Which of the following software cost estimation techniques depends most heavily on the fact that a similar project has been undertaken already and resource requirements can be estimated based on this previous project:

 a Bottom-up estimation

 b Analogy

 c Algorithmic models

 d Expert judgment

5-3 Which program design technique focuses on transformation processes that change either the structure of data or the information content of data:

 a Data structure design

 b Functional decomposition

 c Inside-out design

 d Data flow design

5-4 The transaction analysis data flow program design strategy is most likely to be used when:

 a The system processes many different transaction types

 b A common validation and update method applies to most transactions

 c A central "transform" can be identified

 d The number of efferent streams of input data exceeds the number of afferent streams

5-5 During the analysis and design phase, the number of modules on which a programmer should focus at any one time is:

 a 3–6 modules

 b No less than 10 modules

 c Only one module

 d Dependent on the overall size of the program

5-6 Module strength is measured by:

 a The number of interfaces between modules

 b The frequency with which data is passed across an interface

 c The time needed to execute a module

 d The internal cohesiveness of the elements in a module

5-7 Module strength is maximized when the elements of the module have only:

 a Classical interdependencies

 b Information interdependencies

 c Functional interdependencies

 d Procedural interdependencies

5-8 External coupling occurs when:

 a Modules pass a data structure as an argument between them

 b Modules access the same data structure existing in a shared area

 c Modules access the same data elements existing in a shared area

 d Only data elements are passed as arguments between modules

5-9 A criticism of the data flow approach to program design is:

 a It is not a top-down design method

 b There is no assurance that different programmers will derive the same design for a problem

 c It leads to inefficient programs

 d It works best for online programs rather than batch programs

5-10 In the data structure approach to program design, the following diagram represents:

a An iteration component
b A sequence component
c An atomic component
d A selection component

5-11 In the data structure approach to program design, the following data structure will be represented by:

02 DOLL-CENTS PIC9(4)V99.
02 FRANC-CENTS REDEFINES DOLL-CENTS PIC 9(4)V99.

a An iteration component
b A sequence component
c An atomic component
d A selection component

5-12 Which of the following is *not* an allowable control structure in structured programming:

a Conditional repetition
b Unconditional branch
c Simple sequence
d Selection based on a test

5-13 Pseudocode is needed because:

a High-level design cannot be expressed in code that is compilable
b It ensures the "GO TO" statement is not used
c It is easy to use by unskilled programmers
d It provides an informal way of expressing a design

5-14 Top-down testing proceeds:

a After the program stubs have been designed
b Concurrently with top-down design
c As soon as the first lower-level module is compiled
d After proofs of program correctness have first been attempted

5-15 Design and code inspections differ from structured walk-throughs in that they are:

a Less formal to carry out
b Use a peer group review process
c Do not use a trained moderator
d Have more extensive follow-up procedures

5-16 Adaptive maintenance must be undertaken when:

a Logic errors are discovered
b The program must be tuned to decrease resource consumption
c Execution time is unacceptable
d User needs change and the program must be altered

5-17 Research on operating systems suggests that the time between successive releases:
a Decreases exponentially over time
b Remains relatively constant
c Increases exponentially over time
d Varies erratically

5-18 A chief programmer team primarily is:
a A project-based organization structure
b An adaptive team with a flat structure
c A function-based organization structure
d An organization structure oriented toward low uncertainty tasks

5-19 In a chief programmer team the backup programmer:
a Ensures the resources needed for recovery are working
b Must be capable of assuming the chief programmer's duties at any time
c Ensures all program documentation is up to date
d Codes and tests only the lower-level modules

5-20 The internal component of the program production library used by a chief programmer team contains:
a Job control statements
b Test results
c Compilation results
d HIPO documentation

5-21 In an adaptive team the leader is:
a The chief programmer
b The programming manager
c The person having most expertise with the task at hand
d No one—an adaptive team never has a leader

5-22 Controlled decentralized programming teams probably work best when:
a Information flows must occur from the inside out
b Only senior programmers are employed on the project
c The programming task is large and difficult
d Projects must meet tight deadlines

5-23 Control problems arise with a system programming group because:
a It is impossible to enforce separation of duties
b Creativity is destroyed when controls are exercised
c They must always use the machine when production systems are operating
d It is difficult to evaluate their work

5-24 HIPO charts appear to be deficient as an analysis and design aid because:
a They do not have an adequate numbering system
b They do not lead into the design method
c They are too cryptic
d They do not support top-down decomposition

5-25 An example of a software testing aid is:
a A macro facility
b A shorthand preprocessor
c A text editor
d A trace

5-26 Output analyzers:
a Generate test data
b Detect differences between test results and expected results

c Check all logic paths have been tested
d Both (*b*) and (*c*) above

EXERCISES AND CASES

5-1 Construct a controls matrix where the columns show "what can go wrong" in the programming process and the rows show the controls that can be exercised over the programming process. In each element of the matrix, rate how cost-effective you think each control would be at reducing the expected losses from each cause of the loss. Use a 5-point scale where a score of 5 represents high cost-effectiveness and a score of 1 represents low cost-effectiveness.

5-2 You are the manager of internal audit of Coverit Corporation, a large insurance company. One day you receive an urgent letter from the controller expressing his concerns about some organizational changes that are about to occur in the data processing department. He has received a memorandum from the manager of data processing explaining that in the future all new information system projects will be designed and implemented using the chief programmer team approach. The controller is concerned that the organization structure of the chief programmer team violates a fundamental internal control principle, namely, effective separation of duties. He asks you to evaluate the chief programmer team approach with respect to the basic internal control principles that he believes must be maintained.

Required: Prepare a brief report that provides the analysis requested and give a recommendation as to whether you think the organizational change proposed should be allowed to proceed.

5-3 Since program development and implementation is a major phase in the system development process, the auditor may carry out an evaluation as a member of the design team or in an ex post review capacity (refer to Chapter 4). For *each* of these types of audit evaluation, make up a list showing the major sources of audit evidence on the overall quality of the program development and implementation process.

5-4 The chief programmer team or the adaptive team are not always the most effective and efficient ways to organize programmers. These structures should be used only when there is a high level of uncertainty surrounding the programming task. If the programming task is straightforward and well-defined, traditional organization structures should be used. Comment.

5-5 Make a list of those activities in the program development and implementation phase that directly impact the asset safeguarding and data integrity objectives. As an external auditor, briefly outline how you would evaluate each of these activities.

5-6 Slipup Corporation is a large, decentralized manufacturer of sliding doors and windows. It is based in Brisbane, but it services the southeast Asian market as well as Australia. The company uses information systems technology aggressively, both for its internal data processing requirements and as a strategic means of improving its service to customers. For example, it has a sophisticated manufacturing control system, and it provides a free service to potential customers by using an interactive system to estimate window and door requirements in light of ventilation, insulation, building capacity needs, etc.

So far the company has purposefully restricted the use of microcomputers by its managers because top management has feared it will be unable to adequately control systems developments within the organization. Nevertheless, they recognize that substantial advantages can be obtained by using microcomputers, and they have authorized a series of studies that will recommend guidelines on how microcomputers should be acquired and used within the corporation.

Required: You are the chief internal auditor for Slipup. As part of the series of studies on microcomputers that have been authorized by top management, you have been asked to prepare a set of standards that govern testing, production release, and maintenance of software developed by end-users. These standards will provide guidance to managers who develop their own applications using microcomputers and fourth-generation software. Prepare an outline of the standards you will recommend in your report to management. *Note:* Be sure to restrict yourself only to the testing, production release, and maintenance phases.

ANSWERS TO MULTIPLE CHOICE QUESTIONS

5-1 c	5-7 c	5-13 a	5-20 a
5-2 b	5-8 c	5-14 b	5-21 c
5-3 d	5-9 b	5-15 c	5-22 c
5-4 a	5-10 a	5-16 d	5-23 d
5-5 a	5-11 d	5-17 c	5-24 b
5-6 d	5-12 b	5-18 a	5-25 d
		5-19 b	5-26 b

REFERENCES

Adams, Donald L. "A Survey of Test Data Generators," *EDPACS* (April 1973), pp. 5–9.

Baker, F. T. "Chief Programmer Team Management of Production Programming," *IBM Systems Journal*, vol. 11, no. 1, 1972, pp. 56–73.

Belady, L. A., and M. M. Lehman, "A Model of Large Program Development," *IBM Systems Journal*, vol. 15, no. 3, 1976, pp. 225–252.

Bergland, G. D. "A Guided Tour of Program Design Methodologies," *IEEE Transactions on Computers* (October 1981), pp. 13–37.

Boehm, Barry W. "Software and Its Impact: A Quantitative Study," *Datamation* (May 1973), pp. 48–59.

Boehm, Barry W. "Software Engineering," *IEEE Transactions on Computers* (December 1976), pp. 1226–1241.

Boehm, Barry W. *Software Engineering Economics* (Englewood Cliffs, NJ: Prentice-Hall, 1981).

Boehm, Barry W. "Software Engineering Economics," *IEEE Transactions on Software Engineering* (January 1984), pp. 4–21.

Böhm, C., and G. Jacopini. "Flow Diagrams, Turing Machines and Languages with Only Two Formation Rules," *Communications of the ACM* (May 1966), pp. 366–371.

Brooks, Frederick P., Jr. "Why Is the Software Late?" *Data Management* (August 1971), pp. 18–21.

Canning, Richard G. "Issues in Programming Management," *EDP Analyzer* (April 1974*a*), pp. 1–14.

Canning, Richard G. "The Search for Software Reliability," *EDP Analyzer* (May 1974*b*), pp. 1–14.

Canning, Richard G. "Progress in Software Engineering: Part 1," *EDP Analyzer* (February 1978*a*), pp. 1–13.

Canning, Richard G. "Progress in Software Engineering: Part 2," *EDP Analyzer* (March 1978*b*), pp. 1–13.

Canning, Richard G. "The Analysis of User Needs," *EDP Analyzer (January 1979a),* pp. 1–13.

Canning, Richard G. "The Production of Better Software," *EDP Analyzer* (February 1979*b*), pp. 1–13.

Dijkstra, Edsger W. "The Humble Programmer," *Communications of the ACM* (October 1972), pp. 859–866.

Elshoff, James L. "An Analysis of Some Commercial PL/1 Programs," *IEEE Transactions on Software Engineering* (June 1976), pp. 113–120.

Fagan, M. E. "Design and Code Inspections to Reduce Errors in Program Development," *IBM Systems Journal,* vol. 15, no. 3, 1976, pp. 182–211.

Freiman, F. R., and R. D. Park. "PRICE Software Model—Version 3: An Overview, *Proceedings of the IEEE–PINY Workshop on Quantitative Software Models,* IEEE Catalog No. TH0067-9, October 1979, pp. 32–41.

Glass, Robert L. "Real-Time: The 'Lost World' of Software Debugging and Testing," *Communications of the ACM* (May 1980), pp. 264–271.

Howes, Norman R. "Managing Software Development Projects for Maximum Productivity," *IEEE Transactions on Software Engineering* (January 1984), pp. 27–35.

Jackson, Michael A. *Principles of Program Design* (New York: Academic Press, 1975).

Lientz, B. P., and E. B. Swanson. "Characteristics of Application Software Maintenance," *Communications of the ACM* (June 1978), pp. 466–471.

Lientz, B. P., and E. B. Swanson. *Software Maintenance Management* (Reading, MA: Addison-Wesley, 1980).

Lientz, B. P., and E. B. Swanson. "Problems in Application Software Maintenance," *Communications of the ACM* (November 1981), pp. 763–769.

McGowan, Clement L., and John R. Kelly. *Top-Down Structured Programming Techniques* (New York: Petrocelli Charter, 1975).

Mantei, Marilyn. "The Effect of Programming Team Structures on Programming Tasks," *Communications of the ACM* (March 1981), pp. 106–113.

Mills, Harlan D. "Software Development," *IEEE Transactions on Software Engineering* (December 1976), pp. 265–273.

Myers, G. J. *Reliable Software Through Composite Design* (New York: Petrocelli Charter, 1975).

Myers, G. J. "Composite Design Facilities of Six Programming Languages," *IBM Systems Journal,* vol. 15, no. 3, 1976, pp. 212–224.

Naftaly, Stanley M., Michael C. Cohen, and Bruce G. Johnson. *COBOL Support Packages: Programming and Productivity Aids* (New York: Wiley, 1972).

Nassi, I., and B. Shneiderman. "Flowchart Techniques for Structured Programming," *ACM Sigplan Notices* (August 1973), pp. 12–26.

Page-Jones, Meiler. *The Practical Guide to Structured Systems Design* (New York: Yourdon Press, 1980).

Putnam, L. H. "A General Empirical Solution to the Macro Software Sizing and Estimating Problem," *IEEE Transactions on Software Engineering* (July 1978), pp. 345–361.

Sackman, H., W. J. Erickson, and E. E. Grant, "Exploratory Studies Comparing Online and Offline Programming Performance," *Communications of the ACM* (January 1968), pp. 3–11.

Stay, J. F. "HIPO and Integrated Program Design," *IBM Systems Journal*, vol. 15, no. 2, 1976, pp. 143–154.

Triance, J. M., and J. F. S. Yow. "MCOBOL—A Prototype Macro Facility for Cobol," *Communications of the ACM* (August 1980), pp. 432–439.

Turner, Joshua. "The Structure of Modular Programs," *Communications of the ACM* (May 1980), pp. 272–277.

Van Leer, P. "Top-Down Development Using a Program Design Language," *IBM Systems Journal*, vol. 15, no. 2, 1976, pp. 155–170.

Warnier, J. D. *Logical Construction of Programs* (New York: Van Nostrand Reinhold, 1974).

Weinberg, Gerald M. *The Psychology of Computer Programming* (New York: Van Nostrand Reinhold, 1971).

Yourdon, Edward. *Techniques of Program Structure and Design* (Englewood Cliffs, NJ: Prentice-Hall, 1975).

Yourdon, Edward, and Larry L. Constantine. *Structured Design: Fundamentals of a Discipline of Computer Program and Systems Design*, (Englewood Cliffs, NJ: Prentice-Hall, 1979).

Zave, Pamela. "The Operational Versus the Conventional Approach to Software Development," *Communications of the ACM* (February 1984), pp. 104–118.

DATA RESOURCE MANAGEMENT

ANSWERS TO MULTIPLE CHOICE QUESTIONS
REFERENCES

Increasingly, organizations are recognizing that data is a critical *resource* and that the effective management of data is necessary for its ongoing existence and use. Consequently, they have sought technical and administrative solutions to the problems of how to manage the data resource. Technical solutions have been provided primarily through the acquisition of database management systems (DBMSs) and data dictionary/directory systems (DD/DS). Administrative solutions have been sought through the establishment of two new organizational roles: the data administrator (DA) and the database administrator (DBA).

This chapter discusses the motivations for establishing the DA/DBA roles within organizations. It examines the functions that should be performed by the DA/DBA and the factors that contribute to effective performance of their roles, especially the organizational positions of the DA/DBA and the availability of a DD/DS as a support tool. Because of the substantial influence that the DA/DBA have over the quality of the data resource, the chapter highlights the various audit implications of these roles. Finally, several control problems posed by the existence of the DBA role are identified and some remedial measures examined.

MOTIVATIONS TOWARD THE DA/DBA ROLES

It is not necessary for a computer installation to be using a database management system to institute DA/DBA roles. The term "database" simply implies a centrally *planned* and *controlled* collection of mechanized data. The need for DA/DBA roles arises when an organization makes a commitment to the centralized planning and control of data rather than allowing its planning and control to be dispersed across a number of users of data.

Centralized planning and control does not necessarily mean *physically* centralized planning and control nor a *physically* centralized database. It is quite possible planning and control will be delegated and decentralized in the normal manner. Similarly, it is quite possible a distributed database may be a more effective and efficient way of processing data within the organization. Centralized planning and control simply implies ultimate responsibility for the database is vested in an organization role—the DA/DBA.

For management to commit an organization to centralized planning and control of data and for users to relinquish control over data to a central authority on an ongoing basis, certain objectives must be accomplished in managing the database (see Everest [1976]):

Objective	Explanation
Sharability	A fundamental objective of database management is that the database be shared. This means multiple users of the database with different processes should have access to the same data at virtually the same time.
Availability	Availability means the database should be available to users when it is needed, where it is needed, and in the form it is needed. This implies diverse languages and usage modes should be available to satisfy diverse user needs.
Evolvability	Evolvability means the database must be able to change in response to changing needs. It implies not only the ability to expand but also the ability to contract.
Database integrity	Database integrity means the data in the database must be unimpaired, complete, pure, etc. Maintenance of database integrity is especially critical in a shared data environment. An error in data affects all users.

These objectives are laudable, but their accomplishment causes several problems. Sharing data among various users inevitably means conflict will arise among these users. For example, one user may need a data structure that facilitates fast batch processing. Another user may need a data structure that facilitates fast online access to data. The data structure that each user needs may be unsatisfactory from the viewpoint of the other user. Users cannot pursue their individual goals oblivious to the needs of other users; otherwise, suboptimization of the organization's overall goals may result. In the event of conflict, compromise must take place. A primary objective of the DA/DBA roles is to perform a mediating function to help achieve this compromise (Figure 6-1).

Achieving the other objectives of managing the database requires someone to have a global knowledge of organizational requirements. Maintaining the availability of the database means user requirements for education, documentation, and access tools must be examined continuously. Presumably not all needs can be satisfied. Choices must be made subject to resource constraints. Achieving evolvability means current requirements for database use must be tempered by future requirements. For example, a suboptimal data structure may have to be designed for current use to avoid costly restructuring in the future as the number of users expands and different needs have to be satisfied. Data integrity controls must be built that satisfy the requirements of future users of the data as well as current users. It is the DA's and DBA's responsibility to adopt the global perspective of organizational needs required to achieve these objectives.

Table 6-1 provides an overview of the DA's and DBA's responsibilities. These responsibilities will be discussed shortly in more detail. Clearly, however, they are onerous. Indeed, the emergence of two organizational roles instead of one reflects the extent of these responsibilities. Historically, a single role appeared first. In light of experience, however, a single role proved inadequate for two

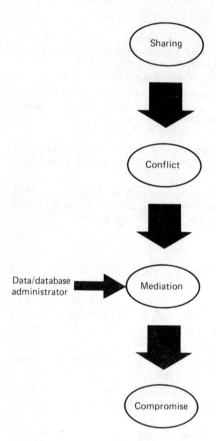

FIGURE 6-1
The chain of events produced by the sharability objective of database management. (*Adapted from Everest [1976]; by permission of McGraw-Hill Book Company.*)

reasons. First, it became clear that two different types of skills were needed to be able to perform the role competently. A set of administrative skills was needed to handle managerial and policy matters and to interact effectively with users of the database. A set of technical skills also was needed to handle the detailed design work and to tune the database so it could be used efficiently. Few people have both sets of skills. Second, the amount of work to be performed by the role grew to the extent that often it was necessary to partition the role. In particular, as the volume of end-user computing in organizations grew, substantially more support had to be provided to database users who were not data processing professionals. Consequently, two roles have emerged rather than one: the DA to handle administrative and policy matters, and the DBA to handle technical matters.

TABLE 6-1
DATA ADMINISTRATION/DATABASE ADMINISTRATION RESPONSIBILITIES

Function	DA responsibilities	DBA responsibilities
Defining data	Specifying logical (user-oriented) data definition	Specifying physical (computer-oriented) data definition
Creating data	Advising users on data collection procedures; specifying validation and editing criteria	Preparing programs to create data
Redefining/ restructuring data	Specifying new logical data definition	Specifying new physical data definition; changing physical data definition to improve performance
Retiring data	Specifying retirement policies	Implementing retirement policies
Making database available to users	Determining end-user requirements for database tools; testing and evaluating end-user database tools	Determining programmer requirements for database tools; determining database optimization tools required; testing and evaluating programmer and database optimization tools
Informing and servicing users	Answering end-user queries; educating end-users; establishing and promulgating policy information and high-level (logical) documentation	Answering programmer queries; educating programmers; establishing and promulgating low-level (physical) documentation
Maintaining database integrity	Developing and promulgating organizationwide standards for database definition control, existence control, access control, update control, concurrency control, and quality control; assisting end-users to formulate application controls	Implementing database definition controls, existence controls, access controls, update controls, concurrency controls, and quality controls; assisting programmers to design and implement application controls
Monitoring operations	Monitoring end-user patterns of database use	Monitoring programmer patterns of database use; collecting performance statistics; tuning the database

SOME AUDIT CONSIDERATIONS

If an organization has made a commitment to centralized planning and control of data and has instituted the DA and DBA roles within its management control framework, the audit function is impacted in three ways. First, since many of the communications in a database environment are channeled through the DA and DBA, they are important sources of information on strengths and weaknesses within the environment. Second, the DA and DBA provide important administrative and technical information that the auditor needs to know and in some cases database tools that the auditor needs to use. For example, the DA may make available to the auditor documentation describing the data structures in the database, and the DBA may provide assistance with software that will extract data from the database. Third, since the ongoing existence of a database environment is directly dependent on the quality of its DA and DBA, the auditor must have a sound knowledge of the functions that both roles should perform so the incumbents' performance can be evaluated.

FUNCTIONS OF THE DA/DBA

Since the DA and DBA roles in organizations are fairly recent, the functions they perform are still evolving. Various publications have proposed normative guidelines for establishing the roles (for example, GUIDE [1977] and Weldon [1981]); nevertheless, several research studies show that the roles differ considerably among organizations and that the functions they perform are changing rapidly (for example, Kahn [1983], Gillenson [1982], and McCririck and Goldstein [1980]).

The following sections examine five major functions that the DA/DBA must perform (see Everest and Weber [1979]). Although there is considerable overlap between the DA and DBA roles, the discussion below also highlights where they differ. In addition, even though these roles may exist in the absence of a DBMS, the discussion below assumes one exists to facilitate performance of the roles.

Defining, Creating, and Retiring Data

When a user requires data that does not currently exist, the life cycle of data commences. The first step is to define the data needed. There are three types of definition required (see Tsichritzis and Klug [1978] and Nijssen [1983]); each definition reflects a different "view" of the database (Figure 6-2):

Description/view	Nature
External schema	The external schema is the grammar that describes a particular user's view of the data/knowledge in the database. It defines a subset of the total database, and it restricts a user to accessing only that defined subset.

Description/view	Nature
Conceptual schema	The conceptual schema is the grammar that describes the entire database from a logical perspective. It defines all object types in the database, all association types between object types, and all integrity constraints on object types and their association types. In essence, it is the amalgamation of all the external schemas into a complete, accurate, and consistent whole.
Internal schema	The internal schema is the grammar that describes how data/knowledge is stored in the database. It defines the records, fields, access paths, and coding schemes used to represent the object types and association types of the conceptual schema.

To illustrate these notions, Figure 6-3 shows the three schemas for a simple database. The external and conceptual schemas have been modeled using a technique called NIAM (see Verheijen and Van Bekkum [1982]). A personnel clerk views the database in terms of a person object type and a department object type, an association type relating a person object type and a department object type, and a constraint indicating that a person can belong only to one department while a department can have many employees. Similarly, a payroll clerk views the database in terms of a person object type, a salary object type, and an association type relating a person object type and a salary object type, and a constraint indicating a person can have only one salary while a salary can apply to many employees. These two views are combined into the overall conceptual schema. The conceptual schema, in turn, is mapped into a record structure with three fields: person, department, and salary.

FIGURE 6-2
Database definition: schemas and their mappings.

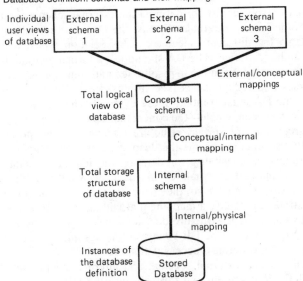

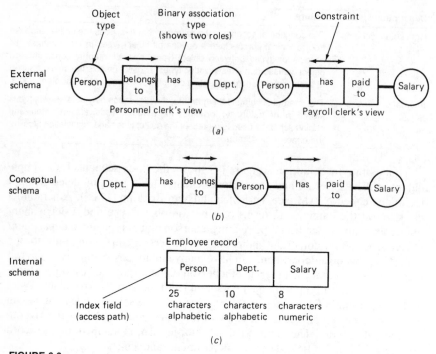

FIGURE 6-3
Three levels of database definition: (a) external schema; (b) conceptual schema; (c) internal schema.

The DA takes primary responsibility for defining the external schemas and conceptual schema. To define the external schemas, the DA must consult all users of the database so the different object types, association types, and integrity constraints can be identified. The DA should use a formal methodology to elicit these elements of the definition to resolve semantic ambiguities and to detect inconsistencies and redundancies (see, for example, Vermeir and Nijssen [1982]). Next, the DA must combine these external schemas into an accurate, complete, and consistent whole—the conceptual schema. In essence, the external schemas represent the surface structure semantics of the stored database; the conceptual schema represents the deep structure semantics.

The DBA takes primary responsibility for defining the internal schema. Once the conceptual schema and external schema have been defined, they must be mapped onto storage media so they can be accessed and used efficiently. The DBA strives to identify a mapping that will meet performance objectives. To some extent, storage structure decisions may be made by the DBMS automatically. Nevertheless, the DBA may still have some latitude in specifying indices to be used, orderings, access paths, etc.

Once the conceptual schema, external schema, and internal schema have been designed, their definitions are entered formally into the DBMS via the data definition language of the system. DBMSs vary in terms of the completeness of their data definition languages. For example, some permit only coarse representations of the conceptual schema, so the DA must seek other means to maintain a more complete definition. A DD/DS (discussed later in this chapter) may be employed for this purpose. Whatever the means of definition used, the DA and DBA take joint responsibility for entering the definitions into the system. The DA tends to focus on entering the conceptual schema and external schema definitions; the DBA tends to focus on entering the internal schema definition.

After the new definitions have been established, the database now must be *populated* with data according to these definitions—that is, specific instances of data must be created that conform with the definitions. Again, both the DA and DBA take joint responsibility for populating the database. The DA advises users on procedures for collecting data and, in particular, validation and editing criteria that should be applied to the data. Also, where different users have maintained files on the same data item or they have an interest in the same data item, the DA designates who will be responsible for assembling instances of the data item and how differences between alternative versions of the data item are to be reconciled. The DBA takes responsibility for preparing the programs needed to introduce the data to the database. The DBMS may provide facilities in this respect, or special programs may have to be designed and written. Again, careful attention must be given to the validation and editing procedures needed in the programs to ensure the quality of the data used to populate the database.

As user needs change, the existing definitions may require modification. A major task that arises when data redefinition must be undertaken is to determine the impact of the redefinition on the database environment. The redefinition may affect some or all existing programs and users. To the extent that a comprehensive data definition is maintained by the DA and DBA, determining the consequences of a redefinition is easier. The respective responsibilities of the DA and DBA are much like those for the data definition and creation phases. The DA works primarily with the users to formulate a modified conceptual schema and external schema; the DBA determines the changes needed to the internal schema, works out the effects of the redefinition, and establishes how the changes can be accomplished.

The final phase in the life cycle of data is retirement. Policies must be formulated to provide guidelines on when data is to be retired and how long it is to be retained. The DA is responsible for formulating these policies and advising users on their implications and application to specific data items. The DBA is responsible for implementing these policies and executing retirement and retention procedures for specific data items.

Making the Database Available to Users

Users of the database need various tools to interrogate and update the database. These tools have to be purchased or developed. Moreover, since user needs change over time and enhanced or new tools become available, someone must monitor the needs of the user population, remain aware of the current tool technology, and ensure required tools are available on a timely basis.

Both the DA and DBA have responsibility for making the database available to users. The DA usually has the better knowledge of user needs and can determine requirements for end-user tools. The DBA usually has the better knowledge of tools that would improve the efficiency with which the database can be used. Thus, both the DA and DBA must remain aware of the technology that impacts their respective functions.

Irrespective of whether a tool is purchased or developed, it must be evaluated carefully before an investment is made in acquiring the tool. Then it must be tested comprehensively before it is released for production use. Even if the initial purchase cost or development cost of a tool is minor, subsequent costs may be high if use of the tool leads to poor decisions or corruption of the database. The DA and DBA must evaluate costs and benefits from a global perspective, not just the up-front costs of obtaining the tool. Similarly, because of the potential damage caused by an erroneous tool in a shared data environment, thorough testing before production release is a necessity. Both the DA and DBA must assume responsibility for evaluation and testing of tools.

Informing and Servicing Users

As the focal points in a database environment, the DA and DBA are responsible for informing and assisting users, and educating and training users. These activities are accomplished in the normal ways. Users must know the current status of the database and any changes made to supporting systems. For example, they need to know if a portion of the database has been damaged or a new availability tool has been purchased or developed.

To inform and service users, the DA and DBA must establish a viable communications system. There are a number of means; for example, documentation, memoranda, electronic bulletin boards, and system messages. Some typical examples of documentation needed are:

1 A dictionary of data names, cross-referenced to associated data names
2 Semantic descriptions of data elements
3 Physical storage information to aid efficient use of data
4 Data retention information
5 Reference and user manuals

A memorandum system must inform users on such matters as:

1 Potential hazards or loss of integrity of the database
2 New standards implemented

3 New user tools available
4 Training courses to be given

Maintaining Database Integrity

To maintain the integrity of the database, the DA and DBA must undertake six control measures: (a) definition control, (b) existence control, (c) access control, (d) update control, (e) concurrency control, and (f) quality control.

Definition Control Definition controls seek to establish correspondence between the database and its definition at all times. The DA takes primary responsibility for developing and promulgating organizationwide data definition standards. Furthermore, the DA takes primary responsibility for monitoring end-users for compliance with these standards. The DBA takes primary responsibility for the technical aspects of definition control. The DBA must ensure that neither a program nor a procedure could destroy the correspondence between the database and its definition. For example, application system programs or end-user developed programs should not be permitted to manipulate pointers (the storage structure level) in the database in case a defined access path is destroyed.

Existence Control The DA and DBA protect the existence of the database by establishing suitable backup and recovery procedures. In conjunction with users, the DA determines backup and recovery requirements. For example, the DA determines how long users can tolerate the whole database being unavailable or a segment of the database being unavailable. The DBA then designs and implements backup and recovery controls that attempt to ensure these requirements are met.

Access Control Access controls prevent inadvertent or unauthorized disclosure of data in the database. Access controls take many forms: passwords, physical locks on terminals, voice prints, etc. Various levels of access controls are needed for data items, groups, and files. To prevent irregularities, separation of duties should be applied so that the person responsible for assigning users a level of access authorization is not the same person who implements the access controls. In this light the DA might perform the former function, and the DBA might perform the latter function.

Update Control Update controls restrict update of the database to authorized users. Update authorization takes two forms. The first form permits only addition of data to the database. The second form allows a user to change or delete existing data. Various refinements on these update forms exist. For example, a user may only be permitted to add data to the end of a file. Again, it is beneficial to separate duties by having the DA assign the level of update authorization to users and the DBA implement the level assigned.

Concurrency Control Data integrity problems arise when two update processes are allowed access to the same data item at the same time. For example, an order entry process may be updating the inventory quantity-on-hand data item at the same time as a warehouse receipts process is updating this data item. The database may end up in an inconsistent state. Hopefully the DBMS automatically handles concurrency problems. However, some DBMS may provide only a partial solution, and human intervention may be required to schedule processes to prevent concurrency problems from arising or to implement recovery actions if the database is corrupted. Since these problems are technical, the DBA assumes primary responsibility for enforcing concurrency control. Chapter 14 discusses these matters further.

Quality Control Quality controls ensure the accuracy, completeness, and consistency of data maintained in the database. Included within this set of controls are traditional measures such as program validation of input data and batch controls over data in transit through the organization. Both the DA and DBA share joint responsibility for quality control over the database. Again, the DA tends to address policy matters and to assist end-users. For example, the DA may formulate standard check digit procedures or develop standard validation tests that must always be applied to a particular data item. The DBA assists in implementing quality control policies and monitors the database for compliance with these policies.

Monitoring Operations

Finally, the DA and DBA must monitor operations and performance within the database environment. Ongoing monitoring enables the DA and DBA to identify areas where effectiveness and efficiency can be improved. For example, in light of user access patterns, it may be possible to improve response times by redesigning a data structure or a storage structure. Similarly, a change in the way users interrogate the database may indicate that a new type of query language is needed.

Effective monitoring of the database environment relies in part on the ingenuity and experience of the DA and DBA. At any one time, only a few aspects of the environment can be monitored successfully. The DA and DBA must be able to identify areas where there are potential difficulties, determine the appropriate performance statistics to be collected, and then devise suitable measurement procedures. In some cases monitoring simply may involve collecting statistics on the types and frequency of user requests against the database. In other cases it may involve more complex efforts to measure user satisfaction with the database.

In part, the integrity of the database depends on users being able to use the database effectively and efficiently. A typical response when users encounter difficulties is that they attempt to circumvent controls which they perceive to inhibit them. Unfortunately, any short-run gains obtained using this strategy often lead to long-run disasters. Thus, the future integrity of the database is dependent on the ability of the system to respond in time to changing user needs. Perceiving the required changes necessitates monitoring the database on a timely basis.

ORGANIZATIONAL ISSUES

The preceding sections have adopted a normative perspective of the DA and DBA roles; that is, they have discussed what these roles *should* be accomplishing in organizations to provide auditors with a basis to evaluate these roles. Unfortunately, the situation in practice is not as clear-cut as the normative descriptions imply. Both roles are relatively new, and several unresolved difficulties remain. The following sections examine four such difficulties: ensuring the roles are effective, placing the DA role in the organizational hierarchy, placing the DBA role in the organizational hierarchy, and accommodating the effects of decentralized data processing on the DA and DBA roles.

Ensuring DA/DBA Effectiveness

A research study by Kahn [1983] indicates that it may not be easy to ensure that the DA and DBA roles are effective even when they appear to have reasonable autonomy, power, and support. She surveyed 56 organizations and the state of their practice with respect to the DA and DBA roles. In brief, some of her findings were as follows:

  1 Organizations with both a DA and DBA role were more likely to use data management standards than organizations with a DBA only or neither a DA nor DBA. She examined four classes of standards pertaining to (*a*) data dictionaries, (*b*) data definitions, (*c*) database/file design, and (*d*) general data management activities.

  2 Organizations with both a DA and DBA perceived policy issues relating to the data resource to be more important than organizations with a DBA only or neither a DA nor DBA.

  3 Two factors seem to affect whether both the DA and DBA roles will be present in organizations: (*a*) the size of the organization—large organizations tend to have both a DA and DBA, medium-size organizations tend to have only a DBA, and small organizations have neither role; (*b*) the reporting level of the chief information officer—both a DA and DBA were more likely to exist if the chief information officer was placed higher in the organizational hierarchy. Interestingly, the industry in which the organization was engaged had no effect on the likelihood of a DA or DBA role being present. Prior research had hypothesized that the DA and DBA roles were more likely to be present in service-related industries—banking, insurance, etc.

4 The DA role was undertaken by a small and young organizational group. Most groups had four or fewer employees and had been established for only a few years.

5 Most DA groups reported directly to the chief information officer. Furthermore, where both a DA and DBA role existed, they tended to be separate, both were on the same organizational level, and both reported directly to the chief information officer.

6 Kahn's most surprising results, however, relate to the success and effectiveness of the DA and DBA roles. Most respondents considered the DA and DBA roles were adequately funded in their organizations and most felt they were relatively successful; but the roles seemed to be only marginally *effective*. Of 17 DA/DBA activities that Kahn examined, she found only two that were being accomplished effectively by most respondents: procedures for data restoration and maintaining data integrity. Furthermore, there was no consensus on the factors that had inhibited the effectiveness of the DA/DBA roles. Only one factor was considered significant by most respondents: management's lack of understanding of the DA role. As a result, Kahn concluded that the cost effectiveness of the DA role needs to be carefully monitored, as it is still unclear whether the ongoing presence of the role in organizations can be justified.

7 On the basis of Kahn's findings, therefore, it cannot be assumed that ensuring the effectiveness of the DA/DBA roles is a straightforward matter. Although educating management on the nature of the roles may help to some extent, it is still unclear what other factors inhibit the effectiveness of the roles. Thus, auditors should be careful when evaluating the roles. They should attempt to see the roles have sufficient authority and responsibility, yet they should not assume the existence of the roles is a panacea for data management problems.

Placement of the DA Role

Aside from the issue of functions to be performed, perhaps the most critical decision facing organizations that wish to implement the DA and DBA roles is where they will place the roles in the organizational hierarchy. Given the policy making, standard setting, and mediation functions that both roles must perform, it is unlikely they will be successful unless they are positioned strategically within the organizational hierarchy.

In terms of the DA role, Ross [1981] proposes three alternatives: (*a*) as a staff function within the offices of top management, (*b*) as a new office reporting to the controller's department, and (*c*) as an office within the data processing department reporting directly to the chief information systems executive. He favors the first alternative (Figure 6-4). If the DA reports to the controller, users of the database may perceive the primary functions of the DA to be monitoring and the issue of sanctions. Thus, users may not adopt a positive attitude to the management of data. If the DA is situated in the data

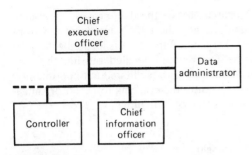

FIGURE 6-4
Organizational placement of the DA role.

processing department, users may be sceptical of the DA's independence. If the DA performs a staff function at the top management level, however, the necessary authority, responsibility, and independence should ensue.

Placement of the DBA Role

In terms of the DBA role, there are even more options than the DA role as to where the DBA should be located within the organizational hierarchy. Weldon [1981] argues that, at least initially, the DBA should be placed within the data processing department. She identifies five possibilities: (*a*) an advisory DBA performing a staff function for top data processing management, (*b*) a project/ support DBA who reports to the manager of a project development group, (*c*) a functional/support DBA who reports to a manager of support services within the data processing department, (*d*) a consultant DBA who occupies a line position on the same level as the manager of application development or the manager of computer operations, and (*e*) a manager DBA who is more senior than the managers of system development or operations.

The situation is even more complicated, however, when a DA role also exists in the organization and the relationship of the DBA to the DA must be considered. One alternative is to have the DBA report to the DA. However, this arrangement is problematical if the DBA is located *within* the data processing department and the DA is located *outside* the data processing department. Nevertheless, because of their joint responsibilities, some type of arrangement for enabling close interaction needs to be set up. If the DBA does not report directly to the DA, they must liaise in some way, and this relationship may involve an arrangement that cuts across established lines of authority and responsibility within the organization.

Whatever the organizational location chosen initially, ultimately the DBA must occupy a position that is not subordinate to any functional or project group. Otherwise, the DBA will not be able to perform a mediation function effectively since users will perceive the DBA to lack independence. Figure 6-5 shows two possible locations that provide the necessary independence. If the DBA reports directly to the DA, a clear communication path exists between the two roles. However, if the DA is located outside the data processing organization, the DBA will be located similarly and the DBA's technical functions may be inhibited as a result. On the other hand, if the DBA is located within the data processing department and the DA remains located outside the data processing department, the technical functions are facilitated but coordination between the two roles is inhibited. Currently there seems to be no organizational arrangement for both roles that is free of difficulties.

Effects of Decentralization of Data Processing

Choosing the location of the DA and DBA roles becomes even more difficult when an organization pursues a policy of decentralized data processing. In some ways the objectives of database management and the objectives of data processing decentralization seem in conflict. On the one hand, centralized planning and control of data is the objective. On the other hand, dispersal of data processing functions so they are close to users is the objective. A reconciliation is possible, however, if it is recognized that standards must apply

FIGURE 6-5
Organizational placement of the DBA role: (a) DBA reports to DA; (b) DBA reports to chief information officer.

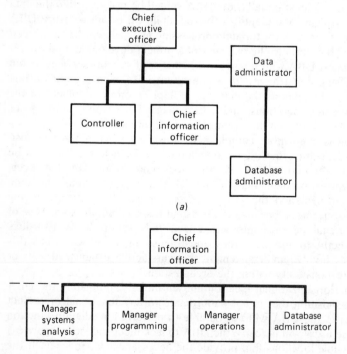

to data communicated among decentralized groups. This situation is no different from two machine vendors agreeing on a common communications protocol so their machines can communicate with each other.

It is important, therefore, in a decentralized data processing environment to partition data into two sets: data that will remain strictly within the confines of the localized processor and data that will be communicated to at least one other group within the organization. In the former case, the data can be managed locally; that is, the design of the data, control over using the data, etc., can be undertaken where it is stored. Hopefully, however, general data management guidelines have been promulgated throughout the organization and the local group adheres to these guidelines. In the latter case, local use of data must comply with the policies and rules established for the shared data by a central authority. In other words, local use must acquiese to the instructions of a higher group so that all users of the shared data items can make effective and efficient use of the database. This does not imply that shared data must be *stored* centrally. Where the data is stored physically is another matter, one determined primarily by efficiency considerations.

If data in a decentralized organization is managed in this way, some alternatives for locating the DA and DBA roles become clearer. Large decentralized groups may have their own DA and DBA to manage local data. However, these local DAs and DBAs must comply with standards established by a corporate DA and DBA for organizationwide data. Indeed, they would be responsible for enforcing these standards among local users.

Alternatively, if local groups are not sufficiently large to support their own DA and DBA, a centralized DA or DBA might perform a staff function. That is, the centralized DA or DBA acts in an advisory role and performs the data management tasks required for local data. In addition, they would be responsible for ensuring the local group understands and complies with standards established for shared data.

Thus, decentralization of the DA and DBA roles can be considered in the same way as decentralization of other roles within the organization. A clear distinction must be made between what can be done locally without detrimental effects to the organization and what must be done on a standardized basis for the good of the overall organization. Where global standards must be enforced, the DAs and DBAs must have a mechanism for meeting and agreeing on the standards that will apply to the entire organization. Again, conflict probably will arise, and the corporate DA/DBA then needs to perform a mediation function. Similarly, the corporate DA/DBA takes ultimate responsibility for ensuring corporate data standards are enforced in all localities.

Perhaps the most difficult decentralization problems arise in organizations where end-user computing is employed widely. With multiple end-users designing and creating their own databases using high-level languages, it becomes especially difficult to enforce corporate standards. If the end-user databases constitute local databases, failure to enforce standards may not be so serious, although it may have implications for effective and efficient use of local

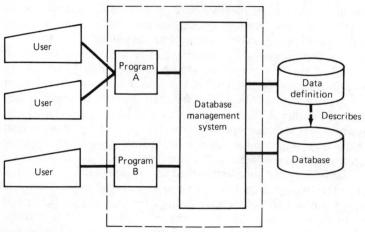

FIGURE 6-6
Using a separate data definition to achieve evolvability and integrity.

data by the end-user. Failure to enforce standards with respect to corporate data, however, is a serious concern. Multiple, conflicting versions of data arise, and it becomes more difficult to protect the integrity of shared data. In an end-user environment, therefore, a critical function of the DA and DBA is to develop and promulgate data standards for end-users and to ensure compliance by end-users with these standards.

DATA DICTIONARY/DIRECTORY SYSTEM (DD/DS)

Recall that two of the major objectives of database management are evolvability and integrity. There are several ways of achieving these objectives, but a primary means is to separate the definition of data from the data itself and from the programs that use that data (Figure 6-6). By separating the definition of data from instances of the data, certain types of changes can be made to the definition without affecting the stored data. For example, it may be possible to alter a user's "view" of the data without modifying the stored data. Similarly, by separating the definition of data from the programs that use the data, certain types of changes can be made to the definition without affecting the programs that use the data. For example, storage structures can be changed without having to alter program source code and to recompile programs. Finally, a separate data definition permits control to be exercised over the definition more easily.

Ideally, a single, complete definition would be maintained by the DBMS. Historically, however, this single, complete definition has not emerged as a common and essential feature in DBMSs. The technical problems to be overcome have been substantial. Consequently, other facilities have been developed to supplement the basic definition provided in order to circumvent the difficulties that have arisen as a result of an incomplete data definition. The most important facility to emerge is the DD/DS.

Elements of a DD/DS

The data elements needed to define a database are often called "metadata"—they are data about data. As discussed earlier, three types of metadata are needed: conceptual schema metadata; external schema metadata; and internal schema metadata. If the data definition maintained by the DBMS does not contain all these elements, it will be inadequate to meet all the needs of users and their associated programs. In general, existing DBMS have provided weak facilities for defining conceptual schemas and only moderate facilities for defining external schemas. DD/DS have been developed to provide more powerful facilities for defining the external and conceptual schemas. In addition, they also may provide the internal schema needed to access the data. Hence, their name—the dictionary aspects describe what data exists and what it means, and the directory aspects describe where the data is stored and how it can be accessed.

Figure 6-7 shows the major functional capabilities provided by a DD/DS. A data definition language processor allows the DA/DBA to create or modify a

FIGURE 6-7
Major user facilities in a data dictionary/directory package.

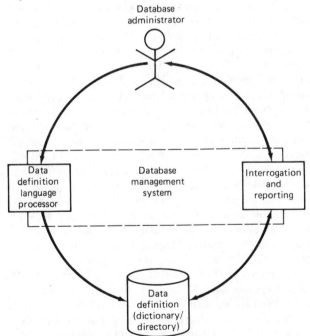

Database administrator

Data definition language processor

Database management system

Interrogation and reporting

Data definition (dictionary/ directory)

```
/-DISPLAY RECORD SUPPLIER
   CREATED.........  6MAR85  11:01:05
   LAST UPDATED.....  6MAR85  11:01:09
   DESCRIPTION......
   An accredited source of goods or services:
   A Supplier is any organization to whom purchase order
   may be addressed whether internal (Central Stores) or
   external (Third Party)
   ENTITIES........  SUPPLIER
   KEYS............  KEY KSUPPLIER IS
                          SUPPLIER-NUMBER
                          DUPLICATES ARE NOT ALLOWED
                     KEY KSUPPLIERINDEX IS
                          ASCENDING SUPPLIER-NAME
                          DUPLICATES ARE NOT ALLOWED
   STRUCTURE........  ITEM SUPPLIER-NUMBER
                      ITEM SUPPLIER-NAME
                      ITEM SUPPLIER-ADDRESS
                      ITEM SUPPLIER-TOWN
                      ITEM SUPPLIER-COUNTY
                      ITEM SUPPLIER-POSTCODE
```

FIGURE 6-8
Listing of metadata elements from a data dictionary package. (*International Computers Limited.*)

data definition. It performs validation tests on the definition provided in an attempt to ensure the integrity of the metadata is preserved. It also exercises controls to prevent unauthorized access to or manipulation of the metadata. An interrogation and reporting language allows the DA/DBA to make enquiries on the data definition. For example, two reports provided are a listing of metadata elements (Figure 6-8) and a cross-reference or where-used report showing the relationships between metadata elements, programs, and users (Figure 6-9).

Unfortunately, although DD/DS have solved some problems, they have produced others. On the one hand, they have led to a more complete definition of data that facilitates information requirements analysis, database design, database use, programming, maintenance, and documentation. Moreover, some DD/DS facilitate evolvability since they can be used by several DBMS; thus, an organization using one of these DD/DS reduces the impact of a change from one DBMS to another DBMS. On the other hand, the existence of two separate definitions—one maintained by the DD/DS and the other by the DBMS—produces the inevitable control problems. These problems are confounded if the DD/DS does not allow users to share data definitions but instead requires users to maintain their own separate definition of the same data.

Difficulties also arise if the DD/DS is used passively rather than actively in a DBMS environment. A *passive* DD/DS is one that is not used by the DBMS to gain access to and to manipulate data. It services primarily the dictionary needs of users. Thus, the data definition maintained by the DD/DS and the data definition maintained by the DBMS are clearly separate. An *active* DD/DS is one that is used directly by the DBMS to gain access to and to manipulate data.

```
/-ENQUIRY USAGE RECORD SUPPLIER
USED BY ELEMENTS
                              PROPERTY DETAILS
    INDEX                     ICL9IDMSGOODSSCI0001
                                *INDEX-FOR
    REPORT-PROGRAM            ALLSUPPLIERS
                                *VIEW
    REPORT-PROGRAM            FORMATTEDOSORDS
                                *VIEW
    REPORT-PROGRAM            LOWSTOCKWITHORDS
                                *VIEW
    SCHEMA                    GOODSCH
                                *RECORDS
    SET                       ORDERS
                                *OWNER
    STORAGE-SCHEMA           GOODSSC
                                *RECORDMAP
    EXCHANGE                  FIND-SUPP
                                *SINGULAR-VIEW
    EXCHANGE                  FIND-SUPPLIER
                                *SINGULAR-VIEW


    ELEMENTS USED
                              PROPERTY DETAILS
    ENTITY                    SUPPLIER
                                *ENTITIES
                                (SKELETON ENTRY)
    ITEM                      SUPPLIER-ADDRESS
                                *STRUCTURE
    ITEM                      SUPPLIER-COUNTY
                                *STRUCTURE
    ITEM                      SUPPLIER-NAME
                                *STRUCTURE
    ITEM                      SUPPLIER-NUMBER
                                *STRUCTURE
    ITEM                      SUPPLIER-POSTCODE
                                *STRUCTURE
    ITEM                      SUPPLIER-TOWN
                                *STRUCTURE
    ENQUIRY COMPLETED
```

FIGURE 6-9
Where-used list from a data dictionary package. (*International Computers Limited.*)

Thus, with an active DD/DS it is more likely that a consistent data definition will exist.

Audit Aspects of a DD/DS

There are three implications for the auditor when an organization uses a DD/DS. First, if the organization uses the DD/DS properly, the auditor can have increased confidence in the reliability of controls over data and application systems. Second, by establishing a centralized database definition using a DD/DS, the organization faces a new set of exposures that may have serious consequences if the database definition or the DD/DS is lost or corrupted. Thus, controls must be established over the database definition and the DD/DS. Third, the existence of a DD/DS facilitates the audit process.

Enhanced Data and System Reliability   By allowing centralized control to be exercised over data, a DD/DS enhances control over data and application systems. Responsibility for data definition functions is not dispersed across the individual data processing personnel who are responsible for various application systems. Instead, the DA and DBA take responsibility for determining the data definition and use the DD/DS to enforce the definition across individual application systems. Since the data definition is not embedded in individual application programs, hopefully the authenticity, accuracy, and completeness of the data definition is enhanced and, as a consequence, the integrity of data increases also.

Use of a common database definition and DD/DS also enhances control over the system development process. Some of the benefits obtained are:

1 Assists planning, requirements analysis, database design, and maintenance through being able to determine the effects of change on users, programs, and data.

2 Facilitates programming by reducing the effort required to establish the database definition. The database definition may be copied into programs, or a program may access the database definition directly.

3 Enhances documentation through the dictionary capabilities of the DD/DS.

4 Enforces common validation criteria as validation criteria are associated with data items rather than being embedded in the programs that access the data items.

Control Aspects   The database definition is a critical master file within the installation, and the DD/DS is a critical program. Both should be subjected to rigorous security, backup, and recovery controls. If the database definition were lost or destroyed, the operations of the organization would be severely impaired. If the integrity of the DD/DS were corrupted, the database definition could be corrupted and the database may be corrupted as a result. Thus, duplicate copies of the database definition and DD/DS need to be stored off site, and a log of changes to the database definition needs to be maintained. In addition, access and validation rules should be established via the DD/DS for the database definition, and the integrity of the DD/DS itself needs to be protected via program library controls, modification controls, etc.

If an organization commits itself to establishing a database and using a DD/DS to support the database, the auditor has to ensure that this commitment extends to all users of the database. One of the costs of centralized control is that individual users may have to compromise in terms of their own needs.

Furthermore, they must be willing to accept common protocols such as data item naming and numbering conventions. If individual users are not willing to compromise and to accept common protocols, they will seek ways to circumvent database controls. Ultimately they may be successful, and the sharability, availability, evolvability, and integrity objectives of database management will not be achieved.

Usage Aspects   The auditor is also a user of the database definition and the DD/DS. For example, the DD/DS enables the auditor to retrieve structural information needed for generalized audit software to be able to access the database. The nonstructural information provided by the DD/DS is also useful. For example, the auditor can examine the adequacy of validation criteria applied to various data items if this information is stored in the database definition. Or, if the auditor wants to trace a data item's path through an application system, the DD/DS provides information on the programs that use the data item, the files where the data item is stored, and the reports where the data item is printed. In this way various types of impact analyses can be undertaken.

CONTROL OVER THE DATABASE ADMINISTRATOR

Even a cursory examination of the functions that should be performed by the DA and DBA shows that these roles provide a position of unique power within the database environment. This power can be used to the organization's advantage or it can be abused. On the one hand, centralizing certain functions to be performed in a database environment improves communication, coordination, and control. On the other hand, vesting substantial power in a single organizational position runs contrary to the fundamental principles of sound internal control.

Perhaps the major control concerns relate to the DBA position. Although both the DA and DBA have substantial administrative powers, the DBA also exercises certain technical powers that allow irregularities to be perpetrated. Consequently, the following sections examine control weaknesses that often surround the DBA position and some remedial measures that can be undertaken. Nevertheless, some of the discussion applies to the DA role, also.

Control Weaknesses

Beside the control problems that can result from improper role performance by the DBA, two other aspects of the DBA's position represent direct threats to data integrity. First, the existence of the DBA role at least partially violates the traditional control principle of separation of duties. Second, the DBA has available tools which, though necessary for the performance of various functions, also can be used to override established controls.

Inadequate Separation of Duties Traditionally, separation of duties has been used to prevent any one individual from having sufficient power to perpetrate a fraud, or as a check on the correct performance of one person's duties by other personnel. For simple systems having well-defined processes and few interfaces with other systems, this fundamental principle of internal control causes few problems. However, as systems become more complex, the number of interfaces among subsystems increases, the risk of error in the communication process increases, and separation of duties can cause rather than prevent control problems. Control is increased in complex systems by simplifying processes and decreasing the number of interfaces existing among subsystems.

The concept of a DBA arose in response to the problems presented by the complexity of a database environment. A DBA position reduces the number of interfaces needed among the users of a database by channeling communications through a single point, thereby increasing control. A tradeoff must be made with the decreased control caused by vesting substantial power in a single position.

Availability of Tools to Override Database Integrity Since the DBA has available tools to set up many of the controls needed over the database, the corresponding power exists to override these controls. For example, tools exist to establish various levels of access and update authorization, find out user passwords, restructure the database, etc. The DBA can assign to a program a level of access and update authorization that will override all other controls. Confidential data can be examined by finding out a user's password. Access paths can be eliminated to remove records from an audit trail. Database tools must be used only for their intended purposes.

Remedial Measures

Control over the DBA presents many of the same problems that arise with controlling any senior position within the organization. Primary emphasis must be placed on administrative controls, though a set of technical controls are available, depending on the sophistication of the hardware and software used within the database environment. The extent of the controls used depends on cost-benefit considerations.

Assign Appropriate Seniority to the Position As discussed previously, to be able to function effectively and efficiently, the DBA must hold a senior position within the computer installation's organizational hierarchy. Individuals who attain the position must be considered trustworthy and must have been subject to the scrutiny that all senior personnel should undergo. Standard control procedures should be applied such as background checking, interviewing, and bonding. Further, the position should be reviewed regularly and the person holding the position evaluated.

TABLE 6-2
POSSIBLE BREAKDOWN OF AUTHORITY AND RESPONSIBILITY
OVER DATABASE SERVICING TOOLS

Function	Person responsible
Storage of source code, listings, and documentation	Installation librarian
Object code	Program librarian
Use of database tools	Database administrator
Log of uses of database tools	Operations manager
Update and maintenance	Programming manager

Separate Duties to the Extent Possible Careful thought should be given to how the duties of the DBA can be separated without unduly impairing the functions of the role. If a DBA *group* exists rather than a single DBA, different functions may be assigned to different members of the group. For example, different personnel might be responsible for monitoring, data retirement, design of access controls, establishment of access controls, etc. Supervisory or review controls also might be exercised over the DBA by the DA.

Another basis for separating duties is to separate authority to use a database servicing tool from the authority to store and maintain the tool. Table 6-2 presents a possible breakdown of authority and responsibility over database servicing tools. The installation librarian has responsibility for safeguarding the source code and documentation for the tools. Only the programming manager can gain access to this source code and documentation for update and maintenance purposes. Source code may not be available if the tool has been supplied by a DBMS vendor. The program librarian exercises control over the object code. Release of the object code for use might require the joint authority of the operations manager and the DBA. The operations manager should have responsibility for safeguarding any machine logs maintained on activities related to database servicing tools.

Maintain Logs Two types of logs can be kept to record the activities of the DBA: (*a*) manual logs and (*b*) machine logs. Manual logs record such activities as the DBA's requests for access to the database, the use of servicing tools, the DBA's and operations manager's requests for object code from the program librarian, the programming manager's requests for source code listings and documentation from the installation librarian, and the return of source code listings and documentation to the installation librarian. Where possible, machine logs should record similar activities to provide an independent check on the manual logs. For example, the operating system should keep a log of the DBA's access to the database.

Periodically the auditor should check the correspondence between the two logs and attempt to detect any unauthorized activity. For example, when the DBA uses a servicing tool, the auditor should check to see an unauthorized copy of the object code was not made. Similarly, if a maintenance programmer retrieves a copy of source code from a program file, the auditor should check to see no other copies were made.

Training and Rotation of Duties If the size of the installation warrants a DBA group rather than a single DBA, control can also be exercised through training and rotation of duties. Training gives several personnel the capabilities needed to perform a required task, thereby allowing duties to be rotated among the members of the DBA group.

SUMMARY

Two key elements in the management control framework of a computer installation are the DA and DBA. Organizations establish DA and DBA positions when they give full recognition to data as an important resource and when they make a commitment to centralized planning and control of data.

The existence of DA and DBA positions impacts the audit in several ways. First, the DA and DBA provide the auditor with information on strengths and weaknesses within the database environment. Second, the DA and DBA provide the auditor with administrative and technical information necessary for the auditor to be able to carry out the evidence collection and evaluation functions. Third, since proper performance of the DA and DBA roles is critical to maintaining asset safeguarding, data integrity, effectiveness, and efficiency in a database environment, the auditor must know what functions the DA and DBA should perform as a basis for evaluating their roles.

The DA and DBA perform five major functions: (a) defining, creating, and retiring data, (b) making the database available to users, (c) informing and servicing users, (d) maintaining database integrity, and (e) monitoring operations and performance. They act as mediators when the sharing of data produces conflict among users. This mediation role necessitates a position of independence. Thus, the DA and DBA should report directly to a manager who is not responsible to any functional or project group within the organization.

The position of power held by the DA and DBA and the availability of servicing tools needed to perform DBA functions create special control problems. Several remedial steps can be undertaken to increase control, for example, separating duties to the extent possible with the position and maintaining logs to record activities relating to the DBA role.

REVIEW QUESTIONS

6-1 What are the objectives of database management? Why are data and database administrators needed to help accomplish these objectives?

6-2 Is it necessary for a computer installation to be using a database management system before it institutes data and database administration roles? Support your answer.

6-3 Sharing of data among multiple users inevitably produces conflict among the users. What parts do the data and the database administrator play when conflict arises?

6-4 Why has both a data administration role and a database administration role emerged in organizations that use a database management system instead of just one role? Do you think both roles will continue, or will they be combined or disappear?

6-5 What implications does the existence of either a data administration role or a database administration role have for the conduct of an audit? Is either role more important than the other from the viewpoint of conducting the audit?

6-6 Briefly describe the differences among the conceptual schema, the internal schema, and the external schema. For each type of schema, identify whether it will be the data administrator or the database administrator who takes primary responsibility for its definition.

6-7 The coarseness or fineness of the conceptual schema is a function of the completeness of the data definition language in a database management system. Explain.

6-8 What is meant by populating the database? What steps should the data administrator and the database administrator take to preserve data integrity when the database is being populated?

6-9 When data redefinition is undertaken, what are the respective responsibilities of the data administrator and the database administrator?

6-10 How might the database administrator "comprehensively test" a new availability tool acquired for database users?

6-11 Why should the data administrator and the database administrator be responsible for informing and servicing users and not someone else be responsible for this function in a database environment?

6-12 Briefly explain the data administrator's and the database administrator's responsibilities with respect to:
  a Definition control
  b Existence control
  c Access control
  d Update control
  e Concurrency control
  f Quality control

6-13 Give three performance statistics that the database administrator may collect to improve performance within a database environment.

6-14 Briefly describe Kahn's [1983] empirical findings with respect to:
  a Effectiveness of the DA and DBA roles
  b Adequacy of funding for the DA and DBA roles
  c Likelihood of the existence of both the DA and DBA roles
  d Perceived importance of database policy issues

6-15 Why should the data administrator report to top management in a staff function capacity rather than report to the controller or the chief information officer?

6-16 To maintain independence the database administrator must hold a senior position within the organizational hierarchy of the computer installation. Explain.

6-17 What impact does decentralization of data processing have on the roles of the data administrator and the database administrator?

6-18 What impact might end-user computing have on the roles of the data administrator and the database administrator?

6-19 Briefly explain the nature of a data dictionary/directory system. What is the relationship between a data dictionary/directory system and the database definition?

6-20 Briefly explain the nature of metadata. Why is it critical that a database management system have strong capabilities for defining metadata?

6-21 What is the difference between an active data dictionary/directory system and a passive data dictionary/directory system? Why would the auditor be concerned with whether a computer installation is using an active or a passive data dictionary/directory system?

6-22 How can a centralized database definition and a data dictionary/directory system enhance control over the system development process?

6-23 Why is it important to exercise control over a data dictionary/directory system? List three control procedures that might be used.

6-24 Why is obtaining support from programmers and systems analysts for a data dictionary/directory system sometimes difficult? Why is it important to obtain their support? How might their support be obtained?

6-25 How is the auditor a user of the data dictionary? How might the auditor's use of the data dictionary give insight into the problems of other users?

6-26 Explain how the position of the database administrator both strengthens and weakens control. Briefly explain the nature of the tradeoffs involved.

6-27 Give three examples of tools that database administrators need to perform their functions but which can also be used to override database integrity.

6-28 There are two types of remedial measures that can be used to increase control over the database administrator: (a) administrative controls and (b) technical controls. Explain the nature of each set of controls and give an example of each. Which set of controls do you think will be the more effective and why?

6-29 Briefly explain how separation of duties can be used to increase control over the database administrator.

6-30 What types of logs should be kept on activities relating to the database administrator? How does the operating system assist in maintaining logs? What alternatives are available to the auditor if the operating system does not maintain logs?

6-31 How can the auditor use logs to examine the activities of the database administrator?

6-32 In responsibility and authority over database servicing tools, what role should the following individuals play:
  a Installation librarian
  b Operations manager
  c Program librarian

MULTIPLE CHOICE QUESTIONS

6-1 A *full* database administration position usually is established when:
  a Management recognizes data to be a critical organizational resource

b A database management system is purchased

c Management decides to integrate application system files

d Project controllers begin to make suboptimal decisions with respect to data

6-2 Which of the following is *not* a reason why the data administration role emerged subsequent to the database administration role:

a It is difficult to find individuals who have both managerial and policy skills as well as technical skills

b The amount of work that the database administrator had to perform was often too great for a single role

c Database administrators had proved to be unsuccessful at performing the mediation function

d With the growth in end-user computing, more support had to be provided to database users who were not skilled data processing professionals

6-3 Which of the following is *not* a way in which the data administrator and the database administrator impact the auditor:

a They provide administrative and technical information that the auditor needs to know

b They provide database tools that the auditor needs to use

c They act as a mediator when conflict arises between management and the auditor over database issues

d They are a source of information on control strengths and weaknesses in the database environment

6-4 The grammar that describes all permitted states and transitions of the deep structure semantics stored in the database is the:

a Internal schema

b Logical schema

c External schema

d Conceptual schema

6-5 The database administrator has primary responsibility for defining the:

a Internal schema

b Logical schema

c External schema

d Conceptual schema

6-6 When the data administrator performs the data definition function, the first step is to:

a Determine whether some database users have already established in the database at least some of the data items needed

b Design a logical structure that attempts to mirror the user's real world view of the data

c Use the data definition language to model the data structure needed

d Formulate the storage structure needed

6-7 Which of the following functions is most likely to be performed by the data administrator:

a Determining the effects of database redefinition on the internal schema

b Formulating data retention and retirement policies

c Preparing the data validation programs needed to populate the database

d Both (*a*) and (*c*) above

6-8 To make the database available to users, the data administrator and the database administrator must:

    a Monitor changing user needs with respect to interrogation and update facilities needed

    b Purchase or develop database tools to support database use

    c Undertake comprehensive testing of any database tools that are purchased or developed

    d All the above

6-9 A memorandum system in a database environment should document:

    a Semantic descriptions of database elements

    b Data retention information

    c Potential short-term hazards that have arisen for users of the database

    d Storage structure designs that have been used

6-10 In a database environment, traditional program validation is an example of:

    a A quality control

    b An existence control

    c A concurrency control

    d An access control

6-11 Which of the following control functions is most likely to be performed by the data administrator:

    a Ensuring neither a program nor a procedure could destroy the correspondence between the database and its definition

    b Determining backup and recovery requirements

    c Implementing access controls that have been assigned to database users via an access control mechanism

    d Ensuring concurrency controls are in place and working

6-12 The database administrator monitors the operations of the database because:

    a The price of generality is increased overhead, so performance must be monitored carefully if the system is not to degrade quickly

    b In part the integrity of the database is dependent on users' being able to use it efficiently

    c In a database environment all responsibility for performance monitoring must be subsumed within the database administration role

    d Both (*a*) and (*b*) above

6-13 Which of the following results was obtained by Kahn [1983] in her empirical study of the data administration and database administration roles:

    a Most data administration groups that she studied reported directly to the controller

    b Both the data administration and database administration roles had been only marginally effective in the organizations she studied

    c The data administration and database administration roles had been inadequately funded

    d Organizations with a data administration role only were most likely to implement and use data management standards

6-14 Data administrators are more likely to be successful in their role if they report to:

    a Top management in a staff capacity

    b The controller in a staff capacity

    c The chief information systems officer in a line capacity

    d The controller in a line capacity

6-15 The database administrator should be responsible to:

    a Top management outside the computer installation

b The manager in charge of systems analysis and programming

c The EDP manager

d The controller

6-16 Which of the following guidelines applies to the data administration and database administration roles in a large decentralized organization that performs diverse functions:

    a The data administrator and database administrator in each division should be completely autonomous

    b The database administrator assumes a more important role than the data administrator

    c The data administrator role should always be centralized but the database administrator role can be decentralized

    d Data management standards must be developed for shared data and promulgated throughout the organization

6-17 Which of the following best describes the concept of metadata:

    a Data about data

    b Logical definitions of data that are not stored in the database

    c Definitional information that applies to shared databases but not partitioned, localized databases

    d Logical constraints that apply to the conceptual schema

6-18 A *passive* data dictionary/directory system is one that is used:

    a By the database management system to retrieve and manipulate data but not to define data

    b Only by the centralized data administration group and not by any decentralized data administration groups

    c As an optional facility that is made available to users of the database

    d To define data only but not to gain access to and to manipulate data when the database management system is being used.

6-19 Which of the following is *not* an advantage of using a data dictionary/directory system:

    a Facilitates programming by reducing the effort required to establish the data definition

    b Helps to enforce common validation criteria

    c Determines the optimum storage structure to use for the conceptual schema

    d Facilitates data requirements analysis for a new application

6-20 Which of the following should *not* be a control exercised over use of the data dictionary:

    a Ensure a numbering and naming convention is adopted for data items even in decentralized organizations

    b To increase security, use separate data directory/dictionary packages for structural information and storage and access information

    c Establish access controls over all metadata

    d Provide off-site storage for the data dictionary/directory

6-21 The existence of the database administration role tends to violate the traditional internal control principle of having:

    a Clear lines of authority and responsibility

    b Proper procedures for authorization

    c Physical control over assets and records

    d Adequate segregation of duties

6-22 Match each of the following functions relating to database servicing tools with the role that should be assigned responsibility for the function:

I Storage of source code   A Database administrator

II Log of tool use   B Installation librarian

III Use of tool   C Programming manager

IV Tool update and maintenance   D Operations manager

a I-B, II-D, III-A, IV-C
b I-C, II-B, III-A, IV-D
c I-D, II-C, III-B, IV-A
d I-B, II-A, III-C, IV-D

6-23 Which of the following activities carried out by the database administrator is unlikely to be recorded on a machine log maintained by the operating system or by the database management system:

a Access to the database
b Change of a password
c Disclosure of a password to an unauthorized user
d Deletion of a database record

EXERCISES AND CASES

6-1 You are the external auditor for Dumpadollar National Bank, a large bank within the metropolitan area. Dumpadollar has an extensive online realtime update database system.

One of the controls exercised by the data processing management of Dumpadollar is to print out each day a listing of all sensitive utility programs used. This data is obtained from the operating system log. The listing is checked to detect any unauthorized use of these utility programs.

During a review of this log, you notice that Delores Sleek, Dumpadollar's database administrator, had used a pointer maintenance utility on the database. This utility is capable of adding, deleting, or modifying the pointers that establish the logical relationships between records on the database.

You are concerned about unauthorized use of this utility and you express your concern to Harry Thompson, the data processing manager. He explains that sometimes a pointer in the database is corrupted and that Delores is the only person with sufficient knowledge of the database to be able to correct the pointer. When you ask how often a corrupted pointer occurs, Harry informs you that Delores reports the occurrence of one about once a week. When you ask why a corrupted pointer occurs, Harry says he does not know and that you will have to talk with Delores.

Required: Write a brief report to your supervisor documenting why you are concerned about the current situation and informing her what action you now intend to take.

6-2 Some organizations are now moving toward the establishment of a *quality assurance function*. This function has responsibility for the overall integrity of data (and systems) within the organization.

A major reason for setting up this function often is the use of a database management system. In a database environment the traditional "ownership" of data by particular users diminishes or is lost. Data is shared and joint responsibility exists for the integrity of a data item. Unfortunately, one user of a data item may not recognize the integrity requirements of another user; for example, whereas personnel files are notorious for being out of date, it is rare to find a payroll file out of date. Often a payroll section demands a higher level of data integrity in its files than a personnel section. When personnel data is shared, the integrity of the data must meet the minimum level of integrity demanded by the user with the most stringent requirements.

Required: Write a brief report outlining the nature of the interface you think will occur between the quality assurance function and the database administration function in an organization.

6-3 To improve access times to its database, an organization purchases higher density disks. The database administrator is given the responsibility of converting the database from the old disk packs to the new disk packs.

Required: As the internal auditor for the organization, what items would you look for in the conversion plan proposed by the database administrator? Highlight any differences between the conversion plan for the database and the conversion plan that should have been prepared if the organization was converting traditional application system files to higher density disks.

6-4 Wowem Corporation manufactures a wide range of clothing apparel. Wowem is a decentralized organization where different divisions have responsibility for the manufacture and distribution of major product lines.

The corporation uses a database management system for its data processing. The DBMS allows a tree data structure to be created. Wowem's responsibility accounting system has been set up using the DBMS so it has the following tree data structure:

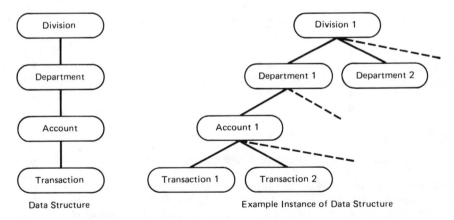

Data Structure   Example Instance of Data Structure

In a major effort to arrest its declining profitability, Wowem undertakes an extensive reorganization of its divisions. Existing product lines are assigned to different divisions, and different departments are assigned to different divisions. As a consequence of this reorganization, the database has to be reorganized.

Required: Wowem's database administrator is responsible for the reorganization of the database to reflect the new lines of responsibility. As the internal auditor for Wowem, you have been asked to review and evaluate the reorganization plan prepared by the database administrator. Make a list of the major items you think should exist in the plan if data integrity is to be preserved during the reorganization process.

6-5 Savers Surety is a large investment house that provides a wide range of investment services for its clients. For some years, Savers has been a pioneering and innovative user of a high-level programming language that has allowed its staff to interact directly with the company's centralized database. For example, investment managers have used the language to prepare various types of analyses on client portfolios or market trends.

The management of Savers has restricted use of the language in two important ways. First, users have not been permitted to download copies of the database (or sections of the database), perform update and retrieval operations, and then upload the database with the data on which they have been working. Second, users have not been permitted to define new data items and store them in the database without the express permission of the data administrator.

Savers has now embarked upon a policy of providing its staff with powerful microcomputers in an attempt to improve productivity. As a consequence, top management has been under substantial pressure to relax the restrictions on downloading/uploading data and defining data since many users are now arguing the real payoffs will occur if they can work on localized copies of data.

Required: You are the data administrator for Savers. Top management asks you to provide a brief report outlining the major policy issues that have to be resolved with respect to data integrity if the restrictions are relaxed.

ANSWERS TO MULTIPLE CHOICE QUESTIONS

6-1 a	6-7 b	6-13 b	6-19 c
6-2 c	6-8 d	6-14 a	6-20 b
6-3 c	6-9 c	6-15 c	6-21 d
6-4 d	6-10 a	6-16 d	6-22 a
6-5 a	6-11 b	6-17 a	6-23 c
6-6 b	6-12 d	6-18 d	

REFERENCES

Adams, Donald L. "System and Audit Aspects of a Data Dictionary," *EDPACS* (May 1976), pp. 1–14.

Allen, Frank W., Mary E. S. Loomis, and Michael Y. Mannino. "The Integrated Dictionary/Directory System," *Computing Surveys* (June 1982), pp. 245–286.

American Institute of Certified Public Accountants, Canadian Institute of Chartered Accountants, and Institute of Internal Auditors. *Report of the Joint Data Base Task Force* (New York: American Institute of Certified Public Accountants, 1983).

Canning, Richard G. "The 'Data Administrator' Function," *EDP Analyzer* (November 1972), pp. 1–14.

Canning, Richard G. "A New View of Data Dictionaries," *EDP Analyzer* (July 1981), pp. 1–12.

CODASYL Programming Language Committee. *Data Base Task Group Report* (New York: Association for Computing Machinery, 1971).

Date, C. J. *An Introduction to Database Systems*, 3d ed. (Reading, MA: Addison-Wesley, 1981).

EDP Auditors Foundation. "Report on an EDPAF Project Entitled Effective Controls and Audit Methodologies in a Data Base Environment," *The EDP Auditor* (Winter 1982/83), pp. 1–22.

Everest, Gordon C. "Database Management Systems Tutorial," in Gordon B. Davis and Gordon C. Everest, eds., *Readings in Management Information Systems* (New York: McGraw-Hill, 1976), pp. 164–187.

Everest, Gordon C., and Ron Weber. "Database Administration: Functional, Organizational, and Control Perspectives," *EDPACS* (January 1979), pp. 1–10.

Gillenson, Mark L. "The State of Data Administration—1981," *Communications of the ACM* (October 1982), pp. 699–706.

GUIDE International Corporation. *Data Administration Methodology* (Chicago, IL: GUIDE International Corporation, 1978).

Kahn, Beverly K. "Some Realities of Data Administration," *Communications of the ACM* (October 1983), pp. 794–799.

Kroenke, David. *Database Processing* (Chicago, IL: Science Research Associates, 1977).

Leong-Hong, Belkis W., and Bernard K. Plagman. *Data Dictionary/Directory Systems: Administration, Implementation and Usage* (New York: Wiley, 1982).

Lyon, John K. *The Database Administrator* (New York: Wiley, 1976).

McCririck, Ian B., and Robert C. Goldstein. "What Do Data Administrators Really Do," *Datamation* (August 1980), pp. 131–134.

Nijssen, G. M. "From Databases towards Knowledge Bases," in *DBMSs—A Technical Comparison* (Maidenhead, Berkshire, England: Pergamon Infotech State of the Art Report 11:5, 1983), pp. 113–131.

Perry, William E. *Auditing Data Systems* (Carol Stream, IL: EDP Auditors Foundation, 1981).

Plagman, Bernard K., and Gene P. Altshuler. "A Data Dictionary/Directory System Within the Context of an Integrated Corporate Data Base," *AFIPS Fall Joint Computer Conference* (Montvale, NJ: AFIPS Press, 1972), pp. 1133–1140.

Ross, Ronald G. *Data Dictionaries and Data Administration: Concepts and Practices for Data Resource Management* (New York: AMACOM, 1981).

Tsichritzis, D. C., and A. Klug (eds.). "The ANSI/SPARC DBMS Framework Report of the Study Group on Database Management Systems," *Information Systems*, vol. 3, 1978, pp. 173–191.

Tsichritzis, D. C., and F. H. Lochovsky. *Data Models* (Englewood Cliffs, NJ: Prentice-Hall, 1982).

Verheijen, G. M. A., and J. Van Bekkum. "NIAM: An Information Analysis Method," in T. W. Olle, H. G. Sol, and A. A. Verrijn-Stuart, eds., *Information Systems Design Methodologies: A Comparative Review* (Amsterdam: North-Holland, 1982), pp. 537–589.

Vermeir, D., and G. M. Nijssen. "A Procedure to Define the Object Type Structure of a Conceptual Schema," *Information Systems*, vol. 7, 1982, pp. 329–336.

Weber, Ron. "Review of John K. Lyons' 'The Database Administrator'," *EDPACS* (February 1978), pp. 9–17.

Weldon, Jay-Louise. *Data Base Administration* (New York: Plenum Press, 1981).

Wiederhold, Gio. *Database Design* (New York: McGraw-Hill, 1977).

SECURITY ADMINISTRATION

CHAPTER OUTLINE

The security administrator in a data processing organization is responsible for matters of *physical* security that affect the computer installation. In other words, the security administrator attempts to ensure that the physical facilities in which systems are developed, implemented, maintained, and operated are safe from threats that affect the continuity of the installation or result in a loss of the installation's assets. Of course, physical security and application security go hand in hand. If the controls established to preserve physical security fail, application controls must then be invoked in an attempt to protect individual application systems (Figure 7-1). For example, a remote terminal may be physically protected by installing it in a locked room. If an intruder gains access to the room, the application system then must be protected via the access controls present in the operating system, the database management system, and the application programs.

The chapter proceeds as follows. The first section discusses some of the organizational considerations that arise in establishing a security administration function. The second section describes the steps to be undertaken in carrying out a security program for the EDP installation. Some major threats to physical security and remedial measures that can be undertaken are described in the third section. Finally, the fourth section describes two controls that must be in place when all else fails: a disaster recovery plan and adequate insurance coverage.

ORGANIZATIONAL CONSIDERATIONS

Depending upon the size of an organization, the security administration function may occupy four possible positions within the organizational hierarchy. In small organizations that use turnkey systems—that is, hardware and software systems that have been purchased as a package rather than developed in house—there may be no data processing staff and, as a consequence, no one obvious to assume the role of security administrator. Nonetheless, security administration in a small organization is just as important as it is in a large organization. For example, a small business that processes all its accounting records on a microcomputer could be forced into liquidation if a malicious employee were to destroy its critical master files and backup and recovery facilities were not available. Someone must be responsible for security. Possibly the person who has overall responsibility for data processing in the organization is the best choice since computer systems developments and the associated security needs then can be considered in a coordinated way.

If an organization has its own data processing staff but insufficient work exists to justify an ongoing, separate security administrator position, responsibility for security matters may be vested in the operations manager (see Chapter 8). Since the operations manager is responsible for the day-to-day running of hardware and software systems, physical control over these facilities seems a natural extension of these responsibilities. As operations

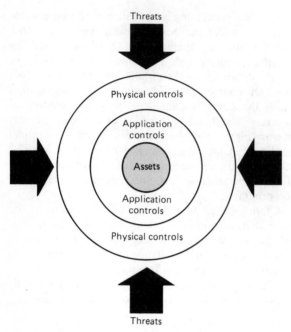

FIGURE 7-1
Asset safeguarding through control layers.

managers must have an in-depth knowledge of the physical facilities, anyway, they are in an excellent position to assess the security needs of the installation.

In large organizations there may be sufficient work to justify a separate security administration position. In some cases the security administrator may report directly to the data processing manager or to the executive in charge of information systems in the organization. In other cases the *computer* security administrator may report to an executive who assumes overall responsibility for *all* security matters with the organization; that is, computer security is just one aspect of the total organizational security that must be managed. The advantage of the former structure is that responsibility for security matters is vested in individuals who are close to computer technology and computer operations. The advantage of the latter structure is that computer security is more likely to be well integrated with the overall security measures adopted by the organization.

Whatever the particular organizational structure used, top management must define carefully the responsibilities and authority of the person who is to perform the security administration role. Auditors must evaluate whether management has given adequate consideration to these matters and ensure that the decisions made are documented in a formal job description. Furthermore, they must assess whether the position has been set up in such a way that the duties are difficult to compromise by either the incumbent or other parties.

CONDUCTING A SECURITY PROGRAM

A security program is a series of ongoing, regular, periodic evaluations conducted to ensure that the physical facilities of a computer installation are safeguarded adequately. The first security evaluation conducted may be a major exercise; the security administrator has to consider an extensive list of possible threats to the organization, prepare an inventory of assets, evaluate the adequacy of controls, implement new controls, etc. Subsequent security evaluations may focus only on changes that have occurred, perhaps in light of the purchase of new hardware, the relocation of the installation to a new site, a new threat, etc. Nevertheless, even in the absence of visible changes, security evaluations need to be repeated periodically to determine whether covert changes have occurred that necessitate modifications to controls. Thus, the essence of a security program is *regular* appraisal of installation security, not just a once-off or infrequent evaluation of safeguards.

The following sections describe six major steps to be undertaken when evaluating installation security: (*a*) preparation of a project plan, (*b*) identification and valuation of assets, (*c*) threats identification, (*d*) exposures analysis, (*e*) controls adjustment, and (*f*) report preparation. While the security administrator assumes major responsibility for performing these steps, the assistance of many individuals within the organization may be required because of their expertise with respect to the various types of assets, threats, exposures, and controls that exist. The auditor's concerns are to see that these steps are performed competently on a regular basis, the results of the reviews are documented, and management takes appropriate action in light of the results.

Preparation of a Project Plan

It may seem an obvious requirement that a security evaluation should commence with the preparation of a project plan. Unfortunately, security evaluations are a mine field for the unwary. There is a tendency to get bogged down in the detail of the review unless strict constraints are imposed upon the conduct of the review. If the objectives of the review are not kept clearly in mind, too much work will be undertaken that has only marginal benefits. In due course this detail may be appropriate, but at the outset the security manager may wish to adopt a phased approach to the program. The initial evaluations deal with critical areas; when these are sorted out, lesser concerns can be addressed.

The project plan for a security evaluation encompasses the normal items that should be present in any project plan:

1 Objectives and scope of the evaluation
2 Tasks to be accomplished
3 Organization of the project team
4 Resources budget
5 Schedule for task completion

These items should be documented formally to provide working guidelines for the review team. Standard tools such as GANTT charts and WBS (work breakdown structure) charts can be used to assist the documentation and communication processes (see Chapter 3).

Like all plans, a security evaluation project plan is useful only if actual progress is monitored against the plan. The security manager must collect data on the status of tasks and the associated resource consumption as a basis for detecting deviations from the plan.

Identification and Valuation of Assets

The first major step in a security evaluation is to identify the assets that exist in the computer installation and to value these assets. This can be a difficult step. The assets resident in a computer installation are not always obvious since they are in electronic form. Nevertheless, it is important to prepare a complete inventory since the omission of an asset may result in a set of exposures being overlooked that ultimately may lead to a loss being incurred.

There are seven major categories of assets that the security manager must investigate:

Asset category	Examples
Personnel	Analysts, programmers, operators, clerks, guards
Hardware	CPU, disk drives, printers, terminals, concentrators
Applications software	Debtors, creditors, payroll, general ledger
System software	Compilers, utilities, interpreters, DBMS
Data	Master files, archival files, transaction files
Facilities	Furniture, office space, filing cabinets
Supplies	Negotiable instruments, tapes, disks, preprinted paper

With each category, the security administrator must prepare a comprehensive list of assets. The difficulty is to know the level of aggregation at which to work. Consider, for example, the problem of preparing an inventory of application programs. In a large installation there may be several thousand programs. On the one hand, for backup purposes a complete inventory of these programs is necessary. On the other hand, valuing each program is an onerous task. Thus the programs may have to be grouped in categories to facilitate valuation.

Valuing the assets is also a difficult step. Parker [1981] points out that the valuation may differ depending upon who is asked to give the valuation, the way in which the asset may be lost, the period of time for which it is lost, and the age of the asset. In terms of who values the asset, an asset may be more useful to some individuals than to others. For example, an end-user who employs a generalized retrieval package more frequently than programmers is more likely to assign a higher value to the package. In terms of how the asset is lost, the accidental loss of an asset may be less serious than the loss that arises through an irregularity. For example, while the accidental destruction of a customer master file may be serious, management may be more concerned if it is stolen by a competitor because of the way in which the file can be used against them. In terms of the time period of loss, for most assets the loss becomes more serious as use of the asset is denied for a longer period. For example, if it is difficult to replace a piece of hardware quickly, management may value it more highly than other hardware that has a higher capital cost but which, nonetheless, can be replaced immediately. In terms of the age of the asset, most assets deteriorate with age. For example, management may be less concerned about a competitor gaining access to an old customer master file than they would be if it were the current version of the file.

Several techniques can be used to assign a value to an asset. In some cases users may be able to provide a dollar valuation for the asset. For example, if an item of hardware can be replaced quickly and easily, they simply may value it at its acquisition cost. In general, however, precise dollar valuations are hard to assign. For example, it is often difficult to determine the loss of customer goodwill that occurs when system failure leads to a degradation in service, or to estimate the lost revenues that result when a competitor steals proprietary software. In these types of situations, indirect valuation techniques have to be used. A formal procedure such as the Delphi method might be used in an attempt to get management consensus on an asset valuation. Alternatively, management may be asked to value an asset on some type of scale where, say, a score of 1 represents a low value and a score of 10 represents a high value. Courtney [1977] suggests another technique whereby users are asked to value assets on a logarithmic scale. They assign a rating, v, to an asset based on their estimate of the dollar value as a function of the base 10. Thus, an asset valued around $100 would be assigned a v of 2; an asset valued around $1 million would be assigned a v of 6. Using this technique, managers are not forced into making fine discriminations between assets based on value.

When undertaking the asset valuation task, the security manager must be careful that the evaluation does not flounder because it is too onerous for users. The primary objectives of asset valuation are to develop users' sensitivity to the possible consequences of a security threat and ultimately to enable an estimate to be made of the amount that can be justified as expenditure on safeguards. The task of asset valuation should be pursued only to the extent that these objectives are accomplished satisfactorily. Otherwise, inordinate resources can be devoted to this phase of the program.

TABLE 7-1
MAJOR THREATS FACING A COMPUTER INSTALLATION

Category	Subcategory	Examples
Unreliable systems	Hardware failure	Power outages
		Circuitry failure
		Disk crashes
	Software failure	Erroneous operating system
		Erroneous update program
	Personnel failure	Intoxicated employees
		Poorly trained employees
Disasters	Natural	Extreme temperature
		Gases
		Liquids
		Living organisms
		Projectiles
		Earth movements
		Electromagnetic discharges
	Financial	Lawsuit
		Bankruptcy
		Strikes
Hostile action	External	Sabotage
		Espionage
	Internal	Fraud
		Theft
		Malice

Threats Identification and Probability Assessment

A threat is some action or event that can lead to a loss. During the threats identification and probability assessment phase of a security review, the security manager attempts to flesh out and evaluate all the threats that may affect the physical security of the computer installation. These threats are considered in terms of their likelihood of occurrence and the assets that may be lost, damaged, or destroyed as a result.

Browne [1979] identifies three major categories of threats that the security manager must consider. Table 7-1 shows examples of specific threats within each category. The first category includes threats that arise because systems are unreliable. For example, if the hardware frequently malfunctions, engineers must be called in constantly to undertake repairs, application systems must be frequently rerun, and personnel become frustrated and fatigued. Consequently, controls tend to become lax, and other threats that arise are more likely to compromise physical security. For example, serious damage results from a fire because the computer room is in an untidy state, or an intruder takes advantage of lax access controls to pose as an engineer and steal vital master files.

The second category includes threats that arise as a result of natural or financial disasters. Table 7-1 shows the seven types of natural disasters identified by Parker [1981]: extreme temperature, gas, liquids, living organisms, projectiles, earth movements, and electromagnetic discharges. The effects of these sorts of disasters are obvious and immediate. Financial disasters, on the other hand, undermine controls over the long run such that other threats take effect on the assets of the installation. For example, lawsuits can stretch management to the extent that they pay little attention to controls. Fire extinguishers may not be serviced regularly, as a result, and a major fire may have disastrous consequences. Similarly, a series of strikes may undermine employee-employer relationships such that lax execution of controls results.

The third category includes threats that arise as a result of hostile action toward the organization and the computer installation. At first glance these threats may seem somewhat removed from reality. There is substantial evidence to show that today this is not the case. Industrial espionage now appears to be a major activity. Similarly, the pirating of software and data files is widespread.

Having identified the threats that face the installation, the security manager next must attempt to estimate their likelihood of occurrence. In some cases, statistical data may be available; for example, an insurance company may be able to provide information on the probability of a fire given the nature of the installation. Similarly, analyses have been undertaken on cases of computer abuse that give insights into the nature of perpetrators, the types of abuses perpetrated, and the schemes used to perpetrate the abuse. Allen [1976], for example, analyzed 150 cases of computer fraud and found inter alia that (a) the most common type of fraud varied depending upon the type of organization, (b) the most common way to perpetrate fraud was to manipulate transactions, (c) managers and clerks were caught taking much more than computer specialists, and (d) collusion among managers was less than collusion among clerks.

However, often the security manager must elicit the probability of the occurrence of a threat from users or management. For example, it may be difficult to obtain an honest answer on the likelihood that financial disaster will undermine physical security, but management is probably the best source of this information. As with asset valuation, formal elicitation techniques like the Delphi method might be used to estimate the likelihood of the occurrence of a threat.

To some extent the nature and value of the assets held within the computer installation affect the likelihood of the occurrence of a threat. If an installation has many high-value, proprietary software packages, for example, it is a prime target for piracy attempts. Thus, the identification and valuation of assets also assists the threats identification and probability assessment phase. The motives that underlie some types of threats are easier to determine in light of a good understanding of the assets held by an organization.

Exposures Analysis

The exposures analysis phase is perhaps the most difficult phase within a security evaluation. It comprises three major tasks: (a) identification of the controls in place and an assessment of their reliability, (b) evaluation of the likelihood that a threat will be successful given the reliability of the controls that are in place, and (c) assessment of the loss that will result if a threat circumvents the controls that are in place. Once these tasks are accomplished, the installation's exposures can be determined. An exposure is simply the expected loss that will occur, given the reliability of the existing control system. In other words, it is a residual (Figure 7-2). It is rarely cost-effective to implement and operate controls to the extent that no exposures exist. Instead, the objective is to reduce exposures to an acceptable level. If exposures are not at an acceptable level, either new controls must be implemented or the existing control system must be modified.

Consider, then, the first task: identifying the controls in place and assessing their reliability. Perhaps the easiest way to perform this task is to use one of the many questionnaires designed to assess physical security (see, for example, Browne [1979] and FitzGerald [1981]). These questionnaires contain extensive control checklists that the security manager can use to determine systematically whether a control is missing. If a control is not present, the security manager then must evaluate its relevance to the installation. For example, a security manager would pay little heed to the controls needed to reduce structural damage caused by earthquakes if the installation was sited in an earthquake-free area. However, relevant controls that are missing must be noted, and even when a control is in place, its reliability still must be assessed. For example, fire extinguishers may be present, but if they have never been

FIGURE 7-2
Exposures—intentionally or unintentionally uncontrolled threats.

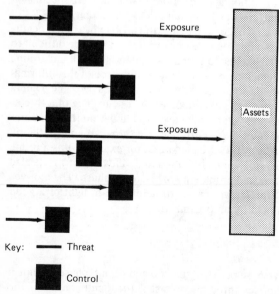

Key: ▬▬▬ Threat

■ Control

serviced, they may be useless in the event of a fire. Thus, the fundamental audit task of assessing the reliability of controls through observation, inquiry, testing, etc., still must be carried out by the security manager.

Once controls and their associated level of reliability have been determined, their ability to safeguard the assets in the installation must be assessed. To accomplish this task, the security manager considers each of the assets or categories of assets identified during the second phase of the review, considers each of the threats identified during the third phase of the review, and assesses the likelihood of the threat circumventing the controls to affect the asset. Parker [1981] suggests that the security manager might write scenarios to describe how threats could compromise controls. These scenarios then can be considered by management to assess their realism (see Table 7-2).

TABLE 7-2
SCENARIO ANALYSIS OF EXPOSURES

Threat:	Malicious damage to minicomputer by operator
Existing controls:	1 Two operators always present 2 Background check carried out before hiring operators
Control weaknesses:	Ongoing psychological stability of operators is not assessed regularly in a formal way
Scenario:	An operator who becomes psychologically unstable could destroy the minicomputer when the other operator leaves the computer room temporarily. Alternatively, the unstable operator may be able to overpower the other operator to carry out the damage.
Probability of occurrence:	Less than 1 in 10,000 a year
Loss that would occur:	$400,000—replacement cost of machine
Assessment:	Exposure is acceptable as costs of carrying out psychological testing exceed $40 per year. The effect of this type of testing on employee morale is also a serious concern.

Once the likelihood of a threat's being successful has been identified, the loss that will result if the threat is successful must be determined. The value of the assets determined in the second phase of the review provides the basis for this assessment. The security manager must determine whether the full value of the asset will be lost or whether the loss will be partial. The expected loss with respect to each threat and each asset can be calculated. For example, given the controls that exist, if the likelihood, p, that a fire will destroy the computer room in any one year is .0001, and the loss, L, that will occur as a result is $4 million, the expected loss each year, EL, with respect to the fire threat and the computer room assets is $400; that is, $EL = p \times L$. The exposure, therefore, is $400.

Unless the security manager is careful, the review can falter badly when the above tasks are performed. Again, there is a tendency to be distracted by details. Somehow the evaluation must be left at a level of aggregation that ensures the tasks are manageable yet at the same time provides sufficient insight into the exposures that exist. The analysis can be facilitated in several ways. First, assets and threats can be categorized and the category rather than the individual asset or threat considered. Second, the materiality of an asset and the significance of a threat should always be kept in mind. Whereas major assets or threats may be analyzed in depth, minor assets and threats may be subjected to a cursory analysis only. Third, it seems best if security enhancements are undertaken in phases. The questionnaires presented in Browne [1979], for example, contain three levels of questions: the first level addresses controls that are basic to most organizations; the second and third levels address controls needed to safeguard assets from threats that are less likely to occur, although the losses incurred may be highest if these threats circumvent controls.

Controls Adjustment

In light of the exposures analysis, the security manager must evaluate whether each exposure is at an acceptable level. Formally, this means the security manager must determine whether any controls can be designed, implemented, and operated such that the cost of the control is less than the reduction in expected losses that occurs by virtue of having the control in place and working. In other words, the benefits of a control that arise because it reduces expected losses from threats must exceed the costs of designing, inplementing, and operating the control (see, also, Chapter 22).

How the security manager makes this decision is in large part a matter of judgment, experience, and training. To some extent, guidance can be obtained from the control questionnaires used to review the state of security during the exposures analysis phase. Controls identified as missing via the questionnaires are candidates for inclusion in a revised controls system. The security manager also might consult security managers in similar installations to determine control profiles that are used commonly. These profiles represent the combined experience and judgments of others who have faced similar problems and, as such, may provide important insights into controls that will be cost-effective. Still another strategy for identifying new controls needed is to analyze the scenarios developed during the exposures analysis phase. These scenarios may suggest the types of controls that will be cost-effective against a threat. In addition, they provide a tangible basis for considering how the control will work to reduce exposures, thereby making the cost-benefit analysis more concrete. Finally, Parker [1981] presents 20 ''principles'' that he argues should provide the formal basis for selecting controls. For example, he argues that controls should place minimum reliance on realtime human intervention, they should have failsafe defaults, and they must not rely on design secrecy for their effectiveness. Proposed safeguards can be evaluated against these principles to determine the likelihood of their success.

The controls adjustment phase also includes consideration of existing controls. The security manager needs to examine whether an existing control should be terminated or modified in some way to make it more cost-effective. The bases used for selecting new controls also can be used to evaluate the status of existing controls. For example, a scenario analysis might show deficiencies in procedures for evacuating the installation in the event of fire. These deficiencies may make obvious the way in which the existing evacuation procedures should be modified to reduce the exposure.

Security Report Preparation

The final phase in a security review is the preparation of a report for management. This report documents the findings of the review and, in particular, makes recommendations as to new safeguards that should be implemented and existing safeguards that should be terminated or modified.

Like all reports to management, often the most difficult part is getting the recommendations accepted. The level of acceptance depends upon the extent to which management agrees with the criticality of the exposures identified and whether they perceive the recommended safeguards are economically, technically, and operationally feasible. Again, scenarios are a useful technique for increasing management's sensitivity to the exposures identified. They provide a tangible basis for management to evaluate how concerned they should be about an exposure. With respect to the feasibility of the safeguards recommended, the onus is on the security manager to demonstrate that the safeguards are within the installation's capabilities to design, implement, and operate.

The security report also must include a plan for implementing the safeguards recommended. Both the seriousness of the exposure to be rectified and the difficulty of implementing the remedial safeguards must be considered. If possible, the most serious exposures should be addressed first, but then the ease with which a safeguard can be installed or modified should determine the order of implementation. To the extent that some safeguards are interdependent and management decides not to implement them all, a contingency plan must be available to establish a revised control configuration.

MAJOR SECURITY THREATS AND REMEDIAL MEASURES

The previous section described a general methodology for evaluating physical security within a computer installation and selecting and implementing controls. This section briefly discusses some of the major security threats that face installations and protective measures that are often taken (Figure 7-3). While the subject of physical security is complex and somewhat situation specific, there is still a set of threats that are the concern of most installations and a set of controls implemented as basic safeguards.

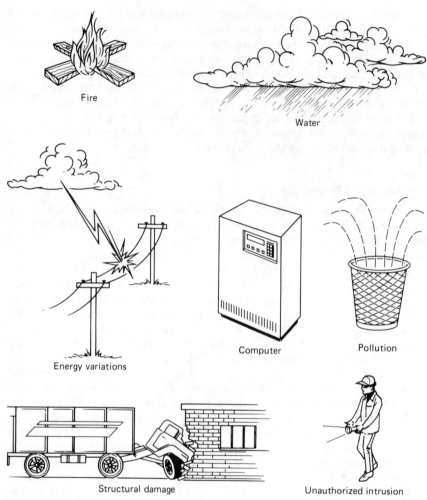

Fire

Water

Energy variations

Computer

Pollution

Structural damage

Unauthorized intrusion

FIGURE 7-3
Major threats to a computer installation.

Fire Damage

Fire is often the major threat to the physical security of a computer installation. Loss from fire can be substantial. A fire in the Pentagon destroyed $6.7 million worth of hardware and over 7000 magnetic tapes. A fire in First Data Corporation's computer installation in New York City destroyed over $2 million worth of hardware.

Some countries have various public service and government organizations that provide advice on fire protection measures. However, the implementation of a specific system usually requires specialist advice. Some major features of a well-designed fire protection system are:

1 Both automatic and manual fire alarms are placed at strategic locations throughout the installation.

2 An automatic extinguisher system exists that dispenses the appropriate suppressant: water, carbon dioxide, halon.

3 The appropriate types of manual fire extinguishers exist at strategic locations throughout the installation.

4 A control panel shows where in the installation an automatic or manual alarm has been triggered.

5 Beside the control panel, master switches exist for power (including air conditioning) and the automatic extinguisher system.

6 The building has been constructed from fire resistant materials, and it is structurally stable when fire damage occurs.

7 Fire extinguishers and fire exits are marked clearly.

8 When a fire alarm is activated, a signal is sent automatically to a permanently manned station.

The security administrator should arrange regular inspections of all fire protection systems. Proper use of these systems requires staff training and periodic drills. The procedures to be followed during an emergency should be documented.

Water Damage

Water damage to a computer installation can be the outcome of a fire; the extinguisher system sprays water that enters hardware, or water pipes may burst. However, water damage results from other sources: cyclones, tornadoes, ice. In 1974, the city of Brisbane experienced freak flooding as the Brisbane River burst its banks. Several computer installations were submerged completely.

Some of the major ways of protecting the installation against water damage are:

1 Where possible have waterproof ceilings, walls, and floors.

2 Ensure that an adequate drainage system exists.

3 Install alarms at strategic points within the installation.

4 In flood areas have the installation above the high-water level.

5 Have a master switch for all water mains.

6 Use a dry pipe automatic sprinkler system that is charged by an alarm and activated by the fire.

7 Cover hardware with a protective fabric when it is not in use.

Again, regular inspections and regular drills are essential if the disaster plan is to be operational when a situation of potential water damage arises.

Energy Variations

Energy variations take the form of increases in power (spikes), decreases in power (brownouts), or loss of power (blackouts). Voltage regulators protect hardware against temporary increases in power; circuit breakers protect the hardware against sustained increases. Batteries will provide power if a temporary loss occurs; however, a generation plant is needed for sustained losses in power. The level of protection needed depends on the utility company's ability to maintain an uninterrupted power source and the likelihood that other disasters will occur (e.g., earthquake) that would destroy the power source.

Power is needed not only to keep the hardware running but also to maintain an acceptable environment for the hardware, that is, an environment that is dust-free and relatively constant with respect to temperature and humidity. Thus, careful assessment of the likelihood of unacceptable energy variations is essential to the ongoing operations of the installation.

The security administrator has two major responsibilities relating to the maintenance of the energy source for the installation. First, the availability of power should be monitored on an ongoing basis. Abnormal power fluctuations may mean the reliability of the power source has to be reassessed. Second, the impact of any new energy consumer (e.g., new hardware) on the existing power supply must be assessed. The resulting energy drain may mean the existing power source is inadequate and alternative sources have to be considered.

The design of security for the installation must provide for the possibility of total loss of power. For example, certain controls such as doors may fail-safe on a power loss. It must be possible to deactivate these controls manually. To the extent that other safeguards such as alarms and extinguisher systems do not have their own independent power source, the security of the installation may be compromised.

Structural Damage

Structural damage to the installation can occur in several ways: earthquake, wind, mud, snow, avalanche. It may be an outcome of some other disaster such as fire. Some installations are more prone to structural damage than others, for example, those situated in an earthquake region.

Preventing disaster from occurring because of structural damage is primarily an engineering problem. In the design of a building, the structural stresses that might be placed on a building are considered. However, if a computer is to be housed in the building, the design engineers should be notified so they can provide for any special structural requirements.

If there is some choice on where the computer is to be housed, the site chosen should be the least prone to structural damage, for example, away from a floodplain or an earthquake region. Similarly, it is better to house the computer on an upper floor of a building. It is less susceptible to damage by floods. It also makes unauthorized intrusion more difficult.

Within the installation, hardware and storage cabinets should be secured so they will not tip easily if structural stress is placed on the building, for example, when vibrations occur during an earthquake. If a disk storage cabinet falls, the damage to a disk can be sufficient to make its contents unreadable.

Pollution

The ongoing operations of a computer depend upon a pollution-free environment. The major pollutant is dust. Dust arises if there is inadequate filtering of air passing through the air conditioning system or if it is allowed to accumulate on equipment, floors, etc. However, there are some more subtle forms of pollution. Extensive damage to a central processor resulted when a cheese sandwich was left on the unit. It melted with the heat generated by the unit and the cheese seeped onto the electronics.

Several steps can be taken to avoid polluting the installation. Regular cleaning of ceilings, walls, floors, storage cabinets, and equipment is necessary. Vacuuming is especially important, particularly in areas where dust collects, as under raised floors. Dust collecting rugs can be placed at entrances. Floors can be treated with special antistatic compounds. Dust generating activities—for example, paper shredding, decollation, or bursting—should be carried out well away from the computer room. Foodstuffs can be prohibited in certain areas such as the computer room, especially where pests such as rodents and insects may cause problems. Regular emptying of wastepaper baskets prevents dust from collecting.

In general, pollution is minimized by having good housekeeping procedures. Good housekeeping procedures also facilitate the orderly running of the installation. Some are essential if disaster procedures are to be carried out effectively and efficiently. For example, if exits are blocked, personnel may be unable to evacuate the installation quickly enough when a fire occurs.

Unauthorized Intrusion

Unauthorized intrusion takes two forms. The intruder physically may enter the installation to steal assets or carry out sabotage. Alternatively, the intruder may eavesdrop on the installation by wiretapping, installing an electronic bug, or using a receiver that picks up electromagnetic signals. One other form of eavesdropping is visual eavesdropping. The intruder may photograph sensitive information or use a telescope to view the information.

Physical intrusion can be inhibited or prevented by erecting various barriers. The building that houses the computer may be protected by a wall or fence. Doors and windows of the building should be secured. Sometimes air conditioning ducts allow unauthorized entry to the building; the intruder simply has to gain access to the roof of the building (perhaps via the fire escape) and crawl through the ducts. The security administrator must ensure these are not potential sources of exposure for the installation.

Alarms and guards can be used to detect an unauthorized intruder. Martin [1973] discusses various types of security devices and systems that signal the presence of an intruder. However, ultimately these defenses may be compromised: a guard may be bribed or a security device deactivated. The last lines of protection are the safes, vaults, or filing cabinets used to store the installation's assets, for example, the program and data files. Even these may not withstand the threats posed by a saboteur intent on destruction.

An intruder also may attempt to enter the installation using the normal means. A receptionist placed at the entry to the installation can challenge unidentified visitors and provide advance warning of unauthorized intrusion. A badge system can be used to identify the status of personnel within the installation: permanent staff or visitors. All visitors should be escorted by a permanent staff member. Unescorted visitors or persons without a badge should be questioned as to their presence in the installation. A security check might be performed before a visitor is issued a badge.

Eavesdropping breaches the privacy of data. It may be used by an intruder to obtain a password. It may be used to obtain the signals transmitted to an output device. Sometimes these signals can be deciphered to obtain sensitive sales information, geological survey information, engineering design information, etc. Short [1974] reports a case where a van with equipment for receiving and processing electromagnetic signals was parked next to an unshielded computer center. The printer in the van produced the same output as the installation's printer.

Various devices are available to detect the presence of bugs. The security administrator periodically may employ a security firm that possesses these devices to examine the installation.

In a communications network the points most likely to be wiretapped are the junction boxes and the private branch exchange. It is very difficult to wiretap a communications line once it leaves the building in which the computer is housed. The line may be underground, signals may be sent via microwave, several thousand channels may be multiplexed together (see, further, Martin [1973]). Thus, the security administrator should ensure the junction boxes and private branch exchange are secure.

The covers on hardware inhibit much electromagnetic emission. In general, most emission occurs with peripherals, for example, printers and terminals. Some vendors now specifically design their hardware to minimize electromagnetic emission. Shields can be placed around peripherals to further inhibit emission. It is best to keep equipment with high emission levels away from the walls of a building.

Visual eavesdropping can be prevented in several ways. Cameras should not be allowed in the installation. Some installations have no windows; however, staff may object to the absence of natural light. If windows do exist they can be shielded by blinds or curtains. Visual display units and printers can be placed strategically so it is impossible for an intruder outside the building with a telescope or a camera with a telescopic lens to view or photograph output.

CONTROLS OF LAST RESORT

In spite of the safeguards implemented, a computer installation still may suffer a disaster; a control may fail or a threat may occur which management has not considered or which management has decided to accept as an exposure. When disaster strikes, it still must be possible to recover operations. In this situation there must be two controls of last resort: (*a*) a disaster recovery plan and (*b*) adequate insurance.

Disaster Recovery Plan

A disaster recovery plan or computer contingency plan is a plan set up to enable a computer installation to restore operations in the event of a disaster. In a survey of 150 companies conducted by Cerullo [1981], he found only 2 companies among the 75 companies which responded that had a comprehensive disaster recovery plan. However, no companies had tested their plan. This is a sobering finding in light of Browne's [1979, p. 51] conclusion: "An examination of computer center disasters shows that in all cases where reasonable recoveries were made, there was a prepared emergency plan coupled with strong vendor support." As always, planning is a difficult cognitive activity, especially when it must be undertaken for circumstances, like disasters, that seem very remote.

Cerullo [1981] argues that a comprehensive disaster recovery plan comprises four parts: (*a*) an emergency plan, (*b*) a backup plan, (*c*) a recovery plan, and (*d*) a test plan. The following sections briefly examine the nature, content, and preparation of each of these parts of the plan.

Emergency Plan   The emergency plan specifies the actions to be undertaken immediately when a disaster occurs. Management must identify those situations that would require the plan to be invoked: major fire, major structural damage, etc. The actions to be initiated may vary somewhat depending upon the nature of the disaster that occurs. For example, some disasters may require that all personnel leave the installation immediately; others may require that a few, select personnel remain behind for a short period to sound alarms, shut down equipment, etc.

If an installation undertakes a comprehensive security review program, the threats identification and exposures analysis phases of the program will enable those situations that invoke the emergency plan to be identified. Each will be an exposure; that is, it will be a threat for which management has decided that controls will not be cost-effective. Management has decided to accept the risk, and the disaster recovery plan is the final basis for limiting the extent of the risk.

Once the situations that evoke the plan have been identified, Cerullo [1981] argues that four other components of the emergency plan must be developed. First, the plan must show who is to be notified immediately upon the disaster's occurring—management, police, fire department, medicos. Second, the plan must show any actions to be undertaken within the installation—shutdown of equipment, removal of files, termination of power. Third, evacuation procedures must be specified. Fourth, return procedures must be specified. In all cases, the personnel responsible for the actions must be identified and the protocols to be followed must be specified clearly.

Backup Plan   The backup plan specifies the location of backup resources, the site where these resources can be assembled and operations restarted, the personnel who are responsible for gathering the backup resources and restarting operations, the priorities to be assigned to recovering the various systems, and a time frame in which recovery of each system must be effected. The plan needs continuous updating as change occurs. For example, as personnel with key responsibilities in executing the plan leave the installation, the plan must be modified accordingly. Indeed, it is prudent to have more than one person knowledgeable in a backup task in case someone is injured when the disaster occurs.

Perhaps the most difficult part in preparing a backup plan is ensuring that all critical resources are backed up. The following resources must be considered:

Resource	Nature of backup
Programs	Inventory of applications and system software stored off site.
Data	Inventory of files stored off site.
Hardware	Arrangements with vendor, trade association, or other company with same equipment for backup support.
Facilities	Arrangements with vendor, trade association, or other company to house resources during recovery process.
Supplies	Inventory of critical supplies stored off site with list of vendors who provide all supplies.
Documentation	Inventory of documentation stored off site.

Resource	Nature of backup
Personnel	Arrangements with vendor, trade association, other company to provide personnel to support recovery in the event employees are injured or killed.

The selection of backup sites is an important decision. These sites must be close enough to enable easy pickup and delivery of backup resources, yet they must be sufficiently distant to make it unlikely that both the installation and the backup sites would be destroyed in a single disaster. This is a difficult objective to achieve in some cases; for example, in an earthquake region, nearby backup sites are just as prone to disaster as the installation if a major earthquake occurs.

The recovery component of the backup plan needs careful consideration. Personnel will be responsible for tasks that they conduct infrequently. Furthermore, they may be working under stress in an unfamiliar environment. The backup plan must assist them as much as possible by providing concise, complete, clear instructions on the recovery procedures they are to accomplish.

Recovery Plan Whereas the backup plan is intended to restore operations quickly so the installation can continue to service the organization, the recovery plan sets out how the full capabilities of the installation will be restored. It is difficult to be specific in terms of how recovery is to be effected because this will depend upon the circumstances of the disaster. Rather, the recovery plan should identify a recovery committee that will be responsible for working out the specifics of the recovery to be undertaken. The plan should specify the responsibilities of the committee and provide guidelines on priorities to be followed. For example, the plan may designate that certain members of the committee are responsible for hardware replacement; and it might designate the critical applications to be recovered first depending upon where in the business data processing cycle the disaster occurred.

It is critical that the personnel who comprise the recovery committee understand their responsibilities. Again, the problem is that they will be required to undertake unfamiliar tasks. Periodically they must review their responsibilities so they are prepared should a disaster occur. If one of the committee members leaves the organization, a new member must be appointed immediately and must become familiar with responsibilities.

Test Plan The final component of a disaster recovery plan is a test plan. The purpose of the test plan is to identify deficiencies in the emergency, backup, or recovery plans or in the preparedness of the organization and its personnel in the event of a disaster. It must enable a range of disasters to be simulated and specify the criteria by which the emergency, backup, and recovery plans can be deemed satisfactory.

Periodically, test plans must be invoked; that is, a disaster must be simulated and the installation required to follow backup and recovery procedures. Unfortunately, organizations are often unwilling to carry out a test because of the disruption that occurs to daily operations and the fear that a real disaster may arise as a result of the test procedures.

To facilitate testing of disaster recovery procedures, a phased approach can be adopted. First, the disaster recovery plan can be tested by desk checking and inspection and walkthroughs, much like the validation procedures adopted for programs (see Chapter 5). Next, a disaster can be simulated at a convenient time, for example, during a slow period in the day. Personnel also might be given prior notice of the test so they are prepared. Finally, disasters may be simulated without warning at any time. These are the acid tests of the organization's ability to recover from a real catastrophe.

Insurance

The residual risks (exposures) that remain after controls have been designed and implemented can be handled in three ways (see National Computer Centre [1974]). First, the organization can bear the risk itself and treat any loss as part of normal operations. Second, the risk can be shared through a trade association or some other means, for example, an agreement among members to provide each other with backup facilities. Third, the risk can be transferred contractually via insurance.

Data processing insurance often is a complex affair. There are few standard policies, and usually an organization must negotiate the specifics of a contract with an insurance company. The security manager must ensure that the following areas are covered:

Insurance area	Explanation
Equipment	Covers repair or acquisition of hardware. Varies depending upon whether the equipment is purchased or leased.
Facilities	Covers, e.g., reconstruction of the computer room, raised floors, special furniture.
Storage media	Covers the replacement of the storage media plus their contents—data files, programs, documentation.
Business interruption	Covers loss in business income because the organization is unable to trade.
Extra expenses	Covers additional costs incurred because the organization is not operating from its normal facilities.
Valuable papers and records	Covers source documents, preprinted reports, documentation, and other valuable papers.

Insurance area	Explanation
Accounts receivable	Covers cash flow problems that arise because the organization cannot collect its accounts receivable promptly.
Malpractice, errors, and omissions	Covers claims against the organization by its customers, e.g., claims made by the clients of a service bureau for lost processing or claims made as a result of a computer crime.

Once an insurance policy has been written, the security manager must take care to ensure that the responsibilities of the installation under the policy are fulfilled. These responsibilities may be onerous. For example, the installation may be required to have an up-to-date, comprehensive disaster recovery plan. In addition, it usually is responsible for notifying the insurer of any substantive change in risk. Just what constitutes a substantive change in risk may be unclear. It usually includes a change in the hardware configuration, but the position with respect to changes in software and data files may be uncertain. Nonetheless, the onus falls on the installation to ensure the policy is not voided because it fails to fulfill a condition of the policy. In this respect a regular security review helps determine whether insurance coverage is adequate and whether the installation is fulfilling its responsibilities.

If the organization acts as a service bureau or uses a service bureau for some of its processing, special care must be taken to establish responsibilities for safeguards as a basis for determining the types of insurance needed. The following matters must be considered:

1 What liability does the service bureau have for malpractice, errors, and omissions?

2 What liability does the service bureau have for failure to deliver promised service?

3 Who owns each of the programs and data files maintained by the service bureau?

4 What are the respective responsibilities of the service bureau and customer for backup?

Each of these matters needs to be addressed contractually and the insurance needed to cover the residual exposures obtained.

SUMMARY

The responsibility for designing and implementing controls to safeguard the physical security of a computer installation is vested in a security administrator. Depending upon the size of the organization, the security administrator may be the person responsible for data processing operations or may occupy a position that reports to the operations manager, the data processing manager, or an executive responsible for all security matters in the organization.

The major task to be undertaken by the security administrator is the formulation and conduct of a security program. A security program comprises security reviews undertaken on a regular basis. Each security review involves six steps: (a) preparing a project plan, (b) identifying and valuing assets, (c) identifying threats, (d) analyzing exposures, (e) determining controls adjustments needed, and (f) preparing a report containing recommendations to improve security. In conducting each review, the security administrator should pay special attention to the major types of threats that may compromise physical security in the installation: fire, water, energy variations, structural damage, pollution, and unauthorized intrusion.

In the event that physical security is compromised, there must be two controls of last resort to enable operations to be restored eventually. A disaster recovery plan must specify backup and recovery procedures to be undertaken when disaster strikes. Adequate insurance also must be available to cover the extra costs associated with restoring normal operations.

REVIEW QUESTIONS

7-1 Briefly describe the primary responsibility of the security administrator.

7-2 For the following types of organizations, who is likely to perform the role of the security administrator:
a A medium-sized organization that has its own data processing facility
b A small organization that uses a microcomputer for its data processing
c A large organization that has multiple data processing installations

7-3 Briefly define what is meant by a security program. What are the six major steps that must be undertaken during the conduct of a security program?

7-4 Why is it important that a project plan be prepared for a security program? Who should be responsible for preparing the plan? Who should be responsible for approving the plan?

7-5 Briefly explain the nature of the "aggregation" problem during the assets identification and valuation phase of a security program. What basis can be used to choose the "right" level of aggregation?

7-6 Why might the value of an asset differ depending upon who is undertaking the valuation? If different values are assigned to the same asset, which value should the security administrator use when valuing the asset?

7-7 Briefly describe *two* techniques that can be used to value assets. What are the relative strengths and limitations of the techniques you identify?

7-8 What is meant by a threat? Identify the *three* major classes of threats that face a computer installation and give an example of each.

7-9 Give *two* techniques that the security manager can use to estimate the likelihood of the occurrence of a threat. Under what situations would one of your techniques be used in preference to the other?

7-10 Briefly describe the *three* major tasks that must be undertaken during the exposures analysis phase of a security program.

7-11 How are internal control questionnaires useful during the exposures analysis phase of a security program?

7-12 Briefly explain how scenarios analysis might be used in the exposures analysis phase of a security program. Under what circumstances is scenarios analysis likely to be most useful?

7-13 Using probability theory, briefly explain how the security manager calculates the expected losses from an exposure.

7-14 What activities are undertaken during the controls adjustment phase of a security program?

7-15 Briefly describe the contents of the security report prepared at the conclusion of a security program. From the viewpoint of having recommendations accepted, what is the most critical aspect of the security report?

7-16 As the auditor of a computer installation, you decide to check the adequacy of hand-held fire extinguishers within the installation. List the major points you would cover in your review.

7-17 What is the purpose of covering hardware with a protective fabric when it is not in use?

7-18 Briefly discuss the responsibilities of the security administrator with respect to maintenance of the energy supply within a computer installation. Why is it important that a master switch exist that can terminate supply of energy to all facilities (including the air conditioning) within the installation?

7-19 Outline the steps an auditor might undertake to determine whether an installation can withstand structural damage.

7-20 Briefly describe *two* problems that can be caused by the presence of dust within a computer installation. What controls can be exercised to limit the effects of pollutants in the computer room?

7-21 From a security viewpoint, what advantages accrue from having no windows in the computer installation, providing only one entrance, and placing the installation on an upper floor of the building?

7-22 Briefly describe *two* ways in which data integrity may be violated using an electronic bug. Where in a computer installation are bugs most likely to be placed?

7-23 What are the most vulnerable points in a data communications network with respect to wiretapping? What actions can the security administrator take to prevent or inhibit wiretapping?

7-24 What are the controls of last resort? Briefly explain the nature of each.

7-25 Briefly describe the major components of an emergency plan.

7-26 Briefly describe the major components of a backup plan. Identify the *seven* major classes of resources that the backup plan must cover.

7-27 What considerations affect the choice of a backup site?

7-28 Briefly describe the major components of a recovery plan. Why are the responsibilities of the recovery committee an important component of the plan?

7-29 What are the purposes of a test plan in a disaster recovery program? Why does a "phased approach" facilitate testing of disaster recovery procedures?

7-30 How can residual risks be controlled in a computer installation?

7-31 Identify the *eight* major areas that must be covered by a data processing insurance policy. What are the security manager's responsibilities once the insurance policy has been agreed upon and signed?

7-32 Why is bonding of data processing employees an important control?

MULTIPLE CHOICE QUESTIONS

7-1 If an organization has its own data processing staff but insufficient security work exists to justify a separate security administration position, responsibility for security matters might be vested in the:
   a Controller
   b Computer operations manager
   c Systems analysis manager
   d Internal auditor

7-2 A security program is:
   a A one-shot investigation to determine the state of physical security in a computer installation
   b A specialized piece of software used to monitor and control access to the computer installation
   c The evidence collection and evidence evaluation procedures used by the auditor to evaluate physical security within a computer installation
   d A series of ongoing, regular, periodic evaluations conducted to ensure that the physical facilities of a computer installation are safeguarded adequately

7-3 For the following steps in a security program, what is the most likely sequence in which they will be conducted?

   I Controls identification
   II Risk analysis
   III Assets valuation
   IV Threats identification

   a I, III, IV, II
   b IV, III, II, I
   c III, IV, I, II
   d I, IV, II, III

7-4 Which of the following is usually *not* a component of a security evaluation project plan:
   a Organization of the project team
   b Risk analysis method to be used
   c Resources budget
   d Schedule for task completion

7-5 In terms of valuing an asset for security evaluation purposes, which of the following statements is most likely to be false:
   a Accidental loss of an asset will be more serious than a loss that arises through an irregularity
   b Losses become more serious as use of the asset is denied for a longer period
   c The value of an asset varies across users of the asset
   d Management will be less concerned about competitors gaining access to an old version of a master file

7-6 The primary objective of the asset valuation phase in a security evaluation is:
   a To develop users' sensitivity to the possible consequences of a security threat
   b To determine an accurate monetary value for all assets
   c To obtain agreement among users on the loss that will result from a successful threat
   d To determine the controls needed to protect the asset

7-7 Match the following threats to the threat category in which they belong:

I Disk crash   A Unreliable system
II Fraud   B Disaster
III Lawsuit   C Hostile action
IV Intoxicated employee
a I-A, II-B, III-C, IV-B
b I-B, II-C, III-B, IV-A
c I-A, II-C, III-C, IV-B
d I-A, II-C, III-B, IV-A

7-8 Empirical research on computer fraud indicates:
a The incidence of fraud is about the same as the incidence of errors
b The most common way to perpetrate a fraud is to alter application programs
c Managers and clerks have been caught taking much more than computer specialists
d Most cases of computer fraud have arisen through management collusion

7-9 An exposure is:
a Any threat that may eventuate
b Any threat for which no controls have been implemented
c The expected loss that will occur, given the reliability of the existing control system
d The expected loss that will occur prior to implementing any controls

7-10 Which of the following activities is *not* a task during exposures analysis:
a Identifying the source of threats to the assets
b Assessing the losses that will result if a threat circumvents the controls that are in place
c Assessing the reliability of the controls that are in place
d Evaluating the likelihood that a threat will be successful given the controls that are in place

7-11 During a security evaluation, an internal control questionnaire is most useful in undertaking which of the following tasks:
a Assessing the reliability of the controls that are in place
b Identifying the new controls needed to enhance security in the installation
c Identifying the exposures that exist
d Identifying the controls that are in place

7-12 Which of the following tasks is most facilitated by scenario analyses:
a Identifying controls and their associated level of reliability
b Identifying how threats can circumvent controls
c Determining the assets to be protected
d Calculating the probability of threat occurrence

7-13 Reducing exposures to an acceptable level means:
a All controls implemented are totally reliable
b Residual threats have been eliminated
c Threats for which no control exists have a low probability of occurrence
d The costs of implementing and operating further controls exceed the reduction in expected losses that will occur

7-14 Which of the following should *not* be used as a basis for determining new controls that might be implemented to reduce exposures to an acceptable level:
a Choose controls that emphasize design secrecy
b Examine the control profiles used in similar installations
c Analyze the scenarios developed during the exposures analysis phase

    d Review the answers to questions on the internal control questionnaires completed during the exposures analysis phase

7-15 Which of the following is *not* a component of the final security report presented to management:

    a Recommendations on existing safeguards that should be changed

    b A singular recommendation on the control configuration that, in the opinion of the project team, must be implemented

    c A plan for implementing the safeguards recommended

    d Scenarios describing the nature of some exposures identified

7-16 In general, the major disaster threat to a computer installation is:

    a Structural damage

    b Visual eavesdropping

    c Fire

    d Water damage

7-17 The purpose of a voltage regulator is to:

    a Protect hardware against temporary increases in power

    b Protect hardware against sustained power surges

    c Compensate when brownouts occur

    d Protect the contents of memory when a blackout occurs

7-18 Which of the following controls would be most useful as a means of reducing losses from at least some types of threats that would result in structural damage to a computer installation:

    a Voltage regulator

    b Housing the computer on the upper floor of a building

    c Fail-safe doors

    d None of the above

7-19 Which of the following is not a control to prevent pollution:

    a Prohibition of food in the computer room

    b Filters on air conditioning

    c Confining decollation to the computer room only

    d Placing antistatic rugs at doorways

7-20 In a communications network, the points most likely to be wiretapped are:

    a The private branch exchange

    b The lines outside the installation

    c Junction box

    d Both **a** and **c** above

7-21 The unchecked emission of electromagnetic signals is a concern because:

    a The signals can be picked up and printed on a remote device

    b The signals interfere with the correct functioning of the central processor

    c Noise pollution levels increase as a result

    d They facilitate visual eavesdropping

7-22 Which of the following plans specifies the actions to be undertaken immediately when a disaster occurs:

    a The backup plan

    b The recovery plan

    c The restart plan

    d The emergency plan

7-23 Which of the following is *not* a component of the emergency plan:

    a Personnel to be notified upon the occurrence of a disaster

    b Evacuation procedures

    c Restart priorities

    d Equipment shutdown protocols

7-24 Which of the following is *not* a component of the backup plan:

    a Site where resources can be assembled and operations restarted

    b Procedures for periodically testing that recovery can be effected

    c Priorities to be assigned to recovering the various systems

    d Personnel who are responsible for gathering the backup resources

7-25 The primary purpose of the recovery plan is to:

    a Specify precisely how recovery will be effected

    b Identify which applications are to be recovered immediately

    c Identify a recovery committee that will be responsible for working out the specifics of the recovery to be undertaken

    d Specify how backup is to be assembled for recovery purposes

7-26 Residual risk is:

    a The risk that cannot be handled by the installation and will not be handled by an insurance company

    b The risk remaining after risks have been controlled by system design, installation of security measures, and regular security audits

    c The risk that must be treated as a cost of doing normal operations

    d The risk not covered in the insurance policies for data processing assets

7-27 Business interruption insurance covers:

    a Additional costs incurred because the organization is not operating from its normal facilities

    b Costs involved in reconstructing the computer facility

    c Claims made by customers because the organization cannot service its customers

    d Loss in business income because the organization is unable to trade

EXERCISES AND CASES

7-1 Money Mover (MM) is a public electronic funds transfer network with its head office and major computer switch based in Melbourne. The company has computer switches in each capital city throughout Australia that are linked into a national communications network. Approximately 150 financial institutions—banks, building societies, credit unions—use the network to provide automatic teller machine and point-of-sale services to their customers.

    MM has only been in operation for three years, but during that time it has been very successful. When Australia began to deregulate its financial markets in 1985 and foreign banks began to enter the marketplace, MM obtained substantial new business since it could offer these financial institutions immediate electronic funds transfer services.

    As a consultant specializing in computer controls and audit, you have been hired by the managing director of MM to examine the state of controls within the electronic funds transfer system. She explains to you that an increasing number of potential customers are requesting some type of independent assurance that controls within the system are reliable. Accordingly, she has decided to initiate a controls review of the entire system so that a third-party "letter of comfort" can be provided to potential customers.

    The initial part of your controls review focuses on the main switch in Melbourne. As part of your review you examine the status of disaster recovery planning for the switch. In terms of short-term recovery, controls appear to be in place and working. Backup tapes for all data and programs are stored both on site and off site to enable recovery if programs and data are lost for some reason. In addition, protocols for short-term recovery are well documented, and operators seem familiar with and well trained in these protocols. From time to time they have to exercise these protocols because some temporary system failure occurs. Since MM claims to offer its customers 24-hour service, all personnel recognize the criticality of being able to recover the system accurately and completely on a timely basis.

When you examine controls over long-term disaster recovery, however, the situation is different. There is no long-term disaster recovery plan, nor are operators and other personnel trained in recovery protocols for a major disaster. For example, it is uncertain how MM would recover from a fire that destroyed the switch or an event that caused major structural damage to the switch.

As a result of your findings, you meet with the managing director to find out why controls in this area are so weak when controls in other areas seem strong. She is surprised by your concern about long-term disaster recovery. She argues that for three reasons it is not cost-effective to prepare a long-term disaster recovery plan and to practice recovery protocols on a regular basis. First, she believes it is useless having a long-term disaster recovery plan because, in the event of a major disaster, timely recovery is impossible anyway. She points out that it would take several days for the telephone company to reconfigure all the data communications lines to another site. Even if MM had another switch available immediately, it could not operate during this period. Second, she argues that long-term disaster recovery cannot be practiced because MM's customers would not tolerate a decrease in their service levels while disaster recovery exercises were carried out. Unless the recovery protocols are practiced regularly, she argues, they are useless. Third, she contends that eventual recovery will not be a problem anyway. Operations can simply be transferred to another switch in one of the other capital cities. While the telephone company reconfigures data communications lines to the other switch, backup files can be flown to the site with plenty of time to spare. She argues that the customers of MM recognize they will not be able to use their electronic funds transfer facilities during the recovery period, but they accept this situation as a risk of doing business. The only other alternative, she argues, is to replicate all switching facilities in each capital city, and this clearly is not cost-effective.

Required: Outline how you intend to respond to the managing director's comments in your report to the board of directors on the state of controls in MM's computer operations.

7-2 Read the case description above on the Money Mover public electronic funds transfer system. The following details apply to the review you are conducting on the state of controls within the company.

As part of your review of physical access controls over the Melbourne switch site, you note one day during a visit that one of MM's system programmers has a card key that provides him with access to the computer room. You interview the operator and you find out that all system programmers have similar keys.

As a result of this finding, you interview the managing director to find out why system programmers have access to the computer room. She argues that they need this access because they are often called in at any hour of the day or night to correct problems "on the fly" that customers are experiencing with the system.

For example, customers may be having problems with a communications line, and the system programmer has to diagnose the problem and correct it as soon as possible so continuous service can be maintained.

You explain to the managing director that you are concerned about the possibility of system programmers undertaking unauthorized activities, particularly if they come in during the middle of the night when no one else is present in the computer room. She laughs and says that system programmers can carry out unauthorized activities any time they want because of their in-depth knowledge of the system, and accordingly it is useless to exercise any type of physical access controls over them. Besides, she argues, there are certain compensating controls over system programmers. First, she has pointed out to the system programmers their responsibility for preserving system security and that they will be fired immediately if any breach of security is discovered. Second, since MM employs only four system programmers, it will not be hard to pinpoint responsibility if any sort of irregularity occurs.

Required: In light of the managing director's responses, how will you now proceed with your investigation? What will be the likely implications, if any, of your current findings for the report you will present to the board of directors?

7-3 You are a security consultant who has been employed by First Singaporean, a large bank based in Singapore, to examine the adequacy of security controls over a new site that it has just established to house all its data processing facilities. At first glance, the new facilities seem impressive. The bank has purchased an old warehouse, and it has extensively refurbished the warehouse in an attempt to set up a secure facility. The location of the warehouse and its purpose is known to only a small number of people who are employees of the bank. These individuals have signed a secrecy agreement in relation to the operations and location of the warehouse.

As part of your review of physical controls, you examine the adequacy of controls to prevent and detect fire. When you tour the computer room, you notice that there are no hand-held fire extinguishers placed at strategic locations throughout the room. You question the operations manager about this apparent weakness. He assures you that this is not a control weakness. He informs you that a sophisticated heat detection system has been set up in the computer room which will detect even the smallest fire. As soon as a fire is detected, an extinguisher system will dump gas suppressant into the room after a 30-second delay. Operators have been instructed to clear the room immediately the alarm sounds since the suppressant is somewhat toxic. Consequently, he argues, hand-held extinguishers are not needed. Indeed, they would be dangerous, as they may cause operators to delay their exit from the computer room when the alarm sounds. When you interview several operators about the fire evacuation procedures outlined by the operations manager, it is clear they are familiar with the procedures and that they are practiced regularly.

Required: At this stage, what are your conclusions about the adequacy of the controls described by the operations manager? How will you now proceed in terms of your investigation of fire prevention and detection controls for the computer room?

7-4 You have recently been appointed as internal auditor for Mincomp, a large Dallas-based service bureau that offers specialized systems for companies in the oil industry. Mincomp supports a wide range of systems covering engineering applications for exploration activities and accounting applications for managing a drill site. The main customer base is in the southern states of the United States, but Mincomp also has a large number of international users because of the high quality of its systems.

As one of your initial jobs, you undertake a review of security over the service bureau operations. During a tour of the computer room, you notice several large racks containing some 4000 magnetic tapes. Periodically, the operators on duty are removing a tape and loading it onto the system or unloading a tape and replacing it in the racks. You also notice that one of the system programmers is working at a console, and she is also loading tapes onto and unloading tapes off the system.

As a result of your observations, you interview the operations manager. You question him on three issues. First, you express your concern that a separate tape library has not been established with a librarian in charge of the library. He replies that the operators could not do their job if they had to continually go to a separate tape library and to make a formal request for tapes from a librarian. He "reminds" you that this is a 24-hour service bureau operation and that customers can request that one of their tapes be loaded quickly at any time. Operators must respond immediately. Second, you question him about the presence of the system programmer in the computer room. Again, he points out the nature of Mincomp's operations. He argues that system programmers are employed to respond immediately to any problems that a customer is experiencing; consequently, they need 24-hour access to the computer facilities if they are to do their job effectively and efficiently. Moreover, he argues that only operators and system programmers are provided with card-key access to the computer room, so entry to the computer room is restricted to a small number of individuals. Third, you question him about the large number of tapes in the racks. He agrees with you that the number is large, even given the size of Mincomp's customer base. He informs you that the tapes have been "left over" from a conversion operation that occurred when Mincomp changed its hardware about a year ago. About 60% of the tapes were for the previous machine. Nevertheless, they have been retained in the computer room in case any aspect of the conversion has to be redone. He points out that Mincomp may not discover an error in one of the new tapes until a customer uses the tape. Sometimes customers might not access a particular tape for several years. Some aspect of the conversion may have to be redone if an error is discovered.

Required: From a security perspective, evaluate the adequacy of the responses provided to you by the operations manager. How will his responses affect the conduct of the remainder of your security review?

7-5 Assemblit, Inc., is a medium-sized parts manufacturing company based in London with distribution outlets in the major cities throughout Great Britain. As a member of the external audit team of the company, you have gathered the following information on the company's operations:

1 All the company's major application systems are computerized; some are online realtime update and some are batch.

2 The company uses a database management system. The DBMS was purchased initially to aid bill-of-materials processing (online realtime update system), but now it is used extensively with other applications.

3 All the company's sales outlets have online access to the head office machine, and source data is captured at the terminals in each sales outlet.

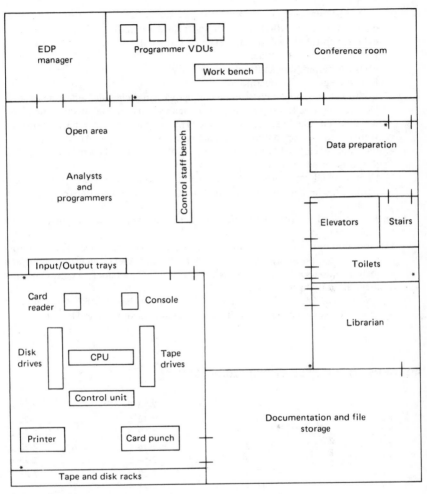

*Fire extinguishers
FIGURE 7-4
Floor plan—Assemblit computer installation.

4 The computer runs six days a week, two shifts a day. Sunday and the third shift are available for "hands on" development and testing by programmers and analysts; however, during normal operations only the operators and the system programmer have access to the computer room. Access is controlled using a card lock system.

5 Assemblit's computer is located in the basement of its head office. A floor plan is attached (see Fig. 7-4).

6 The following DP staff are employed:
a DP manager
b Eight analysts

    c 15 programmers
    d Seven operators (three-four per shift; shifts rotated)
    e Four control clerks (day and evening shifts only)
    f One system programmer
    g One librarian (day shift only)
    h Three key-to-disk operators

7 Control clerks and analysts set up daily processing schedules a day in advance.

8 During the week, programmers and analysts use visual display units for development and maintenance work. The company has purchased powerful software to support online programming work.

9 Program development and maintenance work must be authorized by the analyst in charge of an application system.

10 Copies of all tape files and disk files are taken twice a week for backup purposes. The backup files are stored on site in a special fire resistant vault room.

11 The vendor has promised to provide backup hardware within a few days if an emergency occurs.

12 Input/output is placed in trays just outside the computer room. The operators collect input periodically. Every hour the control clerks pick up output and forward it to users. Users reconcile input to output and notify a control clerk if there are any discrepancies.

Required: On the basis of the information you have so far, write a short report for your manager indicating suspected control weaknesses.

ANSWERS TO MULTIPLE CHOICE QUESTIONS

7-1 b	**7-8** c	**7-15** b	**7-22** d
7-2 d	**7-9** c	**7-16** c	**7-23** c
7-3 c	**7-10** a	**7-17** a	**7-24** b
7-4 b	**7-11** d	**7-18** b	**7-25** c
7-5 a	**7-12** b	**7-19** c	**7-26** b
7-6 a	**7-13** d	**7-20** d	**7-27** d
7-7 d	**7-14** a	**7-21** a	

REFERENCES

Adams, Donald L. "Recovery from a Data Center Fire," *EDPACS* (April 1974), pp. 9–11.

Allen, Brandt. "The Biggest Computer Frauds: Lessons for CPAS," *Journal of Accountancy* (May 1977), pp. 52–62.

Browne, Peter S. *Security: Checklist for Computer Center Self-Audits* (Arlington, VA: American Federation of Information Processing Societies, 1979).

Canning, Richard G. "Protecting Valuable Data—Part 1," *EDP Analyzer* (December 1973), pp. 1–13.

Canning, Richard G. "Protecting Valuable Data—Part 2," *EDP Analyzer* (January 1974), pp. 1–14.

Canning, Richard G. "The Security of Managers' Information," *EDP Analyzer* (July 1979), pp. 1–13.

Carroll, John M. *Computer Security* (Los Angeles, CA: Security World Publishing Co., 1977).

Cerullo, Michael J. "Accountants' Role in Computer Contingency Planning," *The CPA Journal* (January 1981), pp. 22–26.

Copeland, Eric A., and James M. McClure. "Information Systems Contingency Planning—A Business Approach," *The EDP Auditor*, 1984, vol. 1, pp. 25–31.

Courtney, Robert H., Jr. "Security Risk Assessment in Electronic Data Processing Systems," *Proceedings of the 1977 National Computer Conference* (Montvale, NJ: AFIPS Press, 1977), pp. 97–104.

FitzGerald, Jerry. "EDP Risk Analysis for Contingency Planning," *EDPACS* (August 1978), pp. 1–8.

FitzGerald, Jerry. "Developing and Ranking Threat Scenarios," *EDPACS* (September 1978), pp. 1–5.

FitzGerald, Jerry. *Designing Controls into Computerized Systems* (Redwood City, CA: Jerry FitzGerald and Associates, 1981).

Gerberick, Dahl A. "Security Risk Analysis," *EDPACS* (April 1979), pp. 1–11.

Gross, Steven E. "Data Center Security," *EDP Auditing* (Pennsauken, NJ: Auerbach Publishers, 1978), Portfolio 72-03-03, pp. 1–20.

Hoffman, Lance J. *Modern Methods for Computer Security and Privacy* (Englewood Cliffs, NJ: Prentice-Hall, 1977).

IBM Corporation. *Security, Auditability, System Control Publications Bibliography*, 2d ed. (New York: IBM Corporation, 1985).

Jarocki, Stanley R., and Erick J. Novotny. "Data Security/Privacy Requirements in Federal Bureaux," *The EDP Auditor* (Summer 1979), pp. 35–66.

Johnson, Norman L. "Computer Security and Control," *The EDP Auditor* (Fall 1983), pp. 59–72.

Krauss, Leonard I., and Aileen MacGahan. *Computer Fraud and Countermeasures* (Englewood Cliffs, NJ: Prentice-Hall, 1979).

Kuong, Javier F. *Computer Security, Auditing and Controls* (Wellesley Hills, MA: Management Advisory Publications, 1974).

Madnick, Stuart E. *Computer Security* (New York: Academic Press, 1979).

Martin, James. *Security, Accuracy, and Privacy in Computer Systems* (Englewood Cliffs, NJ: Prentice-Hall, 1973).

Molnar, Louie A. "Recovery Control Standards," *The EDP Auditor* (Fall 1983), pp. 11–18.

Murray, W. H. "Security Considerations for Personal Computers," *IBM Systems Journal*, vol. 23, no. 3, 1984, pp. 297–304.

National Computing Centre. *Where Next for Computer Security?* (Manchester: NCC Publications, 1974).

Parker, Donn B. *Computer Security Management* (Reston, VA: Reston Publishing Company, 1981).

Ruder, Brian, and J. D. Madden. *An Analysis of Computer Security Safeguards for Detecting and Preventing Intentional Computer Misuse* (Washington, DC: Institute for Computer Sciences and Technology, National Bureau of Standards, 1978), Report No. C13.10:500-25.

Ruthberg, Zella G. "Risk Assessment and Managerial Analysis," *The EDP Auditor* (Fall 1980), pp. 31–43.

Scherf, John Arthur. "Computer and Data Security: A Comprehensive Annotated Bibliography," *Data Security and Data Processing Volume 4 Study Results:*

Massachusetts Institute of Technology (New York: IBM Corporation, 1974), pp. 223–300.

Short, G. E. "Threats and Vulnerabilities in a Computer System," *Data Security and Data Processing Volume 5 Study Results: TRW Systems, Inc.* (New York: IBM Corporation, 1974), pp. 25–73.

Sleeper, Richard C., and William P. Davis. "Data Processing Risk Insurance: Part I," *EDPACS* (November 1973), pp. 11–14.

Sleeper, Richard C., and William P. Davis. "Data Processing Risk Insurance: Part II," *EDPACS* (December 1973), pp. 7–10.

Sleeper, Richard C., and William P. Davis. "Data Processing Risk Insurance: Part III," *EDPACS* (January 1974), pp. 7–12.

Sperduto, James M. "Disaster Recovery Planning," *The EDP Auditor* (Summer 1983), pp. 29–34.

State of Illinois. "Recommended Security Practices," *Data Security and Data Processing Volume 3 Part 2 Study Results: State of Illinois* (New York: IBM Corporation, 1974), pp. 245–380.

Summers, R. C. "An Overview of Computer Security," *IBM Systems Journal*, vol. 23, no. 4, 1984, pp. 309–325.

Van Tassel, Dennis. *Computer Security Management* (Englewood Cliffs, NJ: Prentice-Hall, 1972).

Wong, K. K. *Computer Security Risk Analysis and Control: A Guide for the DP Manager* (Manchester: NCC Publications, 1977).

CHAPTER **8**

OPERATIONS
MANAGEMENT

ANSWERS TO MULTIPLE CHOICE QUESTIONS

REFERENCES

Operations management is responsible for the daily running of hardware and software facilities so that production application systems can accomplish their work and development staff can design, implement, and maintain systems. Though there are some variations across organizations, the operations group within a data processing installation undertakes seven major functions:

1 Computer operations

2 Communications network control

3 Data preparation

4 Production work flow control

5 File library

6 Documentation library

7 Performance monitoring

In addition, in smaller installations, operations management may take responsibility for installation security (see Chapter 7); and, when top management and EDP management are planning for the resources needed to support future operations, they will seek the advice of operations management.

In some ways, the functions of operations management appear routine and mundane. If they are not carried out properly, however, some serious consequences can occur. For example, well-designed program controls can be compromised if an operator uses a console terminal to alter the state of the computer's internal memory; well-designed program code will execute inefficiently if there is an undesirable job mix in the machine; a disgruntled operations employee can severely damage or destroy the assets of an installation.

Perhaps the most serious difficulties arise, however, with the dispersal of operations functions throughout the organization as microcomputers proliferate. Operations management functions must still be performed, but it is difficult to exercise effective control over these functions since responsibility for executing the functions may be vested in the individuals who operate the microcomputers. Often they seem unaware of the importance of the functions. Nevertheless, someone must be appointed to act as the operations manager, and in a microcomputer environment this person has responsibility for establishing operations standards, promulgating these standards throughout the organization, and ensuring the standards are enforced.

Each section of this chapter examines one of the seven functions of operations management in more detail. Some of the difficulties posed by the use of microcomputers in organizations are highlighted. It is emphasized, however, that these difficulties pertain to *how* operations management functions should be implemented and not *whether* they should be implemented.

COMPUTER OPERATIONS

Controls over computer operations govern the ways in which computer operators conduct the daily running of systems in either test or production mode on the hardware/software system available. Three sets of controls must exist: (*a*) those that prescribe the functions computer operators should perform; (*b*) those that prescribe how hardware, software, and data are to be used; and (*c*) those that prescribe how hardware is to be maintained.

Operator Protocols

There are two sources of information on the protocols that computer operators should follow. First, a *standards manual* details both methods and performance standards for computer operators. The contents of the manual include, for example, procedures for starting up and closing down the machine, actions to be taken upon a system's crash, disaster procedures, prescribed work flow patterns, and descriptions of prohibited activities. For large systems, the manual also includes such items as standard times for mounting and dismounting storage media and procedures for working in a multiuser environment. Many of these protocols are provided by the hardware/system software vendor; others must be developed by the installation. Second, *application system run manuals* detail the procedures to be followed during production running of each system and the resource consumption that can be expected if the system is operating normally. Thus, the standards manual prescribes procedures that are common across application systems; run manuals prescribe procedures that are specific to an application system.

From an audit viewpoint a major concern is the existence and enforcement of standards that prevent computer operators from carrying out unauthorized modifications to programs or data. With small systems, achieving this control objective can be difficult. How, for example, can traditional internal control procedures like separation of duties be exercised when an operator is using a microcomputer? These sorts of problems are compounded when the system software available on the microcomputer enables only a weak level of access control to be exercised. Consequently, reliance must be placed on compensating controls, for example, hiring high-quality staff or careful checking of control totals. In many cases, also, the person who developed the system operates the system, so there is little incentive to undertake improper activities.

With large systems, traditional internal control systems still apply: rotation of operator duties, use of two or more operators on a shift, compulsory vacations, proper training. In addition, several other steps can be taken to safeguard assets and protect data integrity. First, operators can be prevented from having free access to file and documentation libraries. The less an operator knows about the detailed logic in a system, the harder it is to carry out unauthorized modifications to that system. Furthermore, if operators can gain access to program, data, and procedure (job control language) files only for production purposes, it is harder to carry out unauthorized modifications to these files. Second, under normal circumstances, operators should be prohibited from using system resources that enable direct "fixes" to be carried out to programs, data, or procedures, that is, alterations that are not part of the normal production maintenance or modification processes. System resources that allow direct fixes take various forms: these include instructions that can be entered at a console terminal or programs that operate in privileged mode. Third, the duties of operators should be restricted purely to the running of systems. They should not be responsible for attempting to correct programs or data when an application system fails; this is the responsibility of the project manager for the application. Furthermore, their knowledge of programming should be sufficiently limited so they cannot easily carry out modifications to program code. From a control viewpoint, career paths that allow operators to receive programming training while they still act as operators are suspect.

The record of operator activities is the operating system log. Periodically the log should be examined by the operations manager to check operator compliance with standards. Thus, it is important that operators cannot compromise data recorded on the log. Alterations to the log must not be permitted and, if the log is disabled, management must determine whether unauthorized activities have occurred. In some installations where security is especially critical, the log might be located on a storage device located at a different site from the computer room.

Machine Utilization

Controls over machine utilization seek to ensure that the computer is used only for authorized purposes and that consumption of system resources is efficient. With small systems, these objectives are often difficult to achieve. Microcomputers might be given to individuals to improve their personal productivity. How they then use the machine can be difficult to determine and to control. For example, contrary to organizational policies, they might use the microcomputer for private consulting purposes. Nonetheless, other sorts of exposures that occur with large systems tend to be less serious when microcomputers are used. For example, there are fewer concerns about unauthorized modifications to systems since microcomputer operators are often the individuals who also developed the systems they are running. Ultimately, probably the best control that can be exercised over small systems machine ultilization is management supervision.

With large systems, a more extensive set of controls must be established to ensure the machine is used efficiently and used only for authorized purposes.

Production systems should run according to a predetermined schedule set up by applications project managers and the operations manager. Thus, a substantial part of the consumption of system resources should be authorized in advance. In addition, provision also must be made in the daily run schedule for other types of activities: systems reruns, system crashes, program development activities. Nevertheless, it usually is still possible to determine deviations from normal operations even though unscheduled activities must be undertaken. Operators should prepare various daily routine reports for the operations manager, for example, reports on completed and uncompleted jobs, a report on downtime, a report on unused machine time. These reports are based on data contained on the system log. The operations manager can then examine these reports for exception conditions.

To ensure systems resources are used only for the purposes intended, authority must be given for all program executions. In the case of production systems operating on a regular schedule, the computer operations manager can authorize their execution; for example, the operations manager may sign a daily schedule of systems to be run. In the case of programs being developed, the programmer responsible for the program can authorize compilation and test runs, though the operations manager must still authorize whether development and testing is to be carried out during a specific time block or in background mode while production systems are running. If a program fails during production running because of some type of hardware or system software error, the operations shift supervisor can authorize the rerun.

Maintenance

Maintenance of computer hardware is either preventive or remedial in nature. Preventive maintenance occurs on a regular basis and includes routine tests and inspections as well as replacement of components. Remedial (repair) maintenance occurs on demand when a machine component fails.

Maintenance often is performed by an outside party. Usually the hardware vendor recommends a maintenance schedule; however, the relative amounts of preventive and remedial maintenance always can be traded off against each other. More frequent preventive maintenance means less frequent repair maintenance. Management's problem is to minimize the total cost of both preventive and remedial maintenance (Figure 8-1).

An important factor affecting the frequency with which preventive maintenance is carried out is the location of the computer installation. For example, if the installation is at some remote mining site, repair maintenance may involve several days of waiting while an engineer is flown to the site. The downtime may be intolerable. Thus, more frequent preventive maintenance may be carried out to reduce the likelihood of repair maintenance being needed. Conversely, if the computer installation is sited in a large city with ready access to engineers, management may undertake less preventive maintenance and bear the costs of repair maintenance if and when it is needed.

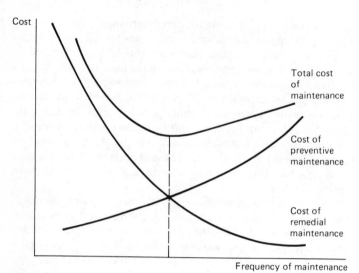

FIGURE 8-1
Tradeoff between preventive and remedial maintenance.

As a basic control, the operations manager should periodically review various maintenance reports prepared by the maintenance engineer and operators, for example, the amount of downtime that has occurred, the amount of time consumed by preventive and repair maintenance, and the amount of maintenance incurred by each hardware unit. This information is important to replacement decisions and to identifying abnormal maintenance cost deviations.

Like system programmers, maintenance engineers cause some difficult control problems for management. Engineers have available to them special hardware and software tools that allow them to bypass the various controls implemented in hardware and software. These tools are necessary if maintenance is to be carried out effectively and efficiently. Nevertheless, their misuse may mean integrity violations will occur. Pinchuk [1974], for example, describes the engineering tools available for one hardware/software system configuration and the ways in which these tools can be used to compromise controls.

It is difficult to know how much effort should be expended on controlling engineers and what types of controls should be instituted over their activities. Little empirical evidence is available to show whether they are a major source of integrity violations in computer systems. Perhaps this is because the technical expertise required to detect any integrity violation is high. Perhaps it is because the number of violations is small.

In spite of the difficulties involved in monitoring the activities of maintenance engineers, several basic controls should be exercised. Another engineer might be employed (perhaps a consultant engineer) to evaluate the work of the primary engineer. If more than one engineer is employed, duties should be rotated. Unfortunately, these policies can result in higher maintenance costs since it takes some time for an engineer to get to know the idiosyncracies of a particular machine. Nonetheless, they ensure a backup engineer exists if the primary engineer is unavailable.

If the engineer carries out concurrent maintenance—that is, maintenance during normal production running—if possible, sensitive programs and data should be unloaded from the machine. This inhibits any attempt to violate system integrity. Engineers also might be required to sign a "nondisclosure" agreement in case sensitive data is exposed in the normal course of duties. With each change of engineer, management should carry out some background checking to assess the likely integrity of the engineer.

COMMUNICATIONS NETWORK CONTROL

If an organization's data processing facilities include either a long-haul or local area communications network, the operations function will have responsibility for managing the daily running of the network. Usually this is accomplished via a network control terminal and specialized communication system software. These facilities can be used to manage the network itself, devices connected to the network, and programs and files that support the operations of the network (Figure 8-2).

Using the network control terminal, operators must regularly monitor the operations of the network. Many different types of incidents require operator intervention. For example, a communications line may fail, a program may terminate abnormally, message queues may consume all the storage space available, unauthorized messages on a line may be identified, and unacceptable line error rates may occur. Operators must be able to reconfigure the network to accommodate these situations. Typical functions that can be performed with a network control terminal are:

1 Starting and terminating lines and processes
2 Monitoring network activity levels
3 Renaming communications lines
4 Generating system statistics
5 Resetting queue lengths
6 Increasing backup frequency
7 Inquiring as to system status
8 Transmitting system warning and status messages
9 Examining data traversing a communications line

Similar functions can be executed with respect to individual terminal devices that are connected to the network—for example:

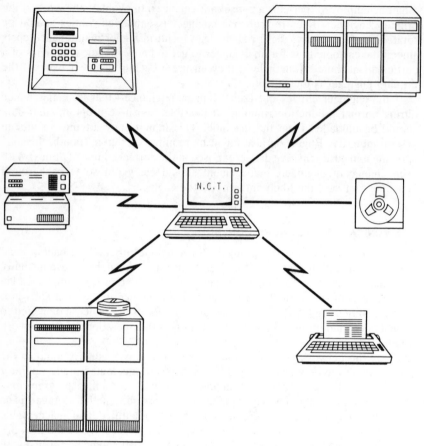

FIGURE 8-2
Management of a communication network using a network control terminal.

1 Starting up or closing down a terminal
2 Inquiring as to terminal status
3 Down-line loading data or programs
4 Generating control totals for terminal devices such as automatic teller machines and point-of-sale devices
5 Sending and receiving terminal warning and error messages

The network control terminal also allows operators to access and maintain various data files required by the data communications software. For example, a terminal identification file designates which terminals are legitimate devices within the network so that the communications software can check the authenticity of a terminal when it attempts to send or to receive messages. If new terminals are added to the network or existing terminals are removed, this file must be updated by the network operator. Similarly, the network control terminal may allow access to various transaction logs so the operator can determine the events surrounding a particular incident in the network.

From an integrity perspective, the network control terminal is a critical component within the network. Its misuse could result in substantial disruption to the system or in unauthorized activities going undetected. Accordingly, several controls must be exercised over operator use of the network control terminal:

1 Only senior operators who are well trained and have a sound employment history should perform network control functions.

2 To the extent possible, network control functions should be separated and duties rotated on a regular basis.

3 The network control software must allow access controls to be enforced so each operator is restricted to performing only certain functions.

4 The network control software must maintain an inviolate audit trail of all operator activities.

5 Operations management must regularly review the audit trail to determine whether unauthorized network operator activities have occurred.

6 If multiple network control terminals are used, network control functions should be partitioned and restricted to a particular terminal.

7 Documented standards and protocols must exist for network operators.

8 Operations management must regularly review network operator activities for compliance with standards and protocols.

The need for control also applies to the activities of engineers who maintain the network. As with mainframe maintenance, engineers have available to them special hardware and software that enables them to bypass the controls implemented in the network. It is difficult to prevent them from undertaking unauthorized activities and to detect any unauthorized activities when they do occur. The types of compensating controls described earlier—rotation of duties, supervision, etc.—must also be exercised over network engineers.

In addition to these asset safeguarding and data integrity concerns, proper management of the network is essential to attaining system effectiveness and system efficiency objectives. If, for example, workloads are not balanced throughout the network, response times may be slow, which in turn may inhibit the effectiveness of management decision making.

DATA PREPARATION

Historically, all source data for application systems was sent to a data preparation section for keypunching and verification before it was entered into a computer system. Many computer systems now provide online update facilities whereby system users enter source data directly at a terminal, thereby obviating the need to key data to cards, tape, or disk. Most microcomputer-based systems, for example, require the operator to key the data directly into the system rather than requiring it to be provided on, say, a diskette or cassette tape. Nevertheless, key preparation of data via key-to-card, key-to-tape, and key-to-disk equipment is still used extensively in many application systems. In these systems, responsibility for data preparation activities usually is vested in operations management.

To ensure an effective and efficient data preparation function, operations management must address four issues: (*a*) design of the keying tasks and keying environment, (*b*) training of data preparation personnel, (*c*) maintenance of data preparation equipment, and (*d*) backup and recovery of data preparation resources and input data. The following sections briefly examine each of these responsibilities.

Design of Keying Tasks/Environment

Two important aspects that affect the speed and accuracy with which source data is converted to machine-readable form are the design of keying tasks and the design of keying environments. Poor decision making in either area can lead to major bottlenecks in the throughput of data, high operator turnover because of job dissatisfaction, and employees experiencing job-related illnesses. Ultimately these problems can affect the reliability of controls that preserve data integrity and safeguard assets.

In general, to relieve operator boredom, keying tasks should be no longer than an hour. Operators also must be able to perceive an end to a task. If source documents continue to arrive, operators get further behind in their work, and frustration and loss of confidence cause inaccuracies and decreased keying speed. Following the sociotechnical system design principles described in Chapter 4, the design of keying tasks might be left to the operators themselves. For example, Hackman et al. [1975] describe how the job satisfaction of keypunch operators was increased by working with them to increase the variety of the work, the meaningfulness of the work, etc.

Four aspects of the task environment affect keying speed and accuracy. First, the lighting in the data preparation area must be adequate without causing glare. This factor is especially important, given that operators may be reading poorly prepared source documents or looking at visual display screens for prolonged periods. Second, acoustically the environment must be neither too noisy nor too quiet. On the one hand, careful choice of carpets, paneling, screens, and flooring is needed to reduce noise levels. On the other hand, key-to-tape and key-to-disk devices now make an audible click to break the silence so the operator can maintain a keying rhythm. Third, the layout of the data preparation area must be uncluttered to facilitate the flow of work. Layout considerations include space, amenities, and the position of keying devices. Fourth, ergonomically designed office equipment should be used to reduce repetition strain injury (RSI). For example, visual display screens should be nonreflective and positioned at a comfortable viewing distance, and chairs and tables should be adjustable to allow operators to maintain good posture.

Since keyboards and visual displays are now used so extensively in many organizations, operations management needs to monitor carefully the productivity and health of employees. If operators begin to experience eye problems, posture-related injuries, or possible radiation effects, the keying environment may have to be redesigned. If keyboards and visual displays are physically dispersed throughout the organizations, environmental design standards need to be prepared, promulgated, and enforced.

Operator Training

Management sometimes has the impression that data preparation tasks are easy and require little training. In some cases this is a reasonable assumption. Often, however, proper training produces significant improvements in the speed and accuracy with which data preparation is carried out. It should not be assumed that high-quality data preparation will be achieved simply by providing a good typist with a new device. Using the full capabilities of the data preparation device often requires extensive training. Today, many organizations are involved in teaching keying skills and experimenting with new keying techniques and keyboard formats, some of which seem capable of improving keying speed and accuracy.

Maintenance of Data Preparation Equipment

As with the hardware in the computer room, a regular maintenance schedule must be established for data preparation equipment. The equipment vendor typically recommends a schedule; management must ensure compliance with this schedule. Any abnormal problems that are experienced with particular equipment can be identified if regular maintenance is carried out and regular maintenance reports are prepared.

Backup and Recovery

The data preparation section often accepts responsibility for storing the data files submitted as input to the computer. Source documents are returned to the user after they have been keyed to cards, paper tape, magnetic tape, or disk, while the storage media on which the source data has been keyed often is returned to the data preparation section. These media constitute backup in case input files are lost or corrupted, and, as such, they must be stored securely. The operations manager and applications project manager must decide how long the data will be retained. Once the retention period has expired, the data must be destroyed in a secure manner; for example, punch cards can be shredded and

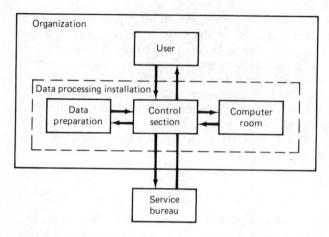

FIGURE 8-3
Control section as the focal point for data flow in computer data processing.

magnetic tapes can be degaussed or overwritten. Input data can be just as valuable as a master file to a competitor or a person wanting to perpetrate a fraud.

Operations management also must ensure that backup exists for data preparation equipment. Often the focus is on ensuring that backup exists for the hardware and software used in the computer room. However, these resources will stand idle if they have no input data to process. Usually it is easy to find suitable backup for data preparation equipment. Nevertheless, if the equipment has its own data validation capabilities (e.g., as with key-to-disk devices), operations management must ensure that backup copies of the data validation software also exist (see, further, Chapter 9).

PRODUCTION WORK FLOW CONTROL

Production work flow control in a computer installation is the responsibility of a control section. The control section manages the flow of data between users and the installation, between data preparation and the computer room, and between the installation and a service bureau facility (Figure 8-3). If a separate control section is set up, it is also more difficult for operators and data preparation personnel to collude and to perpetrate a fraud—for example, by altering input data. The following sections examine three major functions that must be performed by the control section: (*a*) quality assurance, (*b*) query answering, and (*c*) transfer pricing/chargeout control.

Quality Assurance

The control section facilitates the orderly flow of data to and from the computer installation and within the computer installation itself. A typical cycle starts with the receipt of input for some application system from users. The control section checks to see that this input is in order by scanning it for reasonableness and completeness and by checking control totals. If the input passes this quality assurance check, it is entered into a log and dispatched either to the computer room if it is already in machine-readable form or to data preparation if it must be keyed to cards, tape, or disk.

Once data preparation is complete, the control section collects the source data and machine-readable data and checks to see all data for the production run has been prepared. It also may be responsible for preparing any job control language parameters needed for the run. While job control language commands that remain constant should be stored on a secure procedures file and invoked at application system run time, others have to be prepared prior to processing since they vary from run to run. For example, the parameters specifying the job priority or expected run time may need to be altered. The machine-readable data and job control language commands are then dispatched to the computer room for processing.

After production running of an application system, the control section collects the output and machine-readable data from the computer room. It scans the output for completeness and any obvious errors and checks basic control totals. It also reviews the operating system messages to determine whether any problems have occurred during processing. For example, the control section will check to see whether a job has terminated abnormally and whether the correct program, data, and procedures files have been loaded. The system output and source data are then returned to users, and the machine-readable data is returned to the data preparation section.

If data must be sent to a service bureau for application system processing, similar control procedures are exercised over the collection, dispatch, and return of data. In addition, the control section evaluates the service bureau charges to determine their reasonableness and accuracy. Since the application is being processed remotely, it is also essential to communicate clear, accurate, and complete instructions to the service bureau to reduce the likelihood of operator errors.

Periodically, the control section should undertake an in-depth quality assurance review of data processing in each application system. This review involves a detailed check of the authenticity, accuracy, and completeness of input, processing, and output. For example, a sample of computations might be recalculated, the quality of reports might be assessed, and the reliability of input validation procedures might be evaluated. These reviews should be conducted on a regular, cyclical basis. In larger installations, they may be the responsibility of a separate quality assurance group that also has responsibility for evaluating and checking compliance with all standards established by the installation.

Query Answering

As the focal point for the flow of work through a computer installation, the control section takes responsibility for answering queries from users and data processing personnel about the status of work. Users have a range of concerns that they may direct, at least initially, to the control section: lost input or output, error messages that cannot be understood, ineffective reports, the need for a new processing schedule, poor turnaround times, etc. From a control perspective, these concerns must be addressed quickly and completely since they may reflect problem situations that ultimately will affect the integrity of processing. The control section may need to direct these queries to other sections in the computer installation to obtain the required response.

Transfer Pricing/Chargeout Control

If the computer installation uses a transfer pricing or chargeout system, the control section often has responsibility for billing users, collecting receipts (or initiating internal transfers of funds), and following up on unpaid accounts. In this light it must carefully monitor the chargeout system to ensure that charges are accurate, complete, and understandable by users (see, also, Chapter 3). In addition, it must be able to answer user queries on any charges made. Because of its close daily contact with the chargeout system, the control section may be able to alert management when transfer prices are not motivating users to employ computer resources efficiently or when dissatisfaction is arising among the user community with the level of charges or transfer pricing scheme being used.

If the computer installation is incurring charges itself because an outside service bureau is being used for data processing, as discussed earlier, the control section has responsibility for checking the authenticity and accuracy of invoices received. Again, because it has close daily contact with these charges, the control section may advise management if it considers these charges to be unreasonable or it believes that better opportunities exist elsewhere.

FILE LIBRARY

Managing the organization's library of machine-readable files involves three functions. First, files must be used only for the purposes intended. Control must be exercised over program files, data files, and procedure (job control language) files. Second, the storage media used for files must be maintained in correct working order. Third, a file backup strategy and file retention strategy must be implemented.

Within the data processing department, responsibility for managing files is vested in a file library section. If an organization uses microcomputers, however, file management responsibilities also must be discharged by the individuals dispersed throughout the organization who employ microcomputers in their work. Unfortunately, because many microcomputer users have no formal training in data processing, the need for secure storage, careful handling, and backup of files often is not realized. Diskette files, for example, may be kept in unlocked desk drawers, and backup copies may not be made until a major file is lost and it cannot be recovered.

The following sections describe the functions that should be performed by the file library section in the data processing department. While the functions to be exercised by microcomputer users are not as elaborate, nevertheless the general control principles that motivate the functions described below still apply. To assist microcomputer users, an organization should formulate standards for file library management and promulgate them throughout the organization.

Use of Files

A large computer installation may have several thousand files. It is a substantial management problem to ensure correct control and use of these files. A basic prerequisite for effective and efficient management is an orderly filing system. The filing system must encompass procedures for storing and retrieving the files and storage media and maintaining records of events that occur to the files and the storage media.

Files should be stored in a secure room adjacent to or near the computer room to facilitate the issue of files for processing and their return upon completion of processing. Like the computer room, the file storage room must have a stable environment: constant temperature, no dust, etc. Many types of cabinets are available for secure storage of files.

Files should be issued only in accordance with a predetermined application systems run schedule or on the basis of an authorized requisition. In the case of the authorized daily run schedule, the file librarian retrieves the files, transports them to the computer room, and collects them periodically after the application systems have been run. In all other cases file librarians must check that a person who requests a file is authorized to use the file; they must then issue the file only if that person has an authorized requisition. Otherwise, improper modifications may be made to programs, data, or procedure files.

To keep a record of all events that occur to files, a log must be maintained. The log contains information such as:

1 Name of file
2 Programs that access the file
3 Persons authorized to use the file
4 Person ultimately responsible for the file
5 Version number of the file
6 Creation date
7 Scratch date

8 Serial number of storage medium, e.g., tape number
9 Backup requirements
10 Place where backup is stored
11 History of uses—date issued, to whom, for what purpose, date returned

The log serves two purposes. First, it facilitates routine, daily operations. For example, if a file is requested for production purposes, it must be retrieved from its storage location and several checks performed: the person requesting the file is authorized to use it; the file is to be used for an allowed purpose; there are no special "hold" instructions on the file. Second, the log provides the basic source data for management reports on file use. Periodically, various exception reports might be prepared, for example, issues of files to persons other than those listed as authorized to use the file.

It is difficult to manage files effectively and efficiently without a support computer system. In the case of *program* files, librarian packages have been developed that provide several types of functional capabilities:

Functional capabilities	Examples
Update capabilities	Addition, modification, deletion of program source code; implementation of temporary changes to source code; resequencing source code; editing capabilities, e.g., global change of a particular character string; insertion of special documentation records
Integrity capabilities	Access control over programs through the use of passwords; each source program assigned a modification number and version number; each source statement has an associated creation date; encryption and data compaction facilities; automatic creation of backup
Report capabilities	Listing of additions, deletions, modifications; index of programs and their attributes, e.g., programmer, size, purpose; report on storage space utilization by library

In the case of *data* files and *procedure* files, many organizations have written their own library systems, although several commercial packages are also available.

Care must be taken when the retention dates of files expire and they are issued as scratch files. In some computer systems, scratching simply means the header information for the file is changed; however, the data in the file is not overwritten. Thus, the program that next uses the file simply can read the data relating to the previous application and the privacy of the data is violated. However, for some peripheral devices a scratch command causes the device's control unit to disconnect the device from the channel and, under microprogram control, to overwrite data on the file. If the device does not undertake this action, sensitive data should be destroyed before the file is issued as a scratch file. Magnetic tape files can be demagnetized (degaussed). Disk files can be sanitized; that is, the data on the file can be overwritten.

The placement of multiple files on a single storage medium may cause control problems. The system must ensure that a program reading one file cannot backspace itself into another file and read sensitive data. Thus, the placement of files on storage media should be managed carefully. Sensitive files might be allocated sole use of a storage medium if there is some risk of a program reading outside file boundaries.

Periodically, an audit of the file library should be undertaken to review internal controls over file use. The auditor can conduct basic physical inventory procedures to determine whether the actual inventory of files matches the records maintained by the file librarian. The auditor should be alert to the possibility of excess inventory in the form of magnetic tapes that hold obsolete files, missing data files, damaged storage media, files that have exceeded their retention date, etc. Basic compliance test procedures also can be undertaken on such functions as the issue of files, the removal of files to backup, the secure storage of files, and the prompt purging of files that have exceeded their retention date.

Maintenance of Files

Magnetic storage media periodically require cleaning and recertification. A log must be kept on each storage medium used indicating:

1 Serial number of the storage medium
2 Location
3 Files stored on the medium
4 Maintenance instructions
5 History of failures—read/write errors
6 Maintenance record—cleaning, recertification
7 History of uses—date issued, to whom, for what purpose, date returned

If tapes and disks are sent outside the organization for cleaning and recertification, care must be taken to erase any sensitive data contained on the media. If the worn ends of magnetic tapes are to be clipped, degaussing should be undertaken first in case the clippings contain sensitive information. An unauthorized person may retrieve the clippings from a trash can and examine the data recorded on the clippings. As a further protective measure, the clippings can be destroyed.

Various file management reports can be prepared from the maintenance log; for example:

1 Listing of media requiring maintenance
2 Media experiencing an abnormal number of read/write errors
3 Media that should be retired from use

On the basis of these reports, management may decide to move files from one storage medium to another. For example, critical master files might be stored only on new disk packs. If a disk pack starts to experience an abnormal number of read/write errors, files on the disk may be moved to another disk. Older storage media might be used for backup purposes only.

Again, requirements for cross-reference data—for example, files with storage media—highlight the need for a computer system to support file library functions. The system needed is relatively simple; however, the volume of data on file usage that must be processed in even a moderately sized installation makes computer support a necessity.

Backup and Retention of Files

As discussed in Chapter 7, the security administrator has responsibility for formulating a backup and recovery plan for all files. The file library section, in turn, has responsibility for implementing this plan. In conjunction with the security administrator, the file librarian may choose a suitable off-site storage location for backup files—for example, a commercial storage facility or the data processing center in another organization—and a secure means of transporting backup files to this site to ensure the files will not be damaged or improperly accessed during transit.

With the exception of temporary work files, a backup decision must be made for each file. The type of backup (see Chapter 14) and the frequency of backup must be determined. Typically this decision is made by the application systems project manager, who also may seek the advice of the file librarian. Once these decisions have been made, they must be stored in the file library system as part of the basic descriptors for the file. The file library system then provides reports indicating when a file should be removed to a backup site, how it should be removed, and when it should be retrieved.

The file library section also has responsibility for implementing the retention plan prepared for each file. This plan must take into account any statutory requirements that apply to the retention of data (e.g., tax) and the needs of the organization itself (e.g., to answer customer queries). Again, the application systems project manager typically specifies how long data for any application is to be retained, although EDP management should specify any overriding policies that apply to retention periods.

Files should be purged promptly when their retention date expires. Otherwise, excess files begin to accumulate, and it becomes more difficult to manage the file library effectively and efficiently. In addition, more storage media must be purchased to accommodate these files. In the case of magnetic tapes, the fire risk increases as a result since more inflammable objects are held within the computer facility. Prompt purging of data also reduces the risk of privacy violations occurring through inadvertent disclosure of data as old files are released as scratch files.

The adequacy of backup procedures and retention procedures for files should be evaluated regularly. The auditor might simulate a disaster for a particular application system to determine whether backup files can be obtained and the system recovered on a timely basis. As discussed earlier, basic physical inventory audit procedures should examine whether files are being purged promptly when their retention date expires.

DOCUMENTATION LIBRARY

The organization's computer systems documentation library contains the documentation supporting all systems used by the organization: application system documentation, program documentation, operator run manuals, and user manuals. The documentation library also may be the site where standards manuals are kept and maintained, records of memoranda are kept, and books and journals are kept.

As with the file library, responsibility for exercising control over the documentation library is vested in a special section within the data processing department and, if the organization uses microcomputers, the individuals dispersed throughout the organization who employ microcomputers in their work. Again, while the functions of the documentation librarian in the data processing department are more elaborate, the basic control principles that motivate these functions still apply to microcomputer users. The organization should develop standards for control over documentation and promulgate these standards throughout the organization.

As a basis for understanding how the documentation library should be controlled, consider the three major functions performed by the documentation librarian in the data processing department: (*a*) ensuring documentation is stored securely, (*b*) issuing documentation to authorized personnel only, and (*c*) maintaining adequate backup for documentation. Secure storage can be achieved by having documentation stored in cabinets in a separate room. A log of issues and returns of documentation should be kept. Special authority might be needed to obtain some types of documentation, for example, the programming manager's authority to obtain program documentation and a project manager's authority to obtain system documentation.

Providing adequate backup for documentation can be a difficult task. It is easy to copy a magnetic file for backup. It is also relatively easy to make additional copies of initial documentation for backup. However, keeping backup documentation up to date in light of changes can be an onerous task, simply because it is often awkward and unwieldy to amend program listings, flowcharts, textual descriptions, etc. It is not uncommon to find good backup for files on magnetic media and poor backup for documentation.

One solution to the problem of maintaining up-to-date backup for documentation is to store documentation on magnetic media. The widespread availability of word processing equipment and computer text processors makes this means of backup for documentation available to many computer installations. When documentation is altered, the master cassette, diskette, etc., is updated and a copy made for backup purposes. Maintaining documentation on magnetic media also has other advantages:

1 Facilitates amendments and production of revised hard-copy documentation; consequently, the time needed and labor costs incurred to carry out amendments should be reduced.

2 If documentation is maintained online, provides increased accessibility to information. The auditor must then assess whether or not adequate access controls have been installed (see Chapter 9).

3 If the word processing system is connected to a communications network, facilitates distribution of documentation (e.g., user manuals) and amendments to authorized users. The auditor must then assess whether or not adequate communications controls have been installed (see Chapter 12).

4 An audit trail of accesses to the documentation can be maintained by the system that manages use and control of the documentation.

5 Allows automation of controls over documentation; thus, the documentation is less susceptible to corruption through human error.

Another solution to the problem of backup of documentation is to microfilm the documentation. However, this can be a time-consuming process. It is not likely to be cost-effective to produce new microfilm every time documentation is changed. Thus, the backup usually will be somewhat out of date.

Individual microcomputer users also must ensure that documentation is stored securely, access is restricted to authorized personnel, and adequate backup is provided. Again, there is a tendency to leave microcomputer documentation in desk drawers and to disregard the need for backup. Some microcomputer systems are just as critical to the organization as the applications systems that are run on the mainframe. The losses that could result from unauthorized access to or destruction of microcomputer system documentation should be considered and suitable controls designed and implemented.

PERFORMANCE MONITORING

The primary objective of the data processing function is to achieve the goals of system users at minimum cost. To some extent this goal is achieved by high-quality system design and implementation. However, it also depends upon providing a suitable hardware/software configuration on which systems can run. In this respect, operations management must continuously monitor the performance of the hardware/software configuration to ensure that systems are being processed efficiently, an acceptable response time or turnaround time is being achieved, and an acceptable level of uptime is occurring. This monitoring extends not only to the hardware/software configuration existing within the data processing department but also to other configurations (such as minicomputers and microcomputers) dispersed throughout the organization. While the costs of inefficiency may be small for an individual minicomputer or microcomputer, the aggregate costs of inefficiency for the organization may be substantial. These overall costs must be evaluated carefully.

Chapter 21 provides a detailed discussion of some of the instruments that can be used to monitor the performance of a hardware/software configuration and the various measurements that might be taken. Chapter 24 discusses how the measurements can then be assimilated to evaluate overall system efficiency. It is the operations manager's responsibility to devise a plan for monitoring system performance, to identify the data that must be captured to accomplish the plan, to choose the instruments needed to capture the data, and to ensure the instruments are correctly implemented in place and working. The performance monitoring plan and its execution varies considerably depending upon many factors—for example, whether a large mainframe or a set of microcomputers is being evaluated. Moreover, the plan and its implementation have to be reconsidered periodically in light of configuration changes or changed patterns of system use.

On the basis of the performance monitoring statistics calculated, operations managers must make three decisions. First, they must evaluate whether the performance profile indicates the possibility of unauthorized activities occurring. For example, abnormal workloads during a night shift may reflect that an analyst or programmer is using system resources for private consulting purposes. Second, they must determine whether, in light of user needs, system performance is acceptable. If system performance is not acceptable, they must diagnose why this is the case. It may reflect poor job scheduling that is resulting in undesirable job mixes being run. It also may indicate the need for hardware and system software to be reconfigured to avoid particular resource bottlenecks. Finally, it may indicate that more hardware and system software resources are needed. In this respect, careful, regular monitoring of performance facilitates capacity planning. Given the substantial leadtimes that can exist in acquiring and implementing many hardware and system software resources, resource deficiencies must be identified early if the resources are to be available when they are needed.

From an audit perspective, it is important that operations management monitors performance properly and makes competent hardware and system software decisions on the basis of the statistics collected. Recall, Chapter 1 pointed out the relationship between poor system performance and poor controls. If users are frustrated by inadequate system performance, they may circumvent controls in an attempt to decrease resource consumption. As controls degrade, asset safeguarding and data integrity are threatened.

SUMMARY

Operations management has responsibility for the daily running of hardware and software resources. Specifically, it performs seven major functions: (*a*) operation of the hardware and software; (*b*) communications network control; (*c*) data preparation; (*d*) production work flow control; (*e*) control over the data, program, and procedures file library; (*f*) control over the documentation library; and (*g*) performance monitoring.

While these functions appear somewhat routine and mundane, their proper performance is critical if effective controls are to be exercised over the assets of the organization. The operations manager must ensure that methods and performance standards exist for each function, high-quality personnel are hired to perform each function, adequate training for these personnel is provided, and the personnel comply with the standards established.

REVIEW QUESTIONS

8-1 What is the role of operations management with respect to long-range planning within the data processing installation? What expertise qualifies them to play this role?

8-2 Why has the introduction and use of microcomputers in organizations made the operations management role more difficult? Give an example of how microcomputers have made the role more complex.

8-3 Give two items in the computer room standards manual and two items in an application system run manual that an auditor may examine from a control viewpoint. Briefly explain why these items are of interest.

8-4 Give a *specific* example of how a direct "fix" made at a console terminal by an operator may compromise controls within an application system. What controls can be used to prevent direct fixes from occurring and to detect them when they do occur?

8-5 Briefly explain why it is undesirable to allow operators to authorize reruns of application systems.

8-6 The mix of jobs in a machine usually is chosen to minimize resource contention among the programs that are executing. Is there any reason a mix of jobs might be chosen from the viewpoint of maintaining data integrity?

8-7 For the following activities, indicate who is responsible for authorizing machine resources to undertake them and briefly indicate why they are responsible:
a Regular execution of an application system
b Program testing
c Production application system reruns
d Program compilations

8-8 Briefly explain the difference between preventive and repair maintenance. Why might an EDP manager decide to increase the amount of preventive maintenance undertaken on a machine?

8-9 Give two routine decisions that operations management should make on the basis of data contained on the maintenance log.

8-10 Briefly describe two ways in which an engineer might violate data integrity within a computer installation. Give three controls that might be exercised over the engineer to inhibit or prevent the integrity violations you describe.

8-11 What is the overall purpose of the network control terminal in a communications network? Give three specific functions that can be performed by an operator using the network control terminal.

8-12 Why is a network control terminal a threat to the overall security of a data processing installation? What controls should be exercised to try to ensure that the network control terminal is used only for its intended purposes?

8-13 Why is it critical that a communications network operate efficiently if data integrity is to be maintained? Give a specific example of how an inefficient network can lead to a breach of data integrity.

8-14 Briefly describe some guidelines that should be followed to reduce operator boredom in the design of keying tasks undertaken in the data preparation function.

8-15 What is repetition strain injury (RSI)? Why should operations management be concerned about RSI? Give four aspects of the keying environment that must be considered if RSI is to be prevented.

8-16 What responsibilities does operations management have with respect to backup and recovery in the data preparation function?

8-17 Briefly explain the control section's responsibilities with respect to the source documents for an application system. Why does the control section have these responsibilities?

8-18 After source documents for an application system have been keyed to magnetic media, what actions are undertaken by the control section to prepare the application for production running? When the output from the application system is produced, what actions are then taken by the control section?

8-19 Why is the control section a focal point for queries within the data processing installation?

8-20 What are the control section's responsibilities with respect to transfer pricing charges in terms of:
a Users of the data processing installation's services?
b The data processing installation as a user of an outside service bureau's services?

8-21 Briefly explain why operators should not take responsibility for the file library. In a small installation where there is insufficient work for a separate file librarian position, who might take responsibility for the file library?

8-22 Briefly explain the two major purposes of a file library log. Why is it sometimes advantageous to have a computer system to support the maintenance of this log?

8-23 What security considerations apply to the storage of files for:
a A mainframe computer with a large number of users?
b A microcomputer with only one user?

8-24 From a control perspective, list *four* benefits of using a librarian package for the maintenance of program files.

8-25 List the major steps to be carried out in the audit of the file library function.

8-26 What is meant by degaussing and sanitization? Briefly explain the purposes of degaussing and sanitization as control procedures.

8-27 Briefly explain the purposes of maintaining a history of read/write errors for magnetic storage media.

8-28 Briefly explain the responsibilities of the file library section with respect to backup and retention of files in a data processing installation. How do the responsibilities of microcomputer users differ if the users look after their own files?

8-29 What is the purpose of preventing *operators* from having access to program documentation? To what extent should *programmers* be prevented from obtaining access to program documentation? Why should management periodically review the log showing accesses to program documentation?

8-30 Why is it generally more difficult to provide backup for documentation as compared with files? Give two strategies for facilitating the backup process for documentation.

8-31 Briefly describe the responsibilities of operations management with respect to performance monitoring. What decisions does an operations manager make on the basis of the performance monitoring data that is collected?

MULTIPLE CHOICE QUESTIONS

8-1 Which of the following is *not* a function of operations management:
 a Performance monitoring
 b Application system postaudits
 c File library
 d Production work flow control

8-2 In organizations where microcomputers are used extensively, the functions of operations management relating to the microcomputers should be:
 a Still performed by the operations manager responsible for the mainframe computer
 b Determined by and left to the individuals who use the microcomputers
 c Formulated by the person who develops the application system for the microcomputer
 d Formulated by the operations manager and promulgated as a standard throughout the organization

8-3 To assist operators, application system run manuals should contain:
 a Program source code
 b User instructions for preparing source code
 c Expected resource consumption
 d Program flowcharts

8-4 A direct fix is a:
 a Program alteration made using the console terminal
 b Modification to a program carried out correctly on the first attempt
 c System malfunction that is corrected automatically by the operating system
 d Program modification that an operator is authorized to make

8-5 The mix of jobs in a machine should be chosen to:
 a Minimize resource contention among executing programs
 b Ensure all programs are processor-bound
 c Ensure minimum turnaround time for all output
 d Both a and c above

8-6 If a machine error causes an application program to fail during normal production running, the authority to rerun the program should be given by the:
 a Operations manager
 b Application project manager
 c Program librarian
 d Operations shift supervisor

8-7 Maintenance engineers pose some difficult control programs because:
 a They often have a high level of programming skills
 b They have available special hardware/software tools that enable them to breach data integrity
 c As a work group they tend to have high staff turnover so vital experience on a particular machine is lost quickly
 d They sometimes need application program controls to be relaxed so they can do their work

8-8 Which of the following functions *cannot* be performed using a communications network control terminal:
   a Resetting message queue lengths
   b Closing down a terminal
   c Correcting a hardware error in a modem
   d Generating a control total for a point-of-sale device

8-9 Which of the following activities should *not* be permitted when operators use a communications network control terminal:
   a Renaming a communications line
   b Down-line loading a program
   c Altering the audit trail to correct an error
   d Examining data traversing a communications line

8-10 Control over data preparation is important because:
   a It is often a major cost area taking about 50% of the data processing budget
   b It can be a major bottleneck in the work flow in a data processing installation
   c High error rates in this area are the norm
   d The work is boring so high turnover always occurs

8-11 Which of the following guidelines applies to the design of keying tasks to increase the effectiveness and efficiency of the data preparation function:
   a Keying tasks should be no longer than an hour
   b To the extent possible, operators should always key the same application system's data
   c Keying tasks should be precisely defined
   d All of the above are applicable guidelines

8-12 Which of the following design guidelines is used to reduce repetition strain injury:
   a Ensure the key preparation area is brightly lit so keyboard operators can read source documents easily
   b Ensure all seats are at a uniform height so all keyboard operators get used to a common position
   c Choose keyboards that require some pressure to activate so operators can hear an audible click
   d Choose a work station table that has been ergonomically designed

8-13 Which of the following statements applies to backup of data preparation resources:
   a It is a low priority in the security plan since backup equipment is readily available
   b The primary resource to be considered is hardware
   c Care must be taken to back up software
   d It need not be considered if the rate of preventive maintenance is increased

8-14 Which of the following is *not* a function of the control section:
   a Dispatching input to the computer room
   b Scanning output for reasonableness
   c Follow-up on unpaid accounts if a transfer pricing scheme is being used
   d Altering source data to correct input errors

8-15 Which of the following activities would *not* be performed by control section personnel when they collect the output of a batch application system from the computer room:
   a Checking basic control totals
   b One-to-one reconciliation of input with output
   c Checking to see whether any programs terminated abnormally

    d Scanning the output for obvious errors

8-16 Which of the following is *not* a capability of a librarian package:

    a Determining those programs that have inadequate documentation

    b Addition, modification, and deletion of source code

    c Encryption of source code

    d Creating indexes of programs and their attributes

8-17 The purpose of degaussing magnetic tapes before the ends are clipped is to:

    a Indicate which section of the tape should be clipped

    b Delete sensitive information so data privacy is protected

    c Transfer information to another tape

    d Encrypt the information to preserve data privacy

8-18 Sanitization is the process of:

    a Overwriting data on disk

    b Fumigating the computer room to reduce the risk of damage being caused by insects

    c Cleaning a magnetic tape

    d Recertifying magnetic media after an abnormal number of read/write errors have occurred

8-19 Which of the following decisions most likely could *not* be made on the basis of file management reports prepared from the maintenance log:

    a Whether to move files from one storage medium to another to reduce read/write errors

    b Whether a storage medium should be retired

    c Whether a master file should be stored on a particular storage medium

    d Whether a program has updated the correct version of a master file

8-20 Which of the following actions should be undertaken when a file retention date expires:

    a The storage medium on which the file resides should be retired from use

    b The file should be removed to archival storage

    c The file should be purged

    d The file should be retrieved from backup storage

8-21 Which of the following is *not* an advantage of using word processors to maintain documentation:

    a Facilitates amendments to application system user documentation

    b Copies of documentation can be transferred electronically to remote locations

    c Alterations to program flowcharts can be made easily

    d Increased data privacy through the availability of access controls

8-22 Which of the following is *not* a function of the documentation librarian:

    a Ensuring documentation is stored securely

    b Modifying system documentation in light of changes made to program code

    c Issuing documentation to authorized users

    d Maintaining adequate backup for documentation

8-23 Which of the following is an advantage of maintaining documentation on microfilm:

    a The backup documentation will always be up to date

    b It is easy to modify documentation maintained on microfilm

    c It is easier to store documentation on microfilm than documentation on magnetic media

    d None of the above are advantages to storing documentation on microfilm

8-24 Which of the following decisions most likely *cannot* be made on the basis of performance monitoring statistics that are calculated:

a Whether the system being monitored has provided users with a strategic advantage over their competitors

b Whether new hardware/system software resources are needed

c Whether unauthorized use is being made of hardware/system software resources

d Whether resource bottlenecks are occurring

EXERCISES AND CASES

8-1 You are on the internal audit staff of Brownem, Inc., a large producer of suntanning oils and creams and other health and beauty products. Your organization's main computer installation has a file library consisting of 5000 reels of tape and 1000 disk packs.

Required: The internal audit manager asks you to help formulate an audit plan for the file library. He asks you to prepare a memorandum outlining:

1 The objectives of the audit

2 The major controls to be examined and evaluated and how they relate to the audit objectives

3 The means of evidence collection to be used

8-2 You are the external auditor for Scarem, Inc., a medium-sized manufacturer of burglar alarm systems. The company uses computer systems extensively to support all its accounting and manufacturing applications. In addition, it uses the computer to support various word processing and text processing applications, and the management and staff are avid users of electronic mail, electronic diaries, etc. Overall, there is sufficient work for the computer to work on a six day per week 24 hour a day basis.

When you examine the assignment of operators to shifts, you note that only one operator is present for the late night and early morning shifts. You raise the potential control problems that can result from this policy with the operations manager and the EDP manager. However, they argue that one operator can easily run the machine during these periods, and they see no reason why they should incur the expense of having another operator present during these shifts.

Required: List the control weaknesses you pointed out to the operations manager and the EDP manager. How will you respond to their arguments in support of using only one operator on the late night and early morning shifts?

8-3 Recently, the data processing installation in your organization has purchased a word processing system to facilitate update and maintenance of program, system, and user documentation. Master copies of documentation will be stored on diskette. A single hard copy report of the latest version of the documentation also will be maintained for day-to-day use by authorized installation staff.

Required: As a member of the EDP audit staff of your organization, the EDP audit manager asks you to consider the consequences of the change from a *data integrity* viewpoint. He asks you to prepare a brief report that considers:

a Whether or not anything could go wrong with the new documentation system that eventually could lead to corruption of data integrity in the organization's database.

b If so, what controls could be implemented in the new system to reduce the expected losses from this threat to an acceptable level.

8-4 Bleecker Street Blues Corporation is a large New York–based organization involved in the production and distribution of video recordings, primarily for jazz and rock musicians. For several years the company has actively encouraged its management to use microcomputers, and it has purchased a large number of portable microcomputers that managers can take with them when they travel or when they decide to work at home. Several managers have developed some very successful applications using a fourth-generation language that the company has purchased. For example, one manager has developed a system to identify target audiences for advertising based on various characteristics of the video recording and known purchasing patterns of consumers throughout the United States.

As the manager of internal audit for the company, one day you are called to a "crisis" meeting with the president of the company. Several weeks ago he had fired one of his senior managers as a result of several major confrontations that had developed. Unfortunately the manager had designed and implemented some especially successful microcomputer application systems that the president wanted his successor to use. However, while the new manager could load the systems onto a machine, she was unable to understand them sufficiently well to be able to use them. She could find no documentation to support the systems, and she was particularly concerned about modifications that periodically would have to be made to the systems to reflect changing market circumstances.

As a result of these problems, the president had called the old manager to ask him to provide the documentation for the systems. The old manager had informed the president that no documentation existed. Moreover, he argued that even if documentation was available, it belonged to him since he had developed the systems in his own time at home. In addition, he threatened to sue the company if it used the systems he had developed.

As a consequence of the ex-manager's threats, the president had sought legal advice on the ownership of the systems. He had also undertaken a cursory investigation of the state of documentation supporting other microcomputer systems that had been developed by various managers. He was disturbed to see that virtually no documentation existed for the systems that had been developed.

In light of the serious problems that have occurred, the president asks you to advise him on the actions that should be taken to prevent further difficulties from arising. In particular, he asks you whether he should prohibit managers from developing microcomputer systems except with the assistance of staff from the data processing department. In this way, he argues, some assurance might be obtained about the quality and availability of documentation, and the ownership of the systems would also be well defined.

Required: Write a brief report outlining the strategies you believe Bleecker Street Blues should follow in relation to documentation for its microcomputer systems.

8-5 You are the chief internal auditor for a large public utility that has used computer systems for many years in most areas of its operations. One day you are called to a meeting with the general manager, the EDP manager, and the computer operations manager (who is responsible for all data preparation activities in your organization). The general manager indicates she has called the meeting to discuss a crisis that has arisen with respect to data preparation activities in the utility. She provides statistics that show over the last five years there has been a threefold increase in workers compensation claims paid by the utility to data preparation staff because of repetition strain injury (office trauma). In addition, she indicates that morale among keyboard operators is at an all-time low since several operators who have been with the utility for over ten years have been forced to give up their jobs as a result of RSI. Other difficulties have also arisen: the utility is in conflict with several unions over RSI problems; there has been a major loss in productivity in the data preparation area; the error rate for keyed data has risen dramatically, and customers are complaining vociferously about errors in their accounts.

The general manager points out that part of the problem lies in the poor office environment in which the keyboard operators work. Since the utility purchased and installed equipment before the problems of RSI became known, operators have been working for too long with poorly designed furniture, improper lighting, too few rest breaks, etc. She also argues that some managers in the utility have adopted an intolerant attitude toward workers who have shown symptoms of RSI.

In an attempt to overcome the problems that have arisen, the general manager indicates she has called in a consultant ergonomist to advise her on office redesign. However, she points out that the ergonomist can only provide long-run solutions to the problems that have arisen. It will take some time to purchase new equipment, redesign office layouts, etc. In the meantime, some action must be undertaken to restore productivity levels and to reduce data preparation error rates. In this light she seeks your advice on short-run strategies that might be followed to help alleviate the problems that have arisen.

Required: Prepare a brief report for the general manager outlining the courses of action you recommend to help increase productivity and to reduce error rates in the data preparation function.

ANSWERS TO MULTIPLE CHOICE QUESTIONS

8-1 b	8-7 b	8-13 c	8-19 d
8-2 d	8-8 c	8-14 d	8-20 c
8-3 c	8-9 c	8-15 b	8-21 c
8-4 a	8-10 b	8-16 a	8-22 b
8-5 a	8-11 a	8-17 b	8-23 d
8-6 d	8-12 d	8-18 a	8-24 a

REFERENCES

Adams, Donald L. "A Survey of Library System Packages," *EDPACS* (July 1973), pp. 4–8.

Adams, Donald L. "Library System Packages—Revisited," *EDPACS* (February 1974), pp. 7–10.

American Institute of Certified Public Accountants. *Controls Over Using and Changing Computer Programs* (New York: American Institute of Certified Public Accountants, 1979).

Blanding, Steven F. "Auditing JCL Standards," *EDP Auditing* (Pennsauken, NJ: Auerbach Publishers, 1983), Portfolio 72-03-07, pp. 1–11.

Brass, Barry S. "The Auditor's Responsibility in Performance Evaluation," *EDP Auditing* (Pennsauken, NJ: Auerbach Publishers, 1983), Portfolio 72-03-08, pp. 1–15.

Butler, Johnny. "Computer Operations Audit—Some New Areas," *EDPACS* (June 1974), pp. 5–8.

Canning, Richard G. "The Upgrading of Computer Operators," *EDP Analyzer* (September 1974), pp. 1–13.

Cardenas, Alfonso F. "Data Entry: A Giant Cost," *Journal of Systems Management* (August 1973), pp. 35–42.

Eva, Keith D. "EDP Auditing and Off-Site Storage," *The EDP Auditor* (Summer 1983), pp. 41–45.

Hackman, J. Richard, Greg Oldham, Robert Janson, and Kenneth Purdy. "A New Strategy for Job Enrichment," *California Management Review* (Summer 1975), pp. 57–71.

McNurlin, Barbara C. "The Automated Office: Part 1," *EDP Analyzer* (September 1978), pp. 1–13.

McNurlin, Barbara C. "The Automated Office: Part 2," *EDP Analyzer* (October 1978), pp. 1–13.

Moeller, Robert R. "Auditing DP Service Costs and Pricing," *EDP Auditing* (Pennsauken, NJ: Auerbach Publishers, 1983), Portfolio 75-01-30, pp. 1–8.

Moore, Richard A., Benjamin F. Rose, and Thomas J. Koger. "Computer Generated Documentation," *Journal of Accountancy* (June 1975), pp. 82–86.

Murray, William Hugh. "Security Procedures for Program Libraries," *Computers and Security*, vol. 1, 1982, pp. 201–209.

Perry, William E. "Auditing the Data Library," *EDP Auditing* (Pennsauken, NJ: Auerbach Publishers, 1983), Portfolio 72-03-06, pp. 1–10.

Pinchuk, P. L. "TRW Evaluation of a Secure Operating System," *Data Security and Data Processing Volume 6 Evaluations and Installation Experiences: Resource Security System* (New York: IBM Corporation, 1974), pp. 223–300.

Stokel, Kathryn J. "How to Audit Program Library Control Software," *EDPACS* (May 1980), pp. 1–10.

Weston, Stephen S. "Program Library Control and Security," *EDPACS* (September 1979), pp. 1–9.

THREE

THE APPLICATION
CONTROL FRAMEWORK

Application system controls seek to ensure that individual application systems safeguard assets, maintain data integrity, achieve their objectives, and process data efficiently. Application system controls differ from management controls in four ways. First, hardware and software usually exercise them rather than people. Second, they apply to data and the processing of data rather than the system development, modification, and maintenance processes. Third, their existence in *each* application system is a cost-benefit question. The existence of management controls, on the other hand, depends on cost-benefit questions relating to the *whole* set of application systems. Fourth, they tend to focus on safeguarding assets (reducing expected losses from unauthorized or inadvertent removal or destruction of assets) and maintaining data integrity (ensuring data is authorized, complete, and accurate). Nevertheless, systems effectiveness and efficiency are also their objectives; for example, an output distribution control may exist so an application system meets a timeliness requirement, and an audit trail control may exist to provide data on resource consumption by an application system.

On the basis of the evaluation of the management control framework, the auditor may decide to evaluate application controls for two reasons. First, the auditor may hypothesize that control weaknesses exist in a specific application system. For example, it may be that certain management controls were not applied in the development of an accounts payable system. Second, the auditor may wish to test a hypothesis about weaknesses in specific types of controls within application systems. For example, system testing standards for communication controls may be considered to be deficient. Thus, the auditor examines a sample of application systems having communication facilities to test this hypothesis.

The next seven chapters examine in detail the application control framework. The chapters follow a natural sequence: the flow of data from its source through processing to storage to its eventual output.

Chapter	Overview of contents
9 Boundary Controls	Access controls; cryptographic controls; personal identification numbers; plastic cards; audit trail controls; existence controls
10 Input Controls: Data and Instruction Input	Data capture methods; data preparation methods; data preparation devices; direct entry devices; input devices; source document design; data entry screen design; data code controls; check digits; batch controls; instruction input; audit trail controls; existence controls
11 Input Controls: Validation and Error Control	Data input validation checks; design of the data input validation program; control over data input; a generalized data input system; instruction input validation checks; audit trail controls; existence controls
12 Communication Controls	Communication subsystem exposures; controls over component failure; controls over subversive threats; audit trail controls; existence controls
13 Processing Controls	Processor controls; real memory controls; virtual memory controls; operating system integrity; application software controls; audit trail controls; existence controls
14 Database Controls	Access controls; application software controls; concurrency controls; cryptographic controls; file handling controls; audit trail controls; existence controls
15 Output Controls	Inference controls; presentation controls; production and distribution controls; audit trail controls; existence controls

BOUNDARY CONTROLS

The boundary subsystem establishes the interface between the would-be user of a computer system and the computer system itself. When a user sits down at a terminal, switches the terminal on, dials up the computer, connects the telephone handset to a modem, and begins the initial handshaking procedures with the operating system, boundary subsystem functions are being performed. Similarly, when a customer walks up to an automatic teller machine and begins the initial question-answer session during which the machine attempts to establish the identity and authenticity of the customer and what the customer wants to do, boundary subsystem functions are being performed. Once boundary subsystem functions are complete, the user can commence to use the resources of the system.

Boundary subsystem controls have one primary purpose: to establish the identity and authenticity of would-be users of a system. Historically, boundary controls have been considered relatively unimportant. They amounted to little more than passwords that often were publicly known anyway. However, two factors have led to a marked increase in the strength of boundary controls. First, the increasing use of distributed systems has resulted in users being physically dispersed so that it is more difficult to rely on close contact with users and separation of duties as a means of exercising control over the actions they undertake. Second, the rapid growth of electronic funds transfer systems places onerous requirements on systems to identify and authenticate the parties who exchange monies. Today, therefore, boundary controls are some of the most complex controls to be found in computer systems.

This chapter examines some of the major types of controls exercised in the boundary subsystem. First, it describes the general characteristics of an access control mechanism. While access controls are used in several subsystems, typically they are encountered initially in the boundary subsystem. Next, several controls that are critical in electronic funds transfer systems and distributed systems are examined. In particular, cryptographic controls, personal identification numbers, digital signatures, and plastic cards are discussed. Finally, audit trail and existence controls within the boundary subsystem are described.

ACCESS CONTROLS

Access controls usually are a minor problem when only one person uses the resources of a computing system (provided that separation of duties exists). Access control simply amounts to excluding anyone else from using the system, for example, by physically barring access to the system. There may be cases where the computing resources used are so critical that they justify this form of access control. Certain defense installations fall into this category. However, given the processing power of current computing systems, typically a single person can use only a small proportion of the available capabilities. Absolute access control of the type described above is an expensive strategy.

The trend in current computing technology is toward increased sharing of resources. This is achieved by having a single computer simulate the operations of several computers. Each of the simulated computers is called a "virtual machine." Virtual machines allow more efficient use of resources through decreasing a single computer's idle capacity. In a virtual machine environment, however, it is a major design problem to ensure each virtual machine operates as though it were completely unaware of the operations of other virtual machines. Increased scope exists for unintentional or malicious damage. A design flaw may result in one virtual machine unintentionally violating the integrity of processes and data belonging to another virtual machine. Furthermore, because it is difficult to completely isolate virtual machines from each other, one virtual machine may be used intentionally to attempt unauthorized access to another virtual machine.

In a shared resource environment the auditor has two concerns about access controls. First, the auditor must determine whether or not the access control mechanism used within the computer installation is capable of preventing unauthorized access to and use of resources. Since the access control mechanism normally is embedded within the operating system or the database management system, assessing the capabilities of the access control mechanism can be a complex task. Second, given the capabilities of the access control mechanism, for any particular application system the auditor must determine whether or not the access controls chosen for that system suffice. Since the sufficiency of the application system access controls depends directly on the capabilities of the access control mechanism, the following sections discuss the major features that should exist in an access control mechanism.

Functions of an Access Control Mechanism

An access control mechanism associates with identified, authorized users the resources they are permitted to access and the action privileges they have with

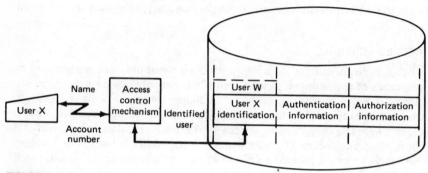

FIGURE 9-1a
Identification process.

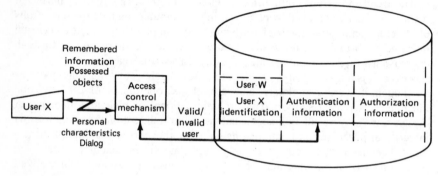

FIGURE 9-1b
Authentication process.

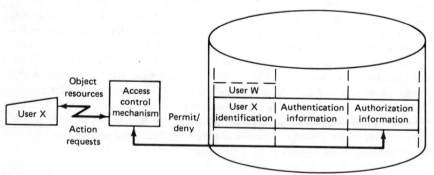

FIGURE 9-1c
Authorization process.

respect to those resources. The mechanism processes users' requests for resources in three steps (Figure 9-1). First, users identify themselves to the mechanism, thereby indicating their intent to request use of system resources. Second, users must authenticate themselves, and the mechanism must authenticate itself. Authentication is a two-way process. Not only must the mechanism be sure it has a valid user, users also must be sure they have a valid mechanism. This matter is discussed in more detail later in the chapter. Third, users request specific resources and specify the actions they intend to undertake with the resources. The mechanism accesses previously stored information about users, the resources they can access, and the action privileges they have with respect to those resources; it then permits or denies the request.

Identification and Authentication Users identify themselves to the access control mechanism by providing information such as a name or account number. This identification information enables the mechanism to select from its file of authentication information the entry corresponding to the user. The authentication process then proceeds on the basis of the information contained in the entry, the user having to indicate prior knowledge of this information.

Users may provide four classes of authentication information:

Class	Examples
Remembered information	Name, account number, passwords
Possessed objects	Badge, plastic card, key
Personal characteristics	Fingerprint, voiceprint, hand size, signature
Dialog	Through/around the computer

Each authentication class has its inherent weaknesses. Consequently, any particular authentication scheme may use several methods to counteract some of these weaknesses; for example, a user may need a key to a terminal and also have to provide a password. Auditors must understand the weaknesses in each class of authentication information.

The primary problem with *remembered information* as an authentication method is that it can be forgotten. A password is probably the most common method used to authenticate users yet it is a good example of an authentication scheme fraught with problems. First, users tend to choose passwords that are easy to remember. Saltzer and Schroeder [1975] report that a study of 300 self-chosen passwords for a typical time-sharing system showed over 50% of the passwords were short enough to guess by exhaustion, or they could be derived from some attribute of the user; for example, the user's name or birth date. Various schemes have been proposed to overcome this difficulty. Everest [1985] suggests using a mathematical function known to both the user and the system; for example, $z = 4x + 3y + 7$. When the user signs onto the system, the access control mechanism supplies the exogenous values, say, $x = 3$ and $y = 6$. The user must respond with the correct value for the endogenous variable, in this case 37. Saltzer [1974] suggests having the access control mechanism generate random passwords that are pronounceable so there is less temptation for users to write them down. Barton and Barton [1984] suggest that users select passwords based on some piece of information that they hold in long-term memory; for example, the first letter in each word of the title of a favorite song.

The second major defect of passwords is that many access control mechanisms associate passwords with resources instead of associating them with users. Consequently, instead of users having to remember just a single password, they must remember every password associated with each resource they wish to use. This strategy causes several problems. Since most users will have to remember several passwords (some perhaps even hundreds of passwords), a strong incentive exists for users to record the passwords somewhere, thereby increasing the risk of exposure. In addition, the access control mechanism often can exercise only a coarse level of access authorization. For example, if a database administrator wished to exercise access control in a database at the data item level, in some cases this may involve users of the database having to know several hundred passwords. Consequently, access control probably would have to be exercised at a higher level; for example, a user does or does not have access to a file in the database. Finally, administrative procedures for an access control scheme where passwords are associated with resources are awkward and unwieldy. If the administrator responsible for assigning passwords suspects a password is no longer secure, a new password must be assigned and all users of the existing password notified. This may be a very time-consuming process, especially if a password must be changed often.

An alternative scheme is to associate passwords with users rather than resources. Each user has a single password, and associated with each password is a list of entries showing the resources that the user is permitted to access and the action privileges that the user has with respect to these resources. With this scheme, users can change their passwords as frequently as they desire without affecting other users. The access control mechanism must perform more functions since it must couple passwords with access control lists. Nonetheless, passwords are more secure since a user has only one to remember, and the password can be changed easily when the user suspects it is no longer secure.

The primary problem with *possessed objects* as a means of authentication is that they can be lost or stolen. Aside from the inconvenience caused, however, the access control mechanism easily should be able to handle lost or stolen possessed objects. Provided the user immediately notifies the administrator responsible for access controls that the object has been lost or stolen, the access control mechanism can be instructed to reject all further requests for resources made using the object. Moreover, it should log any attempts made to use the object, sound an alarm, and perhaps refuse to eject the object from the reading device.

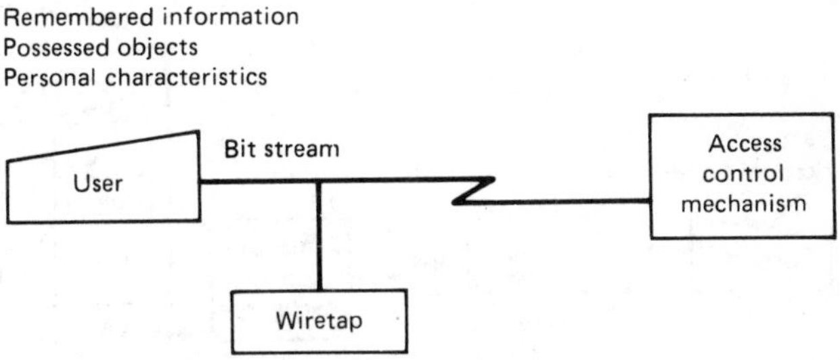

Remembered information
Possessed objects
Personal characteristics

FIGURE 9-2
Using a wiretap to violate the integrity of authentication information.

So far the primary problem with using *personal characteristics* as a means of authentication is that the mechanisms used to read personal characteristics still make errors: they may accept an unauthorized user or reject a legitimate user. Nevertheless, the reliability of the devices is improving.

Passwords, possessed objects, and personal characteristics all have a further weakness. The authentication information eventually is reduced to a bit stream and transmitted to the computer. A would-be penetrator simply has to intercept the bit stream to break security (Figure 9-2). Thus, it is critical for communication lines to be secure if the integrity of authentication information is to be preserved.

To some extent the above problem can be overcome by using *dialog* as a means of authentication. If dialog *through* the computer is used, the user first stores a set of personal characteristics, for example, spouse's name, birth date. When the user signs on, the access control mechanism randomly selects several characteristics from the set of stored characteristics and questions the user about their values. A would-be penetrator has to intercept dialogs over a period and try to construct the set of stored characteristics. Dialog *around* the computer simply involves a security officer asking the questions rather than an access control mechanism.

In all cases users must be sure they are not providing authentication information to a foreign access control mechanism. A penetrator can "masquerade" as a system's access control mechanism, capture a user password, simulate a system crash, and then ask the user to sign on again, this time to the valid access control mechanism.

Saltzer and Schroeder [1975] describe one method for preventing masquerading (Figure 9-3). It requires a terminal be equipped with enciphering circuitry. The terminal user first signs on, bypasses the circuitry, and supplies identification information. The access control mechanism uses the identification information to look up a secured encryption key assigned the user. The access control mechanism then loads the key into its encryption device and starts dialog with the user. In the meantime the user has loaded the encryption key at the terminal, activated the enciphering circuitry, and stands ready for the first response from the access control mechanism. If both the user and the

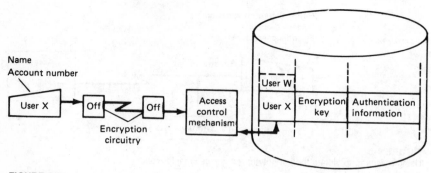

FIGURE 9-3a
User identification in a two-way authentication process.

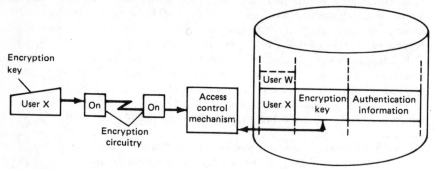

FIGURE 9-3b
Activation of encryption circuitry and load of encryption key by both user and access control mechanism in a two-way authentication process.

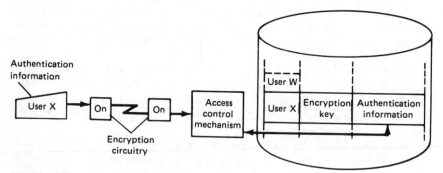

FIGURE 9-3c
Encrypted dialog in a two-way authentication process.

access control mechanism hold the same key, some form of dialog can proceed; otherwise, the user receives an unintelligible bit stream.

To preserve the integrity of authentication information, it should be stored in encrypted form. If passwords are used, for example, a one-way transformation might be employed to convert the cleartext password into ciphertext. Even if a perpetrator discovers the encryption algorithm and the encryption key, the cleartext password is still difficult to recover from the ciphertext password.

Even after having signed on to the system successfully, periodically users should be asked to reauthenticate themselves. This protocol attempts to reduce the exposures that arise when a user fails to sign off after a session is complete and an unauthorized party simply continues under the same session. The access control mechanism also should force users to change their authentication information periodically to reduce the chances of it being compromised.

Object Resources   In a generalized access control mechanism, all resources must be named since the mechanism must couple users with the resources they are permitted to use. Resources can be classified into four types:

Resource classification	Examples
Hardware	Terminals, printers, processors, disks
Software	Application system programs, generalized system software
Commodities	Processor time, storage space
Data	Files, groups, data items

It is important that the access control mechanism have a means of identifying the authenticity of the object resources it provides to a user. One technique used to perpetrate an irregularity is to substitute one object resource for another. For example, a perpetrator may create a program containing fraudulent code with the same name as a system utility. When the operating system calls the system utility, it may be "fooled" into loading the fraudulent program rather than the utility. If the program needing the utility works in trusted mode, the utility might then be used to give the perpetrator special privileges. This irregularity is called a "Trojan horse." To prevent it being perpetrated in the above manner, somehow it must be possible to assign object resources a unique identity that cannot be copied.

Action Privileges   The action privileges assigned a user depend on the user's authority level and the type of resource requested for use. In most cases a user is or is not permitted to use a *hardware* device. There are some refinements. A user may be permitted to use a terminal only in display mode, or the user may not be able to use the light pen attached to the terminal.

Similarly, a user may or may not be able to use a *software* resource. Again, various refinements exist. Some users may be permitted to make copies of the source or object code of a program. Some may only be permitted to view the source code at a terminal. Others may only be allowed to activate the program.

Commodity resources are measured quantitatively. If a user has permission to use a commodity, the amount of the commodity that the user can consume must be specified. Thus, a user is assigned so many seconds of processor time, so many tracks of disk space, a certain number of input/output channels that can be used at one time, etc.

The most complex action privileges relate to the use of *data* resources. Some of the action privileges needed are:

1 Read
   Direct read
   Statistical or aggregate data only
2 Add
   Insert
   Append
3 Modify (write)

These action privileges should apply at an aggregate level and at a detailed level. For example, they may apply at the level of a file so that all the contents of the file are subject to the action privileges assigned the file. Alternatively, they may apply to data items (fields) within a file, different data items within the file having different action privileges assigned.

Conway et al. [1972] also point out the need to distinguish between data independent and data dependent action privileges. Data independent action privileges do not depend on the content of the object data; for example, a user is given or denied access to a salary field in a payroll record. Data dependent action privileges are conditional on the content of the object data; for example, a user has access to a salary field only if it is under $15,000 per year.

The notion of conditional action privileges applies more generally than just data resources. For example, users may be authorized to use greater than two tape units only if the internal memory consumed by their program is less than 10,000 words.

Still another variation on conditional action privileges relates to output. Users may not be permitted access to data depending on the results of a query they specify. This type of control is especially important in maintaining the privacy of individuals' data where statistical databases are used. Chapter 15 discusses these matters further.

One of the most important restrictions on action privileges is a temporal restriction. Users may be granted action privileges only between certain times; for example, they may be permitted to use a terminal and to access a file only during normal working hours. This type of restriction inhibits unauthorized activities outside supervised periods.

Implementing an Access Control Mechanism

The previous sections have outlined the major elements of an access control mechanism. Given the current state of technology, however, a full implementation of this model is extremely costly. In practice, some tradeoffs must be made; overall control must be decreased to reduce costs and improve performance. Unfortunately, systems designers have often placed primary emphasis on performance and paid scant attention to control. Consequently, some widely used systems have serious access control deficiencies. To some extent these deficiencies have been overcome with supplemental software—the so-called access control software (see, for example, Dallas [1983] and Molloy [1983]). When access controls are dispersed across several components, however, the inevitable problems of coordination and control arise.

For any particular computer installation, the auditor's problem is to evaluate whether the tradeoffs made in the access control mechanism are reasonable, given the overall control requirements of the installation. To aid this evaluation, the following sections discuss some of the problems encountered in implementing an access control mechanism.

Open versus Closed Environment An access control mechanism can implement either an open or a closed environment. In an open environment, the mechanism allows users access to a resource unless authorization information specifies the user *cannot* access the resource. In a closed environment, the mechanism will not allow a user to access a resource unless prior authorization information has been provided that specifies the user *may* access the resource. While an open environment allows for an easier implementation of an access control mechanism, only in a closed environment can effective control be exercised over users.

Approaches to Authorization There are two approaches to implementing the authorization module in an access control mechanism: (*a*) a "ticket-oriented" approach and (*b*) a "list-oriented" approach. Conceptually, the distinction between the two approaches can be seen by considering the authorization function in terms of a matrix where the rows represent users, the columns represent resources, and the elements represent the action privileges that each user has with respect to each resource (Figure 9-4). In a ticket-oriented approach to authorization, the access control mechanism assigns users a ticket for each resource they are permitted to access. The mechanism operates via a *row* in the matrix. For each user, a vector of resources that the user can access is maintained together with the action privileges that the user has with respect to each resource. This approach is sometimes called a *capability* system to indicate that a user is assigned a capability with respect to each resource. In a list-oriented approach, the mechanism associates with each resource a list of users who can access the resource and the action privileges that each user has with respect to the resource. That is, the mechanism

Resource User	File X	Editor	File Y	Program 5
User A	Read	Enter		
User B	Statistical Read Only	Enter		Enter
User C		Enter	Append Only	
User D		Enter		Read Source Code Only

FIGURE 9-4
Authorization matrix in an access control mechanism.

operates via a *column* in the matrix. Chapter 13 further explains these approaches in terms of an access control mechanism for virtual memory blocks.

Each implementation approach has its advantages and disadvantages. With a ticket-oriented or capability system, the primary advantage is run-time efficiency. When a user process is executing, its capability list can be stored in some type of fast memory device. When the process seeks access to a resource, the access control mechanism simply looks up the capability list to determine whether the resource is present in the list and, if so, whether the action the user wants to undertake is allowed.

There are several problems with a ticket-oriented system, however. First, it is difficult to revoke capabilities. If the "owner" of a resource initially allows another user to access the resource and then decides to revoke this privilege, the owner must somehow gain access to this user's capability list to delete the capability. Second, a related problem is that the other user may give the capability to access the resource to still other users—that is, the capability may have been propagated. The owner now must determine whether all propagated capabilities are to be revoked, also. Third, even if the owner of the resource revokes a user's capability, the user still may be able to obtain the capability from another user simply by issuing a request for the capability. This issue is discussed further below in terms of the dynamics of authorization.

The primary advantage of a list-oriented system is that it allows efficient administration of capabilities. Each user process has a pointer to the access control list for a resource. Thus, unlike the ticket-oriented system, capabilities for a resource can be better controlled since they are stored in the one place. To determine who has access to a resource, the access control list simply needs to be examined. Similarly, to revoke access to a resource, a user's entry in the access control list simply needs to be deleted.

Unfortunately, a list-oriented system is inefficient during process execution since the access control list for each resource must be examined each time the process seeks access to a resource. Unlike a ticket-oriented system, size constraints limit the extent to which all access control lists can be stored in some fast memory device. To overcome this problem, access control mechanisms may use a combination of ticket-oriented and list-oriented techniques. Capabilities are stored permanently in access control lists so they can be administered efficiently. As a process executes, however, a temporary capability list is created in primary memory. When a process requests access to a resource, the access control mechanism first examines the temporary capability list to see whether the capability is present. If the capability is not present, the mechanism then examines the access control list for the resource. If the capability is present in the access control list, the mechanism loads the capability into the temporary capability list so further access to the access control list is not required.

Size of Protection Domains   The level of protection that an access control mechanism affords a system depends on the size of the protection domain it enforces. In terms of Figure 9-4, the size of a protection domain depends upon how "finely" the rows and columns of the authorization matrix can be specified. If small protection domains can be enforced, for example, a user may constitute a program subroutine and a resource may constitute a data item in a record.

Small protection domains are a desirable goal in access control mechanisms. They allow the *principle of least privilege* to be enforced; that is, at any time a process has been assigned only the necessary and sufficient set of privileges for it to be able to accomplish its purpose. Thus, the risk of the process performing unauthorized actions on a resource is minimized.

Achieving small protection domains, however, is a difficult design problem. As the rows and columns of the authorization matrix are specified more finely, the size of the matrix grows and efficient implementation of the matrix becomes more difficult. Moreover, the access control mechanism now must provide a mechanism for fast *switching* between protection domains. As users and resources are specified more finely, protection domains change more quickly as a system executes its processes.

Conditional Action Privileges   Conditional action privileges can be implemented using special run-time fetch and store functions. Conway et al. [1972] define four sets of functions needed within an access control mechanism:

$$F_t = \text{translation time fetch function}$$
$$S_t = \text{translation time store function}$$
$$F_r = \text{run-time fetch function}$$
$$S_r = \text{run-time store function}$$

The functions F_t and S_t are used for unconditional action privileges and can be generated as object code at compile time. The functions F_r and S_r are used for conditional action privileges. They are called at execution time and apply a Boolean test to determine whether or not action privileges will be granted for the input resources, or in the case of statistical databases, the output results.

Dynamics of Authorization Some difficult implementation problems arise in the area of authorization dynamics. Saltzer and Schroeder [1975] present two cases. First, consider the question of whether user A can access resource Z. A simple check of an entry in the authorization matrix is insufficient. It may show user A has no action privileges with respect to resource Z. However, a further question must be asked: Does user B have action privileges with respect to resource Z, and can user A request user B to assign these action privileges to user A? Furthermore, is the assignment temporary (perhaps leaving no audit trail) or permanent? More complex chains of authorization can be illustrated. Second, what should happen if user B revokes user A's action privileges with respect to resource Z while A is using the resource? If user A is allowed to continue, an integrity violation may occur. If user A is aborted, it may cause substantial disruption. Both these cases demonstrate the need for an external agent—for example, a data administrator—who has a global view of the access authorization needs of the installation, and who can perform a mediating function when conflict arises.

CRYPTOGRAPHIC CONTROLS

Cryptographic controls are becoming increasingly important controls in computer systems as it becomes more difficult to prevent unauthorized access to data. They are used in several subsystems. However, since they underlie several important boundary controls like passwords, personal identification numbers, and digital signatures, they are examined here. Chapter 12 extends the discussion of cryptography to communications controls, and Chapter 14 examines the application of cryptography to databases.

Nature of Cryptography

Cryptology is the science of secret codes. It incorporates the study of cryptography and cryptanalysis. *Cryptography* deals with systems for transforming data into codes (cryptograms) that are meaningless to anyone who does not possess the system for recovering the initial data. *Cryptanalysis* deals with techniques for illegitimately recovering the critical data from cryptograms. The person who designs a cryptographic system (*cryptosystem*) is called a *cryptographer*. A *cryptanalyst* is the antagonist or opponent of a cryptographer.

Cryptography primarily protects the privacy of data. Access and communication controls fail for a variety of reasons: an operating system flaw, a hardware or software fault, misrouting of transmitted data, masquerading, wiretapping. If unauthorized access to data occurs, cryptography renders the data useless.

Cryptographic Techniques

A cryptographic technique transforms (encrypts) data (known as plaintext) into cryptograms (known as ciphertext). The strength of a cryptographic technique is measured in terms of its work factor, that is, the time and cost needed for a cryptanalyst to decipher the ciphertext.

There are three classes of techniques for enciphering plaintext: (*a*) transposition ciphers, (*b*) substitution ciphers, and (*c*) product ciphers. The following sections provide brief introductions to these techniques. Kahn [1967] and Sinkov [1968] give more comprehensive treatments.

Transposition Ciphers Transposition ciphers use some rule to permute the order of characters within a string of data. For example, a simple transposition rule is to swap the position of characters in consecutive pairs. Thus the message:

PEACE IS OUR OBJECTIVE

would be coded as:

EPCA ESIO RUO JBCEITEV

Note that spaces have been counted within a character pair.

Even the more complex transposition ciphers are an easy target for the cryptanalyst. They protect the privacy of data only against the casual browser. When the privacy of data is critical, transposition methods should not be used.

Substitution Ciphers Substitution ciphers retain the position of characters within a message and hide the identity of the characters by replacing them with other characters according to some rule. The key-word Caesar alphabet is an example of a substitution cipher. Using this cipher a key first must be chosen, say, UNCOPYRIGHTABLE (see Van Tassel [1972]). Given the 26 letters of the alphabet, the ciphertext for each letter is derived in the following manner. The first 15 letters of the alphabet are replaced by the key letters. The remaining 11 letters are replaced by those letters not contained in the key, proceeding from the beginning of the alphabet to the end. Thus, the alphabet and its corresponding ciphertext are:

Plaintext: A B C D E F G H I J K L M N O P Q R S T U V W X Y Z
Ciphertext: U N C O P Y R I G H T A B L E D F J K M Q S V W X Z

The message:

PEACE IS OUR OBJECTIVE

would be coded as:

DPUCP GK EQJ ENHPCMGSP

Again, this type of encryption method could be broken easily by a cryptanalyst.

Many other substitution ciphers including the much stronger vigenère and Vernam systems were widely used before the advent of computers (see Kahn [1967]). However, these systems can be broken fairly easily using a computer and again would be of use only for preventing the casual browser from violating the privacy of data.

Product Ciphers   Product ciphers use a combination of transposition and substitution methods. Research has shown that product ciphers are strong; that is, they are resistant to cryptanalysis. Today, product ciphers are the major method of encryption used. The remaining discussion deals only with this class of ciphers.

Choosing a Cipher System

A cipher system has two components: (*a*) an encipherment method or algorithm that constitutes the basic cryptographic technique, and (*b*) a cryptographic key upon which the algorithm operates in conjunction with plaintext to produce ciphertext. Shannon [1949] lists five desirable properties of a cipher system:

Property	Explanation
High work factor	The cipher should be difficult for the cryptanalyst to break.
Small key	The cryptographic key should be small so it can be changed frequently and easily.
Simplicity	Complex cipher systems can be costly.
Low error propagation	Some types of ciphertext depend on previous ciphertext generated for a message. If a chained encryption method is used, corruption of a single bit of ciphertext will cause subsequent decryption to be in error (see Ehrsam et al. [1978]).
Little expansion of message size	Some cipher systems introduce noise into a message to hinder use of statistical techniques to break a code. These techniques examine single-letter frequencies, double-letter frequencies, etc.

Shannon shows these properties cannot all be achieved simultaneously when encrypting natural language. Computer cryptographic methods have traded off either smallness in the key or simplicity in the algorithm. Those cipher systems that use a simple algorithm and a long key are called long-key systems; those that rely on a known algorithm for their strength are called strong-algorithm systems.

In effect the system designer's choice of a cipher system has now been abrogated. During 1977 the National Bureau of Standards (NBS) in the United States accepted as a standard an algorithm developed by IBM. This algorithm is known as the data encryption standard (DES). Both software and hardware implementations of the algorithm exist (see Bright and Enison [1976] and Lennon [1978]).

The DES is a strong-algorithm cipher system. Long-key systems cannot be broken by a cryptanalyst if the key is random and equal in length to the number of characters in the message to be encrypted. However, in most commercial data processing systems a long-key approach is impractical because of the volume of data traffic that occurs. Keys need to be relatively short, of fixed length, and capable of repeated use. For these reasons the NBS chose the strong-algorithm approach. The DES uses a 64-bit key: the algorithm uses 56 bits and 8 bits are parity. The algorithm converts a 64-bit (8-character) block into a 64-bit block of ciphertext by passing through 16 rounds of encipherment.

Public-Key Cryptosystems

One of the major disadvantages of conventional or private-key cryptosystems is that the parties to a communications session must share a common, secret key. The key is used for both encryption and decryption purposes. Ensuring the secure distribution of the key to all parties who need it is a difficult task.

To help overcome this problem, Diffie and Hellman [1976] proposed a new cryptosystem where the encryption and decryption processes were asymmetric; that is, different keys were needed to encrypt and decrypt a message. Moreover, the keys were reversible in the sense that either one could be used to encrypt a message and the other could be used to decrypt the message. By allowing one key to be public and then keeping the other private, a sender S could transmit a message to a receiver R under R's public key, and R could then decrypt the message under R's private key (Figure 9-5). Security efforts, therefore, focus only on the private key that does not have to be distributed.

Several public-key cryptosystems have been proposed. The most widely known is a scheme proposed by Rivest, Shamir, and Adleman [1978], now called the RSA scheme after its founders. The major disadvantage of public-key cryptosystems is that they are slow relative to the processing time required for private-key cryptosystems. Nevertheless, their application is becoming more widespread and faster systems are emerging.

FIGURE 9-5
Public-key cryptosystem.

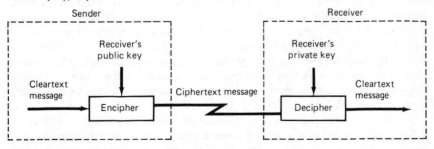

Key Management

In both strong-algorithm and long-key systems, maintaining the secrecy of the cryptographic key is of paramount importance. It cannot be assumed that the algorithm will remain secure. In the case of the DES, the algorithm is publicly known.

To ensure the secrecy of the keys used in cryptography, a system for managing them must be established. Key management involves three functions: (a) key generation, (b) key distribution, and (c) key installation. From an audit viewpoint, evaluating key management is the most critical aspect in assessing the reliability of a cryptosystem.

Key Generation Management of the key generation function involves addressing two questions. First, what keys must be generated? Second, how should these keys be generated? These are relatively complex questions to answer. The following paragraphs provide only a brief introduction to the topic (see, further, Ehrsam et al. [1978] and Matyas and Meyer [1978]).

To examine the question of what keys must be generated, consider a data processing system having a shared database and teleprocessing facilities. At one extreme only one cryptographic key might be used within the system. All data passes through a cryptographic facility, and system users need not concern themselves with encryption processes. This approach has the advantage of simplicity. However, it has several disadvantages. First, the approach only protects the privacy of data against unauthorized parties external to the system. If internal users gain unauthorized access to another user's data, since they have access to the cryptographic key, they can decipher the ciphertext. Second, the approach is susceptible to attack by a cryptanalyst. If the cryptanalyst somehow can submit plaintext to the system (perhaps through illegally obtaining a valid password), and then obtain the corresponding ciphertext (perhaps through wiretapping), the probability of discovering the key is high. Since the key is not specific to a particular terminal session or file, once it is discovered all other users are exposed. Third, the approach does not guard against hardware or software faults such as misrouting a message during data transmission.

To overcome these problems, Ehrsam et al. [1978] suggest another approach that uses multiple keys. They define two classes of keys: (a) key encrypting keys (used to encipher other keys) that remain relatively stable over long periods, and (b) data encrypting keys (used to encipher data) that are time varying and dynamically changing. The latter class of keys remain in existence only as long as the data they protect.

To illustrate the use of a multiple-key cryptosystem, consider a communication session between a host computer and a terminal. Two key encrypting keys are needed: a host master key and a terminal master key. Only a single data encrypting key, a session key, is needed.

The cryptographic protocol for the communication session proceeds as follows. The host master key and the cryptographic algorithm reside in a cryptographic facility that is inaccessible except for encryption/decryption purposes. The host master key exists in the clear (in plaintext); for protection, keys outside the facility are encrypted using the host master key. A copy of the terminal master key exists at the host and the terminal. At the host the terminal master key is encrypted under the host master key. When a session commences, a session key is generated dynamically. The host first decrypts the terminal master key and then encrypts the session key under the terminal master key. The session key encrypted under the master key is then sent to the terminal where it is decrypted. Communications with data encrypted under the session key can then proceed.

The above protocol, in fact, contains a cryptographic weakness that can be overcome through the use of multiple host master keys. The protocol can be modified easily to handle the storage and retrieval of data in a database and communications between two host computers. These matters are left for further study (see Ehrsam et al. [1978], Lempel [1979], Merkle [1978], Popek and Kline [1979], and Simmons [1979]).

Once a decision has been made on what keys must be generated, a decision can be made on how the keys will be generated. In a multiple-key cryptosystem, Matyas and Meyer [1978] suggest generating the host master key by throwing dice or tossing a coin. It is critical this key be generated by a completely random process. All other keys can be generated using a pseudo-random number generator.

Key Distribution The method used to distribute keys throughout the cryptosystem depends on the type of key that must be distributed. Since data encrypting keys are encrypted under key encrypting keys, they can be transmitted through the system over the normal communication paths. Even if they are intercepted by an unauthorized person, they are useless to the person because they are in encrypted form.

Different methods must be used to distribute key encrypting keys throughout the system as they are not protected by encryption. Any of the normal external channels can be used: courier, registered mail, telephone. The key might be fragmented and the different fragments sent over different paths so it would require collusion before a key is compromised. Whatever the method chosen it must be reliable; maintaining the secrecy of key encrypting keys is essential to maintaining the overall secrecy of the cryptosystem.

Key Installation If a key is not generated internally to the cryptosystem, it must be installed physically at the relevant node, for example, a host master key at the host computer and a terminal master key at the associated terminal.

The method used to install the key depends on the hardware/software architecture of the cryptographic facility used. If hard-wired entry of the key to the cryptographic facility is possible, it will be entered by setting switches or dials. If only indirect entry is possible, the key first must be read into memory and a special command then invoked to load it into the cryptographic facility.

Since the cryptographic facility should prevent direct reading of a key once it has been loaded, tests must be undertaken to ensure the key residing in the facility is the one intended. In the case of a host master key, an encrypted value under the key can be computed externally to the system and compared with the result obtained internally to the system using the encrypt function. In the case of terminal master keys, it is important both the host and the terminal have identical versions of the key installed. Some type of handshaking procedure can be designed whereby the host expects a certain value to be transmitted from the terminal that can only be transmitted if the host and terminal have identical keys.

PERSONAL IDENTIFICATION NUMBERS (PINs)

A technique now widely used to authenticate individuals is a PIN. A PIN is simply a type of password; it is a secret number assigned to an individual which, in conjunction with some means of identifying the individual, serves to verify the authenticity of the individual. PINs have been adopted by financial institutions as the primary means of verifying customers in an electronic funds transfer system (EFTS). Typically, customers insert a plastic credit or debit card in some device (identification) and then enter their PIN via a PIN keypad (authentication).

The privacy of PINs is critical. In EFTS, for example, privacy violations can have disastrous consequences. Assume that someone wiretaps a communication line and somehow manages to discover the PINs of many customers. Counterfeit plastic cards could then be produced and, using the PINs obtained, unauthorized withdrawals or charges could be made to customer accounts. Customers would not discover the situation until they inquired on their account balance, received a statement, or received an account overdrawn notification. The initial loss would be the vast sums of money that could be removed from the system. The consequential losses, however, could be more serious. Once the fraud became public, customers might deny transactions recorded in the system. These denials could be genuine because customers have forgotten transactions that they had undertaken, or they may be fraudulent as dishonest cardholders attempt to take advantage of the chaos. In addition, major administrative costs would be associated with discovering the extent of the fraud and handling customer inquiries and complaints. The loss of customer goodwill might be irreparable.

PIN privacy is the joint responsibility of the customer and the institution that relies on the PIN for customer authentication. Customers can be educated to some extent to protect their PINs carefully. Perhaps they are more impressed, however, if they perceive the importance attached to PIN privacy by the issuing institution. In this light, therefore, the following sections examine controls over the management of PINs.

PIN Generation

There are three methods of generating PINs: the first two methods have the institution generating the PIN and conveying it to the customer; the third has the customer generating the PIN and conveying it to the institution.

1 *Derived PIN:* Using this method, the institution generates a PIN based on the customer's account number (or some other identifier). The account number is transformed via the cryptographic algorithm and cryptographic key to produce a PIN of fixed length. The primary advantage of this method is that the PIN need not be stored. When customers enter their PINs, the reference PIN is regenerated based on the entered account number so the validity of the entered PIN can be assessed. The disadvantage is that new account numbers must be issued to customers if their PINs are lost or compromised. Moreover, the cryptographic key cannot be changed without changing all customers' PINs.

2 *Random PIN:* Using this method the institution generates a random number of fixed length to be the PIN. The advantage of this method is that PINs are not tied to account numbers; thus, the PIN can be replaced without having to change the account number. The disadvantage is that the encrypted PIN must be stored for reference purposes in the issuer's database. Thus, the database must be secure against unauthorized access.

3 *Customer-selected PIN:* Using this method, customers choose their PINs to be associated with their accounts. The advantage is that they can choose PINs that are meaningful and easy to remember. Unfortunately, this characteristic is also a shortcoming. Customers tend to select a word or number that is significant—for example, a spouse's name or a birthdate. In addition, as with random PINs, the PIN must be stored somewhere.

Besides choosing the PIN generation method to be used, the institution also must decide on the nature and length of the PIN to be used. PINs can be numeric, alphabetic, or a combination of both. Alphabetics are more useful when customer-selected PINs are employed since a meaningful combination of characters can be chosen. For example, the customer can be instructed to think of two meaningful but unrelated words and combine the first two characters of each if a four-character PIN is used.

As the length of a PIN increases, it is more difficult to determine it by trial and error. However, longer PINs slow down the PIN entry process and increase the overheads associated with PIN verification. Typically, PINs are four to six characters in length. With a four-digit PIN, on average it takes 5000 attempts to determine the PIN through trial and error. If the number of PIN entry attempts is limited before the card is retained and the account closed, the likelihood of an imposter successfully guessing the PIN is low.

PIN Issuance and Delivery

The method of PIN issuance and delivery depends in part on the method used to generate PINs. If the institution generates either a derived PIN or a random PIN, the PIN is conveyed to the customer using a PIN mailer. A PIN mailer is a two-part form where the first part contains only the customer's name and address for mailing or identification purposes and the second part contains only the customer's PIN (Figure 9-6). PIN mailers are either given to customers

FIGURE 9-6a
First part of two-part PIN mailer (*SG10 Building Society*).

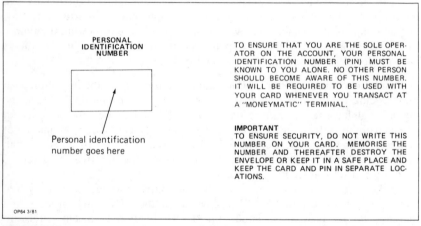

FIGURE 9-6b
Second part of two-part PIN mailer (*SG10 Building Society*).

when they open their accounts or mailed to customers subsequently. If they are mailed subsequently, they should not be mailed with the customer's card. Furthermore, even if the card and PIN are mailed separately, they should not be mailed at the same time in case both are delivered together and they are fraudulently intercepted.

If customers select their PINs, there are four ways in which they can convey their PINs to the institution:

1 *Mail solicitation:* Using this method, the institution mails a PIN mailer plus an opaque return-address envelope to the customer. The customer tears off and discards the first part of the PIN mailer. The second part contains a reference number cryptographically generated from the customer's account number plus a box in which customers are instructed to write their chosen PIN. Customers insert the completed second part of the PIN mailer in the return-address envelope and mail it back to the institution. They are admonished not to put their name and address or account number on the envelope or the PIN mailer. Upon receipt of the envelope at the institution, at least two employees who were not responsible for the initial mailing open the envelope and enter the encrypted reference number plus the chosen PIN into the system via a secure terminal. The PIN mailer is then destroyed. At no stage can the chosen PIN be associated with a customer's account number.

2 *Telephone solicitation:* Using this method, customers call a telephone number after they have received their PIN mailer and selected a PIN. The encrypted reference number provided on the second part of the PIN mailer plus the PIN are keyed in or spoken to an audio-response system. Again, customers are admonished to provide only their reference number and their chosen PIN. At the institution, at least two employees who were not responsible for the initial mailing listen to the recorded PINs, enter them at a secure terminal, and then erase the recording.

3 *PIN entry via a secure terminal:* Using this method customers present themselves at the institution and enter their chosen PIN at a secure terminal. Their cards are mailed or given to them initially. When they request PIN entry, they must prove their identity to an official of the institution who then activates the terminal into PIN selection mode. Customer identification is required in case the card has been stolen. Alternatively, the institution can issue an initial PIN that can be changed by the customer. Using this method, intervention by an official is not required since knowledge of the initial PIN is taken as proof of identity.

4 *PIN entry at the issuer's facility:* To simplify the PIN solicitation process, the customer may be required to select a PIN at the time an account is opened. This approach also enables the encrypted PIN to be stored on the card prior to its issue. Again, a PIN mailer can be used, only this time the first part contains the customer's account number in cleartext form and the second part contains the cryptographically derived reference number plus a space for inserting the chosen PIN. The customer privately chooses a PIN, places the second part in an opaque envelope, and deposits it in a special mailbox provided for this purpose. The first part containing the account number is submitted with the account application. Later, the system decrypts the reference number, associates the chosen PIN with the account number, encrypts the PIN, and stores it securely with the account number. Alternatively, customers can enter their chosen PINs themselves via a secure terminal at the issuer's facility.

Whatever the PIN issuance and delivery technique used, it is especially important to exercise control over PIN mailers. It is desirable for the PIN mailer printer to be an integral part of a secure cryptographic facility. To activate the printer, it should be necessary for two independent employees to submit their own secret identification number to the facility. In addition, dual control must be exercised over the dispatch and receipt of PIN mailers.

The customer also should be notified when a PIN has been established for their account number, though they should not be notified of the PIN itself. If customers have not taken any actions to establish a PIN and they receive such notification, they should be instructed to contact the issuer institution immediately.

PIN Validation

The usual procedure upon PIN entry is to allow the customer a certain number of attempts to submit a valid PIN before the card is retained and the account is closed. This procedure is somewhat disputed. With a four-digit PIN, on average it would take considerable time to obtain the PIN through trial and error. If the card is retained, procedures must be established for safeguarding and returning the card to reduce the likelihood of employee irregularities. Moreover, cards can be reproduced anyway so a determined imposter would not be deterred. From the customer's viewpoint, it is frustrating to have a card retained after two or three attempts at PIN entry. The customer may have a temporary memory loss which might be overcome if several attempts at PIN entry can be made. If only a small number of attempts are allowed, there is an incentive to write the PIN down somewhere as a memory aid. It seems best to allow a reasonable number of PIN entry attempts (say, 5 to 10), to close the account after the limit has been reached, and not to retain the card. A further control is to limit the amount of money that can be transacted in any one day under the PIN.

There are two ways of validating a PIN upon entry: local PIN validation and interchange PIN validation. Local PIN validation is undertaken when the PIN is entered at a terminal controlled by the PIN issuer. Interchange PIN validation occurs when the PIN is entered at a terminal controlled by an institution other than the PIN issuer and this institution is a joint participant in an EFTS. The following sections describe how each type of validation may be undertaken.

Local PIN Validation   Local PIN validation can be undertaken in an online or offline mode. In online mode, validation occurs at the issuing institution's host computer; that is, the terminal transmits the PIN to the mainframe for verification purposes. Two options are available. First, the terminal encrypts the entered PIN and sends it to the host. The host decrypts the PIN under the terminal key, encrypts the PIN under the host key, and then compares it with either a stored PIN or a PIN derived cryptographically from the account number. Second, if the encrypted PIN is stored on the card used for identification purposes, the stored encrypted PIN and the entered PIN encrypted under the terminal key can be transmitted to the host. The host decrypts the entered PIN under the terminal key and then encrypts it under the host key for comparison with the encrypted PIN obtained from the card.

In offline mode, the terminal validates the entered PIN. This means that either the encrypted PIN must be stored on the card or the PIN must be a cryptographic function of the account number. In both cases the terminal must have the master key under which PINs are encrypted by the institution. Consequently, offline validation creates greater exposures for the institution since the master key must be distributed to each terminal and compromise of one terminal puts all PINs at risk.

Interchange PIN Validation   In an interchange environment, a fundamental principle is that PINs must be validated by the issuing institution and not the acquiring institution. Otherwise, compromise of any terminal in the EFTS exposes the PINs of all participants in the network. Thus, the acquiring terminal must encrypt the PIN under its own key and send the transaction to a switch for routing to the issuing institution. Since the transaction may pass through several nodes before it reaches its destination, the PIN may be decrypted and encrypted several times under various interchange keys. To identify genuine PIN entry errors, a PIN checkdigit may be used that can be validated by the acquiring terminal. In this way, a miskeying, for example, can be identified quickly.

PIN Transmission

Unless the privacy of a PIN can be assumed when it is transmitted over some medium, it must be encrypted prior to transmission. The cipher generated must be unique for each transmission of the PIN; otherwise imposters who wiretap a communication line may substitute the encrypted PIN in a transaction they generate on an account number with an invalid PIN. Similarly, imposters may open a valid account and passively wiretap the communication line to determine the ciphertext generated upon submission of their PIN. Once another customer's PIN generates the same ciphertext, they could use their own PIN against that customer's account number to initiate fraudulent transactions.

A unique cipher can be obtained by making the encrypted PIN value a function of some data item that changes with each transaction, for example, a terminal-generated sequence number. Alternatively, a different cryptographic key can be used for each transmission. The new cryptographic key is generated cryptographically as a function of the old key. Since the host knows the initial key and the cryptographic generation function, it can update the terminal key upon each transmission from the terminal. These techniques also prevent fraudulent replay of a transaction whereby a terminal is isolated from its host and a previously approved transaction is replayed as a new instance of the transaction.

PIN Processing

The only kind of processing that needs to be undertaken on a PIN is encryption and decryption of the PIN and comparison of an entered PIN with a reference PIN. Once entered, the PIN should be encrypted immediately by a secure cryptographic facility, and thenceforth it should never exist in the clear except inside a secure cryptographic facility. Whenever an entered PIN must be compared with a reference PIN, the encrypted versions rather than the clear versions of the PINs should be compared.

PIN Storage

If a PIN is not a cryptographic function of the account number and the cryptographic key only, it must be stored for reference purposes. In addition, it may be necessary to store a PIN as part of the audit trail maintained at a terminal or a node in a network. The audit trail may be required to enable the transit of transactions between network nodes to be verified at a later stage, or it may be part of a store-and-forward facility in a communication network.

Whenever a PIN is stored, it must be encrypted and, to prevent substitution of the PIN, it must be encrypted as a function of the account number. That is, the encrypted PIN is derived from the cleartext PIN, the cryptographic key, and the account number (or some other card- or account-related data). Either reversible or irreversible encryption can be used on the PIN. Reversible encryption has two advantages. First, the cryptographic key can be changed periodically to reduce the likelihood of compromise. Second, customers' PINs can be reissued if they forget them. The disadvantage is that the cleartext PIN can be determined from the ciphertext PIN if the cryptographic key is compromised. This disadvantage is overcome by irreversible encryption. However, forgotten PINs cannot be recovered when irreversible encryption is used. Furthermore, the cryptographic key used in irreversible encryption must be retained for the life of the PIN, which increases the risk of compromise. To make compromise more difficult, reversible encryption might be applied to the ciphertext PIN generated via irreversible encryption.

Once short- or long-term storage of a PIN is complete, the storage medium should be degaussed or overwritten immediately. This cannot be accomplished unless careful records are kept of the locations at which PINs are stored. In general, however, it should be impossible to recover either cleartext or ciphertext PINs by scavenging the residue on storage media.

PIN Change

If customers are permitted to change their PINs, the change must be performed through the issuer's system and not any other system in the interchange environment. As discussed earlier, other networks simply should provide a secure carrier service from the viewpoint of the issuer institution in an EFTS.

PIN change can be accomplished using the same techniques (described previously) for PIN generation, issuance, and delivery. In the case of a derived PIN, the issuer must change one of the parameters used to generate the PIN. In the case of a random PIN, a new random number is generated. In the case of a customer-selected PIN, the customer simply chooses a new PIN. Changed derived or random PINs are then communicated to the customer via a PIN mailer. Changed customer-selected PINs are solicited (either) by mail or telephone or entered at a secure terminal after the customer receives the cryptographically generated reference number. If the PIN is stored on the identification card used, the card must be reissued. In all cases the customer should be notified independently that a PIN change has occurred, and clear instructions should be printed on a notification letter advising the customer to inform the issuer immediately if a PIN change had not been requested.

PIN Replacement

PIN replacement occurs when PINs are forgotten or compromised. If PINs are forgotten, it is better to reissue the same PIN since customers find it easier to recall the old PIN rather than to memorize a new PIN. Moreover, identification cards do not have to be reissued if PINs are stored on the cards. Customers are reminded of their PINs by sending out a PIN mailer prepared and dispatched under the secure conditions described previously.

If a PIN is exposed, the extent of the exposure determines the actions that must be taken. If all PINs are at risk, a new cryptographic key must be chosen and new PINs issued to every customer. Clearly, the consequences are serious when all PINs are exposed. However, if only a single PIN is exposed, a new PIN has to be issued. The procedures for issuing a new PIN are the same as those for a PIN change.

PIN Termination

PIN termination occurs when customers close their accounts, new PINs are issued, or PINs are destroyed accidentally. Whenever accounts are closed or new PINs are issued, all trace of the deactivated PINs should be removed from the system. If PINs are destroyed accidentally through, say, a hardware failure, a backup copy of the PIN file is required to restore the system. The backup copy of the PIN file must be kept under strict security.

DIGITAL SIGNATURES

When messages are exchanged via letters or contracts are written and exchanged, the sender of the letter and the parties to the contract sign their names to the documents used. The signature serves two important purposes. First, it establishes the authenticity of the individuals involved. Of course, signatures can be forged; so additional measures to establish authenticity are often used. Second, it prevents the sender of a letter or a party to a contract disavowing the letter or denying they were a party to the contract.

Establishing the authenticity of individuals and preventing the disavowal of messages or contracts are still critical requirements when data is exchanged in electronic form. Indeed, given that the parties are often physically remote and sometimes in conflict with each other, these requirements become even more important. A counterpart is needed for the analog signature used on documents. In computer systems this counterpart is the digital signature. Unlike an analog signature, however, a digital signature is simply a string of 0s and 1s rather than a line drawn on a page. Furthermore, digital signatures are not constant like analog signatures—they vary across messages; and, unlike analog signatures, it should be impossible to forge a digital signature.

Public-Key Approaches

Digital signatures can be established using either private-key or public-key cryptosystems. To date, however, the private-key approaches tend to be somewhat awkward and unwieldy (see, further, Meyer and Matyas [1982]). Thus, public-key approaches are more popular.

Public-key cryptosystems can be used to establish secret messages, signed messages, and signed, secret messages (see Denning [1983]). Chapter 12 examines secret messages in more detail, but it is useful to see the transition from secret messages to signed messages to appreciate how public-key cryptosystems can be used to establish digital signatures.

If a sender S wants to send a *secret* message M to a receiver R using a public-key cryptosystem, S first obtains the public key Pu_R of R. Next S encrypts the message M under R's public key and sends the encrypted message $Pu_R(M)$ to R. R decrypts $Pu_R(M)$ using R's private key Pr_R. Thus, $Pr_R[Pu_R(M)]$ $\rightarrow M$. Since Pu_R is known, there must be enough uncertainty about M for the secrecy of M to be maintained. Otherwise, M can be discovered by enciphering various candidates for M under Pu_R until the ciphertext matches that produced for M. A variable quantity, such as a random number generated by S, can be appended to M and stripped off after M is deciphered.

To send a *signed* message to R, S encrypts M under S's private key Pr_S. The encrypted message $Pr_S(M)$ can be deciphered by R using S's public key. Thus, $Pu_S[Pr_S(M)] \rightarrow M$. It is difficult for R to forge a message and claim it was sent from S since, without knowing Pr_s, it is impossible to produce ciphertext which, when decrypted under Pu_s, will be meaningful. Thus, Pr_s attaches a digital signature to M that authenticates S as the originator of the message. Note, however, that since Pu_s is public, the cleartext M can be recovered by anyone and so the secrecy of M is not preserved.

To send a *signed, secret* message to R, S undertakes the following steps (Figure 9-7):

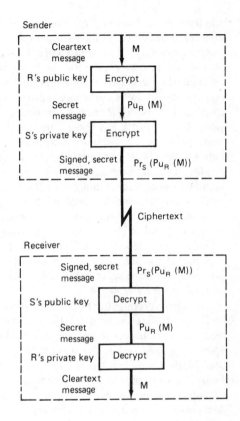

FIGURE 9-7
Cryptosystem for signed, secret messages.

1 Encrypts the message under R's public key. The ciphertext $Pu_R(M)$ is produced. This preserves M's secrecy since only R can decipher the message using R's private key Pr_R.

2 Encrypts the ciphertext $Pu_R(M)$ under S's private key. The ciphertext $Pr_S[Pu_R(M)]$ is produced. This attaches a digital signature to the message.

To retrieve the message, R undertakes the following steps:

1 Deciphers $Pr_S[Pu_R(M)]$ under S's public key. Thus, $Pu_S[Pr_S(Pu_R(M)] \rightarrow Pu_R(M)$.

2 Deciphers $Pu_R(M)$ under R's private key. Thus, $Pr_R[Pu_R(M)] \rightarrow M$.

Only if M is meaningful is the authenticity of S as the sender of the message established. Moreover, only if M is meaningful is R assured that the message M has not been altered in transit. Again, R cannot forge a message from S. If a dispute over message authenticity arises, R must reveal Pr_R to an arbitrator and demonstrate that a ciphertext message decrypted under Pu_s is then meaningful when decrypted under Pr_R. For this to occur, the message must have been encrypted under Pr_s, which supposedly is known only to S.

Unfortunately, there are two disadvantages to the above scheme for sending signed, secret messages. First, as discussed earlier, public-key cryptosystems are still slow compared with private-key cryptosystems. Second, in case a dispute arises over message authenticity, R must maintain a copy of $Pr_s[Pu_R(M)]$. Note, R cannot reproduce the message on the basis of $Pu_R(M)$ since R does not know Pr_s. If the audit trail of messages must be accessed frequently—say, for inquiry purposes—decryption operations will introduce high overheads. R can reduce these overheads by storing the cleartext M [or $Pu_R(M)$ if stored message secrecy is required], but storage overheads are now incurred since both M and $Pr_s[Pu_R(M)]$ must be retained.

To help overcome the problem of speed, one approach is to use a private-key cryptosystem in conjunction with a public-key cryptosystem. When a session between S and R commences, S transmits a session key K_S to R encrypted under R's private key Pr_R. R applies its private key Pr_R to $Pu_R(K_S)$ to retrieve K_S. Messages are then encrypted and decrypted using K_S. This system preserves message secrecy but it does not provide a signature as R could forge a message under K_s.

To help overcome the problem of storage overheads, a technique described by Davies [1983] can be used. First, S computes a checksum C for message M using h, a publicly known one-way hashing function, and I, an initial seed. Thus, $C = h(M,I)$. For the scheme to be useful, the size of C must be smaller than M; for example, C might be a single, 64-bit block. Next, S encrypts C and I under S's private key. R deciphers $Pr_s(C,I)$ under S's public key to retrieve C and I. S then sends the message M encrypted under R's public key. R decrypts this message $Pu_R(M)$ using R's private key. Finally, R computes C using h, M, and I to determine whether the computed C matches the value of C sent by S. If the C's match, the authenticity of S is established.

Note, R need retain only the message M [or $Pu_R(M)$ if stored encryption is required] and the signature $Pr_s(C,I)$. S cannot disavow the message M if R can recompute C. Thus, storage space requirements are reduced. Note, also, that h must be a one-way function to prevent an eavesdropper applying Pu_s to $Pr_s(C,I)$ and then taking the inverse $h^{-1}(C,I)$ to obtain M. In addition, to prevent message forgeries, it must not be possible to produce the same C from another message M' and the same I. Otherwise, R can encrypt M' under Pu_R and claim it was sent by S.

Arbitrated Schemes

Even with digital signatures, a sender S wishing to renege or disavow a contract can simply make their private key Pr_s public and claim the message has been forged. To prevent S adopting this strategy, an arbitrator A can be introduced as a mediator when S sends a message M to a receiver R. The arbitrator fulfills the role of a witness in a conventional contract.

Arbitrated schemes can be used for both private-key and public-key digital signature systems (see Akl [1983]). The following protocol illustrates an arbitrated scheme with a public-key approach:

1 S first computes $C_1 = Pu_R[Pr_s(M)]$. This provides a signed, secret message for R from S.

2 S then computes $C_2 = Pr_s(m')$, where m' is the concatenation of m (m = sender's name, receiver's name, message sequence number) and C_1.

3 S now sends the pair (m, C_2) to an arbitrator A.

4 A deciphers C_2 by applying S's public key. Thus, $Pu_s(C_2) \rightarrow m'$ where m' = m, C_1.

5 A authenticates and validates the message sent from S by comparing the m obtained from deciphering C_2 with the m sent in the pair (m, C_2).

6 A now computes $Pr_A(M')$, where $M' = m$, C_1, time and date of receipt, verification stamp.

7 A sends $Pr_A(M')$ to R.

8 R deciphers $Pr_A(M')$ using A's public key. Thus, $Pu_A[Pr_A(M')] \rightarrow M'$. R checks the verification stamp provided by A and the time and date of receipt.

9 Next, R deciphers C_1 by first applying R's private key and then applying S's public key. Thus, $Pr_R(C_1) \rightarrow Pr_s(M)$, and $Pu_s[Pr_s(M)] \rightarrow M$.

The above scheme has the following advantages. First, S, R, and A do not have to share any information prior to the communications session taking place. Second, messages cannot be dated incorrectly, even when Pr_s is compromised. Third, the content of the message is not known to A. Fourth, collusion is prevented, except between S and A. Both could claim Pr_s and Pr_A had been compromised and a fraudulent message sent to R. However, given the low probability of both Pr_s and Pr_A being compromised at the same time, both S and A would have substantial difficulties establishing their credibility.

Some Exposures

Digital signatures are exposed when either fake public keys are used or private keys are compromised. The former case could occur, for example, if a perpetrator P actively wiretapped a communications line, intercepted a request from a sender S to a key server K for receiver R's public key, and returned a fake public key to S. P could then decipher messages from S sent under the fake public key. The latter case could occur, for example, through poor key management. The private key might not be generated and installed using a secure cryptographic facility.

Two countermeasures can be used to help overcome the problem of fake public keys. The first requires the key server K to issue a public key inside a signed certificate. Assume, for example, that S requests R's public key from K. K encrypts R's public key and a time stamp T under K's private key. Thus, K transmits the message $Pr_K(T, Pu_R)$ to S. S deciphers the message using K's public key Pu_K. The time stamp validates the currency of the certificate since a wiretapper may replay an old certificate containing a public key for R where the corresponding private key has been compromised.

The second countermeasure is to have mass distribution of public keys. Keys might be issued periodically in an official directory, or they could be published in a widely read newspaper. Updates could be printed periodically, say, daily or weekly.

To help overcome the problem of a private key being compromised, a signature certificate can be used. The following protocol is an adaptation of one provided by Denning [1983] to send a signed, secret message with certificates:

1 S generates a seed I and computes a checksum C using a one-way hashing function h. Thus, $C = h(M,I)$, where M is the message to be sent.

2 S signs the checksum. Thus, $X = Pr_s(C,I)$.

3 S sends X to the key server K and requests K to send a public key certificate for R, the receiver of the message, and a signature certificate for X.

4 K computes the following:

   a $P = Pr_K(T_1, Pu_R)$—public key certificate for R

   b $G = Pr_K(T_2, Pu_s, X)$—signature certificate for X

   where T_1 and T_2 are time stamps.

5 K sends P and G to S.

6 Using K's public key, S deciphers P and G and checks the time stamps T_1 and T_2. Thus:

   a $Pu_K(P) \rightarrow T_1, Pu_R$

   b $Pu_K(G) \rightarrow T_2, Pu_s, X$

7 S computes the ciphertext $Pu_R(M)$.

8 S transmits the ciphertext message $Pu_R(M)$ and the signature certificate G to R.

9 R deciphers the message and the signature certificate:

   a $Pr_R[Pu_R(M)] \rightarrow M$

   b $Pu_K(G) \rightarrow T_2, Pu_s, X$

10 R checks the time stamp T_2 for currency.

11 R then validates S's signature by computing:

   a $Pu_s(X) \rightarrow C,I$

   b $C = h(M,I)$.

The retrieved C and the computed C should match.

A more serious situation occurs if the key server's private key is compromised. The perpetrator can now forge public key certificates such that the contents of a message intended for a receiver can now be deciphered. Even more serious is a situation where some user's private key is also known. The perpetrator can now forge signature certificates as well. Thus, the perpetrator can take any message and make it legally binding on the user whose private key has been compromised. The perpetrator simply computes a checksum for the message, signs the checksum, and issues a signature certificate (as in steps 1 to

4 above). While the probability of key compromise might be small, nevertheless the consequences are so serious that a mechanism for detecting compromises and recovering from compromises must be established.

PLASTIC CARDS

Whereas PINs are used for authentication, plastic cards are used for identification purposes, although cards may store information used in the authentication process. Control over plastic cards, therefore, is an essential element of the overall set of boundary controls exercised in electronic funds transfer systems. The following sections briefly examine controls over five phases in the life cycle of a card: (*a*) application for the card, (*b*) preparation of the card, (*c*) issue of the card, (*d*) use of the card, and (*e*) return/destruction of the card.

Application for a Card

Unsolicited cards should never be mailed to a customer. The risk of interception and improper use of the card is too high. Instead, cards should be issued only on the basis of a properly completed application form. The application form must state clearly the duties and responsibilities of the customer who holds the card and the issuing institution. Customers have to understand fully the liabilities they incur when possessing a card before they make application for a card.

Upon receipt of the signed application form, the veracity of the customer must be checked—creditworthiness, previous credit card refusals, etc. When all relevant information has been gathered, a supervisor checks the associated documentation and either approves or refuses the issue of a card to the customer.

Preparation of the Card

Once an application has been approved, a card can be prepared. This involves embossing name, account number, and expiration date information on the card, and writing similar information on the magnetic stripes on the back of the card. Typically, the magnetic stripe contains three tracks for writing information, but institutions vary in terms of which tracks they use and the information they write on the tracks. Some institutions use a "smart" card, that is, a card which contains a microprocessor. The capabilities of the microprocessor vary, but it might contain information such as the customer's PIN, account balance, and a record of transactions made. This information is secure in that it cannot be read or changed. Thus, the microprocessor allows a certain amount of validation to occur at the terminal where the card is entered rather than having to transmit validation requests to a host.

Basic inventory control procedures should be exercised over the stock of plastic cards. Blank cards must be effectively controlled. The number of blank cards issued must correspond to the number of approved applications. Spoiled cards should be destroyed under dual control and the event properly documented as a basis for issuing another blank card. Encoding equipment must also be controlled. If an outside card vendor is used to prepare cards, some assurance should be obtained that the vendor exercises effective controls over card preparation. In this light, a third-party audit report might be required. When an outside vendor is used, shipment of applications and receipt of cards must be carefully controlled.

Issue of the Card

Controls over the issue of cards seek to ensure that the card arrives safely in the hands of the authorized customer. At the outset, the mailing of cards must be carefully controlled to ensure that all cards which have been prepared on the basis of an authorized application are dispatched to customers. A dishonest employee should not be able to intercept a card prior to its mailing.

Emory [1983] suggests three controls to help ensure cards reach customers once they have been mailed. First, premailers might be used to detect invalid addresses. Second, registered or certified mail might be used to those postal areas where there is a high rate of mail loss or mail theft. Third, when a large number of cards is to be mailed, postal authorities might be notified so they can ensure effective control over the mailing exists.

Controls also must exist over returned cards. Cards should be mailed in envelopes with a return address that does not identify the issuing institution. Returned cards should be controlled and investigated by a group not responsible for the initial mailing of the cards or the day-to-day operations of the system. If, after some period, the address of a customer cannot be identified, the card must be destroyed under supervision.

Use of the Card

Controls over card use seek to ensure that customers safeguard their card so it does not fall into unauthorized hands. If a card is lost or stolen, the information on the card can be "skimmed"; that is, the information on the magnetic stripe can be read and a fraudulent card produced with the same information. If the authorized card is then returned to the customer, the existence of a fraudulent card may not be identified until unauthorized withdrawals of monies have occurred.

The primary control to be exercised over card use is customer education. The issuing institution must make substantial efforts to alert customers to the importance of safeguarding their cards. It is also important that the issuing institution shows, through example, that it regards security over cards as an important matter. If customers perceive the issuing institution takes card security seriously, they may be motivated to exercise careful control over their cards themselves.

Card Return/Destruction

Although the policy may be difficult to reinforce, some organizations require customers to return their cards if they close their accounts. Before customers can close their accounts, they must present their cards. Of course, to avoid the inconvenience of returning cards, customers may withdraw all monies from their accounts and leave the accounts dormant. Nevertheless, if cards are returned, proper records must be kept of the return, and careful control must be kept over the destruction of cards. It should not be possible for an employee to remove a returned card and use it for unauthorized purposes.

AUDIT TRAIL CONTROLS

Recall, Chapter 2 identified two types of audit trail that must exist in each subsystem: (a) an accounting audit trail to show the source and nature of data and processes that update the database; and (b) an operations audit trail that maintains a record of attempted or actual resource consumption within a system. The following sections briefly discuss each type of audit trail for the boundary subsystem.

Accounting Audit Trail

All activities undertaken by the boundary subsystem should be recorded in the accounting audit trail so the source and nature of all changes to the database can be identified. The following sorts of data must be kept:

1 Identity of the would-be user of the system
2 Authentication information supplied
3 Resources requested
4 Action privileges requested
5 Terminal identifier
6 Start and finish time
7 Number of sign-on attempts
8 Resources provided/denied
9 Action privileges allowed/denied

This data allows management or the auditor to recreate the time series of events that occurs when a user attempts to gain access to and employ system resources. Periodically the audit trail should be analyzed to detect any control weaknesses in the system.

Public audit trails are an important control in systems where digital signatures are used for authentication purposes. Denning [1983] identifies three events that should be recorded in the public audit trail:

1 Registration of public keys
2 Registration of signatures
3 Notification of key compromises

Only the key server can record these events. Moreover, while all parties to the system can access the audit trail, they can do so only via the key server. As an additional control to prevent unauthorized modifications to the audit trail, Denning [1983] suggests that it be stored sequentially on a write-once device such as an optical disk. Each event is time stamped by the key server, and entries are recorded in ascending order by time.

The public audit trail is used in the following ways. First, any user can register a public key with the key server. The key server validates this registration by sending back the public key to the user encrypted under the server's private key. The user decrypts the certificate under the server's public key to check the validity of the public key received by the server. Second, any user in the system can request another user's public key. The server simply obtains the latest public key from the audit trail and sends it inside a certificate to the user who requests the key. Third, signature certificates provided by the key server are recorded in the audit trail so a particular private key is bound to a public key at a point in time. Finally, users notify the key server when their private keys are compromised, and the key server writes a key compromise message on the audit trail. The user's liability for messages signed under the compromised key is then limited.

Operations Audit Trail

Much of the data collected in the accounting audit trail also serves the purposes of the operations audit trail. For example, auditors might investigate whether users are having difficulty with the sign-on protocol in an online realtime system. An examination of the number of sign-on attempts may indicate the protocol is difficult to use. Similarly, an analysis of start and finish times for the boundary subsystem may indicate that substantial resources are being spent in carrying out identification and authentication functions.

EXISTENCE CONTROLS

If the boundary subsystem fails, would-be users of a computer system cannot establish an interface to the system they seek to use. Failure can occur in any of the boundary subsystem components: circuitry in a terminal may malfunction, the access control software may fail, an automatic teller machine or point-of-sale device may malfunction, a dial-up modem may fail, a cryptographic facility may start to operate incorrectly, a voice response system may fail, etc.

In some ways, existence controls in the boundary subsystem are simpler than those in other subsystems. If failure occurs during subsystem processing and it is possible to recover—for example, an operating system crash occurs—existence controls in many boundary subsystems do not attempt to restore processing to the point of failure. Instead, users must commence the sign-on process again. This usually imposes little cost on the user since boundary subsystem functions are accomplished quickly. Furthermore, it protects against a situation where the original user has left and been replaced by another user.

If a hardware component fails, often a duplicate component is available; for example, another terminal or automatic teller machine can be used. Where duplicate hardware is not readily available, however, regular maintenance acts as a preventive control. In some cases, careful control must be exercised over maintenance activities. For example, if an automatic teller machine fails late at night in a high-crime area, maintenance should not be undertaken until the following day.

SUMMARY

The boundary subsystem is responsible for establishing the interface between a would-be user of a system and the system itself. The primary purpose of controls in the boundary subsystem is to identify and to authenticate users and to assign them action privileges.

Several major types of controls are used in the boundary subsystem. First access controls prevent unauthorized access to and use of resources. For example, plastic cards and personal identification numbers are a primary means of identifying and authenticating users in electronic funds transfer systems. Digital signatures can also be used to prevent messages being forged or disavowed. All these controls rely to some extent on cryptographic techniques to preserve the integrity of data transmitted between one user and another. Second, as with all subsystems, events in the boundary subsystem must be recorded in an audit trail. If digital signatures are used, a public audit trail might be employed to record public keys, signature certificates, and key compromises. Third, existence controls must also be provided to restore the boundary subsystem in the event of failure.

REVIEW QUESTIONS

9-1 Briefly describe the functions of the boundary subsystem. Give two components that perform basic activities in the boundary subsystem.

9-2 Why are boundary subsystem controls becoming more important? Do you expect this trend to continue? If so, why?

9-3 What is meant by an access control? Why are boundary controls needed in most computer systems? Can you think of any computer systems that might purposely decrease the level of access control they exercise?

9-4 What functions should an access control mechanism perform? Give two components in a computer system where the auditor is likely to find an access control mechanism, and describe the types of resources the access control mechanism is likely to protect.

9-5 Outline the advantages and disadvantages of associating passwords with resources rather than users.

9-6 Distinguish between identification and authentication. Is there a relationship between the two? In setting up an authentication scheme, what would be the major factor(s) influencing you to choose personal characteristics in preference to possessed objects as a means of authentication?

9-7 Explain why authentication should be a two-way process: the computer authenticating itself and users authenticating themselves.

9-8 To gain unauthorized access to a file, you decide to carry out a masquerading scheme. Why is it important the terminal user not know you have carried out the scheme? How would you attempt to prevent the user from knowing you have carried out a masquerading scheme?

9-9 Why might passwords be stored after they have been encrypted using a one-way transformation? Can you think of any disadvantages to this scheme?

9-10 Why should an access control mechanism periodically ask users to reauthenticate themselves? How might users be asked to reauthenticate themselves?

9-11 Why is it important that object resources be identified uniquely in a computer system and that the identity of each object resource cannot be forged?

9-12 Which object resource typically has the most complex action privileges applying to its use? Briefly explain why this is the case.

9-13 Briefly explain the difference between conditional and unconditional action privileges. Give two examples of fields in an accounts receivable file where conditional action privileges might be required.

9-14 What is the difference between a closed and an open environment when access controls are to be exercised? From a control perspective, which type of environment is more preferable? Why?

9-15 Briefly explain the difference between a "ticket-oriented approach" and a "list-oriented" approach to access authorization. Outline the relative advantages and disadvantages of each approach.

9-16 What is meant by a "protection domain"? Why are small protection domains desirable? What performance requirement does the implementation of small protection domains place on an access control mechanism? How are small protection domains related to the principle of least privilege?

9-17 Briefly explain how the dynamics of authorization can make it difficult to determine whether a user has access to a particular resource at a point in time.

9-18 Define the following terms:
a Cryptology
b Cryptography
c Cryptanalysis
d Cryptogram

9-19 Briefly explain the difference between transposition ciphers, substitution ciphers, and product ciphers. Which type of cipher is used most often in cryptosystems? Why?

9-20 What is meant by the "work factor" for a cipher system? Explain the relationship between the work factor and the size of the cryptographic key.

9-21 Briefly explain the difference between a strong-algorithm cryptosystem and a long-key cryptosystem. Why did the National Bureau of Standards choose a strong-algorithm cryptosystem for the data encryption standard?

9-22 Briefly explain the nature of public-key cryptography.

9-23 What functions must be carried out in cryptographic key management? Why is the evaluation of key management probably the most important aspect of evaluating a data processing installation's use of cryptography?

9-24 Briefly explain the relative advantages and disadvantages of generating and using a single key versus multiple keys in a cryptosystem.

9-25 How does the architecture of a cryptographic facility affect the method used to install cryptographic keys?

9-26 Outline any differences in the methods used to distribute key encrypting keys and data encrypting keys.

9-27 Briefly explain the difference between derived PINs, random PINs, and customer-selected PINs. What are the relative advantages and disadvantages of each type of PIN?

9-28 How does the method of PIN issuance and delivery differ depending on the method used to generate PINs?

9-29 Briefly explain the nature of each of the following methods for eliciting PINs from customers:
   a Mail solicitation
   b Telephone solicitation
   c PIN entry via a secure terminal
   d PIN entry at the issuer's facility

9-30 Briefly explain the difference between local PIN validation and interchange PIN validation. Why is a PIN checkdigit useful when interchange PIN validation must be used?

9-31 Why is it important that a unique cipher be generated each time a PIN is transmitted over a communication line? How might this be accomplished?

9-32 When an encrypted PIN must be stored for reference purposes, why must it be stored as a function of the account number to which it applies? Briefly discuss the relative advantages of using reversible versus irreversible encryption for storing the PIN.

9-33 What is a digital signature? Why are digital signatures needed in data communication systems? How are digital signatures used to send signed, secret messages?

9-34 Briefly explain the problems that arise with speed and storage overheads when public-key cryptosystems are used for digital signatures. Give a way in which each of these problems might be overcome.

9-35 Why are arbitrated digital signature schemes sometimes needed?

9-36 In terms of the access control mechanism used in an electronic funds transfer system, what function does a plastic debit or credit card fulfill? Why should cards be issued only after a formal application has been received and approved?

9-37 Why must basic inventory control procedures be used over the stock of plastic cards? If cards are produced by an outside vendor, what can the auditor do to obtain some assurance about the reliability of control procedures over cards?

9-38 Why should plastic cards and PIN mailers never be mailed at the same time to a customer? What is the purpose of using premailers prior to mailing a PIN or a card? What actions should be taken by the issuing institution if a card is returned because the customer's address is no longer current?

9-39 Why is customer education such a critical control in the use of plastic cards in an electronic funds transfer system?

9-40 Give *four* data items that might be recorded in the accounting audit trail and *two* items that might be recorded in the operations audit trail for the boundary subsystem.

9-41 Why are existence controls in the boundary subsystem often somewhat simpler than existence controls in other subsystems?

MULTIPLE CHOICE QUESTIONS

9-1 The class of authentication information to which a password belongs is:
a Possessed objects
b Personal information
c Remembered information
d Dialog information

9-2 A major problem that arises if an access control mechanism associates passwords with resources rather than users is:
a Substantial processing time is needed to exercise access control
b Users must remember multiple passwords rather than a single password
c Control can be exercised at only a very fine level of authorization
d None of the above

9-3 A primary problem with using personal characteristics for authentication purposes is:
a Falsifying personal characteristics is easy
b The mechanisms used to read personal characteristics are still unreliable
c They can be lost or stolen
d The authentication process is too slow

9-4 The most complex action privileges relate to:
a Hardware resources
b Commodity resources
c Software resources
d Data resources

9-5 Data dependent action privileges are conditional upon:
a The user supplying the correct data
b The way in which the data is stored
c The content of the object data
d The existence of a privacy lock

9-6 If an access control mechanism is implemented in an open environment, it allows users to access a resource:
a Unless authorization information specifies users cannot access the resource
b Only if authorization information specifies users can access the resource
c Without having to supply authentication information
d With all action privileges always being assigned

9-7 Which of the following statements applies to a capability-based approach to authorization:
a The mechanism associates with each resource a list of users who can access the resource together with the action privileges that each user has with respect to the resource
b The mechanism assigns capabilities to a user as a function of the class into which the user's password falls

    c The mechanism assigns privileges to users only if they know the password for each resource

    d The mechanism associates with each user the resources they can access together with the action privileges they have with respect to each resource

9-8 Relative to the ticket-oriented approach to authorization, the primary advantage of the list-oriented approach to authorization is:

    a It allows efficient administration of capabilities

    b It is efficient during process execution

    c Access control lists can be stored on some type of fast memory device to facilitate access to the list

    d It permits smaller protection domains

9-9 To be able to implement the principle of least privilege effectively, it is necessary to have:

    a A ticket-oriented approach to authorization

    b Small protection domains

    c A list-oriented approach to authorization

    d An open environment as the basis of granting access privileges

9-10 The person who designs a cryptosystem is called a:

    a Cryptographer

    b Cryptanalyst

    c Cryptologist

    d Cryptogenist

9-11 The type of cipher having the highest work factor is the:

    a Substitution cipher

    b Transposition cipher

    c Product cipher

    d Transcription cipher

9-12 Which of the following is *not* a desirable property of a cipher system:

    a Simplicity

    b Small key

    c Low error propagation

    d Low work factor

9-13 The DES is an example of a:

    a Short-key cipher system

    b Strong-algorithm cipher system

    c Long-key cipher system

    d Both a and b above

9-14 A key encrypting key:

    a Is time varying and dynamically changing

    b Constitutes the session key when interaction occurs

    c Remains relatively stable over long periods

    d Is used to load the algorithm into the cryptographic facility

9-15 The primary advantage of a derived PIN is:

    a It is easy to remember

    b It does not have to be stored so preserving privacy is easier

    c Lost or forgotten PINs can be replaced without having to change the account number

    d Changing the cryptographic key has no implications for existing PINs

9-16 Which of the following methods of obtaining customer-selected PINs does not require the cryptographic generation of a reference number to initially associate the PIN with the customer's account number:

a PIN entry via a secure terminal
b Telephone solicitation
c PIN entry at the issuer's facility
d Mail solicitation

9-17 Which of the following methods of validating PINs seems to result in the fewest control problems:

a Allow only a small number of PIN entry attempts, close the account when the limit has been reached, and retain the card
b Allow a reasonable number of PIN entry attempts, close the account after the limit has been reached, but do not retain the card
c Allow a reasonable number of PIN entry attempts, close the account after the limit has been reached, and retain the card
d Allow a small number of PIN entry attempts, do not close the account after the limit has been reached, but retain the card used to initiate the PIN entry

9-18 If interchange PIN validation is used in an EFTS, a fundamental principle is:

a The PIN should always be validated by the card acquiring institution
b The acquiring institution should encrypt the entered PIN under the issuer's key and not its own key
c The PIN should always be validated by the card issuing institution
d To reduce PIN exposure, a single interchange encryption key should be used throughout the network

9-19 Which of the following controls applies to PIN transmission:

a The cipher generated must be unique for each transmission of the PIN
b The PIN must always be encrypted under the issuer's key
c Different PINs must never generate the same ciphertext for transmission
d The PIN checkdigit should not be stripped off before the PIN is encrypted for transmission

9-20 When a PIN must be stored for reference purposes, it must be stored in:

a Cleartext form in case the PIN has to be reissued at some stage because the customer has forgotten their PIN
b Ciphertext form produced only from a reversible encryption algorithm
c Ciphertext form produced only from an irreversible encryption algorithm
d Ciphertext form that is a function of the account number

9-21 To send a *signed* message to a receiver when a public-key cryptosystem is used, the sender encrypts the message under the:

a Sender's private key
b Receiver's public key
c Sender's public key
d Receiver's private key

9-22 An arbitrator is used in a digital signature system to prevent:

a The receiver disavowing that they received the message
b The sender disavowing the message by making their private key public and claiming that the message was forged
c Collusion between the sender and the receiver
d The receiver forging a message using the sender's private key

9-23 Which of the following situations is likely to lead to more serious exposures in a digital signature system:

a Compromise of a receiver's private key

b Compromise of a sender's private key

c Compromise of a key server's private key

d Use of a fake public key

9-24 Which of the following actions should *not* be undertaken when plastic debit/credit cards are issued:

a Mail the cards in an envelope that does not identify the name of the issuing institution

b Make two different groups responsible for the mailing of cards and the investigation of returned cards

c Use premailers to detect invalid addresses

d Mail the card and the PIN mailer together in a registered envelope

9-25 The "best" control that can be exercised over card use by the customer is:

a High customer penalties if careless use leads to a fraud using the card

b Education of the customer as to the importance of card security

c Limiting the amount of money that can be withdrawn or charged to an account using the card

d Periodically changing the PIN associated with the card

9-26 Which of the following events is *not* recorded on a public audit trail in a digital signature system:

a Registration of public keys

b Registration of signatures

c Notification of key compromises

d Modifications to private keys

EXERCISES AND CASES

9-1 You are the manager of the internal audit of a savings and loan association that has decided to install a bill payment by telephone system for its customers. The system will allow customers to telephone a number to enter the system, record bill payment transactions that they wish to make within the next 30 days, and transfer funds between savings and checking accounts. A voice feedback system instructs customers on how to complete each step of a transaction; for example, record the date of a payment and the amount to be paid. Note, all data is entered using a Touch-Tone telephone.

Required: The data processing manager has asked you to advise her on the access controls you think should exist in the system. Prepare a brief report with your recommendations. Be sure to consider how the system will ensure:

a It is dealing with a valid customer

b It is allowing customers to transfer funds to or from authorized accounts only

c Customers do not overdraw accounts

d Payments are made only to creditors that the customer has authorized

9-2 Global Airways is a major airline company based in Los Angeles. It has a computer system dedicated to reservations and ticketing operations. Over 1000

terminals scattered throughout the United States are connected to the computer in the company's head office.

You are a member of the external audit team examining access and communications controls within the reservation and ticketing system. You are amazed to find the system does not use passwords as an access control. When you question the data processing manager why this is the case, he informs you that passwords are unnecessary. He explains that each terminal connected to the computer is given a unique identification number. This number is stored in a table within a secure area of the operating system. A terminal must supply this identification number with each message it sends and the system will respond only to a valid identification number. The identification number is sent automatically by a terminal since it is hard-wired in the terminal.

He further explains that a password system had been tried previously and abandoned. Each reservation and ticketing clerk had been given a unique password. However, since multiple clerks often used a single terminal, the system was too awkward and unwieldy as clerks had to continuously sign on and sign off. The system caused major problems during rush periods.

Required: Write a brief report identifying what could go wrong, if anything, with the current system that would result in the company losing assets or violation of data integrity in the system occurring.

9-3 First International Bankco of Illinois is a large Chicago-based bank. As the manager of internal audit, you are called one day to a meeting with the controller.

The bank has operated for some time now automatic teller machines (ATMs). However, several major problems have arisen with customers' use of the ATMs. The controller outlines the following difficulties:

a Currently the bank issues each customer a plastic card containing the customer's account number (magnetically encoded) and a personal identification number (PIN). Unfortunately, customers have been writing their PINs on their cards; consequently, when customers have lost their cards or their cards have been stolen, unauthorized withdrawals of funds have occurred. The number of unauthorized withdrawals is increasing.

b The ATMs allow a customer three attempts to enter the current PIN; then they lock the card in the machine. Many customers seem to forget their PINs. Recently, an irate customer tried to retrieve his card using a crowbar.

c The bank currently mails cards and PINs to new customers. Recently, mail has been stolen and unauthorized withdrawals of funds have occurred.

Required: The controller asks you to consider the problems and propose some solutions. Write a brief report outlining your recommendations.

9-4 The following situation happened to a friend of mine.

One weekend she was leaving to go to a beach resort with her husband. Since she was short of money, she asked her husband to stop at an automatic teller machine belonging to a building society so she could withdraw money from her account. When she arrived at the ATM, she had a memory lapse and was uncertain about her personal identification number (PIN). She tried one number, which failed. She tried a second number, and this number failed, also. To her surprise, however, the ATM then informed her that it was retaining her plastic account card. It then provided her with a telephone number to call to report her difficulties.

Since neither she nor her husband had much cash on them and they were entertaining a guest for the weekend, she was somewhat annoyed and distressed. Upon arriving home, she called the telephone number given to her by the ATM. A recorded message asked her to state her name and telephone number and to report her problem. The recorded message also indicated that a representative of the building society would return her call as soon as possible.

Prior to calling the telephone number given to her, my friend had looked up her correct PIN in a file that she maintained. In her confusion and frustration over having lost her card, she disclosed her PIN upon reporting her difficulty. After hanging up, she realized that she no longer had her card, nor was her PIN secure.

When no one returned her call after an hour, she borrowed some money from her parents and left for the coast. On the Monday morning, she was waiting as the building society branch opened its doors. She asked immediately to see the manager, and she told her what had happened. The manager then went through a tray containing some 25 cards that had suffered the same fate that weekend. She informed my friend that her card was not in the tray of captured cards. After further searching, my friend's card still could not be found.

My friend then indicated the problem that existed because she had disclosed her PIN and asked why no one had returned her telephone call. She was told that it was the building society's policy to assist people on a weekend only when an ATM malfunctioned. Customers who lost their card because they had forgotten their PIN had to wait till the Monday.

Required:

a Upon discovering her card was "lost," my friend initiated a series of steps to protect her account. What steps would you have advised her to undertake?

b Do you think the building society's system provides reasonable protection over customer accounts? If not, what changes would you recommend, and why?

9-5 Chen Chui was the computer systems manager at the Memorial Sloan-Kettering Cancer Center in New York City. When he logged into the system one Monday, he discovered that $1500 worth of billing records were missing and that five new unauthorized accounts had been established on the system. He immediately removed the unauthorized accounts and changed all the system passwords. Several weeks later, however, he found that an intruder once again had broken into the system. Furthermore, the intruder had established a program within the system that captured every password entered and made it available to the intruder. After this discovery, Chen called the FBI.

The FBI discovered that Sloan-Kettering had been the victim of a group of young computer hackers. The group had used various techniques to break into over 60 computer systems that offered dial-up access. It was nicknamed "the 414 gang" after the telephone area code of the city (Milwaukee) in which the group members were based. With the increasing availability of cheap home computers, the group's activities were symptomatic of a more widespread problem.

Passwords are supposed to prevent unauthorized access to computer systems. However, unless a system has a good access control mechanism and passwords are managed properly, the system may not withstand sustained attempts at unauthorized access. Programs are now available, for example, that will work methodically through a list of telephone numbers, dialing each number until a telltale computer modem signal is detected, and then systematically trying all combinations of characters until a valid password is discovered. If they are logged off after a certain number of invalid attempts, they will simply try again, perhaps at a later time so as not to arouse suspicion.

To counteract unauthorized access in dial-up systems, a piece of hardware called a "port protection device" has now been developed (see, for example, Delmage [1985]). Port protection devices are hardware units placed between the dial-up telephone lines and the computer. They offer various security capabilities. Simple devices allow a large number of password combinations, disconnect the caller after a certain number of invalid access attempts, and alert a security manager when attempted security violations appear to be occurring. More complex devices offer call-back facilities whereby a user first enters an identification code and the device then disconnects the user and calls back the user at an authorized number. In addition, some devices hide the system's communications ports. For example, they do not emit the telltale modem signal that can be detected by automatic calling devices. Instead, they emit a synthesized voice that requests an identification code. If the user enters a valid code, the device then passes control over to the system's access control mechanism.

Required: Port protection devices still do not overcome the basic limitations of passwords as a means of authentication, nor are they protection against someone who wiretaps a dedicated communication line and submits identification and authentication information over the line. Discuss.

ANSWERS TO MULTIPLE CHOICE QUESTIONS

9-1 c	9-8 a	9-15 b	9-21 a
9-2 b	9-9 b	9-16 a	9-22 b
9-3 b	9-10 a	9-17 b	9-23 c
9-4 d	9-11 c	9-18 c	9-24 d
9-5 c	9-12 d	9-19 a	9-25 b
9-6 a	9-13 d	9-20 d	9-26 d
9-7 d	9-14 c		

REFERENCES

Akl, Selim G. "Digital Signatures: A Tutorial Survey," *Computer* (February 1983), pp. 15–24.

Barton, Ben F., and Marthalee S. Barton. "User-Friendly Password Methods for Computer-Mediated Information Systems," *Computers and Security*, vol. 3, 1984, pp. 186–195.

Branstad, Dennis K., and Miles E. Smid. "Integrity and Security Standards Based on Cryptography," *Computers and Security*, vol. 1, 1982, pp. 255–260.

Bright, Herbert S., and R.L. Enison. "Cryptography Using Modular Software Elements," *Proceedings of the 1976 National Computer Conference* (Montvale, NJ: AFIPS Press), pp. 113–123.

Bright, Herbert S., and William E. Perry. "Computational Cryptography and Security," *EDPACS* (September 1977), pp. 1–8.

Conway, R.W., W.L. Maxwell, and H.L. Morgan. "On the Implementation of Security Measures in Information Systems," *Communications of the ACM* (April 1972), pp. 211–220.

Dallas, Dennis A. "Auditing a TSO Environment," *EDP Auditing* (Pennsauken, NJ: Auerbach Publishers, 1983), Portfolio 76-01-03, pp. 1–14.

Davies, Donald W. "Applying the RSA Digital Signature to Electronic Mail," *Computer* (February 1983), pp. 55–62.

Delmage, Sherman. "No Tresspassing," *Digital Review* (March 1985), pp. 31–34.

Denning, Dorothy E. "Protecting Public Keys and Signature Keys," *Computer* (February 1983), pp. 27–35.

Denning, Dorothy E. "Digital Signatures with RSA and Other Public-Key Cryptosystems," *Communications of the ACM* (April 1984), pp. 388–392.

Diffie, W., and M.E. Hellman. "New Directions in Cryptography," *IEEE Transactions on Information Theory* (November 1976), pp. 644–654.

Ehrsam, W.F., S.M. Matyas, C.H. Meyer, and W.L. Tuchman. "A Cryptographic Key Management Scheme for Implementing the Data Encryption Standard," *IBM Systems Journal*, vol. 17, no. 2, 1978, pp. 106–125.

Emory, William A., Jr. "Auditing Electronic Funds Transfer," *EDP Auditing* (Pennsauken, NJ: Auerbach Publishers, 1983), Portfolio 71-04-09, pp. 1–14.

Everest, Gordon C. *Database Management: Objectives, System Functions, and Administration* (New York: McGraw-Hill, 1985).

Fitzgerald, Kevin J. "Passwords—A False Sense of Security?" *5th National EDP Audit Conference* (Melbourne, Australia: EDP Auditors Association, 1983).

Gladney, H.M. "Administrative Control of Computing Service," *IBM Systems Journal*, vol. 17, no. 2, 1978, pp. 151–178.

Gladney, H.M., E.L. Worley, and J.J. Myers. "An Access Control Mechanism for Computing Resources," *IBM Systems Journal*, vol. 14, no. 3, 1975, pp. 212–228.

Hoving, Per L. "To Install an Access Control System, Activities and Checklists," *Computers and Security*, vol. 2, 1983, pp. 163–170.

Kahn, David. *The Codebreakers* (New York: Macmillan, 1967).

Knuth, Donald E. *The Art of Computer Programming, vol. 1: Fundamental Algorithms,* 2d ed. (Reading, MA: Addison-Wesley, 1973).

Lempel, Abraham. "Cryptology in Transition," *Computing Surveys* (December 1979), pp. 285–303.

Lennon, R.E. "Cryptography Architecture for Information Security," *IBM Systems Journal*, vol. 17, no. 2, 1978, pp. 138–150.

Matyas, Stephen M., and Carl H. Meyer. "Generation, Distribution, and Installation of Cryptographic Keys," *IBM Systems Journal*, vol. 17, no. 2, 1978, pp. 126–137.

Merkle, Ralph C. "Secure Communications over Insecure Channels," *Communications of the ACM* (April 1978), pp. 294–299.

Meyer, Carl H., and Stephen M. Matyas. *Cryptography: A New Dimension in Computer Data Security* (New York: Wiley, 1982).

Molloy, Carol G. "Improving CICS Controls with Guardian," *EDP Auditing* (Pennsauken, NJ: Auerbach Publishers, 1983), Portfolio 76-01-04, pp. 1–11.

Popek, Gerald J., and Charles S. Kline. "Encryption and Secure Computer Networks," *Computing Surveys* (December 1979), pp. 331–356.

Rivest, R.L., A. Shamir, and L. Adleman, "A Method for Obtaining Digital Signatures and Public-Key Cryptosystems,'' *Communications of the ACM* (February 1978), pp. 120–126.

Saltzer, Jerome H. ''Protection and Control of Information Sharing in Multics,'' *Communications of the ACM* (July 1974), pp. 388–402.

Saltzer, J.H., and M.D. Schroeder, ''The Protection of Information in Computer Systems,'' *Proceedings of the IEEE* (September 1975), pp. 1278–1308.

Serpell, Stephen C. ''Cryptographic Equipment Security: A Code of Practice,'' *Computers and Security*, vol. 4, 1985, pp. 47–64.

Shannon, Claude E. ''Communication Theory of Secrecy Systems,'' *Bell System Technical Journal* (October 1949), pp. 656–715.

Simmons, Gustavus J. ''Symmetric and Asymmetric Encryption,'' *Computing Surveys* (December 1979), pp. 305–330.

Sinkov, A. *Elementary Cryptanalysis: A Mathematical Approach* (New York: Random House, 1968).

Van Tassel, Dennis. *Computer Security Management* (Englewood Cliffs, NJ: Prentice-Hall, 1972).

Willett, Michael, ''A Tutorial on Public Key Cryptography,'' *Computers and Security*, vol. 1, 1982, pp. 72–79.

INPUT CONTROLS: DATA AND INSTRUCTION INPUT

Components in the input subsystem are responsible for bringing information into a system. This information takes two forms: first, it may be raw data to be processed and perhaps applied against the database; second, it may be instructions to direct the system to execute particular processes, update or interrogate particular data, or prepare particular types of output. Both types of information input must be validated. Any errors detected must be controlled so input resubmission is authentic, accurate, complete, unique, and timely.

This chapter examines controls over the capture, preparation, and entry of data and instructions into a system. The next chapter examines input validation and error control. Overall, the controls discussed in both chapters are critical for three reasons. First, in most computer systems the largest number of controls exists in the input subsystem. Consequently, auditors spend substantial amounts of time assessing the reliability of input controls. Second, activities in the input subsystem often involve substantial amounts of routine, sometimes monotonous, human intervention. Thus, they are error-prone. Third, the input subsystem is often the target of fraud. Allen [1977] studied 156 cases of computer fraud and found that 108 of these cases involved addition, deletion, or alteration of an input transaction.

DATA CAPTURE METHODS

Data capture involves identifying and recording events that are relevant to the ongoing operations of an organization. Three methods of data capture exist: (*a*) document-based data capture; (*b*) direct entry data capture; and (*c*) hybrid data capture, which is a combination of document-based and direct entry methods. Historically, document-based data capture has been used most frequently since the technology needed to support direct entry and hybrid methods has been costly. These costs are decreasing quickly, however, and direct entry and hybrid methods are now widely used.

Document-Based Data Capture

Document-based data capture involves recording events on paper or some related medium such as cards. The data recorded on the document may or may not be in machine-readable form. For example, customers may mark a card with a pencil to indicate the bets they wish to make on a horse race (Figure 10-1). This data is in machine-readable form since it can be read by an optical mark sensing device. Alternatively, data may be transcribed onto a source document that then has to undergo some type of keyboarding operation to convert it into machine-readable form.

Whenever document-based data capture methods are used, some type of data preparation activity also is undertaken. For example: source documents on cards are scanned for reasonableness; batches are prepared and control totals are calculated; data items that are not in machine-readable form undergo some type of keyboarding operation. In addition, inevitably a delay occurs between recording the event of interest and processing the event.

The primary advantages of document-based data capture are ease and flexibility. Document-based data capture simply involves preparing source

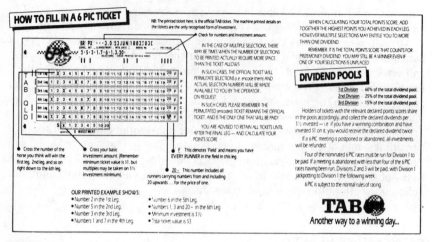

FIGURE 10-1
Document-based data capture using marked cards. (*Used by permission, T.A.B.*)

documents that are preprinted, premarked, prenumbered, etc., and training users to record events on these documents. Documents can be readily distributed close to the points of data capture. Moreover, expensive data capture and input devices are not needed at each location where data capture occurs. However, document-based data capture methods often require substantial amounts of human intervention. Consequently, they can be costly and error-prone.

Direct Entry Data Capture

Direct entry data capture involves immediate recording of an event as it occurs using an input device. Transcription of the event to a source document is not an intermediate step. Often immediate processing of the event also occurs, although in some cases the data may be stored for later processing. A variety of input devices may be used to record the event; for example, a visual display terminal, a speech recognition unit, a Touch-Tone telephone, a process control device, a mouse, a digitizer.

Since data preparation activities are eliminated, direct entry data capture reduces the amount of human intervention needed in the data capture process. Consequently, the risk of clerical or operator errors decreases. In addition, the system can facilitate any human intervention needed by providing immediate feedback during the data capture process. For example, input instructions can be displayed on a screen at a lower light intensity than data keyed in by an operator, and immediate validation of data can be undertaken to provide operators with feedback on data capture errors. Direct entry data capture is often costly, however, because extensive hardware and software support is needed. If many data capture points exist, it may be too costly to provide direct entry facilities at each location.

Hybrid Data Capture

Hybrid data capture methods use a combination of document-based and direct entry techniques. The "documents" used store partial information (usually constant data) about the event to be recorded. For example: a universal product code is preprinted on containers; customer account information is stored on the magnetic stripe at the back of a plastic debit or credit card; employee identification information is stored magnetically on a badge. Additional information about the event (usually variable data) is entered directly via a terminal. For example: bank customers use an automatic teller machine to key in the amounts they wish to withdraw from their accounts; after having used a wand scanner to read the bar code that identifies a product, sales clerks use a point-of-sale device keyboard to enter data about the tender offered—cash, checks, or coupons.

Like direct entry data capture, hybrid data capture methods reduce the amount of human intervention needed in the data capture process, thereby decreasing the risk of errors. Indeed, even less intervention is required since constant information (such as a product code or account number) does not have to be keyed into the system. Moreover, as "documents" like smart cards are used increasingly, even variable information may not have to be keyed into the system. Data stored on the document may be updated after each transaction and read directly from the document when the next transaction occurs (see Chapter 9). The hardware and software needed to support hybrid data capture methods are still costly, however, although costs are decreasing rapidly.

DATA PREPARATION METHODS

If the data capture process does not record events immediately in machine-readable form, some type of data preparation activity must be undertaken. Data preparation activities comprise one or more of the following tasks:

1 *Converting data to machine-readable form:* Some or all data items on a source document may have to be converted to machine-readable form. For example: the amount field on a bank check has to be encoded so it can be read by a magnetic ink character recognition device; a sales order document has to be keyed to tape or disk so it can be read by an order entry program.

2 *Converting data from one machine-readable form to another:* To speed up the input process, data may be converted from a slow input medium to a fast input medium. For example, documents read by an optical character reader may be written offline to a magnetic tape that is later read by an input program.

3 *Preparing batches and control totals:* Source documents may be assembled into batches and various control totals calculated before the batches are keyed to some machine-readable medium (e.g., tape) or read by some input device (e.g., an optical character reader). Machine-readable data produced as a by-product of data capture activities at different locations may be collected and read jointly by an offline input device. For example, rolls of paper tape produced as a by-product of cash register operations may be collected from all cash registers in a particular store and written to a single magnetic tape.

4 *Scanning for authenticity, accuracy, completeness, and uniqueness:* Source documents may be reviewed to determine whether they have been submitted by an authorized person, whether the data appears accurate and complete, and whether duplicate source documents have been submitted. In light of this review, data may be added, deleted, or modified.

5 *Verifying data converted to machine-readable form:* Verification is a duplicate process whereby source data already keyed to machine-readable form is rekeyed to check the accuracy of the initial keying. It is a costly control because it duplicates work. Consequently, it should be used only for critical fields where errors are difficult to detect with an input validation program.

The timing and location of data preparation activities vary considerably. Often they take place after data capture (Figure 10-2a). For example, data is captured on a source document in handwritten form, documents are then

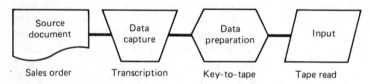

FIGURE 10-2a
Input sequence: data capture, data preparation, and data input.

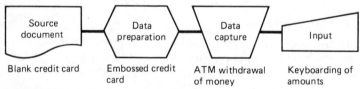

FIGURE 10-2b
Input sequence: data preparation, data capture, and data input.

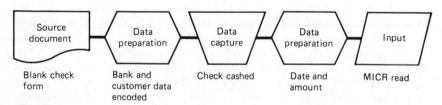

FIGURE 10-2c
Input sequence: data preparation, data capture, data preparation, and data input.

batched, and they are then keyed to tape or into the system using an online terminal. Sometimes data preparation occurs before data capture (Figure 10-2b). For example, credit cards, tags, turnaround documents, and badges all require data preparation before their distribution. On still other occasions, data preparation occurs both before data capture and after data capture (Figure 10-2c). For example, before their distribution, bank checks are encoded with various data items that identify the bank and the customer. When a check is cashed, the date and the amount is encoded onto the check so all data items can be read by magnetic ink character recognition equipment.

DATA PREPARATION DEVICES

Many different types of devices are now used to convert source data to machine-readable form and to undertake verification of data that has already been keyed. The following sections briefly describe the more popular devices. The discussion focuses on those features of the devices that enhance asset safeguarding, data integrity, system effectiveness, and system efficiency.

Keyboard Devices

Keyboard devices are still used extensively to prepare data for input to the computer. However, there has been a shift away from using cards as the storage medium to using magnetic storage such as tapes and disks.

Cards Some modifications have been made to the traditional keypunch (key-to-card) and verifier machines to improve efficiency and to assist in maintaining data integrity. An important innovation is the buffered combination keypunch/verifier known as a card data recorder. Buffering permits data to be stored until keying of a card is complete. The data then is punched automatically as the operator commences to key data for a new card.

Buffered keypunch/verifiers offer several advantages:

1 Fast correction of conscious keying errors. About 80% of all keying errors made are conscious errors; that is, the keypunch operator is aware of the error as soon as it is made.

2 About a 25–30% faster keying rate than unbuffered keypunch/verifiers.

3 Card layout can differ from the source document layout to facilitate data capture by the user and data preparation by the operator.

In addition to the advantages obtained through buffering, the following features improve keying efficiency and help maintain data integrity:

1 Automatic creation and checking of check digits

2 Automatic preparation of control totals for designated fields to allow batch control checking

3 Programming capability to allow automatic selection of different card formats, automatic insertion of constant data, zero and blank filling of fields, left or right justification of data punched in fields, and high-speed skipping over blank columns

4 Preparation of statistics on number of cards punched, keystrokes made, and errors corrected

As an input medium, cards have as their major advantages ease of handling and visibility of the data stored. They have several disadvantages:

1 Cards damage easily through mishandling or improper storage.

2 Compared to other data preparation methods, cards are slow because they are labor intensive and use mechanical rather than electronic equipment.

3 Cards are bulky, heavy, and their storage sometimes difficult.

4 Cards are not a reusable storage medium.

Paper Tape For most applications, other storage mediums have superseded paper tape. However, in some areas it is still useful; for example, data input from a typewriter terminal.

Compared to cards, paper tape is lighter, less bulky, and sometimes faster to prepare and read. However, it has the same disadvantages as cards. In addition, correction of keypunch errors is more difficult because paper tape is a continuous medium. Corrections are made in several ways. The tape can be spliced, but this is time-consuming and causes jams in paper tape readers. Some keypunch machines produce an error punch over the character in error. The paper tape reader ignores characters having an error punch. Paper tape verifiers produce a new reel of tape containing correct data from the original reel used as input and new data where an error on the original reel has been identified.

Magnetic Tape Key-to-tape devices allow source data to be keyed directly to a magnetic tape that can be read by a computer. Both stand-alone and clustered devices exist. A stand-alone device has its own tape recording unit. A clustered device has several keyboards with a multiplexor reading alternately from each keyboard. Clustered devices are less expensive than stand-alone devices, but before they can be justified they require applications where large amounts of the same type of data are being keyed.

Since key-to-tape devices are buffered, they offer all the usual advantages: fast and easy correction of conscious errors, automatic skipping of columns, zero or blank filling, left and right justification of data entered into certain fields. When a device writes a buffer to tape, it performs checks to ensure the buffer has been written correctly; for example, a parity check and a read-after-write check. Verification simply involves switching the device to verification mode. Correction of errors occurs immediately by overwriting the character in error.

Key-to-tape devices have several different and optional characteristics. Some provide a display showing the last character entered. Others provide a full display of the record entered. A printer can be attached to the device to provide hard copy output. Records can be retrieved using a search facility. Check digit verification can be carried out. The devices also will gather various statistics: number of keystrokes, number of errors made. Various offline devices exist to support key-to-tape devices; for example, a tape pooler and a communications controller so data can be sent over long distances.

Key-to-tape devices offer several advantages over traditional keypunch equipment: records are not restricted to 80 characters, less mechanical movement, less operator intervention as cards do not have to be loaded and unloaded, faster input to the computer. Though key-to-tape devices are more expensive than key-to-card devices, they allow faster data preparation and data entry. Currently, as a rule of thumb, about three key-to-tape devices replace four key-to-card devices.

Magnetic Disk   The natural extension of key-to-tape devices is key-to-disk devices. Key-to-disk devices feature: (*a*) multiple keystations attached to a single processor, (*b*) validation and editing capabilities performed by the processor, (*c*) a supervisor's control station, and (*d*) a magnetic tape unit for output of data that has been keyed, edited, and validated.

The number of keystations available with a key-to-disk device varies; small systems have about eight keystations and large systems have in excess of 60 keystations. A keystation consists of a keyboard and a panel display or visual display. The display shows the data entered, and a cursor or light indicates any data identified as being in error. A keystation can be used for initial input of data or verification. One keystation can perform verification while another performs input, providing some time lag exists between entry and verification.

Data validation and editing is performed by a program stored in the processor. The system vendor usually supplies generalized software for validation and editing, but users also can write their own routines. Validation and edit capabilities are fairly comprehensive (see, also, Chapter 11), but the available memory sometimes imposes limitations so that some validation and editing still must be carried out by the input program in the mainframe. When the validation and edit program identifies an error, it locks the keyboard, sounds an alarm, and indicates the field or character in error on the display.

The supervisor's control station controls data input to the system and data output from disk storage to magnetic tape for input to the mainframe. The supervisor assigns buffer storage to keystations, allocates areas on disk, assigns batch numbers, monitors system statistics, and determines when data should be dumped from disk to tape.

Key-to-disk devices offer the same advantages as key-to-tape devices. The major additional advantage is the validation and editing capabilities provided by the processor. If communication facilities are attached to a key-to-disk system, in effect the system constitutes a frontend terminal that can be placed at some remote location. Data can be captured and entered close to its source, thereby enabling timely identification and fast correction of errors made.

The major disadvantages of key-to-disk equipment relate to the consequences of device failure. Not just one but several keystations become inoperable. Data that has been already keyed may be lost. Key-to-disk systems are also costly. However, cost is decreasing; key-to-disk is now a strong competitor with key-to-card and key-to-tape systems.

Cassette   A variation on key-to-tape devices is key-to-cassette devices. The major advantage of cassettes over tape is ease of handling. Spooling and tape loading are unnecessary with cassettes. Because cassettes are much smaller in size than tapes, they also can be transported readily or sent through the mail. They are easier and more economical to store than magnetic tapes.

Diskette   Diskettes (floppy disks) are replacing cassettes as a data storage medium. Their major advantage over cassettes is that they allow fast direct access to data. There are no significant cost differences. However, one disadvantage of diskettes is low reliability. Because the read/write heads make contact with the diskette surface, compared to a conventional magnetic disk, recording errors are more likely to occur.

By-Product Devices

Data is prepared by some devices as a by-product of other activities; for example, cash registers produce paper tape or journal tape suitable as input to an optical character reader, accounting machines produce paper tape or magnetic tape, electric typewriters produce punched cards or cassette tape.

There are several advantages to producing data in machine-readable form as a by-product of other processes. First, no special operator training is necessary for data preparation equipment. Second, by-product data preparation reduces further data preparation activities. For example, if data entered onto a source document is typewritten, keypunching of data from the source document is unnecessary. Third, in the absence of machine failure, there is exact correspondence between data on the sales invoice or ledger card and data in machine-readable form. However, most by-product methods of data preparation are being superseded. For example, cheap minicomputers and microcomputers have replaced many accounting machines. Many documents previously typewritten now are produced by the computer.

Turnaround Document Devices

Turnaround documents reduce the time and effort needed for data capture, preparation, and entry and the risk of input errors occurring. However, they are susceptible to either accidental or malicious damage. Four types of turnaround documents are used: (*a*) tags, (*b*) punched/marked cards, (*c*) plastic cards/badges, and (*d*) documents. The following sections briefly describe their nature and the devices used to prepare them.

Tags   Tags are used primarily in retail stores where they are attached to the item to be sold. Information about the item price, style, department, and supplier is printed, prepunched, or premarked on the tag. Thus, the tag provides information to potential customers and salespersons as well as being in machine-readable form. Tags are prepared in different ways: with a special device that is online to the computer, a special keypunch, or a special device that uses magnetic tape as input. Multipart tags are sometimes prepared. The return of one part denotes receipt of an item; another part the sale of an item.

Punched/Marked Cards   Cards can be prepunched or premarked before their distribution as a turnaround document. For example, in a payroll system a punched card can be produced for each employee using an online card punch. The foreperson writes details about hours worked by an employee on the card. The card is then returned so this additional data can be punched onto the card using a keyboard device. Similarly, cards can be produced with constant information marked on the cards. Additional information can be marked on the card by an employee, and the cards can then be read using an optical mark sensing device.

Plastic Cards/Badges   Special devices are used to prepare the plastic cards or badges used in many online terminal devices. For example, the plastic debit and credit cards used by financial institutions are prepared by a machine that reads a magnetic tape containing customer details and produces as output a card with some details embossed on the card and other details encoded on the magnetic stripe at the back of the card. Badges are produced in a similar way. In both cases, the data magnetically encoded on the card or badge does not have to be keyed into the computer system. Instead, it is read by an input device directly from the card or badge.

Documents   Documents are the most flexible form of turnaround document. Data is preprinted, premarked, or encoded before the document is distributed. Many different types of devices can be used to transcribe the data onto the document. For example: a typewriter may produce typeface that can be read by an optical character reader; an encoder may print bank and customer information on a bank check; a printer may produce output using a machine-readable font. If further information is captured, it is marked, handwritten, typewritten, or encoded on the document. The document is then read using some type of pattern recognition device such as an optical character reader.

DIRECT ENTRY DEVICES

Direct entry devices support direct entry data capture. They allow data to be entered straight into the computer system without any intermediate data preparation step having to be taken. In some cases, however, direct entry devices may also be used as data preparation devices. For example, typewriter terminals and visual display units can be used to key data captured on source documents to a disk. Nonetheless, data preparation activities do not use the full set of input opportunities available with direct entry devices.

The following sections describe some of the more popular direct entry devices used in accounting applications. Other direct entry devices, such as voice recognition units, process control devices, light pens, joysticks, and the mouse, are left for further study.

Terminals

There are two types of terminals: (*a*) typewriter terminals, and (*b*) visual display units (VDUs). Typewriter terminals provide only hard copy printed output. VDUs provide visual output on a display screen. In addition, they have various other features and options; for example, paging and scrolling capabilities, detachable printers, light pens, joysticks for moving graphic displays in any direction, unpluggable keyboards so different keyboards can be attached, a mouse for cursor movement and data entry.

The typewriter terminal was the first major step toward online use of the computer. It provides several advantages. First, it allows data upon capture to be immediately available for processing. Second, it reduces the effort involved in capturing, preparing, and entering data. Third, in many cases it decreases the input error rate. Less scope exists for clerical error because human intervention is reduced. Data can be validated upon entry and feedback immediately provided to the operator so errors can be corrected. Verification of data is rarely necessary. The computer can be used to guide the terminal operator during data entry by providing instructions and answering queries.

VDUs provide additional advantages to those listed above for typewriter terminals. The absence of mechanical movement with a VDU results in faster and quieter keying of data. The display assists the operator to reduce data capture and preparation errors in several ways. Source documents used for data capture can be displayed at low light intensity as background data. Data entered by the operator can be displayed at a high light intensity (double brightness) as foreground data. A cursor (moveable dot, upward arrow, dash) indicates the next character to be entered so the operator clearly sees what point has been reached in the input task. The cursor also can be repositioned to insert, delete, or change data, or made to blink to indicate a character or field in error.

VDUs become "intelligent terminals" when they have minicomputers or microprocessors attached that provide validation, editing, and storage capabilities independent of the main computer. Thus, a VDU can be offline but the user has the same facilities as if the VDU were online. Data that has been validated and edited can be stored (e.g., on cassette tape) and forwarded to the mainframe during quiet periods.

Point-of-Sale Terminals

Productivity and data integrity in supermarkets and retail stores has been considerably enhanced by point-of-sale data input devices. In the case of supermarkets, the technology permitting these advances is a fixed laser checkout scanner capable of reading premarked codes on an item for sale. In the case of retail stores, it is a handheld wand. The wand either reads codes optically or it reads magnetically encoded tickets.

The nature of supermarket and retail store selling operations is different. The salesclerk in a supermarket spends most time at the point of sale, whereas the salesclerk in a retail store spends most time selling rather than checking items out. Another difference is the complexity of the transactions that occur. In a supermarket environment transactions are relatively straightforward: an exchange of tender for the total cost of the items purchased. In a retail environment a large number of different types of transactions exist. Antonelli [1975] reports some retail stores have over 600 combinations of sales transactions; for example, discount, COD, layaway, partial payment, multiple charge plans. Correct recording of a retail store transaction is confounded by the fact that most sales occur during a two-month period of the year when large numbers of temporary staff are employed. The cost of training is significant and the risk of error high. Thus, a point-of-sale terminal for supermarkets differs from a point-of-sale terminal for retail operations.

Compared with cash registers, the major advantages of using supermarket point-of-sale devices are:

1 Optical scanning of a premarked code, for example, the universal product code (UPC), enables faster throughput of items.

2 Increased accuracy in pricing items since a minicomputer retrieves prices from a price file based on an item's unique code.

3 Reduced price marking upon receipt of an item and upon change of the item's price; the price need only be marked on the shelf and not on the item itself.

4 Improved customer satisfaction since a display shows the item and its price as it is checked out; a more detailed customer receipt is printed automatically.

5 Improved control over tender since the terminal controls the cash drawer, automatically dispenses change and stamps, and handles any type of tender—cash, checks, coupons, or food stamps.

6 Automatic check authorization.

7 Better inventory control and shelf allocation through more timely information on item sales.

8 Better information on item advertising effectiveness, the performance of new items, and customer preferences for different brand names.

Retail store point-of-sale terminals have similar advantages. However, an important function of a retail store terminal is to display instructions to salesclerks to guide them through the variety of transaction types that can occur.

Point-of-sale devices present problems when hardware failure occurs. The terminals typically are connected to a store controller that, in turn, is connected to a host computer. Hippert et al. [1975] describe various methods of increasing the reliability and availability of the terminals. If failure occurs the terminal usually can act as a stand-alone register.

Automatic Teller Machines

Automatic teller machines (ATMs) permit customers of a financial institution to initiate transactions on their accounts without having to deal directly with an employee of the financial institution. Typical features on an ATM include a keyboard and customer display, a depository, a bill dispenser, a receipt printer, a card capture tray, a time-of-day clock, a journal tape to record individual transactions, control total counters, a security alarm, and a facility for entering cryptographic keys. Customers often can initiate a wide range of transactions including withdrawals, deposits, transfers, payments, enquiries, and messages to the financial institution.

ATMs provide several important controls. First, they are designed to be physically secure. Since at any time they may contain large amounts of cash, they have the same antitheft features as a safe. Nevertheless, it is important to locate ATMs in relatively secure environments so customers are not mugged when they are undertaking transactions and the ATM cannot be removed physically from the premises. In this respect, camera surveillance might be undertaken, and heat, motion, and sound detectors might be installed.

Second, ATMs provide independent records of the transactions undertaken via their journal tapes and control total counters. Thus, it is difficult for someone to make unauthorized withdrawals of cash or to remove a captured card without being detected. The journal tapes and control total counters also provide a means of independently reconciling transactions at the ATM with the record of transactions maintained by an electronic funds transfer system (EFTS). If a financial institution is using a public EFTS, for example, these independent ATM records provide a means of identifying unauthorized or accidental alterations to the audit trail of transactions maintained by the public EFTS.

Third, ATMs usually provide some type of facility for entering a crypto-graphic key. In some cases the key is entered via a keyboard or a set of dials. In other cases the key is loaded via a cassette. The cryptographic key is used to encrypt and decrypt transactions sent to and received from an EFTS switch or a host computer. The initial key that is loaded may be only a temporary key in that the EFTS may roll over the key on a random basis to reduce the risk of key compromise.

Perhaps the most critical component of an ATM device is the software that drives the device. This software performs many functions including display of output to guide customers through their transactions, formating of transactions so they can be processed by an EFTS switch or host computer, downloading of new cryptographic keys, maintenance of control totals, and activation of the ATM to dispense money. The software also may determine whether daily withdrawal limits have been exceeded and whether money can be dispensed to the customer. If device control software is not secure, fraudulent modifications can be carried out so an ATM dispenses all cash when the software recognizes a particular card.

INPUT DEVICES

After data has undergone a data preparation phase to ensure it is in a form suitable for machine processing, input devices are used to read the data into the application system. The following sections briefly describe the major types of input devices used and the controls incorporated in these devices to ensure they perform their functions reliably. The discussion on two devices used for input—magnetic tape units and disk units—is deferred until Chapter 14 as these devices are used extensively in the database subsystem. Since most input devices now function reliably, however, the auditor's primary concern is that a regular maintenance schedule for these devices be maintained. Nonetheless, the auditors should understand what types of errors will be prevented, detected, and corrected by controls in input devices.

Card Readers

Card reader malfunctions occur for three reasons: (*a*) cards are warped or defective in some way; (*b*) mechanical components have failed so that cards do not move across the read stations in the correct position or during the correct timing intervals; and (*c*) electronic components have failed so that the photoelectric cells or brushes in the read station fail to sense the card correctly. In some cases the malfunction is confined to a single card; the card reader rejects the card and sends it to a separate hopper for correction. In other cases the card reader ceases to function; for example, a card jam occurs that prevents further cards being read.

To detect card reader malfunctions, four types of controls are used:

1 *Dual read:* The card is read twice by two different read stations or the same read station and the results of each read are compared.

2 *Hole count:* The card is read twice and a count of the holes in each column and row made during each read is compared.

3 *Echo check:* The central processor sends a message to the card reader to activate the read function and the card reader returns a message to the central processor to indicate it has been activated.

4 *Character check:* The card reader checks that the combination of holes read represents a valid character.

If a malfunction is confined to a single card, usually all valid cards are written to tape or disk and the rejected card is submitted at a later stage. Controls must be exercised to ensure the reasons for the rejection are determined and the card is resubmitted for processing. If the malfunction terminates the read function completely, input processing must be redone when the problem is corrected.

Magnetic Ink Character Recognition (MICR) Devices

The popularity of MICR arises from its extensive use by the banking industry for processing checks. MICR requires characters to be encoded on a document using a special type font and special magnetic ink. Reading takes place by the device sensing the presence or absence of magnetic ink in a character matrix. The character is identified by the pattern formed in the matrix. In some cases a character passing under the read head may be slightly out of position and a "folded" character is sensed. The reader shifts a folded character vertically and attempts to identify it as a member of the valid set of patterns.

MICR offers several advantages:

1 High reading rates (up to 1600 documents per minute), and low error rates for documents of varying size, thickness, and condition.

2 Documents can be sorted at the time of reading; for example, by account number within bank number.

3 Some devices permit some input validation to be carried out; for example, sequence checking, accumulating, and printing batch totals.

4 The MICR type font can be read easily by humans.

There are two major disadvantages to using MICR. First, it is time-consuming to correct rejected or damaged documents. Second, low error and rejection rates require high-quality printing and ink. The magnetic ink loses much of its magnetism soon after encoding. To minimize read errors and rejections, documents must be handled infrequently.

Optical Character Recognition (OCR) Devices

Three types of OCR devices are available: (a) document readers, (b) page readers, and (c) journal tape readers. The primary difference between a document reader and page reader is the size of the document that can be read; document readers accept smaller size documents than page readers. Journal tape readers accept narrow rolls of paper usually produced by a cash register.

Data for input to an OCR device can be prepared in a variety of ways: typewritten, offset, printed by computer, handwritten. A multitude of type fonts is acceptable. However, in general, the less expensive the OCR device, the fewer the number of fonts it can read. Handwritten characters must be printed carefully and conform to a certain style. Flexibility in the types of fonts and handwriting styles that can be read is not always desirable. Besides being less costly, an OCR device that accepts only one type font and a restricted handwriting style generally has a lower error and rejection rate.

OCR input offers several advantages. First, the fonts that OCR devices read are read easily by humans. Second, to aid data capture and preparation, instructions can be printed on the source document in a dropout color that cannot be read by an OCR device. Third, by minimizing data capture and preparation, OCR is useful for high-volume input. Document readers can process about 400 documents per minute; page readers are slower. Wu [1975] reports the use of OCR for credit card billing by one U.S. oil company resulted in an increased cash flow of $25,000,000 during the first six months of operation.

However, the success of OCR has been limited. OCR devices are still relatively expensive and their reliability lower than other input devices. A major factor determining the success or failure of OCR is the quality of the input system design. A simple switch from keypunches to OCR often is unsuccessful. Using OCR to full advantage may require complete redesign of the input system.

Optical Mark Sensing Devices

Optical mark sensing devices read marks instead of alphanumeric characters. As with OCR equipment, the marks may be preprinted, typewritten, handwritten, or computer-produced. The position of the marks on the document or card indicates their alphabetic or numeric value.

In spite of the greater flexibility and sophistication of OCR devices, optical mark sensing still has its place. It is especially useful for low-volume, exception data entry. For example, a salesperson marks an order form to indicate the number of items ordered; an employee marks a timesheet to indicate normal and overtime hours worked. In both cases constant information is preprinted on the document in a dropout color. Providing the data captured is straightforward, data preparation usually is easy and few errors are made after a little practice.

If the data to be captured is diverse and volatile, optical mark sensing generally is unsuitable as an input method. Since data must be coded as a pattern of marks, diverse data requires many different codes. This increases the risk of clerical error and slows the data capture and preparation processes. If data is volatile, frequent changes to preprinted forms may be necessary. For example, if product lines are preprinted on a sales order form and these lines are volatile, the forms must be changed constantly. Again, the risk of clerical error increases.

SOURCE DOCUMENT DESIGN

Source documents are the forms used to record data that has been captured. A source document may be a piece of paper, a turnaround document such as a punched card, or an image displayed on a VDU for online input of data.

Source document design can be a complex matter. For example, in the case of documents to be read by a pattern recognition device, the design depends on technical characteristics of the device such as its trim and skew tolerance. However, the auditor must understand the fundamentals of good source document design. As a basic data input control, a well-designed source document achieves several purposes:

1 Increases the speed and accuracy with which data can be recorded
2 Controls the work flow
3 Facilitates preparation of the data in machine-readable form
4 For pattern recognition devices, increases the speed and accuracy with which data can be read
5 Facilitates subsequent reference checking

Source document design occurs after carrying out source document analysis. Source document analysis determines what data will be captured, how the data will be captured, who will capture the data, how the data will be prepared and read into the machine, and how the document will be handled, stored, and filed. Once these requirements have been determined, three decisions can be made: (a) the medium to be used for the source document, (b) the makeup of the source document, and (c) its style and layout.

Choice of Medium

The medium used for source documents usually is paper. Other media such as cards may be used. The following choices must be made:

Choice	Considerations
Length and width	Amount of data to be captured; compliance with organization standards; processes and devices that use the form, e.g., typewriters, mailing in window envelopes, file storage
Grade and weight	Amount of handling; retention period; where, when, and by whom the document will be completed, e.g., truck drivers at a loading bay versus clerks in an office

Choice of the wrong length and width or grade and weight can cause a variety of problems; for example, inability to manipulate the document in a typewriter, fast deterioration of the document in storage, frequent tearing of the document when being completed.

Choice of Makeup

The choice of makeup depends on the number of copies of the form required and how it will be completed. There are four types of makeup: (a) padding, (b) multipart sets, (c) continuous forms, and (d) snap-apart sets. Wooldridge [1974] discusses in detail the relative advantages and disadvantages of the different types of makeups. Choice of the wrong makeup results in input errors occurring through documents tearing, and data being too lightly written to be read.

Choice of Layout and Style

The layout and style of a source document probably is the most important factor affecting the number of data capture and preparation errors made. Some general design guidelines follow:

1 *Preprint wherever possible:* Preprint all constant information on a source document. If only a limited number of responses is appropriate to a question, preprint the responses and have the user tick the correct responses or delete those that are inappropriate.

2 *Provide titles, headings, notes, and instructions:* A title clearly identifies the purpose of the source document. Headings break up the document into logical sections. Notes and instructions assist the user to complete the document. Where codes are used, preprint their meaning on the form so the user does not have to rely on memory or waste time referencing manuals.

3 *Use techniques for emphasis and to highlight differences:* Different type fonts such as italics and boldface give emphasis to different parts of the form. Heavy thick lines or hatching highlight important fields. Different colors facilitate distribution of different copies of the form. Background colors emphasize special sections of the document; for example, those for office use only.

4 *Arrange fields for ease of use:* Design the document to be completed in a natural sequence from left to right, top to bottom. Group related items together. The sequence of fields should follow the work flow; the most used fields on the left of the document, those usually used in the center, and those seldom used on the right.

5 *Where possible provide multiple choice answers to questions to avoid omissions:* Figure 10-3a shows how this technique can be used. Instead of asking users to remember all the business subjects they studied, provide a list they can check.

6 *Use boxes to identify field size errors:* Figure 10-3b shows how this technique highlights field overflow or underflow.

7 *Combine instructions with questions:* Figure 10-3c shows how this technique overcomes possible confusion.

8 *Space items appropriately on forms:* Correct spacing of fields on forms is particularly important if responses are to be typewritten. Incorrect spacing results in manual shifting of the document in the machine and too many tab stops.

9 *Design for ease of keying:* Have the order in which fields are keyed follow the order of field placement. Figure 10-3c shows how column numbers

Good	Bad
	List the business subjects
Check the business subjects you have studied	you have studied

Good		Bad
☐ Accounting	☐ Management	
☐ Data Processing	☐ Business and Society	
☐ Commercial Law	☐ Management Science	
☐ Taxation	☐ Marketing	
☐ Microeconomics	☐ Industrial Relations	

FIGURE 10-3a
Using multiple choice to prevent omissions.

Good	Bad
Social Security Number ☐☐☐ – ☐☐ – ☐☐☐☐	Social Security Number _____

FIGURE 10-3b
Using boxes to prevent field size errors.

Good	Bad
4 9	
Date: ☐☐☐☐☐☐	Date: _____
Y Y M M D D	

FIGURE 10-3c
Combining instructions with questions.

can be preprinted with a field to show operators the keying positions of characters.

10 *Prenumber source documents:* Prenumber source documents so it is possible to account for every document. If each document has a unique serial number, input transactions can be sorted by serial number and breaks in the sequence of numbers identified.

11 *Conform to organization's standards:* An organization should have a forms control section responsible for overall forms design standards; for example, numbering and color conventions, placement of the organization's logos, retention requirements, ordering and stockkeeping requirements. Ensure the source document design conforms to these standards.

DATA ENTRY SCREEN DESIGN

If direct entry data capture is used or source documents are keyed directly to magnetic media using some type of visual display device, high-quality screen design must be accomplished if data entry errors are to be avoided and effectiveness and efficiency objectives are to be achieved. Galitz [1980], for example, reports that CNA Insurance estimated an extra 14 worker-years would be needed if poor screen design resulted in users having to spend an extra 20 seconds per screen in a system that processed 4.8 million screens per year.

Although in many ways screen design is still an art, many design guidelines have now emerged based on experience with alternative designs. The primary factor that causes screen designs to vary is whether the screen is used for direct entry data capture (no source document) or input of data already captured on a source document. The following sections provide a brief introduction to screen design issues (see, further, Galitz [1980]).

Screen Organization

Screens should be designed so they are uncluttered and symmetrically balanced. All the information needed to perform a task must be on a screen, yet users should be able to identify quickly the information they require. Where multiple screens must be used to capture a transaction, the screens should be broken at some logical point. Symmetry can be achieved by grouping like elements together, balancing the number of elements on both sides of the screen, ensuring that elements are aligned, and using blank space and line delimiters strategically.

If a screen is used for direct entry data capture, the layout of elements on the screen must mirror the way in which data is obtained during the data capture task. If the screen is used for source document data entry, however, the screen must be an image of the source document on which the data is first captured and transcribed. In the former case, the screen guides users through the data capture process. In the latter case, users should be able to keep their eyes on the source document during the keying process and have to view the screen only when some problem is encountered.

An important objective in screen design is consistency. Users develop facility with a particular design. Consequently, if possible this design should be used repeatedly across applications. For example, certain parts of a screen should always be used to display instructions for completing the screen, error messages, instructions for screen disposition, and status messages.

Caption Design

Captions indicate the nature of the data to be entered in a field on a screen. Design considerations include structure, size, type font, display intensity, format, alignment, justification, and spacing. Again, the primary factor affecting the design of captions is whether the screen is used for direct entry data capture or input of data already captured on a source document.

In terms of structure and size, captions must be fully spelled out if a screen is used for direct entry data capture. Since the screen guides the user during the data capture process, the meaning of the captions must be unambiguous. If data entry is based on a source document, however, captions can be abbreviated since users can refer to the source document to obtain the full meaning of a caption. In general, abbreviated captions should be 3–8 characters in length.

Uppercase type font should be used for all captions to distinguish them from data entered by a user. To further differentiate captions and data entry fields, different display intensities can be used. Since captions are the primary focus during data entry, they should have a higher display intensity than the data entered by users.

Captions should always precede their associated data entry field on the same line as the data entry field. One exception to this guideline is where multiple data entry fields relate to the same caption. In this case, the data entry fields should be stacked under the caption. For example:

SALESPERSON: _____   PREVIOUS OCCUPATION

: _____

: _____

: _____

Note, also, where the caption and data entry field appear on the same line, the caption is followed immediately by a colon, and at least one space exists between the colon and the data entry field. Where the data entry fields are stacked, however, the colon immediately precedes the data entry field, and a separating space is not used between the colon and the data entry field.

If direct entry data capture is used, captions should be aligned vertically in columns. Within a column, justification depends on the relative sizes of captions used within the column. If the caption sizes are approximately equal, left justification should be used. Where caption sizes vary considerably, right justification should be used. For example:

NAME: _____   ORDER LINE NUMBER: _____

AGE: _____   PRODUCT: _____

STATUS: _____   SUPPLY WAREHOUSE: _____

If the screen is used for entry of data already captured on a source document, however, alignment and justification are dictated by the source document. The screen design should be an image of the source document.

Both horizontal and vertical spacing around captions are important to attaining an uncluttered screen. For horizontal spacing, direct entry data capture screens should have a minimum of five spaces between the longest data entry field in a column and the leftmost caption in an adjacent column. Source document screens should have a minimum of three spaces between a data entry field and the following caption. For vertical spacing, direct entry data capture screens should have a blank line every fifth row; that is, captions and the associated data entry fields should be clustered in groups of five. Source document screens should mirror the vertical spaces found on the source document.

Data Entry Field Design

Data entry fields should immediately follow their associated caption either on the same line or, in the case of a repeating field, on several lines immediately below the caption. At least the starting character of the field should be identified, and in many cases it is useful to indicate the size of the field by using an underscore character or some other character. As each new character is entered into the field, the existing character is replaced.

Where direct entry data capture screens are used, completion aids reduce keying errors. For example, if a date must be entered, either the caption or the field size characters can be used to indicate the date format:

DATE (YYMMDD): _____   DATE: YYMMDD

Where source document screens are used, completion aids are not needed since the user can refer to the source document for completion instructions.

Tabbing and Skipping

Galitz [1980] argues that automatic skipping to a new field should be avoided in data entry screen design for two reasons. First, with an automatic skip feature, users may make a field size error that remains undetected because the cursor simply skips to a new field. Second, in many applications, data entry fields often are not filled anyway so the user must still tab to the next field. Rather than having users decide whether tabbing is needed, it is simpler to require them always to tab to the next field.

Color

In a data entry screen design, color can be used to aid in locating a particular caption or data item, to separate areas on the display, or to indicate a changed status (e.g., an error situation). Color appears to reduce search time for an item on a screen and to motivate users better because the screen is more interesting. Nonetheless, poor use of color can distract or confuse users by implying that similarities or differences exist among captions or data items on the display when this is not the case. Some general design guidelines are:

1 Use color sparingly and consistently
2 Use only a few colors that are widely spaced along the visual spectrum
3 Consider the visibility of the color in the context of the environment, e.g., the glare of overhead lighting
4 For data entry screens that are used for prolonged periods, avoid overuse of bright colors that cause fatigue
5 Consider the cultural implications of the colors used—in different cultures the same color can have different meanings
6 Consider the implications of color for users who are color blind

Response Time

During data entry, the response time is the interval that elapses between entry of a data item and the system's indication that it is ready to accept a new data item. As with response times for all types of interactive tasks, the response time for data entry should be reasonably constant and sufficiently fast to sustain continuity in the task being performed by the user. Chapter 15 addresses these matters further.

Within a transaction, response time should be reasonably fast—say, two to four seconds. When data entry for a transaction has been completed, the user will tolerate a longer response time. Fast response times are required if data is being keyed from a source document since the user will not want their keying rhythm broken by response delays. If a dedicated source document is not being used, users will tolerate a slower response time as they move from one data item to another.

Display Rate

The display rate is the rate at which characters or images on a screen are displayed. It is a function of the speed with which data can be communicated between the terminal and the computer (baud rate).

Data entry screens require a fast display rate. Users are unwilling to wait long periods while captions and images are displayed on a screen. They seek to enter data quickly into the system, especially if it is being keyed from a dedicated source document. Thus, data entry screens require high baud rates.

"Help" Facility

A "help" facility may be useful when data entry is not based upon a dedicated source document. If users are uncertain about the nature or format of the data to be entered into a particular field, they may ask the system to provide information to assist them. This information might give a more complete explanation of the nature of the data item and the format for entry of a particular value. It may also describe the validation rules that apply to the item. A help facility is especially important if inexperienced or novice users will submit data to the system.

DATA CODE CONTROLS

Data codes have two purposes in computer systems. First, they uniquely identify an entity or identify an entity as a member of a group or set. Textual or narrative description does not always uniquely identify an entity; for example, two people may have the same name. Second, for identification purposes, codes often are more efficient than textual or narrative description, since they require a smaller number of characters to carry a given amount of information.

Design Requirements

Badly designed codes affect the input process in two ways. First, they are error-prone. Second, they cause data recording and keying processes to be slow and inefficient. A well-designed coding system achieves certain objectives:

Objective	Explanation
Flexibility	Easy addition of new items or categories.
Meaningfulness	Where possible, a code should indicate the values of the attributes of the entity.
Compactness	Maximum information conveyed with a minimum number of characters.
Convenience ✓	A code should be easy to assign, encode, decode, and key.
Evolvability	Where possible, a code can be adapted to changing user requirements.

Data Coding Errors

Data coding errors are one of six types:

1 *Addition:* An extra character is added, e.g., 87942 coded as 879142.

2 *Truncation:* A character is omitted, e.g., 87942 coded as 8792.

3 *Transcription:* A wrong character is recorded, e.g., 87942 coded as 81942.

4 *Transposition:* Adjacent characters are reversed, e.g., 87942 coded as 78942.

5 *Double transposition:* Characters separated by more than one character are reversed, e.g., 87942 coded as 84972.

The notion that length may be important derives from the work of Miller [1956] who argues humans can hold in short-term memory only about five to nine (average seven) "chunks" of information and process them effectively. This theory has been supported by many empirical studies on coding systems (see, for example, Conrad [1959] and Chapdelaine [1963]). In general, the idea of breaking up long codes into chunks by using hyphens or slashes is well-accepted as a means of reducing coding errors.

If alphabetic and numeric characters are to be mixed in a code, the error rate is lower if the alphabetics are grouped together and the numerics are grouped together. Thus, a code such as ABN653 is less prone to error than a code of A6B53N. From the viewpoint of keypunching, the former code is better also. The latter code breaks the rhythm of keying by interchanging alphabetics and numerics. The alphabetic characters I, J, O, Q, and Z also should be avoided since often they are misread.

Types of Codes

Even given the general design guidelines specified above, the choice of a coding system for an application system is not always clear-cut. The following sections briefly discuss the various coding systems available and their relative advantages and disadvantages.

Serial Codes   Serial coding systems assign consecutive numbers (or alphabetics) to an entity irrespective of the attributes of the entity. Thus, a serial code uniquely identifies an entity; however, the code indicates nothing further about the entity; for example, the category of items in which it belongs. The major advantages of a serial code are the ease with which a new item can be added and conciseness. The code presents problems when the file of items is volatile; that is, significant numbers of additions and deletions occur. Deleted items must have their codes reassigned to new items; otherwise, significant gaps in the sequence occur and the code is no longer concise.

As another disadvantage, a serial code often conveys no information about the characteristics of the entity to which it is assigned. However, in some ways this lack is also an advantage. Consider a database management system environment where there is sharing of data and the number and types of users and their needs are in a state of flux. Different users may wish to view data differently. A code that presumes one view of data may be inappropriate for certain users. Thus, a serial coding system may contribute better to the evolution of the system.

Block Sequence Codes   Block sequence codes assign blocks of numbers to particular categories of an entity. The primary attribute on which entities are to be categorized must be chosen, and blocks of numbers assigned for each value of the attribute. For example, if account numbers are assigned to customers on the basis of the discount allowed each customer, a block sequence code would be:

101 R. Allen
102 J. Smith   } 3% discount allowed
103 M. Clarke
.
.
.

201 S. Elders   } 3½% discount allowed
202 M. Ball
.
.
.

301 K. Kline
302 G. Brown   } 4% discount allowed
303 F. Water

Block sequence codes have the advantage of giving some mnemonic value to the code. Nevertheless, there are problems in choosing the size of the block needed (and the remedy if overflow occurs) and ensuring blocks are not too large so wasted characters occur and the code is no longer concise.

Hierarchical Codes   Hierarchical codes require selection of the set of attributes of the entity to be coded and their ordering in terms of importance. The value of the code for the entity is a combination of the values of the codes for each attribute of the entity. For example, the following hierarchical code for an account breaks up into three components (expenditure within departments within divisions):

C65   /   423   /   3956
Division Department   Type of
number   number   expenditure

Hierarchical codes usually are more meaningful to their users than are serial or block sequence codes. They also carry more information about the entity to which they are assigned. Nevertheless, sometimes they present problems when change occurs. If in the example given above a change to the organizational structure occurred and department 423 was assigned to a different division C25, new codes would have to be learned and the master file altered and resequenced.

Association Codes   Association codes go by a variety of names: significant digit codes, mnemonic codes, alphabetic derivation codes. With an association code the attributes of the entity to be coded are selected and unique codes assigned each attribute value. The codes may be numeric, alphabetic, or alphanumeric. The code for the entity is simply a linear combination of the different codes assigned the attributes of the entity. Unlike a hierarchical code, the order in which the codes for the attributes occur in the overall code does not necessarily imply some type of hierarchical relationship. The following is an example of an association code assigned a shirt:

SHM32DRCOT
where   SH = shirt
        M = male
        32 = 32 centimeters, the neck size
        DR = dress shirt
        COT = cotton fabric

Association codes have high mnemonic value; they carry substantial information about the entity they represent. However, they quickly become long. Since often a full set of characters is not used for each character position, they are not concise.

CHECK DIGITS

In some cases errors made in transcribing or keying data can have serious consequences. For example, keying the wrong account number for a creditor may result in a payment being made to someone who has no legal claim on the assets of the organization. Keying a wrong part number may result in a large quantity of incorrect parts being sent to a job. One control used to guard against these types of errors is a check digit.

Calculating Check Digits

A check digit is a redundant digit(s) added to a data code that enables the accuracy of other characters in the code to be checked. The check digit may act as a prefix character, a suffix character, or it may be placed somewhere in the middle of the code. The last alternative is sometimes used for credit cards so that if a blank plastic card is stolen, it is difficult for a forger to work out a valid account number.

There are many ways of calculating check digits. A simple way is to add up the digits in a number and assign the result as a suffix character. For example, if the code is 2148, the check digit is $2 + 1 + 4 + 8 = 15$. Dropping the tens digit, the check digit will be 5 and the code 21485. However, this check digit does not detect a very common kind of coding error, namely, a transposition error. The incorrect code 2814 still produces the correct check digit.

To overcome this problem a different method of calculating a check digit can be used. Given, again, the code 2148, the steps are:

1 Multiply each digit by a weight. In this case the weight used will be 5-4-3-2; that is, 2 for the units digit, 3 for the tens digit, 4 for the hundreds digit, and 5 for the thousands digit, viz:

$$8 \times 2 = 16$$
$$4 \times 3 = 12$$
$$1 \times 4 = 4$$
$$2 \times 5 = 10$$

2 Sum the products $= 42$.

3 Divide by a modulus. In this case the modulus 11 is chosen.

$$\frac{42}{11} = 3 \text{ with remainder } 9$$

4 Subtract the remainder from the modulus and the result constitutes the check digit.

$$11 - 9 = 2$$

5 Add the check digit to the code as a suffix. The result is 21482.

The check digit can be recalculated upon keying to detect a coding or keying error, or upon reading the data into the computer. The recalculation for the above code proceeds as follows:

1 Multiply each digit by its corresponding weight. The check digit takes a weight of 1.

$$2 \times 1 = 2$$
$$8 \times 2 = 16$$
$$4 \times 3 = 12$$
$$1 \times 4 = 4$$
$$2 \times 5 = 10$$

2 Sum the products = 44.

3 Divide by the modulus

$$\frac{44}{11} = 4$$

4 If the remainder is zero, there is a high probability the code is correct.

If the code contains alphabetics, a check digit can still be calculated. Each alphabetic must be assigned a number according to some rule.

EFFICIENCY OF CHECK DIGIT METHODS

Table 10-1 shows the relative efficiency of different check digit methods at detecting various types of errors. The percentages given refer only to the combination of digits that can produce an erroneous code that the check digit will detect. Of course, in practice the different types of errors are unlikely to occur with the same frequency. For example, Beckley [1967] reports that one study found the frequency of errors to be as follows:

Transcription	86%
Single transposition	8%
Double transposition and random	6%

However, he points out that other factors can affect error frequency; for example, whether the codes are typed or handwritten.

One difficulty that arises when choosing a check digit system with modulus 11 or greater is that two check digits rather than one are required. For example, if modulus 11 produces a remainder of 1, a check digit of 10 is required. The overhead of having a two-character check digit instead of a one-character check digit may be unacceptable. There are several solutions to the problem. First, codes generating a check digit of 10 or more are declared illegal and cannot be used. With modulus 11, for example, 9% of possible codes are unavailable. Second, a special character (say, an alphabetic) can be used to represent a check digit that exceeds nine. This approach causes problems if only numeric codes are desired. Finally, Campbell [1970] suggests a scheme whereby two sets of weights are used. When a check digit of 10 or more is calculated using the first set of weights, an alternative check digit is calculated using the second set of weights. When the check digit is validated and a nonzero remainder is obtained, the second set of weights must then be used to see whether the check digit is valid according to this set of weights.

When to Use Check Digits

Check digits involve overhead in terms of a redundant character carried at least partially through the system and extra computation needed to calculate and check the check digit. Therefore, use of check digits should be limited to critical fields.

TABLE 10-1
EFFICIENCY OF DIFFERENT MODULI FOR CHECK DIGITS

Modulus	Range weights that may be used	Max. length of number without repeating weight	Weights used	Tran-scription	Single trans-position	Double trans-position	Other trans-position	Random
					Percentage errors detected			
10	1–9	8	1-2-1-2-1	94.5	100	Nil	50.0	90.0
			1-3-1-3-1	100	88.9	Nil	44.5	90.0
			7-6-5-4-3-2	88.2	100	88.9	89.8	90.0
			9-8-7-4-3-2	94.5	100	88.9	72.2	90.0
			1-3-7-1-3-7	100	88.9	88.9	88.9	90.0
11	1–10	9	10-9-8.....2	100	100	100	100	90.9
			1-2-4-8-16, etc.	100	100	100	100	90.9
13	1–12	11	Any	100	100	100	100	92.3
17	1–16	15	Any	100	100	100	100	94.1
19	1–18	17	Any	100	100	100	100	94.7
23	1–22	21	Any	100	100	100	100	95.6
31	1–30	29	Any	100	100	100	100	96.8
37	1–36	35	Any	100	100	100	100	97.3

Source: Adapted from Daniels and Yeates [1971]. Used by permission. The National Computing Center.

Manual calculation or checking of check digits should be avoided. The process is time-consuming and error-prone. For new codes the check digit should be precalculated and assigned as part of the code. Where possible, the computer should assign new codes with their check digits.

Checking of check digits should take place only by machine; for example, during keying or by an input program. To save storage space the check digit can be dropped once it has been read into the machine and recalculated upon output. The tradeoff here is storage space versus processing time.

BATCH CONTROLS

Some of the simplest and most effective controls over data capture, preparation, and entry processes are batch controls. Batching is the process of grouping together transactions bearing some type of relationship to each other. Various controls then can be exercised over the batch to prevent or detect errors.

There are two types of batches: physical batches and logical batches. Physical batches are groups of transactions that constitute a physical unit. For example, source documents can be spiked and tied together. Logical batches are groups of transactions bound together on some logical basis, rather than being physically contiguous. For example, different clerks may enter transactions into a system using an online terminal. Each clerk keeps control totals of the transactions that she/he has entered. The input program logically groups transactions entered on the basis of the clerk's identification number, and after some period has elapsed, prepares control totals for reconciliation with the clerk's control totals.

Controls over Batches

Controls over batches have two purposes: (*a*) to ensure the accuracy and completeness of their content, and (*b*) to ensure they are not lost during transportation. Two documents are needed to help achieve these purposes: a batch cover sheet and a batch control register.

A batch cover sheet (Figure 10-4) for a physical batch contains some or all of the following information:

1 A unique batch number

2 Control totals for the batch

3 Data common to the various transactions in the batch, e.g., transaction type

4 Date when the batch was prepared

5 Information on errors detected in the batch

6 Space for signatures of personnel who have dealt with the batch, e.g., the person who prepared the batch, the person who checked the batch, the person who keyed the batch, the person who filed the batch

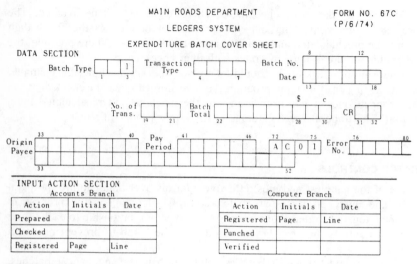

FIGURE 10-4
Batch cover sheet. (*Main Roads Department, Queensland, Australia.*)

For a logical batch, only some of this information may be recorded. For example, a clerk simply may keep a record of the transaction amounts entered into the system over the time period during which batch control totals are computed.

Control totals calculated for a batch are one of three types:

Control total type	Explanation
Financial totals	Grand totals calculated for each field containing dollar amounts
Hash totals	Grand totals calculated for any code on a document in the batch; e.g., the source document serial numbers can be totalled
Document/record counts	Grand totals for the number of documents or records in the batch

To check control totals, either the input validation program, or in some cases the data entry device, recomputes the total. Discrepancies arise through incorrect calculation of a control total, insertion or removal of documents, changes made to fields, or incorrect keying.

A batch control register (Figure 10-5) records the transit of physical batches between various sections or departments within an organization. Each person responsible for handling batches has a batch register. The register is signed each time a batch is received or dispatched. The person who brings the batch or takes the batch away countersigns the register. In some cases the person taking over responsibility for the batch also checks its contents; however, this procedure is costly.

MAIN ROADS DEPARTMENT

LEDGER SYSTEM

BATCH CONTROL REGISTER

FORM 67A
(P/1/75)

DATE _____

PAGE _____

LINE	IDENTIFICATION			CONTROL		VALIDATION RESULTS				G.C.S. BATCH No.	VERIFIED	TRANSFER TAPE No.	ERASE DATE
	TYPE	BATCH No.	DATE	No.	AMOUNT		No.	AMOUNT	DATE				
1						A							
						R							
2						A							
						R							
3						A							
						R							
4						A							
						R							
5						A							
						R							
6						A							
						R							
7						A							
						R							
8						A							
						R							
9						A							
						R							
10						A							
						R							
11						A							
						R							
12						A							
						R							
13						A							
						R							
14						A							
						R							
15						A							
						R							
16						A							
						R							
17						A							
						R							
18						A							
						R							
19						A							
						R							
20						A							
						R							

ACCOUNTS BRANCH   TIME DESPATCHED.................

COMPUTER   TIME RECEIVED.................

FIGURE 10-5
Batch control register. (*Main Roads Department, Queensland, Australia.*)

Batch Design

Batch design involves choosing the size and nature of the batches to be used. Three major design guidelines should be followed:

1 Have the batch small enough to facilitate locating errors if batch controls do not balance.
2 The batch should be large enough to constitute a reasonably sized unit of work.
3 The batch should constitute a logical unit; for example, a group of documents all containing a single transaction type.

INSTRUCTION INPUT

Ensuring the quality of instruction input to a computer system is a more difficult objective to achieve than ensuring the quality of data input. Data input tends to follow standardized patterns. The errors or irregularities that are likely to occur usually can be anticipated. During instruction input, however, users often attempt to communicate complex actions that they want the system to undertake. On the one hand, the input subsystem needs to provide considerable flexibility so users can accomplish their processing objectives. On the other hand, it needs to exercise careful control over the actions they undertake. The languages used to communicate instructions to the system tend to trade off flexibility with control.

Job Control Languages

Job control languages (JCLs) are used to define the tasks to be performed by a computer in a batch processing environment. They specify, among other things, the programs to be executed, the files to be used, the input/output devices needed, the amount of primary and secondary storage required, the amount of central processor time needed, the actions to be undertaken if a job terminates abnormally, and the accounts to be charged for resource consumption.

JCLs tend to be either statement-oriented languages or parameter-oriented languages. Statement-oriented languages provide a large number of commands that have few parameters attached to each command. Thus, errors tend to occur in the statement specification rather than the parameter specification. Parameter-oriented languages use a small number of commands, each command having a large number of parameters. Thus, errors tend to occur in the parameter specification rather than the statement specification.

Irrespective of the type of JCL used, instructions specified in a JCL tend to be error-prone. To accommodate the range of data processing tasks that must be undertaken, JCLs must be flexible; unfortunately, this flexibility leads to complexity. Accordingly, many organizations have developed JCL standards to assist users to write JCL statements and to help others (such as operators, auditors, and managers) to understand these statements. In a review of JCL input procedures, auditors must assess the quality of these standards and evaluate the reliability of the controls used to ensure compliance with these standards.

Chapter 8 indicated the importance of protecting JCL files from unauthorized modifications once those files have been established. Unauthorized modifications allow fraudulent programs or data files to be loaded or data to be dispatched to an unauthorized destination. Program and data library controls should be exercised over JCL files once they have been established and tested to ensure their authenticity, accuracy, and completeness.

Menu-Driven Languages

In interactive systems, the simplest way of providing instructions to a system is via a menu-driven language. The system presents users with a list of options, and users choose an option in some way—for example, they type in a number to indicate their choice, they position the cursor on the selection and hit the carriage return key or press a button if they are using a mouse, they use a light pen, they touch the screen with their finger.

In general, few errors are likely to occur using menu-driven languages. Galitz [1980] argues that numbers rather than alphabetics should be used to designate the list of choices, and that the list of numbers should start with one rather than zero. If possible, the numbering system should be consistent across screens and applications; that is, the same number should apply to the same action choice if the action choice appears on different screens. The range of choices on a single screen also should be limited. Hierarchies of menus can be used to allow the user to increase the specificity of their choice (Figure 10-6).

Effectiveness and efficiency issues are important when menu-driven languages are used. Whereas menus facilitate use of the system by novices, they inhibit fast use of the system by experts. There are various ways to assist the expert user. Menu-driven languages can be used in conjunction with command languages (discussed below) so the user can select either a menu option or specify a command name. A menu of menu names can be used to allow the user to drop through a hierarchy of menus to a particular menu. Backtracking features should exist to enable users to return to higher level menus, particularly if they wish to restart a series of choices.

Question-Answer Dialogs

Question-answer dialogs are used primarily to obtain data input. The system asks a question about the value of some data item and the user responds. Nevertheless, question-answer dialogs also can be used to obtain instruction input in conjunction with data input. For example, Figure 10-7 shows the user wants a project to be evaluated using the net present value technique. The entry of "NPV" then directs the system to ask for particular types of data input.

If the answers to be provided in a question-answer dialog are not clear, users will make errors when they provide instruction (or data) input. A well-designed

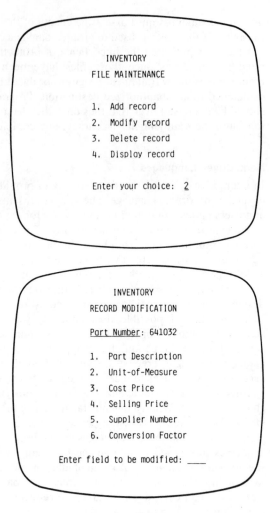

FIGURE 10-6
Menu-driven interactive language.

question-answer dialog makes clear the set of answers that are valid. In those cases where the required answers are not obvious, a help facility can be used to assist inexperienced users.

As with menu-driven languages, effectiveness and efficiency issues are a primary concern. Question-answer dialogs are most useful when users are moderately experienced. For inexperienced users, the answer to be provided may not always be obvious. For experienced users, the alternating sequence of question and answer may be slow and frustrating. The dialog might permit experienced users to stack answers—that is, provide multiple answers at the same time—or to change to another language mode.

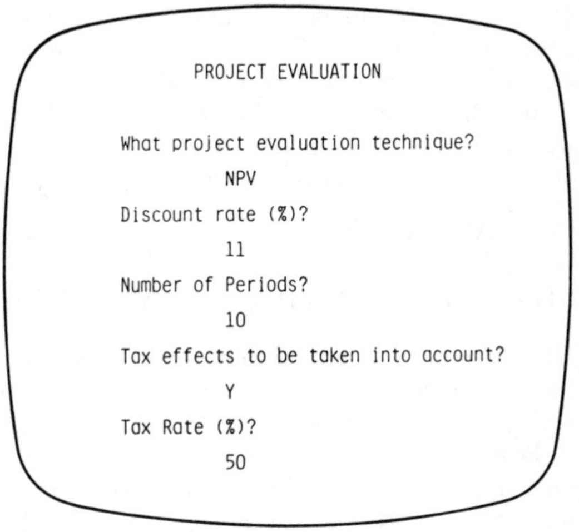

```
                      PROJECT EVALUATION

              What project evaluation technique?
                            NPV
              Discount rate (%)?
                            11
              Number of Periods?
                            10
              Tax effects to be taken into account?
                            Y
              Tax Rate (%)?
                            50
```

FIGURE 10-7
Question-answer dialog.

Command Languages

Command languages require a user to specify a command to invoke some process and a set of arguments that specify precisely how the process should be executed. For example, SQL is a database interrogation language that uses a command language format. To print the customer numbers of those customers who had more than 10 transactions over $200, the following SQL solution would be specified:

SELECT	CUSTNO
FROM	TRANS
WHERE	AMOUNT > '200'
GROUP BY	CUSTNO
HAVING COUNT	(*) > '10';

In this example, "SELECT" is a command and "CUSTNO" is an argument.

Two major decisions must be made in the design of a command language: first, whether to use a large number of commands with a small number of arguments or a small number of commands with a large number of arguments; and second, whether to use keywords or position to specify the arguments. These decisions affect the ease with which users can employ the language and the number of errors that they are likely to make.

In general, it appears better to use command languages with a small number of commands and a large number of arguments. Inevitably, users seem to employ only a small subset of the commands available in a command language—perhaps because they have difficulty remembering all the commands—and so it seems better to make these commands powerful by providing an extensive list of arguments. Furthermore, to permit more effective and efficient use of command languages, command names should be meaningful and it should be possible to truncate them to reduce typing effort (see, for example, Benbasat and Wand [1984]).

Whether arguments should be specified by keywords or position seems to depend on the user's expertise with the command language. Presumably, with a little experience most users would prefer to type:

COPY MYFILE YOURFILE

instead of

COPY FROM = MYFILE TO = YOURFILE

Of course, as argument lists become longer, remembering the position of each argument and whether it is mandatory or optional becomes more difficult. Consequently, keyword specification of arguments may then be preferred.

Prompts and defaults reduce the number of errors made using a command language. For example, if users cannot remember the arguments associated with a command, they should be able to type a "?" (or press some other key) to obtain a prompt from the language on each argument required. Similarly, a command language reduces typing effort if it supplies the likely value of an argument as a default. For example, some spreadsheet command languages use the position of the current cell as the default value in many commands. The default can simply be overwritten if it is not the value required.

Forms-Based Languages

Forms-based languages have users specifying commands and data in the context of either some input or output form. For example, Figure 10-8 shows a command issued in the Query-by-Example database interrogation language to print the stock item number located in warehouse 1. Note how the input commands are provided in the context of an input form that mirrors the relation in the database. Similarly, if the output were some type of graph, users might employ a light pen to select a command that indicates they want the scales of the axes to be changed.

Forms-based languages may be successful if users solve problems in the context of input and output forms. In these cases the syntax of the language corresponds to the ways users think about the problem and, as such, input errors are reduced and the languages tend to be used effectively and efficiently. Once the functions to be performed do not map easily into the context of input and output forms, however, the languages tend to be awkward and unwieldy to use.

Natural Languages

Natural language interfaces are still primarily the subject of substantial research and development efforts. Nevertheless, a few commercial products

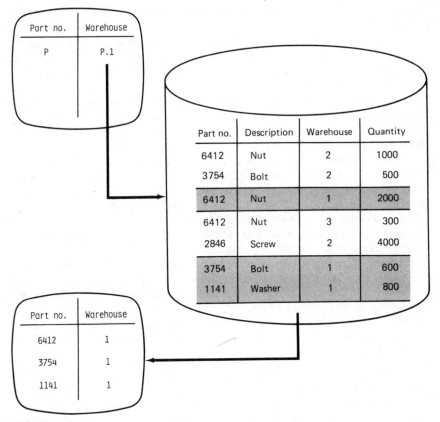

FIGURE 10-8
Forms-based language illustration of Query-by-Example.

are now available, so auditors may confront them in selected application domains and be required to evaluate their capabilities from an asset safeguarding, data integrity, effectiveness, and efficiency perspective.

The ultimate goal of research on natural language interfaces is to enable free-form natural language interaction to occur between users and the machine, perhaps via a speech production/recognition device. Whereas in certain types of applications this may be a laudable objective, it is still unclear whether natural language is the best form of interface for all types of applications. In particular, the sorts of applications that tend to concern auditors may not be suitable applications for natural language interfaces.

Current natural language interfaces have several limitations:

1 They do not always cope well with the ambiguity and redundancy present in natural language. For example, the meaning of the sentence "Time flies." is different depending on whether "time" is the noun and "flies" is the verb or vice versa.

2 Substantial effort must be expended to establish the lexicon for the natural language interface. Users must define all possible words they may use, and this work must be redone each time a new application domain is to be accessed via natural language.

3 Even minor deviations outside the lexicon established for the application domain can cause problems. Users may be unaware of the precise boundaries of the domain and be inhibited in the commands they issue in case they traverse these boundaries.

4 If the database with which users interact is subject to frequent definitional changes, natural language interfaces may quickly become problematical. The lexicon must be able to evolve in light of definitional changes. Currently, easy evolution of the lexicon is technically a difficult problem to solve.

5 Users may be unaware of the ambiguity that can exist in natural language responses that the system gives to the commands they issue. For example, the query "How many stores in Tasmania had price overrides for sales of windsurfers?" may evoke a response of "none." However, no stores in Tasmania may be selling windsurfers, and so the response may be misleading.

6 It is still unclear whether the wordiness of natural language does not lead to ineffective and inefficient interaction with the system, at least for certain types of applications. If users wish to express commands in a formal, constrained, or abbreviated way, a natural language interface should be able to accept this form of input.

Until these technical problems have been overcome, auditors should be cautious in their evaluation of natural language interfaces. If it is critical that absolute precision be attained in the command and data input supplied to a system and in the responses obtained from a system, other types of interfaces should be considered.

Direct Manipulation Interfaces

Some of the newer forms of interfaces to systems employ direct manipulation to enter commands and data. Shneiderman [1983] identifies three attributes of a direct manipulation interface: (a) visibility of the object of interest; (b) rapid, reversible, incremental actions; (c) use of direct manipulation devices rather than command language syntax to manipulate the objects of interest. Some examples of direct manipulation interfaces are:

1 *Electronic spreadsheet:* Users see a visual image of the spreadsheet and its associated cell values. They can alter cell values by using a mouse to move the cursor to the cell to be altered and then keying in the new value. The results of the change are immediately apparent as all dependent cell values adjust.

2 *Spatial data manager:* Users see a graph or a map at one level of detail. They can "zoom" to lower or higher levels of detail using a joystick.

3 *Electronic desktops:* Users see an image of a desktop with an in-basket, an out-basket, a trash basket, a set of files, a Rolodex name-and-address file, etc. They can manipulate these objects using a mouse, a joystick, or some type of pointing device. For example, files to be deleted can be moved to the trash basket.

Direct manipulation interfaces seem to offer substantial advantages: users appear highly motivated to master the system; they enjoy learning and exploring the more powerful aspects of the system; they work effectively and efficiently; and they quickly gain confidence in using the system. Perhaps the most substantial drawback is finding the appropriate image or icon of the object to be manipulated. For many types of accounting data, for example, it is difficult to think of an appropriate icon to use: How should the payment of an accounts receivable be portrayed pictorially? Nevertheless, whenever direct manipulation can be used, from an audit perspective it seems to provide a higher-quality interface than traditional language-oriented interfaces.

AUDIT TRAIL CONTROLS

With the data input and instruction input functions, the audit trail in the input subsystem maintains the chronology of events from the time data and instructions are captured until they are entered into the system.

Accounting Audit Trail

In the case of data input, audit trail controls must maintain data about the origin of a transaction for explosion purposes. If document-based data capture is used, the audit trail data should be present on the source documents that are prepared. For example, the source document should show who prepared the document, who authorized the document, when it was prepared, what account or record is to be updated, what standing data item is to be updated, and the batch number of the physical batch in which the document is to be included.

If direct entry data capture is used, the audit trail data should be stored on magnetic media. In some cases it may also be printed if a hard-copy record of the input is used for other purposes; for example, a sales order acknowledgement may be printed for customers when orders are received via the telephone and entered directly at a terminal. With direct entry data capture, the input program must attach certain audit trail data to the input record; for example, the identity of the terminal operator, the identity of the terminal, the time and date of input, and a unique reference number for the transaction that will be carried through the system.

If a hybrid method of data capture is used, audit trail data must be recorded on magnetic media. In some cases it may be present on source documents or printed documents, depending on the nature of the hybrid data capture method used. For example, if the "source document" is a carton with the universal product code, a point-of-sale device provides a printed list of items purchased by a customer. The original listing is given to the customer, and a duplicate copy is usually retained by the vendor. In addition, the point-of-sale device must attach audit trail data to the input transaction—for example, the time and date of entry, the identity of the terminal operator, and its own identifier.

In the case of instruction input, the input subsystem must retain a record on magnetic media containing such data items as the originator of the instruction, the type of instruction and its arguments, the results produced, the terminal identifier, and the time and date of entry of the instruction. Sometimes a hard-copy record of the instruction is available. For example, it may be a JCL statement that is submitted initially on a coding sheet, or the instruction may have been submitted using a typewriter terminal, in which case a printed copy of the interaction between the user and the system will be available.

Operations Audit Trail

Since the input subsystem often involves labor-intensive activities, operations audit trail data is an important means of improving the effectiveness and efficiency of the subsystem. Some of the types of operations audit trail data that might be collected are:

1 Time to key in a source document at a terminal
2 Number of read errors made by an OCR device
3 Number of keying errors identified during verification
4 Frequency with which an instruction in a command language is used
5 Time taken to execute the same instruction using a light pen versus a mouse

By analyzing this data, error-prone input activities can be identified and remedial action taken. For example, the time taken to enter data on a screen may indicate that more user training is needed or a screen redesign is necessary. Similarly, a comparison of times taken to enter the same data or instruction using different devices may be used to encourage users to employ the more efficient device.

EXISTENCE CONTROLS

Existence controls in the input subsystem are critical since it may be necessary to return to the raw data input if transaction log files are lost. If, for example, the current version of the database is destroyed and the log of transactions that has updated the database since the last dump is also destroyed, it is necessary to reload the last dump of the database and to reprocess the raw data captured and entered into the system since that dump.

To protect source documents from loss or destruction, they should be stored in a secure manner. If possible, a duplicate copy of source documents also should be stored off site. This backup copy might be prepared as part of a multipart form completed at the time of data capture. If the log of input transactions is then lost, recovery can be effected by simply rekeying data from the original source documents or the backup version of the source documents.

If a transaction listing is produced as a by-product of direct data entry, the transaction listing can be used to rekey input if the log of input transactions is lost. Thus, transaction listings should be sorted securely and, if possible, backup copies should be sorted off site. If no transaction listing is produced, however, existence controls over the log of input transactions are critical. If the log is lost and recovery must be undertaken, terminal operators will have to try to recall what input they have keyed into the system. Thus, the log of input transactions should be stored on a secure and reliable device. Moreover, dual recording of the log might be undertaken at two physically separate locations (see, also, Chapter 14).

Existence controls for instruction input are often less critical than those required for data input. If an instruction evokes an update to the database, it will be recorded anyway as part of the input transaction log. If it does not affect the database—for example, it is simply an interrogation of a data item value— recovering the record of the instruction input may be less important. Nonetheless, recovering instruction input should not be dismissed as unnecessary. Sometimes it may be important to identify who interrogated a database when possible security problems are being investigated or when the database is found to be in an erroneous state.

SUMMARY

Controls over data input and instruction input are especially important to the auditor for three reasons. First, often the largest number of controls exist in the input subsystem and so auditors must spend substantial time assessing the reliability of these controls. Second, data and instruction input involves large amounts of human intervention and is often routine, monotonous, and error-prone. Third, research suggests that the input subsystem is often the target of irregularities.

Evaluating controls over data capture, data preparation, data input, and instruction input is a complex problem for the auditor. A large number of different combinations of data and instruction input methods exist, and each of these methods has different strengths and weaknesses. The auditor must have a good understanding of the different methods to be able to evaluate their capabilities and drawbacks.

With respect to data input, many additional controls are needed to preserve integrity. These include good source document design, good data entry screen design, selection of an appropriate data coding method, choice of a check digit method for key fields, and choice of appropriate batch controls.

REVIEW QUESTIONS

10-1 From an audit perspective, why are controls over the input subsystem often more critical than controls over other subsystems?

10-2 Classify each of the following types of data capture as either document-based, direct entry, or a hybrid approach:

a A salesperson uses a card dialer Touch-Tone device to input data from a remote location about a sale to a customer.

b A manager makes alterations with a light pen to a cost-volume-profit chart displayed on a VDU.

c An investment analyst receives a magnetic tape containing stock prices from the stock exchange for input to her financial modeling package.

d A warehouse receiving clerk speaks into a voice recognition device to update a file containing information on the status of various inventory bins.

e A salesclerk removes a punched card attached to a product to designate sale of the product.

f A digitizer is used to read an architect's drawings for input to a computer-aided design application.

10-3 Briefly describe the relative advantages of hybrid data capture over direct entry data capture and the relative advantages of direct entry data capture over document-based data capture.

10-4 Briefly describe the different times at which data preparation can occur during the input process. In each case give an example.

10-5 Briefly describe the five tasks that may be undertaken during the data preparation phase of the input process. Be sure to highlight the control activities that are performed in each task.

10-6 List three control features of a buffered keypunch/verifier data preparation device. Why are these devices disappearing as a means of preparing source data for input to computer systems?

10-7 From a control perspective, briefly describe the relative advantages and disadvantages of key-to-tape versus key-to-disk data preparation devices.

10-8 What impact has the availability of cheap microcomputers had on the data capture and data preparation processes?

10-9 List four types of turnaround documents that can be used for data capture and give an example of an application where each might be used. What are the advantages and disadvantages of using turnaround documents for data capture?

10-10 From a data integrity perspective, what are the advantages of using a VDU instead of a typewriter terminal?

10-11 List the major types of data capture and data preparation errors that may be made by (*a*) a checkout clerk in a supermarket, and (*b*) a sales clerk in a retail store. Which of these errors might be prevented using point-of-sale devices?

10-12 List the major control features of an automatic teller machine (ATM).

10-13 Briefly explain the nature of each of the following controls that are used in card readers:

a Dual read

b Hole count

c Echo check

d Character check

10-14 What has been the primary application for MICR? What control does a MICR device exercise when it identifies a folded character?

10-15 Briefly distinguish between document readers, page readers, and journal tape readers. From a control perspective, what are the advantages and disadvantages of OCR devices?

10-16 What major characteristics of an application system affect whether optical mark sensing is likely to be useful as a means of obtaining input?

10-17 What impact can the following source document design decisions have on the level of data integrity achieved in an application system:
  a Choice of the medium to be used
  b Choice of the layout to be used

10-18 From a control perspective, briefly explain the importance of each of the following source document design guidelines for layout and style:
  a Arrange fields for ease of use during data capture.
  b Where possible, use boxes to delimit field sizes.
  c Prenumber source documents.
  d Combine instructions with questions.
  e Where possible, provide multiple choice answers to questions.

10-19 What is the primary factor affecting the design of data entry screens? Explain why this factor is important. How, for example, does it affect the organization of a screen?

10-20 Briefly explain the design guidelines that apply to captions in terms of:
  a Structure and size
  b Type font and display intensity
  c Format
  d Alignment
  e Justification
  f Spacing

10-21 What techniques can be used to indicate the size of a field on a data entry screen?

10-22 From a data integrity perspective, why is it desirable to have a data entry operator always tab to a new field on a data entry screen rather than having the cursor automatically skip to a new field when the previous field is full?

10-23 Briefly explain the advantages of using color in the design of data entry screens. What design guidelines apply to:
  a The number of colors that should be used
  b The spacing of colors on the visual spectrum
  c The choice of bright colors versus muted colors

10-24 Distinguish between the response time and the display rate for a data entry screen. How does the use of a dedicated source document in data entry screen design affect the display rate and response time that must be achieved?

10-25 If data entry screen design is based on a dedicated source document, how useful is a "help" facility?

10-26 What attributes of a data code affect the likelihood of a recording error being made by a user of the code? Briefly outline some strategies to reduce error rates that occur with data codes.

10-27 Distinguish between the following types of data coding errors:
  a Truncation and transcription
  b Transposition and double transposition

10-28 List the four types of data codes—serial, block sequence, hierarchical, and association—in increasing order of:
  a Mnemonic value

    b Compactness

    c Flexibility for expansion

10-29 What is a check digit? Calculate the check digit for the number 82942 using the weights 1-2-1-2-1 and modulus 10. Show, also, that the check digit you have calculated is correct.

10-30 Briefly describe three solutions to the problem of having a check digit result that is greater than one digit—that is, a check digit that is greater than 9. Point out any disadvantages to the solutions you suggest.

10-31 Briefly discuss the distinction between a physical batch and a logical batch. Are there any differences between the controls that can be exercised over physical and logical batches?

10-32 Briefly explain why it is best not to have different transaction types within the same batch.

10-33 Briefly explain the difference between the following types of batch control totals: (*a*) document count, (*b*) hash total, and (*c*) financial total. For each type of control total, give an example where the application of the control total to the batch would *not* be useful or appropriate.

10-34 List three factors that affect the design of a batch and outline how they affect the design.

10-35 List four types of information typically placed on a batch cover sheet. Briefly explain the purpose of each piece of information you list for the overall control of the batch.

10-36 Briefly explain the difference between a statement-oriented job control language and a parameter-oriented job control language. Why do many organizations develop and promulgate standards for job control languages?

10-37 In general, are novice users more likely to make errors with a menu-driven language or a question-answer dialog? Briefly explain your answer.

10-38 From a data integrity perspective, why does it seem better to use a command language with a small number of commands and a large number of arguments? How can errors in the specification of arguments then be reduced?

10-39 What is the major limitation of using a forms-based language as a means of specifying commands in a computer system?

10-40 Briefly explain the limitations of natural language interfaces with respect to:

    a Ambiguity of commands

    b Establishing the lexicon

    c Ambiguity in responses

    d Changes to the database definition

10-41 What is meant by a direct manipulation interface? From a data integrity perspective, what is the major advantage of using a direct manipulation interface?

10-42 Give *four* items that would be common in the audit trails for data captured using (*a*) document-based data capture, (*b*) direct entry data capture, and (*c*) hybrid data capture.

10-43 Why is the operations audit trail for the input subsystem so important to improving the effectiveness and efficiency of a computer system?

10-44 Existence controls for instruction input are often less critical than existence controls for data input. Explain.

MULTIPLE CHOICE QUESTIONS

10-1 Which of the following is *not* an advantage of document-based data capture:
   a Simplicity
   b Flexibility
   c Little human intervention is required
   d All the above are advantages

10-2 Relative to document-based data capture, which of the following is *not* an advantage of using direct entry data capture:
   a If many physically dispersed data capture points exist, direct entry data capture is cheaper
   b Feedback on errors made is faster
   c Transaction processing occurs sooner
   d Data capture instructions can be better tailored to the experience and knowledge of the user

10-3 The primary difference between direct entry data capture and a hybrid method of data capture is:
   a Direct entry data capture is always faster
   b Hardware costs with hybrid data capture are lower
   c Terminal operators require less skill when hybrid data capture is used
   d Some type of document is used when hybrid data capture is used

10-4 The primary purpose of using some type of terminal during hybrid data capture is to:
   a Request "help" assistance on how to capture the data
   b Enter variable information about the event to be recorded
   c Enhance security over the data capture process
   d Enter constant information about the event to be recorded

10-5 Which of the following activities is undertaken during data preparation:
   a Correcting errors identified during the input validation phase
   b Converting data that has been captured into machine-readable form
   c Identifying and recording economic events that are relevant to the ongoing operations of an organization
   d Recording data on source documents so it can be keyed to some type of magnetic medium

10-6 Which of the following sequences of activities best describes the input process when a store uses a point-of-sale device to record the sale of some type of grocery item:
   a Data capture, data preparation, data input
   b Data preparation, data input
   c Data preparation, data capture, data input
   d Data capture, data preparation, data capture, data input

10-7 Which of the following is *not* a capability of a buffered keypunch:
   a Stored input validation capabilities
   b Preparation of statistics on number of cards punched, keystrokes made, and errors corrected
   c Automatic correction and checking of check digits
   d Card layout can differ from source document layout

10-8 Compared to key-to-tape devices, which of the following is likely to be an advantage of using key-to-disk devices for data preparation:

a Clustered devices can be used with key-to-disk equipment
b Key-to-disk equipment is cheaper
c Key-to-disk devices offer a search facility for automatic retrieval of records
d Key-to-disk devices tend to have a more powerful processor

10-9 A disadvantage of diskettes as a storage medium is:
a Low reliability
b Expensive
c Slower access than cassettes
d Spooling is necessary with diskettes

10-10 Which of the following is *not* an advantage of capturing data in machine-readable form as a by-product of some other type of activity:
a Reduced data preparation activities
b Data input devices are not needed
c Reduced operator training
d Better correspondence between documents and machine-readable data

10-11 The success of OCR has been limited because:
a It is less flexible than MICR
b It cannot read offset printing
c OCR devices have high expense and sometimes low reliability
d Both (*b*) and (*c*) above

10-12 A retail store tag can be used to record information on:
a Product type
b Price
c Department
d All the above

10-13 Optical mark sensing should *not* be used if:
a Only low-volume, exception data is to be captured
b The marks must be handwritten
c The data to be captured is diverse and volatile
d Instructions have to be printed on the source document

10-14 Which of the following is *not* likely to be a control capability in an automatic teller machine:
a Automatic recording of transactions on a secure journal tape
b Encryption/decryption capabilities
c A security alarm
d Built-in programmable data validation capabilities

10-15 The nature of retail and supermarket selling operations is different in that:
a Supermarket transactions are more complex than retail store transactions
b The sales clerk in a supermarket spends most time checking items out rather than selling
c Greater amounts of training are needed for supermarket checkout clerks
d Both (*a*) and (*b*) above

10-16 Which of the following is *not* a control to detect card reader malfunctions:
a "Folded" character check
b Echo check
c Dual read
d Character check

10-17 A factor affecting the grade and weight of paper chosen for a source document is:

 a The conditions under which the source document will be completed
 b Whether or not window envelopes must be used
 c Whether or not a dropout color is to be used
 d The amount of data to be captured

10-18 In the layout of a source document:
 a To prevent users being confused, keying instructions should never appear on the form
 b Instructions should not be combined with questions
 c Fields should follow a natural sequence from left to right and top to bottom
 d Instructions should always be printed in a dropout color

10-19 The primary factor affecting the design of a data entry screen is:
 a The amount of data to be collected on the screen
 b The expertise and experience of the keyboard operator
 c How frequently the screen will be used
 d Whether or not the screen is to be based on a dedicated source document

10-20 If a screen is used for direct entry data capture, it should be organized to:
 a Be an image of the source document on which the source data is first captured and transcribed
 b Mirror the way in which data is obtained during the data capture task
 c Place alphabetic information to the top of the screen and numeric information to the bottom of the screen
 d Both (*a*) and (*b*) above

10-21 Which of the following is *not* a design guideline for captions on a data entry screen:
 a Always use uppercase type font
 b Fully spell out captions if direct data entry is being used
 c Captions should always precede their associated data entry field
 d Always left-justify captions

10-22 Which of the following is *not* a design guideline for data entry field design on a screen:
 a Tab automatically to the next field when the current field is full of data
 b In the case of a repeating field, stack each instance of the field below the caption
 c Identify at least the start of each field with a special character
 d Provide completion aids when direct entry data capture is used

10-23 Which of the following is *not* a design guideline for using color on a data entry screen:
 a Use colors sparingly
 b Always use bright colors so differences are highlighted
 c Use colors that are widely spaced along the visual spectrum
 d Consider whether a color has any cultural implications

10-24 Under what circumstances will a data entry screen keyboard operator tolerate the slowest response time:
 a The transition between one screen and the next screen
 b The transition between one field and the next field
 c When data entry for a transaction has been completed
 d When keying is based on a dedicated source document

10-25 If the product number A5723 is coded as A2753, this is an example of a:
 a Truncation error

b Double transposition error

c Random error

d Transcription error

10-26 A strategy for reducing coding errors is to:

a Have only numeric codes

b Have no more than four characters in a chunk of information

c Group alphabetics together and numerics together if a mixed alphabetic-numeric code is used

d Reduce the mnemonic content of the code to avoid confusing users

10-27 The code AJB/156/7G is most likely to be an example of a(n):

a Hierarchical code

b Block sequence code

c Alphabetic derivation code

d Serial code

10-28 Given the code 7215, modulus 13, and the weights 2-1-2-1, the check digit is:

a 1

b 10

c 0

d 3

10-29 Which of the following guidelines should *not* be used when designing a batch:

a The batch should constitute a logical unit such as single transaction type

b Have the batch small enough to facilitate locating errors

c Have the batch large enough to constitute a reasonable size unit of work

d Minimize the amount of information that is recorded on the batch cover sheet

10-30 In reviewing a data processing installation's use of a job control language (JCL), the auditor's primary concern is:

a The installation has developed and enforced JCL standards

b A statement-oriented JCL has been chosen in preference to a parameter-oriented JCL

c A JCL that specifies parameters using keywords rather than position is used

d The JCL has not been placed under the control of the database administrator

10-31 Novice users are most likely to make errors when they use a:

a Menu-driven language

b Command language

c Question-answer language

d Forms-based language

10-32 To reduce errors, it is better to use a command language that has:

a Specification of arguments using keywords

b A small number of commands with a large number of arguments

c A large number of commands with a small number of arguments

d Few default values in the argument list

10-33 Which of the following is a strength in the use of a natural language interface to a database:

a It copes well with the ambiguity and redundancy inherent in natural language

b The lexicon evolves easily to cope with new words

c Changes to the database have minimal effects on lexicon

d None of the above are advantages

10-34 Which of the following is a limitation in the use of direct manipulation interfaces:

a They are error-prone

     b It is sometimes difficult to choose an appropriate icon
     c Users take some time to gain confidence in their interactions with the system
     d It is difficult to work efficiently using a direct manipulation interface
10-35 Which of the following data items is likely to be most useful as part of the operations audit trail (rather than the accounting audit trail) for the input subsystem:
     a The identity of the person who prepared a source document
     b The logical batch number of a direct entry transaction
     c The number of keying errors identified during verification
     d The identifier of a terminal at which a transaction was entered

EXERCISES AND CASES

10-1 Consider a medium-size insurance company. Fill in the elements of the following controls matrix for the company where the elements represent the cost-effectiveness of the controls at reducing the expected losses from the causes of loss. Assume a score of 5 represents high cost-effectiveness and a score of 1 represents low cost-effectiveness. Justify your rating for any score above 3.

Controls \ Cause of loss	Removal of assets	Destruction of assets	Unauthorized data	Incomplete data	Ineffective systems	Inefficient systems
Appropriate data capture method						
Appropriate data preparation method						
Appropriate data entry method						
Good source document design						
Good interactive language design						
Good data code design						
Check digits						
Batch controls						

10-2 Buildit Corporation is a construction engineering firm with offices scattered throughout Australia in the capital cities and major country cities and towns. Engineers on a job complete source documents to record various information about the job; for example, direct material and direct labor costs, overhead, progress made, and deviations from plans. These source documents then are batched in the various offices and sent to the head office in Sydney for processing.

When the source documents arrive in Sydney, they are keypunched on cards. Currently a high keypunching error rate exists. Because the source documents are completed under adverse conditions, keypunch operators often find them illegible. The problem of errors is confounded further because error reports must be sent back to the respective offices for correction. By the time an office tracks down the responsible engineer, the time delay between completion of the source document and error notification may be several weeks. Often the engineer has difficulties in remembering the circumstances surrounding the data.

Required: The problem has grown to sufficient proportions that Buildit's management has formed a task force group to develop possible solutions. As the manager of internal audit they have asked you to participate as a member of the task force group. Prepare a report outlining some alternative recommendations that may be acceptable. Briefly describe the relative advantages and disadvantages of your proposed solutions. You should at least consider the possibility of redesigning the source documents or having data prepared in the various offices. In the latter case, most district offices could support about three card keypunches on a full-time basis. Note, also, that data communications costs in Australia are high.

10-3 Your company has just installed five key-to-disk devices. Each of these devices has 30 keystations attached to each processor. The key-to-disk devices will be used in the conventional way: keying batches of source documents. The data processing manager is concerned about a device failure since all 30 keystations will be affected and data previously keyed may be lost. He has asked the internal audit manager to examine the problem and she has asked you to prepare a report. Outline a scheme(s) for backup and recovery after device failure. Be sure to describe any advantages or disadvantages of your scheme(s).

10-4 Design an order form that can be used by a wholesaler as a turnaround document and input to an optical mark sensing device. The wholesaler distributes these forms each month to its retail customers. The order form must provide for the following fields:

Field	Picture	Comments
Customer account no.	9(6)	Binary marks preprinted by computer
Customer name and address	X(80)	Four lines of X(20), preprinted by the computer for display in a window envelope
Month number	9(4)	Binary marks preprinted by computer
Product description	X(30)	Preprinted by the computer; some products change from month to month; allow for up to 50 products
Order quantities	9(2)	Marks to be made by hand by the customer; up to 99 units of a product can be ordered
Comments	X(100)	Information for the customer preprinted by the computer; e.g., availability of new products, special discounts available

Briefly indicate any data integrity problems you think may result with your design.

10-5 A supermarket chain in a large city is considering the installation of point-of-sale equipment. One of management's concerns is backup and recovery if hardware or software failure occurs. The chain has 20 supermarkets in the city. The proposed hardware configuration is to have the terminals in a store (normally about 10 checkout lanes) connected to a store controller, which in turn is connected to a host processor at the chain's head office. As the manager of internal audit for the chain, management has asked you to prepare a brief report outlining some possible backup and recovery strategies that can be used in the event of hardware/software failure (*Hint:* Refer to Hippert et al. [1975]).

10-6 For each of the following cases, choose a medium and makeup for the source document to be completed so as to minimize keying errors caused by illegible writing, a torn form, etc.:

   a a traveling salesperson completes orders in the field and mails the orders to head office for keying and input to an invoicing system

   b a foreperson on a production floor completes employee time sheets for keying and input to the payroll system

   c truck drivers provide data on deliveries made to customers for keying and input to an invoicing system

   d a clerk at the front desk of an insurance company provides data on claims made by customers for keying and input to a claims system

10-7 Suggest some ways in which the following source document, an employee timesheet for a job costing system, might be improved to reduce data capture and preparation errors:

Produceit Company ⓟ			Daily Time Sheet			Form No: 4SP-66	
Employee Name: _____							
Employee Number: _____				Date: _____			

Hours			Machine		Stage of Completion	Comments
Regular	Overtime	Job Number	Number	Hours	Stage of Completion	Comments

Foreperson's Signature _____

10-8 Comment on the quality of the following display. Clerks provide data for an invoicing system describing where orders are to be sent.

#87AB649531G

INVOICE TO: SHIP TO:

WEIRDO T-SHIRTS, INC.   WEIRDO T-SHIRTS, INC.
895 COLLING STREET   895 COLLING STREET
MELBOURNE. VIC. 3743   MELBOURNE. VIC. 3743

IS THE ABOVE INFORMATION CORRECT AND, IF SO,
IS SHIPMENT REQUIRED IN < 10 DAYS?

10-9 Calculate check digits for the following:

Code	Modulus	Weight
753642	10	1-2-1-2-1
43196	11	6-5-4-3-2
841975	37	1-3-7-1-3-7

How would you have calculated the check digits if each of the above codes had contained some alphabetic characters?

10-10 The following journal entry transaction is keyed for input into a general ledgers system. Indicate, with reasons why, those fields where you would use a check digit and those fields you would verify:

Record type
Account number
Transaction code
Description
Amount
Source document number

ANSWERS TO MULTIPLE CHOICE QUESTIONS

10-1 c	10-10 b	10-19 d	10-28 d
10-2 a	10-11 c	10-20 b	10-29 d
10-3 d	10-12 d	10-21 d	10-30 a
10-4 b	10-13 c	10-22 a	10-31 b
10-5 b	10-14 d	10-23 b	10-32 b
10-6 c	10-15 b	10-24 c	10-33 d
10-7 a	10-16 a	10-25 b	10-34 b
10-8 d	10-17 a	10-26 c	10-35 c
10-9 a	10-18 c	10-27 a	

REFERENCES

Akresh, Abraham D., and Michael Goldstein. "Point-of-Sale Accounting Systems: Some Implications for the Auditor," *Journal of Accountancy* (December 1978), pp. 68–74.

Allen, Brandt. "The Biggest Computer Frauds: Lessons for CPAs," *Journal of Accountancy* (May 1977), pp. 52–62.

Anderson, Lane K., Raymond A. Hendershot, and Robert C. Shoonmaker. "Self-Checking Digit Concepts," *Journal of Systems Management* (September 1974), pp. 36–42.

Antonelli, D.C. "The Role of the Operator in the Supermarket and Retail Store Systems," *IBM Systems Journal,* vol. 14, no. 1, 1975, pp. 34–45.

Beckley, D.F. "An Optimum System with 'Modulus 11'," *The Computer Bulletin* (December 1967), pp. 213–215.

Benbasat, Izak, and Yair Wand. "Command Abbreviation Behavior in Human-Computer Interaction," *Communications of the ACM* (May 1984), pp. 376–382.

Berk, M.A., C.W. Dunbar, and G.C. Hobson. "Design and Performance Considerations for the Retail Store System," *IBM Systems Journal,* vol. 14, no. 1, 1975, pp. 64–80.

Carey, L. Chester. "The Quality Form," *Journal of Systems Management* (June 1972), pp. 28–30.

Campbell, D.V.A. "A Modulus 11 Check Digit System for a Given System of Codes," *The Computer Bulletin* (January 1970), pp. 12–13.

Chapdelaine, P.A. *Accuracy Control in Source Data Collection* (Ohio: Headquarters, Air Force Logistics Command, Wright-Patterson Air Force Base, 1963).

Conrad, R. "Errors of Immediate Memory," *The British Journal of Psychology* (November 1959), pp. 349–359.

Coughlin, Clifford W. "The Need for Good Procedures," *Journal of Systems Management* (June 1974), pp. 30–33.

Crannell, C.W., and J.M. Parrish. "A Comparison of Immediate Memory Span for Digits, Letters, and Words," *The Journal of Psychology* (October 1957), pp. 319–327.

Daniels, Alan, and Donald Yeates. *Systems Analysis* (Palo Alto: Science Research Associates, 1971).

Davis, Gordon B., and Margrethe H. Olson. *Management Information Systems: Conceptual Foundations, Structure, and Development,* 2d ed. (New York: McGraw-Hill, 1984).

Davis, Gordon B., Donald L. Adams, and Carol A. Schaller. *Auditing and EDP,* 2d ed. (New York: American Institute of Certified Public Accountants, 1983).

Evans, Hugh S. "Where to Use Optical Mark Systems," *Journal of Systems Management* (March 1973), pp. 8–13.

Galitz, Wilbert O. *Human Factors in Office Automation* (Atlanta, Ga.: Life Office Management Association, 1980).

Haga, Clifford I. "Procedures Manuals," *Ideas for Management* (Cleveland: Systems and Procedures Association, 1968), pp. 127–154.

Hauck, Edward J. "Be Kind to Your Data Codes," *Journal of Systems Management* (December 1972), pp. 8–12.

Hippert, R.O., L.R. Palounek, J. Provetero, and R.O. Skatrud. "Reliability, Availability, and Serviceability Design Considerations for the Supermarket and Retail Store Systems," *IBM Systems Journal,* vol. 14, no. 1, 1975, pp. 81–95.

McEnroe, P.V., H.T. Huth, E.A. Moore, and W.W. Morris. "Overview of the Supermarket System and the Retail Store System," *IBM Systems Journal*, vol. 14, no. 1, 1975, pp. 3–15.

Martin, James. *Design of Man-Computer Dialogues* (Englewood Cliffs, NJ: Prentice-Hall, 1973).

Mason, John O., and William E. Connelly. "The Application and Reliability of the Self-Checking Digit Technique," *Management Advisor* (September-October 1971), pp. 27–34.

Metz, W.C., and D. Savir. "Store Performance Studies for the Supermarket System," *IBM Systems Journal*, vol. 14, no. 1, 1975, pp. 46–63.

Miller, George A. "The Magical Number Seven, Plus or Minus Two: Some Limits on Our Capability for Processing Information," *The Psychological Review* (March 1956), pp. 81–97.

Miller, L.A. "Natural Language Programming: Styles, Strategies, and Contrasts," *IBM Systems Journal*, vol. 20, no. 2, 1981, pp. 184–215.

Miller, Robert B. "Response Time in Man-Computer Conversational Transactions," *Proceedings of the 1968 AFIPS Fall Joint Computer Conference* (Washington: The Thompson Book Company, 1968), pp. 267–278.

Owsowitz, S., and A. Sweetland. *Factors Affecting Coding Errors* (Santa Monica, Calif.: The Rand Corporation, 1965). Rand Memorandum RM-4346-PR.

Rocke, Merle G. "The Need for Data Code Control," *Datamation* (September 1973), pp. 105–108.

Savir, D., and G.J. Laurer. "The Characteristics and Decodability of the Universal Product Code," *IBM Systems Journal*, vol. 14, no. 1, 1975, pp. 16–34.

Shneiderman, Ben. "Direct Manipulation: A Step Beyond Programming Languages," *Computer* (August 1983), pp. 57–69.

Shneiderman, Ben. "Response Time and Display Rate in Human Performance with Computers," *Computing Surveys* (September 1984), pp. 265–285.

Shultis, Robert L. "'Playscript'—A New Tool Accountants Need," *NAA Bulletin* (August 1964), pp. 3–10.

Sprague, Ralph H., Jr., and Eric D. Carlson. *Building Effective Decision Support Systems* (Englewood Cliffs, NJ: Prentice-Hall, 1982).

Staggs, Earl W. "Maybe It's Your Forms," *Journal of Systems Management* (March 1972), pp. 8–12.

Wooldridge, Susan. *Computer Input Design* (New York: Petrocelli Books, 1974).

Wu, Margaret. *An Introduction to Computer Data Processing* (New York: Harcourt Brace Jovanovich, 1975).

INPUT CONTROLS: VALIDATION AND ERROR CONTROL

Input validation controls are used to identify errors in data or instructions before the data is processed or the instructions are executed. In the case of data, input validation controls can be exercised at various stages in the flow of data through the input subsystem: during data preparation if the data preparation device provides programmed data validation capabilities; during input when data is read by a card reader, paper tape reader, etc.; during direct entry of data at a terminal if the terminal is intelligent or it is online to a computer (Figure 11-1). In the case of instructions, input validation occurs as the user interacts with the system, or, if job control language instructions are being submitted, at the time the operating system reads the instructions.

DATA INPUT VALIDATION CHECKS

In general, data should be validated as soon as possible after it has been captured and as close as possible to the source of the data. There may be occasions when, from a cost or efficiency viewpoint, validation should be delayed. For example, validating some fields requires referencing a master file. If the master file is stored as a sequential file, this validation check is difficult to perform unless data is entered or sorted in the same sequence as the master file. Nevertheless, to the extent that the time lag between data validation and

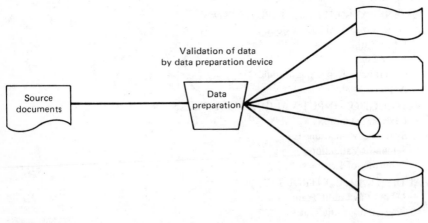

FIGURE 11-1a
Validation of data during data preparation.

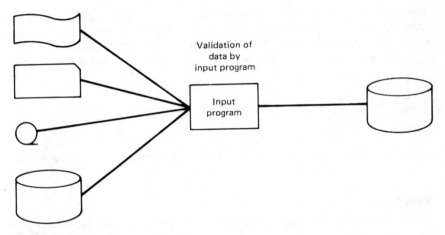

FIGURE 11-1b
Validation of data by input program.

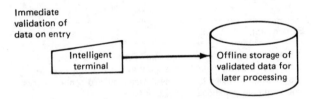

FIGURE 11-1c
Use of an intelligent terminal for offline validation and storage of data.

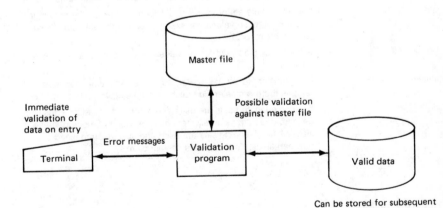

FIGURE 11-1d
Use of an online terminal for data validation.

data capture can be reduced, it is easier for personnel who capture, prepare, and enter data to correct errors. The circumstances surrounding the data are still fresh in their minds, and the effort required to correct the data is minimal.

Controls to check the validity of input data can be exercised at four levels:

1 Field checks
2 Record checks
3 Batch checks
4 File checks

The following sections examine each of these types of checks in more detail.

Field Checks

With a field check the validation logic applied to the field in the input validation program does not depend on other fields within the record or other records within the batch. The following field checks can be applied:

Field check	Explanation
Missing data/blanks	Is there any missing data in the field? For example, if a code should contain two hyphens, though they may be in a variable position, can only one be detected? Does the field contain blanks when data always should be present?
Alphabetics/numerics	Does a field that should contain only alphabetics or numerics contain alphanumeric characters?
Range	Does the data for a field fall within its allowable value range?
Set membership	If a permissible set of values is defined for a field, is the data in the field one of these values, for example, one of the valid transaction types for a record?
Check digit	Is the check digit valid for the value in the field (see, also, Chapter 10)?
Master reference	If the master file can be referenced at the same time input data is read, is there a master file match for the key field?
Size	If variable length fields are used and a set of permissible sizes is defined, does the field delimiter show the field to be one of these sizes? If fixed length fields are used and spaces are defined between fields, do the spaces contain blanks?

Record Checks

With a record check the validation logic applied to a field depends on the field's logical interrelationships with other fields in a record. The following record checks can be applied:

Record check	Explanation
Reasonableness	Even though a field may pass a range check, the contents of another field may determine what is a reasonable value for the field. For example, $35,000 may fall within the range of salaries paid but it is not a reasonable salary for lower-level managers.
Valid sign–numerics	The contents of one field may determine which sign is valid for a numeric field. For example, a cash payment transaction should always have a negative sign for the amount field.
Size	If variable length records are used, the size of the record is a function of the sizes of the variable length fields. The permissible size of variable and fixed length records also may depend on a field indicating the record type.
Sequence check	If during input logical records require more than one physical record and a sequence number is entered in each physical record, do the physical records follow the required order?

Batch Checks

Batch checks apply validation logic to fields and records based on their interrelationships with controls established for the batch. Whereas field and record checks can always be undertaken, batch checks are not always possible. For example, in an online system, clerks may enter single transactions as they occur rather than accumulate them in batches of the same type and enter them at a later stage. If single transactions are entered, the only type of batch checking that can occur is logical batch checking, that is, where the computer sorts the transactions entered by the clerk over the processing period and prepares control totals for each transaction type. At the end of the processing period these totals are reconciled with the clerk's control totals. On the other hand, if data is entered as a batch with a batch header record containing certain control information, the following types of checks can be performed:

Batch check	Explanation
Control totals	Does the accumulation of a field reconcile with a financial total or hash total specified on the batch header? Does the number of records in the batch agree with the number specified on the batch header?
Transaction type	If the batch transaction type is entered on the follower records, does it agree with the transaction type specified on the batch header?
Batch serial number	If the batch serial number is entered on the follower records, does it agree with the batch serial number on the batch header?
Sequence check	If a sequence number is on follower records, do the follower records occur in the required order?
Size	If there is an absolute limit to the number of follower records in the batch, is this limit exceeded?

File Checks

File checks ensure correct files are input to a production run of an application system. These checks are especially important for master files where reconstruction may be difficult and costly. The following types of file checks can be applied:

File check	Explanation
Internal label	Is the name of the file correct?
Generation number	Is the correct generation of the file being used?
Retention date	Has the retention date on the file expired?
Control totals	A record within the file may contain control totals that can be checked. This record is updated at the end of each run and the control totals reported. On the next run users supply a parameter value to the update program to check the control totals on the file.

DESIGN OF THE DATA INPUT VALIDATION PROGRAM

A well-designed data input program ensures that the quality of data entering an application system is high, and it facilitates correction and resubmission of errors. If extensive validation, editing, formatting, and encoding must be performed, good design is essential if the program is to be efficient. If large volumes of input data must be processed, efficiency considerations may be paramount.

The auditor is especially interested in three aspects of the design of the data input validation program:

1 How is data validated?
2 How are errors handled?
3 How are errors reported?

Data Validation

Experience and ingenuity play a large part in being able to specify all the kinds of errors that are likely to occur in input data. The system specifications usually give a programmer some indication of errors to be expected. However, other errors the programmer anticipates through experience, for example, checking the sequence of records that will "always" be in sequence.

It is sometimes easiest to start the design of the validation routines by specifying what should be correct and then identifying deviations that may occur. This activity also aids the program design process since logic that should be grouped in modules can be identified (see, also, Chapter 5). This aspect of the design process should be documented for later use by maintenance programmers and auditors.

Errors should be ordered by their likelihood of occurrence. Ideally, the input program checks for all possible errors. However, hopefully not all code needs to be executed during production running. It is inefficient to check for rare errors first. The cost of comprehensive validation routines should be storage space and not processing efficiency; that is, though program logic always consumes memory space, it need not be executed always if the program is well-designed.

Valid codes or values should be stored in tables in the program and not exist as literals in the procedural section of the program. This facilitates changing the program when codes or values change. The procedure section should reference only variable names.

The input program must identify as many errors as possible in a record or batch. It is frustrating for users to correct one error only to find that another exists. Even when an error has been identified, the program must continue to search for other errors.

There should be no closed routines in an input program. A closed routine exists when a program assumes the existence of a condition if other conditions do not exist. For example, if a program checks for five possible values in a field, a closed routine exists when the program checks for four values and assumes the existence of the fifth value when the other tests fail. Thus, a sixth value is not anticipated. The program should check all possible values and invoke a general error routine if a value other than those permitted is found.

One of the more onerous requirements in writing an input program is ensuring its ability to recover when errors occur. If the program gets "out of step," it may start to read valid records as errors. For example, if the program assumes 50 records follow a batch header record, and in a particular batch read by the program only 49 exist, it should not read the 50th record—a new batch header—as a follower record, signify the current batch is in error, and then process further batches in error because they have no batch header. The program must recognize the 50th record as a new batch header, signify the current batch is in error, and recommence validation for the new batch.

Where possible the input program should correct errors automatically. If an error has to be corrected manually, the likelihood that a further error will be made is increased. Processing is delayed also while the error is corrected. If the input program can correct the error, the chance of further errors is reduced and processing can continue without interruption.

Documentation of the input program is essential. It takes two forms. First, external documentation must exist providing details about the program. Second, comments must occur liberally throughout the program explaining what each validation routine accomplishes. A decision-table preprocessor is especially helpful in documenting the program. Often the validation routines are amenable to coding as decision tables. The decision-table preprocessor ensures correct generation of processing logic and provides useful documentation of the logic involved in the validation routines by automatically inserting comments in the form of decision tables throughout the program.

Handling of Errors

Once errors have been identified in the input data, the validation program must report the errors and exercise careful control to ensure the errors are corrected.

If *immediate validation* of input data occurs—that is, data is validated as it is keyed, for example, at a visual display during direct data capture or at a key-to-disk device during data preparation—upon identifying the error the program should not proceed until the users correct the error, cancel the transaction, or indicate the erroneous transaction is to be written to an error file. The action taken depends on the nature of the error and the user's knowledge of the cause of the error. For example: if users discover the transaction is not allowed for the type of record to be updated, they should cancel the transaction; if users can identify the reasons for an error, they should correct the data immediately; if data preparation operators cannot identify the reason for an error, they should write the transaction to an error file.

If *delayed validation* of input data occurs—that is, data is validated after it has been entered into the system or converted to machine-readable form—errors must be reported and then written to an error file. Upon receiving the error reports, users must identify the reasons for errors, correct the data, and resubmit the data for validation once again.

An important means of controlling errors is a circulating error file (Figure 11-2). Any error that is not corrected immediately should be written to this file. The error file reduces the risk of users forgetting to correct and resubmit data. If errors are not cleared off the error file within a reasonable time period, the input validation program should remind users that the errors still await correction.

Depending on the type of errors identified, either a single record or an entire batch must be written onto the error file. If an error is identified at the field or

FIGURE 11-2
Use of an error file for data validation.

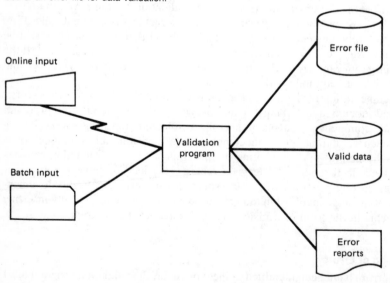

record level, only the record need be written onto the error file. If an error is identified at the batch level, however, the entire batch must be written onto the error file. The data input validation program must recognize whether the correction submitted applies to a record or a batch. Perhaps the simplest way to handle batch corrections is to require resubmission of the entire batch rather than to allow selected correction of fields or records in a batch on the error file.

The user must decide on the number and types of errors that can be tolerated before further processing of data through the system should be stopped. If the data input validation program identifies too many errors, it may not be worthwhile updating master files or producing output that depends on the input data. For example, if a master file contains information on welfare benefits to be paid, all notifications to cease payment must be processed correctly before a check printing run is undertaken. Otherwise, welfare recipients will be overpaid. If an error file is used, data can be submitted and resubmitted until all errors are cleared off the file. Update and report runs can be delayed until no errors remain.

Reporting of Errors

Errors must be reported by the input validation program in a way that facilitates fast and accurate correction of the errors. The program must clearly identify the cause of the error and provide adequate cross-references to permit retrieval of source documents if they are needed.

Screen Error Messages   When immediate validation of input data occurs, errors can be signaled via a buzzer or bell. The cursor also can be made to flash to show the data item in error. An error message should then be displayed to indicate the nature of the error and possible corrective actions that might be undertaken. Error messages must be:

1 *Clear and concise:* Messages should use short, meaningful, and familiar words, avoid the passive voice, avoid contractions and abbreviations, and issue instructions in the sequence to be followed.

2 *Courteous and neutral:* Messages should avoid familiarity, be polite and instructive, avoid humor or condemnation, and assist the user to solve the problem even if repeated errors are made.

The input validation program also might provide various levels of error messages: short-form messages for experienced users and more detailed explanations for novice or infrequent users.

Printed Error Reports   When delayed validation of input data occurs, errors must be shown on printed reports. As data is read and validated, any errors identified are written to a report file. In some cases this report file must be sorted before printing to facilitate error correction. For example: all errors for

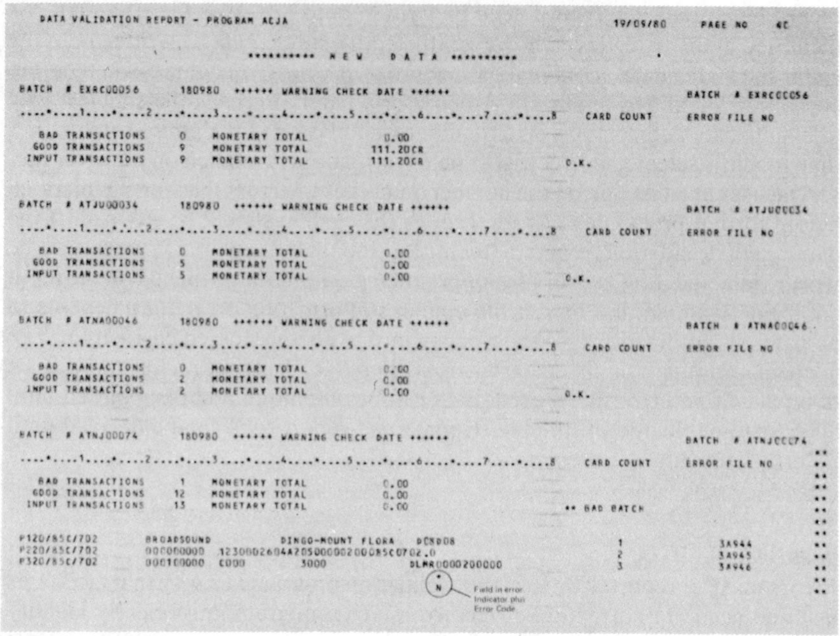

```
DATA VALIDATION REPORT - PROGRAM ACJA                                          19/05/80     PAGE NO    4C

                        ********** N E W   D A T A *********                  .

BATCH  # EXRC00056      180980  ****** WARNING CHECK DATE ******                             BATCH  # EXRC00056
....*....1....*....2....*....3....*....4....*....5....*....6....*....7....*....8   CARD COUNT   ERROR FILE NO

   BAD TRANSACTIONS     0   MONETARY TOTAL            0.00
  GOOD TRANSACTIONS     9   MONETARY TOTAL          111.20CR
 INPUT TRANSACTIONS     9   MONETARY TOTAL          111.20CR          O.K.

BATCH  # ATJU00034      180980  ****** WARNING CHECK DATE ******                             BATCH  # ATJU00034
....*....1....*....2....*....3....*....4....*....5....*....6....*....7....*....8   CARD COUNT   ERROR FILE NO

   BAD TRANSACTIONS     0   MONETARY TOTAL            0.00
  GOOD TRANSACTIONS     5   MONETARY TOTAL            0.00
 INPUT TRANSACTIONS     5   MONETARY TOTAL            0.00            O.K.

BATCH  # ATNA00046      180980  ****** WARNING CHECK DATE ******                             BATCH  # ATNA00046
....*....1....*....2....*....3....*....4....*....5....*....6....*....7....*....8   CARD COUNT   ERROR FILE NO

   BAD TRANSACTIONS     0   MONETARY TOTAL            0.00
  GOOD TRANSACTIONS     2   MONETARY TOTAL            0.00
 INPUT TRANSACTIONS     2   MONETARY TOTAL            0.00            O.K.

BATCH  # ATNJ00074      180980  ****** WARNING CHECK DATE ******                             BATCH  # ATNJ00074
....*....1....*....2....*....3....*....4....*....5....*....6....*....7....*....8   CARD COUNT   ERROR FILE NO

   BAD TRANSACTIONS     1   MONETARY TOTAL            0.00
  GOOD TRANSACTIONS    12   MONETARY TOTAL            0.00
 INPUT TRANSACTIONS    13   MONETARY TOTAL            0.00            ** BAD BATCH

P120/85C/702      BROADSOUND            DINGO-MOUNT FLORA   DC8008                    1           3A944
P220/85C/702      000000000  12300026 04A20500000200085C0702.0                        2           3A945
P320/85C/702      000100000  C000          3000         DLMR0000200000                3           3A946
                                                             *
                                                             N
```


FIGURE 11-3
Input validation report. (*Main Roads Department, Queensland, Australia.*)

a given transaction type may be sorted together, or the errors to be corrected by a particular user may be sorted together.

The report should clearly identify the field in error by printing indicators such as upward arrows or asterisks under the field (Figure 11-3). In some cases it may be worthwhile printing a blown-up version of the record so the field in error can be identified easily.

Space should exist on the error report for the signature of the person correcting the error, the date of correction of the error, and the number of the batch in which the corrected version of the transaction has been resubmitted. This helps ensure all errors are corrected, corrections are not duplicated, and an audit trail exists for corrected errors.

Where possible the error report should be designed to act as a turnaround document for resubmitting corrected errors. For example, a monetary transaction may not have a match for its account number on the master file. Rather than have the person responsible for correcting the error recopy the correct information onto a new source document, thereby increasing the risk of transcription errors, space can be provided on the error report for inserting the corrected account number (Figure 11-4). However, this method of resubmitting corrected errors can be awkward for keyboard operators. Clear keying

```
   PROGRAM ACBB                        NON-MATCHING RECORDS REPORT                          21/06/78
                                                                                           PAGE  2
 TYPE BATCH   ORIG   DOCUMENT    JOB NUMBER      • CO        JOB        TRANSN   CR   DOC   RESUB   • TRAN   ERR RECOV
                                                 •TYP      NUMBER      AMOUNT INDIC    NO   FROM    • DATE  BATCHBATCH
                                                 •1-2       3-19       20-28  29-30  31-38 39-48   • •
 TRMS   1169 8183    287435   MRD13640  NO DIGIT• 81 MRD  13640  - 8   000001400        287435     •21/06/78
 TSMS   1175 1A/6/78 305854   MRD13945-3 INVALID• 81 MRD  13945 - 8    000001370        305854     •21/06/78
 EXSV   73716 00000000        PM10808   NO DIGIT• 81 PM   10808 - 0    000010500        EX73716    •21/06/78
 TSMS   1196 M2208   T291909  PM11600-2 INVALID• 81 PM   11600 - 8     000043219        T291909    •21/06/78
 CLDO   2221 6M181C           PM11650-9 INVALID• 81 FM   11605 - 9     000123600        6M181C     •21/06/78
 CLDO   2211 MO306            PM11863-1 INVALID• 81 PM   11863 - 9     000004674        MO306      •21/06/78
 EXSV   73713 00000000        PM11937-1 INVALID• 81 FM   11937 - 6     000000420        EX73713    •21/06/78
 TSDI   1153 8328    150672   PM12379-7 INVALID• 81 PM   12379 - 9     000025571        150672     •21/06/78
 EXSV   73716 00000000        PM12463-8 INVALID• 81 PM   12463 - 9     000021527        EX73716    •21/06/78
 TSMS   1176 5/6/78  292850   PM13394-5 INVALID• 81 FM   13394 - 8     000042750        292850     •21/06/78
 CLDO   2206 CY4715           PM13449-5 INVALID• 81 PA1  13499 - 5     000000737        CY4715     •21/06/78
 TSMS   1176 5/6/78  292850   PM13544-4 INVALID• 81 PM   13544 - 4     000000950        292850     •21/06/78
 TRMS   1184 86520   273109   PM13590-9 INVALID• 81 PA1  13590 - 8     000006300        273109     •21/06/78
 TRMS   1186 828/78  T289827  PM13824-3 INVALID• 81 PM   13824 - 9     000008550        T289827    •21/06/78
 TRMS   1190 8355    T265166  PM9005-4  INVALID• 81 PM   90005 - 4     000001350        T265166    •21/06/78
                                        Corrected  • 81 C601/3085/1    000292918 CR  CSSSP
                                        Field

                                              NUMBER    TOTAL TRANSACTION AMOUNT
                   MATCHING RECORDS           3966         1920660.02
                   NON-MATCHING RECORDS         40           14437.92
                   COMPUTER SUSPENSE A/C        40           14437.92
                   NON MONETARY TRANSACTIONS    72

                              THIS IS THE END OF THE REPORT
```

FIGURE 11-4
Validation report for use as turnaround document. (*Main Roads Department, Queensland, Australia.*)

instructions must be printed on the report. For example, column numbers for each field can be printed as a heading on the top of the report.

Using the error report as a turnaround document for resubmission of errors is especially useful if large volumes of errors occur and the personnel responsible for correcting errors are under heavy workload pressures. This situation often arises during conversion from a manual system to a computer system (see, also, Chapter 4). The manual system records may contain many errors, and a backlog of errors requiring correction and resubmission develops. Using the error report as a turnaround document reduces workloads and the probability of new errors arising.

It is important that the error messages printed clearly state the nature of the errors. Where possible, printing error codes instead of error messages should be avoided. Users may incorrectly interpret a code, or if the documentation of codes is out of date, users may waste time looking for errors that do not exist. Wooldridge [1974] suggests printing a detailed key to the codes at the end of an error report if codes are used instead of error messages. This also simplifies the change procedure needed when a code is altered or a new error type is added.

User manuals do not have to be changed; only the input program needs to be modified.

At the end of the error report, summary statistics should be printed for the transactions processed and the different types of errors identified. Control totals should show the total number of transactions processed and any monetary amounts involved. The frequency of each error type also should be printed. This allows the control section to check all data has been processed and to identify abnormal numbers of errors.

CONTROL OVER DATA INPUT

Careful control must be exercised over input data to ensure (a) all data is entered into a system, (b) all errors are corrected, (c) errors are corrected once only, and (d) changes in the patterns of errors are identified. These duties are the responsibility of users and the data processing installation's control section (see, also, Chapter 8).

Registers and control totals are the basic means of ensuring that all data enters a system. The input program must be able to display or to print a report showing all logical or physical batches processed and their associated control totals. This report must be reconciled against registers of all data submitted for processing maintained by users or the control section. For example, terminal operators may maintain a list of all transactions entered into a system during direct entry data capture. Periodically they may request the system to print control totals that they can reconcile against their registers. The input program may calculate controls totals on the basis of a logical batch associated with each 15-minute period that the operators used the system.

The primary means of ensuring that all errors are corrected and corrected only once is the circulating error file. If the error is not corrected on a timely basis, the input program should remind users the error is outstanding. Once the error is corrected, it should be removed from the error file so duplicate resubmissions are rejected. In addition, if error reports are provided, corrected errors should be initialed on the error reports. Similarly, if source documents are used to record error corrections, they should be stamped to indicate cancellation once the contents have been prepared in machine-readable form.

Statistics on the frequency of different errors are useful for three reasons. First, they may indicate the need for training in the user area responsible for submitting the data. Second, they may indicate that the input subsystem needs to be redesigned. Third, they may enable the input program to be rewritten so it is more effective and efficient. For example, it may be possible to correct more errors automatically, or the tests for errors may be reordered so more frequent errors are recognized first.

A GENERALIZED DATA INPUT SYSTEM

To enhance control over data input, some organizations have developed a generalized data input system. A generalized data input system provides

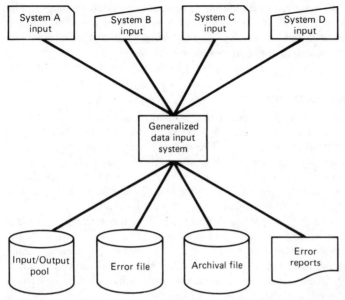

FIGURE 11-5
Using a generalized data input system for validation of data.

centralized management of the data validation processes needed for the installation's portfolio of application systems.

Several factors motivate the use of a generalized data input system. First, much commonality exists across application systems in the functions needed for processing and validating input. Rather than continue to rewrite these processes for each new application system, a generalized system providing parameter-driven processes can cater to the specific requirements of each application system. Second, a generalized input system allows the development and modification of input validation routines for application systems to be accomplished quickly. However, generality incurs a cost in terms of processing overheads. Third, use of a generalized data input system ensures a consistent standard is achieved for the input validation processes used in individual application systems. Fourth, having a single system maintain files of valid data and errors increases control within the installation.

A generalized data input system consists of five major components (Figure 11-5):

1 Generalized validation module
2 Input/output pool
3 Error file
4 Generalized reporting module
5 Archival file

All components of a generalized data input system are shared resources. The system must permit simultaneous input and validation of data by multiple application systems. Similarly, the files and reporting system must be available simultaneously to multiple application systems.

Generalized Validation Module

Because many of the validation processes needed in application systems are common across application systems, it is possible to write generalized programming code for these processes. These processes are then invoked via parameters that specify the specific validation needs of a particular application system. For example, a parameter may specify that a range check is needed for field GROSS-PAY and that the limits are $500 and $3000. The range check is a generalized routine; the limits are parameter-supplied values.

Besides providing generalized validation processes, the generalized validation module must permit specific validation processes to be written. Some validation processes involve complex logic that cannot be handled using generalized code. In other cases the generalized module performs validation too inefficiently. The generalized validation module must allow user-written routines to be stored, and these routines to be invoked at run time.

Input/Output Pool

The generalized data input system dumps valid data into an input/output pool. The file is called a "pool" because it is periodically filled with data, and at various times the "plug" is pulled to remove some or all of the data. The pool file holds valid data temporarily until the data is selected for application system processing.

When an application system is to be run, the generalized data input system's retrieval routines select data from the pool and funnel it off to the application system. Data for the application system can be selected on several bases: all data, data up to a certain date, or by transaction type. If the application system's processing follows a definite schedule, this schedule may be stored in the generalized data input system and the system programmed to call and activate automatically the application system according to this schedule.

Error File

A generalized data input system's error file stores all errors detected by the validation module. As with the pool, all errors (transactions) are given a unique application system identifier. Resubmissions of corrected errors are validated, and successful resubmissions are cleared off the error file. The generalized input system recognizes an unsuccessful resubmission, leaves the old error on the error file, and prints a message denoting the failed transaction as an unsuccessful resubmission and the reasons for failure.

Generalized Reporting Module

The format of error reports is common across most application systems. Similarly, the error messages needed are common. Variable information can be obtained from the parameter values supplied to the generalized input system by the user. For example, if an error message states a range test has been violated, the upper and lower limits can be printed from the parameter values supplied. Other information is standard on all error reports. For example, control totals that enable input to be reconciled with the data processed should always be provided.

Because of these commonalities, a generalized data input system can also provide a generalized reporting module. Using the module means the installation must establish standards for reporting errors. This is desirable from a control perspective. However, the generalized reporting module should also allow user-written report modules to be supplied when the generalized module cannot cater to the reports needed.

Reports need not be generated for every validation run. They can be stored and a number of reports combined or generated separately in a single run. Thus, data might be validated and submitted to the generalized input system throughout a day. Reports generated are stored and printed during the night shift for use the following day. This function also can be performed by spooling software. Report files generated may be kept for a short period as backup for hard copy reports.

Archival System

When data on the pool has been used by all application systems that need the data, it must be written to an archival file. The archival system contains routines for retiring data and retrieving data. Data may be retrieved for all application systems, a specific application system, a certain time period, or a specific application system run. Retrieval from the archival file may be needed for backup and recovery purposes.

There are two major advantages of having a single archival file for the installation. First, instead of having to provide backup for each application system's input data, only the archival file needs to be backed up since it contains all the input data for each application system. Second, the archival file provides data that enables historical trends to be analyzed. For example, the growth in volume of a particular type of transaction might be examined to determine whether a new method of input may be more efficient.

INSTRUCTION INPUT VALIDATION CHECKS

Like data input, instruction input entered via a job control language or interactive dialog also must be validated. Usually the auditor has little concern in this area if the language has an extensive user base and it is written by a reputable vendor. The language will have been tested comprehensively before production release, and any hidden bugs tend to be discovered and corrected quickly during the first few months of operation. Nonetheless, the auditor should understand the types of validation that should be carried out by a job control language or interactive dialog and the way in which errors should be reported as a basis for evaluating the quality of the language and the likelihood of user errors being made.

Lexical Validation

During lexical validation, the language evaluates each "word" entered by a user. Three types of words can be encountered: (*a*) identifiers (labels, variables); (*b*) terminals (operators, reserved words); and (*c*) literals (numerical constants, strings). Since words are formed from characters, the language must establish rules whereby strings of characters are recognized as discrete words. Usually this recognition occurs via boundary characters and delimiters. In many languages, for example, a space or an operator (*, /, [+], [−]) serves to delimit a word.

To illustrate lexical analysis, assume the following command is entered by a user:

SELECT name
FROM employee
WHERE salary >'15000'

The lexical analyzer in the language would read the command, character by character, and attempt to identify the words entered. For example, it would see that a space terminates the characters S, E, L, E, C, and T and that the character string 'SELECT' is a reserved word within the language. Similarly, the operator '>' terminates the variable 'salary', and the constant 15000 is delimited by the quotes symbol. If the lexical analyzer cannot recognize a valid word, it must print or display an error message so the user can undertake corrective action.

Syntactic Validation

During syntactic validation, the language reads the string of words identified and validated by the lexical analyzer and attempts to determine the sequence of operations that the string of words is intended to invoke. For example, an instruction issued in an interactive command language might be:

INTEARN = (OLDBAL + DEPOSITS − WITHDRAWS)*INTEREST

The parentheses imply a particular sequence of operations, namely:

Add DEPOSITS to OLDBAL
Subtract WITHDRAWS from the result
Multiply the results by INTEREST
Store the result in INTEARN (interest earned)

Without the parentheses the first action invoked might be to multiply WITHDRAWS by INTEREST.

The syntax analyzer validates the syntax of an instruction by *parsing* the string of words entered to determine whether it conforms to a particular rule in the grammar of the language. Thus, the quality of syntactic validation depends on having a formal and complete description of the grammar on which the language is based and on making a good choice with respect to the parsing scheme chosen. Otherwise, errors in an instruction entered may not be identified or the error message displayed or printed may not be meaningful.

Semantic Validation

During semantic validation, the language completes its analysis of the meaning of the instruction entered. The boundary between syntactic validation and semantic validation is often obscure; but during semantic validation the language might check, for example, whether two variables that are to be multiplied together are numeric types and not alphabetic or alphanumeric types. Similarly, the language might prevent a comparison of two numeric values that would be meaningless, for example, the salaries of employees with their weight.

The quality of semantic analysis depends on how well the constraints (logical restrictions) surrounding the data on which the language operates can be expressed. Database management systems that provide extensive data definition facilities, for example, allow high-quality semantic validation to be performed. The language can check that the operations to be undertaken on data items or the results produced conform to the constraints expressed for the data items in the data definition.

Reporting of Errors

The guidelines for reporting errors that were discussed earlier for data validation apply also to instruction validation. Error messages must communicate to users as completely and meaningfully as possible the nature of errors made during instruction input. Because the instructions that users enter may be variable and complex, substantial time can be lost if error messages do not allow users to pinpoint errors quickly. Furthermore, if the language fails to identify an error, unbeknown to users, results may be produced that are meaningless.

AUDIT TRAIL CONTROLS

Audit trail controls relating to input validation and error control maintain the chronology of events from the time data is validated to the time data is corrected (if it is in error) and deemed acceptable to enter either the communication subsystem or the processing subsystem.

Accounting Audit Trail

When data is validated, a time and date stamp should be attached so the timeliness of data validation and error correction and resubmission can be assessed. In some cases it may also be useful to attach a processing reference to indicate the program or module that performed the validation tests. In a distributed system, for example, input validation software may be replicated and executed at multiple sites. It may be important to know which instance of the software performed the validation tests, particularly if doubts exist about consistency among replications.

If the input validation program identifies an error, it must generate and attach a unique error number to the data in error unless the data can be corrected immediately. This error number must be associated with the data until it is corrected. It must be printed out or displayed on reports, entered on source documents used to correct the error, keyed in at a terminal if the data is subsequently retrieved from the error file and corrected interactively, etc. In this way the path of the erroneous data can be traced until the time of its correction.

Operations Audit Trail

The operations audit trail should maintain a record of the nature and number of errors made during data and instruction input, the resources consumed to detect and correct errors, and the elapsed time between error identification and error correction. Some of this data will be maintained already in the accounting audit trail—for example, the nature and number of errors made during data input. Other data has to be collected specifically for the operations audit trail— for example, the amount of central processor time used to detect particular types of errors. Periodically the operations audit trail should be analyzed to determine whether users need retraining, specific types of data input or instruction input need to be redesigned, or input validation programs need to be rewritten.

EXISTENCE CONTROLS

Existence controls must enable input validation programs and files of valid data and erroneous data to be reestablished in the event of destruction or loss. It is especially important to maintain backup copies of programs that may be dispersed across multiple input devices, for example, the input validation programs used by key-to-tape and key-to-disk devices to validate the different sorts of application source data. Whereas copies of input validation programs that run on the main machine typically are made automatically as part of the overall backup strategy, the need to make copies of programs that execute on data preparation devices or stand-alone microcomputers may be forgotten. It is pointless recovering the primary database, update and report programs, etc., if the means of validating input data cannot also be recovered on a timely basis.

SUMMARY

Data input controls are applied at four levels: (a) fields, (b) records, (c) batches, and (d) files. Field validation logic assesses the integrity of data within individual fields. Record validation logic uses interrelationships among fields in a record to assess the integrity of data within a record. Batch validation logic uses batch controls supplied on a batch header record to assess the integrity of data within a batch. File validation logic attempts to ensure the correct file is used as input to an application system.

The design of the data input program involves three major decisions: (*a*) how data will be validated, (*b*) how errors will be handled, and (*c*) how errors will be reported. As long as benefits exceed costs, the program should detect as many errors as possible. These errors must be written onto an error file so they are not lost because system users fail to correct them. Error reports must explain clearly the nature of errors detected and provide control totals for checking whether all data has been processed.

Control over data input is the responsibility of both the application system users and the data processing installation's control section. Both groups must ensure all data enters the system, errors are corrected, and data is entered only once. Periodic analysis of errors should take place to determine whether (*a*) users are continually making the same error and (*b*) the effectiveness and efficiency of the input validation program can be improved.

To enhance control over data input, a data processing installation can use a generalized data input system. A generalized data input system provides a generalized module for validating data, an input/output pool for storing valid data, an error file, a generalized reporting system, and an archival system.

Instruction input controls are applied at three levels: (*a*) the lexical level; (*b*) the syntactic level; and (*c*) the semantic level. Lexical validation assesses whether the words used in a language are valid. Syntactic validation assesses whether the sequence of operations requested is valid, given the grammar of the language. Semantic validation assesses whether the sequence of operations requested is valid, given the meaning of the words used.

Audit trail controls relating to data validation and error control maintain the chronology of events from the time data is validated until the time data is corrected, if it is erroneous, and it enters other subsystems. Existence controls restore the input validation programs and the file of valid and invalid data in the event of loss.

REVIEW QUESTIONS

11-1 As a general rule, data should be validated as soon as possible and as close as possible to the source of the data. Briefly explain the rationale behind this rule. Give one exception to the rule.

11-2 Without giving examples, briefly explain the *nature* of:
  a Field checks
  b Record checks
  c Batch checks
  d File checks

11-3 Distinguish between a range check and a reasonableness check. Why is a reasonableness check not a field-level check?

11-4 Briefly distinguish between a size validation check at the field level and a size validation check at the record level.

11-5 What problems does a master reference check normally pose for input validation? Briefly discuss the variables that would influence your decision to include or not to include a master reference check in a data input validation program.

11-6 Why is the check for a valid sign on a numeric field not a field-level check?

11-7 Distinguish between a logical batch and a physical batch. For online data entry, are there any situations where it would be impossible to exercise control using a logical batch?

11-8 For a magnetic tape file, briefly explain any difficulties surrounding the use of control totals as a *file* level check.

11-9 Why should a program check the generation number and retention date of a file used as input to the program?

11-10 Briefly explain why knowledge of the frequency of possible errors is important to the programmer writing the data input validation program.

11-11 What is meant by a "closed routine" in program logic? Briefly explain the problems that can arise if closed routines are used in data input validation programs.

11-12 A data input validation program should identify as many errors in a record as possible and not terminate validation of the record after only one error has been discovered. Why?

11-13 Briefly explain how a data input validation program can get "out of step." What are the consequences of a program getting out of step?

11-14 Briefly distinguish between immediate validation of input data and delayed validation of input data. Under what circumstances does each type of input validation usually arise?

11-15 Briefly explain the nature of a circulating error file. From a control viewpoint, what are the advantages of using a circulating error file during the data input validation process?

11-16 Give *two* examples where a large number of errors or certain types of errors in the input data may result in further processing through the application system being stopped.

11-17 Briefly describe *two* guidelines that apply to the design of screen-based error messages.

11-18 Suggest *two* techniques that can be used in the design of error reports to prevent errors from being corrected and resubmitted more than once.

11-19 Briefly explain the advantages of printing the key to all error codes used in an error report at the end of the report.

11-20 Why should control totals and summary statistics for the different types of errors be printed at the end of an error report?

11-21 How are registers and control totals used to ensure that all data is entered into a system? Be sure to explain their use in the context of an online realtime update system.

11-22 In an input system, why is it possible that corrections to errors may be submitted more than once? How does a circulating error file prevent further errors from arising as a result of duplicate error corrections being submitted?

11-23 Briefly explain the features of the validation module in a generalized input system. Why is it necessary to permit user-written subroutines to be invoked within the module?

11-24 In a generalized input system, briefly explain how the input/output pool and the error file facilitate continuous submission of data to an application system.

11-25 How does the "reminder" system function for an error file? Should resubmitted errors that again fail validation tests be written onto the error file? Explain.

11-26 Briefly explain the advantages of having a single input/output pool file, error file, and archival file in a data processing installation. What are the disadvantages? Should all application systems in the data processing installation use the generalized input system?

11-27 Briefly explain the features of the reporting module in a generalized data input system. If spooling software is available, would it be necessary to provide a system that stores reports for later printing?

11-28 Outline the functions of the archival system in a generalized data input system.

11-29 Briefly explain the nature of lexical validation of instruction input. How does the lexical analyzer handle (*a*) identifiers, (*b*) terminals, and (*c*) literals?

11-30 What is the function of the syntax analyzer in the instruction input validation system? What is meant by "parsing the string of words entered"?

11-31 Briefly explain the nature of semantic validation in an instruction input validation system. What factors govern the quality of semantic validation in an instruction input validation system?

11-32 Briefly describe the purpose of the accounting audit trail for (*a*) data input validation and (*b*) instruction input validation.

11-33 What are the purposes of the operations audit trail for (*a*) data input validation and (*b*) instruction input validation?

11-34 Briefly explain the nature of the existence controls that must be implemented for data validation and instruction validation resources in the input subsystem.

MULTIPLE CHOICE QUESTIONS

11-1 A check for missing data/blanks is an example of a:
a Record check
b Set membership check
c Field check
d Batch check

11-2 A check for valid sign (numerics) is an example of a:
a Record check
b Batch check
c Field check
d Alphabetics/numerics check

11-3 The purpose of an input validation sequence check is to:
a Check that input files are loaded in the correct order
b Check that multiple physical records for a single logical record follow the required order
c Check that the transaction type is always the first data item on a follower card
d Check that the batch serial number is in ascending order

11-4 The purpose of a retention date for a magnetic tape file is to:
a Enable files with the same generation number to be distinguished
b Indicate when the file should be recovered from production activities
c Prevent the file from being overwritten before expiry of the retention date
d Prevent the file from being read before expiry of the retention date

11-5 A closed routine in a program is a routine that:
a Accumulates a self-checking control total as it updates individual data items

    b Requires users to supply a ticket before it can be invoked

    c Ensures that data submitted as input is valid before it will accept data for processing

    d Assumes the existence of a condition if other conditions do not exist

11-6 The purpose of using a circulating error file for data that the input validation program identifies as erroneous is to:

    a Have a basis for issuing reminders if errors are not corrected

    b Ensure that data is not lost

    c Simplify processing in the input validation program

    d Both (*a*) and (*b*) above

11-7 Which of the following guidelines should *not* be followed in the design of screen error messages:

    a Personalize error messages so the user relates more easily to the system

    b Make error message concise

    c Provide multiple levels of error messages to allow for different levels of experience among users

    d Avoid humor in error messages in case the user takes offense

11-8 Which of the following guidelines should *not* be followed in the design of printed error reports:

    a Do not print out messages indicating batches of data that have been accepted as correct

    b If possible, use error reports as a turnaround document

    c Clearly identify the field in error by printing asterisks or upward arrows under the field

    d Both (*a*) and (*b*) above

11-9 The purpose of printing a list of error codes and their meanings at the end of an error report is to:

    a Reduce the amount of training that has to be given to users on how to interpret error reports

    b Simplify the change procedure when an error code is altered or a new error code is added

    c Save printing time for the error report

    d Make the error report more readable

11-10 During the data input process, the primary purpose of registers and control totals is to:

    a Ensure errors are corrected and corrected only once

    b Ensure all data enters the system

    c Enable changes in the patterns of input errors to be identified

    d Identify which types of input resources are being consumed so the efficiency of input validation processes can be improved

11-11 To prevent corrections to errors from being submitted more than once:

    a After errors have been corrected, the error reports should be discarded

    b Data input validation programs should highlight the situation by showing input control totals do not balance

    c Corrected errors should be initialed by the person correcting the error

    d Only one person should be responsible for correcting errors in any application system

11-12 Which of the following is *not* an advantage of a generalized data input/output system:

a Allows the development and implementation of input validation routines for batch application systems to be accomplished quickly

b Provides a single control point for data input

c Facilitates use of the same input data by multiple application systems

d Ensures the most efficient consumption of processing resources

11-13 Which of the following is *not* a function performed by a generalized data input system:

a Immediate update of all application system master files

b Periodic removal of data to an archival file

c Storage of all errors on a single circulating error file

d Periodic generation of reports on valid and invalid data submitted for each application system that uses the input/output pool

11-14 During lexical validation of instruction input by an interactive dialog, which of the following "words" would be classified as a literal:

a A reserved word in the dialog

b A mathematical operator

c A label

d A numerical constant

11-15 Which of the following is *not* a function of the syntax analyzer in an interactive dialog:

a Identifies the sequence of operations to be performed

b Classifies identifiers as either labels or variables

c Identifies whether the string of words entered conforms to a grammatical rule

d Executes a parsing rule on the instructions submitted as input by the user

11-16 Which of the following would be identified as an error during semantic validation of instruction input by an interactive dialog:

a Use of a reserved word as a literal

b A missing parenthesis in a mathematical equation

c Addition of a numeric variable and an alphabetic string

d Failure to delimit a numerical constant by a quotes symbol

11-17 Which of the following data items is more likely to be written to the operations audit trail and not the accounting audit trail during data input validation:

a An error number to uniquely identify the error

b A processing reference to uniquely identify the program performing the validation tests

c The central processing time used to correct each type of error identified

d The time and date at which the error was identified

11-18 Which of the following input subsystem validation components often needs special attention because it is not automatically taken into account as part of the backup strategy for the data processing installation:

a The validation programs run on data preparation devices

b The circulating error file

c The file of valid data

d The syntax analyzer in an interactive language run on a mainframe machine

EXERCISES AND CASES

11-1 You are an internal auditor participating in the design phase of a new order filling system. The programmer responsible for the design of the input validation program asks your opinion on whether or not the input validation tests proposed for customer orders are satisfactory. Customer orders are batched and keyed to tape. The validation tests proposed are:

Field \ Validation tests	Missing data	Must be numeric	Must be alphabetic	Valid range	Check digit	Valid code	Valid sign	Valid batch number
Record code						X		
Customer number		X		X	X			
Salesperson number		X				X		
Purchase order number	X							
Part number	X				X			
Quantity ordered	X	X					X	
Price instructions			X			X		
Batch number		X						X

The following data on the fields is relevant to your decision:

Field	Description
Record code	Must be the value "04"
Customer number	Numeric value that must range between 01000 and 90000
Salesperson number	Must be one of 50 numeric values
Purchase order number	Five character field; first character is alphabetic, last four are numeric
Part number	Alphanumeric field
Quantity ordered	Four character numeric
Price instructions	Alphabetic; only four codes are valid
Batch number	Four character numeric

Required. Write the programmer a brief report with your comments on the validation tests.

11-2 Huymans & Co. is a Dutch civil engineering firm based in Amsterdam. It performs construction work throughout Western Europe. The firm employs 2000 people at various offices and construction sites.

As an internal auditor for the firm, you are investigating controls over personnel change of status processing in the computer payroll system.

The various offices and sites send personnel change of status information to the personnel department in the head office. Change of status source documents are prepared after the supporting documentation has been checked. The source documents are batched and two control totals are calculated: a hash total of the employee numbers in the batch and a document count. Periodically a clerk collects the batches and takes them to data processing to be keyed to tape.

When the control section in data processing receives the batches, each batch is logged in a register. The batches are then keyed, verified, and submitted for processing.

The input program performs a comprehensive set of validation checks and prints a report showing the rejected batches. This report, together with the batches, is returned to the personnel department. A clerk in the personnel department checks to see all batches have been stamped as keyed, and gives the rejected batches report to another clerk who is responsible for correcting and resubmitting the batches. As each batch is corrected and resubmitted, the clerk initials the batch entry on the rejected batches report. Periodically the personnel manager reviews the rejected batch reports.

Required: Prepare your working papers and indicate:

a any control weaknesses that exist

b the possible consequences of these control weaknesses

c some remedial measures

11-3 Refer to case 9-1. Using the bill payment by telephone system, customers enter the following data:

a customer number

b account number

c creditor number

d amount to be paid creditor in cents

e date when amount is to be paid

An automated teller requests each data item on a step-by-step basis. After the date when amount is to be paid has been entered, the teller asks for a new creditor number. Note, creditor numbers must be authorized for customers. They must write or telephone the savings and loan association at a prior time, and new creditor numbers for the customer will be entered into the system. Customers also have special instructions that they can enter using the Touch-Tone telephone; for example:

a by entering #9# when a creditor number is requested, the customer terminates data entry

b by entering #8# they can obtain their account balance

c by entering #4# the automated teller will repeat the last transaction entered

Required: Identify the types of data entry errors that a customer could make. What controls could be used to detect these data entry errors?

11-4 The following card provides input from employee timecards to a payroll system:

Field	Picture
Employee number	9(6)
Regular hours	9(2)
Overtime hours	9(2)
Expenses/commissions	9(4).9(2)
Sick time	9(2)
Vacation time	9(2)

What field and record validation checks do you suggest should be performed on the card? Make up any parameter values you need for your tests but make sure they are reasonable. All fields are fixed length.

11-5 The following batch record and follower record are used to update the master file for a job costing system. The master file contains accounts that are the responsibility of each manager of a job:

a Batch Record

Field	Picture
Record type	A(1)
Batch number	9(4)
Transaction type	X(4)
Number of records in batch	9(2)
Financial control total	9(6).9(2)
Date of preparation	9(6)

b Follower Record

Field	Picture
Record type	A(1)
Transaction type	X(4)
Account number	X(12)
Amount	9(4).9(2)
Transaction date	9(6)

Required: Suggest any validation checks you think appropriate. Make up any parameter values you need for your tests but make sure they are reasonable. All fields are fixed length.

ANSWERS TO MULTIPLE CHOICE QUESTIONS

11-1 c	11-6 d	11-11 c	11-15 b
11-2 a	11-7 a	11-12 d	11-16 c
11-3 b	11-8 a	11-13 a	11-17 c
11-4 c	11-9 b	11-14 d	11-18 a
11-5 d	11-10 b		

REFERENCES

American Federation of Information Processing Societies. *Security: Checklist for Computer Center Self-Audits* (Arlington, VA: American Federation of Information Processing Societies, 1979).

Best, Peter J., and Peter G. Barrett. *Auditing Computer-Based Accounting Systems* (Sydney: Prentice-Hall of Australia, 1983).

Canadian Institute of Chartered Accountants. *Computer Control Guidelines* (Toronto: The Canadian Institute of Chartered Accountants, 1970).

Canadian Institute of Chartered Accountants. *Computer Audit Guidelines* (Toronto: The Canadian Institute of Chartered Accountants, 1975).

Chambers, Andrew D. *Computer Auditing* (Sydney: CCH Australia, 1981).

Corrick, Delroy L. *Auditing in the Electronic Environment: Theory, Practice and Literature* (Mt. Airy, MD: Lomond Publications, 1981).

Davis, Gordon B., Donald L. Adams, and Carol A. Schaller. *Auditing and EDP*, 2d ed. (New York: American Institute of Certified Public Accountants, 1983).

Davis, Keagle W., and William E. Perry. *Auditing Computer Applications: A Basic Systematic Approach* (New York: Wiley, 1982).

EDP Auditors Foundation, Inc. *Control Objectives* (Carol Stream, ILL: EDP Auditors Foundation, 1983).

Edwards, John D. *Accounting and Management Controls for Computer Systems* (Sydney: CCH Australia, 1980).

Jancura, Elise G., ed. *Computers: Auditing and Control*, 2d ed. (New York: Petrocelli/Charter, 1977).

Jancura, Elise G. *Audit & Control of Computer Systems* (New York: Petrocelli/Charter, 1974).

Jancura, Elise G., and Robert V. Boos. *Establishing Controls and Auditing the Computerized Accounting System* (New York: Van Nostrand Reinhold, 1981).

Mair, William C., Donald R. Wood, and Keagle W. Davis. *Computer Control & Audit*, 2d ed. (Altamonte Springs, FL: The Institute of Internal Auditors, 1976).

Porter, W. Thomas, and William E. Perry. *EDP: Controls and Auditing*, 4th ed. (Belmont, CA: Wadsworth, 1984).

Watne, Donald A., and Peter B. B. Turney. *Auditing EDP Systems* (Englewood Cliffs, NJ: Prentice-Hall, 1984).

Woodridge, Susan. *Computer Input Design* (New York: Petrocelli Books, 1974).

CHAPTER **12**

COMMUNICATION CONTROLS

440

The communication subsystem is responsible for transmitting data among all the other subsystems within a system or for transmitting data to or receiving data from another system. Its physical manifestation may be a cable (channel) linking a disk drive with a central processor, or it may be a complex configuration of minicomputers and communication lines linking remote computers that must interact with one another.

This chapter examines the controls that can be established within the communication subsystem to preserve asset safeguarding and data integrity. While effectiveness and efficiency objectives are critical within the communication subsystem, they can be considered only in passing since they are complex and warrant separate volumes (see, for example, Cypser [1978] and Doll [1978]). The focus, here, is on controls to reduce losses from failure in the subsystem components and deliberate attempts to subvert the authenticity and privacy of data traversing the subsystem components.

COMMUNICATION SUBSYSTEM EXPOSURES

There are two major types of exposures in the communication subsystem. First, data may be lost or corrupted through component failure. Second, a hostile party (intruder) may seek to subvert data being transmitted through the subsystem. The following sections examine each type of exposure in more detail.

Component Failure

The primary components in the communication subsystem are (*a*) communication lines—for example, twisted pair, coaxial cables, fiber optics, microwave, satellite; (*b*) hardware—for example, ports, modems, multiplexors, switches, concentrators; and (*c*) software—for example, packet switching software, polling software, data compression software. Each of these components may fail such that data is lost or corrupted or routed incorrectly through the network and perhaps displayed to a person who is unauthorized to view the data.

In a communication line, errors arise because *noise* is present. Noise is the random electric signals that occur which degrade performance in the line. There are two types of noise: white and impulse. White noise arises through the motion of electrons. It increases as a function of absolute temperature. Impulse noise arises for a variety of reasons: atmospheric conditions, faulty switching gear, poor contacts. Noise increases as more data is transmitted over a communication line. If the public telephone exchange network is used for data transmission, line errors increase during peak periods because the increased traffic produces additional noise.

Hardware and software failures can occur for many reasons: circuitry failure, a disk crash, a power surge, insufficient temporary storage, program bugs, etc. The failure may be either temporary or permanent, and it may be either localized or global. An intermittent failure in a modem may corrupt a bit pattern only in short bursts—a temporary failure. An operating system may crash for some unknown reason and the operator may be unable to restart it on a timely basis—a permanent failure. Terminal failure may affect only the user of the terminal—a local failure. Failure in a concentrator, however, affects all users connected to the concentrator—a global failure.

Subversive Threats

In a subversive attack on the communication subsystem, an intruder attempts to violate the integrity of some component in the subsystem. For example, invasive or inductive taps can be installed on telephone lines using, say, a data scope. An invasive tap enables the intruder either to read or to modify the data being transmitted. An inductive tap monitors electromagnetic transmissions and allows the data to be read only. Similarly, satellite signals can be read by a ground receiver over a wide geographic area, although modifying satellite transmission is more difficult.

Subversive attacks can be either passive or active (Figure 12-1). In a *passive* attack, intruders attempt to learn some characteristic of the data being transmitted. They may be able to read the contents of the data so the privacy of the data is violated. Alternatively, although the content of the data itself may remain secure, intruders may read and analyze the cleartext source and destination identifiers attached to a message for routing purposes, or they may examine the lengths and frequency of messages being transmitted. These latter attacks are known as *traffic analysis,* and they can provide an intruder with

FIGURE 12-1
Subversive threats to the communication subsystem.

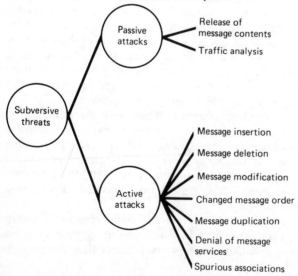

important information about messages being transmitted. For example, analysis of source and destination identifiers may provide insights into troop movements in a military application, or they may provide sales information in a commercial application. Similarly, the lengths and frequency of messages may indicate the types of messages being transmitted.

There are seven types of *active* attack. First, intruders may insert a message in the message stream being transmitted. For example, in an electronic funds transfer system (EFTS), they may add a deposit transaction for their account. Second, intruders may delete a message being transmitted. For example, they may remove an account withdrawal transaction from the message stream being transmitted. Third, intruders may modify the contents of a message being transmitted. For example, they may increase the amount field in a deposit transaction. Fourth, intruders may alter the order of messages in a message stream. For example, they may change the sequence of deposit and withdrawal transactions to affect interest charged or earned on their account. Fifth, intruders may duplicate messages in a message stream. For example, they may copy deposit transactions for their account. Sixth, intruders may deny message services between a sender and a receiver by either discarding messages or delaying messages. This attack is similar to a message deletion attack. However, message deletion is a transient attack on an established association between a sender and a receiver, whereas an attack that denies message services prevents the association from being established in the first place. It might be used by a competitor to severely impair the day-to-day operations of an organization. Finally, intruders may use techniques to establish spurious associations so they are regarded as legitimate users of a system. For example, they may play back a handshaking sequence previously used by a legitimate user of the system. Chapter 9 discussed this type of attack in some detail; thus, it will be considered only briefly in this chapter.

CONTROLS OVER COMPONENT FAILURE

Previous chapters have already discussed some of the important controls that can be used to prevent, detect, or correct component failures that affect the communication subsystem: thorough testing of programs, adequate maintenance of hardware, well-trained operators, well-practiced backup and recovery procedures, etc. The following sections examine some additional controls that tend to be specific to the communication subsystem.

Treatment of Line Errors

Since a bit pattern can be corrupted during transmission through noise occurrence, an important design decision is the way in which line errors will be detected and corrected. Cypser [1978] reports data from four surveys carried out in the United States and the United Kingdom to determine transmission error performance. Bit error rates spanned a range from 1 in 1000 to 1 in

1,000,000. Particularly when public lines are used for data transmission, the designer should assume a wide range of line error rates will be encountered.

The effects of line errors can be catastrophic. Martin [1972] uses the following example to show how a database can be corrupted quickly by line errors. Consider an online database where transactions arrive with one bit in every 100,000 bits in error. Assume a record is updated 100 times a month, and if one of 20 five-bit characters is in error, an update error occurs. After six months, approximately 4500 records will be in error. Certain line errors may have more serious effects than others. For example, if a transaction-type code field is corrupted, erroneous shipments of inventory may be made or a record deleted from the database by mistake. Thus, controls must be implemented to detect and correct line errors.

Error Detection   Line errors can be detected by either using a loop (echo) check or building some form of redundancy into the message transmitted. Consequently, the quality of data transmitted increases at the cost of reduced throughput over the communication line. The design problem is to balance the cost of reduced throughput with the costs of undetected errors.

A *loop check* involves the receiver of a message sending back the message received to the sender. The sender checks the correctness of the message received by the receiver by comparing it with a stored copy of the message sent. If there is a difference, the message is retransmitted with suitable line protocol data to indicate the previous message received was in error. In fact, the message received may have been correct; instead, the receiver's retransmission of the message back to the sender may have been corrupted.

Since a loop check at least halves the throughput on communication lines, normally it is used on full-duplex (simultaneous two-way communication) lines or where communication lines are short. If lines are short, the high protection afforded data transmission using a loop check may justify the costs of the extra channel capacity needed. On full-duplex lines, the return path is often underutilized anyway so it can be used for error detection purposes.

Redundancy takes the form of error detection codes. Three major types of codes exist: (*a*) parity checking codes, (*b*) M-out-of-N codes, and (*c*) cyclic codes.

Both vertical and horizontal *parity checks* can be used: a vertical parity check applies to a character, and a horizontal parity check applies to a string of characters. It is dangerous to use only vertical or horizontal parity checking. Martin [1970] quotes figures from an International Telegraph and Telephone Consultative Committee (CCITT) study on the lengths of bursts of noise. The figures show a high probability (40–50%) that a burst of noise will corrupt more than one bit in a character. Thus, a single parity check (vertical or horizontal) will not detect an error if the corrupted bits compensate. Indeed, there is about a 30% chance that a single parity check will fail. A combination of vertical and horizontal parity checking affords greater protection against line errors.

In *M-out-of-N codes,* characters must be represented by a fixed number of

1 and 0 bits in a character. For example, if a 4-out-of-8 code is used, the bit string for a character must comprise four 1 bits and four 0 bits. If the bit string received does not conform to this requirement, a line error has occurred. Martin [1970] argues an M-out-of-N code offers only a marginal improvement over a single parity check. Unfortunately, bursts of noise often oscillate, thereby causing one bit to change in one direction and a nearby bit to change in the opposite direction. Thus, a string 10 may change to a string 01 and the M-out-of-N code would fail to detect the error. Experiments carried out within IBM show the percentage of undetected errors with a single parity check to be about 1.9 times greater than an M-out-of-N code. However, the M-out-of-N code has more redundancy. A 4-out-of-8 code allows 70 characters to be represented, whereas 128 characters are possible when only one bit is used as a parity check.

Cyclic codes or polynomial codes are more complex than parity checking codes or M-out-of-N codes, but they offer a higher degree of protection against line errors. Peterson and Brown [1961] provide a detailed explanation of how to calculate cyclic codes. The way in which cyclic codes are generated can be chosen to minimize the number of undetected errors, given the characteristics of the particular communication line used. Even though cyclic codes are more complex than parity or M-out-of-N codes, the circuitry needed for decoding and encoding is relatively simple.

Error Correction   Once line errors have been detected, they must then be corrected. Two methods are used to correct errors: (*a*) error correcting codes and (*b*) retransmission of data in error.

Error correcting codes enable line errors to be detected and corrected at the receiving station. However, in general, to be able to carry out error correction, large amounts of redundancy are required in the messages transmitted. There is also a danger the attempted correction of an error will be carried out incorrectly. For these reasons, detection of errors and retransmission usually is chosen as the error correction strategy in preference to error correcting codes.

If *retransmission* is used to correct errors, a decision must be made on how much data is to be retransmitted. It may be as small as a character or as large as a batch of several records. Retransmission of a small quantity of data has two advantages. First, it is faster to retransmit a small amount of data than a large amount. Second, the buffer storage required to hold the message until correct transmission has occurred is small. The major disadvantages of using small amounts of data for retransmission arise because error detection codes are less efficient for small amounts of data (greater amounts of redundancy are required) and more line control characters are needed.

Error correction through retransmission requires special logic (line protocols) to indicate the correct or incorrect receipt of a message. The ASCII ACK-NAK logic is an example. An ACK signal is transmitted by the receiver if the message received is correct. A NAK signal is transmitted by the receiver if the message is incorrect. In some cases the sender waits for either an ACK or NAK signal before transmitting the next message. In other cases the sender continues to transmit messages while awaiting an ACK or NAK signal. If a NAK signal is received, the sender might go back to the message sent in error and retransmit messages from that point.

Noise also may corrupt the control characters used for retransmission in an error detection and correction system. An odd-even record count enables such errors to be detected. For example, consider the situation in which control characters are corrupted and two messages appear to the receiver to be a single message. Assume the control character for the first message was odd. The control character for the second message, an even number, has been corrupted. Thus, when the receiver identifies a third message having an odd-numbered control character, it will recognize a message is missing and an error has occurred.

Improving Network Reliability

Besides using hardware and software to detect and correct line errors, a communication network can be designed to reduce the likelihood of line errors and system failure occurring and to minimize the effects of line errors and system failure when they do occur. The following sections discuss how the choice of modems, communication lines, multiplexing/concentration techniques, network topology, and network control software affect overall network reliability.

Choice of a Modem In general, computer hardware uses and generates discrete, direct current (dc) binary signals. These signals can be transmitted over wires up to about 5–6 kilometers in length. However, if transmission is needed over a longer distance, the signals become so distorted that they cannot be decoded. Communication lines that allow digital transmission of binary signals over much longer distances have been developed and are being used increasingly. Nevertheless, much data transmission still occurs through converting digital signals to continuous analog signals (Figure 12-2). The device that accomplishes this conversion is called a modem or data set.

Modems have two major purposes: (a) to reduce the line errors caused by noise and (b) to increase the speed of data transmission. A tradeoff must be

FIGURE 12-2a
Digital signal.

FIGURE 12-2b
Analog signal.

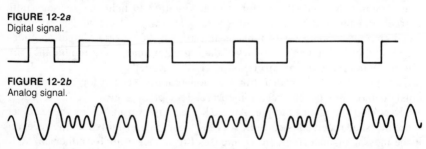

made in accomplishing these objectives. Faster data transmission means a greater number of line errors occur although, hopefully, more throughput is still attained. Also, Carroll [1977] points out that three undesirable control situations arise as noise increases. First, an increasing amount of data must be retransmitted, which increases the probability of unauthorized interception. Second, increased noise can be used to camouflage unauthorized activities. Third, to overcome the noise, the sender must increase signal power, which increases free-space emission from the line and the ease with which an inductive wiretap can be carried out. Thus, control and throughput requirements must be balanced.

Modems work by varying either the amplitude, frequency, or phase of an analog signal to represent a digital signal (Figure 12-3). Noise affects the performance of the three modulation methods differently. Both theoretical and empirical research results show that phase modulation outperforms frequency modulation and frequency modulation outperforms amplitude modulation in terms of the number of line errors that arise. Furthermore, if the analog waveform is generated having more than two states so that dibits or tribits are encoded for faster throughput, phase modulation typically is used since it withstands noise better than the other forms of modulation. Unfortunately, phase modulation costs more than either frequency or amplitude modulation.

Besides noise, line errors are also caused through the presence of *distortion*. Two forms of distortion exist. Attenuation distortion is the unwanted change in waveform that results through decreases in the magnitude of current, voltage, or power in a signal being transmitted. Delay distortion occurs when different waveform frequencies are delayed by different amounts. There are two ways of controlling distortion: (*a*) line conditioning and (*b*) modem equalization. Line conditioning is the process by which a carrier makes a communication line conform to certain quality characteristics. It is discussed in the next section. Modem equalization is the process by which a modem compensates for distortion.

Modem equalization is especially important in controlling line errors when public lines are used for data transmission. Since any line might be chosen for transmission in a public network, the user has no prior knowledge of the specific characteristics of the line. The line cannot be conditioned. However, modems for public lines can be purchased with circuitry for dynamic equalization, a process that measures the characteristics of the line in use and performs automatic adjustment for attenuation and delay distortion.

For control of line errors, it is also an advantage if a modem can transmit at different speeds. As transmission speeds increase, the effects of noise are more pronounced. A modem with different speeds can recognize when high levels of noise exist and transmit at a slower rate to reduce the effects of this noise. Furthermore, if a private line is used for data transmission, where possible, modems that have automatic or semiautomatic dial-up capabilities should be used. Thus, if the private line fails, the modem will (automatically) transfer data transmission over to the public network.

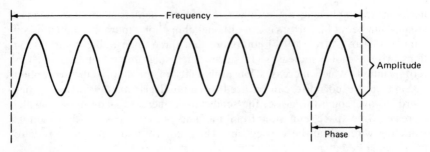

FIGURE 12-3a
Wave form characteristics.

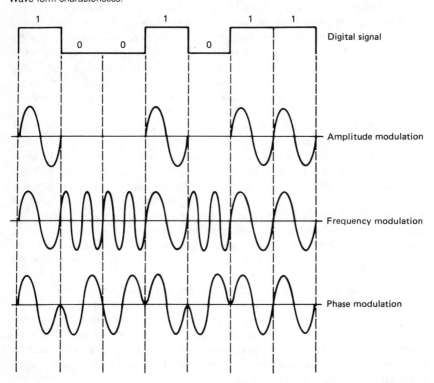

FIGURE 12-3b
Modulation techniques.

Choice of a Communication Line A major factor affecting the reliability of data transmission is whether the communication line chosen is a public line or a private line. Public lines use the normal public switching exchange facilities. Users have either no or only partial control over the lines allocated to them for data transmission. In some cases, users can specify the characteristics of the lines they require. The switching center will then allocate a line having those characteristics. Private lines are lines that are dedicated to service a particular user.

For small amounts of data transmission (generally, less than a few hours per day), public lines are cheaper than private lines. However, as usage increases, private lines become cheaper than public lines. Moreover, private lines have two other major advantages. First, in general, they allow higher rates of data transmission. Second, private lines can be conditioned; that is, the carrier ensures the line has certain quality attributes.

The network designer also should consider whether digital transmission should be used instead of analog transmission. Digital lines are not as widely available as analog lines; however, available services are increasing. The primary advantage of digital transmission is that it is more reliable than analog transmission. Analog lines require linear amplifiers that amplify both the signal and any noise present on the line. Digital lines use nonlinear repeaters that do not pass on certain types of noise. Since noise levels are lower, faster data transmission can also be accomplished.

Other technologies that offer increased speed and higher reliability are becoming increasingly available, for example, satellite transmission, microwave, and optical fiber (laser) transmission. Optical fibers have a major advantage in that they preclude the possibility of wiretapping. No technology is available for tapping light waves; furthermore, splicing cables and making connections to the glass strands used in optical fiber transmission is difficult. However, optical fiber transmission can be used only over short distances since the light loss that occurs when signals are transmitted through glass is high.

Choice of a Multiplexing/Concentration Technique   Multiplexing and concentration techniques allow the bandwidth or capacity of a communication line to be used more effectively. The common objective is to share the use of a high-cost transmission line among many messages that arrive at the multiplexor or concentration point from multiple low-cost source lines.

Multiplexing techniques use static channel derivation schemes to assign capacity on a fixed, predetermined basis. A multiplexor has the same input and output bit rate. The two common multiplexing techniques used are frequency-division multiplexing and time-division multiplexing. The former technique divides a single bandwidth into several smaller bandwidths that are used as independent frequency channels (Figure 12-4a). The latter technique assigns small, fixed time slots to a user during which the user transmits the whole or part of a message (Figure 12-4b).

Concentration techniques use schemes whereby some number of input channels dynamically share a smaller number of output channels on a demand basis. Thus, concentration techniques smooth the traffic flow in a network, and since the number of input channels exceeds the number of output channels, they must be able to handle message queues that develop and choose the "best" path for messages to traverse. The three common concentration techniques are message switching, packet switching, and line switching. In

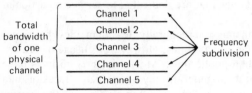

FIGURE 12-4a
Frequency division multiplexing.

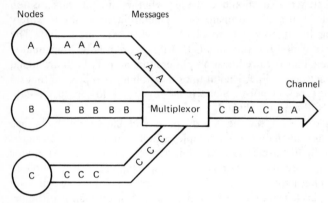

FIGURE 12-4b
Time division multiplexing.

message switching, a complete message is sent to the concentration point and stored until a communication path can be established with the destination node. In packet switching, a message is broken up into small, fixed-length packets, and the individual packets are routed individually through the network depending on the availability of a channel for each packet. In line switching or circuit switching, a device establishes temporary connections between input channels and output channels where the number of input channels exceeds the number of output channels. Responsibility for handling queues that develop falls back on the source node.

Multiplexing and concentration techniques impact system reliability in several ways. First, since these techniques make more efficient use of channel capacity, at least some available channel capacity can be allocated for backup purposes. Second, concentration techniques can route a message over a different path if a channel fails. Third, multiplexing and concentration functions often are incorporated into an intelligent frontend processor that performs other functions such as message validation and protocol conversion which otherwise would increase the workload of, and reliance on, the mainframe. Fourth, as critical components in a network, multiplexors and concentrators must be chosen that have a high mean-time-between-failure (MTBF).

Multiplexors and concentrators also help to protect data against subversive attacks. It is more difficult for a wiretapper to disentangle the myriad of messages passing over a channel connected to a multiplexor or concentrator. Conversely, sophisticated intruders gain access to more data if they have suitable hardware and software and can determine the multiplexing or concentration techniques used.

Choice of a Network Topology   In simple terms a network topology specifies the location of nodes within a network, the ways in which these nodes will be linked, and the data transmission capabilities of the links between the nodes. Specifying the optimum topology for a network is a problem of immense complexity.

Consider some of the design constraints that apply to the choice of a network topology. First, an overall cost constraint exists. Usually a maximum limit is specified for the cost per bit of information transmitted. Second, throughput and response time constraints exist. Communication of messages between different points in the network must be achieved within a certain time. Third, availability and reliability constraints exist. The network must be available for use at any one time by a given number of users. If a component of the network fails, alternative routing of messages or alternative hardware and software may be needed. The problem of determining an optimum topology is the subject of current research. Computationally feasible algorithms for determining an optimum are still evolving. Because of the complexity of the problem, the approach so far is still heuristic to some extent.

Figure 12-5 shows some of the possible topologies (configurations) for a network linking seven terminals to a host computer. Figure 12-5a is one extreme. It achieves high reliability since any one terminal is not dependent on the functioning of another terminal or a communication link other than the one that links it to the host computer. Line costs are high, however, because of the total length of line needed.

Figure 12-5b is another extreme. Here a multidrop line has been used to reduce line costs. However, the network is extremely sensitive to failure in a component of the network. For example, failure in a line segment affects all terminals further down the line.

Figure 12-5c is an intermediate case. Here a communication controller and a concentrator have been used. Line costs are lower than the first extreme but higher than the second. However, the communication controller and the concentrator add to the cost of the overall network. Presumably they have been used to reduce the load on the host computer and to improve line utilization, thereby permitting faster throughput and improving response time and system availability. Network reliability is lower than the first extreme but higher than the second. Failure in the controller or concentrator affects all terminals connected to the controller or concentrator. Failure in the line segment linking the controller or concentrator to the host computer does more damage than failure in a line segment linking a terminal to the controller or concentrator.

In light of the above considerations of line costs and reliability, several common types of network topology have emerged, each giving higher priority

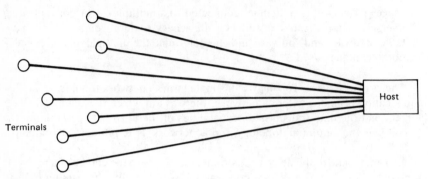

FIGURE 12-5a
Network using point-to-point lines.

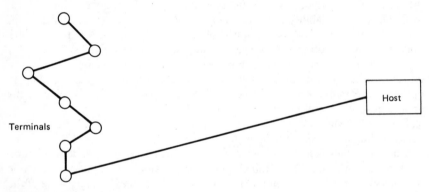

FIGURE 12-5b
Network using a multidrop line.

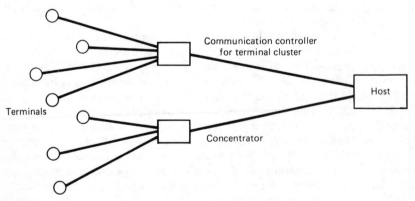

FIGURE 12-5c
Network using communication controller and concentrator.

to different objectives. Again, two polar extremes exist: (*a*) a ring network and (*b*) a completely connected network. A third topology, the intermediate case, is a star network. Of course, unconstrained network topologies can also be used in which the network configuration is not restricted in the way it grows.

Figure 12-6*a* shows a ring network. In this case, communication lines link a number of host computers. These host computers may be small frontend machines, major processors, communication controllers, etc. The ring network reduces line costs by providing only the minimum number of links required to allow communications between any pair of host computers. To reduce costs further, communications may be unidirectional (simplex). However, a ring network has low reliability since failure in a host or a communication link may prevent communications between any two host computers. To some extent this problem can be overcome by allowing communications to be bidirectional (half-duplex or duplex).

Figure 12-6*b* shows a completely connected network. It increases network reliability by providing a direct link between any two host machines. Failure in a communication link or host simply means that messages have to be rerouted.

FIGURE 12-6*a*
Ring network.

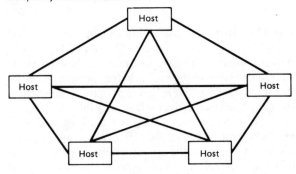

FIGURE 12-6*b*
Completely connected network.

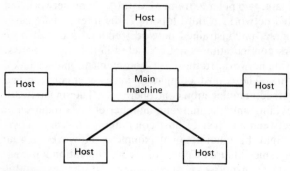

FIGURE 12-6c
Star network.

However, compared to a ring network, line costs are high and more complex message switching facilities are needed.

Figure 12-6c shows a star network. Each host is linked directly to a main machine. The main machine performs message switching functions. Thus, line costs are lower than those for a completely connected network, and communications between two hosts are more direct than communications in a ring network. Compared to a ring network, failure in a host or communication link is less critical. However, failure in the main machine is disastrous.

In all cases, network reliability is increased by providing alternative routes for messages through either using more communication channels or instituting more complex switching devices. If message switching is used to increase network reliability, several controls must exist to ensure a message that must be switched is not lost. First, it is important that the message switching device has a store-and-forward capability in case the receiving station is busy or down and the message must be transmitted at a later time. Second, all messages must have a unique identifier—a message number, an originating terminal number, a user number or password. Third, messages should be transmitted promptly to reduce the risk of loss. Thus, fast throughput in a message switching system is critical from a control viewpoint.

Choice of Network Control Software The reliability of a network can be enhanced considerably through the acquisition and use of high-quality network control software. Good network control software will provide detailed information about the status of all components in the network, for example, whether a line is up or down, whether a terminal is active, the length of message queues, the error rate on a line, the density of traffic over a line, and the adequacy of store-and-forward file space. By carefully monitoring the network using ·the software, an operator can detect problems before they affect reliability and take preventive or remedial actions. For example, the operator may shut down a line or a concentrator, implement an alternative polling schedule for a cluster of terminals, allocate more storage for queues, change the priority status of a network user, or disconnect a terminal that seems to have been compromised. Since network control software is very powerful, careful control must be exercised over its use. A malicious or fraudulent employee could use it to severely disrupt network operations, destroy or change critical data, change network access privileges, etc. Only senior employees should be permitted to use the software. Furthermore, the functions within the software might be segregated so that only a subset of functions is assigned to any one employee.

CONTROLS OVER SUBVERSIVE THREATS

There are two types of controls over subversive threats to the communication subsystem. The first type seeks to establish physical barriers to the data traversing the subsystem. The second type accepts that an intruder somehow can gain access to the data and seeks to render it useless when a privacy violation occurs. Chapter 7 discussed some of the former type of controls that might be used. Carroll [1977] also describes several technical controls that can be used to prevent or detect wiretapping or to reduce electromagnetic emissions from communication lines. In most applications today, however, it must be accepted that an intruder will be able to gain access to the data traversing the communication subsystem. Often the data is sent over public networks or it is sent via satellite or microwave where it is difficult to prevent access to the data from being obtained. Accordingly, the following sections focus on the second type of control, that is, controls that seek to render the data useless if it is intercepted by an intruder. The fundamental technique used is encryption (see, also, Chapter 9). However, other types of controls also must be employed in conjunction with encryption to counteract subversive threats. Table 12-1 provides an overview of the controls to be discussed.

Link Encryption

Link encryption protects all data traversing a communication link between two nodes in a network (Figure 12-7). The two nodes must share a common encryption key. The key may be common to all nodes in the network, in which case it is easy to establish a communication session between any two nodes but it is difficult to protect the privacy of the key. Alternatively, each node must know the keys of all other nodes with which it communicates, in which case the keys are more secure but key management is more difficult.

Link encryption reduces expected losses from traffic analysis. With link encryption, the message and its associated source and destination identifiers can be encrypted. Thus, a wiretapper has difficulty determining the sender and receiver of a message. In addition, it is possible to mask frequency and length patterns in data by maintaining a continuous stream of ciphertext between two nodes.

TABLE 12-1
CONTROLS OVER SUBVERSIVE THREATS

Type of attack	Control
Release of message contents	Link encryption End-to-end encryption
Traffic analysis	Link encryption
Message insertion	Message sequence numbers
Message deletion	Message sequence numbers
Message modification	Stream ciphers Error propagation codes Message authentication codes
Changed message order	Message sequence numbers
Message duplication	Unique session identifiers Message sequence numbers
Denial of message services	Request-response mechanism
Spurious association	Secure authentication

Since each node must be able to decrypt a message to determine where it should be forwarded, link encryption cannot protect the integrity of data if a node in the network is subverted. As always, encryption and decryption should be performed by a secure cryptographic facility that is tamperproof. Thus, even if an intruder subverts a node in the network, the integrity of cryptographic operations is still protected.

End-to-End Encryption

Link encryption has several limitations (see, further, Voydock and Kent [1983]). First, as discussed earlier, if an intermediate node in the network is subverted, all traffic passing through the node is exposed. Second, as a related issue, high costs may have to be incurred to protect the security of each node in the network. For example, security personnel may have to be present, physical barriers may have to be constructed, and regular security reviews may have to be undertaken. Third, to the extent that the users of a public network

FIGURE 12-7
Link encryption.

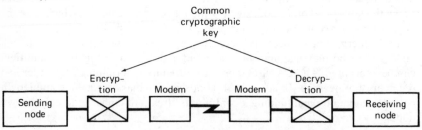

rely on link encryption, network owners may incur high insurance costs to protect themselves against damages resulting from security violations. Fourth, it is difficult to work out a transfer pricing scheme for allocating link encryption costs to users, particularly if some users argue they do not need protection.

To help overcome these problems, end-to-end encryption can be implemented. End-to-end encryption protects the integrity of data passing between a sender and a receiver, independently of the nodes that the data traverses. Thus, a cryptographic facility must be available to each sender and receiver since each now takes responsibility for implementing cryptographic protection. End-to-end encryption can be refined further to implement *association* encryption, whereby each "session" between a sender and a receiver is protected.

Although end-to-end encryption reduces expected losses from active or passive attacks when an intermediate node is subverted, it provides only limited protection against traffic analysis. At a basic level, the source and destination identifiers attached to a message exist in the clear when end-to-end encryption is used since the encrypted message must be routed through the network. Several techniques are available for reducing the level of precision with which traffic analysis can be carried out when end-to-end encryption is used, but ultimately traffic analysis cannot be prevented entirely. Consequently, link encryption sometimes is used in conjunction with end-to-end encryption to reduce exposures from traffic analysis.

Stream Ciphers

There are two types of ciphers: block ciphers and stream ciphers (see, further, Denning [1982]). With *block* ciphers, fixed-length blocks of cleartext are transformed under a constant fixed-length key (Figure 12-8). The Data Encryption Standard (DES) provides this mode of encryption via its electronic code book (ECB) mode. With *stream* ciphers, cleartext is transformed on a bit-by-bit basis under the control of a stream of key bits. There are various ways of generating the stream of key bits, but a widely used technique is to make the key bit stream a function of an initialization value, an encryption key, and the generated ciphertext. Figure 12-9 shows this method as implemented in the DES cipher block chaining (CBC) mode. The cleartext is first partitioned into fixed-length blocks. Next, the first cleartext block is added (modulo 2) to this block. The result is enciphered and the ciphertext produced is added (modulo 2) to the next cleartext block to be enciphered once more. The process continues iteratively.

Stream ciphers have two important characteristics. First, they make it more difficult to analyze patterns in ciphertext. In block mode, each enciphered block is independent of each other block. A cryptanalyst can examine character frequency patterns to break the cipher. Stream ciphers, however, create interbit dependencies. Thus, patterns are masked from the cryptanalyst. Second, because interbit dependencies exist, changes to ciphertext propagate to subsequent ciphertext. If data is corrupted via a burst of noise on a line, at

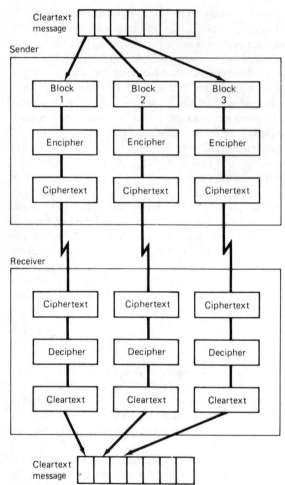

FIGURE 12-8
DES electronic code book (ECB) mode.

least some of the subsequent ciphertext will be unreadable. Or, if a wiretapper undertakes an active attack and modifies data in transit, again, at least some of the subsequent ciphertext will be affected. Stream ciphers, therefore, reduce expected losses from passive attacks and active attacks.

Error Propagation Codes

Unfortunately, use of a stream cipher alone is not sufficient to prevent all types of message modification. Assume, for example, a message is partitioned into fixed-length blocks. Assume, further, that the CBC mode of encryption is applied to the message. Voydock and Kent [1983] show how a cryptanalyst can

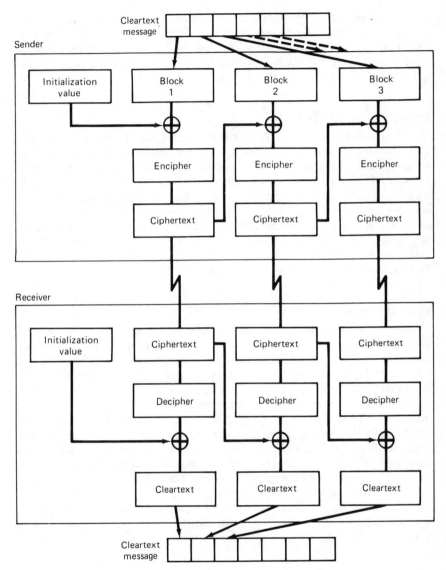

FIGURE 12-9
DES cipher block chaining (CBC) mode.

change the order of blocks within a message so that the receiver of the message does not detect it. This type of attack can also be undertaken successfully on other types of stream ciphers.

To protect the integrity of the message, a suitable error propagation code must be used. The code must be sensitive to the order of bits in the message so that a change to the order of blocks has a high probability of being detected.

Several common error propagation codes, such as longitudinal parity checks, are unsuitable for this purpose since it is fairly easy for a cryptanalyst to determine changes to the ciphertext that will produce the same error detection code. Peterson and Weldon [1972] describe error detection codes that are sensitive to bit order.

Message Authentication Codes

In EFTS, a control used to identify changes to a message in transit is a message authentication code (MAC). The MAC is calculated by applying the DES algorithm and a secret key to selected data items in a message or to the entire message. The MAC field is then appended to the message and sent to the receiver, who recalculates the MAC on the basis of the message received to determine whether the calculated MAC and the received MAC are equal. If the calculated MAC and the received MAC are not equal, the message has been altered in some way during transit. The transmitted message could be in the clear, or only selected data items in the message (such as the personal identification number [PIN]) might be encrypted.

Message Sequence Numbers

Message sequence numbers are required to detect any attack on the *order* of messages being transmitted between a sender and a receiver. An intruder may delete messages from a stream of messages, change the order of messages in a stream, or duplicate legitimate messages. In each case the receiver does not obtain messages in the order generated by the sender.

If each message contains a sequence number and the order of sequence numbers is checked, these attacks will not be successful. It must be impossible, however, for the intruder to alter the sequence number in a message. Controls to prevent message modification have been discussed already: stream ciphers, error propagation codes, and message authentication codes. Furthermore, to prevent message duplication (playback), sequence numbers must not be reused during a communication session between a sender and a receiver. A unique identification number must be established for each communication session, and within this identification number each message sequence number must be unique.

Request-Response Mechanisms

A request-response mechanism is used to identify attacks by an intruder aimed at denying message services to a sender and a receiver. Recall, this type of attack is a form of message stream modification whereby the intruder deletes messages passing over the communication line or delays them for a prolonged period. If the parties to a communication session are not continuously communicating with each other, the receiver cannot detect that a message should have arrived from the sender. The *sender* may be able to detect that the receiver has not obtained the message since no acknowledgment has been returned by the receiver, but in some cases the sender may have no means of notifying the receiver that the communication channel has been broken. For example, in certain high-security applications, the sender may not be able to place a telephone call to the receiver to notify the receiver of the attack.

With a request-response mechanism, a timer is placed with the sender and receiver. The timer periodically triggers a control message from the sender, and since the timer at the receiver is synchronized with the sender, the receiver must respond to show the communication link has not been broken. To the extent that the timing signals can be generated with a pattern that is difficult to determine, the intruder finds it harder to undertake temporary undetected attacks that deny message service. In addition, the intruder must not be able to provide valid responses to the control messages. Otherwise, the sender believes the channel is still open, and the receiver is unaware that message services have been denied. Thus, those controls discussed in Chapter 9 and earlier in this chapter that establish the authenticity of the response must be applied to the request-response mechanism.

AUDIT TRAIL CONTROLS

The audit trail in the communication subsystem maintains the chronology of events from the time a sender dispatches a message to the time a receiver obtains the message.

Accounting Audit Trail

The accounting audit trail must allow a message to be traced through each node in the network. Some examples of data items that might be kept in the accounting audit trail are:

1 Unique identifier of the source node
2 Unique identifier of the person/process authorizing dispatch of the message
3 Time and date at which message dispatched
4 Message sequence number
5 Unique identifier of each node in the network that the message traversed
6 Time and date at which each node in the network was traversed by the message
7 Unique identifier of sink node
8 Time and date at which the message was received by the sink node
9 Image of message received at each node traversed in the network

Given that a message should not be changed as it traverses a node in the network, keeping all the above information may seem pointless. Indeed, if a message traverses a public network or interchange network, the owner of the network may not be willing to maintain or to supply the audit trail information. Nevertheless, the audit trail information is needed if a message is lost in the network or if it is suspected that a node has been compromised or it is malfunctioning and unwanted changes are occurring to the message. As always, what audit trail information should be kept and how long it should be kept is a cost-benefit decision.

Operations Audit Trail

The operations audit trail in the communication subsystem is especially important, as the performance and, ultimately, the integrity of the network depend on the availability of comprehensive operations audit trail data. Using this data, a network supervisor can identify problem areas in the network and reconfigure the network accordingly. Some examples of data items that might be kept in the operations audit trail are:

1 Number of messages that have traversed each link
2 Number of messages that have traversed each node
3 Queue lengths at each node
4 Number of errors occurring on each link or at each node
5 Number of retransmissions that have occurred across each link
6 Log of errors to identify locations and patterns of errors
7 Log of system restarts
8 Message transit times between nodes and at nodes

As discussed earlier in the chapter, the availability of high-quality network control software is essential to a network supervisor's being able to make effective use of the operations audit trail. While substantial operations audit trail data may be available, often it is not readily accessible nor is the data presented in a form that permits effective decision making. Good network control software will access the relevant operations audit trail data and provide meaningful reports that allow the network supervisor to maintain or to improve the performance of the network.

EXISTENCE CONTROLS

Recovering a communication network if it fails poses some difficult problems. Many of the components in the network are complex, and the location and nature of the failure are often difficult to determine. The status of the network upon failure also may be difficult to assess. Message fragments are dispersed throughout the network at various stages of processing. Ensuring complete and accurate recovery of all messages in flight is a complex affair. It is also difficult to provide backup for all network components. Some network components may be geographically remote. It may be too expensive to provide redundant components at remote locations, yet the network may be severely disrupted when long lead times are required to recover these remote components after they fail.

Some of the backup and recovery controls that should be implemented have been discussed earlier in this chapter when network reliability was considered: automatic line speed adjustment by modems based on differing noise levels; modems on private lines having automatic or semiautomatic dial-up capabilities for the public network; choice of a network topology that provides alternative routes between the source node and the sink node; acquisition and use of high-quality network control software. Some additional backup and recovery controls are:

1 Where possible, place redundant components (e.g., modems) and spare parts throughout the network.

2 Use equipment with in-built fault diagnosis capabilities.

3 Acquire high-quality test equipment (e.g., data scopes with extensive diagnostics).

4 Ensure adequate maintenance of hardware and software, especially at remote sites.

5 Ensure adequate logging facilities exist for recovery purposes, especially where store-and-forward operations must be carried out in the network.

Since recovery can be a highly complex process that must be executed under severe time pressures, it is essential that well-trained personnel with high technical competence operate the network. They must be provided with well-documented backup and recovery procedures either for a warm start (partial failure) or for a cold start (total failure). Given that multiple, physically dispersed components may have to be recovered in a coordinated way, a control site must exist for reporting all problems in the network and for managing personnel involved in the recovery process. Network backup and recovery procedures must be practiced regularly.

SUMMARY

Communication controls seek to preserve the integrity of data passing between one subsystem and another subsystem. Integrity may be violated for two reasons. First, a component failure may occur in the subsystem; for example, noise may occur in a communication line or hardware or software may fail. Second, a hostile party may subvert data passing through the subsystem; for example, the privacy of data may be violated through passive wiretapping or unauthorized changes to data may occur through active wiretapping.

Expected losses from component failure can be reduced in several ways. Error detection and error correction mechanisms can be established to reduce the effects of noise on a communication line. Network reliability can be increased through choosing a high-quality modem, choosing a high-quality communication line, careful choice of an appropriate multiplexing or concentration technique, choosing a network topology that provides some redundancy, and choosing network control software that allows the status of the subsystem to be monitored closely so remedial actions can be taken when problems arise.

REVIEW QUESTIONS

12-1 What is meant by noise on a communication line? What factors affect the amount of noise that exists on a line? What are the effects of noise?

12-2 Briefly distinguish between a passive threat and an active threat to the communication subsystem. Identify each of the following as active threats or passive threats:
a Traffic analysis
b Denial of message service
c Release of message contents
d Changed message order
e Message insertion

12-3 Explain the difference between a loop check and redundancy as a means of detecting errors on a communication line. What are the relative advantages and disadvantages of each approach?

12-4 Briefly explain the difference between a parity check and an M-out-of-N code. Which method detects more errors on a communication line?

12-5 Give an example of where error correcting codes might be chosen in preference to retransmission as a means of error correction.

12-6 Noise on a communication line may corrupt the special control characters needed for transmission and retransmission of data. Briefly describe a method that can be used to detect errors in control characters.

12-7 Why is the choice of a modem an important consideration in the design of a reliable network? Outline some desirable control features of a modem used on a private line.

12-8 Briefly explain the difference between amplitude, frequency, and phase modulation. Compare the three methods of modulation in terms of cost and the number of line errors that arise.

12-9 Briefly describe the two types of distortion that can arise on a communication line. Give two ways in which distortion can be controlled.

12-10 From a control perspective, why is it useful if a modem can transmit data at different speeds?

12-11 Briefly explain what is meant by line conditioning. Why are public lines not conditioned?

12-12 Why might a network designer choose to use digital transmission instead of analog transmission?

12-13 From a control viewpoint, what are the advantages and disadvantages of (*a*) optical fibers and (*b*) satellite transmission?

12-14 Briefly explain the difference between multiplexing and concentration techniques. List two multiplexing techniques and three concentration techniques.

12-15 Briefly explain how multiplexing and concentration techniques impact system reliability.

12-16 What is meant by the topology of a network. List five factors that you would consider as a designer in choosing a network topology.

12-17 From a control perspective, list the advantages and disadvantages of the following topologies: (*a*) ring, (*b*) completely connected, and (*c*) star.

12-18 If a network uses message switching, what controls must exist to ensure that a message is not lost?

12-19 Why is high-quality network control software important to maintaining the integrity of a communication network?

12-20 Why is encryption an important means of protecting the integrity of data passing over public communication lines? Is encryption also useful as a means of protecting data passing over private communication lines?

12-21 Distinguish between link encryption and end-to-end encryption. What are the relative strengths and limitations of link encryption versus end-to-end encryption?

12-22 Distinguish between block ciphers and stream ciphers. What are the relative strengths and limitations of block ciphers versus stream ciphers?

12-23 Explain the nature of a message authentication code (MAC). Why are message authentication codes often used in electronic funds transfer systems?

12-24 Expected losses from which types of threats can be reduced by using message sequence numbers? Why must encryption controls be used in conjunction with message sequence numbers?

12-25 Briefly explain the nature of a request-response mechanism. Why is it unlikely that request-response mechanisms would be used extensively in commercial data communication systems?

12-26 What is the purpose of the accounting audit trail in the communication subsystem? List four items that might be contained in the accounting audit trail for the communication subsystem.

12-27 How does the operations audit trail in the communication subsystem assist network supervisors in their decisions on how to reconfigure the network to improve efficiency? List three data items that network supervisors might retrieve from the operations audit trail.

12-28 Why is it difficult to provide backup for all components that might be used in a communication network?

12-29 Why is it especially important that operations personnel be well-trained with respect to backup and recovery procedures for a communication network?

MULTIPLE CHOICE QUESTIONS

12-1 Which of the following conditions leads to an increase in white noise:
  a Faulty switching gear
  b Atmospheric conditions
  c Poor contacts
  d Temperature increases

12-2 Which of the following types of subversive attacks on a communication network is a passive attack:
  a Message modification
  b Denial of message service
  c Traffic analysis

   d Changed message order
12-3 Which of the following types of redundancy controls offers the highest protection against line errors:
   a Polynomial codes
   b Longitudinal parity
   c M-out-of-N codes
   d Latitudinal parity
12-4 The purpose of an odd-even record count is to:
   a Detect errors in ACK-NAK logic
   b Identify corrupted control characters used during transmission
   c Designate whether odd or even parity has been used
   d Minimize the amount of retransmission needed
12-5 Which of the following usually is *not* a purpose of a modem:
   a Reduce line errors caused by noise
   b Produce encrypted messages
   c Convert digital signals to analog signals
   d Increase the speed of data transmission
12-6 The type of modulation method that performs best in terms of the number of line errors that arises is:
   a Phase modulation
   b Analog modulation
   c Frequency modulation
   d Amplitude modulation
12-7 Which of the following is *not* a desirable control feature in a modem:
   a Dynamic equalization
   b Automatic dial-up capabilities
   c Multiple transmission speeds
   d Attenuation amplification
12-8 A communication line that prevents wiretapping is:
   a A digital line
   b A conditioned line
   c An optical fiber line
   d A satellite line
12-9 Packet switching is an example of a:
   a Multiplexing technique
   b Line conditioning technique
   c Concentration technique
   d Modulation technique
12-10 Which of the following is *not* a control benefit that arises as a result of using concentration techniques in a communication network:
   a There is a reduction in the amount of data available to a wiretapper
   b Messages can be routed over a different path if a link in the network fails
   c More channel capacity is available for backup purposes
   d It is more difficult to disentangle messages passing over a communication channel
12-11 In network topology, maximum reliability is achieved using a:
   a Star network
   b Completely connected network
   c Ring network
   d Multidrop line network

12-12 Which of the following is *not* a desirable control when message switching is used in a communication network:

a Store-and-forward capability

b Fast transmission of a message once it arrives at a node

c Facility to change queue sizes at a node

d Automatic message purge facility when maximum queue size at the node is exceeded.

12-13 Which of the following is an advantage of using link encryption:

a It protects messages against traffic analysis

b Individual nodes in the network do not have to be protected

c The exposure that results from compromise of an encryption key is restricted to a single user to whom the key applies

d The costs of using link encryption can be easily assigned to the users of the link

12-14 End-to-end encryption provides only limited protection against a subversive attack that uses:

a Message insertion

b Traffic analysis

c Spurious associations

d Change of message order

12-15 A stream cipher:

a Transforms fixed-length blocks of cleartext

b Uses a constant fixed-length key

c Transforms cleartext on a bit-by-bit basis

d Produces ciphertext blocks that are independent of one another

12-16 When encryption is used in the communication subsystem, the primary purpose of an error propagation code is to protect against:

a Release of message contents

b Spurious associations

c Denial of message services

d Change of message order

12-17 A message authentication code is used to protect against:

a Changes to the content of a message

b Traffic analysis

c Release of message contents

d Exposures that arise when PINs are transmitted in the clear

12-18 Which of the following controls protects against message sequence numbers being altered:

a Error propagation codes

b Stream ciphers

c Message authentication codes

d All the above

12-19 A request-response mechanism is most likely to be used in a:

a System where the receiver and sender are in constant communication with each other

b Military data communication system where data transmission is spasmodic

c Commercial data communication system that transmits sensitive data

d Data communication system that does not use encryption to protect the data being transmitted

12-20 Which of the following data items is most likely to appear in the operations audit trail and not the accounting audit trail for the communication subsystem:
a Time and date at which message dispatched
b Unique identifier of the source node
c Queue length at each network node traversed by the message
d Message sequence number

EXERCISES AND CASES

12-1 During 1984–85, the credit union industry in Australia considered various ways of improving the electronic funds transfer services that it offered to its members. Most credit unions already provided automatic teller machines for their members to use. However, the ATMs were connected only to the local mainframe machine at the credit union's head office. Thus, members could only transact business at an ATM owned by their credit union. If a member traveled elsewhere within Australia, therefore, credit union services were limited.

In an attempt to remedy this situation, many credit unions decided to connect their ATMs to a public electronic funds transfer network. In addition, they agreed to share ATM facilities throughout Australia. In principle, therefore, a member could go to any ATM in Australia owned by a credit union, use their membership card to gain access to the ATM, and carry out deposit or withdrawal transactions. Since the ATM was controlled by the public electronic funds transfer system, a switch in the system would identify the credit union to which the member belonged and route the transaction to the member's own credit union computer for approval and processing. Although the topology of the public electronic funds transfer network changed from time to time in light of cost-benefit considerations, one configuration used is shown in Figure 12-10.

To illustrate processing, assume that you belonged to the XYZ credit union in Brisbane. If you wanted money while you were visiting Sydney, you would go to any ATM connected to the credit union network. Using your membership card, you would activate the ATM, enter your PIN, and then key in a withdrawal

FIGURE 12-10
EFTS configuration.

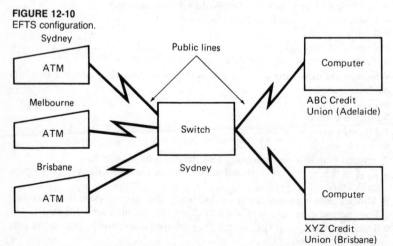

transaction. The ATM would then send the transaction to a switch in the public electronic funds transfer network which, in turn, would route the transaction to the XYZ credit union computer in Brisbane for approval and processing. The XYZ credit union computer would identify and authenticate you, examine whether you had sufficient funds in your account to cover the withdrawal amount, and send a message back to the switch either approving or denying withdrawal of the funds. The switch would then send a message to the ATM that you had used to initiate the transaction.

Required: Identify *four* exposures that arise as a result of the shared ATM configuration. Identify some controls that you believe should be present to reduce expected losses from these exposures to an acceptable level. Note, do *not* list exposures that existed before the use of the shared ATM configuration.

12-2 You are the external auditor for Centnet Pty. Ltd., a public electronic funds transfer network that operates switches in the capital cities of all states in Australia. Since Centnet has a large number of customers that transmit substantial volumes of data, it has been cost-effective to link the switches by private data communication lines. In addition, Centnet has several customers that use point-of-sale facilities, and the private lines are needed to reduce the occurrence of line errors and speed up data communications traffic.

One day you are called to a meeting with the managing director of Centnet. He informs you that he is considering purchasing some data communications capacity on Aussat, Australia's communications satellite. In particular, he is seeking to establish a link initially between Sydney and Perth to act as backup for the terrestrial link. If the terrestrial link fails, data communications traffic will be switched immediately to the satellite so that services to customers can be maintained. Transponder capacity will be purchased off Telecom, Australia's telecommunications authority.

Although his initial investigations indicate the satellite backup link will be cost-effective, the managing director is concerned there may be some significant control issues that he has not considered. Since he knows you have recently spent substantial time studying the implications of satellite communications for auditing, he asks you to advise him on any control matters he should take into account. In addition, he is concerned about any implications of the proposed move for the audit, especially any increased costs that will occur.

Required: Write a brief report advising the managing director of the effects of his proposal to use satellite communications as backup for the Perth-Sydney link on (*a*) controls and (*b*) the audit.

12-3 Centnet Pty. Ltd. is a public electronic funds transfer network that operates switches in the capital cities of all states in Australia (see 12-2 above). Since much of the data transmitted throughout the network is sensitive, it is necessary to encrypt the data to preserve its privacy and to prevent and detect unauthorized alterations.

To implement encryption facilities throughout the network, Centnet uses secure encryption devices (black boxes). These black boxes are placed at each end of a communication line. They store the encryption key, and they perform encryption/decryption functions. Before a new customer can use the network, Centnet must install a black box at the customer's site. Thus, when the customer sends data to a Centnet switch, it is encrypted by the black box before transmission. Similarly, when a customer receives data from a Centnet switch, it is decrypted before it is processed on the customer's computer.

Each customer in the network chooses his or her own encryption key. During the initial installation of a customer on the network, the customer is asked to generate randomly a 16-digit key. The customer is advised strongly to generate the key as two separate 8-digit parts. Each part should be known only by one customer employee; that is, no customer employee should be privy to the full key. Once the key has been generated, each part should be securely stored by the customer.

To install the key in the black boxes, the two customer employees who know the separate parts of the key must attend a Centnet office. The key is installed using a secure terminal to which a black box is first attached. Behind closed doors, one customer employee enters the first part of the key into the secure terminal. After the entry is completed, the second customer employee enters the second part of the key in the same manner. Thus, Centnet employees do not know the keys entered by customers, nor does any customer employee know the full key.

After key entry has been completed, the contents of the black box are copied securely into two other black boxes. Thus, three black boxes ultimately hold the encryption key. One is then installed at the Centnet switch, the second is installed at the customer site, and the third is kept for backup purposes.

Required: You have just been hired as the external auditor of Centnet. As a basis for undertaking your first audit, write a brief report outlining (*a*) the exposures you will consider in your evaluation of the key management system and (*b*) the tests you will undertake to evaluate the reliability of controls within the key management system.

12-4 You are the partner-in-charge of EDP auditing for a large public accounting firm. One of your clients is a major insurance company that is a mature user of data processing. The company is based in Minneapolis, but it has offices scattered throughout the United States. You receive an invitation from the chairman of the company's audit committee to participate in a meeting on the company's proposed move to a distributed system. The company is contemplating distributing both its database and its processing.

The primary reason for the meeting is a debate that has arisen between the vice president of internal audit and the vice president of data processing about whether or not the move to distributed processing is beneficial from a control perspective. The vice president of data processing argues that the major security problem facing the company is the risk of wiretapping by unknown parties. Substantial information is sent via satellite from terminals located in the company's offices. He argues that a distributed system will minimize the amount of information that has to be communicated, thereby reducing the expected losses from data integrity violations. The vice president of internal audit argues, on the other hand, that the primary security problems arise from within the company in the form of unauthorized actions by employees. He argues a single centralized site is much easier to control.

Required: The chairman of the audit committee asks you to prepare for him a report outlining your own feelings on this matter. He also asks you to identify the types of information that the committee would have to obtain to try and resolve the debate.

12-5 To provide more extensive services to their customers, financial institutions in some countries are becoming increasingly involved in using interchange network facilities. In an interchange network environment, one network agrees to pass on and to receive data from another network. For example, a group of financial institutions connected to a common communications network may agree to have their network connected to a second communications network that services another group of financial institutions. Communications between the networks will occur across a gateway switch. In this way, the facilities offered by both groups of financial institutions can be used by the customers of any institution that is a member of either group. For example, a customer of a financial institution in one group can use the ATM facilities of a financial institution in the other group (see 12-1 above). The network to which the transaction receiving institution belongs will then route the transaction to the gateway switch, which, in turn, will route the transaction to the customer's own financial institution. A transaction authorization or denial message will then be routed back via both networks to the transaction receiving institution.

A significant problem with interchange network environments is the reliance that each individual network in the interchange must place upon the reliability of controls in each other network in the interchange. If controls are weak in one network, the integrity of data in all other networks participating in the interchange is at risk. For example, if encryption controls in one member network are weak, the PINs of the customers of financial institutions belonging to other member networks may be compromised. Aside from the monetary losses that may occur, the damage done to the goodwill of each financial institution that participates in the interchange may be irreparable.

Required: Assume you are the external auditor for a financial institution belonging to a network that is about to be connected to another network in an interchange environment. If the integrity of data in your client's data processing is partially dependent on the reliability of controls in other institutions and networks that are not your client's, how will you formulate an audit opinion? *Note:* It is unrealistic to expect that other institutions and networks will allow you to visit them to collect evidence on the reliability of their controls.

ANSWERS TO MULTIPLE CHOICE QUESTIONS

12-1 d	12-6 a	12-11 b	12-16 d
12-2 c	12-7 d	12-12 d	12-17 a
12-3 a	12-8 c	12-13 a	12-18 d
12-4 b	12-9 c	12-14 b	12-19 b
12-5 b	12-10 a	12-15 c	12-20 c

REFERENCES

American Institute of Certified Public Accountants. *Audit Considerations in Electronic Funds Transfer Systems* (New York: American Institute of Certified Public Accountants, 1979).

American National Standards Committee. *Financial Institution Message Authentication X9.9* (Washington, DC: American Bankers Association, 1982).

Branscomb, L. M. "Computing and Communications—A Perspective of the Evolving Environment," *IBM Systems Journal*, vol. 18, no. 2, 1979, pp. 189–201.

Bryant, P., F. W. Giesen, and R. M. Hayes. "Experiments in Line Quality Monitoring," *IBM Systems Journal*, vol. 15, no. 2, 1976, pp. 124–142.

Carroll, John M. *Computer Security* (Boston: Butterworth, 1977).

Champine, George A. *Distributed Computer Systems* (Amsterdam, The Netherlands: North-Holland, 1980).

Cypser, R. J. *Communications Architecture for Distributed Systems* (Reading, MA: Addison-Wesley, 1978).

Davies, D. W., and W. L. Price. *Security for Computer Networks* (New York: Wiley, 1984).

Davies, D. W., D. L. A. Barber, W. L. Price, and C. M. Solomonides. *Computer Networks and Their Protocols* (New York: Wiley, 1979).

DeMillo, Richard, and Michael Merritt. "Protocols for Data Security," *Computer* (February 1983), pp. 39–50.

Denning, Dorothy E. *Cryptography and Data Security* (Reading, MA: Addison-Wesley, 1982).

Digital Equipment Corporation. *Introduction to Local Area Networks* (Maynard, MA: Digital Equipment Corporation, 1982).

Dolan, William J., Don L. Sneary, and Ray M. Whitworth, "Planning for the Impact of EFT Systems on Internal Controls and Audits," *Arthur Andersen Chronicle* (April 1976), pp. 48–59.

Doll, Dixon R. *Data Communications: Facilities, Networks, and System Design* (New York: Wiley, 1978).

Emory, William A., Jr. "Auditing Electronic Funds Transfer," *EDP Auditing* (Pennsauken, NJ: Auerbach, 1983), Portfolio 71-40-09, pp. 1–14.

Ford, J. B. "Enhanced Problem Determination Capability for Teleprocessing," *IBM Systems Journal*, vol. 17, no. 3, 1978, pp. 276–289.

Frazer, W. D. "Potential Technology Implications for Computers and Telecommunications in the 1980s," *IBM Systems Journal*, vol. 18, no. 2, 1979, pp. 333–347.

Greguras, Fred M. "Corporate EFT: Vulnerabilities and Other Audit Considerations," *Retail Control* (November 1981), pp. 47–62.

Hansen, James V. "Audit Considerations in Distributed Processing Systems," *Communications of the ACM* (August 1983), pp. 562–569.

Hecht, H. "Fault-Tolerant Software for Real-Time Applications," *Computing Surveys* (December 1976), pp. 391–407.

Holley, Charles L., and Sheila S. Fitzgerald. "Auditing Electronic Funds Transfer Systems," *The Internal Auditor* (June 1982), pp. 16–20.

Hubbert, James F. "An Audit of a Realtime System—A Case Study," *EDPACS* (December 1979), pp. 1–8.

Lee, Gerald W. "Auditor Concerns with EFTS," *CA Magazine* (February 1982), pp. 36–41.

Leiss, Ernst L. *Principles of Data Security* (New York: Plenum Press, 1982).

Lindup, Ken. "Auditor's Key Role in Strengthening Network Defenses," *Accountancy* (October 1984), pp. 76–77.

Lorin, H. "Distributed Processing: An Assessment," *IBM Systems Journal*, vol. 18, no. 4, 1979, pp. 582–603.

Louderback, Peter D. "Electronic Funds Transfer Systems," *World* (Spring 1975), pp. 9–14.

Lyons, Norman R. "Segregation of Functions in EFTS," *Journal of Accountancy* (October 1978), pp. 89–92.

McGlynn, Daniel R. *Distributed Processing and Data Communications* (New York: Wiley, 1978).

Martin, James. *Design of Real-Time Computer Systems* (Englewood Cliffs, NJ: Prentice-Hall, 1967).

Martin, James. *Teleprocessing Network Organization* (Englewood Cliffs, NJ: Prentice-Hall, 1970).

Martin, James. *Systems Analysis for Data Transmission* (Englewood Cliffs, NJ: Prentice-Hall, 1972).

Martin, James. *Security, Accuracy, and Privacy in Computer Systems* (Englewood Cliffs, NJ: Prentice-Hall, 1973).

Meyer, Carl H., and Stephen M. Matyas. *Cryptography: A New Dimension in Computer Data Security* (New York: Wiley, 1982).

Merkle, Ralph C. "Secure Communications Over Insecure Channels," *Communications of the ACM* (April 1978), pp. 294–299.

Parker, Donn B. "Vulnerabilities of EFT Systems to Intentionally Caused Losses," in Kent W. Colton and Kenneth L. Kraemer, eds., *Computers and Banking: Electronic Funds Transfer Systems and Public Policy* (New York: Plenum Press, 1980), pp. 91–102.

Peterson W., and D. Brown. "Cyclic Codes for Error Detection," *Proceedings of the IRE* (January 1961), pp. 228–235.

Peterson, W., and E. Weldon. *Error Correcting Codes*, 2d ed. (Cambridge, MA: The MIT Press, 1972).

Popek, Gerald J., and Charles S. Kline. "Encryption and Secure Computer Networks," *Computing Surveys* (December 1979), pp. 331–356.

Richardson, Dana R. "Auditing EFTS," *Journal of Accountancy* (October 1978), pp. 81–87.

Rivest, Ronald L., and Adi Shamir. "How to Expose an Eavesdropper," *Communications of the ACM* (April 1984), pp. 393–395.

Rushby, John, and Brian Randell. "A Distributed Secure System," *Computer* (July 1983), pp. 55–67.

Schaller, Carol A. "The Revolution of EFTS," *Journal of Accountancy* (October 1978), pp. 74–80.

Stallings, William. "Local Networks," *Computing Surveys* (March 1984), pp. 3–41.

Toppen, R. "Infinite Confidence: 'The Audit of Data Communication Networks'," *Computers and Security*, vol. 3, 1984, pp. 303–313.

Voydock, V. L., and S. T. Kent. "Security Mechanisms in High-Level Network Protocols," *Computing Surveys* (June 1983), pp. 135–171.

Waldron, Dorothy, and Leslie D. Ball. "The Bottomless Line on Checkless Banking," *Technology Review* (February 1980), pp. 43–52.

PROCESSING CONTROLS

MULTIPLE CHOICE QUESTIONS
EXERCISES AND CASES
ANSWERS TO MULTIPLE CHOICE QUESTIONS
REFERENCES

The processing subsystem is responsible for computing, sorting, classifying, and summarizing data. Its major components are the central processor in which programs are executed, the real or virtual memory in which program instructions and data are stored, the operating system that manages system resources, and the application programs that execute instructions for specific user requirements. This chapter examines controls that enhance the reliability of each of these four components. In addition, it describes audit trail and existence controls for the processing subsystem.

PROCESSOR CONTROLS

Historically, the central processing unit has been the most important resource to allocate in a computer system. It executes program instructions that are fetched from primary memory. These instructions usually are executed sequentially by increasing order of memory address, but instructions can be skipped or repeated using special branching instructions. In this way a program can call subroutines, undertake logical tests, and perform loops, or the operating system can transfer use of the processor to another program. Breaks in the strict sequence of executing instructions by increasing memory address are called interrupts. When an interrupt occurs, the state of the existing process being executed must be saved while control is transferred to another process. When control reverts to the initial process, its state must be restored in the processor.

Managing a processor so it performs effectively, efficiently, and reliably is a complex affair. Nevertheless, usually auditors have little concern about processor management unless some problem is brought to their attention via, say, a review of maintenance logs. Techniques for processor scheduling and use have evolved considerably so performance is rarely a problem. In addition, errors are usually detected immediately and, since most errors are transient, they are corrected before processing proceeds. For example, a *validity check* may be executed to see that the instruction to be performed belongs to the set of valid instructions. If the instruction is erroneous, the processor may reload the instruction and attempt to execute it once again.

Processors often restrict the set of instructions they will execute for a program depending upon the *state* that applies to the program. For example, an instruction that causes the system to load a register with a new value is a critical instruction from a security perspective. It could be used by an unauthorized process to change the contents of a boundary register so the process can gain access to memory locations belonging to other processes. Clearly, use of this instruction needs to be restricted to trusted processes.

Traditionally, processors have executed instructions in one of two states: (a) a supervisor state for privileged users (such as the operating system) that allows any instruction to be executed; and (b) a problem state that typically applies to user programs in which only a restricted set of instructions can be used. The processor determines the state of the program it is executing by referencing some type of secure indicator such as a privilege state bit. This bit is set by a trusted process when transitions between states occur. For example, if a user program issues a supervisor call, the trusted process hands control of the processor over to the operating system and sets the privilege state bit to "on." When the operating system returns control to the user program, the trusted process reinstates the user program in the processor and sets the privilege state bit to "off."

Some computer systems now use more than two execution states to assess the legitimacy of an instruction. For example, a *multiple state machine* may have a kernel state, a supervisor state, and a problem state. The kernel state is the most trusted state, and it is reserved for a small nucleus or core of the operating system that performs the most sensitive functions. The concept of a kernel is discussed later in this chapter.

REAL MEMORY CONTROLS

The real memory of a computer system comprises the fixed amount of primary storage in which programs or data must reside for them to be executed or referenced by the central processor. Controls over real memory seek to detect and correct errors that occur in memory cells and to protect areas of memory assigned to a program from illegal access by another program.

Error Detection and Correction

Errors occur in a memory cell if electronic circuitry malfunctions or some type of random disturbance affects the storage components. For example, extremes of temperature may cause a memory component to function unreliably such that the bit pattern stored in the component is corrupted. Often the error is transient so its effects are temporary. If failure is permanent, the component will have to be replaced.

To detect errors in a memory cell, parity bits are often used. Each time the contents of the cell are referenced, the parity of the contents is computed and compared with the stored parity bit. If the computed and the stored parity bit are different, an error is signaled and some type of error correction procedures may be attempted. Many memory systems now also use Hamming codes, which enable both error detection and error correction to occur (see, for example, Pohm and Smay [1981]).

Access Controls

Early computer systems required real memory to be allocated contiguously to a single user. For the period of processing, only the user's application program and the operating system resided in memory. To prevent the user's program from corrupting the operating system, a single boundary register was implemented in hardware in the central processing unit (Figure 13-1). Each time the user's program referenced a memory location, the processor checked to ensure the memory cell was not within the boundary of the operating system. When a user program needed to access operating system facilities—for example, input/output facilities—a special supervisor call instruction was used.

Single user systems use machine resources inefficiently. For example, if the user program is waiting for a disk pack to be loaded, the processor is idle. To overcome these inefficiencies, most computer systems now allow multiple jobs to reside in real memory at any one time so one job can take advantage of the time when another job is idle. In multiuser systems, however, not only must the operating system be protected from a user program, each user program must be protected from other user programs.

In a multiuser system, real memory can be allocated to a job on a contiguous or a noncontiguous basis. If real memory is allocated contiguously, a set of boundary registers can be used to protect the operating system and the various jobs. For example, in Figure 13-2 one boundary register contains the lower memory boundary of the current active job and another boundary register contains the upper memory boundary. Alternatively, one boundary register can contain the lower memory boundary and the other boundary register can store an offset to indicate the size of the memory partition occupied by the current

FIGURE 13-1
Real memory protection in a single-user, contiguous storage allocation system.

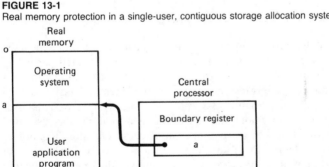

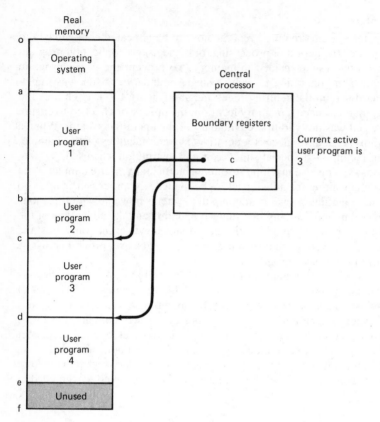

FIGURE 13-2
Real memory protection in a multiuser, contiguous storage allocation system.

active job. Again, these hardware protection mechanisms check that a memory reference by the current active program is confined to its allocated partition.

If noncontiguous storage allocation systems are used, lock and key mechanisms can be employed to protect the areas of real memory assigned to a program. For example, in Figure 13-3 the operating system assigns user program 2 a key called *A* to unlock the various areas of real memory assigned to the program. Without the key a program cannot access a memory location in the area. Sometimes a hierarchy of keys may be used whereby some keys can unlock several different areas of memory. For example, the operating system may be assigned a key called *Z* that will unlock any area of memory.

Control can be extended to each memory location if a location is "tagged" with extra descriptive information. For example, the tag can be used to indicate that the location contains data and not an instruction or that data is an integer and not a real number. In this way the processor avoids errors in that it does not treat data as an instruction or vice versa or it does not attempt to undertake

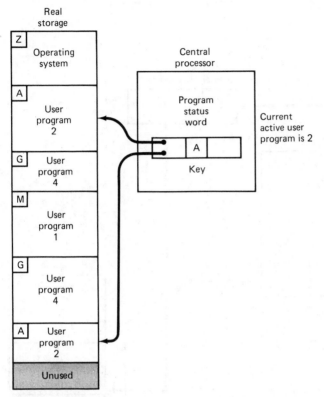

FIGURE 13-3
Real memory protection using locks and keys in a multiuser, noncontiguous storage allocation system.

arithmetic operations in mixed mode. Of course, providing protection at the level of a storage location is costly since considerable extra storage is required to record the protection attributes.

VIRTUAL MEMORY CONTROLS

Virtual memory exists when the addressable storage space is larger than the available real memory space. To achieve this situation, some type of mechanism must exist that maps virtual memory addresses into real memory addresses. An executing program references virtual memory addresses; the mechanism then translates these addresses into real memory addresses.

Conceptually, a virtual memory address can be represented as a block number, b, and a displacement, d. When a program references a virtual memory location (b,d), the addressing mechanism first looks up an address translation table to obtain the real memory address of the start of the block in

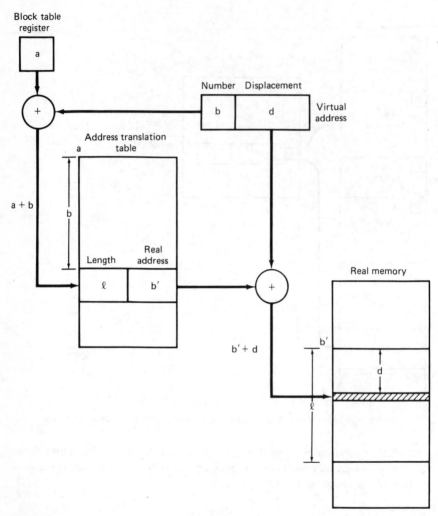

FIGURE 13-4
Virtual memory address translation.

which the virtual memory location resides. It then adds the displacement to this starting address to obtain the real memory address of the virtual memory location that has been referenced (Figure 13-4). This basic mechanism is used irrespective of whether the blocks are fixed length (pages) or variable length (segments) or whether variable length blocks are broken up into several fixed length blocks (combined segmentation/paging systems).

Two types of controls can be exercised over a block of virtual memory. First, when the executing process references a virtual memory location (b,d'), the addressing mechanism checks that the displacement d' is within the boundaries of the block—that is, $d' \leq d$. Thus, the process cannot reference a memory location outside the block. Second, an access control mechanism checks that the action the process wants to undertake on the block is within its allowed set of privileges. For example, if the process is only allowed to read the block and it issues a write instruction, the access control mechanism must prevent the instruction from being executed.

Either a ticket-oriented approach or a list-oriented approach can be used to control the actions a process wants to undertake on a virtual memory block (see Chapter 9). Figure 13-5 shows a ticket-oriented access control system. The access control mechanism starts out with a capability that allows it to access a secure password table. If Smith provides the correct password, she will be

FIGURE 13-5
Simple capability access control system.

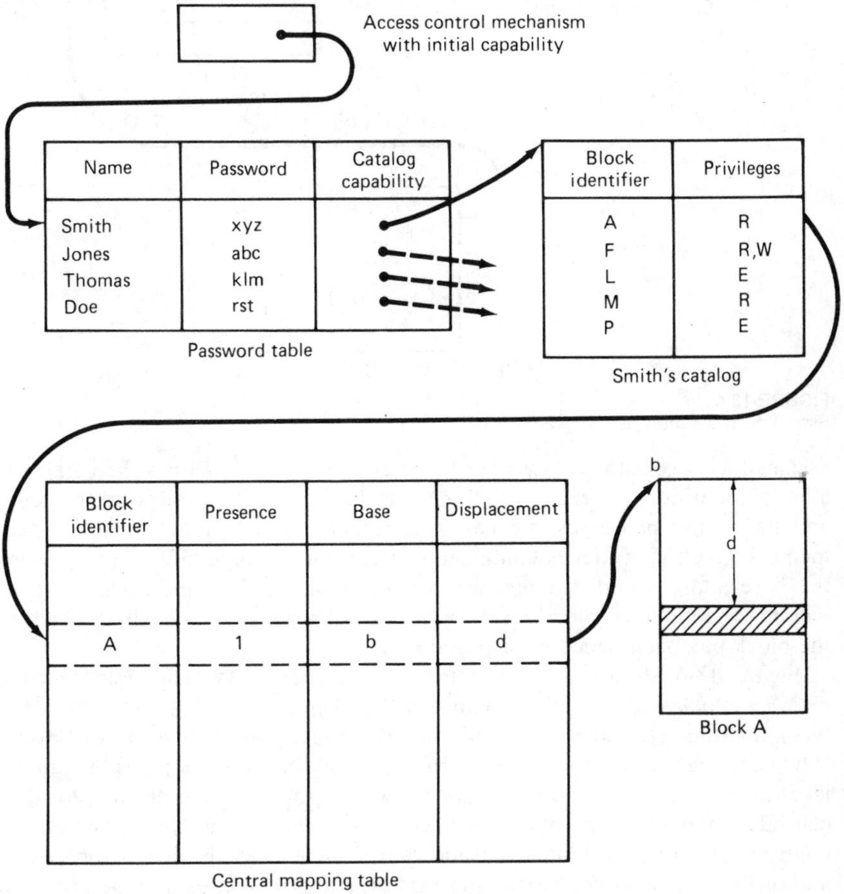

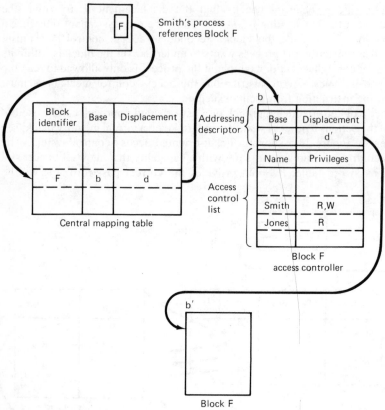

FIGURE 13-6
Simple access control list system.

assigned a process that allows her to access her catalog. Within the catalog is a list of identifiers for each virtual memory block that she is allowed to access and the action privileges she has with respect to each block. Each virtual memory block identifier is contained in a central mapping table that provides the base address and displacement for the block and an indicator to show whether the block is in real memory or in auxiliary memory—that is, whether the block has been paged in or paged out.

Figure 13-6 shows a list-oriented access control system. Each virtual memory block has associated with it a list of processes that can access the block and the action privileges that the process has with respect to the block. When a process wants to access a virtual memory block, it specifies the unique identifier of the block and the actions it wishes to undertake on the block. A central mapping table points to the access controller for the block. The access controller, in turn, contains the address of the block, the list of processes authorized to access the block, and lists of action privileges assigned to each process. Unless an identifier for the process is contained in the access controller and the action requested is in the list of authorized action privileges for the process, the process can proceed no further.

In essence, the addressing mechanism establishes a protective wall around the virtual memory block and the access control mechanism establishes a single door through the wall that is guarded. Unfortunately, not all systems force access to the block through the secure door. They may have loopholes that allow a process to alter a displacement value after it has been checked such that $d' > d$ and access to another block can be obtained; or they may not protect the capability lists that designate the action privileges a process has with respect to a block so that the process can illegally change its capabilities. In this sense, holes exist in the protective wall and the integrity of the block may be corrupted as a result. For example, if the block contains confidential data, its privacy may be violated, or if the block contains a proprietary program, an illegal copy may be made.

OPERATING SYSTEM INTEGRITY

The operating system is the set of programs implemented in software, firmware, or hardware that permits sharing and use of resources within a computer system. The primary resources to be shared are processors, real memory, auxiliary memory, and input/output devices. To enhance usability, the operating system must manage these resources so they are available to each user; however, each user must be able to execute a job without regard to other users.

For various reasons, historically, auditors have paid little attention to the audit of operating systems (see, for example, Williams [1984]): they have considered the operating system to be a low-risk area; few have had the expertise to carry out an operating system audit; they have considered operating system flaws to be endemic and, consequently, have focused on compensating controls.

It is unlikely that the operating system can be ignored for too much longer, however. As more computing facilities are shared among an increasingly larger number of users, the integrity of the operating system becomes a critical issue. If controls in the operating system can be circumvented, basic application controls may be rendered useless and many users may be affected. Moreover, Williams and Lillis [1985] argue that auditors have seriously misjudged the importance of operating systems for the overall reliability of controls. They found, for example, that EDP managers attribute greater security risks to the operating system than auditors.

The following sections provide an introduction to the nature of a secure operating system, the factors that underlie operating system integrity, and the threats and flaws that lead to a violation of operating system integrity. Since the integrity of operating systems is still a major research area, however, auditors should recognize that many issues remain unresolved. The bibliography to this chapter contains several references for the reader who wishes to pursue the topic further.

Nature of a Secure Operating System

For an operating system to be secure, it must achieve *five* goals (see Stepczyk [1974]):

1 The operating system must be protected from user processes. A user process must not be able to halt system running, destroy essential information, take control of the system, or change the system in any way.

2 Users must be protected from each other. One user must not be able to corrupt another user's process or data.

3 Users must be protected from themselves. A user process may consist of a number of distinct modules, each with its own memory area and files. One module should not be able to corrupt another module.

4 The operating system must be protected from itself. Since the operating system also consists of a number of distinct modules, one module should not be able to corrupt another module.

5 The operating system must be protected from its environment. In the event of an environmental failure (power, flood, etc.), the system should be able to bring operations to an orderly halt to enable recovery at a later stage.

Whether or not the operating system achieves these goals depends upon the security policy it enforces and how it has been designed, implemented, verified, and tested. Unfortunately, many operating systems contain some type of flaw that results in only partial accomplishment of these goals.

Functional Requirements

To protect the integrity of the resources that it manages, a secure operating system must enforce a particular *security policy*. A security policy defines the ways in which the resources in a computer system may be accessed and used. Much of the research on operating system integrity has been concerned with specifying precise security policies that ensure resources are not accessed and used in an unintended way. It has been especially difficult to determine whether a particular security policy ultimately does not allow unauthorized access to and use of a resource.

The security policies formulated so far tend to fall into one of three categories (see, also, Landwehr [1981]):

1 *Access policies:* These policies focus on those conditions that are necessary for a process to be given access to a resource, irrespective of the content of the resource. The access control matrix examined in Chapter 9 is an example of a formal model used to represent a particular access policy.

2 *Flow policies:* These policies focus on the flow of information among objects or resources in a computer system. For example, a flow policy would specify the conditions under which a program was allowed to copy the contents of one file into another file. Denning [1976] describes a formal model that can be used to analyze flow policies.

3 *Inference policies:* These policies focus on the conditions under which a process is permitted to make inferences about protected data. Inference policies are important when a user is allowed to undertake statistical inquiries on a database that contains sensitive information. Chapter 15 examines inference policies in more detail.

To illustrate the nature of a security policy, consider the structure often used for military purposes. Information is classified according to four levels: unclassified, confidential, secret, and top secret. Within each classification, security compartments also exist. For example, within a top secret classification, two compartments called "nuclear" and "NATO" may be used. Individuals are not permitted to access information within a security level unless they have obtained clearance for that level. Furthermore, even if they have clearance for a level, they are not allowed access to a compartment within the level unless they can demonstrate a "need-to-know" the information within the compartment. This policy implements a principle called the "principle of least privilege"—that is, individuals are given the minimum resources required for them to be able to perform their job.

Several formal security models attempt to describe this policy so it might be implemented successfully within a computer system. For example, a model developed by Bell and La Padula [1973] focuses on the *static* aspects of the policy. They define four modes of access to a resource: (a) read only—a user can read an object but not modify it; (b) append—a user can write an object but not read it; (c) execute—a user can execute an object but not read or write it; and (d) read/write—a user can either read or write an object. For a system to be in a secure state, two properties must hold:

1 *Simple security property:* A user cannot read an object that has a classification which is at a higher level than the clearance level held by the user. This property prevents a user viewing an object (such as a data file) that they are not entitled to see.

2 **-Property (pronounced "star" property):* A user cannot modify an object unless the classification level of the object is equal to or greater than the clearance level of the user. This property seeks to prevent a problem called the Trojan horse in which a program called by another program attempts to undertake unauthorized activities; for example, it may attempt to make an illegal copy of a file.

Similarly, Denning [1976] has proposed a formal model that attempts to represent the *dynamic* properties of the military security policy described above. Instead of focusing on the access to an object, she requires that all information transfers obey a set of flow rules. These flow rules are derived from and based upon a mathematical structure called a lattice.

Several other security policies have been proposed and formal models developed to represent and study the properties of these policies (see Landwehr [1981]). Moreover, research on formal security models is continuing because computer users, such as the military, have substantial needs for secure computer systems. The auditor should recognize, however, that until the conceptual issues surrounding secure computer systems have been solved, security weaknesses must exist in any implemented computer system.

Design Approaches

Historically, the mechanisms responsible for enforcing a security policy have been dispersed throughout various parts of the operating system. Inevitably this approach has led to inconsistencies and omissions and the consequent integrity weaknesses. In an attempt to remedy these problems, some operating system designers now advocate an approach to operating system design called the *kernel* approach.

The security kernel approach to operating system design is based upon the concept of a reference monitor. A reference monitor is an abstract mechanism that checks each reference by a subject (user, program, process) to an object (file, device, user, program, segment) to ensure that the reference complies with a security policy (Figure 13-7). A security kernel is the hardware/software/firmware mechanism that implements a reference monitor.

The motivation for following the kernel approach to operating system design is that it concentrates all the security-relevant features of the operating system into a single mechanism. This mechanism can then be *isolated* from all other processes in the system so it is tamperproof. In addition, hopefully the kernel will be a small mechanism so it is possible to *verify* mathematically that the kernel indeed implements the security policy. Nonetheless, the kernel must be *complete* in that it mediates *all* accesses by a subject to an object.

From a security perspective, one of the critical aspects of a kernel is the set of *trusted processes* that it provides. Trusted processes are processes not bound by all the security rules implemented in the kernel. They are provided to allow a trusted person, such as a system administrator, to tailor a security policy to the specific needs of a data processing installation. For example, system administrators need access to a trusted process for them to be able to

FIGURE 13-7
Reference monitor abstraction.

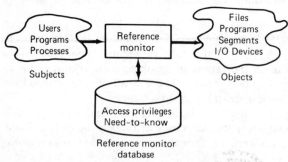

maintain the secure table used by the kernel to determine the access class of each user. Since trusted processes can be used to corrupt the integrity of the system, auditors need to examine carefully the controls exercised over their use.

Few current operating systems have been designed using the kernel approach. Unfortunately, it has been difficult to achieve efficient implementations of kernel-based operating systems. To some extent, efficient implementations require the redesign of current hardware components, and this will take some time to eventuate. Unless an operating system is based on a kernel design, however, it is difficult to verify security mechanisms, to ensure they are complete, and to isolate them from tampering by all other processes.

Implementation Considerations

The prescriptions for implementing a secure operating system generally follow the top-down design, structured programming principles discussed in Chapter 5. Basically the system is specified as a hierarchy of layers corresponding to different levels of abstraction. At the top level is a formal specification of the security policy to be enforced. Various intermediate levels specify progressively more detailed design of the kernel. The lower levels provide formal specifications for the programming language in which the system is to be implemented.

In an attempt to ensure the various levels of specification are accurate and complete, substantial research has been undertaken on the development of automated specification and verification systems (see Cheheyl et al. [1981]). These systems typically comprise the following components: (a) specification language processors—enable the functions provided in a given set of programs to be stated precisely and concisely; (b) verification condition generators—take a program and a set of assertions about a program as input and produce formulas to show the two are consistent; (c) theorem provers—take formulas and prove the truth or falsity of theorems.

Unfortunately, practical use of automated specification and verification systems is still limited. Consequently, Landwehr [1983] argues that operating systems should be implemented using a well-understood, well-supported compiler for a high-level language. The compiler must allow different modules to be compiled separately, and it must generate efficient code if the overhead associated with security functions is to be acceptable.

The extent to which current operating systems have been designed using a layered approach and implemented using a high-level language varies considerably. Auditors must attempt to understand how the operating system they are evaluating has been designed and implemented as a basis for determining the reliance they will place upon the integrity of the system itself and its ability to enforce controls over application systems.

Operating System Integrity Threats

Operating system integrity threats may occur accidentally or be deliberate in nature. Accidental threats include hardware or software failures that cause the system to crash or process erroneously. A user also may undertake some unexpected procedure that the operating system cannot handle or handles incorrectly. These failures breach data integrity by corrupting data or violating the privacy of data. A system crash may result in sections of memory being dumped on various output devices in an uncontrolled manner. As a consequence, user passwords may be exposed.

Deliberate threats to operating system integrity usually aim at unauthorized removal of assets or breaching data integrity by violating data privacy. Deliberate threats occur in various ways. First, privileged personnel abuse their powers. For example, field engineers or system programmers use the special utilities provided them to examine system directories and user files. Second, special devices are used to detect electromechanical radiation or wiretap communication lines. Third, a would-be penetrator actively interacts with the operating system to determine and exploit a flaw in the system.

Some of the major known methods of penetrating operating systems follow:

Penetration technique	Explanation
Browsing	Involves searching residue to gain unauthorized access to information. The residue may be magnetic media such as memory or disk storage, or wastebaskets containing discarded printouts, printer ribbons, etc. In these ways passwords and other sensitive information are obtained.
Masquerading	Involves carrying out unauthorized activities by impersonating a legitimate user of the system or impersonating the system itself. In the latter case the penetrator sends a message to an operator that looks like a system-generated message. The operator undertakes some action that results in a penetration.
Piggybacking	Involves intercepting communications between the operating system and the user and modifying them or substituting new messages. A special terminal is tapped into a communication line.
Between lines entry	A penetrator takes advantage of the time during which a legitimate user still is connected to the system but is inactive. As with piggybacking, the penetrator connects a special terminal to a communication line.
Spoofing	A penetrator fools the user into thinking he/she is interacting with the operating system. For example, a penetrator duplicates the logon procedure, captures a user's password, simulates a system crash, and requests the user to repeat the logon procedure. The second time the user actually logs on to the operating system.
Trojan horse	Can be accomplished by a "system hacker" providing a utility for use by all other users. When the utility is executed by a program in privileged mode, it assigns the hacker's password the highest privilege level available on the system (see, further, Parker [1976]).

Operating System Integrity Flaws

Operating system penetrations result because integrity flaws exist in operating systems. Abbott et al. [1976] describe seven major integrity flaws often found in current operating systems:

Integrity flaw	Explanation
Incomplete parameter validation	The system does not check the validity of all attributes of a user's request. For example, the user requests an address outside the area allocated to the user's program and the system fails to reject the request.
Inconsistent parameter validation	The system applies different validation criteria to the same construct within the system. For example, the user is able to create a password containing blanks but is unable to change or delete the password because the system regards it as illegitimate.
Implicit sharing of data	Part of the operating system's work space is a subset of the space allocated to the user program. The operating system reads in other user's passwords to this space that can be accessed by the user program.
Asynchronous validation	If the operating system permits asynchronous processes, the user takes advantage of timing inadequacies to violate integrity. For example, a user requests an I/O operation and the operating system validates the user parameters. The system finds the channel needed is busy and issues an interrupt. The user then changes the address for the I/O operation to an address outside the valid work space. The system returns control to an illegal address.
Inadequate access control	The operating system performs incomplete checking, or one part of the system assumes another part has performed the checking. For example, a user loads a program with the same name as a system routine and the operating system does not check to see the program is from the system library. Thus, a user routine supplants a system routine.
Violable limits	System documentation states limits, e.g., the maximum size of a buffer. However, the system does not check to see if these limits are exceeded and runs erroneously when they are exceeded.
Exploitable logic error	A system bug is discovered which can be exploited to place the user in privileged mode.

Unfortunately, it is not always easy for auditors to obtain information on integrity flaws in the operating systems they are evaluating. In some cases, published information is available (see, for example, Paans and Bonnes [1983]). In many cases, however, the information is not disseminated. The following statement indicates one group of researcher's attitude toward publishing information on operating system security (Abbott et al. [1976], italics added):

The authors of this document have attempted to write in a way that provides as much information as possible to those responsible for system security while at the same time minimizing its potential usefulness to someone who might misuse the information. It is generally acknowledged that the security provisions of most current operating systems can be broken by an experienced programmer who has spent much time working with the system and has a very detailed understanding of its inner workings. The guidance used in the preparation of this document was that it should not increase the number of people who know all the details needed to effect a security penetration. *Many details about specific security flaws have not been included in this report either because there is no reasonable enhancement to correct the flaws or because exploitation of the flaw could be carried out by someone with relatively little additional detailed information about the system.* (Quoted by permission, the National Bureau of Standards. Note: The quote does not represent necessarily the position of the U.S. government.)

If auditors are to evaluate operating system integrity effectively, therefore, they must develop their own expertise on penetration methods and flaws and formulate their own approach to the audit of operating systems (see, further, Linde [1975], Weber [1975], Gallegos and Kocot [1985], Ferrey [1985], Leonard [1985], and Coyle [1985]).

APPLICATION SOFTWARE CONTROLS

In the processing subsystem, application software computes, sorts, classifies, and summarizes data specific to an application system. It should perform a set of validation checks to identify processing errors when they occur. Furthermore, it should be designed in such a way to avoid processing errors in the first place.

Validation Checks

Processing validation checks primarily ensure computations performed on *numeric* fields are authorized, accurate, and complete. The processing involved with alphabetic or alphanumeric fields typically is minimal: an existing field value is replaced or data is inserted in a field when a new record is created. Because the types of processing performed on data vary considerably, it is difficult to describe generally the validation checks that should be applied. Nevertheless, the following are common:

Level of check	Type of check	Explanation
Field	Overflow	Overflow may occur if a computational field (perhaps in working storage) is not zeroized initially. In COBOL, for example, a special overflow clause is available.
	Range	An allowable value range may apply to the field.

Level of check	Type of check	Explanation
Record	Reasonableness	The contents of one field may determine the allowable value for another. For example, after an employee's allowable deductions have been calculated for payroll, they may be checked to see if they fall within a valid range of values, given the employee's position within the organization.
	Sign	The contents of one field, for example, the record type field, may determine which sign is valid for a numeric field.
File	Crossfooting	Separate control totals can be developed for related fields and crossfooted at the end of a run. For example, for payroll, control totals can be calculated for gross pay, deductions, and net pay. At the end of processing, net pay should equal gross pay less deductions.
	Control totals	Run-to-run control totals can be developed and compared with the results of a run. For example, if the current balance of an accounts receivable file is $100,000 and the incoming transactions consist of $10,000 debit and $8,000 credit, the new balance of the file should be $102,000. The last record on the transaction file used as input to the master file update program may be a control record showing the totals for the debit and credit entries. The master file update program can use these control totals to check the accuracy of its computations.

As always, the costs of performing a validation check should be compared with the benefits derived. For example, if a payroll program computes individual pays correctly, it is difficult to conceive how a crossfooting error can occur. Nevertheless, the computer used may be an old machine that occasionally suffers undetected memory or parity errors, thereby resulting in a corrupted field.

Some Matters of Programming Style

The auditor should be aware of some traps for the unwary or inexperienced programmer that can result in incomplete or inaccurate processing of data. These traps can be avoided through good programming style. The experienced analyst and programmer specifically designs test data to create the underlying conditions for these traps and to check that the program handles these conditions correctly. The following sections describe some elements of good programming style that help avoid these traps and ensure authorized, accurate, and complete processing of data.

Handle Rounding Correctly Rounding problems occur when the level of precision required for an arithmetic calculation is less than the level of precision actually calculated. For example, the interest on a bank account may be calculated to five decimal digits. However, only two are required to record the lowest monetary amount; that is, a cent. If the remaining three decimal digits simply are dropped, an interest calculation made on the grand total of account balances may not agree with the sum of the individual interest calculations. Thus, uncertainty surrounds the accuracy of the processing performed by the interest calculation routine.

An algorithm for handling this problem is well-known. The auditor should check to see the algorithm has been used for two reasons. First, it may not be known by the inexperienced programmer. Second, a minor modification to the algorithm provides an easy means to perpetrate a fraud. Figure 13-8 shows the algorithm for handling the rounding problem. Consider the following three examples of how the algorithm works for an interest rate of 3.25%:

1	Existing accumulator balance	−.00815
	Old account balance	1,351.62
	Interest calculated	43.92765
	New account balance	1,395.54765
	Rounded account balance	1,395.55
	New accumulator balance	−.0105 (−.00235 −.00815)
	Final account balance	1,395.54
	Final accumulator balance	−.0005
2	Existing accumulator balance	.00917
	Old account balance	650.23
	Interest calculated	21.13248
	New account balance	671.36248
	Rounded account balance	671.36
	New accumulator balance	.01165 (.00248 + .00917)
	Final account balance	671.37
	Final accumulator balance	.00165
3	Existing accumulator balance	.00002
	Old account balance	2,911.20
	Interest calculated	94.614
	New account balance	3,005.814
	Rounded account balance	3,005.81
	New accumulator balance	.00402 (.004 + .00002)
	Final account balance	3,005.81
	Final accumulator balance	.00402

Depending on the balance in the accumulator, some accounts are rounded up and others are rounded down. By using this method, the interest calculated on the grand total of the old account balances plus the grand total of the old account balances will equal the sum of the new account balances.

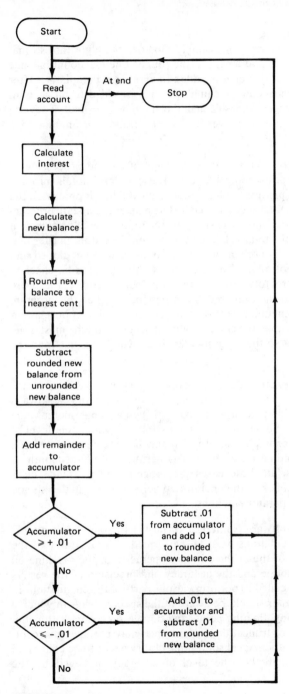

FIGURE 13-8
Algorithm for interest rounding calculations.

To perpetrate a fraud a programmer simply modifies the algorithm so that when the condition occurs to add a cent to the rounded new account balance (i.e., accumulator $\geq$ + .01), this cent is added to another accumulator. After processing is complete this second accumulator then is added to an account specially created by the programmer. Though the amounts are small, if several hundred thousand accounts exist, over a year the fraud can amount to a reasonable sum.

Print Run-to-Run Control Totals At each stage during the processing of data, a program should print control totals. These control totals provide evidence that the program processed all the input data and that it processed the data correctly. For example, an accounts receivable master file update program should show the total value of input transactions, the total value of accounts on the input master file, and the total value of accounts on the output master file. Similarly, even if the data is nonnumeric, hash totals can be developed and summed to produce control totals. These control totals can then be checked against user-prepared control totals to determine whether the correct files were used as input, whether all data entered the program, whether the program dropped a record, etc. Sometimes control totals are supplied as input parameters to a program; for example, the current value of accounts on the master file may be submitted as input so the program can check whether it has read the correct input file.

Minimize Operator Intervention As a general rule, programs that minimize operator intervention are less prone to processing errors. Operators can always make mistakes when providing input for a program such as a parameter value or an alternate start point. Sometimes it is impossible to avoid some level of operator intervention; for example, the program may have to be activated at a different start point depending on whether it is performing end-of-month or end-of-quarter procedures. In these cases the program must provide clear instructions and clear feedback to the operator. Where possible, it also should check the validity of the operator's actions.

Understand Hardware/Software Numerical Hazards In some applications, complex mathematical calculations must be performed. The accuracy of the results may be a function of the arithmetic idiosyncracies of the machine on which the computation is done and the accuracy and precision of the results obtained from subroutines called to perform various parts of the calculation. In these situations a programmer should be aware of the specific ways in which a machine handles fixed point, floating point, and double precision arithmetic. Certain types of round off or truncation, for example, may produce unacceptable results. Similarly, a mathematical subroutine library needs to be calibrated so a user can determine whether the level of accuracy achieved by the algorithms is acceptable.

Use Redundant Calculations If complex mathematical calculations must be performed, programmers should consider whether redundant calculations should be implemented. Often, two different sets of equations can be used to obtain the same results or an additional calculation can be undertaken to check a result. If programmers are uncertain about the arithmetic idiosyncracies of machines or the accuracy and precision of called subroutines, redundant calculations can provide some assurance that the results obtained are acceptable.

Avoid Closed Routines As discussed in Chapter 11, closed routines should not exist in a program. The program should check for all possible values in a field rather than assume the existence of a particular value if all other tests fail. This strategy avoids carrying out incorrect processing on the basis of assumed values that do not, in fact, exist.

AUDIT TRAIL CONTROLS

The audit trail in the processing subsystem maintains the chronology of events from the time data is received from the input subsystem to the time data is dispatched to the database, communication, or output subsystems.

Accounting Audit Trail

The accounting audit trail should provide the auditor with a capability to trace and to replicate the set of processing performed on an input data item. This means the auditor must be able to uniquely identify the process executed on a data item and to understand the process. Process identification is facilitated by printing the process identifier (name and version number) on any output reports or storing the identifier in an audit trail record together with the input and output data items. Process understanding requires that an up-to-date set of documentation be available which can be referenced by the auditor as a basis for any replication work.

The execution of a process may lead to the creation of a triggered transaction. Triggered transactions arise when a process identifies that a set of data items has a particular value and generates a new transaction as a result. For example, as a consequence of a stock withdrawal transaction, the quantity-on-hand of a stock item may fall below the reorder level. When a reorder program recognizes this situation, it generates a purchase requisition containing the economic order quantity for the stock item. Similarly, a process may recognize that the input values in a sales transaction mean a sales commission has to be calculated. The process generates a commission payment as a result.

The audit trail for the triggered transaction must contain the set of data items that caused the transaction to arise, the identifier of the process that produced the triggered transaction, and the data item values for the triggered transaction. Again, this data may be printed on a report or stored in an audit trail record in the database.

To replicate the results of complex processes, a set of intermediate results

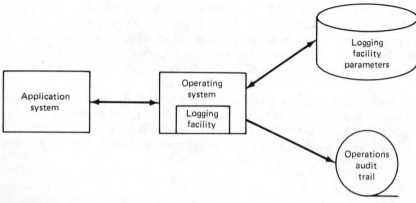

FIGURE 13-9
Parameter-driven operating system logging facility for operations audit trail.

and the values of any standing data items used may have to be printed or stored in the audit trail together with the set of input and output data item values. For example, a program may perform a set of complex calculations to determine the average cost of inventory items. The calculations may be complex because stock movements are frequent and currency conversions are required (overseas suppliers are used). An audit trail of intermediate results and the values of standing data items used (for example, currency conversion factors) may assist the auditor to verify the accuracy of the computations performed.

Operations Audit Trail

Of all subsystems, perhaps the most extensive operations audit trail data is maintained in the processing subsystem. Data for the operations audit trail is usually easy to collect since most operating systems provide a facility to create a comprehensive log of events that occur during system execution. This facility is often parameter-driven. Users specify what data should be logged for each application system and store these requirements as operating system parameters. The operating system then invokes the necessary logging facilities for each application system depending upon the parameter values (Figure 13-9). Unfortunately, the flexibility provided by these facilities can be their downfall. There is a temptation to log too much data and, as a consequence, the system overhead incurred can be high. Even with careful logging, Schaller [1976] reports that increases in system overhead of between 2 and 5% are common.

Content of the Operations Audit Trail   In general, four types of data are collected in the operations audit trail. The first type is resource consumption data. This data identifies which user consumed the resource, what process consumed the resource, and when the resource was consumed. The following types of resource consumption are monitored:

Resource category	Examples
Hardware	CPU time used, peripherals used, main memory used, secondary storage space used
Software	Compilers used, subroutine libraries used, file management facilities used
Data	Files accessed, frequency of access to data items, way in which data used, i.e., deleted, inserted, modified
Personnel	Number of tapes/disks mounted and unmounted, number of operator program starts

Typically, users can specify whether they want this data collected at the level of application system running, program running, subroutine running, or sometimes even program step running. Obviously, the lower the level specified for collection of the data, the more data generated and the more overhead added to system running.

Resource consumption data can be used for many management and audit purposes, for example:

1 *Billing:* The data provides the basis for charging users for the resources they consume. The data also may form the basis for the installation's lease or rental payments on some resources. Auditors can use the data to check whether correct billings, lease, or rental payments are made.

2 *Performance evaluation:* The extent to which resources are used efficiently can be examined. The time required for an application program, subroutine, or system software program to process one transaction can be calculated. This may suggest the logic in the program or subroutine needs to be restructured, or more efficient system software needs to be purchased. Hardware utilization can be examined. A particular input/output channel may be the cause of a bottleneck. Program mixes in a multiprogramming environment may have to be changed to eliminate the bottleneck. Some devices may be underutilized. Chapter 21 discusses these matters in more detail.

3 *Potential integrity breaches:* Certain resource consumption data indicates potential system integrity violations. For example, checks can be made on when a program was run, how many times a program was run, the duration of program running, who initiated the program run. Any variations in the norms for these factors may indicate unauthorized activities are being carried out. Data also can be extracted on who accessed files, who copied files, who renamed files, etc., to determine whether the users and activities are authorized. Files used over a period can be checked against the installation's authorized list of files to see whether any foreign files exist. Any process that was terminated abnormally also can be investigated to determine the reasons why.

The second type of operations audit trail data that can be collected relates to attempted integrity violations. The logging facility may be used to create an audit trail entry for all attempts to use resources that failed. For example, if a process seeks illegal access to a segment, the logging facility may record this event. These entries can then be extracted from the log to determine whether an abnormal number exists.

The third type of operations audit trail data that can be collected is hardware malfunctions. For example, memory parity errors may be recorded by the logging facility. An abnormal number may indicate that a memory component needs to be replaced.

Finally, the operations audit trail can be used to record user-specified events. The logging facility may allow users to write their own programs to collect operations data. It will invoke these programs when the user-specified event occurs. For example, the completion of a program step or the occurrence of a particular transaction type may be recorded. This capability is also useful to auditors. It allows auditors to embed audit evidence collection modules in the logging facility and to collect data on the state of controls in an application system at the same time as application system processing occurs. Careful control must be exercised over this facility, however, as user-specified routines can also be employed to modify or to delete data that is accessed or written by an application system while it is running. These matters are discussed further in Chapter 19.

Interrogating the Operations Audit Trail Interrogating the operations audit trail maintained by an operating system involves four major steps (Figure 13-10):

1 Specifying audit objectives
2 Extracting data from the operations audit trail necessary to meet these objectives
3 Sorting the data into the required order
4 Formatting and presenting the results

In the past, auditors often have experienced some difficulty in interrogating the operations audit trail. The log may contain a multitude of data items and record types, voluminous data spanning several tapes or disks, data that has been encoded and compacted to reduce storage space requirements, data requiring some editing before it is in a form suitable for use, etc.

To help overcome these problems a number of vendors have developed generalized packages that can be used by both management and auditors to interrogate the operations audit trail (see, further, Adams [1977]). These packages produce a set of standard reports using the operations audit trail data. Management or the auditor simply has to specify as parameters to the program what reports they require. The packages then extract the necessary data, sort the data in the required order, and format and present the results. Typical reports that the users of these packages can obtain automatically are:

1 System user billing report
2 Hardware utilization report

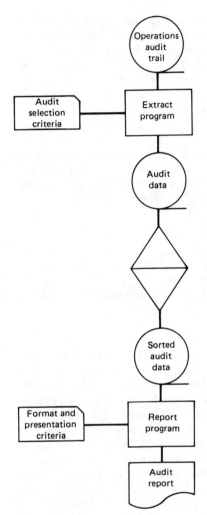

FIGURE 13-10
Interrogating the operations audit trail.

3 Program resource consumption report
4 Hardware malfunction report
5 Program run schedule report
6 Programmer resource consumption report
7 Report on programs abnormally terminated

Even if generalized software is not available for the operations audit trail of a particular machine or operating system, to some extent the auditor can overcome the problems of interrogating the operations audit trail by using generalized audit software (see Chapter 16).

Some Control Issues The existence of software that records data for the operations audit trail sometimes poses control problems for the auditor. The software may permit the user to modify or delete records accessed by an application system during production running, or modify or delete records written to the operations audit trail (see, also, Perry and Adams [1974]). For example, if the software allows the user to declare a run-time exit so a user subroutine can be invoked, this subroutine may be able to carry out unauthorized activities on data, especially if the subroutine can run in the operating system's privileged mode.

There are various ways of detecting and preventing unauthorized use of the logging software. For example, users may be prevented from writing their own subroutines without special authority. Use of user subroutines can be monitored with the logging software to detect any unauthorized activity.

EXISTENCE CONTROLS

The primary existence control exercised in the processing subsystem is a checkpoint/restart facility. It is a short-term backup and recovery control in that it enables a system to be recovered if failure is temporary and localized.

Nature of Checkpoint/Restart Controls

If a program fails for some reason before it reaches normal termination, some of the processing carried out by the program may still be accurate and complete. It is desirable not to have to repeat this valid processing during the recovery process. A checkpoint/restart facility allows an operator to restore a program to some prior valid intermediate point in its processing and to restart the program from that point. Thus, use of a checkpoint/restart facility is especially important for programs that consume substantial resources and take a long time to execute since valid processing does not have to be redone.

Checkpoint/restart recovery cannot be undertaken for all types of program failure. In some cases, completely redoing the processing run may be the only means of recovery. For example, if a program contains a serious logic error, the error has to be corrected and all processing redone. However, the following three examples show where a checkpoint/restart facility is useful as a means of recovering from localized damage or abnormal termination of a program:

1 A hardware error occurs that is not expected to recur if processing is repeated. For example, a processor error may be corrected by replacing circuitry and restarting the program at a previous checkpoint.

2 An operator error may mean partial reprocessing of transactions is necessary. For example, with a multireel file the operator may load the incorrect version of the third reel. Thus, the first two reels have been processed correctly, and the error can be corrected by restarting processing at the beginning of the third reel.

3 A program may be abnormally terminated for some reason. For example, it may have to be rolled out to allow a higher-priority program to operate, or it may be terminated because the operator recognizes an impending hardware failure.

4 Long-term or global failure, such as the physical destruction of the data processing installation, means that other existence controls have to be invoked, for example, the controls described in Chapter 7.

Functions of a Checkpoint/Restart Facility

A checkpoint is taken when the contents of memory are dumped onto a log file. The contents of control registers, buffers, working storage, etc., must be flushed and stored to represent the system state at a point in time. Furthermore, the positions of all active files also must be recorded so these files can be repositioned on their respective devices if program restart is needed. For example, the current block number of an input tape file must be recorded if the tape is to be repositioned correctly when the program is restarted at the checkpoint.

Information written on a log file as part of a checkpoint/restart facility must be secure—that is, it must be impossible for a programmer to access this information and to change it. Otherwise, the memory access controls described earlier in this chapter may be circumvented. For example, a programmer may change an address offset after it has been checked by the access control mechanism to gain unauthorized access to another program's memory block.

For checkpoint/restart facilities to be used as a basic control in systems, however, they must be effective and efficient. The facility must be capable of setting checkpoints at high speed and recovering and restarting systems at high speeds. In this respect, use of reentrant programs facilitates the checkpoint/restart process. If a program is used in several systems and it is a reentrant program, multiple copies of the program do not have to be kept in memory. Instead, only a single copy of the program needs to reside in memory, and a segment is then created for each application to contain the variable data specific to that application. When a checkpoint is taken, only this variable data needs to be written to the log file rather than the entire program.

A checkpoint/restart facility also must be flexible from the viewpoint of both programmers and operators. Programmers must be able to initiate checkpoints in several ways, for example, by transaction count or elapsed time. Operators should be able to easily accomplish a return to a checkpoint and a restart of the system from that checkpoint. If a checkpoint/restart facility is not flexible, there will be a tendency not to use it.

Finally, a checkpoint/restart facility must preserve the integrity of the recovery process. On the one hand, it automates at least part of the recovery process and so it reduces the likelihood of error. On the other hand, it must exercise careful control over recovery procedures if it is to be successful. For example, if different files must be mounted on a tape or disk device, the facility must check that the files mounted are the correct files. In addition, to avoid error, programmers and operators should have minimal responsibilities for checkpoint/restart processes. Programmers should be able to initiate checkpoints through simple commands, for example, a call statement to a system utility. Operators also should have utilities available to them that perform most of the restart activities needed.

Audit of Checkpoint/Restart Facilities

The auditor needs to perform five checks on a data processing installation's checkpoint/restart facilities. First, the checkpoint/restart facilities available should be adequate for the installation's needs. These needs vary depending on such factors as the average length of processing runs and whether the installation primarily supports complex online applications or simple batch applications. Second, the checkpoint/restart facility used by an installation should be secure; that is, the facility itself and the logs which it uses should be protected by an access control mechanism from unauthorized access. It should not be possible to circumvent standard access controls by exploiting security weaknesses in the checkpoint/restart facility. Third, the auditor must evaluate whether checkpoint/restart facilities are implemented in those programs where they are needed—that is, those programs that consume substantial resources or those that would involve complex recovery procedures if they failed. Fourth, documentation on the checkpoint/restart facilities should exist, in terms of both the facility itself and the programs where it has been installed. Finally, checkpoint/restart facilities should be tested periodically to determine whether or not they work.

SUMMARY

Processing controls prevent, detect, and correct errors from the time data is received from the input subsystem to the time data is dispatched to the database, communication, or output subsystems. They seek to enhance the reliability of the central processor on which programs are executed, the real or virtual memory in which instructions and data are stored, the operating system that manages system resources, and the application programs that execute instructions to meet specific user requirements.

Controls over the central processor restrict instruction execution to the set of valid instructions provided by the processor and the set of instructions allowed by the state in which a program is executing—supervisor, kernel, etc. Controls over real and virtual memory are primarily concerned with restricting access to authorized processes and allowing only those actions that have been assigned to the process.

The extent to which an operating system can protect its own integrity and the integrity of the resources it manages is a function of the security policy it enforces, the way it has been designed and implemented, and the way it has been verified and tested. Operating system integrity is still a complex research area. Currently, the best operating system design approaches seem to be those that employ capability-based addressing and kernel-based access control mechanisms.

Application programs protect the integrity of data in the processing subsystem by exercising a set of validation checks on the data they process and the actions they perform. The reliability of the application programs themselves can be enhanced by ensuring they conform to certain principles of programming style that seek to reduce the likelihood of processing error.

Audit trail controls in the processing subsystem should allow the auditor to trace and to replicate the set of processing performed on a data item. In addition, the operating system often provides a facility to maintain a comprehensive operations audit trail of resource consumption in the processing subsystem.

The primary existence control exercised in the processing subsystem is a checkpoint/restart facility. If temporary and localized failure occurs, a checkpoint/restart facility allows a system to be restarted at some intermediate point in its processing.

REVIEW QUESTIONS

13-1 What are the major *functions* of the processing subsystem? What are the major *components* of the processing subsystem?

13-2 What is the function of a validity check in the central processing unit? If a validity check identifies an error, what corrective action is usually taken?

13-3 How does the existence of a multiple state machine enhance control within the central processing unit?

13-4 What factors cause errors in a real memory cell? How are errors often detected?

13-5 Distinguish between the real memory protection mechanisms used in a multiuser, contiguous storage allocation system and a multiuser, noncontiguous storage allocation system.

13-6 How does a "tagged" architecture enhance control over real memory cells?

13-7 Briefly explain the nature of virtual memory. How does the addressing mechanism work in a virtual memory system?

13-8 Briefly distinguish between a ticket-oriented and a list-oriented approach to access control over a virtual memory block.

13-9 Give two reasons why auditors historically have ignored undertaking operating system audits. Are these reasons likely to remain valid in the future?

13-10 List the *five* goals that a secure operating system must achieve.

13-11 What is meant by an operating system security policy? Why must the auditor attempt to understand the security policy that the operating system attempts to enforce?

13-12 In terms of operating system security policies, briefly explain the difference between access policies, flow policies, and inference policies.

13-13 What is the relationship between security compartments, the "need-to-know" policy, and the principle of least privilege?

13-14 Briefly explain what is meant by a reference monitor. What is the relationship between a security kernel and a reference monitor?

13-15 Briefly explain the nature of trusted processes within a security kernel. Why do trusted processes need special attention during the audit of an operating system?

13-16 What is the purpose of an automated specification and verification system in the implementation of an operating system?

13-17 Briefly explain the nature of the following types of operating system penetration techniques:
  a Browsing
  b Piggybacking
  c Trojan horse

13-18 Briefly explain the nature of the following types of operating system integrity flaws:
  a Incomplete parameter validation
  b Implicit sharing of data
  c Asynchronous validation

13-19 Briefly explain the nature of the following types of application program validation checks:
  a Overflow check
  b Range check
  c Reasonableness check
  d Sign check
  e Crossfooting check
  f Control total check

13-20 What is the purpose of minimizing operator intervention during application system processing?

13-21 What are hardware/software numerical hazards? In what types of application systems should the auditor be concerned about hardware/software numerical hazards?

13-22 Why is it sometimes useful to employ redundant calculations in a program? In what types of programs would redundant calculations be most useful?

13-23 What data must be available in the accounting audit trail so the auditor can uniquely identify the process that has been executed on an input data item and the functions performed by that process?

13-24 What is a triggered transaction? What implications do triggered transactions have for the accounting audit trail in the processing subsystem?

13-25 What component in the processing subsystem usually collects data for the operations audit trail? How is this component activated to collect particular kinds of data?

13-26 List the *four* categories of events that are recorded on the operations audit trail. Which category is likely to have the most entries? Briefly explain why.

13-27 What interest does the auditor have in the way in which resource consumption data is used to bill users?

13-28 List two types of events that the auditor might wish to monitor using the exit facilities in the operations audit trail logging facility. Briefly explain why these events are of interest to the auditor.

13-29 Briefly explain why generalized software is useful in assisting the auditor to retrieve data from the operations audit trail. What factors might influence the auditor not to use generalized software for at least some retrieval operations?

13-30 Outline the control problems posed by the existence of an operations audit trail logging facility that allows user exits. Give *two* strategies for overcoming these control problems.

13-31 Briefly explain the nature of checkpoint/restart controls. What situations may arise where checkpoint/restart controls are needed?

13-32 How is a program checkpoint accomplished? Why is it necessary to know the position of all files being used by the program when a checkpoint is taken? When restarting the program, how is a repositioning of files accomplished?

13-33 From an audit perspective, what are the important requirements of a checkpoint/restart system? How can the auditor determine the adequacy of checkpoint/restart facilities?

MULTIPLE CHOICE QUESTIONS

13-1 A multiple state machine is one that provides:
a Multiple types of validity checks in a single state
b A mechanism for executing different programs in different partitions
c Different execution states as a basis for assessing the legitimacy of an instruction
d Different levels of capability to allow the machine to run in degraded mode

13-2 Memory errors primarily are detected through:
a Valid character checks
b Read-after-write checks
c Equipment checks
d Parity checks

13-3 In which type of real memory access control system is a lock and key mechanism most likely to be used:
a Single-user, contiguous storage allocation system
b Single-user, noncontiguous storage allocation system
c Multiple-user, contiguous storage allocation system
d Multiple-user, noncontiguous storage allocation system

13-4 Which of the following types of checks is *not* performed by a virtual memory addressing mechanism:
a The address translation table is examined to determine the real memory address for the block number of the virtual memory address
b The real memory address that corresponds to the virtual memory address is checked to see that it contains zeros
c The displacement is checked to see that it is within the boundaries of the block
d The actions to be undertaken on the block are checked to determine whether they are within the allowed set of actions

13-5 The difference between a security kernel and a reference monitor is that:
a The security kernel is a hardware/software/firmware implementation of a security policy while a reference monitor is an abstract representation of a mechanism to enforce a security policy

b The reference monitor is the component in the security kernel that handles access to the resources to be protected

c A reference monitor is used to protect resources in a single state machine whereas a security kernel is used to protect resources in a multiple state machine

d A reference monitor enforces a flow security policy whereas a security kernel enforces an inference security policy

13-6 Which of the following statements about trusted processes is false:

a They are all implemented within a security kernel

b They are not bound by all the security rules implemented within the kernel

c They are used to tailor a security policy to the specific needs of a data processing installation

d For all practical purposes they can be ignored by the auditor since their operational integrity is guaranteed by the kernel

13-7 Which of the following operating system penetration techniques takes advantage of the time during which a legitimate user is still connected to the system but is inactive:

a Between lines entry

b Piggybacking

c Trojan horse

d Spoofing

13-8 If an operating system uses a subset of the memory allocated to a user program for a work space, this integrity flaw is called:

a Violable limits

b Inconsistent parameter validation

c Implicit sharing of data

d Browsing

13-9 Match the following:

I Field check	A Control total
II Record check	B Sign test
III File check	C Overflow check
	D Crossfooting check

a III-C; II-D; I-B; II-A
b I-C; II-B; III-A; III-D
c II-A; III-B; I-C; I-C
d III-D; I-C; II-B; II-A

13-10 In the processing subsystem, hardware/software numerical hazards arise because of:

a Incorrect program design

b Transient memory errors

c Round off and truncation strategies used

d Use of closed routines

13-11 Which of the following report presentation orders would most likely be used for the accounting audit trail in the processing subsystem:

a Time stamp within destination identifier

b Transaction date within destination identifier

c Account number within date

d Source identifier within destination identifier

13-12 Which of the following events is most likely to be included on the accounting audit trail for the processing subsystem:
a Program start time
b Attempted integrity violation
c A hardware malfunction
d A triggered transaction

13-13 Which of the following would *not* be a report that typically could be produced by the generalized software that is available to interrogate the operations audit trail:
a Hardware utilization report
b Account implosion report
c Program run time report
d Report on programs abnormally terminated

13-14 The software used to maintain the operations audit trail can cause control problems because:
a It can be used to modify or delete records accessed by an application system during production running of the system
b It often is complex and error-prone
c It is powerful yet easy to use even by a computer novice
d Empirical evidence shows it is often the target of fraud

13-15 Checkpoint/restart facilities would *not* permit recovery from which of the following errors:
a Loading the wrong tape reel in a multireel file
b Loading the wrong version of the update program
c A temporary hardware error
d A power loss

13-16 From the viewpoint of maintaining data integrity, which of the following functions provided by a checkpoint/restart facility is subject to the highest exposures:
a Use of reentrant code to facilitate efficient checkpointing and restarting
b Checkpoint initiation via transaction count or elapsed time
c Storage of memory contents on a log file
d Automatic repositioning of files for restart purposes

EXERCISES AND CASES

13-1 Sunshine Credit Union is a small credit union based in San Diego. In the past financial year it has moved from manual data processing to using the services of a computer service bureau to carry out its data processing. The bureau provides a popular generalized package to support the data processing needs of credit unions.

Since the move to the bureau, the directors of the credit union have appointed a new director of financial services, David Swan, with a view to improving the services offered to members. At the outset, Swan undertook a thorough review of the accounting systems with the objective of streamlining the systems and improving controls. In particular, he took advantage of the access controls provided within the credit union package and set up a system of passwords to restrict the action privileges of each employee to those commensurate with their responsibilities.

Swan still had some doubts about controls within the credit union package used by Sunshine, although the system appeared to provide good controls and to restrict the activities of credit union staff to their assigned action privileges. Consequently, since he had no training in data processing, he hired an EDP audit consultant, Helen Webb, to examine controls within the system.

At their first meeting, Webb indicated that she was familiar with the operating system used by the service bureau, but she was not familiar with the package used to carry out the basic data processing. Nevertheless, as an initial step she asked Swan to sign on at a terminal and to show her the system. Once he had signed on, she asked him to attempt to call up the system editor. Swan indicated that he did not understand what she meant by the editor as he had never used the program before. She pointed out the nature of the editor and gave him the command to invoke the editor. Swan noted her concern when the editor was successfully activated. Next she asked him to attach the editor to a specific file, and she gave him the command to carry out the action. Again, he noted her concern when the system indicated the command had been successfully executed. When he queried her about her obvious concerns, she indicated that the editor had been successfully attached to the password file. Finally, Webb asked Swan to attempt to invoke two other programs. She gave him the commands to use, and again the system indicated that the programs were available for use. When Swan asked Webb about the nature of these two programs, she indicated they were the copy and delete utilities provided by the operating system.

Required: Why is Webb concerned about the results obtained so far? What exposures does Sunshine face? Given that Sunshine is using a service bureau for its data processing activities, what actions would you recommend be taken to overcome the problems that exist?

13-2 Consider the following controls evaluation table where the columns represent control objectives for the processing subsystem and the rows represent controls that can be exercised to obtain these objectives.

Controls (good programming practices)	Authorized processing only	Complete processing	Accurate processing
Handle rounding correctly			
Print run-to-run control totals			
Minimize operator intervention			
Understand numerical hazards			
Use redundant calculations			
Avoid closed routines			

Required: Consider an invoicing application system for a medium-size distributor of shoes. Fill in the elements of the table where each element represents your opinion on the cost-effectiveness, in general, of each control with respect to each control objective. Assume a score of 5 represents high cost-effectiveness and a score of 1 represents low cost-effectiveness. Be prepared to justify your ratings.

13-3 For some years your organization has operated a minicomputer to process both its accounting and engineering applications. Much of the data processing has been carried out in batch mode, but recently some new generalized accounting packages have been implemented that facilitate online entry and retrieval of data. In addition, the engineers within your organization are making increasing use of online, interactive programs to help them in their work.

With the shifting emphasis from batch data processing to online data processing, management is considering the purchase of a new operating system that will facilitate online, interactive processing rather than batch processing. Currently, two alternatives are being considered, and there is substantial debate within your firm over which operating system should be chosen.

Required: You are the manager of internal audit within your firm. The data processing manager has approached you over the conflict that exists on which operating system should be purchased. He points out that no one has yet considered how well each of the operating systems enforces security over data processing resources, even though many of the systems used within the firm are very sensitive applications. Consequently, he asks you to assist him by preparing a report that evaluates the two alternatives from a control perspective. Outline the major steps that you will take in your investigation.

13-4 You are an EDP audit specialist in a firm of external auditors. You are currently working on the audit of a new client that operates a large data processing facility with distributed databases and distributed processing. As part of the audit, you are examining controls over the operating system used by your client. You discover that the client has made a substantial number of in-house modifications to the operating system code. When you express your concerns about this situation to the vice-president in charge of information systems, he indicates that these modifications are needed to improve efficiency within the system. He points out the complexity and size of the data processing operations and the need to have an efficient operating system if adequate services are to be provided by the online and data communication facilities.

When you report your findings to your partner, he expresses serious concerns about the integrity of the operating system, particularly in light of some of the sensitive accounting applications that are used by the client. Consequently, he asks you to investigate the matter further.

After conducting a series of interviews with system users and data processing staff, you conclude that the need for in-house modifications to the operating system probably can be justified. However, your investigations show that the modifications are typically carried out by two system programmers who are the resident experts on the operating system code. Unfortunately, neither of these programmers is supervised adequately. Moreover, the programming manager argues it is impossible to review their work anyway because no one else has sufficient expertise in the operating system code.

Required: When you report the results of these further investigations to your partner, he is even more concerned about the integrity of the system. He asks you to prepare a brief report outlining some controls that might be implemented as a basis for ensuring the integrity of the operating system code. He indicates that he will use your recommendations in the letter on internal control weaknesses that he is preparing for the client's audit committee.

13-5 The data processing department in your organization has recently purchased a checkpoint/restart facility to support their batch processing operations. While batch systems are only a small part of the applications portfolio in your organization, nevertheless there are several systems run overnight that consume substantial resources. Furthermore, these systems must meet tight production schedules. The checkpoint/restart facility was purchased in light of problems caused by power fluctuations. The utility company has indicated that periods of unstable power supply are likely to continue because of heavy demands being imposed upon them by several new industrial plants that have recently opened in the area.

As the internal auditor within your organization, you decide to investigate the reliability of the checkpoint/restart facility. In a series of tests that you conduct, the facility performs according to specifications. However, as you are about to conclude your tests, you find that you can easily access the contents of the log file maintained by the facility using the editor provided within the operating system.

Required: What exposures exist in light of the flaw that you have discovered in the facility? Given that you cannot prohibit use of the facility, what control recommendations would you make to try to reduce the likelihood of losses from the exposure?

13-6 Consider Figure 13-8. Draw the flowchart for the algorithm that you could use to perpetrate a fraud using the round down technique. Assume you are working with a program that calculates interest earned on a bank's customer account master file.

ANSWERS TO MULTIPLE CHOICE QUESTIONS

13-1 c	13-5 a	13-9 b	13-13 b
13-2 d	13-6 d	13-10 c	13-14 a
13-3 d	13-7 a	13-11 a	13-15 b
13-4 b	13-8 c	13-12 d	13-16 c

REFERENCES

Abbott, R. P., J. S. Chin, J. E. Donnelley, W. L. Konigsford, S. Tokubo, and D. A. Webb. *Security Analysis and Enhancements of Computer Operating Systems* (Washington, D.C.: Institute for Computer Sciences and Technology, National Bureau of Standards, 1976), Report No. NBSIR-76-1041.

Adams, Donald L. "Audit Uses of SMF Reporting and Analysis Software,"*EDPACS* (April 1977), pp. 1–11, 16.

American Federation of Information Processing Societies. *Security: Checklist for Computer Center Self-Audits* (Arlington, VA: American Federation of Information Processing Societies, 1979).

Ames, Stanley R., Morrie Gasser, and Roger R. Schell. "Security Kernel Design and Implementation: An Introduction," *Computer* (July 1983), pp. 14–22.

Anderson, Douglas A. "Operating Systems," *Computer* (June 1981), pp. 69–82.

Attanasio, C. R., P. W. Markstein, and R.J. Phillips. "Penetrating an Operating System: A Study of VM/370 Integrity," *IBM Systems Journal*, vol. 15, no. 1, 1976, pp. 102–116.

Bell, D. E., and L. J. La Padula. "Secure Computer Systems: A Mathematical Model," ESD-TR-73-278, vol. 2, ESD/AFSC, Hanscom AFB, Bedford, MA, MTR-2547, vol. 2, Mitre Corporation, Bedford, MA, November 1973.

Bonyun, David A. "The Use of Architectural Principles in the Design of Certifiably Secure Systems," *Computers & Security*, vol. 2, 1983, pp. 153–162.

Cheheyl, Maureen Harris, Morrie Gasser, George A. Huff, and Jonathan K. Millen. "Verifying Security," *Computing Surveys* (September 1981), pp. 279–339.

Conway, R. W., W. L. Maxwell, and H. L. Morgan. "On the Implementation of Security Measures in Information Systems," *Communications of the ACM* (April 1972), pp. 211–220.

Coyle, Robert J. "Auditing the MVS Operating System," *EDP Auditing* (Pennsauken, NJ: Auerbach Publishers, Inc., 1985), Portfolio 75-04-30, pp. 1–12.

Crook, B. H., A. P. Smithies, and J. H. Raeburn. "Program Rerun Facilities in Magnetic Tape Systems," *Proceedings of the Fourth Australian Computer Conference* (Adelaide: Australian Computer Society, 1969), pp. 159–165.

Davies, C. T. "Data Processing Spheres of Control," *IBM Systems Journal*, vol. 17, no. 2, 1978, pp. 179–198.

Deitel, Harvey M. *An Introduction to Operating Systems*, rev. 1st ed. (Reading, MA: Addison-Wesley, 1984).

Denning, Dorothy E. "A Lattice Model of Secure Information Flow," *Communications of the ACM* (May 1976), pp. 236–243.

Denning, Dorothy E., and Peter J. Denning. "Data Security," *Computing Surveys* (September 1979), pp. 227–249.

Denning, P. J. "Fault-Tolerant Operating Systems," *Computing Surveys* (December 1976), pp. 359–390.

Donovan, J. J., and S. E. Madnick. "Hierarchical Approach to Computer System Integrity," *IBM Systems Journal*, vol. 14, no. 2, 1975, pp. 188–202.

Ferrey, Jeffrey. "Auditing the Operating System," *EDP Auditing* (Pennsauken, NJ: Auerbach Publishers, Inc., 1985), Portfolio 75-04-20, pp. 1–11.

Gallegos, Frederick, and Rodney Kocot. "A Program for Auditing Operating Systems," *EDP Auditing* (Pennsauken, NJ: Auerbach Publishers, Inc., 1985), Portfolio 75-04-10, pp. 1–15.

Landwehr, Carl E. "Formal Models of Computer Security," *Computing Surveys* (September 1981), pp. 247–278.

Landwehr, Carl E. "The Best Available Technologies for Computer Security," *Computer* (July 1983), pp. 86–100.

Leonard, David M. "Auditing VM/SP," *EDP Auditing* (Pennsauken, NJ: Auerbach Publishers, Inc., 1985), Portfolio 75-04-40, pp. 1–12.

Linde, Richard R. "Operating System Penetration," *Proceedings of the National Computer Conference, 1975* (Montvale, NJ: AFIPS Press, 1975), pp. 361–368.

Linden, Theodore A. "Operating System Structures to Support Security and Reliable Software," *Computing Surveys* (December 1976), pp. 410–445.

McGee, W. C. "The Information Management System IMS/VS Part V: Transaction Processing Facilities," *IBM Systems Journal*, 16 (April 1977), pp. 148–168.

Paans, Ronal, and Guus Bonnes. "Surreptitious Security Violation in the MVS Operating System," *Computers & Security*, vol. 2, 1983, pp. 144–152.

Parker, Donn B. *Crime by Computer* (New York: Charles Scribner's Sons, 1976).

Patrick, Robert L. *Performance Assurance and Data Integrity Practices*, U.S. Department of Commerce, National Bureau of Standards, NBS Special Publication 500-24, Washington, DC, January 1978.

Perry, William E., and Donald L. Adams. "SMF—An Untapped Audit Resource," *EDPACS* (September 1974), pp. 1–8.

Pohm, A. V., and T. A. Smay. "Computer Memory Systems," *Computer* (October 1981), pp. 93–110.

Saltzer, J. H., and M. D. Schroeder. "The Protection of Information in Computer Systems," *Proceedings of the IEEE* (September 1975), pp. 1278–1308.

Schaller, Carol A. "Auditing and Job Accounting Data," *Journal of Accountancy* (May 1976), pp. 36–42.

Schroeder, Michael D., and Jerome H. Saltzer. "A Hardware Architecture for Implementing Protection Rings," *Communications of the ACM* (March 1972), pp. 157–170.

Short, G. E. "Threats and Vulnerabilities in a Computer System," *Data Security and Data Processing Volume 5 Study Results: TRW Systems, Inc.* (New York: IBM Corporation, 1974), pp. 25–73.

Stepczyk, F. M. "Requirements for Secure Operating Systems," *Data Security and Data Processing Volume 5 Study Results: TRW Systems, Inc.* (New York: IBM Corporation, 1974), pp. 75–205.

Weber, Ron. "An Audit Perspective of Operating System Security," *Journal of Accountancy* (September 1975), pp. 97–100.

Williams, David J. "Operating Systems Audits: Their Importance and Use," *Accounting and Business Research* (Autumn 1984), pp. 367–372.

Williams, David J., and Anne Lillis. "EDP Audits of Operating Systems—An Exploratory Study of the Prior Probabilities of Risk," *Auditing: A Journal of Practice and Theory* (Spring 1985), pp. 110–117.

DATABASE CONTROLS

CHAPTER OUTLINE

SUMMARY
REVIEW QUESTIONS
MULTIPLE CHOICE QUESTIONS
EXERCISES AND CASES
ANSWERS TO MULTIPLE CHOICE QUESTIONS
REFERENCES

The database subsystem provides functions to define, create, modify, delete, and read data in an information system. Historically, the primary type of data maintained has been *declarative* data—that is, data that describes the static aspects of real-world objects and the associations among these objects. For example, a payroll file and a personnel file store information about the pay rates for each employee, the various positions within an organization, and the employees who have been assigned to each position. More recently, however, the database subsystem has been used to maintain *procedural* data—that is, data that describes the dynamic aspects of real-world objects and the associations among these objects. For example, the database may contain a set of rules describing how an expert portfolio manager makes decisions about which stocks and bonds to choose for investment purposes. When both declarative and procedural data are stored, the database is sometimes called the *knowledge base* to reflect the greater ''power'' of the data maintained in the database subsystem.

The database subsystem is currently experiencing substantial change among the components that undertake the basic activities performed in the subsystem. Initially, the major components in the database subsystem were the application programs that defined, created, modified, and deleted data, the operating system that performed the basic input/output operations to move data to and from various storage media, the central processor and primary storage in which these activities were performed, and the storage media that maintained the permanent or semipermanent copy of the data. However, to achieve the objectives of database management outlined in Chapter 6 and to provide effective and efficient processing of procedural knowledge, some dramatic changes have occurred to the components used by the database subsystem. For example: the activities previously performed by application programs and operating systems have been migrated to database management systems; special database machines have been developed to support the database subsystem; expert systems have been developed to support the processing of procedural data.

This chapter examines controls in the database subsystem. It discusses the policies and mechanisms needed to prevent unauthorized access to and use of the database, the ways in which application programs, operating systems, and database management systems ensure database functions are carried out accurately and completely, cryptographic controls used to preserve the privacy of data, file handling controls to prevent accidental destruction of data, the audit trail used to maintain a record of events in the subsystem, and the methods used to restore the subsystem in the event of loss.

ACCESS CONTROLS

Access controls in the database subsystem seek to prevent unauthorized access to and use of data. As with all subsystems, access controls are established by first specifying a security policy for the subsystem and then choosing an access control mechanism that will enforce the policy chosen (see, also, Chapter 9).

Choosing a Security Policy

The security policy in the database subsystem specifies the data that subjects can access and the action privileges that subjects have with respect to that data. In the database subsystem, *four* types of security policy can be invoked (see, also, Fernandez et al. [1981]):

1 *Name-dependent access control:* Under this policy, subjects either have access to a *named* data resource or they do not have access to the resource. If subjects have access to a data resource, the action privileges that they have with respect to the resource must also be specified. For example, in the personnel database shown in Figure 14-1, the payroll clerk can read only the names of persons, their location, and their salary. On the other hand, the personnel clerk can read and modify the names of persons, their salary, their location, and their home address. Neither the payroll clerk nor the personnel clerk can access a person's work performance rating. This type of access control is also known as content-independent access control.

2 *Content-dependent access control:* Under this policy, subjects are permitted or denied access to a data resource depending on the contents of the data resource. For example, in the personnel database shown in Figure 14-2, the personnel clerk is not permitted to access the salary of an employee if it exceeds $30,000. Content-dependent access controls depend only on the values of the particular data object that a subject is attempting to access at a point in time.

3 *Context-dependent access control:* Under this policy, subjects are permitted or denied access to a data resource depending upon the context in which they are seeking access to the data resource. For example, in the personnel database shown in Figure 14-3, personnel clerks are not permitted access to the names of employees whose salaries exceed $30,000 unless they are seeking to execute some type of statistical function (such as calculating the average) on the salary data item values.

4 *History-dependent access control:* Under this policy, subjects are permitted or denied access to a data resource depending upon the time series of accesses to and actions that they have undertaken on data resources. For example, payroll clerks may not be allowed to read the names of employees

Personnel database

Name	Location	Salary	Home address	Performance rating
Smith	Production	28000	16 Park St., Anytown	2
Jones	Accounting	22000	2 Odd St., Anytown	4
Brown	Marketing	32000	26 Small Lane, Somewhere	1
Thomas	Research	34000	84 March St., Anytown	1

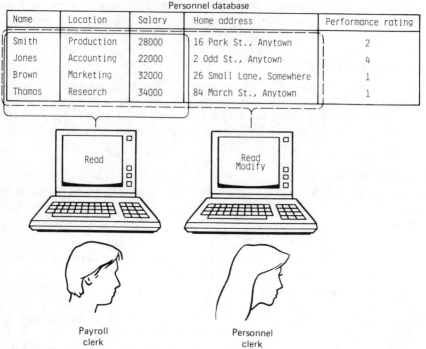

Payroll
clerk

Personnel
clerk

FIGURE 14-1
Name-dependent access control.

who have salaries over $30,000. However, they may not be prevented from reading salaries if they do not access the employee name data item. To circumvent the access restriction, clerks could access the location and salary data items and print out the individual values for both data items. Next, they could access the location and name data items and print out the values for both data items. If the sequence in which both requests were satisfied was the same, the names and salaries of employees could then be matched easily. History-dependent access controls would prevent this type of illegal access to data resources from occurring.

The security policies described above are listed in order of increasing difficulty to enforce. Clearly, history-dependent access controls place onerous demands on the access control mechanism. For example, how long must the access control mechanism remember the time series of access requests that a subject has made on the data resources within the database? Similarly, context-dependent access controls may require that action privileges be expressed as a function of complex Boolean expressions that specify the conditions under which the action privilege will be granted. Finally, the complexity of the security policies increases as the *granularity* of the data

Personnel database

Name	Location	Salary	Home address	Performance rating
Smith	Production	28000	16 Park St., Anytown	2
Jones	Accounting	22000	2 Odd St., Anytown	4
Brown	Marketing	32000	26 Small Lane, Somewhere	1
Thomas	Research	34000	84 March St., Anytown	1

Read
Modify

Personnel
clerk

FIGURE 14-2
Content-dependent access control.

objects on which the access controls are exercised becomes finer. For example, it is easier to enforce access controls at the file level than at the data item level.

Choosing an Access Control Mechanism

Unfortunately, data processing installations often have little discretion over the way in which security policies are implemented via the access control mechanisms available to the database subsystem. Usually, the access control mechanism provided in the operating system or the database management system cannot be altered easily by the installation. Nonetheless, data processing management and auditors still must consider the control strengths and weaknesses of the various access control mechanism implementations that might be used.

A major factor affecting the reliability of the access control mechanism is the extent to which it is located in a single component or multiple components. As discussed in Chapter 9, the reliability of an access control mechanism is increased if it can be embedded within a single component—the kernel of the operating system. If a single component is used, it is easier to protect the

Personnel database

Name	Location	Salary	Home address	Performance rating
Smith	Production	28000	16 Park St., Anytown	2
Jones	Accounting	22000	2 Odd St., Anytown	4
Brown	Marketing	32000	26 Small Lane, Somewhere	1
Thomas	Research	34000	84 March St., Anytown	1

Personnel
clerk

FIGURE 14-3
Context-dependent access control.

integrity of the access control mechanism itself, and it is more likely that a single, consistent security policy will be enforced over each resource within the system.

Unfortunately, practical constraints often dictate that the access control mechanism be distributed across several components. As the functions to be performed by the access control mechanism increase, the size of the kernel also increases. Thus, efficient implementations of the kernel become more difficult to achieve. In this light, Fernandez et al. [1981] point out some fundamental differences exist between the access rules to be enforced over data resources and the access rules to be enforced over other resources within a computer system; for example, more objects must be protected in the database subsystem, data objects usually have a longer life, and finer levels of granularity must be permitted with data objects. Consequently, they advocate establishing a separate access control mechanism for the database subsystem. If this approach is used, however, auditors then must determine whether access controls can be circumvented by taking advantage of inconsistencies or loopholes that exist in the interfaces among different access control mechanisms.

When a database is distributed, it is even more difficult to ensure that the integrity of the access control mechanism is maintained and that a complete and consistent set of access control rules is enforced throughout the data processing system. Irrespective of whether the database is replicated at multiple sites or partitioned with different sections being distributed to different sites, multiple access control mechanisms are often used to support each replication or partition of the database. If the database is replicated, the same access control rules must be enforced at each site. Thus, the system must somehow ensure that the access control rules are always applied consistently across all data resources. If the database is partitioned, the system must somehow route requests to access a data resource to the access control mechanism that possesses the access control rules for that data resource. In each case, maintaining the integrity of access controls places onerous demands on the system hardware/software that supports the access control mechanism.

APPLICATION SOFTWARE CONTROLS

As with the processing subsystem, the integrity of the database subsystem is in part dependent on the controls that have been implemented in any application programs that process transactions against the database. Even though the database management system rather than the application software may directly access and update the database, the database management system is still dependent on the application software to pass across a correct sequence of commands and update parameters and to take appropriate action when certain types of exception conditions are identified. Accordingly, the following sections describe various update protocols and report protocols that may be implemented in application programs to protect the integrity of the database.

Update Protocols

Update protocols in application software seek to ensure that changes to the database reflect changes to the real-world objects and associations that the data in the database is supposed to represent. Designing update protocols that preserve the integrity of the database yet are simple and robust to change has been a notoriously difficult problem (see, for example, Dwyer [1981] and Inglis [1981]). The following sections describe some of the major logical requirements that the protocols must handle.

Sequence Check Master and Transaction Files   In a typical batch update run the transaction file is sorted just prior to the update of the master file. It seems superfluous, therefore, for the master file update program then to check the sequence of the master file and transaction file during processing. Nevertheless, several conditions may cause the master file or transaction file to get out of sequence. First, some "patching" of a master file or transaction file may occur because of an update error. If a data or program error exists, rather than reprocess all the data, a utility program may be used to correct the error existing on the master file or transaction file. Patching often occurs during the changeover from one system to another when data has to be cleaned up. If patching occurs incorrectly, files can get out of sequence. Second, an erroneous update program may insert records in incorrect sequence on the master file. Third, on rare occasions a sort utility package processes erroneously (perhaps after modification) or a hardware/system software error goes undetected.

Ensure All Records on Files are Processed   If correct end-of-file protocols are not followed in a program, records may be lost from either a master file or transaction file. A common error is to close the transaction file upon reaching the end of the master file, and, less frequently, to close the master file upon reaching the end of the transaction file. In the former case there may be new records for insertion after the last record on the old master file. In the latter case, if a new physical version of the file is to be created (e.g., as with a magnetic tape file), existing master file records are lost. Correct end-of-file protocols can be complex if multiple transaction files and master files are processed concurrently.

Process Master File Changes before Updates   Multiple transactions may occur for a single master file record, for example, several monetary transactions for an accounts receivable record plus a change of address transaction. It is important that any master file record insertions, deletions, or changes be made before other types of transactions are processed. Otherwise, several types of errors can occur, for example, billing a customer at a wrong address, continuing to pay an employee after termination, or failing to pay an employee who has just been hired. The system should be designed so transaction codes cause changes to a record to sort before other types of transactions, such as monetary updates.

Maintain a Suspense Account   Whenever monetary transactions are involved, the master file update program should maintain a suspense account—generally the last account on the master file. The suspense account is the repository for monetary transactions that mismatch the master file. These mismatches occur for several reasons; for example, an account number may be coded incorrectly or a new account may not be inserted on the master file correctly. If monetary items are not charged to a suspense account, they may be lost because someone fails to correct the mismatch. The master file update program must accumulate the monetary effects of mismatches throughout processing and charge the net amount to the suspense account at the end of processing.

Report Protocols

Report protocols in application software seek to provide information to users of the database that will enable them to identify errors or transaction mismatches that have occurred when the database has been updated. The following sections briefly describe the nature of three such protocols.

Print Control Data for Internal Tables (Standing Data) Many programs have internal tables that they use to perform various functions. For example: a payroll program may have an internal table of pay rates that it uses to calculate gross pays; a billing program may have an internal table of prices that it uses to prepare invoices. These internal tables, or standing data, are components in the database subsystem.

Maintaining the integrity of these tables is critical since the effects of an error can be substantial. For example, an error in a table of prices may mean several thousand customers are underbilled for merchandise that they receive. It may be too costly to recover the monies lost; furthermore, the organization may not want the error to be known publicly because of an adverse reaction by shareholders, creditors, etc. Consequently, any changes to internal tables (e.g., updating a pay rate) should be checked carefully for accuracy and completeness. A common report protocol for standing data, therefore, is to print out internal tables after they have been changed so users can validate the changes made for accuracy and completeness.

Even if no changes are made to standing data, internal tables may still be printed out after each program run to enable users to check whether unauthorized changes have been made to the data. If the table is large and a decision is made not to print the table after each run, some type of control total (such as a hash total) can still be calculated for the table and reported. Users can then check this control total to determine whether it differs from the previous control total calculated for the data.

Print Run-to-Run Control Totals Chapter 13 discussed the need to calculate and print run-to-run control totals as a basis for identifying errors in the processing subsystem. Run-to-run control totals are also a useful means of identifying errors or irregularities in the database subsystem. For example, they may signal that a record has been dropped for some reason from a master file that has been updated.

Print Suspense Account Entries As discussed earlier, monetary update transactions that mismatch a master file must be written to a suspense account. To ensure these transactions are ultimately cleared to their correct accounts, a suspense account report must be prepared after each update run showing the transactions that were posted to the suspense account. The mismatches must also be written to an error file and removed as they are corrected. Reminders should be issued if they are not removed promptly (see, also, Chapter 11).

CONCURRENCY CONTROLS

A major function of the database subsystem is to allow different users of the database to share the same data resource. Otherwise, multiple versions of the data resource must be maintained to support different users, and inevitably inconsistencies among the different versions of the data resource will arise. Unfortunately, sharing data resources produces a new set of problems that must be handled by the database subsystem if data integrity is to be preserved. The following sections outline the nature of these problems and the various strategies that can be used to overcome them.

Nature of the Shared Data Resource Problem

The following example shows the problems that can arise when several programs are allowed to access the same data concurrently. Consider an inventory application where a salesclerk and a receiving clerk are online to the inventory master file. Moreover, they are allowed concurrent access to the file. Figure 14-4 shows a time sequence of events that can occur whereby data integrity is violated. A supplier delivers 100 units of good XYZ and the receiving clerk accesses the inventory master file to update the record for XYZ. Input/output routines copy an image of the existing record into the receiving program's buffer, and the program commences to update the image of the record. At the same time a customer places an order for 175 units of XYZ and the salesclerk accesses the inventory master file to update the record for XYZ. Input/output routines copy an image of the record into the program's buffer. In the meantime the receiving program completes its update and returns the buffer image of the record to the master file. The sales program carries out its update and returns the buffer image to the master file. Instead of the inventory record showing 425 units, it shows only 325 units. Thus, the record understates the true value of inventory on hand. This may lead to excessive inventory ordering and extra costs of storage space, obsolescence, lost interest, etc.

Data integrity problems caused by concurrent processes are not confined to update programs. Read-only programs can produce erroneous results if they operate concurrently with an update program. For example, a read-only program may be producing a trial balance for an accounts master file. If an update process is concurrently posting debit and credit entries to the accounts, only one side (e.g., the debit) of a double-entry transaction may be posted prior to the read-only program accessing the records to be updated. Thus, the trial balance will not balance.

The obvious solution to data integrity problems caused by concurrent processes is to lock out one process from a data resource while the resource is being used by another process. However, this solution can cause a system to come to a halt because of a situation called deadlock or the "deadly embrace."

The Problem of Deadlock

Figure 14-5 shows the problems that can arise when one process is allowed to lock out another process from a resource. At time t process P acquires exclusive control of data resource 1 and process Q acquires exclusive control of data resource 2. At time $t + 1$ process P makes an additional request for data

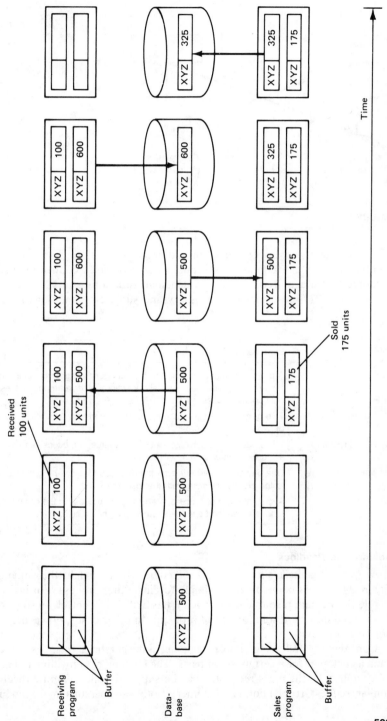

FIGURE 14-4 Concurrent processes as a threat to data integrity.

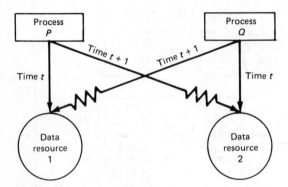

FIGURE 14-5
A deadlock situation.

resource 2 and process Q makes an additional request for data resource 1. Neither process can continue until one process releases control of the data resource that it acquired at time t. A deadlock situation results.

Everest [1974] describes the necessary and sufficient conditions for deadlock to occur:

Condition	Explanation
Lockout	A process can exclude another process from using a resource. Note, a read-only process may not wish to exclude other read-only processes, only update processes.
Concurrency	Two or more processes can compete concurrently for exclusive control of two or more resources.
Additional request	While holding exclusive control of a resource, a process can request exclusive control of another resource.
No preemption	One process cannot force another process to release a resource prior to the process finishing with the resource.
Circular wait	A circular chain of processes exists, each process in the chain holding a resource needed by the next process in the chain.

Solutions to Deadlock

How can a deadlock situation be resolved? At first thought the situation in Figure 14-5 might be resolved by simply forcing either process P or process Q to release the data resource over which it has exclusive control. In some cases this indeed may be a solution to the problem. In other cases, however, it may not be a solution.

Consider the following simple example. Salesperson 1 receives a request from a customer for a certain set of parts. The customer is unwilling to take the order unless all the parts requested can be supplied. Salesperson 2 receives a similar request from another customer. Both salespersons make an initial

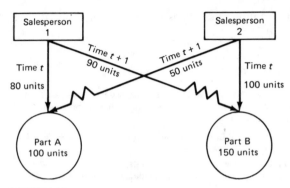

FIGURE 14-6
Inventory example of a deadlock situation.

inquiry of the database to determine whether sufficient inventory exists for all the parts requested (a read-only process). Recognizing that inventory may be depleted in the meantime because of other orders, they both commence to place their orders. Figure 14-6 shows the situation that may result. Assume part A and part B are required in both salesperson's orders. Salesperson 1 acquires exclusive control of part A's record first and decreases the existing stock of 100 units by 80 units. At the same time salesperson 2 acquires exclusive control of part B's record and decreases the existing stock of 150 units by 100 units. At time $t + 1$ a deadlock situation results. Consider what would happen if salesperson 1's program was allowed to preempt salesperson 2's program. After accessing part B's record, salesperson 1's program would find only 50 units (150–100) of part B available since salesperson 2's program already had updated part B's record. Thus, salesperson 1's order would have to be canceled in its entirety since 90 units of part B are required.

The same situation results if salesperson 2's program is allowed to preempt salesperson 1's program. Unless the updates of one program are undone before the other program continues, both customer orders are lost, whereas only one order need be lost. The problem arises because the database is in an inconsistent state when the preemption occurs.

Rolling back the changes made by one program can be difficult. Shipping notices, invoices, etc., may have been prepared by the program that is preempted, and these messages have to be canceled. The degree of complexity is affected by how far the program needs to be rolled back. Further, there is the question of which program should be preempted. Different criteria for making this choice may be used (see, for example, Fossum [1974] and McGee [1977]).

Preventing Deadlock
Recognizing a deadlock situation and recovering from a deadlock situation may consume substantial system resources. A more desirable strategy is to prevent

deadlock from occurring. Prevention of deadlock can be accomplished in four ways (see, further, Everest [1974]):

Strategy	Explanation
Presequence processes	For those processes where a deadlock situation may result, an external administrator must presequence them to prevent their running concurrently.
Preempt resources	One process may force another process to give up control of a data resource.
Preorder resources	To prevent a circular chain of requests, data resources are preordered. Resource requests made by a process must follow this preorder.
Preclaim resources	A process must obtain exclusive control over all resources that it needs before using them.

None of these strategies is entirely satisfactory for preventing deadlock. In an online realtime environment, presequencing resources may be impossible and result in the database being unavailable on a timely basis for users. The problems of rolling back changes to the database under a preemption strategy already have been discussed. Preordering data resources may be extremely difficult, if not impossible. A process may require data resources in an order that violates the preorder, or forcing programs to request data resources according to the preorder may degrade system performance substantially. Under a preclaim strategy a process may be blocked indefinitely from proceeding because it is unable to acquire all the resources it needs. Currently it is impossible with existing hardware to lock all the resources needed simultaneously. Thus, a process must lock needed resources sequentially. If the process fails on the first attempt because a resource is locked already, it must be backed out and the locking process attempted again. To prevent an "accordion effect" from occurring indefinitely, a single locking mechanism for all processes is needed, and a process must acquire higher locking priority each time it fails to lock needed resources.

Two-Phase Locking

In spite of the difficulties of preventing, detecting, and correcting concurrency and deadlock problems, a standard "solution" to the problem now seems widely accepted. This solution, called *two-phase locking*, applies to a *transaction* that is being processed against the database. A transaction constitutes a short sequence of interactions with the database that represents some meaningful unit of activity to a user. For example, in the context of the inventory application described previously, it would represent the sequence of operations needed to retrieve the relevant inventory records that satisfy the customer's request and to update them with the amounts ordered. More precisely, however, a transaction must have *four* properties (see Haerder and Reuter [1983]):

1 *Atomicity:* All actions taken by a transaction must be indivisible. Either all actions undertaken by a transaction are manifested in the current state of the database or nothing is allowed to occur.

2 *Consistency:* A transaction must preserve the consistency of the database. The effects of a transaction are not reflected in the database until it *commits* its results. That is, all changes are first made in a temporary workspace until they can be written permanently, as an indivisible unit, to the database. Commitment is a two-phase process. During the first phase, the system writes the changes in the temporary workspace created for the transaction to some type of secure storage. If failure occurs during this phase, no harm has been done since the changes have not been applied to the database. During the second phase, the system copies the changes from secure storage to the database. If failure occurs during this phase, the new values of the database are recovered from secure storage. In either case, the transaction leaves the database in a consistent state.

3 *Isolation.* The events that occur within a transaction must be transparent to other transactions that are executing concurrently. In other words, no type of interference among transactions can be permitted. Special techniques, called *synchronization techniques,* have been developed to preserve transaction isolation (see Kohler [1981]).

4 *Durability.* Once the results of a transaction have been committed, the system must guarantee that the changes survive any subsequent failure of the database. Existence controls (discussed later in this chapter) are needed to achieve transaction durability.

Two-phase locking handles a transaction using the following protocol. First, before a transaction can read a data item, it must "own" a "read-lock" on the data item. Similarly, before a transaction can write a data item, it must own a "write-lock" on the data item. This rule implements a (partial) preclaim strategy for preventing deadlock. Second, different transactions are not allowed to own "conflicting" locks simultaneously. In essence, this rule means that two transactions can own read-locks on the same data item but a read-lock and a write-lock or two write-locks are not permitted to occur simultaneously. Recall, inconsistent results can be obtained if two processes concurrently read and write a data item or two processes concurrently write a data item. It does not matter, however, if two processes concurrently read a data item. Third, once a transaction releases ownership of a lock, it cannot obtain additional locks. Release of a lock gives another transaction the opportunity to obtain control over the data item and the consistency of results can no longer be guaranteed. Thus, a transaction should commit its database changes before it releases its locks.

Two-phase locking, therefore, has a growing phase and a shrinking phase. During the *growing phase,* the transaction acquires locks without releasing locks. Once the transaction releases a lock, it enters the *shrinking phase* and it must proceed irrevocably to release all its locks. Locks could be released because the transaction has committed its updates or, if a preclaim strategy has been used, it has been unable to acquire all the locks it needs.

Distributed Database Concurrency Controls

In many cases, concurrency and deadlock problems will be infrequent (see, for example, Munz and Krenz [1977]). As the sharing of data among multiple users increases, however, the likelihood of these problems arising also increases. In addition, if a decision is made to distribute a database, concurrency and deadlock problems can become a major threat to database integrity unless the database management system has suitable controls. In the case of a replicated database, the system must somehow ensure that all versions of a data item are kept in a consistent state. This involves locking all instances of the data items needed before update operations can proceed. In the case of a partitioned database, the location of the data items needed must be identified and locks somehow activated over the data items. Conceptually, the approach seems straightforward; however, achieving efficient implementation of concurrency controls is another issue.

To illustrate how concurrency controls might be implemented for a distributed database, consider the two-phase locking scheme described above for a centralized database. At least three strategies can be used to implement the scheme. Under the first strategy, a two-phase *scheduler* must be constructed to process and to enforce the locking protocols. The scheduler for each data item is placed at the location where the data item is stored. In a partitioned database, a transaction must acquire a read-lock or write-lock by first locating the scheduler for the data item requested and then activating the lock. In a replicated database, schedulers are also replicated and stored with each version of the data item. If a read-lock is requested, the transaction need only request the lock at the most convenient scheduler. If a write-lock is requested, however, the transaction must request the lock of all replications of the scheduler for the data item needed.

Under the second strategy, one version of the data item and its associated scheduler is designated as the primary copy. Before accessing a data item, a transaction must acquire the lock for the primary copy. The location of the primary copy is chosen to try to optimize throughput in the system. Transactions access a directory to determine the location of the primary copy.

Under the third strategy, schedulers are located at a single, centralized site. Transactions know that they must access the schedulers for all data items in the database, irrespective of where the data items are located. This strategy simplifies scheduler management, but greater communication costs are incurred since all transactions must access a central site.

Bernstein and Goodman [1981] describe other strategies for handling concurrency and deadlock problems in a distributed system. Unfortunately, the area is very complex, and it may be difficult for the auditor to determine whether the concurrency controls implemented in a distributed database management system will maintain the integrity of data under all situations where resource conflicts arise.

CRYPTOGRAPHIC CONTROLS

So far, the major work undertaken on cryptography relates to its use in authentication and data communication systems (see Chapters 9 and 12). Its use in protecting the privacy of databases is less evolved. Nonetheless, several cryptographic schemes have been developed to protect the integrity of databases and to enable the secure transfer of files between one computer and another computer.

Portable storage media, such as removable disk packs and magnetic tapes, can be protected by implementing a secure encryption device in a disk drive controller or tape drive controller. The data is automatically encrypted each time it is written and decrypted each time it is read. While this type of encryption protects the privacy of data if the storage medium is stolen, it does not protect one user's data from another user since the cryptographic key used for encryption/decryption purposes is common to all users.

If there is little sharing of data among system users, individual users may protect their own files using a personal cryptographic key. They must present this key to the system when they wish to perform operations on their files. This system is unsatisfactory, however, when data is shared. The owner of the file must make the key known to other users who require access to the file, and as the key becomes more widely known, the risk of key compromise increases.

Alternative cryptographic schemes have been devised where data must be shared (see, further, Meyer and Matyas [1982] and Davies and Price [1984]). These schemes enable data to be protected at a host computer and secure transfer of files to be accomplished between one host and another host. In essence, they rely on a hierarchy of cryptographic keys to protect the keys themselves and the data encrypted under the keys. A *file key* is used to encipher data in a particular file. A *secondary key* is used to encrypt the file keys for the files owned by a particular user. This secondary key creates a protection domain that applies to a number of files, each having its own cryptographic key. The file keys encrypted under the secondary key can be stored in the header records of the files to which they apply so they can be retrieved easily each time the file needs to be accessed. The file keys are secure since they are encrypted under the secondary key. Finally, a *master key* is used to encrypt the secondary keys. Thus, the master key can be changed without having to reencrypt all data in the database—only the encrypted versions of the secondary keys need to be changed. To read a file, a user must have access to the secondary key. Access to the secondary key can be protected using the standard access control mechanisms described earlier in the chapter.

FILE HANDLING CONTROLS

File handling controls are used to prevent the accidental destruction of data contained on a storage medium. They are exercised by hardware, software, and the operators who mount and dismount the storage media used for the database.

Several types of data may be stored in the header and trailer records for a file as a basis for determining whether the correct file is being accessed by a program. The following sorts of data are common:

Internal data item	Nature
Internal label	Specifies the name of the file; used by the program accessing the file to check that it has the correct file.
Generation number	There may be several versions of a file with the same name; used by the program accessing the file to check that it is accessing the correct version.
Retention date	Prevents the contents of a file being overwritten before a specified date.
Control totals	A record within each file may contain control totals that can be checked. This record is updated at the end of each run and the control totals reported. On the next run, users supply a parameter value to the update program to check the control totals on the file that is being updated as a basis for ensuring the correct file is being accessed.

Several hardware controls are available to prevent accidental erasure of information. File protection rings can be used to protect magnetic tapes. To enable data to be written to a magnetic tape, a plastic ring must be inserted into the recess at the back of the tape reel. If the ring is removed, data cannot be written to the tape. Similarly, disks can be protected by activating a read-only switch on the disk drive, and diskettes can be protected by covering up a small notch on the side of the diskette with an adhesive strip. Unfortunately, a disk pack or diskette may contain multiple files, and if data must be written to one of the files, read-only protection cannot be activated on the other files.

To assist operators to load the correct files, external labels can be stuck on the outside casing of files. These labels may contain the name of the file, the creation date, and a code to indicate whether the file is a master file, transaction file, or work file. External labels are not a substitute for internal labels, however, since human error during operations procedures is inevitable.

AUDIT TRAIL CONTROLS

The audit trail in the database subsystem maintains the chronology of events that occur either to the database definition or to the database itself. The full set of events must be recorded: creations, modifications, deletions, and retrievals.

Otherwise, it may be impossible to determine how the database definition or the database attained its current state, or who, via a retrieval transaction, relied upon some past state of the database definition or the database.

Accounting Audit Trail

To maintain the accounting audit trail in an application system, the database subsystem must undertake three functions. First, it must attach a unique time stamp to all transactions that are applied against the database definition or the database. This time stamp has two purposes: (a) it confirms that a transaction ultimately reached the database definition or the database; and (b) it identifies a transaction's unique position in the time series of events that has occurred to a data item in the database definition or the database. As a result, the audit trail can be either imploded or exploded (Figure 14-7). Under *implosion*, each transaction can be traced from its source to the data item on which it operates: the transaction's source identifier enables its origin to be traced unambiguously; its destination identifier designates the data item against which it is supposed to be applied; and the time stamp inserted in the transaction by the database subsystem confirms that the transaction ultimately took effect on the database definition or the database. Under *explosion*, the time stamp can be sorted within the destination identifier for the transaction so that the chrono-

FIGURE 14-7a
Implosion purpose of an accounting audit trail.

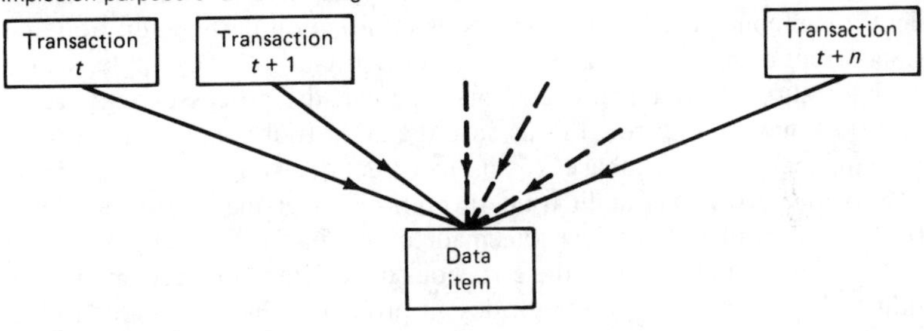

FIGURE 14-7b
Explosion purpose of an accounting audit trail.

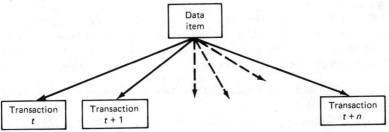

logical sequence of events that has occurred to a data item can be reconstructed.

Second, the database subsystem must attach beforeimages and afterimages of the data item against which a transaction is applied to the audit trail entry for the transaction. If the transaction modifies an existing data item value, the value of the data item before it is updated and the value of the data item after it is updated must be stored in the transaction's audit trail entry. In the case of insertion, deletion, and retrieval transactions that do not change an existing data item value, a flag can be set to indicate that only the afterimage or beforeimage is relevant. These beforeimages and afterimages have two purposes: (a) they facilitate inquiries on the audit trail in that the effects of the transaction on the database definition or the database can be determined immediately from the audit trail entry; and (b) they provide redundancy for the time stamp in that fraudulent deletion of an audit trail entry or fraudulent alteration of a time stamp can be detected via a mismatch between the afterimage of some transaction and the beforeimage of the subsequent transaction.

Third, since audit trail entries require permanent or semipermanent storage, the database subsystem must provide facilities to define, create, modify, delete, and retrieve data in the audit trail. Note that, in general, the audit trail should not have to be modified; it is meant to be a true history of what happened to the database. However, two situations can arise where modifications to the audit trail are necessary. First, the application system updating the database processes data erroneously and, as a result, the audit trail is a history of incorrect operations on the database. Undoing the erroneous results is not sufficient if someone accesses the erroneous information in the audit trail and makes incorrect decisions on the basis of this information, for example, sues a customer for supposedly unpaid accounts. Second, the processes that create the audit trail may be in error. In this case the audit trail is not a true history of what happened to the database. Again, incorrect decisions may be made on the basis of the erroneous audit trail. In both cases, it may be desirable to modify the audit trail so later decisions made on the basis of data contained in the audit trail are not affected by the erroneous data. Unfortunately, modifying the audit trail presents some difficult design problems since an audit trail of modifications to the audit trail must also be maintained—an audit trail for an audit trail. Weber [1982] discusses these issues further and presents some design recommendations.

In terms of the database subsystem supporting permanent or semipermanent storage of the audit trail, perhaps the most difficult problems arise in accommodating the effects of changes that occur within an application system. Consider the implications of the following types of changes on the audit trail:

1 A new data item is defined in the database definition and data collected to populate the database.

2 An existing data item is deleted from the database definition and data no longer collected for that data item.

3 The name used for a data item is changed.

4 A change of measurement scale occurs for a data item, for example, conversion from pounds to kilograms.

5 The coding system used for a data item changes, for example, conversion from a numeric to an alphanumeric code.

6 The key used to encrypt a data item is changed.

All these changes affect the various operations that have to be performed on the audit trail. The addition or deletion of data items from the database definition may mean the data structure and the storage structure used for the audit trail have to be changed. Problems arise when a user wants to retrieve data from the audit trail for a time period during which some change has occurred that has affected the audit trail. For example, suppose a user wishes to examine all transactions that have updated an account during a particular financial period, but the code used for that account has changed during the period. If the user is unaware of the change of code for the account, only a subset of transactions for the account may be retrieved. Ideally, the system that supports the audit trail automatically will identify that a change has occurred and provide users with the full set of transactions, or at least alert users to the change that has invalidated their query specification.

The problems posed by system change are general problems. They are the motivation for research in areas such as database management systems. Various solutions have been proposed, all having their advantages and disadvantages. For example, as discussed in Chapter 6, one solution is to separate the definition of data from the processes that access the data. Using this technique the processes are more robust to changes in the data structure or storage structure of the database. Binding the data definition to the process occurs at some point prior to accessing the database (see Everest [1985]).

Figure 14-8 illustrates this technique applied to the audit trail. A generalized audit trail system accepts output from the various application systems within the computer installation. This output might be dumped in an input/output pool and selectively retrieved periodically by the generalized audit trail system. The definition of the audit trail is separate from the processes that access the audit trail. The audit trail definition maintains the history of definitions for data existing in the audit trail. When a process requires access to the audit trail, the generalized audit trail system binds the audit trail definition to the process. In some cases more than one definition may be bound to the process. For example, if a retrieval process requests data for a period during which the audit trail definition has changed, the generalized audit trail system will change the definition bound to the process when the process accesses data created under the changed definition.

Operations Audit Trail

The operations audit trail in the database subsystem maintains the chronology of resource consumption for each event that occurs to the database definition

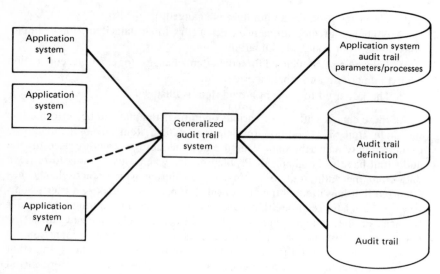

FIGURE 14-8
Generalized audit trail system.

or the database. On the basis of the operations audit trail the database administrator can make two decisions. First, in light of response times or resource consumption to apply transactions against the database, it may be necessary to reorganize the database (see, for example, Sockut and Goldberg [1979]). Reorganization may involve establishing new access paths via indexes or pointers, clearing out overflow areas, assigning data to faster storage devices, etc. Second, resource consumption data may indicate that the processes that apply transactions to the database definition or the database need to be restructured or that new processes need to be acquired or written. For example, the database administrator may determine that a new database management system would better meet the needs of the organization or that update programs have to be rewritten so they are more efficient when they update the database.

EXISTENCE CONTROLS

In many computer systems, the most complex set of existence controls are needed in the database subsystem. They must restore the database in the event of loss. The loss may be localized or global: a file or portion of a file may be damaged or the entire database may be destroyed. Irrespective of the extent of the loss, existence controls must be capable of restoring the database quickly to its state at the point of failure.

The whole or portion of a database can be lost through *five* types of failure:

1 *Application program error:* Application program errors usually cause only localized damage specific to the file they are updating. More widespread damage can occur, however, if the program starts to process pointers incorrectly, reads records from other files, and attempts to update these records. The program should be written to recognize this situation quickly and to halt processing.

2 *System software error:* Even though system software may be extensively tested, an operating system, file copy utility, database management system, etc., may contain dormant errors. The extent of the damage that results to the database depends on the nature of the system software and the way in which it is used. For example, an error in an operating system can cause damage to the whole database since the operating system services all programs. An error in a utility may cause damage only to the file on which it is used. Nonetheless, the extent of the damage also depends on whether the utility is used on a small section or a large section of the database and how often it is used by different application systems.

3 *Hardware failure:* In spite of the high reliability of hardware, failure still occurs: a processor or memory error sometimes happens; a communications network fails because of a faulty terminal, a dataset generating spurious interrupts, or a multiplexor getting into a continuously busy state; a read/write arm drops onto a disk surface and scores a concentric circle on the disk, thereby destroying file control tables, indexes, etc.; an input/output channel starts to write blocks incorrectly. Depending on the nature of the error, damage to the database can be localized or global.

4 *Procedural error:* There are many forms of procedural error that can damage a database: an operator can load an incorrect version of a program or mount an incorrect file; programs can be run out of sequence; a user may supply an incorrect parameter for an update run; a master file may be incorrectly scratched. Again, depending on the nature of the error, damage to the database can be localized or global.

5 *Environmental failure:* Various types of environmental failure can occur: flood, fire, sabotage, etc. Environmental failure often results in extensive damage to the database. Off-site storage of files is essential to restoring the database from many types of environmental failure.

Establishing existence controls in the database subsystem means that both a backup strategy and a recovery strategy must be chosen. All *backup strategies* involve maintaining a prior version of the database and a log of transactions or changes to the database. If an update program creates a new *physical* version of a file, the previous version of the file and the file of transactions used to update the file can be used for backup purposes. If update occurs in place, periodically a dump of the database must be taken and a log of changes to the database since the dump must be maintained.

Recovery strategies take two forms. First, the *current* state of the database may have to be restored if the entire database or a portion of the database is lost—for example, through failure of a physical device. This involves a *rollforward* operation using a prior version or dump of the database and a log of transactions or changes since that version or dump. Second, a *prior* state of the database may have to be restored because the current state of the database is invalid—for example, through an erroneous program having updated the database incorrectly. This involves a *rollback* operation to undo the damage. The current state of the database and a log of transactions or changes are used to restore the database to a previous valid state.

The following sections discuss the various forms of backup and recovery that can be used to restore a damaged or destroyed database. It will become clear that these strategies differ primarily on the basis of their frequency and comprehensiveness of dumping versus their frequency and comprehensiveness of logging. More frequent dumping permits fast recovery of the database; however, logging normally incurs less system overhead. Thus, tradeoffs must be made between dumping and logging. In all cases, the descriptions of the backup and recovery strategies given below focus on *transaction-oriented* database recovery. Like concurrency controls, the concept of a transaction is central to the nature of existence controls. Below the transaction level, a particular backup and recovery strategy can be implemented in various ways. At the subtransaction level, however, the concern is primarily with efficiency rather than maintenance of data integrity (see, further, Haerder and Reuter [1983]).

Grandfather, Father, Son

The grandfather, father, son strategy involves using the previous version of a master file and the update transactions used to create the current file to re-create the current master file if it becomes damaged. There are two requirements for using the strategy. First, the input master file to an update run must be kept physically intact; that is, both changed and unchanged records must be written onto a new file. Second, the transaction file from the update run must be kept. Re-creation simply involves redoing the update run.

The current version of the master file is called the son, the previous version the father (Figure 14-9). The grandfather file is the input file to the run that created the father. The grandfather is kept as backup for the father. If for any reason the father cannot be read—for example, it has been accidentally destroyed or a parity error has occurred—the update run to create the father must be reprocessed. Thus, the strategy involves keeping three generations of the master file and the previous and current versions of the transaction file. It is critical that the different files be stored in different places so that all files are not lost if environmental failure occurs.

The major advantage of this strategy is its simplicity. There are four disadvantages: (*a*) it precludes update in place, (*b*) the file is not available to other processes during recovery, (*c*) concurrent processes cannot update the file, and (*d*) if the update process consumes substantial resources and damage

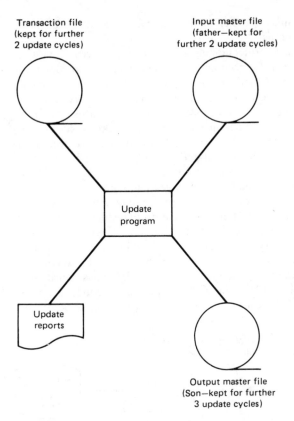

FIGURE 14-9
Father and son in a grandfather, father, son backup strategy.

is localized, recovery is expensive. Thus, the strategy is most useful for batch sequential systems.

Dual Recording

Dual recording involves keeping two completely separate copies of the database and updating both simultaneously (Figure 14-10). The two copies should not be maintained at the one physical location. One copy of the database must be stored remotely to protect against environmental failure. To protect against hardware failure, a second processor has to be used. If failure occurs, switches are set and the second database (and processor) becomes the primary database.

This strategy must be used if it is critical that the database be continuously available as, for example, in an online reservations system. In these cases the losses resulting from the unavailability of the database exceed the costs of maintaining duplicate resources.

Dual recording affords little protection against a procedural error, a system software error, or an application program error. These errors corrupt both databases. Thus, a second backup and recovery strategy must be used to recover from these types of errors. The dual recording strategy assumes procedural and software errors will not occur. In some cases this is a reasonable assumption. For example, in an online reservations system the software often has been extensively tested and widely used so that it is "error-free." Further, procedures are well-defined and also have been extensively tested and widely used. Constancy is a feature of these systems. New processes and procedures are introduced with much caution.

Recovering a database after hardware or environmental failure may or may not be difficult depending on (a) the length of time during which the database is unavailable and (b) the number of update transactions that have occurred during that period. Two recovery strategies can be used. First, at a convenient time a copy of the intact database can be taken, which becomes the secondary database. Update processes must be denied access to the database during the copy, so it must be performed in an off-peak period. Second, a log of transactions being processed against the intact database can be kept and

FIGURE 14-10
Dual recording strategy with remote storage of frontend processor, primary processor and primary database, and duplicate processor and duplicate database.

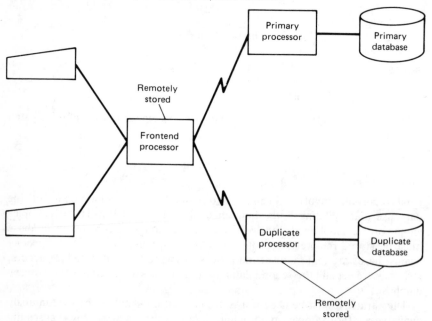

processed against a previous dump of the damaged database. This strategy is used if it is important to recover the damaged database quickly and it will be some time before an off-peak period is available to undertake a copy of the intact database. Update transactions are copied onto the log concurrently, with the log being processed against the damaged database. For the damaged database to be able to catch up to the intact database, processing of the log must be faster than the rate at which transactions are written to the log.

Dumping

Dumping involves copying the whole or a portion of the database to some backup medium—typically, magnetic tape. Recovery involves rewriting the dump back onto the primary storage medium and reprocessing transactions since the dump was taken. Users may be responsible for resubmitting transactions from the time of the dump. Alternatively, a log of transactions may be kept between dumps. If users are responsible for resubmitting transactions, they must know at what time each dump is taken, or they must be informed of the time of the last dump taken prior to the failure of the database.

Either a physical dump or a logical dump may be taken. A *physical dump* involves reading and copying the database in the serial order of the physical records, for example, track by track. In some cases physical boundaries define the space occupied by a file and dumping may be selective. In other cases the physical location of a file is unknown. If the installation uses a database management system and the data is shared, records in a file may be intermingled with records from other files in any particular physical area. In this case, selective recovery of a file may be impossible.

Logical dumping involves reading and copying the database in the serial order of the logical records in a file. When recovering the database, it is not necessary to rewrite the records back into their previous physical locations. Instead, the storage space occupied by the damaged file is freed up, and the dump can be written onto the database wherever available space exists.

Logical dumping becomes complex if data is shared and records are members of several files. Consider, for example, the problems posed by a multilist file organization. In Figure 14-11, record AB is a member of two lists, A and B. Assume an erroneous program updates list A and damages record AB. Recovering AB using only a logical dump of list A is insufficient unless record AB is written back into its previous physical location. Otherwise, list B contains a corrupted record, and furthermore, two copies of record AB now exist on the database. For logical dumping purposes, the two lists must be considered as a single file.

Physical dumping is faster than logical dumping. However, whether recovery is faster from a physical dump or logical dump depends on the nature of the damage. Physical dumping facilitates global recovery of the database. It is useful in the event of environmental failure or the failure of a physical device. Logical dumping facilitates selective recovery of the database. It is useful in the

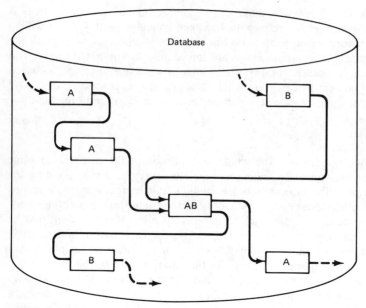

FIGURE 14-11
Multilist to illustrate some problems with a logical dump backup strategy.

event of damage to the database by an erroneous update program or erroneous system software.

If physical dumping is used as a backup strategy, physical reorganization of the database cannot occur between dumps unless the whole database is reorganized and recovered. Partial reorganization means that pointers in a file or on another device may be invalid if, for example, a disk has to be recovered because of physical failure.

Dumping is only a partial backup strategy. It restores the database to a valid state prior to the time of failure. However, the effects of transactions after the dump up to the point of failure still must be recovered through users resubmitting data or the system maintaining a log of transactions or changed images of records on the database. Recovery can be complex when several different update programs are authorized to update the record. Recovering the record if failure occurs means transactions from multiple sources must be recaptured or several programs have to be rerun to restore the database.

Dumping can consume substantial resources. Large databases may take hours, even days, to dump (see, for example, Severance and Lohman [1976]). For some computer installations the time required to take a full dump of the database may be intolerable.

Logging

Logging involves recording a transaction that changes the database, an image of the record changed by the update action, or the change parameters resulting from the update action. Requiring users to resubmit transactions to recover the database may not be a viable strategy for several reasons. First, the downtime required for users to resubmit all transactions may be unacceptable. Second, recovering the database may require transactions to be resubmitted in a specified order. For example, if a bank account fluctuates between a debit and a credit balance and interest is charged on debit balances, the time sequence for the resubmission of transactions to the account is important. If users have not recorded transactions in a time sequence or there are multiple sources of input, obtaining the required time sequence for resubmission of transactions may be impossible. Third, transaction data may not be received directly from a user. It may be generated automatically by a program or received from another computer (perhaps another organization's computer). In these cases some form of logging must occur.

There are four basic types of logging strategies:

1 Logging input transactions
2 Logging beforeimages of the record changed
3 Logging afterimages of the record changed
4 Logging change parameters

Each logging strategy has different advantages and disadvantages and the strategy or combination of strategies chosen depends on the requirements of the application. Whatever logging strategy is chosen, the log file must never be buffered or blocked. If the system crashes and the contents of memory are lost, the log file is not current if the contents of the buffer have not been written to the log.

Logging Input Transactions Using this strategy for recovery involves reprocessing update transactions from the time of the last dump up until the time the database was damaged. To be able to select the relevant transactions from the log, a time and date-of-processing identifier must be stored with each transaction. If selective recovery of the database is to be attempted, a file and program identifier also may be needed for the transaction.

A major problem with this strategy is determining how the input transactions should be reprocessed. One method is to have a special recovery update program that reads the log and updates the database in the same way the various application programs perform updates. This program would be stripped of much of the logic contained in the application update programs. For example, it would not need logic to generate reports or handle transactions that did not change the database. The recovery update program would be very large if a large number of application update programs exists in the installation. As a further disadvantage, someone must ensure correspondence always exists between the recovery and application update programs. All modifications to application update programs must be incorporated in the recovery update program.

A second method of recovery is to read the log and have a master program call each application update program as a transaction for that application program is read. This involves storing a program identifier with each transaction on the log. Everest [1985] suggests a recovery flag be used to modify the normal operations of the application update programs. The recovery flag inhibits the regeneration of reports, error messages, etc. Instead, special control total reports can be produced for verifying the accuracy and completeness of the recovery process.

In some cases recovery is speeded up by sorting like transactions together. For example, all the transactions for a particular application update program can be sorted together or all the transactions for a particular record can be sorted together, their effects summed, and a single update processed against the database. A tradeoff must be made between the costs of sorting and summing the effects of the transactions and the cost of reprocessing all the transactions. Sorting the transactions also may reduce update time through minimizing disk head movement. However, sorting cannot be undertaken if a particular time sequence of transactions is important to database integrity, for example, as with the interest calculation on a bank account in the example previously discussed.

If a user is submitting transactions from an online terminal, a message must be printed to tell the user the last successful transaction processed and perhaps the time at which the transaction was processed. This is especially important if the user has to resubmit transactions because only partial recovery can be accomplished using a transaction log. It is also helpful if the system prints the user a message when a transaction has been processed unsuccessfully. In this way the user knows when the transaction has been logged successfully and when the master file has been updated successfully.

A decision must be made on when to log transactions. All transactions input to the system may be logged or only those transactions processed successfully may be logged. If the first alternative is adopted, the effects of unsuccessful transactions (for example, those that fail a validation test) must be inhibited or the user warned when a recovery process is to be undertaken. Otherwise, duplicate error messages for unsuccessful transactions can be confusing. These problems do not arise if only successful transactions are logged. However, as Everest [1985] points out, this strategy is deficient in providing a complete audit trail. One solution is to log successful and unsuccessful transactions on separate files and process only the file containing the successful transactions during recovery (Figure 14-12).

Logging Beforeimages Logging beforeimages of the database is a strategy designed to facilitate rollback of the database. Each time a record is to be

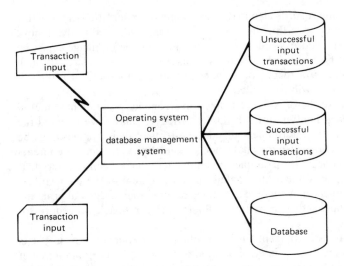

FIGURE 14-12
Separate logging of successful and unsuccessful input transactions for recovery and audit purposes.

updated its image before the update is logged. If an erroneous program updates the database, rollback occurs to the point where the erroneous program commenced processing. The log is read backward and the beforeimages are used to replace the existing records on the database. As the log is read backward, the last beforeimage read for a record up to the point where the erroneous program commenced processing is the state of the record just prior to the program's commencing processing (Figure 14-13).

Beforeimages also can be used for rollforward by applying them to a previous dump of the database. For those records that have been changed since the dump, their status is recovered up to the point where the last transaction for these records has not been processed. This is usually an unacceptable loss of data integrity for most financial information systems.

It is beneficial to log the transaction for the record with its beforeimage. Since the erroneous program must be corrected and the transaction reprocessed, logging the transaction with the beforeimages facilitates recovery.

Adding or deleting records on the database can cause several beforeimages to be taken and logged. If a record is chained to other records, the addition or deletion of the record involves updating pointers in other records within the chain. For example, Figure 14-14 shows a multilist file where one record within the multilist is to be deleted. This record is a member of three lists: A, B, and C. The pointers in the lists go in only one direction. Deleting the record means a beforeimage of the deleted record must be taken. Also, beforeimages of the records that point to the deleted record must be taken since the pointer addresses in these records must be updated. Four beforeimages are needed.

Adding or deleting records also may cause some reorganization of a file, for example, moving an overflow record to the home address if the record occupying the home address is deleted. Again, multiple beforeimages must be taken for all records changed. Similarly, if indexes have to be updated through addition or deletion of a record or a changed value in the field of a record, multiple beforeimages will be needed.

If some time passes before it is recognized an erroneous program has entered the system, rollback is often difficult. Other processes may have updated the damaged records in the interim period and the effects of their changes must be preserved. Some actions also may have been taken on the basis of the contents of the damaged records; for example, inventory may have been reordered. It can be difficult, if not impossible, to determine the extent of the damage that has resulted. Recovery may involve a systems programmer directly altering the contents of the damaged records rather than using a rollback procedure for recovery.

Concurrent processes present further problems for rollback. Even if it is recognized that a program is in error while it is running, the program may not have locked out other processes from the file it is updating. Consequently,

FIGURE 14-13
Removing the effects of an erroneous program using beforeimages.

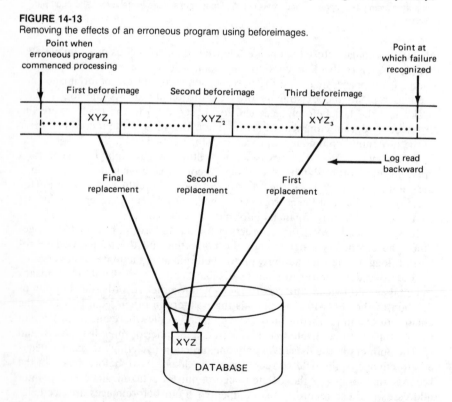

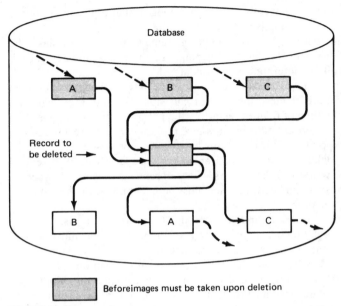

Beforeimages must be taken upon deletion

FIGURE 14-14
Example where multiple beforeimages must be logged upon update.

other processes may have read or updated records already processed by the erroneous program. Thus, programs concurrently reading the data will produce erroneous results. Programs concurrently updating the data will operate on incorrect data item values. As soon as an error is recognized in a program, other processes must be locked out from the data that has been damaged. Someone (the database administrator) must be responsible for determining the extent of the damage and the likely effects of the damage. Other users of the database have to be warned of the condition that exists in case they have accessed the damaged records. A decision then must be made on whether rollback can be accomplished. If too many updates have occurred since the erroneous update, other means of restoring database integrity may have to be used.

Logging Afterimages Logging afterimages of the database is a strategy designed to facilitate rollforward of the database. After a record has been updated by a transaction, its image is copied onto the log. If, for example, a physical device fails, recovery is accomplished by rolling forward using the latest dump of the database and replacing the dump version of the record with afterimage versions from the log. The log is read forward and the latest afterimage version read for a record constitutes the status of the record before the database was damaged. As with beforeimages, the unique location of each record must be stored with its afterimage on the log so that replacement of the dump version can be accomplished.

Recovering the database to the point of damage is useless unless the programs operating on the database at the point of failure also can be restarted. It may be difficult to determine what updates have been accomplished. If pointers have to be updated, not all the maintenance may have been undertaken at the point of failure. Unless the system can store the status of registers, buffers, etc., at the time of failure, restarting the programs may be impossible. Recovery then has to occur to a point where programs can be restarted—for example, a checkpoint—and transactions have to be reprocessed.

Additions or deletions of records on the database can cause several afterimages to be written to the log. As with beforeimage logging, this occurs when pointers must be updated, indexes must be maintained, or the database undergoes reorganization.

If an erroneous program updates the database, rollback also can be accomplished, though the logic involved can be complex. The log must be read backward and the afterimages used to replace the database version of the record. If a record has been updated several times, more than one afterimage will exist. The afterimage for a record addition will have no previous version on the database. This presents no problems as the afterimage is written to an address and the previous contents of the address are irrelevant (it should be free space). The complexity arises when the point where the erroneous program entered the system is reached. One more afterimage of each record damaged must still be obtained prior to this point. The recovery program must continue to read the log backward and flag the database record when it is replaced by one more afterimage to prevent any further replacements. The problem is to determine when all the required afterimages have been obtained. The log can be read back until a dump is reached, and providing the recovery program can determine which records still require an afterimage (e.g., by maintaining a table or searching for unflagged records), the dump version of the record can be used to obtain the afterimage. Further complexities surround record deletes. There will be no afterimage for a deleted record. The recovery program can identify a delete if an update occurred to the record after the dump and prior to the delete. However, if no update occurred, the dump version of the record is the required version. The recovery program somehow must identify this situation. In general, because of the complexities involved, using afterimages for rollback should be avoided.

Logging Change Parameters Frequent reorganization and update activity involving a high number of record additions and deletions may mean heavy logging overheads. If records in the database are linked by pointers, multiple beforeimages and afterimages must be taken. The log quickly becomes very large and the processing overheads become very high. One strategy used to help overcome these problems is to log the parameters of the change. Consider, for example, a record in which only the pointer field is to be updated. Rather than copy the whole image of the record, only the unique identifier of the record and the pointer field to be changed might be copied. Information showing the position of the pointer field in the record must also be copied, for example, its start character position. The recovery process is slightly more complex but less storage space is consumed on the log.

Residual Dumping

As an alternative to logging and taking a periodic full dump of the database, Everest [1976] suggests a backup strategy that he calls residual dumping. The primary motivation for residual dumping is the overhead involved in taking a full dump of the database. A log is insufficient for complete backup protection. If only a log is available for recovery, the possibility exists of having to examine all the entries on the log since the creation of the database. A dump avoids this problem by making it unnecessary to look back at the log prior to the dump. Nevertheless, dumps are costly in three ways: (*a*) they may take substantial time to accomplish, (*b*) the database is unavailable during the dump, and (*c*) dumps waste resources in that they are not selective. A record may be logged and dumped within a short period, resulting in redundant backup.

Residual dumping involves logging records that have *not* been changed since the last residual dump. Thus, records that have not been subject to an update action (and thereby logged) since the last residual dump are logged. Residual dumping is used in conjunction with a beforeimage and afterimage logging strategy. Residual dump records are flagged to show their beforeimage and afterimage are the same.

If a rollforward operation is required, recovery involves going back to (but not including) the second last residual dump taken. The recovery operation starts with an empty database and progressively fills the database by writing afterimages to the database. How far the database must be rolled forward depends on whether or not the status of all the various processes could be saved at the point of failure. Consider Figure 14-15. If at the point of failure the status of all processes could be saved, recovery starts immediately after residual dump 1 and continues up to the point of failure. Between residual

FIGURE 14-15
Rollforward recovery for a residual dump backup strategy.

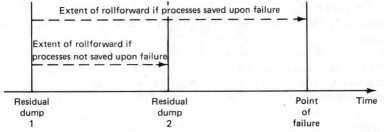

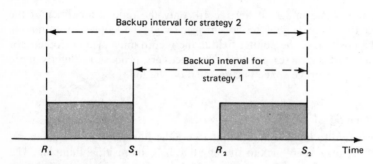

FIGURE 14-16
Residual dumping as a background operation.

dump 1 and residual dump 2, the database is populated with the afterimages of all changes made to the database during this period. Just prior to residual dump 2, the database contains the latest state of all records that have been changed during the period (some of the records may have been changed multiple times). The "empty slots" still remaining in the database because some records have not been changed are then filled with residual dump 2. After residual dump 2 has been read and the dump records written to the database, a complete copy of the database exists. If the status of processes could not be saved at the point of failure, once residual dump 2 has been written back to the database a checkpoint exists at which all processes can be restarted. If the status of all processes could be saved at the point of failure, the rollforward operation continues up to the point of failure.

Residual dumping has no impact on a rollback operation. Beforeimages are utilized in the normal way to effect recovery. Residual dump records are ignored.

Rather than lock out concurrent update processes while residual dumping takes place, a residual dump can be undertaken as a background activity. Thus, residual dumping takes place over an interval while concurrent update processes are running. Again, a rollback operation is no different. However, what now constitutes the backup interval for a rollforward operation? Consider Figure 14-16. If the first residual dump extends over time period R_1 to S_1, when the second residual dump commences at R_2, should records not changed since R_1 or S_1 be logged? Both strategies are viable. With strategy 1, if records older than S_1 are logged, the backup interval is from S_1 to S_2. With strategy 2, if records older than R_1 are logged, the backup interval is from R_1 to S_2. Note that for strategy 2 the backup interval is longer but fewer records are dumped. With strategy 1 a record that has not been updated between the two residual dumps still will be dumped again during the second residual dump, thereby resulting in duplicate backup. With strategy 2 a record that has not been updated between residual dumps will not be dumped again during the second residual dump. Thus, inactive records will be dumped every alternate residual dump. Again, the frequency of dumping is related inversely to recovery time.

If residual dumping occurs as a background operation and other processes are not excluded from updating the database, it is critical that checkpoints of all programs be taken at the end of a residual dump. If a rollforward operation is required and checkpoints cannot be taken when the database is damaged, it may be impossible to recover. There is no synchronization point for the database and the processes operating on the database. If checkpoints of programs cannot be taken at the time of damage, recovery involves rolling forward to the end of the last residual dump and reestablishing the status of programs in progress at that point in time. Transactions then must be reprocessed up to the time of failure.

Everest [1976] discusses five advantages of a residual dump strategy compared with a traditional dump and log strategy. First, concurrent update processes are not excluded from the database during residual dumping. For large databases that take several days to dump, residual dumping may be the only feasible backup strategy. Second, residual dumping results in less duplicate backup, since a record will be logged only once unless it has been updated more than once. Third, residual dumping offers greater flexibility in leveling system workloads. Residual dumping can take place as a background operation and be assigned a low priority. Further, the time and period of residual dumping can be varied. Fourth, residual dumping simplifies the recovery process, since only a single log file is needed. A dump file is not needed. Fifth, if residual dumping occurs on a logical basis, reorganization of the database can occur without having to take physical dumps before and after the reorganization.

Differential Files

Severance and Lohman [1976] have suggested using a differential file technique to facilitate backup and recovery operations. A differential file is a file of changes made to the database. Rather than apply the changes to the database,

FIGURE 14-17
Differential file technique for backup and recovery.

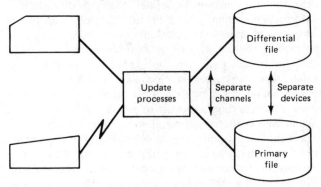

the database is left intact and updates are stored on a differential file. Access times increase but update costs decrease as changes to records (treated as new record additions) do not have to be written back onto the master file. The differential file is stored on a separate device and channel so that instruction overlap occurs to the maximum extent possible and access times are minimized (Figure 14-17). In due course as the size of the differential file grows, the changes are applied to the database because the overheads of maintaining and accessing the file become excessive. There are several advantages of a differential file, some of which relate to backup and recovery:

Advantage	Explanation
Reduces database dumping costs	Since the primary file remains unchanged, only the differential file need be dumped.
Facilitates incremental dumping	If additions to the differential file can be allocated sequential addresses on secondary memory and still be accessed (e.g., via an index or hashing algorithm), only the physical section of the device containing these changes to the differential file need be dumped for backup.
Permits realtime dumping and reorganization with concurrent updates	By building a differential-differential file (i.e., a second differential file), dumping the first differential file, or reorganization of the primary file and first differential file, can occur concurrently with update. The differential-differential file can be held in main memory if the time for dumping is short.
Facilitates rollback	The primary file constitutes beforeimage versions of updated records.
Facilitates rollforward	More frequent dumping can be undertaken since it is inexpensive to dump a differential file.
Reduces the risk of serious data loss	The small critical area of the differential file can be stored on a highly reliable device or duplexed.

SUMMARY

The database subsystem provides functions to define, create, modify, delete, and read data in an information system. Several major types of controls are implemented in the subsystem to improve the reliability of components used in the subsystem and to protect the integrity of data stored in the database. Access controls regulate the actions taken on data items based on data item names, the content of data items, the context in which data items are accessed, and the history of previous actions taken on data items. Application programs should use certain update and reporting protocols to prevent and detect data integrity violations. When data is shared among multiple users, concurrency controls must exist to prevent inconsistent updating or reading of the database. Cryptographic controls can be used to preserve the privacy of data in the database. File handling controls reduce the likelihood of accidental erasure of data. Audit trail controls maintain a chronology of all events that occur in the subsystem. Finally, existence controls must be implemented to restore the database in the event of loss. Of all subsystems, the most complex existence controls are implemented in the database subsystem.

REVIEW QUESTIONS

14-1 Briefly describe the difference between declarative data and procedural data. What type of data is maintained in a knowledge base?

14-2 Outline some of the changes that have been occurring to the components that perform the functions needed in the database subsystem.

14-3 What is a security policy? Distinguish between the following security policies:

  a Name-dependent access control

  b Content-dependent access control

  c Context-dependent access control

  d History-dependent access control

14-4 Which type of security policy is the most difficult to enforce? Why? How does the level of granularity affect the complexity associated with implementing a security policy?

14-5 What are the advantages of having an access control mechanism implemented in a single component? What are the disadvantages? In practice, why is the access control mechanism for the database subsystem often separated from other access control mechanisms?

14-6 Briefly distinguish between a replicated and a partitioned database. How does replication or partitioning of the database affect the implementation of the access control mechanism in the database subsystem?

14-7 How is it possible for a master file to get out of sequence? If a transaction file is sorted prior to a master file update, why is it necessary to check the sequence of this transaction file in the master file update program?

14-8 What types of errors in the database subsystem are avoided by careful design and implementation of end-of-file protocols?

14-9 The record type for an accounts receivable transaction file is four characters long. Give transaction codes for debtors master file record insertions, deletions, modifications (e.g., address changes), and monetary transaction updates so the transactions will sort in the correct order for master file updating.

14-10 Monetary transactions that mismatch the master file accounts should be posted to a suspense account and an error file. Describe how the suspense account should be cleared.

14-11 What is standing data? Why is standing data often critical in an application system? Describe a control often used to help maintain the integrity of updates to standing data.

14-12 What types of errors or irregularities in the database subsystem would be identified by run-to-run control totals?

14-13 Besides posting transaction mismatches to a suspense account, a suspense account report should also be printed. Why?

14-14 Briefly describe the data integrity problems that can be caused by concurrent update processes. Why might a read-only process want to exclude a concurrent update process?

14-15 How can lockout lead to deadlock? What problems can arise if preemption is used to break deadlock without rolling back the preempted processes?

14-16 Briefly describe the necessary and sufficient conditions for deadlock and the nature, advantages, and disadvantages of the strategies that can be used to prevent deadlock.

14-17 Briefly describe the nature of two-phase locking. If two-phase locking is used to prevent a deadlock situation, what properties must the transactions have if two-phase locking is to be successful?

14-18 Briefly distinguish between the growing phase and the shrinking phase in a two-phase locking strategy.

14-19 Briefly describe *three* strategies that can be used to implement concurrency controls in a distributed database subsystem.

14-20 What problems arise when cryptography is used as a control in a shared database environment? How can these problems be overcome, at least to some extent, using a hierarchy of cryptographic keys?

14-21 Briefly describe the nature of file handling controls. What control objectives are accomplished using:
  a Internal file label
  b Retention date
  c File protection ring
  d External file label

14-22 Distinguish between the implosion and the explosion purposes of an accounting audit trail for the database subsystem. Use an accounts payable system to illustrate your answer.

14-23 After a transaction has updated a data item in the database, why must beforeimages and afterimages be attached to these transactions prior to their storage in the audit trail for the database subsystem?

14-24 What functions must the database subsystem provide to support maintenance of the audit trail? Briefly explain why each of these functions is needed.

14-25 What types of changes to an application system pose difficulties for maintenance of the audit trail? Illustrate your answer with some specific examples.

14-26 How might a database administrator use the operations audit trail maintained for the database subsystem?

14-27 Briefly describe the types of failure that may lead to partial or entire loss of the database.

14-28 Distinguish between a rollforward and a rollback operation. For each type of operation give *two* examples of failures that would lead to the operation being undertaken.

14-29 What conditions must exist before a grandfather, father, son backup strategy can be used? Briefly discuss the advantages and disadvantages of the strategy.

14-30 The dual recording backup strategy does not allow recovery of the database from all types of failure. Briefly describe the situations where recovery cannot be accomplished.

14-31 With a dual recording strategy, explain the various methods available for "catching up" the primary copy of the database if it fails and the secondary copy must be used. Discuss the advantages and disadvantages of each strategy.

14-32 Explain the differences between logical dumping and physical dumping. What are the relative advantages and disadvantages of each method of dumping? Explain how a logical dump of a hashed (random) file would be undertaken.

14-33 Consider a file that consists of simple lists, that is, records that are chained to only one head-of-list record. If the pointer from the head-of-list record to the first record in the list is corrupted, what implications will this have for a logical dump backup strategy? What implications will it have for a physical dump backup strategy?

14-34 Why is dumping only a partial backup strategy?

14-35 Briefly describe the various types of logs that can be used for recovery purposes. Why might a combination of logging strategies be used for recovery purposes?

14-36 Discuss the tradeoffs made between more frequent dumping versus more frequent logging.

14-37 What are the differences (if any) between a grandfather, father, son backup and recovery strategy and a dump and log backup and recovery strategy?

14-38 If beforeimages and afterimages are stored on a log file, apart from audit trail considerations, why might transactions still be logged?

14-39 Briefly describe the various methods of reprocessing transactions for recovery purposes. Outline the problems that arise when data is shared and multiple processes concurrently update the database.

14-40 Explain why it is important to preserve the time series of transactions when recovering the database rather than to sort the transactions into an order that speeds recovery.

14-41 When logging input transactions, why it is necessary to distinguish between transactions that have been processed successfully and those that are in error? If this distinction is not made, during the recovery process, what actions must be taken?

14-42 Briefly explain the process of rolling back the database using beforeimages of the records in the database. Why is it necessary to take beforeimages of records in a list file that are moved because of a physical reorganization to the file?

14-43 Discuss the various situations that complicate a rollback recovery operation and make recovering the integrity of the database difficult, if not impossible. What actions can be taken to restore the integrity of the database in these situations?

14-44 Explain the problems of using afterimages to roll back the database. Why might a decision have been made not to log beforeimages, even though the problems of rolling back the database were recognized at the outset?

14-45 Briefly explain the rationale behind logging change parameters rather than beforeimages and afterimages.

14-46 Briefly explain the residual dumping backup and recovery strategy. Is it necessary to log both beforeimages and afterimages of records changed using a residual dumping strategy?

14-47 Explain how rollforward and rollback operations are accomplished using residual dumping.

14-48 If residual dumping occurs as a concurrent process with update processes, why is it necessary to periodically take checkpoints of the status of processes in operation?

14-49 What would the backup period be if residual dumping occurs on a continuous basis; that is, a new residual dump starts immediately on completion of the current residual dump?

14-50 If the database is recovered from a residual dump using a rollforward operation, what date of last change should be given to the records in the database? Discuss what will happen when the first residual dump is taken after the recovery.

14-51 Briefly explain the concept of a differential file. What advantages does a differential file have for backup and recovery purposes?

MULTIPLE CHOICE QUESTIONS

14-1 If a personnel clerk is not permitted to access the names of employees whose salaries exceed $30,000 unless they are seeking to perform some type of statistical function on the salary data items, this is an example of:
  a Content-dependent access control
  b History-dependent access control
  c Context-dependent access control
  d Name-dependent access control

14-2 Which security policy is the most difficult to enforce:
  a Name-dependent access control
  b Context-dependent access control
  c Content-dependent access control
  d History-dependent access control

14-3 When comparing the access rules to be enforced over data resources with the access rules to be enforced over other resources within a computer system, which of the following is false:
  a More objects must be protected in the database subsystem
  b A separate kernel needs to be established for the database subsystem
  c Data objects usually have a longer life than other computing resources
  d Finer levels of granularity must be permitted with data objects

14-4 Incorrect end-of-file protocols tend to result in:
  a Transaction file records not being processed
  b Standing data being corrupted
  c Programs getting into loops
  d The incorrect internal label being inserted into the header record on a file

14-5 Master file record changes should be processed before updates to:
  a Ensure execution times are efficient
  b Prevent changes from being dropped from the transaction file
  c Ensure updates are based on the latest information
  d Ensure the order of the master file is preserved

14-6 A suspense account should exist to:
  a Act as a repository for monetary transactions that mismatch the master file
  b Allow postings if a forward invoicing facility is provided for customers
  c Signal when end-of-period processing can be carried out
  d Store the control total for the monetary value of the master file

14-7 Which of the following is an example of standing data:
  a Raw material issues
  b A pay rate
  c Name and address data items
  d A quantity sold

14-8 Which of the following is *not* a condition for deadlock to arise:
  a Additional request
  b Circular wait
  c Lockout
  d Preemption

14-9 If an external party orders processes that use the same resources so they do not run concurrently, this strategy for preventing deadlock is called:
  a Preordering

b Presequencing

c Preemption

d Preclaiming

14-10 Using a preemption strategy to break deadlock is not always a satisfactory solution because:

    a The database may be in an inconsistent state

    b No basis exists for determining which process will be preempted

    c The strategy will not work when three or more processes reach a deadlock situation

    d The rollback caused may itself produce a deadlock situation

14-11 Which of the following properties of a transaction is *not* required for a two-phase locking strategy to work:

    a Isolation

    b Atomicity

    c Consistency

    d Temporality

14-12 Which of the following is most likely to cause localized damage to the database:

    a Application program logic error

    b Error in the access routines of the database management system

    c Fire in the computer room that occurs around midmorning

    d Operator procedural error whereby the database is loaded as a scratch file

14-13 In a grandfather, father, son backup strategy, the son is kept:

    a For another two update cycles

    b For the same number of cycles as the transaction file

    c For another three update cycles

    d Until transactions have been written to an archival file

14-14 Which of the following is *not* a disadvantage of the grandfather, father, son backup and recovery strategy:

    a Precludes update in place

    b Consumes substantial resources to effect global recovery

    c File is unavailable during recovery

    d Cannot be used where concurrent processes update the file

14-15 Dual protection affords protection against:

    a A procedural error

    b A system software error

    c An application program error

    d A power loss

14-16 Relative to physical dumping, logical dumping:

    a Is a faster backup strategy

    b Is slower when localized recovery is needed

    c Causes fewer problems with multilist file organizations

    d Is more appropriate when concurrent update of the database is permitted

14-17 Which of the following is *not* a purpose of logging:

    a To obviate the need for a dump

    b To provide a record of transactions in the time sequence in which they occurred

    c To reduce the downtime needed for resubmission of the transactions

    d To facilitate both rolling forward and rolling back the database

14-18 Which logging strategy facilitates rollforward of the database:

     a Logging input transactions
     b Logging beforeimages
     c Logging valid transactions only
     d Logging afterimages

14-19 A purpose of separating successful input transactions from unsuccessful input transactions on a log is to:
     a Avoid control total problems when the data must be reprocessed for recovery
     b Avoid duplicate error messages that might cause confusion as recovery occurs
     c Facilitate preserving the time sequence of the successful transactions only
     d Allow both a rollforward and a rollback operation to occur

14-20 If beforeimages are used to roll forward the database, the database is recovered up to the point where:
     a All input transactions have been processed
     b The last transaction for all records changed since the last dump has not been processed
     c The last transaction for the last record changed prior to failure has not been processed
     d The last transaction for all records in the database has not been processed

14-21 Which of the following is *not* a problem when rollback is needed as a means of recovery and concurrent update processes have altered the damaged database:
     a All processes that update the corrupted data items must be identified so they can be locked out when an error is discovered
     b It is difficult to determine the consequences of error so the effects of the damage can be undone
     c Rollback may be pointless if too many other processes have accessed the data in error before the error has been discovered
     d Rollback cannot be accomplished if afterimages have been damaged

14-22 Relative to logging afterimages, logging change parameters:
     a Permits faster recovery
     b Causes less processing overheads
     c Consumes less storage space
     d Reduces the problems caused by multilist files

14-23 Residual dumping involves logging records that have not been changed since the:
     a second-last residual dump
     b last full dump
     c last residual dump
     d second-last full dump

14-24 If a rollforward operation takes place using a residual dump, recovery involves:
     a Going back to but not including the second-last residual dump
     b Going back to and including the last residual dump
     c Going back to the last full dump since a residual dump does not facilitate rollforward
     d Going back to but not including the last residual dump

14-25 The purpose of taking a checkpoint, if possible, when a system crashes is to:
     a Avoid having to use a log for recovery
     b Enable processes to be restarted when recovery has been effected
     c Know where on the log the rollback operation must commence
     d Clear the program buffers of all records contained in the buffers

14-26 Which of the following is a disadvantage of residual dumping:
a There is less flexibility in leveling system workloads
b There is more duplicate backup
c It cannot take place as a background operation
d Recovery is more complex than with a physical dump

14-27 A differential file facilitates rollback because:
a The primary file constitutes beforeimage versions of the updated records
b Record changes and beforeimages can be assigned to a high-speed storage device
c The differential file constitutes beforeimage versions of the updated records
d It is easier to identify which users of the database have been affected by the corrupted records

EXERCISES AND CASES

14-1 The dollar control totals for a master file update run are correct for the input transaction file and the input master file; however, the output master file control total is incorrect. List the possible reasons why the control total may be incorrect. Further, explain how you would check to see whether the reasons you advance are the cause of the error. Since your time as an auditor is a scarce resource, you also should list the reasons according to their probability of being the cause of the error.

14-2 As the manager of internal audit for Streaker Products, a manufacturer of running shoes and related athletic goods, you are called one day to a meeting with the controller, the data processing manager, and the accounts branch manager. The data processing manager is furious. He explains that the accounts receivable master file update program has been dropping records from the master file progressively over the last six months. The error has only just been discovered. He complains that reconstructing the master file is going to be costly; furthermore, the company has lost revenue because the accounts receivable records have been lost. He is upset because the accounts branch has failed to check the control totals reported by the program. If this had occurred, the error would have been discovered earlier.

The accounts branch manager is equally upset. She complains that her branch is understaffed and her clerks have had little time to check anything. Furthermore, she argues that the error occurred because a change to the update program was not tested properly. This is the data processing manager's fault, not hers!

Required: The controller asks you to write a brief report for her explaining:
a How the master file might be reconstructed
b How the revenue lost from failure to bill customers might be recovered
c How this event can be prevented in the future

14-3 Pieces and Parts, Ltd., is a diversified manufacturing company based in New York. However, it has manufacturing facilities throughout the country. The company is contemplating changing its centralized data processing operations to distributed data processing operations. The plants will operate more effectively and efficiently if each has its own data processing facilities.

A major question to be answered if the company uses distributed processing is whether or not the company's database should be partitioned and the different partitions allocated to the plants most likely to use them, or whether or not replicated copies of the entire database should be sent periodically to each plant.

Required: As the head of the internal audit department, management has asked you to identify the advantages and disadvantages of partitioning versus replicating the database from the viewpoint of ensuring accurate and complete processing of data.

14-4 The unique code for a ledger account is 6/35/321, where:

6 = division number
35 = department number
321 = expenditure item

Suppose a major reorganization occurs and department 35 is assigned to division 2. Thus, the ledger account code now is 2/35/321. Because of the nature of the data, an audit trail of transactions operating on the ledger account must be kept for six years. During that time it is possible clerks and internal auditors may access the audit trail.

Required: Briefly describe two ways of alerting users of the audit trail to the change that has occurred if they retrieve data that spans the change. List the advantages and disadvantages of each method you propose.

14-5 You are an internal auditor participating in the design phase of a new online accounts receivable system. Customer accounts will be updated automatically with data captured using point-of-sale devices. The customer service department will have terminals to create new accounts, debit customer accounts, inquire as to the status of accounts, and make alterations to adjust any errors identified in accounts.

When you receive the design of the audit trail, you notice that the system designer has not provided for storing before- and afterimages of the account balance with transaction records. When you ask him about this omission, he explains that he has made this choice to save storage space, since the manager of data processing has expressed concerns about the effects on the availability of mass storage that the system will have.

You explain to the designer that the customer service department will need to know the status of an account balance at various points in time to answer customer queries. He answers that all transactions for an account are chained to the account, and that obtaining an account balance is simply a matter of adding up all transactions after the transaction that is subject to the inquiry and subtracting this amount from the current account balance. He explains that this algorithm will be in the retrieval program.

Required: Evaluate the designer's answer from an audit viewpoint. Can you think of any reasons why before- and afterimages still should be stored with the transaction in spite of the storage constraint problem?

14-6 Feetfirst Inc. is a major manufacturer of boots and shoes. It has diverse types of data processing systems including straightforward batch systems, online realtime update systems, and some application systems (some of which are also online realtime update) that use a database management system. The company does not use telecommunications; all terminals are located at the head office.

The internal audit manager is concerned that an audit has never been conducted to evaluate the adequacy of the company's backup and recovery procedures. As a member of the internal audit staff, he asks you to prepare an audit plan so an evaluation can be undertaken.

Required: Outline an audit plan for evaluating Feetfirst's backup and recovery operations. Your plan should include: (*a*) a statement of audit objectives, (*b*) an outline of compliance testing procedures, (*c*) an outline of substantive testing procedures.

14-7 You are the head of a consulting firm that specializes in EDP audit and control. One day you are approached by a representative of the shareholder group of an organization that has recently gone bankrupt. The reason for the bankruptcy was a fire that destroyed the organization's data processing installation. The backup and recovery procedures for the installation were inadequate; consequently, the organization could not reestablish its critical data files. The representative explains that the shareholders are contemplating legal action against the external auditors of the organization. The shareholders feel that it was the responsibility of the external audit firm to identify the inadequacy of backup and recovery. The shareholders are concerned, however, that the external audit firm has made it clear that the evaluation of backup and recovery procedures was not necessary to assess the adequacy of the financial statements and, as such, was not the responsibility of the external auditor. Thus, the shareholders seek your advice on the wisdom of pursuing legal action.

Required: Write a brief report for the shareholders advising them on the course of action they should take and whether or not their lawsuit is likely to be successful.

14-8 The Convict Savings Bank is a large bank based in Sydney with branches scattered throughout Australia. The bank uses an online realtime update system for its customer accounts system. The branches are connected via a telecommunications network to a centralized database in the head office. The bank uses a database management system for its database.

As a member of the external audit firm of the bank, you are reviewing the adequacy of backup and recovery procedures for the online realtime update system. During an interview with the database administrator, she explains to you that when a system crash occurs, the computer operators attempt to restart the system immediately because downtime is intolerable with the system. Since the database management system used by the bank establishes relationships between entities via pointers, you express your concern to her about the possibility of pointers in the database not having been updated (that is, an update is in progress) when the crash occurs and the database being in an inconsistent state. The database administrator concedes this point. Nevertheless, she argues that it is a relatively minor problem. When the system is restarted, tellers are supposed to check whether the last transaction they submitted was posted. If it was not posted, they resubmit the transaction. An inquiry transaction also will identify inconsistent or corrupted pointers. If the database is in an inconsistent state, since it is unlikely another transaction will occur for the customer's account during that day, backup and recovery is left until the night shift.

Required: Write a brief report for your manager commenting on the adequacy of backup and recovery procedures for the online system. Make any suggestions that you feel would improve the adequacy of backup and recovery procedures for the system.

14-9 Bits-and-Pieces Inc. is a parts retailing firm that has an online realtime update system for its sales system. Clerical staff enter sales transactions and the customer accounts file and parts inventory file are updated immediately.

As the manager of internal audit for Bits-and-Pieces, one day you are called to a meeting with the controller and data processing manager. The controller explains that during the previous day a system crash occurred at 3 p.m. Recovery was started immediately; however, during the recovery process, for the first time ever, a log tape error was encountered. The result was that transactions up to 11 a.m. only could be recovered. Clerical staff were asked to resubmit their transactions from 11 a.m. onward. Unfortunately, new transactions (those that occurred after 3 p.m.) also were submitted because the downtime required for resubmission of old transactions was intolerable. As a consequence, new transactions depleted some stock items to a zero balance before old sales transactions on those stock items were reposted. Thus, sales had been made of inventory where stockouts existed.

Required: The controller is concerned about the loss of customer goodwill that may occur. At this time the cause of the log tape error is unknown. However, he asks you to prepare a brief report outlining your thoughts on how a similar disaster might be prevented in the future. Of course, a log tape error is always possible, though it is usually a rare occurrence.

ANSWERS TO MULTIPLE CHOICE QUESTIONS

14-1 c	14-8 d	14-15 d	14-22 c
14-2 d	14-9 b	14-16 c	14-23 c
14-3 b	14-10 a	14-17 a	14-24 a
14-4 a	14-11 d	14-18 d	14-25 b
14-5 c	14-12 a	14-19 b	14-26 d
14-6 a	14-13 c	14-20 b	14-27 a
14-7 b	14-14 b	14-21 d	

REFERENCES

Bernstein, Philip A., and Nathan Goodman. "Concurrency Control in Distributed Database Systems," *Computing Surveys* (June 1981), pp. 185–221.

Bjork, L. A., Jr. "Generalized Audit Trail Requirements and Concepts for Data Base Applications," *IBM Systems Journal,* vol. 14, no. 3, 1975, pp. 229–245.

Canning, Richard G. "Recovery in Data Base Systems," *EDP Analyzer* (November 1976), pp. 1–11.

Chandy, K. Mani, and Charles H. Sauer. "Approximate Methods for Analyzing Queueing Network Models of Computing systems," *Computing Surveys* (September 1978), pp. 281–317.

Davies, D. W., and W. L. Price. *Security for Computer Networks* (New York: Wiley, 1984).

Delobel, C., and W. Litwin, eds. *Distributed Data Bases* (Amsterdam: North-Holland, 1980).

Drake R. W., and J. L. Smith. "Some Techniques for File Recovery," *The Australian Computer Journal* (November 1971), pp. 162–170.

Durchholz, Reiner, and Hart J. Will. "The Impact of Data Base Management Systems (DBMS) Standardization on Auditing," *Computers & Standards,* vol. 1, 1982, pp. 49–59.

Dwyer, Barry. "One More Time—How to Update a Master File," *Communications of the ACM* (January 1981), pp. 3–8.

Everest, Gordon C. "Concurrent Update Control and Database Integrity," in J. W. Klimbie and K. L. Koffeman, eds., *Data Base Management* (Amsterdam: North-Holland, 1974), pp. 241–270.

Everest, Gordon C. "Residual Dump Backup Strategy for Large Databases," Working Paper MISRC-WP-76-04, Management Information Systems Research Center, University of Minnesota, Minneapolis, MN, 1976.

Everest, Gordon C. *Database Management: Objectives, System Functions, and Administration* (New York: McGraw-Hill, 1985).

Fernandez, Eduardo B., Rita C. Summers, and Christopher Wood. *Database Security and Integrity* (Reading, MA: Addison-Wesley, 1981).

Fikes, Richard, and Tom Kehler. "The Role of Frame-Based Representation in Reasoning," *Communications of the ACM* (September 1985), pp. 904–920.

Fossum, Barbara M. "Database Integrity as Provided for by a Particular Data Base Management System," in J. W. Klimbie and K. L. Koffeman, eds., *Data Base Management* (Amsterdam: North-Holland, 1974), pp. 271–288.

Gal, Graham, and William E. McCarthy. "Specification of Internal Accounting Controls in a Database Environment," *Computers and Security,* vol. 4, 1985, pp. 23–32.

Gauss, Edward J. "Built-In Checklist Reduces File Destruction," *Communications of the ACM* (February 1981), p. 73.

Genesereth, Michael R., and Matthew L. Ginsberg. "Logic Programming," *Communications of the ACM* (September 1985), pp. 933–941.

Greenwald, Bruce M., and Gary Oberlander. "IRS Audits of EDP Systems," *Management Accounting* (April 1975), pp. 13–15.

Haerder, Theo, and Andreas Reuter. "Principles of Transaction-Oriented Database Recovery," *Computing Surveys* (December 1983), pp. 287–317.

Hayes-Roth, Frederick. "Rule-Based Systems," *Communications of the ACM* (September 1985), pp. 921–932.

Hinxman, Anthony I. "Updating a Database in an Unsafe Environment," *Communications of the ACM* (June 1984), pp. 564–566.

Inglis, J. "Updating a Master File—Yet One More Time," *Communications of the ACM* (May 1981), p. 299.

Kim, Won. "Highly Available Systems for Database Applications," *Computing Surveys* (March 1984), pp. 71–98.

Kohler, Walter H. "A Survey of Techniques for Synchronization and Recovery in Decentralized Computer Systems," *Computing Surveys* (June 1981), pp. 149–183.

Le Gore, Laurence B. "Smoothing Data Base Recovery," *Datamation* (January 1979), pp. 170–180.

McGee, W. C. "The Information Management System IMS/VS Part V: Transaction Processing Facilities," *IBM Systems Journal* (April 1977), pp. 148–168.

McHugh, Arthur J. "EDP and the Audit Function," *Accounting Education* (November 1978), pp. 34–54.

Meyer, Carl H., and Stephen M. Matyas. *Cryptography: A New Dimension in Computer Data Security* (New York: Wiley, 1982).

Munz, R., and G. Krenz. "Concurrency in Database Systems—A Simulation Study," in D. C. P. Smith, ed., *Proceedings of the SIGMOD International Conference on Management of Data* (New York: Association for Computing Machinery, 1977), pp. 111–120.

Oldehoeft, Arthur E., and McDonald, Robert. "A Software Scheme for User-Controlled File Encryption," *Computers and Security,* vol. 3, 1984, pp. 35–41.

Sayani, Hasan H. "Restart and Recovery in a Transaction-Oriented Information Processing System," in Randall Rustin, ed., *ACM SIGMOD Workshop on Data Description, Access and Control* (New York: Association for Computing Machinery, 1974), pp. 351–366.

Severance, Dennis G., and Guy M. Lohman. "Differential Files: Their Application to the Maintenance of Large Databases," *ACM Transactions on Database Systems* (September 1976), pp. 256–267.

Sockut, Gary H., and Robert P. Goldberg. "Database Reorganization—Principles and Practice," *Computing Surveys* (December 1979), pp. 371–395.

Verhofstad, J. S. M. "Recovery Techniques for Database Systems," *Computing Surveys* (June 1978), pp. 167–195.

Weber, Ron. "Audit Trail System Support in Advanced Computer-Based Accounting Systems," *The Accounting Review* (April 1982), pp. 311–325.

CHAPTER **15**

OUTPUT CONTROLS

CHAPTER OUTLINE

The output subsystem provides functions that determine the content of data that will be provided to users, the ways in which data will be formatted and presented to users, and the ways in which data will be prepared for and routed to users. The major components of the output system are the software that determines the content, format, and timeliness of data to be provided to users, the various hardware devices used to present the formatted output data to users (e.g., printers, terminals, plotters, voice synthesizers), and the hardware, software, and personnel that route the output to users.

This chapter examines controls in the output subsystem. First, it discusses how inference controls can be used to filter the output that users are permitted to see. Next, it describes various formatting and presentation controls that can be implemented to improve the effectiveness and efficiency of output production and use. Controls over the preparation and distribution of output are then examined. Finally, the audit trail and existence controls that should be implemented in the output subsystem are described.

INFERENCE CONTROLS

The access control models examined in previous chapters have permitted or denied access to a data item based on the name of the data item, the content of the data item, or some characteristic of the query or time series of queries made on the data item (see, for example, Chapter 14). In some cases, however, it may be desirable to grant access to a data item but to restrict the type of information that can be derived from accessing the data item. This situation arises especially with statistical databases. Sensitive and confidential data items, such as medical history data items, are maintained in the database. Furthermore, access to each data item is needed to provide statistical summaries of the information contained in the database. However, it must not be possible for anyone to deduce information about specific data item values on the basis of a query. Otherwise, the organization that owns the database may be sued by the individuals who supplied the specific data item values in confidence.

Inference controls over statistical databases seek to prevent *four* types of compromise that can occur: (*a*) positive compromise—the user determines the value of a particular data item; (*b*) negative compromise—the user determines that a data item does *not* have a particular value; (*c*) exact compromise—the precise value of a data item can be determined; and (*d*) approximate compromise—the data item value cannot be determined precisely but it can be determined with sufficient precision to violate the privacy of data. The following sections provide an introduction to two major types of inference controls used to prevent these compromises from occurring: (*a*) restriction controls and (*b*) perturbation controls. Denning and Schlörer [1983] provide a more detailed discussion of these two types of controls and their strengths and limitations.

Restriction Controls

To illustrate the nature of restriction controls, consider the simple database shown in Figure 15-1. Assume that the salary information of individual

Name	Sex	Position	Salary
Brown	M	Manager	35,000
Charles	F	Manager	35,000
East	M	Secretary	16,000
Gordon	M	Clerk	17,000
Harris	M	Consultant	29,000
Jones	F	Consultant	31,000
Long	F	Secretary	15,000
Martin	M	Consultant	32,000
Proud	F	Clerk	18,000
Reid	F	Manager	34,000

FIGURE 15-1
Payroll database where salary is confidential.

employees in the database is considered to be confidential yet statistical analysis of salary information is to be allowed. Furthermore, assume the query language that operates on the database allows the full range of Boolean operators to be used (and, or, not) and it provides an extensive set of statistical functions (count, sum, average, standard deviation, skewness, etc.).

In the absence of inference controls, compromise is easy. The following queries determine the salary of Jones:

Question: How many employees are female and a consultant?
Answer: 1.
Question: What is the average salary of all people who are a female and a consultant?
Answer: $31,000.

Since Jones is the only person in the database who is a female and a consultant, determining her salary is straightforward.

A simple restriction control might be used in an attempt to prevent the compromise. For example, assume that the following rule is enforced by the output subsystem: Do not respond to a query if fewer than k records satisfy the query. Suppose that $k = 2$. The set of queries used above to determine the salary of Jones now would not be satisfied by the output subsystem.

Unfortunately, even with this restriction, compromise of the database is still easy. Consider the following queries:

Question: How many people are consultants or *not* consultants?
Answer: 10.
Question: How many people are *not* (female and a consultant)?

Answer: 9.

Question: What is the total salary paid for all people who are consultants or *not* consultants?

Answer: $262,000.

Question: What is the total salary paid for all people who are *not* (female and a consultant)?

Answer: $231,000.

The salary of Jones can now be determined by subtracting $231,000 from $262,000. Clearly, the restriction imposed upon the query set size is inadequate as a means of preventing compromise of the database.

To counteract this compromise, a further restriction might be imposed upon the query set size. Suppose the following rule is enforced by the output subsystem: Do not respond to a query if greater than $n - k$ records satisfy the query. The set of queries used above now would not be satisfied by the output subsystem.

Unfortunately, this restriction is still inadequate as a means of preventing compromise of the database. Using a technique called the "tracker," Jones' salary can still be determined. Assuming that $k = 2$, consider the following set of queries:

Question: How many people are consultants?

Answer: 3.

Question: How many people are males and consultants?

Answer: 2.

Question: What is the total salary paid for all people who are consultants?

Answer: $92,000.

Question: What is the total salary paid for all people who are male and consultants?

Answer: $61,000.

Again, Jones' salary can easily be determined by subtracting $61,000 from $92,000. Thus, the two restrictions imposed upon the query set size are still inadequate as a means of preserving the integrity of the database.

The basic idea behind a tracker is to pad the original query with a set of auxiliary attributes so the restrictions on query set size can be circumvented. By eliminating the effects of the auxiliary attributes from the answer, the result for the original query can then be determined. Formally, the tracker can be represented as follows (see Schlörer [1975]). Let F be a *characteristic formula* defined over the database. Informally, F can be considered to be any logical query expressed as a combination of data item names and Boolean operators. Suppose, now, that someone undertaking interrogations on the database knows that a person P can be uniquely characterized by the formula F. Suppose, further, that F can be decomposed into two other formulas, $F1$ and $F2$, such that $F = F1 \land F2$. The *individual tracker, T,* of person P can now be

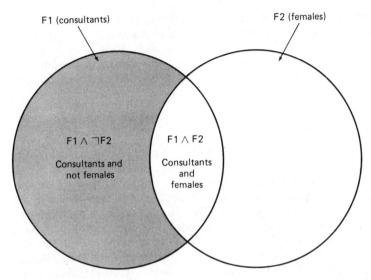

FIGURE 15-2
Venn diagram for a tracker.

represented by the formula $F1 \wedge \neg F2$. The database can be compromised using the following formula:

$$\text{Count}(F) = \text{count}(F1) - \text{count}(F1 \wedge \neg F2)$$

provided that the query set size restrictions are not violated—that is:

$$k \leq \text{count}(F1 \wedge \neg F2) \leq \text{count}(F1) \leq n - k$$

To illustrate how the tracker works, consider the Venn diagram shown in Figure 15-2. The set $F1$ comprises all individuals who are consultants. The set $F2$ comprises all individuals who are females. The intersection of the sets $F1$ and $F2$ comprise the individuals who are consultants and females. In this case it is known that this set comprises only one individual, namely, Jones. Thus, the set $(F1 \wedge \neg F2)$, the shaded area in Figure 15-2, identifies the individuals who are consultants and males. By subtracting the set of consultants who are males from the set of all consultants, the set of consultants who are females can be identified. In other words, the record for Jones can be selected. Note that since the set of consultants who are males comprises two individuals and the set of all consultants comprises three individuals, the query set size restrictions are not violated.

The problem with individual trackers is that a new tracker must be found for each individual in the database. However, Schlörer [1975] has shown that a *general tracker* can be constructed that will work for anyone in the database. Moreover, in one medical database he discovered that 98 percent of the records could be identified using no more than 10 attributes. Thus, trackers can often be constructed fairly quickly, and as a result query set size restrictions provide only limited protection against database compromise. Other more powerful, but less efficient, restriction controls must be used in conjunction with limits on the query set size if database compromise is to be prevented (see, further, Denning and Schlörer [1983]).

Perturbation Controls

Perturbation controls introduce some type of noise into the statistics calculated on the basis of records retrieved from the database. Compared with restriction controls, they seek to allow more statistics to be calculated on the database. However, they result in an information loss associated with the variance of the perturbed statistic around the true value. This information loss is manifested as bias or inconsistency in the results obtained. Bias refers to the difference between the average value of the perturbed statistic and the value of the true statistic. It should be zero or a small value. Inconsistencies arise when different statistics contradict each other or some type of nonsense value is returned as a result of the query. For example, the value obtained from row addition of a table may not equal the value obtained from column addition, or the query may return a real number when only integers are possible (3.62 people satisfy the query).

Perturbation controls can be exercised on either the *records* used as input to a statistical function or the *results* obtained after a statistical function has been computed (see, further, Denning and Schlörer [1983]). *Record-based* perturbation controls calculate a statistic on the basis of a random sample of records that satisfy the query, or they calculate a statistic after some type of error term has been added to the data in the records that satisfy the query. Under either scheme, the same result must be returned if a query is repeated. Otherwise, users will be faced with inconsistent results. Moreover, if the same result is not returned when a query is repeated, the database can be compromised through an *averaging attack*. If a random sample of records has been taken or the error term has been generated with a zero mean, the database user simply repeats the query a large number of times and takes the average of the results to obtain the true value (or a close approximation of the true value).

Results-based perturbation controls introduce an error term after the true statistic has been calculated; that is, the statistic is first computed on the basis of all records that satisfy the query and the result is perturbed with some error term. Results-based perturbation controls primarily differ in terms of the way in which they generate the error used to inoculate the results. For example, some systematically round the result to the nearest integer multiple of a fixed rounding base. If, say, the result is 28 and the fixed rounding base is 5, the result presented to the user would be 30. Other schemes randomly round the results to the next highest or next lowest integer multiple of a fixed rounding base. Again, the different schemes vary in terms of their abilities to protect the privacy of data, the information loss they produce, and their relative cost to operate.

PRESENTATION CONTROLS

Presentation controls govern the ways in which information is communicated to decision makers via the output subsystem. Primarily they seek to ensure that decision makers can effectively use the information provided to them. Nonetheless, they also seek to ensure that the integrity of information communicated to decision makers is preserved and that the output subsystem provides the information efficiently.

Presentation controls take two forms. First, design standards must be established to guide the choices made on how data will be presented to users. Second, a monitoring mechanism must be established to evaluate the quality of the choices made. When auditors examine the ways in which data is communicated to users in the output subsystem, they obtain evidence on how well presentation controls are functioning. Consequently, they must understand when high-quality output presentation decisions have been made by system designers.

The following sections examine *five* choices that determine how output will be communicated to users: (*a*) the choice of output content, (*b*) the choice of output medium, (*c*) the choice of output format, (*d*) the choice of output layout, and (*e*) the choice of output turnaround time or response time. To assist the auditor to evaluate how well these choices have been made in the output subsystem, some basic design guidelines are described below.

Content Controls

Choosing the content of an output report involves determining the set of data items to be presented in the report. This choice implies that certain other decisions have been made, either consciously or subconsciously, about various attributes of the data to be presented:

Content attribute	Impact on output quality
Accuracy	Output quality decreases with decreasing accuracy. Accuracy implies a known, accepted measurement scale—either a nominal, ordinal, interval, or ratio scale.
Age	Output quality decreases with increasing age. Age is a function of (a) the interval between the occurrence of an event and its measurement, and (b) the delay between measurement and the issuance of a report.
Relevance	Output quality increases with increasing relevance. Relevance is defined in terms of the decision to be made. More relevant information is more informative.

Content attribute	Impact on output quality
Summarization	Output quality depends on the adequacy of any summarization procedures used. Formal summarization procedures include computing totals and undertaking statistical inferences. Informal summarization procedures rely on subjective bases to reduce the amount of data presented to users.
Filtering	Output quality depends on the adequacy of any filtering procedures used. Filtering blocks certain data from reaching a decision maker. It can be used to reduce the information load on a decision maker. Alternatively, it can be used to hide facts from or distort facts presented to a decision maker.
Modification	Output quality depends on the adequacy of any modification procedures used. Modification distorts the meaning of a message by altering the message. Like filtering, it can be used to reduce the information load on decision makers or to hide facts from or distort facts presented to decision makers.

Output content quality requirements expressed in terms of accuracy, age, relevance, summarization, filtering, and modification vary across application systems. Improved quality usually means increased costs. Moreover, tradeoffs among the content attributes often must be made. For example, in a strategic planning system a decision maker may be willing to trade off the accuracy of information received against the age of the information.

Medium Controls

The mediums used to present output to a decision maker include paper, visual displays, voice, and microform (microfilm or microfiche). Choosing the right medium is important because it affects how easily decision makers can use output and how likely they are to make errors when they use output.

Compared with a visual display, paper output is permanent and portable; it does not disappear when the terminal is turned off, and it can be transported to any location where it is needed. In addition, if the decision task requires users to flip back and forth through a report, perhaps for cross-referencing purposes or to gain a total "picture" of the problem, printed reports often are more easily used than a visual display. Scanning a visual display report in a disjointed manner requires users to input some instruction to obtain the relevant page. Users sometimes experience a "peephole" effect; that is, they start to feel that the contents of the database can be reviewed only in very small pieces (see Lancaster and Fayen [1973]). To some extent this effect can be mitigated if the output subsystem provides a "windowing" facility; that is, it allows users to view multiple parts of the database concurrently on the one screen (Figure 15-3). Moreover, if users proceed through a report in an orderly fashion or examine several different short reports, perhaps as they work with the computer in an interactive problem-solving mode, visual displays may be

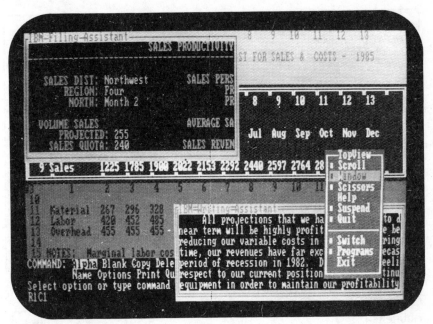

FIGURE 15-3
Windowing facility to help alleviate the "peephole" effect. (*Courtesy, International Business Machines Corporation.*)

preferred because they are faster and quieter and allow users to maintain continuity in thought.

Voice output and microform have more selective uses than paper output or visual display output. Voice output is useful when only a short, sharp response needs to be given to a decision maker and when the user's hands are otherwise occupied so they cannot handle a report or type at a terminal. For example, voice output may be used to assist workers on a production line. Microform is used to provide long-term, permanent storage for large volumes of output. For example, the audit trail for an accounting system may be stored on microfiche; a large volume of transactions can be stored compactly yet users can still access the transactions fairly easily via a microfiche reader.

Format Controls

The primary formats used to present output are tables and graphs. Choices must also be made on the type of print font and size of print font to be used and whether color or monochrome output is to be provided.

Tables classify and order data for reference purposes. Graphs indicate patterns or trends in data (Figure 15-4). In spite of the intuitive appeal that graphics seem to have for system designers, Ives [1982] points out there is little

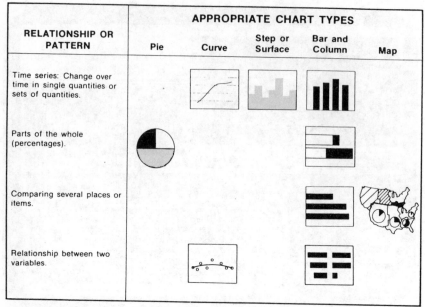

FIGURE 15-4
Choosing the appropriate graph to illustrate a pattern or trend in data. (*From Paller et al. [1980]; reproduced by permission, Integrated Software Systems Corporation.*)

empirical evidence to show that graphics increase managerial productivity or allow users to make higher-quality decisions. Indeed, poor graphics design can substantially inhibit managerial decision making.

Only a small number of type fonts should be used to present a table or graph and, in many cases, only a single type font should be used. Different forms of the type font (bold or light) can be used to highlight different levels of text. Similarly, in most cases the size of the type font should be kept constant. If variations in the size of the type font are used, they should be simple and obvious.

Like graphics, color has substantial intuitive appeal as a means of presenting output. Nonetheless, like graphics there is little empirical evidence to show that color improves managerial productivity or decision making and, like graphics, poor use of color can have an adverse effect on decision making quality (see Ives [1982]). Only a few colors should be used on any output form, and the colors chosen should be widely spaced along the visual spectrum so they are easily discriminated (see, also, Chapter 10).

Layout Controls

The layout of a report determines how much data will be placed on a page or screen and where the data will be placed. If the user simply references a report and makes a decision, if possible, all data relevant to the decision should be placed on a single page or screen. If the user is working in an interactive mode and sequentially making a series of decisions, only data relevant to a specific decision or a single idea should be displayed. Often it is worthwhile partitioning a display into several fixed areas (windows), for example, a main work area (about two lines), a diagnostic area (about one line), and a fixed response area (about four lines).

The layout of a report is a major determinant of response time performance in an online system and the costs of printed output and the turnaround time in a batch system. In an online system the response time deteriorates as more data must traverse a communication line to support output reports. In a batch system the layout of a report affects the amount of stationery that must be used, the print time, and the turnaround time. Given that many organizations spend substantial amounts on data communication services and that paper is no longer a cheap and plentiful resource, important benefits can accrue from careful report layout design.

Two layout strategies can be used to reduce output display time or print time. First, data in a report can be eliminated or compressed so fewer pages are needed for a report. Figure 15-5b shows a revised version of Figure 15-5a; it is more difficult to read but it is more efficient in terms of the display time or the printer time required. Second, in the case of printed output, the layout of a report can be changed to take advantage of the way in which printers skip lines. The greater the number of lines to be skipped, the lower the average time per line for skipping. Printers take several lines to accelerate to their maximum speed. Thus, it is more efficient to skip several lines at a time than to skip a single line. Figure 15-6a shows an accounts receivable statement with a sales message positioned to have more visual impact than the same message in Figure 15-6b; however, Figure 15-6b is more efficient in terms of print time. Preprinting data on forms also may allow the printer to skip a greater number of lines.

Layout decisions also involve choosing the ways in which data is ordered and grouped on a page or display and the ways in which data is displayed on a graph. These decisions are important because they can bias users' perceptions of the significance and meaning of the data. For example: users tend to pay more attention to the early items in a report so the most important items should appear first; users will perceive items that are grouped together to be similar even if this is not the case; the incorrect choice of a scale for a graph can hide an important trend.

Timing Controls

Output must be presented on a timely basis if it is to be used effectively by decision makers. In a batch system, users accept that there will be some delay before the output requested is received. Nevertheless, they have a perception of what is a reasonable delay. Variations outside reasonable bounds may result in their losing track of the decision to be made.

```
EQUIPMENT UTILIZATION REPORT    MONTH    APRIL    PAGE 36 of 94

EQUIPMENT NO.    765A
DESCRIPTION:     BULLDOZER 124 HP
```

JOB NO	HOURLY RATE	HRS WORKED	DATE	DOLLAR CHARGE	TOTAL CHARGE
113	35.00	3	0401	105.00	
113	35.00	2	0404	70.00	
113	35.00	4	0405	140.00	315.00
261	35.00	4	0402	140.00	
261	35.00	1	0404	35.00	
261	35.00	1	0405	35.00	
261	35.00	5	0408	175.00	385.00
═══					
421	35.00	5	0415	175.00	455.00
			EQUIPMENT TOTAL		4065.00

FIGURE 15-5a
Equipment utilization report with high readability.

```
EQUIPMENT UTILIZATION REPORT    MONTH    APRIL    PAGE 36 of 94

EQUIPMENT NO.  765A   DESCRIPTION: BULLDOZER 124 HP   HOURLY RATE   35.00
```

JOB NO	HRS WORKED	DATE	$ CHARGE	TOTAL
113	3	0401	105.00	
113	2	0404	70.00	
113	4	0405	140.00	315.00
261	4	0402	140.00	
261	1	0404	35.00	
261	1	0405	35.00	
261	5	0408	175.00	385.00
══				
421	5	0415	175.00	455.00
			EQUIPMENT TOTAL	4065.00

```
EQUIPMENT NO. 9421C   DESCRIPTION: BACKHOE      HOURLY RATE 10.00

  –
  –
  –
```

FIGURE 15-5b
Equipment utilization report redesigned to improve print time.

MOONSHINE, Inc.
P.O. Box 261
HAPPYVILLE, Q. 40612.

Please change address below if incorrect	Account No.	Month Ending	Past Due	This Month	Amount Due
	49–1253	871130	61.00	201.00	201.00
Mr. H. S. Smithies		Please write in amount of payment enclosed →			
16 Uranda St.					
The Range Q. 45617					

Please pay by due date
Terms: 30 days

Detach and enclose top portion with payment

Date	Invoice No.	Details	Debit	Credit
		Opening Balance	61.00	
871102	41724	4 CASES JONATHON WHISKEY	40.00	
871104	53219	8 CASES XXXX BEER	56.00	
871115	53240	2 CASES OBLITERATION GIN	18.00	
871121	76431	2 CASES RITEOFF RUM	22.00	
871126	76478	5 CASES TORTURE TEQUILA	65.00	
871126	30872	PAYMENT – THANK YOU		61.00
		XMAS SPECIAL – 10% DISCOUNT ON BEER		
Month Ending	871130	Your Ref: Payment Made	Amount Due	201.00

FIGURE 15-6a
Accounts receivable statement with sales message positioned to achieve effect.

In an interactive system, response time performance is a major factor affecting the quality of decisions made. Sudden drops in problem-solving ability have been noted when response times exceed a given magnitude. Miller [1968] accounts for this result in terms of two psychological needs that users have when they interact with computer systems. First, humans expect a response to a communication within 2 to 4 seconds, even if the response is simply to acknowledge receipt of a message. Second, humans cluster their activities into logical groups and become frustrated if they are delayed in completing a cluster of activities. Once a cluster of activities is completed, however, psychological closure occurs and a delay in response time is more likely to be tolerated.

Response times can also be too fast. Users pick up the pace of a system, and they may feel pressured to make fast decisions to the detriment of overall problem-solving effectiveness (see, also, Shneiderman [1984]). Constancy in response times is desirable, and in some cases forced temporal spacing between responses may be needed. Some output subsystems also allow users to choose a parameter value to determine the response time that will be provided.

MOONSHINE, INC.
P.O. Box 261
HAPPYVILLE, Q. 40612.

Please change address below if incorrect

Mr. H. S. Smithies
16 Uranda St.
The Range Q. 45617

Account No.	Month Ending	Past Due	This Month	Amount Due
49-1253	871130	61.00	201.00	201.00

Please write in amount
of payment enclosed →

Please pay by due date
Terms: 30 days

Detach and enclose top
portion with payment

Date	Invoice No.	Details	Debit	Credit
		Opening Balance	61.00	
871102	41724	4 CASES JONATHON WHISKEY	40.00	
871104	53219	8 CASES XXXX BEER	56.00	
871115	53240	2 CASES OBLITERATION GIN	18.00	
871121	76431	2 CASES RITEOFF RUM	22.00	
871126	76478	5 CASES TORTURE TEQUILA	65.00	
871126	30872	PAYMENT – THANK YOU		61.00
		XMAS SPECIAL – 10% DISCOUNT ON BEER		
Month Ending	871130	Your Ref: Payment Made	Amount Due	201.00

FIGURE 15-6b
Accounts receivable statement with sales message repositioned to improve print time.

PRODUCTION AND DISTRIBUTION CONTROLS

Production and distribution controls seek to ensure that output is not lost or corrupted and that the privacy of output is not breached during its preparation and its routing to users. If the output is lost or corrupted, severe disruption can occur to the operations of the organization. For example, if customer bills are destroyed and the organization does not have a suitable backup and recovery facility, cash flow difficulties may arise. If the privacy of output is violated, the organization can suffer losses in several ways. First, the output may contain data that enables unauthorized access to the organization's computing resources. Jerry Schneider used this technique to gain access to Pacific Telephone's computer system. He sifted through trash cans and retrieved discarded output that provided him with the data needed to penetrate the system (see Chapter 1). Second, output data may be sold to a competitor. Trade secrets, patents, marketing data, credit information, etc., would all be valuable to a competitor. Third, output data may be used to blackmail an organization. For example, a criminal could threaten to expose sensitive trust data unless money is handed over.

Two major factors affect the choice of the production and distribution controls needed over output: (*a*) the sensitivity of the data reported and (*b*) whether the output is produced by a batch system or an online system. The first factor determines how much should be spent on output controls. The second factor determines the number and types of controls needed.

In general, a batch system requires more production and distribution controls over output than an online system. Batch output involves some kind of hard-copy report production. More intermediaries are needed between the production of a batch report and its eventual receipt by a user. For example: operators are responsible for loading the relevant programs and files, loading the stationery needed for a report, and printing the report; clerical staff are responsible for decollating, bursting, collating, and distributing reports.

In an online system, output is printed, displayed, or copied to a terminal. The terminal user interacts directly with the machine to obtain the output required. No intermediaries are needed. From a control viewpoint, the major concerns are preventing an unauthorized person from intercepting the transmission of data from the machine to the user, unauthorized viewing of output displayed at a terminal, and unauthorized removal of output by copying data to a terminal that has a removal storage device.

The following sections examine production and distribution controls over batch and online output. The primary focus is the production of report output. Nevertheless, the basic control principles described also apply to other kinds of output—for example, microform output.

Controlling Batch Output

Controls can be exercised over batch output through carefully designing reports and carefully managing the reports throughout all aspects of their creation, distribution, and use. Good report design facilitates the orderly flow of reports through the output process. Good management ensures adherence to the control procedures laid down for the output process.

Table 15-1 shows the information that should be included in a well-designed report to facilitate its flow through the output process. The title page contains information that assists operators and control section personnel to perform their work. In an environment where large numbers of reports are produced, this information is especially important. If the same report is produced several times a day, or a report program has to be rerun for some reason, confusion can arise if each instance of a report is not identified uniquely.

The information on the detail pages of a report prevents the unauthorized removal of data from the report. A person wishing to prevent a fraud from being discovered may remove a page containing exception information. Certain pages of a report may be especially valuable to a competitor. Page numbering and end-of-job markers prevent the undetected removal of a page. Even if the report is split because the printer runs out of paper, the user still can determine if pages were removed by checking that page numbers are continuous.

TABLE 15-1
CONTROL INFORMATION TO BE INCLUDED IN A WELL-DESIGNED REPORT

Control information	Position in report	Purposes
Report name	Title page	Permits immediate identification of report.
Time and date of production	Title page, detail pages	Prevents confusion if report produced several times per day or if for some reason the report has to be produced again, e.g., an error in a program.
Distribution list (includes number of copies)	Title page	Allows operator to check that correct multipart stationery has been used. Facilitates distribution of report by control section.
Processing period covered	Title page	User can see what data has been included in the report. Control section can check against data submitted.
Program producing the report	Title page	Permits immediate identification of originating system/program.
Security classification	Title page	Alerts operators/control section as to sensitivity of data contained in report.
Retention date	Title page	Indicates date before which the report should not be destroyed.
Method of destruction	Title page	Indicates if special procedures to be followed for disposal of report.
Page heading	Detail pages	Shows content of report pages.
Page number	Detail pages	Prevents undetected removal of a report page.
End-of-job marker	Immediately after last entry, last page of report	Prevents undetected removal of last page of report.

Figure 15-7 shows all the possible stages through which a batch report may pass during the output process. All reports may not pass through every stage; for example, a report may be printed directly rather than spooled, a single copy report does not need decollating, some reports may not need bursting. However, identifying all the stages through which a report may pass provides a basis for logically grouping the controls that should be applied to the output process.

The following sections examine the controls that should exist at each output stage. Whether or not a control is implemented, however, depends, as always, on cost-benefit considerations. The full set of controls may be implemented only for reports containing very sensitive data.

Controls Over Stationery Supplies   Computer installations use a wide variety of stationery types: for example, plain stationery for management reports, preprinted invoice stationery for billing customers, preprinted check stationery for employee and creditor payment. Careful control must be exercised over all stationery supplies; however, control of preprinted stationery is especially

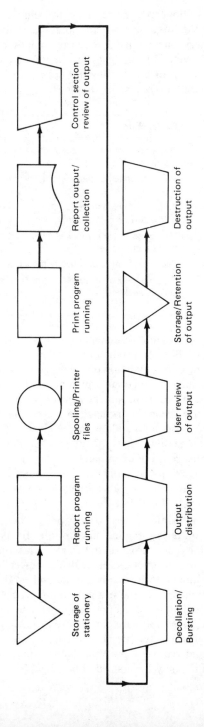

FIGURE 15-7
Stages in the output process for batch reports where controls can be applied.

important. Preprinted stationery can be used to remove assets from an organization or cause the organization considerable embarrassment. For example, check stationery can be used to write unauthorized checks. To destroy an organization's goodwill among its customers, invoice stationery can be used to bill its customers for goods they did not purchase. The following controls help prevent unauthorized use of stationery:

Control	Explanation
Maintain an inventory system for stationery	Helps account for all purchasing, receipt, and use of stationery.
Store stationery in a secure location	Prevents unauthorized destruction/removal of stationery.
Control access to stationery supplies	To prevent unauthorized use of stationery, operators should not be able to gain direct access to stationery supplies.
Where possible use preprinted stationery	Preprinted stationery makes it more difficult to forge reports, notices, checks, etc.
Prenumber preprinted stationery	Facilitates control over use of preprinted stationery.
Store signature stamps at different physical location from that of stationery inventory	Prevents unauthorized use of signature stamps, e.g., use on stolen checks.

Controls Over Report Program Running Auditors have three concerns when they examine controls over production running of a report program. First, they must ensure the correct version of the program has been loaded and activated. They should have formed an opinion on the likelihood of this happening when they examined management controls over program libraries. Second, auditors must ensure operators have not used the console to make direct alterations to the program residing in memory. Third, large report programs should have checkpoint/restart facilities; auditors must ensure these facilities have not been misused. For example, by restarting at a checkpoint, an operator may have obtained duplicate copies of a section of a report. Evidence on these questions can be obtained by examining the console log.

Controls Over Spooling/Printer Files If a report program cannot write directly to a printer, the output is spooled and a printer file is created; that is, system software causes the report program to "think" it is writing to the printer when actually it is writing to magnetic tape or disk storage. When the printer becomes available, spooling software reads the file and produces the report.

The presence of an intermediate file in the printing process causes several control problems. Printer files provide opportunities for unauthorized modification and copying of reports. Software can be used to change the value of a field in the printer file. The printer file can be copied. Some copies may be authorized for backup and recovery purposes; others may be unauthorized. Spooling software facilities may be abused. For example, spooling software

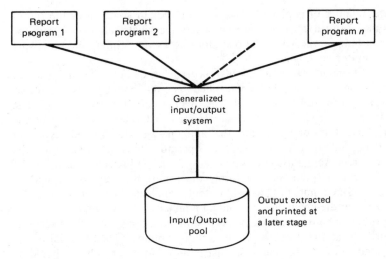

FIGURE 15-8
Use of the input/output pool for temporary storage of output.

allows the operator to return to a prior point on the printer file and restart printing should the printer malfunction. Some spooling software allows the operator to request a different number of copies of a report than the number specified by the programmer. Both these facilities can be used to obtain unauthorized copies of a report. The auditor must ensure:

1 The contents of printer files cannot be altered.
2 Unauthorized copies of printer files are not made.
3 Printer files are printed only once.
4 If copies of printer files are kept for backup and recovery purposes, they are not used to make unauthorized copies of reports.

Control also can be enhanced by using the input/output pool for temporary storage of output (see Chapter 11). Spooling software can write printer files to the pool, or application system programs can invoke the facilities of the generalized input/output system to write output to the pool (Figure 15-8). Output can be printed at a later time when a printer is available or a report is required. Instead of having to exercise controls over multiple files, only use of the input/output pool needs to be controlled.

Controls Over Printing Controls over printing have two purposes: (*a*) to ensure only the required number of copies of reports are made and (*b*) to prevent operators from scanning sensitive data printed on reports.

Various steps can be taken to control the number of copies of a report printed. To avoid having to dispose of extra copies of a report made through operator error, the operator's manual for an application system should state clearly the number of copies of a report required. In some cases the report program may print a console message specifying what stationery should be loaded, halt temporarily while the operator checks the printer, and reactivate upon an operator command.

To prevent unauthorized copies of reports from being made, the issue of stationery to operators should be controlled. The number of pages in a report usually varies from run to run; however, over a period of time the average number of pages produced can be determined. The clerk in charge of the stationery inventory can estimate the amounts of the different types of stationery needed for a period (say, an operator shift) and issue only the amount required. Actual usage can be checked against budgeted usage. In the case of preprinted, prenumbered forms the report program can provide a control total of the number of pages of output, which can be reconciled against the difference in the beginning and ending number on the forms.

New printer ribbons are also a means of obtaining copies of at least sections of a report. On its first cycle a printer ribbon contains a clear imprint of the pages printed. As with stationery the distribution of printer ribbons should be controlled. Further, operators should be prevented from bringing their own stationery and printer ribbons into the computer room.

Often operators see at least sections of a report. Operators check paper alignment, head of form positioning, etc. They may scan the first few pages of a report to check all is well. In the case of sensitive data it may be necessary to prevent operators from seeing any report contents. This can be accomplished in several ways. The report can be printed at a remote printer. A security officer can stand by the printer while the report is printed. The report program can print several covering pages to allow operators to perform printer housekeeping functions before the contents of the report are printed. However, sufficient stationery must be loaded so these housekeeping functions do not have to be performed again at some intermediate stage during report printing when the report contents would be visible to the operator. Special multipart stationery can be purchased with the top copy colored black so printing cannot be read. For example, pay advice slips can be printed in this way to preserve the privacy of payroll data. Employees simply tear off the unreadable top copy of the pay slip and the duplicate copy contains the readable pay details (Figure 15-9). Wooldridge [1975] suggests completely filling a print line with characters so the report user has to apply a template to a page to detect report characters from characters used to camouflage the report contents. This technique protects the privacy of report contents against casual perusal by an unauthorized party but would not prevent a determined attempt to violate data integrity.

Report Collection Controls   Once reports have been printed, they should be collected promptly by control section staff. All output can be placed in a locker and collected periodically. Reports should not be left to accumulate in the computer room, where they may be lost or their contents perused by an unauthorized person.

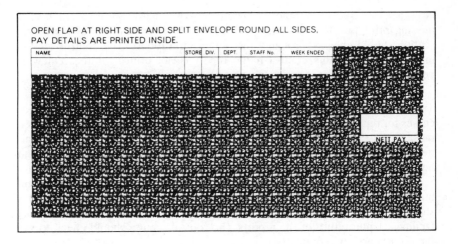

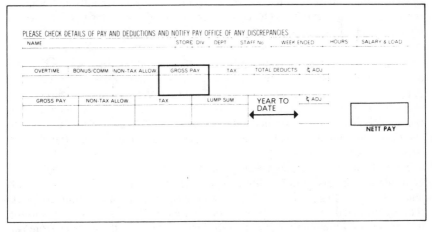

FIGURE 15-9
Protecting data privacy with multipart forms. (*Moore Paragon Australia Ltd.*)

The computer operations manager may prepare a list of all reports to be produced during an operator shift. Control section staff can use this list to determine whether any reports are missing when they collect output from the computer room.

Control Section Output Review Controls Unless a report contains highly sensitive data that only users are allowed to read, the computer installation's control section should perform two checks on output reports produced. First, the control section should scan reports for obvious errors, for example, fields containing unreasonable values, format errors, missing data. These errors may have been caused by a report program bug or a hardware error such as a missing print position. Second, periodically on a random basis the control section should check thoroughly the output on a report. The control section may not exercise this control if the report is not critical or the review is performed by users (see, also, Chapter 8).

Decollation/Bursting Controls Though the decollation and bursting processes for reports are straightforward clerical activities, the personnel involved must be trustworthy. When performing the processes, clerks have opportunities to peruse the contents of reports. For highly sensitive data, decollation and bursting might be performed by the report users.

There must be no opportunities for clerks performing decollation and bursting to make photocopies of reports or remove pages from reports. Reports should be transported directly to and from the decollation and bursting facilities. Upon return of the reports, the control section should check to see the reports are still complete.

It is important to dispose of the carbon paper removed from multipart reports in a secure manner. The carbon paper contains an imprint of the report contents and can be read easily.

Report Distribution Controls After decollation and bursting, reports can be distributed to users. There are various ways to ensure only authorized users obtain the reports. Control section staff can deliver the reports directly to users. Reports can be placed in lockers, only authorized users having keys to the lockers. A courier service can be used to deliver reports to remote locations. For highly sensitive reports, users may have to pick them up in person and sign for them.

Special care must be taken where a large number of copies of a report must be produced and distributed. Often a user name and address file is maintained, and to facilitate distribution of the report the file is printed on gummed labels that are attached to individual copies of the report. Because of changes in the user population the number of copies of the report required may vary from run to run. In these cases maintaining the integrity of the name and address file is critical. If an unauthorized party inserts a name and address record on a file, a gummed label will be produced and a copy of the report distributed.

User Output Review Controls Users should perform reviews of output similar to those carried out by the control section to detect errors in reports. However, because users are more familiar with the application area, they are better able to detect errors. Users also should provide feedback to the computer installation on ways in which reports could be made more effective.

Output Storage/Retention Controls When reports are no longer useful, they should be destroyed. They still may contain information valuable to a competitor. As with magnetic files, a retention date must be determined for each report. Various factors affect the retention date assigned, for example, the need for archival reference of the report, taxation legislation specifying a minimum retention time for the report, privacy legislation specifying a maximum retention time for the report. Until the retention date has expired, reports should be filed and stored in a secure location.

Output Destruction Controls   Report destruction can be accomplished easily using a paper shredder. As retention dates expire, reports should be transported in a secure manner to the shredding facility. Aborted report runs and discarded stationery also should be shredded to prevent any unauthorized use.

Controlling Online Output

Figure 15-10 shows the three areas where control must be exercised over online output. An unauthorized person can intercept report data being transmitted over a communication line, view a report being displayed or printed at a terminal, or make a copy of the output on a terminal storage device such as a diskette.

Chapter 12 described the controls needed to prevent an unauthorized person from gaining access to and using data transmitted over communication lines. The line can be made physically secure so wiretapping cannot be carried out. However, if data is transmitted over a public line, it is impossible to make the line physically secure. Encryption then can be used to render the data useless to anyone without the cryptographic key who gains access to the data.

Unauthorized viewing of data can be prevented in several ways, for example, placing each terminal in a separate room, using hoods on terminals, displaying reports at a low light intensity, positioning terminals so users sit with their backs to a wall. For the novice terminal user, these measures also reduce

FIGURE 15-10
Control points for online output.

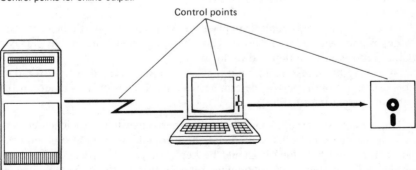

the "fishbowl" effect, that is, the tendency for these users to feel their inadequacies in interacting with the system are being viewed publicly (see Lancaster and Fayen [1973]).

When intelligent terminals are connected to a system and these terminals have their own storage devices, it is easier to remove data from the system. The data can be downloaded to the terminal and copied onto the storage medium. For example, users may access a file and copy the file to a hard disk or diskette at their terminal. Whereas previously the data had to be viewed at a screen or printed if a copy was to be made, now copies of large volumes of data can be made quickly and transported off site.

If the system crashes, users should be asked to sign on again if the system is unavailable for some time. Users may leave a terminal if they have to wait too long for the system to come up again. If, when the system comes up, it continues to print the report being displayed at the time of the crash, the person then sitting at the terminal may be an unauthorized party.

AUDIT TRAIL CONTROLS

Audit trail controls in the output subsystem maintain information about the events that occur from the time the content of output is determined to the time the output is presented to users.

Accounting Audit Trail

The accounting audit trail shows *what* output was presented to users, *who* received the output, and *when* the output was received. This information can be used for various purposes; for example:

1 If an erroneous data item is discovered in the database, it may be necessary to determine who relied on the data item via an output report to make a decision.

2 Periodically the content of reports may need to be scanned to determine whether controls have been circumvented and privacy violations have occurred.

3 Even with access controls in place and working, it may still be necessary to determine whether those users who ultimately gained access to data via output reports were authorized to do so.

4 It may be necessary to determine when a user gained access to a data item via an output report to determine whether a decision was made on the basis of current information.

Unfortunately, perhaps more than any other subsystem, efficiency considerations in the output subsystem dictate how complete the audit trail information can be and how long it should be kept. Many data processing systems produce a large number of voluminous reports. It is costly to maintain images of these reports on magnetic media for audit trail purposes. Often they are kept only for a few days, primarily for backup and recovery purposes. In some cases they may be dumped to microfiche or microfilm to provide a permanent or semipermanent record of their contents. For audit trail purposes, however, microform records are more difficult to access and manipulate than records maintained on magnetic storage media.

It is usually less costly to maintain a record of the output responses to online queries. The responses to online queries are often short and cryptic; indeed, the nature of online interrogation of a database precludes the preparation of lengthy reports. Furthermore, hard-copy versions of online output may not be made or not be kept and, as a consequence, the audit trail may provide the only record of the output presented to the user.

For some types of output, techniques for the design and implementation of the accounting audit trail are still evolving. For example, the nature of the accounting audit trail that should be maintained for graphics and image output or voice output is still unclear. On the one hand the raw data used to provide the graphics, image, and voice output may be sufficient. On the other hand it may be difficult to reproduce an exact replica of the graphics, image, or voice output from the raw data, and in some cases an exact replica may be needed for audit trail purposes.

Operations Audit Trail

As indicated earlier in this chapter, the production of output can consume substantial resources—expensive output devices may be required to produce graphs and images, paper consumption may be high, large amounts of machine time may be required to produce image output, substantial storage space may be required for archival storage of reports. The operations audit trail maintains a record of the hardware and software resources consumed to produce the various types of output. In addition, it may record data that enables the print time, response time, and display rate for output to be determined. This data can then be analyzed as a basis for improving the timeliness of output production and for reducing the amount of resources required to produce the output. For example, the operations audit trail may record the time at which a user enters a command to interrogate a database, the time at which the retrieved data has been assembled to format and present a report, and the time at which the last character of output is provided to the user. Analysis of this data may indicate that more efficient formatting software is needed.

EXISTENCE CONTROLS

Output can be lost or destroyed for a variety of reasons; for example, a report can go astray in the mail, customer invoices can be stolen, reports can be destroyed in a fire. In some cases recovery of the output is simple to accomplish; in other cases it is difficult or impossible. The following factors affect the ease with which output recovery can be accomplished:

1 Availability of report files
2 Whether a status or transaction report must be recovered
3 Whether in-place update has been used
4 Whether loss is partial or total

Many computer systems do not write output directly to an output device; instead, they write the output to a magnetic tape file or disk file, and the file is later dumped to the output device. This strategy, called "spooling," allows more efficient use of output devices since the devices can be driven at maximum speed (they are not slowed down by other types of processing that must occur). Furthermore, spooling creates *virtual* output devices—for example, a program can write simultaneously to multiple printers via the spool files when, in fact, the installation has only one real printer.

Spool files also facilitate backup and recovery of output. If output is lost or destroyed, obtaining a new copy of the output is straightforward if the spool file for the output is still available. The spool file can once again be written to the output device. However, using spool files for backup and recovery purposes usually requires active intervention by the person responsible for backup and recovery. Spooling systems keep output files for a limited period. Many work with a fixed size spool file; once the spool file is full, the system returns to the start of the file and begins to overwrite the existing information. Spool files often fill up quickly; consequently, they may be available only for a limited time as a backup and recovery resource.

Two strategies that can be employed to enhance output existence controls are (*a*) to use larger spool files so they are overwritten less frequently, and (*b*) to retain the spool files for longer periods. Unfortunately, many data processing installations produce large volumes of output, and the overheads incurred in retaining larger or more spool files to facilitate (hopefully) infrequent recovery of lost or destroyed output would be unacceptable. Nonetheless, spool files can be used *selectively* to facilitate output backup and recovery operations. Output might be assigned a criticality rating based upon its importance to the organization, and the period for retention of spool files could be based upon this criticality rating.

A second factor that affects the ease with which backup and recovery can be accomplished is the nature of the report to be recovered. Reports show either *status* information—for example, the quantity-on-hand of various inventory items—or *transaction* information—for example, customer purchases throughout a given period. Of course, a single report can show both types of information. From a recovery viewpoint, the two types of information pose different problems. On the one hand, status information is constantly changing; for example, the quantity-on-hand of an inventory item is frequently updated as stock is received or sold. If a status report must be recovered, therefore, the prior values of different data items have to be retrieved. Some type of beforeimage or afterimage and a time stamp for the data item values must be kept. On the other hand, transaction information usually is not updated; consequently, recovering a report that contains transaction information often is easier to accomplish. Nonetheless, storage costs preclude the indefinite retention of transaction information, so the time period for easy recovery usually is limited.

As a related issue, recovery of output is more difficult when in-place update occurs. Consider, for example, a simple batch processing run where master files are updated with transaction files and prior versions of the master files are not overwritten. Recovery of report output is straightforward: status information can be obtained from the prior versions of master files; transaction information can be obtained from the period transaction files; in some cases combined status and transaction information may have to be obtained by redoing the update run. If in-place update occurs, however, prior versions of status information are overwritten. Beforeimages and afterimages of status information must be kept. In addition, status information at a point in time and transaction information for a period often are not collected together conveniently on the one file. Instead, a time stamp must be attached to data, and recovery of report output involves selecting and sorting data on the basis of time stamps.

Finally, partial recovery of output is facilitated if a checkpoint/restart facility is used. Consider, for example, the implications for recovery if a hardware error causes a program that prints customer invoices to abort. In the absence of a checkpoint/restart facility, the entire invoice production run may have to be redone. This can be costly if large volumes of printed stationery have to be discarded and destroyed and prior versions of master files have to be recovered to restart the run. If a checkpoint/restart facility is used, however, recovery can be accomplished by returning to a prior checkpoint and restarting the run from that checkpoint (see Chapter 13).

SUMMARY

The output subsystem provides functions that determine the content of data that will be provided to users, the ways in which data will be formatted and presented to users, and the ways in which data will be prepared for and routed to users.

Five sets of controls are exercised over these functions. First, inference controls are used to filter the output that users are permitted to see. They are especially important in regulating access to statistical databases where users are allowed to obtain summary information about data but the privacy of individual data items must be preserved. Inference controls work by either restricting query set sizes or perturbing the input or output of a statistical function.

Second, presentation controls govern the ways in which information is communicated to decision makers. They impact the choice of the output content, the output medium, the output format, the output layout, and the output turnaround or response time. Via design standards and a monitoring mechanism, primarily they seek to ensure that users can employ output effectively and efficiently.

Third, production and distribution controls seek to ensure that output is not lost or corrupted or that the privacy of data is not violated during its preparation and its routing to users. The most extensive controls apply to batch reports since greater numbers of people are involved in production and distribution activities. Online reports require fewer controls since a smaller number of intermediaries are involved in the output process.

Finally, like all other subsystems, the output subsystem requires a set of audit trail controls and a set of existence controls. Audit trail controls maintain the chronology of events from the time the content of output is determined to the time the output is presented to users. Existence controls enable output to be recovered in the event of loss.

REVIEW QUESTIONS

15-1 Briefly describe the nature of inference controls. What are the *four* types of compromises of statistical databases that inference controls seek to prevent?

15-2 Briefly describe the nature of restriction controls. Why is a restriction on the minimum size of the query set an inadequate means of preventing a compromise of privacy in the database?

15-3 Briefly describe the nature of a "tracker." What is the distinction between an individual tracker and a general tracker?

15-4 Briefly describe the nature of perturbation controls. How do perturbation controls differ from restriction controls?

15-5 Briefly distinguish between record-based perturbation controls and results-based perturbation controls. What are the relative strengths and limitations of record-based perturbation controls versus results-based perturbation controls?

15-6 Briefly describe the nature of presentation controls. What are the two basic forms that presentation controls take?

15-7 Identify *five* factors that must be considered when choosing the content controls to be exercised over output.

15-8 Briefly describe the nature of medium controls.

15-9 When a visual display is used to present output, what is meant by the "peephole" effect? How does the peephole effect impact the quality of decision making and maintenance of data integrity? Suggest some ways of overcoming the peephole effect.

15-10 On the basis of the research undertaken so far, what effects do graphics and color have on the accuracy with which information system users make decisions?

15-11 How will partitioning of visual display output into several fixed windows improve maintenance of data integrity?

15-12 Reducing output display time or output print time sometimes means reducing the readability of reports. Explain.

15-13 How do layout decisions affect the meaning and significance that users attach to the different items contained in a report?

15-14 For visual display output of reports, what factors determine the amount of information that should be present on a single visual display?

15-15 Briefly explain how the following conditions may affect the quality of decisions made by a user working at an online terminal:
a A very fast response time
b A very slow response time
c A response time subject to large variations

15-16 What are the purposes of output production and distribution controls? What factors affect the choice of the output production and distribution controls used?

15-17 Why does a batch reporting system usually require more output production and distribution controls than an online reporting system?

15-18 Why is it important for each page of a report to have a heading and a page number? What is the purpose of printing an end-of-job marker immediately after the last entry on a report?

15-19 Briefly describe the major elements of an inventory system for computer stationery. Give three advantages that will accrue from having the inventory system you describe. Are there any disadvantages?

15-20 Briefly explain how checkpoint/restart facilities in a report program can be used to obtain unauthorized copies of a report. Suggest a method for detecting the unauthorized use of checkpoint facilities.

15-21 Outline some controls that could be instituted to prevent alteration of fields on a printer file produced as a result of spooling. What controls could be used to ensure a printer file is printed only once?

15-22 Why do printer ribbons and carbon paper present control problems? Suggest ways in which the problems presented can be overcome.

15-23 Briefly describe *four* techniques that can be used to prevent an operator from perusing the contents of a report during the printing process. For each technique, give an example report where the technique might be applied.

15-24 Briefly explain the difference between decollation and bursting. What output control problems arise as a result of the decollation and bursting activities?

15-25 Why should the control section in a data processing installation review output prior to its distribution to users? List three problems that the control section might identify with output.

15-26 Outline some of the controls that should exist over a user name and address file from which gummed labels are printed and attached to reports to facilitate their distribution. Assume the reports contain sensitive data that should not fall into the hands of unauthorized users.

15-27 List three requirements that may affect retention requirements for reports. What should be done with reports once their retention date expires?

15-28 Are there any differences in the controls needed for an output process where batch reports are (a) printed on paper and (b) written on microfilm? List the differences you identify.

15-29 From an output control perspective, briefly explain why it is sometimes necessary to require a user to sign on again when an online system crashes. When would it *not* be necessary to repeat the signon procedure again after a system crash?

15-30 How can unauthorized viewing of data displayed at an online terminal be prevented?

15-31 What control problems arise when users can download data from a central database to an intelligent workstation?

15-32 How are spool files useful for backup and recovery purposes? From a backup and recovery viewpoint, what factors determine how long a spool file should be kept?

15-33 The ease with which backup and recovery of output can be accomplished depends upon whether the output shows status information or transaction information. Explain.

MULTIPLE CHOICE QUESTIONS

15-1 With respect to statistical databases, inference controls seek to prevent:
a Unauthorized addition, modification, or deletion of a data item
b Incorrect deductions by users based on the contents of the database
c Privacy violations
d Access to detailed data when summary data is available

15-2 Which of the following statements about trackers is false:
a They pad the original query so the restrictions on query set size can be circumvented
b Privacy violations obtained via trackers can be prevented by specifying *both* a minimum query set size and a maximum query set size
c General trackers can be constructed that will work for anyone in the database
d Trackers often can be constructed fairly quickly

15-3 Compared with restriction controls, perturbation controls:
a Allow fewer statistics to be calculated on the data contained in the database
b Eliminate biases or inconsistencies that arise as a result of implementing inference controls
c Are not subject to averaging attacks
d Result in an information loss associated with the variance of the perturbed statistic around the true value

15-4 Which of the following statements about record-based perturbation controls is false:
a They calculate a statistic on the basis of a random sample of records that satisfy the query
b They calculate a statistic after some type of error term has been added to the data in the records that satisfy the query
c They can be compromised through an averaging attack if the error term is generated from a distribution with a zero mean
d They introduce an error term after the true statistic has been calculated on the basis of the data in the records that satisfy the query

15-5 Match the following:

I Contents choice   A   Windows
II Medium choice   B   Microform output
III Format choice   C   Accuracy
IV Layout choice   D   Graph
a I-C; II-B; III-D; IV-A
b II-B; III-A; I-C; IV-D
c III-B; IV-D; II-A; I-C
d IV-A; III-C; II-D; I-B

15-6 Which of the following factors does *not* affect print time:
a The number of lines that can be skipped
b With a line printer, the width of the line
c The clarity (sharpness) needed in report output
d The extent to which data is preprinted

15-7 In an interactive system, the quality of decision making depends upon the system:
a Always providing a response in about one second
b Eliminating all forms of delays
c Clustering activities in groups of seven, plus or minus two
d Delaying a response when psychological closure occurs in the problem solving task

15-8 In general, a batch system requires more output controls over reports than an online system because:
a Batch output is more complex than online output
b There are more intermediaries involved in producing and distributing batch output
c Only managers typically receive online reports so less misuse is likely
d The only way to breach the privacy of online reports is to wiretap the communication line

15-9 On a batch report, the control information that prevents undetected removal of the last page of the report is the:
a End-of-job marker
b Page number
c Security classification
d Page title

15-10 Preprinted stationery causes special control problems because it:
a Can be used in an unauthorized way to embarrass the organization
b Is usually handled by only a few people so the risk of collusion is higher
c Is easier to forge than negotiable instruments
d Prevents the use of spooling software to provide backup and recovery controls

15-11 A control problem that arises with spooling software is that:
a Relative to normal reporting software it is easier to carry out unauthorized modifications to spooling software
b It is error-prone because the software is highly complex
c It can be used to obtain an unauthorized copy of a report
d Encryption functions are rarely available to protect the integrity of the software

15-12 With respect to output, which of the following is *not* a function of the control section in a data processing installation:

a Scanning reports for obvious errors

b Detection of missing print positions

c Detailed checking of report content to ensure accuracy and completeness

d Registering user complaints about report output

15-13 Which of the following is *not* a control problem with respect to the decollation and bursting activities associated with batch output:

a Clerical staff have an opportunity to peruse sensitive reports

b Unauthorized removal of carbon paper permits the privacy of reports to be violated

c Undetected removal of pages from a report may occur if there is no end-of-job marker

d Unauthorized pages can be easily substituted for valid pages in the report

15-14 The "fishbowl" effect describes:

a The tendency for novice users at a workstation to feel their activities are being viewed publicly as they interact with the system

b The tendency for users to feel they can view only parts of the database in very small pieces

c The long-term effects felt by personnel working in high-security data processing installations

d The tendency for a malicious party to be able to guess the contents of a report even if only a small part of the report is viewed

15-15 Downloading of data to a workstation may be prevented in order to:

a Reduce the risk of the communication line being wiretapped

b Decrease the likelihood of unauthorized viewing of data occurring at a terminal

c Reduce the risk of data being lost if the system crashes

d Reduce the ability of users to make unauthorized copies of data and remove them off site

15-16 Which of the following factors makes the output recovery process easier:

a Lack of use of spool files

b Transaction data to be recovered instead of status data

c In-place update rather than batch update is used

d Use of checkpoint facilities avoided

EXERCISES AND CASES

15-1 Ubend, Inc., is a large wholesaler of plumbing parts based in Sydney with outlets in the major cities and towns in New South Wales. Each outlet sends all its transactions to the head office for computer data processing, and the head office returns to the outlet summary hard copy reports plus microfiche reports on all the transactions processed. The outlet uses these microfiche reports to answer customer queries on charges to the accounts, determine whether vendors have been paid, etc.

You are a member of the external audit team examining controls over output with the head office computer system. Your manager-in-charge has listed, among others, the following objectives for the audit:

a Ensure report data cannot be lost.

b Ensure report data cannot be stolen.

c Ensure unauthorized access to report data cannot occur.

d Ensure report data is retained for seven years to fulfill statutory requirements relating to tax.

Required: Your manager-in-charge asks you to brief him on any *differences* in controls you think would be needed for the hard copy versus microfiche reports so the control objectives will be achieved.

15-2 First South Australian State Bank recently has installed a new network for teller operations in its 500 branches throughout the state. Teller machines in each branch are connected to a branch controller, and the controllers are connected to the head office machine. While some processing has been distributed to the controllers, the customer account master file still remains centralized.

Unfortunately, the network is unreliable. Furthermore, the problems are not being solved quickly since the bank data processing staff are blaming the machine vendor and the machine vendor is blaming the bank data processing staff.

One consequence of the unreliable network is the submission of duplicate transactions by tellers. The network often goes down for only a few minutes. Tellers are supposed to check whether the last transaction they submitted was posted to the account by submitting an inquiry when the network comes up. Unfortunately, customer lines are long because of the network unreliability and tellers often simply resubmit the last transaction to save time rather than initiate an inquiry. Thus, the same transaction sometimes is processed twice.

Required: Assuming the unreliability of the network continues, what controls would you implement to prevent duplicate transaction processing?

15-3 Rosendale Savings and Loan has recently installed a management information system to support its loan officers. When a customer makes application for a loan, the loan officer uses a terminal to inquire about the customer's financial status based on information in the association's database. The association purchased color-graphic terminals to use with the new system. The color capabilities of the terminal are used to highlight various information: for example, the loan officer detects a credit balance in an account because it is printed in red, and a debit balance is printed in green; colored bar charts are used to show the trend in account balances over the last five years.

Required: Some major errors have resulted in making loan decisions based on information provided by the system. The system has been checked carefully and no errors have been detected in the processing logic. The data processing manager is perplexed. Have you any suggestions to make on what might be wrong and what actions might be undertaken to correct the problems occurring?

15-4 Savecents Ltd. is a major retailing company with stores scattered throughout the United States. Each month the company's head office mails to all stores sales information that management considers to be highly confidential. Store managers are responsible for the reports. They must follow prescribed procedures for preserving the privacy of the information contained in the reports; for example, when a new report is received, the old report must be shredded.

As the manager of internal audit for the company, the controller has expressed some concerns to you about whether store managers are following carefully the procedures defined to preserve the privacy of the reports. She asks you whether it is possible to gain some assurance that the procedures are being followed. Furthermore, she asks you whether any control procedures might be installed to detect any deviation from the procedures.

Required: Write a memorandum to the controller advising her how you intend to obtain assurance that the managers are following the procedures. You also should advise her on any extra control measures that might be implemented to ensure the managers comply with the privacy procedures. (*Note:* Savecents has a communications network linking all its stores, but many reports are mailed to the stores to save communications costs and reduce the risks of privacy violations occurring during data transmission.)

15-5 Heavy Metal Mystique (HMM) Ltd. is a large Montreal-based company involved in most aspects of the rock music industry—for example, the identification and promotion of artists, record and compact disk production, tour management, and the production of videotapes. Because of the nature of the industry in which HMM is engaged, it faces an environment that is highly uncertain. Accordingly, it is organized along decentralized lines with substantial autonomy given to the individual divisions.

Even though most of the data processing carried out within HMM is decentralized, it maintains a critical centralized database containing key information that is used throughout the company. This database is accessed by many users for both update and retrieval purposes.

For several years the company has actively promoted end-user computing. Top management see information systems as being a key strategic tool enabling managers to keep abreast of the volatile market faced by the company. To support end-users, an information center was established. As an indicator of the success of end-user computing within HMM, the size of the information center has grown rapidly as its services have been increasingly demanded.

Required: You are the manager of internal audit for HMM. One day you are approached by the vice-president in charge of all information systems for the company concerning a request that has been made to him by the manager of the information center. He has been asked to allocate funds to purchase a natural language query system that will be made available to all end-users within the firm. The system is expensive, but the information center manager has argued that it will enable end-users to make more effective use of the company's databases and, in particular, the data maintained in the centralized database. Because of the criticality of the centralized database and the need for end-users to formulate accurate and complete queries to retrieve information on which to base their decisions, the vice-president is concerned about the possible effects of using the system on data integrity. He asks you to write a brief report outlining any concerns you have about the integrity of output if the system is acquired and used.

15-6 Social welfare fraud and tax evasion are major problems faced by governments. To combat these problems, some departments within the United States government have undertaken "computer matching." Computer matching involves comparing data in different databases to identify inconsistencies that may indicate some type of irregularity. In 1986 the Australian government supported the introduction of the Australia card to combat fraud and tax evasion. This card was the basis for a national identification scheme that would enable the government to keep track of its financial dealings with Australian citizens. *Required:* Write a brief report outlining the implications, if any, for the output controls that should be implemented in government computer systems if computer matching or a national identification scheme are permitted.

ANSWERS TO MULTIPLE CHOICE QUESTIONS

15-1 c	**15-5** a	**15-9** a	**15-13** d
15-2 b	**15-6** b	**15-10** a	**15-14** a
15-3 d	**15-7** d	**15-11** c	**15-15** d
15-4 d	**15-8** b	**15-12** c	**15-16** b

REFERENCES

Axelrod, C. Warren. "Reduce Computer Printing Costs," *Journal of Systems Management* (December 1977), pp. 30–33.

Caldwell, John. "The Effective Reports Crisis," *Journal of Systems Management* (June 1975), pp. 7–12.

Davis, Gordon B., and Margrethe H. Olson. *Management Information Systems: Conceptual Foundations, Structure, and Development,* 2d ed. (New York: McGraw-Hill, 1985).

Denning, Dorothy E., and Jan Schlörer. "Inference Controls for Statistical Databases," *Computer* (July 1983), pp. 69–82.

Feltham, Gerald A. *Information Evaluation* (Sarasota, FL: American Accounting Association, 1972).

Fernandez, E. B., R. C. Summers, and C. Wood. *Database Security and Integrity* (Reading, MA: Addison-Wesley, 1981).

Galitz, W. O. *Human Factors in Office Automation* (Atlanta, GA: Life Office Management Association, 1980).

Hansen, Morris H. "Insuring Confidentiality of Individual Records in Data Storage and Retrieval for Statistical Purposes," *Proceedings of the 1971 AFIPS Fall Joint Computer Conference* (Montvale, NJ: AFIPS Press, 1971), pp. 579–585.

Huber, George. "Organizational Information Systems: Determinants of Their Performance and Behavior," *Management Science* (February 1982), pp. 138–155.

Ives, Blake. "Graphical User Interfaces for Business Information Systems," *MIS Quarterly* (December 1982), pp. 15–47.

Lancaster, F. W. *Information Retrieval Systems: Characteristics, Testing and Evaluation,* 2d ed. (New York: Wiley, 1979).

Lancaster, F. W., and E. G. Fayen. *Information Retrieval On-Line* (Los Angeles, CA: Melville Publishing Company, 1973).

Martin, James. *Design of Man-Computer Dialogues* (Englewood Cliffs, NJ: Prentice-Hall, 1973).

Miller, Lance A., and John C. Thomas, Jr. "Behavioral Issues in the Use of Interactive

Systems," *International Journal of Man-Machine Studies* (September 1977), pp. 509–536.

Miller, Robert B. "Response Time in Man-Computer Conversational Transactions," *Proceedings of the 1968 AFIPS Fall Joint Computer Conference* (Washington: The Thompson Book Company, 1968), pp. 267–278.

Mock, Theodore Jaye. *Measurement and Accounting Information Criteria* (Sarasota, FL: American Accounting Association, 1976).

Paller, A., K. Szoka, and N. Nelson. *Choosing the Right Chart*, USSCO Graphics, Integrated Software Systems Corporation, 10505 Sorrento Valley Road, San Diego, CA 92121, 1980).

Rouse, William B. "Design of Man-Computer Interfaces for On-Line Interactive Systems," *Proceedings of the IEEE* (June 1975), pp. 847–857.

Schlörer, Jan. "Identification and Retrieval of Personal Records from a Statistical Database," *Methods Information Mediation* (January 1975), pp. 7–13.

Shneiderman, Ben. "Improving the Human Factors Aspect of Database Interactions," *ACM Transactions on Database Systems* (December 1978), pp. 417–439.

Shneiderman, Ben. *Software Psychology: Human Factors in Computer and Information Systems* (Cambridge, MA: Winthrop Publishers, 1980).

Shneiderman, Ben. "Response Time and Display Rate in Human Performance with Computers," *Computing Surveys* (September 1984), pp. 265–285.

Wilkinson, Bryan. "Controlling Output Distribution," *EDP Auditing* (Pennsauken, NJ: Auerbach Publishers, 1978), Portfolio 74-02-01, pp. 1–12.

Wooldridge, Susan. *Computer Output Design* (New York: Petrocelli/Charter, 1975).

PART **FOUR**

EVIDENCE COLLECTION

To evaluate the quality of an application system the auditor needs to collect evidence. Various techniques and tools have been developed to aid this evidence collection function. Some primarily gather data on how well assets are safeguarded or on a system's ability to maintain data integrity; others are useful for collecting data on system effectiveness; still others gauge processing efficiency; and some even have eclectic capabilities. The auditor's problem is not a shortage of evidence collection techniques to use. Rather, it is knowing what technique or set of techniques is best to use for a given system or program.

The next six chapters describe the various evidence collection tools and techniques developed to gather data on whether systems safeguard assets, maintain data integrity, achieve their objectives effectively, and process data efficiently. The focus is on the nature of the tools and techniques, methodologies for using the tools and techniques, and the relative advantages and disadvantages of the tools and techniques.

Chapter	Overview of contents
16 Generalized Audit Software	Functional capabilities and limitations of generalized audit software; audit tasks that can be accomplished; managing an audit software application; accessing complex data structures; purchasing audit software
17 Other Audit Software	Industry-specific audit software; spreadsheet audit software; high-level languages; system software; specialized audit software; decision support software; control of audit software
18 Code Review, Test Data, and Code Comparison	Methodology of program source code review; designing, creating, and using test data; source and object code comparison

Chapter	Overview of contents
19 Concurrent Auditing Techniques	Nature of concurrent auditing techniques; types of concurrent auditing techniques; design and implementation of concurrent auditing techniques; relative advantages and disadvantages of concurrent auditing techniques
20 Interviews, Questionnaires, and Control Flowcharts	Designing, conducting, and analyzing an interview; design and use of questionnaires; reliability and validity of questionnaires; constructing a control flowchart; advantages and disadvantages of control flowcharts
21 Performance Monitoring Tools	Objects of measurement; general characteristics of performance monitoring tools; types of tools available; data integrity issues

GENERALIZED AUDIT SOFTWARE

A major tool available to the auditor for collecting evidence on the quality of an application system is generalized audit software. Generalized audit software provides a means to gain access to and manipulate data maintained on computer media. The auditor obtains evidence directly on the quality of the records produced and maintained by the application system. In turn the quality of the records reflects the quality of the system processing these records.

This chapter discusses why generalized audit software was developed, the major functional capabilities and limitations of audit software, and those factors that over time affect the usefulness of audit software. The bases for managing an audit software project are discussed. Techniques for accessing complex data structures are described and evaluated. Finally, the chapter discusses an approach to acquiring audit software and some of its futures.

MOTIVATIONS FOR GENERALIZED AUDIT SOFTWARE DEVELOPMENT

A generalized audit software package is a program providing powerful data retrieval, data manipulation, and reporting capabilities specifically oriented to the needs of auditors. The primary motivation for developing this software is the set of problems caused by the diversity of computerized information processing environments that confront the auditor.

In a manual system important sources of audit evidence are the records showing the various transactions undertaken by the organization and their resulting effects on the organization. This hard-copy evidence can be examined readily by the auditor. In a computer system this evidence exists on magnetic media and can only be examined using a program to extract or dump the contents of files. The problem is that external auditors (if not internal auditors) must deal with systems having diverse characteristics: different hardware and software environments, different data structures, different record formats, different processing functions. With resource constraints it is often impossible to develop specific programs for every system that will extract, manipulate, and report data required for audit purposes. For this reason generalized software has been developed that is capable of handling a wide variety of different systems. The tradeoff made is processing efficiency for the ability to develop quickly a program capable of accomplishing audit objectives in a new environment. In many cases the loss in processing efficiency is more than compensated by savings in labor hours required for developing audit software capabilities for specific computer systems.

A second major motivation for developing audit software is the need to develop quickly an audit capability in light of changing audit objectives. Both external auditors and internal auditors face situations where new audit objectives must be developed or existing audit objectives change. Generalized audit software facilitates adaptation by the auditor when these changes occur.

A third major motivation for developing audit software is the need to provide audit capabilities to auditors relatively unskilled in the use of computers. In the past many auditors have had little training in computers. Most generalized audit software packages can be used by auditors who are not computer audit specialists; thereby the computer audit capabilities of these auditors are extended.

FUNCTIONAL CAPABILITIES

Generalized audit software allows the auditor to use a high-level, problem-oriented language to invoke functions to be performed on computer files. The auditor must comply with the various syntactic and semantic rules of the language; that is, rules governing the combination of words or terms that can be used in the language, and rules governing the meanings ascribed to the words and legitimate combinations thereof included in the language. Typically, preprinted input specification sheets are supplied with the software package, and the auditor completes these specification sheets to be keyed and input to the software. Some packages allow the auditor to provide terminal input. The package examines input for syntax and semantic errors but, as with programming language compilers, certain logic errors cannot be recognized. After errors identified have been corrected, the package attempts to carry out the functions invoked. Table 16-1 shows the major functions included in generalized audit software packages. The following sections provide a brief description of these functions.

TABLE 16-1
MAJOR SETS OF FUNCTIONS GENERALLY AVAILABLE IN GENERALIZED AUDIT SOFTWARE

Set of functions	Examples
File access	Capabilities to read different record formats and different file structures, especially sequential, index sequential, and random; multiple files can be read simultaneously
File reorganization	Sorting and merging files
Selection	Boolean and relational operators available, e.g., A AND (B OR C); A EQ 2500; A GT 3000
Statistical	Varies from sampling every *n*th item to capabilities supporting attributes and variables sampling
Arithmetic	Full set available: addition, subtraction, multiplication, division
Stratification and frequency analysis	Capabilities to classify data according to certain criteria
File creation and updating	Capabilities to create and update work files based on the installation's files
Reporting	Editing and formatting of output

File Access

The file access functions enable files having different record formats and file structures to be read. Records may have fixed or variable formats. Typically, the file structures that can be read are sequential, index sequential, and random, although some packages now provide access to more complex structures such as trees and networks. Several files usually can be read simultaneously by generalized audit software.

File Reorganization

The file reorganization functions allow data to be sorted into different orders and data from different files to be merged onto one file. Sorting capabilities are necessary for a variety of purposes; for example, reporting data in a specified order or comparing data on two files. Merging capabilities are needed if data from separate files is to be combined on a separate work file.

Selection

Generalized audit software provides powerful selection capabilities for extracting data that satisfies certain tests. Typically, the Boolean operators AND, OR are provided as well as the relational operators EQ, GT, LT, NE, GE, LE; that is, equal to, greater than, less than, not equal to, greater than or equal to, and less than or equal to. Complex queries containing nested tests can be formulated. Brackets establish precedence. For example, the query (PAY GT 12000 AND (OVERTIME GE 2000 OR ALLOWANCES EQ 6)) would extract employee records where pay is greater than $12,000 per year and overtime is greater than or equal to $2000 per year, or employee records where pay is greater than $12,000 and the allowances classification is category 6.

Statistical

The statistical capabilities of generalized audit software vary from primitive to sophisticated. At a basic level every nth record can be selected. However, several packages provide comprehensive attributes and variables sampling capabilities. In some cases functions exist supporting financial analysis; for example, regression and financial ratio analysis. Alternatively, the audit software may be designed to provide input to separate statistical and financial modeling software.

Arithmetic

Generalized audit software provides the full set of arithmetic operators enabling work fields to be computed. the arithmetic accuracy of data to be checked, control totals to be produced. etc. For example, net pay calculations for a payroll file can be recomputed or files can be crossfooted.

Stratification and Frequency Analysis

The software provides varying capabilities with respect to stratification and frequency analysis. If stratification and frequency analysis capabilities are provided, frequency tables and bar charts (histograms) can be produced. For example, the frequency of accounts receivable balances in certain classes can be determined: $0–$200, $200.01–$400, $400.01–$600, etc. The distribution of accounts receivables balances is an important determinant of the type of sampling method chosen.

File Creation and Updating

Some generalized audit software packages allow work files to be created and updated. The auditor uses the software to extract the data needed for audit purposes from the application system files. By using the work file for audit purposes, the auditor causes minimum interference to normal application system processing.

Reporting

Finally, the software can produce reports containing information useful to the auditor. These reports can be formatted in different ways. Edit criteria can be applied; for example, zero suppression and addition of dollar signs.

AUDIT TASKS THAT CAN BE ACCOMPLISHED

The functional capabilities of generalized audit software can be combined in different ways to accomplish several audit tasks:

1 Examine the quality of data
2 Examine the quality of system processes
3 Examine the existence of the entities the data purports to represent
4 Undertake analytical review

The following sections examine the ways in which these tasks can be accomplished.

Examine the Quality of Data

The auditor can use the functional capabilities of generalized audit software to examine the existence, accuracy, completeness, and consistency of data maintained on files. Some examples follow. Records for various fixed assets can be retrieved to see if, in fact, the records exist. The calculation of sales discounts can be checked for accuracy. The address field in an accounts receivable file can be examined to see if it contains blanks. Records on the personnel file and payroll file can be compared for consistency.

The auditor examines the quality of data maintained on application system files for two reasons. First, the quality of the data reflects the quality of the application system that processes the data. For example, if the address fields in debtors' records contain blanks, the auditor must question the adequacy of the validation processes contained in the system. Second, the quality of data reflects the quality of the personnel who developed and maintain the application system, and the quality of the personnel who use the system. If the data is low in quality, the application system processing the data may be poorly designed, poorly implemented, or poorly maintained. If this situation has been allowed to continue, the quality of the personnel who use the system must be questioned. Also, it is possible that even though the system is well-designed, implemented, and maintained, the data supplied by users is low in quality.

Examine the Quality of System Processes

Besides the methods described above, the auditor can examine more directly the quality of both the manual and computer system processes in other ways. Even though the quality of system data is high, the quality of system processes may be low from the viewpoint of achieving the objectives of the organization. For example, upon using generalized audit software to age an accounts receivable file, the auditor may find substantial numbers of overdue accounts. This attribute of the data reflects adversely on both the computer system and the manual system. The computer system may not be producing timely information for control over debtors. The manual system may have inadequate debt collection facilities.

Similarly, the auditor may use generalized audit software to prepare inventory turnover statistics for obsolescence analysis. This analysis highlights inadequate management of inventory and enables the auditor to prepare recommendations for improvement. Generalized audit software provides powerful capabilities for producing management reports useful for various kinds of analyses that reflect on the quality of system processes.

Mair [1975] describes another way of using generalized audit software to examine the quality of system processes via the *parallel simulation* technique. Parallel simulation involves the auditor writing a program to replicate those application processes that are critical to an audit opinion and using this program to reprocess application system data. The results produced are compared with the results produced by the application system and any discrepancies identified. For example, Figure 16-1 shows a parallel simulation program reprocessing transaction data against a master file and producing a new master file. Generalized audit software then compares the master file produced by the parallel simulation program with the master file produced by the application system and generates a report of discrepancies.

The parallel simulation program can be written in any programming language; however, because generalized audit software is a high-level, problem-oriented language, it allows fast development of a program that will accomplish the audit functions required. Since parallel simulation runs are often one-off runs, processing efficiency usually is not a major consideration.

There are several steps involved in constructing a parallel simulation program. First, the auditor must obtain an understanding of the functions performed by the application system. Second, the auditor must identify those functions where reliability is critical to an audit opinion. Third, the auditor constructs a parallel simulation program. Fourth, the auditor runs the program. Finally, the auditor evaluates the results produced. Discrepancies indicate a flaw in either the simulation program or the application system processes.

Examine the Existence of the Entities the Data Purports to Represent

Data may exist, be accurate, complete, and consistent; however, it may have no real world correspondence. It may represent a bogus insurance policy or an inventory item that no longer exists. The auditor must determine the existence of entities that the data purports to describe.

The statistical sampling capabilities of audit software allow the auditor to investigate the existence of the entities described by the data. The auditor can use the software to automatically generate confirmation notices for accounts receivable, select inventory for observation, circularize creditors for accounts payable, etc. Further, the software can print reports to facilitate the sampling process; for example, for observation purposes sort inventory items selected in

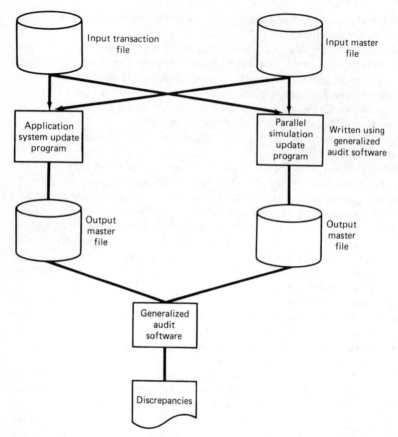

FIGURE 16-1
Example use of the parallel simulation technique.

the sample by their physical location. The statistical sampling capabilities of audit software allow the auditor to make a probabilistic statement about the existence of the assets and equities that the data describes.

Undertake Analytical Review

Analytical review is the process of obtaining key ratios and totals from an organization's data for comparison with previous years' ratios and totals or industrywide ratios and totals. The information obtained from analytical review is used to support or question preliminary audit conclusions based on system reviews and other substantive tests.

Generalized audit software supports analytical review in several ways. It can be used to extract data required for analytical review and prepare various ratios and totals. If the package provides regression analysis capabilities, it can be used to examine firm and industry trends. It can be used to extract and prepare information in suitable form for input into other financial analysis and modeling packages.

FUNCTIONAL LIMITATIONS

To use generalized audit software effectively and efficiently, the auditor must understand both the capabilities and the limitations of the software. The following sections examine three limitations of generalized audit software that cause it to be only a partial solution to the auditor's problems with evidence collection for computer systems. These deficiencies are:

1 Generalized audit software permits only ex post auditing and not concurrent auditing.

2 Only limited capabilities exist for verifying processing logic.

3 It is difficult to determine the application system's propensity for error using generalized audit software.

Ex Post Auditing Only

Generalized audit software enables evidence to be collected only on the state of an application system after the fact. The software examines the quality of data after it has been processed. Even if the auditor uses parallel simulation, the results produced by the parallel simulation program are checked against a set of existing results produced by the application system. Thus, some time lag exists between an application system error occurring and its identification. In some cases this elapsed time may be substantial if the application system is not audited on a regular basis.

For some types of systems the timely identification of errors may be critical. Consider, for example, a situation where multiple online users access a shared database. Unless an error in a data item is discovered quickly, it may permeate the database and cause several incorrect decisions to be made. It is important to quickly identify and correct the error. Chapter 19 discusses the use of concurrent auditing techniques that permit evidence to be collected, and sometimes evaluated, at the same time as system processing occurs. The auditor must use specialized audit software rather than generalized audit software to implement these techniques.

Limited Ability to Verify Processing Logic

In general, the tests performed with generalized audit software involve "live" data; that is, data captured and processed by the application system. The limitations of using live data for testing application systems are well known. The data may not test the exceptional condition that occurs. It is important to know whether the application system will handle this condition. To overcome this problem, parallel simulation can be used with test data as input to both the application system and the parallel simulation program. Chapter 18 further discusses these matters.

Limited Ability to Determine Propensity for Error

Systems can be designed and implemented in a manner that allows them, at least to some extent, to cope with change. Alternatively, they can be designed and implemented so they are inflexible and degenerate quickly when change occurs. For example, writing programs using a structured programming discipline permits programs to be modified quickly in light of change. The ability of the system to cope with change is a concern of the auditor. The auditor can obtain little evidence on this issue by using generalized audit software. The evidence must be obtained in other ways: reviewing the management control framework, examining system designs and program code, etc.

INSTALLATION/AUDIT GROUP MATURITY ISSUES

There is some constancy in the usefulness of generalized audit software for the external auditor. The external auditor continually confronts different information processing environments where a need exists for software having generalized capabilities to cope with these different environments. For the internal auditor, however, the usefulness of generalized audit software may change over time. Audit needs may not remain constant for two reasons. First, the computer installation's life cycle imposes changes on the means of achieving audit objectives for the installation. Second, the internal EDP audit group itself experiences a life cycle throughout which the needs and capabilities of the group change.

Impact of the Installation Life Cycle

Chapter 3 discussed the phases in the life cycle of a computer installation: initiation, expansion, formalization, and maturity. Two aspects of the life cycle impact the audit group's tasks and the usefulness of generalized audit software: (a) the changing types of systems developed by the installation throughout its life cycle, and (b) the changing levels of control exercised by management over the activities of the installation.

As the installation matures, the systems it develops and maintains change in two ways. First, the systems tend to stabilize. Second, there is a tendency to move toward more complex systems: database management systems, online realtime systems, data communications systems. As systems stabilize, there are fewer problems for the auditor in coping with changed file structures, record formats, etc., and the audit objectives for the systems also stabilize.

This increased stability may motivate the auditor to develop specialized audit software so the overheads incurred by the installation because of the audit function are reduced. As a further motivation toward using specialized audit software, the usefulness of ex post auditing declines in more complex information processing environments. There is a greater need for concurrent auditing to identify errors on a timely basis.

Maturity also means control objectives for systems stabilize. During the formalization phase, the controls absent from application systems during the expansion phase are built into systems. The auditor has increasing involvement in the system development life cycle to provide guidance on the design of controls. Thus, the auditor has more scope for designing controls and performing novel tests on these controls.

Impact of the Audit Group Life Cycle

The audit group also experiences a life cycle consisting of three phases: initiation, expansion, and maturity (see Chapter 25). Two aspects of this life cycle impact the usefulness of audit software: (a) the increasing stability of control objectives for application systems, and (b) the growing capabilities of the EDP audit group.

Generalized audit software is most useful during the early stages of the group's life cycle. At this time, control objectives for application systems are unclear and the group's computer or audit expertise may be low. The group may be subject to pressures to institute EDP audit procedures quickly. In the past it has been common for management to respond to crisis situations by setting up an EDP audit group. Generalized audit software provides a means for the audit group to respond quickly to demands for application system audits. The group can gain access quickly to data and change audit programs in light of experience or changing audit objectives.

However, when the audit group matures, its tasks, objectives, standards, and expertise have stabilized. The group may be carrying out efficiency auditing as well as effectiveness auditing. Application system audits are conducted on a regular basis. The group seeks to reduce the overhead costs caused by auditing so it develops specialized audit software to take over the functions previously performed by generalized audit software.

MANAGING A GENERALIZED AUDIT SOFTWARE APPLICATION

Managing a generalized audit software application closely follows the steps needed for properly managing the development of any software project. Since these steps have been discussed extensively in Chapter 5, the following sections provide only a brief discussion of their applicability to the management of an audit software application.

There are five steps involved in managing an audit software application:

1 Feasibility analysis and planning
2 Application design
3 Coding and testing
4 Operation
5 Evaluation and documentation of results

Feasibility Analysis and Planning

When an auditor recognizes a potential opportunity for using audit software, feasibility analysis should be undertaken to see if the likely benefits will exceed the costs. The likely benefits depend on the audit objectives that the audit software application will help achieve. For example, audit software may be used to extract a statistical sample for substantive testing. The value of the substantive test in part depends on the assessed reliability of the internal control system. If the internal control system is weak, the value of the substantive test is higher than if the internal control system is very strong.

When considering the costs of an audit software application, some of the factors to be considered are:

Cost factor	Explanation
Adequacy of installation documentation	Substantial costs can be incurred through the installation having incomplete or inaccurate documentation of its systems and files. The auditor may code up an audit software program incorrectly, undertake useless runs because record formats have been changed, etc.
Complexity of application system and files	If the application system is complex, coding up a parallel simulation program using audit software may be costly. Some complex file structures or record formats present access problems for audit software. These problems may take substantial time to overcome.
Labor costs for auditor	These costs are for the auditor's time expended through all stages of the audit software application.
Technical and administrative advice	Besides the auditor, other personnel may expend time on the application. The auditor may need technical or administrative advice from installation personnel.
Computing costs	These costs include testing and operating costs, running dump utilities to examine the format of records on a file, etc.
Supplies	These costs include tapes, stationery such as confirmation forms, and forms for documenting the application.

Once estimates of costs and benefits have been obtained, a budget and a timetable should be prepared. Decisions then can be made on whether the application should proceed and whether resource deficiencies exist.

Application Design

This stage involves the detailed design of the audit software application. The major steps are:

Design step	Explanation
Obtain detailed understanding of installation application system	This understanding can be obtained through reviewing the application system documentation, flowcharting the application system, preparing decision tables, etc.
Design output reports required	The output reports constitute some of the working papers for the audit. It is critical to see all the information required for the audit is output in a convenient form.
Prepare file definitions	The files to be accessed and any work files to be created must be defined.
Define the logic of the audit software program	The logic should be flowcharted or described in decision tables.
Define supplementary data needed	Reference (look-up) tables for the audit software may have to be designed.
Prepare a test plan	Testing may be undertaken using a test deck or live data. Chapter 18 discusses the various techniques for testing programs.
Desk check logic	When the logic of the audit software application has been designed, it should be desk-checked to see if audit objectives are met.

Once the design has been prepared, it should be reviewed and evaluated against the budget and timetable prepared during the feasibility analysis stage.

Coding and Testing

After the design has been prepared, the preprinted generalized audit software specification sheets are completed. On these sheets the auditor describes the commands necessary to invoke the functions provided in the software. Any data (constants) the software needs for processing also must be described. Before the sheets are keyed in machine-readable form, they should be desk-checked to see they comply with the design specifications.

After the specification sheets have been keyed, they are input to the audit software package, which checks the accuracy of syntax and certain semantics. The package produces an error and diagnostics report, and the auditor must correct the problems identified before proceeding. When the package produces no further diagnostics, the auditor can undertake test runs to check the accuracy of the processing logic specified. Logic errors then must be corrected.

Operation

Once the coding and testing stage is complete, the auditor should make a final check to see no changes have been made to the application system that would impact the audit software program; for example, a change to a record format. The processing time schedule then must be confirmed with the operations manager of the installation and the audit software application run.

Evaluation and Documentation of Results

Upon obtaining the audit software reports, the output should be reviewed to check for any errors and determine whether audit objectives have been attained. Respecification and rerunning of the program may be necessary.

The documentation and results must be incorporated into the audit work papers along with any suggestions for improvements in future runs. The costs and benefits of the application should be compared with the budget. Finally, any files created that may be needed for future use should be secured.

ACCESSING COMPLEX DATA STRUCTURES

One of the problems sometimes confronting the auditor who uses generalized audit software is gaining access to more complex data structures than sequential, index sequential, and random structures. Typically, this problem has arisen when the auditor must gain access to the data maintained by a database management system. Database management systems use a variety of data structures, some of which are complex: tree, network, inverted list, and multilist (for a discussion of these structures, see Goldstein [1985]).

Accessing Methods: Advantages and Limitations

Litecky and Weber [1974] identify three methods of using generalized audit software to access complex data structures, especially those maintained by a database management system:

1 Extract a sequential file for use with generalized audit software.

2 Use generalized interface routines to map the more complex data structures into the simpler data structures used by generalized audit software.

3 Include specialized access routines in generalized audit software that can handle complex data structures.

These solutions also can be applied to situations where the complex data structures are maintained by a procedure-oriented language such as COBOL. An installation does not always use the facilities of a database management system.

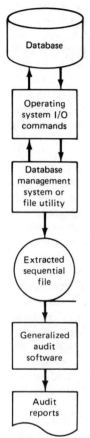

FIGURE 16-2
Extracting a sequential file from complex data structures for use by generalized audit software.

Extracting a Sequential File Rather than directly access complex data structures, the auditor can have an intermediate file prepared for use with generalized audit software. The facilities of the database management system or a file utility can be used to restructure data in a complex data structure as a flat file (Figure 16-2). Records on the file contain only data relevant for the auditor's purposes.

The primary advantage of this approach is its simplicity. Further, it may be the only viable approach for an external auditor to use when the generalized audit software package will not operate on a client's hardware/software configuration. This is a problem as several database management systems operate on a wider variety of hardware/software configurations than many generalized audit software packages.

The approach has several disadvantages. First, unless the auditor develops the routine for extracting the sequential file, there is a risk the integrity of data on the file has been violated. For example, generalized audit software might be used to prepare confirmations from the file. Asset records purposely not included on the file would not be confirmed. Second, the auditor does not take advantage of processing efficiencies offered by the data structures; for example, faster access to records through indexes and pointers. Third, the auditor loses a means of obtaining a deeper understanding of the installation's database management system and its application systems. By dealing directly with complex data structures, the auditor obtains a better appreciation of the problems posed for data integrity by the structures and the problems faced by the user in accessing and maintaining the structures.

Using Generalized Interface Routines One means commonly used to access complex data structures maintained by some database management systems is generalized interface routines. These routines are called host language extensions and have been built to obviate the need for programmers to write the programming code necessary to access and maintain complex data structures. To access a data structure, the program calls the routine, supplies record identification and access parameters, and the routine simply "presents" the program with the retrieved record. For addition, modification, or deletion activities, the program again supplies the change parameters to the routine, and the routine carries out the required maintenance to the data structure. The most commonly used database management systems, TOTAL, IMS, SYSTEM 2000, ADABAS, and IDMS, all provide host language extension facilities for programming languages such as COBOL and FORTRAN. Several audit software packages now have "libraries" of host language extensions for the major database management systems. These libraries are maintained by the audit software vendor. Figure 16-3 shows the overall approach.

Even if a database management system is not used, providing the installation develops and uses standard sets of access routines across application systems, these routines can be used by generalized audit software to access complex data structures. It is only when different application systems have their own specialized access routines that problems arise for the auditor who uses audit software.

The primary advantage of this approach is that the auditor through the host language extensions gains direct access to the database. An intermediate file does not have to be created. The auditor gains a better appreciation of integrity and usage problems experienced with the data structures.

The primary disadvantage surrounds some awkward and unwieldy query processing that can result with tree and network data structures. For generalized audit software to be capable of performing queries on trees and networks, these structures must be flattened. The method to be used for flattening the structure and specifying the query on the flattened structure can be a difficult problem. The whole issue of the relationship between the data structure and the query language that operates on the data structure is a complex issue and it is left for further study. Weber [1977] provides an extended discussion of this issue in an audit context.

Using Specialized Access Routines In some cases, for the auditor to be able to use generalized audit software to directly access complex data structures, specialized access routines have to be included in the audit software package. This occurs under two situations. First, the installation does not use a standard set of access routines or a database management system to maintain the data structures. Specialized access routines are embedded in the application system. For example, a COBOL program maintains its own indexes and pointers for the multilist file that it updates. Second, the database management system being used by the installation is a self-contained database management system; that is, a system that does not provide host language (programmer) facilities, only nonprogramming generalized facilities. Thus, the access routines are built into the database management system, often regarded as proprietary by the system vendor, and generally unavailable for use. Everest and Weber [1977] discuss these systems more fully.

Figure 16-4 shows this solution method for accessing complex data structures. Its primary advantage is processing efficiency. If the auditor frequently audits critical application systems containing specialized access routines, the audit software vendor may be requested to incorporate these access routines into the software. Alternatively, if the audit software package provides a user own-coding routine call facility, the access routines may be invoked using this facility.

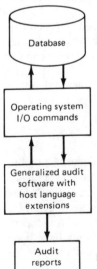

FIGURE 16-3
Including host language extensions in generalized audit software to access complex data structures.

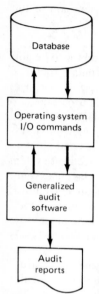

FIGURE 16-4
Including specialized access routines in generalized audit software to access complex data structures.

There are several disadvantages of using this method. First, in the case of self-contained database management systems, the vendor may not supply the information necessary for the modifications. Second, the modifications may be costly and perhaps only relevant to a single application system. Third, the auditor is responsible for ensuring the access routines are updated if they are changed.

Other alternatives for accessing the data should be considered. The sequential file approach can be used. In the case of self-contained database management systems, many of the functions required by the auditor are available in the system's generalized retrieval language (see, further, Weber [1975]). The auditor should consider using the database management system itself rather than generalized audit software for evidence collection purposes.

Auditor Independence Issues

When the auditor does not use an independently controlled generalized audit software package to directly access complex data structures, but instead has a sequential file extracted or uses database management software for evidence collection purposes, questions sometimes are raised about whether the auditor maintains independence. Some would argue the auditor compromises independence by relying on the installation's software. This software may have been modified so the auditor can no longer rely on the integrity of the data obtained using the software.

This argument is false for two reasons. First, independence is well-accepted as a "state of mind." It is an independence in attitude that is required. Second, even if the auditor uses generalized audit software with host language extensions, or generalized audit software with embedded access routines to access the database, reliance still is placed on certain of the installation's software; namely, the integrity of the host language extensions and the integrity of the operating system input/output routines. In the end, to ensure the integrity of the evidence collection process, the auditor would have to stop and restart the hardware, load an independently controlled operating system, an independently controlled generalized audit software package, and perhaps an independently controlled database management system. Even this is not an inviolable process. The microcode of the machine could have undergone unauthorized modifications.

Jenkins and Weber [1976] suggest three methods that can be used to determine whether critical installation software has been modified:

Method	Explanation
Blueprint approach	Obtain from the vendor a copy of the installation's operating system and database management system object code, and compare this with the version used by the client to determine discrepancies. Some are unwilling to supply such "blueprints."
Hash total approach	The auditor obtains a hash total of the object code of the installation's critical software and rechecks this total each time the software is used.
Test data approach	Test data is developed to test the critical modules in the database management system or operating system to see if their integrity has been violated.

These approaches are not trouble-free. The installation may make legitimate modifications to an operating system or database management system to improve efficiency or provide facilities not existing in the software. Thus, blueprints and hash totals must be updated and test data must be modified.

In deciding which approach to adopt to access complex data structures, the auditor should consider the costs and benefits of each approach. All have their various advantages and disadvantages. Different approaches may be appropriate at different times.

PURCHASING GENERALIZED AUDIT SOFTWARE

The purchase cost of most audit software packages is not very high. A basic package costs as low as $5000. However, optional modules may be available with the purchase; for example, interfaces to different database management systems and data dictionaries. These options usually cost extra. The final cost of a package can range up to about $30,000. There may also be an ongoing license fee.

Because of the relatively low cost of purchasing an audit software package, there is a temptation to regard the purchase as an unimportant matter. However, the purchase cost is not the only cost of using audit software. If the "best" audit software package has not been acquired, there are the ongoing

TABLE 16-2
SOME MAJOR GENERALIZED AUDIT SOFTWARE PACKAGES AND THEIR VENDORS

Package	Vendor
ACL	ACL Services
Audassist	Alexander Grant & Co.
Audex 100	Arthur Andersen & Co.
Audit	U.S. Department of Commerce
Audit Analyzer	Program Products
Audit Reporter	Burroughs Corporation
Auditaid	Seymour Schneidman & Associates
Auditape	Deloitte Haskins & Sells
Auditec	Carleton Corporation
Auditpak II	Coopers & Lybrand
Auditronic	Ernst & Whinney
Cars	Sage Software Products
Computer File Analyzer	Price Waterhouse & Co.
Dyl-Audit	Dylakor
EDP Auditor	Cullinane Corporation
Mark IV Auditor	Informatics
Pan Audit	Pansophic Systems, Inc.
Probe	Citibank
Score-Audit	Programming Methods, Inc.
Strata	Touche Ross & Co.
S2190	Peat Marwick Mitchell & Co.

opportunity costs of not having acquired an audit software package that allows the most effective and efficient auditing. Further, some audit groups have found they need to purchase more than one audit software package to accomplish their audit objectives. The level of effort devoted to the evaluation and acquisition of an audit software package should be appropriate for the expected costs, both purchase and opportunity costs.

A large number of generalized software packages is available for purchase by the auditor for use as audit software. Some of these packages were developed specifically as audit software. Others are generalized retrieval packages that auditors have found useful for audit purposes. Table 16-2 lists some of the packages available. The following sections discuss the major differences existing among the packages and describe the steps that should be undertaken when purchasing the software.

Major Differences among Generalized Audit Software Packages

Audit software packages differ on three bases: (*a*) semantics, (*b*) syntax, and (*c*) operating environment. The semantics of the software are the functions that the software can perform. The syntax of the software is the set of rules governing the combination of words or terms used to activate the software. The operating environment is the hardware/software configuration on which the software will run.

Semantics   A large number of functions is common across audit software packages. However, two areas of differences exist. First, some software provide generalized functions tailored for specific industries; for example, banking or insurance. Second, some software provide capabilities for accessing complex data structures.

Industry-specific audit software is now starting to emerge. It takes the form of a generalized audit software package modified to better suit the industry or an audit software package specifically written for the industry. For example, one audit software package written specifically for the banking industry provides generalized functions that check for a low or zero interest rate in an account record, overdrawn accounts, dormant accounts, incorrect loan payment schedules, and suspected kiting. (Kiting involves a customer drawing a check against uncollected funds in an account.) The auditor simply activates these functions by supplying parameter values; for example, the number of months of inactivity required before an account is considered dormant.

Some of the optional modules that can be acquired with generalized audit software packages are interfaces to database management systems and interfaces to other special purpose packages that use complex file structures. For example, some audit software packages provide interfaces to bill-of-materials packages used for manufacturing applications. Bill-of-materials packages typically use complex data structures such as networks.

Syntax   The syntax of audit software takes two basic forms. First, it may require the auditor simply to answer a set of questions in checklist form. Second, to accomplish a task it may require the auditor to undertake some coding in the audit software language.

The first syntax form is the higher-level syntax form and the easiest to use. It may involve the auditor giving a yes or no response to a question; for example, should a field be totaled? It may involve the auditor supplying parameter values for a predefined function; for example, defining the class intervals for frequency analysis. Three examples of this syntax form are:

1 SORT REQUIRED (Y OR N) ☐
                          35
(Explanation: The auditor inserts a Y or N in the box and this value will be keyed in column 35 of a record.)

2 POPULATION SIZE ☐☐☐☐☐☐☐☐☐☐
                   41   50

SAMPLE SIZE   ☐☐☐☐☐☐☐☐
                   51   58
(Explanation: For a statistical sampling routine, the auditor supplies the population size and sample size required.)

3 CONFIRMATIONS (Circle One)

A	Positive Reply
B	Negative Reply

36

(Explanation: The auditor chooses whether the confirmation notices should be printed in positive form or negative form.)

The second syntax form is a lower-level syntax and more difficult to use. However, it provides greater flexibility in allowing different audit tasks to be accomplished. It is used, typically, to specify selection expressions in terms of Boolean and relational operators and for arithmetic expressions. Two examples of this syntax are:

```
1 | W  0  4 | M  U  L | W  0  5 | W  0  6 |
  1       3 4      6 7      9 10     12
```

(Explanation: Field W04 is multiplied by field W05 and the result is placed in a work field labeled W06.)

2 SELECT: PAY.GT.'15000'.AND.STATUS.EQ.'MGR'
(Explanation: This is a free format selection expression containing Boolean and relational operators.)

Typically, audit software packages use both forms of syntax. If the package is intended for use by the auditor with little computer knowledge, it will contain more of the first syntax form. Conversely, if the package is intended for use by a computer audit specialist, it will contain more of the second syntax form. The second syntax form allows more audit tasks to be performed. Also, it usually permits greater processing efficiencies to be attained. However, this is not always the case. An industry-specific audit software package may process more efficiently because unneeded functions have been eliminated. It may also use mainly the first syntax form because flexibility is not a major requirement.

Operating Environment In general, the greater the variety of hardware/ software configurations on which an audit software package will run, the greater will be its processing inefficiencies. Vendors of audit software have made one of two design choices. Some have designed and implemented their packages to run on only a few makes of machines; namely, those makes most often used for accounting applications—IBM, Burroughs. To attain processing efficiency, they have written their packages in the assembly code of these machines. Other vendors have designed and implemented their packages to run on a wide variety of configurations. Consequently, they have written their packages in a high-level language—ANS COBOL. The tradeoff is portability versus efficiency. Whether or not portability is a critical requirement depends on the needs of the audit group. Internal auditors may be concerned only with having a package that will operate on their particular hardware/software configuration. External auditors need packages that will operate on diverse configurations.

Selecting a Package

The steps that should be followed in selecting an audit software package are the same as those that should be followed in selecting any software package (see Vallabhaneni [1985]). Two major steps are involved: (a) evaluation, and (b) acquisition. The depth in which these steps are carried out depends on the likely benefits and costs of using the software. The selection process itself can be costly. It must be tempered by cost-benefit considerations.

Evaluation   The objective of the evaluation stage is to select a generalized audit software package that best meets the needs of the audit group. The following steps should be undertaken:

1 *Plan and initiate the project:* This step involves setting up the project team to undertake the information gathering and information evaluation phases and preparing a budget for the project—required completion date, labor, overheads, etc.

2 *Determine audit needs:* The project group must determine the needs of the audit group that the package must satisfy; for example, functions required, hardware/software configurations on which the package must operate, complexity of language syntax permitted.

3 *Determine constraints:* Constraints take several forms; for example, the dollar amount available for purchase, limitations on the amount of memory and the number of peripherals that the package can use, training time permitted.

4 *Collect and evaluate information on available packages:* The purpose of this step is to select from the list of packages that may satisfy the needs and constraints, those that will be subject to an in-depth evaluation. Information on packages can be obtained from vendors. At various times surveys of audit software are published (see, for example, Sobol [1983]). Different software information houses (e.g., Auerbach and Datapro) provide feature analyses and user survey reports on some audit software packages. Existing users of a package should be consulted. A feature comparison checklist must be prepared and a set of feasible alternatives selected.

5 *In-depth study:* The in-depth study determines in detail a package's strengths and weaknesses. Detailed information on a package must be gathered and evaluated. A technical evaluation must be carried out. Benchmark tests may be necessary. Proposed contract terms must be understood and evaluated.

6 *Cost-benefit analysis:* After the in-depth study, the costs and benefits of the packages can be evaluated and a final selection made.

Acquisition Acquisition of an audit software package involves two steps: (*a*) negotiating a contract with the vendor, and (*b*) final acceptance testing. The contract is a critical element in the final purchase decision. It must specify agreements on prices, payments, delivery, installation, modifications, maintenance, improvements, training, use, penalties, liabilities, termination, etc. Legal advice should be sought if necessary.

In some cases an acceptance test is not necessary. Satisfactory benchmark tests may have been carried out. A free-trial period may be available or a short-term lease/rental contract has been negotiated. If any major doubts still remain about the performance of the package, an acceptance test provides a means of confirming or dispelling these doubts.

SOME FUTURES OF GENERALIZED AUDIT SOFTWARE

Generalized audit software was developed during the late 1960s and early 1970s when data processing activities were dominated by a few makes and models of mainframe machines. Since then, the software has been modified and enhanced in some areas—for example, access to databases and improved sampling capabilities—but, in general, the functional capabilities provided by the software have remained fairly stable. Perhaps this stability manifests the quality of the initial designs embodied in generalized audit software; perhaps it manifests the costs and overall impossibility of modifying and enhancing the software to keep up with changing technology. Whatever the reasons for the stability, surveys of the frequency with which different EDP audit tools and techniques are used by auditors continue to report that generalized audit software is a major evidence collection tool (see, for example, Tobinson and Davis [1981] and Reeve [1984]). Moreover, auditors expect to continue to use generalized audit software as a major evidence collection tool for the forseeable future (see Reeve [1984]).

Nonetheless, advances in technology have taken their toll on the usefulness of generalized audit software. Insofar as accounting applications are now executed on a vast range of hardware/software configurations that encompass mainframes, minicomputers, and microcomputers, the domain of generalized audit software ought to have expanded correspondingly. This has not been the case. Although there have been several developments relating to minicomputers and microcomputers, generalized audit software is still restricted primarily to a few makes and models of mainframe machines. Moreover, few generalized audit software packages allow auditors to work interactively. Often auditors must now look elsewhere for tools and techniques that will help them gather evidence (see Chapter 17).

It is not clear whether the problems posed for generalized audit software by the diversity and rate of change of the technology can be overcome in a cost-effective way. For many years, Will [1983] has argued that auditors should use a common, standardized Audit Command Language (ACL). Such a language would provide some degree of transparency to technological change if different vendors agreed to provide the language among the suite of software that they made available to support a particular machine. For whatever reason, however, ACL is still not available on a widespread basis, and so auditors must continue to seek other solutions when generalized audit software cannot be used as an evidence collection tool.

SUMMARY

Generalized audit software provides an important means for the auditor to gain access to and to manipulate data maintained on computer media. However, the effective and efficient use of the software requires an understanding of both its capabilities and limitations. The benefits and costs of using the software depend in part on the maturity of the audit group and the maturity of the computer installation being audited. The benefits and costs also depend on how well an audit software project is managed.

Accessing complex data structures may present some problems for using generalized audit software. However, alternative methods for accessing these data structures are available. The choice of a method is situation-dependent.

When purchasing generalized audit software, the audit group should follow the standard procedures that are now well-established for purchasing any software package. Though the different audit software packages have many common features, there are sufficient differences to warrant careful evaluation before a purchase decision is made.

In spite of rapid changes in computer technology, generalized audit software will still remain a useful evidence collection tool in many situations. However, auditors will have to rely increasingly on other types of software to collect evidence on the reliability of controls in a system.

REVIEW QUESTIONS

16-1 Briefly discuss the motivations for developing generalized software specifically for audit purposes. Even though generalized retrieval software already existed before audit software was developed, why did auditors prefer to develop their own software packages?

16-2 What is a generalized audit software package?

16-3 Without using the examples in the chapter, give two examples of how each of the following functional capabilities of audit software might be used by the auditor:
a File reorganization
b Statistical
c Arithmetic
d Stratification and frequency analysis

16-4 Briefly explain the difference between a Boolean operator and a relational (conditional) operator used in a selection expression for generalized audit software. Be sure to explain their different purposes from an audit perspective.

16-5 What are the auditor's purposes in using generalized audit software to examine the quality of data maintained on application system files?

16-6 Briefly explain the parallel simulation technique. What is the purpose of using parallel simulation? Outline some of the advantages and disadvantages of using this technique for audit purposes.

16-7 If the auditor confronts a hardware/software configuration on which available generalized audit software will not run, how can the activities normally carried out with audit software be accomplished?

16-8 Why does generalized audit software have only limited capabilities for verifying the processing logic of an application system and the propensity of the application system for error?

16-9 Discuss the advantages of using generalized audit software when an organization first forms an EDP audit group. What factors may cause a decline in the usefulness of generalized audit software as the audit group matures?

16-10 Briefly discuss the impact that complex systems have on the usefulness of generalized audit software.

16-11 When using audit software, why is it important that the installation personnel responsible for the application system being audited be consulted and their cooperation solicited?

16-12 Briefly outline the contents of the audit work papers for an audit software application. Why is it important that the application be documented properly?

16-13 As the manager of an audit software application, what factors would you look for as warnings that the costs of completing the application may exceed the benefits and/or the budget?

16-14 When might it be necessary to keep the files created during an audit software application for a future period's work? Give an example.

16-15 Briefly explain what is meant by the host language extensions of a database management system. How can host language extensions be used in generalized audit software to gain access to complex data structures such as trees and network?

16-16 When confronted with the problem of using generalized audit software to access complex data structures, for each of the following solutions give an example of where you would choose the solution in preference to the two others:
a Extract a sequential file
b Use generalized interface routines
c Use specialized access routines
Briefly justify your selection.

16-17 Some auditors claim that to maintain independence an auditor must always use an independently controlled audit software package to access a database. Why is this a moot point?

16-18 Audit software must interface with other software, for example, the operating system, to carry out its functions. Briefly describe some techniques the auditor can use to determine whether unauthorized modifications have been made to this software. Outline the advantages and disadvantages of each technique.

16-19 Even though audit software may be relatively inexpensive to purchase, why is it important that alternative packages be evaluated carefully before a purchase decision is made?

16-20 Select two currently available audit software packages and list their differences on the basis of:

a Syntax

b Semantics

c Operating environment

16-21 Find an industry-specific audit software package and list those functions included in the package that are not available in a generalized audit software package.

16-22 Select a generalized audit software package and try to find information that describes the advantages and limitations of the package.

16-23 Briefly describe the activities you would carry out during the in-depth study of an audit software package that you are considering for purchase.

MULTIPLE CHOICE QUESTIONS

16-1 Which of the following was *not* a motivation for developing generalized audit software:

a Need to develop an audit capability in light of changing audit objectives

b Provide an audit capability for auditors relatively unskilled in the use of computers

c Provide certain semantic capabilities specific to the auditor's needs

d Unavailability of any other form of generalized interrogation software that could undertake audit functions

16-2 Which of the following file structures is likely to be the most difficult to access using generalized audit software:

a A sequential file structure

b An index sequential file structure

c A network file structure

d A random (hashed) file structure

16-3 The expression PRICE LE 20 OR (PRICE GT 50 AND DISCOUNT LE 5) OR PRICE EQ ZEROS would extract products from a file that have a price:

a Less than or equal to 20, or a price greater than 50 and at the same time a discount less than 6, or a price equal to zero

b Less than 20 or greater than 50 and in either case a discount less than 5, or a price equal to zero

c Less than or equal to 20 and discount less than or equal to 5, or a price greater than 50 and discount less than or equal to 5, or a price equal to zero

d Less than 20, or a price greater than 50 and at the same time a discount less than 5, or a price equal to zero

16-4 A functional capability likely to exist in generalized audit software but unlikely to exist in other generalized interrogation languages is a:

a Boolean expression capability

b Statistical sampling capability

   c File reorganization capability

   d Merge capability

16-5 Parallel simulation involves the auditor:

   a Writing a program to replicate completely an application program

   b Using the random number capabilities of generalized audit software to simulate financial transactions for a period through a large number of iterations

   c Writing a program to replicate those application processes that are critical to an audit opinion and using this program to reprocess application system data

   d Using generalized audit software to perform a parallel run during the implementation of a new application system

16-6 Which of the following basic functional capabilities in generalized audit software would the auditor use to examine whether the entities that the data represents do, in fact, exist:

   a Statistical sampling capability

   b Stratification and frequency analysis capability

   c Analytical review capability

   d Arithmetic capability

16-7 Which of the following is *not* a functional limitation of generalized audit software:

   a Permits ex post auditing only and not concurrent auditing

   b Difficult to determine an application system's propensity for error using generalized audit software

   c Limited capabilities for verifying processing logic

   d Limited capabilities to recompute critical arithmetic expressions

16-8 For the audit group's life cycle, generalized audit software is most likely to be useful:

   a Late in the life cycle when the group has matured

   b During the early stages of the group's life cycle

   c When the group confronts a technologically complex computer system

   d During those stages when the group starts to undertake effectiveness auditing

16-9 A generalized audit software package validates the input parameters provided by the auditor to identify:

   a All syntactic errors only

   b All semantic errors only

   c All syntactic errors and all semantic errors

   d All syntactic errors and some semantic errors

16-10 In a generalized audit software application, evaluation and documentation of results primarily comes after the:

   a Operation phase

   b Feasibility analysis and planning phase

   c Coding and testing phase

   d Application design phase

16-11 A disadvantage of extracting a sequential file to obtain access to a complex data structure using generalized audit software is:

   a Few utility programs are available to perform the extraction

   b The approach is complex and error-prone

   c It is sometimes difficult to ensure the integrity of the file that is extracted

d It is usually difficult to prepare the file in a format that is suitable for input to generalized audit software

16-12 The host language extensions approach to accessing a complex data structure involves the auditor:

   a Rewriting the source code of generalized audit software in the host language of the database management system used

   b Incorporating the host language extensions in the generalized audit software package

   c Using the host language extensions to bypass the database management system used

   d Using the host language extensions instead of generalized audit software to formulate the interrogation needed

16-13 The primary advantage of using specialized access routines incorporated in generalized audit software to access a complex data structure is:

   a Simplicity

   b Efficiency

   c Audit independence assured

   d More comprehensive query facilities available

16-14 The blueprint approach to determining whether critical data processing installation software has been modified involves:

   a Using a standard test bed to determine whether the integrity of critical modules has been corrupted

   b Obtaining a copy of program source or object code from a vendor for comparison with the installation version of the program

   c Comparing the source code with the vendor-supplied documented specifications for the program

   d Checking a hash total of the existing version of the software against a standard hash total

16-15 The argument that the auditor's use of a database management system or a high-level language for interrogation purposes violates independence is suspect because:

   a The auditor has statutory backing for independence

   b It is almost impossible to violate the code of a database management system or a high-level language

   c Auditors can have their work reviewed to determine whether their independence has been violated

   d Even using generalized audit software, the auditor still relies on other hardware/software components to preserve the integrity of data extracted from files

16-16 It is important to evaluate competing generalized audit software packages when making a purchase decision because:

   a Even though the purchase cost may be small, a wrong decision can lead to excessive operational costs and to auditors being unable to attain their objectives

   b Even for those makes of machines that traditionally are not used for commercial purposes, a large number of generalized audit software packages can be purchased

   c The purchase cost of generalized audit software is very high

d The capabilities of generalized audit software change radically each year so vendor support is critical

EXERCISES AND CASES

16-1 Livalife Insurance is a large insurance company with offices scattered throughout the United States and over 1000 independent agents. As a member of the external audit team, during the year-end work you are called to a meeting with your manager. He explains that he is concerned about the activities of one agent who seems to have submitted an abnormal number of change of address forms for her clients. All the change of address forms give a single new address; namely, the agent's home address. On many of the policies taken out by the agent's clients, personal loans have been obtained. Your manager explains that he is concerned that the agent may be illegally obtaining policy loans on her clients' policies, unbeknown to her clients.

Required: Explain how you could use generalized audit software to find out whether the agent has been illegally taking out policy loans on her clients' policies. Assuming the agent has been acting illegally, what controls would you recommend instituting to prevent this type of fraud happening again?

16-2 For the following inventory file, list the audit objectives that you could accomplish using generalized audit software:
part number
part name
part description
bin location
unit price
unit cost
unit measure
quantity on hand
quantity on order
item activity
special prices allowed

16-3 For the following fixed assets file, list the audit objectives that you could accomplish using generalized audit software:
fixed asset number
fixed asset description
fixed asset classification
location
responsible manager
maintenance schedule
purchase price
purchase date
vendor information
depreciation method
current depreciated value
salvage value
depreciation account
taxable value

insured value
insurance vendor

16-4 The following payroll input detail file has been obtained from time card data. List the audit objectives you could accomplish using generalized audit software:
employee number
regular hours
overtime hours
expenses
commission payments
sick time
vacation time
leave time without pay

16-5 Suppose accounting data for a project is maintained in a tree structure of the following form (*Note:* there can be multiple projects, jobs, and transactions):

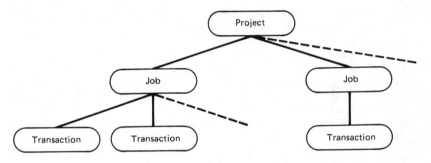

Find a currently available audit software package which will allow access to a tree structure and code up the following query. For project number BC6493, print out any inventory transactions that are less than $50 or greater than $1000 for any jobs numbered between A100 and A199.

16-6 For the previous question, how would you extract a sequential file containing the data you need for your query on the tree structure? Using the audit software package you have selected previously, code up the query again, this time applied to the sequential file you have extracted.

16-7 For the previous two questions, briefly discuss any problems you had in formulating the query under both approaches. Discuss the advantages and disadvantages of each approach.

16-8 Since software is now available to allow files to be uploaded from a microcomputer to a mainframe or downloaded from a mainframe to a microcomputer, it does not matter that the generalized audit software package used by an auditor will not run on a microcomputer. The auditor will still be able to gain access to any microcomputer file that is relevant to an audit. Discuss.

16-9 Obtain documentation on the capabilities provided in a popular database management system package designed for microcomputers. Write a brief report indicating the extent to which the functions listed in Table 16-1 are provided within the package. Describe the benefits and limitations the auditor is likely to encounter in using the database management system to examine the quality of data maintained in the database.

ANSWERS TO MULTIPLE CHOICE QUESTIONS

16-1 d	16-5 c	16-9 d	16-13 b
16-2 c	16-6 a	16-10 a	16-14 b
16-3 a	16-7 d	16-11 c	16-15 d
16-4 b	16-8 b	16-12 b	16-16 a

REFERENCES

Adams, Donald L., and John F. Mullarkey. "A Survey of Audit Software," *Journal of Accountancy* (September 1972), pp. 39–66.

Beitman, Lawrence. "An Audit Software Program Base," *EDPACS* (March 1984), pp. 6–8.

Everest, Gordon C., and Ron Weber. "Data Base Supported Systems and the Auditing Function," *Auerbach Information Management Series: Data Base Management* (Pennsauken, NJ: Auerbach Publishers, 1977).

Goldstein, Robert C. *Database Technology and Management* (New York: Wiley, 1985).

Henitz, Michael J. "What Internal Auditors Should Know About Selecting Audit Software," *The Magazine of Bank Administration* (December 1981), pp. 27–35.

Holmes, W. N., and P. M. Stanley. "An Interactive Package for Teaching EDP Audit," *Australian Computer Journal* (May 1984), pp. 54–59.

Jenkins, A. Milton, and Ron Weber. "Using DBMS Software as an Audit Tool: The Issue of Independence," *Journal of Accountancy* (April 1976), pp. 67–69.

Litecky, Charles R., and Ron Weber. "The Demise of Generalized Audit Software Packages?" *Journal of Accountancy* (November 1974), pp. 45–48.

McCourt, Vaughn W. "Guidelines for Audit Software Documentation," *EDP Auditing* (Pennsauken, NJ: Auerbach Publishers, 1985), Portfolio 74-03-04, pp. 1–15.

Mair, William C. "Parallel Simulation—A Technique for Effective Verification of Computer Programs," *EDPACS* (April 1975), pp. 1–5.

Neumann, Albrecht J. *Features of Seven Audit Software Packages—Principles and Capabilities* (Washington, DC: U.S. Government Printing Office, 1977), S.D. Catalog No. C13.10:500-13.

Perry, William E. "Audit Software: Planning," *EDP Auditing* (Pennsauken, NJ: Auerbach Publishers, 1985), Portfolio 74-03-10, pp. 1–11.

Perry, William E. "Audit Software: Development and Execution," *EDP Auditing* (Pennsauken, NJ: Auerbach Publishers, 1985), Portfolio 74-03-11, pp. 1–9.

Perry, William E. "Audit Software: Review amd Implementation," *EDP Auditing* (Pennsauken, NJ: Auerbach Publishers, 1985), Portfolio 74-03-12, pp. 1–8.

Pleier, Joseph R. "Computer-Assisted Auditing," *EDP Auditor* (1984), pp. 13–20.

Reeve, R. C. "Trends in the Use of EDP Audit Techniques," *Australian Computer Journal* (May 1984), pp. 42–47.

Rodman, Joseph E. "Identifying Potential Audit Software Applications," *EDPACS* (November 1985), pp. 6–9.

Sobol, Michael T. "Comparing Audit Software," *Computer Security Manual* (Northboro, MA: Computer Security Institute, 1983), pp. 5.26–5.28.

Tobinson, Gary L., and Gordon B. Davis. "Actual Use and Perceived Utility of EDP Auditing Techniques," *EDP Auditor* (Spring 1981), pp. 1–22.

Vallabhaneni, S. Rao. *Auditing Purchased Software: Acquisition, Adaptation, and Installation* (Altamonte Springs, FL: The Institute of Internal Auditors, 1985).

Weber, Ron. "Audit Capabilities of Some Database Management Systems," Working Paper MISRC-WP-75-05, Management Information Systems Research Center, University of Minnesota, Minneapolis, 1975.

Weber, Ron. "Implications of Database Management Systems for Auditing Research," in Barry E. Cushing and Jack L. Krogstad, eds., *Studies in Accounting No. 7: Frontiers of Auditing Research* (Bureau of Business Research, The University of Texas at Austin, 1977).

Will, H. J. "ACL: A Language Specific for Auditors," *Communications of the ACM* (May 1983), pp. 356–361.

Wooldridge, Susan. *Software Selection* (Philadelphia: Auerbach Publishers, 1973).

CHAPTER **17**

OTHER AUDIT SOFTWARE

CHAPTER OUTLINE

INDUSTRY-SPECIFIC AUDIT SOFTWARE

SPREADSHEET AUDIT SOFTWARE

HIGH-LEVEL LANGUAGES

SYSTEM SOFTWARE

    Reasons for Audit Use of Utility Software

    Audit Categorization of Utility Software

SPECIALIZED AUDIT SOFTWARE

    Reasons for Developing Specialized Audit Software

    Development and Implementation of Specialized Audit Software

DECISION SUPPORT SOFTWARE

CONTROL OF AUDIT SOFTWARE

SUMMARY

REVIEW QUESTIONS

MULTIPLE CHOICE QUESTIONS

EXERCISES AND CASES

ANSWERS TO MULTIPLE CHOICE QUESTIONS

REFERENCES

Software constitutes a major means of evidence collection for auditors. The previous chapter examined generalized audit software and its usefulness as an evidence collection tool. This chapter examines other types of software that the auditor may find useful throughout various phases of the evidence collection process. In some cases the software has been developed specifically to assist

EDP auditors; in other cases it has been developed primarily for other users but its functional capabilities also make it a useful audit tool.

INDUSTRY-SPECIFIC AUDIT SOFTWARE

Some types of audit software packages are now available that are oriented toward a specific industry in which an auditor works. In a sense, the packages are still *generalized* audit software packages since they provide auditors with a high-level language that can be used to invoke a wide range of functions. However, they differ from the types of software discussed in Chapter 16 in two ways. First, since they are oriented toward a particular industry, they provide high-level commands that invoke common audit functions needed within the industry. For example, in the banking industry, they might use a single command to invoke logic that would check for account kiting. If generalized audit software were used to check for kiting, several commands may be required to express the logic needed for the various tests. Second, industry-specific audit software may run on a smaller number of hardware/software configurations than generalized audit software. Indeed, industry-specific audit software may have been developed to access the data maintained by a *specific* generalized application package that is in widespread use within the industry. Accordingly, the file definitions, record definitions, and field definitions used by the application package may be incorporated in the audit software package—that is, they do not have to be defined by the auditor each time the audit software package is run.

The CAPS package is an example of an industry-specific audit software package (see Kendalls Consulting [1986]). It has been designed for auditors of financial institutions (primarily auditors of credit unions and building societies) and, as such, it provides high-level commands to invoke functions that they will need. In addition, CAPS has been written to access the data maintained by two widely used generalized application packages within the finance industry. Indeed, CAPS cannot be used unless auditees employ either of these two packages for their basic application processing. If the auditee uses one of those packages, however, CAPS provides seven major sets of audit capabilities:

1 *Loan arrears audit:* CAPS can be used to evaluate the movements in loan arrears on an individual member's loan balance throughout a specified period. For example, a report is provided showing any case where a new disbursement has occurred in spite of the loan being in arrears. Using this type of information, the auditor can assess the auditee's controls over loan arrears.

2 *Interest audit:* This module recalculates all interest on member loans and savings accounts to provide an independent check on calculations carried out by the application package.

3 *Term deposit interest audit:* This module recalculates total term deposit interest to a specified date to provide an independent check on calculations carried out by the application package.

4 *Member ledger balances audit:* This module provides several functions that assist the auditor to evaluate the veracity of member ledger balances. For example: it provides summarized information on each loans, savings, and investments ledger; it allows stratified sampling of member ledger balances for confirmation purposes; and it provides routines to statistically evaluate the results of a confirmation of members.

5 *Member ledger transactions audit:* This module examines ledger transactions for evidence of unusual circumstances. For example: it identifies transaction values outside a specified range; it identifies when a disproportionate number of a particular transaction type has occurred; and it selects transactions randomly for audit scrutiny.

6 *Member biographical audit:* This module examines the reasonableness of various demographic and personal data held about a member. For example: it looks for member names without vowels (unusual names); it tests for post codes (zip codes) outside a particular range; and it tests for members who have a post office box number as a primary address.

7 *Dormancy audit:* This module identifies member accounts that are dormant and which, as a consequence, bear a greater risk of fraudulent or unauthorized transactions remaining undetected for some time. The module retains a separate file of dormant accounts and provides a report on changes to the file when subsequent dormancy audits are conducted.

The primary advantages of an industry-specific audit software package over a generalized audit software package are that it will run more efficiently and that it will be easier to use since it incorporates higher-level functions. The primary disadvantage is that it has a more limited domain than generalized audit software. As such, industry-specific audit software tends to be more useful for internal auditors or for external auditors who perform a large number of audits within a specific industry.

SPREADSHEET AUDIT SOFTWARE

Spreadsheet audit software has been developed in response to problems that have arisen as a result of using spreadsheet software for financial modeling purposes (see, further, *InfoWorld* [1985]). Specifically, some organizations have incurred serious financial losses because their managers have based decisions on erroneous spreadsheet models. To reduce the risk of an erroneous spreadsheet model being developed and implemented, several steps can be undertaken (see, also, Grushcow [1985]): someone other than the developer of the model should test the model; all parameter values (for example, interest rates) should be placed in a single area of the spreadsheet; and absolute values should be placed in cells rather than embedded in formulas. In addition, spreadsheet audit software can be used to document the spreadsheet model and to check certain logic within the model.

```
          :        -A-       :             -B-                      :
 1        : 'Sales Forecast :                                      :
 2        : '#5 Linen        : 'Binders                            :
 3        :                  :                                      :
 4        :                  : "1st Q.                             :
 5        : 'Region:         :                                      :
 6        : 'Eastern         : 8320+B24  <8320>                    :
 7        : 'Western         : 2437                                :
 8        : ---------------- : ---------------------------------- :
 9        : 'Total           : @SUM(B4..B8)  <10757>              :
10        :                  :                                      :
11        :                  :                                      :
12        : 'Sales Forecast :                                      :
13        : 'Average Unit    :                                      :
14        : 'Selling Price   :                                      :
15        :                  : "1st Q.                             :
16        : 'Region:         :                                      :
17        : 'Eastern         : +B6*$C$14  <665184>                :
18        : 'Western         : +B7*$C$14  <194838.15>             :
19        : ---------------- : ---------------------------------- :
20        : 'Total           : @SUM(B15..B19)  <860022.15> :
```

FIGURE 17-1a
Spreadsheet audit software cell documentation report. (*Courtesy, Consumers Software, Inc.*)

Typical of the functions provided by spreadsheet audit software are the following:

1 *Cell documentation:* Some spreadsheet software does not provide a facility to print out a report showing the contents of all cells. Instead, the contents of cells must be examined on a cell-by-cell basis using a special instruction that displays the contents of a cell on the visual display screen. Spreadsheet audit software can be used to print the numeric constants, alphanumeric values, and formulas contained in the spreadsheet cells (Figure 17-1a).

2 *Worksheet map report:* Some spreadsheet audit software packages print reports that provide a global view of the contents of the worksheet. They represent the type of contents of each cell with a symbol. By scanning the symbols, a spreadsheet user may detect a particular pattern or configuration of symbols that reflects an error (Figure 17-1b).

3 *Circular reference checker:* A circular reference occurs when a formula in one cell references a value calculated by a formula in another cell which, in turn, depends on a value calculated by the formula in the first cell. In other words, the results are indeterminate because each formula depends on a value calculated by the other formula. With the use of spreadsheet audit software, circular references will be detected and reported (Figure 17-1c).

4 *Macro documentation:* A spreadsheet macro comprises a set of spreadsheet commands that can be invoked by a single command within the spreadsheet model. Spreadsheet audit software can be used to document the contents of macros used within the spreadsheet as a basis for checking the veracity of their logic (Figure 17-1d).

```
File MAPSAM.WKS  ** Range <ALL> [A1..AB32] **
LEGEND: F Formula    .Integer      +Real       m macro    b blank
          Text Left  ^ Text Center  " Text Right  \ Repeat
                          A
         ABCDEFGHIJKLMNOPQRSTUVWXYZAB
     1 : """"""""""""""""""""""""""""" :
     2 :                               :
     3 : '.........................FF :
     4 : '.........................FF :
     5 : '.........................FF :
     6 : '.........................FF :
     7 : '.........................FF :
     8 : '....................@F :
     9 : '.........................FF :
    10 : '.........................FF :
    11 :\\\\\\\\\\\\\\\\\\\\\\\\\\\\\\:
    12 : 'FFFFFFFFFFFFFFFFFFFFFFFFFFFFF :
    13 :\\\\\\\\\\\\\\\\\\\\\\\\\\\\\\:
    14 : '.........................FF :
    15 : '.........................FF :
    16 : '.........................FF :
    17 : '.........................FF :
    18 : '.........................FF :
    19 : '.........................FF :
    20 : '.........................FF :
    21 : '.........................FF :
    22 : '...........................' :
```

Overwritten Formula?

FIGURE 17-1b
Spreadsheet audit software worksheet map report. (*Courtesy, Consumers Software, Inc.*)

```
Circular References:
Cells: A24 -> A22 -> A24
                              Check!
Functions:
@AVG: F6..F7 F17..F18
@SUM: B9..C9 B20..E20 E6..E7 E9 E17..E18

Ranges:
B4..B8: B9
C4..C8: C9
E4..E8: E9
[E.SALES]
B6..D6: E6..F6
[W.SALES]
B7..D7: E7..F7
B15..B19: B20
```

FIGURE 17-1c
Spreadsheet audit software cross-reference report showing circular references. (*Courtesy, Consumers Software Inc.*)

Spreadsheet audit software cannot be used with all spreadsheet packages. Typically, only the spreadsheets maintained by a few of the major spreadsheet packages can be accessed using the software. Thus, if an important model or financial application has been implemented with spreadsheet software which produces files that cannot be accessed by spreadsheet audit software, auditors must use other means to assess the veracity of the spreadsheet model. The ease with which this assessment can be made depends on the quality of the

```
Listing of \S
*B2: /XMC2~
 B3: /XQ~

References:
<xm> [C2]

Menu at [C2]
SAVE   GRAPH   PRINT

Option: SAVE
Prompt: SAVE THE WORKSHEET AS "FORECAST"
 C4: /FSFORECAST~R{ESC}{ESC}{ESC}{ESC}~

Option: GRAPH
Prompt: SAVE A GRAPH CALLED "FORECAST"
 D4: /GSFORECAST~R{ESC}{ESC}{ESC}{ESC}~

Option: PRINT
Prompt: PRINT THE WORKSHEET TO THE PRINTER
*E4: /XCE7~
 E5: /PPG{ESC}{ESC}{ESC}~

References:
<xc> [E7]                          Where's the
                                   subroutine?
Listing of [E7]
```

FIGURE 17-1d
Spreadsheet audit software macro documentation report. (*Courtesy, Consumers Software, Inc.*)

spreadsheet documentation capabilities incorporated into the spreadsheet package.

HIGH-LEVEL LANGUAGES

In recent years, auditors have increasingly used other high-level languages besides generalized audit software to gain access to data. In particular, many auditors are now using fourth-generation languages and generalized statistical software as basic evidence collection tools (see, for example, Dallas [1984] and McMenamy [1984]).

Fourth-generation languages have proved useful to auditors for several reasons. First, most of the functions incorporated in a generalized audit software package are also included within a fourth-generation language. Indeed, this was the case even with the early versions of database management system software (see Weber [1975]). Second, many auditors find that fourth-generation languages are more user friendly than generalized audit software. This finding reflects the fact that fourth-generation languages were designed and implemented much later than most generalized audit software packages. Accordingly, they were intended for online, interactive use rather than batch use, and the designers could take advantage of enhanced knowledge about and more extensive experience with features that lead to better user interfaces.

Finally, if a data processing installation already uses a fourth-generation language, the auditor may encounter fewer operational difficulties in using the language. Inevitably, problems seem to arise when a software package that is not part of the installation's standard operating environment is loaded and executed.

Auditors have become more frequent users of statistical packages as increasing reliance has been placed on analytical review as a diagnostic tool in the conduct of an audit. In generalized audit software packages, the statistical capabilities provided usually are fairly basic. They are oriented toward compliance testing and usually some types of substantive testing. However, analytical review often relies on other statistical models, some of which are complex and require substantial computational support. For example: auditors who undertake time series modeling need various types of linear and nonlinear regression models; auditors who develop bankruptcy prediction models need discriminant analysis models. Several current statistical packages offer very powerful modeling capabilities, and these capabilities are continually being enhanced. Moreover, the user interfaces are friendly, and they are modified regularly to take advantage of technological developments that will assist the user—for example, color graphics.

For both fourth-generation languages and statistical packages, the widespread deployment of microcomputers has contributed significantly to their increasing use by auditors. With suitable utility software, auditors can download a copy of the data they need. The microcomputer versions of fourth-generation languages and statistical packages can then be employed to access and manipulate the data and to prepare reports. In this way, auditors can work in a standardized environment. Providing a download utility is available, auditors continue to use familiar microcomputer hardware and software, thereby avoiding some of the exigencies that arise when multiple hardware/software configurations are encountered.

SYSTEM SOFTWARE

System software comprises the programs that are used generally throughout a data processing installation to support the development, implementation, operation, and use of application systems. For example, system software includes operating systems, database management systems, compilers, interpreters, telecommunications monitors, query languages, sort packages, dump packages, test data generators, file comparison software, and merge packages.

Although all types of system software may be employed by auditors from time to time, a special subset of system software is especially useful for evidence collection purposes. The programs in this subset are often called *utility* programs. It is difficult to define precisely what constitutes utility programs, but, in general, they have two distinguishing characteristics. First, the functions they perform usually are less global than those performed by other system software. For example, a sort package usually is called a utility; a compiler usually is not considered to be a utility. Second, as a consequence of the first difference, utilities generally are smaller in size than other system software.

Reasons for Audit Use of Utility Software

For any given data processing installation, the extent to which the auditor can use utility software to collect evidence depends in part on the types of utility software available. Most hardware vendors supply a wide range of utilities for use with their machines. However, some of this software is not free. The installation must decide whether or not to purchase it. Further, a large number of independent software vendors actively compete to supply supplementary or replacement software. The availability of system software also depends on other factors, for example, the size of the machine used by the installation. In general, there are fewer utility packages available for minicomputers and microcomputers than the larger machines.

The stimulus to use utility software as an audit tool comes from a number of sources. The following sections discuss some of the major reasons why the auditor may choose to use utility software as a means of collecting evidence.

Unavailability of Generalized Audit Software Most generalized audit software packages have been designed to run on IBM hardware/software configurations. This situation simply reflects IBM's dominant share of the market in commercial data processing and the difficulties involved in designing and maintaining audit software that will run on a variety of configurations.

However, inevitably auditors have to evaluate installations using hardware/ software configurations on which generalized audit software will not run. In some countries, for example, Australia, IBM does not dominate the market to the extent it does in the United States. With the rapid growth in the use of minicomputers and microcomputers, the unavailability of generalized audit software that runs on these machines may be a problem confronted increasingly by the auditor. Moreover, at least in some cases, it is unlikely generalized audit software vendors will make major attempts to increase the availability of their packages on new hardware/software configurations. Increased availability means increased maintenance costs, decreased efficiency, and a greater risk of the integrity of the software being compromised. Neither does it seem likely the major machine vendors will implement generalized audit software for their configurations. A task force group within the American Institute of Certified Public Accountants once developed a set of common computer audit software specifications that they hoped the major machine vendors might implement. There has been little progress toward widespread implementation of these specifications. Thus, for those configurations on which generalized audit software will not run, utility software may be the major tool available for evidence collection purposes.

Functional Limitations of Generalized Audit Software With a few exceptions (generally in the statistical sampling and analytical review areas), the set of utility software packages available often provides a wider range of functional capabilities than generalized audit software. Chapter 16 discussed the various functional limitations of audit software: ex post auditing only, limited ability to verify processing logic, limited ability to determine the propensity for error (see, also, Will [1978] and Weber [1978b]). With utility software, often these limitations are overcome. For example, utility software exists that permits the collection of audit evidence concurrently with application system running. Utility software includes a number of testing tools (for example, test data generators) that permit verification of processing logic and allow the auditor to determine the likelihood of errors occurring. Unlike generalized audit software, utility software sometimes runs in privileged mode to gather various evidence; for example, data relevant to assessing operational efficiency.

Efficiency Considerations Because audit software is generalized software, often it consumes more resources to perform a task than the utility software written for a particular hardware/software configuration. In some situations the costs of this inefficiency may be unacceptable. Large volumes of data may have to be processed so the increased costs become substantial. If the auditor uses software to perform a task repeatedly, again, over time the sum total of the costs caused by the inefficiency may be substantial. Though utility software may be somewhat more difficult to use than generalized audit software, the auditor may be unable to accept the increased costs caused by the processing inefficiency of generalized audit software.

Facilitates Use of Other Audit Tools Utility software includes programs that sort data, merge files, copy files, delete files, dump files, convert files produced by one machine into a form suitable for reading by another machine, restructure files, etc. These functions facilitate the use of other evidence collection tools. The following examples show how utility programs can be used to assist generalized audit software applications:

1 If generalized audit software is to compare data on two files, the files must be sorted in the same order.

2 Generalized audit software may be able to read only a small number of files simultaneously. Data on several files can be merged.

. 3 Generalized audit software may be unable to traverse a network data structure. A utility can be used to flatten the network into a sequential file.

4 If generalized audit software will not run on the hardware/software configuration of the installation being audited, a copy of the files to be examined can be made and these files then converted to a form suitable for processing on the hardware/software configuration on which the audit software will run.

5 Several records of a file can be dumped so the auditor can check the format of these records before the audit software application is run.

6 After an audit software run is complete, the work files created can be deleted.

Assists Development of New Audit Tools In some cases specialized audit software is needed for evidence collection purposes (discussed later in the chapter). When these tools must be developed and implemented, the process follows the steps described in Chapter 5. Further, the auditor can use the various software development aids described in Chapter 5 to assist in the production of high-quality software.

Audit Categorization of Utility Software

A major problem often confronting the auditor is identifying utility software that will fulfill an audit purpose. In any installation a large number of utility programs may exist. The documentation for these programs often is scattered and of varying quality. Usually it is written with the programmer rather than the auditor in mind. Thus, in some cases though the software may be well-documented, it may be difficult for the auditor to understand the purposes of the software and how to use the software. Effective and efficient use of utility software may require specialization within the EDP audit team.

To facilitate the EDP auditor's search for appropriate utility software, some machine vendors now have compiled listings of their utility software that are useful for audit purposes (see, for example, IBM [1981]). The software descriptions typically still are oriented toward the programming user and are couched in the jargon of the vendor; however, the listings are a convenient reference aid for the auditor. With the increased security consciousness of recent years, some software vendors also now highlight any audit and control features of their utility software in the documentation they produce for this software.

The following sections categorize and discuss utility software under five headings:

1 Programs that facilitate the auditor's understanding of application systems within an installation

2 Programs that facilitate gathering evidence on the quality of data within an installation

3 Programs that facilitate gathering evidence on the quality of other programs within an installation

4 Programs that facilitate development and implementation of specialized audit software

5 Programs that gather evidence on the efficiency (productivity) of an installation

The categorization scheme used here is not unique; other schemes have been used to classify utility software from an audit perspective (see, for example, Adams [1975]). The scheme below focuses on major functions the auditor will perform. As with most categorization schemes, there is some overlap of categories. Further, many of the programs listed have been discussed in previous chapters or will be discussed further in later chapters; they are listed here to illustrate the nature of the categories and for completeness. Whether or not some of the programs listed should be classified as "utilities" also might be debated. Again, both the terms "utility software" and "system software" are imprecise.

Software to Facilitate System Understanding   A major problem confronting the auditor during the evidence gathering phase is the question of how to gain quickly an understanding of the programs and data within the installation being audited. Understanding program logic always has been a problem. However, with the increasing use of database management systems and the move away from sequential, index sequential, and random files to more complex data structures such as trees and networks, understanding data (especially the relationships between data items) is a growing problem.

The standards established by all professional auditing bodies stress the importance of the auditor understanding the system to be audited. The following utilities, designed primarily to assist the programmer maintain documentation on systems, also assist the auditor to understand programs and data within application systems. As a consequence, the use of other evidence collection techniques should be better directed.

Utility	Function
Flowcharter	Produces flowcharts from program source code.
HIPO charter	Provides automated hierarchy plus input-process-output diagrams. Auditors can request a listing of HIPO charts for a program so they can better understand the functions performed by the program (see, also, Chapter 5).
Hierarchy charter	Produces hierarchical function charts from structured code. A module and its associated lower-level modules are diagrammed. The interfaces between modules (via PERFORMs, GO TOs, etc.) are indicated on the hierarchy chart.
Execution path mapper	Shows all the execution paths through a program by referencing paragraph names.
Cross-reference lister	Provides cross-reference listings for programs showing where a label (field) is referenced in a program.
Data structure charter	Produces charts from the database definition showing the structure of data within the database.
Transaction profile analyzer	Analyzes the characteristics of data updating the database, e.g., volume of a particular transaction type.
Data dictionary	Describes the characteristics of all data items in the database. Facilities exist for selective retrieval of data from the data dictionary.
Text manager	If system documentation is stored on magnetic media (word processing), text managers allow selective retrieval of text (based on key words) from the documentation.

Software to Facilitate Assessing Data Quality   Utility programs that facilitate testing the quality of data within an installation assist the auditor in two ways. First, some utilities allow the auditor to test the quality of the data directly. For example, batch and online query facilities perform the same function as generalized audit software. Second, some utilities facilitate the use of other evidence collection tools. For example, a sort package can be used to order data for report purposes. The following utilities are widely available:

Utility	Function
Query facility	Batch and online query facilities allow selected retrieval of data from a variety of data structure types.
Data structure conversion	Maps one data structure into another; e.g., a tree or network data structure into a flat (sequential) file.
Pointer validation utility	Searches storage structures that use pointers for invalid pointers; e.g., child nodes in a network that do not point back to their parent node (see, further, Thomas et al. [1977]).
Data manipulation utilities	Perform sundry functions, e.g., sort, merge, copy (selective copy), create, modify, delete, reorganize, format conversion, rename.
Dump/lister	Printing (sometimes with partial editing) of file contents.
Data comparison utility	Compares two sets of data and lists the differences.

Software to Facilitate Assessing Program Quality   These utilities allow the auditor to test a program's ability to maintain data integrity. The testing takes two forms. First, the validity of existing program logic is assessed. Second, the ability of the program to withstand abnormal conditions is assessed; for example, data input with severe outlier values can be submitted to the program. The following utilities developed primarily for programmers also assist the auditor to assess program quality:

Utility	Function
Test data generator	Automatic generation of test files with data having specified attributes. Various data and storage structures can be generated.
Trace	Permits batch or online monitoring of the status of programs as they step through various execution paths.
Online debugging facility	Permits online changes to object code and activitation of programs at selected start points.
Execution path monitor	Indicates whether test data has traversed all execution paths within a program.
Output analyzer	Examines test output for various conditions, e.g., differences between output produced and a prior version of output.
Network simulator	Allows batch or online simulation of a communications network without having to use the network hardware/software configuration.
Terminal simulator	Allows batch simulation of online programs so testing can proceed without the online hardware/software configuration being available.

Utility	Function
Test manager/driver	Manages the overall testing process for a program or set of programs.
Concurrent monitor	Captures selected events as application systems are running.
Source/object code comparison utility	Compares two versions of the source/object code of a program and lists differences.
Change tracker	Monitors changes to program source code libraries. May be a facility within a librarian package.

Software to Facilitate Program Development Sometimes neither generalized audit software nor utility software can be used for audit evidence collection purposes; generalized audit software may not run on the hardware/software configuration, utility software may not provide the required functions, etc. In these situations the auditor may be forced to develop specialized audit software to perform the evidence collection function. When developing this software the auditor has the same objectives as a programmer: fast, accurate development of a program that performs the required functions.

The utilities listed below have been developed to facilitate the program development process. One factor affecting the choice of a utility is the need for the specialized audit program to run efficiently. Many of the utilities described below facilitate fast, accurate development of code. Sometimes the code generated also may consume resources efficiently. However, in other cases the code produced executes inefficiently or consumes substantial real memory. If the auditor needs a one-off program, the program runs for only a short time, or it is run infrequently, efficiency considerations may be relatively unimportant. However, sometimes the motivation to develop specialized audit software is the need for processing efficiency. In these cases the auditor must be careful to use only those utilities that produce efficient code.

Utility	Function
Shorthand preprocessor	Allows source code to be written in an abbreviated form.
Macro	Inserts standard code in a program.
Prompter	Supplies a "menu" for compiler option selection or parameter selection. Some prompters have been developed to facilitate structured programming (see, further, IBM [1981]).
Visual display utility	Permits abbreviated coding for visual display input and output. Manages a library of mock displays for training or experimental work to find the best formats/language for the displays.
Decision-table preprocessor	Converts decision tables into source code.
Library copy	Copies source code from a library into a program.
Text editor	Permits parameter-specified modification of source code.
Tidy	Formats source code so it is more readable.

Utility	Function
Online coding facility	Permits programs to be coded and compiled in an interactive mode.
Report generators	Simplifies coding of reports.
Language subset facility	Restricts source code used to an efficient subset.
Code optimizer	Operates on the source or object code of a program to remove inefficient code.
Volume test facility	Shows the performance of a program under stress.

Software to Facilitate Assessing Operational Efficiency Like the auditor, EDP management is concerned with assessing the operating efficiency of an installation. Consequently, a large number of utilities have been developed to gather and report evidence on how efficiently the hardware and software resources in an installation are being used. Some of these utilities are designed primarily to be used by engineers and system programmers; thus, an auditor may have substantial difficulty understanding the output of these utilities without adequate training in performance monitoring methodologies. However, without the utilities it may be extremely difficult for the auditor to extract and report the data necessary for assessing operating efficiency.

Utilities that facilitate assessing operating efficiency perform three major functions. First, they gather the necessary source data on resource consumption. Second, they calculate statistics that reflect various aspects of operating efficiency on the basis of this source data. Third, they report these statistics in various forms: tables, bar charts, pie charts, histograms, frequency distributions, graphs, etc. Chapter 21 discusses these utilities further; however, some of the major types of performance data collected are:

1 CPU utilization
2 Real memory utilization
3 Secondary storage utilization
4 Channel utilization
5 Communication line utilization
6 Peripheral utilization
7 Task rates
8 Response times
9 Queue lengths
10 I/O buffer excesses and deficiencies
11 I/O concurrency
12 Direct access seek times
13 Paging rates/thrashing
14 Frequency of checkpoints/recovery
15 Storage media read/write errors
16 Effects of changes in memory allocations to tasks
17 Effects of changes in task priorities

18 Deviations from transaction profiles
19 Need for database restructuring/reorganization
20 Performance of hashing algorithms/indexes

SPECIALIZED AUDIT SOFTWARE

Specialized audit software is software written in a procedure-oriented or problem-oriented language to fulfill a specific set of audit tasks. The term "specialized" does not mean the software performs only a narrow range of functions. Indeed, it may perform a large number of audit functions. Rather, specialized means the auditor has developed and implemented software where the purposes and users of the software are well-defined before the software is written. With generalized software, the specific tasks for which the software will be employed and the identity of users will not be known at the outset.

Reasons for Developing Specialized Audit Software

Some internal and external audit groups have now developed extensive libraries of specialized audit software (see, for example, Halper et al. [1985]. Since it is usually more costly to develop and implement specialized audit software than it is to use generalized software, these groups have not embarked upon specialized audit software applications unless they have good reasons. The following sections outline briefly some motivations for developing specialized audit software.

Unavailability of Alternate Software In some cases, generalized software is not available that will perform the functions the auditor requires for evidence gathering purposes. The generalized software needed may not run on the hardware/software configuration being audited; thus, specialized software is the only means of gaining access to the data needed for performing the audit functions required. Alternatively, the data processing installation may not have acquired the generalized software needed by the auditor. If the functions required by the auditor are limited and well-defined, it may be cheaper to develop specialized software than to purchase generalized software.

Functional Limitations of Alternate Software Though generalized software may be available to the auditor, it may have functional limitations that prevent its fulfilling the auditor's needs. Suppose, for example, the auditor wants to undertake some form of statistical sampling or analytical review, and the necessary logic has not been incorporated in either generalized audit software or utility software. If the task is to be accomplished, specialized audit software must be developed.

Efficiency Considerations Since specialized audit software is written specifically to accomplish defined audit tasks, usually it will run more efficiently than generalized software. Over time the cost savings from this increased efficiency may outweigh expenditures on developing the software, especially if the software is run frequently or processes large volumes of data. For example, in a decentralized organization the software might be developed centrally and distributed to multiple sites for use by auditors at those sites. Alternatively, data may be dispatched to a centralized EDP audit facility—a competency center—where it is processed by a group of EDP auditors having high expertise. In both these cases, because of high run frequencies, small cost savings per run may accumulate to large amounts.

Increased Understanding of System If the functional limitations of generalized software prevent the auditor from using this software to obtain evidence about an application system, often it means the application system is complex. One way for the auditor to gain an understanding of the system is to prepare detailed program specifications or write program source code for specialized audit software. Again, for one-off or infrequent audits, the costs may outweigh the benefits of undertaking these activities. However, if the application system is critical and the auditor must evaluate it on an ongoing basis, in-depth understanding of the system is essential to the performance of a high-quality audit.

Opportunity for Easy Implementation Often the development and implementation of specialized audit software will be costly. Further, if there is a high rate of change in either the installation's hardware/software configuration or application systems, specialized audit software may become obsolete quickly and high maintenance costs result. However, opportunities still exist for the easy development and implementation of specialized audit software. For example, some information useful to the auditor also may be useful to the users of the application system. Extracting this information may involve only a relatively simple modification to an existing application system program. Also, if the EDP audit staff has an expert programmer, opportunities for developing small specialized audit programs are more likely to be taken than if no programming expertise exists on the staff.

Increased Auditor Independence/Respect To some extent, if auditors can develop their own software for audit purposes, their independence increases. They have a better understanding of application systems, and they are not dependent on other people for the availability of software for evidence collection purposes. As a consequence, both management and the EDP staff may respect auditors more if they perceive auditors to have sufficient technical competence to write their own programs. Management's confidence in the audit staff performing high-quality work may increase. Improved relationships between the audit staff and data processing personnel also may result.

Development and Implementation of Specialized Audit Software

To ensure high-quality software is produced, the development and implementation of specialized audit software should follow the guidelines discussed in Chapter 5. Auditors at least must take responsibility for managing the programming process; they also may have responsibility for carrying out the various steps in the programming process.

Two types of specialized audit programs can be developed and implemented: (*a*) stand-alone programs and (*b*) modified application system programs. Stand-alone specialized audit software is produced if the application system does not accomplish even partially the audit task to be performed, or it is cheaper to produce a stand-alone program. If the application system partially accomplishes the audit task, say, extracts the necessary data from a file, it may be cheaper to modify the application system program code to perform fully the audit task required.

Specialized audit software can be developed and implemented in three ways. First, the auditor can take total responsibility for developing and implementing the software. To do this the auditor must have the necessary programming skills; however, this approach provides the auditor with a high level of control over the programming process. Second, programmers in the installation to be audited may write the software. If specialized audit software also provides information useful to the application system users, they may be willing to bear some part of the development and implementation costs of the software. Third, an outside software vendor may prepare the software if the auditor is concerned about maintaining the integrity of the software. Though the costs may be higher, using the services of an independent third party provides extra assurance that integrity violations have not occurred.

Even though installation personnel or an outside programmer may code, test, debug, and document specialized audit software, the auditor still has responsibility for preparing program specifications, managing the programming process, performing acceptance testing, and preparing user documentation. Unless the auditor performs these tasks, reliance cannot be placed on the integrity of the program.

DECISION SUPPORT SOFTWARE

Both auditing researchers and auditing practitioners have recognized increasingly that many of the evidence collection and evidence evaluation decisions made by auditors during the conduct of an audit are very complex. This awareness has been heightened by the continuing emergence of more complex computer systems that auditors must examine and evaluate. Accordingly, in recent years more research has been undertaken on software that will assist auditors to make various evidence collection and evidence evaluation decisions. This software contrasts with the software examined so far in this chapter and the last chapter in that the focus is the *decision* to be made rather than the *data* to be collected on the reliability of controls. Since the software seeks to support auditors who must make semistructured and unstructured decisions, it is sometimes called auditor decision support software. This section reviews some of the software developed so far and shows how it supports evidence *collection* decisions; Chapter 22 examines the software once again and shows how it supports evidence *evaluation* decisions. In both cases, however, it should be recognized that the software being described is still in the research and development stages so its use is not widespread.

Some of the earliest auditor decision support software developed were simulation programs that auditors could use to model an internal control system (see Burns and Loebbecke [1975] and Weber [1978a]). From an evidence collection viewpoint, the software facilitated making an important decision, namely, *where* resources should be directed during the evidence collection phase. By undertaking sensitivity analysis with the software, it was possible to determine which internal control points were critical to the overall reliability of the system. In light of this information, auditors then could determine where to focus their evidence collection efforts. Chapter 22 discusses the simulation modeling approach of internal control systems in more detail.

A somewhat different form of simulation modeling software has been developed by Garner and Pinnis [1984] to determine whether the past activities of a system have complied with the standards established for the system. Deviations from the norm direct the auditor's attention to those areas where further evidence must be gathered and more in-depth investigation must be carried out.

To illustrate the nature of their software, assume that the auditor is attempting to evaluate whether the computer operations group has complied with the standards established for running application systems. To aid in this evaluation, the auditor could develop and use a simulation model in the following way (see, further, Garner and Pinnis [1984]):

1 *Determine the scope and purpose of the model:* In this case the purpose of the model is to evaluate the reliability of the computer operations group. To gather evidence in support of this objective, the auditor might choose to focus on the time series profile of resource consumption for a particular application system over, say, a three-month period.

2 *Determine the composition and form of the model:* In this step the components of the model would be identified and the relationships between the components would be specified. For the application chosen, the components would include the programs used and their version numbers, the files accessed and their version numbers, the time slots in which the programs should have been executed, the operational mix of jobs in the machine when a program was run, and the volume of input submitted. The relationships would include which files should be accessed by which programs, which programs should be executed in which time slots, and which operational mix should be present in which time slot.

3 *Collect information to determine the model parameters:* Both static and dynamic data and both deterministic and probabilistic data must be collected to build the model. A static data item would be a program name; a dynamic data item would be a file version number. A deterministic data item value would be a file version number (it increases by one after every update run); a probabilistic data item would be the volume of input submitted to a program (represented by a probability distribution in the model). The source of this data would be operational standards, run schedules, systems documentation, historical records, etc.

4 *Build the modeling software and run it:* Once the model has been specified, it can be implemented and executed to produce the time series of resource usage that should have occurred within the system.

5 *Compare the model output with actual resource usage:* Actual resource usage can be obtained by extracting the relevant data from the operating system log.

Garner and Pinnis [1984] indicate that practical experience with the model has identified the following sorts of irregularities: use of test files in production, jobs not run to schedule, unreported runs of a production job, program inefficiencies, and use of nonstandard file names. Of course, deviations between the predicted time series of resource usage and the actual time series of resource usage require follow-up; but the model enables auditors to direct their evidence gathering efforts to where problems are likely to have occurred.

To assist auditors to know *what* evidence they should collect when an error or irregularity has been identified, Garner and Tsui [1985a] have developed a questionnaire generator. The questionnaire generator is an expert system; that is, it is a program developed using artificial intelligence tools and techniques that encapsulates the knowledge of experts about a problem domain and that can reproduce this expertise when confronted with a particular problem. In the case of the questionnaire generator, questions about errors and irregularities are not "prestored" in the knowledge base of the expert system. Instead, "knowledge items" are extracted from experts about errors or irregularities, and the expert system assembles these knowledge items into questions when it is presented with a particular type of error or irregularity. In this way, the questionnaire generator can respond flexibly to new types of errors and irregularities presented to it by a user and it can be updated easily to reflect new types of knowledge. To illustrate how the system works, Figure 17-2 shows an example of an interaction between an auditor and the questionnaire generator.

Perhaps the most extensive system so far constructed to assist auditors to analyze and evaluate internal control systems is The Internal Control Model (TICOM) system developed by Bailey et al. [1985]. Like the questionnaire generator system discussed previously, TICOM relies on artificial intelligence tools and techniques to enable auditors to model an internal control system and to ask questions about the status of internal controls. These two tasks are handled by two sets of programs: (*a*) an Internal Control Descriptive Language

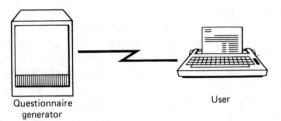

Questionnaire
generator

User

There is no authorization control
for claiming procedure

Is the performance of authorization
procedure reliable?
Are you satisfied with the status
of authorization procedure?
Have you identified the initiator
of authorization procedure?

Reimbursement of claim has
ignored policy guidelines

Who is the endorser of policy
guidelines?
Have you identified the nature
of policy guidelines?
Where is the location of policy
guidelines?

FIGURE 17-2
Example interaction with questionnaire generator expert system. *(From Garner and Tsui [1985a];
adapted by permission, The EDP Auditors Foundation, Inc.)*

(ICDL) compiler that allows an auditor to describe the characteristics of an
internal control system and that produces as output a model of the internal
control system and (*b*) a query language that allows an auditor to assess
whether internal control objectives have been met.

To illustrate the nature of TICOM, Figure 17-3 shows the set of ICDL
commands required to describe a subset of activities in a purchasing and
payments system. An auditor might then ask the following sorts of questions
about the internal control system (see Bailey et al. [1985]):

Question: Who has the authority to fill out remittance advices?

Response: The stores clerk.

Question: What is required before a remittance advice is prepared by the
stores clerk?

Response: The stores clerk must get the mail and the remittance advice must
be missing.

Question: What happens if the mail does not contain a remittance advice?

Response: The stores clerk fills one out.

In this way, the auditor can make an assessment of whether an overall internal
control objective (such as segregation of duties or adequacy of documentation)
has been met. In light of this assessment, the auditor might then seek more

evidence about the functioning of the internal control system to confirm or to refute a hypothesis about an internal control strength or weakness.

To assist auditors to determine the consequences of a control failure identified by an audit test, Hansen and Messier [1984] propose the use of a relational database management system to represent the complex relationships among controls, their locations, vulnerabilities resulting from their absence, and possible exposures. Again, while the primary purpose of their system is to assist auditors in the *evaluation* of system reliability, it provides important information that may influence auditors in making a decision about *where* they should collect evidence on the reliability of controls.

FIGURE 17-3
ICDL task description in TICOM for a task activity. *(From Bailey et al. [1985]; used by permission, The American Accounting Association.)*

Flowchart representation   TICOM commands (ICDL)

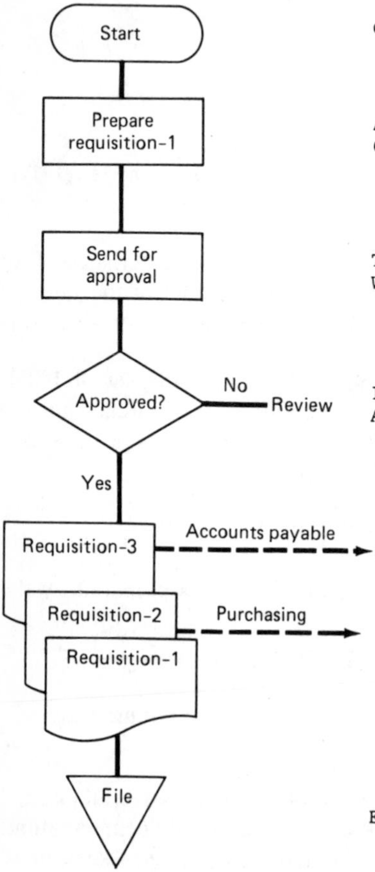

```
   ╭─────────────╮          GET REQUISITION-1 FROM REQUISITON SUPPLY;
  (    Start      )
   ╰─────────────╯

  ┌─────────────┐           ASSIGN SOURCE, DATE, ITEMIZED-DESCRIPTION
  │   Prepare   │           OF REQUISITION-1;
  │requisition-1│
  └─────────────┘

  ┌─────────────┐           TRANSFER REQUISITION-1 TO MANAGER;
  │  Send for   │           WAIT FOR REQUISITION-1;
  │  approval   │
  └─────────────┘

        No
  ◇ Approved? ◇──── Review   IF REQUISITION-1 APPROVAL NOT EQ
                             AUTHORIZATION-CODES THEN REVIEW;

       Yes

            Accounts payable
┌──────────────┐              ELSE
│Requisition-3 │ ─ ─ ─ ─ ─ ─      COPY REQUISITION-1 GIVING REQUISITION-2,
└──────────────┘                  REQUISITION-3
  │Requisition-2│  Purchasing
  └─────────────┘              TRANSFER REQUISITION-3 TO ACCOUNTS-PAYABLE
    │Requisition-1│            TRANSFER REQUISITION-2 TO PURCHASING CLERK
    └─────────────┘            PUT REQUISITION-1 INTO REQUISITION FILE
                               END-IF;

       ▽ File ▽                END TASK
```

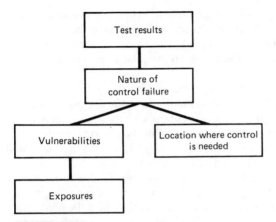

FIGURE 17-4
Relationships that can be explored in the relational decision support system proposed by Hansen and Messier [1984].

To illustrate the nature of this system, Figure 17-4 shows a set of relationships that auditors may wish to pursue. At a basic level in the system, the results of tests on various controls are stored as relational "tuples" within the system. These test results derive from various evidence gathering activities carried out by auditors—use of generalized audit software, test data, embedded audit modules, etc. When auditors detect a control failure during an examination of this data, they first use the system to determine the nature of the failure. For example, the database may show a control failure has been identified in light of tests carried out on inventory transactions. A database query indicates that the nature of the failure is the absence of a transaction journal for the set of inventory transactions. Next, the auditor uses the system to determine vulnerabilities that arise as a result of the control failure. The system indicates the possible vulnerabilities are message loss, message alteration, message insertion, and message duplication. To determine the possible exposures that arise from each of these vulnerabilities, the auditor again submits a query to the system. The system indicates, for example, that exposures which arise from message loss include erroneous record keeping, fraud, statutory sanctions, and excessive costs. Finally, if the auditor is sufficiently concerned about the size of expected losses from these exposures, a query can be submitted to determine the locations where a transaction journal should be used as a control. The system may indicate that it should be used at terminals, switches, concentrators, and frontend processors.

CONTROL OF AUDIT SOFTWARE

If the auditor does not have full control over any software used for evidence collection purposes, the issues of audit independence discussed previously in

Chapter 16 about the use of database management systems as an audit tool again must be considered. Somehow the auditor must gain assurance that the software has not been modified in an unauthorized way—for example, by introducing a Trojan horse that will result in an irregularity remaining undetected.

If the auditor establishes and maintains an independently controlled library of audit software, unauthorized modifications to the software are less likely to occur. The library can be protected via access controls, or the auditor can hold the storage medium on which the software resides. For the external auditor the library provides an additional advantage: the audit is not constrained by the availability of software in the installation to be audited.

Unfortunately, reliance on an independently controlled library of audit software sometimes is impractical, especially for external auditors. Auditors may confront a hardware/system software configuration for which they have no audit software. Moreover, maintenance of the library may be prohibitively expensive, as some of the software needed may have a high purchase or licensing cost. Thus, auditors may be forced to rely, at least in part, on software made available to them by the data processing installation they are auditing.

If this is the case, some type of assurance must be obtained that the software has not been modified in an unauthorized way. Chapter 16 discussed ways in which this assurance might be obtained: the blueprint approach, the hash total (checksum) approach, and the test data approach. Recall, however, that these approaches are not foolproof. If, for example, unauthorized modifications have occurred to the operating system or to the machine microcode, undetected violations of processing integrity will still occur. In this light, the auditor must evaluate the reliability of management controls to assess the likelihood of these types of unauthorized modifications having occurred.

SUMMARY

Besides generalized audit software, the auditor may find other types of software useful for evidence collection purposes. Industry-specific audit software has been developed to provide high-level audit functions that the auditor will find useful in carrying out audits in particular industries. In addition, it may take advantage of the widespread use of certain application packages within the industry. Spreadsheet audit software can be employed to evaluate the integrity of financial models or accounting applications developed via a spreadsheet package. High-level languages, such as those provided in fourth-generation software or statistical software, can be used instead of generalized audit software when the auditor finds they provide easier access to data or a more comprehensive range of functions. System software, especially utility software, often can be employed to gain an understanding of the system to be audited, to assess data quality, to assess program quality, to facilitate development of other evidence collection software, and to assess operational efficiency. The auditor may develop specialized audit software when other software is unavailable to perform an audit function or the other software is functionally limited or operationally inefficient. In addition, use of specialized audit software also can improve the auditor's understanding of an application system, increase auditor independence, and improve management's and data processing personnel's respect for the auditor. Finally, auditors may employ decision support software to obtain help with the semistructured and unstructured parts of their decision making during the evidence collection phase.

Whenever auditors use software for evidence collection purposes, they must attempt to ensure that unauthorized modifications to the software have not occurred. Some level of assurance can be obtained by comparing the software with a blueprint, recalculating a hash total or checksum for the software, undertaking tests on critical modules, or examining an operating system log for unauthorized activities. Nonetheless, these techniques still provide only limited assurance that unauthorized modifications have not occurred. The processing integrity of any audit software is still dependent on the integrity of other system components used in the data processing installation—for example, the operating system.

REVIEW QUESTIONS

17-1 Briefly explain the nature of industry-specific audit software. How does it differ from generalized audit software?

17-2 What are the relative advantages and disadvantages of industry-specific audit software versus generalized audit software?

17-3 What factors have motivated the development of spreadsheet audit software? Is spreadsheet audit software likely to be a useful tool for the external auditor?

17-4 Briefly describe the typical sorts of functions provided by a spreadsheet audit software package.

17-5 Briefly explain the nature of a high-level programming language. How are high-level programming languages useful to the auditor?

17-6 Briefly explain the nature of utility software. Give three factors that affect the availability of utility software within a data processing installation.

17-7 What problems does the use of minicomputers and microcomputers for accounting applications present for the auditor performing the evidence collection function?

17-8 Is it likely that generalized audit software will be available on a wider range of hardware/software configurations in the future? Explain.

17-9 Briefly explain the major ways in which utility software can be used by the auditor to facilitate evidence collection.

17-10 Give an example of an evidence collection task where the external auditor might consider using utility software in preference to generalized audit software. Outline how the external auditor might go about finding out whether or not there is a utility program available in the data processing installation that will perform the evidence gathering task.

17-11 How might the auditor use the following utility packages during the evidence collection phase of an audit:

a Transaction profile analyzer

b Data structure charter

c Pointer validation utility

d Volume test facility

17-12 Briefly explain the nature of specialized audit software.

17-13 Outline a function that is unlikely to be performed by generalized audit software or utility software, thereby forcing the auditor to develop a specialized audit program.

17-14 Why is it likely that more specialized audit software will be developed if an organization develops a competency center, that is, a centralized EDP audit facility having highly skilled EDP audit staff?

17-15 Briefly explain how the development and implementation of specialized audit software can increase an auditor's understanding of a complex application system.

17-16 Briefly explain why the auditor might develop and implement specialized audit software to age accounts receivable and analyze inventory turnover.

17-17 Compared to using generalized audit software and utility software for evidence gathering purposes, give two disadvantages of developing, implementing, and using specialized audit software.

17-18 How might the development and implementation of specialized audit software affect the auditor's relationships with management and data processing personnel?

17-19 What factors would affect the auditor's decision to modify application system program code versus write specialized stand-alone programs to perform audit evidence gathering tasks?

17-20 Outline the ways in which specialized audit software can be developed and implemented. List the relative advantages and disadvantages of each method.

17-21 Briefly describe three techniques the auditor can use to determine whether or not a specialized audit program written by a third party complies with its specifications.

17-22 If, in the data processing installation to be audited, programmers or third parties code, test, and debug a specialized audit program, what are their responsibilities with respect to documenting the program? Explain.

17-23 Briefly explain the nature of auditor decision support software. How does it differ from generalized audit software?

17-24 How can simulation software be used to provide decision support for the EDP auditor?

17-25 Briefly explain the nature of a questionnaire generator. Why does the questionnaire generator developed by Garner and Tsui rely on expert system techniques as the basis of its design and implementation?

17-26 Briefly explain the nature of the TICOM system. How does it provide decision support for the EDP auditor?

17-27 How can a relational database be used to assist auditors in their evaluation of system reliability?

17-28 Outline the advantages and disadvantages of both external auditors and internal auditors building independently controlled libraries of audit software. How can they independently control these libraries?

17-29 If auditors do not maintain an independently controlled library of software that they use for evidence collection and evidence evaluation purposes, how can they be sure that the software they use has not been modified in some unauthorized way?

MULTIPLE CHOICE QUESTIONS

17-1 Compared to generalized audit software, which of the following is unlikely to be true of industry-specific audit software:

a It will perform its functions more efficiently than generalized audit software

b Commands will be easier to specify using industry-specific audit software

c It will run on more makes of machines and more software packages within the industry

d It is less likely to be robust across changes made to application software used within the industry for which it was designed

17-2 The purpose of a worksheet map report provided by a spreadsheet audit software package is to:

a Show the detailed contents of each cell in the spreadsheet

b Identify cells in the spreadsheet where circular references appear to have occurred

c Show the detailed contents of each cell in the spreadsheet that contains a formula

d Provide a global view of the contents of the worksheet by showing the nature of the contents of each cell within the spreadsheet

17-3 Which of the following has *not* been a reason why auditors have used high-level languages instead of generalized audit software to perform evidence gathering functions:

a They contain a wider range of functions specifically oriented toward audit use

b Their interfaces are more user friendly

c Fewer operational problems are encountered when they are used

d They allow access to databases maintained on microcomputers

17-4 Which of the following types of system software is likely to be most useful to the auditor as a means of collecting evidence:

a Utility software

b The operating system

c Software drivers

d Assemblers and compilers

17-5 Which of the following is a reason for using system software instead of generalized audit software for evidence collection purposes:

a Independence will be breached if both internal and external auditors use the same generalized audit software package

b There are functional limitations to generalized audit software

c Utility software to accomplish the auditor's task is more widely available

d The instructions for using utility software are often better documented

17-6 Which of the following tasks would probably be most difficult to accomplish using utility software:

a Merging data on two files

b Dumping several records to check their format

c Selecting a statistical sample for circularization

d Flattening a tree data structure to produce a sequential file

17-7 A hierarchy charter primarily would be useful in helping an auditor to:

a Assess data quality in an application system

b Evaluate the efficiency of an application system

c Understand an application system

d Develop and implement specialized audit software

17-8 Which of the following utilities can be used to directly examine the quality of data in a database:

a Tidy facility

b Test manager/driver

c Trace

d Pointer validation utility

17-9 Which of the following utilities can be used to directly examine the authenticity, accuracy, and completeness of program logic:

a Transaction profile analyzer

b Output analyzer

c Prompter

d Text manager

17-10 Which of the following utilities is likely to be the most useful in the development of specialized audit software:

a Text editor

b Data comparison utility

c Librarian package

d Volume test facility

17-11 A prompter is a utility that:

a Permits abbreviated coding of visual display input and output

b Supplies a menu for compiler option selection

c Indicates likely logic errors in a program

d Permits online monitoring of a program's status

17-12 A language subset facility is a utility that:

a Inserts standard code into a program

b Allows source code to be written in abbreviated form

c Converts syntax with the same meaning to a common command

d Restricts source code used to an efficient subset

17-13 A data structure charter is a utility that:

a Produces a storage structure definition from the data structure definition

b Produces charts from the database definition showing the structure of data within the database

c Provides a cross-reference to data in the program procedure division

d Converts one data structure into another data structure

17-14 A terminal simulator is a utility that:

a Permits batch simulation of online programs

b Allows online simulation of a communications network

c Simulates the operations of terminals under stress

d Permits visual display interaction to be coded on a temporary test basis

17-15 Specialized audit software differs from utility software in that:

a Specialized audit software performs more functions

b Utility software is more efficient

    c Specialized audit software has been developed for specific purposes

    d Specialized audit software is better documented

17-16 Which of the following is *not* a reason for having installation personnel instead of the auditor write specialized audit software:

    a The auditor may lack the expertise to write effective and efficient software

    b The software may also be useful to data processing personnel

    c Communications between the auditor and data processing staff are improved

    d The time-consuming task of preparing program specifications is alleviated

17-17 For evidence collection purposes, auditor simulation decision support software is useful because it:

    a Indicates the important controls on which the auditor should focus during the evidence collection phase

    b Determines the type of evidence that the auditor should collect to evaluate the reliability of an internal control

    c Indicates whether the auditor should use a compliance or substantive test approach to evaluating internal controls

    d Indicates whether controls are likely to fail probabilistically or deterministically

17-18 Which of the following functions is *not* provided in TICOM (The Internal Control Model):

    a Production of a formal model of the internal control system

    b Automatic generation of questions the auditor should ask to assess whether internal controls are reliable

    c Query capability to respond to questions about whether internal control objectives are being met

    d Facility to describe tasks performed in an accounting system

17-19 Which of the following could *not* be determined using the relational auditor decision support system proposed by Hansen and Messier:

    a Results of tests carried out on an internal control

    b Vulnerabilities that arise as a consequence of an internal control failure

    c Locations where a particular internal control is needed

    d Likely materiality of the overall error that arises as a consequence of all the individual internal control errors

EXERCISES AND CASES

17-1 As the manager of internal audit for a company, you are called one day to a meeting with the controller. The controller explains that a programmer has discovered accidentally some fraudulent code in an audit program written by a member of your staff. The audit program examined sales transactions as they were input to an online system and detected any unusual transactions that occurred so they could be examined by the audit staff. Unfortunately, the program also altered transactions for customers who seem to be relations of the auditor who wrote the program.

    The controller asks you how this situation has arisen. You explain that your staff is small and overworked, and the auditor who wrote the program was the only member of your staff who could program.

Required: The controller asks you to prepare a brief report giving some recommendations to prevent a similar fraud from occurring in the future.

17-2 You are the manager of internal audit for a company that uses a database management system for its applications systems. The database management system maintains a log, which includes all transactions that update the database.

One of your junior auditors asks you to approve a budget for $2000 so a program can be written to compare the log tape with the transaction files for the various application systems that use the database management system. You ask why the amount required is so high for a simple comparison program. He explains that the data is formatted and compressed in strange ways on the log tape and difficulties have been experienced on previous occasions when attempts have been made to read the tape.

Required: On the basis of the information given, what are your feelings on whether or not to have the program written? What errors or irregularities do you think the program might identify that other controls would not identify?

17-3 Consider an online realtime update system that has over 1000 terminals scattered in remote locations and connected to a central machine. One task of the EDP audit group is to ensure that all terminals connected to the central machine are authorized and that the actual privileges allocated a terminal user correspond to the documented privileges.

Required: Where in the system would an auditor obtain the information needed to check that the terminals are authorized and the privileges assigned users are valid? Why would specialized or utility software probably be needed to obtain this information? What information would be needed?

17-4 Some external auditors claim they spend up to two-thirds of their time documenting controls in computer systems so they have a basis for evaluating these controls.

Required: Identify some utility software or specialized software that might be written to facilitate the documentation process carried out by the internal auditor. Should the external auditor be responsible for preparing the internal controls documentation for audit evaluation purposes?

17-5 The parts inventory master file for the manufacturing organization you are auditing is set up as a network data structure. The generalized audit software package available to you will not access network data structures. Moreover, it will not run on the machine that your client is using. However, you consider it important that the quality of the data in the parts inventory file be evaluated for audit purposes.

Required: Assume that you can run your generalized audit software package on a microcomputer that is available to you. Outline how you might use utility software to overcome the problems you are facing.

17-6 In 1986 a construction company filed a product liability lawsuit against a major developer and vendor of spreadsheet software. The company had prepared a bid on a construction project using the spreadsheet software. Unfortunately, $250,000 of general and administrative costs were omitted from the final bid. The bid was accepted and, as a result, the company incurred a substantial loss on the contract.

In the lawsuit filed, the construction company claimed that the software vendor was responsible for the loss because the instructions in the user manual were unclear. The software vendor, in turn, argued that it could not be made responsible for mistakes made by the users of its products. Furthermore, the software vendor argued that users had means at their disposal to check the accuracy of results and that users should validate the models they prepared using the spreadsheet software.

Required: To what extent do you think the type of problem described above would have been avoided if the internal auditors in organizations that used spreadsheets extensively regularly checked the veracity of spreadsheet models with spreadsheet audit software? In general, what steps would you recommend organizations take to reduce the likelihood of erroneous spreadsheet models being designed, implemented, and used? Be sure to consider the behavioral feasibility of your recommendations.

17-7 One of the important technological developments that is currently occurring is the emergence of powerful portable microcomputers. As compact, high-quality visual display screens and improved mass storage technology become available, portable microcomputers are gaining stronger acceptance in the marketplace.

It is not obvious whether the widespread availability of portable microcomputers will stimulate or inhibit the growth of different types of audit software. On the one hand it may mean that a few major packages dominate the marketplace. On the other hand it may mean that a large number of audit software packages are developed to cater to the different needs of auditors.

Required: Write a brief report indicating your beliefs about the effects of portable microcomputers on the ways audit software will evolve in the future. Be sure to provide the arguments in support of your beliefs.

ANSWERS TO MULTIPLE CHOICE QUESTIONS

17-1 c	17-6 c	17-11 b	17-16 d
17-2 d	17-7 c	17-12 d	17-17 a
17-3 a	17-8 d	17-13 b	17-18 b
17-4 a	17-9 b	17-14 a	17-19 d
17-5 b	17-10 a	17-15 c	

REFERENCES

Adams, Donald L. "Alternatives to Computer Audit Software," *Journal of Accountancy* (November 1975), pp. 54–57.

Arthur Young and Co. *The Arthur Young Audit Computer* (New York: Arthur Young and Co., 1981).

Bailey, Andrew D., Jr., Gordon Leon Duke, James H. Gerlach, Chen-en Ko, Rayman D. Meservy, and Andrew B. Whinston. "TICOM and the Analysis of Internal Controls," *The Accounting Review* (April 1985), pp. 186–201.

Black, Robert W., Jr. "Systems Maintenance Program (SMP)," *EDP Auditor*, vol. 1, 1984, pp. 33–35.

Brodie, Don G. "Use of a Microcomputer to Assist in Systems-Based Auditing," *EDPACS* (August 1985), pp. 1–6.

Burns, David C., and James K. Loebbecke. "Internal Control Evaluation: How the Computer Can Help," *Journal of Accountancy* (August 1975), pp. 60–70.

Canadian Institute of Chartered Accountants, *Computer Audit Guidelines* (Toronto: The Canadian Institute of Chartered Accountants, 1975).

Cash, James I., Jr., Andrew D. Bailey, Jr., and Andrew B. Whinston. "A Survey of Techniques for Auditing EDP-Based Accounting Information Systems," *The Accounting Review* (October 1977), pp. 813–832.

Chandler, John. "Expert Systems in Auditing: The State-of-the-Art," *The Auditor's Report* (Summer 1985), pp. 1–4.

Dallas, Dennis A. "SAS as an Audit Tool," *EDP Auditing* (Pennsauken, NJ: Auerbach Publishers, 1985), Portfolio 74-02-20, pp. 1–13.

Dallas, Dennis A. "SMF as an Audit Tool," *EDP Auditing* (Pennsauken, NJ: Auerbach Publishers, 1985), Portfolio 74-03-03, pp. 1–11.

Franklin, Bruce. "A Set of Software Tools for Auditing IBM Data Bases," *EDP Auditor*, vol. 3, 1985, pp. 13–21.

Gallegos, Frederick. "Microcomputers in Auditing: An Overview," *EDP Auditing* (Pennsauken, NJ: Auerbach Publishers, 1985), Portfolio 74-02-10, pp. 1–6.

Garner, B. J., and J. Pinnis. "Modelling as an Audit Technique," *Australian Computer Journal* (May 1984), pp. 48–53.

Garner, B. J., and E. Tsui. "Recent Advances in Computer Audit Research," *EDP Auditor*, vol. 4, 1985a, pp. 3–16.

Garner, B. J., and E. Tsui. "Knowledge Representation for an Audit Office," *Australian Computer Journal* (August 1985b), pp. 106–112.

Godier, Dwayne P. "Automated Audit Risk Analysis," *EDP Auditor*, vol. 2, 1984, pp. 21–28.

Grushcow, Jack. "Avoid These Common Spreadsheet Errors," *Lotus* (July 1985), pp. 59–63.

Halper, Stanley D., Glenn C. Davis, P. Jarlath O'Neil-Dunne, and Pamela R. Pfau. *Handbook of EDP Auditing* (Boston: Warren, Gorham, Lamont, Inc., 1985).

Hansen, James V., and William F. Messier, Jr. "Expert Systems for Decision Support in EDP Auditing," *International Journal of Computer and Information Sciences* (October 1982), pp. 357–379.

Hansen, James V., and William F. Messier, Jr. "A Relational Approach to Decision Support for EDP Auditing," *Communications of the ACM* (November 1984), pp. 1129–1133.

IBM Corporation. *Auditability Catalog* (New York: International Business Machines Corporation, 1981), Publication no. G320-6563-0.

InfoWorld. "Spreadsheets: Avoiding Bottom-Line Disaster," February 11, 1985, pp. 26–30.

Kendalls Consulting. *CAPS Users Manual* (Brisbane: Kendalls Consulting, 1986).

Kleinberg, Eugene R. "Computer-Based Productivity Tools," *EDP Auditing* (Pennsauken, NJ: Auerbach Publishers, 1985), Portfolio 74-03-06, pp. 1–12.

Knight, Sherry D., and Steven E. Yoder. "Seven Audit Software Programs: How They Perform", *Computers in Accounting* (May-June 1985), pp. 20–26, 28, 30–35.

Marshall, David, and Michael J. McMullan. "Micro-Based Auditing Goes Public," *CA Magazine* (August 1985), pp. 58–65.

McMenamy, Edward L. "Data Analysis and Audit–Try SAS," *EDP Auditor,* vol. 4, 1984, pp. 27–44.

Martin, James. *Application Development without Programmers* (Englewood Cliffs, NJ: Prentice-Hall, 1981).

Perry, William E. "Audit Aspects of Utility Programs," *EDPACS* (October 1975), pp. 1–8.

Sobol, Michael I. "New Features of SMF," *EDP Auditing* (Pennsauken, NJ: Auerbach Publishers, 1985), Portfolio 74-03-20, pp. 1–5.

Socha, Wayne J. "Microcomputers for Auditors," *EDP Auditing* (Pennsauken, NJ: Auerbach Publishers, 1985), Portfolio 71-04-10, pp. 1–12.

Thomas, D. A., B. Pagurek, and R. J. Buhr. "Validation Algorithms for Pointer Values in DBTG Databases," *ACM Transactions on Database Systems* (December 1977), pp. 352–369.

van den Berg, Bram, and Hans Leenaars. "Advanced Topics in Computer Center Audit," *Computers and Security,* vol. 3, 1984, pp. 171–185.

Weber, Ron. "Audit Capabilities of Some Database Management Systems," Working Paper MISRC-WP-75-05, Management Information Systems Research Center, University of Minnesota, Minneapolis, 1975.

Weber, Ron. "Auditor Decision Making on Overall System Reliability: Accuracy, Consensus, and the Usefulness of a Simulation Decision Aid," *Journal of Accounting Research* (Autumn 1978), pp. 368–388.

Weber, Ron. "On Some Aspects of Audit Software Attributes and User Needs," *Proceedings of the Eighth Australian Computer Conference* (Canberra: Australian Computer Society, 1978), pp. 1781–1794.

Will, Hart J. "Discernible Trends and Overlooked Opportunities in Audit Software," *The EDP Auditor* (Winter 1978), pp. 21–45.

CHAPTER 18

CODE REVIEW, TEST DATA, AND CODE COMPARISON

CHAPTER OUTLINE

This chapter discusses three evidence collection techniques used primarily to assess the quality of program logic. *Code review* involves the auditor reading

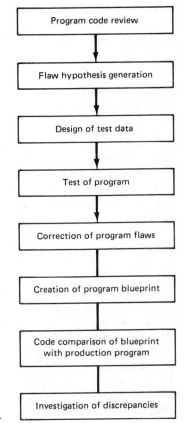

FIGURE 18-1
Integrated use of code review, test data, and code comparison for evidence collection purposes.

program source code listings to determine whether unauthorized code exists and to generate hypotheses about potential errors in the logic. If the auditor is sufficiently skilled, code review also indicates potentially inefficient code and code that does not meet its objectives. *Test data* involves the auditor using a sample of data to assess whether logic errors exist in a program and whether the program meets its objectives. Again, the skilled auditor also can use test data to assess whether a program runs efficiently. *Code comparison* involves the auditor comparing two versions of the source or object code of a program; one version—the blueprint—has known attributes, and the auditor determines whether the other version has the same attributes. This technique has been discussed briefly in previous chapters. It is discussed more fully in this chapter.

Use of the three techniques sometimes follows a natural sequence (see Figure 18-1). First, the auditor reviews program code to generate hypotheses about erroneous code or code that is inefficient or does not meet its objectives. Second, the auditor uses test data to test these hypotheses. Any deficiencies found in the program logic then are corrected. Third, once the auditor is satisfied with the quality of the program code, this version of the program becomes a blueprint. At a later time, production versions of the program can be compared against this blueprint to determine whether any discrepancies exist.

FACTORS THAT LOWER PROGRAM QUALITY: SOME EMPIRICAL EVIDENCE

Code review and test data can be very time-consuming evidence collection techniques to use. They should be applied where they will have most effect; that is, where there is most likely to be erroneous, unauthorized, ineffective, or inefficient code. Unfortunately, in spite of the enormity of the programming effort worldwide, relatively little is known about where the problem areas in programs lie. The studies described briefly below represent some of the few attempts to obtain empirical evidence on this issue.

Boehm et al. [1975] examined the errors discovered during the implementation of a large (100,000 lines of source code) software project. They classified the errors into two broad types: (a) design errors—those arising because the software did not comply with user requirements, and (b) coding errors—those arising because specifications were implemented incorrectly. Of the 224 errors found, 64% were design errors and 36% were coding errors. Further, of the 54% of errors found during or after acceptance testing, 45% were design errors and 9% were coding errors. On average the time taken to diagnose and correct design errors was twice the time required for coding errors.

Additional analysis undertaken on the errors indicated the nature of the design errors and the nature of the coding errors. The design errors arose primarily because of interface problems between the code and the database, input/output devices, and system users. The coding errors arose primarily because of incorrect computation, indexing, or control flow.

Endres [1975] studied the errors made in modifying IBM's DOS/VS operating system to produce Release 28; this release contained some of the most extensive changes ever made to the system. Of the 432 errors discovered when system modules were integrated and a system test (as opposed to a program test) was carried out, 46% were design errors and 38% were coding errors. The remaining 16% were a curious mixture; for example, they included spelling errors in system messages. Endres preferred not to classify them as design or coding errors.

Further analysis of the errors indicated the nature of the design and coding errors. The design errors arose primarily because the problems to be solved when implementing operating systems lack structure. The coding errors that arose were typical of assembly language programming: problems with initialization, addressability, name referencing, and counting and calculating. Interestingly, 85% of the errors that occurred could be corrected by changing only one module. Supposedly, major sources of errors in operating systems (and programs generally) are the interfaces between program modules. At least for this example the empirical evidence contradicts preconceived notions (see, also, Chapter 5).

Rubey et al. [1975] analyzed data from several studies that had collected program error statistics (see, also, Hartwick [1977]). Of 1202 errors discovered, they found 98% were identified by the programmer who coded the software; 2% were discovered during independent testing. Further analysis was undertaken on the errors discovered during independent testing. The errors were classified into 10 categories. The largest category, incomplete or erroneous program specifications, constituted 28% of the total errors discovered. Thus, design errors were again the major factor that lowered program quality. Major categories of coding errors were erroneous data accessing (10%), erroneous decision logic or sequencing (12%), and erroneous arithmetic computations (9%).

From an audit viewpoint, two tentative conclusions can be drawn from these studies about how evidence collection techniques such as code review and test data should be applied. First, if the techniques rely on the integrity of program specifications, a large percentage (possibly 50%) of program errors will be missed (see, also, Mills [1976]). Coding errors may be identified; design errors will be missed. Second, when applying the evidence collection techniques the auditor should pay special attention to three areas of program code: data accessing, sequencing and control, and computation and indexing (see, also, Boehm [1973]). These areas seem especially prone to coding errors. However, since these conclusions are based on a limited number of studies, further empirical evidence is needed to assess their general validity.

Presumably, also, the more times a program is used for production running, the more likely it is that design errors will be discovered and corrected. Thus, the auditor may have more confidence in the integrity of the specifications of older programs. However, it is also more likely that fewer coding (logic) errors exist in older programs.

PROGRAM SOURCE CODE REVIEW

Auditors use program source code review when they are unwilling to treat a computer program as a black box. Some evidence collection techniques permit only inferences to be made about the quality of code in a computer program. For example, generalized audit software can be used to examine the quality of data produced by a program. The quality of data reflects the quality of program code; however, little can be said about whether or not unauthorized or inefficient code exists (see, further, Chapter 16).

Objectives of Code Review

Code review has five specific objectives: (a) to identify erroneous code, (b) to identify unauthorized code, (c) to identify ineffective code, (d) to identify inefficient code, and (e) to identify nonstandard code. The following sections discuss briefly each of these objectives.

Identify Erroneous Code   The use of code review to identify erroneous code is well established. Chapter 5 discussed this purpose under various headings: desk checking, structured walk-throughs, design and code inspections. The empirical evidence discussed earlier in the chapter suggests that coding errors are still a major cause of low-quality programs. The auditor can use code review to determine whether or not the code complies with the program specifications.

Identify Unauthorized Code   Without directly examining a program's source code, it is unlikely that unauthorized program code will be identified. Unauthorized code normally is triggered by a specific data value or combination of data values; for example, an account number or an account number and date combination. A fraudulent programmer may modify a program so it does not print out an overdrawn account. Transactions having a certain account number and date value may be excluded from normal data validation processes. Unless the auditor submits test data having these specific values, the unauthorized code will not be identified. Code review also may deter a programmer from inserting unauthorized code in a program.

Identify Ineffective Code   Ineffective code is code that does not achieve its objectives. The ineffectiveness of code can be gauged at two levels. First, the auditor can examine whether the code meets the documented program specifications. Second, the auditor can examine whether the code fulfills user requirements. The empirical evidence discussed earlier in the chapter suggests the documented program specifications and user requirements do not always correspond. Erroneous program specifications are a major cause of low-quality programs.

Identify Inefficient Code   Code review may enable the auditor to identify inefficient segments of code. For example, in a sequence of tests of transaction types, the tests may not have been ordered according to their frequency of occurrence. Consequently, the program executes more of its code than it would have to if the tests were reordered. The auditor also might identify frequent use of instructions that execute inefficiently on the hardware/software configuration on which the program runs.

Identify Nonstandard Code   Nonstandard code takes a variety of forms. It may be code that does not comply with installation standards covering data item names or internal documentation. It may be code that values an asset inconsistently with generally accepted accounting principles. It may be code that does not conform to legal or statutory requirements. In some areas, for example, the valuation of intangible assets or work-in-process inventory, the impossibility or difficulty of observing the entities that the data represents makes it even more important the code be correct (see, also, Burch and Sardinas [1978]).

Readability of Program Code

The use of program source code review as an audit tool assumes that the code reviewed is readable. The readability of the code under review affects how easily the technique can be applied and the likelihood of finding poor-quality code (aside from the lack of readability) using the technique.

In general, how readable is program code? Again, little empirical evidence has been obtained on this question. Elshoff [1976] studied the readability of 120 production PL/1 programs. He concluded that basically the programs in the study were unreadable. A nonprogrammer would be unable to understand any part of them; even an experienced programmer would have great difficulty understanding them.

Elshoff also found the complexity of the data flow and the control flow impaired the readability of the programs. On average, 384 identifiers appeared in a program; 107 were unreferenced, and the remainder were referenced 1195 times throughout the body of the program. One-third of the statements in an average program directed the flow of control; thus, for practical purposes the number of paths through the program was infinite.

As a further measure of complexity, Elshoff counted the number of statements spanned between two references to an identifier. Nearly 13% of the spans exceeded 100 statements. For the average-size program one span began every six statements. Thus, after 100 statements a programmer reading the program would have to remember as many as 16 separate data and control flows.

The extent to which Elshoff's findings are general within the computer industry is unknown. However, they highlight the difficulties an auditor may experience when trying to use program source code review as an evidence collection tool. In a data processing installation, management must insist on the use of standard labeling conventions, code indentation to show the flow of control, internal documentation, etc. Top-down design, top-down coding, and structured coding clearly make program code more readable, as does use of high-level programming languages.

Source Code Review Methodology

Seven steps are involved in the review of program source code:

1 Select the program to be examined.
2 Review the installation's programming standards.
3 Obtain an understanding of the program specifications.

4 Obtain the source code listing.
5 Review the compiler language used for the program.
6 Review the source code.
7 Formulate flaw hypotheses.

The following sections discuss briefly each of these steps.

Program Selection Since program source code review can be a time-consuming evidence collection technique, the programs selected for review should be critical programs within the installation. Risk assessment techniques can be applied to determine the importance of a program for maintaining the overall integrity of an application system. However, not only must the program be critical, it also must be readable. Unless the program is readable, it may be extremely difficult for the auditor to evaluate whether it safeguards assets, maintains data integrity, achieves its objectives, and processes efficiently.

Review Programming Standards By reviewing the programming standards of the data processing installation, the auditor develops a set of expectations about the code to be reviewed; for example, the way labels will be assigned and the way programs will be structured. The standards also may indicate likely deficiencies that will exist in the code—areas where the auditor has to be especially careful. Besides the installation programming standards, standards also may have been established for a particular application system. For example, programmers may be required to include certain documentation as notes in the program code.

Understand the Program Specifications By understanding the program specifications, the auditor is able to ask the question: Does the program do what it is supposed to do? Here the auditor must make a choice as to how an understanding of the program specifications is to be obtained. One alternative is to review the documented program specifications—those used by the programmer as the basis for constructing the code. By reviewing these specifications, the auditor will be able to check the correspondence of the code with the specifications. Further, deficiencies in the specifications may become apparent; for example, an important control may be missing in the specifications.

As a second alternative the auditor can attempt to understand the purposes of the program by consulting wider sources of information. The auditor can interview users of the program to check their understanding of what the program is supposed to do with the functions actually performed by the program. This alternative is more costly to undertake. However, the empirical evidence discussed earlier in the chapter shows erroneous specifications are a major cause of low-quality programs. The auditor must decide whether the likely additional benefits to be obtained from this alternative will exceed the extra costs involved.

Obtain Source Code   The auditor must be careful to ensure the source code listing obtained for the program under review is the current version. The auditor has greater assurance the listing is current if the installation uses a librarian system to maintain program source code. If the auditor has doubts about the currency of the source code, it can be compiled and compared with the object code of the production version of the program. Any discrepancies identified alert the auditor to the fact that the source code is not current.

When obtaining the source code listing, the auditor can use various software tools to facilitate understanding the program; for example, cross-reference listers and flowcharters (see, further, Chapter 17). Use of these tools is especially important if the auditor does not intend to review the entire source code but only selected portions of the code; for example, the computations performed on a particular data item. A cross-reference lister would show where in the program the data item is used.

Review Programming Language Used   Many compiler languages contain nonstandard features incorporated in the compiler to facilitate implementation and testing of a program. For example, some COBOL compilers include verbs that are not ANS COBOL verbs to aid the programmer to debug a program.

Over time, internal auditors will build up experience with the features of the compiler used within their installation. Nonstandard verbs or clauses that pose threats to a program's processing effectiveness, efficiency, or integrity will become known. However, the external auditor confronts many different compilers for the one language. Before undertaking a review of program code, external auditors should examine carefully the documentation for the compiler. They should note any nonstandard features of the language that pose a threat to the quality of programs written in the language.

Review Source Code   Currently, there is little theory or empirical evidence to indicate the "best" way of reviewing program code. Many questions remain unanswered. Do some ways of reviewing code identify more errors than others? Are some ways of reviewing code faster than others? Is the best way dependent on how the code is written (structured)? Should code be reviewed differently if efficiency is the main concern rather than data integrity? Is the effectiveness and efficiency of a code review technique dependent upon psychological and demographic characteristics of the person undertaking the review (see, further, Myers [1978])?

If only a selected portion of the code is to be reviewed, the auditor may simply focus on that section of the code and any interfaces it has with other sections of code. If the entire code is to be examined, one method of review is to focus first on input and output operations and then on processing.

In any programming language, certain verbs are more likely to be used to implement unauthorized code than others. Similarly, use of certain verbs is more error-prone than others. For example, when an auditor examines input/output in a COBOL program, special attention should be paid to the following verbs since they may be used in conjunction with unauthorized code:

COBOL verb	Audit concerns
SELECT	Relates a file to an input/output device. Can be checked to see the program processes only authorized files.
REDEFINES	Permits alternate record formats to be defined for the one file. Selection of a specific format generally is triggered by an "IF" clause. Can be checked to see the data items redefined are authorized data items.
OPEN/CLOSE	Makes a file available and unavailable for processing respectively. Multiple OPEN/CLOSE verbs in a program may mean a file is being made available for unauthorized processing.
COPY . . . REPLACING	Used to change the definition of data items copied into a program from a source library. Can be checked to see the changes are authorized.

In general, during a complete code review of a program, the auditor should determine whether or not the data items and relationships processed by the program are the authorized set of data items and relationships. A cross-reference lister can be used to provide a listing of all data items and relationships (e.g., pointer fields will be listed). Those used within the FILE SECTION of a COBOL program can be checked against the file definitions in the program specifications; those used within the WORKING-STORAGE section must be evaluated independently. If the COBOL report writer facility is used, data items in the REPORT SECTION should be checked against program specifications. Literals and constants used in the PROCEDURE DIVISION must be verified independently.

With respect to processing, the following COBOL verbs (clauses) tend to be used in conjunction with unauthorized code:

COBOL verb	Audit concerns
IF	Typically the major conditional statement used in a program. Can be used to activate an unauthorized section of code when a certain condition is true or false.
GO TO . . . DEPENDING	The GO TO without DEPENDING allows an unconditional branch in the logic flow; with the DEPENDING it provides a conditional branch. The branch may be to an unauthorized section of code.
ALTER	Changes the transfer point specified in a GO TO. The first transfer point may be authorized code; the second may be unauthorized code.
PERFORM . . . UNTIL	The UNTIL statement permits a conditional branch to be carried out with the PERFORM. The branch may be to an unauthorized section of code.
CALL/ENTER	Used to call a subprogram (subroutine). The subprogram may contain unauthorized code. ENTER is used if the subroutine is written in a language other than COBOL.
DISPLAY	Can be used to breach the privacy of data by having the contents of a field displayed on a peripheral, e.g., the console.

COBOL verb	Audit concerns
ACCEPT	Program stops and awaits the input of data from a peripheral, e.g., the console. Can be used to input a code that will cause a conditional test to branch to unauthorized code.
EXAMINE	Used to replace certain occurrences of a given character in a field with another character. May be inserted before and after a validation test so a specific transaction passes the test. The first instance changes the data item value so it passes the test; the second restores the data item to its original value.

Again, a cross-reference lister can be used to identify where in a program these verbs (clauses) are used. However, the auditor should be careful about examining any section of code in isolation. For example, a GO TO may branch to a section of authorized code. Further on in the program, however, the paragraph name referred to by the GO TO may be changed with an ALTER verb.

After examining the flow of logic and control in a program, the auditor may wish to examine any computations performed by the program. As discussed earlier in the chapter, empirical evidence shows computations often are a major source of error in programs. A cross-reference lister can be used to print out the COBOL verbs used for computations: ADD, SUBTRACT, MULTIPLY, DIVIDE, COMPUTE.

The auditor also should pay special attention to any nonstandard verbs used in the program. For example, some COBOL compilers provide various debugging verbs (TRACE, DEBUG) that are not part of ANS COBOL. These verbs could be used to breach the privacy of data.

Formulate Flaw Hypotheses   Once a deficiency in the programming code has been identified, two further steps must be taken. First, the auditor must work out the implications of the deficiency for the effectiveness, efficiency, or integrity of processing. Second, the auditor must formulate a test to determine whether the postulated deficiency does, in fact, exist and the postulated results of the deficiency do, in fact, occur. These steps can be accomplished by careful desk checking of the code. Test data then may be used to verify the flaw hypotheses.

Costs and Benefits of Code Review

The primary advantage of reviewing program source code is that it provides a level of detailed knowledge about a program that is difficult to acquire using any other evidence collection technique. With other evidence collection techniques, inferences must be made about the quality of the code on the basis of some test result. With program source code review, the auditor examines the code directly.

The primary disadvantage of the technique is its cost. Earl [1977] concludes that, on average, an auditor can complete about one code review per day, assuming the average program does not exceed 600 lines of source code. However, the speed with which a program can be read depends on the type of programming language used, the quality of the program code, and the technical competence of the auditor performing the review.

TEST DATA

The use of a sample of data to assess the quality of a program is fundamental to many evidence collection techniques. It is based on the premise that it is possible to generalize about the overall reliability of a program if it is reliable for a set of specific tests.

The term "test data" usually is reserved for a technique where the set of tests is *designed* rather than based on a set of existing production data. In other words, the test data approach means data is created to test specific aspects of a program. The quality of the program is not inferred from the quality of application production data that has been processed already.

The test data technique goes under several names. It is sometimes called test decking. If a comprehensive set of test data is assembled for an application system, often the set is called a test bed. More recently the name "base case" has been used for a test bed and the testing technique called base case system evaluation (BCSE) (see Mullen [1978]). Some other variations of the basic test data technique also are described in the next chapter.

Some Theoretical Considerations

Like program source code review, test data can be used to evaluate the effectiveness and efficiency of a program and to determine whether or not it safeguards assets and maintains data integrity. However, as an evidence collection technique it has been used primarily to assess whether or not a program maintains data integrity. Because the test data technique underlies many of the evidence collection techniques used, several researchers have investigated the theoretical underpinnings of using test data to assess whether programs contain errors. They have addressed two major issues. First, what are the attributes of a *reliable* set of test data for a program? Second, is it possible to generate automatically a reliable set of test data?

Reliable Test Data. Suppose that P is a program for computing a function F whose domain is the set D. Let a finite subset $T \subset D$ be the set of test data used to determine whether P processes correctly; that is, that $P(d) = F(d) \; \forall d \in D$. Then T is defined to be a reliable set of test data for P if:

$$P(x) = F(x) \; \forall x \in T \Rightarrow P(x) = F(x) \; \forall x \in D$$

In other words, T is reliable if it reveals an error in P whenever P contains an error (see, further, Gerhart and Goodenough [1975] and Howden [1976]).

Clearly, the correctness of P can be determined by exhaustively testing P; that is, letting $T = D$. However, some programs have an infinite domain and testing would not terminate. The test data technique attempts to partition the input domain into a set of equivalence classes. By testing an element of each equivalence class, the correctness of the program for all elements of the equivalence class can be inferred. A reliable set of test data contains one element for every equivalence class of the input domain of the program to be tested.

Automatically Generating Reliable Test Data It would be a major break-through in proving the correctness of programs if there was some way of automatically generating a reliable set of test data. Unfortunately, Howden [1976] has proven that a computable procedure H does not exist which, given an *arbitrary* program P, a function F, and a domain D, generates a reliable set of test data T. Currently, the research is attempting to develop reliable test strategies for particular *classes* of programs (see, further, Howden [1976] and Geller [1978]).

Approaches to Designing Test Data

Since the state of the art still does not allow the automatic generation of a reliable set of test data, test data must be designed. In this light it is important for auditors to use a systematic approach to the design of test data. Otherwise, important deficiencies in the program may be missed. Moreover, excessive test data may be designed and used. Often a tendency is to believe that more comprehensive testing will result when a greater volume of test data is created and executed through a program. Unfortunately, a large volume of test data neither ensures that the critical features of the program will be tested nor does it ensure that testing will be carried out in the most economical manner. Given that testing must be carried out under a cost constraint, a systematic approach to test data design helps the auditor to decide on those program features to be tested and those program features that will be omitted from the test run.

Systematic testing methods can be classified in two ways: (*a*) black box or specification-based testing methods, and (*b*) white box or program-based testing methods (see Figure 18-2). *Black box methods* view the program to be tested as a black box; that is, they do not rely on any knowledge of the internal workings of the program. Instead, test data is designed based on knowledge of the functional specifications for the program. *White box methods* rely on knowledge of the internal structure of the program to be tested. Test data design is undertaken after the program listing has been examined. The following two sections provide an overview of each method of test data design (see, further, Gilbert [1983] and Fairley [1985]).

Black Box Test Data Design Methods Black box test data design methods recognize that major sources of program error are design errors and lack of

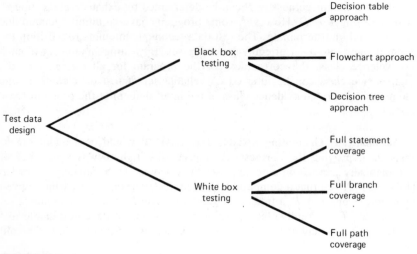

FIGURE 18-2
Approaches to test data design.

conformity of the program code with the program specifications. Accordingly, test data designers who use this approach first seek to understand what the program is supposed to do by eliciting information from knowledgeable users and by examining and evaluating the program specifications. Once they have a clear understanding of the functional requirements for the program, they can then commence to design the necessary test data to evaluate compliance by the program with these requirements.

Three techniques can be used to facilitate test data design under the black box approach: decision tables, flowcharts, and decision trees. *Decision tables* are an important tool for representing the logic of decisions (see, further, Montalbano [1974]). To create a decision table, auditors first must decide what program or section of a program is to be tested. If they decide to follow a top-down approach to testing, the mainline section of the code will be tested first followed by a test of lower-level modules in the program. Once the program or section of code to be tested has been identified, the auditor can begin to formulate a description of the conditions (logic) relevant to the program's correct functioning.

To illustrate the decision-table approach to test data design, assume the auditor interviews a payroll clerk about the payment of sales commissions. The auditor determines that most salespersons are paid a base salary plus 3% of sales if more than 100 units of the product are sold, and 4% of sales if more than 125 units of the product are sold. However, a salesperson can elect to sign a special contract, called a Type A contract, whereby no sales commission is paid until sales exceed 125 units. With a Type A contract, the sales commission is then paid at the rate of 6% of sales.

Assume the auditor decides to test this aspect of the program as sales commissions are deemed a material part of total payroll expense. Table 18-1*a* shows the unreduced decision table constructed by the auditor, and Table 18-1*b* shows the reduced decision table. Montalbano [1974] provides a comprehensive description of the steps to be followed in constructing unreduced and reduced decision tables and the methods that can be used to check the tables for completeness, consistency, and lack of redundancy in the rules. Nonetheless, to provide an intuitive feel for some of these steps, note that the unreduced decision table in Table 18-1*a* contains two rules, 3 and 4, that differ only on the basis of the response to one condition—namely, the sales > 100 condition. Otherwise, in all other respects the rules are the same. Since this condition does not affect the outcome of the actions taken, the two rules can be combined in a reduced form of the decision table. In Table 18-1*b*, rules 3 and 4 are represented as rule 3. Note that a "—" has been used in the response to condition 3 to indicate that the outcome has no effect on the actions to be undertaken. Note, also, that the unreduced form of the decision table contains certain intrarule inconsistencies. For example, in rule 2 it is impossible for condition 2 (sales >125) to be true and condition 3 (sales >100) to be false. This rule could be satisfied only if some form of logic error existed in the program.

TABLE 18-1*a*
UNREDUCED DECISION TABLE

					Rules				
	Sales Commissions	**1**	**2**	**3**	**4**	**5**	**6**	**7**	**8**
Condition stub	Type A contract	Y	Y	Y	Y	N	N	N	N
	Sales > 125	Y	Y	N	N	Y	Y	N	N
	Sales > 100	Y	N	Y	N	Y	N	Y	N
Action stub	Salary = base			X	X				X
	Salary = base + 3% sales							X	
	Salary = base + 4% sales						X		
	Salary = base + 6% sales	X							
	Error		X					X	

TABLE 18-1*b*
REDUCED DECISION TABLE

					Rules			
	Sales commissions	**1**	**2**	**3**	**4**	**5**	**6**	**7**
Condition stub	Type A contract	Y	Y	Y	N	N	N	N
	Sales > 125	Y	Y	N	Y	Y	N	N
	Sales > 100	Y	N	—	Y	N	Y	N
Action stub	Salary = base			X				X
	Salary = base + 3% sales						X	
	Salary = base + 4% sales					X		
	Salary = base + 6% sales	X						
	Error		X			X		

To test the program logic, the auditor simply constructs test data to satisfy each rule in the decision table. If the auditor is unwilling to make assumptions about how the program code has been written, the unreduced form of the decision table should be used. If the auditor assumes that efficient code has been written, the reduced decision table can be used as the basis for the test data design. To illustrate why this is the case, consider rule 3 in the reduced form of the decision table. If the programmer has written efficient code, only the first and second conditions should be tested before the relevant actions are invoked. If the program has been poorly written, the third condition might be tested even though its outcome is irrelevant to the actions to be invoked. Of course, the superfluous code may contain an error, and hopefully test data designed on the basis of the unreduced decision table will identify the erroneous code.

When choosing test data to satisfy each rule, values must be chosen that will test the boundaries of the rule. The boundary values for the first condition in Table 18-1 are easy to choose; an "equal to" value and a "not equal to" value must be used. Choosing the boundary values for condition 2 is slightly more difficult. Breakpoint values must be chosen, and the appropriate breakpoint values depend on the condition and the level of precision used in the program test. In condition 2, it appears that the program is supposed to test an integer value; thus, the appropriate breakpoint values are 125 and 126. If a real number were to be tested, however, the auditor would need to know how many positions after the decimal point were allowed. For example, if condition 2 tested the sales value in dollars and cents, the appropriate breakpoint values would be 125.00 and 125.01. Unfortunately, the level of precision used can only be determined after examining the program code, so black box testing may result in a wrong level of precision being chosen to design the program test.

Table 18-2 shows the test data design for the decision table shown in Table 18-1. Note that two extra parts have been added to the decision table (see, also, Gerhart and Goodenough [1975]). The first part shows the test data design for each rule in the decision table; the second part shows the expected results and whether or not the result was achieved when the program was tested. The two parts are the test data stub and the results stub respectively. Assume that the normal contract for a salesperson is a Type B contract. The base salary for both types of contracts is $10,000. The selling price per unit is $1000. The test data stub shows that test data cannot be designed for rules 2 and 5 since it is impossible to have a data value that is both greater than 125 and less than 100. The "confirmed" row in the results stub shows that the result expected for rule 6 was not obtained. The auditor would have to investigate why this result occurred. An "actual" results row might also be included in the results stub of the table.

In essence, the *flowchart approach* to the design of test data is the same as the decision-table approach. The major difference is the way in which the test is to be documented. The auditor first must decide on the source of the information for construction of the flowchart. Then the program or the section of the program to be flowcharted must be chosen.

TABLE 18-2
REDUCED DECISION TABLE WITH ASSOCIATED TEST DATA AND TEST RESULTS

	Sales commissions	\multicolumn{7}{c}{Rules}						
		1	2	3	4	5	6	7
Condition stub	Type A contract	Y	Y	Y	N	N	N	N
	Sales > 125	Y	Y	N	Y	Y	N	N
	Sales > 100	Y	N	—	Y	Y	N	N
Action stub	Salary = base			X				X
	Salary = base + 3% Sales						X	
	Salary = base + 4% Sales				X			
	Salary = base + 6% Sales	X						
	Error		X			X		
Test data stub	Contract Type	A	A	A	B	B	B	B
	Sales	126	—	125	126	—	101	100
Results stub	Expected Result	17,560	—	10,000	15,040	—	13,030	10,000
	Confirmed	√	—	√	√	—	X	√

Figure 18-3 shows the flowchart for the salary example described earlier. Once the auditor has constructed the flowchart, test data can be designed. The auditor must be careful to design test data for every path through the flowchart. A simple aid to identifying each path is to use different colored pencils to indicate the different paths through the flowchart. As the auditor designs test data for a path, the path should be marked off on the flowchart. The previous discussion on the choice of boundary values also applies to the choice of test data using the flowchart approach.

Similarly, the *decision tree* approach to the design of test data relies on the same underlying principles as the decision table and flowchart approaches. Again, the major difference is in the way the logic to be tested is documented. Figure 18-4 shows a decision tree for the salary example. To design test data, the auditor follows each branch of the decision tree. As with the flowchart approach, a colored pencil can be used to mark off a branch upon completing the test data design for that branch.

The relative advantages and disadvantages of decision tables, flowcharts, and decision trees for test data design are still unclear. The decision-table approach has two major advantages. First, a set procedure exists for ensuring the completeness and consistency of the logic. Second, once the decision table has been constructed, it is easy to design the test data since auditors simply have to follow down a rule (column) in the table. However, for some types of situations, it may be easier to construct a flowchart than a decision table. In some cases, also, auditors may find the graphical properties of a decision tree better facilitate their design of test data than either decision tables or flowcharts (see Ip and Weber [1986] and Vessey and Weber [1986]).

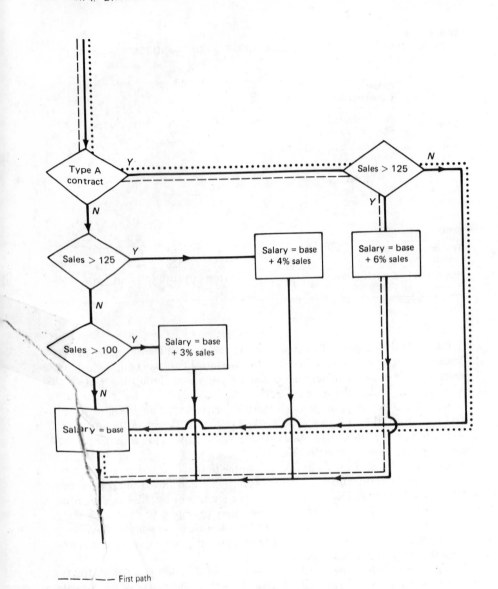

——————— First path

•••••• •••• Second path

FIGURE 18-3
Flowchart for test data design.

White Box Test Data Design Methods   White box test data design methods are based on the premise that significant information about the correctness of a program can be obtained by systematic execution of different paths through the program. Moreover, the approach recognizes that even with substantial prior information about a program, it is still very difficult to predict the actual

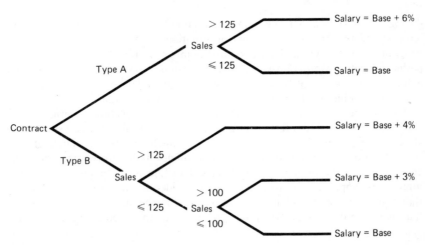

FIGURE 18-4
Decision tree for test data design.

behavior of a program. Accordingly, test data designers who use this approach first seek information about the program by examining a source listing of the program. Having identified critical sections of the source code, they then proceed to design test data to traverse this code. The execution profile of the program is then examined to determine whether errors are present.

Use of a white box test data design approach requires that test data designers specify a test completion criterion. In practice, three criteria are used. The first criterion is *full statement coverage* (Figure 18-5). Under this criterion, the test data design is successful if each program statement is exercised at least once

FIGURE 18-5
White box test completion criteria.

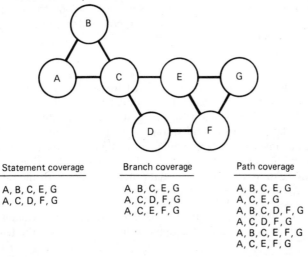

Statement coverage	Branch coverage	Path coverage
A, B, C, E, G	A, B, C, E, G	A, B, C, E, G
A, C, D, F, G	A, C, D, F, G	A, C, E, G
	A, C, E, F, G	A, B, C, D, F, G
		A, C, D, F, G
		A, B, C, E, F, G
		A, C, E, F, G

during the test run. Of the three test completion criteria, full statement coverage testing provides the least information about the correctness of the program. If the program includes a large number of branches and loops, many paths through the program will remain untested. Nonetheless, test data that achieves this criterion is the least costly to design, and in some cases it may still successfully identify the most important errors in a program.

The second white box, test data design, test completion criterion is *full branch coverage*. Under this criterion, the test data design is successful if each statement is executed at least once and each branching path is executed at least once (Figure 18-5). While branch testing provides more information about the correctness of the program than statement testing, unfortunately it is still a limited test approach. Branch testing will not identify an error in the program that results in the incorrect sequence of branches being tested. In addition, it may not identify an incorrect predicate. For example, consider the following set of program statements:

IF TRANTYPE EQ "1" OR TRANTYPE EQ "3"
MULTIPLY AMOUNT BY INTEREST GIVING RESULT.

If test data with transaction type equal to one is executed through the program, the branch will be traversed. However, the program could still be in error since the test perhaps should have been for a transaction type equal to one or four, not one or three. Finally, branch testing may not identify errors in program loops.

The third white box, test data design, test completion criterion is *full path coverage*. Unfortunately, full path coverage is a theoretical ideal since some programs have an infinite number of paths through them. The simple program segment represented by Figure 18-6, for example, has 65,536 possible paths through the segment. Whenever loops are used in programs, the number of possible paths through the program combinatorially explodes. It is this type of problem that has motivated some programming researchers to look for mechanisms that will provide formal proofs of program correctness. In practice, only limited path coverage testing can be accomplished.

Creating Test Data

Once the auditor has designed the test data needed for evidence collection purposes, the next step to be taken is to create test data that complies with the design. This can be a difficult and time-consuming step to complete. Master files may use complex data structures and storage structures that are difficult to create artificially. In some cases a large volume of test data may be required to carry out a comprehensive test. The following sections describe the approaches the auditor can use to create test data that complies with the test data design.

Use Production Data   At least part of the test data required may be available in the form of production (live) data for the application system. Once the test

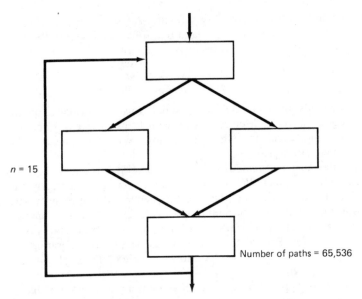

$n = 15$

Number of paths = 65,536

FIGURE 18-6
Program loop with large number of alternative paths through loop.

data design has been formulated, the auditor can use generalized audit software or utility software to select off transaction files and master files data that complies with the design. For example, using the design in Table 18-2, the auditor could formulate a retrieval with generalized audit software to satisfy rule 1; that is, any live transaction for a Type A contract and sales in excess of 125 units would be selected. Similarly, master file records could be selected in the same way. A list of retrievals for which no production data exists must be kept, and test data created for the conditions expressed in the retrievals in some other way.

Use Installation-Prepared Test Data Hopefully, the installation being audited attempts to carry out comprehensive testing of programs. The installation programming and systems staff should have prepared test data to assess the quality of the programs they have designed and implemented. If this test data exists on magnetic media, the auditor can use generalized audit software to select test data that complies with the design.

Develop New Test Data New test data must be created if it is unavailable from either production data or existing test data. One approach to creating new test data is to select data off production or existing test data files that partially fulfills a condition (rule) in the test design and modify those fields in the data that do not comply with the condition. These modifications can be carried out using generalized audit software or utility software. Alternatively, the auditor can code new test data, key in the data, and use software to create the test records.

Automated Aids

Various automated aids that facilitate using test data to gather evidence on the quality of a program have been discussed previously in Chapters 5 and 17. Because of their importance, however, this section briefly reemphasizes the usefulness of some of these aids.

If new test data must be created, a test data generator reduces the time required to develop this data. Providing the auditor specifies correctly the parameter values for the generator, the test data generated will be accurate. This accuracy is important when the auditor has to create test data for complex data structures. Manual creation of test data for complex data structures is an error-prone process. Furthermore, techniques for automatically generating test data are being refined continually (see, for example, Clarke [1976] and Ramamoorthy et al. [1976]).

For a limited set of applications, test data generators also may be able to predict the results that should be obtained when the test data is executed. They also may be able to indicate when these results are not achieved. For example, syntax test case generators have been developed to test out compilers (see, for example, Celentano [1980]). They will randomly generate legal sentences and detect whether the compiler parses these sentences correctly. Some progress also had been made in developing test case generators for graphics software (see Bird and Munoz [1983]). The validity of graphics software is difficult to check since usually it must be verified visually. Nonetheless, graphics test case generators can be used to create large numbers of test cases randomly and to send markers to a screen to indicate the predicted end points of the graphical output. The match between the predicted end points and the actual end points can then be verified visually.

An execution analyzer is an important aid for evaluating the completeness of a test data design. Since an execution analyzer indicates whether a branch through a program has been traversed, the auditor is able to identify unauthorized code and any omissions made in the formulation of the test data design. Before using an execution analyzer, however, the auditor should check that it is able to detect all branches in a program. For example, some analyzers may be unable to detect conditional tests in a subroutine that is CALLed or ENTERed from the main COBOL program. The auditor should also check to see how the analyzer handles such verbs as ALTER.

Whereas an execution analyzer evaluates some of the dynamic properties of a program, static analyzers can be used to evaluate some of the static properties of a program. A static analyzer reads program source code and produces a report on coding errors, questionable coding practices, and deviations from coding standards (see, for example, Fairley [1985]). For example, it can identify sections of code that will never be executed, variables that are not initialized, variables that are initialized but never used, use of instructions that are prohibited according to the installation standards, and mismatches between the parameters passed between one module and another module.

For some complex systems, simulators facilitate the testing process. For example, a network simulator allows testing of a data communications network without having to use the hardware/software configuration of the network. A terminal simulator permits simulation of multiple online terminals without having to use the hardware/software configuration of the online system. In both cases, without simulators the auditor may find it difficult to gather evidence on the quality of programs by using test data.

To evaluate the quality of the human-machine dialog in an interactive system, a dialog test facility can be used (see, for example, Maurer [1983]). A dialog test facility is an interactive debugging tool that allows a programmer or an auditor to (a) examine how predefined panels (screen images) will appear to a user on a visual display so the format of the panels can be verified visually; (b) to monitor the execution of a dialog as it processes a set of test inputs submitted to the dialog; (c) to temporarily halt execution of a dialog so the status of critical variables can be examined; (d) to trace execution of a dialog as it processes a set of test data; and (e) to allow temporary modifications to a dialog so the effects of these modifications can be assessed.

Costs and Benefits of Test Data

The major benefit of using test data as an evidence collection technique is that it allows direct examination of the quality of program code. Well-designed test data tests specifically whether the program complies with specifications. The quality of the code need not be inferred from the quality of production data the program has processed.

Often it is claimed a major benefit of using test data is that auditors require little technical competence with computers to use the technique. For a very simple batch system or an undisciplined approach to the use of test data, this claim may be true. However, as the chapter illustrates, the effective and efficient design and creation of test data and the use of automated tools to support the test data approach requires the auditor to have substantial knowledge of computer technology.

The primary disadvantage of the test data approach is that it is often time-consuming and costly to use. As automated tools to support the approach are improved, this disadvantage may become less important.

The effectiveness and efficiency with which test data is employed also seems highly dependent on the capabilities of the individuals who use the technique. Myers [1978] had three groups of "above average" experienced programmers (average experience was 11 years) test a small program written in PL/1. Subjects in the first group were provided only with the program specifications. Subjects in the second group were provided with the specifications and a source listing. Subjects in the third group were organized into three-person teams and asked to test the program using the manual walk-through/inspection method (see Chapter 5). Each team was provided with the program specifications and a source listing. Myers found none of the groups different in their ability to detect errors; all performed poorly, detecting only about a third of the errors in the program. Further, there was significant variability in the individual results. The walk-through/inspection group took about 2½ times longer than the other groups to complete testing. Myers argues the most effective testing will occur if two programmers are used to test a program independently and their results combined. From his analysis of the types of errors detected and missed, he also concludes that programmers may pay too much attention to normal test conditions and insufficient attention to erroneous input and special conditions; the programmers focused on the program logic rather than input/output anomalies.

PROGRAM CODE COMPARISON

The auditor uses program code comparison for two reasons. First, it provides assurance the software being audited is the correct version of the software. For example, the auditor may wish to check correspondence between an audit version of an application program's code and the production version of an application program's code. Second, it provides assurance any software used as an audit tool is the correct version of the software. For example, the auditor may wish to compare an audit version of a specialized audit program with the installation version of a specialized audit program. If the auditor finds correspondence between the audit version and the installation version of the program, and the program has been tested comprehensively at a prior time, further testing should not be necessary. If the program has not been tested, the auditor obtains assurance the program to be tested is the production version of the program.

Types of Code Comparison

Software is available providing two types of program code comparison: (*a*) source code comparison, and (*b*) object code comparison. With source code comparison the software provides a meaningful listing of any discrepancies between the two versions of the program. Nevertheless, the auditor must obtain further assurance the source code version is the one used in production running.

With object code comparison it is difficult to identify the nature of any discrepancies found between the two versions of object code. Preferably, object code comparison is used to ask the simple question: Are there discrepancies? The major advantage of the technique is that it provides assurance the production version of a program is the authorized one. However, if discrepancies are identified, other techniques must be used to identify the cause of the discrepancies. Since compilers often are modified by their vendors and new releases provided, the auditor must be careful to ensure discrepancies do not arise because the same source code has been compiled with different versions of the compiler.

Use of the Technique

Source code and object code comparison are most effective as an audit technique when they are used in conjunction with each other. Figure 18-7 shows an overall approach to the use of program code comparison. The approach proceeds in the following way. First, the auditor compares the audit version of the program source code with that version the installation contends is the source code used to compile the production object code. Any discrepancies identified between the source code versions must be reconciled. Second, the auditor compiles either the audit or installation version of the source code with the compiler used to produce the production object code. Third, the auditor compares the object code produced with the production version of the object code. Any discrepancies identified mean either the wrong compiler has been used or the auditor has been supplied with the wrong version of the source code or object code.

FIGURE 18-7
Use of code comparison for evidence gathering.

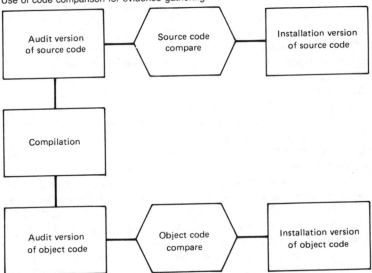

Costs and Benefits of Code Comparison

The code comparison technique is an easy way of identifying changes made to programs. The software that performs code comparison usually is not costly to run. Further, the auditor requires little technical skill to be able to use the software. However, identifying the implications of any discrepancies found in the code requires some knowledge of programming.

The technique is limited in that it does not provide any evidence on the quality of the code being compared unless one version of the code has been thoroughly tested by the auditor.

Code comparison programs also differ in the quality of their output. For example, if two files differ because a block of data (say, documentation text) has been shifted, some programs will show all data in the block as being changed rather than just the beginning and end (probably the more intuitive notion of the change). This may cause the auditor to overlook changes that may have been made within the block (see, further, Heckel [1978]).

SUMMARY

Three evidence collection techniques used primarily to evaluate the quality of program logic are code review, test data, and code comparison. The three techniques can be used together to perform an integrated test of the quality of program code. Code review provides a basis for generating flaw hypotheses about program logic. Test data enables these hypotheses to be tested. Code comparison allows the auditor to test whether the production version of a program used is the tested version.

A major decision that must be made when using code review or test data is how the specifications for the program to be examined will be formulated. Empirical evidence shows design errors are a major source of errors in programs. Thus, if the auditor relies on the documented program specifications as the basis for the code review or test data design, many errors may be missed.

The most effective and efficient ways of performing a code review or designing test data are still research issues. One recommended way of performing a code review is to examine input/output first and then examine processing. Two approaches to designing test data are the black box approach and the white box approach. The former bases test data design on knowledge of the program specifications; the latter requires knowledge of the internal structure of the program.

Software is available to perform either source code or object code comparison. Source code comparison provides a meaningful description of discrepancies between two versions of a program; however, the auditor must obtain assurance the source code examined is the version used to compile the object code. It is difficult to determine the nature of any discrepancies when two object code versions of a program are compared. However, if one of the versions is the production object code, the auditor can test directly whether unauthorized modifications to the code have occurred.

REVIEW QUESTIONS

18-1 Briefly explain the nature of the code review, test data, and code comparison evidence collection techniques. Explain how they can be used as an interrelated set of techniques to examine the quality of a program.

18-2 Briefly outline the findings of the limited empirical research on where errors occur in programs. What implications do these findings have for the use of various audit evidence collection techniques?

18-3 As the auditor of a computer installation, list three factors that would affect your decision on whether or not to rely on the documented program specifications as the basis for code review or test data design for a program.

18-4 Briefly explain how code review can be used to identify ineffective code and nonstandard code in a program.

18-5 Construct a short section of COBOL code to show how you could use the ALTER verb to activate unauthorized code. Briefly explain how your program will work.

18-6 List the attributes of a COBOL program you would examine to see if the code is sufficiently readable for you to be able to carry out code review.

18-7 Briefly explain why it is important to review the documentation for the compiler used within an installation when carrying out program code review.

18-8 Briefly explain the procedures an auditor should follow upon encountering a CALL or ENTER statement during the code review of a program. Which statement usually presents more problems for the auditor in verifying the integrity of code? Explain.

18-9 Give three COBOL verbs that can be used to violate the *privacy* of data, and explain briefly how they can be used. How would the auditor go about detecting the use of these verbs?

18-10 Briefly explain the purpose of the auditor first reviewing input/output instructions when undertaking code review of a program.

18-11 In a COBOL program, what verbs would the auditor review to check any computations performed in the program? What verbs do you think would be the most error-prone?

18-12 Briefly explain what is meant by base case system evaluation. How does it differ from the "normal" test data approach?

18-13 What is meant by reliable test data? Is it possible to automatically generate reliable test data for any arbitrary program?

18-14 Why is it important to design test data before creating test data? What are the advantages and disadvantages of carrying out the design and creation activities concurrently?

18-15 Briefly explain the difference between the black box approach to test data design and the white box approach to test data design?

18-16 Briefly explain the nature of the following three black box approaches to designing test data:
a Decision table approach
b Flowchart approach
c Decision tree approach

18-17 Briefly explain how redundant rules in a decision table are detected and how they are removed. What is meant by interrule and intrarule inconsistency? How are these inconsistencies handled? How can the completeness of a decision table be checked? (*Hint:* See Montalbano [1974]).

18-18 What factors affect whether the auditor uses a reduced form or an unreduced form of a decision table to design test data? If auditors base their test data design on the reduced form of a decision table, why is it then important to use an execution path monitor in conjunction with the program test?

18-19 Why is it important to test the boundary or breakpoint values in a conditional test when test data is being designed? How does the level of precision used in the conditional test affect the test data design for the breakpoint conditions?

18-20 What are the relative advantages and disadvantages of the decision table, flowchart, and decision tree approaches to test data design?

18-21 If a white box approach to test data design is used, briefly explain the difference between the objectives of full statement coverage, full branch coverage, and full path coverage. In practice, which objective do you think auditors are most likely to have when they design test data?

18-22 Briefly explain how the auditor can use production data to create test data. Is production data sometimes still useful even though it does not meet exactly the test data design specifications?

18-23 Are there any hazards in using an execution path monitor to determine whether paths in a program have been traversed? Explain.

18-24 Briefly explain the difference between an execution analyzer and a static analyzer. Which type of analyzer is most likely to be useful to the auditor? Why?

18-25 ''Auditors require limited technical knowledge to use test data effectively as an evidence-gathering tool.'' Discuss.

18-26 Why might an auditor use program code comparison when evaluating the quality of a program?

18-27 Briefly explain the difference between program source code comparison and program object code comparison. What are the relative advantages and disadvantages of each type of code comparison?

18-28 List the reasons why differences may arise between two object code versions of a program.

18-29 What steps can the auditor take to ensure that the integrity of code comparison software has not been corrupted?

MULTIPLE CHOICE QUESTIONS

18-1 Empirical evidence indicates that the largest percentage of errors that occur during program implementation are:
a Coding errors
b Testing errors
c Design errors
d Documentation errors

18-2 From an audit viewpoint, which of the following conclusions can be drawn from empirical studies on program errors:
a Relatively little attention should be given to sequencing and control in the design of test data
b When designing test data, the auditor should be careful about relying on the integrity of program specifications

   c Spelling errors in system messages are often a major problem

   d Erroneous arithmetic computations are the major type of coding error

18-3 Which of the following is most likely to be the motivation for the auditor using program source code review:

   a Generalized audit software is unavailable

   b The auditor believes the program to be reviewed contains inefficient code

   c The program processes only small quantities of data so there is little code available for review

   d The auditor is unwilling to treat the program as a black box

18-4 the limited empirical studies undertaken on the readability of program source code basically have found that:

   a The readability of code in the programs studied increases as the size of logic spans increases

   b Standard labeling conventions do little to enhance the readability of program code

   c Most programs in the studies have been unreadable

   d For practical purposes the number of paths through the programs studied has been finite

18-5 During the conduct of a source code review, the examination of the data processing installation's programming standards occurs:

   a Before reviewing the program's specifications

   b After the source code listing has been obtained

   c Concurrently with the source code review

   d After the programming language used has been reviewed

18-6 The COBOL ALTER verb may be used in conjunction with unauthorized code to change:

   a The contents of an accumulator in working storage

   b The transfer point in a GOTO so the branch occurs to unauthorized code

   c The number of iterations in a PERFORM . . . UNTIL clause

   d The record format of an input file

18-7 Which of the following COBOL computational verbs is likely to be the most error-prone:

   a MULTIPLY

   b SUBTRACT

   c COMPUTE

   d EXPONENTIATE

18-8 The difference between a test deck and a base case system evaluation (BCSE) is:

   a Test data for BCSE is based on production data whereas test data for a test deck is designed

   b BCSE provides more comprehensive test data for a system with known, documented results

   c BCSE test data traverses all execution paths through a program whereas a test deck traverses only a subset of execution paths

   d Test decks correspond more closely to test beds than BCSE

18-9 A reliable set of test data is one that:

   a Reveals an error in a program whenever the program contains an error

   b Traverses all conditional execution paths in the program that it tests

   c Requires no change in spite of modifications made to the program that it tests d Produces consistent results across various executions of the program that it tests

18-10 Which of the following statements best describes the difference between the black box and the white box approaches to test data design:

a The black box approach relies on knowledge of the functional specifications of the program to be tested whereas the white box approach relies on knowledge of the program's internal structure

b The black box approach emphasizes reliable test data design whereas the white box approach emphasizes cost-effective test data design

c The black box approach is oriented toward automatic test data generation whereas the white box approach is oriented toward automatic theorem proving

d The black box approach is oriented toward system testing whereas the white box approach is oriented toward program testing

18-11 The purpose of the results stub in a decision table used for test data purposes is that it:

a Documents the conditions that lead to a particular action

b Shows the rules for different conditional values

c Shows the actions to be undertaken when a rule is satisfied

d Shows the expected and actual results for the test data used for each rule

18-12 Which of the following is *not* an advantage of the decision table approach to test data design:

a A set procedure exists for ensuring the completeness and consistency of the logic to be tested

b It is easy to construct test data once a decision table has been constructed

c Decision tables are a good way of documenting the expected and actual results of test data

d Compared to the flowchart approach, decision tables are a faster way of designing test data

18-13 The objective of full statement coverage in program testing means that:

a Every branching statement in the program is traversed at least once during the test run

b All execution paths in the program are traversed at least once by the test data

c For any statement that is traversed by test data, both the "true" and "false" values are tested

d Each program statement is executed at least once during the test run

18-14 The testing aid that is most likely to identify questionable coding practices used in a program is:

a A static analyzer

b An execution path monitor

c A test case generator

d A test simulator

18-15 Limited empirical evidence on the ability of programmers to design test data suggests that:

a More experienced programmers detect more errors with their test data designs

b Programmers are more successful at detecting errors with test data when they use a white box approach to test data design

c Programmers perform poorly when they design test data, irrespective of their level of programming experience

d The time taken to design test data is reduced if a walk-through/inspection method is used

18-16 Which of the following should *not* cause a discrepancy to be identified when object code comparison is undertaken between a blueprint and a production version of a program:

a The wrong version of the source code has been used to compile the production program

b A block of documentation text has been shifted in the production version of the program

c Different versions of a compiler have been used to compile the blueprint and production code

d A direct fix has been made on one version of the object code

EXERCISES AND CASES

18-1 As the auditor responsible for examining the accounts receivable system within a computer installation, you decide to undertake code review of the program that prints out a list of customers who have exceeded their allowed credit limit. Since the source code is stored in a library and online facilities are available, you use an editor to retrieve all instances of various statements in the program. One of the "IF" statements you retrieve runs as follows:

```
IF ACBAL LE ALLOWBAL
    OR ACNUM EQ C105-6A
        NEXT SENTENCE
    ELSE PERFORM PRINT-ROUTINE
```

You are perplexed by this piece of code. None of the employees within the computer installation has an account with the company numbered C105-6A. Further, you cannot find any customer to whom this account number has been issued yet.

Required: Briefly explain why you are concerned with this piece of code and how you would proceed now.

18-2 You are the auditor in charge of the audit of the payroll system for an organization. One of your staff performs a code review of the input validation program for timecard data. She brings the following section of code to you as she is unable to understand the purpose of the code.

```
EXAMINE HRS-WORKED TALLYING UNTIL FIRST 9
    REPLACING BY 4.
IF HRS-WORKED LT ZERO OR HRS-WORKED GT 60
    PERFORM ERROR-ROUTINE
    GO TO NEW-CARD
IF TALLY EQ 1
    EXAMINE HRS-WORKED UNTIL FIRST 4
        REPLACING BY 9.
GO TO SALARY-CALC.
```

Required: Briefly outline the advice you would give to her.

18-3 The input card for a payroll program contains the following fields:
Employee number
Regular hours
Overtime hours
Expenses
Commission
Vacation time
Sick time
Required: List five tests you might carry out to determine whether the input validation program processes the input data correctly.

18-4 You are the auditor responsible for evaluating an organization's invoicing program. You decide to use test data to test that section of the program relating to sales discounts. During an interview with the sales manager you make the following notes about how the program is supposed to operate:

Providing customers pay within 30 days, they are entitled to a sales discount. If the sales amount is over $5000, a 1% discount applies. If sales are over $10,000, a 1½% discount applies. However, for new customers a salesperson is allowed to override the standard discount. For sales less than or equal to $5000, the salesperson can give a 1% discount, over $5000 a 1½% discount, and over $10,000 a 2% discount. If the customer is the federal government, a 4% discount always applies providing payment is still received within 30 days.

Required: Using both the decision-table and flowchart approach, design test data to test this processing aspect of the program.

18-5 The specifications for a fixed assets program include the following paragraph.

Straight-line depreciation is to be charged on fixed assets at the following rates:

Code no.	Rate
100–199	10%
200–299	15
300–399	20

However, if the fixed asset is located in Alice Springs, a further 5% is to be added to the depreciation rate to allow for the higher deterioration that results from the more severe climate. Further, any asset in the 200–299 code category that produces over 10,000 units per year is to have an extra 2% added to the depreciation rate to allow for the higher deterioration that occurs when the asset produces at above normal output.

Required: Design test data using both the decision-table and flowchart approach to determine whether these specifications have been implemented correctly in the program.

18-6 You are a partner with EDP expertise in a firm of external auditors. Because of your scintillating personality, you win a new client that is a medium-size manufacturing firm which has just gone public.

During the initial planning of the audit, the manager responsible for the audit approaches you about the design of test data to test the client's software. He is a little confused because the client's data processing manager has indicated that all important accounting applications use generalized software packages acquired from well-known software vendors. When the audit manager indicated to the data processing manager that he intended to design test data to test the accounting software, she ridiculed him, claiming that he was proposing a pointless exercise. The data processing manager argued that it was ludicrous to design test data to test out well-known, generalized accounting software and that she would inform her managing director that the auditor was wasting money.

Required: To avert an impending disaster with your client, how would you advise your audit manager about the necessity of undertaking the test data design exercise with the accounting software?

18-7 You are the partner in charge of the audit of a major financial institution. During the last year your client has purchased a fourth-generation programming language and developed a significant financial application using the language.

Required: Your firm is an active user of the test data method to evaluate the quality of programs. However, this is the first time that your firm has encountered a client where an application system that is significant from the audit viewpoint has been programmed using a fourth-generation language. In light of this development, what changes, if any, would you recommend to your firm's standards in terms of how test data should be designed and implemented when your staff encounter systems that have been programmed in a fourth-generation language instead of a third-generation language?

ANSWERS TO MULTIPLE CHOICE QUESTIONS

18-1 c	**18-5** a	**18-9** a	**18-13** d
18-2 b	**18-6** b	**18-10** a	**18-14** a
18-3 d	**18-7** c	**18-11** d	**18-15** c
18-4 c	**18-8** b	**18-12** d	**18-16** b

REFERENCES

Adams, Donald L. "Audit Review of Program Code-I," *EDPACS* (August 1975), pp. 1–5.

Andres, Albert. "An Analysis of Errors and Their Causes in System Programs," *IEEE Transactions on Software Engineering* (June 1975), pp. 140–149.

Baker, F. Terry. "Structured Programming in a Production Programming Environment," *IEEE Transactions on Software Engineering* (June 1975), pp. 241–252.

Bird, D.L., and C.V. Munoz. "Automatic Generation of Random Self-Checking Test Cases," *IBM Systems Journal,* vol. 22, no. 3, 1983, pp. 229–245.

Boehm, Barry W. "Software and Its Impact: A Quantitative Study," *Datamation* (May 1973), pp. 48–59.

Boehm, Barry W., Robert K. McClean, and D.B. Urfrig. "Some Experience with Automated Aids to the Design of Large-Scale Reliable Software," *IEEE Transactions on Software Engineering* (March 1975), pp. 125–133.

Burch, John G., Jr., and Joseph L. Sardinas, Jr. *Computer Control and Audit: A Total Systems Approach* (New York: Wiley, 1978).

Canadian Institute of Chartered Accountants. *Computer Audit Guidelines* (Toronto: The Canadian Institute of Chartered Accountants, 1975).

Celentano, A. "Compiler Testing Using a Sentence Generator," *Software-Practice and Experience*, vol. 10, 1980, pp. 897–913.

Clarke, Lori A. "A System to Generate Test Data and Symbolically Execute Programs," *IEEE Transactions on Software Engineering* (September 1976), pp. 215–222.

Comptroller General of the United States. *Auditing Computers with a Test Deck* (Washington, DC: U.S. Government Printing Office, 1975).

De Millo, Richard A., Richard J. Lipton, and Alan J. Perlis. "Social Processes and Proofs of Theorems and Programs," *Communications of the ACM* (May 1979), pp. 271–280.

Earl, Michael J. "Program Auditing: A New Approach to Computer Audit," *EDPACS* (December 1977), pp. 5–14.

Elshoff, James L. "An Analysis of Some Commercial PL/1 Programs," *IEEE Transactions on Software Engineering* (June 1976), pp. 113–120.

Endres, A. "An Analysis of Errors and Their Causes in System Programs," *IEEE Transactions on Software Engineering* (June 1975), pp. 140–149.

Fairley, Richard. *Software Engineering Concepts* (New York: McGraw-Hill, 1985).

Fitzsimmons, Ann, and Tom Love. "A Review and Evaluation of Software Science," *Computing Surveys* (March 1978), pp. 3–18.

Geller, Matthew. "Test Data as an Aid in Proving Program Correctness," *Communications of the ACM* (May 1978), pp. 368–375.

Gerhart, Susan L., and John B. Goodenough. "Toward a Theory of Test Data Selection," *IEEE Transactions on Software Engineering* (June 1975), pp. 156–173.

Gilbert, Philip. *Software Design and Development* (Chicago: Science Research Associates, 1978).

Hartwick, R. Dean. "Test Planning," *Proceedings of the 1977 National Computer Conference* (Montvale, NJ: AFIPS Press, 1977), pp. 285–294.

Heckel, Paul. "A Technique for Isolating Differences between Files," *Communications of the ACM* (April 1978), pp. 264–268.

Hetzel, W.C., ed. *Program Test Methods* (Englewood Cliffs, NJ: Prentice-Hall, 1973).

Howden, William E. "Reliability of the Path Analysis Testing Strategy," *IEEE Transactions on Software Engineering* (September 1976), pp. 208–215.

Huang, J.C. "An Approach to Program Testing," *Computing Surveys* (September 1975), pp. 113–128.

Ip, Andrew, and Ron Weber. "Decision Trees versus Decision Tables for Audit Test Data Design." *Accounting and Finance* (May 1986), pp. 25–46.

Lauesen, S. "Debugging Techniques," *Software Practice and Experience* (January 1979), pp. 51–63.

Lemos, Ronald S. "An Implementation of Structured Walk-Throughs in Teaching COBOL Programming," *Communications of the ACM* (June 1979), pp. 335–340.

Maurer, M.E. "Full-Screen Testing of Interactive Applications," *IBM Systems Journal*, vol. 22, no. 3, 1983, pp. 246–261.

Mills, Harlan D. "Software Development," *IEEE Transactions on Software Engineering* (December 1976), pp. 265–273.

Montalbano, Michael. *Decision Tables* (Chicago: Science Research Associates, 1974).

Mullen, Jack B. "Defining a Base Case System Evaluation," *EDP Auditing* (Pennsauken, NJ: Auerbach Publishers, 1978), Portfolio 73-01-03, pp. 1–8.

Myers, Glenford J. "A Controlled Experiment in Program Testing and Code Walkthroughs/Inspections," *Communications of the ACM* (September 1978), pp. 760–768.

Myers, G.J. *The Art of Software Testing* (New York: Wiley, 1979).

Orr, Kenneth T. "Systems Design, Structured Programming and Data Security," *IBM Data Security Forum* (September 1974), paper 33 (pages unnumbered).

Power, L.R. "Design and Use of a Program Execution Analyzer," *IBM Systems Journal*, vol. 22, no. 3, 1983, pp. 271–294.

Ramamoorthy, C.V., S.F. Ho, and W.T. Chen. "On the Automated Generation of Program Test Data," *IEEE Transactions on Software Engineering* (December 1976), pp. 293–300.

Rubey, Raymond J., Joseph A. Dana, and Peter W. Biche. "Quantitative Aspects of Software Validation," *IEEE Transactions on Software Engineering* (June 1975), pp. 150–155.

Shomman, Martin L. *Software Engineering: Design, Reliability, and Management* (New York: McGraw-Hill, 1983).

Stanford Research Institute. *Systems Auditability and Control Study: Data Processing Audit Practices Report* (Altamonte Springs, FL: The Institute of Internal Auditors, 1977).

Vessey, Iris, and Ron Weber. "Structured Tools and Conditional Logic: An Empirical Investigation," *Communications of the ACM* (January 1986), pp. 48–57.

Weiss, Harold. "Audit Review of Program Code-II," *EDPACS* (August 1975), pp. 6–7.

Yourdon, Edward. *Techniques of Program Structure and Design* (Englewood Cliffs, NJ: Prentice-Hall, 1975).

CONCURRENT AUDITING TECHNIQUES

REVIEW QUESTIONS
MULTIPLE CHOICE QUESTIONS
EXERCISES AND CASES
ANSWERS TO MULTIPLE CHOICE QUESTIONS
REFERENCES

The previous chapters on evidence collection discussed techniques for gathering evidence *after* application system data has been processed. In some cases ex post evidence collection and evaluation is unsatisfactory. The auditor needs to identify problems in application systems on a more timely basis. For this reason techniques have been developed that collect evidence at the same time as application system processing occurs. These techniques are called "concurrent auditing techniques." This chapter discusses the basic nature of concurrent auditing techniques, the reasons why they were developed, the specific types of concurrent auditing techniques available and their relative advantages and disadvantages, and methods of implementing concurrent auditing techniques.

BASIC NATURE OF CONCURRENT AUDITING TECHNIQUES

Concurrent auditing techniques use two bases for collecting audit evidence. First, special audit modules are embedded in application systems or system software to collect, process, and print audit evidence. Second, in some cases special audit records are used to store the audit evidence collected so the auditor can examine this evidence at a later stage. These records may be stored on application system files or on a separate audit file.

Though evidence collection is concurrent with application system processing, the timing of evidence reporting is a decision for the auditor. If a critical error is identified, the auditor may program the embedded audit routines to report the error immediately. The evidence may be dumped directly to a printer or terminal in the auditor's office. In other cases some time lag will exist between evidence collection and reporting. The auditor uses the special audit records to store the evidence collected during this interim period.

NEED FOR CONCURRENT AUDITING TECHNIQUES

The basic motivation for developing concurrent auditing techniques is the need for more timely evidence collection and evidence evaluation. However, the following sections discuss in more detail why concurrent auditing techniques are becoming more important.

Advanced Systems Require Continuous Monitoring

One characteristic of advanced systems is tight coupling between their subsystems. For example, Figure 19-1 shows a shared database situation where the

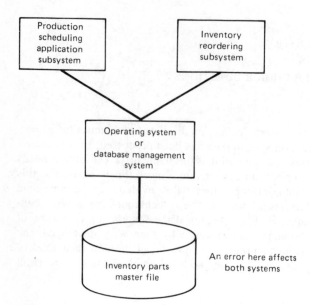

FIGURE 19-1
Tightly coupled subsystems accessing a shared database.

production scheduling and inventory reordering subsystems concurrently access the inventory parts master file. Sharing the database causes these application subsystems to be tightly coupled; that is, each relies heavily on the correct functioning of the other.

Consider the implications of an erroneous update process in one subsystem. Incorrect processing in the production scheduling subsystem may result in the inventory reordering subsystem ordering insufficient inventory, thereby causing stockouts and lost sales; or too much inventory, thereby causing extra costs of obsolescence and storage. Concurrent auditing techniques enable faster identification of errors than ex post auditing techniques. Timely identification of errors is critical to the continuing operations of tightly coupled systems.

Increasing Difficulty of Performing Walk-Throughs

Auditors gain understanding of an application system by taking typical transactions of the system and tracing them through the various logic paths within the system. This also assists in identifying the system's strengths and weaknesses.

Advanced systems make the walk-through process more difficult because a large number of complex logic paths exist. Extensive coupling between different application systems also complicates matters. For example, understanding how a parts master file is updated may mean the auditor has to examine processes in the production scheduling system, inventory reordering system, purchasing system, receiving system, and warehouse system.

Concurrent auditing techniques facilitate the auditor's understanding of advanced systems by collecting all the information normally obtained from a walk-through in the one place. They capture images of a transaction as it traces its way through one particular logic path within a system and write this information to a file. When the auditor then attempts to understand a system and identify its strengths and weaknesses, all the information for different logic paths within the system exists in the one place.

Presence of Entropy in Systems

All systems have a characteristic called entropy (see Davis and Olson [1985]). Entropy is the tendency of a system toward disorder. There is never a question of whether entropy exists. The problem is to identify the *forms* of entropy that are present.

Some common forms of entropy exist in computer systems. One form arises because user information requirements change as the business expands and increased volumes of data have to be processed. These changes may place stress on the existing system design and the system's performance may start to degrade. The situation is further aggravated by hurried system and program maintenance to enable the system to cope with the changes. Errors creep into the system because of incomplete testing.

Because concurrent auditing techniques continuously monitor the system, increasing entropy can be identified at an early stage. They can be used to gather data on error frequencies and system exception frequencies and give advance warning of stresses being placed on the system. Thus, these techniques aid in understanding a system's evolution and assist in decreasing the future occurrence of errors.

Problems Posed by Service Bureaus and Distributed Systems

Sometimes it is difficult for the auditor to be physically present at a data processing installation to gather evidence. For example, a company's data processing may be performed by a service bureau, or data processing may be decentralized in the form of a distributed system. The auditor suffers two difficulties. First, valuable audit evidence cannot be collected because the auditor is unable to simply walk around the installation and gain impressions on the status of the installation's management, any changes occurring, the status of security, etc. Second, it is more difficult for the auditor to carry out data processing necessary for purposes of evidence collection. Even with data communications facilities the auditor may be forced to schedule any computer time required because files must be mounted at a remote installation, or the auditor's use of the system may unacceptably degrade response time.

A partial solution to these problems is to use concurrent auditing techniques.

By embedding audit routines and records into application systems, evidence can be collected and the auditor can examine this evidence at a later stage when files are returned to the installation or time is available on the system for audit use.

TYPES OF CONCURRENT AUDITING TECHNIQUES

There are four major concurrent auditing techniques:

1 Integrated test facility (ITF)
2 Snapshot/extended record
3 System control audit review file (SCARF)
4 Continuous and intermittent simulation (CIS)

The above classification is generic in the sense that a number of specific techniques fall within each category. The specific techniques are simply variations on a basic idea. Furthermore, a technique or combination of techniques can be used to form a concurrent auditing system.

Integrated Test Facility

The integrated test facility (ITF) technique involves establishing a minicompany or dummy entity on an application system's files and processing audit test data against the entity as a means of verifying processing accuracy. For example, if the application is a ledgers system, the auditor sets up a dummy ledger account. If the application is a departmental costing system, the auditor sets up a dummy department.

The auditor submits test data to the application system as part of the normal system data for processing. In the case of a batch system, the auditor completes the system's source documents and submits them through the usual clerical channels. This allows the auditor to examine the quality of both the manual and machine processing within the system. In the case of an interactive system, the auditor keys in data while the system is online. Figure 19-2 shows the methods.

Using ITF involves two major design decisions:

1 What method will be used to enter test data?
2 What method will be used to remove the effects of ITF transactions?

Methods of Entering Test Data Test data can be entered to an ITF application using two methods: (*a*) tagging live transactions, and (*b*) designing new test transactions. The first method involves using the normal transactions of the system and tagging them in some way so that the application system programs recognize them as ITF transactions. Thus, these transactions perform two updates instead of the normal one: one for the application system records and one for the dummy entity. The second method follows the normal procedures described in Chapter 18 for design of test data.

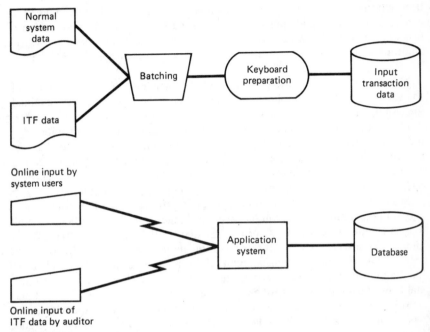

FIGURE 19-2
Submitting ITF data to an application system.

If the first method of entering test data is used, ITF transactions must be identified in some way. There are several alternatives. First, a special identifier field can be used to denote the transaction is also an ITF transaction. Space must be provided on the system's source documents for this field or the transaction tagged at the time of keyboarding. Second, audit software modules can be embedded in the application system's programs to recognize transactions having certain characteristics of interest to the auditor. These modules then select and tag the transactions as ITF transactions. Third, sampling routines can be embedded in the application system programs that tag transactions as ITF transactions. This latter method attempts to select ITF transactions representative of the normal application system processing.

The first method of entering test data has two advantages: (a) ease of use, and (b) testing with transactions representative of normal system processing. It has two major disadvantages. First, using live data may mean the limiting conditions within the system are not tested. Second, because audit modules must be embedded in the application system, the presence of this extraneous code increases the risk of error occurring.

If the auditor uses the second method to enter test data and designs new test transactions, the auditor inserts the dummy entity's unique identifier in the key field of the transaction to denote the transaction as an ITF transaction. The transaction is processed as a normal transaction; no special routines need be embedded in the application system to tag the transaction. Though design of test data can be difficult, this method of entering ITF test data allows the auditor to test systematically all the controls within the application system.

Methods of Removing the Effects of ITF Transactions The presence of ITF transactions within an application system affects the output results obtained; for example, the control totals produced by the system. Unless the auditor discloses that ITF transactions have been used and manual adjustments are then made to output, the effects of ITF transactions must be removed. This can be accomplished in three ways: (a) application system program modification, (b) the auditor submitting reversal entries, and (c) the auditor submitting trivial or immaterial transactions so the effects on output are negligible.

Modifying the application system programs to recognize ITF transactions and not take them into account has two advantages. First, the method is simple to implement. Second, users are not affected by the auditor's activities. The auditor can covertly carry out testing of the application system. However, the method has two disadvantages. First, there is some cost in developing and maintaining the software to recognize the ITF transactions. If the system is stable or few modifications are made that affect ITF transactions, this cost may be relatively low. Second, the presence of extraneous code in the application system increases the risk of data integrity being violated through this code being in error.

If the auditor submits reversal entries to remove the effects of ITF transactions, this method has the advantage of simplicity since no programming costs are involved. It has several disadvantages. First, if the auditor wants to act covertly, the reversal entries must be submitted in the same run. Even then, control totals for the number of transactions processed are affected, and this may cause confusion for application system users. Second, the auditor must ensure the reversals are carried out correctly if data integrity is to be maintained. Third, the method causes problems in a shared database environment. Consider, for example, a company which borrows and lends daily on the short-term money market and which has a computer-based decision support system for its money market managers. This decision support system frequently may access the cash accounts master file during a day and use various fields. If the auditor affects these fields with ITF transactions and the reversal entries have not been processed (the lag may only be a matter of microseconds), this may cause the decision support system to provide wrong information to management, resulting in a costly investment error.

The third method of submitting trivial transactions to "remove" the effects (the effects are not really removed) of ITF test data has the advantages of simplicity and no costs and risks involved with program modification. However, unless users are informed that slight differences in control totals may be due to audit testing, time and effort may be wasted senselessly on trying to identify the source of the error. Even though the amount is trivial, users may be concerned that a logic error is present in the system. The auditor still may have to inform users of ITF testing and so lose covert testing capabilities. Another disadvantage is that it places limitations on the testing that can be carried out. Certain types of limit tests where large amounts are involved cannot be attempted.

Snapshot/Extended Record

For application systems that are large or complex, tracing the different logic paths through the system is difficult. The number of different possibilities can be enormous. The auditor who wants to perform a walk-through of a transaction faces a difficult task. A simple solution to the problem is to allow the computer to perform the walk-through.

The snapshot technique involves taking "pictures" of a transaction as it flows through the system. The auditor embeds software routines at different points within the application system to capture images of the transaction as it progresses through the various stages. To validate processing, the audit routines capture beforeimages and afterimages of the transaction. Figure 19-3 shows how the technique is used to obtain audit evidence at various points in a simple batch system.

A snapshot transaction first must be tagged by the auditor with a special indicator so that the audit software routines recognize it as a transaction for which an audit trail is to be printed. The different snapshot points must be numbered so that the auditor can identify which routine within the application system performed the processing. Audit trail reports must be printed for each snapshot point within the system. Alternatively, the snapshot can be written onto a file for later printing.

A modification of the snapshot technique is the extended record technique. Instead of writing one record for each snapshot point, a large record can be built up consisting of images from each snapshot point and carried through the system (Figure 19-4). This technique has the advantage of collecting all the snapshot data related to a transaction in one place. Again, the extended record can be printed at the end of processing or written away to a file for later printing.

The snapshot and extended record techniques can be used in conjunction with the ITF technique to provide an extensive audit trail. ITF provides a master file record against which the auditor can test the processing of various transaction types. The snapshot and extended record techniques provide the audit trail as each transaction type progresses through the system.

System Control Audit Review File

The system control audit review file (SCARF) technique is the most complex concurrent auditing technique. SCARF involves embedding audit software modules within a host application system to provide continuous monitoring of

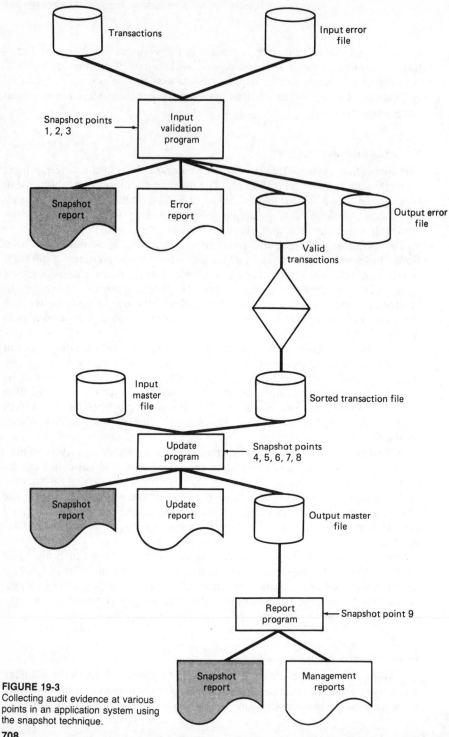

FIGURE 19-3
Collecting audit evidence at various points in an application system using the snapshot technique.

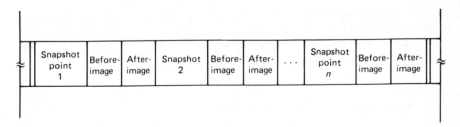

FIGURE 19-4
An extended record used with the snapshot technique.

the system's transactions. These audit modules are placed at predetermined points to gather information about transactions that are of interest to the auditor. The information collected is then written onto a special audit file—the SCARF master file. Periodically the auditor examines the information contained on this file to see if some aspect of the system needs follow-up. Figure 19-5 illustrates the method for a master file update program.

Using SCARF involves two major design decisions:

1 Determining what information will be collected by SCARF embedded audit routines
2 Determining the reporting system to be used with SCARF

FIGURE 19-5
Use of SCARF with a master file update program.

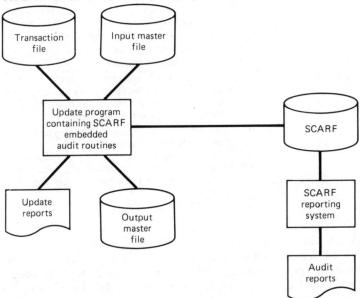

Information to Be Collected by SCARF   The placement of embedded audit routines within the application system depends on the types of evidence the auditor wants to collect. Several types of information can be captured by the routines (see, also, Perry [1974a, 1974b]):

Information captured	Explanation
Application system errors	Ideally an application system contains all the logic necessary to prevent and detect errors that occur. However, it is possible design and programming errors exist from the start, or errors may creep into the system as it is modified and maintained. SCARF audit routines provide an independent check on the quality of system processing.
Policy and procedural variances	Organizations have technical and administrative policies and standards to guide staff in their work. For example, a company may require one of its products to be sold in certain size lots. Industries often have accepted policies and standards to which members of the industry are expected to adhere. SCARF audit routines can be used to check variations from these policies and standards.
System exceptions	SCARF can be used to monitor different types of application system exceptions. For example, certain errors may be allowed within the system provided they are within a specified tolerance. The auditor may wish to examine the frequency with which these errors occur. Salespersons may be given some leeway in the prices they charge customers. SCARF can be used to see how frequently salespersons override the standard price.
Statistical samples	Some of the embedded audit routines may be statistical sampling routines. SCARF provides a convenient way of collecting all the sample information together on one file.
Snapshots and extended records	The printing of snapshots and extended records during normal application system processing may be inconvenient. The snapshots and extended records can be written onto the SCARF file and printed when required.
Performance measurement data	The auditor may use the embedded routines to collect various data useful for measuring or improving the performance of the system. For example, the frequency of certain kinds of transactions can be monitored and programs modified to test for the most frequent kinds of transaction first.

The auditor should give careful consideration to ways in which the integrity of the SCARF embedded audit routines can be maintained. Several measures can be undertaken. Application program listings should not contain the source code of the embedded audit routines. Call statements, only, should exist. The source code should be maintained on a special library file that is the responsibility of the audit staff. Alternatively, the source code can be maintained on the normal program library system and given special security locks to prevent it being read by unauthorized persons. Documentation for the routines should be kept by the auditor or require special authorization for withdrawal from the data processing library.

Structure of the SCARF Reporting System   Determining the structure of the SCARF reporting system involves several design decisions: (*a*) how the SCARF file will be updated, (*b*) sort codes and report formats to be used, and (*c*) the timing of report preparation. If SCARF is to be used in conjunction with ITF and the snapshot/extended record techniques, care must be taken to ensure decisions made on the SCARF reporting system satisfy the requirements of the other techniques.

With respect to the method of updating the SCARF file, one alternative is to have each application system create a temporary SCARF work file that in due course is copied onto the master SCARF file using utility software. This method has the advantage of simplicity and the disadvantages of possible loss of the work file and delay until it has been written to the master file. A second alternative is to allow the SCARF master file to be updated concurrently by several application systems. Since the SCARF file is used primarily for reporting, many of the problems with concurrent update processes, discussed in Chapter 13, do not arise.

Careful thought must be given to the report formats and sort codes used with SCARF. The quality of reporting in part determines the effectiveness with which the evidence collected is communicated to the auditor. The report design should follow the guidelines described in Chapter 15.

The report formats affect the sort codes assigned the SCARF records. Two kinds of sort codes are needed. First, a unique identifier must be assigned the record that identifies it as being needed for the preparation of a specific report. This code enables the records to be selected from the unordered SCARF file. Second, sort codes are needed that are application-specific so data can be presented on the report in some logical order. For example, for a parts inventory audit report, records for subcomponents may have to be sorted by major components, or critical variances detected by the audit modules may be assigned a high priority so they sort to the front of the audit report.

The decision on the length of the reporting period primarily depends on the importance of the audit evidence collected and the costs of generating the SCARF reports. Until report formats and reporting periods stabilize, generalized audit software can be used to prepare reports. Once stability has been attained, report generation can be made automatic. Part of the SCARF reporting system can be a timing facility whereby a file or program table is examined to determine when a SCARF report should be produced.

Continuous and Intermittent Simulation

Koch [1981, 1984] has proposed a variation on the SCARF concurrent auditing technique called continuous and intermittent simulation (CIS). Whereas SCARF requires the auditor to embed audit modules within an application system, CIS requires modification of the database management system used by the application system. The application system is left intact. Instead, when the application system invokes the services provided by the database management system, the database management system indicates to CIS that a service is required, and CIS determines whether it wants to examine the activities to be carried out by the database management system on behalf of the application system (Figure 19-6).

During application system processing, CIS executes in the following way:

1 When the database management system reads an application system transaction, it invokes CIS and passes the transaction across to CIS. CIS then determines whether it wants to examine the transaction further. This decision is made in the same way that SCARF embedded audit routines decide whether to examine a transaction further. For example, the transaction may be selected by CIS on the basis of statistical sampling criteria, or it may be selected because it has been submitted by a certain user. If the transaction is selected, the next three steps are executed; otherwise, CIS waits for a new transaction.

2 The database management system provides CIS with all data requested by the application system to process the selected transaction. This enables CIS to also process the transaction. In other words, CIS replicates application

FIGURE 19-6
Environment for continuous and intermittent simulation *(From Koch [1981]; Reprinted by permission of the* MIS Quarterly, *Vol. 5, No. 1, March 1981. Copyright 1981 by the Society for Information Management and the Management Information Systems Research Center.)*

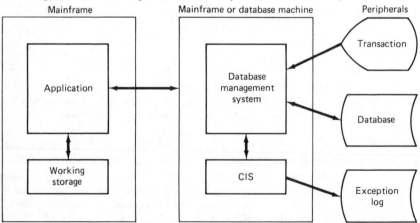

system processing in the same way that a parallel simulation program replicates application system processing (see Chapter 16).

3 Every update to the database that arises from processing the selected transaction will be checked by CIS to determine whether discrepancies exist between the results produced by CIS and the results produced by the application system. If discrepancies exist and they are a serious concern, CIS may prevent the database management system from carrying out the updates requested by the application system. Otherwise, CIS notes the exception and application system processing continues.

4 Exceptions identified by CIS are written to a log file in the same way that SCARF uses an exception log. A reporting system for the log file is also required.

The primary advantage of CIS over the SCARF and snapshot/extended record techniques is that CIS does not require modifications to the application system. Instead, the audit routines are called by the database management system. Of course, the disadvantage is that system software must be modified instead, although presumably the modifications will be less onerous than modifications to the application system.

Koch [1984] also provides a detailed comparison of the relative advantages and disadvantages of CIS versus parallel simulation. The primary advantages of CIS over parallel simulation are: (*a*) like other concurrent auditing techniques, CIS provides an online auditing capability; (*b*) the number of program instructions needed to implement CIS usually will be less than the number needed to implement parallel simulation; and (*c*) the input/output overhead associated with CIS will be less since CIS creates no files aside from an exception log. The primary disadvantage is that CIS often will be more difficult to implement since it executes in an online rather than a batch environment.

IMPLEMENTING CONCURRENT AUDITING TECHNIQUES

When implementing concurrent auditing techniques, the auditor should follow the same steps necessary to achieve any well-implemented system. Since these steps have been described extensively in Chapter 4, the following sections provide only a brief overview and highlight those aspects having special relevance for concurrent auditing.

Perform a Feasibility Study

Concurrent auditing techniques result in overheads for application systems because of the presence of special audit records and embedded audit routines. Sometimes these overheads may be unacceptable; for example, in an online system where response times are critical. The auditor must consider carefully the costs and benefits of using concurrent auditing techniques.

Interact with Groups Affected by Concurrent Auditing

Because of the ongoing support needed for concurrent auditing techniques, they are typically the responsibility of the internal audit staff. However, external auditors should be contacted as they may have requirements that can be met by a concurrent auditing system. In any case they should be informed of progress with concurrent auditing since it will affect their assessment of the reliability of internal control.

Data processing staff may be both developers and users of concurrent auditing techniques. If the audit staff does not have sufficient expertise to be able to program the audit modules required, data processing staff may be made responsible for this task. Concurrent auditing techniques also constitute a useful system testing vehicle for data processing staff.

It is also critical that a viable communications system exists between data processing staff and the audit staff. In the past, one of the major reasons why concurrent auditing techniques have failed is neglect in communicating to the audit staff changes in the application system that affect the concurrent auditing system.

Application system users also must be informed if concurrent auditing affects their normal tasks; for example, the possibility of minor discrepancies existing in control totals because of ITF transactions. Users also may be interested in concurrent auditing techniques as a means of training new staff. This matter is discussed further later in the chapter.

Ensure the Relevant Expertise Is Available

For two reasons, concurrent auditing techniques should be used only after the audit staff has gained some expertise with EDP auditing. First, even if the audit staff has insufficient expertise to perform the programming of the embedded audit modules, at least they still must be able to evaluate the work of data processing staff or consultants who perform the programming. Otherwise, the usual questions of audit independence arise. Second, without EDP audit expertise, it is doubtful whether the auditor will be able to choose those points in a system where audit modules can be placed most profitably. Even with EDP audit experience, auditors first should implement concurrent auditing techniques on simple systems so they gain experience with the techniques.

Ensure the Commitment of Management and Data Processing Staff

If management is not committed to concurrent auditing, they may be unwilling to allocate future resources for its maintenance. If data processing staff are not committed, they may directly sabotage the techniques or contribute to their downfall through neglecting to communicate application system changes to the audit staff.

Make the Necessary Technical Decisions

When implementing concurrent auditing techniques, several key technical design decisions have to be made. For ITF, the test data method to be used and the method of removing the effects of the ITF transactions must be chosen. For snapshot/extended records and SCARF, the auditor must decide on those points in the system where data will be captured and the type of data that will be captured. The structure of the SCARF reporting system also must be determined. For CIS, the transactions whose application system processing will be simulated must be chosen.

Plan the Design and Implementation

Once the necessary technical decisions have been made, the specific design for the concurrent auditing system can proceed and the implementation can be planned. Especially important is the design of the audit support system. This support system includes procedures for follow-up of detected variances, procedures for maintenance of the concurrent auditing system, and standards for documentation of the system, its associated support procedures, and the results produced.

Implement and Test

The normal procedures for orderly and controlled implementation of a system should be used when implementing concurrent auditing techniques. Great care must be taken in testing the techniques. Since an error in a concurrent auditing technique may cause an error in an application system, the continuing support of management, data processing staff, and application system users depends on the techniques being error-free.

Postaudit the Results

After concurrent auditing techniques have been running for some time, the auditor should evaluate the costs and benefits of the techniques. This postaudit identifies weaknesses that possibly can be corrected. It also may lead to the conclusion that concurrent auditing techniques should be scrapped. In addition, the postaudit formalizes the experience gained and establishes guidelines for the design and implementation of concurrent auditing techniques in other application systems.

**ADVANTAGES/DISADVANTAGES OF
CONCURRENT AUDITING TECHNIQUES**

Concurrent auditing techniques provide the following major advantages for the auditor, data processing staff, and application system users:

Advantage	Explanation
Viable alternative to ex post auditing and auditing around the computer	Though the use of concurrent auditing techniques is not widespread (Perry [1977a]), some organizations have successfully implemented the techniques. By using the techniques the auditor need not infer the quality of application system processing through examining only the input and output of the application system. The evidence obtained is more timely and more comprehensive.
Surprise test capability	Using concurrent auditing techniques. the auditor can unobtrusively gather evidence. Because data processing staff and application system users normally are not aware that evidence is being collected, the techniques provide the auditor with a surprise test capability.
Test vehicle for data processing	With respect to the quality of application system processing, data processing staff have the same concerns as the auditors. Those organizations that use concurrent auditing techniques report strong support for the techniques by data processing staff. The auditor must consider trading off some independence for the improved testing capabilities provided to data processing staff by concurrent auditing techniques.
Training vehicle for users	Some organizations use ITF as a training vehicle for new staff. Training need not proceed by simulating the preparation of input data and its submission to the application system. Instead, new staff can prepare data on the system's source documents, submit the data to the application system, and obtain feedback on any mistakes they make via the system's error reports.

In spite of these advantages, widespread implementation of concurrent auditing techniques has not occurred. In the mid-1970s, Stanford Research Institute [1977] found that few organizations were using concurrent auditing techniques. Moreover, they predicted the techniques had questionable future potential. Use of the techniques has increased, but widespread implementation still has not occurred (see, for example, Tobinson and Davis [1981], Reeve [1984], and Skudrna and Lackner [1984]). These findings suggest that concurrent auditing techniques also have significant disadvantages and that auditors should carefully take these disadvantages into account when they are choosing evidence collection techniques to use.

Perhaps the primary disadvantage of using concurrent auditing techniques is the need for auditors to have extensive EDP expertise before they are capable of successfully designing and implementing the techniques. Whether this is a failing of the techniques or the auditors who use them is a moot point. As Perry [1978] points out, a key feature of concurrent auditing techniques is that they provide detailed evidence on the quality of individual programs in the application system rather than general evidence about the application system. However, Stanford Research Institute [1977] appears to believe that investigating individual programs will not be a primary activity of auditors. Instead, they will play a more active role in the system development process. Some experienced EDP auditors would debate this point, so it is an interesting issue for further research.

The costs of implementing concurrent auditing techniques also can be substantial. Stanford Research Institute [1977] found the following costs to be typical:

1 ITF—3–10% of development cost

2 Snapshot—2 weeks planning plus 2½ days programming per audit module

3 Extended records—may be as high as 5% of system development effort

4 SCARF—3-month development effort

The costs of implementing CIS are still unknown as little practical experience has been obtained with the technique. In all cases, however, the costs of implementing concurrent auditing techniques will be less if they are designed and implemented when the application system is initially developed.

Finally, concurrent auditing techniques require an ongoing commitment by the auditors and the organizations using them. Modifications and maintenance to the application system in which they are embedded may mean that changes also have to be made to the concurrent auditing techniques. Otherwise, they may start to collect useless data or cause errors in application system processing.

SUMMARY

Concurrent auditing techniques collect audit evidence at the same time as application system processing occurs. This evidence is written to a file and periodically printed for the auditor to analyze and evaluate. The auditor has control over the time lag between evidence collection and reporting.

Four major concurrent auditing techniques exist. The integrated test facility technique (ITF) involves establishing a dummy entity on the application's system files and processing audit test transactions against the dummy entity. The snapshot/extended record technique involves embedding audit modules in the application system and capturing images of the transaction as it passes through the system. The system control audit review file technique (SCARF) also involves embedding audit modules within the application system and capturing variances and exceptions of interest to the auditor. The continuous and intermittent simulation technique (CIS) replicates application system processing when it is invoked by the database management system and it identifies a transaction that is of interest to the auditor.

The design and implementation of concurrent auditing techniques should follow the system development standards established to achieve effective and efficient application systems. These procedures include the auditor interacting with groups affected by the techniques, a feasibility study, planned implementation and testing, and postaudit. Several key design decisions must be made, including the method of entering test data and removing its effects, the types of variances and exception data to be collected, the points where audit modules will be embedded in the application system, and the structure of the reporting system to be used.

REVIEW QUESTIONS

19-1 Explain the nature of concurrent auditing.

19-2 Why might a cash receipts and payments system be coupled tightly with an investments decision support system? What could be the implications of an error made in either system? How might concurrent auditing techniques assist in preventing errors?

19-3 What is entropy? Data processing installations are often characterized by a high staff turnover. Is this a form of entropy? If so, how can concurrent auditing techniques help arrest entropy?

19-4 What might prevent snapshot and SCARF being used if a service bureau performs routine data processing (e.g., payroll, accounts receivable) for a company? Would there be any restrictions on the form ITF can take if the auditor decides to implement it in the application systems processed at the service bureau?

19-5 Using ITF, what form will the dummy entity take if there are multiple record types on an application system's files? What form will the dummy entity take if there is a single record type of variable length?

19-6 Suppose a file is set up hierarchically; for example, projects within departments within subdivisions within divisions within the company. There may be up to 10 levels within the hierarchy, and because of the nature and size of some of the operations carried out within the company, various levels in the hierarchy can be present or missing. Thus, a large number of possible forms of the hierarchy exists. How would you set up an ITF dummy entity for such a file?

19-7 Discuss some methods of setting up a dummy entity on a file. Outline the advantages and disadvantages of each method depending on whether the file is hierarchical or flat and has fixed length or variable length records.

19-8 Describe the two methods of entering test data for an ITF application and discuss the relative advantages and disadvantages of each method.

19-9 After some time, clerical personnel may start to recognize the code used for ITF transactions and so treat them in a special way; for example, take special care on coding associated source documents such as the batch cover sheet. How can the auditor prevent this occurring?

19-10 Describe the methods of removing the effects of ITF transactions and the relative advantages and disadvantages of each method.

19-11 Outline the difference between the snapshot and extended record techniques.

19-12 In a large system an extended record may grow to a size that is unacceptable because of the size of the input/output buffer required in a program, an installation standard, or system software limitations. What must the auditor do in this situation?

19-13 Describe the SCARF concurrent auditing technique. Discuss how snapshot and SCARF can be integrated.

19-14 A properly written input program should contain the necessary subroutines to validate input data. Why might the auditor also be interested in using SCARF embedded audit modules to check if input data is valid?

19-15 Why might the auditor use a concurrent auditing technique to collect periodically the volumes of different transaction types? When the auditor wishes to "turn off" the collection of this data for a time, how can this be accomplished?

19-16 Who are the groups affected by concurrent auditing techniques and how are they affected?

19-17 Why is it unlikely external auditors will be responsible for implementing and maintaining concurrent auditing techniques in an organization?

19-18 Describe the various design and implementation steps to be undertaken with a SCARF reporting system.

19-19 When report records are selected from the SCARF file and printed, should they then be deleted from the SCARF file? If so, why? If not, what should be the basis for deletion?

19-20 Briefly describe the nature of the continuous and intermittent simulation concurrent auditing technique.

19-21 Briefly describe each of the major steps that must be undertaken during the execution of a continuous and intermittent simulation concurrent auditing technique.

19-22 Give *one* advantage and *one* disadvantage of continuous and intermittent simulation with respect to (*a*) SCARF, and (*b*) parallel simulation.

19-23 What should be the components of the manual audit system supporting a concurrent auditing system? Why is it important to carefully design the audit support system?

19-24 What methods can be used to test a concurrent auditing system? Can the test data used to test the application system be used to test the concurrent auditing system without any alteration being made?

19-25 "If you can't formally document in audit working papers the results of concurrent auditing and the audit analyses undertaken, you shouldn't use concurrent auditing." Agree or disagree?

19-26 What are some of the major factors affecting the cost of concurrent auditing? Which concurrent auditing technique do you think would most likely be more costly? What are the incremental benefits for the added costs of this technique?

MULTIPLE CHOICE QUESTIONS

19-1 Which of the following is *not* a justification for using concurrent auditing techniques:

a Cheaper to implement, operate, and maintain than ex post auditing techniques

b Increasing difficulties of performing walk-throughs

c More timely identification of errors and irregularities needed in advanced systems

d Increasing difficulties of gathering evidence as the number of distributed systems grows

19-2 Entropy, the tendency of a system toward disorder, is present in:

a Only systems with weak controls

b All systems

c Only more advanced systems that are complex

d Only systems with a high level of coupling

19-3 Relative to designing new test data, tagging live transactions in an ITF has the advantage that:

a Special audit routines do not have to be embedded in the host system

b The limiting conditions in the system are more likely to be tested

c Source documents do not have to be redesigned

d Test transactions are more likely to be representative of normal application system processing

19-4 Which of the following advantages is common to submitting reversal entries and submitting trivial transactions as two means of removing the effects of ITF transactions:

a The limiting values in the host system can be tested

b ITF activities are transparent to users

c No costs and risks are involved with program modification

d Control totals are not affected by ITF transactions

19-5 The snapshot technique involves:

a Recording the state of an application system's working storage at a point in time

b Taking pictures of a transaction as it flows through a system

c Evaluating the afterimages of all data items changed for accuracy and completeness

d Providing a filter in the input program through which selected transactions must pass

19-6 The difference between the snapshot technique and the extended record technique is:

a With the extended record technique, an attempt is made to store contiguously the record images collected at different points in the system

b More audit evidence is collected with the extended record technique

c Printing of audit reports in snapshot is immediate upon evidence being collected

d Only afterimages are collected using the snapshot technique

19-7 Which of the following types of information cannot be collected using system control audit review file (SCARF):

a Statistical samples

b Policy and procedural variances

c Lack of internal program documentation

d Performance measurement data

19-8 The purpose of using CALL statements only in the source code of a program to invoke SCARF routines is to:

a Improve the efficiency with which data can be collected

b Highlight those places in a program where a SCARF routine exists

c Obtain the benefits of using structured programming techniques

d Protect the privacy of SCARF routines

19-9 The choice of sort codes in the SCARF reporting system is important because it:

a Determines whether a high-level programming language or a low-level programming language can be used to implement the system

    b Affects the decision on how frequently SCARF reports should be issued

    c Determines whether concurrent update can occur to the report file

    d Determines whether application-specific data can be grouped together in some logical fashion

19-10 Which of the following is the primary difference between SCARF and continuous and intermittent simulation (CIS):

    a CIS is unable to collect data to be used for performance monitoring purposes

    b CIS requires modification of the database management system to collect required data

    c CIS uses generalized reporting capabilities

    d Only tagged transactions can be examined using CIS

19-11 Which of the following functions is *not* performed by the database management system when the CIS concurrent auditing technique is used:

    a It invokes CIS and passes transactions across to CIS for examination

    b It provides CIS with all the data requested by the application system to process the selected transaction

    c It replicates application system processing to determine discrepancies

    d It checks with CIS to determine whether updates to the database that arise from processing the selected transaction should be carried out

19-12 When compared to parallel simulation, which of the following is a disadvantage of the CIS concurrent auditing technique:

    a It is more difficult to implement since it is intended for use in an online rather than a batch processing environment

    b It requires more program instructions to implement than parallel simulation

    c It generates more input/output overhead than parallel simulation

    d The CIS exception log is more difficult to maintain

19-13 Which of the following is *not* a reason for interacting with data processing staff when concurrent auditing techniques are being designed and implemented:

    a The cooperation of data processing staff will be needed if the existence of concurrent auditing techniques is not to be disclosed to application system users

    b Assistance may be needed from the data processing staff to implement concurrent auditing techniques

    c Data processing staff may be users of concurrent auditing techniques for application system testing purposes

    d Data processing staff will need to notify the auditors when changes are made to an application system in which a concurrent auditing technique is embedded

19-14 After studying the use of concurrent auditing in several organizations, Stanford Research Institute concluded:

    a Concurrent auditing techniques were an important breakthrough for auditors as a means of collecting evidence in advanced EDP systems

    b Compared to ex post audit techniques, concurrent audit techniques were a relatively cheap means of collecting audit evidence

    c The future potential of concurrent audit techniques is minimal

    d Concurrent audit techniques would gain acceptance only among internal auditors

19-15 Which of the following is an important disadvantage of concurrent auditing techniques:

a They provide evidence about only a limited set of features in application system processing that interest the auditor

b Only a few types of application systems can accommodate the audit modules needed to collect the evidence

c Few auditors can interpret the output produced by concurrent auditing techniques

d They require a sustained commitment by management, auditors, and data processing staff to their ongoing maintenance and use

EXERCISES AND CASES

19-1 A large diversified company has divisions scattered around the country. These divisions do not necessarily carry out the same kinds of activities. The company has a distributed data processing system to support its operations. Each division has its own costing system but aggregate cost information is transmitted to the head office for centralized planning and control purposes. The costing system is relatively new and the internal audit staff has not examined thoroughly its operations. Because of budget constraints for the current financial year, the audit staff is unable to fly to different divisional locations.

Required: How might the audit staff use concurrent auditing techniques to assist them in a preliminary evaluation of the system before they undertake a detailed investigation for the coming year? Note, this preliminary evaluation may form the basis for deciding which divisions they will then visit.

19-2 The internal audit manager is involved in a debate with management over the implementation of concurrent auditing techniques in a payroll system. She argues the system is a critical system and, as such, there is no need to undertake a feasibility study with respect to implementing the techniques. Further, she points out there are several recurring errors in the system and the source of these errors, as yet, cannot be identified. Management is not so sure of the benefits to be derived from implementing concurrent auditing techniques and they want a detailed feasibility study. Is a detailed feasibility study necessary? Why or why not?

19-3 The internal audit manager has just returned from a course on concurrent auditing techniques and he decides there are many systems where implementing the techniques would be beneficial. He decides to start out with the most critical application system, an online inventory system that supplies information to divisions scattered around the country. How would you advise the internal audit manager to proceed?

19-4 Because of his concern with audit independence, the internal audit manager decides to implement concurrent auditing techniques within an application system and tell as few people as possible. He argues he has an expert programmer on his staff and so he does not need data processing to perform the work. What problems might arise from this strategy?

19-5 With the active support of all groups affected, the audit staff implements its first concurrent auditing system, a SCARF system, in a large ledgers application system. However, on the second day of live operations for the SCARF system, the data processing manager calls the audit manager to complain. She is furious because the SCARF file has already grown to consume an entire disk pack and processing time for the ledgers system has degraded by 15%. She accuses the audit manager of failing to test the embedded audit routines. He argues all the logic was thoroughly tested, and what's more, data processing programmers wrote the routines. What might have happened?

19-6 You are the internal auditor for a company that is implementing a new online realtime update order entry system. Salespersons enter transactions at intelligent terminals, which validate the input data, and a centralized orders master file is updated. The system also is to be integrated with other application systems: inventory, purchasing, billing, accounts payable, cash receipts and disbursements, general ledger.

Required: Identify three economic events that you might monitor using concurrent auditing techniques. Explain what control objectives you hope to achieve by monitoring the events and why you have chosen these events for monitoring purposes.

19-7 As the manager of internal audit for a company, one day you receive a telephone call from the data processing manager. She is upset because a major inventory update run has had to be aborted. The reason why is that some audit modules implemented in the inventory system had commenced to process data erroneously. She points out that this is the fifth time in the last few months that this action has had to be undertaken because of problems with the audit modules.

When you question the junior auditor responsible for the audit modules, he complains that the reason why failures are occurring is because the data processing department has been making changes to the inventory system but failing to notify him of changes that affect the audit modules. He has tried on several occasions to get data processing personnel to send him notification of changes to the inventory system but he has been unsuccessful.

Required: Outline the steps you would follow in an attempt to remedy the problems that have occurred.

ANSWERS TO MULTIPLE CHOICE QUESTIONS

19-1 a	19-5 b	19-9 d	19-13 a
19-2 b	19-6 a	19-10 b	19-14 c
19-3 d	19-7 c	19-11 c	19-15 d
19-4 c	19-8 d	19-12 a	

REFERENCES

Davis, Gordon B., and Margrethe H. Olson. *Management Information Systems: Conceptual Foundations, Structure, and Development,* 2d ed. (New York: McGraw-Hill, 1985).

Koch, Harvey S. "On-Line Computer Auditing Through Continuous and Intermittent Simulation," *Management Information Systems Quarterly* (March 1981), pp. 29–41.

Koch, Harvey S. "Auditing On-Line Systems: An Evaluation of Parallel Versus

Continuous and Intermittent Simulation," *Computers & Security* (February 1984), pp. 9–19.

Mair, William C., Donald R. Wood, and Keagle W. Davis. *Computer Control and Audit,* 2d ed. (Altamonte Springs, FL: The Institute of Internal Auditors, 1976).

Munson, James E. "We Tried ITF—We Like ITF," *EDPACS* (August 1977), pp. 1–3.

Perry, William E. "Try ITF, You'll Like ITF," *EDPACS* (December 1973), pp. 1–6.

Perry, William E. "Concurrent EDP Auditing: An Early Warning Scheme," *EDPACS* (January 1974a), pp. 1–7.

Perry, William E. "Concurrent EDP Auditing: An Implementation Approach," *EDPACS* (February 1974b), pp. 1–6.

Perry, William E. "Snapshot—A Technique for Tagging and Tracing Actions," *EDPACS* (March 1974c), pp. 1–7.

Perry, William E. "Computer Audit Practices," *EDPACS* (July 1977a), pp. 1–9.

Perry, William E. "Skills Needed to Utilize EDP Audit Practices," *EDPACS* (November 1977b), pp. 1–13.

Perry, William E. "Selecting Computer Audit Practices," *EDPACS* (March 1978), pp. 1–11.

Porter, W. Thomas, and William E. Perry. *EDP Controls and Auditing,* 2d ed. (Belmont, CA: Wadsworth, 1977).

Reeve, R. C. "Trends in the Use of EDP Audit Techniques," *Australian Computer Journal* (May 1984), pp. 42–47.

Skudrna, Vincent J., and Frank J. Lackner. "The Implementation of Concurrent Audit Techniques in Advanced EDP Systems," *EDPACS* (April 1984), pp. 1–9.

Stanford Research Institute. *Systems Auditability and Control Study: Data Processing Audit Practices Report* (Altamonte Springs, FL: The Institute of Internal Auditors, 1977).

Tobinson, Gary L., and Gordon B. Davis. "Actual Use and Perceived Utility of EDP Auditing Techniques," *EDP Auditor* (Spring 1981), pp. 1–22.

Weber, Ron. "Auditing Computer Systems Using Integrated Test Facility," *The Australian Accountant* (May 1975), pp. 232–235.

Weiss, Ira R. "Auditability of Software: A Survey of Techniques and Costs," *Management Information Systems Quarterly* (December 1980), pp. 39–50.

CHAPTER **20**

INTERVIEWS, QUESTIONNAIRES, AND CONTROL FLOWCHARTS

CHAPTER OUTLINE

This chapter examines three manual techniques used to collect evidence on the quality of computer systems: interviews, questionnaires, and control flowcharts. Interviews and questionnaires have been widely used evidence collection techniques in manual systems. Their importance has not diminished in computer systems. Particularly during the evaluation of the management control framework, interviews and questionnaires constitute a primary means of testing compliance (see Chapter 2 and, for example, Chapters 3 and 4). Control flowcharting also has been used with manual systems; however, its use is now more widespread because of the general popularity of flowcharting techniques as an analysis and documentation aid in computer systems.

INTERVIEWS

When assessing the quality of a computer system, the auditor may use interviewing for a variety of reasons; for example:

1 Systems analysts and programmers who designed and implemented the system may be interviewed so the auditor can obtain a better understanding of functions and controls within the system.

2 Clerical staff may be interviewed to determine whether or not there are problems in submitting data to the system.

3 Users of the system may be interviewed to determine the impact of the system on their quality of working life.

4 If a fraud is discovered, personnel may be interviewed to try to track down who perpetrated the fraud.

5 Operators may be interviewed to identify systems that seem to consume abnormal amounts of resources at run time.

6 The controller may be interviewed to identify the critical systems within an organization.

Interviews can be used to obtain both qualitative and quantitative information. Ultimately the objective is to elicit frank, complete, and honest answers from a respondent who has more information about a particular topic than the auditor.

A distinction should be made between interviewing and interrogation. The motivation for an interrogation is some type of wrongdoing—a fraud. The respondent often may be antagonistic and uncooperative; possibly the suspected culprit. In an interview, hopefully respondents bear no antagonism toward the interviewer, although this may be the case if respondents believe the auditor will bring about a change that has an unfavorable impact on their work life. Most auditors will perform an interview task. However, effective interrogation requires special skills; it should be left to experts (see, further, Krauss and MacGahan [1979]).

Some Conceptual Issues

Effective interviewing requires the auditor to have a basic understanding of what motivates a person to respond to a question. This knowledge allows the auditor to design better interviews and to identify why problems sometimes arise (see, further, Kahn and Cannell [1966] and Bouchard [1976]).

A respondent's motivation to reply to questions asked in an interview is a function of the extent to which they perceive the interview to be a means of obtaining their own goals. If respondents see the interview as helping them attain their goals, they will respond favorably. If they see the interview as hindering their goal attainment, they may be antagonistic toward the interviewer.

Different interviews require different levels of respondent motivation if the interview is to be successful. Questions vary in the stress they place on the respondent—the amount of time required to answer, the recall effort required, the threats and fears generated, etc. More stressful interviews require higher levels of respondent motivation. The auditor can control the level of stress caused by an interview by limiting the number of difficult questions asked in any one interview, making more stressful interviews shorter, and alleviating any fears that may arise as a result of the interview before the interview is commenced.

In any interview there are two forces that sometimes conflict: the desire of the interviewer to obtain answers to questions on a problem and the desire of the respondent to pursue topics that are of interest to the respondent with a responsible person (the interviewer). Unfortunately the interviewer's task is to try to foster the respondent's interest in the topic of the interview. The interviewer must communicate clearly the purpose of the interview to the respondent, show empathy toward the respondent, and promote a spirit of mutual trust and respect.

Preparing for the Interview

Conducting a successful interview requires careful preparation. The following sections discuss some of the major steps to be taken by the auditor during the preparation phase.

Perform Background Research Before undertaking an interview, the auditor must ensure the information required is not readily available elsewhere; otherwise, respondents may become upset if they consider the interview to be a waste of their time. The auditor should be convinced an interview is the best evidence collection technique to use for the problem at hand.

Background research allows the auditor to become familiar with the organization's policy and terminology relating to the interview topic. Further issues that might be pursued during the interview sometimes are identified. Alternate sources of information also may be found.

Identify the Respondents It is important to identify those personnel within the organization who can provide most information on the interview topic.

Interviews can be costly and time-consuming; wasted effort should be minimized.

Organization charts often are a first source of information on the appropriate respondents. The auditor also might seek the help of senior management when identifying the respondents. It is useful to enlist the help of senior management since they should be aware of any interviews carried out within their area. Further, senior management can introduce the auditor to the respondents (perhaps at a group meeting) prior to the conduct of the interviews so the respondents have advance notice of the reasons for the interview.

Prepare the Interview Content During the preparation phase the auditor should identify clearly the objectives of the interview and make a list of the information to be sought during the interview. If other auditors are conducting interviews, the interview process must be coordinated so a respondent is not asked the same question by different auditors.

After the information sought has been identified, it can be structured in a time sequence for the interview. General information should be requested at the beginning and end of an interview; specific information should be requested toward the middle of an interview. Information requested at the beginning of the interview should not be controversial or sensitive; this allows the respondent time to relax. Information requested at the end of the interview should give the respondent an opportunity to express opinions on central issues. There is a tendency for respondents to leave significant points they wish to make to the end of the interview (see, also, Hartman et al. [1968]).

After the information sought has been structured, the questions to be asked during the interview can be prepared. Formally preparing questions does not mean the interview has to be inflexible. If necessary the auditor must be willing to adapt and diverge from the formal structure.

Either closed or open questions can be used. A closed question requires a yes or no response; thus, closed questions should be used infrequently and only toward the middle of the interview when specific information is requested. In general, open questions should be asked, especially at the beginning and end of the interview. Open questions may lead to closed questions. For example, the open question, "What types of controls do you exercise over the preparation of batches?" may lead to the closed question, "Do you prepare hash totals on document numbers?"

The types of questions formulated for the interview depend on the tasks performed by the respondent and the respondent's seniority within the organization. The tasks performed determine the nature of the information requested. The level of seniority determines whether the questions focus on operational issues or policy issues.

After the interview has been structured and the questions prepared, the auditor should review its content to determine whether it is satisfactory. It may be too long, ask too many difficult questions, require too much respondent recall, ask too many sensitive questions, omit questions that need to be asked, etc. The opinions of other auditors also might be solicited. This review may lead the auditor to restructure or modify questions, or to break the interview into two or more interviews.

Schedule Time and Place of Interview When the auditor has finished preparing the interview content, a respondent can be contacted and the time and place of the interview scheduled. By scheduling the interview in advance, the respondent has time to think about the interview and, if necessary, collect material relevant to the interview.

Lunchtime and late afternoon interviews should be avoided; the respondent is hungry, tired, or concerned with terminating the interview. Midmorning interviews often work well; the respondent is fresh and has had time to clear any urgent business.

If possible, the interview should be conducted at the respondent's work place. The respondent is familiar with the surroundings and has access to any materials needed during the interview. However, a different venue should be chosen if there is a high risk of distractions occurring (e.g., frequent telephone calls) or there is insufficient privacy.

Check the Background of the Respondent Before conducting the interview the auditor should check the background of the respondent. This check may cause the auditor to avoid certain topics in the interview as they may evoke antagonistic responses. Further, if the auditor knows the respondent's biases before the interview, the interview may be directed better to obtain objective responses. The auditor also may be able to couch the interview in terms of the respondent's interests so the respondent is more motivated to answer questions.

Conducting the Interview

At the start of the interview the auditor should reiterate the purpose of the interview so the respondent can confirm the interview to occur corresponds with the arranged interview. The respondent also may have some questions about the objectives of the interview. At this time it is especially important for the auditor to establish rapport with the respondent.

The interview should follow basically the structure established during the preparation phase. During the interview the auditor should apply certain rules of protocol:

1 Minimize digressions from the main purpose of the interview.
2 For the most part be a listener.
3 Allow the respondent some thinking time.
4 Avoid condescension and criticism; be polite.
5 Avoid sarcasm and be careful of humor.
6 Avoid jargon and buzzwords; state clearly the questions.

7 Be attentive and interested.

8 Avoid disagreements and confrontations.

9 Answer courteously the respondent's questions.

10 Maintain a relaxed formality; avoid familiarity.

To facilitate recall of the content of the interview, the auditor may have to maintain a record. Either notes can be taken or a tape recorder used. Tape recorders often make respondents nervous; however, they relieve the auditor of notetaking so the auditor can focus better on the interview. Notetaking keeps the auditor's mind on the interview, especially items to be recorded. However, the time spent on notetaking should be minimized; it may distract the respondent and interrupt the flow of the interview. Whatever recording method is used, the auditor first should ensure its acceptability to the respondent at the start of the interview. The respondent also should have the right to review the transcript of the interview or notes taken during the interview to assess their accuracy.

In some cases the interview might be conducted by two auditors—a tandem interview. Tandem interviews have several advantages (see, further, Bouchard [1976]). First, they allow more efficient use of time; one interviewer can ask questions while the other makes notes. Second, since a respondent has one interviewer's complete attention, increased rapport results. Third, the questioning, recording, and analysis of the interview are more in depth, complete, and accurate. However, since a tandem interview places greater stress on the respondent, they are best used with people whose time is at a premium.

At the end of the interview the auditor should review the material covered with the respondent. Both the auditor and the respondent may wish to clear up ambiguities or omissions. The interview should be concluded promptly but not abruptly.

Analyzing the Interview

As soon as possible after the termination of the interview, the auditor should prepare a report on the interview. Recall of events usually deteriorates rapidly within a few hours of the interview. During the preparation of the report the auditor has two major objectives. First, the auditor attempts to separate fact from opinion. If there is some doubt about the factual content of the information provided, independent verification may be necessary. Where opinion is involved, for verification purposes the auditor may need to show the interviewer a copy of the interview write-up. Second, the auditor attempts to assimilate the information obtained during the interview and determine what it means for the overall objectives of the interview. Is the process well controlled? Has the system decreased the respondent's quality of working life?

Some follow-up may be required after the interview. The auditor may need to contact the respondent to obtain further information or clarify some issues. The respondent may have comments on the auditor's report of the interview.

Information obtained during the interview may cause the auditor to investigate aspects of the system that previously were to be left untouched.

QUESTIONNAIRES

Questionnaires have been used traditionally to evaluate controls within systems. Responses to questions indicate the presence or absence of a control or the nonapplicability of a control. However, questionnaires have other purposes as an evidence collection tool. They can be used to evaluate system effectiveness. For example, Maish [1979] used questionnaires to assess users' overall feelings about an information system. Users were asked about the quality of the information system staff, the quality of data input to the system, the quality of batch output obtained from the system, and the quality of the online part of the system. Lucas [1978] used questionnaires to assess whether users thought a file was up to date, contained relevant information, and was complete. Bostrom and Heinen [1977] used questionnaires to assess a system's impact on the quality of working life of its users.

Questionnaires also may be used to identify areas within an information system where potential inefficiencies exist. For example, operators may be surveyed to determine whether or not they think a system consumes resources inefficiently at run time. Clerical staff who supply input to a system may be surveyed to determine whether or not they think procedures for submission of data can be streamlined.

Design of Questionnaires

Extensive research has been carried out on questionnaire design (see, further, Moser and Kalton [1971]); however, for the most part successful questionnaire design is still an art. The following three sections focus on some major aspects of questionnaire design: (a) design of the questions, (b) design of the response scale, and (c) design of the layout and structure of the questionnaire.

Question Design Three major factors affect the design of the questions for a questionnaire: (a) the respondent group, (b) the nature of the information sought, and (c) how the questionnaire will be administered.

The respondent group for an audit questionnaire may be either the auditors themselves or the users of a system. For example, the well-known internal control questionnaire is completed by the auditor as the evidence gathering task proceeds. However, if the auditor is attempting to elicit attitudes on various attributes of system quality, the respondent group will be the users of the system. For example, customer satisfaction may be surveyed as a measure of system effectiveness; analysts and programmers may be asked their opinions on how easy the system is to maintain and modify. If auditors are the respondent group, questions can be specific, terms can be left undefined, instructions for completing the questionnaire can be minimized, etc.; the auditors should have been trained to use the questionnaire. If the respondent group is the users of the system, these liberties usually cannot be taken.

Questionnaires can be used to obtain either factual information or opinions. A factual question would be: Is there a fire extinguisher in the computer room? An opinion question would be: Do you feel the members of the information system staff are competent? The primary problem in designing factual questions is to ensure the respondent group understands precisely the facts required. Thus, the questionnaire designer may provide different kinds of information (some redundant) on the questionnaire in an attempt to ensure the respondent understands what facts are required. The primary problem in designing opinion questions is to ensure the wording of the question does not bias the response either by leading the respondent or being argumentative. Consider the question: Shouldn't the response time of the system be faster? User responses to this question could be biased positively.

The way in which the questionnaire is administered affects the extent to which questions have to be self-explanatory. If auditors are completing internal control questionnaires themselves, the questionnaire designer can presume the respondent group has substantial prior knowledge of the questionnaire. If auditors administer questionnaires to users, the questionnaire designer may assume the auditor can answer any questions or clarify any ambiguities which arise. However, if the questionnaire is self-administered by the user group, the questionnaire designer must word the questions carefully; the respondent may not be able to ask the auditor for assistance. For example, the auditor may be measuring the effect of an online data communications system on job satisfaction. Users may be dispersed physically over wide areas. The auditor may have to use a mail questionnaire to assess users' opinions on how the system has impacted their job satisfaction.

Though the design of questions depends on the factors described above, some general design guidelines can be given (see, further, Moser and Kalton [1971], Kerlinger [1973], and Bouchard [1976]):

1 *Ensure questions are specific:* The question, "Are controls over input adequate?" is too general to be of much use. The question, "Are hash control totals for batches calculated?" is much more specific. It provides the respondent with a frame of reference to answer the question.

2 *Use simple language and avoid jargon:* In some cases technical terms have a very precise meaning; for example, the auditor should know what the term "encryption" means. However, if the respondent group is the user of an interactive language, the question, "Are the semantics of the language sufficient for you to be able to perform your job?" may cause confusion. The users may or may not know what the term "semantics" means.

3 *Avoid ambiguous questions:* The question, "Does the system allow you to perform your job faster and improve your job satisfaction?" is ambiguous. What does a "no" answer mean? There are several possibilities: the job may be performed faster but job satisfaction remains unchanged, the job may be performed faster but job satisfaction decreases, both the speed with which the task is performed and job satisfaction remain unchanged, job satisfaction may increase but the speed with which the job is performed is unchanged, etc. Questions should focus on a single item; they should be clear and unambiguous.

4 *Avoid leading questions:* Leading questions suggest the answers a respondent should give. For example, suppose a manager is asked about use of an interactive system. The question, "Does your secretary use the system to obtain the information for you?" is unlikely to be answered truthfully. The question may be taken to imply something bad about managers not directly using the system themselves.

5 *Avoid presumptuous questions:* Questions should not presume anything about the respondent. The question, "How often do you use the system?" presumes the respondent uses the system. The respondent may or may not use the system.

6 *Avoid hypothetical questions:* The question, "Would you like the system to provide a faster response time?" is likely to evoke a positive response. Most users would not object to having a faster response time in an interactive system; however, whether they would be willing to pay for a faster response time is another issue.

7 *Avoid embarrassing questions:* At times the auditor may use a questionnaire to obtain information that is personal, delicate, or controversial. Care must be taken to formulate the question in such a way that it does not embarrass the respondent. For example, suppose the auditor is exploring the quality of the system design process within an installation. If the auditor asks system designers, "Do you consider the impact of the systems you design on the user's quality of working life?" a positive response is likely to be obtained. To answer otherwise implies socially unacceptable behavior.

8 *Avoid questions involving extensive recall:* Factual questions involve the respondent recalling information. The accuracy of the response depends upon the extent of recall needed. The question "How many times in January did you use the system?" is unlikely to produce an accurate response if it is asked in the following December, unless the respondent maintains a diary of uses.

9 *Avoid questions about which the respondent has little or no knowledge:* Respondents tend to answer questions on a questionnaire, even when they have little or no knowledge about the subject matter covered by the question. If responses to factual questions are being elicited, respondent ignorance with respect to the question asked may be detected by the auditor. Where opinion is being elicited, however, respondent ignorance may go undetected.

Choosing a Response Scale The type of response scale chosen for a questionnaire depends upon the nature of the question asked. If the question asked requires a factual response, the choice of response scale usually is straightforward. Figure 20-1 shows three examples of response scales that might be used. Typically the scales involve checking a yes or no response or inserting some piece of information; for example, a make of machine.

Disposal of Output:

	Yes	No	N/A
1 Are sensitive reports shredded?			
2 Is disposal of carbon paper secure?			
3 Is disposal of waste paper from computer room secure?			

FIGURE 20-1a
Excerpt from internal control questionnaire.

Fire Protection:
_____ 1 Fire exits marked clearly
_____ 2 Portable fire extinguishers placed at strategic points
_____ 3 Fire drills conducted regularly

FIGURE 20-1b
Excerpt from fire protection checklist.

Hardware Configuration:
Vendor:

_____ Burroughs
_____ Control Data   _____ IBM
_____ Digital   _____ ICL
_____ Fujitsu   _____ Univac
_____ Honeywell
        Other _____

Model: _____
Number of disk drives: _____   Number of tape drives: _____

FIGURE 20-1c
Excerpt from hardware configuration questionnaire.

When opinions or attitudes are solicited, the choice of a response scale is a more complex decision (see, further, Nunnally [1967], Kerlinger [1973], and Brown [1976]). Figure 20-2 shows three types of scales that might be used for questions on various aspects of system effectiveness (see, further, Chapter 23). Figure 20-2a shows a common seven-point scale. Figure 20-2b shows a Likert scale. Responses to individual items on a Likert scale are summed and the average calculated. Figure 20-2c shows a semantic differential scale used to assess users' attitudes toward an information system. Other types of scales can be used; for example, Thurstone scales and Guttman scales (see, further, Moser and Kalton [1971] and Nunnally [1967]). The choice of an appropriate response scale to measure attitudes or opinions requires substantial expertise. Unless the auditor is well-trained in psychometrics, consulting advice should be employed whenever a new questionnaire is to be designed.

Choice of Layout and Structure The layout and structure of a questionnaire impact how accurately the questionnaire will be completed. If the questionnaire is used in a mail survey, layout and structure also affect the response rate (see, further, Bouchard [1976]).

The Job I Perform Offers:

	Low							High
Variety	1							7
Opportunities for learning	1							7
Challenge	1							7

FIGURE 20-2a
Seven-point scale used to assess users' attitudes about the jobs they perform.

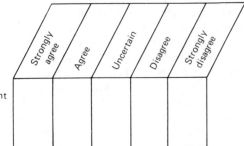

Are technically competent
Design systems with the
user in mind
Deal well with people

FIGURE 20-2b
Likert scale used to assess users' feelings about the information system staff.

The System

1. Pleasant	:__:__:__:__:__:__:__:__:__:__:__:	Unpleasant
2. Ugly	:__:__:__:__:__:__:__:__:__:__:__:	Beautiful
3. Heavy	:__:__:__:__:__:__:__:__:__:__:__:	Light

FIGURE 20-2c
Semantic differential scale used to assess user's attitudes about the system.

The length of a questionnaire affects the morale of the respondent. If a questionnaire is too long, respondents become fatigued. They either refuse to answer the questionnaire or answers given toward the end of the questionnaire become more unreliable.

If the respondent has not been trained to complete the questionnaire, care must be taken to show clearly the flow of questions through the questionnaire, especially if the responses to some questions cause branches to other questions. The questionnaire should appear uncluttered; questions and sections of the questionnaire should be spaced adequately.

Questions placed at the beginning of the questionnaire should be general in nature and place little stress on the respondent. More difficult questions—those that require high recall, are controversial, etc.—should be placed toward the middle and end of the questionnaire.

Reliability and Validity Issues

If a questionnaire is designed to elicit factual information, providing the questions are expressed unambiguously, the responses obtained should be unequivocal. When opinions and attitudes are elicited, however, the auditor faces the problem of designing a questionnaire that is reliable and valid (see, further, Kerlinger [1973]).

A *reliable* questionnaire is one that gives the same measurements over repeated administrations. In other words, assuming all factors are held constant, if a respondent completed the questionnaire twice, the scores obtained on the second administration of the questionnaire would be the same as those obtained on the first administration.

Test-retest reliability is difficult to establish by having respondents complete the questionnaire twice. At the second administration, respondents may remember the ratings they gave at the first administration; thus, the administrations are not independent. It is also difficult to assess whether all other factors remain constant. Nevertheless, the theory of reliability has been researched extensively and techniques for assessing the reliability of questionnaires are well developed (see Nunnally [1967]).

A *valid* questionnaire measures what it sets out to measure. A questionnaire may be reliable but it may not be valid; it may measure something other than the attitude or opinion it is supposed to measure.

There are three major types of validity:

Type of validity	Explanation
Predictive validity	Scores (ratings) on the questionnaire are used to predict some criterion. Predictive accuracy is a measure of validity.
Content validity	How representative are the sample items on the questionnaire of the universe of content? The items on the questionnaire should cover the full range of the attitude or opinion being measured.
Construct validity	What trait does the questionnaire measure? On the basis of theory, associations between scores on the questionnaire and other variables are postulated and these hypotheses are tested empirically.

Again, the theory underlying validity has been researched extensively and techniques for assessing validity are well developed (see, further, Brown [1976]). The American Psychological Association [1966] has issued standards that define reliability and validity criteria that a test (questionnaire) should meet.

Clearly, then, the auditor must be careful when designing questionnaires to elicit attitudes or opinions. Design is not simply a matter of listing questions that the auditor believes to be important. The resulting questionnaire may be neither reliable nor valid, and actions may be taken on the basis of flawed measurements; for example, a system may be redesigned on the basis of an inaccurate measure of the quality of working life of users.

When attitudes must be measured, if possible, the auditor should use a standard instrument. A large number of questionnaires (tests, instruments) have been developed to measure a wide range of attitudes and opinions. For example, if the auditor wishes to measure job satisfaction as part of the evaluation of system effectiveness, Robinson et al. [1969] contains 13 instruments that measure general job satisfaction, five instruments that measure job satisfaction for particular occupations, and eight instruments that measure satisfaction with specific job features. Other collections of instruments are available (see, for example, Chun et al. [1975] and Robinson and Shaver [1969]). These collections also provide discussions of the instrument's validity and reliability, references to its use, the name and address of the publisher of the instrument, and instructions for administering the instrument.

If the auditor must have a new questionnaire developed, the services of a psychometrician should be employed. Until the reliability and validity of the questionnaire have been established, the measures of attitudes or opinions obtained should be interpreted cautiously.

Effective Use of Questionnaires

Even though a questionnaire may be well designed, it may not be used effectively. The auditor must know when to use the questionnaire, how to use it, and what the responses mean.

Mailed questionnaires are useful when the auditor must obtain information from physically dispersed locations. They are a cheap means of collecting data. However, the auditor must be able to ensure a high response rate is obtained. The auditor also must ensure the questionnaire is well designed so response errors are minimal.

Auditors may complete questionnaires themselves during the course of an interview or observation of a system. Questionnaires structure the interview or review process and provide a convenient recording schedule. However, the auditor must be trained to use the questionnaire. Further, if a questionnaire is used on a regular basis, there is a risk the auditor will complete the questionnaire mechanically or copy answers from previous questionnaires.

There is sometimes a problem in choosing the right questionnaire to use. For example, if the auditor wishes to assess a system's impact on job satisfaction, several questionnaires are available. The auditor must evaluate carefully the purposes for which the instrument was designed, how its reliability and validity were assessed, and how well the purposes of the questionnaire correspond with audit purposes.

Care must be taken when questionnaires are administered. A hurriedly completed questionnaire increases the likelihood of response errors occurring. Standardized questionnaires have instructions on how they should be administered. The reliability of the questionnaire depends on these instructions being followed.

The auditor also must know what the responses obtained on a questionnaire mean. For example, what score indicates a high level of job satisfaction exists? When is an internal control system weak? The instructions for standardized questionnaires discuss how scores should be interpreted. If auditors have designed their own questionnaires, they must derive a rule for assigning a global evaluation to the individual or aggregate ratings obtained.

CONTROL FLOWCHARTS

Control flowcharts show *what* controls exist in a system and *where* these controls exist in the system. They have three major audit purposes: (*a*) comprehension—the construction of a control flowchart highlights those areas where the auditor lacks understanding of either the system itself or the controls in the system; (*b*) evaluation—an experienced auditor recognizes patterns on a control flowchart that suggest the presence of either control strengths or control weaknesses in the system; and (*c*) communication—a control flowchart can be used to communicate the auditor's understanding of the system and its associated controls to others. Furthermore, besides their use in audits, control flowcharts can be used in the system development process as a design aid; an analyst can construct a control flowchart as a focal point for the design of controls in a system.

Types of Control Flowcharts

For each type of flowchart that an analyst, designer, or programmer might prepare to understand or to describe a system, a corresponding control flowchart can be constructed. A control flowchart is simply a "normal" flowchart that is stripped of narrative other than the annotations required to understand the controls applied within the system being described via the flowchart.

Four types of control flowcharts facilitate evidence gathering and evidence evaluation activities. First a *document flowchart* can be employed to show controls over the flow of documents through the manual components of a computer system. This type of flowchart has been used for many years by auditors to aid their evaluation of manual systems (see, for example, Arens and Loebbecke [1985]). Typically, the departments or sections through which a document flows are represented as vertical columns on the flowchart, and the flow of documents proceeds from left to right to indicate the passage of the documents through the various departments. Figure 20-3*a* shows a portion of a document flowchart for the manual activities supporting an order entry system. Figure 20-3*b* shows the corresponding control flowchart. Note that most annotations on the document flowchart have been removed from the control flowchart; however, some new annotations have been added to the control flowchart to provide a more complete understanding of the controls being exercised.

Second, a *data flow diagram* can be used to show the controls exercised over the data flows through a system (see, also, Chapter 4). Note, while data flow diagrams focus on data flows rather than control flows, some of the process bubbles in a data flow diagram represent important controls that are exercised to ensure the integrity of data. Moreover, in a set of "leveled" data flow diagrams, the lowest level data flow diagrams show the handling of error and exception conditions (see Gane and Sarson [1979]). The controls narrated on a data flow diagram help the auditor to understand how data integrity is maintained at the logical or functional level in a system. However, a data flow

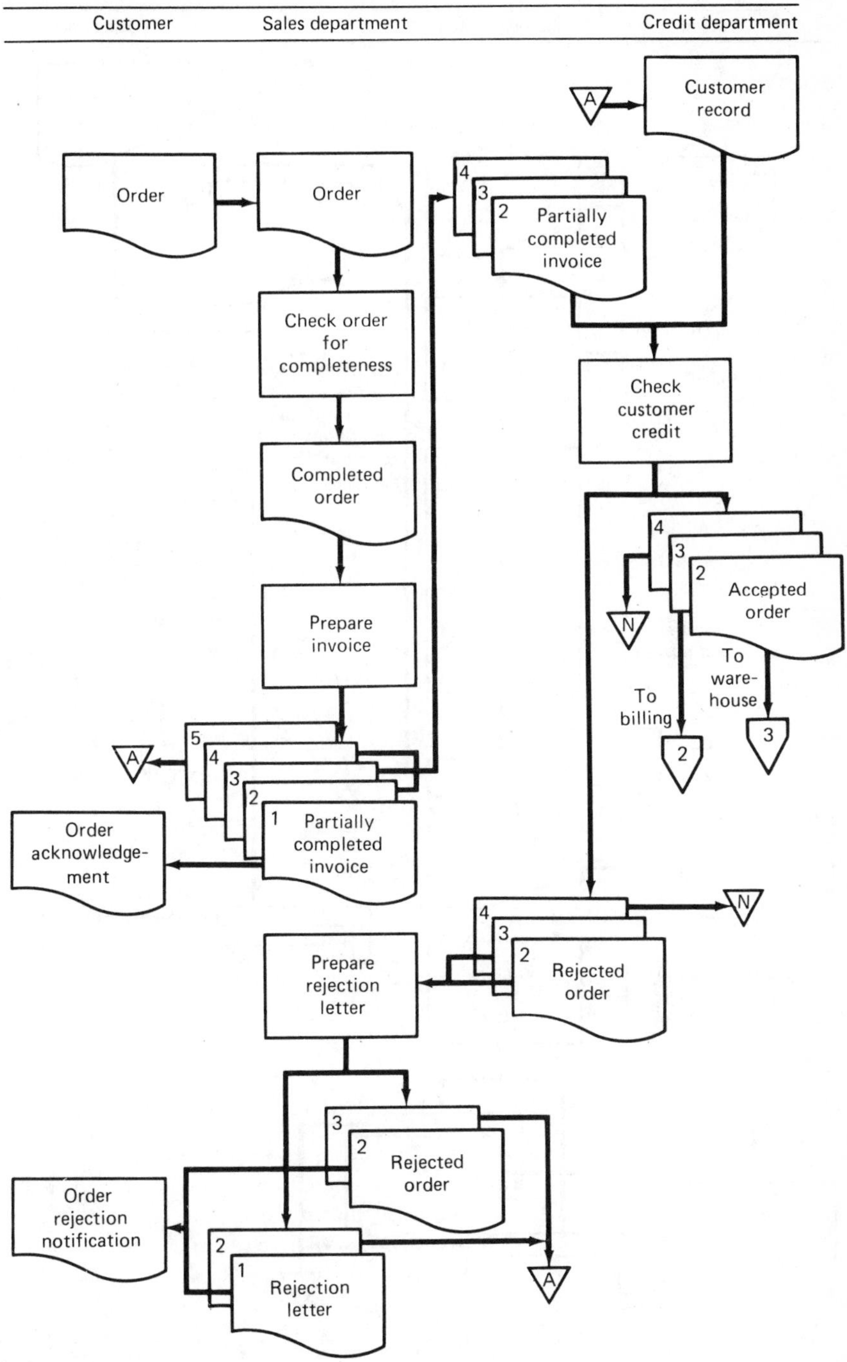

FIGURE 20-3a
Section of a document flowchart for an order entry application.

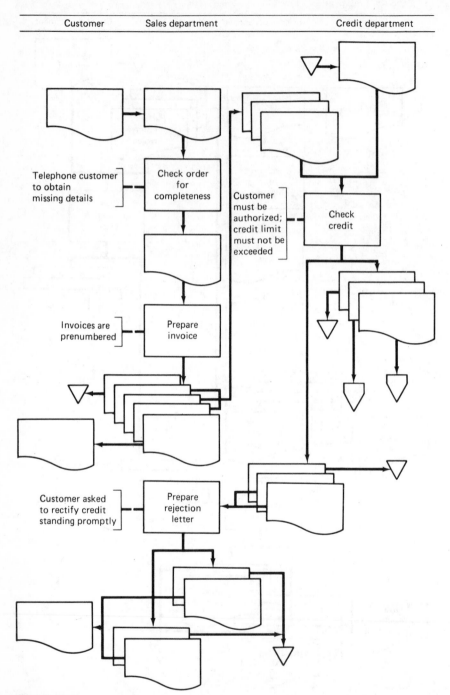

Customer	Sales department		Credit department

Telephone customer
to obtain
missing details

Check order
for
completeness

Customer
must be
authorized;
credit limit
must not be
exceeded

Check
credit

Invoices are
prenumbered

Prepare
invoice

Customer asked
to rectify credit
standing promptly

Prepare
rejection
letter

FIGURE 20-3b
Section of a control flowchart based on a document flowchart for an order entry application.

diagram is not especially useful in understanding the controls exercised at the physical or resource level since it does not show the assignment of data flows, data stores, or processes to the components used to perform the basic activities within the system. Figure 20-4a shows a portion of a data flow diagram for an order entry system. Figure 20-4b shows the corresponding control data flow diagram.

Third, a *system flowchart* can be used to show the controls exercised at the physical or resource level in a system. Since a system flowchart primarily illustrates the flow of data among the major components of a system—the programs, storage media, processors, communication networks, etc.—it can be

FIGURE 20-4a
Section of a data flow diagram for an order entry application.

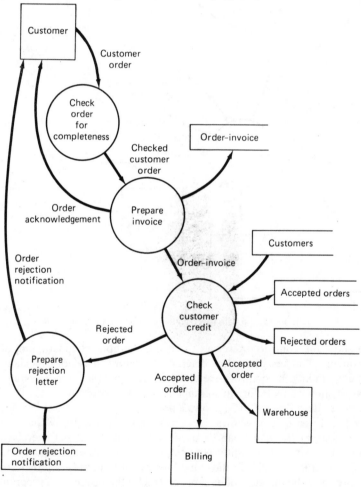

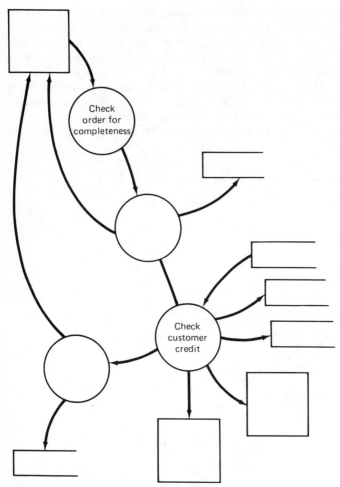

FIGURE 20-4b
Section of a control flowchart based on a data flow diagram for an order entry application.

narrated to show the controls exercised to ensure the correct functioning of these components. Unlike a data flow diagram, therefore, it is not especially useful in understanding the controls exercised at the logical level in a system. Nonetheless, it shows how failure in a component may corrupt the integrity of data within the system. Figure 20-5a shows a portion of a system flowchart for a payroll system. Figure 20-5b shows the corresponding control flowchart.

Fourth, a *program flowchart* can be used to show the controls exercised internally to a program. If the auditor is attempting to understand the detailed workings of a program, especially those modules within the program that are intended to preserve the integrity of data processed by the program, a program

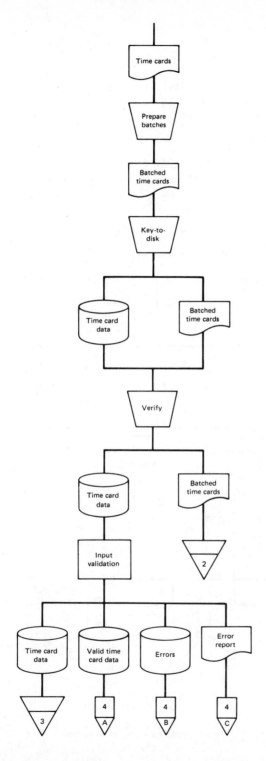

FIGURE 20-5a
Section of a system flowchart for a payroll application.

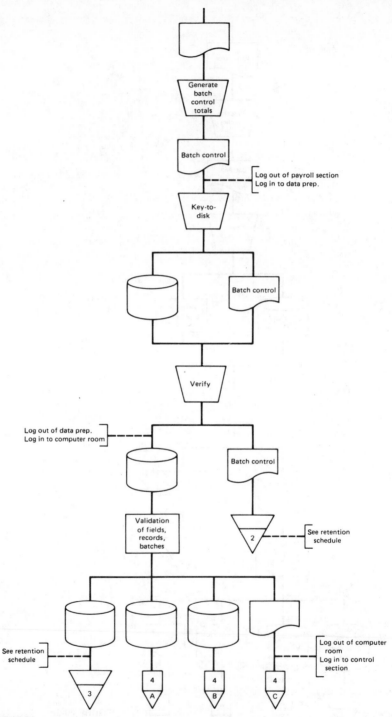

FIGURE 20-5*b*
Section of a control flowchart based on a system flowchart for a payroll application.

flowchart may provide important insights about the controls being exercised. Figure 20-6a shows a portion of a program flowchart for a program that validates time card data submitted to a payroll system. Figure 20-6b shows the corresponding control flowchart.

Constructing a Control Flowchart

There are several steps involved in constructing a control flowchart:

1 Choose the primary flowchart technique to use.

2 Choose the appropriate level of detail at which to work.

FIGURE 20-6a
Section of a program flowchart for a payroll application.

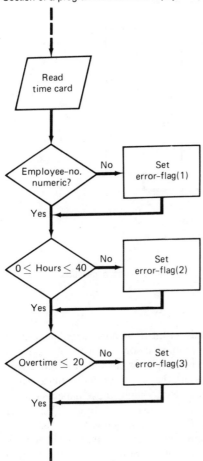

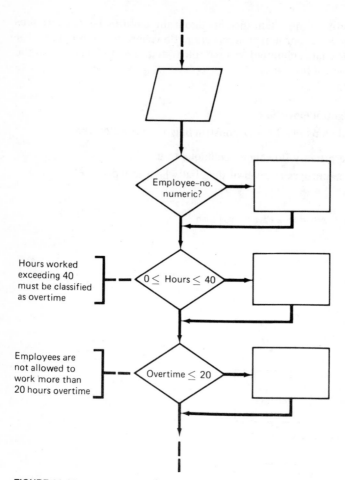

FIGURE 20-6b
Section of a control flowchart based on a program flowchart for a payroll application.

3 Prepare the primary flowchart.
4 Prepare the control flowchart.

As the previous section indicated, the different flowchart techniques have different strengths and weaknesses: they emphasize some aspects of a system and deemphasize other aspects of the system. It is important, therefore, for auditors to identify those aspects of the system that are their main concern and to choose the appropriate charting technique to highlight these aspects.

The preparation of a flowchart may take substantial time. The effort involved should be commensurate with the benefits to be gained from using the flowchart. On the one hand a flowchart must contain sufficient detail for the auditor to be able to judge the quality of controls employed within the system being described. On the other hand, too much detail can obfuscate matters and detract from the auditor spending time on other more productive evidence gathering activities. Unfortunately the ability to choose the right level of detail tends to come only with experience in using the various types of flowcharting methods. Few formal guidelines can be provided.

Once the flowcharting method and the level of detail at which to work have been chosen, the primary flowchart can be constructed. Each of the flowcharting techniques have standard symbols that must be used and basic rules for preparing the flowchart (see, for example, Skinner and Anderson [1966], Gane and Sarson [1979], Chapin [1970], and Halper et al. [1985]). Compliance with these standard symbols and rules for constructing the flowchart is essential if the flowchart is to be used as a vehicle for communicating information to others and if the flowchart must be modified in subsequent audits.

Once the primary flowchart has been prepared, the control flowchart can be constructed. The control flowchart usually should show only the controls exercised within the system; other information about the system should be narrated on the primary flowchart. The major reason for separating controls from other information about the system is to reduce the level of detail on a single flowchart. Of course, if the primary flowchart is sparse, it may be simpler to show controls on the primary flowchart. Moreover, in the absence of a well-drawn primary flowchart, understanding the nature of the controls narrated on the control flowchart will be difficult. Often the auditor can obtain a full understanding of the system only if the primary flowchart and the control flowchart are placed side by side. Deficiencies in the primary flowchart inhibit the auditor understanding details on the control flowchart.

Strengths and Limitations of Control Flowcharts

Unfortunately, the information available on the strengths and weaknesses of the various types of control flowcharting techniques is meager. Given that document control flowcharts have been used extensively by auditors over many years, it would appear they have substantial utility. They are primarily oriented to manual systems, however, so their usefulness may decline as more data processing activities are automated.

Data flow diagrams have been employed by information systems professionals only since the late 1970s. Nonetheless, their use now is widespread since they have proved to be very important tools for communicating the logical flows of data within systems. Their use by auditors, however, is still limited. Auditors still tend to rely on traditional document flowcharts or system flowcharts as the basis for preparing control flowcharts. Presumably this situation will change as auditors become more familiar with data flow diagrams.

When auditors document controls in automated systems, they primarily use system flowcharts as the basis for preparing control flowcharts. The utility of system flowcharts was supported in research by Stanford Research Institute [1977] in which the investigators examined an organization that prepared control flowcharts at a detailed level. The organization reported that system control flowcharts were useful in designing better controls and in communicating the controls existing in a system to personnel who had to become familiar with the system. System control flowcharts were simple to use and required little training time. Nonetheless, Jenkins and Carlis [1975] point out that system flowcharts are not always a good basis for preparing control flowcharts when the system to be described is an event-driven system (like an automated inventory reorder system) as opposed to a data-driven system. Too many activities are represented by a single process symbol on the system flowchart, and the corresponding control flowchart becomes very cluttered and difficult to interpret.

Research carried out by Shneiderman et al. [1977] calls into question the usefulness of program flowcharts and, as a consequence, the usefulness of control flowcharts based on program flowcharts. Experiments were run to test whether program flowcharts aided program composition, comprehension, debugging, and modification. No statistically significant differences were obtained between groups using flowcharts and groups who did not use flowcharts. In some cases flowcharts seemed to hinder rather than help performance. However, several human factors studies support the usefulness of flowcharts at the level of detail typified by program flowcharts (see, for example, Kammann [1975]). Nevertheless, these studies tend to examine whether prose or flowcharts is understood more easily, and they have been carried out using noncomputer tasks. Thus, the utility of program flowcharts and their associated control flowcharts is still a research issue. Perhaps program control flowcharts are useful for the limited set of logic that auditors often want to investigate. Perhaps, however, their utility will continue to decline as use of structured programming techniques becomes more widespread and programmers employ hierarchy charts, decision tables, decision trees, and structured English to document their programs (see, further, Chapter 5).

The primary limitations with all flowcharts are that they are time-consuming to develop and difficult to modify and maintain. Effective use of control flowcharts still requires auditors to have a good understanding of controls within a system; otherwise, control strengths and deficiencies cannot be identified on the flowchart. Only with experience can auditors recognize the patterns that suggest systems are well-controlled or that follow-up work is required.

Some of the difficulties that arise in preparing, modifying, and maintaining control flowcharts may be mitigated as software to support the various types of flowcharting techniques becomes more widely available (see Whitten et al. [1986]). Generalized microcomputer software can also be used to support freehand drawing or graphics applications. The software often provides a library of specialized symbols, or it allows users to create their own symbols and to store them in a library. Symbols can be placed on a screen and joined in various ways using a mouse. Freehand symbols and lines can also be added to the diagram, and the software usually allows the diagrams to be narrated with user-supplied text. The diagrams prepared on the screen can then be printed using a graphics printer, and they can be stored for subsequent use and maintenance.

SUMMARY

Three manual techniques that the auditor can use to collect evidence on the quality of computer systems are interviews, questionnaires, and control flowcharts. These techniques were used before the advent of computers. Their importance has not diminished in computer systems.

Interviews consist of three major phases: preparing for the interview, conducting the interview, and analyzing the interview. Interviews reduce the time required to find out information if someone is willing to provide the answers. However, effective interviewing requires that various rules of protocol be followed carefully.

Questionnaires can be used to elicit factual information or opinion. The most difficult design problems arise when opinion must be obtained. The auditor must be careful to use a questionnaire that is valid and reliable.

Control flowcharts show what controls exist and where they are within a system. An experienced auditor can use control flowcharts to identify both the control strengths and control weaknesses in a system. Nonetheless, control flowcharts are often time-consuming to prepare and difficult to modify and maintain. Software to support freehand drawing and graphics may mitigate some of the difficulties associated with using control flowcharts.

REVIEW QUESTIONS

20-1 Other than those given in the chapter, give an example of how an interview might be used to gather evidence on some aspect of:
   a System effectiveness
   b System efficiency
   c Data integrity
20-2 Briefly explain the difference between interviewing and interrogation. Why should the auditor be careful about becoming involved in an interrogation?
20-3 Why do people respond to questions in an interview? Why is it important the auditor has an understanding of what motivates a person to respond?
20-4 Why do different types of interviews require varying levels of respondent motivation? Give two examples of interviews the auditor might conduct, one that requires a high level of respondent motivation and one that requires a low level of respondent motivation.
20-5 In the structure of an interview, where should general questions be placed? Where should specific questions be placed? Why is placement of questions important?
20-6 Briefly explain the difference between a closed and an open question. What factors affect whether the auditor uses a closed or an open question during an interview?
20-7 Briefly outline the factors that the auditor should consider when choosing a time and place for the interview.

20-8 What is meant by the auditor establishing rapport with the interviewee? Why is rapport important in an interview? Give three ways in which the auditor can set about establishing rapport.

20-9 What can the auditor do if a confrontation situation arises during an interview?

20-10 Briefly explain what is meant by a tandem interview. What are the advantages and disadvantages of a tandem interview? Give an example of where the auditor might use a tandem interview.

20-11 What tasks does the auditor perform during the analysis of an interview? When should the analysis be carried out?

20-12 Why must the auditor consider who will be the respondent group in the design of a questionnaire? What impact does the type of respondent group have on the design?

20-13 How will the characteristics of a self-administered questionnaire differ from the characteristics of a questionnaire administered by the auditor? When should a self-administered questionnaire be used and when should a questionnaire administered by the auditor be used?

20-14 How do response scales differ for questions asked to obtain factual information versus questions asked to obtain attitudes or opinions?

20-15 What is meant by the reliability and validity of a questionnaire? Why must the auditor be concerned with reliability and validity issues?

20-16 What advantages do standardized questionnaires offer the auditor? Does their use have any disadvantages?

20-17 One problem with using the same questionnaire on a routine basis is the problem of "cheating." Explain.

20-18 Give three problems of mail questionnaires. Outline some techniques the auditor can use to overcome these problems.

20-19 What is a control flowchart? What are the purposes of a control flowchart? How does a control flowchart differ from a system flowchart? How does it differ from a program flowchart?

20-20 Briefly describe the nature and purposes of the *four* types of control flowchart that may be constructed.

20-21 Outline the steps that must be undertaken when constructing a control flowchart. Be sure to indicate the critical decisions that must be made at each step.

20-22 For each of the four types of control flowcharts, give a strength and a limitation.

20-23 How might the availability of flowcharting software assist the auditor to prepare control flowcharts?

20-24 A major advantage of control flowcharts is that they can be prepared and used effectively by auditors who have little knowledge of data processing controls. Discuss.

20-25 To what extent is the hypothesized usefulness of flowcharts supported by empirical research results?

MULTIPLE CHOICE QUESTIONS

20-1 Which of the following is a difference between an interview and an interrogation:

a An interrogation requires fewer skills to conduct than an interview

b A respondent in an interview is more likely to be uncooperative than a respondent in an interrogation

  c Interrogations require a shorter period of time to conduct than an interview

  d An interrogation is conducted in light of some type of wrongdoing

20-2 In which of the following situations would an interview be inappropriate:

  a Determining the impact of a system on a user's quality of working life

  b Soliciting the advice of operators on which applications are inefficient

  c Obtaining the opinions of management on the critical systems within the organization

  d Determining from managers how they colluded to carry out a defalcation

20-3 A respondent's motivation to reply to the questions asked in an interview is primarily a function of:

  a Whether or not the questions asked are complex or simple

  b The stress placed on the respondent

  c The extent to which the respondent perceives the interviewer to be a means of obtaining his/her own goals

  d The extent to which the questions asked are interesting

20-4 A tandem interview is an interview conducted:

  a With one respondent and two interviewers

  b With two or more respondents

  c On two or more separate occasions

  d On a regular rotating basis

20-5 In an interview, closed questions should be asked:

  a Toward the beginning of an interview

  b Toward the middle of an interview

  c When a complex topic is being examined

  d When a controversial topic must be addressed

20-6 Which of the following is most likely to be the best time to conduct an interview:

  a Outside normal working hours when the respondent is not interrupted by the pressures of work

  b Over a meal or break so the respondent can relax

  c Midmorning

  d Just after the respondent arrives at work

20-7 Which of the following is *not* a rule of protocol to follow when conducting an interview:

  a For the most part be a listener

  b Use technical terms whenever possible to reduce the time required for the interview

  c Answer all the respondent's questions courteously

  d Avoid familiarity

20-8 Tape recorders should be used in an interview only if:

  a The prior permission of the respondent has been obtained

  b Nonsensitive material is to be covered

  c The respondent does not appear to be nervous

  d The respondent is a senior manager whose time is at a premium

20-9 Which of the following guidelines is most likely to result in the high-quality analysis of an interview:

  a It should be left until some time after the interview so the auditor has time to reflect upon the information obtained

  b The report prepared should be shown to the respondent for comments on accuracy and completeness

    c The auditor's interpretations of the respondent's opinions should not be disclosed to the respondent

    d The analysis should be undertaken by someone other than the auditor who conducted the interview to reduce the likelihood of bias in the write-up to be presented to the respondent

20-10 Which of the following types of questionnaires probably would require the most explanatory information to be included with the questionnaire:

    a An internal control questionnaire completed by auditors

    b A questionnaire completed during an interview

    c A self-administered questionnaire mailed to dispersed application system users

    d A questionnaire requiring factual responses

20-11 Which of the following is *not* a general design guideline for questions to be included in a questionnaire:

    a Limit the responses to all questions to no more than a few alternatives

    b Avoid questions involving extensive recall

    c Avoid hypothetical questions

    d Avoid embarrassing questions

20-12 Which of the following types of response scales typically is *not* used on a questionnaire when opinions are solicited:

    a Guttman scale

    b Semantic differential scale

    c Likert scale

    d Binary scale

20-13 In a questionnaire, more difficult questions should:

    a Be placed toward the middle and end of the questionnaire

    b Require a yes or no response to reduce complexity

    c Leave little room for opinion to reduce the amount of noise in the information obtained

    d Be placed toward the beginning of a questionnaire so respondents are not fatigued when they answer them

20-14 The representativeness of the sample items on a questionnaire in terms of the domain of interest is a measure of its:

    a Construct validity

    b Predictive validity

    c Face validity

    d Content validity

20-15 A reliable questionnaire is one that:

    a Measures what it is supposed to measure

    b Has only a limited number of questions that the respondent must answer

    c Obtains the same responses across repeated administrations of the questionnaire

    d Has been used extensively to measure a construct

20-16 A primary problem with internal control questionnaires used by auditors is:

    a They are prone to high response error rates even after the auditor has received substantial training in their use

    b They are completed mechanically after repeated use

    c They often have low predictive validity

    d They allow no scope for the auditor to offer an opinion

20-17 Which of the following flowcharting techniques is likely to form the basis of a control flowchart that shows controls exercised at the logical or functional level within a system:

a Document flowchart

b Data flow diagram

c System flowchart

d Program flowchart

20-18 In the preparation of a control flowchart, the most difficult decisions are usually associated with:

a Choosing the appropriate level of detail at which to work

b Preparing the primary flowchart

c Narrating controls on the primary flowchart

d Choosing the primary flowcharting technique to use

20-19 After investigating one organization's use of control flowcharts based on system flowcharts, Stanford Research Institute concluded:

a Control flowcharts have little future potential

b The primary problem with control flowcharts is their modification and maintenance

c Control flowcharts were useful as an aid to designing better controls and communicating controls to personnel who were relatively unfamiliar with the system

d Control flowcharts were ineffective unless auditors received substantial training in their construction and use

20-20 Which of the following aspects of control flowcharts requires the most audit experience for their effective use:

a Choosing the right primary flowcharting technique

b Modifying the control flowchart in light of system change

c Narrating controls on the primary flowchart in the correct location

d Recognizing patterns on the control flowchart that signal control strengths and weaknesses

EXERCISES AND CASES

20-1 What problems, if any, exist with the following questions on a self-administered questionnaire given to users to assess their feelings about a system:

a Do you ever have trouble using the system?

b Does your terminal have a fast enough baud rate?

c Would you like graphical reports to be prepared?

d Do you make better decisions using the output of the new system?

e Has the system made many of the tasks you perform trivial?

f On average, how many times per week during the last year has the system been unavailable when you needed it?

g Does your secretary use the system more than you do?

h Has the system caused you to think about changing your job?

i Do you make more errors when preparing input for the new system than you did with the old system?

j How does your husband/wife feel about you using a system that has put some of your work colleagues out of a job?

20-2 The chapter identifies various deficiencies in the following questions:

   a Are the semantics of the language sufficient for you to be able to perform your job?

   b Does the system allow you to perform your job faster and improve your job satisfaction?

   c Does your secretary use the system to obtain the information for you?

   d How often do you use the system?

   e Would you like the system to provide a faster response?

   f Do you consider the impact of the systems you design on the user's quality of working life?

   g How many times in January did you use the system?

   Required: Propose alternatives to the above questions that remedy their deficiencies.

20-3 You are a senior on the external audit team for a bank that has an online realtime update system for its customer accounts file. The customer accounts file uses a network data structure that is maintained by a database management system.

   Required: As part of the evaluation of application controls, your manager decides that you should interview the project manager for the online realtime update system to assess the adequacy of backup and recovery for the system. She asks you to outline the subject matter that you intend to cover in the interview and the chronological order in which you intend to cover the subject matter.

20-4 Design an internal control questionnaire that could be used to evaluate the database administration function.

20-5 Construct a control flowchart for the following system flowchart that shows an online update system used by bank tellers. You should show the controls that you think should be used in the system.

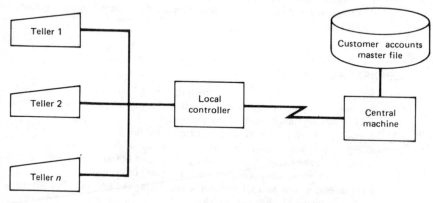

20-6 Draw a data flow diagram to represent the data flows and functions performed when you use an automatic teller machine (ATM) to withdraw cash from your bank account. Assume the ATM is always used in an online realtime update mode. When you have completed the data flow diagram, draw another data flow diagram to highlight the controls that you believe would be performed to safeguard assets and maintain data integrity in the system.

ANSWERS TO MULTIPLE CHOICE QUESTIONS

20-1 d	20-6 c	20-11 a	20-16 b
20-2 d	20-7 b	20-12 d	20-17 b
20-3 c	20-8 a	20-13 a	20-18 a
20-4 a	20-9 b	20-14 d	20-19 c
20-5 b	20-10 c	20-15 c	20-20 d

REFERENCES

American Psychological Association. *Standards for Educational and Psychological Tests and Manuals* (Washington, DC: American Psychological Association, 1966).

Arens, Alvin A., and James K. Loebbecke. *Auditing: An Integrated Approach,* 3d ed. (Englewood Cliffs, NJ: Prentice-Hall, 1985).

Benjamin, Robert I. *Control of the Information System Development Cycle* (New York: Wiley, 1971).

Bostrom, Robert P., and J. Stephen Heinen. "MIS Problems and Failures: Socio-Technical Perspective—Part II: The Application of Socio-Technical Theory," *Management Information Systems Quarterly* (December 1977), pp. 11–28.

Bouchard, Thomas J., Jr. "Field Research Methods: Interviewing, Questionnaires, Participant Observation, Systematic Observation, Unobtrusive Measures," in Marvin D. Dunnette, ed., *Handbook of Industrial and Organizational Psychology* (Chicago: Rand McNally, 1976), pp. 363–413.

Brown, Frederick G. *Principles of Educational and Psychological Testing,* 2d ed. (New York: Holt, Rinehart and Winston, 1976).

Burch, John G., Jr., and Joseph L. Sardinas, Jr. *Computer Control and Audit: A Total Systems Approach* (New York: Wiley, 1978).

Chapin, Ned. "Flowcharting with ANSI Standard: A Tutorial," *Computing Surveys* (June 1970), pp. 119–146.

Chun, Ki-Taek, Sidney Cobb, and John R.P. French, Jr. *Measures for Psychological Assessment* (Ann Arbor: Institute for Social Research, The University of Michigan, 1975).

Clifton, H.D. *Business Data Systems: A Practical Guide to Systems Analysis and Data Processing* (London: Prentice-Hall International, 1978).

Gane, Chris, and Trish Sarson. *Structured Systems Analysis: Tools and Techniques* (Englewood Cliffs, NJ: Prentice-Hall, 1979).

Halper, Stanley D., Glenn C. Davis, P. Jarlath O'Neil-Dunne, and Pamela R. Pfau. *Handbook of EDP Auditing* (Boston: Warren, Gorham & Lamont, 1985).

Hartman, W., H. Matthes, and A. Proeme. *Management Information Systems Handbook: Analysis, Requirements Determination, Design and Development, Implementation and Evaluation* (New York: McGraw-Hill, 1968).

Jenkins, A. Milton, and John V. Carlis. "Control Flowcharting for Data Driven Systems," Working Paper MISRC-WP-76-02, Management Information Systems Research Center, University of Minnesota, Minneapolis, MN, 1975.

Kahn, R.L., and C.F. Cannell. *The Dynamics of Interviewing: Theory, Techniques and Cases* (New York: Wiley, 1966).

Kammann, R. "The Comprehensibility of Printed Instructions and the Flowchart Alternative," *Human Factors* (April 1975), pp. 183–191.

Kerlinger, Fred N. *Foundations of Behavioral Research*, 2d ed. (New York: Holt, Rinehart and Winston, 1973).

Krauss, Leonard I., and Aileen MacGahan. *Computer Fraud and Countermeasures* (Englewood Cliffs, NJ: Prentice-Hall, 1979).

Litecky, Charles R. "EDP Audit Policies of Large Accounting Firms," *The EDP Auditor* (May 1981), pp. 21–27.

Litecky, Charles R. "Effective Interviewing for EDP Audit," *The EDP Auditor*, vol. 4, 1985, pp. 31–39.

Lucas, Henry C. "The Use of an Interactive Information Storage and Retrieval System in Medical Research," *Communications of the ACM* (March 1978), pp. 197–205.

Mair, William C., Donald R. Wood, and Keagle W. Davis. *Computer Control and Audit*, 2d ed. (Altamonte Springs, FL: The Institute of Internal Auditors, 1976).

Maish, Alexander M. "A User's Behavior toward His MIS," *Management Information Systems Quarterly* (March 1979), pp. 39–52.

Moser, C.A., and G. Kalton. *Survey Methods in Social Investigation*, 2d ed. (London: Heinemann, 1971).

Nadler, David A., Philip H. Mirvis, and Cortlandt Cammann. "The Ongoing Feedback System: Experimenting with a New Managerial Tool," *Organizational Dynamics* (Spring 1976): pp. 63–80.

Nunnally, Jum C. *Psychometric Theory* (New York: McGraw-Hill, 1967).

Robinson, John P., and Phillip R. Shaver. *Measures of Social Psychological Attitudes* (Ann Arbor: Institute for Social Research, The University of Michigan, 1969).

Robinson, John P., Robert Athanasious, and Kendra B. Head. *Measures of Occupational Attitudes and Occupational Characteristics* (Ann Arbor: Institute for Social Research, The University of Michigan, 1969).

Sharratt, J.R. *Data Control Guidelines* (Manchester, England: NCC Publications, 1974).

Shneiderman, Ben, Richard Mayer, Don McKay, and Peter Heller. "Experimental Investigations of the Utility of Detailed Flowcharts in Programming," *Communications of the ACM* (June 1977), pp. 373–381.

Skinner, R.M., and R.J. Anderson. *Analytical Auditing* (Toronto: Sir Isaac Pitman, 1966).

Stanford Research Institute. *Systems Auditability and Control Study: Data Processing Audit Practices Report* (Altamonte Springs, FL: The Institute of Internal Auditors, 1977).

Whitten, Jeffrey L., Lonnie D. Bentley, and Thomas I.M. Ho. *Systems Analysis and Design Methods* (St. Louis: Times Mirror/Mosby College Publishing, 1986).

CHAPTER **21**

PERFORMANCE
MONITORING TOOLS

CHAPTER OUTLINE

Performance monitoring tools enable the auditor to obtain evidence on factors relating to system efficiency. The measurements taken are used in two ways. First, for systems that already are operational, they provide the basic data for diagnosis of problems and construction of tuning therapies. For example, data on the frequency of page faults may be used to select a paging algorithm in a virtual storage system. Second, the measurements may be used to estimate the values of parameters in analytical and simulation performance evaluation models of computer systems. For example, to evaluate the effects of a changed hardware configuration on throughput, a simulation model may be constructed. Performance monitoring tools can be used to estimate the characteristics of existing workloads (e.g., service demands) for input to the simulation model. Chapter 24 discusses these matters further.

This chapter provides an overview of performance monitoring tools. The whole subject area of performance monitoring and evaluation has been extensively researched since the early 1970s (see, for example, Kobayashi [1978] and Ferrari [1978]). Consequently, to be capable of using the various performance monitoring tools to carry out performance evaluation now requires substantial expertise. For those EDP audit groups that have responsibility for evaluating system efficiency, either a member of the group must specialize in the area or the services of a consultant must be employed because of the complexity of performance monitoring tools and the consequences of their improper use.

The chapter proceeds as follows. The first section briefly discusses some of the objects of measurement, that is, those factors that affect overall system efficiency. The second section examines the general characteristics of performance monitoring tools. The third section surveys specific types of monitors. Finally, the chapter discusses some implications of performance monitoring for maintenance of data integrity.

THE OBJECTS OF MEASUREMENT

It is not especially meaningful to give a general listing of what objects in a computer system might be measured to evaluate performance. *All* resources in a computer system can be the objects of measurement. For any particular evaluation some subset of the total resources of a system will be measured. The particular subset selected will depend on what aspect of system performance is to be evaluated and whether or not the auditor (analyst) performing the evaluation believes the resources are impacting system performance.

To illustrate these notions, assume the auditor is concerned about the slow response time in an online system. The auditor believes two factors may be causing the slow response time: channel bottlenecks and inefficient algorithms in the online program. To determine whether these factors are a problem, the auditor decides to measure CPU and channel utilization. Two further decisions now must be made. First, the auditor must determine where information on CPU and channel utilization can be found in the system. Various system state memories may be accessible to provide this information, for example, the CPU wait/busy bit, the CPU supervisor/problem state bit, and the channel interrupt bit. Second, the auditor must determine how the information is to be extracted, recorded, and presented. In this case, the auditor may choose a hardware monitor to extract and record the information. A software package then may be used to summarize and present the information, perhaps in graphical form.

GENERAL CHARACTERISTICS OF PERFORMANCE MONITORS

Performance monitors have five basic structural elements (Figure 21-1). The *sensor* detects the occurrence or nonoccurrence of an activity and the magnitude of the activity. The *selector* designates the subset of activities to be measured from the set of all activities that the monitor can measure. The *processor* transforms the data collected into a form suitable for storage and output; for example, it may count the instances of an activity that have occurred over a time period. The *recorder* writes the processed data to the storage medium used by the monitor. The *reporter* summarizes the information stored and presents it to the user of the monitor.

FIGURE 21-1
Structural elements of a performance monitor.

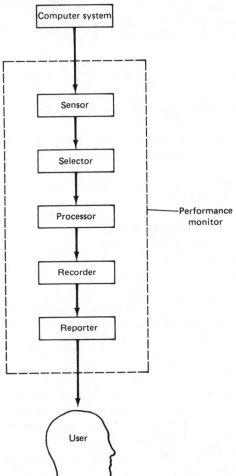

Performance monitors take five types of measurements of resource consumption activities:

Measurement	Explanation
Trace	Recorded sequence of occurrence of activities
Activity duration	Realtime consumed by activity
Relative activity	Ratio of total realtime for the activity to total elapsed time
Activity frequency	Number of times the activity occurs over a given time period
Distribution of activity	Distribution of activity times over some elapsed time period

Not all monitors are capable of making these measurements equally well. Some are designed primarily to measure certain kinds of resource consumption activities. The more expensive monitors usually have greater measurement capabilities. The overall capabilities of a monitor are a function of seven attributes of the monitor:

Attribute	Explanation
Monitor artifact	Extent to which presence of the monitor interferes with the normal operations of the system
Monitor domain (scope)	Set of resource consumption activities that the monitor can detect
Resolution (input rate)	Maximum frequency at which events can be detected and recorded correctly
Input width	Number of bits of input data a monitor can extract and process when an event occurs
Data reduction capabilities	Extent to which data can be summarized before it is stored
Data storage capabilities	Amount of memory available for storage of data
Precision	Number of digits available to represent data

Other factors affect the usefulness of a monitor. For example, the external auditor involved with performance monitoring would be concerned with the number of makes and models of machines on which the monitor will run. Monitors also vary with respect to how easy they are to install and use.

TYPES OF PERFORMANCE MONITORS

There are four types of performance monitors available to measure resource consumption activities: hardware monitors, software monitors, firmware monitors, and hybrid monitors. For each type of monitor, Table 21-1 provides an overview of the attributes that affect their usefulness to the auditor. The following sections discuss in more detail the nature of each type of monitor and their relative strengths and limitations.

TABLE 21-1
ATTRIBUTES OF DIFFERENT TYPES OF MONITORS

Attribute \ Type of monitor	Hardware	Software	Firmware	Hybrid
Monitor artifact	Zero—small	Moderate—high	Moderate—high	Small—moderate
Monitor domain	Moderate	Large	Moderate	Moderate—large
Resolution	High	Low—moderate	Moderate	Moderate—high
Input width	Moderate	High	Moderate	Moderate—high
Data reduction capabilities	Moderate	Substantial	Low—moderate	Moderate—substantial
Data storage capabilities	Moderate—large	Large	Large	Moderate—large
Precision	High	Low—moderate	Moderate	Moderate—high
Portability	Moderate—high	Low—moderate	Low	Low—moderate
Difficulty of installation/use	High	Moderate	Moderate	High

Hardware Monitors

A hardware monitor is a device connected to a host computer (the computer to be measured) that detects pulses in the host computer's electronic circuitry. Assume, for example, that the auditor is interested in the extent of overlap between the operations of the CPU and two channels. Further, the auditor wishes to distinguish between problem state and supervisor state operations in the CPU. Thus, the auditor must monitor four flip-flops in the host computer: the CPU busy/idle flip-flop, the busy/idle flip-flop for channel 1, the busy/idle flip-flop for channel 2, and the problem/supervisor flip-flop for the CPU. Using logical AND combinations of the states of the flip-flops, 12 measurements can be obtained:

1 CPU busy in problem state only
2 CPU busy in supervisor state only
3 Channel 1 busy only
4 Channel 2 busy only
5 CPU in problem state and channel 1 busy
6 CPU in problem state and channel 2 busy
7 CPU in problem state and both channels busy
8 CPU in supervisor state and channel 1 busy
9 CPU in supervisor state and channel 2 busy
10 CPU in supervisor state and both channels busy
11 Both channels busy only
12 CPU busy only

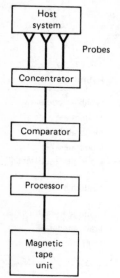

FIGURE 21-2
Structure of a simple hardware
monitor.

Note that measurement 12 is simply the addition of measurements 1 and 2. The
measurements can be printed out as counts or perhaps displayed graphically to
better illustrate the overlap that occurs.

Figure 21-2 shows the basic structure of a hardware monitor. Probes are
connected to the host system. A concentrator reduces the number of cables
from the host system to the monitor. A comparator performs a test on two or
more registers and outputs a pulse depending on the result of the test. The
processor has three major components. A patchboard allows the logic for
different kinds of tests to be specified. Counters are available to count either
event occurrences or the time interval between events. A clock generates
timing pulses. The final component of the monitor is a magnetic tape unit used
to store the measurement data.

Types of Hardware Monitors Ferrari [1978] identifies three types of hardware monitors that exist: (*a*) fixed hardware monitors, (*b*) wired-program
monitors, and (*c*) stored-program monitors.

Fixed hardware monitors are incorporated in the host system at design time.
For example, the system clock and various register displays are fixed hardware
monitors. The contents of these monitors can be displayed at a console or
accessed by programs. The monitors are useful for both measurement and
program debugging purposes. For example, the system clock can be accessed
to determine the start and stop time for a job so system throughput can be
calculated. However, fixed hardware monitors have only limited usefulness for
measurement purposes. Neither the events they monitor nor the actions they
take upon measurement can be controlled by a user.

Wired-program hardware monitors provide the user with some control over the events to be monitored and the actions to be taken on the occurrence of an event. The monitor is connected to the host system via probes onto the circuitry pins of the host computer. Different events can be monitored by changing the placement of the probes on the circuitry pins. The monitor has some type of plugboard or patch panel that allows the user to specify various Boolean functions to be performed on the events monitored, for example, an AND function on a CPU busy event and channel busy event.

The storage capabilities of wired-program hardware monitors vary. Some simply have counters: the contents of these counters are dumped periodically on magnetic tape or disk. Others have random access memory in addition to secondary storage capabilities. The random access memory can be used, for example, to store bit patterns that enter the monitor in parallel or to maintain a histogram of event types as they occur.

Stored-program hardware monitors are driven by sets of microprograms or user-coded programs. An integral part of a stored-program hardware monitor is a minicomputer that controls the operations of the monitor. Thus, the stored-program hardware monitor is the most flexible type of hardware monitor. It allows the user to modify the measurement process during the measurement period depending upon the set of conditions that occur. For example, assume a database management system is partitioned; one part resides in internal memory and the other part on a drum. The auditor wants to evaluate whether the present partitioning could be improved. Other system software also resides on the drum. The map of the drum showing the address ranges for the various system software can be stored in the monitor. When the monitor detects a reference to the drum, it can check the memory reference that is stored in fixed operating system tables that reside in internal memory and compare the address with the drum memory map. If the address falls within the range for the database management system, it increments a counter by one.

Capabilities of Hardware Monitors Because hardware monitors measure electronically the state of a system, they are able to detect very short duration events in a computer system, for example, a change of the CPU from a busy to an idle state. Thus, they are high-resolution tools. They also are able to monitor several events simultaneously, even events occurring on independent hardware units.

Hardware monitors usually have a broad domain; many types of resource consumption activities can be monitored by attaching probes or some type of interface to the circuitry of the system. However, the size of the monitor domain is affected by the architectural design of the system being measured. If the system does not provide access to important measurement points, then the domain of the hardware monitor is restricted. Architectural design to facilitate measurement becomes more important with the more widespread use of large-scale integrated circuits.

Hardware monitors cause little or no artifact and they are often portable.

The monitor functions independently of the host system. Further, it simply recognizes pulses; thus, it can be used on any system that has suitable probe points.

The input width, data reduction capabilities, data storage capabilities, and precision of hardware monitors vary. The input width depends on the number of available probes. The data reduction capabilities and data storage capabilities depend on what logical operations the monitor can perform, the types of secondary storage devices attached to the monitor, and whether or not the monitor has random access memory. Precision is a function of the word length of the counters and storage used by the monitor.

Limitations of Hardware Monitors Effective use of hardware monitors requires substantial expertise. Probes can be connected to incorrect points. Also, care must be taken to ensure stress is not placed on the probe points, which may result in damage to the hardware. To assist with the placement of probes, machine vendors may provide documentation on probe points for their hardware, particularly if they have taken monitoring requirements into account in the design of the hardware. Similarly, the vendors of hardware monitors sometimes provide libraries of probe points for the common types of machine architectures.

Perhaps the major limitation of hardware monitors is their inability to trace software-related events. For example, a hardware monitor cannot detect a program's access to a data structure since it is unable to monitor directly the contents of random access memory. Similarly, it is unable to determine whether a program variable has been modified. These types of capabilities become important when the performance of an individual program must be evaluated. Unless the sequence of state changes that occur within the program can be traced, it is difficult to determine those parts of the program that are executed most frequently and those parts that consume the most resources.

Software Monitors

A software monitor is a program (subroutine, instruction) inserted into the code of a system or another program to collect performance measurement data. If the monitor is incorporated into the operating system, usually the intent is to examine the performance of systemwide functions. If the monitor is incorporated into an application program, the intent is to gather performance data on that specific program.

Software monitors detect the execution of an instruction in a program. Thus, if the instruction results in the modification of a variable, the time series of modifications can be monitored. Similarly, if the instruction results in access to a data structure, the time series of accesses can be monitored. Any event that can be detected by the execution of a program instruction can be monitored.

Figure 21-3 shows the way a software monitor is used. First, instrumentation

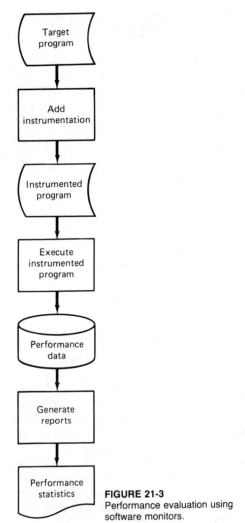

FIGURE 21-3
Performance evaluation using
software monitors.

is added to a target program (the program to be monitored). Either source or run-time instrumentation can be employed. By using source instrumentation, probe points are added manually to the target program, or alternatively a preprocessor reads the source code of the target program and inserts the probe points automatically. By using run-time instrumentation, a probe monitor routine is added to the run-time environment of the target program. Unlike source instrumentation, run-time instrumentation does not require that the target program be recompiled. After instrumentation, the target program is then executed to allow the probes to collect performance data. This data is subsequently analyzed and performance reports are then produced.

Types of Software Monitors There are two types of software monitors: (a) event-driven monitors and (b) sampling monitors. The distinction rests on the manner in which the monitors are activated.

Event-driven software monitors undertake a measurement when some type of event occurs internally to the system or program: for example, a CPU interrupt is generated or a program checkpoint is reached. Assume, for example, the auditor wants to assess the efficiency with which an interactive program executes different decision models that users call selectively to aid their decision-making process. The auditor wants to focus first on those models that are used most frequently and consume most time.

The code below is an excerpt from the interactive program (written in COBOL) and the software monitoring instructions inserted in the program.

WHAT-DEC-MØD.

```
IF DECNØ IS EQUAL TØ 6
CALL CLØCKTIME USING STARTTM
PERFØRM DEC-MØD6
CALL CLØCKTIME USING ENDTM
PERFØRM STATS.
```

The instructions execute in the following way. First, when the interactive program identifies that decision model 6 is required (DECNØ = 6), it calls a subroutine that accesses the system clock to obtain the start time of the execution of the subroutine that performs the processing related to decision model 6. Second, the program performs the subroutine that executes the decision model. Third, when the subroutine returns control, the program again accesses the system clock to determine the finish time of the event. Finally, the program performs a subroutine that writes away to some storage device the decision model number, the start time, and the finish time. At the end of the measurement period the auditor can access this data, determine the number of times a particular decision model was used, plot the distribution of execution times, and calculate relevant statistics such as the mean and variance of execution times for each decision model.

The major device used to collect data in an event-driven software monitor is a checkpoint instruction. These checkpoints may be either permanent or temporary. Permanent checkpoints are always resident in the host system, though they may be deactivated at times. For example, many permanent checkpoints exist in operating systems; the job accounting checkpoints and instructions identify the start and finish of a routine, the resources used, etc. Temporary checkpoints are inserted either manually or automatically in a program only for the measurement period and removed when the measurement period is over.

Sampling software monitors collect performance data when a signal is received from some timing device. The timing device may generate signals randomly or after constant intervals. When a signal occurs, the software monitor accesses system tables to obtain resource consumption data.

Sampling software monitors cause less system interference than event-driven software monitors because they are invoked less often; they sample the population of events rather than measure each event in the population. However, only estimates of the true characteristics of the population of events can be calculated.

The major decision to be made when using a sampling software monitor is how often events will be sampled. The auditor must trade off the benefits of increasing the accuracy of the estimates of resource consumption by more frequent sampling with the increased costs caused by more system interference. Decisions on the sampling rate should be based on (*a*) the frequency with which the event to be measured occurs, (*b*) the required accuracy of the estimates, and (*c*) the costs of measurement, which include both the cost of execution and the cost of system interference.

Capabilities of Software Monitors   The primary advantage of using a software monitor rather than a hardware monitor is the greater flexibility the software monitor usually provides to measure system events. The domain of a software monitor sometimes contains more elements; however, the elements in its domain are more macroscopic events than those in the domain of a hardware monitor, though there is some overlap of domains. With a software monitor, events are detected at the instruction level, whereas events in a hardware monitor are detected at the level of a pulse in the circuitry.

Theoretically, the input width of a software monitor is unlimited. As many checkpoints as the auditor needs to monitor events can be inserted in a program. In comparison, the input width of hardware monitors is limited by the number of probes available. Practically, the input width of a software monitor is limited by the extent of system interference (artifact) that can be tolerated.

In general, software monitors are easier to install than hardware monitors. They are also less susceptible to external interference (for example, accidental removal of probes) than hardware monitors.

Limitations of Software Monitors   Probably the major limitation of software monitors is the artifact they introduce in the system they measure. This artifact takes two forms: time and space. Time artifact occurs because the checkpoint instructions must be executed. Space artifact occurs because the checkpoint instructions must be stored in the machine. In some cases it is possible to correct for this artifact. For example, the time taken to execute a checkpoint instruction may be known and this time can be subtracted from the length of the interval affected by the instruction.

Software monitors also are not as portable as hardware monitors. Whereas in general a hardware monitor can be attached to any CPU, for efficiency reasons a software monitor often must be written in the assembly language of a specific machine; thus, it can run only on that machine. Implementing a software monitor also requires detailed knowledge of the host system or program so the checkpoints can be inserted at the correct place in the code.

A monitor that uses source instrumentation tends to have more disadvantages than a monitor that uses run-time instrumentation. The artifact introduced by a source-instrumented program is usually larger. Monitors that use source instrumentation also are usually less portable; either they require the probes to be inserted manually in the target program or they use a preprocessor to insert the probes that works only with a particular programming language. Finally, it is difficult to implement a sampling procedure to collect data. Source-instrumented monitors are not driven by timing interrupts, so sampling must be restricted to selecting a subset of the events that the monitor detects.

Firmware Monitors

Some instructions used to collect performance measurement data can be implemented as microcode. Firmware monitors operate in a similar way to software monitors. However, they have three major advantages over software monitors. First, the execution time for a microinstruction is shorter; thus, less interference is produced. Second, microinstructions allow access to some hardware indicators that cannot be accessed with a programming language; consequently, the domain of a firmware monitor overlaps both hardware and software monitors (Figure 21-4). Third, firmware monitors have higher resolution.

Relative to software monitors, firmware monitors have several disadvantages. Unlike ordinary program instructions, microinstructions usually have a very constrained space that they are permitted to occupy in the machine; thus, fewer probes can be inserted for monitoring purposes. Since firmware monitors have a high resolution, they can degrade considerably the execution speed of the host system, thereby producing a large monitor artifact. To reduce this artifact, firmware monitors often have low data reduction capabilities. Measurement data collected simply is stored as a trace, and the data then must be summarized at a later time.

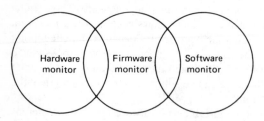

FIGURE 21-4
Relationship between domains (scope) of hardware monitors, firmware monitors, and software monitors.

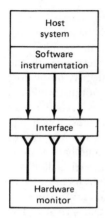

FIGURE 21-5
Basic structural components of a hybrid monitor.

Hybrid Monitors

A hybrid monitor has hardware, software, and perhaps firmware elements. The monitor consists of an external hardware device to receive, process, store, and present data collected by an internal software or firmware component (see Rose [1978]). For example, a microinstruction in a hybrid monitor may be used to output certain bit patterns that can be accessed by a hardware device having probes connected to the appropriate pins in the circuitry.

Svobodova [1976] describes various methods of implementing a hybrid monitor. Special monitor registers can be kept in main memory; software writes the events to be monitored to these registers and the hardware component of the hybrid monitor detects changes to these registers. The monitor also can be installed in a memory bus; again, software detects signals passing along the bus and writes them to registers that are read by the hardware component of the monitor. Whatever the technique used, the basic design principle is the same. An interface exists between the software (firmware) component of a hybrid monitor and the hardware component. The software component writes events monitored as signals to the interface, and the hardware component reads and processes these signals (Figure 21-5). The software component also may control the external hardware component.

Hybrid monitors have two major advantages. First, they reduce the artifact caused by the monitoring process. The domain of hybrid monitors includes the domain of hardware monitors plus some subset of the domain of firmware and software monitors. However, they do not cause as much interference as software and firmware monitors. Second, in general, it is easier to instrument a system with a hybrid monitor than a software monitor. Placement of software probes in the host system can be a complex task. The placement of probes with a hybrid monitor is more well-defined.

The major limitation of hybrid monitors is that they are not able to monitor all the types of events that can be monitored by a software or firmware monitor.

PERFORMANCE MONITORING AND DATA INTEGRITY

Auditors should have two concerns about data integrity whenever a performance monitor is used. First, they must determine whether the monitor has been installed correctly in the host system. Here the concern is with the integrity of the measurements made by the monitor and the integrity of the host system processes after instrumentation. If the host system is not instrumented correctly, the measurements taken will be erroneous and wrong decisions may be made that have serious consequences; for example, an unnecessary change may be made to a hardware/software configuration. Further, the integrity of processes in the host system may be corrupted; again, this could have serious consequences if the host system is the operating system, a compiler, a database management system, or a teleprocessing monitor. Second, auditors must try to determine whether a monitor has been used to violate data integrity. Here the concern is with unauthorized use of the monitor to breach data privacy. The following two sections briefly discuss each of these concerns.

Ensuring Correct System Instrumentation

The proper placement of the probes of a hardware monitor and the checkpoints of a software monitor is a difficult task. Stimler [1974] recommends using test programs to check proper placement of probes with a hardware monitor. If test programs are not available from the monitor vendor, he argues special assembly level programs should be prepared that execute loops of known instructions a predetermined number of times. Resource utilization by these programs should be calculated and compared with measured resource utilization to validate the placement of probes.

Proper placement of checkpoints is facilitated if the auditor uses a software monitor that automatically inserts checkpoints at user-specified locations in the host system. Ferrari and Liu [1975] describe a software monitor that can be used interactively to instrument a program. The monitor automatically inserts the checkpoints that issue calls to either standard predefined measurement routines already included in the monitor or user-coded measurement routines. Further, the monitor checks that checkpoints are not inserted at locations in the host system where they might cause errors, for example, at locations referenced in the program as data and not instructions. Similarly, Power [1983] describes several execution analyzers that can be used to instrument software automatically for performance monitoring purposes.

Some software monitors also validate any user-supplied measurement routines. These monitors impose various restrictions on the code supplied by the user; for example, it must not contain illegal or privileged instructions, it cannot modify itself or other measurement routines, it must not store data or branch into the host system, and it must not contain backward branches (see, further, Ferrari [1978]). Still other types of checks can be applied. For example, the monitor may check whether a checkpoint would cause intolerable interference, thereby destroying the integrity of a time-critical host system process.

Ensuring Maintenance of Data Privacy

Use of a performance monitor within an installation must be controlled carefully. Since monitors have access to lower-level elements within the system hierarchy of resources (for example, memory ports and input/output channels), they can be used to breach the privacy of data. For each user the permitted domain of the monitor must be defined and enforced via access controls (see, also, Chapter 9). Application users should be restricted to monitoring resource consumption of their own processes only. The database administrator may be granted more global privileges to optimize overall resource consumption.

The usual types of access controls should be applied to a monitor. In the case of hardware monitors, physical access to the monitor must be restricted. Even if the hardware monitor is installed permanently in the machine, physical access to its controls should be prevented. Saltzer [1974] expresses his concerns about how the lights and switches on an operator console can be used for unauthorized purposes. In the case of software monitors, access to the monitor should be controlled by the operating system. A log of users of the monitor also can be kept.

The performance monitor itself also must be protected. As a piece of software that may be used widely within an installation, a software monitor is a suitable target for a Trojan horse (see, further, Chapter 13).

SUMMARY

Performance monitoring tools enable the auditor to obtain evidence on hardware and software resource consumption within an installation. This evidence is used as a basis for making decisions on how resource utilization can be improved.

Four types of performance monitoring tools are available: (*a*) hardware monitors, (*b*) software monitors, (*c*) firmware monitors, and (*d*) hybrid monitors. Hardware monitors take measurements through probes attached to the circuitry of the system hardware. Software monitors take measurements through checkpoints inserted into the software that runs on the system. Firmware monitors take measurements through the microcode inserted in the system. Hybrid monitors use an external hardware device to process data collected by an internal software/firmware component. The different types of monitors have varying capabilities with respect to their scope, resolution, input width, data reduction and storage capabilities, precision, portability, and the artifact they produce.

When using a performance monitor, the auditor must ensure that the monitor is installed correctly; otherwise, the measurements taken may be invalid, or the integrity of the host system may be corrupted. When a hardware monitor is used, test programs should be run to determine whether or not the probes have been placed correctly. If possible, a software monitor should be used that automatically inserts user-specified checkpoints into the host program.

Use of a performance monitor also must be controlled. Monitors can be used to breach data privacy. The normal access controls should be applied to monitors. The monitor itself also must be protected against unauthorized modifications.

REVIEW QUESTIONS

21-1 What is a performance monitor? Why does use of a performance monitor require special expertise?

21-2 Give three examples of objects in a computer system that might be measured by a performance monitor. Briefly explain why each of these objects may be measured.

21-3 What constitutes the sensor in (*a*) a hardware monitor and (*b*) a software monitor?

21-4 Briefly explain why it may be necessary to carry out some form of reduction on data collected by a monitor before it is stored. Give two examples of reductions that may be applied to trace measurements.

21-5 Briefly explain why the auditor may be interested in obtaining the distribution of disk seek times for an online realtime program when attempting to improve the efficiency of the program.

21-6 What is meant by monitor artifact? Why is it important for the auditor to know the extent of artifact that a monitor may produce? Is it possible to control for artifact? Explain.

21-7 If an auditor wants to measure the extent of CPU and channel overlap, how can he or she set up the Boolean AND operator required in a hardware monitor?

21-8 Briefly explain the difference between a wired-program hardware monitor and a stored-program hardware monitor. Which type of hardware monitor provides the user with more flexibility? Why?

21-9 Give an example of a fixed hardware monitor and an example of how the monitor might be used during an evaluation of system efficiency.

21-10 Why does a hardware monitor have greater resolution than a software monitor?

21-11 Give two factors that limit the domain of a hardware monitor, and briefly explain how they limit the domain.

21-12 Briefly explain the relative capabilities of hardware monitors and software monitors with respect to input width.

21-13 Briefly explain the difference between an event-driven software monitor and a sampling software monitor. What are the relative advantages and disadvantages of each type of monitor?

21-14 How does a checkpoint instruction in a software monitor work? What is the difference between a permanent checkpoint and a temporary checkpoint? Give an example of each.

21-15 Give two examples of standard (vendor-written) measurement routines you would expect to see in software monitors. Give an example of a measurement routine the user may have to write.

21-16 Briefly explain how a software monitor may be used to measure disk seek time. What type of output might be generated for the user to examine?

21-17 Theoretically, the input width of a software monitor is unlimited; however, practically it is limited by the extent of interference it produces. Explain.

21-18 How do the domains of hardware and software monitors differ? Give an example of an event that would be only in the domain of a hardware monitor, one that would be only in the domain of a software monitor, and one that would be in both domains.

21-19 Briefly explain what is meant by time and space artifact.

21-20 Give two advantages that firmware monitors have over software monitors. What problems may arise because of the high resolution capabilities of firmware monitors?

21-21 Briefly explain the purpose of the interface in a hybrid monitor.

21-22 Why do hybrid monitors produce a lower artifact than software monitors but a higher artifact than hardware monitors?

21-23 What is meant by instrumenting a system for performance monitoring? Why is it desirable for vendors to consider instrumentation during the design stages of a computer system?

21-24 What problems arise during performance monitoring if a system is incorrectly instrumented? How can incorrect instrumentation be detected in a hardware monitor and a software monitor?

21-25 Give two advantages of using a software monitor that instruments a system automatically.

21-26 Why is it important to control who gains access to a performance monitor? Why is a performance monitor a likely target for someone wishing to carry out unauthorized activities in a computer installation?

21-27 Why must the domain of a performance monitor be controlled? Briefly explain how it is possible to limit the domain for different types of users of a monitor.

21-28 In general, why should the operator console not be used for display purposes by a hardware monitor?

MULTIPLE CHOICE QUESTIONS

21-1 The objects of performance measurement are:
a The hardware resources
b System software resources
c All resources in a computer system
d Application system resources

21-2 The structural element of a performance monitor that determines the subset of activities to be measured is the:
a Selector
b Processor
c Sensor
d Reporter

21-3 The type of measurement whereby the realtime consumed by an activity is monitored is called:

a An activity frequency measurement

b A trace measurement

c A relative frequency measurement

d An activity duration measurement

21-4 Monitor artifact is:

a The noise present in the set of measurements taken

b The extent to which the presence of the monitor interferes with the normal system operations

c The extent to which the measurements collected must be recorded in summary form

d The extent to which low-level activities that the monitor cannot detect must be accounted for by an average resource consumption measure

21-5 The set of resource consumption activities that the monitor can detect is called the:

a Monitor resolution

b Monitor precision

c Monitor input width

d Monitor domain

21-6 Monitor resolution indicates:

a The maximum frequency at which events can be detected and recorded correctly

b The percentage of measurements that are likely to be incorrect

c The number of bits of input data that a monitor can extract and process when an event occurs

d The extent to which the monitor can measure high-frequency events

21-7 The hardware monitor component that performs a test on two or more registers and outputs a pulse depending on the result of the test is called a:

a Probe

b Concentrator

c Comparator

d Pulse board

21-8 A register display on a console is an example of a:

a Wired-program hardware monitor

b Fixed hardware monitor

c Firmware monitor

d Stored-program hardware monitor

21-9 The difference between a wired-program hardware monitor and a stored-program monitor is:

a A wired-program hardware monitor does not have a concentrator

b A stored-program hardware monitor does not use probes

c A wired-program hardware monitor never has random access memory

d Wired-program hardware monitors are not driven by microprograms or user-coded programs

21-10 Which of the following is a limitation of hardware monitors:

a Are unable to trace software-related events

b Have high monitor artifact

c Are not portable

d Have limited domain

21-11 Sampling software monitors collect performance data when:
a Some type of event occurs internally to the system or program
b A signal is received from a timing device
c A state change occurs in a register
d A random number generator produces a number that falls within a designated range

21-12 With a sampling software monitor, a decision on the sampling rate should be based on:
a The required accuracy of the estimates
b The cost of monitor artifact
c The frequency with which the event to be measured occurs
d All the above

21-13 Relative to hardware monitors, software monitors have a:
a Smaller artifact
b Smaller input width
c Larger domain
d Higher portability

21-14 Relative to software monitors, which of the following is *not* an advantage of using a hybrid monitor:
a Lower interference
b Greater access to hardware indicators
c More probes
d Higher resolution

21-15 The purpose of the hardware component of a hybrid monitor is to:
a Receive, process, store, and present the performance data collected
b Instrument the host system
c Pass data to the memory bus
d Write the events to be monitored to the storage registers

21-16 Which of the following is a limitation of hybrid monitors:
a Higher artifact than software and firmware monitors
b Smaller domain than software and firmware monitors
c Harder to instrument a system than a software monitor
d Cannot measure any of the events in the domain of a hardware monitor

21-17 Which of the following would *not* occur as a result of incorrect instrumentation of a system for performance monitoring purposes:
a The integrity of processes in the host system is corrupted
b Erroneous measurements are taken
c Privacy violations occur
d The performance monitor is damaged

EXERCISES AND CASES

21-1 As the manager of internal audit for an organization, you are called one day to a meeting with the controller and the data processing manager. The controller informs you that a limited amount of funds has been made available to hire a consultant to carry out some performance evaluation within the data processing department. Since the funds are limited, however, the controller wants the consultant to focus on those application systems where there is most likely to be a payoff. She asks you and the data processing manager to provide her with a list of recommendations on the systems that should be evaluated.

Required: Outline how you would go about determining which systems you would recommend be subject to performance evaluation. Be sure to indicate the variables/attributes of the systems on which you would base your decision.

21-2 As more users are added to an interactive system, response times get longer. The project manager responsible for the system is perplexed because he believes the system should be able to cope with many more users without any noticeable increase in response times. He cannot determine whether the response time problem is hardware- or software-based.

Required: Identify five system activities that might be measured to determine whether the response time problems are hardware- or software-based. Explain the type of measurement you would undertake—trace, activity, duration, etc.—and why you would measure the activities you list in the manner that you specify. For your information, terminals in the system are located in clusters in remote locations. These clusters are connected to a local controller that in turn is connected to a frontend communications controller for the central machine. The software that handles the interactive system consists of a master program that calls subroutines from a library to handle the various functions to be performed in an interactive request.

21-3 Refer to Exercise and Case 21-2. For *each* activity you intend to measure, indicate whether you would use a hardware or software monitor for measurement purposes, and explain the reasons for your choice.

21-4 You are the manager of internal audit for a large company that uses advanced computer systems: distributed, online realtime update, database management, etc. Management of your company has decided that computer operations are sufficiently large that it is worthwhile to employ a full-time person with expertise in computer performance evaluation. This person will be responsible for setting up and carrying out a program of performance review of all computer operations.

Management recognizes that the person responsible for performance evaluations at times will be in a position to breach the integrity of systems. They are concerned that the powers vested in the person not be abused.

Required: Management asks you to write a brief report recommending some controls that might be implemented and exercised over the person to ensure proper performance of duties.

21-5 Grouse and Whistler Credit Union (G & W) is a Vancouver-based credit union set up by a number of skiing clubs to service the financial needs of their members. The management of G & W is aggressive, and they have invested heavily in computer systems as a means of providing their members with a vast and flexible range of services. They are especially proud of their Hot-Dogger online system that allows members to use their own microcomputers to gain access to many of the services offered by the credit union.

In recent months the membership of G & W has been increasing rapidly. Many of the new members are young, upwardly mobile professionals who have access to a microcomputer and who delight in using microcomputers in innovative ways. Accordingly, the demand for the services offered via the Hot-Dogger system has grown substantially.

With the growth in membership and increasing use of the Hot-Dogger system, response time for all online systems has declined. Management has been especially concerned that these slower response times will result in lost goodwill among the members. Consequently, they have authorized the expansion of computer facilities to meet the increased demand for services.

To determine how the computer system should be expanded, an investigation of the existing facilities was carried out by the information systems manager at G & W. On the basis of this investigation she concluded that the primary reason for the declining response times was insufficient disk capacity. She argued that the Hot-Dogger system was now consuming considerable resources and that disk space was the bottleneck.

To rectify the situation, she recommended the purchase of five new disk drives and a disk controller to service the drives. She did not recommend the purchase of a new channel, however, as an investigation of channel utilization had shown that one of the channels in the system was only lightly utilized. The new controller and new disk drives were attached to this channel when they were installed.

The addition of the new controller and new disk drives produced no improvement in response times. In fact, response times continued to decline rapidly. Initially the information systems manager thought that the channel servicing the new controller and new disk drives might now be overloaded. However, performance statistics indicated that the channel was still only lightly utilized.

Required: You are an EDP auditor with expertise in computer performance evaluation. The information systems manager of G & W has asked you to examine her system and to advise her on the problems that exist and the remedial actions that will then be needed. Write a brief report advising her on (*a*) the possible problems that may be causing the poor response times, (*b*) the measurements you intend to take to isolate the problem, and (*c*) the monitoring tools you will use to take the measurements.

21-6 In an effort to decrease the backlog of information systems that need development within your organization, management has supported the growth of end-user computing. So far most developments have been confined to microcomputer applications developed by managers and analysts using widely available microcomputer software. However, end-users have become increasingly sophisticated in their information system needs and their abilities to develop their own systems.

As a result of pressures from several managers who are active in the development and implementation of end-user systems, top management authorized the purchase of a widely used, sophisticated, fourth-generation package to be run on your organization's mainframe. The managers argued that the package would overcome some major limitations they were experiencing in their efforts to develop innovative applications aimed at giving the organization a competitive edge.

The package was installed, and end-users quickly started to experiment with its capabilities. Almost immediately, however, response times and throughput on the mainframe degraded considerably. The information systems manager, who had opposed the purchase of the package in the first place, called for its removal from the system. The end-user managers reacted angrily and argued that he was somehow sabotaging their efforts to use the package. Although no benchmark tests had been undertaken with the package before its purchase and installation, they pointed to its successful use in over 40 other computer centers.

Required: You are the internal audit manager for the organization. Top management has directed the controller to resolve the problems, and he has asked your assistance since he knows you have expertise in computer systems performance evaluation. Write a brief report indicating how you will approach the task, the possible causes of the problem, the type of performance data you will gather, and the tools you will use to gather the performance data.

ANSWERS TO MULTIPLE CHOICE QUESTIONS

21-1 c	21-6 a	21-10 a	21-14 c
21-2 a	21-7 c	21-11 b	21-15 a
21-3 d	21-8 b	21-12 d	21-16 b
21-4 b	21-9 d	21-13 c	21-17 d
21-5 d			

REFERENCES

Anderson, Gordon E. "The Coordinated Use of Five Performance Evaluation Methodologies," *Communications of the ACM* (February 1984), pp. 119–125.

Arndt, Fred R., and G. M. Oliver. "Hardware Monitoring of Real-Time Interactive System Performance," *Computer* (July–August 1972), pp. 25–29.

Baboglu, Ozalp. "On Constructing Synthetic Programs for Virtual Memory Environments," in Domenico Ferrari and Massimo Spadoni, eds., *Experimental Computer Performance Evaluation* (Amsterdam: North-Holland, 1981), pp. 195–204.

Cabrera, Luis Felipe. "Benchmarking UNIX—A Comparative Study," in Domenico Ferrari and Massimo Spadoni, eds., *Experimental Computer Performance Evaluation* (Amsterdam: North-Holland, 1981), pp. 205–215.

Deitch, M. "Analytical Queuing Model for CICS Capacity Planning," *IBM Systems Journal*, vol. 21, no. 4, 1982, pp. 454–470.

Ferrari, Domenico. "Architecture and Instrumentation in a Modular Interactive System," *Computer* (November 1973), pp. 25–29.

Ferrari, Domenico. *Computer Systems Performance Evaluation* (Englewood Cliffs, NJ: Prentice-Hall, 1978).

Ferrari, Domenico, and Mark Liu. "A General-Purpose Software Measurement Tool," *Software-Practice and Experience* (April–June, 1975), pp. 181–192.

Ferrari, Domenico, and Vito Minetti, "A Hybrid Measurement Tool for Minicomputers," in Domenico Ferrari and Massimo Spadoni, eds., *Experimental Computer Performance Evaluation* (Amsterdam: North-Holland, 1981), pp. 217–233.

Fleming, Philip J., and John J. Wallace. "How Not to Lie with Statistics: The Correct Way to Summarize Benchmark Results," *Communications of the ACM* (March 1986), pp. 218–221.

Kobayashi, Hisashi. *Modeling and Analysis: An Introduction to System Performance Evaluation Methodology* (Reading, MA: Addison-Wesley, 1978).

Lucas, Henry C. "Performance Evaluation and Monitoring," *Computing Surveys* (September 1971), pp. 79–91.

Miller, Edward F., Jr. "Bibliography on Techniques of Computer Performance Analysis," *Computer* (September–October 1972), pp. 39–47.

Power, L. R. "Design and Use of a Program Execution Analyzer," *IBM Systems Journal,* vol. 22, no. 3, 1983, pp. 271–294.

Ramamoorthy, C. V., K. H. Kim, and W. T. Chen. "Optimal Placement of Software Monitors Aiding Systematic Testing," *IEEE Transactions on Software Engineering* (December 1975), pp. 403–411.

Rose, Clifford A. "A Measurement Procedure for Queueing Network Models of Computer Systems," *Computing Surveys* (September 1978), pp. 263–280.

Saltzer, Jerome H. "Protection and the Control of Information Sharing in Multics," *Communications of the ACM* (July 1974), pp. 388–402.

Shermer, Jack E., and John B. Robertson. "Instrumentation of Time-Shared Systems," *Computer* (July–August 1972), pp. 39–48.

Stimler, Saul. *Data Processing Systems: Their Performance, Evaluation, Measurement, and Improvement* (Trenton, NJ: Motivational Learning Programs, 1974).

Svobodova, Liba. *Computer Performance Measurement and Evaluation Methods: Analysis and Applications* (New York: American Elsevier, 1976).

PART FIVE

EVIDENCE EVALUATION

Once the evidence on a system has been collected, it must be evaluated. The evaluation process involves the auditor weighting and combining piecemeal evidence to make a global decision on whether a system safeguards assets, maintains data integrity, achieves organizational goals effectively, and consumes resources efficiently.

It is the evidence evaluation process that requires auditors to make the most use of their judgment capabilities. Little is known about how various evidence should be weighted and combined to make a global evaluation. To a large extent, auditors must rely on their intuition and experience when assessing the impact of a system's strength or weakness on the overall quality of the system.

The next three chapters examine the evidence evaluation process for the four major decisions the auditor must make: whether the system safeguards assets, whether it maintains data integrity, whether it is effective, and whether it is efficient. Until more is known about the evaluation process, the chapters can provide only some guidelines to assist making high-quality evaluation decisions. Currently, it is this area that requires the most intensive research effort.

CHAPTER 22

EVALUATING ASSET SAFEGUARDING AND DATA INTEGRITY

CHAPTER OUTLINE

When auditors evaluate how well assets are safeguarded, they attempt to determine whether or not the asset could be destroyed, stolen, or used for unauthorized purposes. When auditors evaluate how well data integrity is maintained, they attempt to determine the completeness, soundness, purity, and veracity of the data. In both cases the auditor is concerned with expected losses given the controls in place.

This chapter examines both the decision on how well assets are safeguarded and the decision on how well data integrity is maintained. It considers these decisions jointly because there is a large overlap in the evaluation methodologies that can be used for each decision.

The chapter proceeds as follows. The first section discusses various measures of asset safeguarding and data integrity that underlie the auditor's judgment process. Next, the chapter examines various qualitative and quantitative approaches to the evaluation decision. Finally, since asset safeguarding and maintenance of data integrity are not costless processes, the chapter considers the evaluation decision within a cost-effectiveness framework.

MEASURES OF ASSET SAFEGUARDING AND DATA INTEGRITY

To evaluate how well assets are safeguarded and data integrity is maintained, the auditor needs some kind of measurement scale. Asset safeguarding and maintenance of data integrity are not all or nothing affairs; assets are safeguarded and systems maintain data integrity to varying degrees.

The measure of *asset safeguarding* that the auditor uses is the expected loss that occurs if the asset is destroyed, stolen, or used for unauthorized purposes. The auditor may assign different probabilities to the different losses that could occur; that is, if there is uncertainty surrounding the size of the dollar losses that result if assets are not safeguarded, the losses can be described via a probability distribution.

The measure of *data integrity* used by the auditor depends on the nature of the data item on which the auditor focuses. In general, the auditor is interested in the extent to which a system of internal control can produce errors. If the auditor is concerned with a monetary data item, data integrity will be evaluated in terms of the *dollar error* that could have been produced. If the auditor is concerned with a quantity figure, say, the amount of an inventory item, data integrity will be evaluated in terms of the *quantity error* that could have been produced. If the auditor simply is concerned with whether or not a data item is in error, say, a name and address record, data integrity will be evaluated in terms of the *number* of data items that might be in error. For these last two cases, however, ultimately the auditor still must translate a quantity error and a number error into a dollar consequence so the cost-effectiveness of controls can be evaluated.

Since most computer systems contain stochastic elements, data integrity must be assessed in terms of a *probability distribution* of possible error. If all errors in computer systems were deterministic, a single point estimate of error

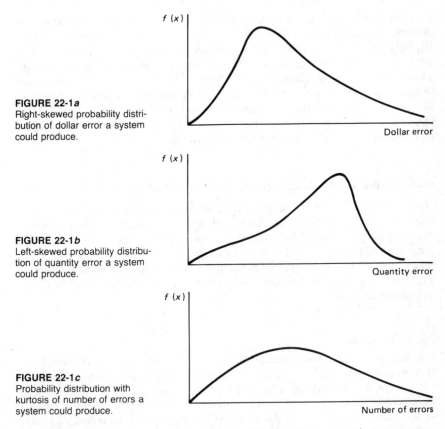

FIGURE 22-1a
Right-skewed probability distribution of dollar error a system could produce.

FIGURE 22-1b
Left-skewed probability distribution of quantity error a system could produce.

FIGURE 22-1c
Probability distribution with kurtosis of number of errors a system could produce.

would suffice. For example, assume the only error that occurs in a computer system is a program error relating to transaction type Z, where a quantity amount is multiplied by $5 instead of $4. Estimating the error produced is simple: the total quantity amount for transaction type Z can be determined and multiplied by the $1 error to obtain the total error.

However, some controls in computer systems fail probabilistically. For example, a clerk randomly may transcribe a wrong amount onto a source document, which the input validation program may be unable to detect. Data communications controls may not detect all errors resulting from noise on a communications line. Thus, the *actual* error produced depends on the nature and seriousness of the errors that occur, the timing of the errors, the ways in which they compound and compensate, the extent to which errors are deterministic or probabilistic, etc. These factors affect the mean, variance, skewness, and kurtosis of the probability distribution of error that could occur.

To illustrate these concepts, Figures 22-1a, 22-1b, and 22-1c show examples of probability distributions of errors that a system might produce. Figure 22-1a shows a probability distribution of error for a dollar data item; note how the distribution is skewed to the right. Figure 22-1b shows a probability distribution of error for a quantity data item; note how the distribution is skewed to the left. Figure 22-1c shows a probability distribution of error for the number of data items that could be in error; note the flatness (kurtosis) of the distribution. Thus, the shapes of the probability distributions of error are important indicators of the risk an auditor faces when making a decision about the materiality of the error that a system could produce. For example, Figure 22-1c shows it is most likely that the error produced will be "small"; however, there is a possibility that a large error could be produced.

QUALITATIVE APPROACHES TO THE EVALUATION DECISION

Historically, auditors have relied upon their experience and know-how to make decisions on how well a system safeguards assets and maintains data integrity. This qualitative approach to making the evaluation judgment is still the most commonly used approach. More recently, however, research has been undertaken on computer systems that will support the auditor's judgment process. The following sections examine both types of qualitative approaches to the evaluation decision.

Auditor Judgment

When auditors make a judgment on the overall reliability of a computer system, their decision making passes through three phases. First, they must identify all the cues or factors that are relevant to their evaluation decision. Second, they must weight these cues as to their importance in affecting the overall reliability of the system. Third, they must combine these cues in some manner to make a global judgment about the overall reliability of the system.

Substantial research has now been undertaken on how well auditors perform each of these decision making phases (see, for example, Libby [1981]). Basically the research confirms more general results obtained elsewhere on the quality of human judgment processes. The following sections briefly review those aspects of the judgment process that are problematical. They also provide some suggestions to help overcome the likely deficiencies in decision making that will arise.

Identifying Relevant Cues As a first step in the evaluation decision, the auditor must attempt to ensure that all relevant cues have been identified. The cues are simply the system characteristics that affect asset safeguarding or data integrity, for example, controls and data volumes for different transaction types. The evaluation process can be flawed badly if important cues are omitted. Unfortunately, research results suggest that auditors may fail to consider all the relevant cues and that they also may avoid searching for cues that contradict their initial assessment of the overall reliability of the system.

A traditional technique used to ensure all relevant cues are considered is a checklist such as an internal control questionnaire. Use of a checklist simply recognizes that auditors may forget to gather evidence on particular aspects of asset safeguarding and data integrity. Checklists have been enhanced and extended in various ways. For example, Chapter 2 illustrated the use of control matrices, which combine checklists of controls with the assets the controls are supposed to protect. Similarly, automated checklists are now available in the form of interactive computer programs that adapt the list of cues to be considered by the auditor based upon information provided by the auditor as evidence gathering and evidence evaluation tasks proceed.

Weighting Relevant Cues   One of the more difficult tasks to perform when evaluating how well a system safeguards assets and maintains data integrity is to determine the relative weighting that should be given to the different internal control cues. For example, what impact does the absence of a control have on data privacy? How sensitive is the overall dollar error rate produced to varying error rates in a system component?

The ways in which the various factors compound and interact to affect asset safeguarding and data integrity are complex. Psychological evidence suggests that decision makers who undertake complex judgment processes often have poor insight into the importance they attach to various cues (see Slovic and Lichtenstein [1971]). They overestimate the importance of minor cues and underestimate the importance of a few major cues.

How can auditor decision making on the relative importance of cues be improved? One way is to use formal quantitative models in conjunction with qualitative models. Formal models are discussed later in this chapter, but an important advantage of using formal models is that they allow sensitivity analyses to be undertaken. For example, changes in the overall reliability of a system can be assessed as error rates in different controls are varied. In this way those attributes of a system that are critical to safeguarding assets or maintaining data integrity can be assessed. Auditors can then focus their attention on those attributes which are critical when they attempt to assign weights to cues.

Another technique for improving decision making is to provide feedback to auditors on the weights they attach to various cues when they make a judgment on asset safeguarding or data integrity. These weights can be determined by using statistical models to regress the auditor's overall judgment with the values of the attributes that affect asset safeguarding or data integrity. For example, the auditor might make a judgment on overall system reliability on a scale ranging from zero (totally unreliable) to one hundred (totally reliable). This rating constitutes the dependent variable in the regression model. For each decision the values of the cues that affect the decision must be determined; these cues are the independent variables in the regression model. For example, the presence or absence of a control can be coded as a binary variable, or an error rate can be coded as a continuous variable.

The beta values for the independent variables provide "objective" measures of the weightings auditors attach to these factors. It is useful for auditors to compare the weightings auditors think they give to factors (subjective weightings) with the objective weightings calculated via the regression model (see, further, Libby [1981]). The divergence of the subjective and objective weights is a measure of the auditors' insight into their decision processes. By knowing the extent of this divergence, auditors can evaluate better the weights they attach to various cues.

Making the Global Judgment One finding consistently appears in research studies that examine the strengths and limitations of humans as decision makers; namely, individuals have only limited abilities to integrate information from various sources to make accurate and reliable overall judgments about complex phenomena. Indeed, as a result of these limitations, formal models are sometimes used in place of humans when a global judgment must be made. For example, many financial institutions now use credit granting models rather than loan officers to decide on whether credit should be given to a customer.

It has been a difficult research task to determine how well auditors perform the global evaluation judgment. Ideally, the quality of auditor decision making on how well a system safeguards assets and maintains data integrity could be assessed by determining the *accuracy* of auditor judgments. Unfortunately, assessing the accuracy of auditor judgments is not a straightforward issue. Inaccurate judgments only become obvious some time after the judgment has been made. Moreover, the judgment must be blatantly wrong for its poor quality to become apparent; for example, a system on which the auditor gives an unqualified judgment eventually fails. For a vast range of intermediate cases, a system that does not safeguard assets or maintain data integrity causes an organization losses, but these losses are not crippling.

In the absence of an accuracy measure, two other measures used to assess the quality of auditor decision making are consensus and consistency. Consensus means different auditors would make the same judgment on how well a system safeguards assets or maintains data integrity. Consistency means the same auditor would make the same evaluation judgment on a system if it were to be evaluated again at a later time and the same internal control conditions applied.

The studies that have been carried out on how well auditors make the global evaluation judgment have produced conflicting results. For example: Ashton [1974] found a high level of consensus among auditors in their judgments on the reliability of an internal control system for payroll; however, Weber [1978] found that auditors were inaccurate when they estimated the range of the probability distribution of error that could be produced by an inventory system. Nonetheless, there now seems to be general agreement among researchers that auditors suffer the same limitations as other humans when they have to make global judgments on the reliability of internal control systems.

To enhance the quality of their decision making, some auditors currently use different types of formal models to assist the judgment process. For example, the research described below on expert systems has been funded in part by audit firms who recognize the difficulties associated with making accurate and reliable global judgments. Similarly, some firms now use computer programs to assist in the evaluation of internal control. These programs recognize critical combinations of controls that lead to strengths or weaknesses in the overall internal control system (see, for example, Deloitte Haskins & Sells [1986]).

To increase judgment quality, auditors can be trained so they are sensitive to some of the problematical aspects of making global judgments on the reliability of internal control. Again, having recognized the error-prone nature of the decision on system reliability, many audit firms now focus on the global evaluation judgment as a major part of their training programs. Auditors are taught techniques to increase judgment accuracy, consensus, and consistency.

Recent research has also examined whether better judgments are made by groups of auditors rather than by individual auditors (see, for example, Trotman [1985]). Group judgments can be made in two ways (see, further, Ferrell [1985]). First, mathematical aggregates of individual decisions can be obtained; for example, the average (mean) judgment of several individual auditors is calculated. Members of the group do not interact with each other when mathematical aggregation is used. Second, behavioral aggregates can be obtained whereby individuals discuss the judgment and agree upon a decision. Various techniques have been developed to improve the quality of group decision making when behavioral aggregates are used, for example, brainstorming, the Delphi technique, the Nominal Group Technique, and the estimate-talk-estimate technique (see, further, Gustafson and Huber [1977]).

Unfortunately, after extensive research on the quality of group decision making in a variety of settings, the results are equivocal. Many factors seem to affect whether the group will be successful, for example, the group size, group communication patterns, and the perceived status of members (see, further, Swap [1984]). Thus, while the initial results in the audit domain are encouraging, much more work needs to be done to determine the circumstances in which auditor group decision making leads to higher-quality judgments.

Global judgments also might be improved if better data reduction techniques were developed to enable auditors to get a better grasp of the overall patterns that exist in the piecemeal data. Unfortunately, little research has been done in this area. Presumably, however, data reduction techniques like filtering, graphical presentation, color, and aggregation must facilitate the global judgment in some way. As more research is undertaken on auditor decision support systems, the types of data reduction techniques that are useful may become apparent (see, also, Chapter 17).

Expert Systems

Auditors have increasingly recognized their limitations as decision makers; consequently, they have sought ways to improve their judgments. The use of quantitative models to improve auditor decision making is described later in the chapter, but in this section the focus is on use of expert systems as a qualitative approach to improved auditor decision making. Recall, Chapter 17 first discussed the use of expert systems in auditing to support the evidence collection process. This chapter now discusses how expert systems can be used to support the evidence evaluation process.

Motivations for Using Expert Systems   As discussed in the previous section, the evidence evaluation judgment is complex and error-prone. For several reasons, expert systems can facilitate and enhance the quality of the decision. First, expert systems make available to a large number of auditors the knowledge typically possessed by only a small number of auditors. By definition, expertise is a scarce resource. When expertise is embodied in an expert system, however, it can be accessed and used by many auditors without the expert's having to be present. Thus, an expert system provides a mechanism for effectively disseminating and operationalizing expertise in the audit domain.

Second, as computer technology evolves even more rapidly in the future, it will be increasingly difficult for auditors to remain knowledgeable across the range of systems that they will confront in an audit. An audit firm might handle this complexity by designating certain auditors as having responsibility for remaining current in a particular technology, embodying their expertise in an expert system, and disseminating their expertise to other auditors in the firm via the expert system.

Third, expert systems provide a mechanism for increasing consensus and consistency in evaluation judgments. Since an expert system can be used to guide an auditor through a series of judgmental steps, it ensures (*a*) important judgments are not omitted; (*b*) the auditor is aware of significant information that may affect a judgment; (*c*) the auditor is alerted to judgmental inconsistencies; and (*d*) the auditor is aware of alternative judgments that might be made on the basis of the evidence available.

Nature of an Expert System   Chapter 17 defined an expert system as a program which encapsulates the knowledge that human experts have about a particular domain and which can reproduce that knowledge when confronted with a particular problem. To emulate human expertise, the system has at least two major components (Figure 22-2). First, domain knowledge elicited from an expert is stored in a "knowledge base." The knowledge base contains well-established facts about the domain of interest and rules that represent the heuristics used by experts to solve problems in the domain. Second, an "inference engine" uses the knowledge base to solve particular problems presented to the expert system. It employs some type of logic to establish interrelationships among facts and rules to reach a conclusion about a problem in the domain of interest.

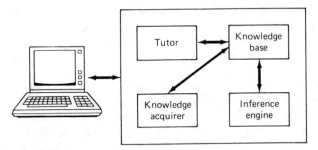

FIGURE 22-2
Major components in an expert system.

In some cases two other components are also present in an expert system (Figure 22-2): (*a*) a tutorial component may be used to provide information to the user of the system about the line of reasoning employed to reach a particular conclusion; and (*b*) a knowledge acquisition component may be used to elicit new knowledge from a user so the expert system can progressively expand its capabilities.

The way in which knowledge bases and inference engines are implemented in expert systems varies considerably, and the ways they *should* be implemented is still a major research issue (see, for example, Waterman [1986]). Nevertheless, to provide a basic understanding of how expert systems can assist the evaluation judgment, Table 22-1 shows some data that might be

TABLE 22-1
EXAMPLE RULES WITHIN KNOWLEDGE BASE OF AN EXPERT SYSTEM FOR ACCOUNTS RECEIVABLE CONTROLS EVALUATION

1.	IF	(a)	batch controls are not used over input data
	THEN		unauthorized changes can be made to cash receipts transactions
2.	IF	(a)	batch controls are used over input data
		(b)	batch controls are not checked
	THEN		unauthorized changes can be made to cash receipts transactions
3.	IF	(a)	batch controls are used over input data
		(b)	batch controls are checked
		(c)	a batch register is not maintained
	THEN		unauthorized changes can be made to cash receipts transactions
4.	IF	(a)	unauthorized changes can be made to cash receipts transactions
		(b)	bank deposits and cash receipts transactions are not independently reconciled
	THEN		an accounts receivable fraud can occur
5.	IF	(a)	an accounts receivable fraud can occur
	THEN		allowance for doubtful debts may be understated
6.	IF	(a)	adequate control is not exercised over credit granting
	THEN		allowance for doubtful debts may be understated

stored within the knowledge base of an expert system that is used to assist the evaluation judgment on accounts receivable systems. Note the peculiar form of this data when compared with the data stored in traditional data processing systems. The form is called a "production rule," and it is characterized by the "if. . .then" representation of the data. Production rules are not the only way of storing knowledge in an expert system, but they appear to be a good way of storing the knowledge that characterizes the audit domain.

To illustrate how the rules in the expert system are used, assume the auditor presents two findings to the expert system based upon evidence collected on a particular accounts receivable system: (a) batch controls are used but not checked within the accounts receivable system and (b) bank deposits and cash receipt transactions are not independently reconciled. Assume, further, that the inference engine in the expert system employs a "forward chaining" strategy to reach conclusions. Using this strategy, the system attempts to deduce new facts about the accounts receivable system by matching the existing facts with the antecedent parts of the production rules. When a match occurs, the consequent part of the production rule is added to the knowledge base as a new fact and the pattern matching activities continue until no new conclusion can be reached.

Given the rules in Table 22-1, the inference engine would proceed sequentially until it reached Rule 2, where some of the facts presented to the expert system match the antecedent part of the rule—the "if" part of the rule. The consequent—the "then" part—of the rule provides a new fact about the accounts receivable system, namely, that unauthorized changes can be made to cash receipts transactions. The inference engine proceeds further looking for a match between the antecedent part of some rule and the facts that it now has available to it within the knowledge base. It would find a match at Rule 4, and as a result it would add a new fact to the knowledge base, namely, that an accounts receivable fraud could occur within the system. Further search would produce a match with Rule 5, and the system would conclude that the allowance for doubtful debts could be understated within the accounts receivable system. Note from Table 22-1 that this conclusion could also be reached on the basis of other facts presented to the system.

Examples of Expert Systems in Auditing Currently, there are only a few expert systems in auditing that assist with the evaluation decision, and these systems are still in the prototype and research stages. Chapter 17 provides a description of some of the major expert systems that have been developed. While their capabilities are still somewhat limited, they indicate the likely nature of future auditor expert systems that will appear. Since there is widespread interest in expert systems among auditors, many new systems are likely to emerge as expert systems technology becomes more refined and more auditors acquire the skills needed to develop these systems.

QUANTITATIVE APPROACHES TO THE EVALUATION DECISION

Quantitative approaches to the evaluation of asset safeguarding and data integrity rely on the development, implementation, and use of formal models of internal control systems to assess the overall reliability of the system. The use of quantitative models is still not widespread, in part because they are sometimes difficult to build, and in part because few auditors have been trained in their construction and use. Nevertheless, an understanding of the different quantitative models provides important insights into the factors that affect the overall reliability of systems. In this light, the sections below examine some deterministic, probabilistic, Bayesian, and simulation models that have been developed to aid the evaluation judgment.

Deterministic Models

Deterministic models may be useful when evaluating part of a system of internal control or obtaining a first approximation of how well a computer system safeguards assets and maintains data integrity.

Consider, for example, the access control mechanism in an operating system. Assume the auditor discovers an integrity flaw in the system that allows, under certain conditions, the privacy of a data file to be violated; that is, the flaw can be exploited so the data file (asset) is no longer safeguarded against unauthorized use. To determine the consequences of the flaw, the auditor might access the system log to determine how many times the flaw has been exploited, assuming, of course, that the integrity of the log has been preserved. Calculating the loss that has resulted because of the flaw involves estimating the loss on each occasion that the flaw was exploited and summing the losses. Thus, the model used in this example is deterministic, provided there is no uncertainty about the losses involved.

Consider, also, a batch computer system. Any errors that the auditor identifies in the programs within the system are deterministic; if a program processes a data item incorrectly, it will always process the data item incorrectly. The auditor simply has to determine the frequency with which the data item occurs and the magnitude of the error that occurs. Audit software can be used to retrieve all instances of the data item from the audit trail so the total error for the data item can be determined. The ways in which different errors compound and compensate, however, still must be considered.

Even if the system to be evaluated contains stochastic elements, a deterministic model still might be used. A *mean value* deterministic model simply replaces each probabilistic element with its mean value. To obtain some idea of the probability distribution of errors that may result, *extreme value* deterministic models can be used; that is, the probabilistic elements can be replaced by their lowest and highest values.

Deterministic models are relatively simple models to construct. The auditor might use them to perform a pencil and paper analysis of how well a system safeguards assets and maintains data integrity. The models provide only limited information, however, about the forms of the probability distribution of error that can be produced when a system contains stochastic elements.

Probabilistic Models

Probabilistic models have more potential than deterministic models for representing the sometimes complex, variable phenomena in systems that affect how well a system safeguards assets and maintains data integrity. In spite of the intuitive appeal of probabilistic models, however, few have been formulated. Moreover, research on probabilistic models continues to be somewhat meager.

In terms of the models that have been proposed, most rely on a subset of applied probability theory called "reliability theory." In essence, reliability theory predicts the likelihood of success or failure in a system when it processes a transaction based on the pattern of past successes or failures in the system or the reliability of individual components within the system.

Two types of reliability models have been constructed to evaluate computer systems. First, macro-based reliability models have been used to predict the likelihood of success or failure based on the profile of past errors for the overall system. Second, micro-based reliability models have been used to predict the likelihood of success or failure based on estimates of the reliability of each component that makes up the system. The next section briefly examines the former type of model; the subsequent section examines the latter type of model.

Macro-Based Reliability Models Macro-based reliability models use statistical model fitting techniques to estimate the likelihood that an error will occur during some time period based on the patterns of past errors that have been discovered in the system. In general, the models assume that the number of

FIGURE 22-3
Pattern of error discovery in systems over time.

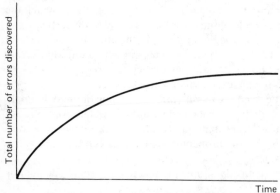

errors discovered over time increases at a decreasing rate (Figure 22-3). This assumption seems reasonable; when a system is first tested, errors are found relatively quickly, but as the testing proceeds, each additional error is harder to find. Provided that records are kept of the error discovery process, the shape of the function that relates the probability that an error will occur to the age of the system can be estimated and predictions made about the likelihood that future errors will occur.

The macro-based reliability models that have been developed fall into several classes (see, further, Goel [1985]):

Class of model	Nature of model
Time between failures models	These models are based on the assumption that the time between successive failures of a system will get longer as errors are removed from the system. The time between failures is predicted to follow a distribution whose parameters depend upon the number of errors that remain in the system during the interval between failures.
Failure count models	These models attempt to predict the number of failures that will occur during a fixed testing interval. As errors within the system are corrected, the models predict that the number of errors discovered during the next time interval will be less.
Fault seeding models	In fault seeding models, errors are introduced into a system that has an unknown number of "indigenous" errors. The system is then tested and the seeded and indigenous errors discovered are counted. On the basis of the proportion of seeded and indigenous errors discovered, estimates can be made of the total number of indigenous errors in the system.

For two reasons, the nature of macro-based reliability models is left for further study. First, it is difficult to appreciate the intricacies of the models without a good background in statistics. Second, researchers in the area are still debating the relative merits of the individual models. The debate surrounds the reasonableness of the assumptions underlying the different models and their relative predictive powers (see, further, Goel [1985]). Thus, auditors who seek to use macro-based reliability models must be well trained in statistics and be familiar with the relative strengths and limitations of each model.

In spite of these difficulties, however, macro-based reliability models are potentially powerful tools for auditors to use when assessing how well a system safeguards assets and maintains data integrity. They require minimum data to make predictions about the likelihood of errors remaining in a system—often only the size of the interval of system execution time that occurs between the discovery of successive errors and a classification of errors discovered as to their materiality. Furthermore, they do *not* rely on evidence gathered about the strengths and weaknesses of individual internal controls within the system, except as a basis for classifying the materiality of the errors that are discovered. The models also can be easily implemented via computer programs.

In this light, auditors can use the models in two ways. First, if auditors have sufficient confidence in the predictive powers of the model, they can make an evaluation judgment without having to rely solely on the difficult task of assimilating piecemeal evidence on the strengths and weaknesses of the individual internal controls within the system. Second, auditors may use the models as analytical review tools. If a model predicts that the likelihood of further errors occurring in a system is high, auditors may focus their evaluation efforts on that system. In addition, they may direct their evidence gathering efforts to obtain more data about the system.

Micro-Based Reliability Models   Micro-based reliability models estimate the overall reliability of a system as a function of the reliability of the individual components and individual internal controls that make up the system. In this respect they mirror the auditor's traditional approach to assessing the overall reliability of a system based upon evidence collected about the reliability of individual internal controls within the system. Knechel [1983] provides a review of these models and indicates that in many ways the assumptions underlying the models are restrictive and their practical usefulness is still questionable. Nevertheless, the models provide important insights into how control strengths and weaknesses can compensate and compound to affect the overall reliability of a system. As such, they help the auditor to understand how the overall evaluation of internal control should be made.

The fundamental ideas behind using micro-based reliability theory to model internal control systems were introduced into the accounting literature by Yu and Neter [1973] and by Cushing [1974]. Yu and Neter used Markov theory as the basis for their model; Cushing based his model on engineering reliability theory. Under certain conditions, Grimlund [1982] has shown that the results produced by both types of models are consistent and reconcilable. Both types of models have also been modified and extended in various ways. Nonetheless, the basic approaches still remain intact.

Since most work has been done on Cushing's model, it will be used to illustrate the micro-based reliability modeling approach to internal control systems evaluation. In this light, consider, first, a simple system where there is one process, a single control, and a single error correction procedure (Figure 22-4a). Assume, also, only one type of error or irregularity occurs within the system. The reliability of the system—that is, the probability the system will not have an error or an irregularity—is calculated as follows:

$$R = p + (1 - p)P(e)P(c)$$

where R = system reliability
  p = probability the process executes correctly
  $P(e)$ = probability the control detects an error or irregularity when one exists
  $P(c)$ = probability an error or irregularity is corrected when the control detects an error or irregularity and one exists

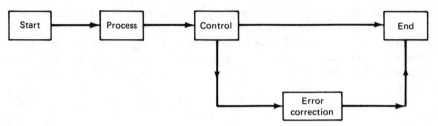

FIGURE 22-4a
System with one process and one control.

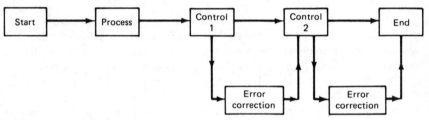

FIGURE 22-4b
System with one process and two controls.

In other words, the reliability of the system equals the probability the process executes correctly plus the probability it executes incorrectly, but the control identifies the error or irregularity and the error or irregularity is corrected.

Consider, first, how the model can be used to assess how well an asset is safeguarded. Assume, for example, the system to be assessed is a fire detection and extinguisher system. Assume the probability $(1 - p)$ of a fire to be .005. In other words, the probability of the "process" executing correctly—there is no fire—is .995. The probability $P(e)$ of the detector system signaling a fire when one occurs is .95. The probability of the system correctly activating the extinguisher and putting out the fire when a fire is signaled and one exists $P(c)$ is .90. Thus, the reliability of the detection and extinguisher system is:

$$R = .995 + (.005)(.95)(.90)$$
$$= .999275$$
$$(1 - R) = .000725$$
$$(R - p) = .004275$$

Note, the probability of a fire occurring even with the detection and extinguisher system $(1 - R)$ is .000725. The detection system may fail to signal a fire, the extinguisher may fail to put the fire out, etc. However, the probability of a fire causing destruction is reduced by .004275; that is, $R - p$.

Consider, also, how the model can be used to assess how well a system maintains data integrity. Assume, for example, the "system" to be evaluated is the keying operation in an application system. The control process is verification of the data that has been keyed. The probability of data being keyed correctly is .9; thus, the probability of incorrect keying $(1 - p)$ is .1. $P(e)$ is the probability .9 that the verifier operator detects a keying error when one exists. $P(c)$ is the probability .95 that the verifier operator corrects a detected error. The reliability of the process R is:

$$R = .9 + (.1)(.9)(.95)$$
$$= .9855$$
$$(1 - R) = .0145$$
$$(R - p) = .0855$$

Note, the probability of an error occurring even with verification is .0145; the verifier operator may omit verifying some incorrectly keyed data, the verifier operator may make the same mistake as the initial keyboard operator, the wrong character may be keyed during the correction process, etc. However, the verification control improves the overall reliability of the process by $R - p$, that is, .0855.

The above example assumes only one type of error or irregularity occurs within the system. For more than one error or irregularity type, the parameters in the formula can be suitably subscripted. Thus, R_i the reliability of the system for the ith error or irregularity type can be computed as follows:

$$R_i = p_i + (1 - p_i)P(e_i)P(c_i)$$

The overall reliability of the system for all error or irregularity types is

$$R = \prod_{i=1}^{n} R_i.$$

For example, if $R_1 = .9$ and $R_2 = .8$, then $R = (.9)(.8)$, that is, .72.

Figure 22-4b shows the case of a simple system where only one error or irregularity type occurs, a single process exists, and two controls operate. Extending the previous key preparation system example, assume the keying device also automatically checks batch totals. However, verification as a second control still would identify compensating errors that were not detected by the batch total check. After the second control point the reliability of the system is:

$$R^2 = R^1 + (1 - R^1)P(e_2)P(c_2)$$

Thus, the reliability of the system after the second control point R^2 is dependent upon the reliability of the system after the first control point R^1. Note in this case only, $P(e_2)$ and $P(c_2)$ are probabilities for the second control point and not the second error type.

More generally, in a single system where $i = 1$, n error or irregularity types

TABLE 22-2
RELIABILITY CALCULATIONS FOR SYSTEM WITH
SINGLE PROCESS, TWO CONTROLS, AND TWO
ERROR TYPES

$p_1 = .8$	$p_2 = .85$
$P(e_{11}) = .85$	$P(e_{21}) = .85$
$P(c_{11}) = .95$	$P(c_{21}) = .90$
$P(e_{12}) = 0$	$P(e_{22}) = .80$
	$P(c_{22}) = .95$

$$R_1^1 = p_1 + (1 - p_1)P(e_{11})P(c_{11})$$
$$= .8 + (.2)(.85)(.95)$$
$$= .9615$$
$$R_2^1 = p_2 + (1 - p_2)P(e_{21})P(c_{21})$$
$$= .85 + (.15)(.85)(.90)$$
$$= .96475$$
$$R_1^2 = R_1^1 + (1 - R_1^1)P(e_{12})P(c_{12})$$
$$= .9615 + (.0385)(0)$$
$$= .9615$$
$$R_2^2 = R_2^1 + (1 - R_2^1)P(e_{22})P(c_{22})$$
$$= .96475 + (.03525)(.8)(.95)$$
$$= .99154$$
$$R = (R_1^2)(R_2^2) = (.9615)(.99154) = .953366$$
$$p = (p_1)(p_2) = (.8)(.85) \qquad = .68$$
$$R - p = .953366 - .68 = .273366$$

can occur and $j = 1, r$ controls exist, the reliability of the system after the jth control for the ith error or irregularity type is:

$$R_i^j = R_i^{j-1} + (1 - R_i^{j-1})P(e_{ij})P(c_{ij})$$

To illustrate the application of this formula, Table 22-2 shows the reliability calculations for a single process system where there are two controls and two error or irregularity types. Note that the second control is unable to identify any of the first error or irregularity type; thus, $R_1^2 = R_1^1$.

By itself a reliability (probability) figure is not especially meaningful. The auditor needs to know what dollar or quantity error a system can produce or how many data items are likely to be in error. For example, if auditors are assessing data integrity and they are dealing with monetary or quantity error types, the effect of error type i on a data item can be calculated by:

$$A_i = Ne_{ir} \times Ve_i \times T_r$$

where A_i = dollar or quantity error produced
Ne_{ir} = average number of errors of type i which remain undetected after r control processes
Ve_i = estimated average dollar or quantity effect of an undetected type i error
T_r = frequency with which the set of r controls is performed

The expected total dollar or quantity error is simply the sum of the individual error effects; that is,

$$A = \sum_{i=1}^{n} A_i$$

If the auditor is attempting to estimate the *number* of data items that are likely to be in error, the formula is:

$$H = \sum_{i=1}^{n} H_i$$

where $H_i = Ne_{i_r} \times T_r$.

Note that A and H are expected (mean) values. Thus, the auditor still must estimate the probability distributions of these variables. The distributions of A and H are a function of the distributions of Ne_{i_r}, Ve_i, and perhaps T_r if T_r is stochastic.

The model described so far also needs further refinement if it is to be used in practice to evaluate how well a system safeguards assets and maintains data integrity. It must be extended to handle the multiple-process case. It also must be extended to handle redundant processes and redundant controls.

Bayesian Models

Bayesian models provide a formal method of revising prior estimates of the reliability of an internal control system on the basis of new information obtained from evidence gathering activities that are undertaken during the course of the audit. Conceptually, the evaluation decision can be considered as a sequential process in which auditors start out with prior estimates of whether the internal control system is reliable and revise these estimates progressively as new evidence comes to hand. At some stage they must cease evidence gathering and reach a decision on the overall reliability of the system.

Bayesian models have been advocated for some time as a means to assist auditors to make evaluation decisions. Auditing researchers have been motivated to examine these models because they are aware of research results obtained elsewhere that show humans perform poorly when they must revise prior estimates of the probability of an event in light of new information received (see, for example, Slovic and Lichtenstein [1971]). Thus, they have sought ways of improving the judgment process (see, for example, Bailey [1981]). The models that have been formulated apply equally well in a manual or a computerized environment.

To illustrate the nature of the Bayesian approach, consider Figure 22-5, which shows the overall evaluation decision faced by the auditor. The internal control system is either reliable or unreliable, and the decision that can be reached is either to accept the system as reliable or to reject it as unreliable.

State of the Internal Control System

		Reliable	Unreliable
Auditor's Decision	Accept	Correct decision	Incorrect decision
	Reject	Incorrect decision	Correct decision

FIGURE 22-5
Decision problem faced by the auditor.

Clearly the auditor wants to reach an accept decision when the system is reliable and a reject decision when the system is unreliable. Unfortunately, in the absence of perfect information, the auditor may make a wrong decision: an accept decision may be made when the system is unreliable, and a reject decision may be made when the system is reliable. Both types of wrong decision are costly. In the former case, the auditor may be sued if the unreliable system leads to liquidation and bankruptcy. In the latter case, the auditor does superfluous audit work, faces conflict with the client, etc.

Assume, at the outset of the audit, that the auditor believes (subjectively) there is a .9 probability of the internal control system being reliable and a .1 probability of the internal control system being unreliable. These probabilities could have been determined in various ways; for example, they may reflect the auditor's prior experience with the system or a judgment made on the basis of a preliminary review of the system. Assume, further, that the estimated cost of accepting an unreliable internal control system is $1,000,000, and the cost of rejecting a reliable internal control system is $50,000. In the absence of further information, the appropriate decision to make can be determined on the basis of the expected losses under both decisions. In the case of the accept decision, it would be (.9)(0) + (.1)(1,000,000)—that is, $100,000. In the case of the reject decision, it would be (.9)(50,000) + (.1)(0)—that is, $45,000. In the absence of further information, the auditor would minimize losses by making a reject decision.

Assume, now, that the auditor undertakes some type of test to evaluate the reliability of controls in the system. For example, suppose the auditor executes a set of test data through the system and evaluates the test results obtained. The test results indicate that the system is reliable. However, since the test data cannot test the system comprehensively, there is some risk that the test results are favorable even though the system may be unreliable. Using a Bayesian approach, the auditor must first estimate the probability of getting a favorable result given the system is reliable and a favorable result given the system is unreliable. These estimates require that the auditor have some knowledge about the reliability of the test; for example, the auditor may have experience with test data design and use.

Assume the auditor concludes that the following estimates apply to the reliability of the test:

$$\text{Probability (favorable|reliable)} \quad = P(F|R) = .8$$
$$\text{Probability (favorable|unreliable)} = P(F|U) = .2$$

Using Bayes' rule, the probability of the system being reliable *given* the favorable test results and the probability of the system being unreliable *given* the favorable test results can be calculated as follows:

$$P(R|F) = \frac{P(F|R)\ P(R)}{P(F)}$$

$$= \frac{P(F|R)\ P(R)}{P(F|R)\ P(R) + P(F|U)\ P(U)}$$

$$= \frac{(.8)(.9)}{(.8)(.9) + (.2)(.1)}$$

$$= .97$$

$$P(U|F) = 1 - P(R|F)$$

$$= 1 - .97$$

$$= .03$$

In light of these revised probabilities, the auditor can now calculate the new expected losses for the accept and reject decisions. For the accept decision, the expected loss is $(.97)(0) + (.03)(1,000,000) = \$30,000$. For the reject decision, the expected loss is $(.97)(50,000) + (.03)(0) = \$48,500$. Thus, the decision now is to accept the system as reliable—a change from the previous decision.

Note, the expected loss under the revised probabilities is $48,500, whereas the expected loss under the prior probabilities is $100,000. Thus, if the test costs more than $51,500 ($100,000 − $48,500), it should not be undertaken. On the other hand, if the costs are less than $51,500, it is worthwhile for the auditor to undertake the test. If the test costs exactly $51,500 to undertake, the auditor is indifferent about proceeding with the test.

As new evidence is gathered on the reliability of the system, the auditor can continue to revise the probabilities of the system being reliable and unreliable using Bayes' rule. At some stage, of course, the benefits of acquiring more evidence will exceed the costs. Bailey [1981] provides a general decision model that enables the auditor to decide what tests should be undertaken and when the auditor should cease undertaking further tests.

Simulation Models

Analytical models should be used whenever possible since the values of the dependent variables can be evaluated usually at low cost over a wide range of values of the independent variables and variations in the structure of the model. However, sometimes analytical models are not mathematically tractable; the equations of the system are not obvious or they may be insolvable. In these cases, simulation often can be used to evaluate the values of the dependent variables. Simulation allows the behavior of the system to be studied over time.

Simulation might be used to evaluate how well assets are safeguarded if the system to be evaluated is complex and there are several levels of controls that can fail stochastically. For example, there may be some probability that a guard will fail to detect an intruder, some probability that a surveillance system also may fail to detect the intruder, some probability that the intruder can crack a safe lock combination, etc., and eventually the intruder gains access to and steals sensitive data files. Often an analytical model can be used to determine the probability of all controls failing. Nevertheless, if controls compound and compensate in different ways, a simulation model may be necessary for gaining insight into the reliability of the system of controls.

The use of simulation to evaluate how well a system maintains data integrity has been suggested by Burns and Loebbecke [1975]. Methodologies for constructing simulation models have been described extensively elsewhere (see, for example, Emshoff and Sisson [1970]); however, the following simplified example illustrates the use of the approach to help solve an auditing problem.

Assume a clerk uses a terminal connected to a minicomputer to perform complex pricing calculations for a product. A counter maintained by the minicomputer shows that in the past year 8000 calculations were performed. During the evidence collection phase the auditor finds that the size of transactions follows a normal distribution, with a mean of 100 units and a standard deviation of 30 units.

The auditor also discovers two errors have occurred during the pricing process. First, an estimated 5% of the time the clerk types the wrong transaction amount as input to the program. The clerk sometimes overstates the amount and sometimes understates the amount. The best description the auditor can give of the error is that it appears to be distributed normally, with a mean of 3 units and a standard deviation of 7 units (overstatements occur more often than understatements). Second, the program contains an error; it prices wrongly if the transaction amount is between 120 and 125 units.

Figure 22-6 shows the flowchart for a simulation program written to estimate the dollar error that could have occurred. Note the program simulates the year's transactions a thousand times. At the end of the simulation the program prints out the probability distribution of total error that might have resulted because of the stochastic error (the clerk typing in the wrong amount) and the deterministic error (the incorrect pricing calculation). Of course, in practice the simulation program needed to evaluate how well a system maintains data integrity usually would be much more complex.

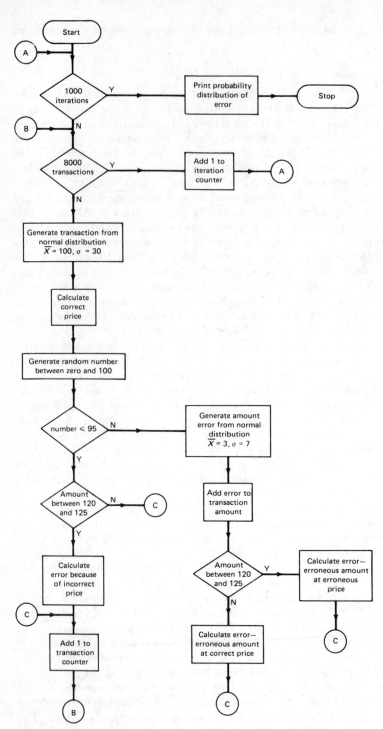

FIGURE 22-6
Flowchart for pricing simulation.

As with analytical models, the accuracy of simulation output is a function of model formulation inaccuracies, solution inaccuracies, and parameter inaccuracies. Techniques for calibrating and validating simulation models are well-developed (see Emshoff and Sisson [1970]). The auditor should be careful not to rely on simulation output until these activities have been performed.

COST-EFFECTIVENESS CONSIDERATIONS

So far the discussion has proceeded without considering the costs of safeguarding assets or maintaining data integrity. However, how well a system of controls safeguards assets or maintains data integrity must be considered within a cost-effectiveness framework. A system might prevent all types of errors or irregularities from occurring but at a prohibitive cost. Always the question must be asked: Do the benefits obtained from having a control exceed the costs of that control?

The following sections outline the elements of a decision model that the auditor can use to evaluate whether a system is cost-effective in its asset safeguarding or maintenance of data integrity. Again, the model provides important insights into this evaluation problem; however, its use is not widespread so little is known about the problems of implementing the model.

Costs and Benefits of Controls

Implementing and operating controls in a system involves four costs. First, initial setup costs must be incurred to design and implement controls; for example, magnetic card door locks must be installed or validation routines must be written into programs. These are one-off costs. Second, execution costs are incurred; for example, the wages of a security officer must be paid or CPU charges arise from executing validation routines. Third, there are costs involved in searching for an error or irregularity, determining whether one exists, and then correcting any error or irregularities that are found. Fourth, costs arise because the controls do not detect some errors or irregularities and these errors or irregularities cause losses; for example, an uncorrected error or irregularity may allow a defalcation to occur. The first cost is the outlay for a system of controls. The last three costs are the ongoing operational costs of a control system.

The benefits derived from having a control system relate to the decreased occurrence of errors or irregularities that results. In some cases errors or irregularities would occur routinely without the control; for example, transposition errors regularly will be made and perhaps remain undetected unless a check digit is used. In other cases the control acts as a deterrent; for example, a burglar alarm may deter unauthorized intruders. The benefits of a control system are calculated when the losses that would result from errors or irregularities that the control system does not detect are compared with the losses that would result from errors or irregularities that an alternate control system does not detect.

Calculating the Ongoing Costs of Control Systems

Perhaps the most difficult part of the evaluation of cost-effectiveness of control systems is assessing the ongoing costs of a system. The reliability approach discussed earlier in the chapter can be extended to provide a basis for calculating these costs. Let C_t be the ongoing costs of a control system in period t. Then:

$$C_t = \sum_{j=1}^{r} Cc_j + \sum_{i=1}^{n} (1 - R_i^r)Ce_i$$

$$+ \sum_{i=1}^{n} \sum_{j=1}^{r} \{R_i^{j-1} [1 - P(s_{ij})][1 - P(d_{ij})] + (1 - R_i^{j-1})P(e_{ij})\}Cs_{ij}$$

where $P(s_{ij})$ = probability the jth control will not signal the ith error or irregularity when an error or irregularity does not exist

$\quad P(d_{ij})$ = probability a failure in the jth control is detected and no action is taken when the control signals an error or irregularity type i and no error or irregularity exists

$\quad Cc_j$ = cost of executing control j

$\quad Cs_{ij}$ = cost of searching for error or irregularity type i, detecting whether it exists, and correcting the error or irregularity

$\quad Ce_i$ = average cost of an uncorrected error or irregularity type i

$\quad R_i^j, P(e_{ij})$ have the usual meaning

In other words, the total ongoing costs of a control system in any period equal the costs of executing the control plus the losses resulting from uncorrected errors or irregularities plus the costs of identifying whether errors or irregularities exist when they are signaled and correcting them if they do exist.

If no controls are implemented, the formula simply reduces to:

$$C_t = \sum_{i=1}^{n} (1 - p_i)Ce_i$$

To illustrate the approach, first, with respect to asset safeguarding, consider again a fire detection and extinguisher system (see, also, State of Illinois [1974]). Assume the probability $(1 - p)$ of a fire in any year to be .005 and the loss Ce that would occur because of the fire to be \$3,000,000. Thus, the expected loss in any one year is $15,000. The maintenance cost of the system Cc is $500 per year. The probability $[1 - P(s)]$ of the detector system falsely signaling a fire and activating the extinguishers is .001. If this occurs, the probability $P(d)$ of detecting the false signal in time before the extinguishers are activated is .5. The probability of the system correctly signaling a fire and activating the extinguishers $P(e)$ is .995. The cost of a cleanup operation after the extinguishers have been activated is $4000.

With the fire detection and extinguisher system, the probability $(1 - R)$ of a fire causing damage is $(1 - p)[1 - P(e)]$; that is, the probability of a fire occurring multiplied by the probability of the detection and extinguisher system not detecting the fire. Thus:

$$(1 - R) = (.005)(.005)$$
$$= .000025$$

The yearly cost of the fire detection and extinguisher system is calculated as follows:

$$C_t = Cc + (1 - R) Ce + \{p[1 - P(s)][1 - P(d)] + (1 - p)P(e)\}Cs$$
$$= 500 + (.000025) (3,000,000) + [(.995) (.001) (.5) + (.005) (.995)] 4000$$
$$= 500 + 75 + [.000498 + .004975] 4000$$
$$= 596.892$$

In other words, the ongoing costs of the fire detection and extinguisher system equal the cost of maintaining the system plus the expected loss which would result from an undetected fire plus the costs of a cleanup operation which results either from incorrect activation or correct activation of the extinguisher system.

Consider, now, use of the model for evaluating how well data integrity is maintained. Assume a simple system where there is one transaction type, one process, two controls, and two possible error types. For example, assume the process is an online update program. The user submits data at a terminal and periodically, with some probability, the user makes two types of error: (*a*) a wrong account number is submitted and (*b*) a wrong dollar amount is submitted.

The program performs two types of validation checks. First, the account is checked against the master file to determine whether or not it is a valid account number. Second, a reasonableness check is performed. Account numbers are coded to indicate the expenditure limits imposed on an account; thus, the program checks that the amount is reasonable given the account number.

Even with the program validation checks, errors still may get through and affect the master file. The wrong account number may be submitted, but it still may be a valid number on the master file. The account number check will not identify this error. However, possibly the reasonableness check will identify

TABLE 22-3
RELIABILITY CALCULATIONS FOR ONLINE UPDATE PROGRAM

p_1(correct account) = .85	p_2(correct amount) = .9
$P(e_{11})$ = .97	$P(e_{21})$ = .0
$P(c_{11})$ = .95	$P(e_{22})$ = .9
$P(e_{12})$ = .25	$P(c_{22})$ = .8
$P(c_{12})$ = .95	

$$R_1^1 = p_1 + (1 - p_1)P(e_{11})P(c_{11})$$
$$= .85 + (.15)(.97)(.95)$$
$$= .988225$$
$$R_2^1 = p_2 + (1 - p_2)P(e_{21})P(c_{21})$$
$$= .9 + (.1)(0)$$
$$= .9$$
$$R_1^2 = R_1^1 + (1 - R_1^1)P(e_{12})P(c_{12})$$
$$= .988225 + (.011775)(.25)(.95)$$
$$= .991022$$
$$R_2^2 = R_2^1 + (1 - R_2^1)P(e_{22})\ P(c_{22})$$
$$= .9 + (.1)(.9)(.8)$$
$$= .972$$
$$R = (R_1^2)(R_2^2) = (.991022)(.972) = .963273$$
$$p = (p_1)(p_2)\ = (.85)(.9)\qquad = .765$$
$$R - p = .963273 - .765 = .198273$$

the error; the dollar amount (submitted correctly) will be unreasonable for the invalid account number.

The reasonableness check also will identify dollar errors that fall outside the allowed range for an account number. However, some amount errors made will fall within the allowed range and remain undetected by the control.

Table 22-3 shows the reliability calculations for the system using the formula discussed earlier in the chapter. Table 22-4 shows example ongoing cost calculations for three alternate control systems: (a) no controls, (b) the account check only, and (c) the account check then the amount check. Note the assumption that the program performs the validation checks correctly; thus, $P(s_{ij})$ the probability of an error signal arising when there is no error is zero. Note, also, the user may not correct an error correctly. Data identified in error and resubmitted in error still may pass the validation checks.

Even with only two controls, two other control systems can be considered. First, a control system using only the *amount* check might be evaluated. Second, a control system using the amount check then the account check might be evaluated. The order of controls could be important when the cost-effectiveness of alternate control systems is considered.

The above procedure provides only the expected (mean) ongoing costs of a control system. Consider, for example, the alternative of no controls shown in Table 22-4. The value 35, the ongoing costs *per transaction*, is an expected value. To illustrate, if A is the event "account error" and B is the event "amount error," then the expected value is calculated as follows:

$$p(A \cap \sim B) = p(A)p(\sim B) = (.15)(.9) \quad = .135$$
$$p(A \cap B) = p(A)p(B) = (.15)(.1) \quad = .015$$
$$p(\sim A \cap B) = p(\sim A)p(B) = (.85)(.1) \quad = .085$$
$$p(\sim A \cap \sim B) = p(\sim A)p(\sim B) = (.85)(.9) = .765$$
$$\Sigma p(E) = 1.000$$

Event	$p(E)$	Cost	Expected cost
$A \cap \sim B$	.135	100	13.5
$A \cap B$	.015	300	4.5
$\sim A \cap B$	.085	200	17.0
$\sim A \cap \sim B$	.765	0	0
			$\Sigma(EC) = 35.0$

TABLE 22-4
ONGOING COSTS FOR ALTERNATE CONTROL SYSTEMS IN ONLINE UPDATE
PROGRAM

$Cc_1 = .01$	$Cc_2 = .02$
$Cs_{11} = 1.00$	$Cs_{21} = -$
$Cs_{12} = 1.25$	$Cs_{22} = 1.10$
$Ce_1 = 100.00$	$Ce_2 = 200.00$
$P(s_{11}) = 1$	$P(s_{22}) = 1$
$P(d_{11}) = 1$	$P(d_{22}) = 1$
$P(s_{12}) = 1$	
$P(d_{12}) = 1$	

1. No controls

$$C_t = (1 - p_1)Ce_1 + (1 - p_2)Ce_2$$
$$= (.15)(100) + (.1)(200)$$
$$= 15 + 20$$
$$= 35$$

2. Account check only

$$C_t = Cc_1 + (1 - R_1^1)Ce_1 + (1 - R_2^1)Ce_2$$
$$+ \{p_1[1 - P(s_{11})][1 - P(d_{11})] + (1 - p_1)P(e_{11})\}Cs_{11}$$
$$+ \{p_2[1 - P(s_{21})][1 - P(d_{21})] + (1 - p_2)P(e_{21})\}Cs_{21}$$
$$= .01 + (.011775)(100) + (.1)(200)$$
$$+ [(.85)(0)(0) + (.15)(.97)]1$$
$$+ [(.9)(0)(0) + (.1)(0)]0$$
$$= .01 + 1.1775 + 20 + .1455$$
$$= 21.333$$

3. Account check then amount check

$$C_t = Cc_1 + Cc_2 + (1 - R_1^2)Ce_1 + (1 - R_2^2)Ce_2$$
$$+ \{p_1[1 - P(s_{11})][1 - P(d_{11})] + (1 - p_1)P(e_{11})\}Cs_{11}$$
$$+ \{R_1^1[1 - P(s_{12})][1 - P(d_{12})] + (1 - R_1^1)P(e_{12})\}Cs_{12}$$
$$+ \{p_2[1 - P(s_{21})][1 - P(d_{21})] + (1 - p_2)P(e_{21})\}Cs_{21}$$
$$+ \{R_2^1[1 - P(s_{22})][1 - P(d_{22})] + (1 - R_2^1)P(e_{22})\}Cs_{22}$$
$$= .01 + .02 + (.008978)(100) + (.028)(200)$$
$$+ [(.85)(0)(0) + (.15)(.97)]1 + [(.988225)(0)(0) + (.011775)(.25)]1.25$$
$$+ [(.9)(0)(0) + (.1)(0)]0 + [(.9)(0)(0) + (.1)(.9)]1.10$$
$$= .01 + .02 + .8978 + 5.6 + .1455 + .00368 + 0 + .099$$
$$= 6.77598$$

The variance of the probability distribution is an important indicator of the riskiness of the cash flows in any period.

Perhaps the most difficult part of using the above model is estimating the probabilities of the various events that can occur. Again, methods of risk analysis can be applied to obtain these probabilities and the associated losses that result (see, for example, Gerberick [1979]).

Controls as an Investment Decision

So far, only the ongoing operational costs of a control system to safeguard assets or maintain data integrity have been considered. When evaluating cost-effectiveness, however, the outlay cost for the control system also must be taken into account.

Whether or not to implement a control system can be evaluated just like any other asset investment decision using the decision models that are well-developed within the finance literature (see, for example, Bierman and Smidt [1975] and Sharpe [1978]). Since control systems so far have been considered only in terms of costs (not benefits), the simple decision rule is to implement that system which has the lowest net present value of costs.

Consider, again, the online update program example discussed in the previous section. Three control systems were considered: (a) no controls, (b) an account check only, and (c) an account check and then amount check. If I_j is the implementation cost of the jth control and k is the required rate of return on an investment for an organization, then TC_m the net present value of the mth control system can be computed as follows:

$$TC_m = \sum_{j=1}^{r} I_j + \sum_{t=1}^{T} \frac{C_t}{(1 + k)^t}$$

The control system having the minimum TC_m should be chosen.

Table 22-5 shows the calculations for the online update program example. Assume the cost of implementing the account check control is $1000 and the cost of implementing the amount check control is $2500. Assume, further, the life of the system is three years, the required rate of return is 10%, and 500 transactions occur per year. Thus, the control system having both the account check and the amount check should be chosen since it has the lowest net present value of total costs.

Obtaining the required rate of return k to carry out the discounting process is a difficult problem. Current finance theory defines k as:

$$k = k_f + \beta(\bar{k}_m - k_f)$$

where k_f = risk-free rate of return
$\bar{k}_m$ = expected rate of return on the market portfolio
β = beta coefficient of a security

TABLE 22-5
NET PRESENT VALUE CALCULATIONS FOR CONTROL
SYSTEM ALTERNATIVES

$I_1 = 1000$
$I_2 = 2500$
$k = 10\%$
$T = 3$ years
Number of transactions per year $= 500$
1 No controls

$$TC_1 = \frac{35 \times 500}{(1.1)^1} + \frac{35 \times 500}{(1.1)^2} + \frac{35 \times 500}{(1.1)^3}$$

$$= 43,520$$

2 Account check only

$$TC_2 = 1000 + \frac{21.33 \times 500}{(1.1)^1} + \frac{21.33 \times 500}{(1.1)^2} + \frac{21.33 \times 500}{(1.1)^3}$$

$$= 1000 + 26,522$$
$$= 27,522$$

3 Account check then amount check

$$TC_3 = (1000 + 2500) + \frac{6.78 \times 500}{(1.1)^1} + \frac{6.78 \times 500}{(1.1)^2} + \frac{6.78 \times 500}{(1.1)^3}$$

$$= 3500 + 8430$$
$$= 11,930$$

The β coefficient of a security indicates the riskiness of returns on the security relative to returns on the market portfolio. The value of β can be obtained by regressing returns on the security against returns on the market portfolio (see Van Horne [1977]).

However, what is β for an investment in a control system? There is no easy answer to this question. One approach to calculating β would be to regress the returns on a security for an organization involved in designing and implementing control systems with the returns on the market portfolio. But there are still further theoretical and practical problems involved in calculating β for multiperiod investments under uncertainty (see Fama [1977]). These matters are left for further study.

As a final point, note also the net present value of cost calculated using the above formula is an expected (mean) value. Recall, there is a probability distribution over the ongoing costs of a control system; thus, there is a probability distribution over the net present value of costs for a control system. The variance of the probability distribution of net present values can be calculated using the following formula (see, further, Van Horne [1977]):

$$\sigma = \sqrt{\sum_{t=1}^{T} \frac{\sigma_t^2}{(1 + k)^{2t}}}$$

where σ_t^2 is the variance of the probability distribution of costs (cash outflows) in period t. The variance of the net present value of costs reflects the risk of the investment in a control system.

SUMMARY

When evaluating asset safeguarding and data integrity, the auditor attempts to determine whether assets could be destroyed, damaged, or used for unauthorized purposes, and how well the completeness, soundness, purity, and veracity of data are maintained. The evaluation process involves the auditor's making a complex global judgment using piecemeal evidence collected on the strengths and weaknesses of an internal control system.

To evaluate how well an internal control system safeguards assets and maintains data integrity, measures of asset safeguarding and data integrity are needed. Common measures are the dollar loss for asset safeguarding and the dollar error, quantity error, and number of errors a system can produce for data integrity. Since a system of internal control usually contains stochastic elements, these measures should usually be expressed probabilistically.

Both qualitative and quantitative approaches can be used when making the evaluation decision. Qualitative approaches rely on various informal techniques that reduce errors in the auditor's judgment process and on expert systems to make available to auditors knowledge about the system that they may not possess. Quantitative approaches rely on deterministic, probabilistic, Bayesian, and simulation models to obtain an estimate of the reliability of the internal control system.

The evaluation of an internal control system must be considered within a cost-effectiveness framework. The implementation, operation, and maintenance costs associated with an internal control system should be assessed in terms of standard return on investment criteria.

REVIEW QUESTIONS

22-1 List three measures of data integrity and give an example of where each measure would be used. Briefly explain why measures of data integrity usually need to be expressed probabilistically.

22-2 Why should the auditor consider the variance of the probability distribution of error that a system could produce?

22-3 What are the three major phases through which the auditor passes when making a judgment on how well a system safeguards assets and maintains data integrity?

22-4 What problems can arise when auditors attempt to identify all the cues that are relevant to a decision on the overall reliability of a system? How can these problems be overcome?

22-5 What problems can arise when auditors attempt to weight the importance of cues that impact the decision on the overall reliability of a system? How can these problems be overcome?

22-6 Briefly explain why it is difficult to assess whether auditors make *accurate* decisions when they evaluate how well an internal control system safeguards assets and maintains data integrity? In the absence of good accuracy measures for assessing the quality of auditor decision making, what other measures might be used?

22-7 When auditors have identified and weighted the cues that are relevant to evaluating system reliability, how well do they make the global evaluation judgment? Can the quality of the global evaluation judgment be improved by using groups of auditors to make the judgment?

22-8 Briefly describe the potential benefits of using expert systems to assist auditors in making the global evaluation judgment.

22-9 What are the *four* major components in an expert system? Briefly explain the purpose of each component.

22-10 Briefly explain the nature and purpose of production rules in expert systems. Give an example of a production rule that might be used in an expert system designed to assess the reliability of an accounts payable system.

22-11 Briefly explain the nature and purpose of deterministic models designed to assist auditors to make the evaluation decision on how well a system safeguards assets and maintains data integrity. Be sure to point out the major strengths and limitations of deterministic models.

22-12 During the test of a program, the auditor discovers that the program incorrectly calculates the discount given for certain types of customers. Outline how the total amount of dollar error that results because of the incorrect calculation could be determined.

22-13 Briefly explain what is meant by a mean value and an extreme value deterministic model for evaluating data integrity. Under what circumstances might the auditor use each type of model?

22-14 In the context of judgments on how well a system safeguards assets and maintains data integrity, what are the relative advantages and disadvantages of deterministic versus probabilistic models designed to assist the judgment?

22-15 Briefly explain the differences between macro-based reliability models and micro-based reliability models for assessing how well a system safeguards assets and maintains data integrity. What are the relative strengths and limitations of each type of model for making the evaluation judgment?

22-16 Briefly explain the nature of the following types of macro-based reliability models:
a Time between failures models
b Failure count models
c Fault seeding models

22-17 In the context of micro-based reliability models of internal control systems, briefly explain *in words* what is meant by the overall reliability of a system of internal control.

22-18 Briefly describe three problems that are encountered if micro-based reliability models are used to assess how well an internal control system safeguards assets and maintains data integrity.

22-19 In a micro-based reliability model, define the following terms:
a R_i
b $P(e_{ij})$
c $P(c_{ij})$
d $(1 - p_i)$
e Ne_{ir}
f T_r
g Ve_i

22-20 Briefly describe the nature of a Bayesian decision making model as it applies to the evaluation of an internal control system. Can the Bayesian approach be used to evaluate the reliability of a single control, a set of controls, or both?

22-21 If $P(F|R)$ is the probability of a favorable test result given an internal control system is reliable and $P(F|U)$ is the probability of a favorable test result given an internal control system is unreliable, give the formula for determining the probability of having a reliable internal control system if a favorable test result is obtained.

22-22 The flowchart in Figure 22-6 shows the simulation program iterating 1000 times. Why is it necessary to iterate 1000 times through the year's transactions? Outline one method the auditor might use to determine whether 1000 iterations is enough.

22-23 What circumstances would lead an auditor to construct a simulation model rather than use a micro-based reliability model to evaluate whether an internal control system safeguards assets and maintains data integrity?

22-24 Why must maintenance of asset safeguarding and data integrity be considered within a data integrity framework?

22-25 Briefly explain the major costs involved in implementing and operating an internal control system. How are the benefits of an internal control system assessed?

22-26 What costs are represented by the following formula:

$$\sum_{i=1}^{n} \sum_{j=1}^{r} \{R_i^{j-1}\,[1 - P(s_{ij})][1 - P(d_{ij})]\}Cs_{ij}$$

22-27 Why is the net present value of costs for an internal control system typically an *expected* value? Why must auditors be careful in dealing with expected net present values only?

MULTIPLE CHOICE QUESTIONS

22-1 The shape of the probability distribution of error that an internal control system could produce is important because it indicates the:
  a Risk an auditor faces when making a decision about the materiality of the error the system could produce
  b Size of the error that the system could produce
  c Number of internal controls in the system that are failing stochastically
  d Level of materiality that should be used to evaluate the error that the system could produce

22-2 Which of the following is *not* a finding obtained from psychological research undertaken on the quality of auditor judgment processes:
  a Auditors often have poor insight into the importance they attach to the various cues on which they base their overall judgment
  b Auditors may avoid searching for cues that contradict their initial assessment of the overall reliability of an internal control system
  c Auditors overestimate the importance of major cues and underestimate the importance of minor cues
  d Auditors often fail to identify all the internal control cues relevant to their overall judgment

22-3 The purpose of an internal control checklist is to:
   a Provide auditors with feedback on the weights they attach to the various internal control cues
   b Help auditors to integrate and combine the internal control cues to make a better global evaluation judgment
   c Indicate the internal controls that are likely to be material to the overall evaluation judgment
   d Help auditors to identify all the relevant internal control cues
22-4 When evaluating the quality of auditor decision making, consensus is a measure of:
   a How accurately several auditors make an evaluation judgment
   b The level of agreement among auditors in their evaluation judgments
   c The extent to which a single auditor would make the same evaluation judgment over time if faced with the same cues
   d The extent to which management agrees with the auditor's evaluation judgment
22-5 Which of the following techniques is least likely to improve the accuracy of auditor judgments made with respect to the weights to attach to various internal control cues:
   a Randomize the way in which reliability evidence on internal controls is presented to an auditor
   b Provide feedback to auditors on the objective weights they used when making an evaluation judgment
   c Form a group mathematical aggregate of individual decisions made on the weights to be attached to the various internal control cues
   d Form a group behavioral aggregate of individual decisions made on the weights to be attached to the various internal control cues
22-6 The component in an expert system that provides information to the user about the line of reasoning used to reach a conclusion is the:
   a Inference engine
   b Knowledge acquirer
   c Knowledge base
   d Tutor
22-7 Which of the following is *not* true about the use of production rules in auditor expert systems:
   a They are used to represent the heuristics employed by auditors to make judgments
   b They are the only technique currently available for storing the kind of knowledge that characterizes the audit domain
   c The antecedent part of a production rule specifies the condition that leads to a particular conclusion
   d They are stored in the knowledge base of an expert system
22-8 To use an analytical model to evaluate how well a system safeguards assets and maintains data integrity, the auditor must be able to:
   a Reduce all estimates of the reliability of controls to a deterministic value
   b Represent the system to be modeled as a closed system
   c Formulate equations showing the relationships between the measure of asset safeguarding or data integrity and the variables that affect these measures
   d Characterize those parts of the evaluation decision that require judgment as a qualitative model

22-9 A macro-based reliability model that attempts to predict the number of failures that will occur in a system during a fixed testing interval is a:
  a Fault seeding model
  b Mean error time model
  c Time between failures model
  d Failure count model

22-10 Which of the following is *not* an advantage of macro-based reliability models over micro-based reliability models for evaluating the reliability of an internal control system:
  a The statistical models that underlie macro-based reliability models are simpler
  b Macro-based reliability models require less data
  c Information on the strengths and weaknesses of each internal control does not have to be collected with a macro-based reliability model
  d They tend to be easier to implement via computer programs

22-11 What is the variable $P(e)$ in the reliability formula:

$$R = p + (1 - p)P(e)P(c)$$

  a Probability of an error
  b Probability of a control signaling an error or irregularity
  c Probability of a control signaling an error or irregularity when one exists
  d Probability that an error discovered is corrected

22-12 Given $R_1 = .7$ and $R_2 = .9$, the overall reliability of the system is:
  a .63
  b .9
  c .7
  d Cannot be determined from the data given

22-13 What is the variable T_r in the following formula that calculates the dollar error produced: $Ne_{i_r} \times Ve_i \times T_r$
  a Tolerance of the rth control
  b Number of errors of type r
  c Frequency with which the set of r controls is executed
  d Total cost of executing the rth control

22-14 Given the following values:

$$
\begin{array}{ll}
p_1 = .8 & p_2 = .9 \\
P(e_{11}) = .9 & P(e_{21}) = .8 \\
P(c_{11}) = .7 & P(c_{21}) = .9 \\
P(e_{12}) = .7 & P(e_{22}) = .8 \\
P(c_{12}) = .9 & P(c_{22}) = .7
\end{array}
$$

The reliability of the system is (to three decimal places):
  a .963
  b .961
  c .980
  d None of the above

22-15 Which of the following is a major reason for using Bayesian models to evaluate the reliability of an internal control system:
  a They are the cheapest analytical model to use
  b They require less information than a macro-based reliability model

      c They provide more accurate results than a simulation model

      d They provide a formal means of revising the auditor's assessment of the reliability of an internal control

22-16 Assume that the auditor is evaluating the reliability of a control. The auditor's prior probability of the control being reliable is .95. However, a test is undertaken and the test result indicates the control is unreliable. Previous experience with the test has shown that the probability of the test producing an unfavorable result when the control is, in fact, reliable is .15, and the probability of the test producing an unfavorable result whent he control is, in fact, unreliable is .9. In light of the test result, the auditor should now assess the probability of the control being reliable as:

      a .24

      b .76

      c .8125

      d None of the above

22-17 Which of the following is a reason to use a simulation model instead of an analytical model to evaluate how well a system safeguards assets or maintains data integrity:

      a Simulation models are cheaper to design, implement, and execute

      b The analytical model needed is not mathematically tractable

      c This cost of the evaluation is reduced over a wide range of values of the independent variable and changes in the structure of the model

      d A general-purpose simulation language is available

22-18 Which of the following is an implementation cost for a control system:

      a Wages of a security officer

      b Cost of an undetected error in a communications line

      c Costs of testing a modification to an access control routine

      d Programming labor costs involved in writing an input validation routine

22-19 What costs are represented by the following formula:

$$\sum_{i=1}^{n} \sum_{j=1}^{r} (1 - R_i^{j-1}) P(e_{ij}) Cs_{ij}$$

      a Total expected costs of identifying whether errors or irregularities exist when they are signaled and correcting them if they do exist

      b Total expected costs of executing the controls

      c Total expected losses resulting from uncorrected errors or irregularities

      d Total expected costs of searching for errors and irregularities when they are incorrectly rejected by the control system

22-20 When evaluating whether an investment in a control system is worthwhile, the term β in the formula used to calculate the discount rate is:

      a The risk-free rate of return

      b Weighted cost of capital of the firm investing in the control system

      c The coefficient obtained when the returns on the security of a firm that designs and implements control systems are regressed against returns on the market portfolio

      d The coefficient obtained when returns on the market portfolio are regressed against the risk-free rate of return

EXERCISES AND CASES

22-1 An auditor wishes to calculate the reliability of a validation program with respect to a particular error type. The probability of a clerk submitting the data item in error is .2. The program can identify the error 80% of the time, and 95% of the time it will be corrected properly by the clerk. What is the reliability of the program with respect to the error?

22-2 Given the following values, calculate the overall reliability of a system having a single process, two error types, and two controls:

$$p_1 = .7 \qquad p_2 = .85$$
$$P(e_{11}) = .8 \qquad P(e_{21}) = .9$$
$$P(c_{11}) = .9 \qquad P(c_{21}) = .95$$
$$P(e_{12}) = .75 \qquad P(e_{22}) = .8$$
$$P(c_{12}) = .6 \qquad P(c_{22}) = .75$$

22-3 Calculate the reliability of the online update program evaluated in Table 22-3 if the amount check is performed before the account check.

22-4 Calculate the value of A, the total dollar error produced in a year by a validation program run monthly if on average the program fails to detect 10 errors and the estimated average effect of each error is $2.

22-5 Calculate the ongoing costs of operating the amount check only and the amount check then the account check for the system evaluated in Table 22-4. Using the data given in Table 22-5, which of the five possible control systems for the online update program would you choose?

22-6 Determine whether or not to invest in the fire detection and extinguisher system described in the chapter if the installation cost of the system is $80,000, the life of the system is 10 years, and the required rate of return is 10%.

22-7 If the fire detection and extinguisher system described in the chapter is installed, show the probability distribution of costs that may occur in any one year.

22-8 Maintaining the privacy of data is a form of asset safeguarding. For an online realtime update system with remote entry terminals and a centralized shared database, list the various controls to preserve privacy that you would examine to assess reliability. Describe the evidence collection technique you would use for each of these controls to assess their reliability. Describe, also, a *formal* model that you could use to assess the *overall* reliability of the internal control system.

ANSWERS TO MULTIPLE CHOICE QUESTIONS

22-1 a	22-6 d	22-11 c	22-16 b
22-2 c	22-7 b	22-12 a	22-17 b
22-3 d	22-8 c	22-13 c	22-18 d
22-4 b	22-9 d	22-14 b	22-19 a
22-5 a	22-10 a	22-15 d	22-20 c

REFERENCES

Ashton, Robert. "An Experimental Study of Internal Control Judgments," *Journal of Accounting Research* (Spring 1974), pp. 143–157.

Bailey, Andrew D., Jr. *Statistical Auditing: Review, Concepts, and Problems* (New York: Harcourt Brace Jovanovich, 1981).

Bailey, Andrew D., Jr., James H. Gerlach, R. Preston McAfee, and Andrew B. Whinston. "An Application of Complexity Theory to the Analysis of Internal Control Systems," *Auditing: A Journal of Practice and Theory* (Summer 1981), pp. 38–52.

Bierman, Harold, and Seymour Smidt. *The Capital Budgeting Decision*, 4th ed. (New York: Macmillan, 1975).

Bodnar, George. "Reliability Modeling of Internal Control Systems," *The Accounting Review* (October 1975), pp. 747–757.

Burns, David C., and James K. Loebbecke. "Internal Control Evaluation: How the Computer Can Help," *Journal of Accountancy* (August 1975), pp. 60–70.

Copeland, Thomas E., and J. Fred Weston. *Financial Theory and Corporate Policy*, 2d ed. (Reading, MA: Addison-Wesley, 1983).

Cushing, Barry E. "A Mathematical Approach to the Analysis and Design of Internal Control Systems," *The Accounting Review* (January 1974), pp. 24–41.

Cushing, Barry E. "A Further Note on the Mathematical Approach to Internal Control," *The Accounting Review* (January 1975), pp. 151–154.

Davis, Randall, and Douglas B. Lenat. *Knowledge-Based Systems in Artificial Intelligence* (New York: McGraw-Hill, 1982).

Deloitte Haskins & Sells. *Auditing with the Microcomputers: A Practical Guide*, 2d ed. (New York: Deloitte Haskins & Sells, 1986).

Emshoff, James R., and Rodger L. Sisson. *Design and Use of Computer Simulation Models* (New York: Macmillan, 1970).

Fama, Eugene F. "Risk-Adjusted Discount Rates and Capital Budgeting under Uncertainty," *Journal of Financial Economics* (August 1977), pp. 3–24.

Ferrell, William R. "Combining Individual Judgments," in George Wright, ed., *Behavioral Decision Making* (New York: Plenum Press, 1985), pp. 111–145.

Fugini, M., and G. Martella. "ACTEN: A Conceptual Model for Security Systems Design," *Computers and Security*, vol. 3, 1984, pp. 196–214.

Gerberick, Dahl A. "Security Risk Analysis," *EDPACS* (April 1979), pp. 1–11.

Goel, Amrit L. "Software Reliability Models: Assumptions, Limitations, and Applicability," *IEEE Transactions on Software Engineering* (December 1985), pp. 1411–1423.

Grimlund, Richard A. "An Integration of Internal Control System and Account Balance Evidence," *Journal of Accounting Research* (Autumn 1982), pp. 316–342.

Gustafson, David H., and George P. Huber. "Behavioral Decision Theory and the Health Delivery System," in Martin F. Kaplan and Steven Schwartz, eds., *Human Judgment and Decision Processes in Applied Settings* (New York: Academic Press, 1977), pp. 145–167.

Ishikawa, Akira. "A Mathematical Approach to the Analysis and Design of Internal Control Systems: A Brief Comment," *The Accounting Review* (January 1975), pp. 148–150.

Ishikawa, Akira, and Charles H. Smith. "A Feedforward Control System for Organizational Planning and Control," *Abacus* (December 1972), pp. 163–180.

Knechel, W. Robert. "The Use of Quantitative Models in the Review and Evaluation of Internal Control: A Survey and Review," *Journal of Accounting Literature* (Spring 1983), pp. 205–219.

Libby, Robert. *Accounting and Human Information Processing: Theory and Applications* (Englewood Cliffs, NJ: Prentice-Hall, 1981).

Misra, P. N. "Software Reliability Analysis," *IBM Systems Journal*, vol. 22, no. 3, 1983, pp. 262–270.

Ramamoorthy, C. V., and Siu-Bun F. Ho. "Testing Large Software with Automated Software Evaluation Aids," *IEEE Transactions on Software Engineering* (March 1975), pp. 46–58.

Schick, George J. "Modeling the Reliability of Computer Software," *Decision Sciences* (October 1974), pp. 529–544.

Schick, George J., and Ray W. Wolverton. "An Analysis of Competing Software Reliability Models," *IEEE Transactions on Software Engineering* (March 1978), pp. 104–120.

Sharpe, William F. *Investments* (Englewood Cliffs, NJ: Prentice-Hall, 1978).

Slovic, Paul, and Sarah Lichtenstein. "Comparison of Bayesian and Regression Approaches to the Study of Information Processing in Judgment," *Organizational Behavior and Human Performance* (June 1971), pp. 649–744.

Sowizral, Henry A. "Expert Systems," in Martha E. Williams, ed., *Annual Review of Information Science and Technology*, vol. 20, 1985, pp. 179–199.

State of Illinois. "Elements and Economics of Information Privacy and Security," *Data Security and Data Processing Volume 3 Part 2 Study Results: State of Illinois* (New York: IBM Corporation, 1974), pp. 23–244.

Swap, Walter C., and Associates. *Group Decision Making* (Beverly Hills: Sage Publications, 1984).

Trotman, Ken. "The Review Process and the Accuracy of Auditor Judgments," *Journal of Accounting Research* (Autumn 1985), pp. 740–752.

Van Horne, James C. *Financial Management and Policy*, 4th ed. (Englewood Cliffs, NJ: Prentice-Hall, 1977).

Waterman, Donald A. *A Guide to Expert Systems* (Reading, MA: Addison-Wesley, 1986).

Weber, Ron. "Auditor Decision Making on Overall System Reliability: Accuracy, Consensus, and the Usefulness of a Simulation Decision Aid," *Journal of Accounting Research* (Autumn 1978), pp. 368–388.

Yu, Seongjae, and John Neter. "A Stochastic Model of the Internal Control System," *Journal of Accounting Research* (Autumn 1973), pp. 273–295.

EVALUATING SYSTEM EFFECTIVENESS

After a system has been operational for some time, it may be subjected to a postimplementation review. A postimplementation review has a twofold purpose. First, it is used to determine whether a system should be scrapped or continued and, if the system is to be continued, whether it should be modified in some way to better meet its objectives. Second, the review evaluates the adequacy of the system development process used to design and implement the system. In light of this evaluation, system development standards may be changed or system development personnel may be counseled.

This chapter focuses on the first objective of a postimplementation review, namely, the evaluation of a system to determine how well it is meeting its objectives. The first section provides a list of overall goals that a high-quality information system must achieve if it is to be effective. The next section describes the evaluation process that the auditor can use to determine how well these goals are being met. Finally, the chapter provides some brief guidelines for improving the auditor's overall judgment on system effectiveness.

GOALS OF AN INFORMATION SYSTEM

What are (should be) the goals of a high-quality information system? This is a frustrating and difficult question to attempt to answer. One answer might be that the overall objective of an information system is to increase the effectiveness of the organization it services. But this response simply shifts the problem; for the next question must be: What are the goals of an effective organization? The goals of an information system and the goals of the organization it serves are inextricably intertwined. Information systems are developed to help an organization meet its goals; thus, whether or not a system is effective must be assessed in terms of organization goals.

Unfortunately there is little consensus on what constitute the goals of an organization. Steers [1977] in his review of the literature on organizational effectiveness shows the diversity of indicators used to measure goal accomplishment. They include profitability, growth, turnover, absenteeism, job satisfaction, stability, flexibility, morale, and readiness. Whether some of these indicators measure goal accomplishment or the state of factors that affect goal accomplishment might be debated. For example, an economist might argue that ultimately the effectiveness of an organization is solely a function of its profitability. Turnover, stability, readiness, absenteeism, etc., all affect profitability. However, an organizational theorist might argue that profitability is too gross a measure of effectiveness. It might be possible, for example, to increase the quality of working life of employees without affecting profitability.

Aside from the debate over what constitutes the goals of the organization, there is also controversy over the approach to be used to evaluate the effectiveness of an organization. Cunningham [1977] identifies seven different approaches to evaluating organizational effectiveness:

Evaluation approach	Explanation
Rational goal model	Evaluates the organization's ability to achieve its formally stated goals.
Systems resource model	Evaluates how well the organization distributes resources to meet the needs of its various subsystems.
Managerial process model	Evaluates the organization's ability to perform various managerial functions that facilitate achieving the overall goals.
Organizational development model	Evaluates how well the organization allows members to achieve their own goals and how well it facilitates their working as a team.

Evaluation approach	Explanation
Bargaining model	Evaluates how well decision makers within the organization can obtain the resources they need to accomplish the tasks they deem important.
Structural functional model	Evaluates how well the organization can respond to a variety of situations and events.
Functional model	Evaluates the usefulness of the organization's activities from the viewpoint of its client groups.

Given the problems, then, of defining organizational goals and in selecting an approach to be used to evaluate how well these goals are being met, it is unlikely that an uncontroversial statement can be made about the goals that an information system should attain or about the approach to be used when evaluating information system effectiveness. In this chapter, the choice of the goals used to evaluate effectiveness and the evaluation approach to be employed simply reflects the biases, experience, and training of the author. In this light, a rational goal approach has been chosen to assess how well an information system attains five major sets of goals (Figure 23-1):

FIGURE 23-1
Major goals of an effective information system.

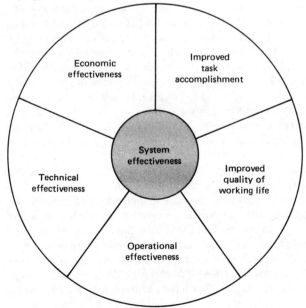

Information system goal	Explanation
Improved task accomplishment	Users of the system should be more productive and produce higher-quality output.
Improved quality of working life	The system should contribute positively to a user's overall quality of life.
Operational effectiveness	The system should be easy to use; it should be used in an appropriate way; it should be used frequently; users should be satisfied with the system.
Technical effectiveness	The system should be supported by the appropriate hardware and software technology.
Economic effectiveness	The benefits of the system should exceed the costs.

The utility of the choices made above is an empirical question, and in a particular context the auditor may determine that another set of goals or another approach to evaluating effectiveness is more appropriate (see, further, Cameron [1986]). Nevertheless, the overall methodology described in the chapter will still apply.

THE EVALUATION PROCESS

Ideally, all information systems should be subjected periodically to a postimplementation review and an assessment of how well they are meeting their goals. However, empirical research has shown that only certain systems undergo postimplementation evaluations (see, for example, Hamilton and Chervany [1981a, 1981b]). The factors that lead to the selection of a particular system for evaluation are still somewhat unclear, but some insight into the decision has been obtained. For example, if management has little doubt about the success of a system, they may not request a postimplementation review. Conversely, if they have doubts about the system, a review may be commissioned. Reviews also may be undertaken for political reasons. For example, managers may have a review undertaken on a system for which they are responsible in order to extract more resources from the organization for their own purposes.

When assessing system effectiveness the auditor carries out two kinds of evaluations: (a) a relative evaluation, and (b) an absolute evaluation. In a relative evaluation the auditor compares the state of goal accomplishment after the system has been implemented with the state of goal accomplishment before the system is implemented. In an absolute evaluation the auditor assesses the size of the goal accomplishment after the system has been implemented.

Relative evaluations can be applied to two goals: (a) improved task accomplishment, and (b) improved quality of working life. With these two goals the auditor attempts to assess what changes have occurred with the implementation of the system. Has task performance improved or deteriorated? Has the quality of working life gone up or down?

Relative evaluations involve six steps:

1 *Identify the attributes of the goal to be measured:* There may be some debate over what attributes of a goal should be measured. In part, the choice may be affected by the cost of measuring various attributes and the perceived importance of these attributes.

2 *Select the measures to be used:* Tools for measuring the attributes next must be chosen. Chapter 20 described how questionnaires and interviews might be used. Data on some attributes may be collected routinely by the organization.

3 *Identify the user group to be measured:* It is important to identify both the primary and secondary users of a system. Improved task accomplishment and increased quality of working life for the primary user group may be attained at a cost of decreased task accomplishment and lowered quality of working life for the secondary user group.

4 *Obtain ex ante measures:* Before the system is implemented, the state of goal accomplishment must be measured.

5 *Obtain ex post measures:* After the system is implemented, the state of goal accomplishment must be measured. The difficulty here is determining what time period should elapse before the measures should be taken.

6 *Assess the change in goal accomplishment:* The ex ante and ex post measures are compared to assess the changes in goal accomplishment. If ex post measures are taken periodically, the time series of changes in goal accomplishment can be plotted.

Absolute evaluations can be applied to three goals: (*a*) operational effectiveness, (*b*) technical effectiveness, and (*c*) economic effectiveness. With these three objectives an ex ante measure of goal accomplishment often cannot be taken; for example, system use cannot be measured before the system is operational. Thus, the auditor must consider an absolute measure of goal accomplishment after the system has been implemented and judge whether the level of accomplishment is satisfactory.

Absolute evaluations follow the same steps to be taken for relative evaluations except that an ex ante measure of goal accomplishment is not taken (step 4) and the process of assessing goal accomplishment (step 6) is different. Initially a judgment must be made on whether the absolute level of goal accomplishment is satisfactory; however, changes in this level over time also may be traced as part of the evaluation process.

Task Accomplishment Objectives

An effective information system improves the task accomplishment of its users. Unfortunately, providing specific measures of task accomplishment that the auditor can use to evaluate an information system is difficult. Performance measures for task accomplishment differ considerably across applications (and sometimes across organizations).

Consider, for example, the ways in which task accomplishment might be assessed for a manufacturing control system, a sales system, and a welfare system that supports counselors in their work. Some of the measures of task accomplishment used for the manufacturing control system might be:

1 Number of units output
2 Number of defective units reworked
3 Number of units scrapped
4 Amount of waste produced
5 Amount of downtime
6 Amount of idle time

For the sales system, some of the measures of task accomplishment might be:

1 Dollar value of sales made
2 Changes in customer satisfaction ratings
3 Amount of doubtful/bad debts that arise
4 Average time for delivery of goods to customer
5 Number of new customers acquired
6 Number of sales made to old customers

For the welfare system, some of the measures of task accomplishment might be (see, also, Kling [1977]):

1 Number of clients successfully counseled
2 Average cost per client
3 Number of clients returning for counseling
4 Client satisfaction ratings of counseling service provided

One of the major problems encountered when evaluating task accomplishment is choosing a measure that is neither too global nor too detailed. In many cases a measure such as profitability probably is too global. It is important to know the factors that affect profitability so they can be manipulated favorably. On the other hand, continuously monitoring, say, 100 measures of task accomplishment would be too detailed a measurement process. The data collection process would be costly. Further, it is doubtful whether the data could be assimilated to assess the impact of changes in the variables monitored on overall effectiveness. The auditor must attempt to identify a small set of indicators that provide most information about goal accomplishment.

It is also important to trace task accomplishment over time. If the system designers have not carried out the process of refreezing (see Chapter 4), users of the system may revert to their old behavior patterns. The level of task accomplishment may fall back to the level existing before the implementation of the system; it may be even lower if the system interferes with these old behavior patterns.

Quality of Working Life Objectives

The Report of a Special Task Force to the U.S. Secretary of Health, Education, and Welfare [1973] claimed fundamental relationships exist between the quality of working life of individuals and their physical and mental health. The report examined, among other things, relationships between work and longevity, work and heart disease, work and peptic ulcers, work and arthritis, work and psychosomatic illness, work and alienation, and work and suicide. The message in the report is clear: the overall welfare of a nation is vitally dependent on the quality of working life of its people.

There is now general acceptance that achieving a high quality of working life for users of a system is a major objective in the design process. There is less agreement on the definition and measurement of the quality of working life. Lawler [1975] argues disputes exist because different groups in an organization have vested interests in how the quality of working life is defined; for example, some consider the quality of working life from a productivity perspective, some from a physical conditions and wages perspective, and some from an alienation perspective.

Even if agreement existed on the attributes of a high quality of working life, some difficult measurement problems remain (see, also, Lawler [1975] and Seashore [1975]). It is not easy to construct a measure that has face validity; that is, one that interested parties perceive to be a legitimate measure. Measurement instruments that have high test-retest reliability are not common. Further, the measure must be objective and verifiable and not subject to manipulation; otherwise, responses may be biased intentionally by a particular interest group. Somehow the measure must take into account that individuals in the same work environment may respond differently; for example, a person who has had several jobs is likely to have a higher level of job satisfaction than a person who is employed for the first time. The time span for measurement also must be chosen; employees subject to poor working conditions may report a high quality of working life if they have high expectations of better things to come.

Surrogate Measures   One way of assessing the quality of working life is to use surrogate measures; that is, measures that act as indicators of the level of the quality of work life existing instead of directly measuring attributes of the quality of working life. Some of the surrogate measures that have been used are (see, further, Macy and Mirvis [1976]):

Measure	Possible definitions
Absenteeism rate	$= \dfrac{\text{total absent days}}{\text{total working days}}$
Tardiness rate	$= \dfrac{\text{total incidents of tardiness}}{\text{total working days}}$
Strike rate	$= \dfrac{\text{total strike days}}{\text{total working days}}$
Work ban rate	$= \dfrac{\text{total work bans}}{\text{total working days}}$
Stoppage rate	$= \dfrac{\text{total stoppages}}{\text{total working days}}$
Grievance rate	$= \dfrac{\text{total grievances}}{\text{average work force size}}$
Turnover rate	$= \dfrac{\text{total turnover incidents}}{\text{average work force size}}$
Accident rate	$= \dfrac{\text{total accidents}}{\text{total working days}}$
Sick rate	$= \dfrac{\text{total sick days}}{\text{total working days}}$
Theft/sabotage rate	$= \dfrac{\text{total theft/sabotage incidents}}{\text{average work force size}}$

Changes in these measures are the outcome of changes in the quality of working life. For example, a lowered quality of working life may cause increased turnover of employees or a greater number of strikes. Thus, to assess the effectiveness of a system, the focus is on how these measures change after the system has been implemented.

There are three advantages of using surrogate measures to assess the quality of working life. First, the measures are objective, verifiable, and difficult to manipulate. Second, the data required for the measures is relatively easy to obtain. Most of the data should be maintained routinely by an organization. For example, the personnel department of the organization should keep records on sickness, absenteeism, strikes, etc. Third, the cost of changes in the measures can be assessed. For example, the cost of absenteeism can be measured by calculating the cost of wages and fringe benefits of replacement workers, the opportunity cost of profit lost during the replacement process, the cost of the personnel department's time in dealing with the absenteeism, etc. (see, further, Macy and Mirvis [1976]).

The major disadvantage of using surrogate measures is that management (or a union) does not always know why the quality of working life has been lowered or raised. What attributes of the quality of working life have been affected by the implementation of a system still must be determined; otherwise, if the quality of working life has been lowered, there is little basis for corrective action. Use of surrogate measures does not alleviate the need to investigate cause-effect relationships.

Direct Measures Direct measures attempt to gauge the levels of the attributes of the quality of working life; thus, a decision must be made on what is meant by a high quality of working life.

Various researchers have proposed different lists of attributes of a high quality of working life (see, for example, Davis and Cherns [1975]). The following list provided by Walton [1975] includes some of the major attributes commonly proposed:

Quality of work life attribute	Explanation
Adequate and fair compensation	The income received from work should meet social standards of sufficiency and bear an appropriate relationship to the income received from other work.
Safe and healthy working conditions	The physical work conditions should minimize the risk of illness and injury. There should be limitations on hours worked.
Opportunity to use and develop human capacities	Jobs should provide autonomy, involve both planning and implementation activities, allow use of multiple skills, and be meaningful. Employees should obtain feedback on their actions.
Opportunity for continued growth and security	There must be ongoing opportunities to develop and use new skills. Employment and income security should exist.
Social integration in the work organization	The workplace should be free of prejudice, allow interpersonal openness, and encourage a sense of community.
Constitution in the work organization	The workplace should preserve personal privacy, allow free speech, provide equitable treatment, and allow due process when disputes arise.
Balanced work role and total life space	Work should be integrated with the total life space; e.g., it should not place unreasonable demands on leisure and family time.
Social relevance of work life	The worker should perceive the workplace to be socially responsible.

Measurement of these attributes is a difficult task. In some cases instruments have been developed and their validity and reliability tested. For example, Hackman et al. [1975] have developed an instrument to measure how well a job matches a worker's needs in terms of variety, challenge, decision making autonomy, opportunities for learning, perceived relevance and contribution, and future prospects. Instruments to measure job satisfaction (as an attribute of the quality of working life) are well developed. Nadler et al. [1976] describe an instrument developed to assess ongoing attitudes in an organization related to job satisfaction, the quality of supervision, and the availability of regular feedback on job performance. However, in general, directly measuring the quality of working life still constitutes a major problem.

Operational Effectiveness Objectives

When assessing operational effectiveness, the auditor examines how well the system meets its goals from the viewpoint of a user who interacts with the system on a day-by-day basis. Many measures of operational effectiveness have been proposed, but four measures have received the most attention from information systems researchers: frequency of use, nature of use, ease of use, and user satisfaction.

Frequency of Use Frequency of use has been employed widely by researchers as a measure of the implementation success of computer systems (see, for example, Schultz and Slevin [1975], Ein-Dor and Segev [1978], and Lucas [1978b]). Intuitively, this relationship is appealing. However, empirical research has produced equivocal results. Some researchers have found a positive relationship between frequency of use and implementation success (see, for example, Danziger [1977] and Robey [1979]); others have found no such relationship (see, for example, Schewe [1976] and Srinivasan [1985]). As a consequence, the auditor should be careful to see that in the context of the information system being evaluated frequency of use appears to be a meaningful measure of information system operational effectiveness.

When measuring information system frequency of use, a distinction must be made between voluntary use and involuntary use (Figure 23-2). In some systems, users can choose whether or not to employ a system to help them with the task that they are performing. In other systems, reports are generated on a routine basis, and users receive the reports unsolicited.

If system use is voluntary, monitors can be built into the system to determine how often the system is invoked by the user to perform a task (see, for example, Lucas [1978a]). If use is involuntary, however, the auditor must

FIGURE 23-2
Types of information system usage.

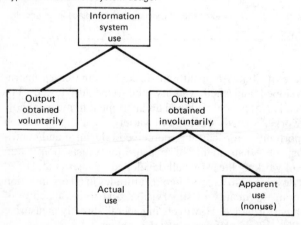

then attempt to determine whether use is "real" or "apparent." Objective evidence of system use might be sought; for example, in some cases it may be clear that system output has been used to make a decision. Alternatively, interviews or questionnaires might be employed to gauge the real use of the system. Unfortunately, the data reported via interviews or questionnaires may not be reliable for various reasons; for example, users may not accurately recall how frequently they use a system, or they may overstate frequency of use to gain favor with management.

Nature of Use   Ginzberg [1978b] has argued that frequency of use often is an inappropriate measure to evaluate system effectiveness. He points to situations where a system is used infrequently yet it is considered to be successful. For example, the act of building a decision support system may provide important insights into how an ongoing problem should be approached, and in this light users may consider the system to be successful even though their day-to-day use of the system may be low.

As a consequence, Ginzberg [1978a] argues that the overall success of a system must be evaluated in terms of the *way* it is used and not just the frequency of use. The way a system is used evokes different types of change in a user's actions. He identifies four different levels of individual change that can occur:

Level of change	Explanation
Management action	The user simply treats the system as a black box and uses the information or solution to the problem provided by the system.
Management change	The user must have an elementary understanding of the system. The user treats the system as a tool that can be applied to find answers to specific problems.
Recurring use of the management science approach	The user develops a fundamental appreciation of the analytical approach used by the system to solve problems. The user attempts to apply this analytical approach to other problems.
Task redefinition	The system causes users to rethink their view of the job, the way in which they perform the job, etc. The user employs the system to help redefine tasks.

Ginzberg [1978a] hypothesizes that different types of systems require different types of change (levels of adoption) if they are to be successful. For example, at one extreme a clerical replacement system such as a payroll system requires only a "management change" level of adoption. At the other extreme a decision support system for portfolio managers requires a "task redefinition" level of change. Furthermore, he argues that attempting to adopt a level of change other than the one appropriate to the type of system at hand is a waste of effort. In essence, Ginzberg's hypothesis is based upon a contingency theory of implementation; successful systems require different levels of adoption depending upon the nature of the system (see, also, Alter [1978] and Moore [1979]).

In an empirical study of 29 systems, Ginzberg [1978a] found evidence to support his hypothesis. He administered a questionnaire to users of the systems to identify the characteristics of the system, the level of change that it evoked, and the perceived degree of success that the system had achieved. Successful systems had evoked the level of change that his theory predicted; unsuccessful systems had not achieved the appropriate level of change.

Consequently, the auditor should be careful not to conclude that a system has high operational effectiveness solely on the basis of its frequency of use. Ginzberg's research suggests that the level of change brought about by the system also must be examined. Users may have no choice but to use the output of a system, but this does not mean that they consider the system to be successful (see, also, Dutton and Kraemer [1978]).

Ease of Use   Maish [1979] found positive associations between a user's feelings about systems and the extent to which the systems were easy to use. Sterling [1974] presents a number of design guidelines to facilitate use of a system; for example, the language of the system should be easy to understand, the system should recognize that it deals with different types of individuals, the system should allow an individual a choice on how to deal with the system, the system should relieve the user of unnecessary chores.

When evaluating ease of use, the auditor again must be careful to identify both the primary and secondary users of a system. A system may have been designed to facilitate use by one class of users with little thought being given to other classes of users. For example, middle managers of an exception reporting system may find the system easy to use; however, the clerical staff who collect the input data may have great difficulty in meeting the data submission deadlines imposed by the system (see, also, Chapter 4).

Questionnaires can be used to evaluate a user's perceptions of how easy a system is to use. Maish [1979] describes a questionnaire he employed to evaluate various attributes of ease of use: terminal location convenience, availability of user instructions, flexibility of reporting formats, ease of error correction, etc. Individual items on a questionnaire will depend on the characteristics of the system used. For example, evaluation of an online system would include questions relating to the interactive language; a questionnaire for a batch system would not include these questions.

User Satisfaction   Because of the difficulties associated with measures of frequency of use, nature of use, and ease of use, some researchers have attempted to develop instruments that will assess a user's satisfaction with a system. The basic tenet that underlies this work is that user satisfaction is highly correlated with system success and, in the absence of good measures of system success, a valid and reliable measure of user satisfaction is a suitable surrogate.

Perhaps the best-developed instrument to measure user satisfaction is the questionnaire developed by Jenkins and Ricketts [1985]. Its use should be restricted to evaluating user satisfaction with turnkey decision support systems. Individual questions in the instrument are based on five underlying dimensions:

Underlying dimension	Issues addressed
Problem finding	Accuracy of report contents; relevance of report contents; adequacy of report contents; clarity of report contents.
Problem solving	Usefulness for identifying and defining problems; usefulness for selecting among alternatives; usefulness for forming solutions to the problems.
Input procedures	Ease of understanding input procedures; ease of using input procedures; capabilities for preventing input errors.
Computer processing	Stability of the system; adequacy of the response time; availability of the system.
Report form	Quality of report format; timeliness of report; mode of presentation; sequence of presentation; adequacy of feedback; relevance of reports.

Unfortunately, instruments to measure user satisfaction are less well developed for other types of computer systems. Ives et al. [1983] provide a review of some of the major instruments that are available and an assessment of their relative strengths and limitations. As Chapter 20 points out, however, the auditor should exercise caution in using any instrument that tries to elicit attitudes, beliefs, or opinions until its reliability and validity have been established.

Technical Effectiveness Objectives

The evaluation of technical effectiveness involves deciding whether or not the appropriate hardware and software technology has been used to support a system. In essence the question asked is: Would a change in the support hardware/software technology enable a system to meet its goals better? The following three sections briefly examine some major aspects of this evaluation process.

Hardware Effectiveness   Chapters 21 and 24 provide detailed discussions of how hardware performance can be evaluated. This evaluation may enable the throughput of the existing configuration to be improved. However, it also may indicate a new hardware configuration is needed; in other words, the benefits of a new configuration would exceed the costs of the change. Since in-depth evaluation of hardware often is a costly and time-consuming process (see, also,

Chapter 3), the regular effectiveness evaluation simply may examine gross measures of hardware performance; for example, system response time, downtime, idle time.

Software Effectiveness The software technology supporting an application system can be evaluated by examining three attributes of application programs: (a) the history of program repair maintenance, (b) the history of program modifications, and (c) run-time resource consumption.

The history of program repair maintenance indicates the quality of logic existing in a program. Repair maintenance is carried out to correct program logic errors. Extensive repair maintenance means inappropriate design, coding, or testing technologies have been used to implement the program—inexperienced programmers have not been supervised adequately, system testing has not been carried out, a top-down design approach has not been used, etc.

There are two reasons why modifications to program specifications occur. First, the designer may formulate incorrect specifications; consequently, the specifications have to be changed and the program logic altered. Second, user requirements may change; the program has to be altered to meet these new user requirements. Incorrect program specifications mean the technology used to develop the specifications should be examined. Frequent modifications to meet changes in user needs may mean the system is inflexible; it has not been designed to accommodate change.

If at run time an application program consumes resources inefficiently, it may mean the logic is structured poorly or the programming language or compiler used is inappropriate for the task to be performed. Again, the auditor should examine the technology supporting these aspects of software implementation; there may be inadequate code review, the installation may be using a poor quality compiler, testing may be inadequate, etc. (see Chapter 5).

The designers and programmers responsible for carrying out program modification and repair maintenance and the operators responsible for running programs are important sources of information on the appropriateness of the software technology used for an application system. Designers and programmers can make judgments on the overall quality of programs; they know whether a program is easy to modify or repair. Operators often can make judgments on whether a program consumes abnormal amounts of resources at run time. These judgments can be elicited using questionnaires or interviews (see Chapter 20).

Independence Goals A major objective in choosing the technology to support an information system is to attain independence within and among the major resources that support the system: hardware, software, and data. Independence is a desired goal for three reasons (see, also, Gilb [1977]). First, it allows a system to be adapted more readily to a future environment. Second, it allows a system to be adapted more readily to multiple existing environments. Third, it allows a system to be adapted more readily to a backup environment.

Halloran et al. [1978] identify six resource relationships where the extent of independence should be assessed:

Resource relationship	Independence criteria
Data—data	The system should minimize data redundancy, "fixed" data, and the number of interrelationships existing between data items.
Software—software	Programs should maximize module strength and minimize module coupling.
Hardware—hardware	Generalized hardware components should be used to reduce interface problems.
Data—software	The definition of data should be maintained independently of the programs that operate on it.
Data—hardware	The definition of data should be separated into a logical definition and a physical definition. The logical definition should remain intact when the hardware on which the data is stored changes.
Software—hardware	To the extent possible, the logical structure and source code of a program should be independent of the hardware on which the program operates.

The development of measures of independence is still a research area. Halloran et al. [1978] provide some guidelines as to the measures that can be used. However, judgment still must be exercised. Designers, programmers, and operators again are important sources of information on the extent of independence existing within and among the resources supporting an application system.

Economic Effectiveness Objectives

When evaluating the economic effectiveness of an information system, the auditor attempts to determine whether the net present value of the investment in the information system is greater than or equal to zero; in other words, the return on the investment in the information system is greater than or equal to the required rate of return. The evaluation involves carrying out three tasks: (*a*) identifying the costs and benefits of the information system, (*b*) valuing these costs and benefits, and (*c*) determining the net present value of these costs and benefits. The following sections provide a brief overview of each of these tasks.

Identifying Costs and Benefits Identifying the costs and benefits of an information system is a difficult task. To some extent, specific costs and benefits depend on the nature of the information system. For example, at least some of the benefits derived from an information system to support welfare counselors would be different from those derived from a manufacturing process control system.

There is also the problem of identifying *all* benefits and costs. The omission of a cost or benefit from a cost-effectiveness analysis may render the analysis

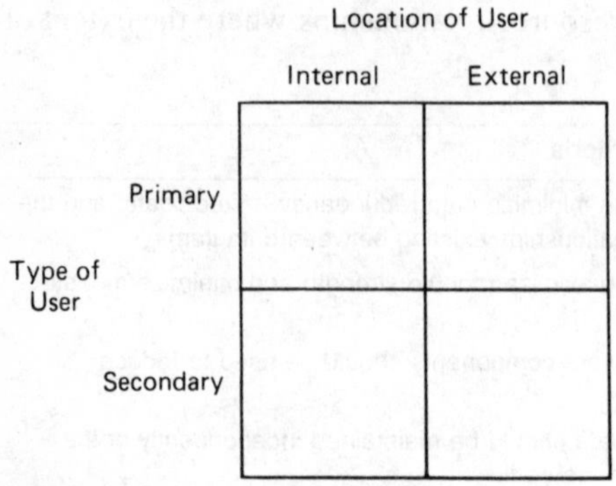

Location of User

Internal   External

Type of
User

Primary

Secondary

FIGURE 23-3
Classification of information system users.

invalid. Two types of costs and benefits present particular problems. First, the intangible benefits and costs of an information system often are difficult to identify as well as value. Does a system "enhance morale"? If so, what is the value of the enhanced morale? Second, externalities or spillover effects often are difficult to identify. For example, if an organization implements an advanced computer system, to what extent is the data processing department now able to hire better computer personnel because of the greater job challenge that exists?

To assist in the identification of *benefits,* the auditor may seek to classify the benefits in different ways. Initially, it may be useful to determine the various categories of users to whom benefits accrue. For example, Figure 23-3 shows users classified according to whether they are internal or external to the organization and whether they are considered to be primary or secondary users of the system. By identifying all potential user groups, the auditor is less likely to omit important benefits that accrue to someone as a result of using the system.

For each user group, benefits might then be classified according to whether they are easy or hard to identify and whether they are easy or hard to value. In Figure 23-4, benefits that fall into quadrants *A* and *D* are usually classified as tangible and intangible benefits, respectively. The nature of benefits that fall into quadrants *B* and *C* is less clear-cut. Again, by classifying the benefits in this way for each user group, auditors reduce the likelihood of omitting an important benefit.

These classification schemes do not work as well when attempting to identify the *costs* of an information system. Unfortunately, most costs that arise from developing, implementing, maintaining, and operating an information system are joint or common costs. In other words, they cannot be attributed uniquely to a particular user or class of users. Instead, they are incurred in the hope that all users of the system may benefit. Nonetheless,

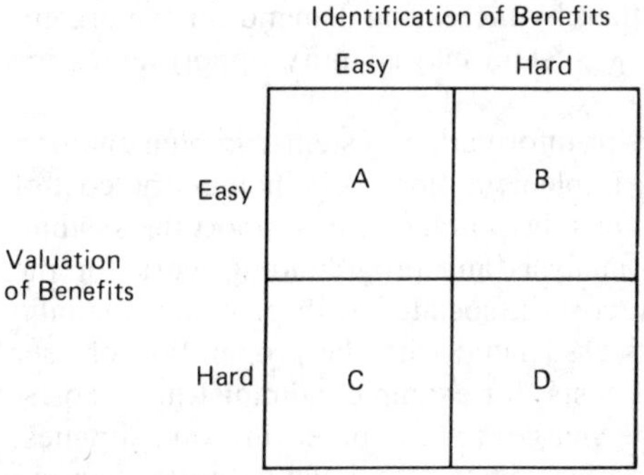

Identification of Benefits

		Easy	Hard
Valuation of Benefits	Easy	A	B
	Hard	C	D

FIGURE 23-4
Classification of information system benefits.

whenever auditors can categorize costs in some way, they should do so as a means of facilitating the complete identification of costs that accrue to the system.

Table 23-1 shows some relatively global classifications of the more tangible benefits and costs of an information system. King and Schrems [1978] present a more detailed listing. Ultimately the benefits of an information system translate into cost savings or revenue increases. Cost savings arise because fewer resources are needed to complete a task or existing resources become more productive. For example, a computerized payroll system eliminates many clerical positions needed with a manual system; a process control system may improve the productivity of machines in the job shop. Revenue increases arise because the demand for existing products increases or the organization is able to expand its markets. For example, a sales system may allow salespersons to

TABLE 23-1
BENEFITS AND COSTS OF AN INFORMATION SYSTEM

Benefits	Costs
Cost savings	Implementation costs
Labor	Hardware/software purchases
Fewer needed	System development costs
More productive	Labor: System analysis and programming
Machines	Hardware usage and supplies
Fewer needed	Documentation
More productive	Overhead
Overhead	Ongoing operational costs
Revenue increases	Hardware usage and supplies
More sales of existing products	Labor
Expanded markets	Program maintenance
	Operations personnel
	Clerical support
	Overhead

improve their service to customers, thereby increasing demand for the organization's products; a strategic planning system may identify opportunities for expanding markets.

Two major types of costs arise with information systems: implementation costs and ongoing operational costs. Implementation costs include the cost of any new hardware and software that must be purchased to support the system, labor costs associated with system analysis and programming work for the system, hardware usage and supply costs associated with program compilations and tests, documentation costs associated with the preparation of user manuals, etc., and various overhead costs, for example, administrative costs. The ongoing operational costs include charges for computer time and supplies, system maintenance costs, clerical support costs associated with data capture and preparation and running the system, and overhead costs.

Valuing Costs and Benefits Once the individual costs and benefits have been identified, they must be valued. The auditor may be involved in several ways in valuing the costs and benefits of an information system. Before the system is implemented the auditor may be asked to assist in estimating the costs and benefits of an information system or act as an objective judge of the quality of these estimates. After the system has been operational the auditor may be involved in the ex post assessment of whether or not the required rate of return was achieved with the investment in the information system.

Ex ante valuation of costs and benefits is the more difficult task; usually there is high uncertainty about the cash inflows and outflows that will arise. Even relatively straightforward costs and benefits sometimes may be difficult to estimate. For example, estimating the clerical support costs may not be simply a matter of calculating wages and salaries for the clerical personnel involved. The auditor may feel the system will have an unfavorable effect on the quality of working life of the clerical staff. Thus, the auditor may want to include an estimate of the extra costs that will arise because of increased staff turnover, higher training costs, strikes, increased absenteeism, etc.

Uncertainty can be incorporated into the cost-effectiveness analysis by expressing the anticipated costs and benefits in the form of a probability distribution. Chapter 22 showed how the probability distribution can be constructed. Assume there are only three operational costs for an information system: labor, machine, and overhead. The auditor estimates that each of these costs will take on one of two possible values with some probability, namely:

Labor		Machine		Overhead	
Cost	Probability	Cost	Probability	Cost	Probability
100,000	.6	7,000	.7	20,000	.8
120,000	.4	8,000	.3	25,000	.2

The resulting joint probability distribution consists of eight mutually exclusive events:

Amount		Probability	
100,000 + 7,000 + 20,000 = 127,000	(.6)(.7)(.8) =	.336
100,000 + 7,000 + 25,000 = 132,000	(.6)(.7)(.2) =	.084
100,000 + 8,000 + 20,000 = 128,000	(.6)(.3)(.8) =	.144
100,000 + 8,000 + 25,000 = 133,000	(.6)(.3)(.2) =	.036
120,000 + 7,000 + 20,000 = 147,000	(.4)(.7)(.8) =	.224
120,000 + 7,000 + 25,000 = 152,000	(.4)(.7)(.2) =	.056
120,000 + 8,000 + 20,000 = 148,000	(.4)(.3)(.8) =	.096
120,000 + 8,000 + 25,000 = 153,000	(.4)(.3)(.2) =	.024
	$\Sigma(p)$ =	1.000

Ex post estimation of costs and benefits usually is less difficult since some costs and benefits are known with certainty, for example, the costs of running a system at a service bureau. In some cases, however, valuation still may be difficult. For example, it may be hard to identify what cost savings or resource increases the system has produced; other factors in the organization that affect costs and revenues may have changed and it may be difficult to disaggregate the effects.

If users cannot estimate the value of a benefit or cost directly, several techniques can be used to assist them with the valuation. First, the auditor might attempt to break the benefit or cost down into smaller components. Users may be able to value the smaller components more easily, and the overall valuation can then be determined as a function of the valuation of these smaller components. Second, the auditor might attempt to simulate a market situation and ask users how much they would be willing to pay an outside vendor to obtain the benefit or to alleviate the cost. A market analogy may help them estimate the value of the benefit or cost. Third, the auditor might provide users with a listing of both tangible and intangible benefits and costs and ask users to rank order the benefits and costs according to their value. Since values can then be attached to the tangible benefits and costs, the values of the intangible benefits and costs may be estimated more easily. Fourth, the auditor might ask users for a range of value estimates, for example, the most optimistic value, the most pessimistic value, and the most likely value. A simulation approach might then be used to determine whether the decision on the economic effectiveness of the system changes under the different values. Finally, it is sometimes worth deferring the valuation of intangibles until after the tangibles have been valued as it may become clear that the decision on the economic effectiveness of the system will not be affected by the value of the intangibles.

Determining the Net Present Value Once the benefits and costs of an information system have been estimated, the net present value of the system can be determined using the formula (see, also, Chapter 22):

$$\text{NPV} = \sum_{t=0}^{n} \frac{B_t - C_t}{(1 + k)^t}$$

where B_t = benefits of information system in period t
C_t = costs of information system in period t
n = life of project in periods
k = required rate of return
As discussed in Chapter 22, k is determined using the formula:

$$k = k_f + \beta(\bar{k}_m - k_f)$$

where k_f = risk-free rate of return
$\bar{k}_m$ = expected rate of return on the market portfolio
β = beta coefficient of a security

Estimating β is still a problem. In this case, conceptually, it is estimated by regressing the returns on a security of an organization involved in designing, implementing, and marketing information systems of the type being considered with the returns on the market portfolio.

Again, as pointed out in Chapter 22, the net present value estimated is an *expected* value. Since there is uncertainty surrounding the benefits and costs of the information system, there is uncertainty surrounding the net present value that will occur. The variance of the probability distribution over the net present values is an important indicator of the risk involved in investing in the information system.

THE GLOBAL EVALUATION JUDGMENT

If dollar values could be attached to all the benefits and costs associated with an information system, the global evaluation judgment would be encapsulated in the assessment of whether or not a system had effectively met its economic objectives. Of course, this is an ideal situation that is rarely achieved in practice. In many systems the problem is that benefits and costs are often hard to identify and even harder to value. Consequently, the global evaluation judgment on system effectiveness is a complex decision that somehow must combine and weight a hodgepodge of information on benefits and costs that have been measured using different scales.

Chapter 22 also discussed the problems of making global judgments about the overall quality of an information system. There several recommendations were made as a basis for improving the quality of the judgment. If a qualitative approach were to be used to make the judgment, several informal strategies could be employed to identify, weight, and combine relevant cues. Furthermore, in some cases an expert system might be available to help with the decision. If a quantitative approach were to be used to make the judgment, the auditor might employ a variety of deterministic, probabilistic, Bayesian, and simulation models.

Unfortunately, few formal models are available to the auditor to assist with the judgment on system effectiveness. Consequently, reliance primarily must be placed on qualitative strategies to improve the quality of the judgment. The techniques described in Chapter 22 can be used: checklists can be employed to ensure the relevant cues are identified; feedback can be provided to auditors on the weights they attach to various cues; auditors can be trained to recognize likely sources of error in their judgments; groups of auditors rather than a single auditor might make the judgment. Hopefully, as more experience is gained with the qualitative aspects of the judgment, expert systems and quantitative models will evolve to support the decision.

As a basis for improving the quality of the decision, it would also be useful if the accuracy of the auditor's judgment could be monitored. Like the judgment on asset safeguarding and data integrity, however, it is difficult, if not impossible, to assess the accuracy of the judgment. Except where gross errors of judgment have been made, poor-quality decisions may not be apparent to management. Again, if management wants to evaluate the quality of auditor decision making, reliance must be placed on surrogate measures of judgment quality such as consensus and consistency.

SUMMARY

The evaluation of system effectiveness involves determining how well a system meets its goals. Perhaps the major problem in making this evaluation is knowing what the goals of an information system should be. Often these goals are left vague and ill-defined when the system is first designed and implemented. Furthermore, it is often unclear how goal accomplishment should be assessed.

In general, a high-quality information system achieves five major goals. First, it improves the task accomplishment of its users by enabling them to be more productive or to achieve higher-quality output. Second, it improves the overall quality of working life of its users. Third, it should be operationally effective in the sense that it is used frequently, it is used in an appropriate way, it is easy to use, and users are satisfied with its characteristics and performance. Fourth, it should be supported by the appropriate hardware and software technology. Fifth, it should be economically effective in the sense that the benefits derived from using the system exceed the costs of implementing, operating, and maintaining the system.

How well the system meets each of these goals first must be assessed; then, a global evaluation must be made. Unfortunately, few formal techniques are available to enhance the quality of this judgment. Consequently, reliance must be placed on informal techniques to ensure that all relevant cues are identified, the cues are properly weighted, and the cues are combined and integrated in an accurate and consistent way.

REVIEW QUESTIONS

23-1 Briefly explain the nature of each of the following approaches to evaluating organizational effectiveness:
   a Rational goal model approach
   b Systems resource model approach
   c Managerial process model approach
   d Organizational development model approach
   e Bargaining model approach
   f Structural functional model approach
   g Functional model approach

23-2 Briefly explain what is meant by each of the following goals for an information system:
   a Improved task accomplishment
   b Improved quality of working life
   c Operational effectiveness
   d Technical effectiveness
   e Economic effectiveness

23-3 Not all systems are subjected to a postimplementation review. Identify *one* factor that increases the probability of a system undergoing a postimplementation review and *one* factor that decreases the probability of a system undergoing a postimplementation review. Briefly justify your answers.

23-4 Briefly explain the difference between a relative evaluation and an absolute evaluation. What goals of an information system are likely to be subjected to a relative evaluation?

23-5 List the steps in a relative evaluation to determine whether a system accomplishes its goals.

23-6 Why is it difficult to give any general listing of task accomplishment objectives for an information system? For each of the following systems give *five* task accomplishment objectives:
   a Personnel system
   b Online insurance system
   c Energy information system

23-7 Briefly explain the problem of choosing too global versus too detailed a measure of task accomplishment.

23-8 Give two reasons why the auditor may wish to trace a measure of task accomplishment over time.

23-9 "Auditors are concerned with controls, not the quality of working life! That should be left to the personnel people in an organization." Discuss.

23-10 Briefly explain why different groups might define a high quality of working life differently. If a dispute arises in an organization over what constitutes a high quality of working life, whose viewpoint should the auditor use as the basis for assessing the effectiveness of an information system?

23-11 Briefly explain why current measurement instruments for assessing the quality of working life still have validity and reliability problems.

23-12 Briefly explain the difference between surrogate measures and direct measures for assessing the quality of working life. List the relative advantages and disadvantages of using each kind of measure.

23-13 Why might frequency of use be an indicator of the operational effectiveness of an information system? Briefly explain how an auditor might measure the frequency of use of:
a An online enquiry system
b A batch reporting system

23-14 Why is it important to distinguish between voluntary use and involuntary use of an information system? How might the auditor identify involuntary use of an information system?

23-15 Why is it important to identify the nature of use of an information system? What type of change (level of adoption) should the following systems evoke if they are to be operationally effective:
a Inventory reordering system
b Accounts receivable system
c System designed to assist short-term money market operators with their investment decisions

23-16 List three attributes of an online enquiry system that would make it easy to use. Similarly, list three attributes of a batch system that would make it easy to use for *secondary* users.

23-17 What factors have motivated the development of instruments to measure user satisfaction as a basis for assessing the effectiveness of an information system? Give two problems associated with employing user satisfaction measures to gauge the effectiveness of an information system.

23-18 Briefly describe three ways in which the auditor can assess the technical effectiveness of the software supporting an information system. Give two major reasons for software sometimes being technically ineffective.

23-19 How does resource independence affect the technical effectiveness of an information system? How can the auditor assess the extent of independence between the software that supports a system and the hardware on which it operates?

23-20 There are two types of data independence:
a Logical data independence (data-software)
b Physical data independence (data-hardware)
How does data independence make a system more technically effective?
How can the auditor assess the extent of data independence in a system?

23-21 Briefly explain what is meant by an externality or spillover effect of an information system. What problems do externalities cause for evaluating the economic effectiveness of an information system? Give an example of an externality that might be caused by an information system that improved utilization of beds in a hospital.

23-22 For each of the following cost categories, give three examples of costs that would be included in the category:
a Ongoing operational costs—overhead
b System development costs—documentation
c Ongoing operational costs—hardware usage
d Implementation costs—overhead

23-23 Briefly explain the difference between an ex ante valuation of the costs and benefits of an information system and an ex post valuation. Which valuation usually is more difficult to perform? Why?

23-24 Consider an invoicing/accounts receivable system. For each of the following categories, identify a user who might fall into the category:

a Primary user who is internal to the organization

b Secondary user who is internal to the organization

c Primary user who is external to the organization

d Secondary user who is external to the organization

23-25 Consider a decision support system used to assist a marketing manager to allocate sales support staff to sales territories. For each of the following categories, identify a benefit that might fall into the category:

a Benefit that is easy to identify and easy to value

b Benefit that is easy to identify but hard to value

c Benefit that is hard to identify but easy to value

d Benefit that is hard to identify and hard to value

23-26 Give two techniques that might be used to assist a user to estimate the value of an intangible benefit or cost that is hard to value.

23-27 One of the parameters in the net present value formula is the life t of the investment. What are the major factors that affect the life of an information system? Give an example of an information system that probably would have a short life and one that probably would have a long life.

23-28 In the global evaluation judgment, is it likely that technical effectiveness might be weighted as being more important for some systems than for others? If so, give an example and explain why.

MULTIPLE CHOICE QUESTIONS

23-1 The evaluation approach that assesses organizational effectiveness in terms of how well decision makers within the organization can obtain the resources they need to accomplish the tasks they deem to be important is called the:

a Bargaining model

b Managerial process model

c Systems resources model

d Functional model

23-2 Which of the following goals, in general, is *not* addressed during the evaluation of *operational* effectiveness:

a Whether the system is easy to use

b Whether users are satisfied with the system

c Whether the appropriate hardware technology has been used

d Whether the system is used frequently

23-3 Empirical research has shown that postimplementation reviews are:

a Rarely undertaken

b Undertaken only for large systems

c Inevitably motivated by user dissatisfaction with a system

d Sometimes undertaken for political purposes

23-4 For which of the following sets of objectives will a relative evaluation usually be easier to undertake:

a Economic effectiveness objectives

b Operational effectiveness objectives

c Quality of working life objectives

d Technical effectiveness objectives

23-5 Quantitative measures of task accomplishment that apply to all systems are difficult to state because:

a They vary considerably depending upon the nature of the organization

b Only global measures of task accomplishment exist

c Task accomplishment measures are subsumed under a profit measure

d Qualitative measures are more appropriate for effectiveness evaluation purposes

23-6 The Special Task Force of the U.S. Secretary of Health, Education, and Welfare [1973] found that:

a The quality of working life in the United States, in general, was high

b Wages and salaries were a primary determinant of a person's perceived quality of working life

c A fundamental relationship existed between the quality of working life of individuals and their physical and mental health

d A poor quality of working life inevitably led to a degradation in the reliability of controls in systems

23-7 Which of the following tends *not* to be a problem when measuring changes to the quality of working life that arise as a result of implementing a computer system:

a Different groups within an organization have vested interests in how the quality of working life is defined

b Few instruments with high validity and reliability are available to measure the level of the quality of working life that exists

c Employees may inflate their ratings of the quality of working life that exists if they have expectations of better things to come

d Experience has shown that employees often refuse to complete questionnaires used to assess the level of their quality of working life

23-8 Which of the following is used as a surrogate measure when attempting to evaluate the level of the quality of working life:

a Adequacy of compensation provided

b Strike rate

c Level of safety in the workplace

d Level of opportunities for personal growth

23-9 A disadvantage of using a surrogate measure to assess the level of the quality of working life is that:

a The measure is not objective or verifiable

b The data supporting the measure is difficult to obtain

c Surrogate measures are not available for every direct measure

d The underlying reasons for any changes to the level of the quality of working life identified via the measure are difficult to determine

23-10 Empirical research has shown that the relationship between frequency of use of an information system and implementation success is:

a Positive

b Equivocal

c Negative

d Negligible

23-11 Which of the following levels of change will a decision support system developed to facilitate top management's strategic decision making have to evoke for it to be successful:

a Task redefinition

b Management change

c Recurring use of the management science approach

d Management action

23-12 The management change level of adoption requires users of an information system to:

    a Treat the system as a black box and use the information or solution to the problem provided by the system

    b Have an elementary understanding of the system so it can be used as a tool to find answers to specific problems

    c Rethink their view of the job and the way in which they perform a job

    d Develop a fundamental appreciation of the analytical approach used by the system to solve a problem

23-13 The primary reason for employing a measure of user satisfaction to gauge the operational success of an information system is that:

    a It is believed user satisfaction is highly correlated with information system success

    b User satisfaction measures are more reliable and valid than frequency of use, nature of use, and ease of use measures

    c A user satisfaction measure is the least costly measure of information system success to obtain

    d User satisfaction measures have a sounder theoretical basis than other measures of operational success

23-14 Program repair maintenance arises because:

    a Program specifications have been prepared incorrectly

    b User requirements change

    c A logic error exists in a program

    d The efficiency of a program must be improved

23-15 By using generalized hardware components, an increase in independence occurs in which of the following resource relationships:

    a Hardware-hardware

    b Data-software

    c Hardware-data

    d Hardware-software

23-16 If the design team for an application system considers including a feature in the system that will produce information on the amount of pollutant dumped into the environment by an industrial process, the potential benefits that accrue to secondary user groups that are external to the organization are likely to be:

    a Easy to identify but hard to value

    b Easy to identify and easy to value

    c Hard to identify but easy to value

    d Hard to identify and hard to value

23-17 Which of the following is an operational cost of an information system:

    a Purchase of system software

    b Perfective maintenance on programs

    c Preparation of user manuals

    d System analysis time devoted to information requirements analysis

23-18 Spillover effects are:

    a The extra overhead costs incurred because the limits on the size of a direct access file have been exceeded b The unanticipated externalities produced by the implementation of an information system

c Any intangible benefit that arises as a result of using an information system

d The error introduced into the cost-benefit analysis of an information system when the cost of capital is not taken into account

23-19 Which of the following strategies is more likely to facilitate a user estimating the value of intangible benefits:

a Lump all intangible benefits together and try to come up with an overall value

b Try to identify a similar system that has already been implemented and determine the value of intangible benefits in that system

c Group similar tangible and intangible benefits together and estimate the value of the group

d Provide users with a listing of both tangible and intangible benefits and ask users to rank order the benefits according to their value

23-20 The net present value of an information system must be determined by discounting the benefits and costs by the required rate of return. To determine the required rate of return, the parameter β must be estimated by:

a Determining the mean of the risk-free rate of return

b Determining the variance of the rate of return on the market portfolio

c Regressing the return on the security of an organization that designs and implements systems of the type being considered with the returns on the market portfolio

d Regressing the return on the security of the organization designing and implementing the system with the return on the market portfolio

EXERCISES AND CASES

23-1 During the evaluation of the economic effectiveness of an information system, you interview the manager of the user department for which the system was developed. You ask her about the benefits obtained from having the system. She responds that all the benefits obtained are intangible; however, she has no doubts that the benefits obtained via the improved decision making of her staff exceed the costs of the system.

Required: Discuss briefly how you would now proceed in the evaluation study.

23-2 You are trying to estimate the likely increases in revenue that will result from a new sales system. Your best estimate of the increased revenue that will result for the two products the system supports is as follows:

Product A		Product B	
Revenue increase	Probability	Revenue increase	Probability
90,000	.7	60,000	.15
115,000	.2	65,000	.3
120,000	.1	70,000	.25
		78,000 .	.25
		80,000	.05

Required: Construct the joint probability distribution of revenue increase you expect to be produced by the system.

23-3 Over one year ago your organization—a travel company—installed a new online realtime update system that allows travel agents to inquire about the available space in hotels, airlines, etc. As the manager of internal audit for the company, management asks you to undertake a postimplementation review of the system to assess whether or not the system has met its objectives. There is some uncertainty in several areas about whether the system has been successful.

You assign two of your staff to undertake a review of the system. After two months you receive a brief memorandum from them informing you that they have completed their review. In the memo they also rate the system on how well it has achieved each of five major sets of objectives. Their ratings are as follows:

Set of objectives	Rating
Task accomplishment objectives	9
Quality of working life objectives	6
Operational effectiveness objectives	8
Technical effectiveness objectives	5
Economic effectiveness objectives	8

Note: The rating is on a 10-point scale; 10 is the highest and 1 is the lowest.

Required: Given only this small amount of information, what is your global assessment of whether or not the system has been successful? Briefly explain your reasons. How would you now proceed to prepare a final report for top management?

23-4 One of the systems in your organization is an old online system that supports advance planning in the marketing department. A variety of data is collected for the system: sales data, general economic indicators, data on competitors, etc. The system produces over 50 reports: some are online and some are batch.

Because the existing hardware/software configuration is becoming saturated with respect to use, management questions whether or not the system can be streamlined. As the manager of internal audit, they ask you to undertake an evaluation of whether or not all the data currently collected to support the system needs to be collected, whether or not all the reports prepared need to be prepared, and whether or not the existing batch and online reports should be changed.

Required: Outline how you will carry out your evaluation task. You should be specific, however, when you describe how you will collect the data needed to answer management's questions.

23-5 Your organization has decided to purchase a database management system and begin to modify existing systems so there is greater sharing of data; for example, the payroll and personnel files will be combined.

Currently there exists an extensive set of standards for carrying out an evaluation of whether systems meet their objectives. However, the standards have been prepared assuming there is no sharing of data among multiple users.

As the manager of internal audit in the organization, management asks you to determine what changes, if any, will be needed to the effectiveness evaluation standards now that a policy of sharing data, wherever it is cost-effective, should be followed.

Required: Prepare a brief report outlining any changes to the standards that you think will be necessary.

23-6 Assume that a postimplementation review (postaudit) of systems in an organization is optional; that is, not all systems necessarily have to be evaluated after they have been implemented. The factor that affects whether or not a postaudit will be undertaken is the level of uncertainty surrounding the effectiveness attributes of a system. This uncertainty may exist in (*a*) the mind of the person responsible for the postaudit decision, or (*b*) the minds of other members of the organization (e.g., top management).

Required: Identify those characteristics of a system that would tend to affect the level of uncertainty surrounding the effectiveness of a system. In other words, why is the person responsible for the postaudit decision or top management more uncertain about the effectiveness of some systems than others?

ANSWERS TO MULTIPLE CHOICE QUESTIONS

23-1 a	23-6 c	23-11 a	23-16 a
23-2 c	23-7 d	23-12 b	23-17 b
23-3 d	23-8 b	23-13 a	23-18 b
23-4 c	23-9 d	23-14 c	23-19 d
23-5 a	23-10 b	23-15 a	23-20 c

REFERENCES

Ahituv, Niv. "A Systematic Approach toward Assessing the Value of an Information System," *Management Information Systems Quarterly* (December 1980), pp. 61–75.

Ahituv, Niv, Malcolm C. Munro, and Yair Wand. "The Value of Information in Information Analysis," *Information and Management,* vol. 4, 1981, pp. 143–150.

Algera, Jen A. "Task Characteristics," in P.J.D. Drenth, H. Thierry, P.J. Willems, and C.J. de Wolff, eds., *Handbook of Work and Organizational Psychology—Volume 1* (New York: Wiley, 1984), pp. 175–195.

Alter, Steven. "Development Patterns for Decision Support Systems," *Management Information Systems Quarterly* (September 1978), pp. 33–42.

Axelrod, C. Warren. *Computer Effectiveness: Bridging the Management/Technology Gap* (Washington, DC: Information Resource Press, 1979).

Bailey, James E., and Sammy W. Pearson. "Development of a Tool for Measuring and Analyzing Computer User Satisfaction," *Management Science* (May 1983), pp. 530–545.

Baroudi, Jack J., Margrethe H. Olson, and Blake Ives. "An Empirical Study of the Impact of User Involvement on System Usage and Information Satisfaction," *Communications of the ACM* (March 1986), pp. 232–238.

Biggs, Stanley F. "Group Participation in MIS Project Teams? Let's Look at the

Contingencies First!'' *Management Information Systems Quarterly* (March 1978), pp. 19–26.

Bostrom, Robert P., and J. Stephen Heinen. "MIS Problems and Failures: A Socio-Technical Perspective—Part I: The Causes," *Management Information Systems Quarterly* (September 1977a), pp. 17–32.

Bostrom, Robert P., and J. Stephen Heinen. "MIS Problems and Failures: A Socio-Technical Perspective—Part II: The Application of Socio-Technical Theory," *Management Information Systems Quarterly* (December 1977b), pp. 11–28.

Cameron, Kim S. "Effectiveness as Paradox: Consensus and Conflict in Conceptions of Organizational Effectiveness," *Management Science* (May 1986), pp. 539–553.

Cameron, Kim S., and David A. Whetten, eds. *Organizational Effectiveness: A Comparison of Multiple Models* (New York: Academic Press, 1983).

Cherns, Albert. "The Principles of Socio-Technical Design," *Human Relations,* vol. 29, no. 8, pp. 783–792.

Cunningham, J. Barton. "Approaches to the Evaluation of Organizational Effectiveness," *Academy of Management Review* (July 1977), pp. 463–474.

Danziger, James N. "Computers and the Frustrated Chief Executive," *Management Information Systems Quarterly* (June 1977), pp. 43–53.

Danzinger, James N., and William H. Dutton. "Computers as an Innovation in American Local Governments," *Communications of the ACM* (December 1977), pp. 945–956.

Davis, Gordon B., and Margrethe H. Olson. *Management Information Systems: Conceptual Foundations, Structure, and Development,* 2d ed. (New York: McGraw-Hill, 1985).

Davis, Louis E., and Albert B. Cherns, eds. *The Quality of Working Life: Volume 1—Problems, Prospects, and the State of the Art* (New York: The Free Press, 1975).

Dutton, William H., and Kenneth L. Kraemer. "Management Utilization of Computers in American Local Governments," *Communications of the ACM* (March 1978), pp. 206–218.

Ein-Dor, Phillip, and Eli Segev. "Organizational Context and the Success of Management Information Systems," *Management Science* (June 1978), pp. 1064–1077.

Gilb, Tom. *Software Metrics* (Cambridge, MA: Winthrop Publishers, 1977).

Ginzberg, Michael J. "Redesign of Managerial Tasks: A Requisite for Successful Decision Support Systems," *Management Information Systems Quarterly* (March 1978a), pp. 39–52.

Ginzberg, Michael J. "Finding an Adequate Measure of OR/MS Effectiveness," *Interfaces* (August 1978b), pp. 59–62.

Guest, Robert H. "Quality of Work Life—Learning from Tarrytown," *Harvard Business Review* (July–August 1979), pp. 76–87.

Guthrie, A. "Attitudes of the User-Managers towards Management Information Systems," *Management Informatics* (October 1974), pp. 221–232.

Hackman, J.R., G.R. Oldham, R. Janson, and K. Purdy. "A New Strategy for Job Enrichment," *California Management Review* (Summer 1975), pp. 57–71.

Halloran, Dennis, Susan Manchester, John Moriarty, Robert Riley, James Rohrman, and Thomas Skramstad. "Systems Development Quality Control," *Management Information Systems Quarterly* (December 1978), pp. 1–13.

Hamilton, Scott, and Norman L. Chervany. "Evaluating I.S. Effectiveness—Part I: Comparing Evaluating Approaches," *Management Information Systems Quarterly* (September 1981a), pp. 55–69.

Hamilton, Scott, and Norman L. Chervany. "Evaluating I.S. Effectiveness—Part II: Comparing Evaluation Viewpoints," *Management Information Systems Quarterly* (December 1981*b*), pp. 79–86.

Ives, Blake, and Margrethe H. Olson. "User Involvement and MIS Success: A Review of Research," *Management Science* (May 1984), pp. 586–603.

Ives, Blake, Margrethe H. Olson, and Jack J. Baroudi. "The Measurement of User Information Satisfaction," *Communications of the ACM* (October 1983), pp. 785–793.

Jenkins, A. Milton, and John A. Ricketts. "The Development of an MIS Satisfaction Questionnaire: An Instrument for Evaluating User Satisfaction with Turnkey Decision Support Systems," discussion paper no. 296, Division of Research, School of Business, Indiana University, 1985.

King, John Leslie, and Edward L. Schrems. "Cost-Benefit Analysis in Information Systems Development and Operation," *Computing Surveys* (March 1978), pp. 19–34.

King, William R., and Jaime I. Rodriquez. "Evaluating Management Information Systems," *Management Information Systems Quarterly* (September 1978), pp. 43–51.

Kling, Rob. "The Organizational Context of User-Centered Software Designs," *Management Information Systems Quarterly* (December 1977), pp. 41–52.

Lawler, Edward E. "Measuring the Psychological Quality of Working Life: The Why and How of It," in Louis E. Davis and Albert B. Cherns, eds., *The Quality of Working Life: Volume 1—Problems, Prospects, and the State of the Art* (New York: The Free Press, 1975), pp. 123–133.

Lucas, Henry C. "Behavioral Factors in System Implementation," in Randall L. Schultz and Dennis P. Slevin, eds., *Implementing Operations Research/Management Science* (New York: American Elsevier, 1975*a*), pp. 203–215.

Lucas, Henry C. *Towards Creative System Design* (New York: Columbia University Press, 1975*b*).

Lucas, Henry C. *Why Information Systems Fail* (New York: Columbia University Press, 1975*c*).

Lucas, Henry C. *The Implementation of Computer-Based Models* (New York: National Association of Accountants, 1976).

Lucas, Henry C. "The Use of an Interactive Information Storage and Retrieval System in Medical Research," *Communications of the ACM* (March 1978*a*), pp. 197–205.

Lucas, Henry C. "Empirical Evidence for a Descriptive Model of Implementation," *Management Information Systems Quarterly* (June 1978*b*), pp. 27–42.

Macy, Barry A., and Philip H. Mirvis. "A Methodology for Assessment of Quality of Work Life and Organizational Effectiveness in Behavioral-Economic Terms," *Administrative Science Quarterly* (June 1976), pp. 212–226.

Maish, Alexander M. "A User's Behavior toward His MIS," *Management Information Systems Quarterly* (March 1979), pp. 39–52.

Manley, John H. "Implementation Attitudes: A Model and a Measurement Methodology," in Randall L. Schultz and Dennis P. Slevin, eds., *Implementing Operations Research/Management Science* (New York: American Elsevier, 1975), pp. 183–202.

Matlin, Gerald L. "How to Survive a Management Assessment," *Management Information Systems Quarterly* (March 1977), pp. 11–17.

Mohrman, Susan A., and Edward E. Lawler III. "Quality of Work Life," in Kendrith M. Rowland and Gerald R. Ferris, eds., *Research in Personnel and Human Resources Management, vol. 2* (Greenwich, CT: JAI Press, 1984), pp. 219–260.

Moore, Jeffrey H. "A Framework for MIS Software Development Projects," *Management Information Systems Quarterly* (March 1979), pp. 29–38.

Mumford, Enid, and Harold Sackman, eds. *Human Choice and Computers* (Amsterdam: North-Holland, 1975).

Nadler, David A., Philip H. Mirvis, and Cortlandt Cammann. "The Ongoing Feedback System: Experimenting with a New Managerial Tool," *Organizational Dynamics* (Spring 1976), pp. 63–80.

Report of a Special Task Force to the Secretary of Health, Education, and Welfare. *Work in America* (Cambridge, MA: The MIT Press, 1973).

Robey, Dan. "User Attitudes and MIS Use," *Academy of Management Journal* (September 1979), pp. 527–538.

Schewe, C.D. "The Management Information Systems User: An Exploratory Behavioral Analysis," *Academy of Management Journal* (September 1976), pp. 577–589.

Schultz, Randall L., and Dennis P. Slevin. "Implementation and Organizational Validity," in Randall L. Schultz and Dennis P. Slevin, eds., *Implementing Operations Research/Management Science* (New York: American Elsevier, 1975), pp. 153–182.

Schultz, Randall L., and Dennis P. Slevin. *Implementing Operations Research/Management Science* (New York: American Elsevier, 1975).

Seashore, Stanley E. "Defining and Measuring the Quality of Working Life," in Louis E. Davis and Albert B. Cherns, eds., *The Quality of Working Life: Volume 1—Problems, Prospects, and the State of the Art* (New York: The Free Press, 1975), pp. 105–118.

Senn, James A. "A Management View of Systems Analysts: Failures and Shortcomings," *Management Information Systems Quarterly* (September 1978), pp. 25–32.

Srinivasan, Ananth. "Alternative Measures of System Effectiveness: Associations and Implications," *Management Information Systems Quarterly* (September 1985), pp. 243–253.

Steers, Richard M. *Organizational Effectiveness: A Behavioral View* (Santa Monica, CA: Goodyear Publishing Company, 1977).

Sterling, T.D. "Guidelines for Humanizing Computerized Information Systems: A Report from Stanley House," *Communications of the ACM* (November 1974), pp. 609–613.

Sterling, T. D. "Consumer Difficulties with Computerized Transactions: An Empirical Investigation," *Communications of the ACM* (May 1979), pp. 283–289.

Walton, Richard E. "Criteria for Quality of Working Life," in Louis E. Davis and Albert B. Cherns, eds. *The Quality of Working Life: Volume 1—Problems, Prospects, and the State of the Art* (New York: The Free Press, 1975), pp. 91–104.

Wetherbe, James C., and V. Thomas Dock. "A Strategic Planning Methodology for the Computing Effort in Higher Education: An Empirical Evaluation," *Communications of the ACM* (December 1978), pp. 1008–1015.

Wood, Robert E. "Task Complexity: Definition of the Construct," *Organizational Behavior and Human Decision Processes* (February 1986), pp. 60–82.

Zammuto, Raymond F. *Assessing Organizational Effectiveness: Systems Change, Adaptation, and Strategy* (Albany: State University of New York, 1982).

EVALUATING SYSTEM EFFICIENCY

The need to evaluate the efficiency of computer systems has now become a contentious issue. On the one hand, several factors have undermined the importance of efficiency evaluations. For example: hardware is cheap relative to labor so it is often more cost-effective to buy extra hardware instead of spending time to improve the efficiency of systems; a substantial amount of computing is now done on single-user microcomputers where efficiency is a minor consideration; to reduce complexity, many large-scale systems have now been broken up into smaller systems and the work assigned to minicomputers where, again, efficiency is less a concern.

On the other hand, however, several countervailing trends have underscored the ongoing importance of efficiency evaluations. For example: microcomputers are being combined into large-scale local area networks where efficiency is a major issue; users of computing systems have become increasingly reliant on national and international data communication systems that provide fast response times; to resolve difficulties in some computing systems, it is unclear just what type of hardware should be acquired to alleviate bottlenecks. For some types of computer systems, therefore, efficiency evaluations *are* needed, and astute data processing management will recognize when the acquisition of more hardware is not a panacea for unsatisfactory system performance.

This chapter discusses methodologies that the auditor can use to determine whether a system is efficient, that is, whether it achieves its objectives in a least-cost manner. Most of these methodologies have been developed within the area that has generally been called "computer performance evaluation." However, as Ferrari [1978] points out, the focus of research in the performance evaluation area is somewhat narrow; it is concerned primarily with system efficiency and not broader performance issues such as ease of use, reliability, or user productivity.

The chapter proceeds as follows. The first section provides an overview of the evaluation process relating to system efficiency. The second section defines several major performance indices used to assess system efficiency. The third section discusses various ways of modeling system workloads. The fourth section discusses various ways of modeling the computer system to be evaluated so experiments can be run to assess the efficiency of the system. Finally, the chapter describes briefly the interrelationships that exist between the workload model used and the system model used.

THE EVALUATION PROCESS

There are two reasons why auditors may become involved in evaluating system efficiency. First, they may be asked to evaluate an existing operational system to determine whether its performance can be improved. For example, it may be possible to decrease the response time of an interactive system by increasing the size of the memory partition allocated to each active user in the system. Second, auditors may be asked to evaluate alternative systems that the data processing installation is considering purchasing, leasing, renting, or developing. For example, management may be attempting to choose between two generalized accounting systems that are available in the marketplace. Auditors

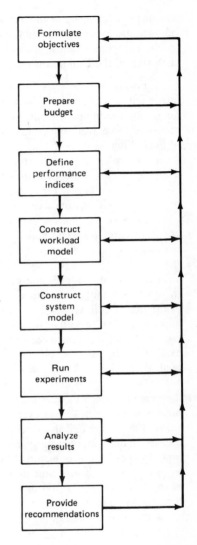

FIGURE 24-1
Major steps in the evaluation of
system efficiency.

may be requested to provide advice on which system is better able to process
the organization's workload.

Whatever the reasons for the evaluation, Figure 24-1 shows the eight major
steps to be taken during an evaluation of system efficiency. Note that at each
step one outcome may be the revision of work done at prior steps. For
example, the formulation of a suitable workload model may be more costly than
anticipated at the outset of the evaluation process; thus, the estimates of the
costs and benefits of the evaluation process may have to be revised. One

possible consequence of this revision may be that the evaluation is terminated because the expected benefits of the evaluation do not exceed the costs.

The paragraphs below provide an overview of the work to be performed at each step in the evaluation process:

1 *Formulate the objectives of the study:* As with all evaluation studies it is important to define the objectives of the study at the start. The objectives determine the boundaries of the system to be evaluated, and they suggest the nature of the performance indices that will be required to assess the efficiency of the defined system. The objectives may be global; for example, improve the performance of the online registration system. They may be specific; for example, improve the CPU utilization. The objectives also should specify the constraints that apply; for example, improve the response time of the interactive system without purchasing any more hardware resources.

2 *Prepare the budget for the evaluation:* Efficiency evaluations can be costly to carry out. The benefits obtained from the evaluation should exceed the costs of the evaluation and the costs of any changes necessary to achieve the benefits. Estimating the costs of the evaluation usually is reasonably straightforward. Unfortunately, estimating the benefits of the evaluation and the costs of changes to achieve these benefits often is difficult. Only after the evaluation is complete will the auditor know whether or not efficiency can be improved, what benefits can be expected from the improved efficiency, and the cost of the changes necessary to achieve the improved efficiency. Ultimately, experience in carrying out efficiency evaluations is a major determinant of quality decisions when the budget for the evaluation is prepared.

3 *Define performance indices:* The performance indices provide the standard against which the efficiency of the system is assessed. What performance indices are chosen for an evaluation study depends on the objectives of the study. For example, if the objective of the study is to improve the timeliness of the output of an interactive system, clearly an index of performance is response time. Response time now must be defined, however; there may be some debate as to whether response time ends upon receipt of the first character of output or the last character of output. If the system is overloaded it may take some time for the output to print so the latter definition may be used.

4 *Construct a workload model:* Figure 24-2 shows a structural model of a

FIGURE 24-2
Structural model of a computer system.

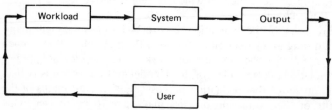

computer system. The performance of a system is some function of the workload the system must process. When evaluating system efficiency the auditor must construct a workload model that is representative of the real system workload. If the system to be evaluated is operational, the workload model may be based on the real workload. If the system to be evaluated is in the design stages, an artificial workload model must be constructed; that is, one based on the expected characteristics of the workload to be processed.

5 *Construct a system (configuration) model:* The performance of the system to be evaluated is studied using a model of the system. Again, if the system is operational, the workload can be processed and the values of various performance indices calculated. However, if the effects of a changed hardware/software configuration are to be determined or the purchase of a new system is considered, some type of artificial model of the changed or new system must be constructed. In essence, the system model maps the attributes of the workload into values of the performance indices chosen.

6 *Run experiments:* Once the workload and system models have been constructed, experiments can be run to determine the values of the performance indices. Sensitivity analyses may be carried out by varying both the characteristics of the workload and the system.

7 *Analyze results:* When evaluating efficiency the auditor hypothesizes certain relationships between the values of the performance indices and the characteristics of the workload and system models. For example, the auditor may hypothesize that varying the time quantum allocated each job in an interactive system will have a major impact on response times, or that changing the device to channel assignment of a system's disk drives will cause a marked change in throughput. Once experiments have been run with these changed parameters and the values of the performance indices determined, the data can be analyzed to determine whether the relationships hypothesized do, in fact, exist.

8 *Provide recommendations:* After the data from the experiments is analyzed, the auditor can make recommendations on how system efficiency can be improved. The recommendations will depend on whether or not the data supported the hypotheses that the auditor postulated about relationships between performance indices and system and workload characteristics, and the relative benefits and costs of changes to improve system efficiency.

PERFORMANCE INDICES

A performance index is a measure of system efficiency; it expresses quantitatively how well the system achieves an efficiency criterion. Performance indices have several functions: they allow users to decide whether a system will meet their needs, they permit comparison of alternate systems, and they show whether changes to the hardware/software configuration of a system have produced the desired effect.

Performance indices must be expressed as a probability distribution. For example, the response time in an online system may have considerable variation—perhaps from one second to one minute or more. If a performance index is expressed only as a mean value, it may hide important information from the user. In the example given, a user may be unaware that at certain times of the day effective problem solving using an online decision model may be inhibited by the slow response time of the system. The mean, variance, and shape of the distribution alert the user to the possibility of these types of problems occurring.

Performance indices also must be expressed in terms of a workload. The response time of an interactive system will vary depending on the number and the nature of the jobs in the system.

Stimler [1974] and Svobodova [1976] provide extensive lists of various performance indices that have been used to assess system efficiency. The following sections discuss briefly only some of the more important and widely used indices.

Timeliness Indices

Timeliness indices reflect how quickly a system is able to provide users with the output they require. The measure of timeliness for a batch system typically is turnaround time. *Turnaround time* is the length of time that elapses between submission of a job and receipt of the complete output. For interactive systems the measure of timeliness is the response time. Typically the *response time* is defined to be the length of time that elapses between submission of an input transaction to the system and receipt of the first character of output.

Timeliness indices must be defined in terms of a unit of work and the priority categorization given to the unit of work. In a batch system the unit of work usually is a job. In an interactive system it may be a job (multiple transactions) or a single transaction. Higher priority units of work are given access first to available computing resources; thus, these units of work should have faster turnaround and response times.

Timeliness indices also are user-oriented performance indices; they reflect the primary concerns of the system user. Other indices discussed below are system-oriented indices; they are the concern of the data processing managers who seek to obtain maximum returns on their investment in hardware and software.

Throughput Indices

Throughput indices are measures of the productivity of a system; that is, they indicate how much work is done by the system over a period of time. The *throughput rate* of a system is the amount of work done per unit time period. The *capability* of a system is the maximum achievable throughput rate. Again, throughput indices must be defined in terms of some unit of work: a job, a task, an instruction, etc. Relative throughput indices can be used to compare the throughput of one system with the throughput of another system (see, further, Stimler [1974]). Note, also, the interdependencies between timeliness indices and throughput indices; in general, the more responsive a system the greater its throughput.

Utilization Indices

Utilization indices measure the proportion of time a system resource is busy. For example, the *CPU utilization* index is calculated by dividing the amount of time the CPU is busy by the total amount of time the system is running. Similarly, *channel utilization* is defined to be the amount of time the channel is busy divided by the amount of time the system is running. Utilization indices may be defined for any hardware, software, or data resource within the system.

WORKLOAD MODELS

A system workload is the set of resource demands imposed upon the system by the set of jobs that occur during a given time period. Conceptually, the workload can be characterized as a matrix. The rows in the matrix are the set of jobs that occur for the time period under consideration. The columns in the matrix are the hardware, software, and data resources of the system. The elements of the matrix are the amounts of each resource demanded by each job. System performance (efficiency) must be defined in terms of a given workload.

When evaluating system efficiency there are several purposes for formulating a workload model. First, using the real workload of the system for evaluation purposes may be too costly. To measure efficiency for a representative workload, the time period for evaluation may be long. Second, the real workload cannot be used if the system to be evaluated is not operational. If the auditor is evaluating competing systems (say, proposed hardware/software configurations for a system yet to be implemented), an artificial workload must be created for purposes of the evaluation. Third, the auditor may want to carry out sensitivity analyses when evaluating system efficiency. If the behavior of the system is to be examined under varying workloads, it may be easier to change the characteristics of a workload model than the real workload to carry out these sensitivity analyses.

The objective of workload model design is to obtain a drive workload (the workload to be used during the evaluation) that is *representative* of the real workload. Unfortunately, what is meant by a representative workload model is still unclear. Ferrari [1972] defines representativeness in terms of the set of performance indices used for the evaluation. A representative workload model is one that produces the same values of the performance indices as the real workload. For example, if a single performance index, throughput rate, is used for the evaluation, the throughput rate values for the workload model and the real workload should be equal. Recall, performance indices often are stochastic variables, so the mean, variance, and higher moments of the distributions of the performance indices for the workload model and the real workload should be compared.

This notion of representativeness may be conceptually useful but it is not always practically useful. For a system that is not operational, the real workload is not yet known; thus, determining the representativeness of the workload model is difficult if not impossible. Even if the values of performance indices for the real workload and the workload model are known, there is the problem of determining whether the workload model will remain representative when the system structure is changed. A workload model is devised to provide a cheaper means of undertaking sensitivity analysis than the real workload; however, the costs of inaccurate performance measurements must not exceed the costs savings obtained by using a model. Ideally, the model's representativeness will be invariant across system structures.

Besides representativeness there are other desirable attributes of a workload model. It should not be costly to construct and use. It should facilitate change to workload parameters. It should be portable across different system structures.

How these attributes of a workload model are obtained is still an extensive research issue. Currently there are few design guidelines. The following sections present an overview of some of the major workload models that have been devised. Following Ferrari [1972], the models are classified as either natural workload models or artificial workload models. The sections also examine briefly how well the models achieve the desired characteristics of workload models discussed earlier.

Natural Workload Models

Natural workload models are constructed by taking some subset of the real workload. There are two methods of obtaining the subset required. First, time subsets can be chosen; the content of the workload model is the same as the real workload but the time interval over which performance indices are calculated is less than the interval for the real workload. Second, content subsets can be chosen; sample jobs from the real workload are selected in some way. Natural workload models sometimes are called *benchmarks*.

If the auditor constructs a natural workload model on the basis of a time subset, the only decision to be made is when the evaluation period should start and end. The start time and duration of measurement should be chosen so as to maximize representativeness and minimize evaluation costs; unfortunately, these objectives conflict.

If the auditor constructs a natural workload model on the basis of a content subset, a decision must be made on how the subset will be selected from all jobs executed within the interval for the real workload. One method is to choose a random sample of jobs from the real workload. Another method is to partition jobs into defined classes and choose at random a job from each class for inclusion in the workload model (see, further, Gaede [1981]). The size of the sample chosen depends on the tradeoff made between representativeness and workload model construction and use costs; smaller samples are less representative but enable cheaper workload models to be constructed and used.

Natural workload models have two major strengths. First, since they are constructed from jobs in the real workload, their representativeness can be high. Second, the cost to construct a natural workload model usually is low; however, this cost increases as the representativeness of the model increases.

A natural workload model has several limitations. Modifications to the workload model are not always easy to make; thus, sensitivity analyses using the model may be difficult to carry out. The operational costs of using the model may be high since they are often less compact than an artificial workload model. Also, natural workload models can be used only if a real workload exists already; the system to be evaluated must be operational.

Artificial Workload Models

If a workload model is not constructed from jobs in the real workload, it is an artificial workload model. The auditor may construct an artificial workload model for several reasons. Some types of system models chosen for evaluation studies are unable to process natural workload models. For example, queuing models can process only an artificial workload model. As discussed previously, if the system to be evaluated is not operational, the real workload is unknown and an artificial workload must be constructed. In general, artificial workload models are more flexible and compact than natural workload models. They facilitate sensitivity analyses and are less costly to use. However, these advantages are attained only at a cost. Artificial workload models usually are more costly to construct, less representative, and less portable than natural workload models.

A large number of different types of artificial workload models have been constructed. They vary widely in their capabilities with respect to representativeness, cost, compactness, etc. To illustrate the diversity that exists, the following sections survey some of the major types of artificial workload models that have been used (see, also, Lucas [1971], Svobodova [1976], Kobayashi [1978], and Deitel [1984]).

Instruction Mixes   An instruction mix specifies the frequency with which different instructions occur or are expected to occur within an application. The mean execution time for a system can be computed using the following formula:

$$\bar{t} = \sum_i p_i t_i$$

where $\bar{t}$ = mean execution time
p_i = probability of the ith instruction being executed
t_i = execution time of the ith instruction

The relative frequencies of the different types of instructions in the mix can be determined in three ways. First, if the system is operational, a trace of instructions in the real workload can be taken and the incidence of the different types of instructions counted. Second, standard instruction mixes such as the Gibson mix can be used (see Svobodova [1976]). Third, the frequencies of the different types of instructions can be estimated on the basis of the expected workload.

An instruction mix is a very limited workload model. It provides a basis for quickly comparing the speeds of different CPU architectures. Also, it is a cheap workload model to use. However, obtaining a representative instruction mix may be difficult. A set of representative programs must be chosen and the frequencies of instructions used estimated or counted. Instruction mixes usually do not take into account instruction overlap nor do they include I/O instructions. Thus, instruction mixes permit only a partial evaluation to be carried out.

Kernel Programs A kernel program is a program or subroutine that has been coded as a representative job within the system to be evaluated. For example, in a scientific installation the kernel may be a matrix inversion routine; in a commercial installation it may be a file updating routine. From the list of instructions in the kernel and the execution times of the instructions in the system being evaluated, the total execution time of the kernel can be calculated; thus, the execution times of two competing systems can be compared.

Instruction mixes and kernel programs have similar strengths and limitations. Kernel programs usually contain more representative instructions; for example, they may include I/O instructions. Like instruction mixes, however, they provide only a first approximation of system efficiency and they are a very limited form of workload model.

Synthetic Jobs A synthetic job is a representative job (or set of jobs) that is coded and executed on the systems being evaluated. Synthetic jobs are similar to benchmarks; however, whereas benchmarks are based on some subset of the real workload, a synthetic job is an artificial workload model. Synthetic jobs usually are prepared because the systems being evaluated are not yet operational so a real workload does not exist.

Provided that the synthetic job used is representative of the real workload, it allows more accurate estimates to be made of system efficiency than instruction mixes or kernel programs. However, synthetic jobs are less compact so they are more costly to develop and use. Synthetic jobs also can be constructed so they are flexible to use. The resources consumed by a synthetic job can be changed by altering its parameters, for example, the number of CPU processing demands and the frequency of disk accesses.

Care must be taken if a synthetic job is used to evaluate alternate hardware/software configurations. Erroneous decisions may be made if synthetic jobs are not written so they execute efficiently on the hardware/software configuration they use. Program structures are not always independent of hardware/software structures.

Probabilistic Workload Models In a probabilistic workload model, resource demands are described by a probability distribution. Various types of distributions may be used, for example, the Poisson distribution, the exponential distribution, and the normal distribution. A time series of resource demands is generated by sampling from the probability distribution.

Probabilistic workload models are used extensively in analytic and simulation studies of computer system performance. The system model used may impose constraints on how the workload model is formulated. For example, if the auditor uses a queuing model to evaluate system efficiency, it is difficult, if not impossible, to obtain a tractable model if the workload model takes into account correlations between service times.

Probabilistic workload models differ in their representativeness of the real workload. To the extent that the workload model is not constrained by tractability requirements imposed by the system model, the workload model has high potential for representativeness. Probabilistic workload models are compact and flexible. Resource demands are described by a probability distribution; changing the workload simply involves changing the parameters of the distribution. Development costs usually are low. However, usage costs depend on how many samples are taken from the distribution when system efficiency is evaluated.

SYSTEM MODELS

To determine whether or not a system can be changed to improve efficiency, the system must be modeled. The modeling process involves specifying the system components, the interfaces between the components, how the system operates, and the functional relationships between outputs and inputs.

Once the system has been modeled, various control parameters in the model can be changed to determine their impact on system efficiency. For example, the auditor may investigate the impact of changes in the priority assigned different jobs, the size of the time slice allocated a job, the amount of memory allocated a job, the device to channel assignment, the paging algorithm used, the number of users allowed to access the system simultaneously, and the maximum allowed paging rate. Using the performance indices discussed earlier in the chapter, the auditor can run experiments to determine the effects of changes in a particular workload or system control parameter when the other parameters are held constant.

One of the more difficult problems in constructing a system model is knowing how to decompose the system into subsystems so the evaluation problem can be conceptualized. In general, the methodologies discussed by Simon [1981] are applicable; the boundaries to subsystems are defined so the relationships between elements of the subsystem are strong and the interfaces between the subsystem to be evaluated and other subsystems are weak. Kobayashi [1978] points out that very often when modeling computer systems to evaluate efficiency, the subsystem boundaries can be identified by major differences in the time interval between events in the subsystems. For example, to evaluate cache memory algorithms, the auditor must work with a subsystem having time intervals of nanoseconds or microseconds. In contrast, if the auditor evaluates I/O scheduling by the operating system, the time interval usually can be expressed in milliseconds. Note that a single event in the latter subsystem may be represented by multiple events in the former subsystem. To evaluate performance of the I/O subsystem, the model should not be defined at the level of the cache memory subsystem; otherwise, it is unlikely that a tractable model will result.

The following three sections provide an overview of the three major types of system models used to evaluate efficiency: (a) analytical models, (b) simulation models, and (c) empirical models. An extensive literature exists relating to each of these models (see, for example, Miller [1972]); thus, the auditor who specializes in this area must undertake substantial further study.

Analytical Models

A variety of analytical models have been developed to evaluate system efficiency; however, queuing models have received the most widespread use. Perhaps the major reasons for this development are the availability of substantial theoretical support for queuing models and the ability of queuing models to represent complex probabilistic phenomena in computer systems.

It is easy to conceive a computer system within a queuing framework. Jobs (customers) make demands on various computer resources (servers). For example, a job submitted by a user at an online terminal will request CPU time, memory, I/O devices, etc. As resource contention among jobs arises, queues result. There will be a queue of jobs waiting for CPU service, an I/O queue, a system software queue, etc.

The output of queuing models includes the timeliness, throughput, and utilization indices discussed earlier in the chapter, as well as such measures as the mean waiting time in a queue, the mean waiting time in the system, the mean number of jobs waiting for service, and the mean number of jobs in the system. Thus, queuing models enable system efficiency to be evaluated and strategies for improving system efficiency to be devised. Often, queuing models are used to focus on a specific resource management problem; for example, hierarchical memory management, channel scheduling, and buffer allocation.

The following sections discuss briefly the major steps to be undertaken when constructing a queuing model to evaluate system efficiency. The sections assume basic familiarity with queuing theory (see, for example, Allen [1975]).

Nevertheless, the discussion is somewhat superficial so the interested reader should consult, for example, Kobayashi [1978], Ferrari [1978], and Sauer and Chandy [1981] for an in-depth treatment of the topic.

Model Formulation   The first step to be taken when using a queuing model to evaluate system efficiency is to formulate the model. This step involves choosing the type of queuing model to be used to represent the system.

The earliest queuing models constructed to evaluate computer systems were simple single-server models (see Graham [1978]). The model consists of a single process (server) and a single queue of jobs (Figure 24-3). Jobs are described by a distribution of arrival times and requested service times. The underlying assumptions of the model are restrictive; for example, the interarrival times and service times are statistically independent, all interarrival times are distributed identically, and all service times are distributed identically. Since there is only one resource queue, the model user has to consider the entire system as a black box. In computer systems where one resource dominates (for example, the CPU), the model may be appropriate. In multiple resource systems, however, its usefulness is limited.

Currently, computer systems are modeled as a network of single resource models (Figure 24-4). Substantial advances have been made in the theory supporting these models (see Denning and Buzen [1978]). Buzen [1978], Bard [1978], and Wong [1978] describe applications of these queuing network models.

The queuing model used may be a closed model, an open model, or a mixed model (see, further, Kobayashi [1978]). In a closed model, for all classes of jobs, the number of jobs in that class is fixed and constant. New jobs are generated internally to the model. In an open model, for all classes of jobs, there exists an external source of jobs. Mixed models have some job classes that are closed and some that are open.

Open models usually are easier to solve mathematically than closed models. Closed models, however, are sometimes more representative of real systems. For example, assuming an infinite population source (open model) is unrealistic for an interactive system where there is a finite number of terminals (see, further, Kobayashi [1978] and Sauer and Chandy [1981]).

Estimating Model Parameter Values   Once the queuing model has been formulated, the values of the parameters in the model must be estimated. If the system to be modeled is operational, the parameter values may be estimated

FIGURE 24-3
Single process/single queue model of a computer system.

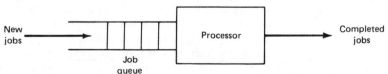

New jobs → | | | | Processor → Completed jobs

Job queue

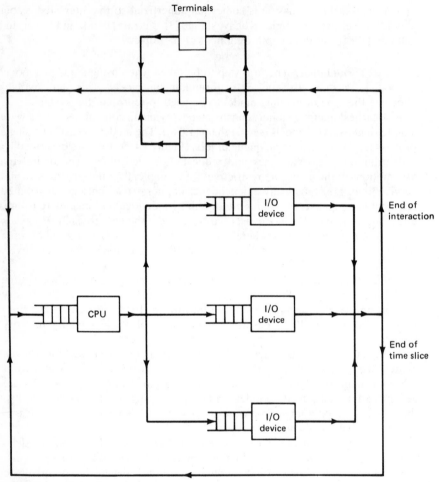

FIGURE 24-4
Queuing network model of a computer system.

from data obtained using a performance monitoring tool; otherwise, the expected parameter values must be used.

The major input parameters to be obtained for a queuing network model are:

Parameter	Explanation
Number of job classes	The jobs in the system must be categorized; for example, as either batch or time-sharing or into different priority classes.
Arrival pattern	The interarrival time distribution for each job class must be specified; for example, a Poisson process may be used.

Parameter	Explanation
CPU queuing discipline	How jobs are scheduled and served by the CPU must be specified, for example, a first-come-first-served basis may be used or a processor sharing (round robin) basis may be used.
Degree of multiprogramming	The number of jobs that can be in the system simultaneously must be specified; this depends on whether a finite or infinite population source has been assumed or a closed or open model has been used.
I/O device routing frequencies	Jobs are processed alternately by either the CPU or an I/O device. The routing frequency for an I/O device is the proportion of total I/O operations executed that apply to that device.
Service time distribution	The service time distributions must be specified for the CPU and I/O devices; for example, exponential distributions might be used.

Solving the Model   Denning and Buzen [1978] survey the formulas used to solve queuing network problems. These solutions can be obtained using exact analysis or approximate analysis (see Muntz [1978]). Exact analysis is used when the assumptions underlying the model are satisfied. Since some queuing model assumptions are restrictive and often may be violated, approximate analysis may be used to solve the model. Approximate analysis also can be used if exact analysis will be too expensive to undertake or alternate more credible models such as simulation will be too expensive to use.

Model Validation and Calibration   Once a queuing model has been constructed, it should be validated to determine how accurately it predicts the values of the various performance indices. If the system to be evaluated is operational, the auditor can compare the results of the queuing model with those obtained using performance monitoring tools. The robustness of the model over changing workloads and changing system parameters also can be examined. If the system to be evaluated is not operational, the auditor must examine the model and its output for face validity.

Validation allows the size of the error in the output of the queuing model to be determined. In light of whether or not the size of the error is acceptable, calibration then might be undertaken. Calibration reduces the size of the output error by reducing or eliminating model formulation inaccuracies, inaccuracies caused by the use of approximate solution methods, and inaccuracies caused by incorrect estimates of parameter values (see, also, Chapter 22).

Simulation Models

The auditor may decide to use simulation to evaluate system efficiency for several reasons. First, an analytical solution may not be available; the model may not be tractable. Second, the system to be evaluated may not be operational; thus, empirical performance measurement cannot be carried out. Third, the simulation model may be used to validate the analytical model. Fourth, simulation may be cheaper to use than empirical performance measurement.

The following sections provide an overview of the steps to be taken when constructing a simulation model to evaluate system efficiency. Stimler [1974], Ferrari [1978], and Kobayashi [1978] provide examples of the use of simulation to evaluate efficiency. They also discuss the theoretical bases underlying the use of simulation methodologies in a performance monitoring context.

Model Formulation It is essential at the start of the design of a simulation model to know how the model will be used for performance evaluation purposes. These objectives impact the design of a simulation model in several ways. They determine the input (workload) parameters, internal (system) parameters, and output variables needed in the model. The output variables to be measured are the performance indices of interest in the evaluation. The input and internal parameters included in the model reflect the auditor's decisions on what variables will be manipulated to determine their impact on the performance indices.

The objectives also determine the level of system detail to be included in the model. Simulations can be expensive to implement and run; therefore, the model should focus only on those variables of interest, and the level of detail in the model should be sufficient simply to produce results that contain an acceptable level of error. If the system to be modeled is the CPU, the simulator must be sufficiently detailed to study instruction execution. However, if the system to be modeled is an application system, the simulator must be formulated at a more macroscopic level.

Simulators differ in their structure depending on whether the auditor focuses on processes or events. If the auditor focuses on processes, time is incremented by constant intervals. If the auditor focuses on events, time is incremented when the simulator changes its state.

Model Implementation When implementing a simulator a choice must be made on how the workload model will be implemented and how the system model will be implemented.

The workload model can be implemented using a probabilistic workload model or a trace. If the auditor chooses a probabilistic workload model, resource requests are generated as random samples from specified distributions. If the auditor chooses a trace, the time series of resource requests for an artificial or operational system must be kept. Trace-driven simulators usually produce more accurate results. The correlations between resource requests by jobs can be preserved, and a more detailed description of the workload is possible. However, traces often are more costly to construct and run than probabilistic models. Further, the simulation results tend to be less accurate when sensitivity analyses involving major modifications to the workload or system structure are carried out.

The major decision to be made when implementing the system model is what simulation language will be used. This choice can have a significant impact on the overall cost of using simulation methodology to evaluate efficiency. Some simulation languages facilitate implementation of event-structured models; others facilitate implementation of process-structured models. Several special simulation languages have been written specifically to facilitate efficiency evaluations of computer systems; for example, CSS, CASE, and SCERT (see, further, Kobayashi [1978] and Ferrari [1978]). These languages contain libraries of performance specifications for the hardware and software configurations of various vendors.

Model Validation and Calibration As with queuing models, validation of simulation models is not always an easy task. If the system being modeled is operational, the values of the performance indices produced by the model can be compared with the values of performance indices for the real system obtained using performance monitoring tools. If the system being modeled is not operational, the auditor must carefully examine the model for face validity. On the basis of the validation results the simulator then can be calibrated.

The auditor also must attempt to determine how robust the model is over changes in the input parameters and system parameters. The simulator must produce accurate results for the range of parameter changes to be made during experiments with the model.

Conduct Experiments Once the auditor is satisfied that the simulator has been adequately validated and calibrated, experiments can be conducted. The values of input and system parameters can be changed to determine their impact on the output performance indices. For example, the auditor can increase the rate at which jobs are submitted to the system to see the effect on throughput. Procedures for analyzing the results produced are discussed further in the next section.

Empirical Models

If the computer system to be evaluated is operational and the auditor can obtain values for the performance indices of interest and the various workload and system parameters of interest, an empirical model can be used to estimate the relationships between the performance indices and workload and system parameters. An empirical model also may be used to estimate relationships between the output of a simulator and changes in its parameters.

The major empirical model used in performance evaluation is the general linear model. The model is a statistical model; both the underlying theory and the practical application of the model are well developed (see, for example, Neter et al. [1985]). In essence, the model considers the system to be a black box. The model estimates the extent to which variations in the independent variables (workload and system parameters) explain variations in the dependent variables (performance indices).

The following sections provide an overview of three forms of the general linear model used to evaluate system efficiency: (a) the analysis of variance, (b) multiple regression, and (c) the analysis of covariance. The sections assume basic familiarity with these forms of the model; thus, the focus of the sections is the application of the model to performance evaluation questions. Huck et al. [1974] provide an introduction to the various forms of the general linear model.

Analysis of Variance The analysis of variance model is used when the workload and system parameters to be changed are measured at a nominal or ordinal level. Assume, for example, the auditor is interested in the effects of changes in the memory size allocation and the page replacement algorithm on the response time in an interactive system. The auditor tries two different memory allocations—10 page frames and 20 page frames—and two different page replacement algorithms—last-in-first-out (LIFO) and least-recently-used (LRU). For a given workload the auditor obtains the response time for 100 jobs using each of the four combinations of memory allocation and paging algorithm; thus, 400 measurements of response time are taken.

Table 24-1 shows the mean response time for each combination (treatment) of the memory allocation and paging algorithm (factors). Analysis of variance allows the auditor to answer three important questions. First, does the memory size allocation and the paging algorithm used interact in a statistically significant way to impact response time? Second, if no statistically significant interaction exists, does the memory size allocation or the paging algorithm used independently impact the response time in a statistically significant way? Third, if the memory size allocation or the paging algorithm does affect the response time, what is the size of the effect?

Table 24-2 shows a hypothetical analysis of variance table for the above example. The table shows that only the memory size allocation has a statistically significant effect on the response time. The size of the effect then can be estimated. From Table 24-1 the point estimate of the difference is 5.584 − 2.335 = 3.249 seconds. However, statistical estimation must be undertaken to determine a confidence interval for the difference between the means (see, further, Neter et al. [1985]).

TABLE 24-1
TREATMENT MEANS FOR TWO FACTOR ANALYSIS OF VARIANCE

		Memory size allocation		
		10 frames	20 frames	Row mean
Paging algorithm	LIFO	5.622	2.306	3.964
	LRU	5.546	2.364	3.955
	Column mean	5.584	2.335	3.9595

TABLE 24-2
ANALYSIS OF VARIANCE TABLE FOR TWO FACTOR EXPERIMENT

Source of variation	Sums of squares	Degrees of freedom	Mean square	F
Memory allocation (A)	215.927	1	215.927	20.541*
Paging algorithm (P)	12.047	1	12.047	1.146
A × P	.999	1	.999	.095
Error	4162.752	396	10.512	
Total	4391.725	399		

* $p < .05$.

Regression A regression model is used when the workload and system parameters to be changed are measured at an interval or ratio level. For example, the auditor may be interested in the impact of the number of simultaneous jobs allowed in the system and the number of logons per hour that occur on the response time of an interactive system. To examine the effects, the following regression model might be used:

$$Y = \beta_0 + \beta_1 X_1 + \beta_2 X_2 + \epsilon$$

where Y = system response time
   X_1 = number of simultaneous jobs allowed in the system
   X_2 = number of logons per hour that occur
   β_j = regression coefficients
   ϵ = error term, normally distributed with constant variance

Using the regression approach, the auditor can test whether the overall model is statistically significant and the individual terms in the model are statistically significant. The variation in response times explained by the independent variables also can be determined, and confidence intervals for the beta coefficients can be estimated.

Assume, using the ordinary least-squares method, the following model is obtained:

$$Y = .342 + .051X_1 + .011X_2 \qquad (R^2 = .24)$$

Assume, also, the overall model is statistically significant and the individual terms are statistically significant. The number of jobs simultaneously in the system (X_1) and the number of logons per hour (X_2) account for 24% of the variation in response times. Further, each extra job in the system adds .051 second to the response time and each extra logon per hour adds .011 second to the response time. The values .051 and .011 are point estimates of the beta coefficients; thus, the auditor may wish to determine a confidence interval for each beta coefficient, say, at the 95% level.

Analysis of Covariance If the auditor investigates the effects of changes to both workload and system parameters, some of which are measured at the nominal or ordinal level and some of which are measured at the interval or ratio level, an analysis of covariance model can be used (see, for example, Friedman and Waldbaum [1975]). The analysis of covariance model can be formulated as a regression model where the variables measured at a nominal or ordinal level can be included as dummy variables (see, further, Neter et al. [1985]). Kobayashi [1978] discusses the use of analysis of covariance for efficiency evaluation purposes.

COMBINING WORKLOAD AND SYSTEM MODELS

When a performance evaluation study is to be carried out, the choice of a workload model and the choice of a system model are not independent decisions. Constraints on the workload model to be constructed affect the system model that can be used, and vice versa. Thus, the auditor should consider carefully how the workload model and the system model will interact before determining the performance evaluation methodology to be used.

Table 24-3 shows the relationships among the various workload and system models examined in this chapter. A benchmark workload model can be used only with a simulation model or an empirical model. Recall, a benchmark is a model of a real workload; thus, it can be used as a trace in a simulation model or as input to an empirical model. Instruction mix and kernel program workload models can be used only with an analytical system model. Indeed, the system model for both workload models is trivial; it simply reflects the probability of each instruction type occurring, and overall performance is assessed as a simple additive model of the different instruction times. A synthetic job workload model can be used either as a trace in a simulation system model or as input to an empirical system model. Finally, probabilistic workload models can be used only with analytical (queuing) system models or simulation system models.

TABLE 24-3
ALLOWABLE COMBINATIONS OF WORKLOAD AND SYSTEM MODELS

System model Workload model	Analytical	Simulation	Empirical
Benchmark		X	X
Instruction mix	X		
Kernel program	X		
Synthetic job		X	X
Probabilistic	X	X	

In some cases the auditor may construct alternative performance evaluation models of a system. Each model is then assessed to estimate its accuracy and its operational costs. The "best" model is then chosen, and experiments are subsequently conducted with the model to determine the performance of the system under varying workloads and system configurations (see, for example, Anderson [1984]).

SUMMARY

The auditor evaluates system efficiency either to determine whether the performance of an existing system can be improved or to assess the relative capabilities of proposed hardware/software configurations to process an installation's workload. The evaluation process consists of eight steps: (*a*) formulate study objectives, (*b*) prepare a budget, (*c*) define performance indices, (*d*) construct a workload model, (*e*) construct a system model, (*f*) run experiments, (*g*) analyze results, and (*h*) provide recommendations.

There are three types of performance indices used to evaluate system efficiency. Timeliness indices measure how quickly a system can process user jobs. Throughput indices measure the productivity of the system. Utilization indices measure how often a system resource is busy.

The major objective in the design of a workload model is representativeness with respect to the real workload. Either natural or artificial workload models can be constructed. Natural workload models are constructed by taking some subset of the real workload; any other type of workload model is artificial.

To assess the impact of workload and system variables on performance indices, a system model must be constructed. The auditor can choose from three types of system models: (*a*) analytical models, (*b*) simulation models, and (*c*) empirical models.

REVIEW QUESTIONS

24-1 Give two factors that have undermined the importance of computer system efficiency evaluations and two factors that have increased the importance of computer system efficiency evaluations.

24-2 Why might EDP auditors be asked to perform an efficiency evaluation of a computer system?

24-3 At the outset of an efficiency evaluation study, why is it important to define clearly the purposes of the evaluation?

24-4 Why is it usually difficult to estimate the benefits of an efficiency evaluation study?

24-5 Briefly explain the difference between a workload model and a system model. To what extent can the workload model be formulated independently of the system model?

24-6 Briefly explain the nature of the three major types of performance indices. For each type, give an example of a specific performance index that might be used in an efficiency evaluation study.

24-7 Why must a performance index usually be described by a probability distribution rather than a single point estimate?

24-8 Even if the system to be evaluated is operational, why might the auditor decide to use a workload model to evaluate system efficiency rather than the real workload?

24-9 What is meant by the representativeness of a workload model? How can the representativeness of a workload model be measured? In practice, why is it sometimes difficult to evaluate the representativeness of a workload model?

24-10 Briefly explain the difference between a natural workload model and an artificial workload model. What are the relative advantages and disadvantages of each type of workload model?

24-11 Briefly explain the difference between constructing a natural workload model on the basis of a content subset versus a time subset. Which model is likely to be more representative of the real workload?

24-12 What is the nature of the *system* model used with an instruction mix workload model? Give three limitations of the output of the system model.

24-13 What is the difference between a synthetic job and a kernel program? How will the system models for these two types of artificial workload models differ?

24-14 Briefly explain the nature of a probabilistic workload model.

24-15 Why is it important to focus on the interevent times when decomposing a system so it can be modeled for efficiency evaluation purposes? When a decision is made on the level of the system to be modeled, how must events in a lower-level system be described in the model?

24-16 What are the attributes of a computer system that allow it to be modeled as a queuing system? Are there any types of computer systems where queuing theory would not provide a useful basis for modeling the system?

24-17 Briefly explain the difference between an open queuing model and a closed queuing model. What factor might cause the auditor to model a computer system as an open queuing model even though a closed queuing model is more realistic?

24-18 Briefly explain the importance of the following parameters in a queuing model of a computer system: (a) number of job classes, (b) arrival pattern of jobs, (c) service time distribution.

24-19 What is meant by the CPU queuing discipline? How does the queuing discipline affect the nature of jobs awaiting service at the CPU?

24-20 Why have queuing theorists been concerned with developing approximate methods for solving queuing models?

24-21 How can the auditor determine which parameters in a queuing model are more important to calibrate?

24-22 Even though the system to be evaluated is operational, why might the auditor use a queuing model of the system for efficiency evaluation purposes rather than a simulation model or an empirical model?

24-23 Briefly explain the nature of a trace-driven simulation model of a computer system. What are the strengths and limitations of a trace-driven simulation? How can a trace be constructed for a system that is not operational?

24-24 What advantage does a simulation package such as SCERT offer over a simulation language such as GPSS?

24-25 Why is it sometimes difficult to evaluate the validity of a simulation model constructed for efficiency evaluation purposes?

24-26 Give two attributes of a simulator that the auditor might examine when assessing the face validity of the simulator as a vehicle for efficiency evaluation purposes.

24-27 Briefly explain how the auditor would conduct experiments with a simulation model that has been constructed for efficiency evaluation purposes.

24-28 Using a simulator, the auditor changes the device to channel assignment to assess the impact on system throughput. How can the auditor determine *formally* whether the change has a significant impact on the performance of the data processing system?

24-29 Briefly explain the nature of an empirical model of a data processing system constructed for efficiency evaluation purposes.

24-30 What factor determines whether the auditor uses analysis of variance, analysis of covariance, or a regression model when constructing an empirical model of a data processing system to evaluate efficiency?

24-31 Identify *two* general questions that can be answered by constructing an analysis of variance model to evaluate system efficiency.

24-32 What information is provided by the beta coefficients that are estimated when a regression model is constructed to evaluate the efficiency of a data processing system?

MULTIPLE CHOICE QUESTIONS

24-1 Which of the following sequence of steps should be used in an efficiency evaluation study:
  a Construct a system model, construct a workload model, define performance indices
  b Define performance indices, construct a system model, construct a workload model
  c Construct a workload model, define performance indices, construct a system model
  d Define performance indices, construct a workload model, construct a system model

24-2 The *capability* of a system is an example of a:
  a Throughput index
  b Utilization index
  c Timeliness index
  d Turnaround index

24-3 Which of the following is an example of a user-oriented performance index (as opposed to a system-oriented performance index):
  a Channel utilization
  b Throughput rate
  c CPU utilization
  d Response time

24-4 A system workload is:
  a The number of jobs in the system at any one time
  b The set of resource demands imposed upon the system by the set of jobs that occur during a given time period
  c The maximum amount of resources that the system can make available at any one time
  d The proportion of time during which the CPU is in a busy state

24-5 A representative workload is one that:
   a Is based on a sample of jobs from the real workload
   b Produces the same values of the performance indices as the real workload
   c Is formulated and used only when the real workload is unavailable
   d Combines both a natural workload model and an artificial workload model for efficiency evaluation purposes

24-6 Which of the following is an example of a natural workload model:
   a A kernel program
   b An instruction mix
   c A benchmark
   d A synthetic job

24-7 Which of the following is an advantage of natural workload models:
   a Their representativeness is high
   b They are always easy to modify
   c They can be constructed even when the real workload does not exist
   d They are always more compact than artificial workload models

24-8 Which of the following workload models is likely to have the highest level of representativeness:
   a A kernel program
   b A cycle count
   c An instruction mix
   d A synthetic job

24-9 Which of the following is a disadvantage of a probabilistic workload model:
   a Lack of compactness
   b Inflexibility
   c Tractability requirements sometimes lower representativeness
   d High development costs

24-10 When modeling a computer system, the boundaries between subsystems can be identified by:
   a The physical differences between each subsystem
   b The presence of some form of channel
   c A major difference in the time interval between events in the subsystems
   d A switch in the nature of the processor, e.g., hardware to software to microcode

24-11 In a queuing model of a computer system, the server is:
   a The CPU
   b An I/O device
   c Memory
   d All of the above

24-12 A problem with using queuing theory to model computer systems is:
   a Closed models, which are more representative of real systems, are harder to solve mathematically
   b Queuing models are somewhat unrealistic ways to view computer systems
   c Only a limited set of performance indices can be investigated using a queuing model of a computer system
   d Queuing models cannot represent the complex probabilistic phenomena that occur in computer systems

24-13 A queuing model where all jobs are generated internally to the model is called:
   a An internal server model
   b A closed model

    c A mixed model

    d An open model

24-14 A round robin strategy describes:

    a An arrival pattern

    b A CPU queuing discipline

    c An I/O device routing strategy

    d A method of multiprogramming

24-15 Approximate analysis may be used to solve a queuing model if:

    a The system to be modeled does not involve online, interactive input

    b An open queuing model has been used to model the computer system

    c A natural workload model has been used

    d Restrictive model assumptions have been violated

24-16 Calibration is the process of:

    a Determining the size of the error in the queuing model output

    b Making an open queuing model more like a realistic, closed queuing model

    c Reducing the size of the output errors by reducing or eliminating various forms of inaccuracies

    d Running a queuing model a sufficient number of times until its output stabilizes

24-17 Which of the following is unlikely to be a reason why the auditor uses a simulation model to evaluate the efficiency of a computer system:

    a Cheaper than a queuing model

    b Used to validate the analytical model

    c The system to be evaluated may not be operational

    d An analytical model may not be tractable

24-18 If the auditor focuses on processes in the design and implementation of a simulation model, time is incremented:

    a When the system changes its state

    b By constant intervals

    c By random intervals

    d When the system invokes a new process

24-19 Which of the following is *not* true of a trace-driven simulation model:

    a It usually produces more accurate results than a simulation based on a probabilistic workload model

    b It usually is more costly to construct and run than a probabilistic model

    c It tends to be less accurate when sensitivity analyses involving major modifications to the workload or system structure are carried out

    d Compared to a probabilistic workload model, it is more difficult to preserve correlations between resource requests

24-20 Which of the following languages is more likely to be chosen to write a simulation for performance evaluation purposes:

    a CSS

    b Simscript

    c Fortran

    d GPSS

24-21 The major empirical model used in performance evaluation is:

    a The general linear model

    b Regression

    c Analysis of variance

    d Analysis of covariance

24-22 If the auditor wishes to evaluate the effects on system response time of a changed CPU scheduling method, a changed channel allocation, and the number of logons that occur each minute, it is most likely that the empirical model used will be:
  a Analysis of variance
  b Factor analysis
  c Analysis of covariance
  d Regression

24-23 Which of the following workload models cannot be used with a simulation system model:
  a Benchmark
  b Kernel program
  c Synthetic job
  d Probabilistic

24-24 Which of the following workload models cannot be used with an analytical system model:
  a Probabilistic
  b Instruction mix
  c Synthetic job
  d Kernel program

EXERCISES AND CASES

24-1 Briefly explain how resource demands are generated in a probabilistic workload model. If the demand for processor time by jobs is distributed normally with a mean of 5 microseconds and a variance of 2.5 microseconds, and the random number generator you use for your workload model is functioning correctly, what percentage of the jobs generated should request more than 7 microseconds of processor time? How could you check that, in fact, this is the case with your workload model?

24-2 The auditor obtains the following results for a regression model used to assess the impact of the number of jobs per hour that request over 5 microseconds of CPU time (X_1) and the number of jobs per hour that require more than one work space in main memory (X_2) on the response time of a system (measured in seconds):

$$Y = .106 + .371X_1 + .402X_2 \quad (R^2 = .16)$$

Required:
  a What is the expected impact on response time of introducing two more jobs into the system that request more than 5 microseconds of processor time?
  b What is the impact on response time of introducing one more job that requests more than 5 microseconds of processor time and four jobs that require more than one work space?
  c What is the expected response time if there are no jobs in the system requiring more than 5 microseconds of processor time or more than one work space.

24-3 Your organization uses an online realtime update system for several of its application systems. Recently, there has been concern over increasing response times with the system. The workload has been increasing; nevertheless, since two of the online realtime update systems are used by clerical staff who deal directly with customers, customer goodwill depends upon fast response times being maintained. One suggestion made by the data processing manager to decrease response times is to see whether the introduction of job priority classes and an increase in the time slice allocated jobs would improve system throughput.

As the internal auditor in your organization having expertise in performance evaluation, management asks you to evaluate the changes proposed by the data processing manager. You decide to evaluate the changes using an experiment.

Required. Outline how you would set up the experiment. Describe how you would determine whether the changes proposed are worthwhile.

24-4 Spreaditround Ltd., is a large fertilizer company with offices scattered throughout the United States. A communications network links the various offices to the head office in Detroit. The offices have online realtime update capabilities to several centralized databases.

Response times in the network have been deteriorating. After an investigation into the possible reasons why response times are increasing, the system programming group suggests two alterations to the network that they feel may remedy the situation. The first option is to purchase a new model of network controller; however, they are uncertain as to which of two models of controller to purchase. The second option is to change the method of polling terminals in the system from roll-call to hub polling.

The system programming group constructs a simulation model of the network and runs the model for 2000 iterations. The first 1000 iterations allow the simulation to stabilize. During the second 1000 iterations, response times for a particular controller-method of polling configuration are measured. The experiment is run four times, one for each controller-method of polling combination.

As the manager of internal audit for Spreaditround, you receive a report from the system programming group on their simulation runs that contains the following table:

TABLE 1
MEAN RESPONSE TIMES IN SECONDS FOR 1000 ITERATIONS OF EACH
CONTROLLER-METHOD OF POLLING COMBINATION

| Method of polling | Type of controller | | Row mean |
	Type 1	Type 2	
Roll-call	5.002	4.157	4.5794
Hub	5.001	3.062	4.0315
Column mean	5.0015	3.6095	4.3055

Required: On the basis of the simulation results, what do you conclude about the proposed changes? If a statistical analysis (ANOVA) of the results was undertaken, what variables do you think would be statistically significant?

24-5 During the design of a new motor vehicle registration system for a state highway department, the systems analysts must decide on the number of terminals that are needed for the clerks who serve customers at the front desk. Customers can come to the counter, pay their registration renewals, and receive their stickers for the coming year. The system also provides answers to queries about registration rates for the different types of motor vehicles, the status of registration on a particular vehicle, etc.

The systems analysts believe that one terminal will serve two clerical staff adequately but they are not sure whether it will serve three without a queue developing, especially during peak periods; for example, around lunchtime.

Required: Outline how you would construct a queuing model to help the analysts with their problem. Note, assume there is excess capacity with the central processor, disks, etc.

24-6 Chuckle and Sue is a medium-sized, Perth-based firm of solicitors who specialize in providing advice to the yachting industry. Twelve months ago the partners decided to install their first computer system to help them process a rapidly increasing volume of accounting transactions and to obtain better management information on the state of their practice. The system that the firm chose comprised a local area network of six microcomputers connected to a 40-megabyte hard disk.

Since the system was installed, the six microcomputers have been used in the following way: one has been used as an update terminal to process transactions against the various ledgers and client files; one has been used as an inquiry terminal by the receptionist/secretary to answer questions from clients; and the other four have been used by the partners to inquire on client files and to print information they need for billing purposes.

Because transaction volumes have been increasing rapidly, the partners decided to add a seventh terminal to the network to act as an update terminal. However, as soon as one of the accounts clerks began to use the terminal to update files, response time in the network degraded significantly. As a consequence, Gloria Chuckle, the senior partner in the firm, approached the computer company that had sold the system to her firm to determine the cause of the problem. A salesperson from the vendor informed her that the local area network configuration was an inappropriate configuration to use if the seventh terminal was to be used as an update terminal. He advised her to sell off the microcomputers and the network and to purchase a minicomputer system that would drive seven terminals.

Required: You are a data processing consultant in the firm of accountants that has Chuckle and Sue as their client. Gloria has approached your partner to seek his advice on the veracity of the information provided by the vendor's salesperson. She is clearly upset by the prospective costs of converting to a new system and the associated disruption that will occur. Your partner asks you to prepare a brief report outlining how you will determine the cause of the problems in the current system as a basis for then deciding on an appropriate solution to the problems.

ANSWERS TO MULTIPLE CHOICE QUESTIONS

24-1 d	24-7 a	24-13 b	24-19 d
24-2 a	24-8 d	24-14 b	24-20 a
24-3 d	24-9 c	24-15 d	24-21 a
24-4 b	24-10 c	24-16 c	24-22 c
24-5 b	24-11 d	24-17 a	24-23 b
24-6 c	24-12 a	24-18 b	24-24 c

REFERENCES

Allen, A.O. "Elements of Queuing Theory for System Design," *IBM Systems Journal*, vol. 14, no. 2, 1975, pp. 161–187.

Anderson, Gordon E. "The Coordinated Use of Five Performance Evaluation Methodologies," *Communications of the ACM* (February 1984), pp. 119–125.

Anderson, H.A., Jr., M. Reiser, and G.L. Galati. "Tuning a Virtual Storage System," *IBM Systems Journal*, vol. 14, no. 3, 1975, pp. 246–263.

Arndt, Fred R., and G.M. Oliver. "Hardware Monitoring of Real-Time Computer System Performance," *Computer* (July–August 1972), pp. 25–29.

Bard, Y. "The VM/370 Performance Predictor," *Computing Surveys* (September 1978), pp. 333–342.

Boyse, John W., and David R. Warn. "A Straightforward Model for Computer Performance Prediction," *Computing Surveys* (June 1975), pp. 73–93.

Buzen, Jeffrey P. "A Queuing Network Model of MVS," *Computing Surveys* (September 1978), pp. 319–331.

Callaway, P.H. "Performance Measurement Tools for VM/370," *IBM Systems Journal*, vol. 14, no. 2, 1975, pp. 134–160.

Chandy, K. Mani, and Charles H. Sauer. "Approximate Methods for Analyzing Queuing Network Models of Computing Systems," *Computing Surveys* (September 1978), pp. 281–317.

Deitel, Harvey M. *An Introduction to Operating Systems*, rev. 1st ed. (Reading, MA: Addison-Wesley, 1984).

Denning, Peter J., and Jeffrey P. Buzen. "The Operational Analysis of Queueing Network Models," *Computing Surveys* (September 1978), pp. 225–261.

Ferrari, Domenico. "Workload Characterization and Selection in Computer Performance Measurement," *Computer* (July–August 1972), pp. 18–24.

Ferrari, Domenico. "Architecture and Instrumentation in a Modular Interactive System," *Computer* (November 1973), pp. 25–29.

Ferrari, Domenico. *Computer Systems Performance Evaluation* (Englewood Cliffs, NJ: Prentice-Hall, 1978).

Ferrari, Domenico, and Mark Lin. "A General-Purpose Software Measurement Tool," *Software—Practice and Experience* (April–June 1975), pp. 181–192.

Friedman, H.P., and G. Waldbaum. "Evaluating System Changes under Uncontrolled Workloads: A Case Study." *IBM Systems Journal*, vol. 14, no. 4, 1975, pp. 340–352.

Gaede, Steven L. "Tools for Research in Computer Workload Characterization and Modeling," in Domenico Ferrari and Massimo Spadoni, eds., *Experimental Computer Performance Evaluation* (Amsterdam: North-Holland, 1981), pp. 235–247.

Graham, G. Scott. "Queueing Network Models of Computer System Performance," *Computing Surveys* (September 1978), pp. 219–224.

Grochow, Jerrold M. "Utility Functions for Time-Sharing System Performance Evaluation," *Computer* (September–October 1972), pp. 16–19.

Huck, Shuyler W., William H. Cormier, and William G. Bounds, Jr. *Reading Statistics and Research* (New York: Harper & Row, 1974).

Kobayashi, Hisashi. *Modeling and Analysis: An Introduction to System Performance Evaluation Methodology* (Reading, MA: Addison-Wesley, 1978).

Kriebel, Charles H., and Artur Raviv. "An Economics Approach to Modeling the Productivity of Computer Systems," *Management Science* (March 1980), pp. 297–311.

Lipsky, Lester, and J.D. Church. "Applications of a Queueing Network Model for a Computer System," *Computing Surveys* (September 1977), pp. 205–221.

Lucas, Henry C. "Performance Evaluation and Monitoring," *Computing Surveys* (September 1971), pp. 79–91.

Miller, Edward F., Jr. "Bibliography on Techniques of Computer Performance Analysis," *Computer* (September–October 1972), pp. 39–47.

Muntz, Richard R. "Queueing Networks: A Critique of the State of the Art and Directions for the Future," *Computing Surveys* (September 1978), pp. 354–359.

Neter, John, William Wasserman, and Michael Kutner. *Applied Linear Statistical Models: Regression, Analysis of Variance, and Experimental Designs,* 2d ed. (Homewood, IL: Irwin, 1985).

Ramamoorthy, C.V., K.H. Kim, and W.T. Chen. "Optimal Placement of Software Monitors Aiding Systematic Testing," *IEEE Transactions on Software Engineering* (December 1975), pp. 403–411.

Rose, Clifford A. "A Measurement Procedure for Queueing Network Models of Computer Systems," *Computing Surveys* (September 1978), pp. 263–280.

Saltzer, Jerome H. "Protection and the Control of Information Sharing in Multics," *Communications of the ACM* (July 1974), pp. 388–402.

Sauer, Charles H., and K. Mani Chandy. *Computer Systems Performance Modeling* (Englewood Cliffs, NJ: Prentice-Hall, 1981).

Shermer, Jack E., and John B. Robertson. "Instrumentation of Time-Shared Systems," *Computer* (July–August 1972), pp. 39–48.

Simon, Herbert A. *The Sciences of the Artificial,* 2d ed. (Cambridge, MA: The M.I.T. Press, 1981).

Stimler, Saul. *Data Processing Systems: Their Performance, Evaluation, Measurement, and Improvement* (Trenton, NJ: Motivational Learning Programs, 1974).

Svobodova, Liba. *Computer Performance Measurement and Evaluation Methods: Analysis and Applications* (New York: American Elsevier, 1976).

Wong, J.W. "Queueing Network Modeling of Computer Communication Networks," *Computing Surveys* (September 1978), pp. 343–351.

PART SIX

SIX

MANAGING THE EDP AUDIT FUNCTION

In the previous twenty-four chapters of this book we have ranged widely over the subject matter of EDP auditing. Clearly the EDP auditor's task is complex. The auditor must know a large number of controls as a basis for evaluating system reliability or designing a system so it safeguards assets, maintains data integrity, achieves its goals effectively, and consumes resources efficiently. Similarly, the auditor must be competent to choose from the large number of techniques available to gather evidence. In light of these complexities, managing the process whereby an EDP audit function accomplishes its own goals effectively and efficiently is a difficult task. Moreover, the constant change associated with data processing technology further confounds the EDP audit management task.

Chapter	Overview of Contents
25 Organization and Management of the EDP Audit Function	Need for a separate EDP audit function; centralization versus decentralization; staffing; training; relationships with other organizational groups; career opportunities; life cycle of the EDP audit group; software support for EDP audit management
26 The Changing EDP Audit Function	Toward professionalism; legal and social influences; the impact of changing technology; research and pedagogy

The final section of this book comprises two chapters. The first presents some guidelines for managing the EDP audit function effectively and efficiently. It identifies some of the contentious areas that confront EDP audit managers. The second discusses some of the possible futures of EDP auditing. Note that the plural form "futures" has been used intentionally. It is impossible to predict with confidence a single future for EDP auditing. Instead, a number of scenarios can be described, all of which are possible. The plural form "futures" denotes the inherent uncertainty surrounding attempts to predict the evolution of any aspect of the data processing industry.

CHAPTER 25

ORGANIZATION AND MANAGEMENT OF THE EDP AUDIT FUNCTION

CHAPTER OUTLINE

The emphasis given to EDP auditing in the accounting literature over recent years sometimes gives the impression that EDP auditing is a function separate and distinct from the traditional audit function. This is a mistaken impression. EDP auditing is an integral part of the total audit function: that part of the function supporting the auditor's judgment on the quality of computer systems. Ultimately the completion of an EDP audit contributes to the overall objectives of an external audit or an internal audit.

The emergence of an EDP audit function, however, has given rise to some controversial organization and management issues. There has been debate on how the function should be integrated with the total audit effort and how the function should be organized and managed. In some cases the issues debated have been resolved; however, there still are many contentious areas.

This chapter examines some of the major organization and management problems and controversies brought about by the existence of the EDP audit function. It assumes familiarity with good organization and management practices for both external and internal auditing (see Arens and Loebbecke [1984] and Sawyer [1973]); thus the chapter only highlights the difficulties that arise when these practices are applied to the EDP audit function.

NEED FOR A SEPARATE EDP AUDIT SECTION

A major question that has arisen when organizing and managing the EDP audit function is whether or not a separate group of computer audit specialists should exist to perform the function. Two issues must be resolved. First, is there a need for computer audit specialists? Second, if computer audit specialists are needed, where should they be placed within the organization hierarchy of the audit group?

Need for Computer Audit Specialists

Three motivations exist for having separate computer audit specialist positions created within the hierarchy of audit organizations. First, someone must be technically proficient to perform EDP audits. Second, audit independence may be increased if auditors are technically proficient with computers. Third, better relations may exist between the audit staff and data processing staff if the auditor is technically proficient with computers.

Technical Proficiency Considerations A fundamental requirement of any audit is that the auditor be technically proficient to carry out the audit. In general, how much knowledge of computers must an auditor have to be able to carry out an EDP audit competently? Further, can the general staff auditor be expected to remain technically proficient in both auditing and EDP?

A debate exists over what level of technical knowledge the auditor must have to be able to perform an EDP audit competently. The debate stems from a deeper issue: what are the responsibilities of an auditor? Some external auditors argue the auditor has neither the time nor the resources available to perform in-depth testing of technologically complex computer systems. It is not the role of the auditor to carry out detailed testing of computer systems. Instead, the external auditor evaluates management controls, examines the work of internal auditors, etc. If expert advice is needed, the services of a data processing professional can be employed. The external auditor simply needs sufficient knowledge of computers to be able to liaise with experts and maintain an independent attitude. It is reasonable to expect general staff auditors to have this level of knowledge.

Various professional organizations of external auditors have taken a different viewpoint. They argue a distinction should be made between the EDP knowledge requirements of a *general* staff auditor and the EDP knowledge requirements of a *computer audit specialist*. For example, both the American Institute of Certified Public Accountants and the Canadian Institute of Chartered Accountants argue all auditors must be able to carry out an audit of a simple batch computer system (see Jancura [1975a, 1975b]). However, beyond that level the services of a computer audit specialist usually are needed.

There is less room for debate over the level of computer knowledge required by *internal* auditors. The substantial growth in the number of organizations that employ computer audit specialists clearly shows management believes high technical expertise is necessary to achieve certain objectives of the internal audit group.

External auditors usually require greater breadth of knowledge about computers than internal auditors since they encounter more different types of systems. At least for some time period the internal auditor examines and evaluates only one or a small number of hardware/software configurations. On the one hand this practice suggests the external auditor cannot be expected to have an in-depth knowledge of computer systems. On the other hand it suggests the need for a separate group of computer audit specialists who can evaluate the variety of configurations confronted. It seems more reasonable to expect internal auditors to have in-depth knowledge of the computer systems they audit; hence, it might be argued there is less justification for a separate group of computer audit specialists in an internal audit department.

Audit Independence Considerations One of the major arguments advanced for having separate computer audit specialists is that it will increase the independence of the audit group. Rittenberg [1977] asked EDP audit managers, heads of internal audit, staff EDP auditors, company management, heads of EDP departments, and external auditors about methods of increasing audit independence. Several of their responses involved arguments for greater technical proficiency on the part of the auditor:

1 Increase technical EDP knowledge   75% of respondents agreed
2 Recruit employees with more
  extensive EDP experience   44% of respondents agreed
3 Set up audit section specializing
  in EDP auditing   32% of respondents agreed

Underlying these responses is the belief that decreased audit independence results from relying on data processing professionals for technical assistance. Some auditors argue this is not the case; it is an independence in *attitude* that is important because to some extent the auditor must always rely on others for assistance.

Relationships with EDP Staff Sometimes the respect of EDP staff for the auditor depends on the auditor's technical proficiency with computers. If the data processing professional sees the auditor has clearly formulated objectives, and further has the technical knowledge to accomplish those objectives, then relationships between the EDP group and the audit group may be enhanced.

Placement of Computer Audit Specialists

Though there now seems to be some agreement that computer audit specialists are needed, a debate still continues over *where* computer audit specialists should be placed within the hierarchy of external or internal audit groups. One side sees the computer audit specialists primarily performing a staff function; that is, providing advice and assistance to the general staff auditor on technologically complex matters (Figure 25-1*a*). The other side sees the computer audit specialist primarily performing a line function; that is, being an integral part of an audit team and assuming responsibility for those parts of the audit that involve the computer (Figure 25-1*b*).

EDP Auditing as a Staff Function There are several arguments given for having EDP audit as a staff function:

1 *Better utilization of EDP audit resources:* Maintaining an effective and efficient EDP audit group requires a heavy commitment to ongoing training. Further, skilled EDP auditors are difficult to hire. In a staff capacity the EDP auditor advises and assists on matters that involve data processing only. This specialization of function improves utilization of a scarce resource.

2 *Greater work satisfaction for EDP auditor:* Since EDP auditors working in a staff capacity will be involved purely with EDP audit work, they should

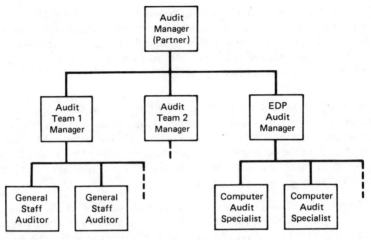

FIGURE 25-1a
EDP auditing as a staff function.

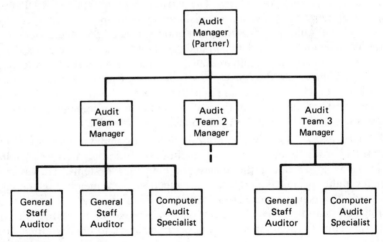

FIGURE 25-1b
EDP auditing as a line function.

have higher job satisfaction. They will not be forced to keep up with the changing technology of auditing as well as data processing.

3 *Organization commitment to EDP auditing more likely:* In a staff capacity the EDP audit group has a separate existence. Thus, it is more difficult for top management to overlook the EDP audit function. A greater ongoing organization commitment to EDP auditing should result.

4 *Facilitates coordination and control:* If EDP auditors exist as a separate group having their own manager, they can be better coordinated and controlled.

5 *Allows increased specialization to cope with complex technology:* Within the EDP audit group, different EDP auditors can specialize in different aspects of computer technology. Especially for external audit groups, this specialization helps ensure someone is always able to cope with the diverse types of complex technology encountered.

EDP Auditing as a Line Function If EDP auditing is a line function, computer audit specialists will be assigned to any audit involving a computer system simply as a member of the audit team performing the audit. Thus, the responsibilities of the computer audit specialist will encompass both EDP audit as well as more traditional audit functions. Three major arguments are given for having EDP auditing as a line function:

1 *Greater goal congruence:* As an integral member of the audit team having full responsibility for completion of an audit, the computer audit specialist should have a better understanding of the overall audit objectives and assume greater responsibility for achieving the objectives.

2 *Facilitates communications:* The existence of a separate EDP audit group sometimes causes friction to arise between computer audit specialists and general staff auditors. The computer audit specialist sees the general staff auditor as being technically deficient and resistant to change; the general staff auditor sees the computer audit specialist as being more interested in technology than accomplishing the objectives of the audit. Consequently, communications between the two groups are inhibited or break down. Having computer audit specialists as a member of the audit team facilitates communications and improves relations between the two groups.

3 *Improves EDP expertise of staff auditors:* If computer audit specialists perform a staff function, general staff auditors tend to abrogate responsibility for decisions made about the quality of computer systems. However, if computer audit specialists perform a line function, each member of the audit team tends to assume more responsibility for each other's decisions. Thus, general staff auditors have an incentive to improve their EDP expertise. Similarly, computer audit specialists have an incentive to improve their audit skills.

CENTRALIZATION VERSUS DECENTRALIZATION OF THE EDP AUDIT FUNCTION

Both internal and external audit groups face a decision on whether or not to centralize or decentralize their EDP audit expertise. If the group decentralizes, still a further decision must be made: how much decentralization should occur?

There is no clear-cut answer to whether or not an EDP audit group should be centralized or decentralized. The following factors influence the decision:

1 If EDP audits must be performed in locations that are dispersed physically, there is a tendency toward decentralization to overcome communications and control problems.

2 If the audit group has a shortage of EDP audit expertise, there is a tendency toward centralization to make more effective use of the limited expertise that is available.

3 If general staff auditors have basic computer training, there is a tendency to have a centralized group of computer audit specialists performing a staff function.

4 If it is difficult to implement computer-assisted evidence collection techniques at physically dispersed locations, there is a tendency to set up a centralized EDP audit group that performs service bureau type functions.

5 Newly formed EDP audit groups tend to be centralized; decentralization occurs as the group matures.

Stanford Research Institute [1977] reports that one form of centralized EDP audit function used by some organizations is a *competency center*. Essentially, a competency center performs EDP audit service bureau functions. General staff auditors can send data files to the competency center to be processed. Computer audit specialists in the center also provide consulting advice. The center has other responsibilities; for example, it develops EDP audit standards to be used generally, refines EDP audit methodologies, and develops, implements, and tests computer-assisted audit techniques. A competency center may be implemented by both internal and external audit groups.

STAFFING THE EDP AUDIT FUNCTION

In most countries staffing the EDP audit function has been a major problem. Historically there has been a shortage of accounting professionals. A similar situation has existed in the data processing field. Finding personnel who have both sets of skills has been very difficult; EDP auditor salaries have reflected the problem.

As a result of the shortage, management has focused on two questions related to staffing. First, how many EDP auditors does an organization need? Second, given that few EDP auditors exist having equal facility with auditing and data processing, should personnel with an auditing background or a data processing background be hired into EDP auditing?

Number of EDP Auditors Required

There is no fixed formula that an external or internal audit group can use to determine how many EDP auditors it should have on its staff. For internal audit groups, Weiss [1977] argues a ratio of about one EDP auditor to every 16½ systems analysts and programmers on average is a reasonable ratio. However, other major factors affect this decision; for example:

Factor	Explanation
Size of the organization	Larger organizations usually have more EDP systems and therefore a greater need for EDP auditors.
Nature of the organization	Some types of business activities require more controls to be exercised than others. For example, banking and public accounting organizations are more likely to require a greater number of EDP auditors than engineering organizations (see, also, the survey by Weiss [1977]).
Extent of EDP use	Organizations making greater use of EDP for their data processing are more likely to require a larger number of EDP auditors.
Types of computer systems implemented	Organizations that have installed complex systems such as on-line realtime systems and database management systems are more likely to need a greater number of EDP auditors than organizations that have only batch computer systems.
Stability of the EDP environment	Mature data processing installations primarily carrying out maintenance work rather than new system development will require fewer EDP auditors.

The number of EDP auditors required by an organization may follow a cyclical pattern. The data processing activities of the organization often stabilize after some period of development, remain stable for a time, and then undergo another major change. For example, the organization may decide to purchase different hardware and software or commence integration of a number of application systems. As development and implementation activity increases, the number of EDP auditors needed also will increase (see, also, Chapter 3).

The number of EDP auditors needed by an *external* audit group depends on the number of clients using computers for their data processing and the complexity of the data processing performed. It also will depend on the level of computer training provided to general staff auditors and whether or not computer audit specialists are centralized or decentralized.

Source of EDP Audit Staff

Since a shortage of EDP auditors exists and few tertiary institutions graduate individuals with both audit and computer expertise, many organizations have been forced to train their own EDP auditors. They have faced a decision on whether to train data processing professionals in auditing or auditors in data processing. There are two issues involved: (a) whether it is easier to train an auditor or a data processing professional in EDP auditing; and (b) who will be the most effective and efficient EDP auditor?

Those who favor training computer professionals as EDP auditors give several reasons. First, they argue that computer professionals already have a solid grounding in computer controls. Systems analysts and programmers are already responsible for designing and implementing controls in systems; thus, they understand what controls are needed in systems. Second, they argue that the technical knowledge required to evaluate computer controls in a system of even moderate complexity can be obtained only through practical experience in the design and implementation of systems. Third, they argue that EDP auditors need more knowledge of computers than accounting; the accounting knowledge required to interact with auditors is less than the computer knowledge required to interact with data processing professionals.

Those who favor training accountants as EDP auditors give two reasons. First, they argue that the overall control philosophy needed to be an effective and efficient EDP auditor is best acquired through training in accounting and auditing. Second, they argue that in most cases the ultimate objective of any type of audit is to make some judgment about the state of the accounting records. Substantial training in accounting and auditing is essential if a quality judgment is to be made.

It is difficult to establish empirically whether personnel who were first trained in auditing or computers make better EDP auditors. Interestingly, Rittenberg [1975] asked both types of EDP auditor whether they perceived auditing knowledge or data processing knowledge to be more difficult to acquire. Those who were trained first in computers thought auditing knowledge was more difficult to acquire; those who were trained first in auditing thought data processing knowledge was more difficult to acquire. In practice it seems organizations generally prefer to train computer professionals in auditing (see Weiss [1977]).

TRAINING

With the advent of the EDP audit function some auditors argue the commitment to continuing education will have to be increased. However, training is a costly activity. Management's problem is to balance the benefits and costs of ongoing education for the EDP auditor. Two questions must be addressed: (*a*) how much ongoing training does an auditor need; and (*b*) what types of training are needed?

Amount of Training Needed

Weiss [1977] found that although some organizations provided 60 or more days of training per year for each of their EDP auditors, about three weeks per year was the average. He argues this amount is insufficient for EDP auditors to keep up with the pace of change in computer technology.

There is very little research evidence to guide management in their decision on the amount of ongoing training needed. Some of the major factors influencing this decision are:

Factor	Explanation
Level of technology used by data processing installation	If the data processing installation to be evaluated by the auditor uses complex technology, the auditor will have to invest more in training.
Changes in the data processing environment	Higher investments in training may be required if the data processing installation to be audited changes the technology it uses.
Maturity of the EDP audit group	As individual EDP auditors gain more experience, they require less training to keep up with computer technology. As an EDP audit group matures, the objectives, standards, methodologies, etc., of the group become stabilized and less training is needed to refine and communicate this knowledge.
Changes in EDP audit objectives	If the objectives of the EDP audit function change, further training may be required to enable these objectives to be met. For example, if an EDP audit group previously has performed only financial audits and it commences to perform operational (efficiency) audits, further training may be needed.

Types of Training Needed

Compared to the question of how much training is needed, somewhat more formal analysis has been undertaken on the types of training an EDP auditor needs. Stanford Research Institute [1977] studied the skill levels needed by EDP auditors to be able to implement and use various EDP audit techniques. SRI identified seven basic areas where the EDP auditor must be competent to be technically proficient:

Knowledge area	Explanation
Data processing principles and concepts	Overview of computer terminology, hardware, software, file processing, system development
Computer application systems structure	Basic understanding of how an application system is developed, implemented, and operated
Computer application systems controls and procedures	Understanding of the controls that can be exercised over all aspects of application system processing
Data management	Understanding of the methods used to define, create, update, and retrieve data; techniques for control and use of data
Computer service center controls	Understanding of controls needed for data processing operations; job scheduling, librarian function, report distribution, data transit controls, etc.
Application system development controls	Understanding of controls needed to ensure development of quality application systems
Computer application programming	Familiarity with a programming language used for commercial purposes; for example, COBOL

TABLE 25-1
EXTENT OF DATA PROCESSING KNOWLEDGE REQUIRED TO ACHIEVE VARIOUS
LEVELS OF EDP AUDIT PROFICIENCY

Knowledge area	Auditor's overall skill level		
	Basic	Intermediate	Advanced
Data processing principles and concepts	Elementary	Substantive	Substantive
Computer application systems structure	Elementary	Substantive	Substantive
Computer application systems controls and procedures	Elementary	Elementary	Substantive
Data management	Elementary	Elementary	Substantive
Computer service center controls	Elementary	Elementary	Substantive
Application system development controls	Nil	Elementary	Substantive
Computer application programming	Nil	Elementary	Substantive

(Adapted from Perry [1977]. Copyright 1977 by the Institute of Internal Auditors, Inc., 249 Maitland Avenue, Altamonte Springs, Florida 32701, U.S.A. Reprinted with permission. Adapted with permission, also, Automation Training Center, Inc.)

Perry [1977] provides an extensive analysis and summary of the SRI findings. His analysis proceeds in two steps. First, he identifies three types of EDP auditor: (*a*) those having basic skills, (*b*) those having intermediate skills, and (*c*) those having advanced skills. Table 25-1 shows the level of proficiency each type of auditor requires in each of the seven knowledge areas identified by SRI. For example, those auditors having basic skills in EDP auditing need not be able to program in any language; those having intermediate skills should be able to write elementary programs; and those having advanced skills should have substantive programming knowledge.

Second, he examines each type of auditor's facility with the different EDP audit techniques. Following SRI he distinguishes between an auditor's ability to *develop and implement* the technique and an auditor's ability to *use* the technique. Table 25-2 provides an overview of the second part of his analysis. Part 4 of this book discussed many of the techniques listed in the table. However, the primary purpose of the table is to illustrate two of Perry's major findings:

1 A substantial number of EDP audit techniques do not require programming skills for their development and implementation or use.

2 For some techniques there is a difference between the skill level needed to develop and implement the technique and the skill level needed to use the technique.

These findings run contrary to a viewpoint often expressed; namely, that auditors need substantial computer knowledge and substantial programming skills to be able to carry out EDP auditing competently. If the SRI results are

TABLE 25-2
SKILL LEVELS NEEDED FOR DEVELOPMENT, IMPLEMENTATION, AND USE OF EDP AUDIT TECHNIQUES

EDP audit technique	Data processing skills needed					
	Basic		Intermediate		Advanced	
	I*	U*	I	U	I	U
Scoring	✓	✓	✓	✓	✓	✓
Test data method	✓	✓	✓	✓	✓	✓
Computer-aided mapping	✓	✓	✓	✓	✓	✓
Audit guide	✓	✓	✓	✓	✓	✓
Extended records	✓	✓	✓	✓	✓	✓
Manual tracing and mapping	✓	✓	✓	✓	✓	✓
Competency center	✓	✓	✓	✓	✓	✓
Integrated test facility	✓	✓	✓	✓	✓	✓
Disaster test	✓	✓	✓	✓	✓	✓
Transaction selection		✓	✓	✓	✓	✓
Audit area selection		✓	✓	✓	✓	✓
Embedded audit data collection		✓	✓	✓	✓	✓
Snapshot		✓	✓	✓	✓	✓
Multisite audit software		✓	✓	✓	✓	✓
Base case system evaluation			✓	✓	✓	✓
Generalized audit software			✓	✓	✓	✓
Terminal audit software			✓	✓	✓	✓
Postinstallation audit procedures			✓	✓	✓	✓
Job accounting data analysis			✓	✓	✓	✓
Code comparison			✓	✓	✓	✓
Computer-aided flowcharting			✓	✓	✓	✓
Simulation/modeling					✓	✓
Parallel operation					✓	✓
Parallel simulation					✓	✓
Special-purpose audit programs					✓	✓
Computer-aided tracing					✓	✓
Systems development life cycle					✓	✓
Systems development control guidelines					✓	✓
Systems acceptance control group					✓	✓

* I = Development and Implementation. U = Use.
(Adapted from Perry [1977]. Copyright 1977 by the Institute of Internal Auditors, Inc., 249 Maitland Avenue, Altamonte Springs, Florida 32701, U.S.A. Reprinted with permission. Adapted with permission, also, Automation Training Center, Inc.)

valid, selective training at an elementary level in certain skill areas enables the EDP auditor to use many EDP audit techniques. In-depth training across skill areas may be reserved only for a select few EDP auditors.

The findings also raise another issue. It now becomes important to establish *which* EDP audit techniques provide the highest payoffs when they are used. If only those EDP audit techniques requiring advanced data processing skills provide high payoffs, then the most cost-effective way of accomplishing an EDP audit may be to use only these techniques and give EDP auditors in-depth training in the knowledge areas required. Alternatively, some EDP audit techniques that require only basic skills for their use may provide high payoffs in terms of audit objectives. Selective training then can take place.

RELATIONSHIPS WITH MANAGEMENT AND OTHER ORGANIZATION GROUPS

One of the major objectives of an *internal* audit group that performs the EDP audit function is to achieve good relationships with the various levels of management in the organization. Good relationships are important for two reasons. First, they facilitate work being accomplished. Second, strong support from top management is a primary factor affecting the auditor's independence. Rittenberg [1977] found EDP audit managers, heads of internal audit, staff EDP auditors, public accountants, and top management unanimous in their rating of top-management support as the primary factor affecting audit independence.

Unfortunately EDP auditors have had their share of problems in establishing good relationships with management and other organizational groups (see, for example, Adamson [1985], Gustafson [1976], and Perry [1976]). The following sections examine some of the types of problems experienced and some strategies for overcoming these problems.

Types of Problems Experienced

Some of the problems experienced by internal EDP auditors in establishing good relationships with management and other organizational groups can be expected because they confront any internal audit group (see Sawyer [1973]). However, there are some characteristics of EDP auditing that cause additional problems:

1 *Pressures on function to develop quickly:* Some primary stimuli for the EDP audit function to develop have been the major cases of computer fraud. Often the establishment of an EDP audit group has been a panic reaction by management. On other occasions it may be a response to problems being experienced with the organization's data processing: the discovery of errors or suspicions of gross inefficiency in the use of computing resources. The problem here is that the situations giving rise to the EDP audit function are stress situations. Consequently, management has high expectations of fast results from the EDP audit group. The EDP audit manager may have to follow a strategy of getting operational quickly and worrying about standards, documentation, etc., at a later stage. The EDP audit group may feel pressured to attack problem areas where they have insufficient expertise. As a result the actual achievements of the EDP audit group may fall below the expected achievements.

2 *Communications problems:* The establishment of an EDP audit group produces a new set of communications problems within the organization.

Management may be unclear on what objectives the group should have. Because of the technology involved, doubts may exist about how to evaluate the function. Data processing management may not understand clearly why the EDP audit group is interfering with their function. Traditional auditors may be uncertain about how they should interact with the EDP audit function.

3 *Frictions produced with other groups:* These communications problems and the changes brought about to work patterns and relationships because of the existence of the EDP audit function often produce frictions between the EDP audit group and other groups within the organization. Data processing personnel may resent their activities being subjected to scrutiny. They may feel the overheads added to their function by the presence of EDP auditors exceed the benefits obtained. Traditional auditors may resent the uncertainty produced about their own function because of the presence of an EDP audit function. They also may perceive characteristics of the EDP auditor and the EDP audit function that violate what they consider to be behavior norms for audit professionals: higher allegiance by EDP auditors to the data processing profession rather than the accounting profession, unacceptable involvement by EDP auditors in the design phase of new systems (thereby violating audit independence), unorthodox audit reporting on design flaws in systems before their implementation rather than after their implementation (again violating audit independence), unduly long time commitments to complete assignments, etc.

Methods of Improving Relations

Many of the problems experienced by EDP auditors with management and other groups within the organization result from the newness of the EDP audit function. To some extent these problems will be resolved as the function becomes more established. In the meantime some remedial steps can be undertaken to alleviate some of the problems that arise:

1 *Promote open communications:* In general, organization theorists believe that conflict in organizations is resolved best through open communications between the parties involved (see, for example, Lawrence and Lorsch [1969]). The EDP audit group must interact heavily with three other groups in the organization: top management, other audit personnel, and data processing personnel. It is important the EDP audit group clearly communicates its objectives and the methodologies to be used to accomplish these objectives to personnel affected by EDP audit activities. These individuals then have an opportunity to debate an issue or seek clarification on an issue that they feel is contentious.

2 *Audit within technical capabilities:* Especially during the formative stages of the EDP audit function, it is important to undertake only those audit tasks that are well within the technical capabilities of the EDP audit group. The success of the group during its early activities is a major factor affecting the attitudes of top management, audit personnel, and data processing personnel

toward the group. If the group performs its function well, it is likely that personnel affected by the group will have a more positive attitude toward the EDP audit function.

3 *Prioritize tasks to be accomplished:* Given the technical capabilities of the group, those EDP audit tasks that can be accomplished should be prioritized. This process helps identify activities where the payoffs are highest. The opinions of top management, data processing management, and audit management should be solicited and priorities formulated in a cooperative manner.

4 *Manage the EDP Audit Function Well:* Relationships with other organizational groups will improve if these groups perceive the EDP audit function to be well managed. Different organization groups compete for the scarce resources of the organization. Poor relationships develop if other groups in the organization believe the resources assigned to the EDP audit function are not used effectively and efficiently.

PROMOTIONAL OPPORTUNITIES FOR THE EDP AUDITOR

A major problem facing management with respect to any group of technical experts is providing promotional opportunities for the members of the group. Finding suitable job positions for technicians often is difficult. Promotion usually requires greater facility with generalist skills rather than specialist skills. However, unless management provides a suitable career path for specialists, morale deteriorates and staff turnover occurs. Thus, the organization suffers losses on its investment in human capital.

Because the EDP audit function is relatively new within organizations, providing career advancement for the EDP auditor is a problem that has received little attention. There is uncertainty about the kinds of promotional opportunities suitable for EDP auditors given their training and experience. Few organizations have experimented with different types of career paths so their relative strengths and weaknesses can be evaluated.

Internal Career Advancement

One set of promotional opportunities for the EDP auditor exists within the EDP audit group. The Institute of Internal Auditors [1974] surveyed 15 organizations and identified eight positions currently used within the hierarchy of the EDP audit group (see, also, Figure 25-2):

Position	Function/Duties
Audit trainee—EDP	Under close supervision assists in collecting and evaluating evidence on small computer systems or segments of large computer systems

Position	Function/Duties
Internal audit specialist—EDP	Under close supervision assists in collecting and evaluating evidence on all types of data processing activities; performs detailed examinations of records where selection and test criteria have been defined
Internal audit analyst—EDP	Under limited supervision conducts audits of all types of data processing activities by following established audit procedures
Assistant internal auditor—EDP	Under limited supervision conducts audits of all types of data processing activities; participates in new projects and special investigations; responsible for analyzing audit evidence, making recommendations, and preparing documentation to support audit findings
Internal auditor—EDP	Under limited supervision performs audits of large complex computer systems
Associate internal audit manager—EDP	Develops standards for conduct of EDP audits; supervises EDP internal audit assignments
Internal audit manager—EDP	Establishes long-run goals for EDP audit group; plans and assigns work and sets performance objectives; responsible for motivating, counseling, and developing staff
Consultant for internal auditing—EDP	Acts in a staff capacity; provides any detailed technical assistance needed to perform audits

Currently few organizations could support an EDP audit group having eight levels in its hierarchy. Often external auditors have only a consultant position for EDP auditors. Many internal audit groups have only a few levels in the hierarchy.

External Career Advancement

Promotional opportunities for the EDP auditor exist outside the EDP audit group. Perry [1974a] gives the following ranking of career paths outside the EDP audit group for an internal auditor; however, an external auditor who leaves public accounting also might take one of these career paths:

1 Database administration
2 Data processing consulting
3 Data processing management
4 Financial management

He lists financial management last since he argues non-EDP management often looks with suspicion on personnel having computer expertise. This outlook is slowly changing. Database administration makes best use of the auditor's training and experience in preserving data integrity (see Chapter 6).

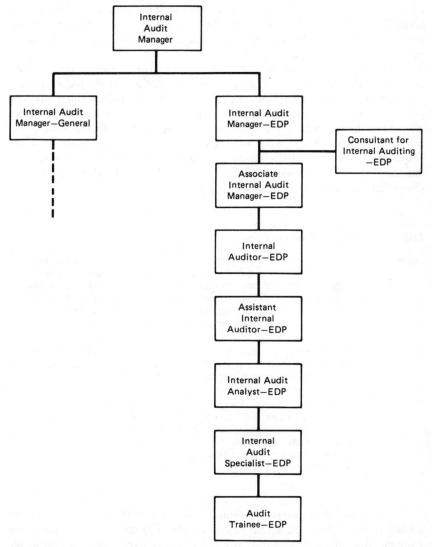

FIGURE 25-2
EDP audit hierarchy within the internal audit department. *(Adapted from the Institute of Internal Auditors [1974]. Copyright 1974 by the Institute of Internal Auditors, Inc., 249 Maitland Avenue, Altamonte Springs, Florida 32701. Reprinted with permission.)*

LIFE CYCLE OF THE EDP AUDIT GROUP

There is at least some evidence to suggest that organizations follow a certain life cycle in their control and use of EDP facilities. Nolan [1973] argues that for computer installations this life cycle can be depicted graphically by an S curve if the size of the computer installation budget is plotted over time (see, further,

Chapter 3). However, an S-curve representation of the life cycle seems to hold generally for all types of organizations. Miller [1978] points out that for all living systems (which includes organizations) the growth curve appears to take a sigmoid or logistic shape.

It is useful for management to identify the stage reached by an organization in its life cycle. At each stage the organization exhibits certain characteristics; consequently, management can anticipate the likely capabilities and limitations of the organization at each stage. With respect to an EDP audit group the stage reached in the life cycle affects decisions on what EDP audit tasks the group can handle competently, what EDP audit techniques it will have sufficient expertise to use, and what controls should be exercised over the group. To illustrate this point, consider the following life cycle stages and their associated characteristics for an *internal* audit group:

Stage	Characteristics of stage
Initiation	Establishment of the EDP audit group; financial audits carried out only on major accounting application systems; controls are lacking; EDP audit objectives have not been clearly formulated; standards do not exist; no formal basis established for assigning priorities to tasks; substantial pressures applied to get work accomplished quickly; lines of authority and responsibility unclear; behavioral problems exist because of uncertainty surrounding interactions with other organization groups
Expansion	More widespread coverage of application systems by EDP audit; expansion sometimes rapid; attempted use of more complex EDP audit techniques; some formalization of objectives, standards, lines of authority and responsibility, etc.; controls still loose
Maturity	Involvement in complex application systems; EDP audit participation in the system development life cycle; concurrent auditing being carried out as well as ex post auditing; operational audits for system effectiveness and efficiency undertaken; objectives and standards have been formalized; well-established interactions with other organization groups; tight project control exists; advance planning undertaken

If the organization experiences some major change in its use of computing facilities, the EDP audit group may pass through these stages again. For example, the organization may attempt a changeover from batch-oriented systems to online systems or change from using centralized systems to distributed systems. The structure, objectives, standards, control procedures, etc., of the EDP audit group also may have to change. New EDP audit techniques may have to be developed and implemented. Existing EDP auditors may have to undertake substantial training in the new technology. The three stages in subsequent iterations of the life cycle may not be as pronounced as those in the first iteration; however, in general the EDP audit group still will exhibit the characteristics of each stage as it adapts to the changes made.

SOFTWARE SUPPORT FOR EDP AUDIT MANAGEMENT

The widespread availability of computers has increased the scope of data processing activities in most organizations. As a result, the scope of audit activities has expanded, and management of the EDP audit function has become increasingly difficult. Accordingly, EDP auditors have looked for ways of automating their own tasks to improve their effectiveness and efficiency. The primary means used have been microcomputers. Standard microcomputer software has been employed on many audit tasks, and specialized audit software has been developed where the standard software has been deficient. As a result of using this software, some audit groups report a 15–25% improvement in productivity (see Gallegos [1984]).

The following sections provide a brief overview of the ways in which microcomputer software has been used to assist the audit. The discussion covers five major functions that are a concern to EDP audit management: audit planning, controlling the audit, documenting the results of the audit, reporting the audit findings, and personnel management.

Planning the EDP Audit

In a large organization, there may be several hundred application systems that an EDP audit group may have to evaluate. Given limited resources, EDP audit management must make a decision on which systems they will evaluate and

TABLE 25-3
EXPOSURES SCORING ANALYSIS/RISK ANALYSIS

		Application systems			
		Accounts payable		Accounts receivable	
Factor	Factor weight (0–100)	Weight (0–10)	Composite weight	Weight (0–10)	Composite weight
No. of financial trans. processed	75	3	225	8	600
Dollar amount of trans. processed	90	5	450	7	630
Online/batch system	40	3	120	3	120
Prior difficulties with system	35	1	35	3	105
Effects of errors on goodwill	80	5	400	7	560
Centralized/distributed system	70	1	70	1	70
Purchased/in-house software	65	1	65	1	65
Total composite			1365		2150

what priority they will assign to the evaluation of each system. One technique used as a basis for this decision is exposures scoring analysis or risk analysis.

Table 25-3 shows a simple example of exposures scoring analysis for several application systems that EDP audit management might be considering examining and evaluating. Basically the technique requires audit management to list the factors that they consider when they determine the criticality of an application system and to assign a weighting to these factors to reflect their importance to the decision. For example, Table 25-3 shows that one of the factors considered by management is the number of financial transactions processed by the system. On a 100-point scale, this factor is given a rating of 75 to reflect its importance relative to the other factors that are considered. Next, each system must be weighted to reflect the importance of that factor to the system. For example, Table 25-3 shows the accounts payable application system has been assigned a score of 3 on a 10-point scale, perhaps indicating that the organization purchases supplies and inventory from only a small number of vendors. Finally, the factor weightings are multiplied by the system weightings to obtain a composite score, and these scores are then added to obtain an overall score for the system.

If many systems must be considered, these calculations can be tedious, particularly if management wants to test the sensitivity of a system's overall score to changes in the factor weightings or the system weightings. The calculations represent a straightforward spreadsheet application and, as a consequence, spreadsheet packages are often used to help with this planning decision. Management first assigns the various weightings to factors and systems; next the spreadsheet package computes an overall score and sorts the systems into rank order of importance on the basis of this overall score. It is then easy to change the weightings and carry out sensitivity analyses. Moreover, the spreadsheet can be stored for later use.

Controlling the Audit

Microcomputer software can be used to help control the audit in two ways. First, spreadsheet software facilitates preparation of a budget and monitoring of progress against the budget. In particular, since EDP audit staff are usually a scarce resource, it is especially helpful with the staff assignment problem— that is, allocating personnel to the various audit tasks to avoid excesses or deficiencies of staff on a job and to ensure that the audit tasks are completed on schedule. Second, either spreadsheet or word processing software can be used to prepare the audit programs used to guide staff in the conduct of an audit. Standard audit programs can be maintained on file, and these programs can be modified in light of the specific audit requirements for a job before distributing the programs to the audit team.

Documenting the Audit

Microcomputer software packages can be used to document the results of an audit in several ways. Standard internal control questionnaires can be established on, say, spreadsheet or word processing files and modified in light of the specific requirements of the audit. Responses to the internal control questions can be entered into the files as evidence is collected, and in some cases software may be available to perform preliminary analyses on the responses provided.

Software packages also are available to provide working paper support for the audit (see, for example, Knight and Yoder [1985]). These packages perform a variety of tasks; for example, they facilitate preparation of trial balances and the production of lead schedules. Moreover, since a substantial amount of information remains constant across audits, they alleviate the time-consuming task of copying items from one set of working papers to another set of working papers.

As discussed in Chapters 2 and 22, control matrices are now frequently used by auditors as a basis for organizing their evidence collection activities and as a means of facilitating the evidence evaluation task. However, large matrices can be awkward and unwieldy to manipulate. Control matrices are an ideal application for spreadsheet software. Standard control matrices can be stored in spreadsheet files and modified in light of the needs of a specific audit. Of course, producing hard-copy versions of control matrices is easy with a spreadsheet package.

Reporting Audit Findings

Word processing software, graphics software, and spreadsheet software are an important means of preparing, assembling, and modifying audit reports. Since various parts of an audit report may be prepared by different auditors, the software allows easy assembly of the entire report and easy editing by someone to ensure a uniform style. The software also allows a high-level, professional presentation of results in a form especially suited for management.

Personnel Management

As the size of the EDP audit staff grows, it becomes more difficult to effectively handle the various aspects of personnel management. For example, as discussed earlier in this chapter, EDP auditors must receive regular, ongoing training if they are to perform their duties competently. It can be an onerous task to collate manually the skill requirements of the EDP audit group, the training needs of individual auditors, and the timing and availability of various training courses. Consequently, some EDP audit managers use microcomputer database packages to store information about their staff as a basis for more effective personnel management.

Personnel data can also be used in the planning and control of an audit assignment. For example, a skills inventory might be reviewed as a basis for allocating staff to a job. Data on job performance might also be collected as a basis for determining whether a job will be completed on schedule and ultimately as a basis for making salary and promotion decisions.

SUMMARY

The emergence of an EDP audit function within organizations has given rise to some controversial organization and management issues. There has been debate over the need for computer audit specialists and a separate EDP audit group, whether the group should be centralized or decentralized, the number of EDP auditors required, whether or not their background should be audit or EDP, and how much and what types of training are needed.

The existence of the function also has caused several other problems. Often data processing personnel and other audit personnel react unfavorably toward the EDP audit function. They resent their work being examined by EDP auditors and the uncertainty surrounding the nature of their interactions with the EDP audit group. The newness of the function, its requirements for expertise, and the smallness of the function cause problems in providing career paths for EDP auditors that will maintain their morale and prevent staff turnover.

To some extent management can deal with these problems by recognizing the EDP audit function passes through a life cycle. By identifying the stage in the life cycle reached by the EDP audit group, management can undertake actions to alleviate some of the problems caused by the group being in a particular stage.

EDP audit managers now frequently use microcomputer software to assist them to manage the EDP audit function. The software is used in five ways: spreadsheet software enables exposures scoring (risk) analysis to be undertaken more easily as a basis for assigning audit priorities; spreadsheet and word processing software facilitate control by allowing budgets and audit programs to be prepared more easily as a basis for monitoring actual progress against planned progress; various software packages are available to assist with the documentation of audit findings; word processing, graphics, and spreadsheet software facilitate preparation of audit reports; and database software can be employed to facilitate personnel management of the EDP audit staff.

REVIEW QUESTIONS

25-1 Briefly explain why some auditors argue it is not necessary for them to have detailed technical knowledge of computer systems. Can external and internal auditors make this argument with equal ease?

25-2 Why do some auditors argue that increased technical competence will increase their independence? Is there a relationship between increased technical competence and an independence in *attitude?*

25-3 Briefly explain the difference in duties between an EDP auditor who performs a line function and an EDP auditor who performs a staff function. Give two arguments for and two arguments against having EDP audit as a staff function.

25-4 Can any stronger arguments be made for having EDP audit as a staff function or a line function depending on whether the group performs external auditing or internal auditing? Explain.

25-5 Briefly explain how the nature of the business performed by an organization will affect the number of EDP auditors it will need to perform the EDP audit function. What types of business activities are likely to require a greater number of EDP auditors?

25-6 What is a competency center? Give three reasons why an *external* audit organization might set up a competency center.

25-7 Give two factors that favor decentralization of EDP audit operations.

25-8 Briefly explain why system maintenance is likely to require less EDP audit effort than system development. Give an example where the reverse situation might apply.

25-9 Give two arguments against and two arguments for recruiting EDP auditors who were previously data processing professionals versus recruiting EDP auditors who were previously general staff auditors.

25-10 Is it likely that external auditors or internal auditors who perform the EDP audit function will need a greater amount of ongoing training in EDP? Outline some of the factors that influence your decision.

25-11 Stanford Research Institute [1977] found that for several EDP audit techniques there was a substantial difference in the knowledge required to develop and implement the technique and the knowledge required to use it. Briefly explain why you think SRI obtained this finding.

25-12 Give two implications for EDP auditor training of Stanford Research Institute's finding that often the level of training needed to develop and implement an EDP audit technique was different from the level of training needed to use the technique.

25-13 With reference to Perry [1977], what is the primary basis for distinguishing between an EDP auditor who has basic skills, one who has intermediate skills, and one who has advanced skills?

25-14 Outline two problems often faced by EDP auditors when the EDP audit function is first established in an organization. For each of these problems, suggest a way in which EDP audit management may seek to overcome the difficulties that arise.

25-15 Give two characteristics of the EDP audit function that often result in problems for EDP auditors in their interaction with data processing personnel and other audit personnel.

25-16 Briefly discuss two major problems experienced in providing a suitable career path for EDP auditors.

25-17 Give two problems that might face a systems analyst/programmer who becomes an EDP auditor for a period of about three years and then returns to the data processing department for career advancement purposes.

25-18 Outline a career path for an external auditor who performs the EDP audit function in a staff (as opposed to a line) capacity. List some of the strengths and weaknesses of your career path.

25-19 List four characteristics of the expansion stage in the life cycle of an EDP audit group.

25-20 A "life cycle" concept implies an iterative process. What types of factors would cause a mature EDP audit group to pass once again through the three stages of initiation, expansion, and maturity?

25-21 Why is a knowledge of the life cycle of an EDP audit group useful to management?

25-22 Briefly explain how exposures scoring (or risk) analysis can be used as an EDP audit planning tool. What types of microcomputer software can be used to assist EDP audit management when they undertake exposures scoring analysis?

25-23 Briefly explain how spreadsheet software can be used to control an EDP audit assignment.

25-24 Outline the types of software support available to assist with the documentation of EDP audit work.

25-25 How can a microcomputer database management package assist with the management of EDP audit personnel?

MULTIPLE CHOICE QUESTIONS

25-1 A major reason for setting up a separate group of EDP audit specialists is to:
  a Remove responsibility for performing audits of computer-based systems from the general staff auditor
  b Examine and evaluate the work of data processing personnel who perform the post-audit function
  c Provide the necessary technical expertise so audits of computer systems can be carried out competently
  d Restore the independence lost by general staff auditors when they become involved with computers

25-2 In Rittenberg's study of design phase participation by EDP auditors, the major way of increasing independence advocated by the respondents was to:
  a Set up an audit section specializing in computer auditing
  b Increase the technical EDP knowledge of auditors
  c Recruit auditors with more extensive EDP experience
  d Foster the auditors' independence in attitude

25-3 Which of the following is a major argument for having EDP auditing as a line function:
  a Facilitates communication between EDP audit specialists and general staff auditors
  b Promotes better utilization of EDP audit resources
  c Makes greater work satisfaction for the EDP auditor
  d Provides a career path for EDP audit managers

25-4 Which of the following is *not* a reason for centralizing the EDP audit function:
  a To facilitate establishing a competency center
  b To overcome communication and control problems that arise when EDP audits must be performed at physically dispersed data processing locations
  c To overcome the difficulties of implementing computer-assisted audit techniques at physically dispersed locations
  d To make more effective use of limited computer audit expertise

25-5 The number of EDP audit staff required by an organization is greater if:
  a Application systems are mature and the organization primarily carries out maintenance work rather than development work
  b The organization centralizes all its data processing functions that previously were dispersed
  c The organization automates some of its computer audit functions that previously were performed manually

   d The organization diversifies and commences activities in financial markets (borrowing and lending of monies)
25-6 In practice it seems as if organizations generally prefer to train data processing professionals as EDP auditors because:
   a It is easier to learn the accounting and auditing knowledge required to perform EDP audits
   b Empirical research shows that data processing professionals trained as EDP auditors perform EDP audits more effectively and efficiently than accounting professionals trained as EDP auditors
   c It has been found that EDP auditing requires little knowledge of accounting anyway
   d Practical experience as a systems analyst/programmer seems to provide the essential technical understanding needed to perform EDP audits well
25-7 On the basis of the Stanford Research Institute study of the types of training that EDP auditors need, Perry [1977] concludes:
   a There is often a difference between the skill level needed to develop and implement an EDP audit technique and the skill level needed to use the technique
   b Most EDP audit techniques require a high level of programming knowledge for their design, implementation, and use
   c The primary skills needed by EDP auditors to use EDP audit techniques effectively and efficiently are systems analysis skills
   d An EDP auditor with only basic skills can use very few EDP audit techniques
25-8 Which of the following is unlikely to be an effective method of improving the relationships between the EDP audit group and other organizational groups:
   a Promoting open communications
   b Keeping careful control over the resources consumed by the EDP audit group
   c Avoiding all conflict situations
   d Auditing within the technical capabilities of the EDP audit group
25-9 The institution of an EDP audit group in response to crisis situations in organizations has resulted in:
   a Ready acceptance of the EDP audit group by other groups within the organization
   b Communication problems between the EDP audit group and other groups because the likely impact of the EDP audit group on the organization is unclear
   c Management being more tolerant of failures by the EDP audit group
   d A disproportionate share of resources being devoted to the EDP audit group relative to other organizational groups
25-10 For career paths outside EDP auditing, Perry argues that best use is made of EDP auditors' skills if they become:
   a Financial managers
   b Data processing consultants
   c Data processing managers
   d Database administrators
25-11 The phase in an EDP audit group's life cycle in which an attempt is made to formalize objectives, standards, and controls is called the:
   a Expansion phase
   b Initiation phase

c Maturity phase

d Recapitulation phase

25-12 Which of the following microcomputer software packages is likely to be most useful when undertaking risk analysis during the planning phase of an EDP audit:

a Spreadsheet software

b Database management software

c Statistical software

d Expert system software

25-13 Which of the following microcomputer software packages is likely to be most useful for EDP auditor personnel management:

a Database management software

b Spreadsheet software

c Word processing software

d Graphics software

EXERCISES AND CASES

25-1 You are the director of internal audit for a large company. One day the president of the company calls you to inquire about the reasons for the high staff turnover in your EDP audit group. She has noted from personnel reports that on average new college graduates who enter EDP audit stay with the company for about a year only before they move to another company. She questions you about the loss of human capital that results. You respond by pointing out that the demand for EDP auditors greatly exceeds the supply so competition for EDP auditors is high.

Required: The president asks you to prepare a report for her outlining some strategies for decreasing staff turnover among the EDP audit group. You are to discuss briefly the strengths and weaknesses of each strategy and make a recommendation on which strategy the company should implement.

25-2 You are EDP manager in the internal audit department for a large retail store chain. Currently you have six EDP audit staff under you who perform a staff function in the internal audit department.

Top management of the chain has decided to change the mode of data processing used from a centralized operation to a decentralized operation. Currently each store in the chain is connected via terminals to a large computer at the head office. Over the next two years minicomputers will be installed in each store. Each store will be responsible for its own data processing and, in general, only summary information will be transmitted to the head office. A communications network will link the minicomputers in each store to the head office computer. Communications will be possible between any store though messages must be sent via the head office computer.

The data processing staff to support the new configuration will still remain centralized at the head office. Standard application system packages will be made available to each store. However, to assist in the implementation of these systems each store will have its own systems analyst/programmer.

Required: The internal audit manager has asked you to assess the impact of these changes on the organization and management of the EDP audit staff.

Prepare a brief report outlining any changes you think are necessary and provide justification for the changes you recommend.

25-3 You are the internal audit manager for a small- to medium-sized company that has well-developed batch computer systems for all major applications. In light of recent cases of computer fraud publicized in the newspapers, management has given you permission to advertise an EDP auditor position (the first in the company) for which you will be responsible.

You receive only two applications for the position. One application is from an existing member of the internal audit staff, a college graduate hired six years ago by the company. He worked first as an accountant for the company, but because of his promise he was transferred to internal audit. He has no experience with computers except one course he took at college and as a user of the output produced by the company's computer systems. However, he has a good knowledge of the company's accounting systems and you feel his abilities and brightness would allow him to acquire the necessary computer knowledge quickly.

The other applicant is from another company with which you are familiar. She is a systems analyst/programmer for the company. Though she has been involved in the design and implementation of accounting systems, she has no formal training in accounting. Her college degree is in mathematics. After you interview her and carry out some discreet background checking with a friend you have who works with her current employer, you believe she would make a very capable employee.

Required: Prepare a brief report for management notifying them whom you have selected for the position. Provide the necessary justification for your decision. Outline what staff development you intend to take with the person you select.

25-4 Corbetto Ltd. is a medium-sized firm that manufactures machines which make meat pies and sausage rolls. It sells its products to bakeries throughout southeast Asia, but its primary markets are in Australia and New Zealand. The company has sales of approximately $9 million Australian and a work force of approximately 100 personnel.

The general manager of the company has aggressively pursued a policy whereby all major application systems are to be computerized as soon as possible. He believes that computer systems have been the major factor behind Corbetto's success. The following systems have already been implemented:

General ledger
Accounts receivable
Accounts payable
Inventory control
Payroll
Order entry
Bill of materials
Material requirements planning
Job costing
Sales analysis

In each case the application has been developed using an off-the-shelf package that Corbetto has purchased from a software vendor. This strategy has allowed Corbetto to minimize the size of its data processing staff and to speed the implementation of its systems. Currently there are only three data processing personnel: a data processing manager, a systems analyst/programmer, and an operator. Nonetheless, all the computer systems have been implemented successfully during the preceding three-year period on a minicomputer that Corbetto purchased. The systems are all online, realtime update systems.

You have just been appointed as the first internal auditor of Corbetto. The job was created by the general manager in light of his belief that the company's operations had become sufficiently complex to justify appointing an independent person who would report to him on issues of asset safeguarding, data integrity, system effectiveness, and system efficiency. You obtained the job primarily as a result of your skills as an EDP auditor.

Required: It is your first day on the job. During a meeting with the general manager, he requests that you prepare a brief report outlining the major projects that you intend to undertake during your first year. In light of the information supplied above and your extensive EDP auditing knowledge, briefly describe the major items that you will include in your report.

25-5 You are the partner in charge of EDP auditing in a large office of a major public accounting firm. You have over 60 EDP auditors who report to you. The firm uses your staff to act as consultants to the various audit teams that undertake the regular audit work for clients. The data processing systems used by clients range from simple systems using microcomputer software packages to large, complex, online, realtime update systems.

Two factors have made it increasingly difficult to manage your staff. First, the size of your staff has grown rapidly. Second, high turnover exists because your staff are frequently attracted to lucrative job offers made elsewhere. Accordingly, you ask one of your staff, who is an expert in microcomputer database management software, to develop a system for your personal computer that will enable you to undertake better personnel management.

Required: The staff member who is developing the personnel management system has asked you to prepare a brief report outlining the major functions that you want in the system. List the types of data that you believe should be maintained in the system and the types of reports you believe it should provide.

ANSWERS TO MULTIPLE CHOICE QUESTIONS

25-1 c	25-4 b	25-7 a	25-10 d
25-2 b	25-5 d	25-8 c	25-11 c
25-3 a	25-6 d	25-9 b	25-12 a
			25-13 a

REFERENCES

Adamson, W. J. "Managing Conflict in the EDP/Auditor Relationship," *The EDP Auditor,* vol. 3, 1985, pp. 1–12.

Arens, Alvin A., and James K. Loebbecke. *Auditing: An Integrated Approach,* 2d ed. (Englewood Cliffs, NJ: Prentice-Hall, 1984).

Beitman, Lawrence. "Writing Effective Audit Reports," *The EDP Auditor*, vol. 2, 1984, pp. 41–43.

Canning, Richard G. "The Internal Auditor and the Computer," *EDP Analyzer* (March 1975), pp. 1–13.

Choo, Freddie. "A Distributed Audit Value Approach for Efficient Audit Resources Allocation in a Distributed Computer Systems Environment," *The EDP Auditor*, vol. 4, 1985, pp. 41–56.

Cutting, Richard W., Richard J. Guiltman, Fred L. Lilly, and John F. Mullarkey. "Technical Proficiency for Auditing Computer Processed Records," *Journal of Accountancy* (October 1971), pp. 74–77.

Deloitte Haskins & Sells. *Auditing with the Microcomputer: A Practical Guide*, 2d ed. (New York: Deloitte Haskins & Sells, 1986).

Federspiel, Christy A. "An Investment in EDP Auditing," *The EDP Auditor*, vol. 1, 1984, pp. 11–18.

Gallegos, Frederick. "Microcomputers in Auditing: An Overview," *EDP Auditing* (Pennsauken, NJ: Auerbach Publishers, 1985), Portfolio 74-02-10, pp. 1–6.

Godier, Dwayne P. "Automated Audit Risk Analysis," *The EDP Auditor*, vol. 2, 1984, pp. 21–28.

Good, Lynn G. "Establishing an EDP Audit Function," *The EDP Auditor* (Fall 1982), pp. 15–31.

Gustafson, L. M. "Improving Relations between Audit and EDP," *EDPACS* (September 1976), pp. 1–8.

Holmes, Fenwicke. "Auditing from the EDP Manager's Viewpoint," *The Internal Auditor* (November–December 1975), pp. 29–34.

Institute of Internal Auditors. *Establishing the Internal Audit Function in EDP: Job Descriptions* (Orlando, FL: The Institute of Internal Auditors, 1974).

Jancura, Elise. "The Auditor's Responsibilities in Examining Computer Processed Records," *International Journal of Government Auditing* (July 1975*a*), pp. 13–17.

Jancura, Elise. "Technical Proficiency Standards for Auditing Computer Processed Records," *Journal of Accountancy* (August 1975*b*), pp. 39–44.

Kneer, Dan C., John D. Wade, and Bruce A. Baldwin. "Necessary Training for EDP Auditors: Feedback from Practitioners and Academicians," *The EDP Auditor*, vol. 4, 1985, pp. 17–29.

Knight, Sherry D., and Steven E. Yoder. "Seven Audit Software Programs: How They Perform," *Computers in Accounting* (May-June 1985), pp. 20–26, 28, 30–35.

Lawrence, Paul R., and Jay W. Lorsch. *Developing Organizations: Diagnosis and Action* (Reading, MA: Addison-Wesley, 1969).

Mair, William C., Donald R. Wood, and Keagle W. Davis. *Computer Control & Audit*, 2d ed. (Altamonte Springs, FL: The Institute of Internal Auditors, 1976).

Miller, James Grier. *Living Systems* (New York: McGraw-Hill, 1978).

Mullen, Jack B. "Developing an EDP Audit Staff," *EDP Auditing* (Pennsauken, NJ: Auerbach Publishers 1979), Portfolio 71-03-08, pp. 1–7.

Myers, Edith. "EDP Auditors: Explosive Growth," *Datamation* (August 1977), pp. 120–121, 124.

Nolan, Richard L. "Managing the Computer Resource: A Stage Hypothesis," *Communications of the ACM* (July 1973), pp. 399–405.

Perry, William E. "Career Advancement for the EDP Auditor," *EDPACS* (August 1974*a*), pp. 1–6.

Perry, William E. "The Making of a Computer Auditor," *The Internal Auditor* (November-December 1974*b*), pp. 11–22.

Perry, William E. "Management Support for EDP Auditing," *EDPACS* (August 1976), pp. 5–9.

Perry, William E. "Skills Needed to Utilize EDP Audit Practices," *EDPACS* (November 1977), pp. 1–13.

Perry, William E. "The EDP Auditor Relationship with DP Management," *EDP Auditing* (Pennsauken, NJ: Auerbach Publishers, 1978), Portfolio 71-02-03, pp. 1–15.

Perry, William E. "EDP Auditor Job Descriptions," *EDP Auditing* (Pennsauken, NJ: Auerbach Publishers, 1979*a*), Portfolio 71-03-06, pp. 1–15.

Perry, William E. "How to Interview an EDP Auditor Candidate," *EDP Auditing* (Pennsauken, NJ: Auerbach Publishers, 1979*b*), Portfolio 71-03-07, pp. 1–12.

Rittenberg, Larry E. "The Impact of Internal Auditing during the EDP Application Design Process on Perceptions of Internal Audit Independence." Unpublished Ph.D. dissertation, University of Minnesota, Minneapolis, MN, 1975.

Rittenberg, Larry E. *Auditor Independence and Systems Design* (Altamonte Springs, FL: The Institute of Internal Auditors, 1977).

Ross, Stephen J. "Evaluating the Performance of Data Security Professionals," *The EDP Auditor* (Winter, 1982/83), pp. 43–45.

Sawyer, Lawrence B. *The Practice of Modern Internal Auditing* (Altamonte Springs, FL: The Institute of Internal Auditors, 1973).

Stanford Research Institute. *Systems Auditability and Control Study: Data Processing Audit and Practices Report* (Altamonte Springs, FL: The Institute of Internal Auditors, 1977).

Verschoor, Curtis C. "Perceptions of the Importance of Computer-Related Competencies of General Staff Auditors," *The EDP Auditor*, vol. 2, 1984, pp. 45–52.

Weiss, Harold. "EDP Audit Job Descriptions," *EDPACS* (March 1974), pp. 7–11.

Weiss, Harold. "Computer Audit Survey," *EDPACS* (September 1977), pp. 8–15.

CHAPTER 26

THE CHANGING EDP AUDIT FUNCTION

Chapter Outline

This final chapter reviews a number of forces acting on the EDP audit function that may cause it to change in some way. These forces have a variety of origins.

Some arise because the society has been focusing critically on the professions and there have been major pressures for change and improvement. Others arise because there has been widespread concern about how computer technology should be used; consequently, there has been more questioning about the global benefits and costs of using computers. Still others arise because technological advancements have not stood still; if anything, at least in some areas of computer technology, the rate of change has increased.

The chapter proceeds as follows. The first section examines moves made by EDP auditors toward increased professionalism. The motivation for and likely outcome of these moves are discussed. The second and third sections review possible changes that may arise because of the enactment of laws and the increased focus of a more informed public on computer use. The fourth section examines some of the major implications of advanced systems for the EDP audit function. Finally, the chapter discusses some changes that must arise if research and pedagogy within the EDP audit area are to be improved.

TOWARD PROFESSIONALISM

In 1969 the EDP Auditors Association was formed in Los Angeles. The Association started out with approximately 100 members. In 1986 it had approximately 9000 members in 48 different countries and 102 chapters in 22 different countries. Although other professional bodies had taken steps to recognize the importance of the EDP audit function (see, for example, Sanchez-Saavedra [1982/83]), the EDP Auditors Association was the first organization formed to cater solely for individuals in the EDP audit area.

Motivations toward Professionalism

During the 1970s the various professions—medicine, law, accounting, etc.—were subjected to intense scrutiny. There was general dissatisfaction with the professions. Both governments and the public questioned whether professionals were overpaid, whether they were performing their duties with sufficient care, whether their ethical and performance standards might not be improved, whether professional organizations had acted in restraint of trade, etc. In essence the professions were asked to be more accountable. Were the benefits of their outputs exceeding their costs? Could these benefits be attained in a cheaper way?

In December 1976 the U.S. Senate Subcommittee on Reports, Accounting and Management issued a report titled: "The Accounting Establishment: A Staff Study." The report was highly critical of the accounting profession. It recommended, inter alia, direct involvement by the federal government in establishing financial accounting standards and auditing standards, promulgating standards of conduct for auditors, and reviewing periodically the work performed by auditors. In other countries the accounting profession was experiencing similar criticisms. For example, in Australia the New South

Wales Attorney General announced his support for an Accounting Practitioner's Act to regulate and discipline the accounting profession, and an Accounting Standards Board that would endorse or reject accounting standards proposed by the accounting profession, company directors, stockbrokers, bankers, and other interested groups.

In November 1977 the U.S. Senate Subcommittee on Reports, Accounting and Management issued a second report titled: "Improving the Accountability of Publicly Owned Corporations and Their Auditors." In this report the Subcommittee tempered the recommendations made in its initial report. It encouraged private reform of the profession rather than mandatory reform as the preferred mode of action. However, the Subcommittee issued a warning that mandatory reform would be forthcoming if private reform was not timely.

Since many auditors were members of the various EDP audit groups that had been formed, they recognized that the criticisms levied at the accounting profession in general soon might focus on EDP auditors (see, for example, Barnes and Bariff [1978]). Thus, there were substantial motivations to seek formal recognition of professional status for EDP auditors.

Throughout the 1980s, the pressure to improve the professional performance of accountants and auditors has continued. In the United States, for example, the Securities and Exchange Commission and the House Oversight and Investigations Subcommittee chaired by Congressman John D. Dingell have subjected the accounting and auditing professions to ongoing scrutiny. Legislators have threatened intervention if they are not satisfied with the profession's own attempts at self-regulation (see, for example, American Institute of Certified Public Accountants [1986]). Consequently, all the professional accounting and auditing bodies have been striving to enhance their professional status and to improve their performance.

EDP Audit Professionalism

The U.S. Taft-Hartley Act identifies five conditions for defining a profession: (*a*) a common body of knowledge, (*b*) standards of competency, (*c*) examination of competency, (*d*) a code of ethics, and (*e*) a disciplinary mechanism (see, further, Canning [1976]). Since its inception, the EDP Auditors Association has been attempting to comply with these requirements. In 1976 the Association formed the EDP Auditors Foundation to take responsibility for education and research within the Association as a basis for professional certification. In 1978 the Certified Information Systems Auditor (CISA) program was established.

Through the CISA program, the EDP Auditors Association attempts to meet the requirements for professionalism in the following ways:

1 *Common body of knowledge:* In 1979 the Foundation undertook a survey of data processing managers, EDP auditors, and educators to identify the types and levels of knowledge that EDP auditors should possess if they were to be considered competent (see, further, Li [1983]).

2 *Standards of competency:* In conjunction with the Educational Testing Service of Princeton, New Jersey, the Foundation developed the CISA

examination as the basis for obtaining certification as an EDP auditor. In addition, recertification is required every three years either via demonstrating that 120 hours of continuing education have been obtained in the three-year period or by retaking the CISA examination (see, further, Weiss [1982]).

3 *Examination of competency:* As discussed above, the CISA examination forms the basis for determining the competency of an EDP auditor.

4 *Code of ethics:* The Foundation has established a code of professional conduct for Certified Information Systems Auditors. In addition, the Association has established a code of ethics for its members.

5 *Disciplinary mechanism:* Violation of the code of professional conduct or the code of ethics may result in revocation of the certificate or revocation of membership in the Association.

Hopefully, certification of information systems auditors will provide a number of benefits. First, the formalization of EDP audit knowledge should result in higher-quality EDP audits being performed. Second, the certification program reduces the information search costs incurred by an employer when seeking out a suitably qualified and competent EDP auditor. The CISA certificate defines the minimum level of skills an employer should be able to expect. If the certificate skill level is too high for the employer's needs, a noncertified EDP auditor can be hired, presumably at a lower salary. Third, if the disciplinary mechanisms of the Foundation and the Association are effective, certification provides a means of penalizing those EDP auditors who violate ethics or perform substandard work.

Nonetheless, these benefits are attained at a cost. Professional organizations must be supported by membership fees. Moreover, to be certified, members normally incur substantial personal costs in both time and money. Thus, the employer must expect to pay for the benefits obtained by the existence of a certification program. Because the certification program is still relatively new, the extent to which both individuals and organizations will be willing to bear the costs is still unclear.

If a certification program is supported by government licensing of the professional, the society also tends to bear costs that ultimately it may deem unacceptable. Licensing enables a profession to restrict entry. It is difficult, if not impossible, for other competing professional organizations to be set up or for the noncertified individual to practice. Thus, consumer choice is restricted. The profession has all the powers of a cartel. It can extract monopoly profits, and the level of output of the services provided usually is less than the level that would be attained in a freely operating marketplace (see, further, Friedman [1962]).

LEGAL INFLUENCES

In the 1970s, two major sets of laws were enacted that have had and continue to have a substantial impact on the EDP audit function. The first set applies to protection of personal privacy. There has been widespread activity internationally with respect to privacy legislation; thus, EDP auditors in many countries have been or potentially will be affected. The second set applies to the ways in which organizations use their funds to conduct business. In particular, the laws seek to prohibit payment of funds to foreign officials and political parties for the purpose of obtaining business. Most legal activity with respect to "foreign corrupt practices" has taken place in the United States. However, the effects of this legislation are examined here because the United States EDP audit function is so large; furthermore, there are many U.S.-based multinational companies affected by the laws relating to foreign corrupt practices.

Privacy Legislation

Data privacy refers to the right to have data protected from inadvertent or unauthorized disclosure. Inadvertent disclosure occurs, for example, when a system crash results and the contents of a user's files are displayed publically at a terminal. Unauthorized disclosure occurs when a person having access rights uses the data for an unintended purpose. Thus, authorization has two dimensions: (*a*) the authority to access data, and (*b*) the authority to use data only for specified purposes.

Scope of Privacy Legislation   Many countries already have enacted privacy laws; for example, Sweden, the United States, West Germany, Denmark, Norway, Canada, France, the United Kingdom, and Austria. Various states have enacted their own privacy laws; for example, Minnesota in the United States and the West German Land of Hesse. There have been a number of specific laws to protect certain kinds of data; for example, New Zealand's Wanganui Computer Centre Act that regulates how police may process and use personal data. Still other countries have given power to various organizations to mediate on privacy issues. For example, in Australia the New South Wales Privacy Committee with limited powers has been successful in resolving a wide range of privacy disputes (see, further, Kirby [1979]). At the international level, the Council of Europe and the Organization for Economic Cooperation and Development have been active in the privacy area.

The forms of legislation passed vary considerably. Some acts apply only to the public sector, some apply only to the private sector, and some cover both sectors. There are differences relating to whether the laws cover only personal data or both personal and organizational data. The means of enforcing the laws are different. Some countries have established powerful supervisory agencies, some rely on the courts, and some have created an ombudsman position. There are still other differences; for example, whether the laws apply to both manual and computer systems, whether they cover transborder data flows, and whether they cover third-party use of data.

However, some emerging principles are common, at least to some extent, in the laws. Stadlen [1979] identifies seven such principles:

1 Individuals should be able to discover the existence and ownership of automated personal data systems. Usually, organizations that establish such systems must register them publicly.

2 Individuals should be able to discover whether information about them exists in a personal data system. Usually, the owner of the system must respond to a request by an individual about whether data on them exists in the system.

3 Individuals should be able to examine data held about them.

4 Individuals should be able to correct or delete data held about them that is inaccurate, outdated, or irrelevant.

5 Data should be collected lawfully and fairly.

6 Data collection on some individual attributes should be prohibited; for example, racial origin, political philosophy, religious views, and sex life details.

7 Special measures over and above the normal computer security measures should be taken to preserve the privacy of personal data.

The extent to which these principles become pervasive or further principles emerge is yet unknown. However, the trends in privacy legislation are relatively clear, and with increasing international flows of data there are pressures toward standardization.

Implications for the EDP Auditor   The scope and extent of the impact of privacy legislation on the EDP auditor depends on the particular form of the legislation existing in the country in which the EDP auditor resides or the form of the legislation applying to the organization audited. However, there are five broad ways in which privacy legislation may impact the auditor:

1 *Need to be familiar with statutes:* Auditing standards generally require auditors to be familiar with statutes affecting the organizations they audit. In the case of privacy statutes, the laws applicable may have both domestic and foreign origins. For example, under the Swedish Data Act the Data Inspection Board must give approval for the release of data about Swedish citizens to foreign countries. The Board occasionally has refused to release permission because it considers the foreign organization to have inadequate security to protect data privacy.

2 *Need to audit for legislative compliance:* Because of the risk of penalties arising under a privacy act, EDP auditors may be responsible for ensuring the organization complies with the statutes. Internal auditors also may be responsible for preparing a privacy impact statement and constructing a comprehensive privacy plan (see, further, Goldstein and Nolan [1975]). In some cases external auditors may have to determine whether there is a possibility of contingent liabilities arising because of noncompliance with an act.

3 *Auditor as a user of personal data:* How privacy legislation will eventually affect the auditor as a user of data is still unclear. In some ways it appears that, because of the statutes, an organization may have to identify its

auditor and the ways in which the auditor will use personal data in advance. Approval for any deviation from these stated purposes may have to be sought. The timing of audits may be affected if substantial lead time is required for notification and approval of deviations from stated purposes. Audit reports also may be delayed if some dispute arises over how the data will be used. If organizations must keep a log of uses made of personal data and individuals have access to data about them on this log, the auditor's ability to carry out confidential investigations is impaired. Further, audit techniques may become widely known and ways of circumventing these techniques devised more readily.

4 *Auditor as a maintainer of personal data:* In the course of an audit the EDP auditor may extract personal data from files for inclusion in working papers. Thus, auditors must ensure that adequate security exists over their own files, just as this security must exist over the files of the organizations they audit. In fact, the organization audited may be unable to transfer personal data to the auditor unless the auditor's files are secure.

5 *Need to evaluate the "fairness" of information practices:* Although privacy legislation may not apply to a specific information practice in which an organization engages, the society now expects that organizations will evaluate their actions for compliance in spirit with privacy principles. For example, in spite of privacy laws that apply to government organizations, the U.S. Government has engaged in the practice of computer matching in which one set of records is compared with another set of records to detect fraud by individuals who receive government benefits. For example, social security beneficiaries have been matched against Medicare records of deceased persons to identify individuals who were receiving payments made to deceased persons. These types of activities have evoked widespread debate over their implications for personal privacy (see, for example, Kusserow [1984] and Shattuck [1984]). From the viewpoint of the EDP auditor, however, the debate signals the need to continually evaluate how information technology is used in an organization in case there are unfavorable implications for personal privacy.

Foreign Corrupt Practices Act

In December 1977 the Foreign Corrupt Practices Act became law in the United States. The act was the outcome of post-Watergate investigations that revealed corporations making illegal domestic and foreign contributions to governments, politicians, and civil servants for purposes of obtaining business.

The act has international importance in that it applies to U.S. multinational firms; thus, EDP auditors involved with these firms in foreign countries are affected. For example, the firm's primary external auditor in the United States has responsibility for ensuring that audits carried out by foreign external auditors comply with the act. Similarly, the firm's management will require foreign internal auditors to ensure the firm complies with the act.

Scope of the Act   The act has two major sections: the Antibribery Provisions and the Accounting Standards Provisions (see, further, McKee [1979]). The Antibribery Provisions make it a criminal offence for a firm under the act to pay a bribe to obtain business. Penalties are prescribed; companies may be fined up to $1,000,000 and individuals fined up to $10,000 and imprisoned up to five years. The Accounting Standards Provisions, in general, require a firm under the act to devise and maintain a sound system of internal control. In a prior study of firms who had made bribes, the SEC found in each case a weak internal control system facilitated the illegal payments.

Implications for the EDP Auditor   In essence, the act does not change the existing responsibilities of both internal and external auditors. Ensuring the firm has a sound internal control system has always been a concern of the auditor. What does change, however, is the risk auditors confront when performing their duties. The penalties for nonperformance of duties are now even higher.

Roberts [1978] argues that in the event of a firm failing to comply with the act, EDP auditors may find themselves subject to a private suit brought by the firm's management. Ultimately, management is responsible for the firm's internal control system. Management might argue, however, that it was technically unable to perform an evaluation of a computer-based internal control system. Thus, it discharged its responsibility by hiring individuals competent to perform such an evaluation; namely, EDP auditors. Though the collection of significant damages from EDP auditors is unlikely, the penalties levied on management for violating the act may be lessened.

As a consequence, greater resources may be devoted to establishing a viable internal EDP audit function. McKee [1979] argues the act will accelerate the trend toward professionalism and certification and strengthen the position of EDP auditors within organizations.

From the auditor's viewpoint, it now becomes more important for a firm under the act to have a sound corporate code of conduct and a sound internal control system. EDP audit resources may have to be shifted away from other areas (e.g., operational audits) to ensure compliance with the act. More extensive auditing also may have to be carried out. Under the act the level of materiality of an error changes. The act prohibits paying "anything of value" as a bribe. What was considered previously as immaterial from an audit viewpoint may now constitute something of value in terms of the act.

SOCIAL INFLUENCES

The ability of organizations to survive depends in part on how well they monitor changing values within the society. Failure to monitor these changing values results in one of two outcomes. First, individuals in the society signal to the legislature via their votes that laws should be enacted to force the organization to comply with their wishes. Second, the organization produces goods or services that the society does not want—at least at the selling price offered. Organizations better attuned to the market's wishes can increase their profitability, usually at the expense of less responsive organizations.

Today the society is forming stronger values about how computers should be used. The ACM Committee on Computers and Public Policy [1974] identified 16 major problem areas that arise because of the interaction between computers and people. All these issues are important to an organization wanting to survive in the marketplace. Ultimately, they infringe upon the characteristics of the products and the prices of these products that the organization offers to consumers.

To identify potential areas of impact of the society's changing values with respect to computers, management of an organization must make some group within the organization responsible for monitoring these changes. As individuals primarily concerned with control of computer implementation and use, more and more the EDP auditor may perform this function. Thus, increasing their awareness of the social influences affecting how computers are used may be an increasingly important part of the EDP auditor's changing job function.

The following two sections examine two major forces within the society that currently appear to have the potential to impact significantly the way organizations will use computers. The first force arises because of a growing concern about the effects of computers on jobs. The second force arises because of a growing concern about the quality of the computer systems that are designed and implemented.

Computers and the Worker

In 1979 the Australian Government made available $.75 million to carry out research on the impact of technological change. The nation had experienced a series of crippling strikes, primarily in the telecommunications industry, over disputes about how new technology (primarily computer technology) should be introduced into organizations. On the one hand unions claimed the technology was resulting in widespread displacement of workers and substantial unemployment. On the other hand employers argued that to remain competitive internationally it was necessary for the technology to be introduced as quickly as possible. In lost output the strikes cost millions of dollars. The strikes also were very controversial and bitter ones. Friendships were lost, work relationships were strained, and some employees at all levels within the organizations involved were ostracized. The social patterns within the organizations had been changed irrevocably.

In the aftermath of the strikes, one of the major questions asked was whether or not the strikes could have been avoided by introducing the technology differently within the organization. The problems caused by technological change are not new. They were experienced by organizations in the nineteenth century when the technological innovations of the Industrial Revolution were introduced. What is clear is that economic survival in the long run depends on technological innovation being accommodated in some way; otherwise, an organization not introducing the technology is driven from the marketplace by an unfavorable cost structure relative to organizations that have introduced the technology. In the Australian situation, however, little evidence showed that organizations attempting to introduce the technology also had planned carefully the implementation of change from a social viewpoint using, for example, some of the strategies discussed in Chapter 4. Further, little evidence showed the unions involved had attempted over the long run to prepare their members for those technological changes that were inevitable.

Although there are many examples like the above where the effect of computer technology on workers has been direct and apparent, in general our understanding of the ways in which computers will impact workers has been poor (see Attewell and Rule [1984]). In the late 1950s, for example, researchers were predicting that computers would have a widespread effect on middle management. Computers supposedly would streamline communications from lower levels of the organization to higher levels of the organization, thereby reducing the need for middle managers to perform information classification, summarization, and filtering functions (see Leavitt and Whisler [1958]).

In the early 1980s, researchers were predicting that computers would change the location and time at which work was performed (see Olson [1982]). Developments in microcomputers, end-user software, and data communications technology would release workers from the constraints of having to be physically present at a particular workplace and having to perform work during specified time intervals. Instead, workers might choose to work at home or at locations near their homes as a means of reducing commuting costs and satisfying other responsibilities such as childcare.

More recently, some researchers have expressed concerns that unequal access to computer technology will result in two classes of workers: one which is "information rich" and another which is "information poor." Since in many economies employment in the information sector has continued to expand relative to other sectors like manufacturing, those workers who are information poor will be disadvantaged when they seek employment.

The reliability of these predictions can only be determined with the passage of time; however, preliminary evidence suggests their accuracy is questionable, at least in the short run. What they underscore, however, is the need for organizations to carefully plan technological changes and to regularly monitor the consequences of technological change. Otherwise, the organizational and social costs may be substantial and the effectiveness and efficiency of information systems may be undermined.

Who will be responsible for planning and monitoring technological changes in organizations? Clearly the diversity of ways in which technological change might be manifested will mean that several individuals with different skills will need to have a planning and monitoring role. As someone concerned with asset safeguarding, data integrity, system effectiveness, and system efficiency, however, EDP auditors are likely to have a major part to play.

Computers and the Consumer

EDP auditors always have been concerned with users' perceptions of the quality of a computer system. Users often provide important insights into the strengths and weaknesses of a system. To date, however, who EDP auditors have considered to be the users of a computer system has been a narrow group. Chapter 4 pointed out the tendency among many system designers (and EDP auditors) to focus on the primary users of a system and not the secondary users who often have the most direct contact with the system. The conception of who constitutes the user group is narrow in still another way. It tends to include only users who are internal to the firm. The external users, the consumers of the organization's product, often are forgotten or ignored. Evidence collection on the quality of a computer system remains internal to the organization. Rarely are the external users consulted. If the internal users are happy with the system and the auditor's tests suggest there are few problems with the system, it is assumed the external users are receiving high-quality output.

There is now some research that shows external users of a computer system are an important source of evidence on the quality of the system. For example, Sterling [1979] surveyed a random sample of members of the Consumer's Association of British Columbia to determine the extent to which they experienced errors in their dealings with computer systems. Of the individuals responding to the survey questionnaire, 40.5% reported they had encountered one or more errors within the preceding 12 months. Eighty-one percent of the errors reported were billing errors involving charges that were not justified, overcharges, etc. Further, 7.2% of the consumers reporting errors gave up trying to correct the errors after initial unsuccessful attempts. Similar results have been obtained in other studies of consumer experiences with computer systems (see, further, Sterling [1979]).

Sterling's study provides some initial evidence of a potential consumer backlash against further moves toward a cashless and checkless society (see, also, Kling [1978]). Respondents in the study reported they often experienced considerable difficulties trying to correct the errors they encountered. The average time spent by a consumer dealing with the organization involved was 2.6 hours, and the average length of time between discovery of the error and its correction was 8 weeks. Further, the consumers reported their experiences trying to correct the error often were unpleasant; some were coerced to pay a disputed amount and some were treated as troublemakers.

One consequence of these experiences was a move by the consumers back to using cash rather than credit to transact business. Such a move is in direct conflict with business organizations that want to move even more to electronic transfer of funds.

It is difficult to understand why such a large percentage of consumers encounter difficulties with well-established systems like billing systems. The design principles for these types of systems are known widely and many standard packages are available. Consumer difficulties also provide direct feedback on errors in the system. Nevertheless, long-run problems still seem to persist. Either organizations are inflexible and not responsive to these problems, the systems are badly designed or badly managed, consumers are at least partially responsible for some of the errors themselves, or the error rate for the systems must be considered normal. Whatever the reasons, it appears there is still considerable scope for improvement of basic computer systems. Further, organizations wishing to introduce new technology that increases the consumer's dependence on correct processing by computer systems may experience problems unless they are able to demonstrate convincingly to the consumer that the benefits of the technology exceed the costs.

The problems described above highlight the need for EDP auditors to ensure they include consumers within the user group they consult on matters affecting data integrity and system effectiveness. Sterling's study shows consumers can provide important information on errors existing within a system, or failure by the system to meet its objectives, at least from a consumer viewpoint. This information might be solicited not only after systems have been implemented and made operational but also during the design phase.

IMPACT OF THE CHANGING TECHNOLOGY

The previous section examined the indirect effects produced on the EDP auditor as a consequence of the impact of the changing technology on the worker and the consumer. This section briefly examines some of the possible *direct* effects of the changing technology. What will be the impact on the EDP auditor of more widespread use of database management systems, data communications, minicomputers and microcomputers, electronic funds transfer systems, online realtime systems, word processing systems, distributed systems, etc.? Clearly, there is a need for futures research in EDP auditing. The development of EDP audit tools and methodologies (e.g., audit software and its use) often has been a slow and painful process. A greater understanding of the implications of future technology for EDP auditing would result in better-directed EDP audit developmental work.

Impact at a General Level

At a basic level it is difficult to see how the changing technology can have any major impact on the role of EDP auditors or fundamental EDP audit methodologies. The auditor will still need to perform the attest function. Furthermore, the auditor will still need to evaluate management controls, application system controls, and the quality of data in an organization's database. These aspects of auditing are invariant across technologies.

Where the impact of the changing technology will be felt is at the margin. At least five possible areas of impact can be identified. First, clearly the auditor will need to understand the new technology. Without this understanding the auditor is unable to make an informed judgment nor adequately perform evidence collection tasks. Second, there may be a greater number of more well-defined levels of EDP audit work. At one extreme an organization may use a complex system implemented in assembly level programming. For this system the auditor will require detailed technical knowledge to audit the system. At the other extreme an organization may use a package where most of the logic has been implemented as read-only microcode. Further, the system may be certified as to the adequacy of its controls and it may contain inbuilt routines for collecting audit evidence. Thus, the auditor may work at a higher level of system detail than current audits. Third, more systems should contain features that facilitate audit work. There is now a heightened awareness of the importance of data integrity. Many vendors emphasize the auditability of their systems during marketing efforts. Fourth, in the short run, system design audits may become increasingly important. Because of the difficulty of changing complex systems, the auditor will need to ensure controls are incorporated during the design phase. However, in the long run, systems may have greater ability to evolve; thus, it may be relatively easy to modify systems to incorporate better controls in light of experience with the system. Fifth, in some areas there will be a scarcity of audit tools. Currently, few generalized audit software packages run on minicomputers and microcomputers. As the makes and models of minicomputers and microcomputers proliferate, the problems caused by the lack of availability of audit tools may become more acute.

Some Specific Areas of Impact

Though the changing technology may have little impact on EDP auditing at a general level, there are many specific ways in which the EDP auditor's work is likely to alter. The following sections provide a brief overview of some technological developments that are continuing to have an effect on the EDP audit function.

Impact of Microcomputers   Microcomputers have already had a widespread impact on organizations and society and on the practice of EDP auditing. The nature of this impact is still not well understood, however, because the changes that have occurred have been so rapid. Furthermore, the likely future effects are still somewhat unpredictable.

Within organizations, microcomputers have allowed more people to have access to computing power. From an EDP viewpoint, this increased access has had both positive and negative implications. On the positive side, many users now better appreciate the strengths and limitations of computer systems and the controls needed to ensure these systems are reliable. On the negative side, deployment of microcomputers within organizations has not been well controlled in several respects. First, many users have now begun to develop their own application systems. Unfortunately, they have often been ignorant of the methodologies needed to produce high-quality systems. This issue is discussed further below. Second, many organizations have exercised inadequate controls over the purchase and use of microcomputers. As a result, the following sorts of problems have arisen: excessive numbers of microcomputers have been purchased; hardware and software have sometimes been purchased for private purposes; many of the applications developed have been ineffective and inefficient; and problems of hardware and software incompatibility have occurred. Third, often users of microcomputers have paid scant attention to "mundane" operational issues such as backup, security, software updates, documentation, etc., until a crisis has arisen. Fourth, lax controls have allowed violation of software copyright. Fifth, training and support needs have been hopelessly underestimated.

Within the society, increased use of microcomputers has also had both positive and negative implications for organizations. Since more people possess greater knowledge about computers, individuals now seem more empathetic toward some of the difficulties faced by an organization when it uses computers. Greater knowledge, however, has led to phenomena such as "hacking" (see Lee et al. [1986]). When knowledgeable outsiders actively try to circumvent controls in an organization's computer systems, additional precautions must be taken to safeguard assets and maintain data integrity.

Growth of End-User Computing Previous chapters in this book have already pointed out that developments in microcomputer technology and high-level software are now allowing users to develop their own application systems. It is clear that this trend will continue. It is also clear that end-user computing must be controlled like any other activity within an organization. Already, lack of control has led to poorly developed systems that have resulted in organizations incurring substantial losses. For example, important decisions have been made using erroneous financial models constructed via spreadsheet programs. The programs contained serious errors because they had not been tested thoroughly.

What is not clear, however, is *how* end-user computing can be controlled effectively. The traditional conflicts between centralized versus decentralized control once again emerge. On the one hand, organizations would like to encourage their staff to use computers creatively. This creativity is unlikely to occur in an environment of tight centralized control. On the other hand, control needs to be exercised over the purchase of hardware and software, the decision on what systems should be developed, the ways in which systems are developed and documented, the ways in which systems are integrated, and the ways in which systems are supported. These types of decisions require a deep knowledge of both good information systems practices and the needs of the organization. To guide the decisions, policies must be developed, promulgated, and enforced throughout the organization. Again, since many of the policy issues that must be addressed relate to asset safeguarding, data integrity, system effectiveness, and system efficiency, the EDP auditor is likely to have an active and ongoing role to play in their development and enforcement.

Impact of Knowledge-Based Systems Substantial research is now being undertaken on the development of intelligent, knowledge-based systems. The forerunners of these systems are today's expert systems. However, the goals for the new generation of expert systems are much more ambitious. For example, with the help of the Japanese government, a consortium of Japanese firms has embarked upon a "fifth-generation" project to develop systems that will (a) act intelligently to support human judgment and decision making, (b) facilitate human-machine interaction via natural language, voice, graphics, images, and documents, (c) support expertise via specialized knowledge bases, and (d) learn, associate, and infer to increase their knowledge-based capabilities. Similar projects have been commenced within the United States, although not of the same magnitude as the Japanese initiative. The technological problems that have to be overcome are enormous, but there are certain to be spinoffs that enable the capabilities of existing expert systems to be enhanced (see, further, Shapiro [1983]).

The use of knowledge-based systems in organizations poses several new control problems for the auditor. If the organization makes critical decisions on the basis of these systems, the auditor will be interested in the integrity of the facts and knowledge embodied in them and the ways in which they make inferences. The *facts* can be verified using traditional audit means. Determining the quality of the *knowledge* embodied in the system, however, is another matter. Since this knowledge represents the heuristics and knowhow possessed by experts, it is unclear how its quality can be assessed. Presumably substantial reliance will have to be placed on the methodologies used to develop these systems. In this light, management should carefully choose the individuals who are given authority to develop knowledge-based systems within the organization.

Important ethical issues also arise as a result of using knowledge-based systems in organizations. For example, Turn [1985] has expressed concerns about the potential of artificial intelligence techniques for eroding personal privacy. Knowledge-based systems might be used to undertake sophisticated surveillance activities and to infer facts about people based on seemingly unrelated data. If an organization has access to large amounts of personal data, auditors eventually may be responsible for ensuring that knowledge-based systems are not used improperly to violate an individual's privacy.

Knowledge-based systems also may enhance the auditor's abilities to gather and to evaluate evidence. Expert auditors recognize covert and intricate patterns in data that manifest control problems. If this knowledge can be incorporated into a computer program, novice auditors have a powerful tool to assist them in their work, and expert auditors have a basis for improved decision-making accuracy, consensus, and consistency.

Growth in Data Communications   The data communications industry continues to experience rapid growth. Major advances are still producing increases in the bandwidth of communication channels and decreases in the unit cost of each bit of information transmitted. For example: satellites now allow low-cost transmission of voice, image, and data; fiber optics have substantially increased the capacity of land-based lines; new digital networks are permitting voice, image, and data to be combined in the one network to enable more effective utilization of transmission facilities.

Reduced data communications costs allow new data processing application systems to be developed which take advantage of the facilities enabling transmission of data between remote sites. Four major application areas that are likely to have an ongoing and significant effect on the EDP audit function are:

1 *Electronic funds transfer systems:* These systems are expanding in terms of the range of services they offer, the distances they cover, and the number of financial institutions and vendors that can communicate with one another.

2 *Office information systems:* These systems are becoming increasingly complex as they use data communications technology to provide widespread electronic mail services, access to corporate databases, and easy transfer of documents and images among individuals in an organization.

3 *Customer electronic services:* Many organizations are now providing electronic services that allow customers to transact business remotely. For example, bank customers may use personal microcomputers in their homes to initiate transactions on their accounts. Similarly, a customer may place orders on a supplier via a terminal at the customer's site which is connected to the supplier's computer system.

4 *Electronic message systems:* Both private and public message systems are allowing large numbers of individuals and organizations to communicate with one another to share information and to transact business. For example, electronic bulletin boards allow users to display a public message requesting some good or service in the hope that some participant within the network will be able to respond to meet the demand.

Five general audit concerns arise as a result of these types of systems becoming more commonplace. First, data communication systems often involve a level of technological complexity not present in a centralized data processing system. They have more components, more interfaces among components, and higher levels of functionality.

Second, exposures are often higher in a data communication system: controls can be circumvented at more points within the system; the control technology needed to prevent, detect, and correct errors and irregularities is somewhat unstable and still evolving; increasingly valuable data is being transmitted over communication lines. Unfortunately, to make the systems easier to use, designers sometimes compromise controls so that users have freer access to the resources available in the system.

Third, data communication systems increase the dependence of system users on one another. In an electronic funds transfer system, for example, a breakdown of controls in one part of the system potentially exposes all users of the system. Clearly, all users cannot undertake control reviews of all other users in the system. Global control standards must be developed, and someone must be appointed to monitor user compliance with these standards. As the networks become larger, however, it is increasingly difficult to obtain the levels of assurance required.

Fourth, privacy issues become more important in data communication systems. For example, in an office information system, documents that were previously secured in filing cabinets are now stored on magnetic media. Unless access controls to these documents are effective, unauthorized copies of the files can be easily made and removed. Similarly, if a home banking system or an electronic mail system uses an insecure communication channel, data traversing the channel may be analyzed surreptitiously to discover facts about the parties using the channel.

Fifth, the ways in which data communication systems can be used may become a concern. For example, if an organization provides a bulletin board system, it may be used as a clearing house for pirated software, stolen data files, illicit sale of compromised passwords, etc. The organization may find itself in an invidious position as it attempts to sort out legitimate use of the system from illegitimate use.

Obtaining satisfactory solutions to these problems is unlikely to be an easy task. Auditors will have to undertake substantial research and to acquire substantial practical experience with data communication systems before suitable controls and audit procedures can be devised.

Determining Needed Changes to Controls and Audit Procedures

Though the changing technology may have little impact on EDP auditing at a general level, at a detailed level the EDP auditor must make and evaluate decisions on the controls and audit procedures that need to be changed when the new technology is introduced into an organization. How can the auditor determine what changes need to be made to controls and audit procedures when an organization changes from using its existing technology to using new technology for its data processing?

Davis and Weber [1986] propose a conceptual model that the auditor can use to think about the consequences of a change to new technology for controls and audit procedures. They argue that a change to new technology occurs because an organization is responding to some stress; for example, a stress to be more

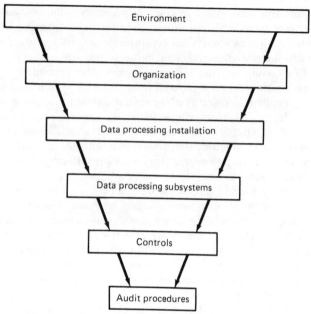

FIGURE 26-1
Stress imposed by higher-level systems on lower-level systems. *(By permission, The Limperg Institute, The Netherlands.)*

responsive to customer demands or a stress to operate more efficiently. The use of new technology helps the organization accommodate this stress and survive. Understanding the impact of a stress on controls and audit procedures involves understanding the nature of the stress itself and the nature of the adjustment processes that are (should be) undertaken by the organization.

Figure 26-1 shows an organization as consisting of various suprasystems, systems, and subsystems. For example, if the organization is considered to be the system, its suprasystem is its environment and its subsystems consist of various functional units, one of which is the data processing installation. A stress imposed by one level of system eventually permeates all the lower levels of systems. For example, if the task environment faced by the organization becomes more uncertain (see Chapter 4), the organization may respond by altering its organization structure. Eventually, pressures may be imposed on the data processing installation to change so management information can be provided on a more timely basis for the new organization structure.

Within this framework, then, of levels of systems, consider the system of audit procedures within an organization. What forces drive a change to audit procedures? Davis and Weber [1986] argue that the suprasystem for the system of audit procedures is the controls system; thus, changes to controls (in response to stress) drive changes to audit procedures.

This relationship can be demonstrated by example. Assume an organization changes from using a batch system to using an online realtime update system for its data processing. Many of the controls exercised over the batch processes disappear; for example, verification of keyed data and batch control registers. Audit procedures used to examine the reliability of these controls are no longer required.

At the next level of systems within an organization, what forces drive changes to controls? Davis and Weber [1986] argue that the suprasystem for the system of controls is the set of computer installation subsystems that exist. Changes to a data processing subsystem drive a change to controls.

Table 26-1 shows a conceptualization of the various data processing installation subsystems within an organization. Consider how a change to the form of the structure or processes within these subsystems drives a change to controls. Again, assume an organization changes from using batch processing to using an online realtime update system for its data processing. The form of the structure and processes in the input subsystem changes from using source document preparation and offline key preparation to online data entry. Consider how controls change as a consequence. Controls such as key verification and dual signature authorization disappear. New controls are needed; for example, checking the validity of the terminal identification number for the terminal used to enter the data.

Given, then, that changes to data processing installation subsystems drive changes to controls and changes to controls drive changes to audit procedures, the auditor's problem is to determine what data processing installation subsystems, if any, are affected in terms of the form of their structure and processes when an organization implements new technology. By identifying what subsystems change, the auditor can determine *where* changes to controls and audit procedures are most likely to occur.

TABLE 26-1
DATA PROCESSING SUBSYSTEMS

Application systems
- data capture/transaction origination
- access (e.g., to programs and data)
- input (terminal transaction entry or offline data preparation and input)
- data transmission
- transaction processing (computation, classification, and summarization)
- update of data for addition, modification, and deletion purposes
- use of system resources (e.g., memory, system software)
- retrieval of data
- output/report preparation and distribution
- output/report use by decision makers

Systems management

Application system design and implementation

Modification and maintenance of application systems

File/database design

Modification and maintenance on file/database designs

Computer operations

Backup and recovery operations

Obviously the specific adjustments made to data processing installation subsystems depend on the form of the stress. At a conceptual level, however, Davis and Weber [1986] propose two "principles" for identifying what subsystems will be adjusted to accommodate a stress. The first principle states that those subsystems "closest to the stress" will be the subsystems that adjust primarily to accommodate the stress. "Closeness" is measured in terms of *functional* closeness; that is, the extent to which a subsystem performs the *function* that must be adjusted to accommodate the stress. The rationale for this principle is that the system consumes less resources to accommodate the stress by adjusting those subsystems closest to the stress. Note, *all* subsystems may be affected in some way by the stress; the principle simply states there is a rank order of effects.

The second principle states that systems will attempt to *localize* the impact of a stress to a subset of subsystems. In other words, when a system undergoes stress and it adjusts to accommodate the stress, it attempts to confine the adjustments to only some of its subsystems. Again, the rationale behind this principle of stress localization is that the system consumes fewer of its resources by accommodating the stress in this way. Recall, also, from Chapter 5 that complex systems survive by maximizing the cohesiveness of their subsystems and minimizing coupling between their subsystems. In this way changes to one subsystem have minimal impact on other subsystems.

To illustrate how these two principles can be applied, assume once again that the organization changes from using batch processing to using an online realtime update system so the data in the database is more current. What data processing installation subsystems will have to adjust to accommodate this timeliness stress? According to the "closeness to stress" principle, all subsystems that inhibit the timely update of the database must be adjusted. According to the principle of stress localization, only a few subsystems will undergo major change. In terms of the example, the input subsystem must be adjusted to allow faster input of data—offline key preparation no longer satisfies timeliness requirements. The access subsystem can be streamlined. Dual signature authorizations constrain the speed of the input process; program access controls can be exercised instead. Similarly, the data capture subsystem can be streamlined. Rather than having clerks perform detailed manual validation of data before data entry, programmed validation checks can be used with immediate feedback on errors. The backup and recovery subsystem also must be adjusted to recover the system more quickly if the timeliness stress is to be accommodated. Other data processing installation subsystems primarily remain unchanged.

Nevertheless, even after having identified where control and audit procedure adjustments must be made, two issues still remain. First, the auditor still must determine the *specific* control and audit procedure adjustments to be made. Unfortunately, at a conceptual level, all that can be said is that this issue is a cost-benefit question. The specific values of the costs and benefits must be determined empirically. Second, even if the auditor makes a "correct" decision on how controls and audit procedures should be adjusted, an incorrect decision on adjustments to be made at high levels of systems can nullify the auditor's decision. For example, an incorrect decision on how a system should be distributed may cause so many behavioral problems that the system fails even with sound controls. Thus, the relationship between stresses and the adjustment processes needed to accommodate these stresses is still a major research area.

RESEARCH AND PEDAGOGY

Two hallmarks of a strong profession are a sound theoretical and empirical knowledge base and well-developed pedagogical support for passing on this knowledge base. Unfortunately, in both areas the record of the EDP auditing profession is somewhat dismal. To date, little theoretical and little empirical research have been carried out within the EDP audit area. Moreover, whereas a fairly extensive literature now exists, it primarily comprises practitioner writings. Thus, the experiences of EDP auditors are reasonably well documented but basic research is lacking.

Ultimately, the speed with which a profession advances depends upon the availability of basic research to support the discipline. Thus, it is important to try to understand the factors that have inhibited research and, if possible, to overcome these factors.

The reason for the dearth of research in the area seems straightforward: in general, academics have not been interested in working on EDP audit topics. However, the reasons why academics have not undertaken research in the area are not so clear. Mavrogeorge [1982] suggests one possibility. He argues that EDP audit research problems tend to be applied or engineeringlike problems. Since universities primarily reward their staff for undertaking basic research, academics do not have an incentive to embark on EDP audit research.

The accounting and auditing professions faced similar problems in their formative years within tertiary institutions. A substantial research base now supports these disciplines, but only after academics made major commitments to try to identify fundamental research issues in these fields and to embark on sustained programs of research. Similar commitments are needed in the EDP audit area if a research base is to develop and its intellectual status is to be improved.

Progress also has been inhibited because the discipline has lacked awareness of relevant research undertaken within other fields. For example, for many years computer scientists have carried out research on operating system integrity, but few references are made to this work within the EDP audit area in spite of its relevance to the discipline. Again, this reflects lack of interest in the area among academics. Since it is the academic side of the profession that usually is most aware of developments in other fields via their reading of journals and their interactions with colleagues, cross-fertilization of ideas will not be forthcoming without more academic participation.

EDP audit pedagogy is in a similar state. Few courses are offered within tertiary institutions to provide training in EDP auditing. Furthermore, those courses that are offered often are not well integrated with the rest of the curriculum. As a result, EDP audit education still comes primarily from on-the-job training and from short courses offered by professional firms, professional bodies, and private training organizations. This situation cannot be allowed to persist if the professional standing of the discipline is to be improved.

Fortunately, some changes are starting to occur. In recent years more funds have been made available by business and the accounting profession to encourage EDP audit research and to support the development of teaching materials. The trend toward professionalism and certification provides an added incentive for tertiary institutions to develop and offer courses in EDP auditing. Hopefully the outcome will be higher-quality decision making among EDP auditors and more effective and efficient production and dissemination of EDP audit knowledge.

SUMMARY

Currently, several forces are at work that may change the EDP audit function. As a result of pressures applied by governments and the public, professions have attempted to improve their standards of conduct and performance and be more accountable. EDP auditors have responded by trying to increase their professionalism by developing a common body of knowledge, a code of ethics, and a certification program.

The legislative process also has impacted the EDP audit function, especially with the enactment of data privacy laws in various countries and the Foreign Corrupt Practices Act in the United States. In some cases privacy laws have extended the EDP auditor's responsibilities to ensure compliance of an organization with the laws. EDP auditors also may be subject to the laws as maintainers and users of data. The Foreign Corrupt Practices Act has increased the possible penalties faced by an EDP auditor who makes a wrong judgment about the quality of an internal control system.

New computer technology has impacted the EDP audit function both indirectly and directly. Indirectly, the effects have occurred because of problems experienced by workers and consumers with changing technology. Organizations need to be increasingly aware of the society's attitudes toward computer use. EDP auditors may perform some part of this monitoring function required. Directly, the effects have occurred because the EDP auditor must evaluate systems based on the new technology. The role of the EDP auditor and the basic audit methodologies remain unchanged; however, the EDP auditor must understand the new technologies, be capable of determining their impact on controls and audit procedures, and ensure that evidence collection tools and techniques have been developed.

Finally, the EDP audit function is changing because research and pedagogy in the area is improving. More research will provide a better-developed theoretical and empirical knowledge base for the function. Improved pedagogy will allow more effective and efficient production and dissemination of this knowledge base.

REVIEW QUESTIONS

26-1 What impact did moves by various governments to regulate the accounting profession have on the development of the EDP audit profession?

26-2 List five identifying characteristics of a profession. What actions have EDP auditors taken to ensure compliance with these characteristics?

26-3 Give two benefits and two costs of professional certification. What problems can arise when professional certification is supported by government licensing?

26-4 List three ways in which international privacy laws differ. What implications do these differences have for EDP auditing in a multinational corporation?

26-5 List four privacy "principles" that are common, at least to some extent, in international privacy laws. Choose one principle and outline how it might affect the EDP audit function.

26-6 What implications do privacy laws have for EDP auditors as maintainers of personal data?

26-7 How may a contingent liability arise because of privacy laws? Why might the EDP auditor be concerned with contingent liabilities when auditing an organization for compliance with privacy laws?

26-8 What implications do privacy laws have for EDP auditors as users of personal data?

26-9 What is meant by computer matching? Why is computer matching a threat to personal privacy?

26-10 The Foreign Corrupt Practices Act does not change the responsibilities of EDP auditors; however, it does change the risks they face. Explain.

26-11 Why does the concept of materiality change under the Foreign Corrupt Practices Act? How might the evidence collection phase of an EDP audit change as a consequence?

26-12 Even though the Foreign Corrupt Practices Act is a United States act, why may it affect foreign EDP auditors?

26-13 Why may the EDP auditor become increasingly involved in monitoring social attitudes toward computers?

26-14 Briefly discuss the dilemma facing management and workers over the introduction of new technology within organizations. What part might the EDP auditor have to play in resolving some of the problems caused by the dilemma?

26-15 What evidence exists to show that EDP auditors may have a narrow conception of who constitutes the user group of a computer system? Give two potential consequences if this focus continues to be narrow.

26-16 How might consumer experiences with batch billing systems affect moves toward further implementation and use of electronic funds transfer systems?

26-17 Briefly describe two ways in which an EDP auditor might better monitor the attitudes of consumers toward an organization's computer systems.

26-18 Why is it unlikely that the changing technology will affect the basic role of EDP auditors and fundamental EDP audit methodologies?

26-19 Why might the changing technology allow the EDP auditor to work at a higher level of detail? Give two implications of the EDP auditor being able to work at this higher level of detail.

26-20 What problems have arisen as a result of inadequate controls over the purchase and use of microcomputers?

26-21 What is meant by "computer hacking"? Why has the phenomenon of hacking occurred? What implications does hacking have for establishment of controls over an organization's computer systems?

26-22 Why must control be exercised over the growth of end-user computing within an organization?

26-23 Briefly describe *three* characteristics of fifth-generation computer systems.

26-24 What control problems arise as a result of an organization using intelligent knowledge-based systems?

26-25 Briefly describe two major trends within telecommunications technology. What implications do these trends have for EDP auditing?

26-26 Identify *one* implication of each of the following technological developments for EDP auditing:
a Growth in electronic funds transfer systems
b More extensive use of office information systems
c Provision of customer electronic services
d Growth in electronic message systems

26-27 Why does privacy often become a more important issue in data communication systems?

26-28 Briefly explain the relationship between the form of the data processing installation subsystem and the form of controls, and between the form of controls and the form of audit procedures.

26-29 How is the principle of stress localization useful when considering the impact of new technology on controls and audit procedures?

26-30 What is meant by futures research? How would futures research aid the development of the EDP audit function?

26-31 Give two reasons why EDP audit research and pedagogy have been slow to develop. Why is it likely that the pace will quicken in the future?

26-32 Briefly discuss why it is necessary for the survival of a profession to have a sound theoretical and empirical knowledge base and an effective means of disseminating this knowledge.

MULTIPLE CHOICE QUESTIONS

26-1 In December 1976 a report titled "The Accounting Establishment: A Staff Study" issued by the U.S. Senate Subcommittee on Reports, Accounting and Management recommended:
a A separate professional group be set up for EDP auditors
b Direct involvement by the U.S. Government in establishing financial accounting standards and auditing standards
c Deregulation of the accounting profession
d The accounting profession should substantially upgrade its knowledge of EDP

26-2 Which of the following is *not* a criterion identified by the U.S. Taft-Hartley Act for defining a profession:
a Code of ethics
b A disciplinary mechanism
c Government-mandated registration
d Common body of knowledge

26-3 Which of the following is *not* an advantage of professional certification:
a Reduces the search costs of employers
b Increased focus on developing a common body of knowledge
c Reduces the advertising costs of professionals
d More widespread consumer choice in terms of the range and quality of services offered by professionals

26-4 Which of the following is *not* a general principle of privacy legislation:
a Individuals should be able to delete data about themselves that is irrelevant
b Data collected on political philosophy or religious views should be subject to special protection measures
c Individuals should be able to examine data held about them
d Organizations must publicly register personal data systems

26-5 The Foreign Corrupt Practices Act impacts the EDP auditor because:
a It changes the level of errors and irregularities that might be considered material
b It makes the auditor responsible for the system of internal control
c It makes the auditor responsible if bribes are not detected
d Some internal audit functions are now likely to be performed by a quality assurance group

26-6 Which of the following predictions made by futurists about the impact of computers on organizations and workers has proved to be accurate:
a Computers would reduce the need for middle management in organizations
b Computers would change the time and location at which work was performed
c Computers would affect employment levels in particular sectors of the economy
d A class of workers who were "information rich" would rapidly emerge

26-7 In a study carried out by Sterling [1979] of a random sample of members of the Consumer's Association of British Columbia, he found:
a About 40% of consumers had encountered one or more errors when dealing with computer systems in the previous 12 months
b Most computer system errors were incorrect name and address errors
c Consumers persisted in trying to correct computer system errors even after their initial attempts were unsuccessful
d Errors were more likely to be corrected in organizations that had a viable internal audit function

26-8 At a general level, it seems that one impact of changing computer technology on the EDP audit function will be:
a The attest duties of auditors will alter
b Application system controls will be less important
c A greater number of more well-defined levels of EDP audit work will arise
d Auditors will have to work at a lower level of detail

26-9 Which of the following outcomes has occurred as a result of the widespread use of microcomputers in organizations:

a Application systems have become more centralized

b Backup and recovery concerns have decreased

c Training and support needs for users have decreased

d Inventory control over hardware and software purchases has been more difficult to exercise

26-10 To exercise control over the growth of end-user computing in organizations, management should:

a Develop, promulgate, and enforce organizationwide policies

b Centralize all hardware and software purchases

c Require that all system development projects be approved by information systems management

d Require that all systems be examined by the internal audit department to ensure that reliable controls have been implemented in the system

26-11 Which of the following will be an impact of using knowledge-based systems in organizations:

a Auditors will be able to reduce their focus on application systems

b Privacy concerns will decrease

c Facts in knowledge-based systems will be easier to verify than facts in application systems

d The integrity of the knowledge embodied in these systems will be difficult to assess

26-12 Which of the following is *not* true about advanced computer systems that use data communication technology:

a They increase the dependence of system users on one another

b They reduce privacy concerns because data becomes decentralized

c They increase the need for control standards

d They reduce each user's ability to maintain the integrity of their own data

26-13 In the stress hierarchy proposed by Davis and Weber [1986], changes to controls are motivated by changes in:

a The organization structure

b The structure of the data processing subsystems

c Audit procedures

d The data processing installation's structure

26-14 The conceptual framework proposed by Davis and Weber [1986] enables the auditor to determine:

a Where control and audit changes are likely to occur

b What control and audit changes will occur

c Which control and audit procedure changes are likely to be cost-effective

d All the above

26-15 The principle of stress localization predicts:

a Changes in controls and audit procedures will occur in those subsystems closest to the stress

b Stress only occurs in the local vicinity of a subsystem

c Systems will attempt to confine the impact of a stress to a subset of their subsystems

d More stress will be experienced in subsystems that are internally cohesive

26-16 Which of the following statements best describes the status of research and pedagogy within the EDP audit field:

a Both research and pedagogy are in a well-developed state
b Substantial research has been carried out but pedagogy is not well developed
c Pedagogy is well developed but basic research is lacking
d Neither research nor pedagogy is well developed

EXERCISES AND CASES

26-1 For the general principles of privacy legislation, identify those aspects likely to impact only the external auditor, those aspects likely to impact only the internal auditor, and those aspects likely to impact both external auditors and internal auditors. Be sure to explain the nature of the impact in each case.

26-2 As auditors we tend to think of the impact of computers on jobs other than our own. Over the next 10 years, to what extent will the computer cause job displacement within the auditing profession? If you believe the displacement will not occur, explain why auditors will be "saved."

26-3 How much do we know about where computers will have an impact over the next 10 years? To what extent is there agreement among the experts? As someone having some knowledge of computers and their capabilities, rate the extent to which computers will cause work displacement in the following jobs over the next 10 years. A score of 10 means high job displacement will occur; a score of 1 means there will be little or no impact.

Real estate salesperson
Medical practitioner (doctor)
Assembly line worker
University academic
Farmer
Auto mechanic
Accounts clerk
Biochemist
Homemaker
Surveyor
Civil engineer

Compare your ratings with other members of your class to determine consensus.

26-4 Using the conceptual framework proposed by Davis and Weber [1986] for considering the impact of new technology on controls and audit procedures, what data processing installation subsystems would be affected (see Table 26-1) when an organization implements a database management system to promote sharing of data? For each subsystem that you list as being affected, explain why you think it will be affected. Furthermore, list some control changes and audit procedure changes that you would expect to arise as a result of the subsystem changes.

26-5 "The data processing installation subsystems that will be affected by a stress imposed upon the data processing installation cannot be determined unless the stress is understood." Explain this statement in terms of a move by a data processing installation from centralized to distributed processing. (*Hint:* You should consider what is meant by distributed data processing.)

26-6 Assume that a financial institution seeks to build an expert system to assist its portfolio managers with their decisions on the equities to choose for investment purposes. Assume, also, that the organization has not previously designed and built an expert system. As the internal auditor for the organization, outline the standards you would recommend to management to cover the design and implementation of the system.

ANSWERS TO MULTIPLE CHOICE QUESTIONS

26-1 b	26-5 a	26-9 d	26-13 b
26-2 c	26-6 c	26-10 a	26-14 a
26-3 d	26-7 a	26-11 d	26-15 c
26-4 b	26-8 c	26-12 b	26-16 d

REFERENCES

ACM Committee on Computers and Public Policy. "A Problem-List of Issues Concerning Computers and Public Policy," *Communications of the ACM* (September 1974), pp. 495–503.

American Institute of Certified Public Accountants. "New Legislation Would Change Auditor Responsibilities," *The CPA Letter,* June 9, 1986, p. 1.

Attewell, P., and J. Rule. "Computing and Organizations: What We Know and What We Don't Know," *Communications of the ACM* (December 1984), pp. 1184–1192.

Bailey, Andrew D., Jr., James H. Gerlach, R. Preston McAfee, and Andrew B. Whinston. "An OIS Model for Internal Control Evaluation," *ACM Transactions on Office Information Systems* (January 1983), pp. 25–44.

Bailey, Andrew D., Jr., James H. Gerlach, R. Preston McAfee, and Andrew B. Whinston. "Internal Accounting Controls in the Office of the Future," *IEEE Computer* (May 1981), pp. 59–70.

Barnes, Stanley H., and Martin L. Bariff. "Professionalism and the EDP Auditor," *The EDP Auditor* (Winter 1978), pp. 4–11.

Bump, Morrison. "A Primer on Software Piracy Cases in the Courts," *Computers and Security* (May 1984), pp. 123–134.

Caelli, W. J. "Privacy and Security in Office Automation Systems," *Australian Computer Journal* (August 1985), pp. 126–130.

Canning, Richard G. "Professionalism: Coming or Not," *EDP Analyzer* (March 1976), pp. 1–12.

Davis, Gordon B., and Ron Weber. *Auditing Advanced EDP Systems* (Altamonte Springs, FL: The Institute of Internal Auditors, 1981).

Davis, Gordon B., and Ron Weber. "The Impact of Advanced Computer Systems on Controls and Audit Procedures: A Theory and an Empirical Test," *Auditing: A Journal of Practice and Theory* (Spring 1986), pp. 35–49.

Everest, Gordon C. *Database Management: Objectives, System Functions, and Administration* (New York: McGraw-Hill, 1986).

Feigenbaum, E., and P. McCorduck. *The Fifth Generation* (Reading, MA: Addison-Wesley, 1983).

Friedman, Milton. *Capitalism and Freedom* (Chicago: The University of Chicago Press, 1962).

Goldstein, Robert C., and Richard L. Nolan. "Personal Privacy Versus the Corporate Computer," *Harvard Business Review* (March–April 1975), pp. 62–70.

Highland, Harold Joseph. *Protecting Your Microcomputer System* (New York: Wiley, 1984).

Kirby, M.D. "Data Protection and Law Reform," *Computer Networks* (June 1979), pp. 149–163.

Kling, Rob. "Value Conflicts and Social Choice in Electronic Funds Transfer System Developments," *Communications of the ACM* (August 1978), pp. 642–657.

Kusserow, R.P. "The Government Needs Computer Matching to Root Out Waste and Fraud," *Communications of the ACM* (June 1984), pp. 542–545.

Leavitt, Harold J., and Thomas L. Whisler. "Management in the 1980's," *Harvard Business Review* (November–December 1958), pp. 41–48.

Lee, John A.N., Gerald Segal, and Rosalie Steier. "Positive Alternatives: A Report on an ACM Panel on Hacking," *Communications of the ACM* (April, 1986), pp. 297–299.

Li, David H. "Common Body of Knowledge for EDP Auditing," *The EDP Auditor* (Summer 1983), pp. 1–17.

McKee, Thomas E. "Auditing Under the Foreign Corrupt Practices Act," *The CPA Journal* (August 1979), pp. 31–35.

Mason, John O., Jr., and Jonathan J. Davies. "Legal Implications of EDP Deficiencies," *The CPA Journal* (August 1979), pp. 21–24.

Mautz, Robert K., Alan G. Merten, and Dennis G. Severance. "Corporate Computer Control Guide," *Financial Executive* (June 1984), pp. 25–36.

Mavrogeorge, Brian. "Identifying Research Needs for EDP Auditing," *The EDP Auditor* (Fall 1982), pp. 33–44.

Maxfield, John F. "Computer Bulletin Boards and the Hacker Problem," *EDPACS* (October 1985), pp. 1–11.

Novotny, Eric J. "Restrictions on the Transnational Flow of Corporate Information: New Challenges for the Auditing Profession," *The EDP Auditor* (Summer 1979), pp. 13–33.

Olson, Margrethe H. "New Information Technology and Organizational Culture," *Management Information Systems Quarterly* (Special Issue 1982), pp. 71–92.

Report of the Secretary's Advisory Committee on Automated Personal Data Systems, U.S. Department of Health, Education and Welfare. *Records, Computers, and the Rights of Citizens* (Boston: The Massachusetts Institute of Technology, 1973).

Roberts, Ray. "Impact on the Auditor of Recent Developments Relating to Internal Control," *The EDP Auditor* (Winter 1978), pp. 12–20.

Ross, Steven J. "What EDP Auditors Will See in the Future," *The EDP Auditor* (Fall, 1983), pp. 27–35.

Ruder, Brian. "Privacy and Data Base Administration," *EDP Auditing* (Pennsauken, NJ: Auerbach Publishers, 1978*a*), Portfolio 73-02-04, pp. 1–12.

Ruder, Brian. "Privacy and the Data Center," *EDP Auditing* (Pennsauken, NJ: Auerbach Publishers, 1978*b*), Portfolio 72-03-05, pp. 1–12.

Ruthberg, Zella G. "Where Will Managerial Controls be Needed in the Year 2000," *The EDP Auditor*, vol. 1, 1984, pp. 1–6.

Sanchez-Saavedra, Susan A. "Measuring the Competency of the EDP Auditor," *The EDP Auditor* (Winter 1982/83), pp. 23–33.

Shapiro, Ehud Y. "The Fifth Generation Project—A Trip Report," *Communications of the ACM* (September 1983), pp. 637–641.

Shattuck, J. "Computer Matching is a Serious Threat to Individual Rights," *Communications of the ACM* (June 1984), pp. 538---541.

Stadlen, Godfrey. "Survey of National Data Protection Legislation," *Computing Networks* (June 1979), pp. 174–186.

Sterling, T.D. "Consumer Difficulties with Computerized Transactions: An Empirical Investigation," *Communications of the ACM* (May 1979), pp. 283–289.

Summers, R.C. "An Overview of Computer Security," *IBM Systems Journal,* vol. 23, no. 4, 1984, pp. 309–325.

Turn, Rein. "Privacy Protection," in Martha E. Williams, ed., *Annual Review of Information Science and Technology* (White Plains, NY: Knowledge Industry Publications, 1985), vol. 20, pp. 27–50.

United Kingdom. *Data Protection Act 1984* (London: United Kingdom Government, Her Majesty's Stationery Office, 1984).

Weiss, Ira. "The Certified Information Systems Auditor Examination: A Description of Exam Development and Analysis of Results," *The EDP Auditor* (Spring 1982), pp. 15–19.

Westin, Alan F., and Michael G. Baker. *Databanks in a Free Society: Computers, Record-keeping and Privacy* (New York: Quadrangle/New York Times, 1972).

NAME INDEX

945

SUBJECT INDEX